The Encyclopedia of JUDAISM

The Encyclopedia of Judaism

EDITOR-IN-CHIEF *Geoffrey Wigoder*

MACMILLAN PUBLISHING COMPANY
New York
Collier Macmillan Publishers
London

Macmillan Publishing Company
866 Third Avenue, New York, NY 10022
Collier Macmillan Canada, Inc.

Library of Congress Cataloging-in-Publication Data

The Encyclopedia of Judaism/edited by Geoffrey Wigoder.
p. cm.
ISBN 0-02-628410-3
1. Judaism—Dictionaries. I. Widoger, Geoffrey, 1922–
BM50.E63 1989 269'.03—dc20
89-8184 CIP

Macmillan books are available at special discounts for bulk purchases for sales promotions, premiums, fund-raising, or educational use.
For details, contact:

Special Sales Director
Macmillan Publishing Company
866 Third Avenue
New York, NY 10022

10 9 8 7 6 5 4 3 2 1

Printed in Belgium

CONTRIBUTORS

Yaacov Adler
Lecturer in Ancient Hebrew Literature, Bar Ilan University, Ramat Gan.
Marc D. Angel, Ph.D.
Rabbi, Spanish and Portuguese Synagogue, Shearith Israel of the City of New York; First Vice-President of the Rabbinical Council of America.
David Applebaum, M.D.
Rabbi; physician, Jerusalem.
Yehuda Bauer, Ph.D.
Professor, Hebrew University, Jerusalem; Chairman, International Federation of Secular-Humanistic Jews.
Adina Ben-Chorin
Researcher and editor, Jerusalem.
Schalom Ben-Chorin
Professor D. Theology h.c., Jerusalem.
Tovia Ben-Chorin
Rabbi, Har-El Synagogue, Jerusalem.
Alexander Carlebach, Ph.D.
Former Chief Rabbi of Northern Ireland. Jerusalem.
Bernard Casper, Ph.D. (the late)
Former Chief Rabbi of South Africa. Jerusalem.
Jonathan Chipman, Ph.D
Rabbi; editor and translator, Jerusalem.
Yosef Dan, Ph.D
Professor of Jewish Studies, Hebrew University, Jerusalem.
Uri Dasberg
Rabbi; researcher, Zomet-Torah and Science Institute, Gush-Etsion.
David Jay Derovan
Rabbi; educator, Jerusalem.
Jackie Feldman, M.A.
Shalom Hartman Institute for Advanced Jewish Studies, Jerusalem.
Sir Monty Finniston, F.Eng. FRS
Industrialist, London.
Seymour Freedman Ph.D.
Writer, Jerusalem.
Albert H. Friedlander Ph.D.
Rabbi, Westminster Synagogue, London.
Theodore Friedman, Ph.D.
Rabbi; former President of Rabbinical Assembly of America, Jerusalem.
David Geffen, Ph.D.
Rabbi; researcher, Jerusalem.
Hanna Goodman
Writer, educator, Jerusalem.
Ilana Goldberg, M.A.
Researcher, Hebrew University, Jerusalem.
Itshak Gottlieb, Ph.D.
Senior Lecturer, Department of Bible, Bar Ilan University, Ramat Gan.
Reuven Hammer, Ph.D.
Rabbi; Founding Director of Seminary of Judaic Studies, Jerusalem.
Shmuel Himelstein, Ph.D.
Rabbi; editor and translator, Jerusalem.
Ida Huberman, M.A.
Lecturer, Beth Berl College, Kefar Saba.
Boaz Huss, M.A.
Researcher, Hebrew University, Jerusalem.
Julian G. Jacobs, Ph.D.
Rabbi; Senior Minister, Liverpool Old Hebrew Congregation.

Louis Jacobs, Ph.D.
Author and Rabbi of the New London Synagogue.
Lord Jakobovits
The Chief Rabbi of the United Hebrew Congregation of the British Commonwealth, London.
Michael Klein, Ph.D.
Professor of Bible and Targumic Literature;
Dean of the Hebrew Union College-Institute of Religion, Jerusalem.
Michael L. Klein-Katz
Rabbi; educator and lecturer. Jerusalem.
Daniel Lasker
Associate Professor, Department of History, Ben Gurion University of the Negev, Beersheba.
Sidney B. Leperer, Ph.D.
Rabbi; Lecturer in Jewish History, Jews' College, London.
Mendell Lewittes, D.D.
Rabbi; Editor of Shanah be-Shanah. Jerusalem.
Sheldon Lilker, D.H.L.
Rabbi; author, Kibbutz Kefar Ha-Maccabi.
Norman Linzer, Ph.D.
Professor, Wurzweiler School of Social Work, Yeshiva University. New York.
Barry Mindel
Translator, Jerusalem.
Chaim Mayerson
Educator and translator, Jerusalem.
Tirzah Meacham, Ph.D.
Department of Near Eastern Studies, University of Toronto, Ontario, Canada.
Moshe Miller
Rabbi; editor and translator.
Aryeh Newman, M.A.
Senior Lecturer, E.F.L. Department, Hebrew University, Jerusalem.
Isaac Newman
Coordinator Hebrew Studies, Middlesex Polytechnic; Rabbi; Barnet, Herts., England.
Avi Ofer, B.A.
Translator and editor, Jerusalem.
Shalom Paul, Ph.D.
Professor, Chairman of the Department of Bible, Hebrew University, Jerusalem.
Chaim Pearl, Ph.D.
Rabbi Emeritus, Conservative Synagogue Adath Israel of Riverdale, N.Y., Jerusalem.
Chaim Rabin, Ph.D.
Professor Emeritus of Hebrew Language, Hebrew University, Jerusalem.
Aaron Rakefet D.H.L.
Rabbi; Professor of Responsa Literature, Gruss Institute of Yeshiva University, Jerusalem.
Aviezer Ravitzky, Ph.D.
Professor of Jewish Philosophy, Hebrew University, Jerusalem.
Uri Regev LL.B.
Rabbi; Director of Israel Program, Hebrew Union College-Institute of Religion, Jerusalem.
Meir Rikin
Researcher, Hebrew University, Jerusalem.
Nissim Rejwan
Journalist, writer specializing in Middle East and Israeli politics and culture, Jerusalem.
Henry Romberg, M.D.
Physician, Jerusalem.
David Rosen
Dean of Sapir Center. A.D.L. Liaison to the Vatican.
Former Chief Rabbi of Ireland. Jerusalem.
Yaakov G. Rosenberg
Rabbi; Vice Chancellor Emeritus of Jewish Theological Seminary. Jerusalem.
Yael Rossing, M.A.
Researcher, Shalom Hartman Institute for Advanced Jewish Studies, Jerusalem.

James Rudin
Rabbi; American Jewish Committee, New York.
Moshe Sachs, Ph.D.
Researcher, Jerusalem.
Fern Sackbach, M.A.
Researcher, Jerusalem.
Eliahu Schleifer, Ph.D.
Associate Professor of Jewish Music, Hebrew Union College-Institute of Religion, Jerusalem.
Abraham Shafir Ph.D.
Lecturer, Department of Bible, Beth Berl College, Kefar Saba.
Mark Elliott Shapiro, M.A.
Editor and translator, Jerusalem.
Suzan Laikin Shifron
Reconstructionist Rabbi, Kefar Saba.
Vivian Charles Silverman, M. Phil.
Rabbi, Central Synagogue, London.
Gabriel A. Sivan, Ph.D.
Writer and lecturer, Jerusalem.
David Solomon Ph.D.
Lecturer, Central Teachers College for Extension Studies, Tel Aviv.
Dora Sowden
Dance critic, Jerusalem.
Shubert Spero, D. Phil.
Rabbi Emeritus, Young Israel Congregation, Cleveland, Ohio. Irving Stone Professor in Jewish Thought, Bar Ilan University, Ramat Gan.
Iris Spero, M.S.L.S.
Librarian, Jerusalem.
Benjamin Stein
Cantor, Jerusalem.
Shafer B. Stollman
Editor, Jewish Agency Publications, Jerusalem.
Sefton D. Temkin, Ph.D.
Rabbi; Professor Emeritus; State University of NY, Albany.
Yoel Tobin Ph.D.
Fellow of the Shalom Hartman Institute for Advanced Jewish Studies, Jerusalem.
Benjamin Zvieli
Rabbi; Former director of religious broadcasting, Israel Radio and Television, Jerusalem.
Moshe Tutnauer
Rabbi, educator, Jerusalem.
Shalva Weil Ph.D.
Institute of Research on Education, Hebrew University, Jerusalem.
Mendel Weinberger
Rabbi, columnist, Jerusalem.
Geoffrey Wigoder, D. Phil.
Editor-in-chief Encyclopedia Judaica, Director, Oral History Department
Institute of Contemporary Jewry, Hebrew University, Jerusalem.
Walter Zanger
Rabbi, author, columnist, and guide, Jerusalem.

EDITORS

Adina Ben-Chorin; Sam Freedman; David Geffen; Evelyn Katrak; Michael L. Klein-Katz; Chaim Mayerson; Linda C. Newman; Susanna Shabetai; Stacy Weiner.

INDEXER

David Jay Derovan

PREFACE

The publication of the *Encyclopedia of Judaism* obviously entailed a consideration and determination of the meaning and scope of "Judaism" for the purposes of this volume. The early Israelites had no comparable term (nor indeed had they a word for "religion" which had to be imported from Persia in the later stages of the Bible [*dat*]). *Torah* ("teaching") was perhaps the closest concept, covering the totality of Jewish belief and practice (with the emphasis usually on the practice).

Abstract theological thinking crystallized only in the classical period under the impact of external schools of thought, notably Hellenistic philosophy, but even this largely disappeared until the Middle Ages. Then, the Jews fell under the influence of Arab thought and now sought to define their creed and codify Jewish practice.

The Hebrew word *yahadut*, meaning "Judaism", first appeared in the Middle Ages but with the advent of Emancipation in the late 18th-early 19th centuries, the term became ambiguous. Jews moving into an open society could retain their Jewish identity while disassociating themselves from all or part of the "religious" heritage, which had not previously been possible. The word *yahadut* now had three meanings, for which English (but not Hebrew) had different words: "Judaism", "Jewishness" and "Jewry". The word "Jewishness" (best known to Western Jews in its Yiddish form — *yiddishkeit*) covers the whole complex of being Jewish, including ethnic and secular elements. "Judaism" is taken as a parallel to "Christianity" in that it refers to what is called the religious tradition, traced back to Biblical times. The truth is that habitually "Judaism/Jewishness" cannot be broken up into its various components; everything is related to the holy, and the efforts to differentiate between the holy and the secular are, for Jews, misleading. Nevertheless, most Jews today accept a certain *de facto* distinction and this volume deals with those aspects which the Western world calls "religious" and confines itself to religious life and development. For example, its biographical entries concentrate on outstanding individuals who have contributed to the development of Judaism. Within the religious context, all facets are covered, although in relation to Jewish jurisprudence, some of the more detailed and technical aspects have been omitted.

Judaism today is highly pluralistic and every effort has been made to give a balanced picture reflecting the various trends and schools of thought and practice. We have been fortunate to enjoy the cooperation of authorities on the many different subjects covered.

A concise work of this nature cannot present full details of every topic; cross-references (indicated by small capital letters) direct the reader to supplementary information in other entries. Bible quotations are usually based on the new translation of the Jewish Publication Society of America but other standard translations have also been used and on occasion the contributor has chosen to supply his own version. Where place names and personal names have a familiar English form, these have been used; otherwise they have been transliterated.

It is hoped that this volume will prove a handy reference and learning tool for laymen and students, opening up the world of inspiration, faith, learning, and experience contained in Judaism.

ABBREVIATIONS

Ar. — Arakhin
Arab. — Arabic
Aram. — Aramaic
ARN — Avot de-Rabbi Natan
AZ — Avodah Zarah
BB — Bava Batra
BCE — before C.E. (BC)
Bekh. — Bekhorot
Ber. — Berakhot
Bik. — Bikkurim
BK — Bava Kamma
BM — Bava Metsia
c. — circa
CE — Common Era (AD)
cent. — century
Chr. — Chronicles
Dan. — Daniel
Dem. — Demai
Deut. — Deuteronomy
Deut. R. — Deuteronomy Rabbah
Eccl. — Ecclesiastes
Eccl. R. — Ecclesiastes Rabbah
Ecclus. — Ecclesiasticus (Ben Sira)
Ed. — Eduyyot
EH — Even ha-Ezer
Er. — Eruvin
Est. — Esther
Est. R. — Esther Rabbah
Ex. — Exodus
Ex. R. — Exodus Rabbah
Ezek. — Ezekiel
ff. — following
Fr. — French
Gen. — Genesis
Gen. R. — Genesis Rabbah
Germ. — German
Git. — Gittin
Gk. — Greek
H̱ag. — H̱agigah
H̱al. — H̱allah
Heb. — Hebrew
H̱M — H̱oshen Mishpat
Hor. — Horayot
Hos. — Hosea
H̱ul. — H̱ullin
Isa. — Isaiah
Jer. — Jeremiah
Josh. — Joshua
JPS — Jewish Publication Society Bible translation
Judg. — Judges
Ker. — Keritot
Ket — Ketubbot
Kid. — Kiddushin
Kil. — Kilayim
Kin. — Kinnim
Lam. — Lamentations
Lam. R. — Lam. Rabbah
Lat. — Latin
Lev. — Leviticus
Lev. R. — Leviticus Rabbah
lit. — literally
LXX — Septuagint
Ma'as. — Ma'aserot
Ma'as. Sh. — Ma'aser Sheni
Macc. — Maccabees
Mak. — Makkot
Makh. — Makhshirim
Mal. — Malachi
Matt. — Matthew
Meg. — Megillah
Mekh. — Mekhilta
Men. — Menaẖot
Mic. — Micah
Mid. — Middot
Midr. — Midrash
Mik. — Mikva'ot
Mish. — Mishnah
Maim. — Maimonides
MK — Mo'ed Katan
Ned. — Nedarim
Neg. — Nega'im
Neh. — Nehemiah
Nid. — Niddah
Num. — Numbers
Num. R. — Numbers Rabbah
Ob. — Obadiah
Ohol. — Oholot
OH̱ — Oraẖ H̱ayyim
Orl. — Orlah
Pes. — Pesaẖim
pl. — plural
Prov. — Proverbs
Ps. — Psalms
R. — Rabbi (title)
RH — Rosh ha-Shanah
Ruth R. — Ruth Rabbah
Sam. — Samuel
Sanh. — Sanhedrin
Shab. — Shabbat

Shek.	Shekalim	*Tem.*	Temurah
Shev.	Shevi'it	*Ter.*	Terumot
Shevu.	Shevu'ot	TJ	Jerusalem Talmud
Sh. Ar.	Shulh̲an Arukh	*Toh.*	Tohorot
Sif.	Sifré	*Tos.*	Tosafot
Sof.	Soferim	*Tosef.*	Tosefta
Song	Song of Songs (Canticles)	*Uk.*	Uktsin
Song R.	Song of Songs Rabbah	*Yad.*	Yadayim (Maim., Yad=Mishneh Torah)
Sot.	Sotah	*Yal.*	Yalkut
Sp.	Spanish	*YD*	Yoreh De'ah
Suk.	Sukkah	*Yev.*	Yevamot
Ta'an.	Ta'anit	Yid.	Yiddish
Tam.	Tamid	*Zav.*	Zavim
Tanh.	Tanh̲uma	Zech.	Zechariah
Targ.	Targum	Zeph.	Zephaniah
TB	Babylonian Talmud	*Zev.*	Zevah̲im

TRANSLITERATION

Hebrew	English	Hebrew	English	Hebrew	English
א not transliterated (e.g., at end of word)					
אַ or אָ or אֲ	a	ו	v	ס	s
אֵ or אֶ or אֱ	e	ז	z	ע	not transliterated
אוֹ or אֹ	o	ח	h̲	פּ	p
אוּ or אֻ	u (as in tool)	ט	t	פ	f
אִי or אִ	i	י	y	צ	ts
בּ	b	כּ	k	ק	k
ב	v	כ	kh	ר	r
ג	g	ל	l	שׁ	sh
ד	d	מ	m	שׂ	s
ה	h (also at end of word)	נ	n	תּ or ת	t

Vowels	Transliteration of Hebrew	Vowels	Transliteration of Hebrew
Hebrew	**English**	**Hebrew**	**English**
—ָ	a	—ֶ	e
short —ָ	o	—ִ	i
—ַ	a	—ֵ	e
וֹ—	o	—ֱ	e
וּ—	u	—ֳ	o
—ֵי —ֵא	é	—ֲ	a

vocal sheva – e

silent sheva – not transliterated

GLOSSARY

(plural and adjectival forms in parentheses)

ADAR: twelfth month of the Jewish religious calendar.

AGGADAH (AGGADOT; AGGADIC): Non-legal portions of the Talmud and Midrash.

AḤARONIM: later rabbinical authorities.

ALÉNU: prayer recited at the end of each daily service.

AMIDAH: prayer of "Eighteen Benedictions" recited in every service.

AMORA (AMORAIM; AMORAIC): sage of the talmudic era.

ARK: Niche or cupboard in synagogue for Scrolls of the Law.

ASHKENAZI(M): Jew of medieval German tradition and descent.

AV: fifth month of the Jewish religious calendar.

AV BET DIN: head of law court.

AVOT: ethical tractate of the Mishnah.

BARAITA: tradition of *tanna* not found in Mishnah.

BAR MITSVAH: attaining by a boy of his religious majority (for a girl, bat mitsvah).

BET DIN (BATTÉ DIN): rabbinical court.

BET MIDRASH: study center, often part of synagogue.

BIMAH: reader's desk or platform in the synagogue.

CONSERVATIVE: movement in Judaism which permits modifications in *halakhah*.

DAYYAN: religious judge.

DIASPORA: Jewish communities outside the Land of Israel.

EASTERN JEWS: Jews in Islamic and Asian lands, not of European origin.

ELUL: sixth month of the Jewish religious calendar.

ERETS ISRAEL: The Land of Israel.

ESSENES: Ascetic movement in Second Temple times.

EXILARCH: Lay head of the Jewish community in Babylon.

FIRST TEMPLE PERIOD: from building of the First Temple c. 950 BCE to its destruction by the Babylonians in 586 BCE.

GABBAI (GABBA'IM): Jewish community official; synagogue warden.

GALUT (GOLAH): Exile, Diaspora.

GAON (GE'ONIM; GEONIC): title given to leading Babylonian sages of the sixth-12th centuries.

GEMARA: commentary on Mishnah incorporated in Talmud.

GENIZAH: depository for worn-out or damaged sacred volumes.

GET: bill of divorcement.

ḤABAD: Ḥasidic movement.

HAFTARAH: reading from the Prophets chanted after the Reading of the Law.

HAGGADAH (HAGGADOT): book from which the traditional "narrative" is recited at the Passover *Seder*.

ḤAKHAM: Sephardi rabbi.

HAKKAFOT: circuits, especially around the synagogue.

HALAKHAH (HALAKHOT; HALAKHIC): Jewish religious law.

ḤALITSAH: ceremony releasing from obligation of levirate marriage.

ḤALLAH (ḤALLOT): white loaf baked for Sabbaths and festivals.

HALLEL: "Psalms of Praise" (113-118) recited on festive occasions.

ḤAMETS: leavened bread.

ḤANUKKAH: festival, commemorating victory of the Maccabees.

ḤASIDIM (ḤASIDIC): adherents of various pietist movements, especially one founded in Eastern Europe in 18th century.

HASKALAH: Jewish Enlightenment movement.

ḤAZZAN: synagogue cantor or "reader".

ḤEDER: primary religious school.

ḤESHVAN: eighth month of the Jewish religious calendar.

HIGH HOLIDAYS: Rosh ha-Shanah (the Jewish New Year) and the Day of Atonement (Yom Kippur).

ḤOL HA-MO'ED: intermediate (semi-festive) days of Passover and Sukkot.

HOSHANA RABBAH: seventh day of the festival of Tabernacles.

IYYAR: second month of the Jewish religious calendar.

KABBALAH (KABBALISTIC): Jewish mystical tradition.

KADDISH: doxology chanted by the reader or mourners in public worship.

KARAITES: sect founded in 8th century CE rejecting the Oral Law.

KASHER: conforming to the Jewish dietary laws (*kashrut*).

KETUBBAH: Marriage contract.

KIDDUSH: "sanctification" blessing on Sabbaths and festivals.

KISLEV: ninth month of the Jewish religious calendar.

KOHEN (KOHANIM): Jew of priestly descent.

KOL NIDRÉ: formula recited on the eve of Day of Atonement.

LAG BA-OMER: Semi-holiday during the Omer period.

LEVIRATE MARRIAGE: marriage of childless widow with husband's brother

LIBERAL: see Reform.

MAFTIR: last portion of the Law read on Sabbaths, festivals, etc.

MA'ARIV: evening prayer service.

MAGEN DAVID: hexagram which became major Jewish symbol.

MAḤZOR: festival prayer book

MASKILIM: adherents of the Jewish Enlightenment (*Haskalah*).

MATSAH: Unleavened bread.

MARRANOS: descendants of Jews of Spain and Portugal who had been forcibly baptised but secretly observed Jewish rituals.

MASORAH (MASORETIC): body of traditions concerning Bible text.

MENORAH: Temple candelabrum which became major Jewish symbol.

MEZUZAH: Container carrying parchment scroll with Torah verses, affixed to doorposts.

MIDRASH (MIDRASHIM; MIDRASHIC): exposition of Scripture, both aggadic and halakhic.

MIKVEH: ritual bath.

MINHAG: local customs; prayer rite.

MINḤAH: afternoon prayer service.

MINYAN: prayer quorum of at least ten adult males.

MISHNAH (MISHNAIC): first rabbinic codification of the Oral Law.

MITNAGGEDIM (MITNAGDIC): "Opponents" of Ḥasidism.

MITSVAH (MITSVOT): religious commandment; honor allocated to a worshiper in synagogue.

MUSAF: additional prayer service.

NASI: President of Sanhedrin.

NE'ILAH: Concluding Service on the Day of Atonement.

NEOLOGY: Reform Jewish trend in Hungary.

NISAN: first month of the Jewish religious calendar.

NOVELLAE (Heb. *ḥiddushim*): rabbinic commentary deriving original conclusions.

OMER: period of semi-mourning between Passover and Shavu'ot.

ORAL LAW: Body of legal rules traditionally given by God to Moses and passed on from generation to generation.

ORTHODOX: subscribing to the beliefs and practices of traditional Judaism.

PHARISEES: Rabbinical movement in Mishnaic times.

PILGRIM FESTIVALS: Passover, Shavu'ot; and Sukkot.

PIYYUT (PIYYUTIM): liturgical poetry.

PROGRESSIVE: Term for Reform Judaism.

PURIM: Feast celebrating the deliverance of Persian Jewry.

RABBANITE: Rabbinical Jew, especially as opposed to Karaite.

RABBI: qualified teacher of Judaism (variants include Rav, Rabban, Reb, Rebbe).

RECONSTRUCTIONISM: movement in US Judaism regarding Judaism as a civilization.

REFORM: movement in Judaism advocating major departures from *halakhah* and traditional belief (also called Liberal).

RESPONSA: authoritative replies to halakhic questions.

RISHONIM: earlier rabbinic authorities.

ROSH HA-SHANAH: New Year Festival.

ROSH ḤODESH: new moon semi-festival.

SADDUCEES: movement of aristocrats and priests in Second Temple times.

SAGES: the early (tannaitic and amoraic) rabbis.

SAMARITANS: people in northern Israel (Samaria) who accepted Mosaic law.

SANHEDRIN: ancient Israel's supreme court.

SAVORAIM: Babylonian scholars in 6th century CE.

SECOND TEMPLE PERIOD: from Temple rebuilding (c.520) to its destruction in 70 CE.

SEDER: home service on Passover eve.

SEFER TORAH: Scroll of the Law.

SEFIROT: mystical concept of ten spheres or emanations through which God manifests Himself.

SEMIKHAH: rabbinic ordination.

SEPHARDI(M): Jew of Spanish-Portuguese tradition and descent.

SEPTUAGINT: first Greek translation of the Bible.

SHABBATEAN: adherent of the pseudo-messianic and heretical movement founded by Shabbetai Tsevi.

SHAḤARIT: morning prayer service.

SHAVU'OT: Festival of Weeks or Pentecost.

SHEḤITAH: ritual slaughter.

SHEKHINAH: the Divine Presence.

SHEMA: "Hear, O Israel" profession of Jewish faith.

SHEMINI ATSERET: festival that concludes Sukkot.

SHEVAT: eleventh month of the Jewish religious calendar.

SHOFAR: ceremonial ram's horn blown on the New Year and other solemn occasions.

SHULḤAN ARUKH: major codification of Jewish law.

SIDDUR: prayer book.

SIMḤAT TORAH: festival of the Rejoicing of the Law.

SIVAN: third month of the Jewish religious calendar.

SUKKOT: festival of Tabernacles, the "Feast of Booths".

TALLIT (TALLITOT): prayer shawl worn by Jewish males.

TALMUD (TALMUDIC): basic codification of Jewish law, comprising the Mishnah and the Gemara.

TALMUD TORAH: religious school.

TAMMUZ: fourth month of the Jewish religious calendar.

TANNA (TANNAIM; tannaitic): sage of the Mishnaic era.

TARGUM: Aramaic translation of Bible.

TEFILLIN: "phylacteries" worn at weekday morning prayers.

TEVET: tenth month of the Jewish religious calendar.

TISHAH BE-AV: Ninth of Av fast day commemorating the Temple's destruction.

TISHRI: seventh month of the Jewish religious calendar.

TORAH: the Pentateuch or Five Books of Moses; Jewish religious teaching in the widest sense.

TOSAFOT: comments on Talmud by successors of Rashi, 12th-14th century (tosafists).

TOSEFTA: collections of tannaitic traditions not found in Mishnah.

TSADDIK: Ḥasidic leader.

TSITSIT: fringes attached to prayer shawl or undergarment.

TU BI-SHEVAT: Semi-festival of New Year for the Trees.

YESHIVAH (YESHIVOT): Babylonian or Palestinian Academy; modern talmudical college.

YOM KIPPUR: Day of Atonement.

ZOHAR: principal work of Jewish mysticism.

AARON Elder brother of MOSES and younger brother of Miriam, whose levitical descent is recorded in the Bible (Ex. 6:16-20, Num. 26:58-59). Aaron was first divinely appointed to act as Moses' spokesman before Pharaoh and the Israelites at the time of the Exodus from Egypt. With his wondrous rod, he overcame Pharaoh's magicians and cast the first three devastating plagues on the Egyptians (Ex. 7-8); subsequently, during the battle with the Amalekites at Rephidim, Aaron and Hur provided Moses with vital support (Ex. 17:10-13). Once the Tabernacle had been constructed, Aaron and his sons became a hereditary priesthood, he himself assuming the office and dignity of Israel's HIGH PRIEST (Ex. 28-29, Lev. 8). Three major crises overshadowed his life: the controversial role that he played, during the absence of Moses, in acceding to the people's demand for a visible god by fashioning the GOLDEN CALF (Ex. 32); the loss of Nadab and Abihu, two of his four sons, after they provoked God's anger by offering "alien fire" in the Sanctuary (Lev. 10:1-2); and the rebellion fomented by Korah, a Levite cousin of Aaron, who aspired to replace him as High Priest (Num. 16). The Torah recounts the grim end of this rebellion and how Aaron's title was miraculously confirmed by the blossoming of his staff (Num. 16:32-35, 17:23-25). However, because of their disobedience at the Waters of Meribah, Aaron and Moses were doomed not to enter the Promised Land (Num. 20:7-13). Stripped of his vestments, which were then donned by Eleazar, his son and successor, Aaron "breathed his last" on Mount Hor (Num. 20:28).

Aaron, the High Priest. From an anthology of texts on the Bible, religion, grammar, astrology, etc. Northern France, c 1280.

The rabbis made Aaron an idealized spiritual figure — not remote and austere like Moses, but one close to the people who reconciled their differences and restored domestic peace. They portrayed Aaron as the biblical ideal of priesthood, a view that inspired Hillel's injunction: "Be a disciple of Aaron, loving peace and pursuing peace, loving your fellow creatures and attracting them to the Torah" (*Avot* 1.12). On the basis of a separate, mystical tradition, Aaron figures among the seven "invisible holy guests" (USHPIZIN) whom observant Jews welcome to their tabernacle on the festival of Sukkot.

ABBAHU (flourished 300 CE). Palestinian AMORA of the third generation, head of the Academy in Caesarea. His position, wealth, and knowledge of Greek made him the recognized spokesman of the Jewish community in Erets Israel before the Roman authorities. A disciple of R. JOHANAN BEN NAPPAḪA, whom he quotes frequently (as he does SIMEON BEN LAKISH), Abbahu was paid great deference by his colleagues. It was at this Academy that the first three tractates of the order *Nezikin* were compiled and later incorporated in the Jerusalem Talmud. Having been proclaimed the state religion of the Roman Empire, Christianity gained many Palestinian adherents in Abbahu's time. He engaged them in lively polemics, and significant aspects of his preaching were leveled against Christian doctrine. From their content, however, it is apparent that some of his polemics were directed not against Christians but against Jewish sectarians (see GNOSTICISM; MINIM). The Jerusalem Talmud records a number of decrees that he issued — enactments that were accepted throughout Erets Israel. As the official representative of the Jewish community, Abbahu traveled extensively both within the country and abroad. He is frequently quoted in the Jerusalem Talmud, occasionally in the Babylonian Talmud as well, and several famous aphorisms are credited to him, e.g., "Be among the persecuted, rather than the persecutors" (*BK* 93a) and "the place where repentant sinners stand the wholly righteous cannot attain" (*Ber.* 34b).

ABBAYÉ (c.280-338 CE). Babylonian AMORA of the fourth generation; together with RAVA, the most prominent of his time. Having lost both of his parents in infancy, Abbayé was raised by an uncle, RABBAH BAR NAH̱MANI, who put a devoted nurse in charge of his ward. Abbayé often quotes her folk wisdom and home remedies. His teachers were Rabbah and R. Joseph. The former was head of the Academy in Pumbedita, a position to which Abbayé eventually succeeded; from R. Joseph, noted for his broad familiarity with the traditions of the *tannaim* and *amoraim*, he received his knowledge of the sources. Abbayé laid greater stress on such knowledge than he did on mere casuistical skill, in which his colleague Rava excelled. From the NEH̱UTÉ Ravina and Rav Dimi he received the teachings of the *amoraim* of Erets Israel, particularly those of JOHANAN BEN NAPPAH̱A. Abbayé's halakhic controversies with Rava are to be found throughout the Talmud. Abbayé was known for his sterling moral character and mild disposition, of which many examples are related. When the *halakhah* was in doubt, he used to say: "Go out and see how people act in such situations" (*Ber.* 45a, etc.). Frequently, Abbayé quotes the popular proverbs current in his time, an indication that he was no sheltered recluse who lived in an ivory tower.

ABLUTIONS Ritual washings that range from immersion of the whole body (*tevilah*) to pouring water over the hands (*netilat yadayim*). The Torah (Lev. 11:30) prescribed total immersion in a natural spring, river, or MIKVEH (ritual bath) to cleanse persons or objects rendered unclean through direct or indirect contact with various sources of impurity (see PURITY AND IMPURITY). These include menstruation, seminal issue, contagious diseases such as gonorrhea and the various kinds of leprosy referred to in the Torah, as well as contact with a corpse or dead animal (Lev. 15:1-28; 22:1-6). Ablution had also to be performed by those attending services in the Temple on various festive and ceremonial occasions, for which they needed to be in a state of ritual purity. It was obligatory for PRIESTS before they officiated or partook of the consecrated food they received as offerings and tithes (Ex. 30:18-21). The HIGH PRIEST underwent five separate immersions on the holiest day of the Jewish year, as part of the Day of Atonement service in the Temple. In some cases, washing the hands and feet or merely the hands fulfilled the requirement.

Copper receptacle with a wide mouth and two handles for the ritual washing of the hands (netilat yadayim) *involving pouring water over the right hand and then over the left. Central Europe, 19th century.*

Since the suspension of the rite of the RED HEIFER, whose ashes were used in the waters of purification in the Temple, the following ablutions have remained in force: ritual immersion by women after their menstrual period or other vaginal discharge of blood and after childbirth; the purification of cooking utensils manufactured by non-Jews; ritual immersion by proselytes on their CONVERSION to Judaism; and washing of the hands before breaking bread (*mayim rishonim*; see GRACE BEFORE MEALS) and after rising from sleep or using the toilet. In all of these cases, immersion or ablution is accompanied by the appropriate benediction which the sages formulated. *Netilat yadayim*, the ablution performed before eating bread, must involve human effort — pouring water over the right hand and then over the left from a wide-mouthed, smooth-brimmed receptacle holding about half a pint. No blessing is required for certain other ablutions that are still practiced: washing a corpse before burial (*taharah*) and one's hands after leaving the cemetery; and washing the hands after touching parts of the body usually covered, after clipping nails and removing the shoes, before prayer and prior to GRACE AFTER MEALS (*Mayim Aẖaronim*) as well as before dipping the greens or *karpas* at the Passover SEDER (a relic of the purification in Temple times). Levites also wash the hands of priests without saying a benediction when the latter are about to recite the PRIESTLY BLESSING in synagogue. Others likewise practice immersion in the *mikveh* on the eve of the Day of Atonement and before Sabbaths and festivals, although the custom is mainly restricted to adherents of H̱ASIDISM. For ritual purposes, a laver is situated in the entrance hall of traditional synagogues.

Hygienic and sacramental considerations both figure in these rites. No ablution is valid unless the person or object involved has been made scrupulously clean beforehand, to insure that no barrier (*ẖatsitsah*) of foreign matter intervenes between the person or object and the purifying waters. Simi-

The Ten Commandments on a Torah Scroll shield. Austria, 1851.

אנכי ה
לאיהיה
לאתשא
זכור את
כבד את
לאתרצח
לאתנאף
לא תגנב
לאתענה
לאתחמד
שבת

וזאת
התורה אשר
שם משה לפני
בני ישראל אלה
החקים והמשפט
והתורת אשר נתן
ה בינו ובין בני

larly, when no water is available for washing the hands before bread, alternative cleaning material (even grass or sand) may be used. The benediction's wording is then changed from "washing the hands" (*al netilat yadayim*) to "making the hands clean" (*al nekiyyut yadayim*).

In the Second Temple period, a number of Jewish sects laid particular emphasis on ritual ablution. These sects included the Hemerobaptists ("morning bathers"), the ESSENES, and the Qumran community (see DEAD SEA SCROLLS AND SECT). It is likely that John the Baptist was close to one of these ascetic groups, and from him the custom of baptism passed into Christianity.

ABOAB, ISAAC (late 14th cent.). Talmudic scholar and preacher who lived in Spain. Aboab is famous for his *Menorat ha-Ma'or* ("Candlestick of Light"), a classic of Jewish religious-moralistic literature. Over 75 editions have been printed since 1514, and the work has been translated into Spanish, Judeo-Spanish, Yiddish, German, and (in part) English. *Menorat ha-Ma'or* was part of a trilogy, but the other two sections, *Aron ha-Edut* ("The Ark of the Testimony") and *Shulḥan ha-Panim* ("Table of Showbread"), have been lost. One of the author's purposes in writing *Menorat ha-Ma'or* was to arrange the AGGADAH systematically for his own preaching. The book became a standard text for preachers and was also read publicly in synagogue.

Following the seven branched lampstand or MENORAH in the Tabernacle (Num. 4:9), Aboab divided his work into seven *nerot* ("lamps") which are further subdivided. The general arrangement is based on three phrases of Ps. 34:15 which are used as headings: (1) "Depart from evil," (2) "Do good," and (3) "Seek peace and pursue it." *Menorat ha-Ma'or* deals with such subjects as avoidance of jealousy, lust, and ambition; adherence to the precepts of circumcision, prayer, honoring parents, charity, and justice; Torah study, penitence, and humility. The author's chief aim was to inspire the masses. He therefore presented the moral and religious truths of Judaism in a popular form through excerpts of beautiful rabbinic sayings and maxims. Inclined toward both philosophy and mysticism, Aboab combines the teachings of MAIMONIDES (whom he often quotes) with certain ideas drawn from the Kabbalah. He also acknowledges the value of non-Jewish wisdom, quoting Plato and Aristotle.

Menorat ha-Ma'or was likewise the title of an ethical work by Israel ben Joseph Al-Nakawa, a contemporary of Aboab. Other members of the Aboab family later distinguished themselves as scholars and preachers, among them **Isaac Aboab da Fonseca** (1605-1693), who as *Ḥakham* of Pernambuco, Dutch Brazil, was the first rabbi in the New World.

ABORTION Four considerations of Jewish law are involved in induced abortion. The most severe consideration is that abortion may involve the prohibition against murder, although it is not regarded as a capital crime. This is so if the foetus is viewed by the *halakhah* as a living being. The Talmudic sources are not conclusive; see Rashi (*San.* 72b) and *Tos. Nid.* 44a, which seem to indicate that the unborn child is not considered as a living being. Additional considerations include the prohibition against inflicting bodily injury, the prohibition against the destruction of human seed, and the prohibition against causing financial or property damage. The father has a property interest in his offspring, and if someone strikes a woman and causes her to miscarry, he would be required to pay pecuniary compensation to the father (Ex. 21:22). All rabbinic authorities agree that for social or economic reasons alone, abortion is contrary to Jewish law.

However, if a woman's life is endangered by the pregnancy the abortion is permitted. The Mishnah (*Ohol.* 7.6) explicitly states that it is permissible to sacrifice a foetus in order to save the mother's life because the life of the mother takes precedence over the life of the unborn child. While most rabbinic authorities will consider permitting an abortion only when the mother's life is endangered, some permit an abortion if it is ascertained that the foetus suffers a severe malformation or genetic disease, such as Tay-Sachs Disease. Others permit an abortion if continuation of the pregnancy would affect the mother's mental health. Furthermore, a lenient position is taken if the foetus is less than 41 days old, since the Talmud asserts that a foetus is not formed until after that period.

ABRAHAM Father of the Jewish people, first of the three PATRIARCHS, son of Terah. As listed in the Book of Genesis, there were ten generations from Adam to Noah and ten from Noah to Abraham. According to Jewish tradition, he was born in the year 1948 after creation (corresponding to 1812 BCE). At first his name was Abram (i.e., "the Father is exalted") but he was subsequently renamed Abraham which the Bible explains as "father of many nations" (Gen. 17:5). His father originally lived in the southern Mesopotamian city, Ur of the Chaldees, but moved to Haran in northwestern Mesopotamia (Gen. 11:31). After Terah's death, God told the 75-year-old Abraham to move with his family — including his wife SARAH — "to the land which I will show you," namely, the Land of CANAAN. God also promised to make him into a great nation, a blessing for all the families of the earth (Gen. 12:1-3).

Abraham's event-filled life included much wandering. After a period in Canaan, the clan was forced to escape a famine and journeyed to Egypt. Later they returned to Canaan but an argument between the shepherds of Abraham and those of his nephew, Lot, culminated in a split, with Abraham settling near Hebron and Lot in the Dead Sea area. When Lot was taken prisoner by invaders, Abraham came to his rescue. Despite this warlike episode, Abraham is depicted essentially as a peaceful herdsman. The Divine

Two Torah Scrolls cases of the 19th century: on the right, in painted wood, from India; on the left, in wood with silver plaques, from Iran.

Map of Abraham's travels by the cartographer Abraham Ortelius. The twenty-two vignettes surrounding the map show the major events of the Patriarch's life, from the time he left Haran to his death. Beginning at the top right, clockwise: Abraham leaves Mesopotamia with his family; God promises Abraham to make him into a great nation; the Patriarch builds an altar to the Lord; God appears and promises Abraham the Land of Canaan; he sets out to Lot's rescue; upon his return, he is greeted by Melchizedek, the king of Salem; God renews his promise to Abraham; the three angels predict that Sarah will bear him a son; the birth of Isaac; Hagar and Ishmael are banished; the covenant with Abimelech; the supreme test: God orders the sacrifice of Isaac; Sarah's death and burial; the marriage of Isaac and Rebekah; Abraham's burial in the Cave of Machpelah at Hebron, next to Sarah. From Additamentum IV Thiatri orbus terrarum, *Antwerp 1590.*

promise of the Land to Abraham is reiterated in a COVENANT ceremony (Gen. 15:7-21). He is also instructed to circumcise himself as a sign of the covenant between him and God, binding on all his male descendants.

When Abraham was in his eighties and Sarah was still childless, she offered her handmaiden HAGAR to Abraham as a concubine, and Ishmael was born of this union. However, he was not regarded as a full heir. Abraham was reassured by God that he would still have a son by Sarah and, when Abraham was 100 and Sarah 90, she bore ISAAC, who was to become his heir, materially and spiritually. After the child had grown, God put Abraham to a supreme test, demanding that he sacrifice Isaac as a burnt-offering on Mount Moriah (Gen. 22:1-2). Abraham was prepared to obey, but at the last moment an angel prevented the sacrifice (see AKEDAH). When Abraham died at the age of 175, he was buried by his two sons in the Cave of Machpelah at Hebron, which he had purchased as a burial place for Sarah.

Rabbinic legend (the AGGADAH) has much to say of Abraham. He was the father of MONOTHEISM, the first person to recognize the existence of the One God, using only his reasoning to come to this conclusion. Once he became convinced of the truth of his belief, Abraham smashed all the idols which his pagan father had manufactured. In order to crush this blatant rebellion against the established order, Nimrod, the Mesopotamian ruler, had Abraham thrown into a fiery furnace, from which he emerged unscathed. Jewish tradition regards Abraham as the epitome of HOSPITALITY and of *ḥesed*, loving regard for others. Traditionally, he instituted the Morning Service.

ABRAHAM BEN DAVID OF POSQUIÈRES (known by the acronym *Ravad*; c.1125-c.1198). French talmudist. A native of Provence and a pupil of Moses ben Joseph of Narbonne and Meshullam ben Jacob of Lunel, Ravad was one of the most important talmudists of his era. A man of wealth, possibly a textile merchant, he supported all the needy students in the *yeshivah* which he established at Posquières, near Nîmes. Famous for his critical glosses (*hassagot*) on ALFASI's legal code, on the *Sefer ha-Ma'or* of GERONDI, and especially on the *Mishneh Torah* of MAIMONIDES, he was known as *ba'al hassagot*, i.e., the critic *par excellence*. He criticized Maimonides belligerently for not giving any explanations or sources in his code of law, and his opposition to codification helped to prevent the Talmud from becoming merely a code. Acquainted also with philosophy, Ravad opposed Maimonides' attempt to construct a system of dogmas in Judaism.

In his commentary on the Mishnah, of which that on two tractates only has survived, Ravad explained obscure passages which are not dealt with in the Talmud. Only a few of his responsa, collected in a work entitled *Temim De'im* ("Perfect in Knowledge"), have likewise been preserved. His commentary on the SIFRA, the tannaitic Midrash on Leviticus, is also extant. Ravad's learning and piety were much admired by Naḥmanides, while Menaḥem Meiri described him as one of the greatest of the commentators. Among his disciples in Posquières were Isaac Ha-Kohen of Narbonne, the first commentator on the Jerusalem Talmud, and Abraham ben Nathan of Lunel, author of *Ha-Manhig*.

ABRAVANEL (ABRABANEL), ISAAC BEN JUDAH (1437-1508). Statesman, Bible commentator, and philosopher. A financier and diplomat, Abravanel was the treasurer of Alfonso V of Portugal; after the latter's death, however, he was falsely accused of conspiracy and in 1483 fled to Toledo, where he entered the service of Ferdinand and Isabella. When he failed in his attempt to reverse the edict expelling the Jews from Spain, he headed the Spanish Jews who went into exile (1492). Settling in Naples, he was again called into royal service. Further misfortunes drove him to Sicily, Corfu, Monopoli, and finally to Venice, where he negotiated a commercial treaty with Portugal.

A pupil of Joseph Ḥayyun, the rabbi of Lisbon, Abravanel was well versed in both talmudic and secular learning. In his lengthy commentary on the Pentateuch and Prophets, he utilizes the works of classical authors and Christian exegetes, also revealing a profound distrust of monarchy. Abravanel was the first Jewish scholar to write introductions to the biblical books and to preface each section with a number of questions or "doubts" which he then attempts to solve, a method borrowed from the Christian scholar Alfonso Tostado. Influenced by Renaissance stress on clarity of expression, he points out faults of style and language in Jeremiah and Ezekiel. His Bible commentaries tend to be diffuse, verbose, and repetitive. Unlike other commentators, who inclined to explain the text verse by verse, Abravanel

Page from an illustrated Haggadah *with a commentary (appearing in smaller letters on the right) by Isaac Abravanel. Central Europe, 1741.*

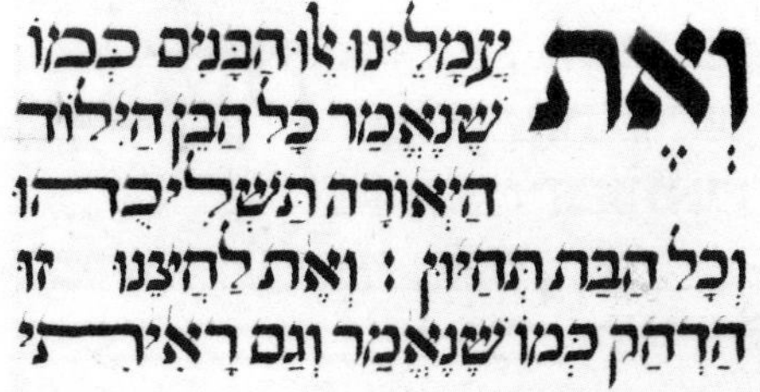
פירוש אברבנל

ואת עמלינו אלו הבנים כמו שנאמר כל הבן הילוד היאורה תשליכהו וכל הבת תחיון : ואת לחצנו זו הדחק כמו שנאמר וגם ראיתי

prefers long dissertations. His approach is primarily rational and philosophical, and he was the first Jewish commentator to adduce social and political factors for an understanding of the Bible.

By the age of 20, Abravanel had completed his first philosophical work, *Ateret Zekenim* ("The Crown of the Elders"), which discusses Divine providence. His *Rosh Amanah* ("The Principles of Faith") defends Maimonides' 13 Principles of Faith against the criticism of Ḥasdai Crescas and Joseph Albo, but he asserts that there are no dogmas in Judaism and that one must believe in the entire Torah with all its precepts and commandments. In order to console those of his fellow Jews who had borne the expulsion and to strengthen their faith in the coming of the Messiah, Abravanel wrote a trilogy comprising *Ma'ayañe ha-Yeshu'ah* ("Wells of Salvation"), *Yeshu'ot Meshiḇo* ("The Salvation of His Anointed"), and *Mashmi'a Yeshu'ah* ("The Announcer of Salvation"). Daring in his attack on the messiahship of Jesus and opposing renegade Jews who treated the Messiah's coming allegorically, Abravanel insisted that the times demanded a living Redeemer whose arrival he anticipated in the year 1503. His other works include commentaries on *Avot*, on the Passover *Haggadah*, and on Maimonides' *Guide to the Perplexed.*

The stateman's eldest son, **Judah Abravanel** (c.1460-c.1535), known in Italy as Leone Ebreo, was the author of a vastly influential philosophical work entitled *Dialoghi di Amore* (1535), modeled on the Platonic dialogues, in which God is identified with Love.

ABULAFIA, ABRAHAM BEN SAMUEL (1240-after 1291). Spanish Kabbalist. When Abulafia was 20, he decided to leave Spain to locate the legendary SAMBATYON river, beyond which, by tradition, the TEN TRIBES still live. While in Italy, he became involved in philosophy, but this stage did not last long, and he moved on to KABBALAH. His specialty was dealing with the mystical significance of letters and GEMATRIA equivalents of words, for he believed that the different combinations of letters and words encompassed within themselves the forces of creation. Abulafia lived an ascetic life, and believed that God had appeared to him. Later, he predicted that the messianic era would begin in the year 1290. In this capacity, he decided that he would convert the Pope, Nicholas III, to Judaism. The Pope had Abulafia imprisoned and brought to Rome, but the Pope's sudden death enabled Abulafia to escape the harsh penalty that had been in store for him. Little is known of his later years, in which he continually wandered, and there is no information as to where he died and under what circumstances. Abulafia regarded his own kabbalism, which combined the esoteric with the rational, as the logical continuation of the philosophical views of Maimonides to whom he ascribed mystical tendencies. His kabbalism was later one of the bases of the 16th century kabbalism of the Safed school.

Illustration from Abraham Abulafia's major work Or ha-Sekhel *("The Light of Intellect"). Manuscript, Italy, 14th century. Vatican Library.*

ACADEMIES The original schools of higher Jewish learning, established in Erets Israel and Babylonia, where both the written Torah and the ORAL LAW were expounded by the rabbinical sages. The earliest recorded mention of systematic "instruction" or "houses of learning" occurs in the Apocrypha (Ecclus. 51.16, 23, 29), where the term "sitting" (Heb. *yeshivah*) is equated with the BET MIDRASH or "house of study" (cf. *Avot.* 2.7). Owing to its seating arrangements, *yeshivah* became the standard designation for a rabbinical Academy (see below); *metivta* was its Aramaic equivalent in Babylonia (*Yev.* 105b).

The rabbis affirmed that such Academies were already in existence during the period of the ZUGOT (scholarly "pairs"; second cent. BCE-early first cent. CE), one of whom served as NASI (Patriarch or president of the Academy) and the other as *av bet din* (head of the great BET DIN or high court). The SANHEDRIN of 71 members which originally held its sessions on the Temple Mount served not only as a high court, but also as a center of rabbinic learning and discussion (i.e., as an Academy or *bet midrash*: TJ *Bétsah* 2.4; *Mid.* 5.4).

Palestinian (Erets Israel) Academies

There is little evidence of organized rabbinic (tannaitic) instruction outside Jerusalem prior to the destruction of the Temple in 70 CE. A minor Academy may nevertheless have been founded in Jabneh (Yavneh), a town lying some 25 miles to the west of Jerusalem. According to the *aggadah*, when the Romans were besieging Jerusalem, R. JOHANAN BEN ZAKKAI arranged to have himself smuggled out of the city in a coffin and brought before Vespasian, the Roman commander. Knowing R. Johanan to be a moderate, Vespasian was prepared to grant his request — "Give me Yavneh and its sages!" (*Git.* 56b).

Johanan proceeded to make Yavneh the first and central point in a network of Academies spreading from Erets Israel to Nisibis in Babylonia and even to Rome. The Academy of Yavneh, both in structure and functions, took the lost Great Sanhedrin of Jerusalem as its model. Other Academies flourished under Johanan ben Zakkai's immediate disciples, notably ELIEZER BEN HYRCANUS (at Lydda) and JOSHUA BEN ḤANANIAH (at Peki'in); later also under AKIVA (Bené Berak), Ḥananiah ben Teradyon (Sikhnin), YOSÉ BEN ḤALAFTA (Sepphoris), and others, down to the Patriarch JUDAH HA-NASI (Beth She'arim). Eleazar ben Arakh founded an Academy at Emmaus, but it had to close for lack of students. R. Akiva, however, a towering and legendary figure, is said to have drawn thousands to his Academy at Bené Berak.

The devastation of central and southern Palestine, as a result of Bar Kokhba's unsuccessful rebellion against the Romans (132-135 CE), led to the dispersal of many scholars, some to Babylonia. A period of reconsolidation began with the Yavneh Academy's transfer to Usha in Galilee (c. 140), this northern region of Erets Israel providing a sanctuary for additional schools and sages. The original Yavneh Academy moved from Usha to Sepphoris (c. 200), with Judah ha-Nasi as its president, and there the MISHNAH was redacted; ultimately this *yeshivah* was relocated in Tiberias (c.235).

The succeeding era was that of the amoraic or talmudic rabbis and their Academies. Tiberias became the central "workshop" of the Jerusalem (or Palestinian) TALMUD. Despite one long period of inactivity (c. 400-520 CE), its Academy managed to survive until a century after the Arab conquest in the seventh century. The remaining Academies of Erets Israel — Lydda, Caesarea, and Sepphoris — all vanished by the end of the fourth century.

In the talmudic period, the functions and authority of the Academy were varied. Together with his senior colleagues, the head of the Academy formed a supreme court of law before which actual cases were tried and decisions handed down. The head of the Academy likewise conferred rabbinical ORDINATION (*semikhah*) on deserving students, and until the Jewish calendar was permanently fixed in 359 he determined the beginning of the New MOON (Rosh Ḥodesh) and the intercalation of a leap year.

As the supreme religious authority of both Palestinian and Diaspora Jewry, the Patriarch would from time to time send messengers, to convey religious instruction to the communities of Erets Israel and Babylonia, and also to raise funds on behalf of the Academies and their students. The amounts received were hardly sufficient for the needs of the hundreds of scholars who, with few exceptions, had to earn their livelihood either as artisans or as farmers, and sessions of the Academy were therefore often held in the evening.

One exclusive right of the Patriarch, exercised later by heads of the Academies, was to enact decrees (see TAKKANAH). These were designed to provide for new situations that had not been covered by existing traditional law. Scholars of the Academies likewise reserved the right to issue prohibitive decrees as a "fence around the law" (see GEZERAH).

From the third century CE, scholars "went down" to Babylonia, where they transmitted the teachings of the rabbis of Erets Israel to colleagues and students in the Diaspora (see NEḤUTÉ). This activity proved especially vital as Jewish life and culture in the Holy Land suffered increasingly from the intolerance of Byzantine Christian rulers. Anti-Jewish measures led to emigration, the closing of Academies, and the abolition of the Patriarchate in 425.

Shortly after the arrival of Mar Zutra III from Babylonia, the Academy of Tiberias reopened its doors in 520. It survived there until 740, when its operations were transferred to Jerusalem, which had been under Arab Muslim rule since 638. The Seljuk conquest (1071), followed by that of the Crusaders (1099), sealed the fate of Jerusalem's revived Academy. Well before the 11th century, however, the Academies of Erets Israel had been eclipsed by those of Babylonia.

Babylonian Academies

Despite the lack of conclusive evidence, it seems probable that in the first century BCE there were already schools of higher learning in Babylonia. The *tanna* Judah ben Bathyra I may have established an Academy in Nisibis during the last days of the Temple (*Pes.* 3b). Ḥananiah, a nephew of Joshua ben Ḥananiah, taught in Nehar Pekod, where he usurped the authority of Erets Israel by announcing New Moon dates and fixing leap years. This high-handed action was nullified, however, by students of R. Akiva who found a temporary refuge in Babylonia after the suppression of Bar Kokhba's revolt.

Under Rav Shila and Abba bar Abba, the Academy of Nehardea was Babylonian Jewry's spiritual center around 200 CE, contact being maintained with Judah ha-Nasi and the Jewish community of Erets Israel. This Palestinian influence strengthened with the return of RAV (Abba Arikha), who had obtained his rabbinic ordination from Judah ha-Nasi. The new Academy which Rav founded at Sura (c.220) was destined to overshadow Nehardea and to remain active for nearly 800 years. Thanks to Rav's reputation as a scholar, it attracted well over 1,000 full-time students and revitalized Jewish learning throughout Babylonia. Rav's contemporary, SAMUEL (Mar), headed the older Academy of

Nehardea, and these two men dominated the first generation of Babylonian *amoraim*. Samuel often deferred to Rav, and it was at Sura that most tractates of the Babylonian Talmud were edited.

Like the Academies of Erets Israel which served as their model, the Babylonian Academies had a dual function: each was simultaneously a study center, a *bet midrash* for the interpretation of Jewish law, and a *bet din* (law court) that tried both religious and civil cases.

Since both teachers and students were unpaid and had to earn a livelihood, those heading the Academies lectured in the early hours of the morning and at night, thus allowing time for students to do their homework and prepare themselves for the next session (*Shab.* 136b). Anyone could be enrolled and at any age, but the highest qualifications were required to be admitted as a teacher. As in Erets Israel, the president of an Academy was voted into office by its scholars, his title being *rosh (ha-)yeshivah* ("head of the session," *Ber.* 57a), but each appointment had to be ratified by the Babylonian EXILARCH. No separate classes were held, all sessions taking place in one lecture hall with the head of the Academy standing on a platform and students occupying rows of seats in front of him, sometimes as many as 24 (*BK* 117a; *Meg.* 28b). Twice a year, during the months of Elul and Adar, thousands of people would gather at one of the Academies to study a talmudic tractate under the *rosh yeshivah's* direction (see KALLAH months).

The Nehardea Academy was destroyed in 259, by Palmyran allies of Rome. Under Samuel's pupil and successor, Judah bar Ezekiel (c. 220-299), it was restored in Pumbedita, where it remained until the ninth century. From then until as late as the 13th century it functioned in Baghdad. Sura flourished especially during the long presidency of Rav ASHI (376-427), under whom it was transferred to Mata Meḫasya.

Several factors combined to promote the ascendancy of the Babylonian Academies in the post-talmudic age, when (from 589) each presiding scholar bore the title of GAON ("Eminence" or "Excellency"). Jewish communities throughout the Diaspora directed their questions to the *ge'onim* of Sura or, in some instances, to those of Pumbedita. This gave rise to the RESPONSA literature, which included not only queries about ritual practice but questions regarding theology, Bible, liturgy, and the interpretation of passages in the Talmud as well. Thanks also to the *ge'onim*, a series of Jewish legal codes reduced the HALAKHAH to a practical guide, unencumbered by talmudic debate. Among these were the *Halakhot Pesukot* attributed to Yehudai Gaon (c. 760) and the HALAKHOT GEDOLOT (c. 825) of later authorship.

There were frequent clashes of authority between the exilarch and the *gaon*. Another source of friction, between the Academies of Sura and Pumbedita, concerned the division of funds for their support which were received from abroad. A question addressed to a *gaon* from the Diaspora would normally be accompanied by a sum of money intended for the students of the Academy and for himself. Ultimately, the problem was solved by making two regions out of the Diaspora and dividing the funds accordingly between Sura and Pumbedita.

The growth of Jewish communities in the medieval West (Spain, Italy, France, and Germany), led by native scholars who had often been trained in the Babylonian Academies, brought about a decline in the prestige and influence of these schools. Western communities gradually ceased turning to the *ge'onim* for instruction and guidance. Before its final eclipse, however, the Academy of Pumbedita had the good fortune to be led by SHERIRA GAON and his son, HAI GAON (998-1038), who brought the Academy to a final period of glory.

For the later Academies, see YESHIVOT.

ACADEMY ON HIGH (Heb. *Yeshivah shel Ma'lah*). Rabbinic concept of an assembly in heaven comprising the souls of all who studied or expounded Torah on earth; they are joined there by the souls of other scholars and righteous people who acquired outstanding merit in this life. There are several references to the *Yeshivah shel Ma'lah* in both Talmud and Midrash (e.g., *Pes.* 53b), where the sages are placed according to their rank and angels are often also included, under the presidency of God. In most respects, the Academy on High parallels the tribunals (SANHEDRIN or BET DIN) on earth, yet the latter's decisions may override those of the former since the Torah "is not in heaven" (*BM* 59b). A phrase used in connection with RABBAH BAR NAḤMANI, that he "was summoned by the Academy on High" (*BM* 86a), became a traditional euphemism for the death of the righteous. A familiar survival of this concept is in the formula recited before KOL NIDRÉ on the eve of the Day of Atonement, citing the permission of both the heavenly and the earthly "tribunals" for prayers to be said with "transgressors."

ACROSTICS Composition, usually poetic, in which sets of letters spell out words or names or appear in a special order. In Hebrew liturgical poetry the lines often begin with successive letters of the Hebrew alphabet or include them in some different order, or spell out the author's name. This ancient literary style finds expression in the Bible (Ps. 111-112, Lam. 1-2), sometimes with the omission of one letter (Ps. 37, 145), and attains its most elaborate form in Ps. 119, where all 22 stanzas are made up of alphabetical verses in the proper sequence. The purpose of this acrostic technique (*notarikon*) was to supply a useful mnemonic, which was of particular value before printing when prayer books were not readily available. A similar didactic aim, employing the alphabetical order in reverse, appears in the *Tikkanta Shabbat* prayer of the Sabbath Additional Service.

Acrostics were much used in liturgical poetry (PIYYUT) of the Middle Ages (e.g., AN'IM ZEMIROT), and especially in the

Acrostics from an initial word-panel for a liturgical poem for Shavu'ot, from a prayer book with commentary. Southern Germany, c. 1320.

Kabbalah. A number of the popular songs and hymns which conclude the Passover *Seder* (e.g., ADDIR HU) follow this old alphabetical system. Elsewhere, acrostics serve to preserve the author's name — that of Mordecai in the *Ḥanukkah* hymn, MA'OZ TSUR, for example, or of Solomon (Shelomoh Ha-Levi) Alkabets in the Sabbath eve hymn, LEKHAH DODI.

A related technique, much employed since medieval times, is the use of acronyms (*rashé tevot*), whereby the initial letters of a name or title are combined to form a word which is used as a standard abbreviation. Some outstanding examples are RASHI (Rabbi Shelomoh Yitsḥaki), Rambam (Rabbi Mosheh ben Maimon or MAIMONIDES), Ramban (Rabbi Mosheh ben Naḥman or NAḤMANIDES), and Ha-Ari (Ashkenazi Rabbi Yitsḥak or Isaac LURIA) or certain acronyms of books by which their author became known. Rabbi Isaiah HOROWITZ is generally called "Shelah" after his book *Shené Luḥot ha-Berit*.

ADAM AND EVE The first couple, progenitors of mankind, whose creation is initially described in Gen. 1:26-30, which relates that God created man — both male and female — in His own image and likeness, endowing mankind with fertility and the power to dominate all other living creatures. Chapters 2-3 of Genesis give a more detailed account of man's creation. First, he is made from the dust of the earth (or ground, Heb. *adamah*) and life is breathed into him; then he is placed in the Garden of EDEN, which it will be his responsibility to tend. God authorizes him to eat all the fruit in the garden, except that on the Tree of Knowledge (of good and evil), for eating that fruit will result in his death. Seeing that "it is not good for man to be alone," God casts a deep sleep on him, takes one of his ribs, and fashions it into a woman — destined to become his "fitting helper." Tempted by the serpent, however, the woman samples the forbidden fruit of the Tree of Knowledge and gives some to her husband. Once having eaten it, the two of them realize that they are naked and proceed to make themselves loincloths out of fig leaves. Confronted with their disobedience, the man blames his wife and she the serpent, and God ordains punishment for all three of them. Only at this juncture is the man (*ha-adam*) specifically named Adam (Gen. 3:17), while he names the woman — his wife — Eve (Heb. Ḥavvah), "mother of all the living" (3:20).

God tells Adam that he will henceforth earn his bread only through toiling "by the sweat of his brow," while Eve is made subject to her husband and condemned to the pangs of childbearing. Eve bears two sons, CAIN AND ABEL, a third son named Seth compensating for Abel when the latter is murdered by Cain.

Various explanations have been proposed for the discrepancies between the two accounts of man's creation given in Genesis. Scholars who accept the Documentary Hypothesis attribute the appearance of twin stories to two distinct sources that were later joined together. More conservative Bible scholars regard the latter story of Adam's creation (Gen. 2) as a detailed elaboration of the previous account. From the Jewish perspective, the story of Adam and Eve explains the intrusion of evil into a world which the Creator had pronounced "very good" (Gen. 1:31); but man's "fall from grace" makes it necessary for him to redeem himself in God's eyes and is very different from the Christian doctrine of "original sin," which insists that man's lost perfection can only be restored through the advent and self-sacrifice of Jesus, the "second Adam."

There are numerous references to Adam and Eve in both the Pseudepigrapha and midrashic literature, the former incorporating a complete work called the *Book of the Life of Adam and Eve*. According to the Midrash (Gen. R. 8.5), God consulted the angels before man's creation was finalized. Some were in favor because of his good qualities, while others were opposed because of his evil propensities. Having secured a majority for His design, the Creator saw that it was implemented. Legends about man's creation are scattered through ancient Near Eastern traditions, but while there are some similarities to the biblical account, the ethical element is lacking (see CREATION AND COSMOLOGY). Many Jewish philosophers tended to allegorize the story of Adam and Eve. In the two separate biblical accounts PHILO detected the creation of two separate beings: an immortal heavenly man fashioned in God's image and his earthly counterpart, the summit of human perfection, who brought about his own mortality. MAIMONIDES, however, saw only one primal man gifted with a developed intellect whose willfulness turned him to the acquisition of practical (rather than theoretical) wisdom. Joseph ALBO made Adam symbolic of mankind,

Eden of the world, the Tree of Life equivalent to the Torah, and the serpent a personification of the evil inclination. In the Kabbalah, Philo's heavenly man reappears as the mystical ADAM KADMON.

RABBINIC VIEWS OF ADAM AND EVE

Adam's dust was gathered from all parts of the world.

A single man was brought forth at creation, indicating that to destroy one human life is to destroy a whole world and to preserve one life is to preserve a whole world, so that no man should ever say to another: "My father was superior to yours!" God's greatness was thereby established, for when a human being uses one die to stamp coins, all of them emerge alike; yet when God stamps men with the die of Adam, each of them is in some way different. Thus all have the right to say: "The world was created for my sake!"

Adam was created from the dust, and Eve from Adam; but henceforth it will be in God's image only — not man without woman, nor woman without man, and neither without the Divine Presence.

A heretic said to Rabban Gamaliel: "Your God is a thief, for is it not written that He caused Adam to fall asleep and then stole one of his ribs?" Gamaliel's daughter promptly told this heretic that she was sending for the police, as thieves had stolen a silver jug from the house, leaving a golden one in its place. "I wouldn't mind such thieves breaking into my house!" said the heretic, to which Gamaliel's daughter replied: "Then why criticize our God? If He took a rib from Adam, it was only to enrich him with a helpmate!"

ADAM KADMON ("primeval man"). Kabbalistic term, known especially for the symbolism of the ZOHAR, expressing the anthropomorphic conception of Jewish mysticism of the divine realm. The divine-emanated hypostases, the SEFIROT, are described symbolically as comprising a huge human-like figure: The three upper ones, *Keter* (crown), *Ḥokhmah* (wisdom) and *Binah* (intelligence), are the head of this figure; *Ḥesed* (love) is the right hand, *Din* (judgment) — the left (and this hand is also the source of earthly evil), *Tiferet* (beauty) is the body or heart, *Netsaḥ* (endurance) — the right leg, *Hod* (majesty) — the left, and *Yesod* (foundation) — the male organ. The feminine element in the divine realm, *Malkhut* (kingdom) or the SHEKHINAH (divine presence), is depicted as a parallel female body.

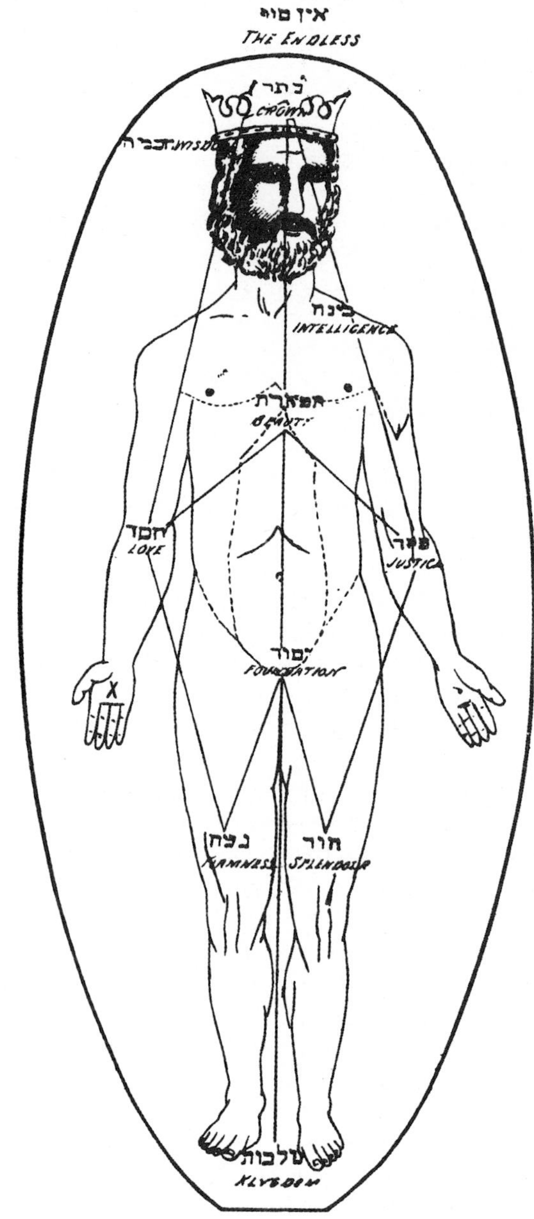

A representation of Adam Kadmon *in* The Kabbalah *by Christian Ginsburg, 1925.*

The concept of *Adam Kadmon* is the Kabbalah's mystical interpretation of the *imago dei* — the creation of Man in the form of God (Gen. 1:26). The figure itself is first presented in a Jewish mystical work in the ancient *Shi'ur Komah* text which belongs to the HEKHALOT and *Merkabah* mysticism, in which the Creator's limbs are described, their names listed, and their gigantic measurements presented. This mystical symbolism is based on the anthropomorphic interpretation of the verses in Song of Songs 5:10-16, where the "lover" is understood to be God Himself. Medieval Kabbalah used extensively the *Shi'ur Komah* symbolism, which may have had some roots in Jewish mystical speculations of the Second Temple period.

Various kabbalists in the Middle Ages and early modern times used this symbol in different ways, some emphasizing its mythical-anthropomorphic meaning and some moderating its mythical impact, using it for the hidden realms within the Godhead.

ADAR (Akkadian: *Addaru*). Twelfth month of the Jewish religious CALENDAR; sixth month of the Hebrew civil year counting from TISHRI. A second month of Adar is included in a leap year (see below). Normally, however, Adar is a month of 29 days coinciding with February-March. Its sign of the zodiac, Pisces the Fishes, was considered by the rabbis unusually propitious. Under its Babylonian name of Adar, this month is several times mentioned in the Bible (Est. 3:7, 13, 8:12, 9:1, etc.; Ezra 6:15) and the Apocrypha (esp. II Macc. 15.36), chiefly because of its many historical associations.

On the third day of the month, with Persian royal assent, the rebuilt Temple in Jerusalem was solemnly dedicated (Ezra 6:14-16). Traditionally, 7 Adar marks the birth and death of Moses (*Meg.* 13b); a minor fast on this date is still observed by Jewish BURIAL SOCIETY officers to atone for any acts of disrespect which they may unwittingly have committed toward the dead. The major holiday in the month is the festival of PURIM on 14 Adar; in Jerusalem and ancient walled cities it is observed on the following day, known as Shushan Purim.

In a leap year, there is a first Adar (Heb. *Adar Rishon*) consisting of 30 days and a second Adar (Heb. *Adar Sheni* or *Ve-Adar*) of 29. All the events commemorated in a regular month are then transferred to the second Adar, including Purim. However, in this case a meager foretaste of Purim known as Purim Katan (the "Minor Purim") is observed on the same dates in Adar I. Leap year complications are overcome by the generally accepted halakhic rule that a BAR MITSVAH or BAT MITSVAH is celebrated in the second Adar while YAHRZEIT and KADDISH observances are held in the first.

Mainly because of Purim, this is a uniquely joyous month in the religious calendar, inspiring the rabbinic dictum that "when Adar comes in, rejoicing is increased" (*Ta'an.* 29a). Judah Maccabee's defeat of the Syrian general Nicanor was originally celebrated as a minor festival on 13 Adar (I Macc. 7.49), this "Day of Nicanor" being specifically mentioned in the Apocrypha as occurring immediately before Purim, "the day of Mordecai" (II Macc. 15.36). In time, however, it gave way to the Fast of Esther (see FASTING AND FAST DAYS), now observed on the same date.

ADDIR BI-MELUKHAH ("Mighty in Kingship"). Alphabetical acrostic hymn, first mentioned in the 13th century, which Ashkenazim chant toward the end of their Passover SEDER ritual. Each of the eight stanzas mentions two Divine attributes and one class of angelic praise; the hymn, also known from its refrain as *Ki Lo Na'eh* ("For to Him praise is becoming"), was inspired by a Midrash (Gen. R. 6.2). In the medieval Franco-German rite, *Addir bi-Melukhah* may have been recited on the first *Seder* night and ADDIR HU, on the second; however, both have long been sung on the two nights. The composer's identity is uncertain, but he probably lived in France or Germany.

ADDIR HU ("Mighty is He"). Alphabetical acrostic hymn of uncertain authorship, probably composed in 14th-century Germany; one of the popular songs which Ashkenazim sing in chorus on Passover eve after completing the formal part of the SEDER service. A Judeo-German (Western Yiddish) version was once popular in Central Europe. Each stanza of *Addir Hu* serves to build up an alphabetical list of the Divine qualities and attributes, while the refrain calls upon God to restore His Sanctuary without delay. A standard Ashkenazi melody, known for centuries, has also entered the synagogue liturgy for HALLEL on Passover, incidentally helping to popularize the hymn among Jews observing other rites (especially in Israel).

ADDITIONAL SERVICE (Heb. *Musaf*). Prayer service added after the MORNING SERVICE on Sabbaths, the New Moon, Pilgrim Festivals, and the High Holidays (Rosh ha-Shanah and the Day of Atonement). On each of these days, the Bible orders the bringing of an additional (*musaf*) sacrifice or sacrifices, to supplement the *tamid* morning sacrifice brought daily throughout the year. The specific SACRIFICES AND OFFERINGS are detailed in Num. 28:9-29:39. Just as the *Shaharit* (Morning) Service is recited in place of the *shaharit* sacrifice, so the *Musaf* ("Additional") Service is recited in place of the *musaf* sacrifices brought on the abovementioned days. According to the Talmud (*Suk.* 53a), however, a *Musaf* prayer was already known in the Second Temple era.

Ideally, the service should take place with a prayer quorum (MINYAN), but it is obligatory even if there is no quorum, in which case one recites it alone. The Additional Service is generally recited immediately after the Morning Service Torah reading (often after a sermon), but this is chiefly a matter of convenience. There is no halakhic reason for reciting the Additional Service at that time, and it is independent of the Morning Service. The *Musaf* prayers may be said any time after sunrise, and should ideally be recited no later than an hour after midday (the halfway point between sunrise and sunset). If one has not said them by the latter time, they may still be recited until sunset.

Half KADDISH is recited before the Additional Service,

which consists of a special AMIDAH prayer, with the standard three preliminary and three concluding benedictions of the *Amidah*. Except for the Additional Service of Rosh ha-Shanah (the New Year), all the *Amidah* prayers contain a single middle blessing. It reflects on the importance of the day, asks God to restore the Jews to their land and Temple, and quotes the verse or verses relating to the *musaf* sacrifice that was offered in the Temple on that particular day. When the New Moon falls on a Sabbath, the normal *Tikkanta Shabbat* section is replaced by a special formulation, *Attah Yatzarta* ("You have created"), which incorporates elements of both days, including the pertinent Bible verses of both.

On Rosh ha-Shanah, the middle section of the *Amidah* comprises three blessings, after each of which the SHOFAR (ram's horn) is sounded (except on Sabbath). These blessings are known as MALKHUYYOT, in which God's kingship is proclaimed; ZIKHRONOT, in which the merits of previous generations are recalled; and SHOFAROT, in which there is a reference to the blowing of the *shofar* on the New Year. Each of these three sections quotes a total of ten Bible verses referring to the topic of that section: three from the Pentateuch, three from the Prophets, three from the Hagiographa, and a final verse from the Pentateuch. The references to the sacrifices brought on that day are included in the *Malkhuyyot* section.

The *Amidah* of each Additional Service is first read silently by the congregation and then repeated aloud by the reader. On the New Moon and the intermediate days of the Pilgrim Festivals, the standard KEDUSHAH is recited in the third benediction; on Sabbaths, the High Holidays and the Pilgrim Festivals (including Hoshana Rabbah), a special extended Kedushah is recited.

Outside Israel, on all holy days except the Sabbath and New Moon, the priests assemble before the Holy Ark to bless the congregation during the last benediction of the Additional Service AMIDAH (see PRIESTLY BLESSING). Should any of these days coincide with a Sabbath, opinions are divided as to whether the priests give their blessing or not. In Israel, priests bless the other congregants at every Additional Service.

On the first day of Passover, a special Prayer for DEW is added to the (*Musaf*) *Amidah*, a similar Prayer for RAIN being chanted on Shemini Atseret. On the High Holidays, extensive *piyyutim* (liturgical poems) — some of a supplicatory nature and others of praise — are added to the reader's repetition of the *Amidah*. An elaborate AVODAH mini-service is read here on the Day of Atonement. The service is usually concluded with ÉN K(E)-ELOHÉNU, ALÉNU, and ADON OLAM, *Kaddish* being recited at least twice before the end.

ADMOR (Heb. acronym of *Adonenu Morenu ve-Rabbenu* — "Our lord, teacher, and master"). Honorific title which Ḥasidic Jews (mainly in Israel) often give to one of their dynastic leaders (see also TSADDIK). In Diaspora communities, the Yiddish title of *Rebbe* is more usual.

ADONAI See GOD, NAMES OF

ADON OLAM ("Lord of the Universe"). Opening words of a popular liturgical hymn. The author is not known, but it has been suggested that *Adon Olam* was written by the 11th-century poet Solomon IBN GABIROL. One of the most popular of all synagogue hymns, it is technically a monorhyme, expressing trust in God, man's one eternal Creator, Guardian, and Redeemer. Ashkenazim observing the German rite first made *Adon Olam* part of their daily worship in the 14th century, but its universal appeal led to the adoption of this hymn by Jewish prayer rites and communities throughout the world. In the traditional prayer book it makes several appearances: at the very beginning of the Morning Service, at the conclusion of the Additional Service for Sabbaths and festivals (when it is usually sung by the congregation), and at the end of the Night Prayers before going to sleep. Ashkenazi congregations, following the practice in the community of Worms, also normally sing *Adon Olam* at the end of the eve of the Day of Atonement service. Their text consists of 12 verses, whereas Sephardim have a longer (16-verse) form of the hymn. In Morocco it is sung at weddings and other festivities. The number of musical settings is vast and impressive, and melodies have been borrowed from a wide variety of sources (not all of them Jewish). Salomone de' Rossi (Italy, 17th century) composed a setting for eight voices, David Aaron de Sola (London) and Solomon Sulzer (Vienna) wrote other famous versions in the 19th century. On festivals, the appropriate melodic tradition or prayer mode (*nusaḥ*) is often employed.

The 19th-century English author, George Borrow, included this translation of *Adon Olam* in his *Lavengro*.

ADON OLAM

Reigned the Universe's Master,
Ere were earthly things begun;
When His mandate all created,
Ruler was the name He won.
And alone He'll rule tremendous
When all things are past and gone,
He no equal has, nor consort,
He, the singular and lone,
Has no end and no beginning;
His the sceptre, might and throne.
He's my God and living Saviour,
Rock to Whom I in need run;
He's my banner and my refuge,
Fount of weal when call'd upon.
In His hand I place my spirit,
At nightfall and at rise of sun,
And therewith my body also;
God's my God — I fear no-one.

ADOPTION Establishment of a parent-child relationship between those not so biologically related. Although Jewish law regards natural parenthood as the primary basis for personal status, and does not consider adoptive parenthood to constitute such a basis, provision is made for adoptive relationships. Thus, according to Jewish law, an individual is permitted to take on responsibility for the physical, emotional, and social wellbeing of a child. In such circumstances, the death of the adoptive parent does not terminate the relationship of obligation and the parent's heirs must continue to care for the child. Furthermore, a rabbinical court is authorized to remove a child from the custody of his or her natural parents if the child's interests are endangered, in accordance with the halakhic principle that the child's welfare and interests are the central factors to be considered in any question related to childcare.

In Jewish law, the adoptive relationship does not totally eliminate the relationship between the adopted child and his or her natural parents, who must continue to provide for the child's needs if the adoptive parent is unable to do so. The adopted child does not automatically inherit from the adoptive parent, who must make special provision in his or her will. Although adoption does not have legal status as constituting a new family relationship, this special provision is effective even if the adopted child is referred to in the will as "son" or "daughter." Because adoption does not alter personal status, no prohibitions regarding marriage or divorce exist between, on the one hand, the adopter and his or her family, and, on the other hand, the adoptee.

In Israeli law, a district or rabbinical court order of adoption severs all rights and obligations between the adoptee and his or her natural parents, while establishing a new and binding legal relationship with the adoptive one(s). Thus, the adoptee is usually considered to be a legal heir and there is no need for a special provision in the adoptive parent's will.

The small number of biblical references — implicit or explicit — to the institution of adoption include Sarah's wish to have a son as the result of her handmaiden cohabiting with her husband (Gen. 16:2); Moses' adoption by Pharaoh's daughter (Ex. 2:10); and Esther's adoption by her uncle Mordecai (Est. 2:7) although the last relationship could be interpreted as foster parenthood.

ADRET, SOLOMON BEN ABRAHAM (known by the acronym *Rashba*; c.1235-1310). Rabbinical authority in Spain. He was a native of Barcelona, where he served as rabbi for half a century. A disciple of Jonah ben Abraham Gerondi and Naḫmanides, Adret wrote prolifically on all branches of rabbinic literature and his works are studied to this day. He produced analytical commentaries (novellae) on 17 talmudical tractates; all of these have been published. His code, *Torat ha-Bayit* ("The Law of the House"), deals mainly with regulations for the Jewish home: dietary laws and laws of family purity. He also wrote a briefer form of this work, summarizing the discussions and the halakhic decisions, which he called *Torat ha-Bayit ha-Katser* ("The Brief Law of the House"). Glosses and notes to this code under the title *Bedek ha-Bayit* ("The Repair of the House") were written by his friend and colleague, Aaron Ha-Levi of Barcelona, and these were in turn vigorously criticized by the author in notes entitled *Mishmeret ha-Bayit* ("The Preservation of the House"). Adret wrote thousands of responsa on all aspects of Jewish law, in answer to questions addressed to him by Jewish communities from northern Europe to Erets Israel. These responsa are thought to have constituted part of the groundwork for the SHULḪAN ARUKH.

Familiar with poetry, Kabbalah, and philosophy, Adret also dealt with philosophical and theological queries. He opposed both the allegorical and the mystical methods of Scriptural exegesis. While acknowledging that many verses in the Bible cannot be taken literally, and that they require interpretation, he insisted that the interpretation accord with tradition. Despite his own knowledge of philosophy, he placed under a ban (*ḫerem*) anyone who studied the subject before the age of 25 years.

A courageous defender of Jewish rights, Adret composed a work refuting the charges of a Dominican monk, Raymond Martini, who in his Latin tract, *Pugio Fidei* ("Dagger of Faith"), had interpreted talmudic and midrashic passages tendentiously, so as to show Judaism in an unfavorable light.

ADULT While the onset of puberty confers the status of adult with regard to most matters, it is impossible to isolate one particular date or event which marks a clear demarcation between childhood and adulthood. So, for instance, women are considered adults at the age of 12 years and one day, whereas men do not achieve adult status until the age of 13 and one day (*Nid.* 5:6; 52a). Puberty was defined as the appearance of two pubic hairs, known in the legal literature as "signs" (*simanim*). The different ages of maturity stem from the rabbis' judgment that puberty begins earlier in women than in men. The process of maturation in women was divided into three stages: a girl from the age of three until the age of 12 was classified as a "minor" (*ketannah*). For six months after the age of twelve, she was classed as a "young woman" (*na'arah*). From 12 years and six months, she was known as an "adult" (*bogeret*). The process for men consisted of only two stages. Prior to age 13 and one day a boy is a "minor" (*katan*) and subsequently an "adult" (*gadol*). One who has reached the required age but has not shown the "signs" is not considered an adult, since he has not reached physical maturity. Thus attainment of adulthood may be deferred for a number of years until the "signs" appear or until positive evidence of sterility is brought forth. Similarly, if the "signs" appear before the mandatory age, they are not recognized. Nevertheless all men and women upon reaching the mandatory age are presumed to have reached maturity. So it is ruled that a young man who has passed the age of BAR MITSVAH is counted for a prayer quorum (*minyan*) even without examination.

Having reached adulthood, the individual is deemed morally responsible for his actions, thus the custom of the father's declaring at the bar mitsvah ceremony that he is no longer liable for any punishment incurred by the behavior of the son (BARUKH SHE-PETARANI). Young adults become responsible for observance of all commandments, and for discharging all communal obligations. Their legitimacy as legal and ritual agents is recognized, and they are held responsible in criminal and civil matters. Here too, however, it is impossible to draw a clear demarcation between child and adult. In spite of the rights and obligations incurred with reaching maturity, it was believed that individuals were not liable for heavenly punishment for sins committed before the age of 20 (*Shab.* 89b). On the other hand, vows, under certain circumstances, were recognized as binding even if taken during the year prior to reaching maturity, and girls were capable of being betrothed at the age of three, boys from the age of nine (*Nid.*5:4-5).

In the State of Israel, both men and women are permitted to marry only from age 17. District courts (not rabbinic) are empowered to permit earlier marriages under unusual circumstances.

ADULTERY (Heb. *ni'uf*). Sexual relations engaged in voluntarily by a married or betrothed woman with someone other than her husband. Since a wife, in biblical times, was considered the possession of her husband, the prohibition against adultery appears in the TEN COMMANDMENTS among those which forbid injury to one's neighbor (Ex. 20:13; Deut. 5:17). Episodes in the Pentateuch, involving Sarah and Abimelech (Gen. 20) and Potiphar's wife and Joseph (Gen. 39:9), reflect the concept that adultery is a sin against God. It is also stigmatized as an act of defilement (Lev. 18:20), and King David is later punished for this offense (II Sam. 12:9ff.). Several biblical passages explicitly prescribe the death penalty for adulterers, both the man and the woman (Lev. 20:10; Deut. 22:22-24; Ezek. 16:38-40). The first nine chapters of the Book of Proverbs contain repeated advice to young men, warning them against the seductive wiles of an unfaithful wife. Married men are urged to maintain conjugal fidelity and not to be enticed by another man's wife, called the "strange woman" (Prov. 2:16, 5:3-20, 7:5ff.). Similar admonitions are found in the Apocrypha (Ecclus. 9.4ff.) Metaphorically, in Scripture, the relationship between God and Israel is frequently portrayed as marriage; the worship of false gods is therefore described as an act of adultery or prostitution (Ezek. 16:15ff.; Hos. 2:4; cf. Ex. 34:15-16, Num.15:39).

On the basis of WISDOM LITERATURE (e.g., Job 31:9-12) and prophetic condemnation (Jer. 5:8, etc.), the rabbis expanded both the moral and the legal implications of marital infidelity. Thus, one who gazes at a married woman with lustful eyes is also called an adulterer (Lev. R. 23.12); likewise the wife who thinks of another man while having intercourse with her own husband. Both the adulterer and the adulteress belong to the category of those for whom eternal punishment is reserved in the hereafter (*BM* 58b). As a crime endangering human society, adulterous conduct is prohibited by the seven NOACHIDE LAWS and is therefore applicable to mankind as a whole; together with idolatry and murder, it constitutes one of the commandments for which a Jew must be prepared to accept martyrdom rather than transgress (*San.* 74a). The method of the biblically ordained penalty of death for this offense is not specified, but the Talmud interprets it as death by strangulation. In Jewish law, however, the death penalty for this (or any other) crime might only be imposed if the offending parties had been duly forewarned and when two witnesses had also given evidence as to their misconduct. A

Joseph and Potiphar's wife *shown in one of a series of woodcuts illustrating the Ten Commandments, by Lukas Cranach (1472-1453). Würtermbergische Landesbibliothek, Stuttgart.*

classic exception to this rule was the woman suspected of adultery who underwent an ordeal known as "the waters of bitterness" to determine her guilt or innocence (Num. 5:12-31; see SOTAH). Halakhic regulations stipulate that a husband may give his wife a bill of DIVORCE when he has good reason to suspect, or proof of the fact, that she has committed adultery. Once the case has been established, such a husband must divorce his unfaithful wife (even if he is willing to forgive her) and she cannot then marry her lover. Any offspring of an adulterous union, termed a *mamzer*, can only marry another *mamzer* or a proselyte (see ILLEGITIMACY). Though severely condemned, relations between a married man and an unmarried woman do not constitute adultery in Jewish law and the child of such a union suffers from no religious disabilities. For the legal aspects of rape, a different type of felony, see SEXUAL OFFENSES. See also HUSBAND-WIFE RELATIONSHIP.

AFIKOMAN See HAGGADAH

AFTERLIFE Although rarely cast into dogmatic or systematic form, Judaism's concept of an afterlife has generally focused upon corporeal RESURRECTION and the immortality of the SOUL. The Bible's treatment of such notions is decidedly vague. Early biblical tradition assumes that when people die they go to *sheol*, the grave (Gen. 37:35), an unclear designation which may mean no more than the burial plot. No hint is given of an afterlife, although Saul's communication with the deceased Samuel (I Sam. 28) implies that the prophet continued to exist after death. Later biblical traditions contain intimations of resurrection, initially of the entire people (Ezek. 37), later perhaps extending to individuals (Dan. 12:2). Prior to the Babylonian exile, however, there is no indication of the existence of a fully developed belief in an afterlife.

Recent scholars have asserted that when this belief did emerge, it was probably through external influences, Persian or Greek. It included the belief in physical resurrection which was held by the PHARISEES but rejected by the SADDUCEES. Some held that such resurrection would be general, others that it would apply only to the righteous. The doctrine of REWARD AND PUNISHMENT began to be applied to life after death as a way of maintaining the belief in God's promise to the righteous (notably the martyrs of persecution in the time of the Maccabees 167-164 BCE) that they would ultimately witness the restoration of Israel. In the words of II Maccabees 12:44 "For if he had not hoped that they that were slain would rise again, it would have been superfluous to pray for the dead."

Jewish devotional literature of the Hellenistic period contrasts *olam ha-ba* "the world to come" with *olam ha-zeh*, "this world" (*Apocalypse of Enoch*, (71:15)). The concept of the immortality of the soul was introduced into Diaspora Judaism at this time under the influence of Greco-Roman culture and is evident in the Wisdom of Solomon (3:1-10, 5:15-16) and extensively developed in the writing of the 1st century Alexandrian Jewish philosopher, PHILO (*Allegorical Interpretation* 1.105-108; *On Sacrifice* 2.5).

Belief in the corporeal resurrection of the dead became so essential to rabbinic ESCHATOLOGY that the Mishnah explicitly states: "All Israel has a portion in the world-to-come" (based upon Is. 60:21) except "one who says, 'There is no resurrection of the dead'" (*San.* 10.1). The rabbinic doctrine concerning reward and punishment in the hereafter is based upon belief in the reunion of the body with the soul before judgment, an article of faith for which the rabbis attempted to find sources in the Bible (*Sif.*, Deut. Finkelstein, 1939, no. 306, p. 341). God's resurrecting power is the theme of the second benediction in the AMIDAH as well as in other prayers of the traditional liturgy.

Aside from the belief in resurrection, however, the rabbis held differing opinions about nearly everything related to the afterlife. They discussed such matters as the fate of those who are neither wholly righteous nor utterly wicked (*Tos. San.* 13:3), the place of the non-Jew in the world to come (the righteous of all peoples, not only Jews, have a place, *ibid.* 13:1), and the relationship of the body to the soul (*Shab.* 152a-b; *Ber.* 18b-19a). Nevertheless, the hereafter never became a central concern. The general disinterest of the rabbis in the subject of the future world is summed up in the statement by JOHANAN BAR NAPPAḤA, a third century sage from Erets Israel, "All the prophets prophesied only about the days of the Messiah; but of the world to come, eye hath not seen it, O God (Is. 64:4)" (*San.* 99a, *Ber.* 34b).

Nevertheless, descriptions approximating the idea of heaven and hell are found in rabbinic writings. The latter was known as Gehinnom (Gehenna) and derives its name from the infamous valley of Ben Hinnom, south of Jerusalem, in which a pagan cult of child sacrifice was conducted during the time of the biblical monarchy. The exact location of Gehinnom varies from the depths of the earth (*Eruv.* 19a) to the heavens or beyond "the mountains of darkness" (*Tam.* 32b). One opinion even holds that its place is found in the self-consuming fire that destroys the wicked. Heaven is referred to as the "Garden of EDEN," which is described variously as an earthly or a heavenly garden. It is also used to express the complete realization of all the ideals the rabbis valued most in this world. So, for example, the Sabbath is an important "one-sixtieth of the world to come" (*Ber.* 57b). The Babylonian scholar RAV said, "In the world to come, there is no eating, no drinking, no begetting of children, no bargaining or hatred or jealousy or strife; rather, the righteous will sit with crowns on their heads and enjoy the effulgence of God's presence" (*Ber.* 17a). Later, the study of Torah became a major occupation for the righteous in the world to come (*Seder Eliyyahu Rabbah*). In general, the rabbis taught that the righteous would receive their reward and the wicked their punishment after death. This requires appropriate behavior on earth as is indicated by Rabbi Jacob: "This world is like a vestibule to the world to come; prepare yourself in the vestibule so you may enter the banqueting hall" (*Avot* 4:16).

Medieval Jewish views of an afterlife embraced the entire belief spectrum. A denial of corporeal resurrection as an essential creed also emerged. Although Judaized folk beliefs narrated frequent encounters with dead souls and visits to the netherworld, it was in the literature of Jewish philosophy and of Kabbalah (MYSTICISM) that the most significant developments took place in Jewish eschatological thinking during this period. SAADIAH GAON (Babylonia, 882-942) sought to reconcile the belief in corporeal resurrection with other ideas in his theology by emphasizing the unity of body and soul (*The Book of Beliefs and Opinions* 6.1, 6.7, 7.113). He posited two resurrections for the righteous: the first, a physical one, when the messianic age begins; the second when they enter the world to come for a purely spiritual existence. The wicked will be condemned to eternal suffering.

The Neoplatonic and Aristotelian philosophers who followed Saadiah elaborated on his thought. Jewish Neoplatonists including Isaac Israeli (d. 955/6), Solomon IBN GABIROL (d. 1058), BAḪYA IBN PAKUDA (11th century), and JUDAH HALEVI (d. 1141) believed that the souls of the righteous ultimately ascend to God to a communion with Wisdom. In contrast, Jewish Aristotelian thinkers' concept of eternity was defined by the "conjunction" of the individual's soul, or acquired intellect, with the universal Active Intellect. The most celebrated Jewish Aristotelian, Moses MAIMONIDES (d. 1205), was severely criticized for having denied corporeal resurrection because of his assertion that "in the world to come the body and the flesh do not exist, but only the souls of the righteous alone" (*Yad, Teshuvah* 3:6). In addition to including the dogma of resurrection as the thirteenth fundamental of the PRINCIPLES OF FAITH, Maimonides defended himself in his *Treatise on Resurrection*. There he distinguishes between the afterlife in the messianic age, when the souls of the righteous "will return to their bodies and...die after enjoying long lives", and the afterlife in the world to come, where the rewarded soul alone enjoyed an eternal and purely spiritual bliss. Some modern scholars have suggested, however, that Maimonides' repeated and dogmatic affirmations of corporeal resurrection were merely concessions to tradition and popular sentiment, and fueled by his fear of being branded a heretic.

In later centuries, Maimonides' position was attacked for its intellectualism (Ḫasdai CRESCAS' *The Light of the Lord*) and for its failure to emphasize that the soul's immortality was bound up in doing, not only knowing, God's will (Joseph ALBO's *Book of Principles*). Albo characterized resurrection as a dogma accepted by our nation," but not "a fundamental or a derivative principle of divine law in general or of the law of Moses in particular" (*ibid.* 1.23).

In contrast with the difficulties encountered by medieval Jewish philosophers with the concept of resurrection, Jewish mystics in the Middle Ages elaborated the details of the resurrected soul's existence in the afterlife and charted their chronology in terms of divine emanations, or SEFIROT. The Spanish scholar, Moses NAḪMANIDES (c.1194-1270), who was influenced by mysticism, expounded upon three distinct worlds that follow this one: a world into which the soul enters to be judged; a future world that ushers in a messianic age of final judgment and resurrection; and the world to come, in which "the body will become like the soul and the soul will cleave to knowledge of the Most High" (*Gate of the Reward*).

The ZOHAR, the classical kabbalistic work, postulated different fates for three parts of the soul, i.e., *nefesh*, *ruaḫ*, and *neshamah*. Only the first two were susceptible to sin and therefore subject to punishment. The pure and unsullied *neshamah*, having existed before the body among the *sefirot*, ascends again to their heights to a special place, *tzeror ha-ḫayyim*, or "bundle of life" (cf. I Sam. 25:29). As a corollary of this, the kabblistic tradition affirmed *gilgul*, or the TRANSMIGRATION OF SOULS after death, originally conceived as a punishment for extraordinary sin.

Paradoxically, *gilgul* came to be viewed as an exemplary act of God's resurrecting mercy, offering souls an opportunity to correct their sins and thus restore themselves as spiritual beings. Later, it became a principle wherein everything in the world, from inorganic matter to the angels, was believed to be in constant flux and metamorphosis.

In the later Middle Ages, the notion of the transmigration of souls became an accepted folk belief which was manifested in the DIBBUK, an errant soul whose sins were so great that it wandered desperately in search of refuge in helpless living bodies whom it would possess and torment until exorcised. Jews in Muslim lands as well as Ḫasidim believe that the souls of the righteous who have passed to the world to come can intercede for the living.

With the change in religious temper that occurred during the Emancipation and Enlightenment, the problem of the afterlife has lost much of its compelling urgency for Jewish theology. Orthodox Judaism maintains the traditional rabbinic belief in resurrection as part of its conception of the messianic age, and accordingly preserves the liturgical references in their original form. In contrast, the early American Reformers expressly rejected "as ideas not rooted in Judaism the beliefs both in bodily resurrection and in Gehenna and Eden as abodes for eternal punishment and reward" (Pittsburgh Platform, 1885).

In general, when the afterlife is considered today, it usually refers to personal immortality, an inheritance left to modernity from the medieval philosophers. In any case, the tendency in Judaism was to stress the obligation in this world, *olam ha-zeh* , and speculations about the afterlife in Judaism were far more marginal than in Christianity or Islam.

AFTERNOON SERVICE (Heb. *Minḫah*, i.e., "meal offering"). The daily afternoon prayer service. It replaced the *tamid shel bén ha-arbayim* (the afternoon offering) which was brought daily in Temple times (see II Kings 16:15). According to the rabbis (*Ber.* 26b), this Afternoon Service was instituted by the patriarch Isaac (cf. Gen. 24:63). The service must be recited, ideally with a prayer quorum (MINYAN), no earlier than half an hour after midday (defined as the midpoint between sunrise and sunset) and no later than sunset. The period of time from approximately 2 1/2 hours before sunset until dusk is called *Minḫah Ketannah*, (the "small" or late *Minḫah*), while that from half an hour after midday to *Minḫah Ketannah* is called *Minḫah Gedolah* (the "great" or early *Minḫah*). The last half of *Minḫah Ketannah* is known as *Pelag ha-Minḫah* and some very observant Jews maintain that it is immediately before this critical point that one should recite the Afternoon Service.

Every Afternoon Service includes Ps. 145 (ASHRÉ), the AMIDAH, the reader's repetition of the *Amidah* (which may be abbreviated if time is pressing), and ALÉNU, with various additions on certain specific days, both in the *Amidah* and during the service itself. No SHEMA is said, however, as the time of day is inappropriate (cf. Deut.6:7). Half-KADDISH is recited before the silent *Amidah*, and the full *Kaddish* before *Alénu*, while the latter is followed by the mourners' *Kaddish*. In the Sephardi ritual, *Ashré* is preceded by the recitation of *korbanot* — an account of the various SACRIFICES AND OFFERINGS that were brought to the Temple.

Generally on weekdays, except those that are special (e.g., the NEW YEAR FOR TREES) or which precede the Sabbath or festive days, the TAḪANUN supplications are read after the cantor's repetition of the *Amidah*.

On Sabbaths and festivals, *Ashré* is followed by *U-Va le-Tsiyyon*, a series of biblical verses commencing with Isa. 59:20. On Sabbaths, a Scroll of the Law is taken from the Ark and the first section of the following Sabbath's portion is read (see READING OF THE LAW). The Torah is also read on fast days and on the Day of Atonement; on the latter occasion, the entire book of Jonah serves as HAFTARAH. In the Afternoon Service preceding the Day of Atonement, the AL ḪET confession is recited after the silent *Amidah*.

On the fast of TISHAH BE-AV, men wear the prayer shawl (*tallit*) and phylacteries (*tefillin*) during the Afternoon Service, to make up for the Morning Service when these are not worn. The *tallit* is also worn on the Day of Atonement

During the repetition of the *Amidah*, the reader and congregation chant the KEDUSHAH responsively in the third benediction. On fast days, prior to the last benediction, the reader recites the PRIESTLY BLESSING, and in Israel, the priests bless other congregants. For convenience, many synagogues delay the Afternoon Service until late in the day, so as to leave only a short interval between afternoon and evening prayers. On Sabbaths, a *se'udah shelishit* ("third meal") helps to bridge this gap.

AGE AND THE AGED The Bible regards long life as a blessing (Isa. 65:20; Ps. 92:15). It gives the instruction to "rise before the aged and show deference to the old" (Lev. 19:32), but does not define "old." That definition is left to the Oral Law: according to tractate *Avot* (5.21), "At sixty one is an elder, at seventy one attains gray-haired old age." The *halakhah* lays down that one must show respect and rise for every person of 70 years or more. There are other views regarding who is included in the category of the "gray-headed": some sages consider the verse as applying only to someone who is both old and wise, while R. Yosé the Galilean sees age as irrelevant and Torah scholarship as the only criterion. In ancient times, the ELDERS were vested with special authority out of respect for their wisdom and experience. There are other definitions of "old" as well, although these do not affect the law concerning respect for elders. Thus, a priest may work in the Temple until he is "old," and the definition of "old" given in this case refers to one whose hands tremble. This same criterion has also been applied by some authorities to disqualify a ritual slaughterer on the basis of his age. Another talmudic definition of an old person is that he cannot stand on one foot and remove his shoe from the other foot while doing so. Old age may also be a question of one's mental state. Thus, the SHULḪAN ARUKH rules that any woman who does not object to being called "mother" is considered to be old (*YD* 189.29), although another view modifies this definition and makes it more objective by regarding as old any woman who is fit to be called "mother" without objecting.

Various laws make specific provision for the old: unleavened bread may be soaked in water for the Passover *Seder* so that the old can consume it, and the old are exempt from going to Jerusalem for the Pilgrim Festivals. An old person who is too infirm to walk without a cane (or anyone else with such an infirmity) is permitted to take his cane with him on the Sabbath, as it is considered to be an extension of his body, whereas a person who does not need a cane would be held to break the Sabbath law by carrying were he to take a cane with him on that day. While there are references to the old as being compassionate, other references suggest that they are not so: an old man may not be appointed to the Sanhedrin (*San.* 36b) because, according to RASHI, "he has forgotten the difficulties of raising children, and is not merciful."

In the Bible, there are three distinct periods of a lifetime, each with its own range of how long people lived. From the creation until Noah, ages of 900 and more were common. In the case of the patriarchs, Abraham lived 175 years, Isaac 180 years, and Jacob 147 years. Sarah, the only one of the matriarchs whose age is recorded, died at 127. Moses lived to 120, which (on the basis of Gen. 6:3) was also seen as the limit of human life; a favorite Jewish greeting is "May you live to 120." Finally, a verse in Psalms closely reflects man's life expectancy even today. "The span of our life is seventy years or, given the strength, eighty years" (Ps. 90:10). The Hebrew word for "strength", *gevurot*, has indeed entered the Jewish vocabulary to represent one who is 80 years old.

The Bible offers long life as a reward for honoring one's parents (Ex. 20:12), for sending away the mother bird before taking its chicks (Deut. 22:7), and for keeping correct weights (Deut. 25:15) or for generally obeying the Torah (Deut. 6:2). Long life is not always viewed favorably, however, Ecclesiastes (12:1) declaring that "those years arrive of which you will say, 'I have no pleasure in them.'"

Care of the aged has always been basic to Jewish life, linked to the plea of the Psalmist: "Do not cast me off in old age when my strength fails, do not forsake me!" (Ps. 71:9). In ancient times, this was closely linked to the commandment of honoring one's parents and the family looked after the elderly. Where there was no family, the aged were cared for by the community as a whole. In recent centuries, the home for the aged (*moshav zekenim*) became an integral feature of Jewish communal life and most communities supported such an institution.

SAYINGS ABOUT THE AGED

If the old say "tear down" and the children "build" — tear down. For the "destruction" of the old is construction; the "construction" of the young is destruction.

If a person studies when he is old, to what may he be compared? To ink written on paper that is blotted out.

For the ignorant, old age is like winter; for the studious, it is harvest time.

An old man in the house is a burden; but an old woman is a treasure.

Do not dishonor the old; we shall one day be among them.

AGGADAH (lit. "narration"). The non-legal elements in classical rabbinic writings. Rabbinic literature is divided into two main parts, called HALAKHAH and *aggadah*. The former includes all the legal discussion and decisions; the latter comprises the rest.

The *aggadah* is restricted to the classical rabbinic period and is found in two main sources, the TALMUD and the MIDRASH. The *aggadah* in the Talmud is interspersed between the legal discussions of the rabbis. Side by side with the talmudic legal argument and search for the *halakhah* are sections about history, philosophy, theology, ethics, and folklore. The Talmud is thus the first source for the *aggadah*, which comprises roughly one third of the talmudic material.

Although there are some midrashic works which concentrate on the legal aspects of Jewish life, most of them are aggadic (see MIDRASH AGGADAH). Because the midrashic literature developed over a period of nearly 1,000 years and was written in several different countries, the midrashic *aggadah* bears evidence of varied influences — not only in the language (Greek words in the Palestinian midrashim and Persian words in the Babylonian midrashim) but also in the philosophical concepts. It is sometimes necessary to distinguish between the authentic rabbinic theology, which subsequently entered the mainstream of Jewish doctrine, and the secondary material which is the result of the impact of Greek, Babylonian, or other external environments.

Since the term *aggadah* refers to the whole corpus of nonlegalistic rabbinic literature, it has a very comprehensive meaning, but is always didactic. First of all, it includes legends, mostly deriving from rabbinic expositions of the Bible and the biographies of rabbis and Jewish heroes. Other elements of *aggadah* are elaborations of the biblical story which provide an imaginative literary extension of the Bible narrative. Then there is a vast literature of Jewish folklore which has no thematic connection with the Bible story or with famous personalities in the post-biblical period; it may deal with ANGELS or DEMONS, or with quaint customs prevalent in some sections of the Jewish community.

There are also philosophical, particularly theological, concepts which are included in the general term *aggadah*. Sometimes these are explicitly stated and then there is no difficulty in identifying and explaining them. This applies particularly in the sphere of ETHICS. For example, the Mishnaic tractate AVOT ("Chapters of the Fathers") is in that class of aggadic works, presenting a number of generally clear teachings about the concept of God, man, Israel, Torah, and the ethical life — all expressed in a clear and popular style. Very often those teachings are indirectly conveyed by a parable and the stories have to be explored in order to discover the implicit moral, since most of them are told without the storyteller

The Hebrew letter Bet *whose form is a subject for a rabbinic* aggadah *(see text).*

Adon Olam, *"Lord of the Universe", the hymn sung at the end of Sabbath and festival services. Italy, 15th-century manuscript.*

[illegible]

אדון

עולם א
אשר מ
מלך ב
בטרם י
כל יציר
נברא ל
לעת נז
נעשה
בחפצו
כל אדון
מלך ש
שמו נ

נקרא" ואחרי ככלות הכל לבדו הוא ימלוך נורא" והוא היה והוא
הוה והוא יהיה בתפארה" והוא אחד ואין שני להמשיל
לו ולהחבירה" בלי ראשית ובלי תכלית ולו העז
והמשרה" והוא אלי וחי גואלי וצור
חבלי ביום צרה" והוא נסי ומנוסי מ
מנת כוסי ביום אקרא" בידו
אפקיד רוחי בעת
אישן ואעירה"
ועם רוחי
גויתי
ה'
לי
לי ולא אירא"

[illegible]

אברהם
אל תשלח
יצחק
ΜΝΙϹΘΟΥϹΙΝ ΥΤΕ
ΧΝΙΤΕΥΚΑΜΝΟΝ
ΤΕϹΤΩΕΡΓΟΝΤΟΥ
ΤΩΜΑΡΙΑΝΟϹΚΑΙ
ΑΝΙΝΑϹΥΟϹ

making his point clear. In reading this genre of *aggadah* it is necessary to inquire why the story is told. It then becomes clear that the piece is to be read not as historically true but as morally true.

There is, in addition, a wide and profound rabbinic theology which derives from comments on a biblical text. For example, as the very first letter of the Hebrew Bible is the letter *bet*, the rabbis ask, "Why does the holy Book start with the letter *bet*, which is not the first letter of the alphabet?" They answer that the *bet* is like a square with one side open. It is closed above, below, and at the back; it is open only in the front. This, they suggest, is to teach that man ought not to inquire what is in the heavens above, or in the netherworld, or what preceded Creation. The only sensible and practical way for man to live is to proceed forward in the one direction which is open to him. Frequently, that type of brief comment is elaborated with an anecdote which expands it into the realm of true literary folklore.

Whereas the *halakhah* remained the law which had to be practiced until it was changed or abrogated by a competent authority, the *aggadah* was held to be nothing more than a personal opinion of its author and had no binding force upon the community. The rabbis refused to base laws on aggadic material, miracle tales, folklore, and legend. However, there is a significant fusion of *halakhah* and *aggadah* which invalidates the strict separation of the two. The ethical teachings of the *aggadah* frequently inform and influence the spirit of the legal *halakhah*, so that the law then becomes more sensitive to the human situation. The modern Hebrew poet and scholar Ḥayyim Naḥman Bialik pointed out that *aggadah* is a refinement of the *halakhah*, while *halakhah* is a codification of the essence of the *aggadah*. In other words, *aggadah* has made the law more ethical and *halakhah* has made the ethics more obligatory.

Efforts have been made to present the *aggadah* in special anthologies. The most noteworthy and thorough work in this field was carried out by the 15th-century Spanish scholar Jacob Ibn Ḥabib, who recognized the vast appeal of *aggadah* to the Jewish masses. He therefore compiled a special edition of the Talmud which excluded all *halakhah* and its discussions and included only the *aggadah*. This volume, entitled ÉN YA'AKOV ("Jacob's Well"), is to this day a popular text in synagogues and study circles. A modern anthology, the *Sefer ha-Aggadah* ("Book of Aggadah," 1910), was compiled by Bialik and Y.H. Rawnitzki. Another major achievement, in English, was *The Legends of the Jews* (7 vols., 1909-38) by Louis GINZBERG.

AGGADAT BERESHIT A homiletical MIDRASH on the Book of GENESIS (see also MIDRASH AGGADAH). It is divided into more than 80 three-part chapters, following the TRIENNIAL CYCLE of Torah readings. Part one of each chapter is an exegetical Midrash on a single verse of the weekly reading from the Pentateuch (normally the opening verse); part two expounds a verse from the prophetical reading; and part three deals more briefly with a verse from Psalms. Internal evidence suggests that it was composed between 900 and 1000 CE. The material is chiefly drawn from the Midrash TANḤUMA (old version). A copiously annotated edition was published by Solomon Buber in 1903; it included a brief commentary by Abraham ben Elijah (son of ELIJAH, GAON OF VILNA), who produced an edition of his own a century earlier (1802).

AGNOSTICISM AND ATHEISM Terms denoting separate positions on the existence or nonexistence of God; since neither is theistic, these outlooks are often confused or misunderstood. The atheist flatly denies that there is a God; the agnostic, while not denying the possibility that God may exist, claims that man has no way of knowing if there is such a Divine power, God's existence or nonexistence being outside the boundaries of rational inquiry.

While there are some Jews today who describe themselves as agnostics, the concept of agnosticism nowhere appears in Jewish religious literature. Gershom Scholem, a world authority on KABBALAH, defined the kabbalists' approach as a "mystical agnosticism," but this applies only to their thinking about the nature of God, which is beyond man's intellectual grasp. For the kabbalists, God certainly exists, but to them He is the ÉN SOF — the indescribable, unknowable Infinite. Similarly, medieval Jewish philosophers headed by SAADIAH GAON adopted the position that "if I knew Him, I would be Him." The kabbalists, however, undoubtedly believed that God can be known in relation to His world of creation.

Atheism is a concept for which there is no equivalent in the Hebrew language, since ancient Israel was part of a world where no one doubted the existence of supernatural forces. The verses in Psalms (14:1, 53:2) popularly translated as "the fool hath said in his heart, There is no God" should not be taken literally as a profession of atheism. "The benighted man [or "knave"] thinks God does not care" is a more accurate translation (cf. Ps. 10:4). It implies contempt for the supreme Judge who watches over human affairs, distinguishing between the benighted and the righteous. For the biblical prophets, whose teaching is focused entirely on God, the issue was not belief or disbelief in God's existence, but whether a man should believe in One God or in many.

Rabbinic sources likewise provide no evidence of atheism among the Jews. The rabbis attacked the *kofer ba-ikkar*, "one who denies the root principle" (*San.* 39a-b; *Tosef. Shev.* 3.6), just as they condemned the man who proclaims *Lét din ve-lét dayyan*, "There is neither judgment nor Judge" (Gen. R. 26.14; Lev. R. 28.1). This means a denial of God's justice, not of His existence. Even the famous heretic, ELISHA BEN AVUYAH, was not accused of atheism but of denying that there is a personal God who "cares" and who dispenses reward or punishment in accordance with human merit.

Akedah (*"binding of Isaac") on the mosaic pavement of Beth Alpha synagogue. Early 6th century.*

The confrontation with atheism, as understood today, began in the Middle Ages, when MAIMONIDES and other Jewish philosophers — like their Christian and Muslim counterparts — formulated various "proofs" of God's existence. Even so, their concept of the atheist was still overshadowed by the MIN or "heretic" who denies God's unity or creative power rather than the likelihood that He exists. Only since the 18th-century Age of Enlightenment have thinkers been called upon to grapple with atheistic contentions in the modern sense and on a more rational basis. Theism is buffeted by numerous schools of thought, the principal challenge stemming from a materialistic view of the universe fostered by scientific investigations. Atheists have proved adept at disputing traditional theistic proofs that there is a God who maintains the harmony of the universe and who determines the fate of mankind.

Jewish theologians of the 20th century also addressed themselves to the questions raised by atheism, many citing Albert Einstein who (while unable to believe in a personal God) affirmed that "the cosmic religious experience is the strongest and noblest driving force behind scientific research" (an echo of the statement of Baruch Spinoza that he could believe in God only as "the sum total of the laws of nature"). Since World War II, Jewish thinkers have also had to contend with the problem of religious doubt and loss of faith resulting from the Nazi HOLOCAUST.

Many Jews in the modern world, although they would define themselves as atheistic or agnostic (and despite being estranged from their ancestral faith and practices), have nevertheless remained Jews since Jewish identity is not only a matter of religious belief but one that involves other commitments as well, including the Jewish people, a cultural tradition, and a Jewish homeland. See also SECULARISM; HUMANISTIC JUDAISM.

AGRICULTURAL LAWS As envisioned in the Pentateuch, the Israelite nation was to be primarily agrarian, and many of its laws relate to agriculture. The CALENDAR and Jewish FESTIVALS are largely related to agricultural seasons. The ORAL LAW, too, deals with agricultural laws at great length, and one entire order of the Mishnah, ZERA'IM — literally, "seeds" — is devoted to different aspects of the topic.

All three pilgrimage festivals, in addition to their historical symbolism, are directly linked to the agricultural year. PASSOVER is "the festival of the spring" (Ex.13:4) and on its second night an OMER — a specific measure — of barley is harvested and brought to the Temple. Several weeks later, SHAVU'OT is the Harvest Festival (Ex.23:16) which marks the end of the barley harvest and the beginning of the wheat harvest. It is also the Festival of the First Fruits (Num.28:26) when the first crops are brought to Jerusalem. SUKKOT is the Festival of Ingathering (Ex.23:16) when the grain is brought from the fields into the barns.

The New Year, Rosh ha-Shanah, also has an agricultural significance (*R.H.* 1:1). Where the Bible prescribes that the crops of trees of a certain age may or may not be eaten, all trees planted in sufficient time to germinate by the New Year are considered to be one year old on that day. Similarly, the Torah commands giving every tenth calf to the priests: all the calves born between one New Year and the next were put together, counted and each tenth one was marked to be given to the priests.

The so-called Gezer Calendar incised on soft limestone with a listing of the year by agricultural tasks: the (two) months of harvest; the (two) months of sowing; the (two) months of late planting; the month of reaping flax; the month of reaping barley; the month of reaping and measuring; the (two) months of (vine) tending; the month of summer (fruit). Eight agricultural activities are listed; since four of them are in association with the plural "months", the latter must indicate a two-month period. In the margin of the calendar are the first three letters of the Hebrew alphabet. This agricultural calendar is dated to the 10th century BCE, and is one of the earliest Hebrew inscriptions known.

The agricultural laws of the Pentateuch are in the category of "commandments (*mitsvot*) dependent on the land," which are obligatory only within the borders of the Biblical Land of Israel. A certain few laws were also imposed by the rabbis on Jews living elsewhere, but generally, the laws outlined below apply only to the Land of Israel.

Certain obligations are imposed on the farmer. When he harvests his crop, he must set an amount aside for the priests as *terumah* ("heave-offering", see SACRIFICES AND OFFERINGS) — (Num.18:11). While the absolute minimum is one stalk per barn, by rabbinic law the *terumah* must be no less than 1/60th of the crop, with the average person giving 1/50th and the magnanimous, 1/40th (*Terumot* 4:3). In addition, the farmer must give 1/10th of the crop to the Levites as the "first tithe" (*ma'aser rishon*) (Num.18:24). In the first, second, fourth, and fifth years of the seven-year *shemittah* (SABBATICAL YEAR) cycle (see below), the farmer must also set aside a tenth of the remaining crop as the "second tithe" (*ma'aser sheni*) (Lev.27:30-31). The second tithe may be eaten only in Jerusalem or, alternatively, may be sold, provided that the proceeds received be brought to Jerusalem, where they may be used only to buy food that will be consumed there. In the third and sixth years of the *shemittah* cycle, the second tithe is known as "the poor man's tithe" (*ma'aser ani*) (Deut.14:28-29) and must be distributed among the poor.

When harvesting his field, the farmer must also make provision for the poor by leaving the *leket* — grain which dropped during the harvesting (Lev.19:9); *shikhehah* — the grain forgotten in the field when the harvest is brought in (Deut.24:19); and *pe'ah* — a corner of the field which must be left unharvested (Lev.19:9).

In the case of trees, the crops of the first three years are known as *orlah* (literally, "uncircumcised"), and may not be eaten. The crop of the fourth year, *neta reva'i* ("the planting of the fourth" year), must be taken to Jerusalem and eaten there, or else the produce may be sold, and the money taken to Jerusalem, where it must be used to purchase other food to be eaten there. From the fifth year onwards, the crop is subject to no further limitations (Lev.19:23-25).

A person kneading more than a specified minimum of dough must separate part of it for the priests (HALLAH).

Just as the mixing of wool and linen in garments is forbidden, so is the sowing of diverse seeds in the same area. Such a crop is known as *kilayim* (MIXED SPECIES), (Lev. 19:19). The mishnaic tractate *Kilayim* lays down rules for the different species involved and the required distance between species in order to avoid a violation of the law. Included in the prohibition is the grafting of the branch of one species onto the tree of another. Also forbidden is the cross-pollination of different species of fruits, although cross-pollination of two strains of the same species is permitted.

Every seventh year is known as *shemittah* ("release"), during which all land must be fallowed (Lev.25:1-5). All fields must be left with access available to all — humans and animals. The Bible promises that those who keep the *shemittah* will be blessed so that the crop of the sixth year will suffice for three years: the sixth year, the *shemittah* year, and the following year, until the new crop is harvested.

The JUBILEE year is proclaimed at the conclusion of seven *shemittah* cycles (Lev.25:8-12). (The Talmud records a dispute on the dating of the jubilee year: was it counted as the first year of the next cycle (yielding cycles of 49 years) or was it a separate year falling after the 49th year of one cycle and before the first year of the next (yielding fifty year cycles)? During the jubilee year, everything is given the chance to begin afresh. All land sold since the last jubilee is returned to the possession of each ancestral family. Hebrew slaves are also freed (see SLAVERY). Thus, in a society where the ownership of land was of paramount importance, each ancestral family, no matter how poor it might have become, was to have its land restored to it in the jubilee year, and was able to make a new start. Under the terms of this law, no land is sold permanently. All that is actually sold is the number of crops until the next jubilee year, after which the land is restored to its original owners.

Unlike agricultural land, houses in cities may be sold permanently, and do not revert to their original owners in the jubilee year. The original owner of such a house nevertheless has the right, within the first year after the sale, to buy back his home (Lev.25:29-30).

Since the destruction of the Second Temple in 70 CE, the agricultural laws have been regarded by most rabbis as binding by rabbinic decree rather than by Torah law. This has resulted in modifications in certain of the rules. As an example, while produce grown in the Land of Israel must still be tithed (see above), the tithe actually taken is only a little over one percent of the total. A special formula, devised by Rabbi Avraham Yeshayahu KARELITZ (known as *Hazon Ish*) is recited, whereby the sanctity of the tithes is transferred to a coin. The 1% of the produce put aside, rather than being given to priests and Levites, must be disposed of in a dignified manner.

Nowadays, the laws of leaving produce for the poor are not in effect, nor must produce be brought to Jerusalem. Fruit of the first four years, however, may not be eaten since this law applies both inside Israel and outside.

The fact that the Sabbatical year is binding only by rabbinic law was the basis for a far-reaching decision of Rabbi Avraham Yitzhak KOOK, the first chief rabbi of Palestine in his monumental *Shabbat ha-Aretz*. As leaving the land fallow each Sabbatical year endangered the existence of the newly-founded Zionist settlements, Kook devised a formula whereby the land was sold to a non-Jew. The land under non-Jewish ownership could then be worked during the Sabbatical year. This ruling aroused a storm of protest throughout the rabbinic world, primarily among non-Zionist elements. The more Zionist rabbis, however, generally endorsed this decision. As Rabbi Kook's decision clearly stated that it was to be considered *ad hoc*, rather than a permanent waiver of the law, the Israel chief rabbinate meets before each Sabbatical year to review the situation, before arranging for the sale of the land.

AGUNAH (lit. a wife "forsaken" or "shut off"; Ruth 1.13). Term applied in Jewish law to a woman who remains "chained" to her husband for life and is denied the option of remarriage either because he refuses to give her a bill of DIVORCE (*get*), or because he is incapacitated from doing so on account of mental illness, or because he has disappeared and his death cannot be established. This situation has always constituted a formidable halakhic problem, since Jewish law does not permit the dissolution of a marriage on mere presumption of death, and only allows a divorce to be executed on instructions received from the husband. The problem is further aggravated on account of the fact that any children of a married woman by someone other than her husband are *mamzerim*, who can only marry converts to Judaism or other *mamzerim* (see ILLEGITIMACY). The "forsaken" husband can obtain relief, however, by receiving dispensation to take another wife (*hetter nissu'in*) from the rabbinical court.

The rabbis, for their part, always considered it a supreme moral obligation to devise every possible solution that might ease the plight of the *agunah*. In talmudic and medieval times, they mitigated the strict laws of evidence, accepting hearsay testimony of death and the evidence of one rather than two witnesses to validate a divorce (*Git*. 3a; *Yev*. 122b). They regarded it as praiseworthy for the husband to deposit a conditional divorce (*Git*. 73a) in the event of illness, especially when the wife had no issue at the time, thus saving her from being bound by the laws of LEVIRATE MARRIAGE (*Ket*. 2b); also in the event of his leaving on a hazardous journey or going into battle (*Ket*. 9b). These were all termed bills of divorce "prompted by love, not hate," i.e., by concern for the wife's situation as a potential *agunah*. The rabbis would likewise annul a marriage if, in their view, its essential basis had been violated (*Ket*. 3a).

With the greater dispersal of Jewry, however, and the abolition of central rabbinic authority, courts after the talmudic era proved increasingly reluctant to utilize these devices. The result was that the *agunah* became an acute problem, especially in times of war, pogroms, and the mass movement of populations. The breakdown of religious homogeneity within the community and the fact that the option of civil divorce was not recognized by *halakhah* complicated matters even more. In the 19th and 20th centuries, rabbinical authority still followed talmudic and medieval precedents concerning Jews drafted into the armed forces, arranging for a conditional divorce that would be activated if they failed to return within a fixed period after demobilization. Rabbis were generally willing to authorize a conditional marriage in the special case of a woman whose brothers-in-law had abandoned Judaism or were otherwise inaccessible. Where the husband died without issue, such a marriage was retroactively annulled (*Sh. Ar., EH* 157.4).

In recent times, the Chief Rabbinate and Chief Chaplaincy of the State of Israel overcame the problems that resulted from a person's death in the Holocaust or disappearance on active service by accepting a liberal interpretation of reliable circumstantial evidence, wherever there was no record of marital discord or suspicion that he might have deserted the wife. For example, all the widows of the Israeli sailors who disappeared when two vessels, the destroyer *Eilat* and the submarine *Dakar*, were lost at sea in 1967-8 were declared free to remarry. Some relief is also provided the *agunah* in Israel's rabbinical courts by awarding high alimony or (in rare cases) by imprisoning the husband when he refuses to grant a divorce. In the Diaspora, efforts have been made by the Conservative movement to insert a clause in the marriage contract that would empower the civil courts to employ sanctions enforcing a *get*. The problem of the *agunah* still remains acute, however, particularly in cases of mental illness or desertion. This has resulted in increasing pressure from Jewish women's organizations aimed at inducing the rabbinate to adopt a radical general enactment that would remove most of the hardships involved. For Reform Jews, who do not consider themselves bound by the *halakhah*, the problem of the *agunah* does not exist.

"One need hardly stress that the *halakhah* [Jewish law] has no interest whatsoever in aggravating the pain and hardship experienced by the *agunah*. The *halakhah*'s only concern is to ensure that the woman involved should not remarry before her existing marital status has duly been voided. It is thus the *halakhah*'s prerogative and, indeed, its sacred duty to take advantage of any legal devices such as conditional marriage and annulment which can achieve this object. For it is the *halakhah*'s underlying purpose to ensure that no woman be denied the option of remarriage, a principle which informs the vast corpus of halakhic literature devoted to the relief of *agunot*."

From a statement by Justice Menaḫem Elon of Israel's Supreme Court, a recognized authority on Jewish law; in *Religious Legislation in the State of Israel*, Tel Aviv, 1968, p. 183.

AḪAI (or AḪA) OF SHABḪA (680-752). Talmudic scholar of the gaonic era. Born and educated in Babylonia, Aḫai migrated to Erets Israel (c.750) when he failed to be elected GAON of Pumbedita and was passed over in favor of one of his students. In Erets Israel he composed the *She'iltot*, the first halakhic work to be written after the close of the Talmud. It consists of 182 halakhic and aggadic discourses in Aramaic on the weekly readings from the Torah. Each *she'ilta* has a fixed arrangement and is divided into five sections, the first of which opens with a few *halakhot* on the theme to be discussed. Section two, after a prefatory formula, introduces two quite simple halakhic questions with arguments pro and con. The third section, preceded once again by a fixed rubric, consists of halakhic and aggadic quotations on the theme of the *she'ilta*; these derive from the Babylonian Talmud. Section four provides answers to the two questions previously raised. The last section (now missing in most of the *She'iltot*) consists of a homiletical discourse. The author drew exclusively on Babylonian sources, for which reason it has been suggested that his intention was to spread a knowledge of the Babylonian Talmud among readers in Erets Israel. The only *gaon* to cite this work was the last, HAI GAON, further evidence that it was unknown in Babylonia for centuries. Not the least importance of the *She'iltot* is the fact that it contains numerous passages and versions of talmudic texts that differ from those in standard editions. In many instances, the former texts provide better readings than the latter.

AḪARONIM ("Later ones"). Designation for those authorities on and codifiers of Jewish law who, from the late Middle Ages, succeeded the RISHONIM or earlier authorities. The dividing line between them is somewhat blurred: one school of thought maintains that the period of the *Aḫaronim* dates from the appearance of the SHULḪAN ARUKH (1565). According to other opinions, however, this period began a century earlier, following the deaths of Jacob MÖLLN and Israel ISSERLEIN, or even in the 11th-12th century (see TOSAFOT). It is, in any case, the *Shulḫan Arukh* that has exerted a predominant influence over the *Aḫaronim*, determining the nature and content of their work as expositors and elucidators of the HALAKHAH. A few *Aḫaronim* nevertheless criticized or even rejected the decisions of Caro; more frequently, they displayed an innovative approach within the existing framework, although most of the *Aḫaronim* tended to content themselves with applying standard rules to new cases in their responsa and novellae.

AHAVAH RABBAH ("[With] abounding love"). Initial words of the benediction which immediately precedes the reading of the SHEMA in the Morning Service. It dates from Second Temple times, being indirectly referred to in the Mishnah (*Ber.* 1.4), where another allusion (*Tam.* 5.1) is taken to indicate that *Ahavah Rabbah* was used to open the daily Temple service of the priests (*Ber.* 11b-12a). Two versions of the blessing were already known then, however, and a conflict arose as to which of these should be recited before the *Shema* (*Ber.* 11b). It is possible that this controversy was based on a difference between Palestinian and Babylonian usage. A compromise was reached many centuries later, whereby *Ahavah Rabbah* was recited in the morning and AHAVAT OLAM, the shorter though similar text, in the evening. *Ahavah Rabbah* thanks God for His loving gift of the Torah, and requests Him to grant Israel spiritual light to understand and obey His precepts. Thanksgiving for Israel's election as God's Chosen People and a prayer for the INGATHERING OF THE EXILES conclude this benediction. The chief differences between *Ahavah Rabbah* and *Ahavat Olam* are most apparent in the Ashkenazi rite, which has preserved their separate opening phrases. Other rituals commence "With everlasting love" (*Ahavat olam*), but there are numerous variations in the text (between Sephardi and Yemenite Jews, for example). For doctrinal reasons, the Reform prayer book has severely curtailed its Ashkenazi prototype.

AHAVAT OLAM ([”With] everlasting love"). Opening words of the benediction which immediately precedes the reading of the SHEMA in the Evening Service. For its liturgical background and details of its counterpart in the Morning Service, see AHAVAH RABBAH. It thanks God for His gift of the Torah and commandments, an eternal heritage in which the Jew can find happiness on earth as well as life in the world to come. There are textual differences among the various rites. Both Ḥasidic Jews and Reform liturgy retain the traditional Ashkenazi text.

AHAVAT YISRA'EL See LOVE OF ISRAEL

AḪOT KETANNAH (literally "little sister", an allusion to Song of Songs 8:8, "We have a little sister," taken by Rashi to refer to the Jewish people). Poem in the Sephardi liturgy, also introduced into some Yemenite and Ashkenazi communities, especially those influenced by the KABBALAH. It is recited just prior to the evening prayer of ROSH HA-SHANAH. Its author, according to the acrostic of the first verses, was Abraham Ḫazzan, perhaps Abraham Ḫazzan Gerondi, a 13th century poet in southern France.

The poem, which consists of nine stanzas, has a single refrain for the first eight stanzas: "Let the (previous) year and its curses end," while the ninth and final verse concludes, "May the (new) year and its blessings begin." In vivid imagery, the poem describes how the Jewish people are in distress; it begs God to "heal their illness" and "to raise up the chief of all nations from its lowly position."

AKDAMUT MILLIN ("Prefatory Words"). Liturgical hymn in Aramaic, consisting of 90 rhymes, recited on SHAVU'OT; it was written by Meir ben Isaac Nehora'i, an 11th-century preacher and liturgical poet of Worms. His name appears after the double alphabetical acrostics heading this poem. *Akdamut Millin* is recited by Ashkenazim only;

some maintain the original practice of chanting *Akdamut Millin* after the first verse of the prescribed Torah reading on Shavu'ot (in Diaspora communities on the first day of the festival). Objecting to this interruption, however, later halakhic scholars ruled that the hymn be recited before the entire Torah reading, and this is now the more usual practice. A song of praise to God, the Creator and Lawgiver, *Akdamut Millin* also glorifies the Jewish people's religious loyalty and concludes with an account of the "eschatological banquet" which will be enjoyed by the righteous in time to come. See also YETSIV PITGAM.

AKDAMUT MILLIN (excerpt)

Could we with ink the ocean fill,
Were every blade of grass a quill,
Were the world of parchment made,
And every man a scribe by trade,
To write the love
Of God above
Would drain that ocean dry;
Nor would the scroll
Contain the whole,
Though stretched from sky to sky!

These verses, based on lines 5-10 of *Akdamut Millin*, are reproduced from *A Book of Jewish Thoughts* by J.H. Hertz (London, 1944), p. 213.

AKEDAH (Heb. *Akedat Yitsḇak*, the "binding of Isaac"). The episode describing the readiness of ABRAHAM to bind his son ISAAC on the altar, as narrated in Gen. 22:1-19. Abraham is subjected to a fearsome test by God, who commands him to take Isaac and sacrifice him as a burnt offering. When, after a journey of three days, Abraham is about to carry out this instruction on Mount MORIAH, his hand is stayed by an angel of the Lord; the angel commands him from heaven not to harm the lad, since God now realizes that Abraham fears Him to the extent that he is prepared to offer up his beloved son. Having noticed a ram caught in the thicket by its horns, Abraham takes the ram and sacrifices it in place of Isaac.

Down the ages, the awesome nature of God's command, as well as the dramatic quality of the story as a whole, evoked much comment and interpretation. PHILO, the first-century Jewish philosopher, interpreted the *Akedah* as a protest against the ancient heathen practice of sacrificing a firstborn son or other child in times of emergency (cf. II Kings 3:27). Though forbidden by Mosaic legislation (Lev. 18:21, etc.) and denounced by the prophets (e.g., Mic. 6:7), such barbarism found its way into ancient Israelite practice during the reigns of Ahaz and Manasseh (II Kings 16:2-3, 21:6). This interpretation is favored by a number of modern Bible commentators.

Homiletical (Midrashic) interpretation of the *Akedah* makes its appearance in the late biblical period, when Mount Moriah was identified with the site on which Solomon built the TEMPLE (II Chron. 3:1).

The Midrash enlarges on the biblical account in a series of legends which heighten its dramatic quality. Inspired, no doubt, by the prologue to the Book of JOB, Midrashic tradition relates that SATAN cast doubts before God on Abraham's piety. Satan charged that despite the great feast which Abraham made in honor of Isaac's birth, he failed to offer a single thanksgiving sacrifice. God counters by declaring that Abraham would even sacrifice his beloved son if He so commanded. Satan thereupon challenges God to do so. Assuming a number of disguises, Satan tries first to dissuade Abraham and then Isaac from obeying the Divine command, but all his efforts fail. Satan finally appears to SARAH and maliciously informs her that Isaac has indeed been sacrificed. On hearing the dreadful news, Sarah is overcome with grief and dies.

In the Midrash, there are two versions of the *Akedah*. In one group of legends, Abraham is the hero (cf. Lev. R 29.8); in the other, it is Isaac, who (though 37 years of age at the time) makes no protest (Gen. R. 56.11).

Virtually all Jewish thinkers through the late Middle Ages interpret the *Akedah* in philosophic terms. To Philo, Abraham's act was the supreme expression of his love of God, the highest form of serving Him. In the era of SAADIAH GAON, some pointed to the *Akedah* as an example of God cancelling His own command, which surely demonstrated the imperfection of His nature. Saadiah replied that all God required of Abraham was a willingness to obey His command. Once Abraham had shown such a readiness, there was no longer any need to carry it out (*Emunot ve-De'ot* 3.9). For JUDAH HALEVI, the testing of Abraham offered a solution to the problem of reconciling God's foreknowledge with man's FREE WILL. The real object of the test was to make actual the potential piety of Abraham, the actual being a higher state than the potential.

MAIMONIDES regarded the *Akedah* as the tenth and most severe of the tests which Abraham faced and withstood (cf. *Avot* 5.3). He also declared that the *Akedah* story presents one of the most difficult theological problems in all of Scripture. What need was there for God, who — being omniscient — already knew that Abraham would stand the test, to actually put him to it? Basing himself on a Midrash, Maimonides replied that the purpose was to make known to the world the height to which man's love and reverence for God must aspire (*Guide* 3.24). Joseph ALBO follows the Maimonidean interpretation and adds that the story is conclusive proof that Abraham served God out of love, not fear.

Jewish liturgy, beginning with Mishnaic sources quoted in the SELIHOT for the penitential season (*Ta'an* 2.4), incorporates references to appeals which God traditionally answered, as He once "answered our father Abraham at Mount Moriah." In the ZIKHRONOT section of the Additional Service *Amidah* for the New Year (Rosh ha-Shanah), Abraham's meritorious act of faith is once more invoked: "Remember in our favor...the merciful promise which You made to our father Abraham at Mount Moriah...How Abraham suppressed his fatherly love in order to do Your will..." The *Akedah* story constitutes the Pentateuchal reading (Gen. 22:1-24) for the second day of the New Year and, according to the Talmud (*RH* 16a), the blowing of the SHOFAR is in remembrance of the ram caught by its horn in the thicket (Gen. 22:13). Sephardim recite a poetic version of the *Akedah* before sounding the *shofar*, while many Orthodox Jews (both Ashkenazim and Sephardim) read the Hebrew text on weekdays after the MORNING BENEDICTIONS.

An Apocryphal reflection of the theme, known to the rabbis, may be seen in the tale of Hannah ("the mother") and her seven martyred sons (II Macc. 7; cf. *Git.* 57b). This no doubt helps to explain why, in the Middle Ages, the *Akedah* served as a paradigm for Jewish martyrdom (KIDDUSH HA-SHEM) — fathers slaying their own children to prevent their forcible conversion to Christianity. During this period, various liturgical poems (PIYYUTIM) were written on the *Akedah* theme, with Abraham as their hero. The theme of self-sacrifice (*mesirat nefesh*) may also have been viewed as a Jewish answer to the Christian doctrine of the crucifixion: there is a legend, first recorded at this time, that Isaac was actually sacrificed and then resurrected from his ashes.

The mystical interpretation of this theme in the ZOHAR is based on legends drawn from the Midrash. Kabbalistic literature, however, associates the date of the *Akedah* not with the New Year but with the Day of Atonement. The reason may well be that the kabbalists regarded Abraham's act as one of expiation and ATONEMENT, the dominant themes of the Yom Kippur liturgy.

Akedat Yitshak was the title given to an extensive commentary on the weekly readings from the Pentateuch, compiled by Isaac ARAMA in 15th century Spain. Though important in Muslim religious thought, the *Akedah* theme chiefly influenced medieval Christian typology, also leaving its imprint on Western art and music.

AKIVA BEN JOSEPH (c. 45-135 CE). Pre-eminent sage of the Mishnaic era, third-generation TANNA, spiritual hero renowned as one of the TEN MARTYRS. A pupil of ELIEZER BEN HYRCANUS and JOSHUA BEN HANANIAH, he left his impress on most tannaitic sources, introducing new methods of Scriptural interpretation, and thus helped to expand the ORAL LAW on a vast scale. Rabbinic tradition pictures Akiva as an ignorant shepherd who, as a mature adult, was encouraged by his loyal, self-sacrificing wife Rachel to leave home to study Torah. Years later, he returned with an entourage of thousands of disciples, telling them that both he and they owed everything to her (*ARN* 6; *Ned.* 50a; *Ket.* 62b-63a). Hence the point of Akiva's dictum, "Who is wealthy? The man who has a virtuous wife" (*Shab.* 25b). The Academy which he established at Bené Berak drew phenomenally large numbers of students, among whom were practically all the leading *tannaim* of the succeeding (fourth) generation, notably SIMEON BAR YOHAI, R. Nehemiah, JUDAH BAR ILAI, Johanan ha-Sandelar, R. MEIR, and YOSÉ BAR HALAFTA. Through them,

The traditional tomb of Rabbi Akiva at Tiberias. The inscriptions include some of the sage's sayings.

Akiva's teachings were transmitted and eventually incorporated in the MISHNAH (where there are more than 270 references to him), in the *Tosefta*, and in the tannaitic Midrashim.

The novelty of R. Akiva's method and approach took various forms. Thus, by means of ingenious but often farfetched interpretation, he was able to sift masses of accumulated rabbinic legal rulings and discover a Scriptural basis for these hallowed practices. In so doing, he wished to demonstrate the organic unity of the Written and Oral Law by proving that the latter was implicit in the former. Akiva's system of HERMENEUTICS likewise displayed an innovative approach. He made every orthographic variation or peculiarity in the Pentateuch serve as a peg on which to hang new and unsuspected meanings. This exegetical method, opposed by ISHMAEL BEN ELISHA, led others to declare that Akiva derived "mountains of legal decision from the crownlets adorning letters of the Torah scroll." Equally novel was Akiva's method of arranging the traditional legal decisions according to their subject matter. This produced an entire semi-codex, termed the "Mishnah of R. Akiva." It is clear that Akiva did not hesitate to revise and alter the existing *halakhah*. JUDAH HA-NASI, the Mishnah's final redactor, paid tribute to his predecessor's achievement, observing that the latter had given shape and order to the halakhic material which he assembled.

Though primarily renowned as a halakhist, Akiva is also credited with some of the most memorable sayings of the AGGADAH. Oustanding among them is his version of the GOLDEN RULE: "'Love your neighbor as yourself' is the Torah's great principle" (*Sifra* to Lev. 19:18). Akiva favored the abolition of capital punishment (*Mak.* 1.10) and used his prestige to insure that the SONG OF SONGS was admitted to the biblical canon, declaring that if "all the Writings are holy, *Shir ha-Shirim* is the holy of holies" (*Yad.* 3.5). He engaged in mystical speculation and, of the four sages who "entered the mystical Garden [PARDES]," was the only one to emerge unscathed by that experience (*Ḫag.* 14b). His concept of the Torah as a heavenly entity preceding the world's existence may well explain Akiva's bid to uncover layer upon layer of hidden meaning in the Bible.

A fervent Jewish nationalist and patriot, R. Akiva gave enthusiastic support to the second war against the Romans, hailing its leader Bar Kokhba, as the long awaited Messiah (132 CE). Others among the sages were more cautious, warning Akiva that the "messianic" deliverer might prove a calamitous disappointment (TJ *Ta'an.* 4.7-8), as in fact transpired. Having defied the Emperor Hadrian's edict outlawing instruction in Torah, R. Akiva was himself arrested and imprisoned. At the venerable age of 90 (or thereabouts), he was finally condemned to death and executed by a gruesome form of torture, the Romans tearing his flesh with iron "combs" at Caesarea. Martyrdom he regarded as the ultimate way of proving his love of God and, with his dying breath, Akiva pronounced the last word (*Eḇad*, "One") of the SHEMA.

SAYINGS OF RABBI AKIVA

Tradition is a protection ("fence") for Torah; tithes are a protection for wealth; vows for abstinence; silence for wisdom.

Before you taste anything, recite a benediction.

He who sheds blood impairs the Divine image.

If a husband and wife are worthy, the *Shekhinah* (Divine Presence) abides with them; if they are not, fire consumes them.

Everything is foreseen, yet freedom of choice is granted. The world is judged favorably, yet all depends on the preponderance of good deeds.

Whoever neglects to visit a sick person is like one who sheds blood.

More than the calf wants to suck, the cow wants to suckle [i.e., the teacher wants to teach even more than the pupil wants to learn].

Beloved is man, for he was created in the image of God.

Do not move to a foreign land, lest you embrace idolatry.

Beware of unsolicited advice.

The judge who passes sentence must fast on the day of execution.

As a house implies a builder, a dress a weaver, a door a carpenter, so the world proclaims God, its Creator.

ALBO, JOSEPH (c.1360-1444). Jewish philosopher who lived in Spain. A student of Ḫasdai CRESCAS, he participated in the Tortosa DISPUTATION of 1413-14. Albo was expert in all branches of Jewish thought, biblical, rabbinic, and philosophical. He was also well versed in Islamic philosophy and in Christian scholasticism, particularly through the writings of Thomas Aquinas.

As a philosopher, Albo is chiefly known for his *Sefer ha-Ikkarim* ("Book of Principles), a four-part work in which the author sets down and expounds the basic teachings of Judaism. He presents Judaism as based on three principles, six doctrines, and eight subsidiary tenets. The three principles are the existence of God, Divine revelation, and reward and punishment. The six doctrines are not fundamentals and one can be a good Jew even without accepting all of them. They are belief in *creatio ex nihilo*, the creation of the universe out of nothing; in the supremacy of Moses as the greatest of the prophets; in the eternal validity of the Law of Moses; in the potential for human perfection through observance of the Divine Law; in the resurrection of the dead; and in the coming of the Messiah. The eight subsidiary tenets are all related to the three cardinal principles, giving them a more detailed description. Above all, Albo emphasizes the binding factor of Divine Law, which is the most perfect kind of law, intended for man's true happiness.

Although critics pointed out that there is little originality in this work and that it is chiefly eclectic, *Sefer ha-Ikkarim* achieved great popularity. A critical edition, with English translation and notes, by I. Husik, was published in five volumes (1929-30).

ALÉNU LE-SHABBE'AḪ ("It is our duty to praise [the Lord of all things]"). Opening words of one of the most ancient Jewish prayers (often called simply *Alénu*). An old tradition asserts that it was composed by Joshua, after his conquest of Jericho, while some have maintained that RAV (third century, Babylon) was the prayer's author. Textual evidence, however, indicates that its origins go back to the period of the Great Assembly in Second Temple times, and that Rav first incorporated it in the New Year liturgy as part of the *Malkhuyyot* section of the Additional Service *Amidah*. With its exalted expression, use of short phrases, and telling parallelisms, *Alénu* resembles the earliest forms of liturgical poetry (*piyyut*). The note of solemnity is emphasized by the rhythmic prose. Despite their differing content, the two paragraphs of this prayer are closely linked affirmations of Jewish belief. The first paragraph emphasizes Israel's unique role as the Chosen People; the second, reiterating God's sovereignty, gives voice to the universalist hope for "a world perfected under the kingdom of the Almighty" — the brotherhood of man combined with a vision of the Messianic Age.

From about the 12th century, *Alénu* was also recited in the weekday Morning Service by Jews living in Western Europe. It eventually formed part of the *Musaf* (Additional Service) *Amidah* on the Day of Atonement and then entered the two remaining (Afternoon and Evening) services for weekdays. This process was largely the result of grim developments affecting the Ashkenazim in medieval times. One involved a blood libel at Blois, near Orleans, which led to the martyrdom of 30-40 Jews who were burned to death there on May 26, 1171. Even the remorseless Christian onlookers could not help being moved by the strains of *Alénu*, which the Jews chose to sing as their defiant hymn of faith; and a 24-hour fast was proclaimed for all the communities in France and the Rhineland by Rabbenu Tam. As a credo, almost on a par with the *Shema*, *Alénu* soon impressed itself on Sephardim and Oriental Jews as well, and it is now read (while standing) at the conclusion of every daily service. Owing to the malice of a German Jewish apostate in 1394, Christian censors later forced Ashkenazim to omit a key phrase in the first paragraph of *Alénu*: "for they [the nations of other lands] prostrate themselves before vanity and emptiness, and pray to a god that saves not." Churchmen regarded this as a slur on their own faith, detecting a reference to Jesus (Yeshu'a) in "a god that saves not" (*el lo yoshi'a*) and a numerological play on his name in the words "vanity and emptiness." Jewish explanations that the entire phrase was a citation from Isaiah (30:7, 45:20), and that its liturgical use predated Christianity, fell on deaf ears. The supposedly offensive wording was, however, preserved in the *Alénu* text of Jews living in the Muslim world. It is still missing from Ashkenazi prayer books in the Diaspora, although some Israeli prayer books have latterly restored the "objectionable" phrase.

On High Holidays, the two paragraphs of *Alénu* are recited separately; at other times, they are read as one continuous prayer by all Jewish communities and an extra verse, *Ve-ne'emar* (Zech. 14:9), is appended. On Sabbaths and festivals, this is usually sung in congregation by Ashkenazim. Kneeling and prostration are acts of worship foreign to Jews, but they do form part of the synagogue ritual on Rosh ha-Shanah and the Day of Atonement during the recitation of *Alénu*. Traditional practice requires the reader to kneel and bow his head to the ground when reciting "for we bend the knee and offer worship"; he is helped to his feet so that they stay together when he continues his repetition of the *Amidah*. In many Orthodox congregations, worshipers make the same gesture of submission. A widespread practice on other days of the year is simply to bow as this phrase is recited. Conservative usage varies; in Reform temples, the Ark is opened on the High Holidays, but kneeling does not take place. Unlike Jews who observe the Sephardi-Oriental rite, Ashkenazim sing the opening lines of *Alénu* to a traditional melody (or "*Mi-Sinai*" NIGGUN) in the Additional Service of Rosh ha-Shanah and the Day of Atonement. The same prayer mode, which may well date from the Middle Ages, is used for KOL NIDRÉ as the Atonement Day solemnities begin.

First paragraph of ALÉNU LE-SHABBE'AḤ (translation by Chaim Raphael)

It is our duty to praise the Lord of all things, to ascribe greatness to the Creator, that He has not made us like the nations of other lands and not placed us like the other families of earth. Our inheritance is different from theirs, our role on earth has been separate [for others bow down to vanity and emptiness, and pray to a god that saves not]; we bend the knee and offer worship and thanks to the supreme King of kings, the Holy One, blessed be He, who stretched out the heavens and laid the foundations of the earth. The seat of His splendor is in the heavens above: the abode of His might in the loftiest heights. He is our God, there is no other; He is our King in truth, beyond compare; and so it is written in His Torah: "Know this day, and take it to your heart, that the Lord is God, in the heavens above and on the earth below; there is no other."

ALFASI, ISAAC BEN JACOB (1013-1103). Talmudic scholar and codifier. Born near Constantine in Algeria, Alfasi studied in Kairouan (Tunisia) and then lived in Fez, Morocco (whence his surname, Alfasi, and his acronym *Rif* = *R*abbi *I*saac *F*asi), where he stayed until 1088. As an old man of 74, he was maliciously denounced to the authorities and had to take refuge in Spain. There, after a short stay in Cordova, he moved to Lucena, where he became head of the *yeshivah* and spent the remainder of his life, founding the Spanish center of talmudic study.

Alfasi played an important role in the transfer of the focus of Jewish scholarship from Babylonia in the east to Spain in the west. His main work is his *Sefer ha-Halakhot* ("Book of

Legal Decisions," also known as "Alfas"), written partly in Arabic. An abridgment of the talmudic literature, it was described by ABRAHAM BEN DAVID OF POSQUIÈRES as "the little Talmud" (*Talmud Katan*). In this work, first printed in 1509, Alfasi omits all aggadic comments, condenses the halakhic discussion, and deals only with practical *halakhot* applicable to his time. Relevant laws, such as those covering *tefillin*, *mezuzah*, and *sefer Torah*, which are not dealt with in separate talmudic tractates but scattered throughout a number of them, are grouped in their respective categories under the title *Halakhot Ketannot* ("Minor Legal Decisions"). Alfasi always gives the final decision of the Babylonian Talmud according to his understanding of that legal code. His work is superior to earlier collections, such as the *Halakhot Pesukot* of Yehudai Gaon and the *She'iltot* of AHAI BEN SHABHA, which are among his sources. It incorporates most of the body of *halakhot* developed by the *ge'onim*. Later scholars were lavish in their praise of the *Sefer ha-Halakhot*. MAIMONIDES declared that Alfasi had surpassed all his predecessors in this great work, while Menahem Meiri regarded him as the greatest of the halakhic authorities.

Alfasi represents a new and different type of Sephardi scholar. Those before him had devoted their attention to wider Jewish and secular studies, whereas Alfasi immersed himself in study of the Talmud. He was the outstanding codifier up to the period of Maimonides and his influence on the subsequent development of the *halakhah* was considerable. He also wrote hundreds of responsa, mainly in Arabic, answering halakhic queries sent to him from many Jewish communities.

AL HA-NISSIM ("For the Miracles"). Prayer of thanksgiving, composed in the talmudic era, recited during the *Amidah* and Grace after Meals on the festivals of HANUKKAH and PURIM. On both these holidays it is followed by an appropriate brief historical account of the reasons for the festival. It thanks God for a miraculous deliverance, whether "in the days of Mattathias the Hasmonean" (Hanukkah) or "in the days of Mordecai and Esther" (Purim). Some modern Orthodox Jews believe that *Al ha-Nissim* and a new paragraph should be recited (in Grace after Meals at least) on Israel's INDEPENDENCE DAY. The Conservative prayer book's introductory formula gives thanks for miracles performed "in other days and in our time," also supplying an Independence Day passage that combines phrases from the Hanukkah text with allusions to Israel's 1948-49 War of Independence.

AL HA-NISSIM

We thank You for the miracles, the redemption, the mighty deeds, and the saving acts You performed, as well as for the wars which You did wage, for our fathers in days of old at this season.

Illustration of Al-ha-Nissim, *the thanksgiving prayer recited on the occasion of the festivals of* Hanukkah *and* Purim. *Hebrew manuscript, Italy, c. 1470.*

AL HET ("For the Sin"). Opening words of the "Great Confession of Sins" recited nine times on the DAY OF ATONEMENT. Each line starts with the words *Al Het*. This liturgical formula — more fully *al het she-hatanu le-fanekha*, "for the sin we have committed before You..." — is of uncertain authorship and was first mentioned in the second century CE. Written in alphabetical acrostics and using the first person plural form, *Al Het* covers a multitude of transgressions between man and man. It is initially recited during the Afternoon Service preceding the Day of Atonement, then in both the silent *Amidah* and the reader's repetition during the KOL NIDRÉ, Morning, Additional, and Afternoon services of Atonement Day, but not in the Concluding (NE'ILAH) Service. Textual variations occur in different prayer rites: Sephardim match one sin to each letter of the Hebrew alphabet, Ashkenazim list two sins for each letter while both

Yemenite and Reform Jews have shorter formulas. The Ashkenazi version is divided into four parts, the first three comprising 44 transgressions and the last their prescribed punishments. After the reader has repeated the concluding lines of each of the first three passages in turn, the congregation responds with *Ve-al kullam* — "And for all these [sins], O God of forgiveness, forgive us, pardon us, grant us atonement." The response is normally sung to a traditional melody. It is also a widespread practice to bow the head and beat one's breast in contrition as each sin is mentioned. Ritual lapses are virtually ignored in *Al Ḫet*. Public confession and use of the plural form stress collective responsibility.

AL ḪET (exerpt)

For the sin we have committed before You
under duress or of our own free will.
And for the sin we have committed before
You by hardening our hearts.
For the sin we have committed before You
unwittingly.
And for the sin we have committed before
You with the utterance of our lips.
For the sin we have committed before You
by unchastity.
And for the sin we have committed before
You whether in public or in private...

ALIYAH ("Going Up"). Term with various connotations in Judaism. (1) Immigrating to the Land of Israel (whereas emigration from Israel is called *yeridah*, i.e., "going down"). The usage is found already in the Book of Genesis (13:1; 46:4). Similarly, King Cyrus of Persia told the exiled Jews that they could "go up" to Jerusalem (Ezra 1:3). Immigration to the Land of Israel for those living outside of it is a religious duty (see Return to ZION). (2) *Aliyah le-Regel* ("going up for the festival") is the Hebrew term for pilgrimage, i.e., going to the Holy Land and to Jerusalem in order to fulfill a religious obligation, but not for the purpose of remaining there (see PILGRIMAGE AND PILGRIM FESTIVALS). (3) *Aliyah la-Torah* ("going up to [the Reading of] the Pentateuch"). The honor of being called to participate in the Reading of the Torah in synagogue (see READING OF THE LAW). (4) Miraculous assumption into heaven, e.g., the ascents attributed to Enoch (on the basis of Gen. 5:23-24) and to Elijah (II Kings 2:11). Rabbinical tradition also ascribed miraculous assumptions to other biblical figures, such as Moses and Baruch, but in general mainstream Judaism was reticent about end-of-life ascents to heaven.

A Yemenite family helped down the plane bringing them on aliyah *(immigration to the Land of Israel) in November 1949, to the new State of Israel.*

ALIYAH LA-TORAH See READING OF THE LAW

ALKABETS, SOLOMON BEN MOSES HA-LEVI (c. 1505-1584). Kabbalist, preacher, and poet; best known for his Sabbath eve hymn LEKHAH DODI. While living in his native Turkey, Alkabets first met Joseph CARO and, following a shared mystical experience, they initiated the custom of studying Torah throughout the night of SHAVU'OT (see also TIKKUN). Having persuaded Caro to leave with him for Erets Israel, Alkabets reached Safed in 1535 and played a leading role in the kabbalistic circle that developed there. Many of his works vanished or were stolen after his death. Alkabets was an impressive and influential mystic; one of his chief disciples, Moses CORDOVERO, became his brother-in-law and the two men seem to have influenced each other doctrinally. The practice of "going out into the fields" around Safed, to welcome the Sabbath with psalms and hymns (KABBALAT SHABBAT), may well have been inspired by Alkabets.

ALLEGORY A literary device employing narrative, an extended metaphor, figurative speech, etc., to convey one idea under the surface of another. Thus, in ancient Jewish sources, allegory was used to heighten the dramatic effect of a particular situation or to symbolize a religio-ethical message. Allegorical interpretation of Scripture likewise reveals unsuspected meanings that transcend the literal sense of a biblical text. Various kinds of allegory are to be found in the Hebrew Bible: personifications of good and evil, wisdom and folly, danger and protection occur regularly in Psalms and Proverbs; Ezekiel's "riddle" of the eagle and the vine (17:1ff.) is an allegory of the first Exile, and his vision of the dry bones (37:1-14) symbolically portrays the nation's restoration to Zion. Ezekiel is a master of this technique, depicting Samaria and Jerusalem as adulterous sisters (23:2-45), but it was also utilized by other prophets to convey Israel's faithlessness (Hos. 1:2-2:15) and the disasters of a foreign invasion (Joel 1:2-2:11).

As opposed to the intentional use of allegory, the reading of allegorical significance into the Torah and other Scriptural passages only emerged wth the development of post-biblical commentary and exposition. It was used in an effort to discover deeper or hidden meanings in the text. This allegorical technique, known as *remez* (lit. "hint" or "allusion"), is one of four traditional methods for the elucidation of Scripture (see PARDES).

Hellenistic influences gave a major impetus to the allegorical approach. PHILO, its classic exponent, strongly advocated following "the rules of that wise architect, Allegory" (*De Somniis*, 2.2). Yet although Philo believed that the patriarchs of Israel exemplified certain archetypal moral qualities, and saw in the deliverance from Egypt an allegory of the individual's emancipation from bodily passions, he never contemplated discarding the literal significance of the biblical stories and observances.

The rabbis, for their part, in the MIDRASH especially, accepted figurative interpretations of Scripture. In the case of ANTHROPOMORPHISMS, for example, where any impression of God's corporeality had to be avoided, they regarded the allegorical meaning as the only legitimate one. A typical example of the allegorical approach is the Midrashic comment on Gen. 11:5 in the story of Babel: "'The Lord went down to look at the city'- Everything is revealed to God, yet He had to go down and see for Himself! The text, however, wishes to point a moral — that one should never pass judgment on mere hearsay, but go first and see for oneself" (*Tanḫuma, ad loc.*).

Occasionally, extensive allegorization can be found in Talmud and Midrash. The rabbis allegorized King Solomon's three biblical books (Song of Songs, Proverbs, Ecclesiastes) as the Three Ages of Man (Song R. 1.10). Sometimes, both the literal and the allegorical views are represented side by side. Thus, while some rabbis in the Talmud tried to pinpoint a date for the story of Job, another sage declared that "it was an allegory — he never existed and it never happened at all" (*BB* 15a). The Song of Songs was interpreted as an extended allegory of the love between God and Israel; as such, it was canonized, although its literal meaning as a hymn to earthly love between man and maid was not entirely superseded.

Allegorical interpretation was adopted by the rabbis as a homiletical (rather than systematic) device for expounding a sacred text. Misuse of this technique impelled later Jewish thinkers to formulate rules limiting its utilization. Perhaps the most succinct of these rules were devised by SAADIAH GAON, who laid down that allegorism was only permitted when the literal meaning contradicted good sense, reason, or other texts, or when allegory had the mandate of rabbinic tradition. The kabbalists nevertheless believed that hidden treasures were to be unearthed in the Torah (Zohar I, 132a) and, while condemning literalism, insisted that "the biblical stories are only the Torah's outer garments" (*ibid.*, III, 152a).

Allegory continued to loom large in medieval Hebrew poetry and fiction, in the theological approach of Baḫya Ibn Pakuda and Maimonides, and in the exegetical methods of Baḫya ben Asher and Naḫmanides. It makes an appearance in liturgy (the ḪAD GADYA Passover *Seder* song) and in sermons, it played a major role in Ḫasidic literature, and it can be found in the tales of modern Hebrew writers such as Shemuel Yosef Agnon.

ALMEMAR See BIMAH

ALPHABET Man first wrote by drawing pictures to represent the objects denoted by words, as in Akkadian (Assyrian and Babylonian) and in Chinese to this day. In Sumerian and Akkadian, however, the signs for certain short words were used as syllable signs, from which other words could be combined. Egyptian employed the initial consonants of one-syllable words to represent consonants. This method was passed to Canaanite and Phoenician, possibly via the harbor city of Gebal, north of Beirut (Ezek. 27:9). The Greek pronunciation of that name, Byblos, came to mean in Greek any written document and, via Latin, developed into the word "Bible." From the Gebal script, that of Ugarit in Syria (15th-14th century BCE) was apparently derived. Hebrew inscriptions prove that this script was also employed by the Israelites and later was known as *ketav ivri* (Hebrew script). A form of it is still used by the SAMARITANS. In most signs of this early writing, the object is still recognizable and they are called by the name of those objects, such as *aleph* = ox, *bet* = house, *mem* = water (depicting waves). This script is found in ancient inscriptions and was still used, even after its replacement, on certain Jewish coins, and in some of the DEAD SEA SCROLLS.

	Hebrew, end of 10th century BCE. From the Gezer Calendar.
	Square Hebrew Script, late 2nd century BCE. From the Dead Sea Scrolls (Isaiah Scroll).
	Rashi Script, first used in the 15th century.
א ב ג ד ה ו ז ח ט י כ ל מ נ ס ע פ צ ק ר ש ת	*Modern Hebrew Square Script.*

On the left: Old Hebrew script used on a coin minted at the time of the second Jewish revolt against Rome (132-5 CE).
On the right: an example of early square script on a fragment of the Book of Samuel from the Dead Sea Scrolls found at Qumran. Israel Museum, Jerusalem.

However, already by the eighth century BCE, inscriptions have been found in letters tending towards a square script. This was called the ARAMAIC script, since it is found in early Aramaic inscriptions. During the Second Temple period, it became the main script for writing Hebrew, where it is called *ketav merubba* (square script). In the Palestinian Talmud (TJ *Meg.* 1.7) and the Babylonian Talmud (*San.* 21b), it is called *Ashuri*. This is usually translated as "brought from Assyria" but this is improbable and more likely should be translated "straight [script]". This remains the standard Hebrew printed script to this day and is used in Scrolls of the Law and other religious documents. The rabbis said that Moses received the Pentateuch in the Hebrew script (see above), but in the time of Ezra it was written in the square script (*San.* 21b).

Cursive scripts also developed over the years. The best-known is called Rashi Script, because it was first used for printing RASHI's commentary in the first printed Hebrew book (*Reggio di Calabria*, 1485). Jews also used the Hebrew letters for writing the vernacular in countries where they lived (see JEWISH LANGUAGES).

The Hebrew alphabet, like Arabic and Syriac of today, does not include indications of the vowels, and these had to be supplied by the reader from his knowledge of the language. Later some letters (*vav* and *yod*) were inserted to indicate certain long vowels. They were inserted in an unsystematic manner and already in the text of the Bible were often omitted.

To assure the reading tradition, systems of vowel signs were developed during the second half of the first millennium CE. These are known as the Babylonian, Erets Israel, and Tiberias systems of punctuation. The first two put above the consonants (supralinear) all the vowel indicators which the Tiberian system put under, over, and inside the letter. Of the three systems, only the Tiberian gained general acceptance. The vowel signs do not, however, appear in a Scroll of the Law or most religious documents. Many printed Bibles contain both the punctuation and the CANTILLATION accents. Actual pronunciation differs in the traditions of various communities. The Yemenite Jews probably retained the pronunciation closest to the original. Certain vowels (as well as the consonant *tav*) are pronounced differently in the Ashkenazi and Sephardi traditions (the latter having been adopted as standard in Israel).

In rabbinic literature, a controversy developed as to whether the vowel-indications in the Bible were revealed by God to Moses or were a subsequent insertion, and, therefore, less reliable. Even slight changes in the pointing can alter the literal, halakhic, or theological meaning of the text. Certain alternative readings of the text were accepted by the rabbis and incorporated in the Masoretic text (see BIBLE), but Orthodox scholars subsequently regarded the entire text, consonants and vowels, as unchangeable. Modern Bible interpretation has frequently suggested changes in the vowels in order to reach a more acceptable meaning without amending the text itself, on the assumption that the vowels, having been inserted at a relatively late date, do not necessarily correspond to the original meaning. Some authorities point to ancient translations as indicating an alternative vocalization. Critical scholars go further and suggest changes in the consonants. The order of the alphabet was determined from its outset; this can be confirmed by alphabetic acrostics found already in the Bible (e.g., Ps. 34; 119; Prov. 31:10-31; Lam.1-4). As the letters of the alphabet were used to indicate NUMBERS, the numerical values of words were used to derive hidden or mystical meanings or for word-play (see GEMATRIA). Mystics, (such as Abraham ABULAFIA) also attached special significance to the very form of the letters of the Hebrew alphabet.

ALROY, DAVID See MESSIANIC MOVEMENTS

ALTAR Place of offerings to God. In biblical times, an altar served several functions. Parts of animal sacrifices and sometimes the whole sacrifice, were placed on it to be burnt and the blood of the sacrifice was sprinkled on its "horns" (the protrusions at its corners). In the early period, before the erection of a Sanctuary or Temple, altars stood in open fields and the sacrifices were brought by non-priests. The Bible records the building of an altar by Noah (Gen.8:20), by the Patriarchs (Gen.12:7; 26:25; 33:20), by Joshua (Josh. 8:30), etc. The altars erected by the Patriarchs were given theophoric names and usually stood near an ancient tree or a pillar of stone, the former called an *asherah*, the latter, a *matsevah*. According to Deuteronomy (16:21-22) both are forbidden. In the early biblical period, an altar could be erected to mark the area in which a memorable historical event had taken place, e.g., Moses' altar at Rephidim where he had defeated the Amalekites (Ex. 17:15) and Saul's marking a victory over the Philistines (I.Sam.14:35).

These popular altars were usually built on the crest of a hill. They were called *bamot* (high places) and were an essential part of Canaanite worship. Repeatedly, the Book of Deuteronomy proscribes such "high places" and calls for the centralization of sacrifice in the "place that the Lord shall choose" (Deut.12:11-14; 14:23; 16:16 etc.). Nevertheless, these were taken over by the Israelites until worship was centralized in the Jerusalem Temple. Even subsequently, there was frequent recourse to such local altars, a custom roundly denounced by the prophets.

After the split in the kingdom, the rulers of the northern kingdom of Israel established altars which were to serve as alternatives to the altar in Jerusalem. An altar could be of either earth or stone. The stones had to be unhewn ones over which no iron tool had been wielded (Ex.20: 21,22). One explanation in the Talmud for prohibiting the use of iron for building an altar is that the altar was created to lengthen man's life whereas iron (the sword) was created to shorten it (*Mid.* 3.4). There were to be no steps leading up to the altar for fear of the officiant's exposing his nakedness (Ex.20:23). The warning against using hewn stones is reported to have been scrupulously observed by Solomon when he built the Temple (I K 6:5). Upon its completion, the altar in Jerusalem was covered with gold (I K 6:22). In addition to the main altar, the Bible (Ex. 30:1-7) commands the building of an altar for the daily offering of incense. This altar was made of acacia wood overlaid with gold and stood before the ARK OF THE COVENANT. Only priests were permitted to approach the altar and offer SACRIFICES.

It was an ancient custom for the altar to serve as ASYLUM for one who had committed murder. The Bible (Ex. 21:14) denies this right to one who "schemes against another and kills him treacherously." Nevertheless, when Joab learned that he had been condemned to death by Solomon for his slaying of Abner, he fled to the Temple and took hold of the horns of the altar (I K 2:28).

The exiles returning from Babylonia first built an altar and only later reconstructed the Temple.

A description of the altar of the Herodian Temple is found in the Mishnah, tractate MIDDOT. It was rectangular, 32 by 32 cubits, and consisted of two receding parts. Access was by a ramp in accordance with the prohibition of approaching it by steps. The Arch of Titus contains in its frieze a sculpture of what is probably the altar of incense being carried away, together with other vessels of the Temple, by Roman soldiers.

The rabbis stressed the altar as a symbol of atonement and after the destruction of the Second Temple, taught that it was to be replaced by the giving of charity. The table in the Jewish home was seen as a substitute for the altar and many customs derived from this identification (Tosef. Sot.15. 11-13).

AL TIRA MI-PAḤAD PITOM ("Be not afraid of sudden terror"). Opening words of a biblical verse sequence (Prov. 3:25; Isa. 8:10, 46:4) which some Orthodox Ashkenazim recite after ALÉNU LE-SHABBE'AḤ. The message of these three verses is that despite malevolent threats and recurrent outrages by hostile forces, the people of Israel can rely on God's protection. *Al Tira* is read silently, by Jews observing the Ḥasidic as well as the traditional Ashkenazi rite, but an arrangement for cantor or soloist and choir is popular in Western (British and Commonwealth) synagogues. There are also non-liturgical folk settings of the second verse, *Utsu etsah ve-tufar...*, "Lay your plot — it shall fail;/ Make your plan — it won't avail;/ For God is with me."

ALTRUISM Concern for or devotion to the interests of others as a matter of principle. In rabbinic terms, an altruist is one who performs a good deed or fulfills a precept disinterestedly or *le-shem shamayim* — "for the sake of heaven." Whether a person is attending to his own needs or to those of the community, he should not concentrate on personal benefit, achieving power, or self-glorification. Similarly, one who occupies himself with Torah "for its own sake" (*li-shmah*) demonstrates his love for God and mankind, and is said to "gladden" both (*Avot* 6.1). According to the rabbis, motivation is all-important: the study of Torah "for its own sake" (i.e., for unselfish purposes) constitutes an elixir of life; when studied for ulterior motives, however, it acts as a deadly poison (*Ta'an.* 7a). Yet, in the words of the Talmud, "man should always occupy himself with Torah study and observance of the precepts, for even if he does not do so altruistically at first, he will do so by persevering in the end." Additional light was shed on this thought by Maimonides: even while mindful of the reward or punishment that his behavior will incur, a man acquires understanding and in the end he will serve God and man purely out of love. From Second Temple times onward, the self-denial and generosity awakened by considerations of *le-shem shamayim* led to self-sacrificing acts "for the glory of God" (see KIDDUSH HA-SHEM).

AMEN A word meaning "truly" or "so be it," used to endorse a hope or wish, but more especially to confirm a blessing, curse, or prayer which one has heard. There are 14 examples of this formula in the Hebrew Bible (Deut. 27:15ff., Ps. 106:48, etc.). In the ritual of the First Temple, as a congregational response to the PRIESTLY BLESSING, *amen* was not used. During and after the period of the Second Temple, it assumed lasting importance in the synagogue liturgy. From the musical service of the Levites and from the prayers and blessings of later Jewish worship, the use of *amen* as a standard response was also adopted by Christians (and, to a lesser extent, by Muslims). Talmudic sources relate that the huge central synagogue of Alexandria drew such a vast congregation that an official had to signal with a flag whenever worshipers needed to respond with *amen* (*Suk.* 51b). According to a rabbinic homily, this term is an acronym for EL MELEKH NE'EMAN ("God, faithful King"; *Shab.* 119b). Both sinful Jews and righteous Gentiles have only to say *amen* once to be saved from perdition (*Yal.*, Deut. 837). In general, the rule is that all prescribed BENEDICTIONS are to be answered with *amen*. It is forbidden to do so, however, when someone pronounces a vain or superfluous blessing, nor may one give this response to a blessing of one's own, except when reciting the benediction for Jerusalem in GRACE AFTER MEALS. *Amen* should be said after each complete sentence of the KADDISH and after each verse of the priestly blessing, the only time that *amen* can be melodically prolonged (cf. *Ber.* 47a). In some Diaspora communities, the response after the last verse of the Priestly Blessing is extended to *amen, ken yehi ratson* — "Amen, may this be God's will!"

AM HA-ARETS (lit. "people of the land"). Hebrew term possessing various connotations in the Bible. It can mean the indigenous population, e.g., of Egypt, Canaan, or Persia (Gen. 42:6; Num. 14:9; Est. 8:17); a Hittite representative council (Gen. 23:7, 12-13); foreign idolators (Deut. 28:10; I Kings 8:43; I Chron. 5:25); and Israelites as well, including both representative leaders (Lev. 20:2) and the lower peasant class (II Kings 24:14). By the Mishnaic period, however, *am ha-arets* was increasingly used in the derogatory sense of an uneducated man whose fulfillment of halakhic regulations could not be trusted, either because of his ignorance or his carelessness. HILLEL declared that "an *am ha-arets* cannot be pious" (*Avot* 2.5); and a pious man (see ḤAVER) of Second Temple times would refrain from eating the produce of an *am ha-arets* farmer, suspecting him of laxity in the separation of tithes (see also DEMAI). According to the rabbis, an *am ha-arets* was remiss in such matters as educating his children and reciting the *Shema* (*Sot.* 22a), neglected the laws of PURITY AND IMPURITY, and might be excluded from the AFTERLIFE (*Ket.* 111b).

Some indication of the animosity displayed on either side may be glimpsed from a series of declarations in the Talmud (*Pes.* 49b) to the effect that such Jews hate scholars, are invalid witnesses, and deserve to be ostracized. Whether these often hyperbolical remarks point to an unbridgeable social gap seems doubtful. R. MEIR showed respect for an *am ha-arets* who had obviously deserved the blessing of long life (TJ *Bik.* 3.3), while a common saying of the time was: "Let the grapes [scholars] pray for the leaves [ignorant folk], since without the leaves there would be no grapes" (*Ḥul.* 92a). The *am ha-arets* disappeared after the end of the tannaitic period. Nowadays, *am ha-arets* means simply an ignoramus, in Jewish religious matters particularly (Yiddish: *amoretz*).

AMIDAH (lit. the "standing [prayer]"). Central element in every prayer service, recited while standing with one's feet together. It is also referred to in the Talmud as *Ha-Tefillah*, "the Prayer" *par excellence*. Ideally, it is said with a prayer quorum (MINYAN), but must be recited regardless of whether or not a *minyan* is available. According to the rabbis, three daily *Amidah* prayers were instituted as replacements for the daily Temple offerings (*Ber.* 26b). The text, ascribed to "the Men of the Great Synagogue" (GREAT ASSEMBLY), was finalized after the Temple's destruction, traditionally in the days of Rabban Gamaliel II (*Meg.* 17b). The term *Amidah* itself appears to have originated in the Zohar.

The *Amidah* comprises a framework of three preliminary BENEDICTIONS known collectively as *Shevaḥ* ("Praise") and three concluding blessings known as *Hoda'ah* ("Thanks"), with a central portion that varies according to the specific occasion and service. The first three benedictions consist of (1) *Avot* ("Patriarchs"), recalling Israel's ancestors and praising the God of history; (2) *Gevurot* ("Mighty Deeds"), alluding to God's saving power as the Master of life, with a reference in the winter months to His bestowal of RAIN (during the summer months, the Sephardi, Ḥasidic, and all Israeli rites substitute a reference to DEW); and (3) *Kedushat ha-Shem* ("the Holiness of God's Name"), a benediction which, during the HIGH HOLIDAYS, is expanded considerably.

The last three benedictions of the *Amidah* are (1) *Avodah* ("Temple Service"), a petition for the Temple worship and offerings to be restored (on New Moons and the intermediate days of Pilgrim Festivals, YA'ALEH VE-YAVO is inserted here); (2) *Hoda'ah* ("Thanksgiving"), an expression of gratitude for God's bounty (on Ḥanukkah and Purim, AL HA-NISSIM is added to thank God for His miraculous deliverance on those occasions); and (3) *Birkat ha-Shalom*, a concluding plea for "the Blessing of Peace." The *Amidah* is phrased throughout in the first person plural, indicating that these are the prayers of all Israel. It concludes with *Elohai netsor* ("God guard [my tongue from evil]"), a prayer formulated in the singular and based on one composed by Mar bar Ravina (cf. *Ber.* 18a), a Babylonian *amora* of the fourth century CE. Here the worshiper requests God's help in not harming or being harmed by others.

The usual weekday *Amidah*, recited at the Morning, Afternoon, and Evening services, contains 13 further benedictions in the middle section, which, with the "framework," give a total of 19 blessings. Originally, there were only 12 benedictions in this section, hence the *Amidah*'s popular title of *Shemoneh Esreh*, "the [prayer of] Eighteen Benedictions." Although a 19th blessing (the BIRKAT HA-MINIM) was added when the *Amidah* text was standardized, this prayer is still referred to as the *Shemoneh Esreh*.

The 13 middle blessings or petitions of the weekday *Amidah* consist of (1) *Da'at* or *Binah* ("Insight"), acknowledging God's gift of discernment to man; (2) *Teshuvah* ("Repentance"), asking Him to influence man to repent; (3) *Seliḥah* ("Forgiveness"), requesting His pardon for man's sins; (4) *Ge'ulah* ("Redemption"), beseeching God's deliverance of Israel from oppression; (5) *Refu'ah* ("Healing"), in which He is asked to relieve the sick (provision is also made here for those so wishing to recite a private prayer for one who is ill); (6) *Birkat ha-Shanim* ("Seasonal Blessing"), a prayer for a bountiful food crop (in the winter, a special request is added for rain); (7) *Kibbuts Galuyyot* ("Ingathering of Exiles"), a plea for God to "sound the great *shofar*" and restore all Jews to the Land of Israel; (8) *Hashavat Mishpat* or *Din* ("Justice"), asking Him to restore Israel's ancient judicial system; (9) *Birkat ha-Minim* ("Against Heretics"), the blessing added after all the rest, which begs God to humble the wicked and foil the plans of those slanderers who would do Israel harm; (10) *Al ha-Tsaddikim* ("For the Righteous"), invoking His compassionate regard for all the House of Israel; (11) *Binyan Yerushalayim* ("Rebuilding Jerusalem"), a prayer for the Holy City (on TISHAH BE-AV, a special passage [*Naḥem*] amplifying this request is added in the Afternoon Service *Amidah*); (12) *Mashi'aḥ* ("Messiah") or *Malkhut Bet David* ("Davidic Kingdom"), expressing the hope for messianic deliverance; and (13) *Kabbalat Tefillah* ("Acceptance of Prayer"), a general plea that God may hear and answer all requests (provision is made in this blessing for those who may wish to offer prayers of their own to God).

Except for the ADDITIONAL SERVICE on Rosh ha-Shanah (the New Year), all Sabbath and festival *Amidah* prayers, as well as the Additional Service on New Moons, have only one extra blessing in addition to the six "framework" benedictions, giving a total of seven. This central blessing, *Kedushat ha-Yom* ("Holiness of the Day"), alludes to the special occasion on which it is recited. In the case of the Additional Service, this central blessing quotes a biblical verse indicating the additional SACRIFICES AND OFFERINGS brought on that day when the Temple stood.

Diverging from the standard *Amidah* pattern of either 19 or 7 benedictions is the Additional Service *Amidah* of the New Year, which contains three central blessings, i.e., nine altogether. These three central blessings are known as MALKHUYYOT ("Sovereignty"), ZIKHRONOT ("Remembrance"), and SHOFAROT (verses on the blowing of the *shofar* or ram's horn). After the seventh benediction of the Day of Atonement *Amidah*, an elaborate *viddu'i* (CONFESSION OF SINS) is introduced.

It is customary to take three steps back and then three steps forward prior to reciting the *Amidah*, and to do the same at its conclusion, when one also bows three times (to the left, right, and front). This gesture symbolizes the worshiper's approach toward and subsequent departure from God's throne. During the first and second from last blessings, it is customary to bend the knees and bow.

When prayers are held with a *minyan*, the silent *Amidah* (except that of the Evening Service) is followed by *ḥazarat ha-shats*, a repetition of the prayer aloud by the congregational reader. The origin of this practice goes back to the days when some were unable to pray, the reader therefore undertaking to repeat it on their behalf. During the third blessing of the repetition, KEDUSHAH is chanted responsively. In the penultimate benediction, as the reader recites *Modim*, congregants read a parallel passage. In the Morning and Additional services, and in the Afternoon Service on fast

Samuel anointing David. From a series of wall paintings on biblical subjects at the 3rd-century synagogue of Dura-Europos.

days, the reader's repetition includes the PRIESTLY BLESSING. In Diaspora communities, this Priestly Blessing is normally chanted by the priests when the Additional Service *Amidah* is repeated on the Day of Atonement, as well as on the New Year and Pilgrim Festivals when these do not coincide with a Sabbath. In Israel, however, priests recite it at both Morning and Additional services on all Sabbaths and festivals; in Jerusalem, the Priestly Blessing is chanted daily.

SOME OF THE RULES FOR SAYING THE AMIDAH

1. The prayer must be recited while standing and facing the Ark (i.e., in the direction of Jerusalem).

2. It must be recited silently by each worshiper, every word being clearly articulated to himself.

3. The feet are placed together as a mark of respect; one begins the *Amidah* by taking three steps forward, as if approaching God, and concludes by taking three steps backward.

4. In the opening benediction, the worshiper must bow his head at the word *Barukh*, bend his knees at the word *Attah*, and straighten up at *Adonai*. The same procedure is repeated in the next to last benediction (at *Modim* and after *Ve-khol ha- Ḥayyim*).

5. If at least six worshipers out of the statutory *minyan* have recited the silent *Amidah* together, it must be repeated aloud and the *amen* response must be given after every benediction.

6. Before commencing his repetition, which is said aloud, the reader must first make sure that the other worshipers have finished their silent *Amidah*.

7. Worshipers may be seated throughout the reader's repetition, except during *Kedushah* in the third benediction, when they take part in the responsive readings.

8. No conversation or interruptions are permitted during the *Amidah*, and it is forbidden to make any kind of noise that might disturb the concentration of others.

9. During the reader's repetition, congregants recite an alternative version of the *Modim* prayer (in the 18th blessing) while the reader recites the original *Modim*, all but the first and last phrases in an undertone.

10. In the Priestly Blessing, which forms part of the penultimate benediction, worshipers respond with *amen* or *ken yehi ratson* after each of the three short verses.

BLESSINGS OF THE AMIDAH

Weekdays

Avot ("Patriarchs")
Gevurot ("God's Might")
Kedushat Ha-Shem ("God's Holiness")
Da'at or *Binah* ("Knowledge and Insight")
Teshuvah ("Repentance")
Seliḇah ("Forgiveness")
Ge'ulah ("Redemption")
Refu'ah ("Healing")
Birkat ha-Shanim ("For a Prosperous Year")
Kibbuts Galuyyot ("Ingathering of the Exiles")
Hashavat ha-Mishpat ("Restoration of Justice")
Birkat ha-Minim ("Against Heretics")
Al ha-Tsaddikim ("For the Righteous")
Binyan Yerushalayim ("Rebuilding Jerusalem")
Mashi'aḇ ben David ("Davidic Messiah")
Kabbalat Tefillah ("Acceptance of Prayer")
Avodah ("Temple Service")
Hoda'ah ("Thanksgiving")
Birkat Shalom ("For Peace")
Elohai Netsor — Concluding Prayers

Sabbaths, New Moon (*Rosh Ḥodesh*) and Pilgrim Festivals

Avot
Gevurot
Kedushat Ha-Shem
Kedushat ha-Yom
Avodah
Hoda'ah
Birkat Shalom
Elohai Netsor

Rosh ha-Shanah
Avot
Gevurot
Kedushat Ha-Shem

(Morning, Afternoon and Evening services):
Kedushat ha-Yom Avodah
Hoda'ah
Birkat Shalom
Elohai Netsor

Additional Service:

Malkhuyyot ("Sovereignty")
Zikhronot ("Remembrance")
Shofarot ("Shofar Verses")
Avodah
Hoda'ah
Birkat Shalom
Elohai Netsor

Day of Atonement
Avot
Gevurot
Kedushat Ha-Shem
Kedushat ha-Yom
Avodah
Hoda'ah
Birkat Shalom
Seder Viddu'i ("Confession")
Elohai Netsor

Amulets from Italy, Kurdistan, Iran, Yemen and Holland, dating from the 17th-19th centuries.

AMORA (plur. *amoraim*; literally, "speaker" or "expounder"). Term designating the sages, both Palestinian and Babylonian, whose period of activity extended from the redaction of the MISHNAH (c.200 CE) to the final redaction of the Babylonian TALMUD (i.e., until about 500 CE). The discussions of these scholars, who comprised eight generations in Babylonia and five in Erets Israel, occupy most of both Talmuds as well as the MIDRASH Aggadah. The *amora*'s authority was limited in that he could not contradict a statement of his predecessors, the *tannaim*, unless he found another one that supported his opinion. The *amoraim* could — and in fact often did — disagree with one another. The basic focus of their debates was the interpretation of the Mishnah. With few exceptions, the views of the *tannaim* presented in the Mishnah nowhere indicate the Scriptural basis of their opinions or the reasoning by which they arrived at them. This task was assumed by the *amoraim*.

After citing a Mishnah, an amoraic discussion often begins with the question: "From where do we know this?" — i.e., on which verse is the halakhic opinion based? (or, alternatively, what is the legal principle underlying the HALAKHAH of the Mishnah?). The latter is couched in terms of specific situations (case law) and does not cite abstract, general principles. The *amoraim*, particularly in the Babylonian Talmud, explain a Mishnaic controversy on the basis of a difference of opinion regarding a general principle, one *tanna* accepting it and another rejecting it. This reading of general principles into the Mishnah led to an enormous expansion of the *halakhah* in amoraic times.

By carefully analyzing the Mishnah, the *amoraim* were able to point out what seemed to be contradictions between two *halakhot* stated there. These contradictions are frequently resolved either by concluding that the *halakhot* represent the opinions of two different *tannaim* or by asserting that they refer to two different sets of circumstances, even though no hint of this appears in the Mishnah itself. A not inconsiderable portion of amoraic analysis is taken up with the effort to identify the author of some anonymous *halakhah* in a Mishnah. The purpose of such identification is to examine cognate statements by the *tanna* so identified, in order to determine whether these opinions are consistent with the one expressed by him in the Mishnah. Frequently, the *amoraim* examine the *halakhah* of the Mishnah in the light of parallel statements in other tannaitic sources. The examination, as often as not, reveals a contradiction between the two. The *amoraim* then proceed to interpret either the Mishnah or the tannaitic sources adduced in order to make them consistent with each other.

While the *amoraim* cultivated both *halakhah* and *aggadah*, some were particularly noted as aggadists and, as a result, were known as "rabbis of the *aggadah*." Other *amoraim* concentrated on halakhic matters. Whereas the Palestinian *amoraim* (like their tannaitic predecessors) bore the title RABBI, most Babylonian *amoraim* were entitled *Rav*. This difference arose because full ORDINATION (*semikhah*) was conferred only in Erets Israel. The Babylonian *amoraim* thus deferred to their Palestinian colleagues, whom they regarded as legitimate successors of the *tannaim*. Palestinian scholars had, in fact, brought Mishnaic texts and early amoraic discussions to Babylonia (see NEHUTÉ). Accordingly, when there was some difference of opinion among the Babylonian *amoraim*, questions were often sent to the ACADEMIES of Erets Israel for a final decision. Between the two countries, upwards of 2,000 *amoraim* have been identified and approximately dated. Others remain unidentified owing to the sparse information about them in the sources. Toward the end of the tannaitic period and throughout that of the *amoraim*, scholars were exempt from both government taxes and the municipal duties incumbent upon citizens. Otherwise, for the most part, the *amoraim* (like the *tannaim* before them) earned their livelihood from a variety of occupations.

The term *amora* has a secondary meaning quite distinct from that described above. Originally, in the Academies, a presiding scholar who, for example, wished to explain a Mishnah to his students, first recited the lesson *sotto voce* to an "*amora*" (interpreter), who would then repeat it aloud for all the students to hear. At times, in the process, the "*amora*" translated it into Aramaic, or (if the scholar had used Aramaic) into Hebrew. Rav HUNA is said to have needed 13 such "*amoraim*," so great was the number of students who came to hear him lecture.

AMOS (mid-eighth cent. BCE). First of the literary or "writing" PROPHETS. A Judean, engaged in raising livestock and growing fruit at Tekoa, he was entrusted with the Divine mission of preaching repentance to sinful inhabitants of the Northern Kingdom of Israel during the reign of Jeroboam II. Having witnessed the demoralization brought about by a hollow, corrupt form of religion and by a wealthy, parasitical ruling class, Amos repeatedly admonished the priests and worshipers at the shrine in Bethel with telling prophecies of their impending doom. Responsibility, not privilege, was meant by the election of Israel: "You alone have I singled out from all the families on earth, which is why I will make you accountable for all your iniquities" (3:2). A generation before Samaria's collapse, he predicted its terrible fate (Amos 3:15, 7:9). The first prophet to invoke the concept of exile (GALUT), Amos likewise foresaw the grim fate of Israel's inhabitants (7:17), warning that true religion cannot be divorced from a just and moral society: "I loathe, I spurn your festivals... If you offer Me burnt offerings or meal offerings, I will not accept them... Spare Me the sound of your hymns, and let Me not hear the music of your lutes. But let justice well up like water, righteousness like an unfailing stream" (5:21-24). The king forced this disturber of the peace to quit the realm (7:10-13) and it was presumably later, in Tekoa, that Amos recorded his prophecies in the

book bearing his name which appears (unchronologically) as the third of the MINOR PROPHETS.

Amos was a great social reformer with a lofty conception of God, humanity, and the ethical imperatives of Judaism. The Book of Amos proclaims a universal God who will no more overlook the transgressions of His own people than He will those of other nations (chapters 1-2). Material prosperity acquired by exploiting the poor and the underprivileged testifies neither to Divine favor nor to man's godly conduct. Man's aim should be to "hate evil and love good, and establish justice in the gate" (chapters 3-6). Amos denounces religious hypocrisy (8:4-6) and stresses the urgency of repentance to avert ultimate calamity (chapters 7-8). An epilogue (chapter 9) contains the vision of a future Golden Age in which social justice and the "fallen Davidic tabernacle" will both be restored when God and His surviving people are finally reconciled.

THE BOOK OF AMOS

1:1 — 2:16	Oracles against foreign nations and against Israel
3:1 — 5:17	Reprimands and reproofs of Samaria
5:18 — 6:14	Prophecies of woe
7:1 — 9:6	Visions (locusts, judgment by fire, basket of fruit) forecasting doom
9:7 — 15	Hope and promise of restoration

AMRAM (BEN SHESHNA) GAON (c. 810-874). Head of the Babylonian Academy of Sura from 858, pupil and successor of Natronai Gaon. He wrote over 200 responsa which shed light on religious conditions among the Jews of his time and on his own personality. One such ruling forbids the taking of interest (even indirectly) from non-Jews. He is chiefly renowned and remembered, however, for his *Seder Tefillot* ("Order of Prayers," c. 860), the oldest surviving Jewish PRAYER BOOK, generally known as *Seder Rav Amram Gaon*. Based on authoritative sources, it was the first work to supply a logical arrangement of the prayers for every occasion in the year, together with complete texts of the LITURGY, applicable laws and customs, and the rules governing Sabbath and festival observance. Though originally intended for the Jewish community of Barcelona, as a trustworthy guide to the synagogue service, Rav Amram Gaon's *Seder* became far more widely influential. Its major impact was on prayer books of the Babylonian (e.g., Sephardi) rite, yet it also served as a model for Ashkenazi rituals such as the *Maḥzor Vitry* (11th cent., France). A comparison of old manuscripts with later printed editions shows that various changes and additions were made to *Seder Rav Amram Gaon* in the course of time.

AMULET Object worn or kept close to one's person as a protection against evil, natural and supernatural. These artifacts are believed, on account of their origin, inscriptions, or special associations, to have the spiritual power or holiness to ward off misfortune (see EVIL EYE). The Talmud mentions the practice of hanging or wearing parchments containing suitable biblical inscriptions as amulets. This raised halakhic questions as to whether such amulets — termed *kamé'ot* in Aramaic — possessed the holiness of Scriptural scrolls, and whether they might be worn outside the home on the Sabbath (*Shab.* 6.2; *Yoma* 84a). While MAIMONIDES opposed reliance on amulets, most other rabbinical authorities permitted their use. Belief in their efficacy was widespread in Eastern Europe and the Orient, particularly after the spread of kabbalistic ideas in the Middle Ages. Special amulets could be prepared for various needs, e.g., to cure BARRENNESS and heal the sick, or to serve as protective talismans during pregnancy and childbirth, as well as for the newly born. Traditional Judaism does not consider the TEFILLIN or MEZUZAH to be amulets in this sense, but there were periods in which these ritual objects assumed talismanic importance among ordinary folk and miniature replicas are worn today as "good luck" charms.

Amulet inscriptions included the PRIESTLY BLESSING (Num. 6:24-26), the Names of God in various permutations, the names given to dozens of angels, and various mystical incantations written either in full or in abbreviation. These inscriptions were often set down on parchment and placed in cases of cylindrical or other shapes; otherwise, they were inscribed on discs of silver or other metals, the latter taking the form of jewelry or pendants worn around the neck. Occasionally, the inscription is woven into a popular design or symbol, but sometimes the symbol accompanies the writing. Popular motifs include the MAGEN DAVID (Star of David), Psalm 67 in the form of a seven-branched MENORAH, the hand (*ḥamsa* in Arabic), squares and rectangles.

Two small cylindrical objects, with a space in the middle through which a string could be threaded, were discovered in 1979 within a tomb on Ketef Hinnom in Jerusalem. When unrolled, they were found to be silver plaques inscribed with the Priestly Blessing. Dating from the mid-seventh century BCE, these silver scrolls constitute the earliest evidence that metal amulets were used and worn during the First Temple period.

ANGEL OF DEATH The angel who takes man's soul from his body. While life and death are for God to apportion, there are occasional biblical references to a host of "destroying angels" (Ex. 12:23; II Sam. 24:16; Isa. 37:36), to a fatal "reaper" (Jer. 9:20), and to wrathful "messengers of death" (Prov. 16:14). Such evil forces begin to act on their own initiative in post-biblical literature, where they are personified as the demon Ashmedai or Asmodeus of the Apocrypha (Tobit 3.8, 17) and as more notorious figures of dread.

According to the Talmud, SATAN, the evil inclination, and the Angel of Death (Heb. *malakh ha-mavet*) are one and the same (*BB* 16a); no mortal can escape the all-seeing angel (*Av. Zar.* 20b), who waits for no man (Eccl. R. 8.8). Thus, "Israel only accepted the Torah so that the Angel of Death should have no dominion over them" (*Av. Zar.* 5a). Such notions gave rise to many folk tales and also to various superstitious practices associated with death, burial, mourning, and even with childbirth (see LILITH). On the strength of the biblical phrase, "righteousness delivers from death" (Prov. 10:2, 11:14), *tsedakah* ("righteousness") was popularly interpreted as Torah study, benevolence, and piety, through which the Angel of Death can be defied and overcome. In Jewish folklore, he was also viewed as a fearsome, death-dealing physician, a notion that inspired a quip by the 12th-century Spanish poet Joseph Ibn Zabara that "both the doctor and the Angel of Death kill, but the former charges a fee" and a sardonic echo by NAHMAN OF BRATSLAV: "It was difficult for the Angel of Death to slay everyone in the world, so he found doctors to assist him." Talmudic legend portrays Joshua ben Levi outwitting the Angel of Death and only consenting to give back his sword when the Almighty decides to intervene (*Ket.* 77b). This inspired Longfellow's poetic version, "The Legend of Rabbi Ben Levi," in *Tales of a Wayside Inn* (1863). By contrast, an allegorical interpretation is given to the Angel of Death who figures in HAD GADYA, the last song concluding the Passover *Seder*. Here, the Angel of Death personifies those medieval (Christian) persecutors whose reign of violence God would finally bring to an end.

ANGELS Heavenly beings. The term "angel" is the standard translation of the Hebrew *malakh*, deriving from the root *lakh* — mission or service — that appears in Ugaritic, Arabic and other Semitic tongues. The original meaning of *malakh* is messenger, and in the Bible the messenger referred to by this name may be a superhuman messenger of God (e.g., Gen. 16:7, 22:11, Ex. 23:20), a human messenger of God such as a prophet (e.g. Haggai 1:13, Is. 42:19), or a human messenger acting as the agent of another human (e.g. Gen. 32:3, Judg. 9:31). In the Bible, then, not every *malakh* is an angel. Moreover, there are various synonyms for mortal as well as immortal messengers, so that not every angel is a *malakh*. In later eras, however, *malakh* became the term referring to superhuman creatures in the service of God and ceased to refer to other types of messengers. Thus, in post-biblical usage, *malakh* is a near equivalent of the English "angel." Angels appear in the earliest chapters of the Bible and in many books, and their existence is taken for granted in Jewish sources of practically every period. Nevertheless, angelology never became a central Jewish concern or even a systematically elaborated branch of Jewish thought.

In the Bible, the existence of angels is assumed. This does not detract from the uniqueness of the One God. Rather it is a function of His transcendence, which implies the need of created intermediaries between the Creator and His World. With the exception of the Book of Daniel (and perhaps Job), angels in the Bible have neither names nor an independent will. Mortals neither pray to nor serve angels in any way (this point is emphasized in Judg. 13:16).

Angels of two types (which are not always completely distinct from one another) appear in the Bible. The first type comprises angels that perform some divinely appointed mission, such as delivering a message from God to a particular man, explicating a prophecy, executing God's decrees, etc. These assume a variety of forms depending on their tasks. They appear most frequently as human beings, and in all cases remain obedient to their Divine mandate. These messenger angels bear names (Gabriel and Michael) and distinct personalities only in the Book of Daniel (see for example, Dan. 8:16 and 10:13) and the Book of Job where SATAN, or the satan, appears as a kind of heavenly prosecutor. It is not clear whether Satan is a proper name or a description of this creature's role (cf. Numb. 22:22). The Bible does not always distinguish clearly between the angel and God. So, for instance, the angel of God calls to Moses from the BURNING BUSH (Ex. 3:2), but the ensuing dialogue is conducted with God Himself. Some scholars see this as indicating that angels were considered to have no independent existence, while others speculate that where original texts had God addressing man directly, later scribes may have been uncomfortable with such boldness and injected an intermediary into the narrative.

The second type consists of the members of the heavenly court who surround God and praise Him (see, for instance, Is. 6:1-7). These are divided into a number of subgroups, each bearing a different name. There are seraphim (Isa. 6:2), cherubim (Ezek. 10:3) *Hayyot* — living creatures (Ezek. 1:5), and *Ofannim* — wheels (of the divine chariot) (Ezek. 1:16).

Angels are frequently mentioned in the post-exilic Books of Ezekiel and Zechariah. Ezekiel contains references to both types of angels, with the notion of a heavenly host or court receiving its greatest biblical elaboration in the first chapter of Ezekiel's vision. On the other hand, chapters 11-39 do not mention angels at all. The entire Book of Zechariah is replete with references to angels.

Contemporary biblical scholarship finds the belief in angels, as such, unique to the religion of Israel and daughter religions. Similarities do exist in other ancient Semitic systems which have heavenly hosts, servants of the gods, etc. However, in systems with numerous gods of various rank and status, such phenomena cannot be considered precisely parallel. The messenger angel seems to be even more exclusively Israelite — a function of the inappropriateness of divine-human encounters becoming daily occurrences. A fully developed belief in created beings that are not human and act in the service of God is probable only in a system that asserts the existence of one all-powerful Creator. Angels are conspicuously absent in large sections of the Bible, most notably in pre-exilic prophecy where only two mentions of angels exist (Isa. 6:2 ff, Hos. 12:5-6). While this has led some scholars to posit an ancient school of dissent on the existence of angels or their importance, others believe that no suitable explanation has yet been proposed. Rabbinic tradition was not unaware of foreign influences upon Israel's belief in angels and mentions that the names of the angels were brought by the Jews from the Babylonian exile (TJ, RH.1:2).

The belief in angels developed in scope and complexity during the Second Temple period. Such development is reflected chiefly in the non-canonical apocryphal literature and the writings of the Dead Sea Sect. Here angels are seen to be numerous, variegated, and discharging a wide range of responsibilities. Angels may fall into different subcategories, and the most important ones have individual names and hierarchical roles (e.g. Enoch 20: 1-8). The explanation generally advanced for this phenomenon is the increasing emphasis upon God's transcendence. During this period, the sense of God's immediate presence and involvement in human affairs, so evident in the pre-exilic biblical narratives, has clearly diminished. Reality is conceived as being more complex and God more distant. His involvement in the world is mediated by a ramified apparatus of servants, assistants and the like. Thus angels are known to become involved in the lives of the righteous (Tobit), and numerous human beings are witness to visions of the heavenly court. Apocalyptic visions are narrated by an angelic spokesman. The Book of Jubilees claims to have been dictated by an angel to Moses. There are angels of the interior, angels of holiness, angels of fire, angels of winds, clouds, hail, etc. There are angels in charge of seasons of the year, and a different angel is in charge of each day (see Jubilees 2:2; 82; 75; 80:1; 60:16-22). The chief angels are known as archangels, and there are various versions of their identity. Among them appear the names Uriel, Raguel, Raphael, Michael, Gabriel, Sariel, Jermiel (see Tobit 12:15, IV Ezra 4:38, I Enoch 20, I Enoch 90:21 ff). There are also fallen angels, who have been seduced to earth, or, while they are on earth, by the beauty of mortal women and who may become involved in various evil pursuits (Enoch 6ff.; Jubilees 4:15; 5:1ff). Satan is portrayed in some sources as a fallen angel, punished for his unwillingness to bow before man (Adam and Eve 12ff), who becomes a kind of independent evil demon (for possible biblical roots of the fallen angel idea, see also Gen. 6:4 whose meaning remains disputed).

During the talmudic period, the existence of angels was taken for granted by scholars and common people alike. In the SIFRA (1:1), for example, Ben Azzai speaks of two categories of angels, clearly assuming their existence as a reality. The Mishnah (a legal work) contains no mention of angels, but other tannaitic sources do. Whereas the importance of angels in rabbinic thinking is clearly less than in apocryphal literature, it would be inconceivable that a literature as broad and colorful as the Talmuds and Midrashim could ignore angels altogether. They contain discussions of the creation of angels (e.g., Gen. R.1:3) and their classification (e.g., *Tanḫ*.B., Lev.39). Angels, moreover, are characters in various aggadic tales and heavenly debates, advocates before the heavenly court of justice, etc. Angels, on the one hand, seem to be superior to man, while on the other, it is asserted that righteous mortals are superior to the ministering angels (e.g. TJ *Shab.* 6:10, 8d). In any case, it is difficult to determine, with regard to any given passage, whether the angels portrayed are truly regarded as existing beings or personified symbols of some idea or value. As in earlier periods, angel worship is nearly unheard of and never normative, this despite (or perhaps because of) the existence of such worship within the Christian church and its approval by contemporary Church Fathers.

Jewish philosophers differ considerably in their conception of the nature and function of angels. PHILO conceives of angels as the incorporeal, rational, and immortal souls which have not entered human bodies. "They convey the bidding of the Father to His children and report the children's needs to their Father." JUDAH HALEVI identifies the angels with the Aristotelian separate intelligences through whose agency God governs the world. For Abraham IBN EZRA, angels are the immaterial, Neo-Platonic "eternal forms," the archetypes of all earthly material things.

For MAIMONIDES, angels are to be identified with the immaterial separate intelligences, although in one context, he identifies angels with prophets. The latter view is already to be found in the Midrash and is supported, to some extent, by Hag. 1:13 and II Chron. 36:15-16. He opposed the common practice of praying to angels for intercession with God.

Angels receive considerable attention in Jewish mysticism which groups them in various categories such as angels of severe judgment and angels of mercy, and evil and ministering angels. Mystical texts also contrast between angels of masculine and feminine qualities (Zohar 1:11 9b; 2:4b). Angels have particular roles in heaven and are arranged into various hierarchies (Zohar 1:11-45). These angels may assume human form or appear as spirits when executing their earthly missions (Zohar 1:34a, 81a, 101a); *Pardes Rimmonim* sect. 24:chap. 11). Every human being has a good angel and a bad one (Zohar 1:144b). Man is accompanied by angels in the world to come as well. There he is met by angels of peace or destruction depending upon his deeds on earth (Zohar Ḫadash to Ruth (1902), 89a). There is also a hierarchy of angels serving the forces of evil. These seduce man to perform evil and then report on his sinful acts (*Pardes Rimmonim* sect. 26, chaps. 1-7). As a result of the extraordinary powers assigned to angels, appeals and supplications were made to angels in AMULETS and incantations despite the opposition of many rabbinic authorities. Mystical conceptions, nevertheless, remain essentially monotheistic.

Silver amulet with a loop at the top, and an inscription in six lines with dividing strips including the names of the angels Michael, Gabriel, Raphael and Uriel. Kurdistan, 19th century.

Various conceptions of angels originating in the Bible and later developed in the apocryphal and aggadic literatures appear in the liturgy. The most common theme is that of angels singing praise to God. The KEDUSHAH prayers of the daily and festival services, for example, are based upon the text of the angels' praises of God that appear in Isaiah (see above). The popular *Shalom Aleikhem* prayer chanted upon returning home from synagogue on the Sabbath eve addresses the two angels that accompany each man. It is believed that such themes began entering the liturgy primarily during the early geonic period under the influence of mystical movements that flourished at the time. In later eras, the themes of angels as members of the heavenly court and singing hymns of praise received extensive elaboration in various religious poems (PIYYUTIM). The 16th century mystics of Safed attributed even greater liturgical significance to particular angels, positing an active role for them in the transmission and processing of prayer.

Modern views of angels tend to interpret Biblical and liturgical references symbolically. Reform Judaism has removed most references to angels from the prayerbook. The Conservatives have retained references, but do not take them literally. Modern Orthodoxy, while not dismissing the notion altogether, also tends to rationalize angels or explain them symbolically, avoiding any fundamental argument regarding their existence. In the more traditional branches of Orthodoxy, particularly those with mystical leanings such as the Ḥasidic and Oriental communities, the belief in angels continues relatively unchanged. (See also ANGEL OF DEATH).

ANI MA'AMIN See PRINCIPLES OF FAITH

ANIMALS, ATTITUDE TO The very first chapter of Genesis postulates human mastery over animals, with God granting man "dominion over the fish of the sea, the birds of the air, the cattle, the whole earth, and every creeping thing" (Gen. 1:26). Ancient civilizations, including Judaism, took it for granted that animal sacrifices were due to the divinity. The Pentateuch laid down an elaborate code of animal SACRIFICES AND OFFERINGS, observed in practice until the destruction of the Temple in 70 CE, for the restoration of which Orthodox Jews continue to pray. At the same time, Judaism adopted a humane attitude toward the treatment of animals and laid down clear guidelines regulating their feeding, the avoidance of disease or needless pain, and limitations on their work. One of the basic injunctions to Noah (see NOACHIDE LAWS) prohibited eating any limb amputated from an animal while it was still alive (Gen. 9:4), evidently a widespread practice at the time.

Other laws derive from a compassion for animals and are designed to protect them from maltreatment, overwork, hunger, and pain. An animal which is threshing wheat may not be muzzled (Deut. 25:4); animals, like humans, must be given a day of rest (Ex. 20:10, 23:12; Deut. 5:14); an ox and an ass may not plow together (Deut. 22:10) for, as various commentators explain, the weaker animal will be dragged along by the stronger; an animal that has fallen under its burden must be helped to its feet (Ex. 23:5; Deut. 22:4); and a lost animal must be returned to its owner (Ex. 23:4). No cow, sheep, or goat may be slaughtered on the same day as its young (Lev.22:28), nor may young birds or birds' eggs be taken away while the mother is present (Deut. 22:6-7). During the Sabbatical year, when all land is to lie fallow, the fields must be left open and accessible to both humans and animals (Lev. 25:6-7). "A righteous man knows the needs of his beast," it is stated in Proverbs (12:10).

These biblical laws were amplified by the rabbis, who classified cruelty to animals as a biblical offense and laid down many regulations aimed at the prevention of suffering to animals (*tsa'ar ba'alé ḥayyim*). They prohibited castration (*Shab.* 111a; cf. Lev. 22:24) and taught that many Sabbath laws could be broken to save an animal's life or relieve it from pain (*Shab.* 128b). A man should not sit down to eat until he has first fed his animals (*Ber.* 40a; *Git.* 62a) and he may not buy an animal unless he can guarantee it an adequate food supply (TJ *Ket.* 4.8). Though not opposed to eating the flesh of "clean" animals, the rabbis laid down rules for ritual slaughter (SHEḤITAH) which, according to many authorities, were based on humane considerations, so as to cause the animals the minimum of pain.

One rabbinic work (*Perek Shirah*) suggests that each animal sings its own psalm of praise to God, while the medieval philosophers Saadiah Gaon and Maimonides are divided over the question as to whether animals go to heaven

(Saadiah-yes; Maimonides-no). Jewish ETHICAL LITERATURE further stresses the duty of kindness to animals.

Animal experimentation is generally approved by Jewish religious authorities, but with the clear proviso that the animals be spared all needless pain and that the experiments must be directed to human benefit. Hunting for food and skins is mentioned in the Bible, without objection, but there is an ingrained Jewish dislike for the hunter. "Savage beasts may be killed, not tortured to death," wrote Aḫai of Shabḫa and hunting for sport is banned by every codifier from Maimonides (*Yad, Melakhim* 6.10) to Ezekiel Landau (*Noda bi-Yehudah*, 1776).

ON KINDNESS TO ANIMALS

Had the Torah not been given to us, we would learn modesty from cats, honest toil from ants, chastity from doves, and gallantry from cockerels!

While Moses was feeding his father-in-law's sheep in the wilderness, a young kid ran away. When he eventually found the kid drinking from a well, Moses realized that it must have been thirsty and would now be tired, so he carried it home on his back. Then God said, "Because you have shown pity for one of man's flock, you will lead My flock — Israel."

"The path of sinners" (Ps.1:1) is staging contests between wild animals and also hunting.

A kindly man does not sell his beast to a cruel person.

One who hunts game with dogs will not feast in the world to come.

While Judah ha-Nasi once sat teaching in Sepphoris, a calf sought refuge with him, mooing as if to say, "Please save me!" "What can I do?" was R. Judah's reaction. "You were created for the slaughterer's knife". As a punishment, he suffered from toothache for 13 years...At the end of that time, a small creature chanced to run past his daughter and she wanted to kill it. "No, leave it alone!" R. Judah told her. "Is it not written that 'His mercy extends over all His works' (Ps.145:9)?" So then it was decreed in heaven: "Because R. Judah had pity, pity will also be shown to him." And his toothache vanished.

AN'IM ZEMIROT ("Sweet hymns shall be my chant"). Opening words of the "Hymn of Glory" (*Shir ha-Kavod*) attributed to Judah he-Ḫasid (d. 1217), a medieval German mystic who traditionally composed the *Sefer Ḫasidim* ("Book of the Pious"). Biblical, rabbinic, and kabbalistic elements are mingled in this song of praise to the Creator, which employs bold and vivid metaphors that come close to anthropomorphism — even if the poet did not mean them to be taken literally. Apart from the prologue (lines 1-4) and the epilogue (lines 28-31), *An'im Zemirot* is an alphabetical acrostic hymn; there are rhyming half-lines throughout and two biblical verses (I Chron. 29:11; Ps. 106:2) are added at the end. It has figured in Ashkenazi prayer books since the 16th century, despite strenuous opposition from Solomon LURIA, who thought *Shir ha-Kavod* too holy for liturgical use. Objections on similar grounds were also voiced by JUDAH LÖW BEN BEZALEL (*Maharal*) of Prague, Jacob EMDEN, and ELIJAH GAON OF VILNA, who felt that this sublime hymn should be reserved for Sabbaths and holy days. Until recently, however, many congregations recited it daily. In most Diaspora communities, *An'im Zemirot* is now recited (before ADON OLAM) at the conclusion of the Additional Service on Sabbaths and festivals, sometimes also at the end of KOL NIDRÉ on the Day of Atonement. Israeli congregations usually recite it before the Reading of Law, at the end of Morning Service on Sabbaths and holy days. After the Ark has been opened, alternate verses are chanted by the reader and congregants. It has become a widespread practice for a boy (or also a girl in non-Orthodox congregations) under the age of 13 to serve as soloist.

AN'IM ZEMIROT

(extract from the verse translation by Israel Zangwill):

Sweet hymns shall be my chant and woven songs,
For Thou art all for which my spirit longs -
To be within the shadow of Thy hand
And all Thy mystery to understand...
In Thee old age and youth at once were drawn,
The grey of eld, the flowing locks of dawn,
The ancient Judge, the youthful Warrior,
The Man of Battles, terrible in war,
The helmet of salvation on His head,
And by His hand and arm the triumph led...
Deem precious unto Thee the poor man's song,
As those that to Thine altar did belong.

ANINUT Hebrew term used to describe the status of a person in MOURNING for a close relative (father, mother, sister, brother, son, daughter, husband or wife) between that person's death and the actual BURIAL. During that period, the funeral arrangements must be the prime concern of the *onen* (i.e., the person in *aninut*), and he is accordingly not only exempt from but forbidden to perform any other regular positive commandments. Thus, for example, an *onen* does not read the *Shema* or pray with *tallit* and *tefillin* (phylacteries) when the proper time arrives. An *onen* is also forbidden to eat meat or drink wine. However, should the period of *aninut* include a Sabbath, these special laws are suspended for the day and the *onen* fulfills all commandments, as he is in any case unable to make arrangements for burial on the Sabbath. By the same token, a person located in a place where he is unable to attend to any funeral arrangements is not considered an *onen* in terms of these laws, and is not exempt from the fulfillment of the commandments.

ANOINTING In biblical times, humans and objects intended for sacred purposes were consecrated by anointment with oil. Anointing was also a ceremony of initiation into royal or prophetic office. For individuals, it consisted of pouring oil from a vessel over the head, for example, of a high priest (Ex. 28:41) or a king (I Sam.10:1; II Sam.5:17). Objects were also anointed to sanctify them; thus Jacob poured oil over the pillar he built on the site of a divine revelation (Gen.28:18) while the entire Sanctuary was anointed upon its completion (Ex. 40:10).

The anointment of a king signified his special qualification for the office and similarly the anointment of a prophet, such as that of Elisha by Elijah (I Kings 19:16) denoted the former's charismatic quality. The English word "messiah" comes from the Hebrew *mashiaḥ* i.e., "the Anointed One" *par excellence*, who, in Jewish tradition, is descended from the line of kings of the House of David.

In the ritual of purification of the leper, the priest who conducted the ceremony anointed various parts of the leper's body (Lev.14:10-18). Here the intention was to purify the leper from his unclean state of leprosy.

According to the rabbis, the oil of anointing that was produced according to a special biblically prescribed formula, was hidden away on the destruction of the First Temple and not even used during the Second Temple period. Anointing played no role in subsequent Jewish ritual.

ANTHROPOMORPHISM (From the Greek words meaning "human form"). The description of God in human terms. There are numerous anthropomorphisms in the Scriptures, e.g. such phrases as "the image of God," "the hand of the Lord," "His outstretched arm," "the eyes of the Lord," or "His footstool." The prevailing view has always been the one expressed in the rabbinic phrase "the Torah speaks in the language of men" (*Ber.* 316); in other words, that the Bible uses such terms because they are the only kind of language which humans can understand. This is a clear affirmation that the biblical anthropomorphisms must not be taken literally, but should be viewed as metaphors to describe the otherwise impossible-to-describe Divine Presence and God's involvement in the history of Israel and of mankind. When the Bible refers to the "outstretched arm" of God, it is taken to indicate something of His power. Similarly, the expression "the eyes of the Lord" is interpreted as a metaphor for Divine omniscience. The first Aramaic translation (TARGUM) of the Bible by Onkelos (first cent. CE) attempted to avoid some of the strongest anthropomorphisms by means of paraphrase. The rabbis of the talmudic period, while frequently using anthropomorphisms homiletically, were also keenly aware of the potential danger to the purely spiritual concept of God, should such anthropomorphisms be taken literally. They therefore had recourse to several phrases which sought to diminish such a possibility, for example, their use of the term *ki-ve-yakhol*, "if it were possible to say this... [of God]," and of SHEKHINAH, *Gevurah, Ha-Makom* (the Divine Presence, the Omnipotent One, the Omnipresent One) as descriptions of God's manifestation which did not involve any physical form.

Illustration in the Birds' Head Haggadah *showing the hand of God giving Moses the Tablets of the Law. Germany, c.1300.*

MAIMONIDES is particularly insistent on the need to understand all biblical anthropomorphisms as metaphors, in keeping with his philosophical system which denies that God has any physical form whatsoever. Even the phrase, "and the Lord spoke," is to be understood in a non-literal way, for God does not "speak"; the verb is therefore only a metaphor pointing to the mystery of the Divine communication with Moses and the people, which is beyond mortal comprehension. The paramount significance for Maimonides of the doctrine of the total spirituality of God, without any shape or form, can be understood from its inclusion in his Thirteen PRINCIPLES OF FAITH. Maimonides' position was not universally accepted. One of his sharpest critics was ABRAHAM BEN

DAVID OF POSQUIÈRE, who wrote that there were scholars greater than Maimonides who believed in the literal words of the Bible ascribing physical proportions to the Divinity (see his comment on *Yad,Teshuvah* 3.7). However, apart from the Kabbalah (Judaism's mystical tradition), the mainstream of Jewish theology follows the Maimonidean teaching that God has no physical form or dimension.

Strictly speaking, these expressions are Anthropathisms, i.e., ascribing human feelings to God as for example: God willed; God repented His oath; God showed his anger or his love, is a related but separate phenomenon. The rabbis of the Talmud used anthropomorphisms extensively, while a modern writer like A.J. HESCHEL uses the concept of "Divine pathos" to emphasize the reality of God's nearness, especially His concern about human affairs.

ANTINOMIANISM (from the Greek, meaning "against the law,"). Term applied to various beliefs which negate the practice of the law as it stands, while stressing instead other values and beliefs. At different times, Judaism has had movements or sects which have been antinomian by nature, although the reasons for these beliefs have not been uniform. One of the earliest of these doctrines was that of PAUL, who negated all the ritual commandments and preached that he who believed in JESUS would be saved. The CHURCH FATHERS, too, felt that the Mosaic law had been superseded with the advent of Jesus. For the Church, the old Covenant had been replaced by a new one — one that abrogated the Jewish law.

Among Jews, too, there were antinomian trends, primarily in the different MESSIANIC MOVEMENTS. Some of these taught that with the coming of the MESSIAH, the law would no longer be in force. Certain movements, such as that of SHABBETAI TSEVI and that of Jacob Frank (see FRANKISTS), not only rejected the law as it stood, but preached doctrines that glorified its deliberate violation. These movements spoke of the virtue of the "holy sinner". Special emphasis was placed upon the deliberate violation of those laws for which the Pentateuchal punishment is KARET — "excision" from the Jewish people. A special blessing was devised to be recited before such actions, "...who permits the forbidden" (*mattir issurim*), which was adapted from the daily blessing recited in the morning service, "...who releases the bound" (*mattir asurim*). The leaders of the Jacob Frank sect went so far as to hold orgies, rationalized as being in accordance with God's will. They considered such acts to be beneficial to the world, bringing *tikkun* — a "healing" or "repair" to the upper, mystical spheres.

The modern Reform movement has also been branded antinomian in its rejection of the traditional law, but the primary basis for its position is its rejection of the belief that the Pentateuch was given directly by God to man. Instead, the Reform movement regards the Pentateuch as being written by man, although inspired by God, and as such, subject to re-evaluation from generation to generation.

ANTI-SEMITISM Term coined in 1879 by Wilhelm Marr, an anti-Jewish propagandist in Germany, to describe hatred of the Jews. The term is a misnomer, since it is used with reference to Jews only rather than to all Semites (including Arabs). Quotations by Latin and Greek writers show that anti-Semitism dates back at least to classical times. The Jews were accused, among other things, of laziness because they rested on the seventh day. As have anti-Semites throughout history, those of ancient times often condemned the Jews and Judaism on the basis of false charges, hearsay, and distorted information. Anti-Semitism was fueled to an extent by the fact that whereas other nations were willing to acknowledge foreign gods in addition to their own, Judaism's staunch monotheism totally rejected the worship of other gods. Moreover, the Jewish code — especially the dietary laws — restricted Jews from engaging in full social intercourse with Gentiles.

With the advent of CHRISTIANITY, which regarded itself as the "new Israel," anti-Semitism entered a pernicious phase that lasted until modern times. Now a Jew's very life was in danger simply because he was a Jew. Christian leaders charged "the Jews" with responsibility for the death of JESUS, claimed that the Jews had been rejected by God, and insisted that the "old Law" of Judaism had given way to the "new covenant" of Christianity. Jews would, therefore, remain permanently subservient until they chose to accept Christianity as a Divine imperative.

In the Muslim world, for other religious reasons, Jews were demoted to second-class citizens and their rights were restricted. Except during certain periods of fanaticism, however, the hatred and persecution never became as intense as

Woodcut illustrating the libel that the Jews take the blood of a Christian child to make unleavened bread for Passover, Germany 15th century.

they did in the Christian world, partly because the Jews were not considered responsible for deicide. Like Christians, Jews were seen as infidels but classified as "people of the Book" who should receive more tolerant treatment than non-monotheists. Nevertheless, Jews were generally subject to repressive and discriminatory laws, compelling them to wear a distinctive badge or costume, for example, or forbidding them to build new synagogues or repair old ones (see ISLAM).

The Middle Ages marked a turn for the worse in Jewish-Christian relations. During the period of the Crusades, beginning in 1096, Europe witnessed vast movements of people on their way to the Holy Land. Scores of Jewish communities that lay in the path of the Crusaders were either wiped out or so reduced that they had to find a haven elsewhere. The Crusades are often pictured in glowing, heroic terms, but they mark one of the darkest periods of Jewish history. Another medieval development was the blood libel, or "ritual murder" charge, based on the fantastic notion that Jews required the BLOOD of Christians for their unleavened Passover bread (MATSAH). If any Christian child disappeared from home during the weeks before Passover, rumors spread by anti-Jewish troublemakers could lead to the massacre of an entire Jewish community.

Many restrictions were placed on Jews under Christian rule. They were not permitted to own land or to belong to guilds. One of the few areas open to them was money-lending (see USURY) a practice forbidden to Christians by canon law. Often, arbitrary taxation would be imposed on the Jews, regardless of their ability to pay. Attempts were also made to bring Jews to abandon their faith by obliging them to listen to conversionist sermons, compelling them to participate in DISPUTATIONS heavily weighted on the Christian side, and even by subjecting them to forced baptism (see MARRANOS).

The later Middle Ages also saw the spread of ghettos named for the first institution of this type which was imposed in Venice (1516). Such ghettos continued to exist in various European towns until the 19th century, and in various Muslim countries (where they were known as *mellahs*) until the mid-20th century. During World War II in Nazi-occupied Europe, the "ghetto" system was revived.

Certain themes appeared repeatedly in anti-Semitic propaganda, the blood libel being only one of several defamatory charges. Jews were also accused of willfully desecrating Christian ritual objects, (especially the host), of harboring lascivious designs on Christian females, and of committing crimes of every type for the sake of money. The wholesale murder of Jews was commonplace for centuries and although the pretext given was taking vengeance on the killers of Christ, a more genuine motivation was the excuse such bloody riots provided for robbing the Jews of their possessions. Tsarist-inspired pogroms in the late 19th and early 20th centuries led to the mass emigration of Russian Jews, especially to the United States and other Western countries.

Anti-Semitism underwent a change in character at the end of the 19th century. Whereas it had previously been religiously motivated (conversion supposedly removing the "stigma" of Jewishness), since the pseudo-scientific theories of Marr, Houston Stewart Chamberlain, and others proclaimed the Jews to be a race, the influence of Jews could only be done away with by eliminating the so-called "Jewish race" entirely. It was this vicious theory that ultimately led to the Nazi HOLOCAUST, and to the fact that even a third generation practicing Christian with one Jewish grandparent might be condemned to the gas chambers.

World War II marked the peak of anti-Semitism: during the years 1939-1945, six million Jews, over one-third of the Jewish people, were put to death in the most brutal fashion.

Anti-Semites have felt no compunction over manufacturing "evidence" against the Jews. A classic example, the notorious "*Protocols of the Learned Elders of Zion*", purported to be the minutes of a secret meeting at which leading Jews conspired to bring the world under Jewish control. As demonstrated by a non-Jewish British newspaperman in 1921, the entire work was fabricated by Tsarist anti-Semites in Russia and plagiarized from a mid-19th century French satire against Napoleon III which had nothing to do with the Jews. Despite this exposure of the *Protocols* as a crude forgery, it was — and still is — widely circulated by anti-Jewish propagandists.

Although the end of World War II marked a decline in anti-Semitism throughout the West, where hostile remarks about Jews became "unfashionable," pogroms swept Poland in 1946. The Soviet Union and other Communist regimes were affected by anti-Semitic campaigns after the war, especially during Stalin's last years. Anti-Jewish feeling and widespread pogroms also erupted in Arab lands, chiefly in reaction to the Israel-Arab conflict. Recent "revisionist" historians have claimed that the Holocaust of European Jewry never took place, neo-Nazi movements gain periodic support, and in recent years anti-Semitism has often been disguised as "anti-Zionism." Since World War II, the Western Christian churches have condemned anti-Semitism and taken steps to eliminate or modify traditional anti-Semitic teachings in their liturgy, textbooks, and catechisms.

APIKOROS See EPIKOROS

APOCALYPSE Literary genre of eschatalogical works about the mysteries of a transcendent world where secret knowledge is revealed through supernatural figures. These mysteries include insights into the nature of God, the celestial beings, and the end of days. Although the term "apocalypse" derives from the Greek, meaning "revelation" or "disclosure" and is first used in Christian writings (Apocalypse of John or Book of Revelation), its forms are well attested in Jewish literature from the third century BCE. These include the biblical Book of DANIEL and other Second

Temple period works such as *4 Ezra, 2 Baruch*, and some sections of *1 Enoch* (second century, BCE), known in full only in Ge'ez (Ethiopic) but mentioned in fragments from the DEAD SEA SCROLLS. Apocalypticism is steeped in the hope of a radically new social order, reflective of the historic realities during which these works were written. The Book of Daniel and sections of 1 Enoch were consciously responding to Jewish persecutions at the hands of the Syrian ruler, Antiochus Epiphanes, which led to the Hasmonean revolt of 168 BCE just as *4 Ezra* and *2 Baruch* appeared in the aftermath of the war against Rome and the destruction of Jerusalem.

All Jewish apocalypses are pseudonymous; i.e., they do not give the names of their real authors but claim to report the revelations of ancient prophetic personalities, such as ENOCH (Gen. 5:24), ABRAHAM, or MOSES, and so are classified as part of the Pseudepigrapha ("falsely ascribed writings"). Since the voice of biblical prophecy had fallen silent and would resume only at the end of days, the apocalyptics believed they were "the last generation" between this world (or, "the rule of wickedness") and the next, when righteousness would reign. The "end of days" is conceived as a cosmic process accompanied by upheavals in nature, when earthly events will be a mere echo of the final war between the forces of good and evil, when "the heavenly host will give forth in great voice, the foundations of the world will be shaken, and a war of the mighty ones of the heavens will spread throughout the world" (Dead Sea Scrolls, Thanksgiving Song). The vision of Israel's redemption, therefore, in contrast with the biblical prophets, is metahistorical, and the Messiah often portrayed as a superhuman being. The inevitability of "the end" leaves little time for normal historical development and so disallows the possibility of changing the course of history through repentance. The ultimate victory of good over evil finds full expression only in the culmination of the process and not at any stage along the way, often manifesting a fatalistic mood.

Although the origins of Jewish apocalypse can be found in biblical prophecy, the two are distinctly different in form and content. Whereas the prophets spoke out with the conviction of Divine inspiration when they interpreted the significant events of their day and aimed at an immediate and active response, the apocalyptics relied upon the authority of venerated biblical personalities for their visions of the past or of the ultimate future. Unlike the prophets, the apocalytics challenged contemporary reality with the hope of a sudden, miraculous Divine intervention which was to redeem and restore Israel. However, the apocalyptic concepts of the Day of the Lord and a new creation, together with allegorical visions interpreted by an angel, are clearly rooted in the prophetic tradition (Zech. 9-14; Is. 65:17; Amos 5:18).

The apocalypses were generally learned works composed by the inner circles of the wise, but at least some, e.g., the Book of Daniel, were intended for a wider audience though they did not arise as folk literature. Some scholars argue that apocalypticism bears a closer resemblance to the so-called WISDOM LITERATURE in Scripture than to the prophets, even though the supernatural wisdom of the apocalypses, dependent upon divine revelation, is clearly not the empirical wisdom of the books of PROVERBS, JOB, and ECCLESIASTES.

Jewish apocalypticism of the pre-talmudic period is characterized by a number of themes which distinguish it from other literary genres: (1) the periodization of history, an idea which defines the world's chronology in divinely set eras or epochs at the consummation of which the messianic era is expected to dawn upon those selected for redemption and Israel will witness a political restoration (cf., the *Apocalypse of Abraham* and the *Similitudes of Enoch*, both of the first century CE); (2) angelology, which explores the several important positions that ANGELS occupy as intermediaries between the heavenly and earthly realms, as guides in apocalyptic journeys and visions, as an active presence in the temptation of humankind to transgress divine decrees, and in the celestial courtroom; (3) secret knowledge, or the kind of ultimate knowledge that is not accessible through scriptural prophecy nor inspired wisdom; (4) other-worldly journeys and heavenly ascents, including a vision of the throne of God and revelations about a personal AFTERLIFE and ultimate judgment (cf., the *Testament of Levi* and *3 Baruch*); (5) a DUALISM which, in contrast to the monistic biblical view of morality defining evil as a mortal choice, posits SATAN as a metaphysical entity who leads a band of angels in rebellion against the supremacy of God and thus originates sin and wickedness.

These major features of apocalypticism having already been shaped in the intertestamental period before 100 CE, they were appropriated by talmudic and midrashic rabbis in an unsystematic and fragmentary fashion. Apocalyptic themes competed for attention amid a wide range of contrasting views on eschatological matters in rabbinic literature. The *tannaim* were wary, however, of the influence of Christian and Gnostic apocalyptic texts, and so warned the people: "These writings and the books of the heretics are not to be saved from a fire but are to be burnt wherever found, they and the Divine Names occurring in them" (*Shab.* 116a).

From the early decades of the seventh century through the tenth century in the Land of Israel and the Near East, apocalyptic literature became recognizable by its messianic speculations and literary themes. In addition to the classical subjects, medieval apocalypses are characterized by a preoccupation with the messianic significance of the upheavals of world empires and with the tribulations and final vindication of the people of Israel. Redemption, instead of being an abstract theory, is understood as an inevitable process that has already begun and, although not completely in Man's control, is divinely scheduled for a future, predictable time.

In subsequent centuries, the influence of such extremely popular works as *Sefer Zerubbavel* (Book of Zerubbabel) is evident in Midrashim, the poetry of Eleazar KALLIR, the philosophy of SAADIAH GAON and MERKABAH MYSTICISM. In the

16th century, particularly as a response to the expulsion of the Jews from Spain and Portugal, messianic apocalypticism sprang up throughout the Mediterranean region. Its authors included, among others, Isaac ABRAVANEL (1437-1508) whose interpretation of the Book of Daniel led him to calculate the year 1503 as the beginning of the messianic age; the anonymous composer of *Kaf ha-Ketoret* (cf. 1500), which interprets the Psalms as battle hymns for the final apocalytic wars; the treatises of a Jerusalem rabbi and kabbalist, Abraham ben Eliezer ha-Levi (1460-1528); and the work of Solomon Molcho (c. 1501-1532), which laid the foundations in the 17th century for the most significant messianic movement in Judaism since the birth of Christianity, Shabbateanism (see SHABBETAI TSEVI). The Book of Enoch is mentioned several times in the ZOHAR thus extending the importance of apocalypticism to an understanding of Kabbalah and Ḥasidism as well.

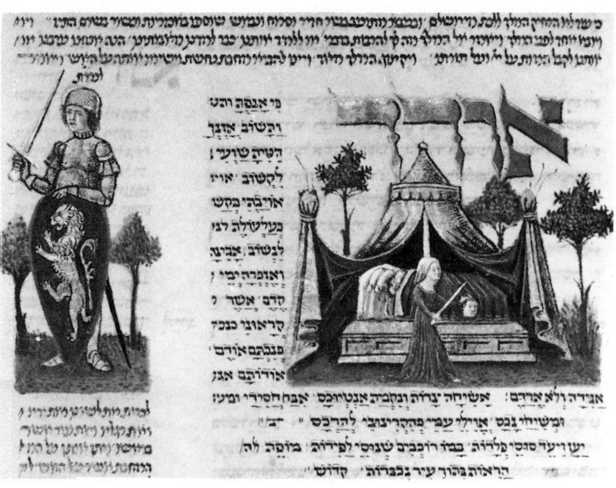

Judith and the head of Holofernes, commander of the Assyrian forces. From an illustration of the apocryphal story of Judith in the Rothschild Miscellany Manuscript, *Northern Italy, 15th century.*

APOCRYPHA AND PSEUDEPIGRAPHA Collections of Jewish writings that date from the Second Temple period and shortly thereafter, which were not included in the Jewish BIBLE Canon. The Apocrypha and Pseudepigrapha, which include various types of literature and express differing viewpoints, were originally written in a number of different languages — Hebrew, Aramaic, and Greek — and in different places: Erets Israel and Egypt. Some of them were preserved because of the sanctity attached to them in various Christian churches, where they were considered as part of the Bible. The Apocrypha and Pseudepigrapha are essential to the study of Judaism in the Second Temple period and for understanding the sources of rabbinic Judaism and the beginnings of Christianity.

The division of these writings into two major groups, known as Apocrypha ("hidden" books) and Pseudepigrapha (books ascribed to a person other than their actual author), results from the way in which these books were preserved and from their standing within the different churches. The apocryphal books are those included in the Greek translation of the Bible, the SEPTUAGINT, and in Jerome's Latin translation, the Vulgate, which were sanctified in the canon of the Greek Orthodox and the Catholic Churches. These apocryphal books include *Tobit, Judith, Baruch*, the *Letter of Jeremiah, the Wisdom of Ben Sira* (*Sirach* or *Ecclesiasticus*), the *Wisdom of Solomon, I and II Maccabees, Esdras* as well as additions to Esther and Daniel. The pseudepigraphal books were preserved by different churches, but were not included in the Christian biblical canon. There is no generally agreed list of the pseudepigraphal works, which include far more books than the Apocrypha. Many pseudepigraphal works have Christian interpolations, some composed by Christians to modify Jewish material of the Second Temple era. The Apocrypha and Pseudepigrapha were rejected by the sages, and are referred to in the Talmud as the *Sefarim Ḥitsonim* ("external books").

The Apocrypha and Pseudepigrapha were preserved not only in Greek and Latin, but also in the languages of various Churches, such as Ethiopian, Armenian, Syriac, and Old Slavonic. Some of these works have survived in their original language — a few in Greek and one (*Ben Sira* or *Ecclesiasticus*), in Hebrew, the latter's original version having been discovered at the end of the 19th century in the Cairo GENIZAH. Remnants of other such works were found among the DEAD SEA SCROLLS, in Hebrew and Aramaic, at Qumran.

The Apocrypha and Pseudepigrapha include various types of literature, most of them paralleling the Bible. There are historical works of great reliability, works which claim to be historical, and fictional works with a didactic and dramatic content; WISDOM LITERATURE and works of a philosophical nature, psalms and revelations, prophecies and works which expand upon the biblical accounts of certain individuals or which retell biblical stories while offering a different stress. Some of the apocryphal writings claim to complete books included in the Bible. These extracanonical works are not of a uniform character, and they represent various different literary genres.

Among the historical works, *I Maccabees* is extremely reliable as a historical source and was originally written in Hebrew. It recounts the history of the HASMONEANS from the ascent of Antiochus Epiphanes to the Syrian throne until the death of Simon the Hasmonean. *II Maccabees*, an abridgment of some large work, concentrates on the campaigns fought by JUDAH THE MACCABEE, also extolling legendary martyrs (as in the tale of Hannah and her seven sons). Originally written in Greek, it is less reliable than *I Maccabees* as a historical source. *III Maccabees*, a pseudepigraphical work, deals not with the history of the Hasmoneans, but with the decrees which Ptolemy, the ruler of Egypt, enacted against the Jews of Alexandria. It is of little historical value and should be regarded as a religious novel. From that point of view, it resembles the letter of ARISTEAS, which tells how Greek (Septuagint) translation of the Bible came into being. This legendary work, written in Egypt, is of an apologetic nature and was intended to show the greatness of the Jewish religion.

Some portions of the Wisdom Literature are attributed to SOLOMON. The *Wisdom of Solomon*, which forms part of the Apocrypha, was written in Greek (evidently in Alexandria) no later than the first century BCE, and was influenced by Hellenistic Jewish philosophy. *Ben Sira* was written in Hebrew (evidently in Jerusalem) around 180 BCE; translated into Greek by the author's grandson, it is included in the Septuagint. *Ben Sira*, which includes proverbs and allegories stylistically resembling the Book of Proverbs, extols wisdom and describes it in anthropomorphic terms. Wisdom Literature, influenced by the style and ideas of Greek philosophy, is also to be found in the Pseudepigrapha. This influence is especially apparent in *IV Maccabees*, which was written in Greek and which combines the principles of Judaism with Greek philosophical ideas, especially those of the Stoics.

Many apocryphal or pseudepigraphical works retell bible stories. The *Book of Jubilees*, which describes the Divine revelations to Moses on Sinai, repeats the Scriptural account from Creation until the first chapters of Exodus, with certain omissions, changes, and additions. *Jubilees* was originally written in Hebrew, fragments having been discovered at Qumran, but the entire book survives only in Ethiopian. "*Biblical Antiquities*" — mistakenly attributed to Philo and therefore known as *Pseudo-Philo* — repeats the stories of the Bible from Adam to David. The *Book of Adam and Eve* deals primarily with episodes involving the first couple after their banishment from the Garden of Eden. *Asenath*, originally written in Greek, is a long work recounting Joseph's marriage to Asenath, daughter of Potiphera, which is mentioned in Genesis. The *Epistle of Jeremiah* and the works attributed to Baruch amplify the biblical text of Jeremiah. The *Ascension of Isaiah*, which contains numerous Christian interpolations, describes the prophet's flight from Jerusalem and his murder by Manasseh. Two books of the Apocrypha known as *I* and *II Esdras* modify or embroider episodes in II Chronicles, the Book of Ezra, and parts of Nehemiah. A special place in the Pseudepigrapha is occupied by the various "testaments" which recount the last words of biblical heroes on their death beds, also including moral and didactic lessons. The major work in this genre is the *Testaments of the Twelve Patriarchs.*

The Apocrypha also includes additions to the canonical text of several biblical books. Thus, the Greek *Additions to the Book of Esther* (also known as *The Rest of Esther*) supply a number of apologetic chapters that give the book a religious dimension and expand its literary content. Among the *Additions to the Book of Daniel* are two works deserving a place on their own: the *History of Susanna* or *Susanna and the Elders*, which describes the attempt made by two lustful old men to incriminate the virtuous Susannah prior to her rescue by the wise young Daniel; and *Bel and the Dragon*, a mocking refutation of idolatry. Others include the *Prayers of Manasseh* and the *Song of the Three Holy Children*, ascribed to Daniel's friends, who were saved from the fiery furnace.

The apocryphal books of *Tobit* and *Judith* resemble *Susanna*, being religious fiction of a didactic character. *Tobit* describes the ideal home life and adventures of a righteous Israelite, carried away to exile in Nineveh, whom the angel Raphael supports in his fight with ASMODEUS. The second book is also a novella, telling the heroic story of Judith, a beautiful and patriotic woman, who manages to behead Nebuchadnezzar's general, Holofernes, thereby saving Israel from the foreign menace. Both works are ancient, dating back to the late Persian era (fourth cent. BCE) or at least to the early Hasmonean period (c. 160 BCE).

Many hymns and prayers are scattered among the Apocrypha and Pseudepigrapha. Some of these are collections which strongly resemble the Book of Psalms. A notable example, the *Psalms of Solomon*, appears originally to have been written in Hebrew. The short *Prayer of Manasseh*, a wicked king who repents and confesses his sins while held captive in Babylon, was only preserved in Greek and Syriac.

Apocryphic literature, made up of books dealing with visions and revelations, constitutes a major genre of the same period. Numerous apocalytic books, ascribed to biblical figures, are included in the Pseudepigrapha. Enoch plays a major role, the two apocalyptic revelations attributed to him being known by the languages in which they were preserved. The Ethiopian *Book of Enoch* (also known as *Enoch I*) comprises a number of works written at different periods. Parts of it were written before the Hasmonean era and some fragments of the book in Aramaic have been found at Qumran. This *Book of Enoch* includes revelations concerning the Day of Judgment, a description of the Messiah, other revelations of Sheol, the Garden of Eden, and the heavens, a symbolic description of Jewish history, and astrological material. The Slavonic *Book of Enoch* is also an apocalyptic work, describing the hero's ascent through the seven heavens and the lives of his descendants until the Flood. It includes cosmological speculations, moral guidance, and prophecies concerning the future. The Slavonic *Enoch* is also composed of diverse elements, and scholars have not reached any conclusions as to its date and provenance. Another such work, which survived in a (Slavonic) Christian form, is the *Apocalypse of Abraham.* Its Jewish original, describing revelations to Abraham by the angel Jehoel, was evidently written in Hebrew after the destruction of the Second Temple. Similarly, the apocalyptic *Esdras* (also known as IV Ezra) seems to have been composed in Erets Israel after 70 CE. Baruch is the supposed author of two apocalyptic works, the Syriac (*II*) *Baruch* and the

Ethiopian (*III*) *Baruch*, which are among the latest of the apocryphal works.

The Apocrypha and Pseudepigrapha were written over a period of 400 years (300 BCE-100 CE). The oldest books date from the end of the Persian era while the last of these works postdate the Second Temple's destruction. Apocryphal literature reflects a wide range of thought during the Second Temple era in two of the largest Jewish centers, Erets Israel and Egypt. Various philosophical streams and religious views are represented and, in a number of the oldest works, a Persian influence is unmistakable. Others betray a Hellenistic influence, some bearing the imprint of Greek (primarily Stoic) philosophy. Most books of the Apocrypha are concerned with the Jewish people and ignore sectarian disputes. A major trend, originating in Egypt, was toward apologetics with a non-Jewish public in mind.

By contrast a number of the pseudepigraphical works show evidence of sectarianism, particularly in *Enoch* and in the *Book of Jubilees*, where there are references to a (solar) calendar differing from the (lunar) one used in mainstream Judaism. The numerous apocalyphic books in the Pseudepigrapha must have originated among circles that believed in the continuity of Divine revelation. The fact that these apocalypses are associated with biblical figures indicates an attempt by those circles to gain Scriptural legitimacy for their writings.

The apocryphal books were not accepted by the rabbis and were therefore preserved only in the Christian churches or in the libraries of the Dead Sea Sect. The one exception is *Ben Sira*, which is quoted in the Talmud. It appears that the sages were mainly averse to apocalyptic literature, as may be seen from their warnings against reading "external books" or searching for hidden meanings (*San. 10.1*) and from their negative comments about *Enoch*. Nevertheless, many of the stories and motifs found both in the Apocrypha and in the Pseudepigrapha also recur in the Talmud and Midrash. PIRKÉ DE-RABBI ELIEZER, a late Midrash dating from the era of the Muslim conquest, includes a good deal of material that stems from the Apocrypha while the ancient mystical HEKHALOT literature develops apocalyptic motifs of similar original. This literature grants an important role to Enoch, hero of the pseudepigraphal revelations. Especially popular during the Middle Ages was *Megillat Antiochus*, the *Scroll of Antiochus* (or *of the Hasmoneans*) dating from geonic times, which drew from *I Maccabees* and was often read on ḤANUKKAH. Since the *Wisdom of Ben Sira* and the *Testament of Levi* were unearthed in the Cairo *Genizah*, it is clear that a number of apocryphal works were preserved among the Jews for a considerable period of time.

Throughout the Middle Ages, Jewish scholars maintained an interest in the apocryphal works which had been preserved in other languages and translated them into Hebrew. The author of Sefer *Yosippon* (*Pseudo-Josephus*), written in tenth-century Italy, (though partly of earlier date) utilized apocryphal works included in the Latin Vulgate. MIDRASH VA-YISSA'U, a medieval reworking of the stories found in the *Testament of Judah* and the *Book of Jubilees*, is based on a translation from Greek or Latin. Medieval Hebrew versions of *Judith* and *Tobit* could also be found. Quotations from the *Testaments of the Twelve Patriarchs* are included in GENESIS RABBATI, a work ascribed to R. Moses ha-Darshan. During the Renaissance, Azariah dei Rossi promoted Jewish scholarly interest in the Apocrypha and Pseudepigrapha by translating the *Letter of Aristeas* into Hebrew. Since the EMANCIPATION era, many such works have been published in Hebrew versions.

APOLOGETICS AND POLEMICS Defense of a credal position and the rebutting of attacks against it. The beginnings of Jewish apologetics are generally dated to the Hellenistic period, when Jewish writers sought to defend Judaism against the criticisms of Hellenism and paganism. Two noted works were Philo's *Apology on behalf of the Jews* and *Against Apion* by the historian Josephus, who vindicated the Jewish religion against the calumnies of an anti-Jewish propagandist, Apion. The Hellenistic Jewish apologists defended themselves against accusations, explained the nature of Judaism, and also counterattacked with a critique of paganism. Apologetics are also to be found in the Talmud and Midrash, often in the shape of fanciful arguments between rabbis and pagans (philosophers, officials, even rulers); the arguments of opponents are cited and then refuted.

The rise of Christianity, and later of Islam, led to an extensive apologetic literature. The argument with CHRISTIANITY can be detected in various passages in both the Talmud and the liturgy, although these were often later deleted by Christian censors. Modern talmudic scholarship has revealed previously unsuspected apologetic (usually anti-Christian) nuances in talmudic texts. When ABBAHU said "If someone tells you 'I am God,' he is a liar; 'I am the son of man,' his end is that he will regret it; 'I am going to heaven' — he will not fulfill it" (TJ *Ta'an* 2.1, 65f), the object of the statement is not spelled out, but its meaning must have been obvious to Abbahu's audience.

In the Middle Ages, Jewish apologists were concerned with answering the attacks not only of other faiths but also of Jewish sects regarded as heretical. The outstanding example was that of the KARAITES, who at one time threatened to become serious rivals to rabbinical Jews. The replies to Karaism, notably by SAADIAH GAON (tenth century), led eventually to a decline in support for their teachings. At this time, Jews were forced by the Church into verbal apologetics which took the form of DISPUTATIONS. Apologetics can also be found in the writings of many outstanding Jewish medieval scholars: David KIMḤI's commentary on the Bible contains many excursuses which are anti-Christian polemics; Judah HALEVI's famous *Kuzari* — based on a supposedly historical disputation between a Christian, a Muslim, and a Jew which persuaded the king of the KHAZARS to embrace Judaism — is in fact a 12th-century Jewish apologetic against Christianity and Islam. Other notable Jewish polemical works included Joseph KIMHI's *Sefer ha-Berit*, which defends Judaism and shows its excellence; the satirical *Al Tehi ka-Avotekha* of Profiat Duran, written in Spain (c.1400); the *Sefer ha-Nitsaḇon* of Yom Tov Lipmann Mülhausen, summarizing an early 15th-century disputation held in Prague; and the outstanding *Ḥizzuk Emunah* of the Karaite Isaac ben Abraham of Troki (16th cent.), which was translated into Latin and was widely read in Christian circles. A widespread apologetic literature also grew up among ex-Marranos settled in northern Europe who sought to persuade others in a similar position of the superiority of Judaism to Christianity. A leading example is Manasseh Ben Israel's *Vindiciae Judaeorum* (1656), which was directed to non-Jewish readers.

Moses MENDELSSOHN's *Jerusalem* (1783) was written as a defense against criticism of his earlier writings and aroused considerable discussion in Christian circles, but his presentation of Judaism proved highly influential in paving the way to the granting of civil rights to Jews.

In the 19th and 20th centuries, "ritual murder" accusations and anti-Semitic manifestations, culminating in Nazism, evoked a certain Jewish apologetic response. However, the advent of Emancipation, the growth of Jewish nationalism and especially Zionism, the post-World War II acceptance of religious and cultural pluralism in major countries of Jewish residence, and the replacement of Jewish-Christian polemics by dialogue have all helped to diminish the role of apologetics in modern times.

APOSTASY Abandoning one's faith to accept another. The Bible acknowledges the possibility of such acts when it warns: "If your brother ... or your closest friend ... entices you secretly, saying, 'Come let us worship other gods'... do not assent or give heed to him ... but take his life" (Deut. 13:7,9-10). All the prophets preach against IDOLATRY, which was not uncommon among the ancient Israelites, though probably not apostasy as generally understood. Those who indulged in idolatrous practices did not break their ties with the religion or the people of Israel.

The first formal account of organized apostasy dates from the period of the HASMONEANS (second century BCE). Under the influence of their Greco-Syrian rulers, many Jews — primarily those of the upper classes — became Hellenized, in the process discarding the religion of their ancestors. Sacrifices were even offered in the Temple in Jerusalem to foreign gods. Under the leadership of the priestly Hasmonean clan, the foreign rulers were driven out and the entire nation reverted to Judaic practice.

Under Roman rule, there were individual Jews who apostatized. Tiberius Julius Alexander, for example, the nephew of PHILO, went over to the enemy and even led a Roman army unit in the siege and subsequent destruction of Jerusalem.

The next major challenge came with the rise of Christianity. At first, the Judeo-Christians remained part of the Jewish people, but eventually they severed their links with Judaism. Once Christian doctrine embraced the Incarnation and the Trinity, concepts which Jews regard as nothing less than idolatrous, the final break proved unavoidable. Early in the Christian era, an extra petition "against apostates and heretics" composed by Samuel ha-Katan, was added to the 18 blessings of the daily *Amidah* prayer, and early versions of this text may specifically have mentioned the Nazarenes or Christians (see BIRKAT HA-MINIM).

The sages make a distinction between a person who apostatizes for material benefit and one who does so out of conviction. They likewise distinguish between those who convert under pressure (*anusim*) and those who do so voluntarily and for ideological reasons (*meshummadim*). HERESY, though excoriated, is judged according to its seriousness. The most famous heretic in the Talmud was ELISHA BEN AVUYAH, never mentioned by name but only as *Aḇer* — the "other one."

During the Middle Ages, especially in Christian lands, pressure was often exerted for Jews to convert, the alternative being death. Whether motivated originally by fear or conviction, some of these converts to Christianity became zealous observers of their new religion. Such *meshummadim* were usually deemed to be experts in Jewish lore and practice, for which reason the Church enlisted them in its war against the Synagogue. Many DISPUTATIONS were enforced upon the Jews in medieval times, and the Christian champion was often a converted Jew. Other converts were recruited to censor Jewish books (see CENSORSHIP). A notorious example was Johann Pfefferkorn (1469-1521?) who, though a butcher of scant Jewish education, was given the responsibility of passing judgment on rabbinic books. Pfefferkorn's attempt to have all copies of the Talmud confiscated or destroyed was unsuccessful.

The great pressure exerted on Jews in Spain (1391-1492) resulted in many converting outwardly, while maintaining their Jewish identity in secret. These Spanish *conversos* or "New Christians" were dubbed "MARRANOS," a term of opprobrium meaning "swine," but among professing Sephardi Jews they were known as *anusim*, "forced converts" (see above). Marranos were the chief victims of the Inquisition in Spain and Portugal: once baptized, any person clinging to Jewish observances was condemned by the Church as a heretic and might perish at the stake.

Less frequently, there were periods when Muslim extremists (e.g. the Almohads in 12th-13th century North Africa and Spain) forced Jews and many Christians to embrace Islam. Many of these *anusim* also led a double life, conducting themselves as Muslims in public while remaining loyal to Judaism in the secrecy of their homes.

Jews in a church in Rome, forced by priests and soldiers to remain seated and listen to a conversion sermon. Watercolor by Hieronymus Hess, 1829.

With the dawning of European Enlightenment and EMANCIPATION, large numbers of educated Jews converted to Christianity, seeing this as the only way to advance in life. The German Jewish poet, Heinrich Heine (1797-1856) termed his baptismal certificate the "entrance ticket to European civilization." Others, contrasting their dismal ghetto existence with the allurements of the "outside world," abandoned Judaism as a matter of genuine conviction: some openly disparaged loyal Jews, a few even propagated ANTI-SEMITISM; conversion was also one way of evading tax levied by Jewish communities.

Traditionally, an apostate is considered dead, to the extent that close relatives even observe all the practices of MOURNING for him. When an apostate actually dies, however, no such mourning period is observed. There are halakhic discussions as to whether a Jew who once converted, and who now wishes to return to the fold, need perform any symbolic act — such as immersion in a ritual bath (*mikveh*) before resuming his former status (although, halakhically, a Jew who converts still remains a Jew). While generally averse to facilitating DIVORCE, Jewish law is lenient in the case of a woman whose husband has apostatized, the assumption being that she would rather be divorced than remain married to an apostate.

Christians have a long record of active missionary work aimed at converting Jews. The missionary (sometimes himself an apostate) was particularly feared and hated by the Jews of Eastern Europe. However, since the HOLOCAUST, the Roman Catholic and some other mainline churches have ceased their missions to the Jews. In the contemporary world, Jewish apostates are not especially numerous, but there are certain fringe groups and CULTS, the "Messianic Jews," for example, and "Jews for Jesus," whose members still consider themselves part of the Jewish people, although Jews tend to classify them as apostates.

ARAKHIN (Evaluations). Fifth tractate of Order KODASHIM in the Mishnah. Its nine chapters deal mainly with the laws of dedicating property, be it animals, produce, or money, to the Temple (cf. Lev.27:1-8, 16-24; 25:25-34). Once dedicated, this property becomes "holy" and may not be used for any profane purpose without being first redeemed. The last three chapters discuss buying, selling, and redeeming dedicated real estate and the special laws which take effect in the JUBILEE YEAR. The subject matter of *Arakhin* is amplified in the Babylonian Talmud and the *Tosefta*.

ARAMA, ISAAC BEN MOSES (c.1420-c.1494). Philosopher and preacher born in northern Spain. He served as rabbi in Tarragona and later in Calatayud; there, in addition to his rabbinic and communal responsibilities, he headed a *yeshivah* (talmudical academy). Arama joined the Spanish exiles in 1492 and died either in Naples or in Salonika. His major work is *Akedat Yitsḫak* ("The Binding of Isaac"), a voluminous philosophical commentary on the Pentateuch containing more than 100 homiletical essays based on the weekly Torah portion. Each essay (or "portal") is divided into two parts, the Investigation and the Exposition. While the latter part became an important homiletical source, it is through the first portion that Arama gained renown as a medieval Jewish philosopher by virtue of his wide examination of all the doctrines and beliefs of Judaism. He demonstrates a comprehensive knowledge of his predecessors, from SAADIAH GAON onward, and also reveals his acquaintance with the early classical Greek thinkers and with their Arab translators. Although MAIMONIDES is his chief guide, Arama nevertheless frequently differs with him, particularly as an anti-Aristotelian who insisted on the primacy of religious faith over reason. While there is little originality in his conclusions, the eclecticism displayed leads him to present what he considers to be the normative theological view. This made him a noteworthy representative of the medieval Jewish mind. Arama's other works include *Ḫazut Kashah* ("A Burdensome Vision"), on the relationship between religion and philosophy; and commentaries on the Five Scrolls and the Book of Proverbs.

ARAMAIC North Semitic language, similar to Hebrew and written with the same square script (see ALPHABET). The first Arameans seem to have lived in the south-eastern part of Mesopotamia in the area of Ur from where Abraham's family originated (Gen.11:31). The tribal name *Kasdim*

The Rema Synagogue in Cracow, Poland, restored after the Second World War.

("Ur of Kasdim") is shown by Akkadian documents to denote speakers of Aramaic, who are called in Akkadian "Kaldu," and later known as Chaldeans.

Aramaic is found in inscriptions from Sam'al, now Zendjirli, in the far north across the Turkish frontier, down to Syria, where Aramean states existed during the period of the First Temple. In Mesopotamia, the Aramaic language spread, partly because it was not written in cuneiform script; the latter was hard to learn and required tablets which needed to be heated and took up space, while Aramaic was written with pens and ink. In the course of time, Aramaic became a link between the multilingual populations of Mesopotamia, and was taken over by the Persians who ruled the Near East after 529 BCE and used Aramaic for their correspondence. In the Bible, parts of the books of Daniel and Ezra are in Aramaic.

Among Jews, Aramaic was employed in the Second Temple period as an international language for contracts, and has remained so until now as the text for marriage (*ketubbah*) and divorce (*get*) documents. It was also used for the mystical texts among the DEAD SEA SCROLLS. There is a controversy whether, at the time, Aramaic replaced HEBREW as the spoken language among the lower classes of the Jewish population of Palestine. This was argued especially by Christian scholars, who assumed that the Gospels had originally been in Aramaic. As evidence, they cited a dozen words quoted in the New Testament, half of which could equally well be Mishnaic Hebrew. It is probable that JESUS, having grown up in Galilee, would have known Aramaic, but since, according to the Gospels, he was expert in the Bible, he must have known Hebrew. This allows no conclusion regarding the language of his preaching.

The TARGUM which accompanied the reading of the Law was an Aramaic translation of the Bible and also a commentary. It was given in Aramaic in order to differentiate between the reading and the comment, lest listeners conclude that the comments were also written in the text. This is confirmed by the later Palestinian Targums (translations of the Bible into Aramaic) which inserted much additional information. At a time when texts could be obtained only in handwritten copies, and only a minority of the people could read, it was important to make clear whether a text was the original or a commentary, and this could be indicated by changing the language. This probably applies to the use of Aramaic in the Palestinian TALMUD. It is more probable that the discussions in the Babylonian Talmud were originally held in Aramaic, though in an educated form of that language, different from those sayings introduced by "as people say," which contain what appears to be a reproduction of ordinary speech.

The use of Aramaic in Mesopotamia diminished in the geonic period (600-1040 CE). After the Muslim conquest in the 7th century, Arabic replaced the local Aramaic (Syriac), also among Jews.

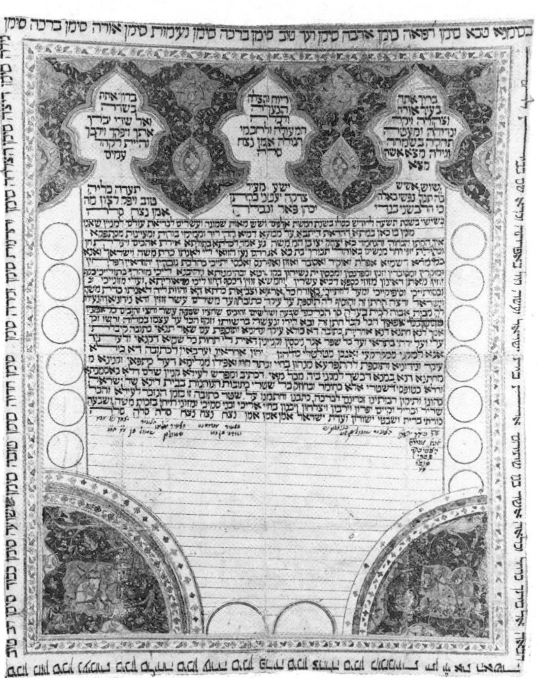

A ketubbah *(marriage contract) written in Aramaic. From Herat, Afghanistan, 1868. Marriage contracts are still written in Aramaic today.*

Several items in the LITURGY are recited in Aramaic to this day, the best known being the KADDISH. KOL NIDRÉ, the introduction of the Day of Atonement, is said in most communities in Aramaic. Some sections of the Passover Haggadah, such as HA LAḤMA ANYA are also in Aramaic. The most outstanding field for the use of Aramaic in the Middle Ages was in Kabbalah, beginning with the ZOHAR (towards the end of the 13th century CE), and many Jewish mystical works were written in Aramaic.

Aramaic, especially that of the Babylonian Talmud, has played a role in the formation of the modern Hebrew vocabulary.

ARCHISYNAGOGOS ("Head of the synagogue"). Greek term used in Hellenistic and Roman times for the official in charge of the synagogue, who also served as head of the Jewish community. His functions were wide-ranging, both in regard to the synagogue building and services and also within the community as a whole. The term is found in many inscriptions, from Erets Israel to Rome, and it was sometimes used as an honorary title bestowed on women and even on children. Other inscriptions have been found mentioning a ***Pater Synagogae*** (Latin: "father of the synagogue") either another form of *Archisynagogos* or else a title of honor given to some congregational worker or benefactor. The designation *Mater Synagogae* ("mother of the synagogue") is also found.

Jewish wedding. Painting by Moritz Oppenheim. Germany, 19th century.

ARISTEAS, LETTER OF Pseudepigraphical work in Greek, written in Alexandria and purporting to be of non-Jewish origin. It is the written source for the tradition according to which the Greek SEPTUAGINT translation of the Bible was composed, on the orders of the Egyptian king Ptolemy II (283-247 BCE), by 72 Judean priestly scholars brought to Alexandria for that express purpose. The impetus for the translation, according to the *Letter of Aristeas*, was the king's desire to complete his 20,000-volume library of the world's wisdom literature which did not as yet include the laws of the Jews, since these were written in "special letters." A translation was thus required, necessitating the cooperation of Eleazar, the High Priest in Jerusalem. Among the envoys sent to Eleazar was Aristeas, the *Letter's* supposed author, who apparently enjoyed much influence at court.

The text recounts Ptolemy's commissioning of the translation, the letter sent to Eleazar and his reply, the gift sent by the king to the High Priest and the delegation's visit to Jerusalem, the welcome extended to the scholars in Alexandria, the conditions under which the translation was prepared, and its reception both within the Jewish community and by the king.

In view of the extremely pro-Jewish tone of the text and the Jewish information which it contains, scholars are generally agreed that this *Letter* — attributed to a disinterested pagan contemporary of Ptolemy II — was written by an Alexandrian Jew at some later period (c.200 BCE). This dating is further supported by various inaccuracies and anachronisms. The document's purpose was to give authority and sanctity to the Septuagint, which the sages of Erets Israel regarded with disfavor, and to clarify the position of the Jews vis-à-vis Greek culture.

ARISTOTELIANISM The works of Aristotle (the fourth century BCE Greek philosopher) in Arabic translation began to exert a major influence upon Jewish thought from the mid-12th century, displacing Neo-Platonism. Known to Jews and Moslems alike as "the philosopher," Aristotle was described by MAIMONIDES as having "reached the highest degree of intellectual perfection open to man, barring only the still higher degree of prophetic inspiration." Aristotelianism is found in the 12th century writings of Abraham IBN DAUD and continued to shape Jewish philosophical thinking through the mid-16th century. In the 13th-14th century, an anti-intellectual countermovement arose, composed of traditionalist and kabbalistic critics, including the esteemed Ḫasdai CRESCAS.

From the ninth century and during the Golden Age of Spanish Jewry, Jews living in North Africa and Moslem Europe had access to Aristotelian literature through abbreviated though accurate Arabic translations, which became available after the 12th century in Hebrew translations by Jews living in Christian Europe. Jews also played an important role in their translation into Latin. Generally, Aristotelian philosophy was wholeheartedly accepted by Jewish medieval thinkers because of its pure, less anthropomorphic God-concept. Its theories of the eternity of the universe and of God as the passive, unmoved Mover, however, were often rejected as they contradicted the traditional Jewish understanding of an active, sustaining Creator.

The Arabic philosopher Al-Farabi's tenth century work, *The Philosophy of Plato and Aristotle*, served not only as a basic orientation for Jews and Moslems of his generation, but influenced the works of MAIMONIDES two hundred years later. Maimonides, the outstanding Jewish Aristotelian, attempted to synthesize Biblical revelations and Aristotelianism. Although Aristotle's reasoned arguments were used scientifically demonstrating such religious doctrines as the existence of God and God's unity, Maimonides concluded that Judaism's traditional position of creation *ex nihilo* had to be derived from prophetic faith alone (*Guide*, 2:15). Motivated by his belief that miracles were possible only if built into the original divine order of the world, Maimonides rejected the Aristotelian concept of the eternity of the universe, i.e., creation as an eternal process and not as a genesis of prime matter. In contrast, however, he negated the traditional notion of individual providence in favor of Aristotle's, claiming that divine intervention operates on behalf of the human species rather than individual. His successors suggested solutions to reconcile religion and philosophy but Maimonides dominated over the next three centuries.

Hebrew translations of the Arabic commentaries of Averroes (1126-1198) served as the Aristotelian source for Jewish thinkers after the 12th century. Some of them, such as Isaac Albalag, objected to the Maimonidean attempts to rely on the conventional account of the creation to refute Aristotle's proofs of the eternity of the world.

Aristotle is one of the few non-Jews to figure in Jewish legend. Josephus records traditions that he was affected by contact with Jews (Josephus, *Apion*, 1:176-182). Several medieval and Renaissance Jewish writers claim that Aristotle actually converted to Judaism and one story even tells of his natural Jewish origin from the tribe of Benjamin. A number of apocryphal notes ascribed to Aristotle brought him esteem in kabbalistic circles.

ARK, SYNAGOGUE (or Ark of the Law). The enclosed structure, freestanding or built into the wall of the SYNAGOGUE, which houses the SCROLLS OF THE LAW. In Hebrew, it is known as the *aron ha-kodesh* ("holy Ark") or *hékhal* ("sanctuary"); in the days of the Mishnah it was called simply the *tevah* ("chest"; *Ta'an* 2.1). Jewish law requires that great honor be paid to the scrolls, on account of their special holiness, by keeping them in a special place which must be beautiful and respected (*YD* 282). The Ark itself then becomes the next holiest component of the synagogue and, while one may sell the pews to purchase an Ark, one may not sell an Ark even to build a synagogue (*Meg.* 26a).

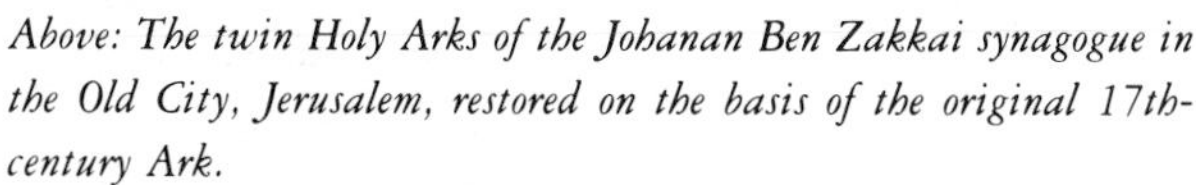

Above: The twin Holy Arks of the Johanan Ben Zakkai synagogue in the Old City, Jerusalem, restored on the basis of the original 17th-century Ark.
Right: Mishkan Israel Synagogue, Hamden, Connecticut, built in 1960. The mosaic above the Ark of the Law is by Ben Shahn.

There is literary and archeological evidence that, in synagogues of the early talmudic period, the Ark was portable; sometimes it was wheeled into the synagogue and placed in a specially designed niche (as at Dura Europos). This feature, as well as the name "Ark" (*aron*), suggests the assigning of a role to the Torah scrolls in the synagogue analogous to that of the two TABLETS OF THE COVENANT in the desert Sanctuary and in Solomon's Temple, which were kept in a portable ARK OF THE COVENANT (Ex. 25:10-16). Indeed, the Bible relates that the original Torah scroll, when completed by Moses, was kept next to or within the Ark in which the stone tablets bearing the TEN COMMANDMENTS were contained (Deut. 31:26; see Rashi *ad hoc*). That this association continued down the ages may be seen from the popular custom of placing a symbolic representation of the Ten Commandments on two tablets above the Ark; an early example can be found in the Sephardi (Portuguese) synagogue of Amsterdam (1675).

Originally, the Torah scrolls may have been placed in a horizontal position within the Ark. From the Middle Ages, however, the dominant practice was to stand them upright, bejeweled and wrapped in ornate mantles (see TORAH ORNAMENTS). To this day, Eastern Sephardim enclose their scrolls in a case (*tik*) which is always kept upright. The Ark itself usually has an embroidered curtain (PAROKHET) in front or within and an ETERNAL LIGHT (*ner tamid*) burning continuously in front or nearby. Larger Sephardi synagogues contained multiple Arks — usually two or three.

Once the Ark was built into the wall of the synagogue and no longer served merely as a "chest" or repository for the scrolls, it began to take on the character of a "sacred portal" giving access to the sanctuary of the Torah. From the 16th century onward, as the focal point of the synagogue, the Ark was given an elaborate, artistic form and its ornamentation was in line with the dominant architectural style of the period. Thus, there is a Gothic-style Ark (1505) from Modena (Museé Cluny, Paris), a Renaissance-style Ark (1550) from Urbino (Jewish Museum, New York), and an elaborately carved and gilded Ark of the Vittorio Veneto Synagogue (1701) in the Israel Museum, Jerusalem, which has been described as "resembling the portal of a classical Greek temple, decorated in baroque style with the addition of some Jewish iconography."

Other notable baroque-style Arks can be seen in the Venetian Ghetto, while oriental-style, 19th century Arks (both European and American) were often topped by domed representations of the Jerusalem Temple. A splendid example of iconography can be found on the delicately carved wooden doors of an 18th-century Polish synagogue Ark depicting birds, animals and floral designs, with the Hebrew inscription (*Avot* 5.20): "Bold as a leopard, light as an eagle, swift as a deer, strong as a lion" (Sir Isaac and Lady Wolfson Museum, Hechal Shlomo, Jerusalem). The Tablets of the Law, supported by a lion on either side, have become a standard feature of Ark design in many contemporary synagogues.

While the space between the Ark and the BIMAH (reader's platform) in the center of the synagogue or next to the opposite wall presented a challenge to synagogue architects from medieval times, those who designed Reform synagogues from the mid-19th century onwards invariably combined the two features. The reader now stood on a dais in front of the Ark, which thereby remained the focus of attention throughout the entire service.

The Ark is placed on the "eastern" wall of the synagogue, which is oriented towards Jerusalem, so that worshipers will face the Torah and the Temple area in prayer (I Kings 8:48). Synagogues in Jerusalem itself face the Temple Mount (see MIZRAḤ).

Whenever a Torah scroll is taken out for the READING OF THE LAW, the Ark becomes the focus of a dramatic ceremony. Adorned with silver crown, breastplate, and finials, the scroll is carried in a procession to the reading desk, amid song and praise, as the congregation stands in respect. During the reading of special prayers, when the Ark doors are opened (see PETIḤAH), worshipers also rise as a mark of respect and stand while the Ark remains open.

ARK OF THE COVENANT (Heb. *aron ha-berit*). A specially designed wooden chest containing the TABLETS OF THE COVENANT fashioned in the wilderness at God's command by the craftsman Bezalel (Ex. 25:10ff., 37:1ff.). It was the most sacred ritual possession of ancient Israel. Originally housed in the SANCTUARY, and later in the First Temple's HOLY OF HOLIES, this Ark was also carried by the Levites (or priests) whenever the Israelite people set out on the march or went to war. It had various designations such as "the Ark of the Pact" (*aron ha-edut*; Ex. 25:22), "the Ark of the Covenant of the Lord" (*aron berit Adonai*; Num. 20:33), "the Ark of the Covenant of the Lord of Hosts enthroned on the cherubim" (I Sam. 4:4), or more simply as "the Ark of the Covenant" (Josh. 3:6) and "the Ark of the Lord" (I Sam. 5:3). Scriptural references indicate that it was in use from shortly after the revelation at Mount Sinai until after the time of Solomon (I Kings 8:6).

Because of its several designations and functions, some critical scholars believe that there may have been different traditions as to its origin and purpose. The Ark of the Covenant described in Exodus was a rectangular chest 2.5 cubits (3 3/4 ft or 1.10 meters) long and 1.5 cubits (2 1/4 ft or 70 cm) in height and width, open at the top. It was made of acacia wood and overlaid with pure gold; the whole upper surface of the Ark also had a covering plate (*kapporet*) of gold, and of one piece with it were two golden figures of a CHERUB which faced each other with outstretched wings. The Tablets of the Covenant were deposited in the Ark, which was then placed in the Sanctuary's Holy of Holies. Moses was told that the Lord would meet with him between the two cherubim.

Bible scholars note that shrines similar to the Sanctuary (Tabernacle) and replicas of creatures similar to the cherubim were also found among other Middle Eastern peoples of antiquity. They, too, deposited important documents in a holy place close to their gods. Unlike these heathen shrines, however, the Israelite Sanctuary contained no image of the deity, while the Ark contained only the two stone tablets — and they were not to be worshiped. Their function was to remind the people of their covenant with God, of His nearness to them, and of His demands on all aspects of their lives. Since the Tablets of the Covenant were housed in the Ark, and since the Lord was visualized as communicating with Moses from the cherubim above it, the *aron ha-berit* attained the highest degree of holiness. Touching it was considered a form of sacrilege liable to kindle Divine wrath (Num. 4:15; I Sam. 6:19).

Biblical tradition also associates the Ark with ancient Israel's wars of conquest. Its presence in front of the people was a sign that the Lord went ahead of them in battle (Deut. 1:30-33). "When the Ark was to set out, Moses would say: 'Advance, O Lord! May Your enemies be scattered, and may Your foes flee before You!' And when he halted, he would say: 'Return, O Lord, You who are Israel's myriads of thousands!'" (Num. 10:35-36). Accordingly, when the Israelites first tried to conquer the land (Num. 14:39-45), Moses

The Holy Ark on wheels, carved on a stone found in the synagogue of Capernaum, on the shore of the Sea of Galilee; dating from the late 3rd or 4th century CE.

warned them not to go "for the Lord is not in your midst." They disobeyed, attacking even though "the Lord's Ark of the Covenant" remained in the camp, and they were dealt a shattering blow. Critical scholarship differs as to whether these verses indicate that the Ark and the Lord were considered one and the same or whether the Ark "symbolized" the Lord's presence.

In any event, it was with the Israelites at the miraculous crossing of the Jordan into the Promised Land (Josh. 3:6ff.) and when the walls of Jericho collapsed (Josh. 6). After the conquest of the land, it was kept in the Shiloh sanctuary, but was taken out occasionally to battles. During Samuel's wars (I Sam. 4-7), its presence in the Israelite camp led the Philistines to tremble, saying: "God has come to the camp" (I Sam. 4:7). Once the Ark fell into the hands of the Philistines, it wrought plague and havoc in their cities; only after the Israelites recovered it were they able to defeat the Philistines (I Sam. 5-7). When King David was bringing the Ark to Jerusalem, a certain Uzzah reached out and grasped it to prevent it from toppling. God struck him down on the spot for his indiscretion (II Sam. 6:6-7; and I Chron. 13:9-10). David later placed the Ark in a special tent (II Sam. 6:17), where it remained until his son, King Solomon, installed it in the Temple he had built in Jerusalem. When the priests brought the Ark into the Holy of Holies, a "cloud filled the House of the Lord... for the glory of the Lord filled the House of God" (I Kings 8:1-11; II Chron. 5:2-14).

Little mention is made of the Ark after the period of Solomon's Temple, the last reference dating from the time of Josiah in the seventh century BCE (see Jer. 3:16-17; II Chron. 35:3). Rabbinic traditions speculate that it may have been hidden by Jeremiah or that it could have been taken to Babylon when the First Temple was destroyed (*Yoma* 53b-54a; TJ *Shek.* 6:1-2, 49c). It was not present in the Second Temple (*Yoma* 5:2). A replica, the Holy ARK (*aron ha-kodesh*), now forms part of synagogues throughout the world. In place of the Tablets of the Covenant, this Ark houses the Scrolls of the Law.

ART Over the generations, Jews in many communities, both in the Land of Israel and the Diaspora, have created works of art. Until the modern era, Jewish artistic activity was restricted to decoration of the SYNAGOGUE and to the beautification of ritual objects used on the Sabbath and festivals, both among the community and within the family circle. These were often examples of folk art, and they served the religious life style of the Jewish individual, family, and society. Non-Jews were also commissioned to create such objects and it is sometimes impossible to determine whether the artist was himself a Jew.

The approach of biblical and rabbinic law to art was always ambivalent. On the one hand, the Bible contains verses which forbid the making of pictures, statues, and "graven" or sculptured images (Ex. 20:4; Deut. 5:8). This prohibition, elaborated in Deut. 4:16-18, applies to the likeness of any person, animal, bird, fish or other living creature, and is aimed against IDOLATRY. On the other hand, detailed expressions of artistry and craftsmanship are given in Ex.31:2-10 where Bezalel is singled out as one "endowed with a Divine spirit" who was commanded to build the SANCTUARY of the wilderness for the God of Israel.

The Sanctuary was made in accordance with a Divine commandment, and its description in the Bible goes into great detail regarding the forms, colors, and materials used in its construction. It was a work of art which served Jewish ritual, as opposed to the GOLDEN CALF which was destroyed as a symbol of idolatry.

Although it is difficult to make an accurate reconstruction of the Sanctuary based on descriptions in the Bible, its motifs became common themes in Jewish iconography. Items such as the pillars, the seven-branched lampstand (MENORAH) and designs woven into the curtain (PAROKHET) of the ARK were repeated in various ritual objects and in arks of synagogues of various eras.

The modest folk character of Jewish art, which often tends to the naive, was a result of both religious and social factors. Fear of drawing and carving likenesses that might serve idolatry was no doubt responsible for these artistic limitations. As opposed to other cultures, in which drawings and statues served as direct objects of veneration and deification to make tangible the sources of holiness, Judaism stressed the decorational role of art, which is classified as "beautifying the commandment" (*hiddur mitsvah*).

The extent to which Jews were forbidden to express themselves artistically changed from era to era in accordance with prevailing conditions. Some rabbis were stringent and others more lenient in interpreting the biblical prohibition. The liberal approach was conditioned by various factors, among them a feeling of spiritual immunity and security on the part of members of the community, as well as the social, political, and cultural environment in which the Jews lived, and the relationship with the authorities.

Archeological research since the beginning of the 20th century has continually unearthed artistic fragments at various sites, such as ancient synagogues in Capernaum and Khorazin in Galilee, and Sardis in Turkey. There are also mosaic floors in old synagogues dating back to between the fourth and the seventh centuries CE, including Ḥammat Tiberias, Bet Alpha, Gaza, Na'aran, and Bet She'an in Israel and Hamam in Tunisia. Most remarkable are the walls of the 4th century synagogue at Dura-Europos in Syria, covered with frescoes of biblical scenes.

The Sages, at various times, laid down what was permitted or forbidden artistically. One of the items forbidden was three-dimensional representation, but a distinction was made between raised, flat, and sunken reliefs. Free sculpture and raised reliefs were considered to verge on idolatry, and Jews therefore developed other techniques such as mosaics, illuminated manuscripts, metal engravings, embroidery, appliqué work and papercuts, as well as flat reliefs on synagogue arks and gravestones. Apart from religious factors, unstable economic and social conditions, recurrent banishments, and heavy fines imposed on the Jews also had the effect of restricting monumental art and of concentrating effort on the decoration of portable objects. Very few ritual objects have survived from ancient times and the Middle Ages. Many must have been destroyed. Alternatively, it is possible that, owing to the limitations imposed upon them by the guilds in Christian Europe, very few Jews were able to make ritual objects of high artistic and aesthetic quality. Among the most common artistic objects are decorations for the Scrolls of the Law (see TORAH ORNAMENTS), and the ESTHER SCROLL (*Megillah*), illuminated manuscripts, ḤANUKKAH lamps, KIDDUSH cups, candlesticks, SPICE BOXES, marriage documents (KETUBBOT) and utensils to be used at the festive table.

Many Jewish craftsmen in Islamic lands engaged in metal work, producing beautiful silver and copper utensils. In Eastern Europe, wherever there were abundant forests, wood carvings of a high standard could be found in many of the synagogues. There were also Jewish artists who painted the walls and ceilings of East European synagogues with bright colors. Unique schools of Hebrew manuscript illumination developed in Spain, Germany, and Italy. Among the books most commonly illustrated was the Passover HAGGADAH. These handwritten books, most of which were commissioned by wealthy families, included pictures and representations of people; in medieval Germany, human figures were sometimes depicted with animal heads so as not to portray the human face. The development of printing in the 15th century did not mark the end of such illustrated volumes.

The decorating of ritual objects is mostly characterized by symmetrical compositions and by a continuous tradition of symbols. Despite the influence of surrounding non-Jewish cultures, the images and symbols are faithful to mainstream Jewish thought and express the common faith prevalent among the community. The motifs most commonly found in ritual objects and on the synagogue Ark were those symbolizing the Sanctuary, the TEMPLE, and Jerusalem. The artistry present in the Temple is only known from descriptions in the Bible and early Jewish sources. It may be assumed that even the earliest extant images of the Temple, such as those on coins of the Bar Kokhba period, were not based on reality but on eyewitness accounts. However, over the course of time, the portrayals (now often idealized) of the Temple structure and its ritual objects became symbols accepted by the Jewish masses and handed down by tradition from one generation to the next. In addition to Temple motifs such as a gate, pillars, the table and showbread, the seven-branched *menorah*, basin, tongs, ram's horn (SHOFAR), and the CHERUB, Jewish visual symbolism was later enriched by new motifs derived from the surrounding culture and integrated within the general system. These motifs, symbolizing links with the past and the physical and metaphysical longing for redemption, included lions, eagles, deer, griffins, and other beasts, signs of the ZODIAC, and carvings on the *ets ḥayyim*, wooden rollers of Torah scrolls .

Until modern times, individual Jewish artists are hardly known, although some of those who designed mosaics, illuminated manuscripts, painted synagogues, or fashioned ritual objects have been identified. Only from the late 18th century, with the period of Emancipation and Enlightenment, did conditions become ripe for such a change. Jews became prominent in general art and some depicted Jewish subjects. The pioneer Jewish artist of the 19th century was Moritz Oppenheim (1799-1882), who worked in Germany and excelled in portraiture, in painting biblical scenes, and in depicting observance of the Jewish festivals in synagogue and home.

The 19th century witnessed the building of magnificent synagogues as previous architectural restrictions were abolished (see SYNAGOGUE). Modern aesthetic values were applied both to synagogue design and to ritual objects. American Jews have pioneered in forms of ritual ornamentation, and many of the greatest US artists — both Jewish and non-Jewish — have contributed to this efflorescence, which combines beauty with holiness.

ARTICLES OF FAITH See PRINCIPLES OF FAITH

ARTIFICIAL INSEMINATION Several references in the Talmud and Midrash are made to the phenomenon of artificial insemination as a rare occurrence, but not as strategy for conception (e.g. *Ḥag* 15a). Still, these references served as a basis for elucidation of the halakhic issues involved in artificial insemination centuries before it was practiced by the medical profession.

Of the halakhic issues involved, the question of the paternal relationship of the donor is central. Most authorities, however, entertain the notion that the donor is indeed recognized as the father of the child that is born in all respects, including the possibility that one fulfills the *mitsvah* of procreation through artificial insemination.

Several restrictions apply to artificial insemination. It has been permitted only on the condition that a woman's husband serves as the donor. However, should artificial insemination have been performed with a donor other than the husband, rabbinic consensus is that the child is not tainted with a status of ILLEGITIMACY (*mamzerut*). The basis of this ruling is that no forbidden physical act occurred between the donor and the woman.

There are authorities who deal with the problem of inseminating a woman during the time of her menstrual impurity (NIDDAH). There is a preference towards insemination after the ritual immersion, if possible, so that conception will occur in a state of ritual cleanliness.

Semen banks, where donors are anonymous, complicate the problem. Halakhic problems also arise when semen of the husband is used to impregnate his widow, especially with regard to the obligation for *ḥalitsah* (rejection of LEVIRATE MARRIAGE).

ARVIT See EVENING SERVICE

ASARAH BE-TEVET See TEVET, TENTH OF

ASCETICISM Practice of self-denial as spiritual discipline. Asceticism, isolation, deprivation, and abstinence have existed as religious values in Judaism from biblical times to the present, although, beginning with the talmudic period, there has been a tendency to oppose extreme asceticism and total withdrawal from the community.

Asceticism in the Bible was expressed in adopting NAZIRITE vows — in refraining from drinking wine and from cutting one's hair for a given period of time. According to the sages, Nazirite vows continued to be taken during the Second Temple period when asceticism played a central place in Jewish religious life. In addition to individuals, there were whole communities, such as the THERAPEUTAE and the ESSENES, that led ascetic lives at this time. At the end of the Second Temple era, asceticism as a religious value and as a means to draw closer to God, is found in the writings of PHILO.

After the destruction of the Second Temple (70 CE) and the failure of the Bar Kokhba revolt (135 CE), various hermitic and ascetic practices spread among the people. "After the Temple was destroyed, the *Perushim* (i.e., ascetics) increased in Israel, and they did not eat meat or drink wine" (*Tosef Sot.* 15:11). Rabbinic Judaism, which sought in the post-Temple period to structure Jewish life around the community, was opposed to these ascetic tendencies. "On the day of judgment a man will have to account for pleasure he has denied himself" (TJ.*Kid.* 4.12). R. Joshua demonstrated to the *Perushim*, who refrained from eating meat because of the cancellation of the daily sacrifice in the Temple, the absurdity of extreme mourning practices: "Should we then not eat figs and grapes, from which the first fruits were brought on *Shavu'ot*? Should we not eat bread...? Should we not drink water which was used as a libation on *Sukkot*?" (*Tosef Sot.* 15:12).

The accepted manner of asceticism in Judaism, from the Talmudic times on, is the public or individual FAST. Individual sages practiced asceticism and deprivation, but the major trend within Jewish law is to oppose extreme asceticism and hermitic practices. This opposition included strong objections to sexual abstinence and celibacy, which were not even enjoined on the Nazirites, although such practices seem to have been part of the regimen in certain Essene groups. Among the rabbis of the Talmud, Ben Azzai was unusual in his celibacy, saying "My soul loves the Torah; let others propagate" (*Yev.* 63b).

The opposition to extreme forms of asceticism continued throughout the Middle Ages, and groups of ascetics, parallel to the Muslim sufis and the Christian hermits and monks, did not form within Judaism. Nevertheless, ascetic tendencies within Judaism never died out entirely, and the impact of Christianity and Islam may be seen in the writings of various authors. The influence of the sufis is particularly apparent in the works of BAḤYA Ibn Pakuda, Abraham, son of Maimonides, and Abraham bar Ḥayya. Other philosophers, such as JUDAH HALEVI and Maimonides, strongly opposed excessive asceticism.

The ḤASIDEI ASHKENAZ (medieval German pietists), possibly under the influence of the Christian ascetices, also saw great value in asceticism. JUDAH HE-HASID and ELEAZAR OF WORMS suggest in their writings that various forms of deprivation can lead to repentance. The Safed kabbalists of the 16th century adopted customs of self-denial, originating with the German pietists, practices which have influenced the ascetic tendencies of Eastern European Jews in recent centuries.

Whereas in Islam and Christianity asceticism was linked to mysticism, in Judaism most of the kabbalists did not practice self-denial. The body and this world are regarded in Kabbalah as reflecting the Divine world, and, therefore, there is no religious value in depriving the body or in separating oneself from everyday life. At the same time, certain mystic streams, such as the HEKHALOT literature and prophetic kabbalah, observed various isolationary practices as a preparation for the achievement of mystic illumination.

ASHAMNU ("We have trespassed"): Opening word of the "Shorter Confession" which is recited ten times on the DAY OF ATONEMENT, from the Afternoon Service preceding Yom Kippur through the Concluding (NE'ILAH) Service. Like AL ḤET, the lengthier CONFESSION OF SINS (*viddu'i*), it is arranged as an alphabetical acrostic, but the last letter of the Hebrew alphabet (*tav*) is employed three times to make up 24 instances of moral wrongdoing. In common with *Al Ḥet*, the *Ashamnu* formula uses the first person plural to emphasize collective responsibility; when reciting it, the practice is to beat one's breast as each sin is enumerated. The traditional text stems from the ancient confession of the High Priest in the Temple on Atonement Day (see AVODAH), but this was later expanded to include a wider range of human failings. There is, however, no mention of offenses such as murder and cruelty, which the sages thought Jews were unlikely to commit. This shorter *viddu'i* is included in the SELIḤOT for the penitential season, starting before Rosh ha-Shanah, and as a result of kabbalistic influence it now also introduces the weekday TAḤANUN prayer in some rites. Here, customs vary: Ashkenazim in Israel, Sephardim, and others recite it in *Taḥanun* on MONDAYS AND THURSDAYS, whereas Ḥasidic Jews recite it daily. Reform Jews say it only on the Day of Atonement, in an abridged version.

ASHAMNU

We abuse, we betray, we are cruel.
We destroy, we embitter, we falsify.
We gossip, we hate, we insult.
We jeer, we kill, we lie.
We mock, we neglect, we oppress.
We pervert, we quarrel, we rebel.
We steal, we transgress, we are unkind.
We are violent, we are wicked, we are xenophobic.
We yield to evil, we are zealots for bad causes.
Siddur "Sim Shalom"

ASHER See TRIBES, TWELVE

ASHER BEN JEHIEL (known by the acronym *Rosh*, and also as *Asheri*; c. 1250-1327). Talmudist and codifier. Born in Germany, he was the most distinguished pupil of R. MEIR OF ROTHENBURG, and, after his teacher's death, assumed the leadership of German Jewry. In 1303 he left Germany, probably as a result of blackmail by the government, which wished to seize his fortune. After reaching Spain and living for a year in Barcelona, he was appointed rabbi of Toledo on the recommendation of Solomon ADRET; there he was destined to become the spiritual authority of Spanish Jewry. His law court was granted full jurisdiction by the government and had the power to impose severe punishments, including the mutilation of informers.

Bringing to Spain the strict and narrow outlook of the Franco-German school, Asher adopted stringent decisions in matters of law. He disseminated in Spain the teachings and methods of the TOSAFISTS, and it was largely as a result of his influence that Spanish Jewry turned from scientific pursuits to talmudic study. He opposed the acquisition of secular knowledge, more especially philosophy, holding that since it is based on critical research it cannot be harmonized with religious tradition. Asher wrote commentaries on four tractates of the Talmud, and glosses, known as *Tosefot ha-Rosh* ("Additions of Rabbi Asher"), on 17 tractates. He was also the author of commentaries on the Mishnah, and wrote over 1,000 responsa which are a major source for the history of Spanish Jewry. His fame rests on his code, *Pisḳé ha-Rosh* ("Decisions of Rabbi Asher"); aiming, like the code of Isaac ALFASI, to show scholars how a legal decision might be derived directly from the Talmud, it omitted all laws not observed outside the Land of Israel. Unlike the *Mishneh Torah* code of MAIMONIDES, it lists all the main opinions with their reasoning and shows how the final decision is reached. Accepted as authoritative by succeeding generations, the *Pisḳé ha-Rosh* formed the basis of the *Tur* code of his son, JACOB BEN ASHER. His ethical outlook, greatly influenced by the ḤASIDÉ ASHKENAZ, finds expression in *Hanhagat ha-Rosh*, one of the best known works of Jewish moralistic literature.

ASHI (c.335-c.427 CE). Babylonian *amora* of the sixth generation. Known also as Rabbana, Rav Ashi was taught by leading scholars of the previous generation, including Rav Papi, Rav Kahana, and RAVA. For some 50 years (375-c.424 CE), Ashi headed the Sura Academy, which he reestablished at nearby Mata Meḥasya and restored to its former glory (see ACADEMIES). The Academy attracted hundreds of students, particularly during the KALLAH months of Adar and Elul. Not until Rav Ashi's time, according to the Talmud, had such learning and prestige been combined in one person since the days of JUDAH HA-NASI. By "prestige" the Talmud no doubt means Ashi's undisputed leadership, cordial relations with the Sassanid (Persian) monarch Shapur II, and personal wealth — a rare phenomenon among the sages. Rav Ashi's enduring fame is linked with his role in editing the Babylonian Talmud. He and Ravina are said to have furnished "the completion of teaching" (*BM* 86a). Traditionally, this has been interpreted to mean that they were the Talmud's coeditors, but more recent scholarship has cast doubt on that interpretation. It seems likely that Ashi and Ravina gathered additional halakhic material and provided the Mishnah's final amoraic exposition, leaving the redaction of the Babylonian Talmud to their successors.

ASHKAVAH See MEMORIAL SERVICES

ASHKENAZI, TSEVI HIRSCH BEN JACOB (c.1660-1718). Rabbi and halakhic scholar known as "Ḥakham Tsevi." Educated by his father and maternal grandfather, both of whom had escaped from Vilna to Hungary during the Cossack rebellion, Ashkenazi wrote his first responsum at the age of 16. He then studied for three years (1676-9) in Salonika and Belgrade, learning Sephardi customs and procedures (a number of which he adopted). The Sephardim honored him as *ḥakham* (sage), a title which he decided to assume together with the surname Ashkenazi. After his return to Buda, the Hungarian capital, Ashkenazi was dogged by misfortune. His wife and child were killed during the Austrian siege of Buda in 1686, he himself managed to take refuge in Sarajevo (where he was appointed *ḥakham*), and not until three years later did he discover that his parents had survived and been ransomed by the Jews of Berlin. His second wife, Sarah, was the daughter of R. Meshullam Zalman Neumark-Mirels, who headed the rabbinical court of Altona, Hamburg, and Wandsbeck. Settling in Altona, he taught there until 1707, when he succeeded his late father-in-law as rabbi of Hamburg and Wandsbeck. He resigned after only two years, however, as the result of a halakhic controversy.

In 1710, Ḥakham Tsevi was elected chief rabbi of the Ashkenazi community in Amsterdam. His collection of responsa, printed there in 1712, met with warm praise from the city's Portuguese rabbis. New troubles arose, however, when Nehemiah Ḥayon, a follower of the arch-heretic SHABBETAI TSEVI, arrived in Amsterdam to seek help from the Portuguese community in distributing his own writings (1713). The Sephardi elders feared that their own rabbi, Solomon Ayllon, had Shabbatean sympathies and therefore asked Ḥakham Tsevi Ashkenazi to issue a ruling. Ḥakham Tsevi decided against Ḥayon, banned his publications, and excommunicated him. Infuriated that he had not been consulted, Ayllon then changed the original conflict into one of Sephardi prestige vis-à-vis the Ashkenazim. The commission which he headed dismissed all charges against Ḥayon; subjected to abusive attacks, Ashkenazi resigned his post in 1714. After visits to London and Emden, he left for Poland and early in 1718 became rabbi of Lemberg (Lvov), where he died four months later.

The volume of responsa entitled *Ḥakham Tsevi* was his major halakhic work. It reflects the author's wandering life and sad experiences, also dealing with unusual questions — such as the alleged Spinozism of David Nieto (the *ḥakham* of London) or whether a GOLEM may be counted in a prayer quorum.

ASHKENAZIM Jews tracing their descent from ancestors who settled throughout northwestern Europe in the early Middle Ages; the preponderant section of world Jewry, long distinguishable from SEPHARDIM and "Oriental" Jewish communities by virtue of their folkways, outlook, cultural heritage, and religious traditions. In the Hebrew Bible, Ashkenaz first denotes a grandson of Japheth and great-grandson of the patriarch Noah (Gen. 10:1-3; I Chron. 1:4-6); it also designates the territory of a (Scythian?) people located north of Mesopotamia (Jer. 51:27). Talmudic sources (*Yoma* 10a), followed by the prayer book of AMRAM GAON (ninth cent.), however, identify Ashkenaz with *Germamia* or *Germania* — and when speaking of the German language or homeland, RASHI likewise employs the term "Ashkenaz." By his time (11th cent.), it had come to mean Lotharingia or *"Lother"* in rabbinic parlance, a region embracing parts of the old Carolingian Empire (northeastern France, Lorraine, Flanders, and the Rhineland) where Jews who spoke Old French or Middle High German were developing a socio-religious life style of their own. Between 1050 and 1300, these Ashkenazi or "German" Jewish communities dominated the whole of France (apart from Provence), England and the Low Countries, Germany west of the Elbe, Switzerland, and northern Italy. Ashkenazim expelled from England (1290) and France (1306, 1394) fled elsewhere, mainly to Germany, Austria, and Poland. Renewed persecution, in both Germany (13th-15th centuries) and Poland-Lithuania (Cossack massacres of 1648-49), drove their

German Jews wearing the Judenhut, *a pointed cap, they were compelled to wear in the Middle Ages.* Regensburg Pentateuch, *c. 1300.*

A Jewish couple from Warsaw. After L. Hollaenderski, Les Israélites de Pologne, Paris, 1846.

descendants to other parts of Europe and even farther afield. One indication of this troubled history is the fact that the surname "Ashkenazi" can now mostly be found among Jews of North African or Turkish origin.

A primary characteristic of medieval Franco-German Jewry was its adoption of liturgical rites deriving from the ancient "Palestinian" (rather than "Babylonian") group. The order and wording of many prayers differed considerably from those recited by Jews in Spain, Portugal, Provence, and the Orient (see LITURGY; NUSAḤ); distinctive forms of liturgical hymn (PIYYUT), elegiac verse (KINOT), and penitential prayer (SELIḤOT) were composed; and the melodic chanting of biblical texts (CANTILLATION) was highly diversified in both Western and Eastern Europe. Legend had it that such traditions were first brought northward to "Ashkenaz" from Apulia, in southern Italy, inspiring a famous quip by Rabbenu Jacob TAM: "For out of Bari shall go forth Torah, and the word of the Lord from Otranto" (cf. Isa. 2:3). The pre-expulsion French and English rite has been preserved in the 11th-century *Maḥzor Vitry* and in the 13th-century *Ets Ḥayyim* compiled by R. Jacob Ḥazzan of London. Its last surviving elements could still be found, until recently, in the ritual maintained by three small Jewish communities (Asti, Fossano, Moncalvo) in northern Italy. Waves of emigration, religious tenacity, and the invention of printing helped the closely related Ashkenazi rite to spread from medieval Rhenish Jewry to Central and Eastern Europe, where it became known as *minhag Polin*, "the Polish rite." With only slight regional variations, this now forms the basis of worship in Ashkenazi synagogues throughout the world. ḤASIDISM, the popular religious movement originating in the 18th century, adopted the rite of Isaac LURIA, Sephardi in part but retaining much Ashkenazi liturgical content. Both the Ḥasidim and their traditional "Opponents," the MITNAGGEDIM, share a common musical heritage in the *"Mi-Sinai" niggunim* — traditional melodies to which various prayers have been chanted in synagogue ever since the Middle Ages.

Whereas the Sephardim evolved a broad (and often more tolerant, "open") cultural form of life, historical circumstances — notably the restrictions imposed by their Christian environment — tended to make the Ashkenazim narrower and more rigorous in their outlook and practice. Talmudic scholarship in the Ashkenazi world became intensified from age to age and from one land of exile to the next. With his vastly influential commentaries on both the Bible and the Talmud, Rashi set new standards of learning; the pietistic and mystical ḤASIDÉ ASHKENAZ of 13th-century Germany fostered a preparedness for martyrdom (KIDDUSH HA-SHEM); and Rabbenu GERSHOM ME'OR HA-GOLAH imposed monogamy on the Jews of Christian Europe and protected women facing an arbitrary divorce. Despite the liturgical and other differences between them, Ashkenazim and Sephardim maintained a fruitful relationship for several hundred years. The works of Rashi and his school were greatly admired in Spain. Among the "Germans" who settled or exerted a personal influence there, MOSES BEN JACOB of Coucy was a highly effective preacher and ASHER BEN JEHIEL enjoyed supreme rabbinical authority. It was the latter's son, JACOB BEN ASHER, who did much to inspire the format of Caro's SHULḤAN ARUKH through the writing of his major legal (halakhic) work, *Arba'ah Turim*. Subsequently, Ashkenazi regulations and practices were added by Moses ISSERLES to the standard (Sephardi) *Shulḥan Arukh* code. Spanish luminaries, in their turn, had a considerable impact on the Ashkenazim: MAIMONIDES appears to have influenced the *Hasidé Ashkenaz*, while he, Abraham IBN EZRA, and the Sephardi masters of the Kabbalah gained a lasting reputation in northern Europe. These reciprocal influences have, to varying degrees, continued down to modern times.

Strict adherence to the HALAKHAH (Jewish Law) became a hallmark of the Ashkenazim. Within the system of communal autonomy which they evolved, the "Council of the Four Lands" (*Va'ad Arba ha-Aratsot*) flourished for two centuries (c.1550-1764) in Poland and Lithuania, regulating all aspects of Jewish communal, economic, and religious life in the future heartland of European ORTHODOXY. The local rabbi often served also as *dayyan* (judge), *av bet din* (head of the law court), or head of a *yeshivah* (rabbinical academy). Torah study was promoted daily, much deference was paid to local CUSTOM (*minhag*), and — despite economic pressures and recurrent persecution — Ashkenazi Jews maintained a rare standard of literacy, to a degree unknown among the surrounding Christian population. The complex "civilization" which thus developed, with its own customs and traditions, legal norms, ethical and religious values, social institutions, and hallowed "way of life," was the vitalizing force that enabled the Ashkenazim to survive and to build up each new community, from Germany to Poland and Russia, and from there to Western Europe, America, the Land of Israel, and other parts of the world. A unique Ashkenazi possession, for more than 1,000 years, has been the YIDDISH language, which served as a *lingua franca* wherever Jews went.

By the 18th century, Ashkenazim outnumbered Sephardim in the world and, by the late 19th century, their mass emigration from Tsarist Russia had changed the complexion of many Jewish communities in the West. On the eve of World War II (1939), Ashkenazi Jews represented 90 percent of the worldwide Jewish population. This overwhelming preponderance, though reduced by the Holocaust, assimilation, intermarriage, and a falling birthrate, still characterizes world Jewry, although Sephardim and Eastern Jews form a slight majority in the State of Israel. Ashkenazim laid the foundations of a centralized CHIEF RABBINATE in Western Europe, the British Commonwealth, and Israel. Movements such as Ḥasidism, the HASKALAH, and Political Zionism were founded and led by them, and this is to a great extent also true of the three major religious trends — REFORM JUDAISM,

NEO-ORTHODOXY, and CONSERVATIVE Judaism. Ashkenazim constitute the dominant sectors of Jewish communities in Europe (except France, where the North African immigration of the 1950s and 1960s has put them in a minority), North and Latin America, South Africa, and Australia.

ASHRÉ ("Happy are they"). First word of a hymn of praise to God that serves as a daily reading from the Book of Psalms in Jewish worship. It comprises two prefatory verses, both commencing with *Ashré* (Ps. 84:5, 144:15), the whole of Psalm 145, and one concluding verse (Ps. 115:18). Bible scholars have devoted much attention to the structural pattern and content of Ps. 145, an alphabetical acrostic omitting a single Hebrew letter (*nun*). Successive verses proclaim God's greatness (1-6), lovingkindness (7-10), majesty (11-13), and unceasing benevolence toward all who revere Him (14-21); repeated use of the word *kol* ("all") emphasizes His immanent sovereignty. An ancient text of Ps. 145, discovered among the DEAD SEA SCROLLS, includes responses indicating that its liturgical use may date from Second Temple times. This text also contains a *nun* verse which appears to fill the gap mentioned above.

According to the rabbis, one who recites this psalm three times daily "is assured of life in the world to come" (*Ber.* 4b). Here, the context strongly suggests that the two introductory (*Ashré*) verses were prefixed to Ps. 145 in the early centuries CE. It is recited twice in the Morning Service; before the Afternoon Service (except in the Ashkenazi rite on the DAY OF ATONEMENT); before NE'ILAH on the Day of Atonement; and prior to SELIḤOT in the penitential season starting before Rosh ha-Shanah. During Morning Service, some Ashkenazim touch their TEFILLIN when reciting verse 16; Sephardim, however, make a symbolic gesture with the palms of their hands. On Sabbaths and festivals, the first and last lines of *Ashré* are usually sung to a traditional melody. In many Western (Orthodox and Conservative) congregations, the entire passage is often chanted responsively or sung by a choir. Reform practice, generally, is to recite it in the vernacular.

ASHRÉ (opening lines)

Ps. 84:5 Happy are those who dwell in Your house: they shall ever be praising You. Selah.
Ps. 144:15 Happy the people that is so favored: happy the people whose God is the Lord.
Ps. 145:1 A Psalm of Praise: by David:
I will exalt You, my God and King, and I will bless Your Name forever and ever.
2 Every day I will bless You, and I will praise Your Name forever and ever.

ASSEMBLY, GREAT See GREAT ASSEMBLY

ASSEMBLY OF NOTABLES See CONSISTORY

ASSIMILATION This familiar word can suggest opposing ideas: there is active assimilation, where a society or individual absorbs forces from outside, which strengthen its own identity and become regarded by later generations as peculiar to that identity; and passive assimilation, where the object allows the outside forces to change or destroy its identity. Jewish history exhibits many instances of active assimilation in such matters as language, music, diet or dress. More often, however, assimilation signifies the replacement of practices sanctified by the Jewish past by others derived from the non-Jewish world and is used as the equivalent of complete absorption. This process is illustrated by the transformation of Jewish life in Europe following the French Revolution. Prior to that event the Jewish communities of Europe had lived as a *corpus separatum*, segregated as to residence, restricted in their occupations, professing a religion which their neighbors regarded with hostility, speaking their own language, living under their own laws. Their position depended on the will of the ruler, but the hope of messianic redemption limited their concern for the politics of their immediate environment and compensated psychologically for the wretchedness of their situation.

Differentiation by inherited status was not suffered by Jews alone, and the philosophers of the 18th century Enlightenment visualized a society in which all men would enjoy the same freedom, live under the same laws, and stand in the same relation to the State. To share the life of the majority it would not be necessary for Jews to embrace the religion of the majority: religion was a matter on which state and society would be neutral.

Moses MENDELSSOHN (1729-1783) was the herald of this ideal for the Jews of Europe; and the French Revolution created political conditions which made its accomplishment possible. Mendelssohn emphasized the importance of secular education and familiarity with the vernacular; the French Revolution conferred on the Jews the status of equal citizens, at the same time dismantling their separate corporate structure, and this became the hallmark of Jewish EMANCIPATION. Official Jewish activity became limited to the religious congregation and, as with other denominations, this was subject to government control.

Educational and political factors speedily undermined the Jew's acceptance of his tradition in such matters as language, dress, and the authority of rabbinic law. Economic opportunity enhanced the claims of the gentile world on the Jews' style of life.

In central Europe, the emancipation of the Jews did not proceed without interruption. In general, civil rights were conceded before political equality, the lifting of the final barriers being retarded by an upsurge of German nationalism.

The metamorphosis of a Ḥanukkah candlestick into a Christmas tree, symbolizing the process of assimilation of Jews as they became wealthier. From the first issue of Schlemiel, a Jewish satiric newspaper, Germany, 1906.

This did not diminish assimilationist tendencies, since among many Jews it stimulated the desire to prove themselves worthy members of the host nation. In the area of religion, it is found as one of the factors influencing the development of REFORM JUDAISM. Likewise it is seen in the NEO-ORTHODOXY which replaced the old traditional Judaism in central Europe.

The situation in eastern Europe raised stiffer barriers against assimilationist forces. The Jews were not an isolated tiny group standing in juxtaposition to a strong indigenous culture; they were one of several ethnic groups, and there was no obvious reason to assimilate to any one of them. The Tsarist government's clumsy attempts at Russification and suspicion of conversionist motives hardened the traditionalist outlook among Jews. Counter-currents developing within the Jewish groups — the desire to cultivate secular knowledge, the spread of Jewish nationalism, adherence to revolutionary groups — weakened the hold of traditional Judaism. It would be far-fetched to attribute to assimilationist forces the westward migration of east European Jews at the end of the 19th century, but the readiness with which very many of the emigrants divested themselves of their traditional garb suggests a susceptibility to those forces.

The United States provided par excellence the "open society" pursued by the Enlightenment. Legal stratification, inherited in Europe from feudal practice, did not exist and ran counter to the political system. Adherence to the Jewish community was a matter of voluntary decision; there was no basis for the traditional community structure, and defection from traditional Judaism was an individual affair. Though Reform Judaism attempted to halt the tide of assimilation it betrayed a strong influence of assimilationist forces, extending eventually to the "Protestantization" of the synagogue.

During the second of the two centuries following the French Revolution the pendulum swung against the liberal society visualized by the Enlightenment, and within the Jewish group the current in favor of cultivating the separate Jewish identity prevailed. The emergence of a Jewish State (1948), supported whole-heartedly by Diaspora communities, is the outstanding witness to this movement. The Jewish cosmopolitan socialist groups disappeared along with the east European communities which sustained them; in the United States Reform Judaism turned away from its assimilationist tendences and cultivated Jewish ethnic identity, while there are sections of ORTHODOXY which use the openness of the American system to recreate something similar to the *corpus separatum* of pre-revolutionary Europe; likewise with some sections of Orthodoxy within the State of Israel.

If assimilation as ideology is disavowed, as practice it is in full force. The post-Holocaust world is hospitable to the Jew, and the evidence, in particular the rate of intermarriage, suggests that large numbers are succumbing to it.

ASTROLOGY Study of the stars in the belief that they influence human affairs. The traditional Jewish attitude concerning the validity of astrology was not unified, although it would appear that most of the great rabbis, certainly through the Middle Ages and even beyond, accepted its validity. The debate about the efficacy of astrology can be traced back to the Talmud (at which time astrology was linked with astronomy). Thus, in *Shab.* 156a, R. Joshua ben Levi states that a person born on a Sunday will be either totally virtuous or totally evil, since on the first day of creation both light and darkness were created. Similarly, birth on any other day of the week implied a list of certain characteristics. R. Ḥanina, disagreeing with R. Joshua ben Levi, does not question the overall hypothesis, but claims that it is the hour of one's birth that determines one's nature, as each part of the day is dominated by the sun or by one of the planets. R. Johanan, on the other hand, rejects the entire idea of propitious times — at least as far as Jews are concerned, and states: "The Jews have no *mazzal*," the word mazzal, which later came to mean "luck," referring to the different signs of the ZODIAC. It was also suggested that Israel lay under the planet Saturn. In general, though, the Talmud assumes that the constellations do play a role in man's fate, but that the Jew has the ability by his actions to overcome what the constellations otherwise decree.

The Talmud has various passages indicating that certain times are more propitious than others. Thus, for example (*Shab.* 129b), Samuel gives detailed rules regarding the dates on which blood-letting is dangerous. When the Talmud asks why people engage in blood-letting on Fridays even though the constellations are inauspicious, the response is that as this has become common practice, "the Lord preserves the simple" (Ps. 116:6). Vestiges of the idea of favorable and unfavorable times are to be found in later Jewish law, e.g., the law that "from the beginning of the month of Av, a Jew involved in litigation with a Cuthean (i.e., a non-Jew) should attempt to postpone it, because it is an inauspicious time" (*Shul.Ar OH* 551:1), since at that time of the year, Jerusalem and the Temple fell.

Among the open proponents of astrology were Saadiah Gaon, who included astrological material in his writings; Solomon IBN GABIROL; Abraham IBN EZRA; and NAHMANIDES. LEVI BEN GERSHON, while endorsing the concept of astrology, claimed that the astrologers were unable to obtain correct readings of the portents in the constellations. Rabbi JUDAH LÖW of Prague was also involved in astrology, and is reputed to have worked with his friend, the astronomer and astrologer Tycho Brahe. The mystical Zohar considers the validity of astrology as axiomatic.

The greatest opponent of astrology was MAIMONIDES, especially in his *Mishneh Torah*, "Laws of Idolatry". There (11:9), Maimonides writes, "One is forbidden to predict (favorable or unfavorable) times, even if he did nothing more than state these lies, for the simple believe that these are true words emanating from the wise. Whoever is involved in astrology and plans his work or a trip based on the time set by those who examine the heavens is liable to be whipped, for it is written (Lev. 19:26), 'You shall not observe times.'" After listing other such activities, Maimonides concludes, "All these matters are lies and deceit, and it was with these that the ancient constellation-worshipers deceived the nations so that they might follow them. It is not proper for Israelites, who are wise, to follow these deceits and to think for an instant that there is any value in them." Furthermore, he asserts, "whoever believes in these matters and similar ones, and thinks to himself that they are true and wise except that they were forbidden (to be engaged in) by the Torah, is but a fool and lacking in sense." Elsewhere, Maimonides notes that those who were involved in astrology were, among others, the Chaldeans and the Egyptians, whereas the great Greek thinkers all rejected astrology as baseless.

One of the few relics of astrology in common use today — although it is unlikely that anyone uses it in its original sense — is the universal Jewish expression, — *mazzal tov* ("good luck") which means literally "may your constellation be a good one".

ASYLUM Place of refuge. The principle of asylum for fugitives was accepted in ancient societies and continued through the Middle Ages. The SANCTUARY, particularly the altar, served as a place of refuge. The Bible sharply limits the right of asylum by declaring: "When a man schemes against another and kills him treacherously, you shall take him from My very altar to be put to death" (Ex.21:14). Despite this Pentateuchal law, both Adonijah and Joab sought asylum by grasping the horns of the ALTAR (I Kings 1:50;2:28). The altar offered only temporary shelter; from there the involuntary killer would be taken under escort to a city of refuge.

The first reference to a city of refuge as asylum for one guilty of involuntary manslaughter is found in Ex. 21:13. A more detailed reference is the command (Num. 35:9-34) to set aside three towns in Transjordan and three in Canaan as cities of refuge for the manslayer. The phrase (Num. 35:6) "to which you shall add forty-two towns" is understood by the Babylonian Talmud to mean that the 48 towns assigned to the Levites (I Chron. 6:39-66) were likewise to serve as cities of refuge. According to the Talmud, the roads leading to them were marked by signposts. Shortly before his death, Moses designated the three cities in Transjordan (Deut. 4:41-43); Joshua did the same for the Land of Canaan (Josh. 20:7).

The institution of cities of refuge is to be understood in the light of an even more ancient institution in patriarchal societies — that of the BLOOD AVENGER. When someone was slain, whether willfully or by accident, it was the duty of the slain man's kinsmen to avenge his blood by killing the slayer.

Stone horned altar found at Megiddo, dated to the 10th-9th century BCE. A person grasping the horns of the altar was granted temporary asylum.

The cities of refuge were intended to offer asylum from the avenger of blood to any person who had caused another's death through accident. In one passage (Num. 35:24), the local assembly is to decide whether the slaying was a case of manslaughter or intentional murder. According to Joshua 20:4, the decision was to be rendered by the elders of the city of refuge after hearing the testimony of the slayer as to the circumstances. Talmudic law ordains that anyone who has slain a fellow-man is to be brought before a court that will try the accused and determine whether or not the slaying was accidental. If it is adjudged to be accidental, the slayer finds asylum in one of the cities of refuge and within its boundaries he must remain until the death of the High Priest (Num. 35:25), after which he can safely return to his native town. It seems probable that the death of the High Priest was regarded as atonement for the innocent blood that had been shed.

The three Pentateuchal passages quoted concerning the cities of refuge differ in their individual emphasis. The Exodus passages stress the distinction between manslaughter and deliberate murder. The passage in Numbers emphasizes the obligation of the slayer to remain within the boundaries of the city of refuge; if he should venture beyond them, the avenger of blood can kill him with impunity. The passage in Deuteronomy stresses that the three cities of refuge in Canaan are to be located in three different parts of the country so as to make them readily accessible.

There is no information as to how the law of the cities of refuge actually operated. They are not mentioned after Joshua, chapter 20. While tractate *Makkot* of the Mishnah and Talmud deals extensively with the subject (flight to a city of refuge is termed exile) there is no real indication that the law was operative either in the Second Temple period or subsequently.

Cities of refuge are to be found in other ancient cultures, but these provided asylum for anyone guilty of slaying another — whether deliberately or accidentally — as well as for defaulting debtors and runaway slaves.

ATTAH BEKHARTANU See CHOSEN PEOPLE

ATHEISM See AGNOSTICISM AND ATHEISM

ATONEMENT (Heb. *kapparah*). A state of reconciliation between the sinner and the offended party prior to forgiveness of the SIN. Whether deliberate or unwitting, the offense must first be expiated — in some instances by the payment of a "ransom" (Heb. *kofer*, i.e., compensation). Judaism views the sinner as one spiritually alienated from God, from his fellow-man, or from his ideal self. Atonement, in the religious sense, means a reversal of the alienation caused by sin whereby the offending party is restored to spiritual "at-one-ment" and ultimately forgiven. Atonement, in Jewish teaching, can only be achieved after a process of REPENTANCE which involves a recognition and admission of the sin, feelings of remorse, restitution to the offended party, and a resolve not to repeat the offense.

Furthermore, the exercise of human freedom is central to atonement. Just as man is free to sin, so he is free to repent, and it is for him to take the initiative in seeking atonement. The Bible and rabbinic literature contain numerous references to God as a merciful and forgiving Sovereign who does not want the death of the sinner, but rather that he return from his evil ways and live (Ezek. 33:11). In Judaism, however, there is no concept of "prevenient grace" whereby God takes the first step. Atonement depends first on the sinner's genuine, wholehearted repentance. Only when that becomes evident in the sinner's conduct does God proceed to the stages of granting atonement and pardon.

In the case of unwitting offenses against the ritual law, the Bible prescribes a sin-offering. This is not viewed as some payment of restitution to an offended God, but rather as a sacrament intended to restore the ideal relationship between man and God, a relationship that had been impaired by man's sin. CONFESSION, as an expression of repentance, always accompanied such SACRIFICES AND OFFERINGS. When the prophets of Israel directed harsh criticism against sacrifice, their real target was not the sacrificial system as such but insincere atonement and the perfunctory way in which the offering was made (Isa. 1:11ff.; Hos. 14:2-3; Amos 5:21ff.; Mic. 6:6-8). No sacrifices could atone for deliberate transgressions, and the concept of a vicarious sacrifice was largely alien to Judaism.

Following the destruction of the Second Temple (and, to a certain extent, even before), PRAYER replaced sacrifice, and propitiatory devotions became the chief means of restoring a broken spiritual relationship. Fasting, GEMILUT ḪASADIM ("kindly acts"), and the giving of charity were recommended paths to atonement (*RH* 18a; *Ta'an.* 16a; *BB* 9a). At this later stage, no priest or other intermediary helps the sinner to expiate his offense. The sinner must stand alone before God, and only God can forgive him. So Rabbi Akiva declared (*Yoma* 8.9): "Happy are you, Israelites! Before whom are you made clean, and who cleanses you? Your Father in heaven."

So important, in the Jewish view, is the concept of atonement to man's spiritual health that a ten-day period is set aside at the beginning of each year so that more deliberate attention can be paid to the exercise of spiritual renewal (see TEN DAYS OF PENITENCE). The climax of this period is Yom Kippur, the DAY OF ATONEMENT, dedicated entirely to prayer and fasting. A distant reflection of the ancient scapegoat (AZAZEL) ritual in the Temple may be seen in the KAPPAROT atonement rite observed by some on the eve of the Day of Atonement whereby an individual's sins are symbolically expiated by a white fowl. The Day of Atonement can help bring atonement, however, only for offenses against God. For those sins committed against one's fellowman, atonement is granted only after the sinner has made full restitution and sought the offended party's forgiveness (*Yoma* 8.9).

ATTAH EḴHAD ("You are One"). Prayer composed in the era of the *ge'onim* (c. 800, Babylonia); the opening sentence is inspired by I Chron. 17:21. In the AMIDAH of the Sabbath Afternoon Service, it forms an introduction to the prayer blessing the Day of Rest and may therefore be compared to *Attah Kiddashta* ("You hallowed...") in the Sabbath Eve Service, *Yismaḥ Mosheh* ("Moses rejoiced...") in the Sabbath morning *Shaḥarit*, and *Tikkanta Shabbat* ("You instituted the Sabbath...") in the Additional Service. *Attah Eḥad* proclaims a threefold link between the One God, His Chosen People, and the holy Sabbath. The belief that Israel's three Patriarchs honored the Sabbath day is found in the Midrash. The language employed here hints at the bliss awaiting observant Jews in the afterlife. Ashkenazim often sing most of this prayer to a well-loved traditional melody.

ATTAH EḤAD

You are One and Your Name is One; and who is like Your people Israel, a nation unique on earth? Glorious greatness and a crown of salvation, a day of rest and holiness, have You given to Your people. On that day, Abraham was glad, Isaac rejoiced, Jacob and his sons rested — a rest granted in generous love, a true and faithful rest, spent in peace and tranquillity, in quietude and safety, a perfect rest in which You delight. Let Your children know and understand that this rest of theirs emanates from You, and by their rest may they sanctify Your Name.

ATTAH HORETA LA-DA'AT ("It has been clearly demonstrated to you"). Opening of a selection of biblical verses recited in both the Evening and Morning services of SIMḤAT TORAH (the Festival of the Rejoicing of the Law) before all the Scrolls of the Law are removed from the Ark. *Attah horeta la-da'at* (Deut. 4:35) introduces a long series of verses (Ps. 136:4, 86:8, 104:31, etc.; the order is not the same in all communities) which are read before the commencement of HAKKAFOT processions around the synagogue. The verses give thanks and praise to God, beseech His acceptance of Israel's prayers, and express the hope that He will redeem His people. Each verse is recited responsively, first by the cantor or prayer leader, and then by all the congregants. According to a time-honored Ashkenazi custom, however, the verses may be allotted to different congregants in turn; they recite them aloud and are answered by the other worshipers. A popular practice, now becoming rare, was for the honor of apportioning the verses to be auctioned half-humorously (and often in Yiddish), with the proceeds going to charity. Ashkenazi Jews the world over sing *Attah horeta* to a traditional melody which contains echoes of the prayer mode used for the reading of the Scroll of Esther on Purim. Sephardim and Jews who observe the Ḥasidic rite also read *Attah horeta*, with a shorter selection of verses, on all Sabbath and festival mornings when the scrolls are taken out of the Ark.

ATTRIBUTES, DIVINE See GOD

ATSERET See SHAVU'OT; SHEMINI ATSERET

AUFRUFEN See READING OF THE LAW

AUTHORITY, RABBINIC Power vested in authorized rabbis governing the religious life of the Jewish people. Judaism's Torah comprises both the WRITTEN LAW and the ORAL LAW. The interpretation of the former and the transmission and application of the latter have always been the prerogative of qualified rabbinic authorities. Jewish tradition maintains that the Oral Law was received by Moses at Sinai and transmitted by him to Joshua. An unbroken chain of tradition then continued with the elders, the prophets, and the men of the Great Assembly (*Avot* 1.1). This tradition was ultimately received and transmitted by the rabbinic sages of each generation.

MAIMONIDES delineated five categories of the Oral Law, all of which are dependent on rabbinic authority. First, the Oral Law includes definitions of terms presented in the Written Law. For example, the Pentateuch states that on the first day of Sukkot one should take "the fruit of goodly trees" (Lev. 23:40), but does not specify which kind of fruit. The Oral Law indicates that the Torah is referring to the *etrog* (citron). This definition and many others have been conveyed faithfully by the rabbis throughout the generations, and may not be disputed.

The second category is known as HALAKHAH LE-MOSHEH MI-SINAI, i.e., laws which are known only from the oral tradition. It includes, for example, the rule that the SCROLL OF THE LAW must be written on parchment and that TEFILLIN must be black.

The third category embraces laws derived by reason, through the use of traditional HERMENEUTICS. This process was utilized by qualified rabbis when the Great Court (*bet din ha-gadol* or SANHEDRIN) in Jerusalem functioned. The rabbis of the Great Court were empowered to legislate, and all Jews were obligated to follow their rulings. According to Maimonides (*Yad, Mamrim* 1.1), "everyone who believes in Moses our teacher and his Torah is obligated to rely and depend on them [the rabbis of the Great Court] for religious matters."

Included in the fourth category are rabbinical decrees aimed at safeguarding Scriptural observance. Rabbis have the power to enact new prohibitions so as to prevent individuals from violating Torah laws (see GEZERAH). The fifth category includes ordinances and customs which enhance religious observance (see TAKKANAH). Rabbis of each generation are authorized to issue decrees that will strengthen the religious life of their communities.

After the Roman destruction of Jerusalem in 70 CE, JOHANAN BEN ZAKKAI established a center of rabbinical authority at Yavneh. Once the Romans had put an end to the Bar Kokhba uprising in 135 CE, the maintenance of a universally acknowledged rabbinic body became much more difficult. With the rise of a large and educated Jewish population in Babylonia, and as a result of increasingly difficult conditions in Erets Israel, rabbinical authority shifted from one main court to a number of leading scholars and ACADEMIES, both in the Land of Israel and in Babylonia. Over the centuries, this process continued wherever Jews settled. Although their authority became more localized or regionalized, outstanding rabbinic leaders gained wide acceptance and their rulings were highly regarded throughout the Jewish world (see POSEKIM; RESPONSA). Such rabbis are popularly known as *gedolé ha-dor*, "great sages of the generation."

The authority of rabbis to determine the HALAKHAH was strongly maintained. The Talmud (*BM* 59b) discusses a certain dispute in which R. Eliezer's opinion was overruled by his colleagues. R. Eliezer caused various wonders to occur in order to validate his stand. A heavenly voice (BAT KOL) even proclaimed that the law was according to R. Eliezer. R. Joshua ben Ḫananiah, however, representing the majority opinion, stated categorically: "The Torah is not in heaven; we pay no attention to a heavenly voice." In other words, once the Torah had been given to the people of Israel, only the rabbis had (and have) the power to determine *halakhah*. No miracles or heavenly voices can be factored into the discussion. Rather, the law must follow the majority opinion of the authorized sages, according to their own best understanding.

Rabbinic tradition lays down that the earlier sages (RISHONIM) have greater authority than the later sages (AḪARONIM). The closer one lived to the time of the revelation at Sinai, the greater his authority. Rabbinic literature tends to glorify the earlier sages, attributing to them superior wisdom and even Divine inspiration, yet actual halakhic practice is based on the rulings of the most recent authorities. The assumption is that the latter sages familiarized themselves with all the teachings of the earlier ones, and were therefore in the best position to apply those teachings to contemporary life.

Although great reverence is shown for the earlier authorities and for one's own teachers, each rabbinic scholar is nevertheless obligated to study the halakhic sources himself. When dealing with cases brought before him, he may not simply rely on the rulings of others to determine the law. If he has valid proofs to reject the decisions of earlier authorities, he may rule differently from them. If he disagrees with his own teacher, he must respectfully present his arguments and refutations to facilitate clarification of the law. He is under an obligation, however, to follow the rulings of his teacher, should the latter reject his arguments.

The issue of rabbinic authority is not confined to *halakhah* or halakhic CODIFICATION, but also extends to AGGADAH and MIDRASH (homiletical interpretations and teachings). One school of thought insists that all the words of the sages are true and may not be discarded: if we do not agree with or understand their words, the fault lies with us, not with them. Isaac ABRAVANEL argued that to admit errors by the sages, even in aggadic statements, is to undermine rabbinical authority. If it is permitted to reject their homiletical observations, the result may be rejection of their halakhic statements as well. However, another school of thought distinguishes between halakhic and aggadic teachings. While there is a clear obligation to follow halakhic rulings by the sages, not all their non-halakhic statements have to be accepted as true. In Kabbalah (Jewish mysticism), rabbinic authority is also an important factor. The Kabbalah presents itself as an ancient "received tradition," preserved by the greatest Jewish sages and transmitted by them to a chosen elite.

Rabbinic authority has thus been a dominant feature in all aspects of Jewish life. Down to the present day, authority rests with those who have received the traditional ORDINATION first granted to a rabbi. The scholarship which such a rabbi acquires and the court of law (BET DIN) on which he serves, or over which he presides (as *av bet din*), enhance that authority.

Historically, there have been a number of attempts to undermine rabbinic authority. During the era of the Second Temple, the SADDUCEES rejected many teachings of the early rabbis (PHARISEES), disputing their authority to determine the *halakhah* and authentic Jewish belief. After the Temple's destruction, these Sadducee opponents disappeared. The KARAITES later split from "rabbanite" Judaism, insisting on the primacy of the Written Law, and SAADIAH GAON championed rabbinic authority against their attacks. While the Karaites did have periods of growth, their influence and numbers declined over the centuries; today, they are a very small group presenting no challenge to rabbinic authority.

During the 16th-18th centuries, crypto-Jews left Spain and Portugal with the aim of returning to Judaism (see MARRANO). Large numbers of them established communities in Western Europe, notably in Amsterdam, Hamburg, and London. Trained from childhood in a Bible-based understanding of Judaism, they needed to be taught post-biblical Judaism's rabbinic interpretations and halakhic rules. Some had difficulty in accepting and adjusting to rabbinic authority, others more rarely rejected it (see Uriel da COSTA; SPINOZA). David Nieto, the Sephardi chief rabbi of London, wrote an important treatise (*Matteh Dan*, 1714) defending the Oral Law and rabbinic authority against such detractors.

The most serious challenge to the traditional rabbinic leadership since the Karaite schism was not so much the blatant heresy preached by SHABBETAI TSEVI and his successors, the FRANKISTS, as the mass appeal of ḤASIDISM — an anti-intellectual, pietist movement that swept Jewish communities in many parts of Eastern Europe from the late 18th century. Ḥasidism deliberately undermined rabbinic authority in order to enhance the prestige of its own spiritual leaders, the *Tsaddikim*. As a result of the ferocious conflict that ensued between Ḥasidic Jews and their traditionalist opponents, it appeared at one stage that the new movement would either split Judaism in two or become yet another ephemeral sect. In the end, however, Ḥasidism adopted a more moderate course, largely reverting to time-honored norms and even surpassing the opposition in its religious conservatism.

The changes brought about by Napoleon's "Great Sanhedrin" in the early part of the 19th century also weakened rabbinic authority in Western Europe (see CONSISTORY). REFORM JUDAISM produced rabbis of a new type who, in addition to implementing liturgical and ritual departures, rejected the authority of both the *halakhah* and the traditional "orthodox" rabbinate. This process was accelerated by Reform SYNODS and conferences held in Germany and the United States. CONSERVATIVE JUDAISM developed as a moderately traditionalist alternative to Reform, acknowledging the principle of rabbinic authority but insisting that Orthodox sages of the time were not adapting the *halakhah* to contemporary needs and situations. While the Reform movement has abandoned halakhic legislation and its arbiters as non-mandatory, Conservatism seeks to update the Oral Law in accordance with the decisions of its own rabbinic leadership. ORTHODOXY maintains a total commitment to rabbinic authority as that concept has been understood and interpreted throughout the ages. Such authority, in the Orthodox view, is only possessed by thoroughly qualified rabbis who fully accept the halakhic tradition and who are therefore part of that tradition.

AUTOPSIES AND DISSECTION Biblical laws include specific legislation promoting respect for the deceased. The underlying philosophy behind these rules is that man was created in "the image of God" (Gen.I:27). Divine creations should be treated with the greatest reverence, even in death.

In addition to an absolute requirement to bury, there is the specific halakhic objection to autopsy based on the biblical prohibition against physically disfiguring or shaming a corpse (*nivvul ha-met*). Both are deduced from biblical verses (Deut.21:22-23). There is also a specific law prohibiting any form of obtaining any sort of benefit from a corpse (*AZ* 29b). Hundreds of responsa dealing with this subject can be found in rabbinic literature. The most prevalent approach taken by the rabbis towards the law of *nivvul ha-met* is that mutilation of a corpse for any reason is strictly forbidden. However, in a case in which an autopsy is needed in a situation involving PIKKUAḤ NEFESH (saving life), the overwhelming need overrides the prohibitions and the autopsy may be permitted. Practical applications of the *pikkuaḥ nefesh* principle might include: the post-mortem removal of organs for transplantation in life-threatening cases, to assess experimental drugs used for other patients, to study serious familial diseases when other living members may be affected, and to collect evidence needed to apprehend a murderer in criminal hearings.

Many responsa deal with the question of permitting total anatomical dissection. A number of authorities decided that a more lenient position may be taken towards limited procedures performed post mortem. Therefore, in cases that require further elucidation by the medical profession, it is preferable to achieve a post-mortem diagnosis by examinations that would limit the disfigurement to the corpse, rather than submitting to a routine and complete dissection. On this basis, limited post-mortem examinations are frequently permitted.

AV (Akkadian: *Abu*). Fifth month of the Jewish religious CALENDAR; 11th month of the Hebrew civil year counting from TISHRI. It is a month of 30 days and normally coincides with July-August; Leo the Lion is its sign of the ZODIAC. Despite numerous references to "the fifth month," there is no specific mention of Av in the Bible; it is often mentioned, however, in rabbinic sources. In Second Temple times, a minor festival was celebrated on 15 Av (see AV, FIFTEENTH OF) and this month had joyful associations. Eventually, however, it was overshadowed by gloom because of the TISHAH BE-AV (i.e., Ninth of Av) fast day commemorating the First Temple's destruction by the Babylonians in 586 BCE and the Second Temple's destruction by the Romans in 70 CE. This date also became linked with many other calamities in Jewish history. According to the rabbis, therefore, "when Av comes in, rejoicing is diminished" (*Ta'an*. 4.6, 29a). From the first day of the month until the day after Tishah be-Av, the THREE WEEKS of mourning which commence on 17 Tammuz reach a climax in the period known as the NINE DAYS. A special HAFTARAH (prophetical portion) is read on *Shabbat Naḥamu*, the first of seven "Sabbaths of Consolation" that follow Tishah be-Av (see SABBATHS, SPECIAL). The death of Aaron is also said to have occurred on the New Moon of Av (Num. 33:38). Euphemistically, this month is referred to as Menaḥem Av (*Menaḥem* means "Comforter") not only because "consolation" is promised after the Nine Days, but also because of the rabbinic tradition that Israel's messianic deliverer will be born on Tishah be-Av.

AV, FIFTEENTH OF (*Ḥamishah Asar be-Av*). Folk festival in Second Temple times, when young bachelors would select their wives from the unmarried girls. According to the Mishnah (*Ta'an.* 4.8), on this day as well as on the DAY OF ATONEMENT, the young women of Jerusalem dressed in white garments which they borrowed (so as not to embarrass the poor ones) and danced in the vineyards, where young men would choose their brides.

The Jerusalem and Babylonian Talmuds give various historical reasons for this festival: it was the day when the tribes, previously forbidden to intermarry (Num. 36:8ff.), were allowed to do so; when the Benjaminites were permitted to intermarry with other tribes (Judg. 21:18ff.); and when those killed at Betar in the Bar Kokhba rebellion could be buried. Most likely, the festival originated in the sacrificial service of the Temple, as 15 Av as the day when trees were no longer chopped down for the fire which burned on the altar; from this date the heat of the sun is not so strong, and there was reason for concern that the trees would not dry out properly. The holiday aspect may well have been adopted from an ancient summer solstice festival.

In *Megillat Ta'anit*, this day is referred to as "the time of the priests' wood," which is how it is called in the Mishnah (*Ta'an. 4.5; Meg. 1.5*), because the Israelites returning from exile in Babylonia did not find any wood in the stockpile. As a result, the prophets of the time decreed that even if the stockpiles were full, people were to donate wood on this day (see Neh. 10:35).

In modern times, the day is only marked by a ban on eulogies or fasting, while the TAḆANUN prayer is not recited after the AMIDAH. Attempts by the new settlements in Erets Israel to turn the day into one of music and folk dance proved unsuccessful.

AV, NINTH OF See TISHAH BE-AV

AVELÉ ZION ("Mourners of Zion"). Term of biblical origin (Isa. 61:3) used to denote certain groups of pious Jews who manifested their grief over the destruction of the Second Temple by the practice of asceticism, and by devoting themselves to prayer for the Redemption. Such "Mourners of Zion" first appeared in 70 CE, and their abstemious way of life was censured by the rabbis (*BB* 60b). While Jerusalem remained under Byzantine control, they made little impression, but their numbers and influence grew from the Arab conquest of the Holy Land in 638 until the 12th century. Abstaining from daily work, as well as from meat and wine, these mystically inclined *Avelé Zion* received financial support from Diaspora communities while they awaited and prayed for the coming of the Messiah. Their population in Jerusalem, during the early Middle Ages (9th-11th centuries), was swelled by immigrant KARAITES who adopted their customs. Other like-minded ascetics were to be found in medieval Yemen, Italy, and Germany. Prominent among the German "Mourners of Zion" was Meir ben Isaac Nehorai, the liturgical poet who wrote AKDAMUT MILLIN. Even later, at the beginning of the 14th century, ASHER BEN JEHIEL still declared that every Jew had a constant obligation "to remember Zion with a broken heart and bitter tears." Since the talmudic era, a few references to the *Avelé Zion* have entered the traditional prayer book. Thus, in the Afternoon Service *Amidah* for TISHAH BE-AV, a special passage concluding the 14th petition asks God to "console the mourners of Zion and the mourners of Jerusalem." A similar phrase is included in the modified Grace after Meals prescribed for a house of mourning. Both at the cemetery and when entering the synagogue on Friday night, mourners are greeted with the formula of condolence: "May the Almighty console you among the other mourners for Zion and Jerusalem."

AVERAH See SIN

AV HA-RAḆAMIM ("Merciful Father"). Requiem for Jewish martyrs and annihilated Jewish communities dating from the era of the First Crusade (1096-1099). The author's identity is unknown, but this memorial prayer reflects the wholesale massacres that took place at that time in the Rhineland and southern Germany, when thousands of Jews were murdered, preferring death to baptism. The *Av ha-Raḇamim* "Dirge of the Martyrs," is only recited by Ashkenazim, and it has formed part of their Sabbath Morning Service ever since the 13th century. There are variations in local custom: some Ashkenazi congregations recite *Av ha-Raḇamim* on the Sabbaths prior to Shavu'ot and Tishah be-Av, as well as at the end of each *Yizkor* memorial service; most say it weekly, however, except on the New Moon (Rosh Ḫodesh), the preceding Sabbath, and one or two other special occasions. It is invariably recited before *Ashré*, when the Torah reading has been completed and the scrolls are soon to be returned to the Holy Ark. Certain German communities followed the practice of reciting *Av ha-Raḇamim* as an accompaniment to long lists of the martyred dead, on Sabbaths during the Omer period between Passover and Shavu'ot. The prayer gives expression to the concept of KIDDUSH HA-SHEM (martyrdom), glorifying those "who laid down their lives for the sanctification of the Divine Name" (Heb. *al kedushat ha-Shem*). However, while God is asked to avenge the blood of such martyrs, grateful reference is also made to "the other righteous of the world" (see ḪASIDÉ UMMOT HA-OLAM), indicating that Jews faced with persecution and massacre did not despair of humanity.

Two other forms of *Av ha-Raḇamim* are associated with the Reading of the Law. One, read on Sabbaths and festivals, implores God to bestow His favor on Zion and rebuild the walls of Jerusalem. The other is recited (in traditional congregations) immediately before the Torah reading; a short liturgical poem composed in 12th-century France, it invokes God's mercy and the promised deliverance of His people.

THE AV HA-RAHAMIM PRAYER

May the Merciful Father who dwells on high, in His mighty compassion, remember those loving, upright, and blameless ones, the holy congregations that laid down their lives as martyrs (for the sanctification of the Divine Name);

who were lovely and pleasant in their lives, and in their death were not divided:

they were swifter than eagles, stronger than lions [II Sam. 1:23]

to do the will of their Master and the desire of their God. May our God remember them for good with the other righteous of the world, and exact retribution for the blood of His servants which has been shed... And in the Holy Scriptures it is said: Why should the heathen say, Where then is their God?

Let there be made known among the nations, in our sight, an avenging of Your servants' blood which has been shed [Ps. 79:10]...

AVINU MALKENU ("Our Father, our King"). Opening words and refrain of the most ancient Jewish litany, recited on penitential and fast days. Its origin may be found in a talmudic passage describing how, during a severe drought, only the prayer of R. AKIVA was answered when he made an impromptu supplication: "Our Father, our King, we have no king beside You. Our Father, our King, for Your own sake have mercy on us!" (*Ta'an.* 25b). This forms the basis of a brief prayer that Sephardim and Yemenite Jews recite, morning and afternoon, in the weekday TAHANUN. From early rabbinic times, as new disasters befell the Jewish people, an expanded litany developed and each additional petition used the same opening words. In the ninth-century prayer book of AMRAM GAON there are 25 lines, which have been incorporated in the Yemenite ritual. Both the order and the number of lines vary in other rites: Sephardim generally recite 32 and Ashkenazim 44 lines. The *Avinu Malkenu* petitions cover a wide range of private and communal anxieties; as well as expressing humility and repentance, they ask for the worshiper's own lack of merit to be weighed in the balance with the righteousness of Israel's saints and martyrs. While God is approached as a loving and protective Father, He is also the King of Kings who demands obedience to His Torah.

The Ashkenazi tradition lays down that *Avinu Malkenu* be recited immediately after the Morning and Afternoon Service AMIDAH during the TEN DAYS OF PENITENCE and on all public fast days (excluding Tishah be-Av). It is not read, however, when these occasions fall on a Friday afternoon or on Sabbaths; when the DAY OF ATONEMENT coincides with a Sabbath, it is only recited in the Concluding (NE'ILAH) Service. Not all of these restrictions are observed by Sephardim, who include *Avinu Malkenu* in their liturgy for *Shabbat Teshuvah*, the "Sabbath of Repentance" (see SABBATHS, SPECIAL). Reform Jews recite the prayer only on Rosh ha-Shanah and the Day of Atonement. In most Ashkenazi congregations, the last line is sung to a traditional melody on the High Holidays. It is customary for the Ark to be opened and for worshipers to stand while *Avinu Malkenu* is recited.

AVINU MALKENU
(Opening Lines)

Our Father, our King, we have sinned before You.
Our Father, our King, we have no king beside You.
Our Father, our King, deal (kindly) with us for Your own Name's sake.
Our Father, our King, nullify all evil decrees against us.
Our Father, our King, frustrate the designs of those who hate us.

AVINU SHE-BA-SHAMAYIM ("Our Father who is in Heaven"). Adoring epithet for God, much favored by the rabbis, which has entered the Jewish liturgy. The concept of a Divine Father has strong roots in the Hebrew Bible (for example, Isa. 63:16; Jer. 31:9; Ps. 103:13; I Chron. 29:10), and from it the talmudic sages derived their idea of Israel's "Father in Heaven" which finds expression throughout rabbinic literature. Piety, the "fear of God," was thus seen as "doing the will of Our Father in Heaven," on whom Jews could safely depend (*Sot.* 9.15).

This father-child relationship was liturgically balanced, however, by the notion of Divine sovereignty and transcendence (e.g., in the AVINU MALKENU supplication). "Father in Heaven, may Your great Name be blessed for all eternity," an adoration that recurs in the Midrashic *Tanna de-Vé Eliyyahu*, may well have been one source of the Christian "Lord's prayer" in the Gospels ("Our Father, which art in Heaven...," Matt. 6:9-13; Luke 11:2-4). Hasidism later extended this affectionate sense of intimacy with God through Yiddish epithets such as *Tatenyu* (i.e., "our Father"). The phrase, *Avinu she-ba-shamayim*, sometimes introduces petitionary prayers in the Jewish ritual.

AVODAH ("Service", "Worship"). Term used in a liturgical context to designate the High Priest's Order of Service in the Temple on the DAY OF ATONEMENT. All the essential details of this ritual are set forth in the Pentateuch (Lev. 16) and elaborated by the rabbis in tractate *Yoma* of the Mishnah and both Talmuds. After a week's spiritual preparation, the

High Priest entered the HOLY OF HOLIES to conduct the annual ceremony of atonement. This involved the sacrifice of a bull as his own sin offering; a threefold CONFESSION OF SINS, invoking God's Ineffable Name (the Tetragrammaton; see GOD, NAMES OF), on behalf of the officiant and his family, the priesthood, and the entire people of Israel; the drawing of lots to decide which of two goats would be chosen as a scapegoat "for AZAZEL" and which for a sacrifice; and a concluding prayer for the nation's welfare. With the Temple's destruction in 70 CE, a version of this *Avodah* was incorporated in the Additional (*Musaf*) Service of Atonement Day. By medieval times, various liturgical hymns were added to make the *Avodah* more elaborate and dramatic.

Acccording to Sephardi and Ḫasidic practice, the *Avodah* begins with a poem arranged in alphabetical acrostics and entitled *Attah konanta olam me-rosh* ("You first established the world"). Its theme, emphasizing man's history of disobedience and need to atone for his sins, resembles that of *Ammits Ko'aḫ* ("Powerful and Mighty"), the equivalent poem in the Ashkenazi rite. Of special importance are the triple confession, *Ve-khakh hayah omer* ("Thus did he say"); *Ve-ha-kohanim ve-ha-am* ("When the priests and the people"), recalling the once-yearly pronunciation of the Ineffable Name; and the congregational response of BARUKH SHEM KEVOD MALKHUTO. These three related passages are quoted from the Mishnah (*Yoma* 6.2). At a designated point in *Ve-ha-kohanim ve-ha-am*, Orthodox Jews (Ashkenazim, Ḫasidim, and some Sephardim) observe the ancient ritual of prostrating themselves and bowing their heads to the ground. This practice is followed by some Conservative Jews as well, but was abandoned by Reform Judaism. Apart from the High Priest's confession, none of the traditional *Avodah* survives in Reform liturgy; most of the Hebrew text has been retained by Conservative Judaism, although the English translation has been modified. A modern orchestral work on the theme is Ernest Bloch's *Abodah: A Yom Kippur Melody*.

AVODAH ZARAH (Idolatry). Eighth tractate of Order NEZIKIN in the Mishnah. Its five chapters deal with the rules and regulations regarding the conduct of Jews towards idolatry and idolators (cf. Ex.20: 3-5; 23:13,24,32,33; 34:12-16; Deut.7:1-5,25,26). Included are the laws forbidding business transactions with idolators, associating with them, using their images, the commandment to destroy idols, and the prohibition against using or benefiting from wine made by idolators. In the fourth chapter, the Mishnah records a discussion between the Romans and the Jewish elders concerning idolatry: "The Romans asked the elders, 'If God has no use for idol worship, why does He not destroy it?' The elders replied, 'If they worshiped a thing for which the world has no use, He would destroy it; but behold, they worship the sun, the moon, the stars and the planets. Shall He make an end of His world because of fools?'" (*Av.Zar.* 4:7). The subject matter is amplified in both Talmuds and the *Tosefta*.

AVOT ("Fathers"). Ninth tractate of Order NEZIKIN in the MISHNAH, also known as *Pirké Avot* ("Chapters of the Fathers"). It is a collection of rabbinic sayings and maxims which emphasize the importance of wise counsel, Torah study, and religious observance in Jewish life. *Avot* is the only Mishnaic tractate with no halakhic or narrative content, and there is no *Gemara* amplifying it in the Talmud. Originally, it comprised five chapters, the first two of which build a "chain of tradition" extending from Moses to the Men of the GREAT ASSEMBLY, from them to the schools of HILLEL and SHAMMAI, and finally down to Rabban GAMALIEL (son of JUDAH HA-NASI who compiled the Mishnah). About 40 tannaitic scholars are also named and quoted in chapters 3-4, but with only three exceptions all of the sayings in the fifth chapter are anonymous. Covering a period of some 500 years (from c. 300 BCE to c. 200 CE), *Avot* presents a wealth of Jewish ethical teachings and ideals, popularly entitled in English the "Ethics of the Fathers." Since Babylonian Jews adopted the custom of reading *Pirké Avot* between the festivals of Passover and Shavu'ot, a sixth (post-Mishnaic) chapter was added for supplementary reading on the last Sabbath before Shavu'ot. Known as the *Baraita de-Rabbi Meir*, after the author of the first saying quoted, this additional chapter was actually entitled *Kinyan Torah* ("Acquisition of the Torah")

Quotation from Avot *inscribed on the carved wooden doors of an Ark of the Law from Poland, 18th century. It reads: "Strong as a leopard, swift as an eagle, springs like a deer, brave as a lion."*

because Torah study constitutes its central theme. In this amplified form, *Avot* was eventually incorporated in the prayer book during the gaonic era.

Sephardim read it (usually at home) from the Sabbath after Passover until the Sabbath preceding Shavu'ot; Ashkenazim complete three reading cycles of *Avot* in synagogue, one chapter at a time being recited on Sabbath afternoons from Passover until the week before the New Year. *Pirké Avot* also gave rise to a minor talmudic tractate, AVOT DE-RABBI NATAN.

ANONYMOUS SAYINGS FROM PIRKÉ AVOT

Seven things characterize a boor and seven a wise man: The wise man does not speak before someone wiser than he; does not interrupt his fellow; does not reply in haste; asks what is relevant and answers to the point; deals with matters in their proper order; says of what he has not heard, "I haven't heard"; and admits to the truth. The opposite of these typifies the boor (5.7).

There are four types of people who give to charity: One who is willing to give but does not wish others to do so — he begrudges others [any applause for their generosity]; One who is willing that others should give but not willing to do so himself — he begrudges himself [what is involved]; One who is willing to give and who wishes others to give — he is a righteous man; One who both refuses to give and wishes others to refuse — he is a scoundrel (5.13).

Any dispute for the sake of heaven will have lasting importance, but one not conducted for the sake of heaven will never endure. The debates of Hillel and Shammai are examples of the first type, the conspiracy of Korah and his supporters is an example of the second (5.17).

He who learns from his colleague a single chapter, law, verse, expression, or even one letter, is obliged to pay him honor (6.3).

How great is the Torah! It assures life to those who fulfill it both in this world and in the world to come, as it is written (Prov. 3:18): "It is a tree of life to those who grasp it, and those who hold fast to it are made happy" 6.7).

AVOT DE-RABBI NATAN ("*Avot*" according to Rabbi Nathan). Extra-canonical tractate of 41 chapters providing an early commentary on and amplification of Mishnah AVOT, including moral sayings by *tannaim* which are absent from *Avot*. This tractate, like the one on which it was based, is entirely aggadic. It often illustrates the sayings of *Avot* with parables and anecdotes drawn from the lives of the sages who are mentioned in *Avot*. The identity of the R. Nathan to whom it is traditionally ascribed remains obscure. A commentary on some old version of *Avot* was produced by a certain Rabbi Nathan (perhaps R. Nathan the Babylonian) who lived in the second-third century CE. Internal evidence suggests that *Avot de-Rabbi Natan* was edited in the late third or early fourth century. The text has come down in two versions, with significant differences. One is found in standard editions of the Babylonian Talmud, following Tractate *Avot* at the end of Order *Nezikin*. The other, consisting of 48 chapters, was first published in full by Solomon SCHECHTER. The work, frequently quoted by post-talmudic authorities, is a prime source for the study of *aggadah*.

AVTALYON See SHEMAYAH

AYIN HA-RA See EVIL EYE

AZAZEL Place in the wilderness to which one of the two he-goats was sent by the High Priest, as part of the DAY OF ATONEMENT service in the Temple in Jerusalem. This goat was to carry "all the sins" of Israel with it (Lev. 16:22) hence the concept of "scapegoat." Preceding this action, the High Priest drew lots over two he-goats, assigning one goat to be sacrificed and the other to be sent away "to *Azazel*" to the wilderness to be killed (v. 8). The derivation of the word is not completely clear; the Talmud suggests that *Azazel* was a craggy cliff, over which the goat was thrown to its death in the wilderness (*Yoma* 67b). According to the sages of the Talmud, the law of the *azazel* is included in the category of *ḫukim*, namely those laws which man's intellect cannot understand (*ibid*).

In the kabbalistic and midrashic literature, *Azazel* is considered to be a composite name for two fallen angels, Uza and Azael, who had come down to earth at the time of Tubal Cain and had become corrupted in their ways. Some commentators, medieval and modern, have suggested that *Azazel* was the name of a desert demon. In modern Hebrew slang "go to Azazel" is the equivalent of the English "go to hell."

AZHAROT ("exhortations, warnings"). Name given to a type of didactic liturgical poem that first appeared in the geonic era. The genre owes its name to the earliest known poem of this type, which begins with the words: *Azharot reshit le-ammekha natata* — "In the beginning You [God] exhorted [gave *azharot* to] Your people." The reference is to a talmudic passage (*Mak.* 23b): "R. Simlai taught: "613 exhortations [commandments] were given to Moses, 365 negative precepts in accordance with the days of the solar year, and 248 positive precepts in accordance with the number of limbs in the human body." The connection between the word *azharot* and the 613 COMMANDMENTS is further implied from the fact that the numerical value of *azharot* in Hebrew is 613. The *azharot* delineate and allude to the 613 Commandments in poetic form. Occasionally, their content diverges from the accepted *halakhah* (as reflected in *Yoma* 8a and elsewhere), but the poems should be viewed as liturgical constructions rather than halakhic statements.

Saadiah Gaon, AMRAM GAON, and Solomon IBN GABIROL were among the many medieval personalities who composed *azharot*. One popular example is attributed to R. Elijah "the Elder," identified with Elijah the prophet. The earlier poems are simple in structure, taking the form of straight alphabetical acrostics. Rhymes and inverted alphabetical acrostics appeared at a later stage.

Azharot were normally recited as part of the Morning Service on SHAVU'OT, the festival celebrating the giving of the Law, but were transferred to the Afternoon Service, presumably because the Morning Service had become too lengthy. As the recitation of *azharot* gained in popularity, other and similar liturgies developed in conjunction with the festivals of Passover and Sukkot, the New Year, Ḥanukkah, and Purim. Today, *azharot* are rarely recited and the entire literature is virtually unknown.

AZULAI, ḤAYYIM YOSEF DAVID (known by the acronym *Ḥida*; 1724-1806). Rabbinic scholar, author, and emissary. He was born in Jerusalem into a well-known kabbalistic family, and studied with the leading rabbis of the community. In the course of his lifetime, Azulai made notable contributions to religious literature in the fields of legal, mystical, and ethical literature, biography, and bibliography. He also took a keen interest in Jewish folk literature. His most important work is the bibliographical lexicon, *Shem ha-Gedolim* ("Name of the Great Ones"), presenting biographies of scholars and analyses of books and manuscripts.

Azulai traveled extensively in Europe, Turkey, and North Africa as a fundraising emissary of the Jewish communities of Erets Israel, notably Hebron. He eventually settled in Leghorn, Italy. His diary, *Ma'agal Tov*, reflects his wide interests as well as his perceptive mind and unusual memory. An outstanding feature are the references to rare Jewish manuscripts and books which he examined in public and private collections. Azulai was a compelling and popular preacher who spoke clearly, disdaining the use of complicated argument. He had strong mystical leanings which imbued his religious outlook and his writings. He was widely acknowledged as the leading Sephardi rabbi of his generation.

B

BAAL (Phoenician and Canaanite: "lord"). The most important of the Canaanite fertility gods, son of El and brother of Anath. As the god of wind and rain, Baal was related to the productivity of the soil, and by extension his cult included animal and human fertility as well. Its strong sexual overtones are attested by the presence of the corresponding female symbol, Ashtoreth.

The worship of Baal was regarded as one of the greatest threats to early Israelite religion, either undermining or perverting the worship of Israel's God. Many biblical references show the extent of its influence; HOSEA addresses the moral and religious ruin which it brought upon the Northern Kingdom of Israel (e.g., Hos. 2:10, 13:1), while JEREMIAH describes this abhorrent worship, including child sacrifice, as occurring at the very gates of Jerusalem (Jer. 19).

The best-known and most detailed biblical episode in which this god figures is the early confrontation between ELIJAH and the 450 prophets of Baal assembled on Mount Carmel (I Kings 18: 19-40). Here, proof of the impotence of Baal is supplied to King Ahab and his Phoenician wife Jezebel, the protectors and followers of an active Baal cult in the Northern Kingdom. It is the God of Israel who has withheld the rain, and it is He who publicly sends down fire to consume and validate the sacrifice of His servant.

Despite that victory over the false prophets, and their physical elimination, Elijah's success in discrediting Baal was short-lived. The attraction of Baal was not easily overcome and his cult proved extremely resilient. The fierce resistance of the Judean kings Hezekiah and Josiah, and their destruction of Baal's altars notwithstanding, Baal worship continued to exert its influence throughout the entire First Temple period.

BA'AL KERI'AH (lit. "master of the reading"). The person who chants the prescribed reading from the Pentateuch whenever this forms part of congregational worship in the synagogue (see READING OF THE LAW). Among Sephardi, North African, and Eastern Jews, the congregational reader (*ḫazzan* or SHELI'AḪ TSIBBUR) normally serves also as *ba'al keri'ah*. In Ashkenazi congregations he is popularly known as a *ba'al koré*. From Second Temple times until the early Middle Ages, each person called to the Torah would recite the appropriate TORAH BLESSINGS, prior to and after the reading, which he would chant himself. By about the ninth century CE, however, large numbers of Jews were no longer capable of reading the unvocalized text with sufficient accuracy, also being unfamiliar with the Masoretic accents (see CANTILLATION). (An exception is the Yemenite community

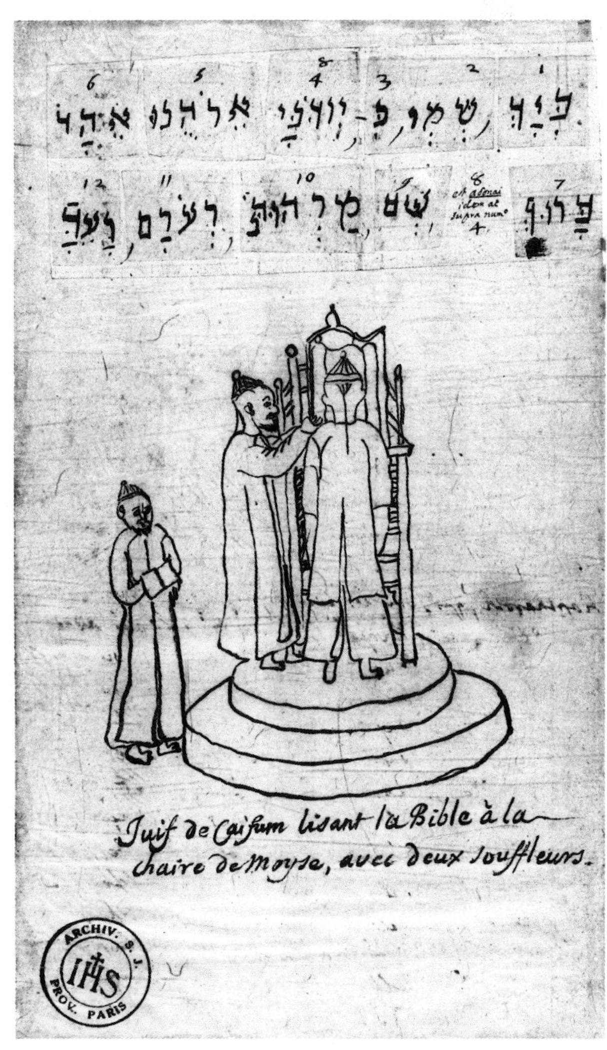

Chinese Jew from Kaifeng reading from the Scroll of the Law. The ba'al keriah *on the left, holds a Torah written with vowels to help the reader. From a 1772 drawing.*

where each individual still chants his own portion.) It therefore became a standard practice for synagogues or communities to appoint a skilled *ba'al keri'ah* who, either as a volunteer or as a paid official, would be responsible for every Torah reading throughout the year.

Nowadays, the *ba'al keri'ah* is often a specialist with professional training who is expected to chant each Torah portion with the highest degree of accuracy. He uses a special pointer (YAD) to guide himself as he reads the text. Although the employment of a *ba'al keri'ah* is a widely accepted practice, even in the most Orthodox congregations, the privilege of reading from the Torah is also granted to learned Jews possessing the necessary skill, to a youngster on the occasion of his BAR MITSVAH, and latterly sometimes to a BAT MITSVAH (in non-Orthodox congregations). Special training programs in various communities now make it possible for Jews of all ages to gain proficiency as Torah readers, instruction also being available in the form of recorded cassettes. This trend has led to a reduction in the number of professional *ba'alé keri'ah* whose services are in demand.

BA'AL SHEM ("Master of the [Divine] Name"). Title given from early medieval times to an alleged wonderworker, someone believed to "possess" the secret of the *Shem ha-Meforash* (Tetragrammaton) and thought capable of using it to perform miracles (see also GOD, NAMES OF). Allusions to *ba'alé shem* (plur.) can be traced from HAI GAON in Babylonia to the ḤASIDÉ ASHKENAZ mystics in medieval Germany and to the leading kabbalists (such as MOSES DE LEÓN) in Spain. Those who originally bore this title tended to be rabbis and talmudists whose "magical" power consisted largely in writing AMULETS bearing various holy names. At a later stage, however, particularly in Eastern Europe, the *ba'al shem* title was assumed by men of a different type who combined PRACTICAL KABBALAH with faith healing, incantations and the sale of amulets with folk-cures. Popular legends were often woven around such personalities, and some were credited with the power of exorcising evil spirits (see DEMONS AND DEMONOLOGY; DIBBUK). In many cases, claimants to the title must undoubtedly have been quacks and impostors, as well as followers of SHABBETAI TSEVI. The modified designation of *ba'al shem tov* ("possessor of a good name") was current even before it was assumed in the 18th century by R. Israel ben Eliezer BA'AL SHEM TOV, the founder of ḤASIDISM. A contemporary of his, Samuel Jacob Ḥayyim Falk (c. 1710-1782), a Podolian adventurer and reputed Shabbatean, won fame and fortune as "the *Ba'al Shem* of London."

BA'AL SHEM TOV, ISRAEL BEN ELIEZER (known as the *Besht*, an acronym of *Ba'al Shem Tov*; 1698-1760). Founder of ḤASIDISM. The major problem in trying to describe the life of this charismatic personality is the lack of reliable documentation. *Shivḥé ha-Besht* (1814-15; *In Praise of the Ba'al Shem Tov*, 1970), an early biography, is crammed with

The bet midrash *(study and prayer room) of Israel Ba'al Shem Tov, the founder of Ḥasidism, in Medzibezh, Podolia.*

legendary material which cannot be disentangled from historical fact. Nevertheless, scholars have been able to reconstruct the essential features of his life and teachings by reading between the lines of the various hagiographies, by studying the very few known contemporary documents, and by piecing together the authentic sayings as they appear in the writings of his disciples.

Israel ben Eliezer was born in the Podolian village of Okup in the Carpathian Mountains. There he earned his living as a school teacher or *shoḥet* (ritual slaughterer), eventually marrying the sister of R. Abraham Gershon of Kutow, a learned and wealthy resident of Brody, who was at first opposed to the match but subsequently became a disciple of the Ba'al Shem Tov. It would seem that before his particular teaching mission, Israel was a healer and miracle worker, who employed combinations of Divine Names — hence the title *Ba'al Shem Tov*, signifying "Master of the Good Name [of God]." His followers, and later Ḥasidic devotees, are more than a little embarrassed by his early career as a mere miracle worker and tend to play down this role, justifiably preferring to see him as a religious teacher with a new, exhilarating message. The fact is that, in villages and townships of the region, there were a number of mystical figures, each with his own circle of disciples. The group surrounding Israel ben Eliezer became the dominant one, however, the others either fading from the scene or being absorbed by Israel's group which, in Ḥasidic parlance, is known as the *ḥavurah kaddisha* or "holy company." From the beginning, Ḥasidic companies were centered on the leader, a guru-type mentor known as the TSADDIK (in this context meaning "saint"). Some scholars have inaccurately portrayed the rise of "Tsaddikism" as a later development in the history of Ḥasidism. Yet the Ba'al Shem Tov was a *Tsaddik* or *Rebbe* (a spiritual leader distinct from the traditional *Rav*), and his disciples and their disciples after them became *Tsaddikim*.

Despite the claims often made by the Ḥasidim themselves, all the evidence points to the fact that the Ba'al Shem Tov was not a profound rabbinic scholar. He was, however, equipped with a good knowledge of the Bible, the rabbinic *aggadah*, and (especially) the Kabbalah, his own teachings making use of their vocabulary. These teachings do not appear to have been presented in anything like a systematic form, but were conveyed in maxims and aphorisms — probably in Yiddish. They were collected and published in the works of his disciples, in Rabbinic Hebrew, and naturally assume the formulation of that particular disciple, as well as his special interpretation of the master's ideas. The result is various interpretations of those ideas, making it somewhat precarious to assert with any degree of confidence that this or that idea is an expression of the Ba'al Shem Tov's original doctrine — presented offhand, as it were, and not in any methodical fashion.

Prominent among these teachings is the idea of DEVEKUT, "attachment" (to God). *Devekut* in Ḫasidism means God being in the mind of the Ḫasid at all times, so far as this is humanly possible. Even when the Ḫasidic Jew is engaged in worldly things, when he eats, drinks, or sees to his business affairs, he should realize that he is doing whatever he does as an act of worship. Torah study must likewise be engaged in as a devotional exercise, namely, the mind of the worshiper is to be on God. The MITNAGGEDIM — opponents of Ḫasidism — inveighed against this aspect of its teaching, seeing in it a denial of Torah study as the supreme religious value: if the mind of the student was on God, rather than on the subject he was studying, he would never master the subject and would, indeed, not be studying at all. This explains the many tales told by the Ḫasidim in which the Ba'al Shem Tov confronts his scholarly opponents and gets the better of them. In one such tale the rabbis, wishing to expose the Ba'al Shem's ignorance, asked him what the procedure should be in the event of one's forgetting the special Rosh Ḫodesh (New Moon) insertion in the liturgy: must one repeat the whole prayer? The Ba'al Shem Tov replied: "One has to repeat the prayer — but I don't know for whom this law was intended, since I will never forget it the first time round, whereas you will forget it the second time as well."

There are also many aphorisms attributed to the Ba'al Shem Tov in which it is implied that the simple Jew with no pretensions to learning, but who is genuinely devout, ranks higher than the learned talmudist who studies with the aim of gaining a reputation for himself. Another maxim of the Ba'al Shem Tov, in the same vein, declares: "If it is highly meritorious, as the scholars affirm, to study that section in the Talmud dealing with the exchange of an ox for an ass, how much more meritorious would it be actually to effect such an exchange in a spirit of devotion." The scholar is only studying the laws governing the exchange; the Ḫasid, with his mind on God, is actually engaged in an act of worship, even when he carries out such a mundane transaction.

The Ḫasidim remark that all the Divine mysteries revealed to the Ba'al Shem Tov were not revealed to him because he was a great scholar, but because he offered his prayers with intense devotion. Reciting one's prayers out of longing for God, and joyous enthusiasm (*hitlahavut*) in the worship of the Creator, is given special emphasis in "Beshtian" doctrine. To facilitate such intense concentration, it is reported that the Ba'al Shem Tov would smoke a pipe before praying so as to make himself ready for contemplation of the awesome act he was about to perform. Gestures, even of a grotesque kind, were allowed during prayer if they helped the worshiper to concentrate. The Ba'al Shem Tov reportedly observed that a drowning man is not ashamed to gesticulate wildly so that others will come to his assistance.

Israel Ba'al Shem Tov had two children — a son, Tsevi Hirsch, and a daughter named Adel (Odel). Very little is related about the son in Ḫasidic lore, but there are many wondrous tales about his daughter, whose own children included Moses Ḫayyim Ephraim of Sudylkow (1740-1800) and Baruch, the *Tsaddik* of Medzibozh (1757-1810), who became the Ba'al Shem's spiritual heir. Adel's daughter, Feige, was the mother of NAḪMAN OF BRATSLAV, but the more important line of succession came through the Ba'al Shem Tov's disciples. They and those who followed them were responsible for the amazingly rapid spread of Ḫasidism: by the beginning of the 19th century, half the Jews in Eastern Europe had been won over to the Ḫasidic movement.

APHORISMS OF THE BA'AL SHEM TOV

What matters is not how many precepts you fulfill, but the spirit in which you fulfill them.

Serve God with joy: a joyful person has an abundance of love for man and all of God's creatures.

If you want to pull your friend out of the mud, don't be afraid of getting a little dirty.

When God wishes to punish a man, He deprives him of faith.

The world is full of wonderful sights and great mysteries, but one small hand in front of our eyes obstructs the view.

There is no room for God in one who is full of himself.

If your son has taken to evil ways, love him more than ever.

When I die, I shall go out of one door and then in through another.

If you wish to live long, don't become famous.

Hearing from some Ḫasidim of the persecution to which they were being subjected in Brody, the Ba'al Shem Tov commented: "Our opponents do this out of religious zeal. Since they derive pleasure from harassing us, in the belief that they are performing a *mitsvah*, why should we deprive them of their enjoyment?"

BA'AL TEFILLAH (lit. "master of the prayer"). The person who conducts public worship in the synagogue. Until the era of the *ge'onim* (sixth cent. CE onward), any Jew possessing the necessary qualifications might be invited to lead the congregation in prayer; thereafter, a musically trained "reader" or professional CANTOR often took over the functions of the *ba'al tefillah*. The term *ba'al tefillah* has become virtually interchangeable with SHELI'AḤ TSIBBUR ("delegate of the community") and is used to denote anyone asked to recite the prayer service on an unpaid, *ad hoc* basis.

BA'AL TEKI'AH ("master of the blowing"). The person who sounds the SHOFAR (ram's horn) in synagogue on Rosh ha-Shanah and at the conclusion of the Day of Atonement. He is also known as a *toke'a* or (according to a popular Ashkenazi misnomer) as *"ba'al-toke'a."* Although any male capable of doing so may sound the *shofar* when a qualified *ba'al teki'ah* is not available, halakhic authorities stipulate that the one appointed should be pious and learned as well as competent. For this reason, preference is given to a worthy prayer leader, mindful of his awesome duty and of the fact that the blessings he is about to recite and the notes he will sound are intended as a fulfillment of the precept on the congregation's behalf. Ashkenazi practice requires the *ba'al teki'ah* to don a white KITEL. After having recited the prescribed benedictions, "to hear the sound of the *shofar*" and SHE-HEḤEYANU, he blows the necessary sequences of *shofar* notes before the Additional Service and during the reader's repetition. A prompter (*makri*), normally the rabbi, stands next to the *ba'al teki'ah* so as to insure that all the notes sounded will be correct. Two additional precautions are an extra *shofar*, in case the blower has difficulty sounding the first, and a substitute "*shofar*-blower" to replace him if he is unable to continue.

A ba'al tek'iah *("master of the blowing"), wearing a prayer shawl and phylacteries, blows the* shofar *(ram's horn) at the Western Wall, Jerusalem.*

BAAL TESHUVAH (or *ḥozer bi-teshuvah*; "one who has returned, repented"). Hebrew term for a penitent who returns to the ways of religion; also applied in recent years to a newly observant Jew. The rabbis showered praise on the *ba'al teshuvah* and made every effort to ensure that he was not handicapped by his previous conduct, forbidding anyone to embarrass him by recalling his sinful past (*Pes.* 119a, *Yoma* 86b, etc.). The Talmud declares that "the place where penitents stand cannot be attained even by the wholly righteous" (T.B. Ber. 34b; see also REPENTANCE).

A contemporary phenomenon is the growth of the "*Ba'al Teshuvah* movement," with possibly thousands of nonobservant Jews accepting Orthodox beliefs and practices. It emerged in the United States, largely as a reaction to the conflicts of the 1960s (which also led to the proliferation of alien CULTS), and in Israel it resulted from the euphoria aroused by the 1967 Six-Day War. Most of those affected belonged to the youthful sector of the population and were attracted to an ultra-Orthodox ideology and way of life. Traditionally, the *ba'al teshuvah* was a Jew who had gone astray but now repented of his wrongdoing. The modern *ba'al teshuvah* is usually not "returning" but adopting a religious life style for the first time. This has given rise to the establishment of special YESHIVOT for *ba'alé teshuvah* in various places, notably in Israel.

BABYLONIAN EXILE See EXILE, BABYLONIAN

BABYLONIAN TALMUD See TALMUD

BACHARACH, JAIR ḤAYYIM BEN MOSES SAMSON (1638-1702). Rabbi and talmudic authority. A descendent of JUDAH LÖW BEN BEZALEL, the *Maharal* of Prague, Bacharach grew up in Leipnik, where his father was rabbi. They moved to Worms in 1650, when Moses Samson became the communal rabbi there. Married at 15, Bacharach spent the next six years studying at his father-in-law's home in Fulda. He was impressed by the messianic claims of SHABBETAI TSEVI, and even after these had proved false still called him "our Teacher." In 1666, Bacharach was appointed rabbi and head of the rabbinical court in Koblenz, but was forced to resign three years later. From 1670 he lived in Worms but once it was occupied by the troops of Louis XIV (1689), he fled to Metz and then wandered from one city to another in the Rhineland. In 1699, prematurely aged and infirm, Bacharach was elected rabbi of Worms. To succeed his grandfather and father in that prestigious office was a long-delayed satisfaction.

That same year (1699), his collection of 238 responsa appeared, bearing the title *Ḥavvot Ya'ir* — a phrase taken from Numbers 32:41 and incorporating the author's name. This volume displays Bacharach's familiarity with mathematics, astronomy, and music, as well as his mastery of rabbinics. The most extensive of his works, it was printed with the help of a relative, Samson Wertheimer, the Viennese court Jew. One responsum discusses the Oral Law, another expresses support for the building of schools and the teaching of pedagogics. Bacharach would not permit an inquirer to cross a river on the Sabbath in order to attend synagogue; he called for a person who had drunk non-*kasher* wine to be punished; and he was offended by a father's wish, expressed in the man's will, that his only child (a daughter) should recite *Kaddish* in his memory. Bacharach felt that if such a request were to be granted, each individual might then choose his own interpretation of the *halakhah*.

BAECK, LEO (1873-1956). Rabbi, religious philosopher, leader of German Jewry and of the world movement for Progressive Judaism. Born in Lissa, then part of Prussia, he studied at the Jewish Theological Seminary of Breslau (Conservative) and at the Hochschule für die Wissenschaft des Judentums in Berlin (Liberal). He served as rabbi in several communities before his appointment to a leading rabbinic post in Berlin, where he taught Midrash and homiletics at the Hochschule.

In his communal leadership, Baeck served as president of the representative body of German Jewry — the *Reichsvertretung* — and as president of the General Association of German Rabbis. Though not a Zionist in the political sense, he recognized the importance of building a strong Jewish community in Palestine as a step forward in the renaissance of Jewish life.

With Hitler's rise to power in 1933, Baeck dedicated his efforts to defending the rights of the Jews in the face of Nazi persecution. He was arrested and interrogated in Gestapo headquarters several times, and with each successive questioning his personal position became more dangerous. Yet he refused many invitations from Jewish communities and institutions outside Germany, feeling a strong obligation to remain with his endangered community and to minister to their spiritual needs as long as there were Jews remaining in Germany. In 1943 he was deported to Theresienstadt concentration camp. There he was an example of great moral courage and saintliness as he tirelessly worked to strengthen the morale of his fellow inmates, lecturing on Judaism and encouraging them in all ways possible to keep alive their hope, faith, and humanity. After the war, he moved to London and became head of the World Union for Progressive Judaism.

Baeck wrote on the philosophy and history of religion. His best known work was *Das Wesen des Judentums* ("The Essence of Judaism," 1936). His philosophy at first stressed the rationalism of Judaism and his expositions of the Jewish faith appear rather apologetic. With the growing influence of the Jewish national movement and the vigorous revival of Jewish life in Palestine, his views were modified. Like Hermann COHEN, Baeck emphasized Judaism as a system of ethical monotheism in which the duties between man and man and the moral and ethical values are central. The ritual laws are not unimportant, but their purpose is to guide one toward the ethical life. Ultimately, the challenge facing the Jew is to redeem the world from evil through the values of justice and love. Israel is the CHOSEN PEOPLE in the sense that God's purpose is for Israel to be loyal to its mission to help mankind by upholding the ultimate ethical values in life.

Baeck also wrote on Christianity, and here he offers a strongly critical assessment of what he calls the "romantic" Christian religion — one very different from the "classical" earthly religion of Judaism, which sees its daily purpose as making this world a better place for all men. His work on the PHARISEES (English translation, 1947) was a pioneering effort to counteract the New Testament bias against and misrepresentation of this important school of rabbinic thought.

BAHIR, SEFER ("Book of Light"). Hebrew mystical treatise written in its present form at the end of the 12th century. It is the first work of the medieval Jewish mystical movement, the KABBALAH, and was written in the form of a classical *Midrash*, each section or group of sections dealing with a homiletical interpretation of biblical verses. Traditionally, it is attributed to the Mishnaic sage R. Neḫunya ben ha-Kanah, who is the speaker in the first section of the book, and who is described as the head of the mystical group in HEKHALOT literature. Other sections are attributed to various talmudic scholars and to fictional figures ("Rabbi Amora"). The author of the *Bahir* made widespread use of the Midrashic form of the parable (*mashal*), often to express paradoxical ideas. The manuscripts and traditional editions of the book do not use any system of chapters or sections. The two modern editions are divided into 130 sections (G. Scholem, in his German translation) or 200 sections (R. Margaliot in his Hebrew edition).

The book *Bahir*'s importance lies in the fact that this is probably the earliest source of the system of the ten Divine hypostases, the kabbalistic SEFIROT, described in the latter part of the book. The Divine world is described as a tree (*ilan*), whose roots are deep within the Godhead and whose branches are turned toward the cosmos. The ten Divine powers include a feminine element, and probably also an evil element on the left side. These symbols became central in the later development of the Kabbalah in 13th-century Gerona and in the ZOHAR, at the end of that century.

The sources of the *Bahir* include some medieval Jewish works, like *Hegyon ha-Nefesh* by Abraham bar Ḫiyya, the Bible commentary by Abraham IBN EZRA, and the Hebrew translation of BAḪYA IBN PAKUDA's *Ḫovot ha-Levavot*. The author used extensively the texts of *Hekhalot* mysticism and the *Sefer* YETSIRAH, giving a new meaning to the old mystical texts. Some gnostic elements may have influenced the symbols of the *Bahir*, either from a Hebrew text which served as a source for the ancient mystics or from non-Jewish gnosticism. No connection has been demonstrated between the *Bahir* and the contemporary gnostic movement of the Cathars in Southern France, or any other specific gnostic sect.

BAHUR ("young man," lit. "chosen one"). Hebrew term possessing various connotations in the Bible, but later applied to a Talmud student, especially one who is unmarried. Although occasionally denoting "chosen warriors" (Jer. 48:15; I Chron. 19:10), it more frequently designates a young man in the prime of life (e.g., Judg. 14:10; Isa. 9:16) or a youth of marriageable age (e.g., Isa. 23:4, 62:5; Jer. 31:12, 51:22). By early rabbinic times, *bahur* had acquired the generalized sense of "a single man," whether as a desirable marriage partner (*Ta'an.* 4.8) or as a presumably older man taking a widow for his bride (*Ket.* 7a-b). From the Middle Ages onward, *bahur* specifically denoted a youthful Talmud student in his early stage of "learning" at a *yeshivah* (rabbinical academy). Having graduated from the traditional HEDER, he was now a *bahur yeshivah* (or *yeshivah bokher* in Yiddish), whereas older, newly married students became known as *avrekhim*. The biblical expression *tiferet bahurim* ("the glory of young men"; Prov. 20:29) was extended to mean youths who were the pride and joy of their community.

BAHYA BEN ASHER IBN HALAWA (known as Rabbenu Bahyé; c.1260-1340). Spanish Bible commentator and mystic. Little is known about his life, apart from the fact that he served as a rabbi and preacher in Saragossa, his instructor in Talmud having been Solomon ben Abraham ADRET. Bahya wrote a number of works, including *Kad ha-Kemah*, an encyclopedic treatise on ethical and philosophical themes; *Shulhan shel Arba*; and a commentary on tractate AVOT. Far more important than these, however, was his *Be'ur al ha-Torah*, a commentary on the Pentateuch written in 1291. This work is distinguished by its scope, the systematic weaving of kabbalistic ideas into the biblical exposition, and a marked tendency to explain textual difficulties by providing vernacular (Spanish, French, or Arabic) equivalents in Hebrew transliteration — a method pioneered by RASHI. Bahya adopts a fourfold approach to Scripture, utilizing "the way of PESHAT" (its "plain" or literal meaning); "the way of Midrash" (i.e., the homiletical approach; see DERASH); "the way of *sekhel*" or intellect (a reasoned or philosophical method); and "the way of *sod*" or mysticism (i.e., KABBALAH). Bahya's fourfold technique, slightly modified, was to become known by the mnemonic PARDES. His commentary gained lasting popularity because of its lucid presentation of Jewish mystical ideas; it was the earliest work of Kabbalah to be printed (1492) and inspired no less than ten different supercommentaries.

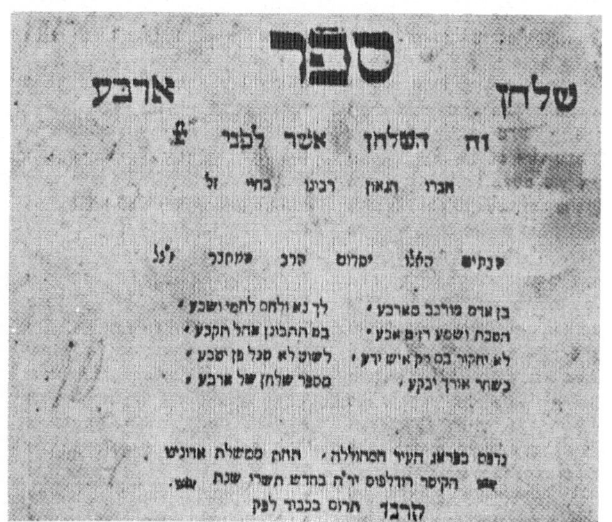

ספר
שלחן ארבע
וזה השלחן אשר לפני ה׳
חברו הגאון רבינו בחיי ז"ל

בן אדם מורכב מארבע · לך נא ולחם לחמי ושבע ·
הסבת ושמע רזים אבע · במה תתבונן אהל תקבע ·
לא יחקור בם רק איש ירע · לשוב לא סכל פן ישבע ·
כשור אורך יבקע · מספר שלחן של ארבע ·

נדפס בפראג העיר המהוללה · תחת ממשלת אדונינו
הקיסר רודלפוס יר"ה בחדש תשרי שנת
קרבן תרום בכבוד לפק

Title page of Shulhan Arba, a work of halakhah *and etiquette relating to meals, by Bahya ben Asher, printed in Prague in 1596.*

BAHYA BEN JOSEPH IBN PAKUDA (11th cent.). Jewish philosopher in Spain. Almost nothing is known of his life, apart from his having been a rabbinical judge (*dayyan*). The work which earned him a distinguished place among medieval Jewish thinkers was his *Kitab al-Hidaya ila Fara'id al-Qulub*, which appeared in 1080. As *Hovot ha-Levavot* ("The Duties of the Heart"), it was translated from the Arabic original into Hebrew by Judah Ibn Tibbon (1161), and in modern times there have been translations into English and other languages. Bahya explains that Jewish religious life can be examined under two headings. These are the duties of practical observance, i.e., performing the commandments of Judaism (e.g., Sabbath, festivals, dietary laws, prayer). Then there are the "duties of the heart" which are associated with man's inner life, and which call for the cultivation and exercise of profound spirituality. This second part of the religious life is no less important than the first, Bahya argues, yet it has been neglected by Jewish teachers in their concentration on the practical observance of Judaism's laws and customs. He seeks to redress the balance by expounding the values of the inner spiritual life of the Jew and those qualities of faith which are necessary for human perfection.

The book is divided into ten "gates" or chapters, each one devoted to a single duty of the heart which is important in the spiritual life. These are acceptance of the unity of God; recognition of the complex universe and all things in it created by an all-powerful God; worship, in a spirit of gratitude, of the one God and Creator; complete trust in God, who is close, ever-present, and able to protect man from the dangers that exist all around him; purity of motive; humility; repentance; self-examination; reasonable asceticism; and love of God. Bahya's philosophy was Neo-Platonic and he was influenced by Islamic mystical writings. For Jews, his book was a pioneering ethical work which became very popular and influential.

BAKKASHOT ("supplications"). Liturgical poems (PIYYUTIM) recited in the Sephardi ritual, originally prior to the daily Morning Service but later only on Sabbath mornings. The tradition appears to have originated in the late 17th or early 18th century, under the influence of the Safed kabbalists. These poems focus on the nature of God, the Sabbath, the redemption of Israel, and such mystical elements as the SEFIROT (emanations) and the SHEKHINAH (Divine presence). Collections of such prayers in Hebrew, Aramaic, and Arabic have been handed down from generation to generation, each adding its own contribution. In the Syrian (Aleppo) and Moroccan traditions, now flourishing in Israel, young and old alike gather in synagogue to chant *bakkashot,* commencing 3 a.m. every Sabbath throughout the winter, from the Sabbath after Simḫat Torah to the Sabbath before Purim.

BAL TASHḪIT (lit. "Don't destroy!"). Expression derived from the biblical law prohibiting the destruction of fruit trees within the domain of a besieged city (Deut. 20:19-20). This law was extended by the rabbis in the form of "a warning not to destroy" anything in God's creation that may prove beneficial to man (*Shab.* 129a; *BK* 91b). Accordingly, vandalism, wastefulness, and all other willful damage to property (including one's own) come under the law of *bal tashḫit.* A person who rips his clothes in exaggerated mourning, who smashes china or furnishings in uncontrollable rage, who squanders his hard-earned money on drink or other vices, may be compared to an idol-worshiper (*Shab.* 105b). In present-day terms, the same law would apply to anyone damaging public transport, vandalizing signposts and public buildings, burning down forests, destroying animal life and natural vegetation, or wantonly harming the ecology.

BA-MEH MADLIKIN ("With what may one kindle [or not kindle the Sabbath lamp]...?"). Opening words of the second chapter of the Mishnaic tractate SHABBAT, recited in the Friday night service. It indicates the types of oil and wick that may lawfully be used for Sabbath lights; when they may be extinguished in an emergency; and the domestic preparations that should be made before the Sabbath commences. As an appendix to this chapter, the rabbis selected a short homiletical passage from the Talmud (*Ber.* 64a), outlining their concept of the Torah's role in fostering world peace. Some authorities, including RASHI, placed *Ba-meh Madlikin* at the end of the Sabbath eve prayers; others held that it should be recited before the service, thus enabling Jews to take care of any last-minute arrangements which they had overlooked in the home. Living in the medieval Christian world, however, Rashi also had a practical consideration in mind: Jews arriving in the synagogue late from work would be able to complete their prayers while *Ba-meh Madlikin* was being recited and could then return home with the other worshipers. The former practice is still maintained by some Ashkenazi congregations in the Diaspora, but a compromise between the two different rulings has been adopted by Sephardim, Eastern Jews, and most Ashkenazim (particularly in Israel), who insert this reading in their prayers after the entrance of the Sabbath (KABBALAT SHABBAT) and before the Evening Service. It is generally omitted when Sabbath eve coincides with the beginning or termination of a festival or with the intermediate days of Passover and Sukkot. Jews adhering to the Ḫasidic rite substitute a passage from the Zohar for *Ba-meh Madlikin.* Some textual changes have been made in the Conservative prayer book.

BAN See EXCOMMUNICATION

BARAITA (Aram. "external teaching"; plur. *baraitot*). Any tannaitic statement not found in the MISHNAH as well as certain amoraic statements in which the Mishnah is explained. Collections of such explanatory *baraitot*, arranged by R. Ḫiyya and R. Oshaya and by Bar Kappara, appear in the TOSEFTA and the MIDRASH HALAKHAH, while many laws found in them are cited in the Talmud. The legal authority of a *baraita* is less than that of a Mishnaic statement; hence, when there is a contradiction between the two, the Mishnah nearly always proves decisive, although there are some exceptions to this rule.

Tannaitic *baraitot* may be divided into various categories. There are those which supplement the Mishnah; or a *baraita* may also quote a *halakhah* not found in the Mishnah; or it may contain a version of a *halakhah* differing from that cited in the Mishnah. These *baraitot* have a distinguishing introductory formula, such as *tanya* ("we have learned this") or *tanu rabbanan* ("the sages taught").

The numerous *baraitot* of amoraic origin are usually either brief explanations of or additions to the Mishnah; unlike the tannaitic *baraitot*, they do not contain differing opinions. Such *baraitot* were not given much weight by the talmudic sages. While most of the *baraitot* are halakhic in nature, a significant number (both tannaitic and amoraic) have an aggadic character.

Certain collections of *baraitot*, dating from the tannaitic period, form special units of their own. Prominent among them are (a) the *Baraita de-Rabbi Meir*, "on acquiring the Torah," which constitutes an extra chapter (no. 6) attached to tractate AVOT of the Mishnah; (b) the *Baraita de-Rabbi Yishma'el* ("of 13 Rules"), which now forms part of the daily Morning Service; and (c) the *Baraita de-Rabbi Eliezer* ("of 32 Rules"), which is often printed after tractate *Berakhot* of the Babylonian Talmud. For further details, see HERMENEUTICS.

BAREKHI NAFSHI ("Bless [the Lord], O my soul"). Opening words of Psalm 104, a hymn of praise to God and the wonders of His creation that has been incorporated in the Jewish liturgy. Ashkenazim recite it after the Sabbath

Afternoon Service, during the period between Sukkot and Passover. The creation theme in general, and this psalm's reference to the lunar cycle (v. 19) in particular, explain the other liturgical use of *Barekhi Nafshi* — after the Additional Service on the morning of New Moon (Rosh Ḫodesh). Sephardim and Eastern Jews read it also before Evening Service on the previous night.

BAREKHU ("Bless!"). Opening word of the formal summons to public worship read twice daily, in both the Morning and the Evening services, when prayers are held with a quorum (MINYAN). The full text is *Barekhu et-Adonai ha-Mevorakh* ("Praise the Lord who is [alone to be] praised"). In answer, the congregation then responds: *Barukh Adonai ha-Mevorakh le-olam va-ed* ("Praised be the Lord who is [to be] praised for all eternity"). The wording of the summons has its origin in the Bible (Ps. 134:1-2, 135:19-20) and the practice of rising to one's feet for *Barekhu* possibly dates from the time of Ezra (Neh. 9:5). This call to worship was discussed in the Mishnah (*Ber.* 7.3) and later standardized in the Talmud (*Ber.* 50a). The same formula is recited by a person called to the READING OF THE LAW, after which congregants give the traditional response. At one time it also introduced GRACE AFTER MEALS, but this was changed in amoraic times to a different formula beginning *Nevarekh* ("let us bless"). The exact purpose of the *Barekhu* invocation has given rise to much debate over the centuries, many questioning God's need of man's praise and blessings. NAḪMANIDES held piety and worship to be for the good of man rather than the Creator; the kabbalists, however, affirmed that prayer releases beneficent influences in heaven, thereby establishing harmony throughout the cosmos; while Samson Raphael HIRSCH declared that by praising God and fulfilling His commandments, man is able to play some part in achieving His design for humanity.

When pronouncing his invocation to prayer, the reader bows at the word *Barekhu*, then honors the Divine Name by standing erect. Congregants do likewise in the response. According to the Sephardi-Eastern and Ḫasidic practice, *Barekhu* is again recited at the end of Morning and Evening services. This custom, for the benefit of latecomers who missed the original call to worship (*Sof.* 10.7), has been adopted also in the Israeli Ashkenazi rite.

BAR MITSVAH (popularly translated as "son of the commandment"). The attaining by a boy of his religious adulthood and responsibility on reaching the age of 13; thereafter, he is counted in the prayer quorum (MINYAN). The Mishnah (*Avot* 5.21) states that 13 is the age for observing the commandments (*mitsvot*). The term *bar mitsvah* (often spelled "bar mitzvah") appears five times in the Babylonian Talmud (*BK* 15a (twice); *BM* 96a; *San.* 84b; *Men.* 93b), but in each case the reference is merely to someone obligated to fulfill the precepts of Judaism. The term utilized in the Talmud for a 13-year-old boy is *bar onshin* — one who is responsible and punishable for his actions. This relates to the legal distinction that at age 13 the male child becomes liable for his own transgressions; no longer does his father bear this responsibility.

A young boy reading from the Scroll of the Law at his bar mitsvah, at the Western Wall, Jerusalem, where this ceremony is frequently held for boys from all over Israel and from the Diaspora.

According to the Talmud, male adolescence begins at the age of 13 years and a day (*Kid.* 16b). Under the age of 13, however, a boy could participate in religious ceremonies as soon as he was able to appreciate their significance. He might be called to the READING OF THE LAW (*Meg.* 23a), wear TEFILLIN, and even fast on the Day of Atonement (*Yoma* 82a). There is no evidence of a bar mitsvah ceremony prior to 1400 and major codifiers of the Oral Law, such as Isaac ALFASI (11th century) and MAIMONIDES (12th century) do not mention it.

By the late Middle Ages, a Jewish minor's participation in religious rituals had become limited. Ashkenazim permitted a boy to wear *tefillin* only after he was 13 years old, and until then he was not entitled to be called to the Reading of the Law. Sephardi communities also imposed restrictions, all of which promoted the development of a formal bar mitsvah ceremony.

The essentials of this ritual were (1) praying with *tefillin* for the first time; and (2) being called to the Reading of the Law. Among East European Ashkenazim, a boy was usually called to the Torah on the first Monday or Thursday after his 13th birthday (according to the Hebrew date), when he would recite the TORAH BLESSINGS and perhaps chant some verses from that week's Pentateuchal reading. In Western Europe, however, a 13-year-old would be called to the Reading at Sabbath morning services. In addition to reciting the Torah blessings, the boy would chant "a portion of the Law" (MAFTIR) and the HAFTARAH reading from the Prophets. This is now the prevailing custom throughout the world. On either a weekday or Sabbath morning, when his son had completed the second Torah blessing, the father would recite a special formula — BARUKH SHE-PETARANI — marking the lad's new status of religious responsibility.

As elaborated in both the Ashkenazi and Sephardi communities, the bar mitsvah ceremony came to include a discourse or talk (*derashah*) by the 13-year-old. This demonstrated his understanding of the rabbinic commentaries and, in some cases, expounded points in talmudic law. The speech was (and usually still is) written by the teacher for the bar mitsvah boy to memorize and deliver.

Additional practices were gradually adopted, some religious and others of a social nature. Once the boy had mastered CANTILLATION as well as Hebrew, he might not only chant his particular section of the Pentateuch but the entire weekly reading (*parashah*) as well. Boys were trained as prayer leaders and, while some conducted the Sabbath eve (*Kabbalat Shabbat*) service on Friday night, others could lead the Sabbath Morning Service. Some Western (Ashkenazi and Sephardi) communities also instituted the reading of a special prayer by the young man while he stood before the rabbi or the Holy Ark. In modern times, it has become customary for the rabbi to address a bar mitsvah boy after the Reading of the Law, and for a MI SHE-BERAKH prayer to be recited on his behalf.

Initially, a bar mitsvah repast for family and friends was tendered after the weekday Morning Service or at the "third meal" (*se'udah shelishit*) eaten after the Sabbath Afternoon Service. Later, this was expanded into a KIDDUSH for all present at the Sabbath Morning Service, which was followed by a family dinner. Nowadays, the bar mitsvah reception or dinner often becomes a lavish social event, the bar mitsvah boy receiving gifts from his parents, relatives, and other guests.

Whereas Ashkenazi tradition permits the bar mitsvah to begin wearing *tefillin* only a month before his 13th birthday, Eastern Sephardim allow him to do so at least six months earlier. In the Moroccan Jewish community, a celebration was traditionally held on the Thursday after the boy's 12th birthday. On the Wednesday night, a party was arranged at home for adults and children; the next morning, services began with the rabbi placing the *tefillin* on the boy, who later read a section from the Pentateuch. Among Syrian, Turkish, and Iraqi Jews, the boy is usually about 12 1/2 when he celebrates his bar mitsvah. In many Eastern Sephardi communities, elaborate Hebrew poems (*piyyutim*) were often written to mark this special occasion. Western Sephardim (Spanish and Portuguese Jews) allow even a youngster of seven or eight to chant the *haftarah*, but only when he reaches the age of 13 years and a day is he permitted to recite the Torah blessings and to chant the *Maftir*.

It is a general practice among Sephardim for a bar mitsvah boy to recite the SHE-HEḨEYANU benediction. Ashkenazi communities in the West have imitated the Sephardi custom permitting youngsters to wear a prayer shawl (TALLIT) in synagogue, even when they are not called to the Torah reading. Both Eastern Sephardim and all communities in Israel maintain another practice — women and girls pelt the bar mitsvah with candies as soon as he has completed his reading from the Pentateuch.

Reform Judaism in the 19th century replaced the bar mitsvah with a CONFIRMATION ceremony for boys and girls in their late teens, but most Reform congregations have since also made room for the traditional celebration. In recent times, the bar mitsvah ceremony has acquired extra importance as an occasion for the young man to affirm his Jewish heritage. All streams of American Jewry utilize the bar mitsvah as leverage for persuading families to join a synagogue and enroll their child either in an afternoon Hebrew school or in a Jewish day school. Many synagogues require five years of religious education prior to bar mitsvah; and according to the regulations of Britain's United Synagogue (Orthodox), no bar mitsvah boy may read *maftir* unless he has passed an examination in Hebrew and Jewish knowledge. For those American Jews who never celebrated their bar mitsvah at 13, courses are now available preparing them to do so as adults.

In Israel, secular kibbutzim introduced various nonreligious types of ceremony. Since 1967, many boys — from Israel and abroad — celebrate their bar mitsvah at the Western Wall in Jerusalem, where they read from the Law on a Monday or Thursday morning. Some hold collective or individual ceremonies in the ruins of the ancient synagogue at Masada.

BARRENNESS A sterile condition, in particular the inability of a woman to conceive and bear children. The Bible regards barrenness in both humans and farm animals as a curse, and one of its blessings is: "There shall be no sterile male or female among you, or among your livestock" (Deut. 7:14). Of the four MATRIARCHS, three — SARAH, REBEKAH, and RACHEL — did not conceive easily. Sarah was 90 years old when she finally bore Isaac; Rebekah was barren for the first 20 years of her marriage, until she finally gave birth to twins; and Rachel, too, did not conceive for many years. Hannah, mother of the prophet SAMUEL, was only blessed with her child after constant prayers and entreaties to God (I Sam. 1). According to the *aggadah*, God deliberately withheld children from some of the matriarchs, so that they might pour out their hearts to Him.

The sages considered a childless person to be "as good as dead" (*Av. Zar. 5a*). A scholar without children was debarred from membership of the Sanhedrin (*San.* 36b), Maimonides explaining that such a man was "apt to lack tenderheartedness." Barrenness in Jewish law is grounds for divorce and, if a wife has not conceived within the first ten years of marriage, her husband should divorce her (*Yev.* 64a) so as to marry another woman by whom he will be able to have children (the wife may also remarry). Some later medieval authorities, however, do not require the husband to divorce his wife if she is barren. In polygamous Jewish societies, a man whose wife had not borne children could take a second wife, even without his first wife's consent. Legally, if a woman has not conceived and the couple moves to the Land of Israel, the ten-year period that must elapse before divorce proceedings can be instituted begins afresh from the date they arrive in the land. Many folk SUPERSTITIONS developed among barren women in their attempts to become pregnant.

BARUCH See APOCRYPHA AND PSEUDEPIGRAPHA

BARUKH DAYYAN HA-EMET ("Blessed be the true Judge"). Abbreviated form of the benediction traditionally recited when one hears bad news (especially of a death), or, in the case of a mourner, when the RENDING OF GARMENTS (*keri'ah*) is performed. The phrase occurs twice in the FUNERAL SERVICE. It is also recited when visiting the ruins of Jewish holy places or the site of a devastated synagogue.

BARUKH HA-SHEM ("Blessed be the Name [i.e., of the Lord]"). Phrase of thanksgiving, equivalent to "Thank God" or "Thank heaven." Sometimes it is extended to *Barukh Ha-Shem yom yom*, "Blessed be the Lord day by day" (Ps. 68:20).

BARUKH SHE-AMAR ("Blessed be He who spoke [and the world came into being]..."). Opening words of the hymn which introduces the PESUKÉ DE-ZIMRA ("Passages of Song") in every Morning Service. An old tradition ascribes it to the Men of the GREAT ASSEMBLY, but its earliest liturgical use (in the prayer book of AMRAM GAON) dates from the ninth century CE. The central theme of this two-part adoration is the manifold activity of God as Creator of the universe and Redeemer of Israel, whom all the righteous should acclaim with song and praise. Only its second part is a benediction commencing and ending with the formula "Blessed are You, O Lord," but the word *Barukh* ("Blessed") occurs no less than 11 times (among 38 words) in the first section. Here, *Barukh she-Amar* immediately precedes the "Passages of Song" in the Ashkenazi and Yemenite rituals; it follows *Hodu* (I Chron. 16:8-36) and various readings from the Psalms in the Sephardi and Ḥasidic rites. When reciting the hymn, worshipers stand and the traditional practice is to avoid all conversation and interruption (other than prescribed responses) from this stage of the Morning Service until after the repetition of the AMIDAH.

BARUKH SHEM KEVOD MALKHUTO ("Blessed be the Name of His glorious kingdom"). Initial words of a doxology stemming from the Bible (Neh. 9:5) which follows the opening sentence of the SHEMA. The complete formula, *Barukh Shem Kevod Malkhuto le-olam va-ed*, has been given various English translations, e.g., "Blessed be His Name, whose glorious kingdom is forever and ever" and "Praised be His glorious sovereignty throughout all time." Rabbinic tradition asserts that the patriarch Jacob first used this response after his sons had made their declaration of loyalty to Israel's God, i.e., the *Shema* (*Pes.* 56a; Deut. R. 2.25). Moses later heard the angels in heaven reciting these words and transmitted them to the Israelites (*ibid.*). As a congregational response, it was substituted for AMEN in Temple worship, especially during the High Priest's Service (AVODAH) on the Day of Atonement, when the people heard him solemnly pronounce the Tetragrammaton (*Yoma* 6.2, 66a; *Ta'an.* 16b). Twice a day throughout the year, in the traditional Morning and Evening services, the six-word formula is recited in an undertone — to separate it from the purely biblical texts that come immediately before and after in the *Shema* (Deut. 6:4, 5-9), because of its association with the angels and as a sign of grief for the destroyed Temple. On the Day of Atonement, however, it is read aloud, since abstaining from food and worldly concerns raises the Jewish people to angelic heights; two other reasons are that this doxology figured in the Temple service and that it is linked with medieval Jewish martyrs.

A number of historical factors account for its early appearance in the liturgy, next to the *Shema* proclamation of faith. They include defiance of Zoroastrian decrees outlawing Judaism in ancient Persia (fifth cent. BCE) and a deliberate negation by the PHARISEES of the servile homage which their religious opponents paid to the gods and emperors of Rome. Thus, in all traditional rites, the formula is read silently at the beginning of the Morning Service, before public worship commences, to indicate acceptance of God's rule only, and later also as part of the *Shema* that heathen persecutors once banned. In Orthodox Ashkenazi practice (followed by Ḥasidic and Conservative Jews), it is also recited after the blessings on donning the phylacteries (TEFILLIN); and, in the Ashkenazi rite, it is repeated three times after *Shema Yisra'el* as a solemn proclamation of Jewish faith at the end of the NE'ILAH Service concluding the Day of Atonement.

BARUKH SHE-PETARANI ("Blessed be the One who has relieved me"). Form of benediction recited by the father of a boy who has been called to the Torah on the occasion of his BAR MITSVAH. The traditional formula is quoted in the Midrash: "A man should be responsible for his son until the boy is 13; he should then say, 'Blessed be He who has relieved me of the punishment due on his account'" (Gen. R. 63.14). The parent of any minor guilty of religious misbehavior would have been liable to punishment, but this was no longer the case once the man's son attained his religious majority. In reciting this formula, the father is not shedding all responsibility for his son, but announcing that the boy has come of age and may now assume the religious duties of an adult. A special MI SHE-BERAKH for the bar mitsvah normally follows this recitation. Conservative Jews tend to omit this benediction in favor of the *Mi she-Berakh* blessing said by the reader, whereas the SHE-HEḆEYANU benediction replaces it in Reform congregations. Some modern Orthodox Jews likewise recite the traditional formula on the occasion of a daughter's BAT MITSVAH.

Nowadays, in popular (Yiddish and Hebrew) speech, *Barukh she-Petarani* is an expression of relief equivalent to "Good riddance!"

BAT KOL (literally in Hebrew, "daughter of a voice," meaning "an echo"). Term generally used in talmudic literature for a heavenly voice which issues forth with Divine pronouncements. It is regarded as being spoken by an angel, especially Gabriel. The *bat kol* speaks succinctly and its message is often derived from a biblical text. According to tradition, a *bat kol* announced that God Himself would bury Moses, and another announced Moses' death. When the prophet Samuel declared that he had never taken a single thing belonging to another person, a *bat kol* corroborated his statement. In a classic confrontation with R. Eleazar, the sages refused to accept his position, although R. Eleazar caused various rules of nature to be broken. Finally, R. Eleazar called upon heaven to intercede, and a *bat kol* issued forth, stating that the law was in accordance with R. Eleazar. The sages, however,rejected even the *bat kol*, explaining that the Torah "is not in heaven." Once it was given to man, only man has jurisdiction over the Torah and even a *bat kol* is disregarded (*BM* 59b). The Talmud goes on to mention that a certain rabbi met the prophet Elijah, who told him that God's reaction had been to exclaim laughingly, "My children have vanquished Me! My children have vanquished Me!"

BATLANIM (Heb. for "men of leisure" or "idlers"; in Yiddish, *batlonim*). Originally, a designation for those with time to spare who could devote all or part of their day to Jewish communal work. From early rabbinic times, no community of size and importance would remain without a minimum of ten scholarly adults (*asarah batlanim*) attending prayers and conducting Torah study (*Meg.* 1.3, 3b, 5a; *San.* 17b; *Ber.* 6b). In his commentary on the Talmud (*San. 17b; Meg. 3b*) RASHI defines the *batlanim* as "ten persons who abstain from all other work in order to be present in synagogue for morning and evening prayers"; elsewhere (*BK* 82a), he adds that they also devote themselves to the affairs of the community, from which they receive support. Until recent centuries, these ten "men of leisure" fulfilled an important role in Jewish communal life, sometimes deciding legal questions. The institution degenerated, however, into the system of paid "*minyan* men" who help make up the necessary quorum for daily services and augment their income by reciting KADDISH for those families lacking any male adult to perform that duty. This largely explains the modern sense of *batlan* as a disparaging term for an idler or ne'er-do-well. In Yiddish parlance and folklore, the *batlon* was a social misfit or half-baked intellectual, and his impractical mode of life was stigmatized as *batlonus*.

BAT MITSVAH (lit. "daughter of the commandment"). A girl who has attained her religious majority which, according to Jewish law, is at the age of 12 years and one day. There are no specific legal requirements for a girl to take part in any religious ceremony marking this occasion. Jewish law merely takes cognizance of the fact that her father may no longer annul her vows and that she is to be considered an independent woman responsible for her own decisions. A ceremonial equivalent of the BAR MITSVAH designed for girls, but not forming part of the synagogue service, appears to have been an innovation of Jacob ETTLINGER, the Neo-Orthodox chief rabbi of Altona in the mid-19th century. This practice spread to other lands and, in the late 19th century, it was approved by a leading Sephardi halakhist, Joseph Ḥayyim ben Elijah al-Ḥakam of Baghdad. His detailed recommendations (*Ben Ish Ḥai*, 1898) included the holding of a banquet and the wearing of a new dress by the bat mitsvah girl so that she could recite the SHE-HEḆEYANU benediction.

Mordecai KAPLAN pioneered the bat mitsvah ceremony, as part of the regular synagogue service, in the USA during the 1920s. Since then, it has become widely popular and is now observed in various ways by most communities. In American non-Orthodox congregations, a 12-year-old girl celebrates her "coming of age" on a Friday night or Sabbath morning: she conducts the service, chants the appropriate reading from the prophetical books (*haftarah*), and in some cases also reads from the Torah and delivers an address on the theme of her attaining Jewish adulthood. In Orthodox synagogues, the bat mitsvah girl's participation in the services is more limited, although she may address the congregation; at a women's *minyan*, however, she will be called to the reading of the Torah and even chant one of the portions together with the *haftarah*. A difference of opinion has arisen in American Orthodox circles as to whether the bat mitsvah ceremony should take place when the girl is 12 or 13.

Ultra-Orthodox Ashkenazim and most Sephardi-Eastern communities are opposed to bat mitsvah celebrations. Their halakhic arguments are rejected, however, by authorities such as Jehiel Jacob Weinberg (*Seridé Esh*, vol. 3) who justify the practice on educational and socioreligious grounds, provided that the bat mitsvah is observed in a manner that will "strengthen Torah consciousness." Outside the USA, the ceremony takes various forms: Reform observance is in line with the American pattern, but Orthodox girls do not participate in synagogue ritual. Instead, on the appropriate Sabbath morning, a bat mitsvah's father is called to the Torah and pronounces the BARUKH SHE-PETARANI benediction; his daughter then recites *She-heḇeyanu*; and the rabbi may either address her in synagogue or at a *Kiddush* reception after the services. Alternatively, the bat mitsvah celebration may take place at home or in the synagogue hall on a weekday. Both Western Sephardim and Orthodox Israelis favor this type of observance, at which the bat mitsvah girl herself often gives a suitable discourse.

The occasion is marked differently in most British Commonwealth and South African communities. After undertaking courses in Bible, Jewish history, laws and customs, etc., the bat mitzvah must pass a test qualifying her to participate in a collective ceremony organized by traditional congregations or Jewish day schools. In Israel, non-observant families arrange a special 12th birthday party with no religious accompaniments, marking the girl's entrance into maturity. Both M'sorati (Conservative) and Progressive (Reform) synagogues enable the bat mitsvah to participate actively in the Sabbath services and, on occasion, to chant the *haftarah*.

Latterly, in the US, some women who never had a bat mitsvah when they were young have a ceremony of their own as adults; this is arranged once they have been prepared by the congregational rabbi or cantor. Another development is the publication of creative liturgy. An entire bat mitsvah service is included in the Reform movement's *New Union Prayer Book* (1975), while the Conservative *Siddur Sim Shalom* (1985) contains a special MI SHE-BERAKH prayer for the bat mitsvah, as well as an insertion in Grace after Meals and (English) readings appropriate for a bat mitsvah ceremony.

BAVA BATRA ("Last Gate"). Third tractate of Order NEZIKIN in the Mishnah. Its ten chapters deal with the laws pertaining to the sale, acquisition, ownership, partnership in, and transfer of real estate (cf. Lev.19: 35-36; Num. 27: 8-11; Deut. 25:12-16). It also discusses laws of inheritance, legal deeds and documents, and the injunction to use exact weights and measures. The subject matter is amplified in both Talmuds and the *Tosefta*.

BAVA KAMMA ("First Gate"). First tractate of Order NEZIKIN in the Mishnah. Its ten chapters deal with the laws of damages and compensation. (cf. Ex.21:18-19, 28-37; 22:1-6; Lev.5:20-26). Distinctions are made between cases where the damage is unintentional or intentional, in the private or public domain, and as to whether or not damage or injury occurred through negligence. The final three chapters deal with cases of damage by theft, violence, and robbery. Originally, this tractate, together with the following two, BAVA METS'IA and BAVA BATRA, formed one complete tractate, but later it was divided into three, hence the name *Bava Kamma* ("First Gate") referring to the first part of this triad. The subject matter is amplified in both Talmuds and the *Tosefta*.

BAVA METS'IA ("Middle Gate"). Second tractate of Order NEZIKIN in the Mishnah. Its ten chapters deal principally with the laws of the acquisition and transfer of property, lost and found property, usury or interest, and trusteeship (cf. Ex.22:6-14, 24-26; Lev.25:14, 35-37; Deut.22:1-4). Also discussed are the sale or lease of property, joint ownership, and the hiring of laborers. The first *mishnah* of the first chapter, starting *Shenayim oḇezin be-tallit* ("Two are holding a cloak..."), is considered one of the classic texts in the study of the Talmud and is often introduced to beginners to acquaint them with the depth of the Oral Law. The subject matter is amplified in both Talmuds and the *Tosefta*.

Opening page of the talmudic tractate, Bava Metsi'a.

BEDIKAT ḤAMETS See LEAVEN, SEARCH FOR

BE-EZRAT HA-SHEM ("With the help of the Name [of God]"). Phrase expressing trust in God (cf. "God willing"). It was not known in ancient times, but by the medieval period it was a standard feature of rabbinic parlance and is now frequently employed by Jews. Among the strictly observant, it most often figures as an abbreviated superscription over the date in correspondence, even when the letter itself is not written in Hebrew. Similar use is made of an Aramaic equivalent, *be-siyyatta di-Shemayya*, "with the help of [God in] Heaven." See also GREETINGS.

BEHEMOTH See LEVIATHAN

BEKHOROT ("First-born"). Fourth tractate of Order KODASHIM in the Mishnah. Its nine chapters deal with the laws of offering or redeeming the three categories of first-born: 1) a mother's first-born male child, who was redeemed by giving five *sela'im* of silver to a priest; 2) the firstling of a clean animal (i.e. ox, sheep, goat) which was sacrificed if without blemish; 3) the firstling of an ass which was redeemed with a lamb or else killed (Ex. 13:2; 11-13; 34: 19-20; Lev.27:26; Num.18:15-18). The Mishnah also discusses the procedure when a blemish is found in a first-born animal, the tithing of animals, and the first-born's special right of inheritance. See also FIRST-BORN, REDEMPTION OF. The subject is amplified in the Babylonian Talmud and the *Tosefta*.

BENAMOZEGH, ELIJAH (1822-1900). Rabbi, theologian, and philosopher. Born in Leghorn, Italy, into a prominent Moroccan Jewish family, he grew up to serve as a rabbi there and to become professor of Jewish thought in the city's rabbinical school. Deeply versed in classical Jewish sources, he wrote works in Hebrew, Italian, and French. Being fully aware of the intellectual trends of the time, Benamozegh was deeply committed to maintaining the integrity of traditional Jewish thought and practice. He presented his exposition of the teachings of Judaism in an intellectual framework which well-educated contemporaries could appreciate. Among his writings are several defenses of the Zohar and the Kabbalah; explanatory notes to the TARGUM Onkelos; and a commentary on Psalms. His commentary on the Pentateuch drew on classical Jewish commentaries as well as on modern biblical research. In Italian, he published a collection of essays on the Essenes and a work of theology, but his most popular book was in French (*Israël et l'humanité*, 1914).

Benamozegh argued that Jewish ethics and Jewish nationalism are intertwined. Jewish ethics is therefore grounded in the reality of human life, not an esoteric, abstract system for other-worldly pietists. By observing the precepts, Jews maintain their total commitment to ethical behavior, through which they are able to convey the universal message of Judaism to the world. Christianity and Islam are heavily in debt to the religious traditions of Israel. The Jewish idea that all of humanity derives from Adam and Eve is at the root of the notion of human equality. Judaism teaches that God created the world, and that all people can be righteous and beloved by God; as a result, everyone has spiritual dignity.

BENEDICTIONS Various blessings which are to be recited on prescribed occasions. *Berakhah*, the Hebrew term for "benediction" (plur. *berakhot*), derives from the same root as *berekh* ("knee"), since "bowing the knee" was an accompaniment to worship and giving thanks or praise to God (Isa. 45:23; Ps. 95:6; Dan. 6:11; II Chron. 6:13). Throughout the Bible, there are numerous references to either God or man being the agent or the recipient of a blessing. Various formulas were evidently current from patriarchal times down to the Mishnaic period, often introduced by the words *Barukh* ("Blessed"), BAREKHU ("Bless...!"), or *Odekha* ("I will praise You"). One of the oldest types of benediction, commencing with the three words *Barukh Attah Adonai* ("Blessed are You, O Lord"), is found in the Bible (Ps. 119:12; I Chron.29:10) and was incorporated in the Jewish LITURGY. Other forms were also used (e.g., in the DEAD SEA SCROLLS), and some latitude was permitted for extempore blessings and praise. A first attempt at standardization seems

The blessing on fragrant herbs. From an illustrated compilation of blessings to be recited on various occasions. Printed in Nikolsburg, Czechoslovakia, 1728.

to have been made by the tannaitic rabbis (c. 90 CE), but this process reached its conclusion only in the talmudic era (after 220 CE).

Of the different blessing patterns that have survived, one short form opens with the "Blessed are You, O Lord" wording, another short form incorporates it in its conclusion, while a third and longer form uses it at both the beginning and the end. In accordance with a rule laid down by the sages (*Ber.* 12a, 40b), no statutory benediction may exclude the mention of God's name (the Tetragrammaton *YHVH* pronounced "*Adonai*") and of His kingship. This decision is believed to reflect the Jewish response to Roman worship of the emperor, introduced by Augustus Caesar at the beginning of the common era; in practice, it meant that all formal benedictions (i.e., apart from those of a private, non-statutory type) must commence as follows: ***Barukh Attah Adonai Elohénu Melekh ha-Olam***, "Blessed are You, O Lord our God, King of the Universe..."

The talmudic ideal, mentioned by R. Meir (*Men.* 43b), is that a Jew should recite 100 blessings daily. Apart from those recited in congregational prayer, such as the "Eighteen Benedictions" of the AMIDAH, three main categories of blessing are enumerated by Maimonides (*Yad, Berakhot* 1-3, esp. 1.4). Included in the first category are all the blessings to be recited before and after eating or drinking and before inhaling spices or perfumes, in gratitude for the pleasure man thereby enjoys. These *Birkhot ha-Nehenin* ("Benedictions for Enjoyment") are traced to sources in the Bible which allude to an expression of thanksgiving before and after eating (I Sam. 9:13; Deut. 8:10). The Talmud adds that "it is forbidden to taste anything before making a benediction," since the bounty and fullness of the earth belong to God (Ps. 24:1) and not offering thanks for their enjoyment is tantamount to stealing from Him (*Ber.* 35a).

SPECIAL BENEDICTIONS

I. *Birkhot ha-Nehenin* :"Benedictions for Enjoyment"
A. Blessings recited over food and drink — *Ha-Motsi leḫem min ha-arets* ("Who brings forth bread from the earth") over BREAD and as GRACE BEFORE MEALS; *Boré miné mezonot* ("Who creates various kinds of nourishment") before eating food other than bread prepared from the FIVE SPECIES of grain; *Boré peri ha-gefen* ("Who creates the fruit of the vine") before drinking WINE or grape juice; *Boré peri ha-ets* ("Who creates the fruit of the tree") before eating grapes and all other fruit that grows on trees or bushes; *Boré peri ha-adamah* ("Who creates the fruit of the ground") before eating vegetables or fruit that grow directly from the earth; and *She-ha-kol niheyeh bi-devaro* ("At whose word all things come into being") before eating or drinking any other foods.

B. Blessings recited after food and drink — *Birkat ha-Mazon* (GRACE AFTER MEALS); *Berakhah Aḫaronah* ("Final Benediction"), recited after a meal in which no bread was eaten but which did include food made from the Five Species of grain, wine or grape juice, or any of the fruits belonging to the SEVEN SPECIES; and *Boré nefashot* ("Who creates many living things"), recited after any other type of food or beverage.

C. Blessings recited over fragrances — chiefly *Boré miné vesamim* ("Who creates various spices"), when inhaling fragrant spices and perfumes; *Boré atsé vesamim* ("Who creates fragrant trees"), when smelling fragrant trees and shrubs or the flowers that grow on them; *Boré isvé vesamim* ("Who creates fragrant plants"), when smelling the fragrance of herbs, plants, or flowers; and *Ha-Noten ré'aḫ tov ba-pérot* ("Who gives a pleasant aroma to fruits"), when smelling fragrant and edible fruit or nuts.

II. *Birkhot ha-Mitsvot*: "Benedictions on the Performance of Commandments"

These blessings, all of which include the *asher kiddeshanu* ("Who has sanctified us with His commandments") formula, may be subdivided into two groups:

A. General — *Al netilat yadayim* ("On washing the hands") for the ABLUTIONS performed before eating bread; on attaching a MEZUZAH to one's doorpost; on erecting a protective rail or wall around a flat roof; when immersing new kitchen utensils in the MIKVEH (ritual bath); on separating ḪALLAH from dough or *terumah* and *ma'aser* (TITHE) from crops grown in the Land of Israel; when donning one's TALLIT (prayer shawl) or TEFILLIN (phylacteries); by the father and the *mohel* at a CIRCUMCISION; and by the father at a Redemption of the FIRSTBORN ceremony.

B. Holy Days — on lighting CANDLES prior to the SABBATH and FESTIVALS and nightly during ḪANUKKAH; when creating an ERUV that will permit cooking for a Sabbath which begins immediately after a festival; before chanting the *Megillah* (Scroll of Esther) on PURIM; on taking the FOUR SPECIES of plants during the Sukkot (Tabernacles) festival; when sitting down in the SUKKAH for the purpose of eating or drinking there; when the SHOFAR (ram's horn) is about to be sounded on Rosh ha-Shanah, the New Year; and prior to beginning the search for LEAVEN shortly before Passover. (These are only representative examples.)

III. *Birkhot Hoda'ah*: "Benedictions of Gratitude or Thanksgiving"

A. On witnessing natural phenomena or having an unusual experience — *Oseh ma'aseh vereshit* ("Who performs the work of Creation"), on seeing lightning, comets and shooting stars, a sunrise, high mountains, great deserts and rivers, or when an earthquake occurs; *She-koḫo u-gevurato malé olam* ("Whose power and might fill the universe"), when hearing thunder or witnessing thunderstorms, tornadoes, and hurricanes; on seeing a rainbow; when seeing the ocean; at the sight of beautiful trees or animals; when seeing curious beasts or strangely formed people (e.g., dwarfs and giants); on seeing trees blossoming for the first time in spring; when visiting the site of a destroyed synagogue or one that has been restored; on visiting a place where a miraculous deliverance occurred (to oneself or others); *She-ḫalak me-ḫokhmato li-yere'av* ("Who has distributed His wisdom to those who revere Him"), the blessing recited when one meets an outstanding Torah scholar; *She-natan me-ḫokhmato le-vasar va-dam* ("Who has given of His wisdom to flesh and blood"), on meeting a person renowned for secular learning; and *She-natan mi-kevodo le-vasar va-dam* ("Who has given of His glory to flesh and blood"), when meeting or seeing royalty and heads of state.

B. Miscellaneous Blessings — e.g., SHE-HEḆEYANU ("Who has kept us alive"), recited when enjoying something for the first time, wearing a new suit or dress, performing a seasonal *mitsvah*, etc.; *Ha-Tov ve-ha-Metiv* ("Who is good and beneficent"), on hearing exceptionally good news; BARUKH DAYYAN HA-EMET ("Blessed be the true Judge"), recited by the newly bereaved or when hearing particularly bad news; and *Asher yatsar etkhem ba-din* ("Who fashioned you with justice"), said on entering a CEMETERY by one who has not visited it for 30 days.

C. Ritual and Liturgical Blessings — *Birkhot ha-Shaḇar* (the MORNING BENEDICTIONS); *Birkat Horim* (the PARENTAL BLESSING); *Birkat Kohanim* (the PRIESTLY BLESSING); KIDDUSH (Sanctification) on Sabbaths and festivals; HAVDALAH at the termination of Sabbaths and festivals; the opening benediction for HALLEL; *Birkat ha-Ḫodesh*, the prayer announcing the New MOON, and *Kiddush Levanah* (blessing the New Moon once it is visible); *Sheva Berakhot* (the "Seven Benedictions" recited under the *ḫuppah* MARRIAGE canopy); the TORAH BLESSINGS said by one called to the Reading of the Law; BARUKH SHE-PETARANI, recited by the father of a BAR MITSVAH boy; and the GOMEL blessing recited in synagogue by one who has escaped danger, recovered from a grave illness, etc., and by a woman who has recovered from childbirth.

A second category of blessings is made up of those to be recited when fulfilling a MITSVAH (commandment), thus demonstrating that God's precepts are acknowledged and obeyed. Such *Birkhot ha-Mitsvot* ("Benedictions on the Performance of Commandments") necessitate the inclusion of an extra formula, after the initial *Barukh Attah* wording mentioned above, which reads: *asher kiddeshanu be-mitsvotav ve-tsivvanu* ("Who has sanctified us with His commandments and commanded us..."), followed by the specific commandment (e.g., "to kindle the Sabbath light" or "to hear the sound of the ram's horn"). All of these benedictions are recited by an individual, in some cases even during public worship, but not every precept (e.g., the giving of charity) requires a blessing when it is fulfilled.

The third category includes *Birkhot Hoda'ah* ("Blessings of Gratitude and Thanksgiving") to be recited on witnessing natural phenomena or special events; it also comprises miscellaneous benedictions of a seasonal, family, or liturgical nature. These express the belief that everything in life, whether it gives rise to joy or sorrow, has its ultimate source in the Creator. Ashkenazim employ the Yiddish verb BENTSHEN to designate the reciting of a benediction, while Sephardim use *benca* or other terms. The response to most (though not all) blessings is AMEN (cf. I Chron. 16:36).

By conscientiously reciting the prescribed benedictions, from first thing in the morning until last thing at night, the Jew takes upon himself a unique form of religious discipline, serving as a constant reminder of his dependence on and indebtedness to God. At the family table, on festive occasions, and in the open air, he or she is capable of transforming a routine act or some unusual experience into the grateful worship and acknowledgment of man's Divine Benefactor. Most of the rules governing benedictions are contained in the Mishnaic tractate BERAKHOT.

BENE ISRAEL ("Children of Israel"). Indian Jews from the Konkan coast of Maharashtra. The Bene Israel claim that they are members of "lost" tribes that reached India, as long ago as 175 BCE (see Ten Lost TRIBES). According to their tradition, their ancestors were shipwrecked off the Konkan coast and lost all their holy books; they only remembered the SHEMA. They lived among the Hindus and adopted several of their customs. When discovered by a Jewish outsider, David Rahabi, possibly in the 18th century, they observed the Sabbath, dietary laws, circumcision, and many of the Jewish festivals, but had no synagogue. *Navyacha San* or the New Year was only celebrated for one day; the rationale for several Jewish fast days appeared to have been forgotten; and Ḫanukkah was unknown since it occurred after the Bene Israel departure from Erets Israel.

From 1750 onward, the Bene Israel embarked upon a process of adjusting to mainstream Judaism. Several factors contributed to their religious revival. They gradually moved from the Konkan villages to Bombay and other cities as their involvement with the British Raj increased. Their first synagogue, named "Gate of Mercy," was established in Bombay in 1796. The Bene Israel were also assisted in their religious life by Cochin Jews from the Malabar coast, who acted as cantors, ritual slaughterers, and teachers. In the second half of the 19th century, the Bene Israel of Bombay were joined by Jews from Baghdad, who served as a reference model of normative Judaism. Paradoxically, the arrival of Christian missionaries in the Konkan from 1810 promoted the Bene Israel rapprochement with world Jewry by introducing them to the Hebrew Bible and other religious texts in Marathi translation.

The Bene Israel population increased from 6,000 in the 1830s to 20,000 in 1948. After the British withdrew from India in 1947 and the State of Israel's establishment in 1948, the Bene Israel began emigrating to Israel with the active encouragement of the Jewish Agency. By 1960, it became clear that certain rabbis in Israel would not marry Bene Israel to other Israelis on halakhic grounds, alleging that there were doubts concerning their Jewishness. In 1962, the Chief Rabbinate issued directives instructing marriage registrars to examine the descent of Bene Israel wishing to marry other Jews. Between 1962 and 1964, the Bene Israel organized a series of strikes and demonstrations involving the whole community to demand status as "full Jews." In 1964, the Chief Rabbinate withdrew its halakhic objections and declared the Bene Israel "full Jews in every respect." During the 1970s there were still cases of individual rabbis refusing to marry Bene Israel. The situation was resolved in 1982, when the two Chief Rabbis, Shlomo Goren and Ovadyah Yosef, issued a directive to marriage registrars reaffirming that the Bene Israel were "Jews in every respect."

BENJAMIN See TRIBES, TWELVE

BEN SIRA See APOCRYPHA AND PSEUDEPIGRAPHA

BENTSHEN (Yiddish, "bless"). Term used by many Ashkenazim to denote the act of reciting a benediction, whenever this is required by Jewish law, especially GRACE AFTER MEALS. Etymologically, the term derives from an Old French verb, *beneïr* or *beneïstre* (cf. Latin *benedicere*), which Yiddish-speaking Jews borrowed in medieval times. A kindred Romance expression (*bençāo*) is current among Jews of Spanish and Portuguese origin. The opening Hebrew phrase in Grace after Meals — *Rabbotai nevarekh*, "Gentlemen, let us pronounce the blessing!" — is sometimes replaced among Ashkenazi Jews by the Yiddish equivalent, *Rabbosay, mir velen bentshen*. The special booklet for Grace and Sabbath table hymns is known as a *bentsher*. There are also other forms of benediction to which the Yiddish term is applied: lighting candles for the Sabbath and festivals (*likht-bentshen*), reciting the prayer blessing the New Moon (*Rosh Ḫodesh bentshen*), taking the FOUR SPECIES on Sukkot (*bentshen lulav*), and giving thanks after surviving a danger or on returning from a long journey (*bentshen "Gomel"*).

BERAḪ DODI ("Hasten, my Beloved"). Opening words of three liturgical poems by different authors, read in some Ashkenazi congregations on Passover (first two days and intermediate Sabbath), which conclude the GE'ULAH prayer immediately before the Morning Service *Amidah*. These words are a quotation from the Song of Songs (8:14) and each poem draws upon the allegorical interpretation of that biblical book, Israel imploring God (the "Beloved") to abandon His "exile," redeem His people, and renew their ancient ties. The first *Beraḫ Dodi* poem, comprising three stanzas and written by Solomon ben Judah ha-Bavli (mid-tenth cent., Italy) is recited on the first morning of Passover; the second, of four stanzas, was composed by Solomon's pupil, Meshullam ben Kalonymus, and is read — by Diaspora congregations only — on the second day; the third *Beraḫ Dodi*, comprising five stanzas and written by Simeon bar Isaac of Mainz (tenth cent.), is recited on the intermediate Sabbath.

BERAKHOT See BENEDICTIONS

BERAKHOT ("Benedictions"). First tractate of Order ZERA'IM in the Mishnah (cf. Deut. 6:4-9; 11:13,18-20; 8:10). Its nine chapters deal with the laws of reading the SHEMA in the morning and evening; the time for reciting the AMIDAH prayer in every daily service as well as creating a proper mood of devotion for it; the blessings recited over different kinds of food; and the recitation of GRACE AFTER MEALS (*Birkat ha-Mazon*). Also included are a chapter explaining the differences between the Schools of Hillel and Shammai in regard to reciting KIDDUSH and HAVDALAH, and a final chapter describing the special benedictions made on various other occasions, e.g., when witnessing natural phenomena (lightning, thunder, earthquake) or upon hearing good or bad news. The subject matter is amplified, with considerable aggadic material, in both Talmuds and in the *Tosefta*.

BERIKH SHEMEH ("Blessed be the [Universal Lord's] Name"). Meditation in Aramaic recited by traditional congregations when the Ark is opened prior to the Reading of the Law on Sabbaths and festivals. A mystical prayer attributed to SIMEON BAR YOḤAI, it reflects basic doctrines of the Kabbalah and is taken from the ZOHAR (II, 206a). Man's role as a Divine agent on earth and his duty to help strengthen all positive forces in the universe are alluded to in an introductory passage, which states that "the gates of mercy are opened and God's love reawakened above when the Torah scroll is taken out of the Ark for congregational reading." The following text combines blessings and supplications with an acknowledgment of God's universal beneficence and kingship, expressing Jewish faith "not in any man or angel, but in the God of truth whose Law and prophets are true." Both Ashkenazim and Sephardim recite *Berikh Shemeh* immediately after the Ark is opened; Yemenite Jews, prior to the actual Torah reading. Some modern Israeli prayer books contain a Hebrew translation.

BERIT MILAH See CIRCUMCISION

BERLIN, NAFTALI TSEVI YEHUDAH (1817-1893). Lithuanian rabbinical leader and head of the Volozhin *yeshivah*, popularly known (from the acronym of his Hebrew name) as the *Netsiv* or "pillar" of Volozhin. Born in Mir, White Russia, he entered the *yeshivah* at 13 and later married the daughter of its principal, R. Isaac of Volozhin. After the latter's death in 1849, his elder son-in-law, R. Eliezer Isaac Fried, became dean with Berlin as his assistant. When Fried died in 1853, a controversy arose over the appointment of Berlin and R. Joseph Baer SOLOVEICHIK as joint principals, some of the student body maintaining that Soloveichik alone should be head. Berlin's strength lay in his thorough knowledge of all rabbinical literature, while Soloveichik's forte was a keen and penetrating method of talmudic analysis. Leading rabbis of the time, R. Isaac Elhanan SPEKTOR among them, were called upon to adjudicate the dispute and they decided in favor of Berlin. He went on to exert a far-reaching influence over the *yeshivah* and the number of students rose to 400 under his tutelage. The Babylonian Talmud was worked through in sequence and explained in accordance with the system evolved by ELIJAH GAON OF VILNA. Berlin shunned *pilpul* (casuistic reasoning), for example, and emphasized the basic meaning of each text by referring to parallel sections of the Jerusalem Talmud and the *Midrash Halakhah*. He also lectured daily, after Morning Service, on the Torah portion of that week. His many published works reflect both his approach and his teachings. They include commentaries on the halakhic Midrashim and his classic explanatory volumes entitled *Ha'amek She'elah* (1861 ff.) on the *She'iltot*, a geonic work attributed to AHAI OF SHABHA. Berlin also published Scriptural interpretations, notably *Ha'amek Davar* on the Pentateuch (1879-80), and detailed responsa on halakhic and philosophical issues, *Meshiv Davar* (1892).

A vigorous communal leader, Berlin openly declared himself on all the major questions of his time. He was an active supporter of the Hibbat Zion ("Lovers of Zion") movement from its very inception and urged observant Jews to swell its ranks and promote Jewish settlement in Erets Israel. Rejecting proposals for the establishment of separatist Orthodox communities (see Samson Raphael HIRSCH, NEO-ORTHODOXY), he insisted that every attempt be made to win over non-Orthodox and irreligious sections of the Jewish people. His last years were clouded by unrelenting tsarist interference in the Volozhin *yeshivah*'s educational program. The Russian authorities called for a limit on the number of hours devoted to Torah study and for the introduction of a secular curriculum. Berlin would not agree to these excessive demands and the most prestigious talmudical academy in Eastern Europe was therefore closed by governmental decree on January 22, 1892. Having been expelled from Volozhin, the *Netsiv* planned to settle in Erets Israel and began attending to his affairs in Warsaw; his death there, some 18 months later, put an end to that dream.

The *Netsiv*'s younger son, **Meir Berlin (Bar-Ilan**; 1880-1949), became one of the outstanding personalities in religious Zionism and a leader of the Mizrahi movement. He lived for a time in Berlin and then, for a decade (1915-26), in New York, where he organized the American Mizrahi and founded the Teachers' Institute that was to be incorporated in Yeshiva University. From 1926, Meir Berlin was active and prominent in Jerusalem. He founded and edited the Mizrahi newspaper *Ha-Tsofeh* (1937-), was an architect of the *Talmudic Encyclopedia* (1947-), and also published several works, notably a volume of memoirs in Yiddish (1933; translated into Hebrew as *Mi-Volozhin ad Yerushalayim*, 1939-40) and a biography of his father (*Rabban shel Yisra' el*, 1943). Israel's modern Orthodox Bar-Ilan University, established in 1955, honors his memory.

BERNAYS, ISAAC (1792-1849). Rabbi and pioneer of NEO-ORTHODOXY. Born in Mainz, he studied at the rabbinical academy of Abraham Bing in Würzburg, where he also became the first German traditionalist rabbi to acquire a university education. This broad cultural background made Bernays an effective opponent of the newly established Reform temple, once he assumed the chief rabbinate of Hamburg in 1821. Objecting to the fact that halakhically unqualified Reformers now styled themselves "rabbis," he adopted the Sephardi title of *Hakham*. Bernays did not restrict himself to launching attacks on REFORM JUDAISM. With the aim of fostering loyalty to tradition, he reinvigorated the Hamburg *talmud torah* school, paid attention to the aesthetics of synagogue worship, delivered impressive German sermons, and formulated a program of Neo-Orthodox belief and observance that would attract young Jewish intellectuals. Writing in 1823, the poet Heinrich Heine (a cousin of Bernays) dubbed him an unconventional, spirited preacher with whom the Reformers compared unfavorably. The revised edition of the Hamburg temple's prayer book aroused Bernays' scathing criticism because it omitted all prayers for the restoration of Zion. His own teachings, not least the concept of a Jewish "mission," influenced Samson Raphael HIRSCH.

BERTINORO, OBADIAH BEN ABRAHAM YARÉ DI (c. 1450-c. 1515). Rabbinic scholar and commentator on the MISHNAH, known also by the acronym *Ra'av* (= Rabbenu Ovadyah mi-Bartenura). Yaré, an anagram of the Hebrew name Ari (or Aryeh), also comprises the initial letters of *Yehi retsu'i ehav* ("Let him be the favorite of his brothers," Deut. 33:24). His surname indicates that his family roots were in the northern Italian town of Bertinoro.

In 1485, he left Città di Castello on a voyage to Erets Israel, and he wrote an account of this journey in three letters to his father, his brother, and an unidentified person. These letters, containing much information of geographical, historical, and cultural interest, are among the best known in Hebrew travel literature. Bertinoro's journey lasted nearly three years, during which time he visited Naples, Salerno, Palermo, Messina, Rhodes, and Egypt. In Erets Israel he passed through Gaza, Hebron, and Bethlehem before reaching Jerusalem. There, with the aid of Nathan Ha-Kohen Sholal, the Egyptian *nagid*, he became head of the small and impoverished Jewish community. Bertinoro succeeded in reorganizing communal life and, after the expulsion of the Jews from Spain in 1492, cultured Sephardi refugees helped to improve conditions still further.

Bertinoro's commentary on the Mishnah, first published in Venice (1548-9), has become as indispensable to Mishnah study as Rashi's commentary has to study of the Talmud. Drawing on Rashi and Maimonides, and writing in a clear, concise style, Bertinoro summarizes the talmudic discussion for those learning Mishnah without Gemara. In certain instances, he also utilized the commentaries of ASHER BEN JEHIEL. No standard edition of the Mishnah is now printed without Bertinoro's authoritative commentary. He also wrote an exposition of Rashi's Torah commentary; a homiletical work on the Book of Ruth; halakhic novellae on those of his teacher, R. Joseph Colon; and various liturgical poems.

BERURYAH (second cent. CE). Wife of R. MEIR and a scholar in her own right; daughter of R. Ḫananyah ben Teradyon. She and her husband lived mainly in or near Tiberias. There are numerous references in talmudic literature to her exemplary virtue, intellectual gifts, and ability to dispute with the sages in halakhic matters. The opinions Beruryah expressed were given the same weight as those of a *tanna*, and on at least one occasion they were accepted by R. JUDAH BAR ILAI.

The Talmud (*Ber.* 10a) relates that ruffians in R. Meir's neighborhood made themselves troublesome to the sage and so provoked him that he wanted to pray for God to punish them. Beruryah intervened and pointed out that Scripture (Ps. 104:35) declares, "Let wickedness cease from the earth," not the wicked. R. Meir then prayed that they should repent, which they did.

Beruryah's life was dogged by tragedy. Not only was her father tortured to death by the Roman authorities, but her sister was forced into prostitution and her brother was killed by bandits. These misfortunes culminated, as the Midrash relates, in the sudden death of her two sons one Sabbath afternoon — a blow which she concealed from her husband until he came home from the Academy when the Sabbath had terminated. Only then did she gently break the news to him, by asking if a precious object deposited with her for safekeeping should be returned to the owner. "Why, of course it should!" Meir replied, whereupon Beruryah showed him their sons lying in the bedroom and comforted her stricken husband by quoting Job (1:21), "The Lord has given, and the Lord has taken away; blessed be the name of the Lord."

BESAMIM See SPICES

BETA ISRAEL See ETHIOPIAN JEWS

BET DIN A court of Jewish law. From the very earliest times, we are told, Moses judged the people "from the morning to the evening" (Ex. 18:13) until advised by his father-in-law, Jethro, to decentralize the system. Judges were then appointed "over thousands, hundreds, fifties, and tens," with the proviso that any case too difficult for the judges to handle would be referred upward, eventually to Moses. The Torah, too, cautioned (Deut. 17:8), "If there arise a matter too hard for you in judgment ... then shall you arise, and get you up into the place which the Lord your God shall choose."

Later, after Israel entered its land, there were judges who were also leaders of the people. Many of the kings also served in the capacity of judges, the classic example being Solomon.

The Talmud indicates that in Second Temple times there were various courts, consisting of three, 23, or 71 judges. Different types of cases were tried by *batté din* (courts) of a specific size, but there was no appeal of a verdict to a higher court. Only where an inferior court was unable to come to a decision on the law was a case referred upward.

Each locality had a court consisting of three judges, which was authorized to rule on civil matters. Each town consisting of 120 or more adult males had a *bet din* of 23 judges (San. 1.6), which was empowered to rule on questions of corporal and capital punishment (*ibid.* 1.4). Cases involving capital crimes required a two-judge majority for conviction. According to one view, Jerusalem had three courts of 23 members, one of which sat at the entrance to the Temple Mount, one at the entrance to the Temple courtyard, and one in the Chamber of Hewn Stone. Finally, there was the SANHEDRIN, which consisted of 71 members. Questions which could not be answered by the local 23-judge courts were sent to the 23-judge courts in Jerusalem and, if these were unable to decide, the question was sent on to the Sanhedrin.

Decisions of the Sanhedrin were final and binding on all of Israel. In fact, should a Torah scholar differ with an announced verdict of the Sanhedrin, he was deemed a *zaken mamreh* — a "rebellious elder" — and was liable to the death penalty.

The Sanhedrin ruled on two basic types of issue: when it decided a question of Jewish law (i.e., legislation), the *nasi* (president) presided, whereas when it acted in trials (i.e., as the highest judicial tribunal), it was headed by the *av bet din* (head of the *bet din*). Certain decisions could only be decided by the Sanhedrin, including proclaiming a person a false prophet, embarking on a non-obligatory war, and declaring a city to be an *ir niddahat* — one that was to be razed because all the residents were idolatrous (San. 1.5). The Sanhedrin also ruled on the appearance of the New Moon, thus deciding when the different festivals would occur.

The judges of the local courts were appointed by the Sanhedrin, based on their probity, their knowledge of the Torah, and the acquiescence of the local populace. The judges of the court at the entrance to the Temple Mount were chosen from among the local judges.

The Sanhedrin may have consisted of the three 23-member courts which met in Jerusalem, plus the *av bet din* and the *nasi*. According to another view, there were only two 23-man courts in Jerusalem, and rather than a 23-man court in the Chamber of Hewn Stone, it was the Sanhedrin, which was a separate entity consisting of 71 judges, which met there.

With the fall of Jerusalem, Johanan ben Zakkai arranged to move the Sanhedrin to Yavneh, where it still maintained supreme authority in all areas of Jewish life, although it was unable to impose capital punishment. This authority, however, was gradually challenged by other Jewish centers as the Babylonian schools emerged as the leading institutions of Jewish learning, and by 425 CE the Sanhedrin in Yavneh had been dissolved.

For a judge to impose a monetary fine, he had to be ordained in a direct line from Moses. The judges outside the Land of Israel, who had not received this ordination, did not have the same authority as those inside the land. They were nevertheless permitted to rule in cases brought before them as they were considered to be acting as *sheliḥim* ("messengers") for the rabbis who had been ordained.

Before emancipation, when Jews lived in their own relatively autonomous communities, the *bet din* would rule on all judicial questions, whether religious, personal status, or civil cases. Even though in most cases the courts were not permitted to impose corporal punishment, they had other punitive weapons at hand, the strongest of these probably being the *ḥerem*, or EXCOMMUNICATION, an extremely severe penalty in the tightly knit Jewish communities of the time. In Spain, under authority of the Spanish king, the *batté din* were given extraordinarily broad powers, including the authority to impose capital punishment. Later, the Council of the Four Lands (mid-16th century to 1764) which controlled Jewish life in Lithuania and Poland, also exerted a tremendous amount of power, especially as the government had given it full powers of taxation. Furthermore, the Council was able to impose the *ḥerem* and assess fines, thus granting it the power to ensure that decisions by the *batté din* would indeed be binding.

With the emancipation of the Jews, the general courts now became open to them, and more and more applied to these courts for remedy. This process was no doubt accelerated as the Jewish community lost its coercive power, and the state took its place. This does not, however, mean that *batté din* no longer exist. They are to be found in almost every center of Jewish life throughout the world. In most countries except for Israel, these *batté din* often deal with questions of *gittin* — DIVORCE according to *halakhah*. In Israel, the *batté din* have considerably broader powers in almost all areas of personal status, including conversions. These powers, though, have come in conflict with those of the secular courts in Israel, and there is an ongoing struggle between the two systems on various questions. A classic instance of this is the question of classifying those converted under non-Orthodox auspices as Jews.

Throughout the world, wherever both parties sign an undertaking to abide by a *bet din*'s ruling, it will consider civil cases between individuals as well. In the United States, there have been state court rulings that the consent by individuals to accept the ruling of a *bet din* is binding by civil law, just as is an agreement to submit to binding arbitration.

BET HA-MIKDASH See TEMPLE

BET MIDRASH (lit. "house of study"). Center for religious learning, often part of a synagogue building or complex. The *bet midrash* has generally served as the primary place for study of the classical talmudic texts and commentaries. It is also generally used for prayers by those who study there. Due to the supreme importance of Torah study, the *bet midrash* is considered to be even more holy than the synagogue, and it is permitted to sell a synagogue in order to buy or construct a *bet midrash*.

Legendarily, the first *bet midrash* was that of Noah's son Shem, and his son Eber. The Midrash lists various biblical figures who are said to have either studied at a *bet midrash* or to have founded one.

One of the earliest known examples was that of the first century BCE sages, SHEMAYAH AND AVTALYON. There was an entrance fee, and when HILLEL, who later became one of the greatest scholars in Jewish history, was unable to afford it, he climbed to the roof to hear the lecture.

During and after the Middle Ages, the *bet midrash* was a standard fixture in each town, usually maintained by the community, where young men would spend their entire day studying the Talmud, while those who worked for a living might attend before or after work to study for a few hours.

Lintel from the bet midrash *of Eliezer ha-Kappar, in the Golan Heights, 3rd century CE.*

Sometimes the *bet midrash* was inside the synagogue which was identified with it. Today, the communal *bet midrash* has almost ceased to exist, although certain synagogues maintain their own *bet midrash*, often during specified hours of the day. Nowadays, each *yeshivah* has a *bet midrash*, which serves as the focal point of all study, and the yeshivah *bet midrash* is often also utilized by members of the local community for study purposes.

In German, the *bet midrash* was known as a KLAUS. The Ḥasidic equivalent was a SHTIBL. In Muslim lands, it was often known simply as "*midrash*".

BET OLAM See CEMETERY

BETROTHAL See MARRIAGE

BÉTSAH ("Egg"). Seventh tractate of Order MO'ED in the Mishnah. Its five chapters deal with the distinction between what is called "work" on the Sabbath and "work" on a festival day (such as the New Year or Passover, etc.) (cf. Ex.12:16; 20:10). The distinction comes out mainly with regard to the preparation of food, which is permitted on a festival day with certain restrictions. The tractate explains the laws of MUKTSEH (things forbidden to be touched on the Sabbath or a festival), the preparation of food on holy days, and the concept of *shevut* (rabbinical restriction against work). This tractate's name is unusual in that it is named after its first word rather than after its subject matter. However, it is also called *Yom Tov* (Festival Day) in keeping with its contents. The text is amplified in both Talmuds and in the *Tosefta*.

BET SHAMMAI AND BET HILLEL (The "House of Shammai and House of Hillel"). Two rival schools of thought which, through their debates and controversies, greatly influenced the development of the ORAL LAW during the last decades of the Second Temple and immediately thereafter. These two schools were established by the foremost sages of that time, SHAMMAI and HILLEL (who was president of the Sanhedrin). Bet Shammai and Bet Hillel probably continued to exist until some time after 100 CE; only a few names of individual teachers have been preserved. Their controversies (316 are recorded) embrace every field of the HALAKHAH, and the opinion of Bet Shammai is usually stated first. Apart from those exceptions listed in the Mishnah (*Ed.* 4, 5.1-4), Shammai's school invariably adopted the more stringent view. Occasionally, Hillel's school changed its position and accepted that of Bet Shammai.

Broadly speaking, there is a fundamental difference between the two schools in their interpretation of Scripture. The Shammaites tend to interpret a biblical verse quite literally, whereas the Hillelites pay greater heed to its underlying purpose. An examination of ancient extra-tannaitic sources (e.g., the Apocrypha) reveals that Bet Shammai almost invariably follows the older *halakhah*, which was noted for its severity. Modern scholars therefore treat the Shammaites as conservatives and the Hillelites as liberals.

Since the mid-19th century, repeated efforts have been made to explain the controversies between the two schools on the basis of sociological factors. The Shammaites came from the wealthy rural aristocracy — a socioeconomic group traditionally noted for its conservatism. The Hillelites, by contrast, represented their own "plebeian" class — the small merchants and artisans who lived in the towns. The Shammaites tended to advocate the older *halakhah*, a case in point being the law of DIVORCE. According to the School of Shammai, a man could divorce his wife only on the grounds of adultery; this view reflects an aversion to divorce, clearly expressed by the prophet Malachi (2:16). Hillel's school, however, granted a husband the right to divorce his wife if he had any serious complaint against her (*Git.* 9.10).

For all their differences, the two schools did not hesitate to intermarry, even though they disagreed about several of the marriage laws. This amicable relationship gave way, through external pressures, to acrimonious debate and even physical violence. Such pressures may well have stemmed from an increasingly oppressive Roman rule (c. 65 CE). Among the Shammaites, this evoked a sharp reaction and galvanized their wish to enact 18 prohibitive measures (*gezerot*) severely limiting contact between Jews and Gentiles. Outnumbering the School of Hillel, Shammai's followers triumphed and the measures were enacted. Some 40 years later, at Jabneh (Yavneh), it was finally resolved that the *halakhah* should always follow the opinion of Bet Hillel. The Talmud (*Er.* 13b) expresses the decision in this way: "For three years, the schools of Shammai and Hillel contended, each insisting that its opinion constituted the *halakhah*. Thereupon, a heavenly voice [BAT KOL] proclaimed: 'Both of them are the words of the living God, but the *halakhah* is according to Bet Hillel.' Why, then, should the Hillelites have been granted the decision? — Because they were pleasant and humble, teaching the opinion of both sides, and always stated Bet Shammai's view before their own."

BIBLE The common English designation for the Hebrew Scriptures. "The Bible" is derived from the Greek *biblia* (lit. "the books"). This term is the precise equivalent of the Hebrew *Ha-Sefarim* ("the books"), which is commonly used to refer to the sacred writings in rabbinic literature. Evidently this usage was widespread even earlier among Hellenistic Jews who translated it into the Greek vernacular.

Other Hebrew names, *Sifré ha-Kodesh* ("the Holy Books") or *Kitvé ha-Kodesh* ("the Holy Writings"), were current from ancient times down to the Middle Ages. These terms underscore two central concepts concerning the text: its Divine inspiration and its definitive written form. The characterization of the Bible as written is complemented by another

term, *Mikra* (lit. "reading"), which highlights the vocal manner of study and points to the fact that the Scriptures were read publicly as part of the liturgical service.

The popular Hebrew designation *Tanakh* is an acronym (TaNaKh) composed of the initial letters of the names of the three divisions of the Hebrew Bible, *Torah* (Pentateuch), *Nevi'im* (Prophets), *Ketuvim* (Hagiographa). The Christian term "Old Testament" is used to distinguish the Hebrew Scriptures from the New Testament.

The biblical text is written in the HEBREW language, with the exception of two words in Genesis (31:47), one verse in Jeremiah (10:11), and sections of the books of Daniel (2:46-7:25) and Ezra (4:8-6:18; 7:12-26), which are in ARAMAIC. The Hebrew of the Bible is not uniform, since it reflects many historical periods and preserves different strata of language, and even different dialects.

Contents The Hebrew Bible consists of three divisions.

1. Pentateuch (*Torah*). This comprises the first five books of the Bible: Genesis, Exodus, Leviticus, Numbers, and Deuteronomy. Jewish tradition ascribed authorship of the entire Pentateuch to MOSES, although the Scriptures themselves make no such explicit claim. This is best explained as an inference from Moses' role as lawgiver, and is most probably based on passages such as Deuteronomy 31:9-12. The basic meaning of TORAH, however, is "instruction" and is in no way limited to legal or ritual prescriptions.

The Five Books constitute a complete uninterrupted narrative beginning with the creation of the world and the patriarchal history, through the Law-giving at Sinai, until Moses' death before Israel's entry into Canaan (see PENTATEUCH). With the increased circulation of the Pentateuch from the times of EZRA and NEHEMIAH, the narrative was divided into five parts, and was conventionally transcribed on five different scrolls for convenience. Thereafter the work became known as "the five-volumed book" (Heb. *Ḫamishah Ḫumshé Torah*, lit. "the five fifths of the Torah"), later, popularly among Jews "the Ḫumash," whose Greek and ultimately English equivalent is "Pentateuch."

The Hebrew names of the Five Books, *Be-Reshit, Shemot, Va-Yikra, Be-Midbar, Devarim*, are derived from the initial words or first significant word of each book. The English titles, on the other hand, are borrowed from the Greek and Latin translations of the Bible and reflect the major theme or content of each book. They, in turn, can be traced back to Hebrew names used for these books as reflected in early rabbinic literature.

2. Prophets (*Nevi'im*). The appellation "Prophets" has been variously explained. The authorship of the books was traditionally ascribed to prophets: "Joshua wrote the book which bears his name...Samuel wrote the book which bears his name and the Book of Judges...Jeremiah wrote the book which bears his name and the Book of Kings..." (*BB* 14b). An alternate explanation is that prophets (e.g., Samuel, Elijah, Elisha, Isaiah) figure centrally in the narrative of the "Former Prophets" (or "pre-classical prophets"), which is essentially an interpretation of Israel's history from the perspective of prophetic teaching.

The second division of the Bible is subdivided into two sections. The name "Former Prophets" applies to the narrative-historical works Joshua, Judges, Samuel (I and II), and Kings (I and II). These form a continuation of the Pentateuch, by picking up the narrative thread where it was cut off. The books of Joshua, Judges, and Samuel trace the history of Israel from the conquest of Canaan and the period of the Judges through the establishment of the Monarchy in the times of Saul and David. The Book of Kings presents a history of the two Kingdoms of Israel and Judah until Jerusalem's downfall in 586 BCE. The narratives were edited to link one book to the next, and the result is a continuous literary work, unfolding in a clear chronological sequence. Their separation into four books may be the product of a later development.

The "Latter Prophets" (or "classical prophets") consists of the books of Isaiah, Jeremiah, Ezekiel and the twelve "Minor Prophets" (Aram. *Teré Asar* — "the Twelve"): Hosea, Joel, Amos, Obadiah, Jonah, Micah, Nahum, Habakkuk, Zephaniah, Haggai, Zechariah, and Malachi. This is an assemblage of works which span the eighth to fifth centuries BCE, i.e., the latter ages of the monarchies of Israel and Judah, the Babylonian EXILE, and the early Second TEMPLE period. The designation "Minor Prophets" refers to the length of the books and not to their relative significance. These shorter books came to be gathered and written together on one scroll to ensure their preservation, and were consequently counted as one book rather than twelve.

Aside from original prophetic utterances preserved and recorded in literary (generally poetic) form, some of the books occasionally contain biographical and historical material pertaining to the lives and activities of the prophets, along with their teachings and public addresses. The order of the first three books as given here, and as present in most manuscripts, is chronological, although some sources deviate from this sequence for various reasons (cf. *BB* 14b). The Minor Prophets were invariably placed at the end of the collection, even though some of the individual prophets predate Isaiah.

3. Hagiographa (*Ketuvim*). The third division of the Bible is a collection of diverse literary genres including liturgical poetry (Psalms and Lamentations); love poetry (The Song of Songs); WISDOM LITERATURE (Proverbs, Job, and Ecclesiastes); historical books (Ruth, Chronicles (I and II), Esther, Ezra, and Nehemiah); and the book of Daniel which mingles history, prophecy, and apocalypse. The all-inclusive Hebrew term *Ketuvim* (lit. "Writings") suits the miscellaneous nature of the corpus. The order of the books in *Ketuvim* was not firmly established, as can be seen by the varying traditions in the Greek Bible as to their sequence and arrangement. Hebrew manuscripts and editions vary as well, though to a

lesser degree. Five of the books of *Ketuvim*, traditionally called the FIVE SCROLLS (*Megillot*), are customarily read in the synagogue on festival days: the Song of Songs on Passover, Ruth on Shavu'ot, Lamentations on Tishah be-Av, Ecclesiastes on Sukkot, and Esther on Purim. Subsequently, these books formed a subgrouping, and were arranged in this order, although an alternate order reflects the relative chronology of their reputed authors. Despite this evident fluidity, the Book of Chronicles came to occupy the final position in the Hagiographa. Scholars have noted the structural affinities between Chronicles and Genesis, the first book of the Bible. Both books relate the beginnings of mankind and end in anticipation of the return to the Land of Israel. Balancing Genesis with Chronicles served to create an overall unifying literary theme for the entire Bible.

Most ancient Jewish sources specify the sum total of biblical books as 24. There is no clear indication whether this number bore special significance, yet it seems to have been derived somewhat artificially by counting the Minor Prophets as one book, Ezra and Nehemiah being regarded originally as one work. The subdivision of Samuel, Kings, and Chronicles into two books each is the product of a later development. A variant reckoning of 22 books is attested to by Josephus (*Against Apion* 1.38-42), probably to be explained by attaching Ruth to Judges and Lamentations to Jeremiah, a practice which has survived in the Greek and Latin translations of the Bible.

The division of the Bible into three distinct corpora would seem to imply a categorization of its contents. However, this does not strictly classify the books according to genre or style. According to the prevalent scholarly view, the division delineates three progressive stages in the evolvement of the Canon (see separate entries on each of the books of the Bible).

Canon The term "canon" refers to the closed and authoritative nature of a corpus of sacred writings. The biblical books are considered binding by various religious communities because of the belief that they have been Divinely revealed or inspired. The concept of canon is central to understanding how the Bible became the focus of Jewish life, making Israel "the People of the Book" and infusing its teachings, values, and national ethic into the fabric of the nation's being.

The word "canon," borrowed from Semitic usage, originally meant "reed" or "cane" (Heb. *kaneh*), and hence "measuring rod." It came to be used in the abstract sense of a measure of excellence, and was thus first applied to the Scriptures by the Church Fathers. Jewish sources also acknowledge the concept of "canon" or "canonicity." This is inferred, on the one hand, by the category of *Sefarim Ḥitsonim* (lit. "External Books," see, e.g., *San.* 10:1), which was applied to all literary works that were not canonical (see APOCRYPHA AND PSEUDEPIGRAPHA), and, on the other hand, by two technical Hebrew expressions — *metamé et ha-yadayim* ("renders the hands unclean"), which refers to the rabbinic injunction that anyone who touched a biblical book contracted ritual uncleanness, and GENIZAH, the storing away of sacred books (and other artifacts) which could no longer be used. These phrases are employed in rabbinic discussions questioning the canonicity of Proverbs, Ecclesiastes, the Song of Songs, and Esther.

It is clear that not all of the literature of ancient Israel has survived, and the Scriptures themselves refer to various contemporary books or records which were lost. Such works are: "The Book of the Wars of the Lord" (Num. 21:14); "The Book of Jashar" (Josh. 10:13, II Sam. 1:18); and "The Chronicles of the Kings of Israel/Judah" (e.g., I Kings 14:19,29). This fact can be partly explained as accident, but nonetheless the idea of a canon implies a process whereby certain books were consciously rejected, while others were considered sacred books and therefore formally canonized. However, many factors operating over time contributed to the gradual recognition of certain works over others. Temple liturgy, by virtue of its cultic function, and other texts related intrinsically to the cult (such as the priestly codes), were revered and carefully transmitted within Temple circles. Narratives which encompassed the national past and testified to God's covenant with Israel soon achieved an elevated rank and were considered a Divine legacy. Prophetic addresses were naturally recorded and preserved by groups of adherents. Sometimes individual books were accepted as canonical, yet were not included in a given corpus for an extended period of time. For example, much of the Psalter was probably in existence and sanctified for centuries before the canonization of the Book of Psalms, let alone the canonization of the Hagiographa. It is important, therefore, to distinguish between the various processes involved. Upon canonization of a book, its literary growth came to an end, and it was henceforth only to be transmitted textually by scribes and copyists. With the canonization of a corpus, a boundary was set and no further books were to be included. In all cases, the common belief in the Divine inspiration of these writings was a prerequisite for canonicity.

The present form of the Canon was determined by a complex historical and literary process. Although sources from the Hellenistic period provide some evidence concerning the latter stages of this process, information for the earlier periods is scant and inconclusive. Therefore, any reconstruction will remain largely a matter of conjecture. The tripartite division of the Canon is considered by most scholars to be the result of a historical development; the three divisions attained canonical status one by one at successive historical stages.

One of the most significant accounts concerning the canonization of the Pentateuch is in II Kings 22-23. In the 18th year of King Josiah's reign (622 BCE), a previously neglected "book of the Torah" (or "Book of the Covenant") was discovered in the Temple by the High Priest and read before the king. The book was immediately recognized as

authentic, and shortly thereafter was read aloud in a national covenant ceremony. The description of the subsequent cultic reform complies exactly with the central instruction of the Book of Deuteronomy, and therefore this event is usually seen as the formal canonization of that book. The next record of a public reading of the Torah, at the time of Ezra (c. 444 BCE), is found in Neh. 8-10. The ceremony is described as taking place in response to the people's demand that "the Book of the Torah of Moses" be read to them. Hence, it must be assumed that the book was known and that its final compilation had already been accomplished in the Babylonian Exile, before the Return to Zion. The request was carried out by Ezra, who is described as a "scribe, expert in the Torah of Moses." Ezra's main contribution was in promoting the teaching and interpretation of the Torah, and elevating it to its unique position in Jewish life.

The second stage of the canonization of the Bible began with the collection of the prophetic literature, which had been preserved since the days of the First Temple, together with the books of Haggai, Zechariah, and Malachi, whose activity was inspired by the events surrounding the Return to Zion and the reconstruction of the Temple. A widely evidenced rabbinic tradition states that these prophets were the last to be endowed with the HOLY SPIRIT (Heb. *ru'aḇ ha-kodesh*). Other sources, too, intimate that the social and religious institution of prophecy was gradually losing its vitality and credibility during the Second Temple period. The prophetic canon was probably sealed before the end of the Persian empire. Moreover, the prophetic corpus betrays no Greek influence and the historical horizon of the books only extends as far as the era of Persian hegemony.

Sources from the Hellenistic period show that the threefold division of the Bible was by then well established. All refer to the Law and the Prophets as such, yet the third category had no commonly recognized name, but was rather given different descriptions, such as "the wisdom of the ancients," "the Psalms and other writings," or "the remaining books." This evidence all points to the fact that the Hagiographa was a rather amorphous group of writings for a considerable length of time after the canonization of the Prophets, and was not finally closed until well into the Greco-Roman period. It is notable that the Hagiographa contains works that were contemporaneous with some of the later prophetic books, but were excluded from the second collection because of their non-prophetic character. On the other hand, some books were written too late to be included. This explains why the Book of Daniel, which contains a great deal of prophecy, was nevertheless included in the Hagiographa, since it is a product of the later Hellenistic period and is also the only biblical book to contain Greek words.

A number of facts seem to indicate that there were divergent canonical traditions in the Jewish community of the late Second Temple period. Some controversy surrounding the canonicity of several books (Proverbs, Ecclesiastes, the Song of Songs, Esther) still reverberates in rabbinic discussions from the tannaitic and amoraic periods (see, e.g., *Yad.* 3.5, *Meg.* 7a). The Book of Ben Sira (Ecclesiasticus) enjoyed a quasi-canonical status in the community until the rabbis explicitly declared it uncanonical (*Tosef. Yad.* 2.13). Many of the original works composed at this period, which might have been possible candidates for inclusion in the Hagiographa, have survived only because of their acceptance within the Hellenistic canon and from there into the canon of the Christian Church. These works (e.g., the Books of Maccabees, Esdras, Enoch, etc.) are known today mainly through the Greek translations. Some scholars consider the Hellenistic canon to reflect a Jewish canonical tradition current in Erets Israel and Alexandria at the time that the Greek translations of the Bible were made. The sectarian community at Qumran appears to have had an entirely different attitude towards the Scriptures. Their collection of writings was much more comprehensive, containing many sectarian compositions unknown before the discovery of the DEAD SEA SCROLLS. As to the normative Jewish canon, talmudic discussions frequently point back to the rabbinic council at Yavneh (c. 90 CE) as the time when final decisions were made concerning the status of the controversial books. Yet the continuing interest in this question on the rabbis' part suggests that even after that event the boundary was not quite fixed, and not until the middle of the second century CE was there unshaken agreement as to the scope of the Hagiographa.

For the large community of "hellenized" Jews in Alexandria, the language of the Bible was no longer familiar as it had been to their ancestors. Around the third century BCE, the community undertook to render the Scriptures into Greek, and the result was the translation known as the SEPTUAGINT. This differs from the Hebrew canon in two major respects (aside from the textual one). It includes many works which were rejected from the normative Jewish canon and considered "external" by the rabbis of Erets Israel. Secondly, the Greek canon preserves a different arrangement of the books. These are distributed among four classes (as opposed to the conventional three): Torah , History, Poetic and Didactic Literature, and Prophecy.

Text The text of the Hebrew Bible, as it is printed in modern editions and as it has been known from the Middle Ages onward, is composed of three graphic elements: (1) the consonants, (2) the vowel signs, (3) the accentuation marks. The last serve as the musical-liturgical reading of the Scriptures and also have an exegetical function in interpreting each verse. Both the vowel signs and the accentuation marks are secondary additions to the consonantal text. They were introduced by the Masoretes in the Middle Ages to preserve the oral tradition of vocalization, pronunciation, and chanting which had always accompanied the written words (see CANTILLATION). In the earlier periods only the consonantal text existed, and the other elements had no graphic representation.

The earliest medieval texts preserved are from the ninth century onward, and they all reflect the textual tradition known as the Masoretic Text. Among manuscripts of this type, many textual variants may be found, but these are largely variations of spelling or of grammatical form, and the majority are of trivial significance. By this time, the text had long become standardized and stabilized by a complex critical process.

In contrast to this uniformity, the prior history of the consonantal text attests to much diversity. The evidence for this derives from a variety of sources (called textual witnesses), but an overview readily reveals that in the early stages of textual transmission many different types of texts were circulating, each exhibiting its own variant readings. These variants are not limited merely to minute particulars such as orthography or grammatical forms, but include more significant divergences, such as different wording, synonymous readings, a different ordering of verses or of entire episodes, an expansive or embellished text versus a laconic one, and occasionally one version may contain information not preserved elsewhere.

The earliest evidence of this type is found within the Bible itself, where several passages are duplicated (yet not without textual divergences) in other books, e.g., the two versions of the Decalogue, Exodus 20:2-14 = Deuteronomy 5:6-19; the Assyrian siege of Jerusalem, II Kings 18:13-20:19 = Isaiah 36-39; the eschatological vision in Isaiah 2:2-4 = Micah 4:1-3; and the parallels between Samuel-Kings and Chronicles. These examples show that wide discrepancies existed in different versions of the text, even when biblical literature was still in its formative stages.

The Samaritan Pentateuch (see SAMARITANS) is a Hebrew text of the first five books of the Bible, which was preserved within the Samaritan community as their canon. This text first came to the attention of European scholars in the 17th century. Although it contains several secondary features which are easily recognized as ideological additions or corrections, its intrinsic nature is not sectarian. Ever since the discovery of prototypes of this text among the Dead Sea Scrolls, it has become clear that it was only one of several types of text current among Jews in Erets Israel in the Second Temple period. Later developments brought about its disappearance from Jewish circles. The text differs from the Masoretic text in its tendency to harmonize inconsistencies or points of variance between different descriptions of the same subject, or between repeated episodes in the narrative. Nonetheless, many of the textual variants have important value.

Another type of textual witness are the ancient translations of the Bible. These often reveal that the original Hebrew underlying the translation was not identical to the Masoretic Text. This evidence is not always clear-cut, however, since the original Hebrew can only be hypothetically reconstructed. The most ancient translation, and therefore the most important, is the Septuagint, which provides rich and varied material invaluable for textual criticism. The Aramaic TARGUM "translations", even those which are literal and not Midrashic, have less importance in this respect. Other early translations are the Latin "Vulgate" and the Syriac "Peshitta."

A page with verses from the Book of Psalms, from the Aleppo Codex, *the oldest complete manuscript of the Bible, dating from the 10th century.*

Of all the textual witnesses, the most important are the biblical scrolls and fragments discovered in caves at the site of Qumran in the Judean Desert in the 1940s and 50s. The discovery of the Dead Sea Scrolls brought to light the earliest extant manuscripts of biblical literature, predating the medieval codices by over a thousand years. Hundreds of fragments were found, representing the whole range of biblical books with the exception of Esther. Some of the older scrolls are written in the paleo-Hebrew script. The scrolls span a period of a few hundred years from the first settlement at Qumran in the third century BCE until its abandonment in 70 CE, with the destruction of Jerusalem by the Romans. They provide direct and unmistakable evidence for the textual reality of the Second Temple period, and since the earlier scrolls were brought to the site from afar, they testify not only for the minority group residing at Qumran but also for the Jewish population of the country at large. Prototypes of all the major textual traditions known to scholars were found at Qumran (Masoretic Text, Samaritan Pentateuch, and Sep-

tuagint), and also texts belonging to independent traditions that cannot be classified along with texts previously known.

The last type of evidence are the many citations of biblical verses in works from the period of the Second Temple (e.g., in Philo, Josephus, the New Testament), including the rabbinic literature containing hundreds of quotations from Scripture, some of which include genuine textual variants.

The rabbinic sources also supply a few descriptions of scribal activities in transmitting the text. One such account tells of several *tikkuné soferim* ("scribal corrections") in the text, another of *maggihé sefarim* ("book revisers"). Also preserved were traditions of an official Temple scroll which was used as a standard for correction. These sources reveal some of the processes which brought about the exclusive preservation of the Masoretic Text. By the end of the first century CE, it had become the only authorized text, while all the other traditions seem to have been neglected, rejected, or forgotten. At this time the text had already become fixed, even to the extent of the number of words and letters. This is indicated by the activities of the *soferim* ("counters"), who established the middle words and letters and the total number of words in each book, and thus created a critical apparatus for the accurate duplication of the text in transmission. The movement from plurality to uniformity was undoubtedly motivated by the idea of canonicity, which had come to emphasize the precise original form of the Divine word. The historical circumstances, namely the national emergency in the first and second centuries CE, enhanced the need for religious and communal solidarity; the unity of the text was one way sought to achieve this.

Scientific Study of the Bible The antecedents of modern biblical scholarship can be found in sources from late antiquity to the Middle Ages, where students of the Bible, whether Jewish, Hellenistic, Christian, KARAITE, or Muslim, addressed themselves to problems arising from contradictions, inconsistencies, or difficulties in the text. An apt example is one of the more radical statements made by a talmudic sage: "The Torah was given scroll by scroll" (*Git.* 60a). While such discussions induced Jewish scholars to develop the principles of HERMENEUTICS with which to resolve such problems in the text, others, such as certain Hellenistic philosophers or Muslim polemicists, wished to aim a critique against the authenticity of the Bible. The medieval exegete Abraham IBN EZRA (1092-1167) is exceptional in this respect, for he appears to have hinted, albeit in obscure and allusive language, at a number of anachronisms in the Pentateuch which could undermine the assumption of Mosaic authorship (for those passages, at least). He also discerned the work of a second prophet in the latter half of the Book of Isaiah.

The emergence of biblical criticism proper in the modern era is associated with the name of Baruch Spinoza (1632-1677), who advocated a rational-historical approach to the Holy Scriptures. He urged that the Scriptures be studied, as any other document, only by reference to their own content and independent of tradition. Pursuing Ibn Ezra's lead, he openly took issue with the hitherto inviolable belief in Mosaic authorship of the Pentateuch. During the ages following Spinoza, biblical scholarship concerned itself primarily with the question of the composition of the Pentateuch. The initial direction was given when scholars noticed the alternation of Divine Names in the Pentateuch and used this as a key to discerning different literary strata. Other scholars expanded this sort of inquiry, employing other criteria, such as differing style, phraseology, theological outlook, doublets, or signs of editorial activity, to unravel the different strands in the narrative. The same methods were also applied to the rest of biblical literature. The culmination of these scholarly efforts was the consolidation of what is known as the Documentary Hypothesis, which isolated four distinct written sources through literary-critical analysis, each of which contained a narrative element and a body of laws which were combined to create the Pentateuch. These are designated the Jahwist (J), so called because of its usage of *Yahweh* for the Divine Name; the Elohist (E), for its use of *Elohim* for God; Deuteronomy (D); and the Priestly Document (P). This, too, was their purported chronological order. After various preliminary recensions, the Torah was supposed to have been finally edited by a priestly editor in the post-Exilic age. Although most of its central theses were propounded before him, the German scholar Julius Wellhausen added historical-evolutionist arguments that gave this theory a persuasiveness and finality which remained uncontested for a long time afterwards. The classical formulation of the Documentary Hypothesis has since been modified, but its essential propositions are still defended by most scholars. Nonetheless, many have criticized it on the grounds that its arguments are circular, that it is based largely on speculative assumptions about the development of religious thought and practice and has thereby forced true evidence to conform to a conjectured historical scheme. The Italian-born Israeli scholar Mosheh David (Umberto) Cassuto disputed the theory in its entirety, while two other Jewish scholars, David Tsevi Hoffmann and Yeḇezkel Kaufman, criticized the dating of the priestly writing to the post-Exilic era and argued that they enjoy even greater antiquity than the Book of Deuteronomy.

The next pivotal shift in biblical scholarship was made by Hermann Gunkel, who examined the prehistory of the written documents, and tried to explore the origins of biblical literature in the phases before it was committed to writing. Gunkel proposed to identify the different genres of literature in the Bible by learning to recognize each one's characteristic forms, patterns, and mood. He believed each genre to be the product of a unique "life setting" (*Sitz im Leben*) or social (and often cultic) context, in which a specific form of literary expression was created and performed at recurrent intervals. This method is known as "Form Criticism." The classification of the Psalms remains Gunkel's most lasting contribution. His work was important in that it gave rise to research in new directions and advanced the study of social and cultic institutions in the biblical period.

In recent years, there has been a growing interest in developing a literary approach to the Bible, which emphasizes the total composition of the text and its artistic unity, rather than its fragmentation and dissection by conventional criticism. The sentiment common to the proponents of this approach is that the "scissors and paste" method of scholarship has been exhausted to its full extent, and that its achievements, however important, are limited in scope, because scholars tended to ignore the relationship between the parts and the whole and did not view the text in its final form as a cohesive structure. This relatively recent trend has produced many penetrating studies in biblical poetics, especially of narrative technique and parallelism in biblical poetry.

The early generation of biblical scholars created their reconstructions of Israel's past without any external knowledge of its contemporary cultural environment, aside from what could be learned from the Bible itself. This contextual void was often compensated for by speculation and theorizing. The archeological discoveries of the 19th and 20th centuries corrected this state of affairs. In the Land of Israel, excavations at important biblical sites such as Hazor, Megiddo, Samaria, Jerusalem, and Lachish have revealed the architecture of royal buildings, common dwellings, fortifications, sanctuaries and altars, water supplies, food utensils, weaponry, agricultural tools, and cultic objects to help paint a picture of Israelite society and of the Canaanites who preceded them. Only a few written documents from Israel have been found, probably because the materials commonly used for writing were perishable. However, in Egypt, Mesopotamia, Syria, and Anatolia, beyond the remains of material culture, a wealth of textual information, stored in ancient libraries or inscribed on monuments, has survived. These texts bring to light the history, languages, and literatures of the surrounding peoples of the ancient Near East. The recovery of these ancient languages has made an immense contribution to comparative Semitic lexicography and has vastly enriched understanding of biblical Hebrew.

Within a short time it became clear that all of the literary forms and genres present in ancient Israel had their parallels in the neighboring cultures, not surprisingly since Israel emerged as a nation long after the civilizations of Egypt and Mesopotamia had reached their peak. It is hard to say whether this is due to a substratum of culture that once dominated the whole region, or to subtle processes of cultural borrowing in both directions over the centuries.

A few examples will serve to demonstrate these parallels. More than six legal collections have been discovered in the cuneiform script, many of which show striking similarities with biblical law. The law dealing with the "goring ox" (Ex. 21:28-32) as a classic case of damages is such an example by way of content. As to structure and style, it was soon noted that the celebrated legal collection of Hammurabi has a historical prologue and ends with admonitions in much the same way as some of the biblical collections of law. The uniqueness of biblical law is that it is derived entirely from the Deity, and does not differentiate between secular and cultic law, but rather comprehends them both in one sphere. The discovery of ancient Canaanite epic literature in the city of Ugarit in northern Syria has shown that biblical poetry inherited much of its language, imagery, structure, and motifs from the Canaanites. Biblical psalmody has many parallels in Egyptian and Mesopotamian hymnology and prayer. The central concept in biblical religion of the covenant between Israel and God has been illuminated by comparisons with the form and contents of Near-Eastern treaties. It seems that the affirmation of loyalty between political entities was adapted in Israel (most typically in the Book of Deuteronomy) to the religious sphere between God and man. One of the most dramatic parallels between biblical and Mesopotamian literature is in the literary traditions about CREATION and especially the FLOOD story (preserved in its most elaborate form in the Epic of Gilgamesh). Despite the similarities in plot and language, the biblical story is markedly different in its moral and didactic viewpoint. Equally illuminating as the quest for parallels is the fact that the Bible does not contain any literature dealing with magic, divination, and astrology, so abundant in the other traditions. This is a clear indication that biblical religion did not tolerate certain pagan forms of communication with the supernatural

Part of the Epic of Gilgamesh *on which the Babylonian version of the Flood is recorded. It is dated to c.2000-1800 BCE. Parallels have been found in Mesopotamian literature with Creation in the Bible.*

Opening page of the Book of Numbers. From the Lisbon Bible, *1483.*

לרע ד פת וסימניהון לא יבקר בין טוב לרע. הוי האמרים לרע טוב. רגליהם לרע ירוצו. רגליהם לרע ירוצו ג קמ וסימ
עלי כל מחשבתם לרע. כי לא תהיה אחרית לרע. מסלף רשעים לרע. וכל למרע דכו פת במב קמ וסימ ולא דבר אבשלום. ושניהם המלכים לבבם למרע

אחזתו לא ימכר ולא יגאל כל
חרם קדש קדשים הוא ליהוה
כל חרם אשר יחרם מן האדם
לא יפדה מות יומת וכל מעשר
הארץ מזרע הארץ מפרי העץ
ליהוה הוא קדש ליהוה ואם
גאל יגאל איש ממעשרו ח
חמשיתו יסף עליו וכל מעשר
בקר וצאן כל אשר יעבר תחת
השבט העשירי יהיה קדש
ליהוה לא יבקר בין טוב לרע
ולא ימירנו ואם המר ימירנו
והיה הוא ותמורתו יהיה קדש
לא יגאל אלה המצות אשר
צוה יהוה את משה אל בני
ישראל בהר סיני

וידבר

יהוה אל משה במדבר סיני
באהל מועד באחד לחדש
השני בשנה השנית לצאתם
מארץ מצרים לאמר שאו

את ראש כל עדת בני ישראל
למשפחתם לבית אבתם במספר
שמות כל זכר לגלגלתם מבן
עשרים שנה ומעלה כל יצא
צבא בישראל תפקדו אתם
לצבאתם אתה ואהרן ואתכם
יהיו איש איש למטה איש ראש
לבית אבתיו הוא ואלה שמות
האנשים אשר יעמדו אתכם
לראובן אליצור בן שדיאור
לשמעון שלמיאל בן צורישדי
ליהודה נחשון בן עמינדב
ליששכר נתנאל בן צוער לזבולן
אליאב בן חלן לבני יוסף לאפרים
אלישמע בן עמיהוד למנשה
גמליאל בן פדהצור לבנימן
אבידן בן גדעני לדן אחיעזר
א בן עמישדי לאשר פגעיאל
בן עכרן לגד אליסף בן דעואל
לנפתלי אחירע בן עינן אלה
קריאי העדה נשיאי מטות
אבותם ראשי אלפי ישראל הם
ויקח משה ואהרן את האנשים
האלה אשר נקבו בשמות ואת
כל העדה הקהילו באחד לחדש
השני ויתילדו על משפחתם

שמות ט מל בתו וסימניהון ויקרא האדם שמות. ויקרא להן שמות. שאו את ראש כל עדת. ואת כל העדה הקהילו
ויהיו בני ראובן בכר ישראל. לבני שמעון. לבני גד. לבני מנשה. לאלה תחלק הארץ. ואתכם ג וסימ ואתכם יהיו. ואתכם עבדי
אבותם ב מל בתו וסימ אלה קרואי העדה. ואת שם אהרן. וכל נגו ובתו דכו במה חס וסימ וכלם בשמות להגיד בית אבתם. גם בעהם ובני בעהם
גם יהודה לאשר

אלף בית מן חד חד מנתרתין תיבותהון לא נסב׳ ו׳ בריש תיבותה ואינון דמט׳ ע׳ בהון׳ ארבעים שנה׳ בן שלשים שנה חד
כל לשון אפס אפי אפיו על כמ״א הראית

sphere. In all the examples cited, the importance of drawing the parallels is in discerning the subtle differences and in highlighting the individual character of each tradition. Then it can be observed how certain elements deviate from the common pattern or were transformed by the monotheistic outlook, giving them a particular Israelite quality.

In Judaism From the period of the Exodus until Second Temple times, the Bible's impact on ancient Israel could mainly be seen in adherence to the Pentateuchal commandments. Thereafter, with the development of a religious "chain of tradition," Jewish life was increasingly dominated by an ORAL LAW that supplemented and vitalized the WRITTEN LAW. Out of rabbinic exposition of the Scriptures two literary currents emerged: the first, rooted in the Pentateuch, laid the foundations of Judaism's religio-legal "way of life," the HALAKHAH, based on 613 commandments (MITSVOT); the second, homiletical and imaginative, gave rise to the AGGADAH and MIDRASH, extending from the weekly Pentateuchal and prophetical readings in the SYNAGOGUE to many other sections of the Bible as well. Rabbinic law prescribed how the Sabbath and festivals were to be observed, establishing rules that governed every aspect of daily life from the cradle to the grave, each *mitsvah* being ultimately traceable to the Pentateuch. Midrashic literature, which looked beyond the "plain" literal meaning of a biblical text, provided much of the impetus for Jewish exegesis and created a vast treasure of legend, anecdote, and folklore, also fostering a Jewish mystical tradition, the KABBALAH.

It was during the hellenistic era that an attempt was first made to combine biblical and advanced secular (Greek) culture. The most important outcome of that short-lived trend was the Septuagint, through which Torah became familiar to Gentiles as the "Law" (*Nomos*), or Pentateuch. Hellenistic Judaism likewise gave birth to the first epic poetry and drama on biblical themes.

A concentration of biblical influences is visible in the synagogue, in its traditional design and mode of worship. Following the Temple's destruction in 70 CE, each Jewish house of prayer became a *mikdash me'at* ("Sanctuary in miniature"). Each daily service replaced one of the daily sacrifices. The ARK containing SCROLLS OF THE LAW (manuscripts of the Pentateuch) replaces the ancient Ark of the Covenant; the PAROKHET ("curtain") hung in front of the Ark, a replica of the TABLETS OF THE COVENANT inscribed with the TEN COMMANDMENTS, the ETERNAL LIGHT, and various forms of candelabra substituting for the MENORAH are other notable reminders of the lost Temple.

Elaborately inscribed biblical verses often formed part of the synagogue's interior design in medieval Spain; nowadays, an appropriate verse may be engraved over the Ark or may embellish the exterior. Hebrew, the language of the Bible, is also the traditional language of prayer. From early rabbinic times, the LITURGY comprised various PSALMS, the SHEMA, other Scriptural passages, the AMIDAH prayer which contains many biblical echoes, benedictions such as the PRIESTLY BLESSING, and the READING OF THE LAW on Mondays and Thursdays, Sabbaths, the New Moon, and all festivals as well as fast days. The HALLEL psalms are recited on Pilgrim Festivals and the AVODAH, the High Priest's Temple ritual, on the Day of Atonement. The rabbi's sermon is usually based on that particular day's Pentateuchal or prophetical reading. The Jew is reminded of the Bible every time he sees the MEZUZAH on his doorpost.

Jewish EDUCATION proceeded from the child's mastery of Hebrew to study of the weekly Torah portion and then to MISHNAH, TALMUD, and the essentials of Jewish law. Prime Jewish interest in and study of the Bible was concentrated on the Pentateuch, seen as the direct word of God, whereas the rest of the Bible, while often directly Divinely inspired (as in the words of the prophets), did not have the same authority. Although conflicting points of view were expressed in regard to dogma, MAIMONIDES defined 13 PRINCIPLES OF FAITH, which in time gained almost universal acceptance. They included the belief "that all the words of the prophets are true," that Moses remains the supreme prophet, that the Torah which he received is the one preserved by Jews, and that it will never be replaced by any other revelation. While Midrashic literature helped Jews to see the partriarchs, prophets, and other biblical figures as real flesh-and-blood people, an increasing emphasis on talmudic and halakhic study made both youngsters and adults inclined to view the Bible from the Talmud's perspective. It was partly in reaction to this trend that the KARAITES mounted their campaign against Judaism's domination by the Oral Law; and it was chiefly as a result of that conflict that Karaism's "Rabbanite" opponents acknowledged the need for an authentic literal approach to Scripture and for an authoritative exposition of the entire Hebrew Bible. This change of emphasis had two vastly important effects: it promoted the development of rabbinic exegesis spearheaded by RASHI and later medieval commentators (see BIBLE COMMENTARIES), and it fostered a biblical Hebrew revival under JUDAH HALEVI and other poets of the Spanish Golden Age.

Except in Italy, where Jewish scholarship and Hebrew culture benefited from the Renaissance, an enforced ghetto existence adversely affected Bible study among Jews from the early 16th until the late 18th century, attention being concentrated on the Talmud and Kabbalah. A change occurred with the emergence of Jewish Enlightenment (HASKALAH) in Europe, and Moses MENDELSSOHN's *Biur*, which enabled German Jews to acquire secular knowledge through reading the Bible in German. This, in turn, led to a jettisoning of the *halakhah* and talmudic discipline by REFORM JUDAISM, which proclaimed its return to biblical inspiration, especially stressing the morality of the prophets; to the Hebrew revival in Eastern Europe; and to an upsurge of Jewish nationalism, in which Hebrew and a new secular approach to the Bible played a vital role.

Carpet page from the Damascus Keter *Bible with micrographic* masorah. *Spain, 13th century.*

Whereas Ashkenazi Jews largely neglected Bible study from the Middle Ages down to the 19th century (and, among the ultra-Orthodox, down to modern times), a different attitude prevailed in the Sephardi-Eastern Jewish world. There, a comprehensive knowledge of the Scriptures was taught, enabling the average Sephardi Jew to quote long biblical passages from memory. Such loving familiarity with the Hebrew Bible remains typical of the North African and Middle Eastern Jewish communities down to the present.

Modern Jewish education, reinforced by translations and commentaries in the the vernacular, has stressed the Bible as a basis of Jewish study. In modern Israel, Bible study is integral to every child's schooling, although different approaches are adopted by the religious and non-religious educational streams. With Hebrew being the national language of Israel, the Bible is an open book to Israelis. Archeology sheds new light on the biblical past, children and new villages or neighborhoods are often given biblical names, an unending stream of books and articles roll off the press, talks on the weekly portion are broadcast each morning, and Bible contests are a popular pastime.

BIBLE COMMENTARY, JEWISH A proper understanding of the text and teachings of the Hebrew Bible has been one of the most assiduously cultivated occupations of the Jewish people. For the first 1,000 years of its history, the people of Israel was mainly occupied with the compiling of the Scriptures. Once the Canon of the BIBLE had been determined, Jews began to expound and interpret their sacred books. Thus, from the period of Ezra (fifth century BCE), almost another 1,000 years were devoted to the systematic development of the law (HALAKHAH) taking its authority from the biblical text, as well as to the AGGADAH (non-legal interpretations, homilies, folklore, moral tales, etc.) also rooted in the Bible.

The biblical text remained the basis of almost all subsequent Jewish literary activity, most of which took the form of direct commentary on the Scriptures. Notable examples of this genre are the allegorical interpretations of PHILO in the Hellenistic period; the writings of Josephus, whose *Antiquities* may be seen as largely a running commentary on the narrative portions of the Bible; the Arabic Bible translation of SAADIAH GAON which helped to counter anti-rabbinical liberalism (see below); outstanding Jewish philosophical works of the Middle Ages, chiefly responding to the religious challenges of ISLAM and CHRISTIANITY; the works of the great medieval Jewish Bible commentators; and the kabbalistic and Ḥasidic products of Jewish mysticism. The importance which Jews always attached to the proper interpretation of Scripture is evidenced by the enormous volume of commentary literature produced throughout the centuries.

According to Jewish tradition, both the WRITTEN LAW (the Pentateuch) and the ORAL LAW were received by Moses at the Sinaitic revelation. Oral teachings were indispensable if the Jew sought the true meaning of a written text; and these teachings eventually grew into the corpus of literature known as the Talmud. A "chain of tradition" was recorded by the Mishnah (*Avot* 1.1): "Moses received the Torah from Sinai and transmitted it to Joshua, and Joshua to the Elders [i.e., the Judges], the Elders to the Prophets, and the Prophets transmitted it to the Men of the Great Assembly."

That GREAT ASSEMBLY was established by EZRA who left Babylonia at the very beginning of the Second Temple period, authorized by Persia's "great king" to place the new and struggling community in Judah on a secure religious basis. In 444 BCE, a great assembly of the people was held at which the Torah was formally read and ratified, Ezra thereby making the Pentateuch the constitution of the new Jewish Commonwealth. This reading was performed in a clear and accurate manner, with the Levites walking among the people to make sure that everyone heard and understood the text that was being recited: "They read in the book, in the Law of God, *distinctly* [Heb. *meforash*]; and they *gave the sense* [of the text] so that the reading would be understood" (Neh. 8:8). Moreover, Ezra also "dedicated himself to *seek* [*li-drosh*] the Law of the Lord..." (Ezra 7:10). The Hebrew verb used here for "to seek" (*darash*) means to investigate the text, to inquire into its meaning; from this same root the rabbis later coined the noun MIDRASH to denote the exposition of Scripture. Systematic Jewish interpretation of the Bible thus dates from the period of Ezra, who headed a line of teachers known as the SCRIBES (*Soferim*).

During the Babylonian EXILE, much of the Hebrew language had been forgotten and this made it necessary for the Scribes to explain the meaning of the Bible text. They therefore translated passages into the Aramaic vernacular, and it was from these translations that there emerged a complete Aramaic version of the Bible, the TARGUM. This was no mere translation of the Hebrew text, however, since it conveyed its traditional interpretation. As such, the Targum is an embodiment of early Bible commentary, a Hellenistic parallel being found in the Greek SEPTUAGINT.

The work of the Scribes was continued by their rabbinical successors, the *tannaim* (see TANNA). Apart from preserving legal (halakhic) traditions, they also transmitted numerous collections of Midrash which were themselves based on varying styles or methods of biblical interpretation, chiefly in the form of a verse-by-verse commentary on the Scriptural text. Altogether, four distinct methods of interpretation emerged, which are known by the acronym PARDES: PESHAT (the "plain" or literal sense); *Remez ("hint"*, i.e., the allegorical interpretation); *Derash* (homiletical deduction); and *Sod* (the mystical or "secret" meaning). Other tannaitic sages laid down the rules (*middot*) to be followed when expounding a biblical text. HILLEL first drew up seven rules, which were expanded to 13 by ISHMAEL BEN ELISHA, and finally to 32 in the days of R. Eliezer ben Yosé the Galilean (see HERMENEUTICS). Two great schools of Midrashic interpretation emerged, the school of AKIVA which carefully (even pedantically) inquired into every word and letter; and that of R. Ishmael, who held that there is no chronological order in the Bible (*Pes.* 6b) and that "the Torah speaks in the language of men" (*Sif.* to Num. 112; cf. *Ber.* 31b). They produced basic Midrashic texts: MEKHILTA to the Book of Exodus, SIFRA to Leviticus, and SIFRÉ to Numbers and Deuteronomy.

From the seventh century, conquering Arab armies diffused not only Islam but also the Arabic language throughout western Asia and North Africa. Arabic soon became the new medium for literary activity, while the Koran's influence on philosophy likewise affected Jewish scholars, widening the horizons of Bible commentary. An important early contribution in this field was made by Saadiah Gaon (882-942), who translated the Bible into Arabic. Among the Jews of the Near East, Saadiah's translation, like the Aramaic Targum before it, came to be studied along with the Hebrew original of each weekly portion. A major impetus for Saadiah Gaon's exegetical work, however, was the need to counter heretical views propagated by the KARAITES, who accepted only the literal meaning of the Torah and rejected the Oral Law. Karaism attacked "Rabbanite" authority and the traditional interpretations, as well as the legal system of the Talmud. Saadiah proved himself an able champion and defender of the rabbinic position; his linguistic and philosophical approach brought a new dimension to Jewish Bible commentary, influencing its course over the next three centuries, when most Jews lived in Arab lands from Persia to Spain.

Linguistic analysis in the interpretation of Scripture dates at least from the amoraic period. Thus, an ancient tradition is quoted by the Talmud (*Meg.* 10b) "that wherever *Va-yehi* ["Now it came to pass..."] appears in the Bible, some chapter of calamities begins." The new cultural challenges facing Spanish Jewry during its Golden Age produced a varied response, one being the use of grammatical tools and techniques for exegetical purposes. In the tenth century, for example, Menahem Ibn Saruk wrote a systematic Hebrew lexicon of the Bible and Judah ben David Ḫayyun's commentary on some biblical books paid great attention to matters of language. Jonah Ibn Janaḫ had no hesitation in declaring that "Scripture can only be understood with the aid of philology."

The philosopher, poet, and grammarian, Abraham IBN EZRA, wrote a brilliant and incisive exposition of many biblical books, seeking to clarify the text and rejecting overfanciful Midrashic interpretations. His commentary is a mine of information in which many forerunners are quoted, either to support his own views or as "authorities" whose opinions should be discounted. Ibn Ezra particularly attacked the allegorizers, Karaites, and those who paid no heed to grammar. He adopted a commonsense approach to textual problems. Among his guarded critical suggestions was the conjecture that Joshua must have written the final verses of Deuteronomy and that the last 26 chapters of the Book of Isaiah were composed by a "second Isaiah" in Babylonia.

David KIMḪI, known by the acronym *Radak*, was a grammarian as well as an exegete. Most of his exegesis was devoted to the Prophets, although his commentary on Psalms became especially popular. Like Ibn Ezra, he quotes a wide range of sources. presenting a wealth of knowledge in an even more lucid style. While concentrating on the "plain" meaning of a text, however, Kimḫi did not neglect Midrashic sources. He also displays much originality, suggesting (for example) that Jephthah's daughter may not in fact have been sacrificed but condemned to remain unmarried (cf. Judg. 11:31, 37-39). There are likewise periodical references to contemporary events, such as the Crusades, and anti-Christian polemics. Kimḫi's exegetical works on the Prophets were destined to appear in print even before the original Hebrew texts; through translation into Latin, they had a major impact on Christian Bible scholarship, helping to shape the English *Authorized Version* of 1611.

In the philosophical and halakhic works of MAIMONIDES (*Rambam*), Judeo-Spanish learning and culture reached an unexcelled high point. Maimonides was not a Bible commentator in the sense of writing a continuous, verse-by-verse exposition of biblical texts, but in his major works — especially in his *Guide for the Perplexed* — he often explained difficult Scriptural terms and passages. Because of his rationalism and his inclination to treat biblical episodes allegorically, Maimonides was subjected to widespread criticism. Such attacks were one element in the anti-Maimonidean polemic that lasted for centuries. An even more decided rationalist was LEVI BEN GERSHOM (Gersonides or *Ralbag*), the 14th-century Provençal philosopher, mathematician, and exegete, whose commentary on the Pentateuch was especially voluminous and controversial.

The opposing trend found an early exponent in JUDAH HALEVI. In his philosophical treatise, the *Kuzari*, one can detect a protest against all rationalization of Scripture. Intent on defending Judaism as well as expounding it, Judah Halevi scorned efforts to twist the literal meaning, adopting an approach to the Bible that was both mystically fundamentalist and intensely nationalistic. A century or more later, NAḪMANIDES (*Ramban*) also refused to accept the human intellect as a capable arbiter of biblical issues. "The whole Pentateuch, from the beginning of Genesis to the last phrase in Deuteronomy, was communicated by God directly to Moses," he insists at the very start of his major commentary on the Pentateuch. While endeavoring to mediate between the two opposing sides in the Maimonidean controversy, Naḫmanides was a pioneer of the mystical interpretation of Scripture. Almost as popular was the commentary of BAḪYA BEN ASHER, which was based on the fourfold expository method of *Pardes* (see above).

Mystical exegesis attained its zenith in the ZOHAR

שמות א

א ואלה שמות בני ישראל הבאים מצרימה את יעקב איש וביתו באו: ב ראובן שמעון לוי ויהודה: ג יששכר זבולן ובנימן: ד דן ונפתלי גד ואשר: ה ויהי כל נפש יצאי ירך יעקב שבעים נפש ויוסף היה במצרים: ו וימת יוסף וכל אחיו וכל הדור ההוא: ז ובני ישראל פרו וישרצו וירבו ויעצמו במאד מאד ותמלא הארץ אתם: פ ח ויקם מלך חדש על מצרים אשר לא ידע את יוסף: ט ויאמר אל עמו הנה עם בני ישראל רב ועצום ממנו:

1. THE TORAH. The passage shown is the commencement of the book of Exodus.

2. TARGUM. The **Targum** is a translation into Aramaic. (The word "Targum" means "translation"). It was made at approximately the end of the 1st Century. The **Targum** of the **Torah** is traditionally attributed to Onkelos, a proselyte to Judaism. It is a fairly literal translation but occasionally contains interpretations.

3. RASHI. Commentary of **Rabbi Shlomo Yitzchaki** (1040-1105). He lived and taught in Troyes, (France). His commentary contains explanations derived from the Talmud and Midrash and often he translates difficult Hebrew words into Mediaeval French.

4. RAMBAN. Commentary of **Rabbi Moshe ben Nachmon Gerondi** (1194-1270) also known as Nachmonides. He was a Spanish Talmudical scholar and physician. A great Talmudist, he was sympathetic towards **Cabalah** (Jewish mysticism).

In 1263, he participated in a public disputation before the King of Aragon. It lasted four days and, although the king sided with him, he was banished. He eventually settled in Palestine.

5. IBN EZRA. Avraham ben Meir (1093-1167) was a poet as well as commentator. Born in Spain, where he lived for a great deal of his life, he travelled in North Africa, Palestine, Persia, Italy

ical, philosophical and scientific, were written in Hebrew.

6. COMMENTARY ON IBN EZRA. The Commentary of **Ibn Ezra** itself presents various difficulties. This "Commentary" on Ibn Ezra's work was written by **Rabbi Shlomo Zalman Netter** in an attempt to render Ibn Ezra more understandable.

7. SFORNO. Obadia Sforno (1475-1550) lived in Italy. He too was a physician by calling. His commentary is largely devoted to a literal explanation of the text.

8. RASHBAM. Rabbi Shmuel ben Meir (1085-1174) was a grandson of the famous Rashi, and also lived in France. In his commentary, he is concerned with the simple meaning of the text. In addition to his commentary on the **Torah,** he also wrote a commentary on most of the "Prophets", ("Neviim").

9. MASSORAH. These are notes and rules concerning the actual text of the Torah. They are concerned with the writing, spacing and paragraphing of the text of a **Sefer Torah.** Observations are also made on the correct vowels of the text. The purpose is to ensure the accuracy and uniformity of text.

The Scholars responsible for the **"Massorah"** are referred to as **"Massoretes".** They lived from about the 6th to the 10th Centuries and their work was done mainly in Tiberias.

A page from Numbers with commentaries, in Hebrew. On either side are explanatory notes and biographies of the commentators, in English. From an educational brochure of the Jewish National Fund, printed in London in the 1930s.

(c.1300). Essentially a kabbalistic Midrash, purporting to have been written by SIMEON BAR YOḤAI, the Zohar is a prolix commentary of parts of the Bible which exerted a vast influence on successive movements in and out of Judaism. A parallel development in the German Jewish medieval world was the type of exegesis cultivated by ELEAZAR BEN JUDAH OF WORMS and other leading figures, whose ascetic and mystical group came to be known as the ḤASIDÉ ASHKENAZ ("German Pietists").

The greatest and most influential Jewish Bible scholar came from that same Ashkenazi environment. R. Solomon ben Isaac of Troyes, better known as RASHI (1040-1135), lived in a Christian world of ignorance and bigotry under the shadow of the First Crusade. His mastery of talmudic and Midrashic sources, his insistence that "a passage should be explained according to its context," his succinct and lucid style, made the Hebrew Bible an open book to laymen and children, earning Rashi the title of *Parshandata* — "Prince of Jewish Commentators," the interpreter *par excellence*. His method was that of a running commentary, seeking to give the plain, unembellished meaning. Logical and concise, he nevertheless introduced Midrashic explanations selectively, also paying attention to Hebrew grammar and citing equivalents in the Old French vernacular of his day to explain difficult terms. Rashi's commentaries enjoyed an unequaled popularity, influencing Kimḥi and other Jewish exegetes; among Jews they still remain the most important Bible commentary. His Pentateuch commentary was the first Hebrew book to be printed (1475) and, through Latin translation, his work had a notable impact on Luther's German Bible (1534).

Another French talmudist, SAMUEL BEN MEIR (*Rashbam*), the grandson of Rashi, laid even greater stress on the plain meaning of a text in his own commentary on the Pentateuch. This literal and rational approach was the hallmark of Rashi's school in 12th-century France, also typifying the commentary of Joseph Bekhor Shor.

The mystical tendency which became dominant in Spain from the late 13th century onward, led to a general deterioration of exegetical scholarship among the Jews. Only one further figure stood out in Spain — Isaac ABRAVANEL, the last great Jewish Bible commentator of the Middle Ages. Known chiefly in his time as a statesman and philosopher, Abravanel seems to have utilized lectures and talks that he delivered as the basis for his Scriptural commentaries, and this would account for their long-winded, repetitious style. Yet there are many virtues and original features in his commentary, which makes judicious use of the homiletical Midrash and shuns the Kabbalah. Abravanel's approach is a rational one; he prefaces each biblical book expounded with an enlightening introduction, raising and then discussing textual problems. He was the first Jewish commentator who made sociopolitical factors one key to an understanding of the Bible. A generation later, in Italy, Obadiah SFORNO produced a commentary on the Pentateuch that was notable for its insight, scholarship, and rejection of mystical interpretations.

Once the ghetto system had been imposed on European Jewish communities from around the mid-16th century, Ashkenazi life became introverted and Bible commentary among the Jews underwent 200 years of stagnation. In Eastern Europe, the main concentration was on the Talmud and Bible study was secondary. At the end of this period, a new type of running commentary on the Prophets and Writings was begun by David Altschuler, a Galician (Polish) exegete, whose son eventually completed it. One portion, entitled *Metsudat Tsiyyon* ("Citadel of Zion"), explains words in the text; *Metsudat David* ("Citadel of David"), the other portion, is devoted to explaining the text itself. Like the commentaries of Rashi, Ibn Ezra, Kimẖi, Rashbam, Ralbag, Naẖmanides, and Sforno, these *Metsudot* always appear in the standard printed editions of the Rabbinic Bible (or *Mikra'ot Gedolot*).

As liberal Christians in Central and Western Europe began supporting the campaign for Jewish EMANCIPATION in the 18th century, Moses MENDELSSOHN also strove to break down the ghetto walls from within, attacking the continued use of a Yiddish "jargon" which he derided, calling upon Jews to speak German instead, and deploring their almost exclusive preoccupation with the Talmud. To promote a true understanding and appreciation of the Hebrew Bible, first among the young and later among adults as well, Mendelssohn set to work on a German translation of the Pentateuch which he had printed in Hebrew characters (then more familiar to most Jews). With the initial assistance of Solomon Dubno and later of Hartwig (Naphtali Herz) Wessely, he added a commentary in Hebrew known as the "*Biur*" (Heb. *be'ur*, "explanation"); its educational impact on German Jewry was enormous, although Ezekiel LANDAU and some other Orthodox rabbis of the time banned the use of this dangerously "modern" commentary.

A direct outcome of Mendelssohn's activities proved to be the HASKALAH or Jewish Enlightenment movement, which

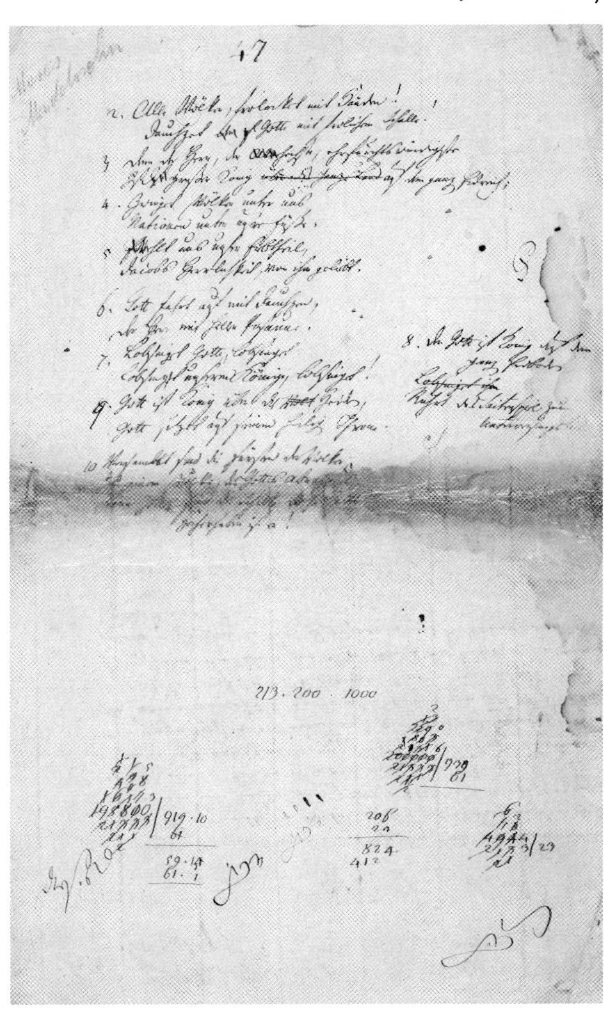

Draft of a translation into German of Psalm 47 in the handwriting of Moses Mendelssohn, whose aim was to promote an understanding of the Bible among German Jewry.

spread from Central to Eastern Europe. *Haskalah* ideas were likewise responsible for the emergence in 1819 of the "Science of Judaism" (WISSENSCHAFT DES JUDENTUMS), which brought Jews to study the Bible using the tools of modern science and rationalism.

Meanwhile, there had been a revival of Jewish Bible scholarship in other parts of Europe. Thus, Samuel David Luzzatto (*Shadal*; 1800-1865), a traditionally minded Italian rabbi and philosopher, helped to promote the study and use of Hebrew while publishing a valuable commentary on the Pentateuch and other biblical books, together with a modern Italian translation. Marked by a reliance on PILPUL (talmudic hairsplitting) as well as by an anachronistic reading of halakhic rules into Scripture, the Bible commentary of Meir Leib MALBIM became especially popular among the Orthodox masses. Malbim set out to demonstrate the essential unity of the Written and the Oral Law.

A modern Orthodox approach to the Bible was evinced by Samson Raphael HIRSCH, who wrote a German commentary to accompany his German translations of the Pentateuch and the Book of Psalms.

Non-Orthodox Jewish scholars were influenced by the Christian schools of Bible scholarship emerging in the 19th century and used the same tools of textual and "higher" criticism. From the mid-20th century, Jewish Bible scholarship (and to some extent general Bible scholarship) became less extreme and returned to more conservative attitudes, under the impact of the greater understanding which derived from a deeper knowledge of the languages, legal systems, religion, and life of the ancient Near Eastern peoples and from the findings of archeology. A prominent role in this new scholarship was taken by scholars at Jerusalem's Hebrew University, including Umberto Cassuto, Moses Hirsch Segal, and Yeḫezkel Kaufman.

BIGAMY See MONOGAMY AND POLYGAMY

BIKKURIM See FIRST FRUITS

BIKKURIM ("First Fruits"). Last tractate of Order ZERA'IM in the Mishnah. Its three chapters deal with the laws governing the FIRST FRUITS of Erets Israel, which in Temple times the farmer had to bring to Jerusalem (cf. Ex. 23:19, 34:26; Deut. 26:1-11). This offering was limited to the SEVEN SPECIES that grow abundantly in the Land of Israel. The Mishnah discusses who is obligated to bring the first fruits, the declaration made upon offering them, the differences between first fruits and other kinds of TITHE, and the colorful processions that took place all over the country when people went up to Jerusalem with their offerings. *Androginos*, a fourth chapter later added to this tractate, deals with some of the legal problems faced by a hermaphrodite in regard to ritual impurity, marriage, and tithes. The subject matter is amplified in the Jerusalem Talmud and the *Tosefta*.

BIKKUR ḪOLIM See SICK, VISITING THE

BIMAH ("rostrum"). An elevated platform with a reader's desk or table from which the READING OF THE LAW and other liturgical functions are conducted in the SYNAGOGUE. Among Ashkenazim, it is known also as the *almemar* (Arabic *al-minbar*, "pulpit" of a mosque) and among Sephardim as the *tevah*, (Heb. "chest" or "box"). Maimonides (*Yad, Tefillah* 11.3) observes that "the *bimah* is erected in the middle [of the synagogue] so that congregants may ascend to read from the Torah and so that those delivering [sermons of] reproof may be heard by all." When the case that contains the Torah scroll (in accordance with Sephardi custom) is set down, it is placed at the center [of the *bimah*], its rear facing the Ark and its front (the side which opens) facing the congregation.

Reading the Torah publicly from a raised structure dates at least from the period of Ezra and Nehemiah (Neh. 8:2-4). The Mishnah (*Sot.* 7.8) refers to the use of such a platform in Second Temple times, and the Talmud (*Suk.* 51b) speaks of a wooden platform being located in the middle of Alexandria's Great Synagogue.

From medieval times, the reader's platform was the focus of activity in Ashkenazi synagogues. It was placed in the center of the building, so that the reader and preacher might be heard by all the congregation. However, this central positioning was not seen as obligatory, and in Spain and Italy the *bimah* was often placed at the far end of the synagogue, against the western wall. The relation between the ARK and the platform became a major architectural consideration in synagogue design, evoking an artistic balance. The most

From left to right: Summer bimah *outside the ancient synagogue of Aleppo, Syria; decorated wood* bimah *in the center of the synagogue (now destroyed) of Zelwa, Poland; raised* bimah, *opposite the Ark, in the Sephardi synagogue of Pesaro, Italy.*

striking emphasis on the platform was achieved in East European synagogues, where four large pillars which supported the roof occupied the center of the building, with the reader's platform between them. In some of the oldest Ashkenazi synagogues, the *bimah* was enclosed within a cage-like structure of wrought iron. In medieval Spain, it was raised on columns high above the worshipers (like the pulpit of a church or mosque), and access was by way of a flight of stairs; the SCROLLS OF THE LAW were placed on the surrounding ledge while portions of the Torah were being read. Customs differed as to whether congregants sat between the platform and the Ark or left this space open. In Muslim lands, the *tevah* was usually in the center, with the congregation sitting around, but in Yemen it was placed close to the Ark and rested on four wooden pillars.

In the 19th century, REFORM JUDAISM moved the *bimah* forward, combining it with the area in front of the Ark and eliminating a separate structure. While halakhic statements could be found to demonstrate that the platform's exact location was a matter of CUSTOM and not law, Orthodox leaders bitterly opposed the innovation. Any break with established tradition was seen as evidence of the Reform movement's assimilationist policies, and a declaration signed by 100 Orthodox rabbis prohibited worship in any synagogue where the *bimah* was not located in the center. However, even some modern Orthodox synagogues eventually modified their design in this way, as a space-saving device, and both Reform and almost all Conservative congregations now place the *bimah* next to the Ark.

In Sephardi synagogues, the *ḥazzan* (reader) usually conducts all of the service from a central reading desk, and his duties are referred to as "passing before the *tevah*" (cf. *Ber.* 5.3). In strictly Orthodox Ashkenazi congregations, much of the service (apart from the Reading of the Law) is conducted from a reader's lectern or *ammud* placed next to or immediately in front of the Ark, hence the expression "to pray [Yiddish DAVNEN] before the *ammud*."

BINDING OF ISAAC See AKEDAH

BIRKAT HA-MAZON See GRACE AFTER MEALS

BIRKAT HA-MINIM ("Benediction against Heretics"). Prayer dating from the Hellenistic era which constitutes the 12th benediction of the weekday AMIDAH. A talmudic reference to the prayer as a "benediction against SADDUCEES" composed at the instigation of R. Gamaliel II (*Ber.* 28b) has led to the widespread and mistaken belief that it was first written some time after 70 CE, and that it was a later addition to the 18 blessings of the daily *Shemoneh Esreh (Amidah)*. More probably, however, it originated among the ḤASIDIM RISHONIM in the second century BCE, during the Maccabean struggle against Jewish traitors who collaborated with the Syrian oppressor (see ḤANUKKAH). New historical circumstances led to various modifications of the text, especially after the Second Temple's destruction, when informers worked for the Roman authorities (*Shab.* 33b), sectarian propaganda increased (*Meg.* 17b), and Judaism's very survival was in question. To expose and isolate dangerous elements within the Jewish camp, R. Samuel ha-Katan then enlarged and adapted the existing petition, directing it against Nazarenes (Judeo-Christians), apostates, slanderers, and other contemporary instigators of Roman persecution (*Tosef. Ber.* 3.25). Though tolerated as a minor sect prior to the rebellion against Rome (68-70 CE), the Judeo-Christians had interpreted those calamitous events as Divine retribution, thereby antagonizing even the most liberal rabbinic opinion.

In its revised form, the *Birkat ha-Minim* was a malediction which no sectarians (MINIM) could recite aloud in synagogue and to which they could not possibly respond *amen*. It thus effectively barred them from public worship and severed their ties with the Jewish people. The text most probably read as follows: "For apostates who have rejected Your Torah let there be no hope, and may the Nazarenes and heretics perish in an instant. Let all the enemies of Your people, the House of Israel, be speedily cut down; and may You swiftly uproot, shatter, destroy, subdue, and humiliate the kingdom of arrogance, speedily in our days! Blessed are You, O Lord, who shatters His enemies and humbles the arrogant."

After the immediate danger had passed, further textual changes were made to take account of later religious developments and historical realities. However, the Jews of medieval France and England still preserved much of the original wording in their ritual until the 13th century at least (see Jacob ben Judah of London, *Ets Ḥayyim*, Vol. 1, ed. Israel Brodie, p. 90). Key phrases also survive in the Yemenite prayer book and, to a lesser extent, in the Sephardi rite. Though never meant to impugn the adherents of other faiths, this malediction was denounced as an attack on Christianity: Abner of Burgos (Alfonso de Valladolid), a 14th-century Spanish apostate, had it removed from the *Amidah* and Christian censors elsewhere demanded various modifications in the text. Such pressures within the Ashkenazi world have resulted in the substitution of "slanderers" (*malshinim*) for "apostates" (*meshummadim*) and of "wickedness" for "heretics" (*minim*); a neutral term, "the arrogant" (*zedim*), often replaces "the kingdom of arrogance" (*malkhut zadon*), which originally stood for Rome; and "Your enemies" sometimes replaces "the enemies of Your people." Reform prayer books, from the mid-19th century onward, tended to omit or modify this petition.

BIRTH "Be fruitful and multiply" (Gen. 1:28) is regarded as the first commandment in the Bible. However, man's first recorded act of disobedience, eating from the Tree of Knowledge, led to a curse being imposed on Eve and her female descendants that they would suffer the pain of childbirth (Gen. 1:16). In biblical times, a woman gave birth in a kneeling position (I Sam. 4:19) or while sitting on a special birthstool (Ex. 16). Midwives were highly esteemed (Ex. 1:17-21). Ezekiel offers an image of a child who is rejected at birth (a prevalent heathen custom), but his description vividly indicates the customary procedure: "When you were born your navel cord was not cut, and you were not bathed in water to soothe you; you were not rubbed with salt, nor were you swaddled" (Ezek. 16:4-5; the use of salt may have been a protection against the EVIL EYE). A woman with many children was regarded as blessed, but BARRENNESS was a curse.

The Pentateuch (Lev.12) imposes certain laws of ritual PURITY AND IMPURITY on the new mother. After giving birth to a male child, she was considered to be ritually impure for seven days. Thereafter, for the next 33 days, she might not enter the precincts of the Temple or handle sacred objects. For the mother of a newborn girl, the number of days was 14 and 66 respectively. In Temple times, when the mother's prescribed "days of purification" had ended, she had to bring a burnt-offering and a sin-offering. Nowadays, however, a woman who has just given birth observes the usual laws of NIDDAH, including immersion in a ritual bath once she is "clean."

Should a woman in childbirth be in mortal danger, Jewish law decrees that her life takes precedence over that of the unborn infant and, if necessary, it is sacrificed to save the mother's life. Once most of the child's body has emerged from the birth canal, however, it is considered to be alive, and the mother's life no longer takes precedence (*Ohol.* 7.6). The modern trend to have the father present at childbirth has been discussed in halakhic literature, which forbids the practice.

In accordance with the general concept of PIKKU'AḤ NEFESH ("danger to life"), the violation of Sabbath laws is not only permitted but demanded by the rabbis in order to save an unborn child. All necessary measures may therefore be taken on the Sabbath in connection with childbirth (*Shab.* 18.3), as laid down subsequently by Maimonides and the *Shulḥan Arukh.* For the first three days after the child's birth, the mother has the status of a person who is in mortal danger; the Sabbath may be violated on her behalf, even if she declares such an action unnecessary, provided that a doctor, a nurse, or even someone moderately knowledgeable in medicine deems the action necessary. During the next four days, the woman is still considered to be in grave danger, but her assurance that certain actions need not be taken in violation of the Sabbath has precedence over the opinion of experts. Over the following 23 days, the new mother is considered to be ill, but not sick enough to be in mortal danger, and only rabbinic (not biblical) decrees may be violated on her behalf on the Sabbath. A non-Jew, however, may perform any action thought necessary for the new mother, including one forbidden by Torah law. Even at this last stage, should serious complications arise, the woman is again considered to be in mortal danger and she must be treated accordingly.

The rabbis followed the Greek scientists in believing that a seven-month-old fetus would survive, and that an eight-month-old would not. The Mishnah (*Bekh.* 8.2) refers to cesarean births, declaring that any FIRST-BORN child delivered in this way does not have the rights or duties of the first-born (nor does any child born subsequently to that mother).

Much folklore and superstition — often of non-Jewish origin — accompanied Jewish birth customs. AMULETS and talismans were placed above the bed of an expectant mother. After the birth, family and friends would gather nightly to say prayers designed to ward off evil spirits, especially LILITH, the female demon who supposedly tries to kill all newborn children.

Among German Jews, it was often the custom for parents of a newborn son to cut a strip from the swaddling cloth in which the infant was wrapped in at the time of his circumcision. It was then embroidred with the name of the child and with good wishes for his future. This cloth, known as a *wimple*, was kept until the boy's *bar mitsvah.* He would use it then for tying the Scroll of the Law and then donate it to the synagogue.

From the Middle Ages onward, Ashkenazi mothers made it a practice to visit the synagogue after their recovery from childbirth and to recite the GOMEL blessing or other prayers

Torah binders made from strips of the swaddling cloth used at the circumcision of a child, embroidered later with good wishes for the future of the infant. Germany, 19th century.

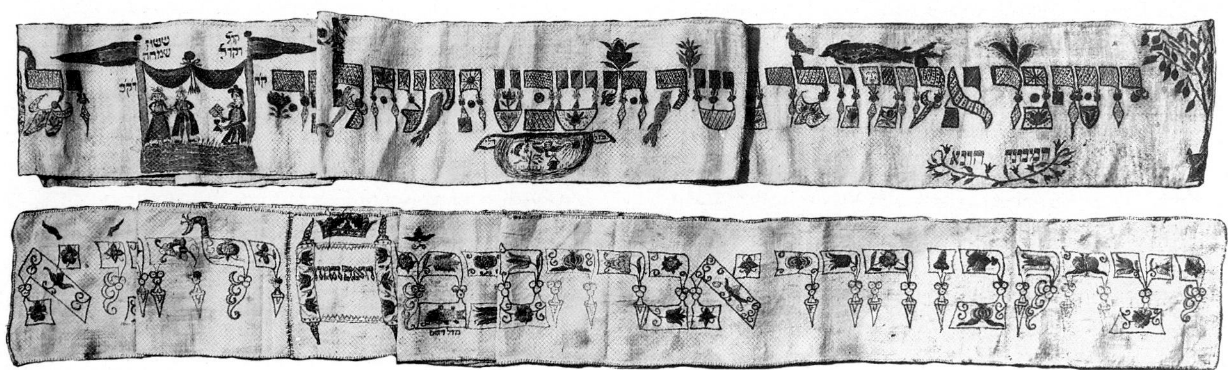

on that occasion. It is also customary for a MI SHE-BERAKH to be recited for the welfare of mother and child.

BIRTH CONTROL The duty to produce offspring is frequently referred to as the first commandment in the Bible, as Adam was commanded "Be fruitful and multiply" (Gen. 1:28). The use of any measure to prevent conception is problematic from the standpoint of Jewish law, as it involves abstaining from a biblical duty. Furthermore, some methods of birth control result in explicitly prohibited acts. The proscription of anatomical methods of sterilization such as vasectomy and tubal ligation is derived from Lev. 22:24. Methods which interfere with a proper seminal emission, such as coitus interruptus, are condemned as "acts of Er and Onan."

In line with this halakhic attitude toward birth control, elective contraception is not permitted. However, the permissible use of some forms of birth control in various mitigating circumstances is discussed at length in the Talmud and responsa literature. Legitimate reasons for contraception usually involve the medical welfare of the woman or of the potential fetus in question. The Talmud discusses three categories of women who may (or must, according to some authorities) use a contraceptive device: a minor below the age of 12 (who was allowed to marry at that time), a pregnant woman, and a nursing mother (*Ket.* 39a).

There are many differences of opinion on the subject of contraception among the later rabbis. When contraception is permitted, the rabbis tend to approve methods which least interfere with the natural sex act. Contraceptives used by women (e.g., diaphragm, IUD) are preferred to the male contraceptive (condom), since the sages rule that women are exempt from the commandment to "be fruitful and multiply." Oral contraceptives are in principle the most acceptable, as they do not interfere artificially with the movement of the sperm, although caution must be exercised lest they upset the menstrual cycle.

BITTER HERBS See MAROR

BITTUL HA-TAMID ("cancellation of the daily offering"). Ashkenazi practice, rooted in the Middle Ages, whereby anyone seeking redress of a grievance might interrupt services in the synagogue in order to focus public attention on the matter. This custom was also (and more generally) known as *ikkuv ha-tefillah* ("delaying prayers") or *ikkuv ha-keri'ah* ("halting the [Torah] reading"). It often involved some moral or judicial wrong committed by a private individual, but no less frequently allowed for the voicing of a protest against high-handed action by the Jewish communal authorities. Women, as well as men, were entitled to this unusual privilege and could thus gain public sympathy and support by dramatizing their plight. Some medieval regulations endeavored to limit the practice, but safeguards were devised for the protection of widows and orphans. During the 19th century, most attempts to invoke this right occurred in tsarist Russia. As a result of Nicholas I's Recruitment Statute (1827), hardhearted communal leaders employed special *khappers* ("snatchers") to kidnap unwary Jewish boys for a 25-year period of service in the army. Desperate mothers would then resort to *ikkuv ha-tefillah* in the hope of releasing their children; some prominent rabbis shamed the offending lay leaders in public and freed the under-age "recruits." All too often, however, this form of religious disruption was so overworked as to prove ineffectual. Though still occasionally invoked among pious Jews, the custom has largely fallen into disuse.

BI'UR ḤAMETS See LEAVEN, SEARCH FOR

BLASPHEMY (Heb. *gidduf, ḥeruf*). Any utterance showing contempt for God or profaning the Divine Name. The Third Commandment (Ex. 20:7, Deut. 5:11) explicitly forbids "taking the Lord's Name in vain" and biblical law, which made it an offense to "revile God" (Ex. 22:27), inflicted the penalty of death by stoning on one who had "cursed" and "blasphemed" in this way (Lev. 24:10-16, 23). Coupled with the prohibition of blasphemy was the admonition not to curse a legitimate ruler of Israel (Ex. 22:27). The rabbis made the prohibition of blasphemy incumbent on all mankind as one of the NOACHIDE LAWS. By Mishnaic times, only a flagrant profanation of the Tetragrammaton — God's "ineffable Name" — incurred the death penalty (*San.* 7.5). A person guilty of a profane utterance involving any other Divine Name was sentenced to flogging (*San.* 56a). The rule demanding two witnesses of the crime often rendered proof of the offense difficult. Consideration was also shown for the repentant blasphemer. As biblical sources already indicate (II Kings 18:37-19:2; Isa. 36:22-37:2), the solemn RENDING OF GARMENTS became a practice observed by anyone who heard God's Name desecrated in public (*San.* 60a). With the decline of Jewish legal autonomy, the original punishment for blasphemy was commuted to *ḥerem* (EXCOMMUNICATION). See also BLESSING AND CURSING; ḤILLUL HA-SHEM.

BLESSING AND CURSING The original meaning of the Hebrew word for "blessing" (*berakhah*) was "gift" or "homage." This explains the Bible's frequent references to man "blessing" God. Man gives God his thanks, praise, and adoration, and in return receives from God His blessing in the form of both physical and spiritual well-being. In addition, the ancients believed in the power of the spoken word to fulfill itself, whether for good (as a blessing) or for evil (as a curse). Blessing or cursing in ancient Israelite culture were significantly different, however, from what obtained in other ancient Middle Eastern cultures. In the latter, it was the inherent, automatic power of the word to affect reality; in the Bible, God's will alone determines the good and the evil. Blessing and cursing are therefore always in the name of God, either explicitly or implicitly.

The first blessing mentioned in the Bible is that conferred by God on the creatures of the sea and the air: "Be fertile and increase" (Gen. 1:22). A similar but more elaborate blessing is bestowed on the man and the woman (Gen. 1:28). Particularly noteworthy is God's blessing of the seventh day of creation and declaring it holy (Gen. 2:3). The first curse in the Bible is God's anathema of the serpent for having enticed Eve to eat of the fruit of the Tree of Knowledge (Gen. 3:14).

One of the specific meanings of Divine blessing, as evidenced by the verses cited above as well as in many other passages (e.g., Gen. 9:1, 17:16), is fruitfulness. The fertility of the earth, increased by rain, is thus implied: "Will I not then open the windows of heaven and pour you out a blessing that there shall be more than enough?" (Mal.3:10). Divine blessing can spell not only material abundance but also spiritual well-being, as implied in God's blessing of Abraham: "All the families of the earth shall bless themselves by you" (Gen. 12:2).

The Bible contains many references to a father blessing his sons and grandsons before his death, and of friends blessing each other on meeting or parting. Examples of the former are Isaac's blessing of Jacob and Esau (Gen. 27:27-29, 39-40) and Jacob's blessing of his grandsons (Gen. 48:8 ff.; 49:25-26). Moses likewise blessed the people on a number of occasions (Ex. 29:43; Deut. 33), while the priest Eli blessed Elkanah and his wife, Hannah, in the name of God (I Sam. 2:20). The traditional response to a friend's greeting is "The Lord bless you!" (Ruth 2:4).

Blessings are pronounced on the people by priests, kings, prophets, and leaders. On the last day of the Sanctuary's inauguration, Aaron blessed the people with uplifted hands (Lev. 9:22) and a threefold formula known as the PRIESTLY BLESSING is given in Num. 6:22-26. This blessing is pronounced to this day in traditional synagogues by the *kohanim*, worshipers of priestly descent. At the dedication of the First Temple, King Solomon (I Kings 8:14, 54-55) blessed "the whole congregation of Israel"; and it was the prophet Samuel's custom to bless the sacrifice brought by the people before they partook of it (I Sam. 9:13).

In the ancient Near East, it was common practice to append a series of blessings and curses, in the name of a god or gods, to the end of a collection of laws. The blessings were intended for those who maintained the laws and the curses for those who violated them. Similarly, the Pentateuch gives a series of blessings and curses following the laws of Leviticus (26:3-46) and Deuteronomy (chapter 28). The maledictory portions of these are known as the TOKHEḤAH ("chastisement").

Like blessings, curses are invoked in the name of God, either explicitly or implicitly. The curse (Heb. *kelalah*) may be pronounced for some past misdeed, as on Cain after his slaying of Abel (Gen. 4:11-12), or it may be uttered conditionally, as when Joshua curses anyone attempting to rebuild the destroyed city of Jericho (Josh. 6:26; cf. Judg. 21:18). Particularly ferocious was the malediction to "blot out the memory of Amalek from under heaven" (Ex. 17:14, Deut. 25:19; see below). A dramatic ceremony, whereby a series of curses is invoked against anyone performing certain forbidden acts, is described in Deut. 27:11-26. Six tribes were to be stationed on Mount GERIZIM for a series of blessings, and six tribes on Mount Ebal to hear and respond AMEN to the curses pronounced by the Levites. Apart from these collective blessings and curses, a number of curses are also directed against individuals and their families — the curse pronounced by Joshua on Achan (Josh. 7:25), for example, and the Divine curse on the house of Eli uttered by a prophet (I Sam. 2:31-34).

The seriousness with which a curse was taken can be seen from an episode in the life of King David, who was roundly cursed — as a man guilty of shedding innocent blood — by Shimei, son of Gera, a member of King Saul's family (II Sam. 16:5-8). On his deathbed, David commanded Solomon, his successor, to bring Shimei's "gray head down to the grave in blood" (I Kings 2:9). It was taken for granted that a curse spoken in the name of God was bound to be fulfilled unless it was nullified by a blessing. When hiring Balaam to put a curse on the people of Israel, Balak, the king of Moab, said: "For I know that he whom you bless is blessed indeed, and he whom you curse is cursed" (Num. 22:6). In the sequel, it is only through God's intervention that Balaam pronounces blessings on Israel rather than curses.

Something similar occurs elsewhere, in episodes concerning two individuals. Jacob, fearing that his deception of Isaac will bring down on him a curse rather than a blessing, is reassured when Rebekah declares that, in such an event, she will take the curse upon herself (Gen. 27:13). An even more direct nullification of a curse by a blessing occurs in the story of Micah, a pious Ephraimite. His mother discovered that 1100 silver shekels had been taken from her, whereupon she cursed the person who had stolen them. When Micah admitted that he had taken the money, she hastened to say "Blessed be my son of the Lord" (Judg. 17:1-2), thus nullifying the curse she had pronounced.

The consuming power of a malediction to destroy an evildoer is graphically described (Zech. 5:3-4) as "the curse which goes out over the whole land... and shall enter the house of the thief... and consume it down to the last timber and stones." This helps explain why, in biblical law, cursing God or the king, a national leader, or one's parents is a crime punishable by death (Ex. 22:27 and 21:17; Lev. 20:9, 24:23). For further information, see BLASPHEMY.

In the talmudic period, blessings giving thanks to God were standardized and categorized (see BENEDICTIONS). The performance of every commandment (MITSVAH) has to be preceded by the appropriate blessing, and just as a benediction is pronounced on receiving good news, so one must also be pronounced on evil tidings (*Ber.* 9.2; *Pes.* 50a). That the biblical concept of the power of blessing and cursing persisted in the talmudic era may be seen from the following statements: "Never underestimate the blessings [or curses] of an ordinary person" (*Ber.* 7a; *Meg.* 15a); "A curse pronounced by a sage, even if groundless, is bound to be fulfilled" (*Ber.* 56a; *Mak.* 11a); and "Rather the curse of Ahijah the Shilonite than the blessing of Balaam the wicked!" (*Ta'an.* 20a).

Cursing was forbidden, unless religiously motivated, and the rabbinic maxim was "Let yourself be cursed, rather than curse [someone else]" (*San.* 49a). However, one expression that has remained current among Jews is *Yimmaḥ shemo* (*ve-zikhro*) — "May his name (and memory) be blotted out!" This phrase, stemming from the Bible (Ps. 109:13; cf. Deut. 29:19, etc.), is usually applied to such persecutors as Haman and Hitler.

BLESSING OF CHILDREN See PARENTAL BLESSING

BLOOD (Heb. *dam*). The vital fluid which, in biblical thought, is the seat of life itself, "for the life of the flesh is in the blood" (Lev. 17:11; cf. Deut. 12:23). This explains the repeated prohibition against consuming the blood of animals or birds (e.g., Lev. 3:17, 7:26, 17:13; Deut. 12:23-25), a law peculiar to Israel in the ancient world. On the basis of Gen. 9:4, this same prohibition was included among the seven NOACHIDE LAWS devolving upon all mankind and the penalty for infringing it was KARET, Divine punishment or "excision" (Lev. 7:27, 17:10-14). The blood of any sacrifice had to be poured out, dashed against the altar (Ex. 24:6, 29:21; Lev. 1:5), and in some instances either poured over the horns of the altar or at its base (Lev. 4:7). The last procedure was followed in the case of a guilt offering brought by a priest (Lev. 4:3-7). That priestly sacrifice was one that involved the sprinking of the blood seven times in front of the Sanctuary's curtain. At the investiture of Aaron and his sons, Moses took some of the consecrated animal's blood from the altar and dabbed it on the lobe of Aaron's right ear, on the thumb of his right hand, and on the big toe of his right foot, then did the same to Aaron's sons (Lev. 8:23-24). The blood of a slaughtered bird was likewise used in purification rites, e.g., that of a leper (Lev. 14:4-7). Non-Israelites were also subject to the general law when resident in the Land of Israel, the blood of any animal or fowl having to be poured out and covered with dust (Lev. 17:12-13; Deut. 12:16, 23-24).

Among the pagan Canaanites, blood was conceived as the food of the gods and as a potent magical element. It is in protest against the former concept that the psalmist voices God's declaration: "Do I eat the flesh of bulls, or drink the blood of he-goats?" (Ps. 50:13; cf. 16:4). This concept is elsewhere reflected in the wild behavior of Elijah's opponents, the prophets of BAAL, who gashed themselves with knives and spears until they were covered with blood (I Kings 18:28), a practice expressly forbidden by the Torah (Deut. 14:1).

In biblical sources, "blood" is often used as a metonym for MURDER. Thus, Abel's blood "cries out from the ground" (Gen. 4:10), homicides are "men of blood" (Ps. 5:7, 26:9, 59:3, etc.), and the criminal's blood "will be upon him" (Lev. 20:9 ff.; Josh. 2:19; Ezek. 18:13). Murdering a guiltless person is called "shedding innocent blood" (II Kings 24:4; Isa. 59:7; Jer. 22:17; Joel 4:19; Prov. 6:17), but God will surely avenge "the blood of His servants" (Deut. 32:43; Ps. 79:10). Blood is also the bond of solidarity uniting a man with his family or tribe, one that gave rise to the practice of avenging a slain kinsman (see BLOOD AVENGER). Unlike the pagan legal systems of antiquity, biblical law does not permit the acceptance of financial compensation for the deliberate taking of a human life (Num. 35:31-34). The shedding of innocent blood "defiles the land" and can only be expiated through the death of the murderer, in keeping with the injunction that "whoever sheds the blood of man, by man shall his blood be shed" (Gen. 9:6). Hence the ceremony of expiation for a murder committed by some person or persons unknown (Deut. 21:1-9), which concludes with the elders of the nearest town washing their hands in token of their innocence. To be finally absolved of bloodguilt, they make the following declaration: "Our hands did not shed this blood, nor did our eyes see it done. Absolve, O Lord, Your people Israel whom You redeemed, and do not let guilt for the blood of the innocent remain among Your people Israel."

Although some of these detailed regulations lapsed with the Temple's destruction, others (of biblical origin, but interpreted and codified by the sages) remain in force and have exerted a major impact on traditional Jewish life. One example is the rite of CIRCUMCISION, which involves a slight loss of blood, the child undergoing this operation being termed in the Bible *ḥatan damim*, "a bridegroom of blood" (Ex. 4:25-26). Even in the case of a child born circumcised, or of a proselyte to Judaism who has already been circumcised for health reasons, the officiating *mohel* allows a symbolic drop of blood to flow. The laws of FAMILY PURITY (based on Lev. 15:19 ff.) declare a woman ritually "unclean" and prohibit normal marital relations during the period of her menstrual flow (or any other discharge of blood from the womb) and for at least a week thereafter (see also NIDDAH).

A direct consequence of the biblical prohibition of blood may be seen in *kashrut* — the Jewish DIETARY LAWS. Apart from stipulating which domestic beasts and fowl are permitted, these laws authorize only SHEḤITAH as the method of slaughter, whereby pain is reduced to a minimum through the swift draining of lifeblood. Any residual blood is then drawn out by a process of soaking and salting, after which the *kasher* meat may be prepared for Jewish consumption. The animal's lifeblood must be covered with sand or earth at the time of slaughter, unless it is collected for use as fertilizer; and the dietary laws even prohibit the eating of an egg in which a blood spot is attached to the yolk.

Strict adherence to these regulations made even the thought of drinking blood abhorrent to the Jew. Pagan charges concerning the eucharist embarrassed the early Christians, who found themselves accused of consuming human flesh and blood. By a grim irony, such baseless accusations were later directed against the Jews of medieval Europe. Malicious preachers, ignorant rabble-rousers, and vindictive Jewish apostates exploited popular fear and superstition, alleging that the blood of a Christian child was an essential ingredient in certain Jewish rites. Furthermore, the periodical coincidence of Easter with Passover led to "ritual murder" charges that pursued Jews down the ages. It was thus alleged that Christian blood was used in the preparation of unleavened bread and wine for the Passover SEDER. Despite the efforts made by popes, emperors, and enlightened scholars to refute these lies, agitators down to the 20th century utilized the disappearance or unsolved murder of a Christian child for the propagation of miracle tales, the torture, execution, or wholesale massacre of innocent Jews, and the confiscation of their property.

BLOOD-AVENGER (or "blood redeemer"; Heb. *go'el ha-dam*). Kinsman required by ancient law to avenge bloodshed. The institution emerged in societies organized on the basis of tribes and clans. It provided that if a member of a clan or family was slain, direct kinsmen or fellow members of the clan were obliged to kill the slayer or, failing that, any member of the slayer's clan. According to the Bible, human blood shed by man requires expiation (Gen. 9:6). If the murder goes unavenged, restitution devolves upon the supreme avenger, God (Gen. 9:5; Deut. 32:43; II Kings 9:7). However, the prime burden and duty of revenge falls on the blood-avenger. The Bible includes several references to this practice, the earliest of which is Lamech's song (Gen. 4:23-24). Gideon slew Zebah and Zalmunna for killing his brothers (Judg. 8:18-21); Joab slew Abner for murdering his brother Asahel (II Sam. 3:27); and Absalom slew Amnon for having raped Tamar, Absalom's sister (II Sam. 13:28ff.). To this day, among Beduin Arabs, the rape and dishonor of a female must be avenged by a member of the raped woman's family, who takes it upon himself to kill the offender.

Aside from providing ASYLUM in cities of refuge for the involuntary manslayer, biblical legislation stipulates that justice be meted out to those guilty of premeditated murder by an established court and not by a blood-avenger. The Talmud (in tractate MAKKOT) endeavors to assimilate biblical ordinances regarding the blood-avenger with the normal judicial procedure against one guilty of murder.

BODY Judaism generally differentiates between the body and the soul. According to the Midrash, man is the link between the earthly — as represented by his body — and the Divine — as represented by his SOUL. Even though the body is sometimes described as the "outer garment" of the soul, it has its own intrinsic value. Man is considered to be the custodian of his own body, not its master, and mutilation of the body is accordingly forbidden by Jewish law. Operations are permitted only by virtue of the overall good resulting to the body. Thus, according to some authorities, plastic surgery for cosmetic reasons is prohibited, unless psychological factors necessitate such an operation. SUICIDE is also forbidden. After death, the body retains its sanctity, hence the opposition by numerous rabbis to AUTOPSY, except where such a step is of immediate life-saving benefit to others. Jewish law forbids CREMATION, even when this was the wish of the deceased; one has no right to his body after his death. This prohibition is also connected with the belief in physical RESURRECTION, which will not be possible if the body has been destroyed.

The body and soul are considered to be jointly responsible for the individual's sinning. To illustrate this point, the Talmud (*San.* 91a) brings a parable of a lame man who managed to steal fruit from a tree while being carried on the back of a blind man. Just as each man individually would be unable to perpetrate such a crime, so neither body nor soul could sin without the collaboration of the other. Unlike certain other systems, Judaism does not regard the body as base. Even the physical evacuation of waste matter justifies a blessing of thanks to God for having created the wondrous complexity of the human body. See also MEDICAL ETHICS.

BOOK OF LIFE (Heb. *Sefer ha-Ḥayyim*). Heavenly "ledger" containing the record of man's deeds and conduct throughout the year. Though found also in ancient Mesopotamian sources, this concept receives only one specific mention in the Hebrew Bible (Ps. 69:29), where the hope is expressed that evil men "may be erased from the Book of Life and not inscribed with the righteous." However, many indirect references to God's "ledger" or "record" can be found elsewhere in the Bible (e.g., Ex. 32:32-33; Mal. 3:16, Ps. 87:6; Dan. 12:1; and especially Isa. 4:3), in the Pseudepigrapha, and in early Christian sources (Rev. 3:5, 17:8, 20:12, etc.). The ethical force of this "Book of Life" (or "Book of the Living") concept was emphasized by the rabbis. JUDAH HA-NASI warned: "Know what is above you — an Eye that sees, an Ear that hears, and a Book in which all your deeds are recorded" (*Avot* 2.1), while AKIVA declared that "the ledger is open, the hand records..." (*ibid.*, 3.16), both of them implying that no one can escape the consequences of his actions and utterances. According to the Talmud (*RH* 16b), three separate ledgers are opened on the New Year, Rosh ha-Shanah: one for the thoroughly wicked, who are immediately condemned to death; a second for the wholly righteous, who are forthwith inscribed and sealed for life; and a third for "intermediate" or average people, whose fate is held in suspense until the Day of Atonement when it is sealed. This talmudic idea has reinforced the underlying message of the annual TEN DAYS OF PENITENCE and of the HIGH HOLIDAYS. The prayer "Inscribe us in the Book of Life" recurs throughout the liturgy of this penitential season (becoming "Seal us in the Book of Life" in the Concluding *Ne'ilah* Service on the Day of Atonement). Wishes for a "good inscription and sealing" are likewise expressed in the traditional GREETINGS for this period. A belief of kabbalistic origin holds that the Divine judgment is only finally sealed on HOSHANA RABBAH (consequently known as "the day of the great seal"). According to Ashkenazi folklore, slips of paper fall from heaven on that day bearing the record of everyone's fate, hence the traditional Ashkenazi greeting on Hoshana Rabbah: "A good seal" or "A good slip" (in Yiddish, *a gute kvitl*).

BREAD (Heb. *pat* or *leḇem*). In ancient Erets Israel, bread was man's "staff of life," the basic staple food. As such, it symbolized an entire meal or one's livelihood, and gave rise to many proverbial expressions. The MANNA was called "bread from heaven" (Ex. 16:4). In biblical times, bread was made from either wheat or barley flour; in the talmudic period, poorer folk made it from either spelt or pounded beans. It was used extensively as an accompaniment to various types of SACRIFICES AND OFFERINGS. In the ordination of AARON and his sons, the offering included "a flat loaf of bread" (Ex. 29:23). In the SANCTUARY, as well as in the TEMPLE, 12 loaves of SHOWBREAD were displayed on a table that stood before the ARK OF THE COVENANT.

Various methods of baking bread were used in the biblical period. The most common was to place the kneaded dough on the sides of an earthenware stove. If the dough was baked before it fermented, the result would be the flat unleavened bread (MATSAH) eaten on Passover. The task of baking bread fell to the wife (Gen. 18:6). In the process of baking, according to Jewish law, a piece of the dough is taken and thrown into the fire; originally this was a gift to the priest (Num. 15:20; see ḤALLAH). There are FIVE SPECIES of grain from which *ḥallah* must be taken: wheat, barley, rye, oats, and spelt.

In talmudic times, the practice began of reciting the *Ha-Motsi* benediction (*Ber.* 38a) prior to eating bread (see GRACE BEFORE MEALS). This benediction is preceded by a ritual washing of the hands (*Netilat Yadayim*; see ABLUTIONS). The blessing obviates the necessity to recite benedictions over other food eaten in the course of the meal with the exception of wine and fruit. Any meal that began with the benediction over bread must be followed by GRACE AFTER MEALS. The rabbis laid down that bread must be handled respectfully, never tossed from one person to another (*Ber.* 50b), and not mingled with other kitchen waste when it grows stale.

On the Sabbath, two loaves (*ḥallot*) baked of white flour are used for the benediction. These two loaves are reminiscent of the double portion of manna (*leḇem mishneh*) which the Israelites gathered in the wilderness on Fridays (Ex. 16:22). The two Sabbath loaves are baked in elliptical form and braided on top. Only one *ḥallah* is required for the benediction on festivals not coinciding with a Sabbath, and other symbolic shapes are given to the loaves on each particular festival. A special embroidered *ḥallah* cover is placed on the loaves, before the *Ha-Motsi* blessing is recited, on Sabbaths and festivals.

Clay figurine of a woman kneading dough. From the Phoenician cemetery in Achziv, Israel, dating to the 6th-4th century BCE.

BREASTPLATE See PRIESTLY GARMENTS

BRIBERY The giving of an illicit present to an official in order to influence him. The Bible forbids the taking of bribes, "for bribes blind the clear-sighted and upset the pleas of those who are in the right" (Ex. 23:8; see also Deut. 16:19). A curse is pronounced on one who takes bribes in a capital case (Deut. 27:25; cf. Ezek. 22:12), and God Himself is depicted as spurning bribes (Deut. 10:17).

Denunciations of bribery are found throughout the Prophets and the Hagiographa. "For I have noted how many are your crimes, and how countless your sins — you enemies of the righteous, you takers of bribes, you who subvert in the gate the cause of the needy" (Amos 5:12). Likewise, it is said of the sons of Samuel that rather than walk in the ways of their father, they took bribes and subverted justice (I Sam. 8:3).

The Talmud and the Midrash shared the biblical abhorrence of bribery. Judges were warned against taking bribes even for the purpose of acquitting the innocent or convicting the guilty (*Sif.* to Deut. 16:19; *Ket.* 105a). Because "bribes blind the clear-sighted," the Talmud concluded that a bribe-taking judge is liable to physically lose his sight (*Pe'ah* 8.9; *Ket.* 105a). Furthermore, it was held that judges must reject even subtle, non-monetary forms of bribery. Thus, the *amora* Samuel disqualified himself from judging the case of a man who had extended his hand to assist him in crossing a river. Even the taking of fees in equal amounts from both parties was allowed only in limited circumstances.

Jewish law regards the one who gives bribes as a transgressor, basing itself on Lev. 19:14: "You shall not... place a stumbling block before the blind" — i.e., one may not lead another to sin (Maim.,*Yad*, *San*. 23.2; *Sh.Ar. ḤM* 9).

BRIDEGROOMS OF THE LAW Titles awarded to the recipients of two special honors on the SIMḤAT TORAH festival (coinciding in Israel with SHEMINI ATSERET), when the annual reading of the Pentateuch is concluded and the cycle begins anew. During the early Middle Ages, it was apparently the custom for one man to chant the final section of Deuteronomy and the opening section of Genesis from the same scroll. By the 12th century, however, this practice had changed: the readings were now divided, two scrolls were employed, and the original "Bridegroom of the Law" (*ḥatan Torah*) was joined by a "Bridegroom of Genesis" (*ḥatan Bereshit*). One "bridegroom" continues to read both passages in the Yemenite tradition. According to standard practice, Deut. 33:27-34:12 is the reading prescribed for the Bridegroom of the Law and Gen. 1:1-2:3 that reserved for the Bridegroom of Genesis. Both honors are now usually allocated on the basis of piety and learning, seniority, or services to the congregation. At one time, the first honor was the rabbi's prerogative and the second that of a warden (PARNAS or GABBAI). In Western Sephardi congregations, voting formerly took place each year to choose the recipients; both Sephardi and Eastern Jews once gave preference to an actual bridegroom — a congregant who had married during the past year. The reader chants elaborate introductory *piyyutim* when each of the two "bridegrooms" is summoned to the Law on the morning of *Simḥat Torah*. With textual variations, these Ashkenazi as well as Sephardi-Eastern poems emphasize the privileges inherent in each title and the blessings accompanying their bestowal.

Customs dating from the Middle Ages include handsome donations to charity by the two "bridegrooms" and their throwing candies to children in synagogue. In Eastern Jewish communities the process was reversed, sweets being scattered over the "bridegrooms" as they went up to and left the reading platform. In Sephardi congregations, the two "bridegrooms" are often seated in special chairs of honor under a canopy. Deputies were sometimes appointed to receive additional, minor honors, one of which (universal among Ashkenazim) involves to this day the spreading of a large woollen prayer shawl (*tallit*) as a canopy over the heads of all small children present ("*kol ha-ne'arim*"), who then repeat the Torah blessings in unison. To keep the revelry within bounds, "for the sake of decorum," strict communal regulations once had to be enforced in certain Western congregations. It was a widespread custom to escort both "bridegrooms" to and from the synagogue with torchlight processions on Simḥat Torah eve, sometimes to the accompaniment of salvoes. Nowadays, a festive *kiddush* or more elaborate meal (SE'UDAH) is usually tendered by the Bridegrooms, all worshipers being invited to partake after the services. In some congregations (e.g., in Italy) the wives of the Bridegrooms of the Law were called "Brides of the Law" (*Kallot Torah*) and were also honored. In contemporary Reform and Egalitarian communities, women, also known as *Kallot Torah*, may be honored with the special readings on Simḥat Torah.

Chairs reserved in the synagogue for the Bridegrooms of the Law.

In many Conservative congregations, it is the practice for the wives of the Bridegrooms to accompany their husbands as they are called to the Torah reading.

BUBER, MARTIN (1878-1965). Theologian, philosopher, educator, and Zionist theoretician. Born in Austria, he lived during his childhood with his grandfather, Solomon Buber, a well-known Midrash scholar from whom he received his introduction to Bible and Talmud studies as well as an enduring love for Judaism.

In the period of his earliest Zionist involvement, Buber associated with Theodor Herzl, but later distanced himself from Herzl's emphasis on political Zionism, believing that the Zionist movement had to be based on a cultural renaissance. He and some of his colleagues helped to establish *Der Jude*, which became a vehicle for the expression of his Zionist views. This Zionist philosophy was expounded as a special kind of humanistic socialism which he described as "the holy way." Buber also advocated a Zionism which would concern itself with the needs of the Arabs and would "develop the common homeland into a republic in which both peoples will have the possibility of free development."

Early in his literary career, Buber began to translate Ḥasidic tales, first in a free adaptation, but later retaining the simplicity and directness of the original stories. He wrote several books on the religious message of HASIDISM. Those which have appeared in English include *For the Sake of Heaven* (1945), *The Legend of the Baal Shem* (1955), *Tales of Rabbi Nachman* (1956), *Hasidism and Modern Man* (1958), and *The Origin and Meaning of Hasidism* (1960). Buber revealed the world of Ḥasidism to Western Jewry, which previously had tended to look on it with a certain disdain.

In 1925, Buber published the first volumes of a new German translation of the Bible, a work which he began with Franz ROSENZWEIG. After the latter's death, Buber continued the work alone and completed it in 1961. The translation seeks to express the original character of the Scriptures by a judicious choice of language and literary style. Buber was appointed professor of religion at the University of Frankfurt, and retained this position until the Nazis rose to power in 1933. For the next few years he devoted himself to teaching Judaism and, as head of the famous Frankfurt *Lehrhaus*, brought spiritual strength to the Jews of Germany through his teaching and encouragement.

In 1938, when it became impossible for Buber to continue his work as a teacher and lecturer in Germany, he left to settle in Palestine. There he was appointed professor of social philosophy at the Hebrew University. Among his many achievements as a teacher at the University was his founding of an Institute for Adult Education which he codirected. Throughout his years in Israel, in addition to his extensive cultural and literary work, Buber remained active in public affairs and continued to advocate a bi-national state in which Jews and Arabs would live and cooperate.

Buber's social and religious philosophy is discovered mainly in his exposition of the relationship between man and his fellow man and God as a dialogue relationship. In his *Ich und Du* ("I and Thou," 1937), Buber differentiates between the I-It relationship and the I-Thou relationship. In the latter there is a dialogue, with mutuality, openness, directness, and human sympathy. These are ultimately the qualities of life which form the basis of all human values. The I-Thou relationship finds its highest expression when it brings man into a revelational contact with God, who is the Eternal Thou.

For Buber, the Bible is the record of Israel's dialogue with the Eternal Thou, and the laws of Judaism are part of the human response to this revelational dialogue. Carried to its logical conclusion, this means that every generation is bound to make its own response in its own dialogue with God. The laws embraced by one generation are therefore not necessarily valid for later generations, since each man has to follow what he believes to be God's law for him. This non-halakhic view of Judaism set Buber at variance with traditional schools of Jewish religious thought.

Martin Buber

Buber's writings, particularly his philosophy expounded in *I and Thou*, have had a wide influence on modern Christian thinkers. He, together with Rosenzweig, was one of the pioneers of the modern Jewish-Christian dialogue, holding that both faiths retain continuing validity in the sight of God, and referring to Jesus as "my brother."

BURIAL Interment of the dead (Heb. *kevurah*) which, according to Jewish tradition, necessitates burying a deceased person in the ground or under stones. This reflects the biblical notion that "dust you are, and to dust you shall return" (Gen. 3:19). In ancient Israel, leaving a CORPSE unburied was considered a horrifying indignity (I Kings 14:11, 16:4; Jer. 22:19). No greater curse was imaginable than that someone's remains should fall a prey to "the birds of the air and the beasts of the earth, with none to frighten them off" (Deut. 28:26). This explains why, in the view of the Talmud (*San.* 46b), the religious obligation to bury the dead can be derived from the respect shown even for a criminal who had been executed by hanging: "His corpse shall not remain all night on the tree, but you must bury him the same day" (Deut. 21:23).

In the Bible, references to burial often accompany the mention of DEATH. Abraham's purchase of the Cave of

Tombs and sarcophagi elaborately decorated in the necropolis of Bet She'arim, dating from the 2nd to 4th centuries CE. The underground tunnels are carved out of the soft chalk rock.

Machpelah, for example, is described at length in connection with the interment of his newly deceased wife, Sarah (Gen. 23). This cave later became the sepulcher in which all of the patriarchs and matriarchs were buried, excepting Rachel. The Bible also relates that Moses was buried in Moab, where (according to rabbinic tradition) God Himself attended to the prophet's interment, leaving the gravesite unknown to men for all time (Deut. 34:6).

Respectful interment of the dead has always been characteristic of the Jewish people. Caves, catacombs, and other types of sepulcher were used in ancient times, although cemeteries or privately owned land are now set aside for Jewish burial. Until the Middle Ages, it was standard practice to reinter the bones of the dead in sarcophagi and then, after about a year, to exhume and give them permanent burial in a crypt or ossuary. This custom was known as "gathering the bones" (*likkut atsamot*). The embalming of Jacob and Joseph (Gen. 50:2, 26) was an Egyptian burial practice which, like CREMATION, is forbidden by Jewish law and shunned by Conservative as well as Orthodox Jews.

The initial responsibility for burying the dead, in accordance with biblical precedent (Gen. 25:9, etc.), falls on the mourners and immediate kinfolk of the deceased. Where there are no surviving relatives, or if the mourners are for some reason unable to make the necessary arrangements, this duty is assumed by others as a communal responsibility. The Talmud stipulates that burying someone who dies without family or friends (*met mitsvah*) should be regarded as a supreme religious obligation. The same applies to an unidentified corpse found along the road: it must be buried as near as possible to where it was discovered (*Meg.* 28b; *BK* 81a). Even a High Priest, normally debarred from having contact with the dead, must attend to the burial of a *met mitsvah* if no one else is available to do so (*Naz.* 7.1). Furthermore, this Jewish concern for speedy interment has no religious limitation: Jews must also attend to Gentiles who are in need of burial, a rule codified in the *Shulḥan Arukh* (*YD* 367.1).

Most Jewish communities of any size have their own BURIAL SOCIETY, the *ḥevrah kaddisha*, a "holy brotherhood" which until recent times was often the first communal institution to be established. Since interment of the dead is considered a positive commandment, all who take part in the funeral (pallbearers, gravediggers, etc.) should themselves be Jewish wherever possible. In special circumstances — on the first day of a festival, for example, when Jews may not perform burial rites — non-Jews are halakhically entitled to discharge the task of burying a newly deceased person. Nowadays, however, this practice is avoided and the interment is usually delayed until such time as Jews are themselves able to take charge of the burial.

"Escorting the dead" ranks among the basic humanitarian deeds (GEMILUT ḤASADIM) for which there will be a reward in the afterlife (*Shab.* 127a), although burial society members who volunteer their services are considered to be performing an "act of true kindness" (*ḥesed shel emet*) for which no reward or reciprocation can be expected. A Jew is obligated to accompany a funeral procession for a short distance (6 feet at least) on the way to the CEMETERY. Such a gesture is allowed to take precedence over other commandments, and failure to do so is considered tantamount to mocking the dead (*Ber.* 18 a; *Sh. Ar., YD* 361.3). The term *halvayat ha-met* or, more popularly, *levayah* (from the Hebrew root meaning "to accompany") denotes both the cortege and the funeral service at the burial ground.

Interment should take place as soon as possible after death. Jewish law permits a delay only in extenuating circumstances, when it is purely in honor of the deceased: to allow time for the shrouds or casket to be prepared, for example, or to enable close relatives far away to reach the appointed place. Even so, a delay of more than 24 hours is unusual in the average Orthodox community. No burial may take place on a Sabbath or the Day of Atonement, and contemporary practice now also disfavors the holding of a funeral on the first and last days of PILGRIM FESTIVALS. In Israel, particularly in Jerusalem, a funeral may take place at night (even after the termination of a Sabbath).

Burial in the Land of Israel has always been considered a desideratum, and some observant Jews living abroad purchase burial plots and make other arrangements in advance for that specific purpose. Otherwise, it is traditional for some earth from the Land of Israel to be placed on the head or under the body of Jews interred in the Diaspora. Importance

List of the months of the Jewish calendar. Poland, 1640.

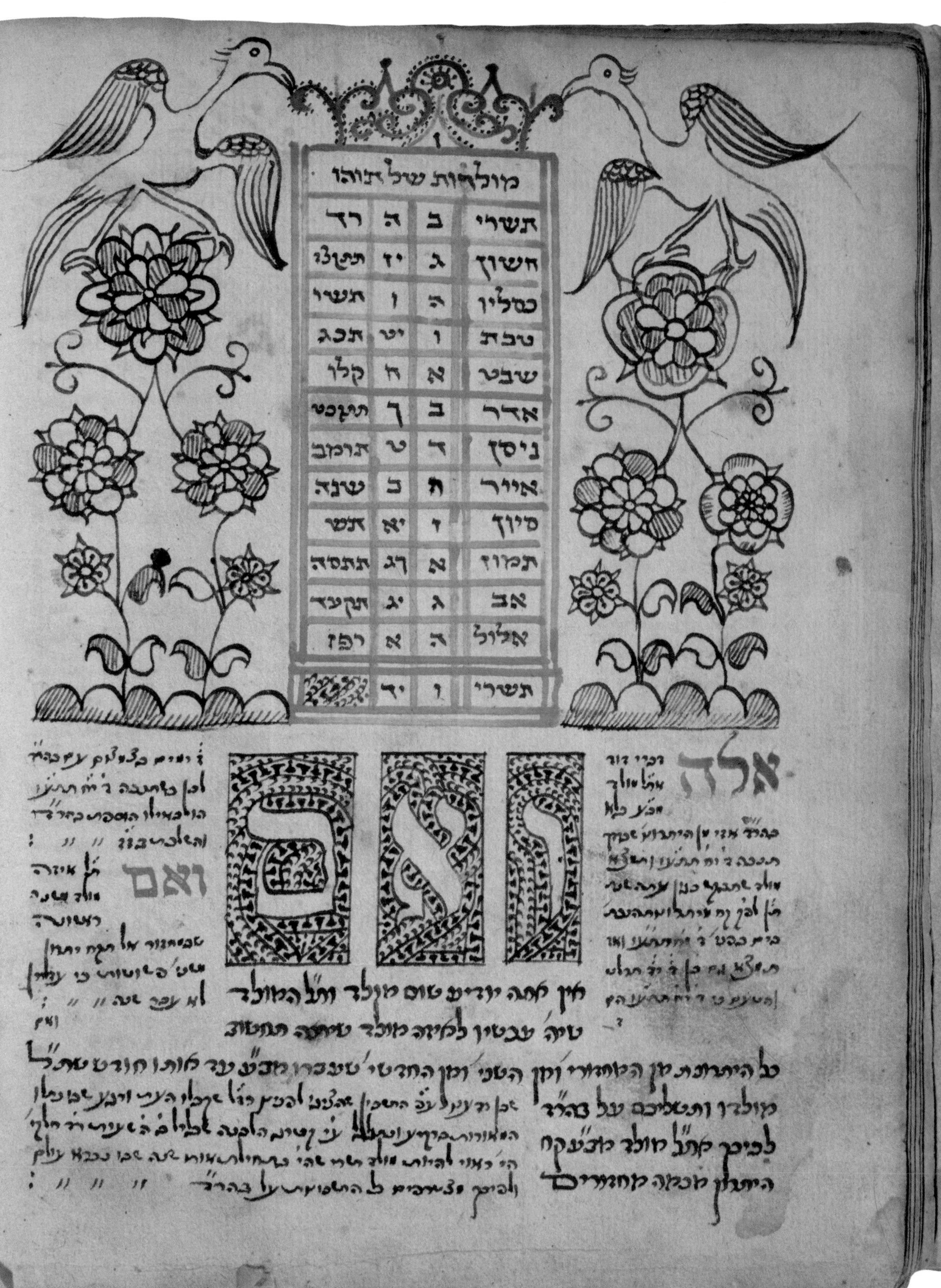

מולדות של׳ תעוהו
תשרי ב ה רד
חשון ג יז תתקנ
כסליו ה ו תשי
טבת ו יט תכג
שבט א ח קלו
אדר ב ך תתקכט
ניסן ד ט תרמב
אייר ח ב שנה
סיון ז יא תש
תמוז א רג תתסה
אב ג יג תקעד
אלול ה א רפז
תשרי ו יד
אלה
ואם

is also attached to burial in KEVER AVOT, ancestral plots in which generations of the same family have been interred. For the traditionally minded, burial in a Jewish cemetery, where the land has been consecrated as a Jewish graveyard, is a matter of religious principle. Alternatively, one portion of a general cemetery may be reserved and kept for a small Jewish community.

Within larger Jewish cemeteries, a special row or section may be reserved for prominent rabbis and scholars, thus insuring that "the righteous and the wicked are not buried next to each other" (*San.* 47a). *Kohanim*, Jews of priestly descent, may not approach a grave or take any active part in a funeral, as they are subject to laws prohibiting their contamination by the dead (see PRIESTS). The traditional practice, therefore, is to set aside either one row or the last plot in a row for the burial of *kohanim*; by placing these next to an avenue or broad pathway in the burial ground, other close relatives of priestly descent are enabled to witness the funeral service and (later) to visit the grave without transgressing the law.

After members of the burial society have taken charge of the body, they prepare it for burial, washing it thoroughly in a process known as TOHORAH (or *taharah,* i.e., ritual purification) and then dressing it in a white linen shroud (*takhrikhin*). Ashkenazim often refer to the place where this is done as the "*taharah* house"; Sephardim occasionally use the terms *reḇitsah* or *reḇitsat ha-met* ("washing of the dead") as substitutes for *tohorah*. Finally, the shrouded corpse is placed either in a coffin or on a bier prior to the funeral service. According to the most ancient practice, still observed in Israel and by some Eastern Sephardi Jews, no coffin is used and burial takes place directly in the earth. A coffin was used, however, for the burial of Joseph (Gen. 50:26) and this type of burial was accepted by talmudic times. Maimonides ruled that Jews should be buried in wooden coffins (*Yad, Evel* 4.4), as is now general practice throughout the Diaspora and, for state and military funerals, in Israel as well. Observant Jews only permit the use of a plain wooden coffin (*aron*), with no metal handles or adornments, lined ornamental "caskets" being prohibited. Following the example of R. Judah ha-Nasi (TJ *Kil.* 9.4), some arrange for holes to be drilled in the base of the coffin so that the body may have more direct contact with the earth. Whether in a coffin or on a bier, the deceased is borne to the grave face upward; adult males are buried wearing their prayer shawl (*tallit*), one of the fringes having been removed or deliberately marred in order to render the prayer shawl unfit. In some Eastern communities, the deceased Jew's phylacteries (*tefillin*) are also buried with him.

Interment in shrouds originated as a measure aimed against social discrimination. Whereas the rich were buried in expensive garments that left the face uncovered, poor people were interred in a cheap winding-sheet that enveloped them completely. To counter this trend, the aristocratic Rabban Gamaliel II (died c. 110 CE) left instructions that he be buried in a simple white linen shroud (*MK* 27a-b; *Ket.* 8b). That example, together with other rules devised to prevent ostentation and embarrassment, helped create a uniform pattern of Jewish burial which remains in force today. Various objections have also been raised by the practice of laying flowers on a coffin or on a grave. Both Sephardi and Ashkenazi Jews in the West consider this to be an emulation of Gentile practice (ḤUKKAT HA-GOY), but Jews in Muslim lands tend to think otherwise. Provided that wreaths or flowers are laid as a mark of respect for the dead, and not as a vulgar display of wealth, some halakhic authorities are willing to sanction the custom (which is generally accepted in Israel).

A marker is placed on the newly-filled grave and a TOMBSTONE should be erected and unveiled at the earliest permissible time, either at the end of the 30-day mourning period (as in Israel) or after 11 months have elapsed (in the Diaspora). Exhumation of the dead is forbidden by Jewish law, unless it is for the purpose of reburial in the Land of Israel or in some ancestral plot (*Sh. Ar., YD* 363.1, 364.5). A limb severed or amputated from a person who is still alive must be buried; this is true also of bodies on which AUTOPSIES or dissections have been conducted or from which organs have been removed for TRANSPLANTS. A stillborn child, or one that died before reaching the age of 30 days, must likewise be interred (although the usual laws of mourning do not apply).

Burial practice among Reform Jews, in the United States especially, differs from that of Ashkenazi and Sephardi traditionalists. Embalming and cremation are generally permitted, many Reform rabbis being willing to hold funeral services at a crematorium. Burial may be delayed for several days; and, where traditional interment in the earth is performed, the deceased is buried in normal clothing (not shrouds), without a prayer shawl, and earth from the Land of Israel is not placed in the casket. No special places are reserved for *kohanim*, nor is any separate arrangement made for suicides or Jews who married out of the faith. See also FUNERAL SERVICE.

BURIAL SOCIETY (Heb./Aram. *Ḥevrah* or *Ḥavurah Kaddisha*, i.e., "Holy Brotherhood" or "Society"). Voluntary group of individuals who look after the needs of the dying and the requirements of the dead. The term originally was used for a general mutual benefit society or for the Jewish community as a whole (and is so used in the YEKUM PURKAN prayer). In Judaism, burial of the dead is deemed a religious commandment (MITSVAH), one that takes precedence even over the study of Torah. To bury someone who leaves no kin is regarded as particularly meritorious, a duty that supersedes other commandments. The burial of the dead was considered to be a duty devolving on the deceased person's surviving relatives. Burial societies are first mentioned in

Two charity boxes: one with inscription Bikur Holim, Italy, 17th century; *the other with inscription* Hevrah Kadishah, Austria, 19th century.

חסד ואמת

Sancta Hebra instituida em Amsterdam; no K.K. de T.T.

No Anno 5465 para lavar Diffuntos por Mismaroth.

MISMARAH Nº

Os'r Isac de Silva

The burial society of Amsterdam summons Isaac de Silva to prepare the body of a deceased for burial. 1705.

amoraic times (*Ket.* 8b, etc) and have been a feature of Jewish communal life ever since. They often number 18 members, as in Hebrew the number 18 spells *H̱ai*, i.e., "life."

The records of some of these societies are available, beginning with the 13th-14th century (Western Europe). It was regarded as a special honor to belong to such a society, and members were often recruited from among the wealthiest and most learned men of the community (in 19th-century England, Sir Moses Montefiore assiduously fulfilled his duties as a member of the Sephardi *H̱evrah Kaddisha*). Members of the "Holy Society" also received special communal privileges. The services provided began with special prayers recited at the bedside of the gravely ill; thereafter, they included ritual washing of the body (TOHORAH), appropriate BURIAL, and visits of consolation to the home of the mourners.

The society had a constitution, usually based on the one drawn up in late 16th-century Prague by JUDAH LÖW BEN BEZALEL. Women were also active in the Society and saw to the last rites of other women. After a burial, the participating members would go to the ritual bath (*mikveh*) and then partake of a meal together. Once a year (on 7 Adar or 15/20 Kislev), the members observed a fast day and recited penitential prayers in atonement for any ritual disrespect of which they might have been guilty toward any of the deceased. After the fast day, all members would hold a feast. A number of these practices are still observed in Orthodox communities.

In 18th-century Lithuania, the community set maximum fees for the services of these societies in order to prevent extortionism. Generally, the cemetery belonged to and was controlled by the burial society. In larger communities, a further society, known as *H̱evrah H̱esed Shel Emet* ("Society of Lovingkindness"), devoted itself to burying dead persons who had left no kin. The burial society is a major organization today and the fees that it collects fund general communal activity. In Western Sephardi communities, the *H̱evrah Kaddisha* members are often known as *lavadores* (i.e., "those who wash [the body]"). Until recently, in the USA, many organizations of Jews originating from the same part of Eastern Europe (known as *landsmanshaften*) had their own burial society. In Israel, separate societies are maintained not only by Ashkenazim and Sephardim, but also (in some cases) by H̱asidim and *Mitnaggedim* within the Ashkenazi group. In many places today, the work of *H̱evrah Kaddisha* members is now remunerated.

BURNING BUSH The plant from which God revealed Himself to Moses in the wilderness of Sinai and instructed him to lead the enslaved Israelites to freedom (Ex. 3:1-10). For the biblical narrator, the extraordinary thing was that this bush should be "all aflame, yet it was not consumed" (3:2). In Deuteronomy 33:16, God is called the one "who dwelt in the bush." Rabbinical commentators, however, were also concerned with the fact that God should have chosen to reveal Himself in a lowly bush rather than a mighty tree. The whole phenomenon has been taken as symbolic of Israel's indestructibility. There is no certainty about the plant's botanical identification, although there have been

A trailing bush in St. Catherine's Monastery in the Sinai is said by the monks to have grown from the original burning bush.

various conjectures (e.g., the jujube tree, the acacia, the bramble), based on Midrashic references or cognate names in Arabic. Perhaps because this vision took place on Mount Horeb, attempts have been made to establish an etymological link between *seneh* ("bush") and *Sinai*. A bush growing in St. Catherine's monastery on the traditional site of Mount Sinai is revered by the monks as the original burning bush.

BURNT-OFFERING See OFFERINGS AND SACRIFICES

BUSINESS ETHICS The Jewish religion, based on the Torah and its revelations, was supported by the debates, sayings, and preaching of recognized authorities in successive eras. The Talmud and subsequent legal transcriptions were concerned with basic rules of conduct in transactions of all kinds (including business dealing) between each man and his neighbor.

These rules, though not all formulated in the written Scriptures, were conceived in such a fashion as to be seen to be fair and just in light of the general ethical standards of Judaism. Business which involved relationships between people was part of the religion. The result can be seen in the flexibility and ubiquity of the Jewish codes of conduct to meet the changing environment and the conditions of Jewish traders throughout the ages. Jews transmitted these codes and standards, practiced and (where necessary) modified them in the various lands of their dispersion.

One of their values was an appreciation of the creation of wealth through labor, on which industry and trading depend. "Six days shalt thou labor" (Ex. 20:9) is part of the Fourth Commandment. "All study of the Torah without work [some productive occupation] must in the end be futile and lead to sin" (*Avot* 2.2). (This raises the question as to whether unemployment is immoral.) "Great is work, for it honors the workman" (*Ned.* 49b).

Wealth acquired without effort, however, is frowned upon: "An estate may be gotten hastily at the beginning; but the end thereof shall not be blessed" (Prov. 20:21). On wealth gained through labor, and transferred through charitable giving to the poor and underprivileged, there is religious guidance.

The Jewish religion was concerned that business actions should be fair both to seller and buyer, and that the outcome of such transactions should be just. The laws of profiteering (*hafka'at she'arim*) had their origin in rabbinic enactments which were intended to prohibit the setting of prices in excess of the customarily accepted rate, even if the buyer was aware of, and agreed to, the inflated price. As defined by the scholars, profiteering included giving short measure (Lev. 19:35; Deut. 25:14-16) and/or charging interest on loans when aiding someone in distress (Ex. 22:24; Lev. 25:35-37; Deut. 23:20-21). Charging reasonable interest on a business investment however, is permissible.

The analogous concept of overreaching (*ona'ah*) was also based expressly on the preservation of a fair and just price. This concept, however, stemmed from a biblical prohibition (Lev. 25:14). The law was fixed that "if the price exceeded the value by one-sixth, the seller must return this part to the purchaser. If the price were higher still, the purchaser might demand cancellation of the transaction. Conversely, if the price were too low, the law applied in favor of the seller" (*BM* 50b).

This is reminiscent — and perhaps even a more stringent application — of the anti-inflationary price controls maintained by various countries at various times in recent years.

There were arguments as to how price control should be exercised. In the Mishnaic period, fixed prices were set by a recognized authority; later, in the talmudic era, market commissioners supervised only measures, not prices. Authority to determine prices was subsequently given not only to the courts, but also to local community representatives. According to Rashi, "the townspeople are authorized to fix prices and measures and workers' wages, which they may enforce by punishment (i.e., fines)." Doubts were even expressed as to whether price inspectors were necessary, on the basis that competition between merchants would stabilize prices.

Various measures were invoked to check profiteering and inflation. For example, it was forbidden to hoard produce brought to the market, since this might cause prices to rise and affect the poor; nor was it permitted to export essential products, since this might also lead to a shortage and raise prices. Today, in Israel, legislative measures contain prices and combat profiteering in essential commodities through laws enforceable by imprisonment, fine, or the closing down of a business. Similarly, other laws regarding property control maximum rental for premises, protect tenants by limiting the right of ejectment to specified grounds, and bar the artificial manipulation of price levels by a monopoly or cartel. These secular laws embody the rabbinic view.

Tsedek (fairness and justice) is the motivation of Jewish business conduct. One must not defraud or cheat people in business (Lev. 19:13, 25:14); mislead a man even verbally (Lev. 25:17); or annoy the stranger and do him injury in trade (Ex. 22:20).

Ḫesed (goodness), however, was an added dimension to these guiding principles, and goodness did not just concern itself with sticking to the letter of the law; it went beyond it in the spirit of the Torah's ethical wisdom, as is found in the Tenth Commandment: "You shall not covet your neighbor's house ... nor anything that is your neighbor's" (Ex. 20:14). Enlarging on this general precept, the rabbis said: "Do not covet another man's possessions, even if you are willing to pay for them." In the light of this interpretation, it would be hard to find ethical justification for many of today's industrial mergers.

Business is concerned with the integration of men, machines, and markets, with money as the binding cement.

On the employment and treatment of labor, biblical Judaism was unambiguous (see LABOR LAWS). It believed in the need and value of work; it also believed in the fair treatment of a worker: not to delay payment of his wages (Lev. 19:13) in those days meant paying him daily. Bondsmen had to be treated humanely (Lev. 25:39ff.) and never in a harsh, unfeeling manner (see SLAVERY). Today, trade unions undertake these responsibilities without the benefit of religious direction, but from early times trade unions were recognized in Jewish law (*BB* 8b).

There were also conditions laid on the Jewish workman who, perceived as a servant of God, had the right to terminate his contract but not to strike. The worker's right to contract out was based on an interpretation of Lev. 25:55, that no one could acquire ownership in a person; a strike, on the other hand, was considered an attempt to change the terms of a contract. This view was modified by Rabbi Avraham Yitsḫak KOOK and others at the beginning of the 20th century, but the strike was given legitimacy only as a means of forcing an employer either to submit a grievance or demand to arbitration, or to adhere to a decision reached through arbitration.

From ancient times, Jews have been closely associated in people's minds with moneylending and, in the modern age, with banking and high finance. On money, and particularly on loans, there were safeguards which even today can be found in civil law. The Torah (Deut. 23:20-21, Lev. 25:35-37, etc.) added a moral dimension. Loans were originally given for charitable purposes and not for commercial gain: no creditor might therefore exact repayment in the seventh year (Deut. 15:2). Ezekiel (18:13) also condemns the taking of interest, and one who never lent on interest deserves praise (Ps. 15:5). Similarly, no one must condemn a poor man when he cannot pay (Ex. 22:24).

The Bible, however, is specific (if discriminatory) about the Jewish position on moneylending and interest. The injunction that it is forbidden to lend on interest to a Jew "waxen poor or of failing means" — or to participate in an agreement involving interest either as a guarantor, witness, or writer of the contract — is to be found, for example, in Lev. 25:35-37. This injunction does distinguish between the Jew and the non-Jew, however, since, although repeated in Deut. 23:20 ("You shall not lend on interest to your brother"), the following verse says, "Unto a foreigner you may lend upon interest."

Whatever the economic rationale may be for this distinction, the rabbis considered that for Jews the verse had a moral implication — that of CHARITY (*tsedakah*), but charity with a difference, as expressed by MAIMONIDES in his *Mishneh Torah (Yad, Mattenot Aniyyim* 10.7-14): "The highest degree, exceeded by none, is that of a person who assists the poor man by providing him with a gift or a loan, or by accepting him into a partnership, or by helping him find employment — in a word, by placing him in a situation where he can dispense with other people's aid." The adoption of this attitude toward aid for Third World countries is an interesting recent development, and the concept may even be extended to politically motivated "caring capitalism."

Jewish law does not approve of the restraint of trade by Jews in community or inter-community transactions, and countervailing measures are listed, short-term and long-term, which can be taken against the boycott weapon, namely, preventing the free exchange of goods. These include organizing consumers not to purchase even if religious practices are embarrassingly involved — for example, when Sabbath observance is hindered by extortionate monopoly pricing.

Jewish communities may not place any restrictions on foreign wholesale trade activities, however, in contrast to certain Arab countries which have long practiced discrimination against Jews. The rabbinic policy is laid down by several authorities, including Asher ben Jehiel (*Rosh*) and Jacob ben Asher.

When finding ethical solutions to modern problems, Judaism looks for solutions that will, if at all possible, reflect biblical morality and rabbinic guidance. If such solutions are not available, because the issues are entirely new and the religion offers no precedent, then, at the very least, the *ad hoc* practices of secular law or institutions should not conflict with the ethical principle of *tsedek* (fairness and justice) on which Jewish law is based. Ideally, however, our code of behavior in a changing world should draw upon the further element of *ḫesed* (goodness).

C

CABALA See KABBALAH

CAIN AND ABEL Two eldest sons of ADAM AND EVE, born after the expulsion from the Garden of Eden. Cain was "a tiller of the soil" and Abel "a keeper of sheep." Both prepared a thanksgiving sacrifice, but God showed a preference for Abel's offering, whereupon, in a fit of jealousy, Cain slew his brother and became the first murderer in history. When confronted by God, Cain says "Am I my brother's keeper?" and to this God replies, "Your brother's blood cries out to Me from the ground!" (Gen. 4:9-10). Cain is banished from civilization, but first a sign is placed on him — not as a felon's brand ("the mark of Cain") but to protect him from roving hunters. The rabbis, while condemning Cain's sin, also saw him as a genuine penitent who was therefore not punished by death. This story reflects the ancient rivalry between the farmer and the nomadic shepherd.

CALENDAR The Creation is the starting point for the year One in the Jewish method of counting the calendar. The first known chronological work is the *Seder Olam*, traditionally ascribed to the 2nd century rabbi, Yosé ben Halafta, but probably a much later composition. This reckons the years from the Creation, a system in popular use by the 9th century. This calculation is based on the biblical genealogical tables, the length of lives as recorded in Scripture, and the creation of the world in six days. By this reckoning the exact year of the Creation was 3761 BCE. Thus the year 1989-90 CE is 5750 in the Jewish calendar. Modern scholars reject this reckoning, arguing that from scientific evidence the world is countless millions of years old.

The Jewish calendar is based on a lunar year of 12 months, each month of 29 or 30 days. The year lasts approximately 354 days. Since the biblical festivals relate to the agricultural seasons of the 365-day solar year, the shortage of 11 days between the lunar and solar years has to be made up. To overcome this problem, a 13th month is added in certain years. In Temple times this was done periodically, after examining the agricultural situation at the end of the 12th month. In a later period the additional month was introduced automatically seven times in a lunar cycle of 19 years; in the years 3, 6, 8, 11, 14, 17, and 19 of the cycle (the year 5749 [1989-90] began such a cycle).

Before the introduction of a fixed permanent calendar the identification and designation of *Rosh Hodesh* — the day of the New MOON — was of crucial importance for the timely observance of festivals during that month. In Temple times, to avoid the possibility of festivals being observed in different communities on different days, the SANHEDRIN in Jerusalem insisted on retaining its centralized and single authority for fixing the date of the new moon as well as for the intercalation of the 13th month of the leap year when they thought it was necessary. Originally, the beginning of the new month was decided after eyewitness evidence to the appearance of the new moon had been accepted by the Sanhedrin. Distant communities were informed of the date by means of a chain of fire signals from one hilltop to another. When this method of spreading the information was exposed to interference by sectarians, the rabbis decided to send out special messengers to the outlying communities on those months which contained festivals. As Diaspora communities might still be in doubt concerning the exact beginning of the month, the rabbis instituted a SECOND DAY of festivals to insure that no mistake would be made.

A major problem was the designation of ROSH HA-SHANAH, the New Year. To prevent the DAY OF ATONEMENT falling on Fridays or Sundays (which would create problems of Sabbath observance) or HOSHANA RABBAH from falling on a Sabbath (for the same reason), the rabbis ordained that the first day of the New Year could not fall on a Sunday, Wednesday, or Friday. Sometimes, the Sanhedrin would deliberately postpone the announcement of the New Year on Tishri 1 for a day, and sometimes for two days.

In 358 the patriarch Hillel II introduced a permanent calendar based on mathematical and astronomical calculations which made the evidence of eye witnesses of the new moon unnecessary. Until the 10th century only slight variations were made to Hillel's calendar. Since then it has remained unchanged. In spite of this, sectarian calendars did exist both before the date of the fixed calendar and even afterwards. The Samaritans, the Sadducees, and the Dead Sea Sect each had their own calendar. In the case of the Sadducees this created a special problem in the dating of the Shavu'ot festival, because of their different interpretation of the biblical command relating to the commencement of the seven weeks to be counted from Passover until Shavu'ot.

THE JEWISH CALENDAR

Name of month	Number of days	Special dates	
Nisan	30	15	First day of Passover
Iyyar	29	5	Israel Independence Day
		18	Lag ba-Omer
Sivan	30	6	Shavuot (first day outside Israel)
Tammuz	29	17	Fast of 17th Tammuz
Av	30	9	Fast of 9th Av
Elul	29		
Tishri	30	1	First day of Rosh ha-Shanah (New Year)
		10	Day of Atonement
		15	First day of Sukkot
Ḫeshvan (Marḫeshvan)	29 or 30		
Kislev	29 or 30	25	First day of Ḫanukkah
Tevet	29	10	Fast of 10th Tevet
Shevat	30	15	New Year for Trees
Adar	29 (30 in leap year)	14	Purim
Adar II	(29 in leap year)		In leap year Purim is celebrated on 14th Adar II

See also entries on each individual month.

The names of the twelve months are of Babylonian origin. The pre-exilic books of the Bible generally identify the months by their numerical order, Nisan being accepted as the first month of the year (see NEW YEAR).

The day in the Jewish calendar begins at sunset and ends at nightfall on the following day. Consequently, the Sabbath starts at sundown on Friday and ends with the appearance of three stars on Saturday night. The same calculation applies to the observance of all holy days (although in rabbinic law the holy day may be welcomed earlier than the onset of sundown since one can always "add from the secular to the holy"). The Talmud finds biblical support for this in the Creation story where at the end of each day the Bible records, "And it was evening and it was morning," in that order (e.g., Gen. 1:5, 8, 13).

The Hebrew date is generally given by indicating the name of the month, the date in that month, and then the year; for example, Tevet 21, 5750. When the year is written in Hebrew letters it is usual to omit the thousands. An alternative method of giving the date is sometimes used by rabbinic scholars by giving the day of the week together with the name of the Bible portion for that week.

In modern times, several attempts have been made in Western countries at general calendar reform. The chief objectives of the reformers are to arrange a calendar with the same number of days in each month so that the same date every year fall on the same day of the week, and that the year be divisible into two equal halves or quarters. The main Jewish objection to calendar reform is that it would break the regularity of a fixed Sabbath day after every six working days; if the reform were accepted it would fall on a different day each year. The last major effort for calendar reform was organized under the auspices of the League of Nations in Geneva in 1931. At that time, it was vigorously opposed by the British Chief Rabbi J.H. Hertz.

CANAAN, LAND OF Standard designation for the Land of ISRAEL from patriarchal times until the Second Temple era. Canaan's name, mentioned in Akkadian documents and in the Tell El-Amarna letters (Egypt, 14th cent. BCE), has biblical associations with the son of Ham and grandson of NOAH upon whom a curse was invoked (Gen. 9:20 ff.). There are repeated allusions to the land and its inhabitants (Heb. *Kena'anim*) throughout the Pentateuch, Joshua, and Judges; God's promise to give Abraham and his descendants "all the Land of Canaan" is likewise reiterated in the Bible (Gen. 17:8; Num. 34:2 ff.; Ps. 105:11, etc.). As a geographical region, however, Canaan is not clearly defined: it was evidently thought to encompass about 6,000 square miles of territory "from Dan to Beersheba" and west of the Jordan river, but the inclusion of other territory (parts of Lebanon, Syria, and Transjordan) was sometimes also mentioned.

From c. 3000 BCE, Canaan's inhabitants were predominantly Semitic tribesmen (Amorites, Canaanites, and Jebusites), although Indo-European invaders (Hittites and the "Sea Peoples" or Philistines) later penetrated the area. "Canaanite" and "Amorite" are synonymous designations for the indigenous population (I Sam. 7:14). They had a fairly advanced civilization, spoke a language akin to biblical Hebrew, and on the eve of Israel's conquest under Joshua owed allegiance to the Egyptian pharaoh. Having defeated no less than 31 petty rulers of Canaan (Josh. 12), the Israelites gradually overcame or absorbed these tribes, but had to contend with the menace of Canaanite idolatry and pagan practices for centuries to come.

CANDLES In ancient times, oil lamps were used for ritual as well as domestic purposes. The lampstand (MENORAH) kindled daily in the Sanctuary, and thereafter in the Temple, used a wick dipped in oil. The Mishnah (*Shab.* 2) discusses the substances that may or may not be used as oils and wicks for kindling the SABBATH light. Generally, it is accepted that any flammable substance which is not malodorous may be used for the Sabbath lights, although R. Tarfon held that only olive oil is permissible. Once candles became common, their use was authorized — always provided that they were not made of tallow, a non-kasher fat (see BA-MEH MADLIKIN).

At least two candles must be used for kindling the lamps (*hadlakat ha-nerot*), in honor of the dual commandment to "remember" and "observe" the Sabbath day (Ex. 20:8; Deut. 5:12). This ceremony, performed before sunset on the eve of Sabbaths and festivals, is thought to symbolize the light and joy shed by God's holy day (Ps. 97:11; Est. 8:16; cf. Prov. 6:23, 13:9). The practice of leaving candles to burn after the Sabbath had commenced was a geonic innovation aimed against the form of observance in vogue among the KARAITES. Lighting the Sabbath candles is traditionally the Jewish housewife's prerogative (*Shab.* 2.6-7), but any other adult member of the family may do it — and pronounce the appropriate benediction — in her absence.

The HAVDALAH ceremony which takes place at the Sabbath's termination includes the lighting of a candle made of at least two intertwined wicks; otherwise, two ordinary candles are used with their lighted wicks held together. This is because the text of the benediction recited over them ("who creates the lights of the fire") alludes to a plural fire.

In the case of ḤANUKKAH lamps, Jewish law gives preference to those using olive oil, since the miracle of Ḥanukkah involved the Temple *menorah* and a small cruse of oil that lasted for eight days. Candles are nevertheless acceptable, and there is even a view that they are preferable, because of the mess that oil lamps often make. A candle is also used in the search for LEAVEN on the eve of Passover, and candles or tapers are sometimes used in a darkened synagogue when the Book of Lamentations and elegies are read on the eve of TISHAH BE-AV. Synagogues customarily have an ETERNAL LIGHT (*ner tamid*) burning in front of the Ark, but there is no halakhic requirement for the use of oil, and the eternal light in many synagogues today is powered by electricity or gas.

Lighting the Sabbath candles before sunset on Friday or on the eve of festivals, is traditionally the housewife's prerogative. At least two candles must be used.

In certain Orthodox circles, it is customary at a wedding for the fathers of the bride and of the groom to accompany the groom down the aisle or to the *Ḥuppah* (see MARRIAGE), each holding a lighted candle. The two mothers then accompany the bride, also holding lighted candles.

A more general practice is lighting candles in rituals connected with the dead, lamps and lights being symbolic of man's SOUL, as reflected in the verse (Prov. 20:27), "The spirit of man is the lamp of the Lord." Candles are thus lit when a person dies (see CORPSE; DEATH), in the house of a bereaved family throughout the seven (*shivah*) days of MOURNING, on the anniversary (YAHRZEIT) of the death of a close relative, and on those days when *yizkor* MEMORIAL PRAYERS for the dead are recited in synagogue. Eastern Jews light candles on the graves of their venerated rabbis. It is also customary for a MEMORIAL LIGHT to be kept burning throughout the Day of Atonement (and in Israel on *Yom ha-Sho'ah*, Holocaust Memorial Day, among other occasions).

CANDLESTICK See MENORAH

CANTILLATION The art of the liturgical chanting of the BIBLE. Jewish liturgical regulations require that various portions of the Bible be read ceremoniously in public services. Portions of the Pentateuch are read at the morning services on Mondays, Thursdays, Saturdays, New Moons, Festivals and the High Holidays (see READING OF THE LAW). Portions from the Prophets are read on Saturdays, Festivals and Holidays (see HAFTARAH). Other books are read on appropriate occasions: The Scrolls of Song of Songs, Ruth and Ecclesiastes are read on the three PILGRIM FESTIVALS, the Scrolls of Esther on Purim and Lamentations on the Ninth of Av (TISHAH BE-AV).

The public reading of the Pentateuch and the Scrolls is usually executed by a professional or semi-professional reader called BA'AL KERI'AH or BA'AL KORÉ (in the Yemenite tradition the Pentateuch is read by laymen), and with the exception of some Reform synagogues, the reading is always chanted. The art of chanting is ancient and may go back to Second Temple times, but the different melodic patterns used by the various Jewish communities developed much later, perhaps during the Middle Ages, and have continued to grow and change ever since.

The cantillation of Scripture is expected to adhere to the signs called *te'amim*. These were developed together with the punctuation signs in Babylonia and Erets Israel during the talmudic and post-talmudic periods; they were first transmitted orally and were later codified in various notation systems, the fullest and most important of which was the one developed by the Masoretic school of Tiberias in the ninth and tenth centuries CE (see MASORAH). The Tiberian sages assigned three functions to the accents (*te'amim*): (a) to show the proper accentuation of the words, (b) to divide the biblical verses properly and thus to help preserve the acceptable interpretation of the text, and (c) to indicate the melodic patterns which should be used with each part of the verse. Due to the last function, the signs are also called *neginot* (melodies). The codices compiled by these scholars (the most famous of which are the Crown of Aleppo, of c. 920 CE, now in Jerusalem, and the Leningrad Codex of c. 1010) have been accepted as the authorized versions of the Hebrew Bible.

The signs of the accents are marked only in the Masoretic codices and in the printed Bibles. They are never copied in the scrolls used for the liturgical reading in the synagogue. In most communities, it is customary to read the portion of the Prophets from a codex or a printed Bible, but the Pentateuch and the five scrolls are read from scrolls (see SCROLLS OF THE LAW; FIVE SCROLLS). In these cases, the reader is obliged to memorize the signs in order to effect a correct cantillation. As a practicing device, modern readers use a book called *tikkun la-korim* which contains the original text as written in the scroll, side by side with the Masoretic version which includes the punctuation and accents, in two parallel columns. An earlier means of overcoming the lack of accents in the scrolls was the use of a prompter (*somekh*) who indicated the accents to the reader by a system of hand signals called cheironomy. Some of the accents may have derived their names from the cheironomical signals that accompanied them. Cheironomy is still in use in some Jewish communities, some preserving the old customs, others inventing new methods.

The Masoretic accents of Tiberias are organized in two graphical systems: one for the Psalms, Proverbs and the central part of Job, and a second system for the other 21 books of the Bible. Only the latter is relevant to the ceremonial reading of Scripture in public. This system contains 29 signs, most of which are written above and some below the letters; one sign follows the relevant word. The signs are classified as (a) Disjunctives, or Lords, which mark the end of verses and divide the latter into phrases, clauses, and sub-clauses; and (b) Conjunctives, or Servants, whose task is to link the words within the division or sub-division of the verse. The Disjunctives are hierarchical, according to the degree of closure which they affect. Their placement in the text was determined by syntactical, exegetical, and musical considerations. considerations.

The signs of the *te'amim* are universally accepted by all Jews. However, their musical interpretation differs from one community to the other. One may speak of eight main musical traditions of cantillation:

1. Southern Arab Peninsula: Yemen and Hadramaut. This is perhaps one of the oldest traditions of cantillation. Theoretically it recognizes all the signs of the *te'amim*, but in practice, some are not used and the style of chanting may suggest that the tradition is based on an earlier system of cantillation, such as was recorded in the Babylonian notation of the seventh century and earlier.

2. The Middle East: Iran, Bukhara, Kurdistan, Georgia, and the northern parts of Iraq. Another old tradition, perhaps based partially on the old Babylonian system of notation, but musically different from the Yemenite tradition.

3. The Near East: Turkey, Syria, central Iraq, Lebanon, and Egypt. This is known as the "Eastern Sephardi Tradition"; it can be heard among some Greek and Balkan communities, and it has become the dominant style of the non-Ashkenazi communities of Israel. The readers of the Pentateuch strive to give musical meaning to each sign, but some of the signs are ignored in reading the Prophets and other books. The musical motives are influenced by the Arabic modes of the *maqam*.

4. North Africa: Libya, Tunisia, Algeria, and Morocco. This reflects the influence of African pentatonic patterns, especially in communities far from the Mediterranean shores.

5. Italy. The ancient tradition of the Italian Jews can still be heard in Rome and in the Roman Jewish community of

Jerusalem. Cheironomy is still used by some of the readers of this tradition.

6. The Sephardi and Portuguese communities of Europe. The so-called Western Sephardim may preserve the main features of the original Sephardi cantillation melodies.

7. Western European Ashkenazim: German-speaking countries, France, some communities of the Netherlands, and England. The tradition, which developed in medieval times, was first recorded in European cantorial manuals of the 19th century.

8. East-European Ashkenazim. The tradition developed out of the Western Ashkenazi cantillation, and has become the dominant style among the Ashkenazi communities of Israel and the English-speaking countries. The Lithuanian version of this tradition is perhaps the most meticulous musical system in existence.

Most of the eight musical traditions have diverse sub-traditions. Considerable musical differences exist among the various countries within one tradition and even various sections of the same country. In addition, each tradition has different melodic patterns for various divisions of the Bible or for different liturgical occasions. Thus, for instance, the East-European Ashkenazi tradition consists of six musical systems: The regular Pentateuch reading; the High Holiday version of the same; the Prophets; the Book of Esther; the Song of Songs, Ruth, and Ecclesiastes; and Lamentations.

SIGNS AND NAMES OF THE MASORETIC ACCENTS ACCORDING TO THE ASHKENAZI, SEPHARDI, AND YEMENITE TRADITIONS

Ashkenazi	Sephardi	Yemenite	The Sign
A. First Class Disjunctives:			
1. *Sof-pasuk (Silluk)*	*Sof-pasuk*	*Sof-Pasuk*	
2. *Etnaẖta*	*Atnaẖ*	*Atnaẖa*	
B. Second Class Disjunctives:			
3. *Segol*	*Segolta*	*Segulta*	
4. *Shalshelet*	*Shalshelet*	*Shalshelet*	
5. *Zakef-katon*	*Zakef-katon*	*Zakef-katon*	
6. *Zakef-gadol*	*Zakef-gadol*	*Zakef-gadol*	
7. *Revi'i*	*Ravi'a*	*Rebia*	
C. Third Degree Disjunctives:			
8. *Tipẖa*	*Tarẖa*	*Tifẖa*	
9. *Pashta*	*Kadma*	*Fishta*	
10. *Pashta* (as above)	*Ṯerei-kadmin*	*Terein-fishtin*	
11. *Yetiv*	*Yetiv*	*Yetiv*	
12. *Zarka*	*Zarka*	*Zirka*	
13. *Munah-legarmeh*	*Shofar-holekh Pasek*	*Shofar-holekh Pesik*	
D. Fourth Degree Disjunctives:			
14. *Tevir*	*Tevir*	*Tobir*	
15. *Geresh*	*Gerish*	*Atei*	
16. *Azla*	*Gerish*	*Atei*	
17. *Gershayim*	*Shenei-grishin*	*Trein-tirsin*	
18. *Telishah-gedolah*	*Talshah*	*Tilsha-yamin*	
19. *Pazer*	*Pazer-gadol*	*Pazer*	
20. *Karnei-farah*	*Karnei-farah*	*Karnei-farah*	
E. Auxiliary Disjunctive:			
21. *Pesi*	*Pasek*	*Pesik*	
F. Conjunctives With Limited Disjunctive Power:			
22. *Telisha-ketannah*	*Tarsa*	*Tilsha-semol*	
23. *Merkha-khefulah*	*Terei-ta'amei*	*Terei-ta'amei*	
G. Conjunctives:			
24. *Merkha*	*Ma'arikh*	*Ma'arakhah*	
25. *Munaẖ*	*Shofar-holekh*	*Shofar-holekh*	
26. *Mahpakh*	*Shofar-mehupakh*	*Shofar-hafukh*	
27. *Kadma*	*Kadma*	*Azel*	
28. *Darga*	*Darga*	*Dirga*	
29. *Yare'aẖ-ben-yomo*	*Yare'aẖ-ben-yomo*	*Yare'aẖ-ben-yomo*	

CANTOR AND CANTORIAL MUSIC In modern usage, the Hebrew term *ḥazzan* is applied to the cantor who leads the SYNAGOGUE prayer service, frequently a paid position. As distinct from the SHELI'AḤ TSIBBUR or the amateur *ba'al tefillah*, the cantor in the Ashkenazi synagogue was usually trained for his function in music, voice, and liturgy, with particular emphasis on vocal ability and, to a lesser extent, improvisation. By contrast, the cantor in the Sephardi tradition adheres very closely to traditional chants and melodies, vocal prowess being of secondary importance.

Originally, the word *ḥazzan* meant a congregational functionary whose duties included supervising children's studies, prayer meetings, etc., the functions fulfilled by a sexton or beadle in the later synagogue, and this is the meaning of the term when used in talmudic sources (see *Sot.* 7.7-8). In talmudic times his many responsibilities included occasional leading of the prayer service, as in the case of any other Jew who was capable of serving as *sheli'aḥ tsibbur*. It was not until the geonic period that a combination of factors — including a desire to add beauty and formality to the service, a decline in the general public's knowledge of Hebrew, and the addition to the prayer service of many liturgical poems (PIYYUTIM) that required a musical setting — led to the institutionalization of the *ḥazzan* as prayer leader. Some of the early *ḥazzanim* supplied both the Hebrew poetry and its appropriate musical rendering.

Formalization of the post led to congregational and rabbinic requirements for the holder, which were not always identical. Whereas the congregations usually sought musical ability and vocal accomplishment, the rabbinic requirements called for a mature man of exemplary character, free of any suspicion of wrongdoing, humble, acceptable to the congregation, possessed of a good voice, and accustomed to regular Torah study. According to a gloss on the *Shulḥan Arukh*, preference should be given to a youngster with a poor voice who understands the prayers over a mature man with a good voice chosen by the congregation, who does not understand the prayers. The rabbis in later times frequently inveighed against the prevalent cantorial practice of repeating words, though usually to little avail.

The style and development of cantorial music in Europe was strongly affected by the social conditions in which the Jews lived. In Western Europe, the partial EMANCIPATION of Jewry exposed both the cantors and the Jewish public at large to the culture and music of the time. As a result, from the early 19th century, most cantors acquired at least some formal musical training and began both to record traditional melodies in standard musical notation and to write choir arrangements for these melodies (see CHOIRS AND CHORAL MUSIC). In addition, talented cantor-composers such as Salomon Sulzer, Samuel Naumbourg, Hirsch Weintraub, and Abraham Baer, and choral director-composers such as Louis Lewandowski, wrote new melodies and choir pieces consonant with traditional modes. The resultant large body of cantorial music (Heb. *ḥazzanut*), characterized by a clear, simple melodic line and mostly devoid of ornamentation, was eminently suitable to the formal services held in the large synagogue buildings characteristic of Western Europe.

Cantorial music in Eastern Europe developed along entirely different lines. Since Jews had lived there in small-town communities from the late Middle Ages onward, with minimal exposure to the culture of the outside world, cantors acquired little more than the rudiments of music notation (if at all), and in general they learned, composed, and taught orally. Youngsters who showed vocal promise were sent to study with practicing cantors and generally began as choristers (*meshorerim*). Gradually they were allowed a few solo parts, and some developed into *ḥazzanim* in their own right. Because East European Jewry was essentially a ghetto-bound religious community, the *ḥazzan* not only served as synagogue precentor, but also as the community's leading musical personality. He was eminently qualified to satisfy the musical needs of such a society, steeped as it was in religious practice and Jewish learning, since his *ḥazzanut* was a melding of prayer and music. As a result, the most popular cantors were those with the finest voices (almost always tenor) who sang new melodies and who were capable of interesting improvisation and spectacular coloratura. Since many of the smaller villages and towns could not afford to keep a good cantor, two new institutions arose: the peripatetic cantor (*"a ḥazzan oyf shabbos"*) and the cantorial concert. A traveling cantor went from village to village and in one of them conducted Sabbath services, for which he was compensated (most often indirectly). Thus, he earned a livelihood and the local populace had, essentially, a Sabbath concert in a religious atmosphere. The best cantors gave actual concerts, with paid admission, a system which continues in the West and Israel to this day. Here, the prayers serve only as a vehicle for the *ḥazzan*'s voice and music.

East European cantorial music is characterized by the prominence given to the solo voice, by complex and sometimes phenomenal coloratura (often improvised), by singable melodies (frequently based on Ḥasidic or folk tunes), and by very simple choir arrangements. Many cantors of this era (mid-18th-late 19th century) were talented composers, but their ignorance of even the rudiments of musical notation meant that their works were not written down (except in part by their students); they were passed on orally, however, and are sung to this day. Some of the best-known cantors of this era were Dovidl Brod, Bezalel Shulsinger ("Bezalel Odessaer"), Joseph Altshul ("Yoshe Slonimer"), Joel Levinsohn (the "Vilner Ballabessil"), Jeruham Blindman ("Yerucham ha-Koton"), and Nissan Spivak ("Nissi Belzer"). The last named was a prolific composer, many of whose works are still popular.

The final part of this era, roughly the last decade of the 19th century and the first two decades of the 20th, became known as the "Golden Age of *Ḥazzanut.*" A number of factors contributed to the enormous popularity of cantorial music, which gave this era its distinctive title. Among them were the appearance of several *ḥazzanim* with truly great voices, the spread of gramophone recordings, and the emigration of large numbers of East European Jews to America, where cantorial concerts provided a tie with the Old World and the *shtetl* culture they knew so well. The most famous cantors of this era were Gershon Sirota, Mordecai Herschman, Zavel Kwartin, and Josef (Yossele) Rosenblatt, known as the "King of Cantors." Sirota and Herschman both had ringing tenor voices of operatic quality. Rosenblatt possessed a tenor voice of unusual range, a phenomenal falsetto, and superb coloratura. He composed almost everything that he sang and recorded most of his selections, as did Herschman and many others. The period between the two World Wars saw a sharp decline in cantorial music, but there was a resurgence in America, Western Europe, South Africa and Israel after World War II. In the USA, the Conservative and Reform movements acted to de-emphasize the central role of the *ḥazzan* and to simplify cantorial music in the synagogue. Some Reform congregations eliminated the cantor entirely, while others used only those with a heavy bass voice. Orthodox communities maintained the florid East European tradition with cantors such as the Koussevitzky brothers, Berele Chagy, Leib Glanz and Pierre Pinchik, as well as cantor-opera singers such as Richard Tucker and Jan Peerce, drawing large audiences.

In more recent years, despite the establishment of cantorial schools in the US and Israel, cantorial music as it developed in Eastern Europe has tended to decline. In some non-Orthodox synagogues, the cantor is resuming his historic position as a synagogue functionary whose primary task is leading the prayer service and whose secondary functions include teaching and choir directing. In the Orthodox community, apart from a few synagogues where the tradition of *ḥazzanut* is still strong, prayers are led on the Sabbath by a *sheli'aḥ tsibbur* and on festivals (especially the High Holidays) by a professional cantor or *ba'al tefillah*. Cantorial concerts are still well attended, but the average age of the audience is high.

CAPITAL PUNISHMENT The Bible mandates capital punishment for a series of crimes, among them kidnaping, murder, idolatry, desecration of the Sabbath, blasphemy, adultery, incest, and various other sexual offenses. Capital punishment was the standard punishment in the civilizations of the ancient Near East, and the Biblical code clearly believed in its value as a deterrent: "And all the men of his city shall stone him with stones, that he die; so shalt you put away the evil from your midst; and all Israel shall hear, and fear" (Deut.21:21). The death penalty was believed also to have a purging effect upon society at large. Thus the institutions charged with dispensing justice were explicitly forbidden to show mercy to those convicted of certain heinous crimes such as murder, kidnaping, and idolatry, and Deuteronomy demands the death penalty on ten separate occasions with the formulation "and you shall root out the evil from your midst."

Two forms of capital punishment are mentioned directly in the Bible, the more common being stoning, which consisted of all the people hurling stones at the condemned until he died. Although stoning seems to have been the standard biblical form of execution following due process of law (see for instance Lev.24:23), on several occasions (e.g. Ex.17:4; Num.14:10; II Chron.10:18) it appears as a spontaneous and almost reflexive expression of communal wrath. Thus, stoning seems to have been the expression of *vindicta popula* predating Sinaitic legislation that remained the presumed form of punishment for severe offenses thereafter.

Burning is the specified punishment for two offenses (Lev.20:14 and 21:9). Burning, however, may not have served as a primary form of execution but rather may have been used to attach a special stigma to a particular offense, the corpse of the offender having been burnt after death by stoning (Josh.7:25). All three cases of burning mentioned in the Pentateuch are related to sexual offenses. Burning too seems to have been a recognized penalty prior to Sinaitic legislation (Gen.38:24).

Apparently to heighten the deterrent power of capital punishment, Deut. 21:22 commands that the body of anyone executed for a capital offense be impaled on a stake and left on public display. The following verse, however, forbids leaving the body on display over night, "for he that is hanged is a reproach unto God; that you defile not your land (ibid.:23)."

By contrast to prevailing Mesopotamian custom according to which an individual could be punished for a crime committed by a member of his family, the Bible limited liability for criminal acts to the perpetrator. Families do not bear collective responsibility for crimes, as is established in Deut. 24:16, "The fathers shall not be put to death for the children, neither shall the children be put to death for the fathers; every man shall be put to death for his own sin [only]." The formulation of this verse suggests that it came to override an existing practice.

Criminal responsibility, and with it capital punishment, extended to animals as well. The ox that gores a human to death (Ex.25:28-29) as well as the animal involved in bestiality (Lev.20:16) are to be put to death. This has no parallel in the ancient Near East and is conceivable only in the religiously-based Hebrew legal code.

Talmudic discussions seem to show a shift in attitude towards capital punishment epitomized by the statement of Rabbis Akiva and Tarfon in the following passage (*Mak.* 1:10). R.Eleazar ben Azariah said that a Sanhedrin that put a man to death even only once in 70 years was considered bloodthirsty. R. Tarfon and R. Akiva said "Had we sat on the Sanhedrin, no one would ever have been executed." The Jewish legal system was clearly confronting the classic tensions regarding the morality and efficacy of capital punishment at this time.

The Talmud indicates, in addition to stoning and burning, two additional forms of execution, slaying (by sword) and strangling. Thus, the Talmud lists four methods of execution, the administration of which was governed by two central principles. The first principle was application of the Biblical injunction of "love your neighbour as yourself" (Lev. 19:17) to the condemned criminal. The operational result of this was the formulation "choose for him the most humane death possible" (*Ket.* 37b, *Sanh.* 45a). The second principle specified that execution be modeled on the taking of life by God: as when God takes a life only the soul is taken while the body remains unharmed, so must the method of execution leave the body unharmed. So, for example, stoning no longer consisted of the convicted offender being stoned to death by the people. The offender was killed by being pushed from a high place. The place was to be high enough that death be instantaneous and low enough to ensure that the body not be mutilated by the fall (*Sanh.* 6:4; 45a).

Not only did Talmudic law revise the methods of execution, it severely circumscribed the court's ability to convict those accused of capital crimes. A few of the limitations were: capital crimes could be tried only before a court of twenty-three; conviction could be obtained only on the testimony of two eye-witnesses; circumstantial evidence as well as hearsay evidence was inadmissable; witnesses related to each other or to the accused by blood or marriage were disqualified; conviction could not be obtained unless the accused had been warned in advance that his crime was punishable by death and unless he acknowledged the warning verbally. (See also Maimonides, *Yad, Sanh.* 12.)

Thus, where the Bible mandates the death penalty for numerous offenses, believes it to be an effective deterrent, cautions against showing mercy to those convicted, and demands its administration in order to purge society of evil, talmudic law renders administration of capital punishment practically impossible. The Talmud, of course, takes its regulations from the biblical text by means of the accepted hermeneutical principles. The traditional view, therefore, is that the talmudic attitude is simply the articulation of the Bible's intent. Recent scholars, however, tend to view the talmudic circumscription of capital punishment as a *de facto* reversal of biblical legislation. In any case, the rabbis, despite their leniency in the administration of capital punishment, reserved the right to use its acknowledged deterrent power even when not mandated by the Bible should the general state of the society or the particular circumstances warrant it (*Sanh.* 46a). Thus Jewish communities, during periods when granted such jurisdiction by the ruling power (e.g., Muslim Spain), continued to administer capital punishment even as punishment for offenses not considered capital crimes by the Bible. The exercise of this power was particularly common with regard to informers (see Maimonides, *Yad, Ḫovel u-Mazzik* 8:10).

Since the death penalty could be administered only by a qualified Sanhedrin, there is no existing Jewish body considered competent to administer capital punishment today.

With the establishment of the State of Israel, the question of the administration of capital punishment by a Jewish court became relevant. Since the new State took over the existing corpus of British mandatory law, the administration of capital punishment was a theoretical possibility. During the first murder trial to be held under Israeli jurisdiction, the chief rabbis notified the Minister of Justice of their opposition to the death penalty in the absence of a qualified Sanhedrin. The death penalty was officially abolished in 1954 in the Penal Code Revision Law. Until that time several death sentences were issued, but none was carried out. The death penalty was retained, however, under the Crime of Genocide (Prevention and Punishment) Law and for treason committed in time of warfare. The prescribed method of execution under the legislation cited is hanging for civilians and shooting for members of the military. In the only instance of capital punishment in the history of the State, Adolf Eichmann, convicted of genocide, was hanged in Ramleh prison in 1962.

CAPTIVES, RANSOMING OF (Heb. *pidyon shevuyim*). A religious obligation to which Jews have given the highest priority since biblical times, in accordance with their interpretation of the commandment: "You shall not stand idly by the blood of your neighbor" (Lev. 19:16). The rabbis considered the ransoming of captives to be one of Judaism's fundamental duties (*BB* 8a-b); for both MAIMONIDES (*Yad, Mattenot Aniyyim* 8.12) and the SHULḤAN ARUKH (*YD* 252.3), failure to act promptly in securing a captive's release is tantamount to shedding his blood. Even a Scroll of the Law could be sold to raise money to ransom captives (*Tos.* on *BB* 8b). At the same time, however, talmudic sages opposed giving way to extortion by paying inflated ransoms (Mish. *Git.* 4.6; TB *Git.* 45a). This is the position taken by Maimonides and most later authorities, such as David IBN ZIMRA (*Radbaz*), who wrote that even where lives may be at stake, a captive's release is not to be secured today if it will endanger another person's security tomorrow. MEIR (*Maharam*) of Rothenburg, when imprisoned in 1286 by the Holy Roman emperor, Rudolf I of Hapsburg, created a precedent by refusing to allow fellow Jews to obtain his release in exchange for a vast sum. He chose to spend the remaining seven years of his life in jail, rather than yield to the imperial extortioner and thereby encourage other despots to kidnap Jewish scholars. Nevertheless, every effort was generally made to liberate Jews sold into slavery or held to ransom. This obligation to redeem captives was usually discharged through a communal fund that gave practical expression to the talmudic dictum: "All Jews are responsible for one another" (*Shevu.* 39a).

Present-day realities, in the form of hijacks and kidnaping, have made the ransoming of hostages a live issue, the price demanded being sometimes political (the freeing of terrorists) and sometimes financial (the payment of a ransom). Authorities have suggested that the thrust of Jewish thinking is to resist the demands of hijackers, even if this runs counter to natural feelings of compassion. If giving way to extortion will place other lives in jeopardy, no exchange is permissible. On the other hand, where the release of hostages in exchange for political prisoners or convicts (or even, as has been the case with Israel, in exchange for the bodies of Israelis held by their enemies) is not likely to endanger public security, every effort should be made to redeem those in captivity.

CARO, JOSEPH BEN EPHRAIM (1488-1575). Greatest Jewish codifier of the 16th century, author of the SHULḤAN ARUKH. Born in Spain or Portugal, Caro was taken as a child to Turkey. He eventually settled in Edirne (Adrianople), becoming an eminent talmudist. In 1536 Caro moved to Safed where he was one of the first four scholars to be ordained by Rabbi Jacob Berab (see ORDINATION). He became head of the local rabbinical court and of an important *yeshivah* (talmudic academy), where his pupils included Moses CORDOVERO.

The *Shulḥan Arukh* is Caro's most famous work, but the *magnum opus* which kept him occupied from 1522 to 1554 was his *Bet Yosef* ("House of Joseph"). Ordination — and the heavenly mentor guiding his actions (see below) — inspired him with a sense of historic mission, as well as the courage to produce a unifying compendium of the ORAL LAW. Though written in the form of a commentary on JACOB BEN ASHER's *Arba'ah Turim* (*Tur*), Caro's *Bet Yosef* is an independent work that traces every law from its source in the Talmud through all stages of its development, discussing the opinions of all authorities before arriving at a decision.

The *Shulḥan Arukh* ("Prepared Table") was originally intended for young students as a digest of his *Bet Yosef*. First published in 1564-5, it follows the *Tur's* structure; each of the four parts is divided into chapters (*simanim*) and then into paragraphs called *se'ifim* ("branches"). Its most serious failing was the lack of reference to Ashkenazi CUSTOM (*minhag*), which often differed from Caro's Sephardi tradition. This fault was repaired by Moses ISSERLES, an outstanding Polish halakhist, whose *Mappah* ("Tablecloth") supplements and annotations made the *Shulḥan Arukh* acceptable to all sections of Jewry. Down to the present day, Orthodox Jews consider the decisions of the *Shulḥan Arukh* to be authoritative.

Caro's other works include supplementary corrections to his *Bet Yosef* entitled *Bedek ha-Bayit*; a volume of responsa, *Avkat Rokhel*; and *Kesef Mishneh*, a now standard commentary on part of MAIMONIDES' *Mishneh Torah*. One of the leading Safed kabbalists, Caro believed himself to be guided by a heavenly mentor (MAGGID) the "Mishnah personified," who revealed to him mysteries and instructions ever since his youth in Turkey. The mystical diary which he wrote later appeared as *Maggid Mesharim*.

Title page of the Shulḥan Arukh, *Joseph Caro's most famous work. Published in Amsterdam, 1698.*

CELIBACY Marriage is a commandment in Jewish tradition and celibacy is deplored. The first positive precept in the Bible is "be fruitful and multiply" (Gen.1:28) and this sets the pattern for Jewish attitudes. Procreation is a holy obligation, and deliberate abstention from marriage has never been condoned; indeed many authorities regard it as a sin. Halakhically speaking, the commandment to be fruitful is binding upon males only, so that female celibacy is less problematic. The biblical NAZIRITE took various vows of abstinence; sexual abstinence, however, was not among them. One exception in the Bible was JEREMIAH who apparently chose to remain celibate due to his unwillingness to bring children into the world to face the impending doom of the Jewish people. According to JOSEPHUS, celibacy was practiced among the sectarian ESSENES. The normative teaching is contained in the saying "He who is without a wife is without joy, without blessing, without happiness, without learning, without protection, without peace; indeed he is no man" (*Yev.* 62b).

One talmudic scholar, Ben Azzai, never married, but he and his colleagues acknowledged that he was an exception. None of the medieval rabbis is known to have been unmarried, and bachelors were not allowed to occupy positions of leadership in the Jewish community. Judaism, moreover, encouraged early marriage to counter sexual temptation.

CEMETERY Area of land designated for the BURIAL of the dead. In biblical times, the general practice was to bury the dead in family sepulchers. The Mishnah (*Sanh.* 6:5) records that executed criminals were not buried in their ancestral burial ground, but were interred in separate cemeteries. Another Mishnah (*B.B.* 2:9) rules that graves should be outside the town. It seems that cemeteries developed during talmudic times. In Rome there were special Jewish catacombs.

The cemetery is known in Hebrew as *bet kevarot* ("place of graves"); *bet olam* ("house of eternity"); and euphemistically as *bet ḫayyim* ("place of the living"). Usually, the land of the cemetery is considered to be holy, and a special CONSECRATION ceremony is held on its inauguration. It is reserved for Jews. The cemetery requires decorum akin to that for a synagogue. On the other hand, the cemetery is a source of ritual impurity (*tum'ah*). Those of priestly descent (*kohanim*) are not allowed to enter a cemetery, except to attend the burial of near relatives whom they are obligated to mourn. Ritual purification is needed by those who have entered a cemetery; today, the custom is to wash one's hands on leaving a cemetery as a symbol of purification. Thus, the cemetery has the paradoxical status of having both elements of consecration and of ritual impurity.

The old cemetery of Vilna, Lithuania, with tombs dating back to the beginning of the 20th century.

The responsibility for establishing a Jewish cemetery devolves on the community, and is one of the first matters to be arranged when a new community is being formed. The Jewish cemetery has generally been purchased and maintained with communal funds, and has been managed by a committee appointed by the community. In recent times, cemeteries have been acquired by communities, synagogues, and burial societies. Private Jewish cemeteries have also come into existence, selling graves to the general Jewish public who do not have burial ground in the non-profit cemeteries.

An ancient custom was to leave cemeteries unadorned by trees and plants. This practice is maintained by the old cemeteries of the communities in Jerusalem, Safed, Tiberias, and Hebron. However, beautifying cemeteries with trees and plants is now a widespread practice among Jews.

Traditionally, a building was erected at the cemetery to serve as a chapel (*ohel*) and sometimes also as a place to prepare the body for burial (see TOHORAH). A wall or fence surrounds a cemetery.

The graves are arranged in rows. Jewish law requires a distance of six handbreadths between graves. Under certain circumstances, the distance may be reduced to a minimum of six fingerbreadths. If necessary, one body may be buried on top of another, if there is a separation of earth the depth of six handbreadths.

Some cemeteries have separate rows for men and for women, and some separate different communities (e.g., Ashkenazim and Sephardim). Some bury in chronological order of death; others have family plots; some have a combination of both practices. Traditionally, certain rows were reserved for rabbis and pious communal leaders. There was also a designated row for suicides (unless adjudged "of unsound mind"), apostates, and notorious transgressors, often near the cemetery wall. The SHULKḪAN ARUKH indicates that a wicked person should not be buried near a righteous person, nor even near a person who was not as wicked. Only a pious person should be buried near another pious person. Enemies should not be buried next to each other.

Graves are generally marked with TOMBSTONES. A widespread Sephardi practice is for the stone to lie flat on the grave (though not in Italy and some other Western lands). The prevalent Ashkenazi practice in the Diaspora is to erect an upright headstone. Rabbi Yehiel Michel Epstein in his *Arukh ha-Shulkḫan* (*YD.* 364:6) ruled against the erection of expensive and elaborate tombstones,. Simplicity is by far to be preferred. Instead of expending large sums on tombstones, the family can better serve the memory of the dead by contributing to charity in his memory.

One should not act in a lightheaded fashion in a cemetery.

It is inappropriate to eat, drink, read, or study there. Animals should not be allowed to graze in a cemetery, and it should not be used as a shortcut or as a place to take a stroll. It is considered mocking the dead to wear phylacteries (*tefillin*) or carry a Scroll of the Law in the cemetery within four cubits of a grave. The Torah can only be fulfilled by the living, so by performing MITSVOT in a cemetery it is as though the dead are reminded of their own deprivation (Maimonides, *Yad Evel* 114.13; *Sh. Ar. YD* 367-8).

There are various customs with regard to visiting the gravesite. Most common are: at the end of seven days of MOURNING; thirty days after burial; annually on the date of death. On such visits, psalms and prayers for the dead are recited.

In many communities, it is customary to visit the cemetery during the month of Elul, prior to the New Year. Some visit on the ninth of Av and the eve of the Day of Atonement. However, the rabbis discouraged overfrequent visiting of cemeteries. A custom in many Sephardi communities has been to bury any worn-out sacred books and artifacts on LAG BA-OMER. Pilgrimages to the cemetery were also common at times of communal distress; people prayed at the graves of the pious seeking God's mercy (*Ta'an.* 16a,23b; Maimonides, *Hilkhot Ta'anit* 4:18).

Among North African Jews, a custom arose known as HILLULA. This was an annual pilgrimage to the grave of a saintly person, whose spirit was believed to continue to exert influence on the affairs of the living. Prayers were offered, seeking the saint's intercession with God for the benefit of those who were praying. The *hillula* was often the occasion for a large gathering at the cemetery. Fires were lit, candles were placed on the grave, prayers were chanted. The event would last through the night, often having a festive quality.

In traditional custom, a person entering a cemetery after an interval of over 30 days recites a blessing acknowledging that God is the master of life and death, and that He will raise us to new life hereafter. It concludes: "Blessed are You O Lord, who revives the dead."

CENSORSHIP Following a DISPUTATION in Paris (1240), all manuscripts of the Talmud were collected and burned. After the disputation of Barcelona (1263), James I of Aragon ordered the Jews to remove from their manuscripts all references found to be objectionable to Christians. The pattern of attacks on Jewish works, especially the Talmud, was to continue for many centuries. From the earliest days of printing, the classical Jewish works have been subject to censorship. The Talmud was burned in Italy after the promulgation of a Papal Bull (1554) which permitted Jews to own other writings, providing they contained no blasphemies against Christianity. Generally, the censors excised any references which were deemed offensive to Christianity. Books thus appeared with entire lines or passages inked out or pages torn out by the censors. Often, the censor was an apostate Jew, since non-Jews were rarely sufficiently well-versed in Talmud and Midrash to perform the task. Many of the apostate Jews were also ignorant. Thus, Johannes Pfefferkorn (1469-c.1521) of Cologne, who was given the authority to censor all Hebrew books except the Bible, and who suggested that all copies of the Talmud be burned, was a butcher, with very little Jewish education. Generally, censorship involved the removal of references to such topics as Christianity, Jesus, and Rome, the last often being understood as a euphemism for the Church. On one occasion, toward the end of the 16th century, an entire tractate of the Talmud, AVODAH ZARAH, was censored out, and the Basle Talmud of that era appears without it.

Jews attempted to anticipate Christian objections and sometimes initiated a pre-censorship examination by the rabbinical authorities who removed passages they felt might offend Christians.

Once the State replaced the Church as supreme authority, various countries instituted their own systems of censorship, one of the most notorious being that of Russia, which existed until the end of the 19th century. Nazi Germany embarked on the burning of all books by Jewish authors, and the 1933 Nazi list of prescribed books included 12,400 titles.

Prayers have also been censored, and the ALÉNU prayer was edited by Ashkenazi Jews themselves, who were frequently attacked for passages which were interpreted as offensive to Christianity.

According to some authorities, the Passover Haggadah contains another example of preventive censorship in the phrase "an Aramean sought to slay my father," where the word "Aramean" (*arami* in Hebrew) may be a euphemism for "Roman" (*Romi*).

In addition to the above instances of censorship, there was also internal Jewish censorship, by the device known as the HASKAMAH, whereby every Jewish text had to be endorsed by a leading rabbi, thereby certifying that its contents were in no way inappropriate morally or in terms of belief.

CHARITY The Hebrew word for charity is *tsedakah*, deriving from the root for "justice." A distinction is made in Jewish sources between charity and *gemilut ḥasadim* (the latter usually translated as "acts of lovingkindness"). *Gemilut ḥasadim* generally includes all types of aid and assistance to others, e.g., lending one's possessions, visiting the sick, and escorting the dead at a funeral. Thus, in actuality, *tsedakah* is but one aspect of the broader category of *gemilut ḥasadim*. The Talmud (*Suk.* 49b) points out the difference between the two concepts: "There are three ways in which *gemilut ḥasadim* exceeds charity: charity can be performed only with one's money, while *gemilut ḥasadim* can be performed with one's body or one's money; charity is only for the poor, whereas *gemilut ḥasadim* is for the poor and the rich; charity can be only for the living, while *gemilut ḥasadim* is for the living and the dead."

> **CHARITY**
>
> A person must be scrupulous in fulfilling the commandment to give charity for this is the sign of a descendant of Abraham.
>
> Israel will be redeemed through acts of charity.
>
> As great as is the commandment of charity, even greater is persuading another to give charity.
>
> Charity is one of the things whose profits man enjoys in this world, but whose principal remains for the world to come.
>
> Charity is equal to all the other commandments combined.
>
> Everyone should give charity; even he who depends on charity should give to those who are even less fortunate.
>
> It is better not to give charity than to do so and shame the recipient publicly.
>
> He who is generous to the poor makes a loan to the Lord.
>
> Nobody is ever impoverished through giving charity.
>
> Do not humiliate a beggar; God is beside him.

The Pentateuch makes clear provisions for the poor, when, based on the agrarian society of the time, it demands that the landowner leave for the poor the gleanings, grain forgotten in the field, and the corner of each field (see AGRICULTURE, LAWS OF). Similarly, in the third and sixth years of the SABBATICAL YEAR cycle, a TITHE had to be given to the poor. Moreover, all financial debts still owing by the sabbatical year were cancelled.

In the Pentateuch, there appears to be a contradiction regarding the poor. While Deut. 15:4 says, "There shall be no needy among you," a few verses later, (15:11) it says, "There will never cease to be needy ones in your land." Various interpretations have been offered to explain the apparent contradiction. Naḫmanides, for example, saw the first verse as the ideal situation, contingent on all Jews' observing the commandments, whereas the second verse reflects the reality — that people are imperfect. It is following the second statement that the Pentateuch commands: "You shall surely open your hand to the poor and the destitute in your land."

According to the rabbis, the manner in which charity is given adds to the value of the deed. R.Eleazar said: "The reward that is paid for giving charity is directly related to the kindness with which it is given" (*Suk.* 49b). Charity, together with prayer and repentance during the TEN DAYS OF PENITENCE, can cancel an adverse Divine decree regarding the coming year. Maimonides, in his *Laws of Gifts to the Poor*, (10:7ff.), notes eight degrees of charity, the highest of which is enabling a poor person to become self-sufficient, as, for example, establishing the person in business. The next highest is giving charity such that the donor and the recipient are ignorant of each other's identity. The lowest of these levels is giving charity to another while visibly showing resentment.

The amount one ought to give to charity (there is a dispute whether the figure is ordained by biblical law, rabbinic law, or by custom) is 1/10th of one's initial capital and 1/10th of all subsequent earnings. The Talmud nevertheless cautions that one should not give more than one fifth of his earnings, for by doing so, he may become destitute and need to be supported himself.

The Talmud defines a poor person entitled to receive charity, as one whose total assets do not exceed 200 *zuz*. The amount that an individual should be given appears to be relative: according to HILLEL (*Ket.* 67b), the person should be given enough for him not to feel deprived of his former lifestyle. Jewish law is also sensitive to needs in specific instances. Thus a farmer whose gross assets may be in excess of the allowable limit, is permitted to receive charity if the alternative would be selling his land at a depressed price. At the same time, a person ought to do everything possible to avoid taking charity; the Talmud counsels, "Make your Sabbath into a weekday (i.e., do not purchase delicacies for the Sabbath) rather than be forced to depend upon human beings." One who takes charity when he has no right to, will ultimately have to accept charity out of need.

The traditional Jewish COMMUNITY contained various organizations that disbursed charitable funds. For example, there were funds for hospitality to wayfarers, funds to redeem those taken captive, to buy Passover supplies for the needy, and to bury the indigent.

Besides the straightforward donation of money to the poor, certain other expenditures are also considered to be charity in the halakhic sense. Thus, if one is of very limited means, his support of his children above the age at which they are deemed capable of supporting themselves is considered charity. The same applies to a person who supports his parents. Donating money to an individual to enable him to study Torah or directly to a Torah institution is also considered charity.

Contemporary rabbinic authorities differ as to whether the purchase of a seat in a synagogue is considered a charitable contribution or merely payment for services rendered.

There are also criteria of priority in the allocation of charity. The general rule states that "the poor of one's own community take precedence." (This rule is further refined to give precedence to the poor members of one's own family.) The poor of the Land of Israel take precedence over the poor of other lands, but whether the poor of the Land of Israel take precedence over the poor of one's own city is a matter of rabbinic dispute. Women take precedence over men.

Every town in which there are Jews is required to have a

charity fund, with at least two individuals appointed to administer it (Maimonides, *Laws of Gifts to the Poor*, 9:1). As the Talmud explains it, the basic charity fund, named *kuppah* — or "the chest" — must disburse a full week's needs to every poor family each Friday. Some cities had an additional fund, named *tamḇui*, which would collect food from various householders and would distribute enough for two meals each evening to those in need. While the *kuppah* was available only to local residents, the *tamḇui* was open to anyone in need, and helped wayfarers who were passing through. There are clear criteria as to who must contribute toward the different needs of the poor. Thus, one who has lived in a town for 30 days must donate to the *kuppah*, while one who has been a resident for three months must contribute to the *tamḇui*.

CHASTITY Abstention from illicit sexual activity (in contrast to VIRGINITY, which is abstention from all sexual intercourse). The Bible warned the Israelites against defiling themselves and their land in the manner "that the nations which I am casting out before you defiled themselves" (Lev. 18:24). Illicit sexual activity such as ADULTERY, incest, sodomy and bestiality — called "the practices of the land of Egypt" — is considered "abhorrent" to God. By refraining from such activity, the Israelites achieve a state of holiness. Maimonides wrote: "No prohibition in all the Torah is as difficult to keep as that of forbidden unions and illicit sexual relations" (*Yad, Issuré Bi'ah* 22:18). Because Joseph resisted seduction by Potiphar's wife (Gen. 39:9), he is called Joseph the righteous. Adultery is one of the three cardinal sins, along with murder and idolatry, for which death, viz. martyrdom, is preferable.

Marriage is the ideal relationship between man and woman. Even in marriage, chastity is required during the NIDDAH period (separation during menstruation and for a time thereafter). An unmarried woman who has not ritually immersed herself since her last period, is also considered a *niddah*. Sexual relations and physical contact are prohibited with her, just as they are with one's wife during this time. One difference at all times is that one may be alone with one's wife, but not with an unmarried woman. The sages, aware of the formidable temptations in the attraction between men and women explained as due to the power of the *yetzer ha-ra*, the evil inclination, recommended early marriage (*Kid.* 29b), diverting unchaste thoughts through Torah study (*Kid.* 30b), and avoidance of too much conversation with women (*Avot* 1:5).

Chastity refers to avoiding illicit sex, not sex *per se*. Permitted sex is intrinsically good, a *mitsvah*, a natural drive inherent in the individual's biological constitution. As such, it is not to be repressed as in certain other cultures, but merely channeled. A husband may not withhold sexual relations from his wife, nor she from him, due to anger or ascetic inclinations, for this is grounds for divorce. MODESTY and constraint govern the marital relationship, which attains a state of holiness through the practice of chastity.

CHERUB (Heb. *keruv* from which the English word is derived; plur. *keruvim*). Type of winged celestial being mentioned frequently in the Bible, either as a Divine messenger (see ANGELS) or as one of a sculptured pair guarding the ARK OF THE COVENANT. Etymologically, "cherub" may be traced to the Akkadian *karubu* or *kuribu* meaning "an intercessor," one who brings man's prayers before the gods. Winged bulls or geniuses are a standard feature of Assyrian monuments, reliefs, and seals, where they often appear ministering to the gods or worshiping a sacred tree. After the expulsion of Adam and Eve, God stationed cherubim east of the Garden of EDEN "to guard the way to the tree of life" (Gen. 3:24). God Himself is portrayed as the "Lord of Hosts enthroned on the Cherubim" (I Sam. 4:4; II Kings 19:15; Ps. 80:2; Isa. 37:16) and He also flies through the air mounted on a cherub (II Sam. 22:11; Ps. 18:11).

Two wooden cherubim overlaid with gold, facing each other with outstretched wings, were placed at either end of the mercy seat above the Ark in the SANCTUARY of the wilderness, thereby serving as God's throne (Ex. 25:18-22, 37:7-9). Cherub motifs were also embroidered on the curtains of the Sanctuary, as well as on the veil separating the "Holy" from the "Holy of Holies" (Ex. 26:1, 36:8; and

A carved ivory cherub with two wings and one face. From Samaria, 9th century BCE.

26:31, 36:35). Two of these figures, each ten cubits (approx. 15 feet) in height with a similar measurement across the wings, mounted guard over the Holy of Holies (I Kings 6:23-28, 8:6-7). Carved reliefs depicting cherubim, palms, and other motifs were also set on all the walls, doors, and panels of the Temple (*ibid.*, 6:29, 32, 35; 7:29, 36). Certain discrepancies are apparent, however, in the various biblical accounts. Each of the two cherubim designed for the Sanctuary and later for Solomon's Temple has one pair of wings and one face (Ex. 25:20; I Kings 6:24, 27), whereas the creatures in Ezekiel's chariot vision have two sets of wings and four faces (Ezek. 1:6, 23). They are also described as having the faces of a man, a lion, an ox, and an eagle (1:10), although the face of a cherub is substituted for that of the ox in a later chapter (10:14). Archetypal portrayals may well account for the fact that each cherub is given two faces only — that of a man and that of a lion — in Ezekiel's Temple vision (41:18-19).

Phoenician cherub motifs likewise decorated Ahab's ivory palace in Samaria, but these (along with the First Temple structure in Jerusalem) fell victim to invading armies. According to rabbinic sources (*Yoma* 21a), no cherubim were re-created for the Second Temple and the term *keruv* was understood to mean "childlike" (*Suk.* 5b; *Ḥag.* 13b). This presumably explains the cherub's subsequent transformation in Christian iconography and Western art, where a beautiful angelic child usually symbolizes Divine justice and wisdom. Cherubim are of peripheral importance in Jewish ritual art, although Maimonides assigned them a place next to the seraphim in his angelic constellation (*Yad, Yesodé ha-Torah*, 2.7).

CHIEF RABBINATE A centralized form of Jewish religious authority developed from the Middle Ages, with functions that were often representative as well as judicial. In medieval Europe, a "chief Jew" (*magister Judaeorum*) was sometimes little more than a tax collector and agent of the crown; in other cases, he might be the head of a rabbinical court (BET DIN), some prominent Jew who was recognized by the government as "crown rabbi," or one serving as both. This system helped to preserve juridical autonomy and led to the establishment of local or more widely recognized chief rabbinates. Thus, a preeminent crown rabbi (*Rab de la Corte* or *Rabi mayor*) of Castile was Ḥasdai CRESCAS; a *Rabbi Mór ("arraby moor")* held office in Portugal for more than two centuries (1278-1497); while Solomon ADRET of Barcelona was known as *Rab d'Espama.* Under the Holy Roman Empire, MEIR OF ROTHENBURG was both a government-appointed *Hochmeister* of the Jews and the community's spiritual authority. Among the Jews of Central Europe, from the 14th century onward, the concept of a "town rabbi" (*mara de-atra*) found expression in the LANDESRABBINER. Two modern examples of politically motivated state appointments are the various Grands Rabbins first imposed on French Jewry by Napoleon (see CONSISTORY) and the office of KAZYONNY RAVVIN ("government" or "official" rabbi) disparaged by the Jews of Tsarist Russia.

In England, the rabbi of London's Great Synagogue enjoyed semi-official status until 1844, when a representative body of delegates elected Nathan Marcus Adler as "Chief Rabbi of the United Hebrew Congregations of the British Empire" (now the British Commonwealth). No parallel institution exists in America: Jacob Joseph, a Lithuanian talmudist, served briefly as chief rabbi of New York's Orthodox congregations (1888-1902), but the experiment did not succeed. Other chief rabbinates exist today in Western Europe (e.g., Belgium, Denmark, France, Holland, Italy, Sweden, and Switzerland), in Eastern Europe (Hungary, Romania and the Soviet Union), and in South Africa, Turkey, and Latin America (Argentina and Venezuela). All of these bodies are Orthodox, apart from the chief rabbinates of Sweden and Hungary (Conservative).

By virtue of the authority conferred on him by the Sublime Porte, a ḤAKHAM BASHI in Istanbul was acknowledged by Jewish communities throughout the Ottoman Empire. During the Turkish period, a Sephardi "Chief Rabbinate of the Holy Land" also began functioning in Jerusalem (see RISHON LE-TSIYYON). Soon after the establishment of Britain's Palestine Mandate, the previous authority was transformed into a dual chief rabbinate headed by Jacob Meir (Sephardi) and Abraham Isaac KOOK (Ashkenazi) from 1921. This system continued, virtually unchanged, after the State of Israel came into being. All the Diaspora chief rabbinates are based on congregational "roof organizations" and are financed by voluntary contributions. The Chief Rabbinate of Israel, however, is a state authority with a governmental budget and exclusive jurisdiction over matters of personal status (marriage, divorce, conversion to Judaism, etc.). The Chief Rabbinate Council functions as a supreme *bet din*, and there are also dual chief rabbinates in Israel's major cities. See also RABBI AND RABBINATE.

CHILDREN Judaism has always placed a high value on bearing and rearing children. The verse, "Be fruitful and multiply" (Gen. 1:28), was considered to be the first commandment in the Bible. The Talmud asserts that one who is childless may be considered as dead (*Ned.* 64b) and compares intentional avoidance of having children to murder (*Yev.* 63b). The commandment to be fruitful, however, devolves upon men only and is regarded as fulfilled once two boys or a boy and girl have been born. A man may marry a woman incapable of bearing children only if he has already fulfilled his obligation or if he has another wife who is presumed fertile (*Maim. Yad, Ishut* 15:7). A couple that remains childless after ten years of marriage is expected to divorce; if infertility is attributable to the woman she forfeits the basic compensation (but not any additional compensation promised) guaranteed in her marriage contract. If infer-

Children at a kindergarten of the Reform movement in Jerusalem, being taught how a religious service is conducted.

tility is attributable to the HUSBAND, he must pay all benefits enumerated in the marriage contract (*ibid.* 15:8). In modern times, divorce of this kind is extremely rare. One interpretation equates the biblical punishment of KARET, being "cut off," with BARRENNESS.

The Bible states that children will suffer for their parents' evil doings "unto the third and fourth generation" (Ex.20:5). However, this was modified by the rabbis (*Ber.* 7a) to refer only to offspring who continue to follow their parents' sins. Children benefit from their parents' righteousness "to the thousandth generation" (Ex. 20:5-6).

The origin of the celebration of SHALOM ZAKHAR, held on the Friday night following the birth of a son, is found in the Talmud. NAMES are given to male children at their circumcision; girls when the father is called to the READING OF THE LAW in the synagogue within a week of the birth. In recent decades, Jews in various western communities originated the custom of celebrating the birth of a daughter with a ceremony known as *Simḥat Bat.*

The child's initiation to Jewish life begins from an early age with the recitation of the SHEMA and blessings and the study of Hebrew and the Pentateuch. The Mishnah states that boys are to study the Bible from the age of five, Mishnah at ten, to perform *mitsvot* at the age of 13, and to study Talmud at 15 (*Avot* 5:21); see EDUCATION. Today, the study of Mishnah and Talmud may begin at younger ages. In previous eras, girls were not given formal schooling, but rather learned their Jewish and domestic responsibilities from their mothers in the home. Although children are exempt from the performance of *mitsvot*, both boys and girls were early introduced to the various rituals so that they would be well accustomed to them when they reached majority — girls at the age of 12 and boys at the age of 13. Traditionally, girls were not encouraged to participate in the various rituals such as TSITSIT, TEFILLIN, TALLIT, etc., from which they were exempt. In nearly all communities, except the extremely traditional Orthodox, this pattern is currently changing, with Reform, Conservative, and Reconstructionist movements taking the lead. Today, girls in virtually all communities attend school.

The filial obligations of children are recorded in the Pentateuch under the rubrics of honor (Ex. 20:12) and reverence (Lev. 19:3). Honor requires the provision of food, drink, and personal needs. Reverence requires that the child not sit in his parent's seat or contradict him in conversation (*Kid.* 31b). The Bible (Deut. 21:18-21) even invoked the death penalty for the REBELLIOUS SON who disregarded his parents and exhibited other extreme forms of anti-social behavior. The predominant opinion in the Talmud claims that the Bible's intent was never actually to bring such a child to execution but rather to express a value judgment upon such actions (*San.* 71a). However, a child is instructed to defy his parents should they order him to transgress the laws of Judaism.

A child born of an incestuous or adulterous relationship is designated a *mamzer* and may not marry into the community (*Yev.* 49a, see ILLEGITIMACY). Such a child is still considered a Jew, however, and is permitted to marry another *mamzer.* The Talmud further states that a *mamzer* who is a Torah scholar is to be accorded higher honor than an uneducated High Priest (*Hor.* 3:8). There is no legal stigma attached to children born out of wedlock.

In practice, the Jewish household has traditionally revolved around the the bearing and rearing of children. Jewish parents the world over aspire to be blessed with God-fearing children and grandchildren and to be able to take pride in their offspring's accomplishments (see also FAMILY; MOTHER; PARENT AND CHILD.

CHILDREN

He who has a son who toils in the Torah is regarded as not having died

Parents must fulfill promises made to children, lest the children learn to lie

Not to have children detracts from God's image

Each child brings his own blessing into the world

He who teaches his son to be righteous is like an immortal

Love all your children equally and have no favorites

What a child says on the street, the parents said at home

Small children can disturb your sleep, big ones your life

The world will be redeemed through the merits of the children

The rich don't have children; they have heirs.

CHILDREN'S PRAYERS AND SERVICES Forms of worship specially devised for, and often conducted by, Jewish youngsters. Teaching children to recite daily prayers has long been an integral part of religious education in the home and, subsequently, at Hebrew school. Among observant Jews, even very small children are taught brief prayers to be recited on waking up in the morning and before going to sleep at night. Such formulas normally include an appropriate benediction and the first three verses of the SHEMA; other passages are added when the child reaches school age. MODEH ANI is then said in the morning, together with the entire first paragraph of the *Shema*, and boys wearing TSITSIT also recite an appropriate benediction. At this stage, an abbreviated version of the NIGHT PRAYER for adults is likewise prescribed, sometimes concluding with all or part of the ADON OLAM hymn. Sephardi Jews permit a small boy to recite one liturgical verse aloud in public worship and a seven-year-old to read the *haftarah* on an ordinary Sabbath (for an Ashkenazi parallel, see AN'IM ZEMIROT).

Reform Judaism, from the mid-19th century, instituted shortened prayer services for boys and girls on Sabbath mornings or afternoons. Prayers were usually recited in the vernacular, although portions of the *Shema*, ALÉNU LE-SHABBE'AḤ etc., were declaimed in Hebrew. In time this system also became popular in the Conservative movement, and special prayer books have been issued by both non-Orthodox trends for use in their "junior congregations" and youth camps. Children's services (for the "under 13s") and youth services for teenagers have likewise become fashionable in some Western (mainly English-speaking) Orthodox congregations. Here they are normally conducted during the Reading of the Law and Additional Service on Sabbaths and festivals, their purpose being to familiarize youngsters with the traditional Hebrew liturgy. Abbreviated, illustrated prayer books for small children have been published by Orthodox sponsors in the USA. The concept of a children's service is virtually restricted to the Diaspora: in Israel, its nearest equivalent is the weekly Sabbath morning service organized by local affiliates of the religious Zionist Bnei Akiva youth movement within the framework of its regular activities. This service follows the modern Orthodox pattern and has also been copied by branches of the movement overseas.

CHOIRS AND CHORAL MUSIC As singers and musicians, Jews have been prominent since antiquity. Many biblical passages allude to a choir of LEVITES enhancing public worship in the Sanctuary, and later in the Temple, where they were accompanied by an orchestra. Centuries later, this choir figured in the purified worship introduced by King Hezekiah (II Chron. 29:25-30). The term *La-menatse'aḥ* ("For the Leader") introducing many of the psalms possibly refers to a choirmaster or musical director. From other biblical passages (I Chron. 16:34, 41; II Chron. 5:13, 7:6, 20:21) it is clear that the HALLEL psalms had pride of place in the repertoire, while the fame of the Levites and their Temple song even aroused comment abroad (Ps. 137:1-3).

The choir of the Second Temple was exclusively male, could only be joined after intensive training, and adhered to the highest musical standards. It comprised a dozen choristers between the ages of 30 and 50, augmented by younger trained voices. An outline of its functioning in the last decades of the Temple is provided by the Mishnah (*Tam.* 7.3-4), which underlines the choir's professional accomplishments. According to the Talmud (*Suk.* 50b-51a; *Ar.* 11a), choral rather than instrumental music distinguished the Temple service. Even before the Second Temple's destruction in 70 CE, however, congregational chanting had begun to replace elaborate chorales in SYNAGOGUE worship, where services were led by a *ḥazzan* (precentor) and no instrumental accompaniment was allowed. Thereafter, and down to the 17th century (or later), a prayer leader often conducted services with two *meshorerim* (auxiliary "singers"), an adult and a boy soprano, and it was this form of chanting that created the pattern for all subsequent congregational worship in Judaism (see CANTOR AND CANTORIAL MUSIC; MUSIC AND SONG).

The next important stage was reached in the late 16th century, when talented Jewish musicians in northern Italy fell victim to the Catholic Counter-Reformation. Excluded from Renaissance culture and banished to various Italian ghettoes, they now displayed a creative interest in the music of the synagogue. Their most enthusiastic supporter was Leone (Judah) Modena, a Venetian rabbi who had earlier established a trained synagogue choir in Ferrara (c. 1605). His polyphonic song techniques, borrowed from Italian art music, paved the way for Salomone de' Rossi, a Jewish colleague of Monteverde at the court of Mantua, whose collected *Songs of Solomon* (1622-23) were an original and ambitious attempt to revive the ancient Levitical tradition. The outstanding pre-modern Jewish composer, de' Rossi, wrote and conducted Hebrew choral works, chiefly "echo-poems," for two eight-voice choirs without instrumental accompaniment. Intended for weddings, special Sabbaths, and festive occasions, they were not intended to replace the traditional chants but to enhance religious ceremonies. Throughout the 17th and 18th centuries, de' Rossi's pioneering musical techniques inspired others to write Hebrew cantatas and choral works in Provence and the Sephardi congregation of Amsterdam as well as in Italy, two or three of the composers, Carlo Grossi of Mantua and Louis Saladin of Avignon (*Canticum Hebraicum,* c. 1690), even being non-Jews.

Meanwhile, East European cantorial and choral music had also begun to make its impact on Western Ashkenazim (e.g., in Amsterdam, c. 1700). The traditional *ḥazzan-meshorerim* combination remained in vogue until the 19th century, by which time sweeping changes were affecting synagogue worship owing to the innovations of REFORM JUDAISM. For the first time, age-old halakhic norms were changed by Israel JACOBSON, who trained boy choristers to sing Lutheran-style hymns with ORGAN accompaniment in Germany (1809-18), a technique which was soon broadened and improved upon by more full-fledged Reform congregations in Central Europe (see MUSIC). This type of choral service utilized women and non-Jewish choristers, instrumental music, and Protestant or Sephardi compositions, largely abandoning the Ashkenazi prayer chants, and gained currency in the United States. At the same time, a more moderate course was pursued by the two leading 19th-century composers of synagogue music, Salomon Sulzer in Vienna and Louis Lewandowski in Berlin, who attempted to find a synthesis between the traditional melodies and the new methods. Their outstanding choral works have had a lasting impact not only on Liberal and Conservative services but on the modern Orthodox liturgy as well.

Both the radical Reform, which dispensed with the cantor, and East European Ḥasidism, which condemned the use of professional choirs, were until recently unaffected by the new Hebrew compositions. Though they were initially derided, "Choir Synagogues" with improved traditional services became part of the East European Jewish scene in the early 1900s, leading cantor-composers and choirmasters such as David Nowakowsky (Odessa) and Abraham M. Bernstein (Vilna) exerting a vast and far-reaching influence. Western Neo-Orthodoxy had accepted the need for aesthetic worship and trained choirs at a much earlier stage; thanks to the efforts of Samson Raphael HIRSCH, Israel Meyer Japhet was able to develop choral services in the Orthodox *Austrittsgemeinde* of Frankfurt. Similar changes took place in Paris and Great Britain.

In the United States, it was an Orthodox Sephardi congregation, Shearith Israel, that organized the first synagogue choir in 1818. Thereafter, until the early 20th century, choral music chiefly owed its development to the initiative of leading Reform temples. They commissioned elaborate "Sabbath Service" works from composers of world rank such as Ernest Bloch, Darius Milhaud, and Joseph Achron, but some of their musical directors (Edward Stark, Lazare Saminsky, and Abraham Wolf Binder) fostered a partial return to more traditional worship with cantor and choir. For various choral and musical improvements to the service, American Orthodoxy was indebted to cantor-composers and choirmasters such as Josef ("Yossele") Rosenblatt, Zavel Zilberts, and Samuel Malavsky, the latter establishing a popular family choir with his two sons and four daughters.

Some US Reform congregations still shun traditional prayer modes and employ non-Jewish singers. Conservative synagogues in the US are increasingly following the Reform example by organizing "mixed" choirs and permitting organ accompaniment on Sabbaths and festivals. Orthodox congregations throughout the world oppose the inclusion of female voices in the synagogue choir. Like their Ashkenazi counterparts, the Spanish and Portuguese congregations in London and New York maintain professionally trained male choirs for Sabbath and festival services. In Israel and other countries, augmented synagogue choirs often appear at cantorial music concerts, drawing large and appreciative audiences.

CHORIN, AARON (1766-1844). Moravian-born pioneer of REFORM JUDAISM in Hungary. As rabbi of Arad (Transylvania) from 1789, Chorin wrote and preached fiercely against customs that he held to be superstitious (e.g. KAPPAROT). While basing his opinions on the Oral Law, Chorin launched ever more radical attacks on traditional practice and it was only governmental intervention that enabled him to retain his post in the face of rabbinical censure. His reformist measures (which he justified with citations from rabbinic authorities) included the abolition of KOL NIDRE on the Day of Atonement; permitting bareheaded worship and services in the (Hungarian) vernacular, as well as the playing of an ORGAN on Sabbaths and festivals; curtailing the *shivah* week of MOURNING; and waiving Sabbath prohibitions against writing and travel. Chorin was also an ardent promoter of secular education and vocational training for young Jews. Religious tradition, in his view, meant that one should "not simply cling to the dry letter of the Law, but be guided by its spirit."

CHOSEN PEOPLE The doctrine in Judaism (also known as election) that God chose the people of Israel from among the nations. The doctrine of the chosen people is closely related to the notion of COVENANT, the contract between God and Israel.

The concept originates with the Divine choice of Abraham and his descendants as recounted in Genesis. God's first communication with Abraham already hints at a unique relationship with God that has implications for the rest of mankind: "I will make of you a great nation...and all the families of the earth shall bless themselves by you" (Gen. 12: 2-3). God's covenant with Abraham is narrated in Genesis 17, and the contractual agreement in which the people of Israel agree to keep God's law (Ex. 19-24) is foreshadowed in God's musing: "Since Abraham is to become a great and populous nation, and all the nations of the earth are to bless themselves by him; for I have singled him out, that he may instruct his children and his posterity to keep the way of the Lord, by doing what is just and right" (Gen. 18:18-19).

At Sinai, the entire people of Israel is invited to affirm the covenant and enter into a special relationship with God: "Now, therefore, if you will obey Me faithfully, and keep My covenant, you shall be My treasured possession among all peoples; for all the earth is Mine; but you shall be unto Me a kingdom of priests, and a holy nation..." (Ex. 19:5-6). Israel, in agreeing to these terms (Ex. 19:7, 24:3, 7), reconfirms Abraham's covenant and renders it binding upon all future generations. Lest the people forget the experience, Moses, shortly before his death, reminds them: "For you are a people consecrated unto the Lord your God, and the Lord your God chose you from among all other peoples on earth to be His treasured possession" (Deut. 14:2).

The doctrine of the chosen people is presumed throughout the Bible, although nowhere does it receive systematic elaboration. No clear reason is offered for Israel's election: on the contrary, "The Lord did not set His heart upon you or choose you because you were more numerous than other peoples — indeed, you were the fewest of all peoples — but it was because the Lord favored you..." (Deut. 7:7-8). Here and in the above citations, the Bible reiterates the unique tension that although the Lord is God of all the nations, Israel is nevertheless singled out. God tells Moses to inform Pharaoh that the Jewish people is His first-born, not His only child (Ex. 4:22; see also Amos 9:7 and Mal. 2:10). Although the perception of a special relationship with God was at the very least a source of pride (Num. 17:6), the Bible does not spare its rebuke of the people of Israel for their transgressions, and informs them that, "I have known only you of all the peoples of the earth; therefore I will visit upon you all your iniquities" (Amos 3:2). Chosenness implied responsibilities towards the other nations (e.g., Gen. 12:3; Ex. 19:6; Deut. 4:6-7; Isa. 49:6), even suffering on their behalf (Isa. 52:13-53:12).

Although the doctrine of Israel's election receives no direct expression in MAIMONIDES' thirteen PRINCIPLES OF FAITH, it has been suggested that its place in Jewish consciousness always maintained the centrality of an "unformulated dogma." The rabbis of the Talmud presumed a system of the most intimate relationship between God and the Jewish people, with R. AKIVA (second century CE) going so far as to assert that the highly explicit love poetry of the SONG OF SONGS was nothing less than a metaphor of the relationship between God and His people (*Yad.* 3.5; *Tosef. Sanh.* 12.10). One rabbinic tradition (based on Ex. 19:8, 24:3,7) credits the Jewish people with choosing God, in that it was the only nation on earth willing to accept the Torah (*AZ* 2b-3a). The most succinct expression of the rabbinic view of election is to be found in the text of the holiday liturgy, "You have chosen us from all peoples; You have loved us and taken pleasure in us, and have exalted us above all tongues; You have sanctified us by Your commandments and brought us near unto Your service, our King; You have called us by Your great and holy Name." The rabbis also subscribed to the biblical perspective that posited God as not only the "patron" of Israel but the God of all nations: "He is our God by making His name particularly attached to us; but He is also the one God of all mankind. He is our God in this world, He will be the only God in the world to come, as it is said (Zech. 14:9), 'And the Lord shall be King over all the earth; in that day there shall be one Lord and His name One'" (*Sif.* on Deut. 6:4).

In later periods, views of chosenness coalesced along two fairly distinct lines. Some medieval and modern thinkers, Maimonides foremost among them, saw election as a matter of duty, not of rights. Sanctity and superiority are promised as a consequence of obedience to the covenant, not granted as an outright gift or presumed as a national prerogative. Transgression brings with it inferiority and decline. The second school, whose chief proponent was JUDAH HALEVI, and which is echoed in ḤASIDISM and the KABBALAH, sees Israel as intrinsically unique and attributes special qualities to Jewish souls. Although the possibility of CONVERSION TO JUDAISM was one factor precluding any racist theory, the emphasis on Israel's election became stronger when historical circumstances and persecutions pressed upon the Jewish community. The treatment that Jews received from their neighbors throughout history did not encourage universalist tendencies, while Christianity's claim to have replaced Israel's covenant and become the "true Israel" further exacerbated exclusivist leanings.

With EMANCIPATION, the doctrine of the chosen people became increasingly problematic. Early Reformers such as Abraham GEIGER sought to retain the notion of election by rational reinterpretation, seeing Israel's mission fulfilled in its dispersion through which it brings God's message to the world. Others emphasized the element of Israel's choice of God and Torah, for which there is a basis in rabbinic thought. The Reform prayer book *Gates of Prayer* (New York, 1975) provides a very broad gamut of alternate worship services for all occasions, from the traditional and particularistic to the universalistic and non-theistic. The idea of chosenness has been reintroduced in the particularistic prayers. For example, the traditional version of the ancient Hebrew prayer ALÉNU LE-SHABBE'AḤ is one of the alternatives offered. A literal translation of the Hebrew is: "We must praise the Lord of all, and attribute greatness to the Primeval Creator, Who has not made us like the nations of the lands, nor established us like the families of the earth. He has not set our lot like theirs, and our destiny like that of all their multitudes... The translation given in *Gates of Prayer* is somewhat modified: "...Who has set us apart from the other families of earth, giving us a destiny unique among the nations."

The idea of chosenness of Israel is, however, preserved in the blessings before the READING OF THE LAW and the HAFTARAH in both the Hebrew and English. Likewise, the traditional passage "You have chosen us" has been restored to the AMIDAH prayer in the festival services.

Most of these elements were excluded from the *Union Prayer Book* which had previously dominated American Reform congregations for over 80 years.

Certain thinkers, most notably Mordecai KAPLAN, repudiated the idea, and his Reconstructionist movement expunged all mention of chosenness from its prayer book. Nevertheless, most contemporary thinkers retain some conception of chosenness and covenant. More traditional circles did not find these ideas difficult, their members daily reciting benedictions which thank God for choosing Israel.

Many Zionist thinkers (though not all), while seeking the "normalization" of Jewish national life, were also intrigued by the biblical appellation "light unto the nations" (Isa. 49:6) and hoped that the State of Israel would develop into some expression of this ideal.

Throughout the generations, the belief in its election has fortified the Jewish people in time of crisis, given a sense of purpose to individual and national life, and motivated the pursuit of moral and spiritual excellence, while rarely degenerating into crass ethnocentricity.

CHRISTIANITY Major world religion which arose out of JUDAISM. Christians believe that Jesus of Nazareth (first century CE) fulfilled the prophetic predictions of the Hebrew Bible as the Christ, a Greek term which translates the Hebrew *Mashi'aḫ* (literally, the anointed; figuratively, savior, MESSIAH). As portrayed in the NEW TESTAMENT, Jesus was the son of Mary, a Jewish virgin whose miraculous conception of Jesus was caused by the Holy Spirit. Jesus attracted a number of Jewish followers (apostles) with his preaching, which called for repentance in anticipation of the long-awaited "Kingdom of Heaven." He criticized the two major Jewish religio-socio-economic parties, the SADDUCEES and the PHARISEES, but seems to have shared many ideas with both groups, especially the Pharisees, and observed the commandments ordained in the Hebrew Scriptures. His "messianic" activity, which was seen as a political threat both to the Roman government in Erets Israel and to the Jewish authorities, led to his crucifixion. Jesus' disappointed disciples were able to reinterpret his messianic calling, giving it spiritual rather than political content, thereby keeping Jesus' movement alive — initially as a Jewish sect — until it developed fully into Christianity.

All the first Christians were Jewish followers of Jesus who believed that he had risen from the dead and would imminently return. Under the influence of PAUL of Tarsus (a Jew who was originally an opponent of Christianity), the new religion expanded to include Gentiles who considered themselves free of the obligation to observe the commandments. Scholars are divided as to when the final break between the two religions occurred, but it was probably some time in the second century as gentile Christianity became the dominant part of the religion. Eventually, the Jewish-Christians became a small minority among Christians, despised by Jews for being Christians, and by Christians for being Jews. They survived for a few centuries.

Early Christians were persecuted by the Romans, but, in the fourth century, the Emperor Constantine made Christianity the official Roman religion. From that time on, Jews who lived under Christian governments were subject to persecution, discrimination, conversionary attempts, expulsions, and massacres. Many Christians believed that the continued existence of the Jews as a separate, legitimate religious entity called into question the truth of Christianity as the successor religion to biblical Israel. They also accused the entire Jewish people with the crime of "deicide," i.e., killing God, (i.e., Jesus) because of the New Testament account of Jewish complicity in the crucifixion. Therefore, while Christians generally recognized the right of Jews to observe their own religion in the hope that they would eventually convert to Christianity, attempts were made to guarantee that a secondary status for Jews was maintained, as if their depressed condition were evidence of divine displeasure. Christian anti-Semitic theory and practice have been major factors in Jewish history. Anti-Jewish stereotypes, even identifying Jews with the devil, became deeply ingrained in the Christians consciousness.

While there are many forms of both Judaism and Christianity, the differences between classical Judaism and classical Christianity may be summarized as follows:

(1) Judaism conceives of God's unity as absolute, with no internal distinction; Christianity maintains a divine trinity of three Persons, the Father, the Son, and the Holy Spirit, all of whom are God, even though the Father generated the Son, and the Father and Son together (according to Western Christianity) caused the procession of the Spirit.

(2) For Judaism, God is incorporeal and can never be visible in human form; while agreeing that God is incorporeal, Christianity sees in Jesus the incarnation (embodiment) of the second Person of the Trinity, the Son.

(3) Although Judaism contains certain concepts of original sin, the preponderance of Jewish opinion holds that individuals can achieve salvation through their own effort; Christianity holds that the sinful nature of humanity, caused by the original sin of Adam, prevents salvation without the intermediacy of the sacrifice of the divine-human messiah.

(4) The Jewish concept of the Messiah is generally a political one: when he comes in the future, he will be a human descendant of David who restores the monarchy, rebuilds the Temple, and gathers in the Jewish exiles from the Diaspora; for Christians, while Jesus the Messiah was fully human, the son of Mary and descendant of David, he was also fully God, and his task was humanity's redemption from the original sin of Adam.

(5) Judaism maintains that the covenant between God and the People of Israel embodied in the Hebrew Scriptures is eternally valid and not to be superseded; observance of the commandments, as understood through Talmudic legislation, is necessary for the personal salvation of the Jews. Christianity believes in a second covenant, between God and all humanity, recorded in the New Testament (as contrasted to the Hebrew "Old Testament") and pronounced by the mission of the divine-human person of Jesus; salvation (available to all humanity) depends on belief in Jesus as the Christ/Messiah, not observance of the commandments.

(6) Since Christians see themselves as the recipients of the new covenant, they believe that they are the true spiritual descendants of Abraham and deserve the name Israel; Jews maintain that they remain the "true Israel," being both the physical and spiritual heirs of Abraham.

Historically, Jews have been the objects of Christian missionaries, who attempted to demonstrate that the Christian approach to the issues outlined above is the correct one. Converted Jews who knew Jewish literature and tradition often stood at the forefront of the conversionary campaigns. Jews, for their part, maintained that Christianity was a false religion, contradicted by the simple words of the Bible and by human reason. Both Jews and Christians wrote polemical works; Jewish anti-Christian compositions included detailed refutations of Christian doctrines and were intended to provide answers to the Christian attack on Judaism. While these works rarely represent the most sophisticated theological thinking of either side, they do indicate the state of popular religion as understood by both advocates and opponents of the two religions (see APOLOGETICS AND POLEMICS).

While the Christian mission to the Jews was usually low-key, it many times took on violent forms, and forced conversions were not an uncommon feature of Jewish-Christian relations. An additional distinctive earmark of the Jewish-Christian conflict in the Middle Ages was the DISPUTATION, a public debate held between representatives of the two religions (most notably Paris, 1240; Barcelona, 1263; and Tortosa, 1413-14). These were usually stage-managed affairs with the anti-Jewish results known in advance. Often the local Christian rulers used such occasions for their internal political purposes. In the modern period, Jews and Christians have often met on more equal terms engaging in dialogue rather than in disputation (see INTERFAITH).

Despite the history of antagonism between Judaism and Christianity, there were often cultural exchanges and mutual influences between the religions. Early Christianity adopted many distinctive Jewish beliefs and practices, such as prayers and baptism, while, at the same time, it was heavily affected by Greek paganism. Medieval Jews were instrumental in the transfer of Greek learning in its Arabic form to Christian Europe. The works of MAIMONIDES were used by a number of Christian thinkers, including Thomas Aquinas. Christianity, for its part, influenced Judaism, both in the area of popular religious practices, and in theology, mainly, but not only, in regard to Jewish mysticism (KABBALAH). The influence of Christianity on Judaism has been especially pronounced in the modern period in Western countries as Jews began to evaluate Christianity more positively and were more willing to borrow consciously from it.

Judaism has traditionally had an ambivalent attitude towards Christians and Christianity. Since Christianity claimed to be the true Israel and heir to the biblical tradition, Jews naturally regarded it as an illegitimate usurper. The Christian beliefs in trinity and incarnation, as well as the cultic use of images, were often seen as proof that Christianity is another form of idolatry. In addition, living under Christian persecution caused many Jews to have an extremely negative view of the majority religion. On the other hand, many Jews were able to distinguish favorably between Christian trinitarian monotheism and idolatrous polytheism. Some (notably JUDAH HALEVI and MAIMONIDES) have even seen positive aspects to the spread of Christianity (and ISLAM), believing that it would help prepare the world for the eventual advent of the true Messiah. Still others, e.g., Franz ROSENZWEIG, taught that Christianity is the proper way for Gentiles to worship God.

Ecclesia *(Church) holding a cross, and* Synagoga *(Synagogue) holding a broken staff, a common motif in medieval Christian art.*

In recent years, many Christians have come to realize that Christian beliefs have often nurtured ANTI-SEMITISM, and were among the factors leading to the HOLOCAUST. The Catholic Church has issued proclamations condemning anti-Semitism and declaring that contemporary Jews are not to be considered guilty of deicide. Catholics and liberal Protestants now rarely seek to convert Jews, and have revised anti-Judaism in the prayers and catechisms, but evangelical Protestants continue their conversionary attempts, and such groups as "Jews for Jesus" are an integral part of their campaign (See CULTS). In general, the evangelical groups have been very supportive of the State of Israel because of their messianic beliefs and eschatological timetable, while Catholics and liberal Protestants have been much less approving. The Eastern Orthodox churches have not changed their teachings concerning the Jews and Judaism and retain traditional prejudices.

CHRONICLES, BOOK(S) OF (Heb. ***Divré ha-Yamim*****).** According to Jewish tradition, Chronicles is the last volume of the HAGIOGRAPHA as well as the last book of the Bible, although in early manuscripts it appears at the beginning of the Hagiographa. In the SEPTUAGINT as well as in the Vulgate, it is included in the historical books, and appears after the Book of Kings. Originally, Chronicles was a single volume and only in the Septuagint was it divided into two, a division which has been preserved to this day. The Septuagint refers to Chronicles as *Paraleipomenon* — "the [Book of] Things Omitted" — since it contains data about the Judean monarchy which was left out of the Book of Kings.

I CHRONICLES

1:1 — 1:54	Genealogical listing
2:1 — 9:1	Lists of the tribes of Israel
9:2 — 9:18	List of the inhabitants of Jerusalem
9:19 — 9:34	List of the Levites and their duties
9:35 — 9:44	List of the inhabitants of Gibeon
10:1 — 29:30	The monarchy during David's time

II CHRONICLES

1:1 — 9:31	Solomon's reign
10:1 — 12:16	Rehoboam's reign
13:1 — 13:23	Abijah's reign
14:1 — 16:14	Asa's reign
17:1 — 20:37	Jehoshaphat's reign
21:1 — 21:20	Jehoram's reign
22:1 — 22:9	Ahaziah's reign
22:10 — 23:21	Athaliah's reign
24:1 — 24:27	Joash's reign
25:1 — 25:28	Amaziah's reign
26:1 — 26:23	Uzziah's reign
27:1 — 27:9	Jotham's reign
28:1 — 28:27	Ahaz's reign
29:1 — 32:33	Hezekiah's reign
33:1 — 33:20	Manasseh's reign
33:21 — 33:25	Amon's reign
34:1 — 35:27	Josiah's reign
36:1 — 36:4	Jehoahaz's reign
36:5 — 36:8	Jehoiakim's reign
36:9 — 36:10	Jehoiachin's reign
36:11 — 36:21	Zedekiah's reign
36:22 — 36:23	The proclamation of Cyrus

The volume begins with a genealogical table from Adam and ends with a prelude to the return to Zion from the Babylonian Exile. It emphasizes the annals of the House of David, from David's ascent to the throne, with particular reference to Solomon's building of the Temple and the history of the 19 kings of Judah from Rehoboam until the destruction of Jerusalem. Of the 20 kings of Israel during the parallel period, only those who had dealings with the kings of Judah — either by fighting against them or as their allies — are mentioned. The book concludes with the proclamation of Cyrus, allowing the Judean exiles to return home, as quoted more fully in the Book of EZRA.

While Chronicles is meant to summarize the historic books of II Samuel and Kings, it includes many details that are not mentioned in these, notably the fact that Solomon was anointed twice (I Chron. 23:1, 29:22), Solomon's visit to Hamath Zobah and the building of storage cities there (II Chron. 8:3-4), as well as details of Pharaoh Shishak's campaign in Judah (II Chron. 12). The author of Chronicles omits negative details which appear in Samuel and Kings — David's misdemeanors, for example, or the fact that Solomon built altars for foreign gods (I Kings 11:7). The chief focus of attention is the Davidic monarchy, which symbolizes the uniqueness and unity of Israel and its observance of the Torah. As a result of this perspective, the book projects an idealized image of the kings of Judah, and especially of David and Solomon. It lays special emphasis on the Temple and its construction, on the role of the priestly house of Zadok, and on the Levites, whose work was organized during David's time.

The sources for the Book of Chronicles are II Samuel and Kings, various genealogies, traditions contained in the records of the kings of Judah and Israel, poetry (especially from the book of Psalms), and the words of various prophets such as Shemaiah, Samuel, and Nathan, as well as the seers Gad and Iddo. According to tradition (*BB* 15a), Ezra wrote "his own book" and most of Chronicles (i.e., around 450 BCE), the work being completed by Nehemiah about a decade later. Despite 19th-century assumptions that Chronicles, Ezra, and Nehemiah formed one sequence (cf. II Chron. 36: 22-23 and Ezra 1:1-3), modern Bible scholars have concluded that there is an essential difference between the pro-Davidic line of Chronicles and the historical perspective of the other two books; that the author of Chronicles merely quoted the beginning of Ezra; and that Chronicles is much the later work, written toward the end of the Persian era but displaying no Hellenistic influence, either linguistically or conceptually.

CHURCH FATHERS Theologians of the early Christian church, who determined the structure of its dogma, lived between the second and eighth centuries, and wrote in Greek or Latin. In general, their attitude was anti-Jewish, laying the basis for many centuries of Christian ANTI-SEMITISM and persecution of the Jews. An exception, to some extent, was Jerome (c.345-c.420), who worked in Bethlehem and prepared the standard Latin Bible translation (the Vulgate), based on the text of the Hebrew Bible. Jerome's Hebrew

Saint Jerome distributes copies of the Vulgate (his translation of the Bible into Latin) to monks who carry it through the world. Tenth-century miniature.

studies angered his fanatical colleagues, who suspected him of adhering to Jewish tenets.

The Greek Church Father John Chrysostom (354-407), bishop of Antioch and later head of the church in Byzantium, was one of the most unrelenting enemies of Judaism. He wrote eight "homilies" or sermons against the Jews in Antioch (386-7), largely to counteract Judaism's hold on many professed Christians. Among other things, Chrysostom maintained that "the Synagogue is not only a whorehouse and a stage for actors, but a den of thieves and a refuge for wild beasts as well." He claimed that "the Jews have no conception of sacred matters and are, in no way, superior to goats and swine, leading debauched and gluttonous lives" (*Adversus Judaeos* I. 3,4,).

The most famous Latin church father Augustine, (354-430) bishop of Hippo in North Africa, exerted a lasting influence on the Church, especially at the time of the Reformation in the 16th century. Though not as violently anti-Jewish as some other patristic writers, Augustine nevertheless declared that God had only kept the Jews alive to bear witness to Christian truth and that they "can never grasp the meaning of Holy Scripture and will forever bear the guilt for the death of Jesus" (*Tractatus adversus Judaeos*).

Ambrose (339-397), the bishop of Milan, accused the Jews of not observing the laws of the Roman Empire and of being enemies of the State. He justified the destruction of a synagogue and berated the Emperor for daring to penalize the Christians who had taken such action against the "enemies of Christ." Cyril (376-444), Patriarch of Alexandria, incited the mob against the Jews and in 415 brought about their expulsion from that one-time great center of Hellenistic Jewry.

Due to the Church Fathers, the Jewish roots of Christianity were suppressed and only the Greek roots were constantly developed. The dogmatic thinking of the Church Fathers was based to a far larger extent on Greek philosophy than on the Hebrew Bible. This led to dogmatism, for instance, concerning the Trinity and the bearer of God. These dogmas were in complete opposition to Judaism and were unknown to the early Judeo-Christian community.

Only during the age of the Reformation did Protestant Christianity find its way back to the Hebrew Bible. However, the disastrous legacy of the Church Fathers has persisted to this day, and presents obstacles to the new dialogue of understanding between Judaism and Christianity.

A first attempt at such a dialogue goes back to the Church Father Justin the Martyr, who was a native of Sichem (Nablus) and who died a martyr's death around 165. In his dialogue with the Jew Tryphon he tried to equate the two ways of believing, the Jewish and the Christian, albeit with missionary intentions.

The historian of the old church, Eusebius (born around 270 in Caesarea) was ill-disposed towards the Jews and influenced Roman legislation adversely.

Although the Church Fathers were anti-Jewish in attitude, they were responsible for the preservation of the writings of the Alexandrian Jewish philosopher PHILO who nearly fell into oblivion among the Jews. Philo's LOGOS (God's word) represents God's emanation, His active reason. However, with the Church Fathers this concept developed into the hypostasis, in the meaning of the Godhead's third person as Holy Spirit; but also due to the incarnation, as God's becoming man in JESUS, the pre-existent Christ. Patterns of thought like these illustrate the influence of Hellenistic Judaism (Philo) in the development of Christianity. At the same time, they stand in direct opposition to normative Judaism, to which the speculations of the church fathers and the church councils remained completely alien.

CITIES OF REFUGE See ASYLUM

CIRCUMCISION (*berit milah*, literally "covenant of circumcision"). The removal of part or all of the foreskin which covers the glans of the penis. In Judaism circumcision is performed on the eighth day of the male child's life in accordance with God's command and as a sign of the COVENANT between God and the descendants of ABRAHAM. It is also peformed upon male converts to Judaism as a sign of their entrance into that covenant.

The biblical roots of circumcision are found in Genesis 17:

> God said to Abraham...such shall be the covenant between Me and you and your offspring to follow which you shall keep; every male among you shall be circumcised. You shall circumcise the flesh of your foreskin, and that shall be the sign of the covenant between Me and you. Throughout the generations, every male among you shall be circumcised at the age of eight days. Thus shall my covenant be marked in your flesh as an everlasting covenant (Gen. 17:10-13).

Circumcision must also be performed upon "the home-born slave and the one purchased from the outside" (Gen. 17:12) as well as upon "a stranger who dwells with you (who) would offer the Passover to the Lord" (Ex. 12:48). The Bible relates that "Abraham was 99 years old when he circumcised the flesh of his foreskin, and his son Ishmael was 13 years old when he was circumcised" (Gen. 17:24-25).

The narrative sections of the Bible contain three additional stories relating to circumcision. In the first, Shechem the Hivite wants to marry Jacob's daughter, Dinah. His brothers object: "We cannot do this thing, to give our sister to a man who is uncircumcised, for that is a disgrace among us" (Gen. 34). In the second story, Zipporah, the wife of Moses, "took a flint and cut off her son's foreskin" when "the Lord encountered him and sought to kill him" (Ex. 4). The third narrative mentioning circumcision is found in Joshua 5. The Israelites had just crossed the Jordan, entering into the promised land, when: "The Lord said to Joshua: Make flint knives and proceed with a second circumcision of the Israelites."

These stories are the basis for differing scholarly theories regarding the origin of circumcision. For traditionalists circumcision is a Divine commandment; a sign of the covenant between God and the Jewish people. They speculate that His reasons for decreeing the removal of the foreskin might be both hygienic (cleanliness) and moral (symbolic control of sexual desires) (Philo).

Critics emphasize that circumcision was practiced by many ancient peoples even before the time of Abraham. They suggest differing theories as to the original reason for this practice; a tribal initiation ceremony and a sign of membership in a particular ethnic group; a magical rite designed to appease angry gods and protect human males from their wrath; a male fertility ritual performed at puberty.

Whatever its origin, circumcision of the foreskin came to be the sign of an everlasting covenant through which God assigned: "the land you sojourn into you and your offspring to come...as an everlasting holding" (Gen. 17;80-11). On the other hand, circumcision of the heart, a term used in Deuteronomy (10:16, 30:6) and by Jeremiah (4:4) was of a more spiritual nature and was not necessarily tied to the land.

At the time of the Maccabees, the practice of ritual circumcision became a matter of great consequence and controversy. Some Jews, apparently ashamed of the ritual, tried to disguise the fact that they had been circumcised; on the other hand the Greek king, Antiochus Epiphanes, forbade its practice. The Maccabees revolted against Antiochus and even went so far as to forcibly circumcise fellow Jews. The Hasmonean king, John Hyrcanus, forced the practice upon peoples whom he conquered (Josephus, *Ant.* 13). Centuries later, the Jews, under Bar Kokhba, rebelled when the Roman emperor proscribed circumcision.

Jewish ritual circumcision requires the removal of the entire foreskin (Heb. *orlah*), fully exposing the glans penis (Heb. *attarah*), and the release of a minimal quantity of blood (Heb. *dam berit milah*). Health permitting, the procedure must be done on the eighth day of life (for example, if the child were born between sunset Monday evening and sunset Tuesday evening, the circumcision would be performed the following Tuesday) by a properly qualified professional who must be an observant Jew (Heb. *mohel*). The ceremony is performed on the Sabbath, festivals, or even the Day of Atonement. Postponement is allowed if there is any question of danger to the child's health. If two male children in a family have died following circumcision, further male children need not be circumcised.

The laws detailing the various aspects of ritual circumcision are drawn directly from biblical sources, from the Sinaitic legislation transmitted in the oral tradition, and from rabbinical enactments. Today, the basic ritual is complemented by many customs which have developed in the course of time. The ceremony is traditionally performed in the presence of a quorum of ten adult Jewish males (Heb. *minyan*). On the morning of the eighth day, the infant is taken from the mother by the godmother who hands him to the godfather (SANDAK). The latter carries the child into the room where the circumcision is to be performed and hands him to the one who will place the child on a chair designated as the Chair of Elijah (Heb. *kisé shel Eliyahu*) (see below). Another takes him from the Chair of Elijah and passes him to the child's father who places him on the lap of the godfather who holds the infant during the ceremony.

The circumcision itself takes only a few seconds, and is performed by a circumciser (*mohel*). Formerly the blood was drawn orally by the *mohel* but now an instrument is used. The infant is handed to the person who will hold him (Heb. *omed al ha-berakhot*) during the naming ceremony. Finally, a special blessing is said over a cup of wine and the child receives his Jewish NAME.

Ritual circumcision implements, and book of rules and prayers for circumcision. Germany, France, and Italy, 18th and 19th centuries.

Circumcision is universally observed by the Jewish people although Reform Jews accept a medical doctor instead of a *mohel*. For his services, the *mohel* usually receives payment, though he often contributes to charity all monies received.

Circumcision is an essential part of conversion to Judaism for males, although if the convert is already circumcised, a ritual drawing of a drop of blood from the site of the circumcision is performed.

The instruments which the *mohel* uses are of very ancient derivation. The knife (*izamel*) is traditionally sharpened on both sides. The shield (*magen*), a thin metal instrument through which the foreskin is passed before it is removed, serves both to protect the glans penis and guide the knife along a safe and proper path. A silver probe is frequently used before the circumcision to loosen up the foreskin which often adheres to the glans penis.

The Chair of Elijah in some countries is the chair upon which the godfather sits during the ceremony but is often a separate chair upon which the baby is briefly placed before the circumcision. The prophet ELIJAH is traditionally invited to every circumcision because he once complained to God "...for the children of Israel have forsaken Your covenant" (interpreted as the practice of ritual circumcision) (I Kings 19:10). According to the Zohar (Gen. 17:10), God replied, "In every case when My sons shall incise this holy sign in their flesh, you (Elijah) shall be invited ...And the mouth which testifies that Israel has forsaken the covenant shall testify that they are keeping the covenant."

The ceremony is followed by a festive meal (*se'udat mitsvah*). At one time this was held in the synagogue (and sometimes still is).

Judaism has never countenanced female circumcision.

CIVIL MARRIAGE According to Jewish law, marriage must be carried out "in accordance with the laws of Moses and Israel." Where the partners to a marriage undergo a civil rather than a religious ceremony, a question arises whether the partners are nevertheless married in accordance with Jewish law. Should the answer be in the affirmative, the two would require a *get* — a halakhic bill of divorce — before being able to marry another person, whereas should the answer be in the negative, no such *get* would be necessary. Basically, the question revolves about the general rule in Jewish law to the effect that no man wishes his acts of intercourse to be extra-marital, and that a man and woman who live together are accordingly presumed to have contracted a valid Jewish marriage through their first act of intercourse — intercourse being one of the three ways of contracting a valid Jewish marriage. This question arose particularly in the Middle Ages, when the Spanish MARRANOS were forced to marry in a Catholic ceremony rather than in accordance with Jewish law.

Opinions have been divided among the greatest rabbinic authorities throughout the centuries. There are those who dismiss the presumption that the first act of intercourse was meant to contract a valid Jewish marriage. In a civil marriage, they argue, the very fact that the couple specifically opted for a civil over a religious ceremony is clear evidence that they have no interest in a halakhically valid marriage. As such, no divorce is needed upon the termination of the relationship. This view, though, would differentiate between those who live in a society where a religious marriage is readily available, so that a civil marriage is *ipso facto* evidence of a desire not to have a religious marriage; and those countries where religious marriage may pose a danger to the participants, in which case the civil marriage cannot be brought as proof of an intention to bypass Jewish law. Another view, while generally agreeing with the absence of a valid Jewish marriage in the case of a civil ceremony, nevertheless requires the couple to have a *get* upon parting. This *get* is not evidence that a valid marriage has taken place, but is meant to be *le-ḥumrah* — as a safeguard. Thus, if the husband is not available to give the *get*, the Jewish court would permit the woman's remarriage without it. Basically, the *get* is meant to serve as a deterrent, for if a *get* is not demanded, those with halakhically valid marriages may jump to the conclusion that a person may marry a second partner without divorcing the first.

Israel itself does not have any mechanism for civil marriages, although it does recognize such marriages when contracted elsewhere. Certain individuals have been attempting to amend the situation by conducting private contractual ceremonies in place of rabbinically sanctioned weddings.

CODIFICATION OF JEWISH LAW Collections of halakhic rulings in concise and systematic arrangement constitute a significant branch of halakhic literature. They are primarily designed to serve as guides for religious practice for laymen as well as for halakhic authorities. They invariably comprise both civil and ritual law, often including moral as well as legal directives. Based upon Torah law as expounded by the rabbinic sages, their authority is commensurate with the reputation of their respective authors.

The earliest rabbinic codes, called *halakhot*, were compiled in the first and second centuries CE by the *tannaim*, and consisted of two categories: those attached to the Scriptural verses from which the *halakhot* were derived; and those arranged according to subject matter. The former are *midrash* (i.e., inferred by rabbinic exegesis), and include the following: MEKHILTA to Exodus; SIFRA to Leviticus; SIFREI to Numbers and Deuteronomy. The latter are *mishnah* (i.e., teaching) and include MISHNAH and TOSEFTA (cf. *Kid.* 49a-b). These *halakhot* were taught orally; additions were made to them by succeeding generations of teachers; and they included various conflicting opinions. In the first decade of the third century, Rabbi JUDAH HA-NASI assembled the leading scholars of his time and had each of them repeat the *halakhot* learned from their teachers. Judah then arranged them in six codices or "orders," each dealing with a different branch of Jewish law. This arrangement is the MISHNAH.

Specific codes were not composed during the Talmudic period (third to sixth centuries). The gaonic period, which began shortly thereafter, saw the computation of a series of halakhic codes, systematic digests of the diffused teachings of the Talmud, and incorporating decisions of the *ge'onim* (see GAON). The *She'iltot* of the 8th century Babylonian scholar, AḪAI OF SHABḪA, was a pioneer of codification. So was HALAKHOT PESUKOT of Yehudai Gaon, head of the ACADEMY in Sura (middle of the eighth century). Despite his blindness, he was able to dictate to his students briefly stated rulings of the Talmud confirmed as HALAKHAH (Jewish law) by his teachers. He was opposed to innovation, and therefore ruled against the introduction of prayers and benedictions not mentioned in the Talmud. His work received wide acclamation and was circulated in many versions. A generation or two later, Simeon Kayyara, basing himself upon the *Halakhot Pesukot*, composed a larger digest called HALAKHOT GEDOLOT, which became the most widely accepted halakhic work of the geonic period, frequently cited by the early rabbinic authorities as absolutely reliable. In the Introduction, Simeon listed the 613 Biblical injunctions (see COMMANDMENTS, 613), the first such listing in rabbinic literature.

The latter half of the geonic period (850-1000) saw a spate of halakhic codes of a different genre; a series of treatises each dealing with the laws of a specific subject. The PRAYER-BOOKS of AMRAM GAON and SAADIAH GAON contained not only the text of the prayers but the laws concerning prayer as well. Saadiah was the most prolific codifier, composing about ten separate monographs on specific areas of the *Halakhah*, such as legal documents, inheritance, trusts, oaths and dietary laws. These works were written in Arabic, at that time the common language of the Jews in the Middle East, North Africa and Muslim Spain. Saadiah's successors in the geonate, Samuel ben Hofni and HAI in particular, composed similar works; the most prominent among them the *Sefer Mekaḫ u-Memkar* ("Book of Buying and Selling") of Hai Gaon. Unfortunately, most of these works are known only from citations in the writings of others or from fragments discovered in the Cairo GENIZAH.

The first of the early Spanish authorities, Isaac ALFASI, introduced a new system of codification. He followed the pages of the Babylonian Talmud, recording only those passages relevant to the practical *Halakhah*, and where necessary the decisions of the *ge'onim*. His work is known as *Hilkhot ha-Rif*, and it soon became the standard code for Sephardi Jewry. Little more than two centuries later, a distinguished Ashkenazi authority, ASHER BEN JEHIEL, followed the style of Alfasi in his code, entitled *Hilkhot* (or *Piskei*, decisions) *ha-Rosh*. His work included the opinions of the many authorities of the 12th and 13th centuries, and soon became the standard code for Ashkenazi Jewry. In between these two luminaries, dozens of digests of Jewish law were composed; the shifts in population from country to country and the introduction of new *minhagim* (customary practices) made such handbooks necessary. The Ashkenazi works included: *Sefer ha-Roke'aḫ* by ELEAZAR OF WORMS; *Sefer Yere'im* by Eliezer ben Samuel of Metz; *Even ha-Ezer* by Eliezer ben Nathan of Mainz; *Sefer ha-Terumah* by Baruch ben Isaac of Worms; *Avi ha-Ezer* (also known as *Sefer Raviah*) by Eliezer ben Joel ha-Levi. The last and most comprehensive of this series is the *Or Zaru'a* of ISAAC BEN MOSES OF VIENNA, a stanch defender of the earlier authorities. Two Ashkenazi codes from this period but of different style are: *Maḫzor Vitry*, a comprehensive prayer book that includes, in addition to the order and text of the prayers, the halakhic rulings concerning prayer. It was composed by Simḫah of Vitry, a disciple of RASHI. MOSES BEN JACOB OF COUCY wrote the *Sefer Mitsvot Gadol* (or *Semag*), an halakhic and homiletic treatment of the 613 commandments.

The contributions of most Sephardi scholars of this period to halakhic literature was not in codes. The reason was that for Sephardim, in addition to *Hilkhot ha-Rif*, the authorative code was the *Mishneh Torah* (also known as *Yad ha Ḫazakah*) of Moses MAIMONIDES. This code was, and remains to this day, the most comprehensive and systematic collection of Jewish law ever written. In contradistinction to all the others mentioned, it encompasses every aspect of Jewish law, including laws in effect only when sacrificial offerings are offered in the Jerusalem Temple, such as the measurements of the Temple to be built and the rules governing a Jewish sovereign. Maimonides' code attracted a host of commentaries, and to this day most halakhic discourses contain one or more references to its rulings. Maimonides also wrote a *Sefer ha-Mitsvot*, a listing of the 613 commandments with brief annotations; another work on the same subject which adds the rationale to these biblical injunctions, is the *Sefer ha-Ḥinnukh*, attributed to Aaron ha-Levi of Barcelona.

Another series of halakhic digests was produced in the third center of medieval talmudic scholarship, the area of southern France called Provence. Among the earliest is the *Sefer ha-Ittim* by Judah ben Barzilai of Barcelona, a digest of laws on the Sabbath and Festivals which contains many citations from the *ge'onim* and influenced succeeding works. These included *Sefer ha-Eshkol* by Abraham ben Isaac of Narbonne; *Sefer ha-Ittur* by Isaac ben Abba Mari of Marseilles; *Orḥot Ḥayyim* by Aaron ha-Cohen of Lunel.

The period of the early authorities (RISHONIM) comes to a close with the appearance of another compendium of Jewish law which became a classic code, the *Arba'ah Turim (Tur* for short) or "Four Rows" of JACOB BEN ASHER, the son of Asher ben Jehiel. Differing from the Mishnah, which is divided into Six Orders and encompasses all aspects of Jewish law, the *Tur* deals only with laws in effect during the period of the Exile, i.e., when the Jerusalem Temple is not in existence. It divides them into four major divisions, as follows: 1. *Oraḥ Ḥayyim* or Way of Life, comprising the laws of prayer, Sabbath and Festivals; 2. *Yoreh De'ah* or Instructor of Knowledge, comprising the dietary laws, the menstruant woman and her purification, and sundry commandments, e.g., honoring parents, circumcision, charity and the laws of mourning; 3. *Even ha-Ezer* or Stone of Help, comprising the laws of marriage, divorce, levirate marriage; and 4. *Ḥoshen Mishpat* or Breastplate of Judgment, with laws concerning courts, judges, witnesses, and all matters of property (contracts, loans, damages etc.). The *Tur* became the basis of the best known code, the SHULḤAN ARUKH, but was not displaced by it; it is still a major reference book for halakhic authorities.

A century later, a much more condensed guide to religious practice appeared, the *Minhagim* of Jacob MÖLLN of Mainz. Appended to it is the *Hilkhot Sheḥitah U-Vedikah* (laws of slaughtering and examining of cattle) of his disciple, Jacob ben Judah Weil.

By the beginning of the 16th century, after a long period of expulsions suffered by both Sephardi and Ashkenazi Jewries, new centers of Jewish life were established; the Sephardim concentrated in North Africa, the Balkans and Erets Israel, and the Ashkenazim in eastern Europe. The newly established communities required new guidance, either by confirming the old practices of their predecessors or legitimizing the new practices which had arisen. By this time the differences between Sephardi and Ashkenazi practices had multiplied, a reflection both of their different ambience and the somewhat different approach to halakhic decisions of their respective religious leaders. Because of the system of PILPUL (casuistic argument) which dominated among the Ashkenazim there was great hesitancy in making clear-cut decisions where earlier authorities had expressed contradictory opinions and the rule adopted was always to follow the more stringent opinion. Force of law was given to many customs which added restrictions in marital relations and to those in mourning. Another factor which had some influence for both Ashkenazim and Sephardim in halakhic decision was the spread of the mystical teachings of the KABBALAH. The needs of the time were met by two eminent talmudists, Joseph CARO, a Sephardi, and Moses ISSERLES of Cracow ("Rema" for short), an Ashkenazi. Each had first written an extensive commentary to the *Tur*, but they then proceeded to condense their works into a concise code with clear decisions. Caro published his code first, following the four-volume structure of the *Tur*, and called it *Shulḥan Arukh*, "a set table" or a handy guide for student and scholar alike. Isserles, seeing that Karo ignored many decisions and *minhagim* of the Ashkenazim — he mostly followed Maimonides' *Mishneh Torah* — decided to add *haggahot*, annotations, to the *Shulḥan Arukh* to set down the Ashkenazi practice. He called these notes *Mappah*, a tablecloth covering the "set table" of Caro. Together, they constitute the authoritative code of Jewish law, the Sephardim following the decisions of Caro, and the Ashkenazim following the decisions of Isserles. The wide acceptance of the *Shulḥan Arukh* did not, however, close the door to continued analysis of all its sources and opinions. This is attested by the number of commentaries which increased with each new edition of the *Shulḥan Arukh*. This proliferation of halakhic material created the need for new digests of Jewish law, so that even the layman could have some handy reference to the requirements of the halakhah in his daily conduct. *Ḥayyei Adam* and *Ḥokhmat Adam* are the respective digests of *Oraḥ Ḥayyim* and *Yoreh De'ah* of the *Shulḥan Arukh* written by Abraham Danzig of Vilna. Solomon Ganzfried of Hungary composed for the layman a handbook of Jewish law which he called *Kitsur* ("Abridgment of") *Shulḥan Arukh*. It became extremely popular and has been published in many editions, with commentaries to bring it up-to-date. A more elaborate review of the *Shulḥan Arukh*, citing the sources for its decisions and not infrequently disagreeing with them, is the *Arukh ha-Shulḥan* of Jehiel Michal Epstein of Novogrudok, Belorussia. Early in the 20th century, a clarification and resolution of the decisions recorded in the *Shulḥan Arukh, Oraḥ Ḥayyim* that gained wide acceptance by halakhic authorities was the *Mishnah Berurah* ("Clear Code") of Israel Meir ha-Cohen Kagan, better known as the HAFETS ḤAYYIM.

A recent digest of the laws concerning the Sabbath and Festivals is *Shemirat Shabbat ke-Hilkhata* of Yehoshua

Neuwirth of Jerusalem, subtitled, "Particular attention given to problems raised in our time."

Sephardi scholars were no less diligent and productive in providing halakhic guidance for their communities. Many dealt with the laws of ritual slaughter, designed primarily to instruct ritual slaughterers. Ashkenazi rabbis also composed such special guides. A rather unusual guide for his time was the *Pe'at ha-Shulḫan* of Israel of Shklov, a disciple of the Gaon of Vilna, who settled in Erets Israel in the early 19th century. It deals with the laws of agricultural products, a subject which had been rather neglected previously.

Another system of codification of Jewish law is an attempt to make accessible to the authority who has to make decisions (*posek*) its voluminous literature, in encyclopedic form, with subject matters arranged according to the alphabet. The first such encyclopedia was composed in the early 18th century by Isaac Hezekiah Lampronti of Ferrara under the title *Paḫad Yitshak*. A bulkier, though somewhat less systematic work, was published in the latter half of the 19th century by Ḫayyim Hezekiah Medini of Izmir entitled *Sedei Ḫemed*. A comprehensive encyclopedia of rabbinic law is the *Entsiklopedia Talmudit* (Talmudic Encyclopedia) appearing in Jerusalem.

COHEN, HERMANN (1842-1918). German philosopher and interpreter of Judaism. The son of a cantor, he originally studied at the Jewish Theological Seminary of Breslau, but turned from rabbinics to philosophy. In 1876, Cohen became professor of philosophy at the University of Marburg and remained there until his retirement in 1912. He then lived in Berlin, where he taught at the Liberal Hochschule für die Wissenschaft des Judentums.

Cohen's main achievements — and his renown as a philosopher — are linked with the Neo-Kantian "Marburg School" which he established and with his theistic belief in the dignity of man. He also found himself doing battle, however, with Treitschke and other German anti-Semites who alleged that the Talmud and Jewish law were "racist," being concerned only with Jews. Cohen's defense of the CHOSEN PEOPLE concept maintained that Judaism is concerned both for the "homeborn" (Israel) and for the "stranger" (mankind in general), that its ultimate religious ideal is the unification of mankind, and that the Jews are "chosen" to help achieve this goal by establishing God's kingdom on earth. In Cohen's earlier system, ethics were central and God merely an idea in religion that fortified the ethical life, as well as a force preserving the universe. Later, when his attitude toward religion changed, Cohen began to see religion and faith in God as vital for the individual's salvation.

His new ideas on religion are chiefly expounded in *Die Religion der Vernunft aus den Quellen des Judentums* ("The Religion of Reason from the Sources of Judaism"). In this book, published a year after his death, Cohen argues that God is not a hypothesis but a reality. Human reason, culture, and everything vital to man are not the products of human thought but have their source in God. Jewish monotheism, he insists, lays stress both on God's *Einzigheit* (moral uniqueness) and on His *Einheit* (absolute unity). Cohen's religious philosophy thus became theocentric: man's ideal should be a wholehearted attempt to imitate God and to approach the ideal of God's own holiness. This man can do more effectively by becoming a copartner with God in perfecting the work of creation. If it is man's task to unify mankind through a humanitarian socialism, it is the Jewish people's specific task to hasten the messianic era by serving as God's agent on earth, living as a model community and working for social justice and universal peace. Cohen therefore rejected Zionism, believing that its national emphasis ran counter to Judaism's universalist ideal.

Despite his liberal and ethical approach to Judaism, Cohen made room in his system for observance of the MITSVAH, the commandment which he traced directly to God, and which he considered it the Jew's duty to accept and obey.

COMMANDMENTS, TEN See TEN COMMANDMENTS

COMMANDMENTS, THE 613 (*Taryag Mitsvot*). The injunctions recorded in the Pentateuch as having been spoken by God to Moses, to be communicated to the Children of Israel. These commandments were to be observed as the terms of the Covenant between God and His people. A third-century *amora*, R. Simlai, postulated that they total 613 ("*taryag*" in Hebrew numerical value), 365 negative (prohibited) actions corresponding to the number of days in a solar year, and 248 positive (duties to be performed) corresponding to the number of limbs in the human body (*Mak.* 23b). These figures, though not mentioned in tannaitic sources, have been accepted by subsequent halakhic authorities as authentic, and are the subject of numerous discussions in classical rabbinic works.

The commandments have been classified into several categories. The Torah speaks of *ḫukkim* (statutes) and *mishpatim* (judgments; Lev. 18:4-5), the former comprising ritual performances characterized as obligations "between man and the Omnipresent" (*bén adam la-makom*), the latter governing relationships "between man and his fellow man" (*bén adam le-ḫavero*). The sages define *mishpatim* as rational laws, such as the prohibitions against murder and theft, which "even if they had not been commanded by God would be adopted by society"; whereas *ḫukkim* are laws which man's reason questions, such as the prohibition against eating the flesh of the pig (Deut. 14:8) or wearing a garment of mixed threads (Deut. 22:11). Concerning the *ḫukkim*, it is written, "I am the Lord. I have decreed them and you have no right to question them" (Lev. 18:5; *Yoma* 67b). The sages made further classifications. There are commandments "dependent upon the Land," i.e., involving agricultural products, and commandments not dependent. The former (for example, tithes which are taken only from things grown in the soil) apply only to produce grown in the Land of Israel; the latter (for example, attaching a MEZUZAH to the doorpost) are observed universally. Some commentators indicate that all the commandments were given to be observed in Erets Israel; those in effect in the Diaspora are observed there so that they will be familiar upon Israel's return to the Land of Israel (cf. *Sif.* to Deut. 11:18).

Another classification distinguishes between "positive commandments observed at specific times" — such as SUKKAH and *lulav* — and those not dependent upon time — such as *mezuzah* and GRACE AFTER MEALS. WOMEN are exempted from commandments which have to be performed at a fixed time, in order to give them flexibility for their household duties, though there are exceptions. Women are also exempt from the commandment to study the Law and commandments associated with sacrificial offerings. Furthermore, a mother is exempt from commandments which a father must perform for his son, such as circumcision and teaching him Torah (*Kid. 34a-36a*). However, women may perform voluntarily commandments from which they are exempt.

Another classification — made by medieval authorities — distinguishes between commandments that are in effect only when the Temple is standing, and those obligatory at all times. Thus all laws concerning sacrificial offerings have not been in effect since the destruction of the Temple. Similarly, the laws concerning Jewish slaves (Ex. 21:6ff.) and the JUBILEE YEAR (Lev.25:8ff.) ceased to apply once the TEN TRIBES were exiled from the northern kingdom of Israel. According to many medieval authorities, the laws of the SABBATICAL YEAR are also no longer in effect as a biblical command; though their restrictions remain as a rabbinic ordinance. It has been estimated that in the period of the Exile, 270 out of the 613 remained in effect.

The earliest numeration of the 613 Commandments was made in the geonic period, in the introduction to HALAKHOT GEDOLOT, probably written by Simeon Kayyara in the ninth century. He first lists 350 negative commandments, grouped according to the severity of the penalties prescribed for their violation; followed by 182 general positive commandments; then 18 incumbent upon priests; and then 65 communal duties arising from various contingencies. Surprisingly, he includes the reading of the Book of Esther on Purim and the kindling of the Ḥanukkah candles, though they are of post-biblical origin.

During this period — and for several centuries thereafter — liturgical poets (*paytanim*) composed AZHAROT (literally "warnings"; the technical term in the Talmud for negative commandments) in which are enumerated the 613 commandments, for recitation on SHAVU'OT, "the time of the giving of our Torah."

In his work on Jewish philosophy, SAADIAH GAON divides the commandments into two main categories: those comprehended by human reason (*sikhliyyot*) and those not so comprehended but dictated by God (*shimiyyot*), and proceeds to subdivide them into various groupings (*Emunot ve-De'ot*). Saadiah also classified the 613 Commandments according to their relationship to the Ten Commandments, and interpreted the command given to the Children of Israel, to inscribe "the words of the Torah on great stones" (Deut.27:3) as a requirement to inscribe the 613 *mitsvot*.

BAḤYA IBN PAKUDA (11th century) designated the commandments performed by visible action as "commandments of the limbs," and those performed inwardly with conscious intention as "duties of the heart" (*ḥovot ha-levavot*), and it is to the exposition of the latter that he devotes the volume so entitled.

MAIMONIDES (12th century), the great systematizer of the halakhah, wrote in Arabic, a *Sefer ha-Mitsvot* ("Book of Commandments"), listing each commandment with a brief notation of its source in Scripture and its exposition in talmudic sources. In his introduction, he sets forth his purpose in composing the volume; namely, to correct the many errors in the listing found in the *Halakhot Gedolot*, which were mistakenly followed by composers of the *azharot*. He also lists 14 principles which guided him in determining his selection. Little less than a century later, NAḤMANIDES wrote strictures on Maimonides' work, coming to the defense of *Halakhot Gedolot*. First questioning the authenticity of the number 613 in view of the many disagreements in the Talmud as to whether a particular ruling is a biblical commandment and hence included in the number, he concludes that the number is an ancient tradition and therefore merits serious examination. Of the many disagreements between Maimonides and Naḥmanides, two are of particular interest. Maimonides claims that PRAYER is a positive commandment of the Torah — the sages having instituted only the obligatory framework and wording — whereas Naḥmanides contends that there is no biblical commandment to pray. On the other hand, where Naḥmanides claims that there is a positive commandment for Jews to settle and possess the Land of Israel, Maimonides does not include this commandment in his listing.

A late contemporary of Naḥmanides also composed an enumeration of the 613, arranging them in the order of their appearance in the Pentateuch. This is the *Sefer ha-Ḥinnukh*, attributed to Aaron ha-Levi of Barcelona. The author first establishes whether the commandment is in effect in exilic times, and which persons are obligated to fulfill it. He then details the manner of performance, invariably following the ruling of Maimonides.

Medieval Ashkenazi scholars also produced volumes enumerating the 613 Commandments, adding the halakhically accepted practice as a handy guide for the observant. One of the Tosafists, MOSES OF COUCY, composed the *Sefer Mitsvot Gadol* ("Great Book of Commandments," *Semag* for short), an elaborate resumé of the halakhic development of the 613, largely based upon Maimonides' *Mishneh Torah*. The *Semag* was widely accepted by subsequent halakhists as authoritative. Somewhat later, Isaac of Corbeil wrote a briefer treatment of the 613 entitled *Sefer Mitsvot Katan* ("Small Book of Commandments," *Semak* for short). He divided the commandments into seven categories, introducing moral as well as purely halakhic guidance. Many of the authors appended to their lists seven commandments of rabbinic origin. Although there are many more than seven, these were singled out because they were instituted in such a formal manner as to require before their performance the recitation of a benediction which acknowledges God as having commanded its performance (*Shab.23a*).

To this day, Jewish legal authorities argue whether a particular obligatory practice is of biblical origin (*min ha-Torah*) or not, and whether women are included in certain obligations or not. For the differences between biblical commandments and those of rabbinic origin, see HALAKHAH; see also MITSVAH.

COMMUNITY, JEWISH The Jews have been organized as a social unit and a distinct people for thousands of years, the earliest such unit being the ancient Hebrew clan. As they changed from a nomadic to an agrarian life style and began to settle in towns, their leadership tended to become urbanized. The ELDERS are identified as leaders of the various towns, especially for the administration of justice. In ancient Israel, towns were also organized in larger territorial or tribal units.

It was during the period of the Babylonian EXILE that the foundations seem to have been laid for self-governing institutions, including the SYNAGOGUE. Other lands of the Diaspora developed similar patterns of autonomy. These institutions combined concepts taken from the experience of sovereignty in Erets Israel with the social structures and ideologies of the Diaspora environment. The synagogue or *bet ha-keneset* ("assembly hall") was not only a house of prayer but also the focus of communal activities; it accommodated the children's school and the study hall (BET MIDRASH) for adults. As early as the second century BCE, Jews living in Alexandria were entitled to their own corporation with a council (*gerousia*) empowered to conduct its affairs according to Jewish law, to build synagogues, and to send to Jerusalem taxes collected for the Temple. In the Roman Empire, Jews could be judged by their own courts and according to their own laws, a system which laid the foundations of a unique legal autonomy that was to characterize Jewish life for almost 20 centuries and to play a major role in Jewish continuity.

The end of the Second Temple period (70 CE) brought about major changes in Jewish communal organization. The two great centers of Jewish life, Erets Israel and (later) Babylonia, were headed by central authorities. The patriarchate, together with the SANHEDRIN, enjoyed this prerogative in Erets Israel. In Babylonia, the EXILARCH, traditionally of Davidic descent, was accorded the highest honor after the Muslim conquest, being close to the Caliph himself. The religious head of the Babylonian community was the GAON and, in their daily life, Jews were bound by *halakhah*. The local community established a way of life that was totally Jewish: synagogues, law courts, schools, philanthropic institutions, and ritual baths formed part of a centralized complex under the control of the exilarch or the *gaon*. In North African communities and in Spain, the head of the community was the *nagid*, a title which in Egypt was retained hereditarily by descendants of MAIMONIDES for over two centuries.

In medieval Ashkenaz (the Franco-German region), communal leadership was exercised by outstanding rabbinical authorities. The community or congregation (KEHILLAH) was often in a defined quarter of the town, sometimes near to the castle of the ruler who afforded the Jews protection. Within the Ashkenazi community, life was also regulated by *halakhah*. As in Babylonia, a multitude of institutions dealt with every aspect of life. The community was responsible for all taxes, both those demanded by the secular authorities and those required for the community chest. Special societies were organized and funds collected for such purposes as the ransoming of CAPTIVES, providing HOSPITALITY to Jewish visitors from other communities, visiting the SICK and caring for the AGED, collecting the DOWRY for a poor bride, taking care of the WIDOW or supervising Jewish BURIAL. The focus of Jewish life was the synagogue with its own many-faceted functions; it was not only the center of worship and religious ceremonies but also the venue of communal assemblies, the law court, and the school, ritual baths and even a "dance hall" for community functions.

Special communal statutes (*takkanot ha-kahal*) laid down the community's constitution, which might be amplified by special ordinances and enactments for everyday life (see TAKKANAH) ranging from economic procedure to sumptuary laws governing dress. Responsible for their enforcement was the court (BET DIN), a panel of religious judges (*dayyanim*)

Seal of the Rousinov Community, Moravia, 19th-20th century. The inscription reads: "Gemeinde Neuraussnitz".

who, in exceptional cases, would issue bans of EXCOMMUNICATION (*ḥerem*) and who — in even rarer instances (e.g., with regard to "informers" who had endangered the community) — might pass sentences of death. The community's president (PARNAS) was recognized by the secular or Church authorities as the official representative of the Jews; he or the local rabbi (see also CHIEF RABBINATE) usually received an official title such as "Master of the Jews" (*Magister Judaeorum*) or "Bishop of the Jews" (*Judenbischof*).

From the 14th century onward, the center of gravity in European Jewry began shifting to Poland, where the community was to gain its most effective autonomy and power. This sometimes took the form of a structure in which the Jewish community of one central town had authority over all smaller communities in the region and became responsible for serving them. It was in Poland-Lithuania that the centralized and powerful Council of the (Four) Lands (*Va'ad Arba ha-Aratsot*) functioned as a sort of Jewish parliament.

In the Ottoman Empire, central authority was vested in a chief rabbi, the ḤAKHAM BASHI, who was recognized by the Sublime Porte as the Jewish community's representative. Each province of the Empire had its own chief rabbi, and in Egypt the *ḥakham bashi's* office replaced that of the *nagid*.

This traditional pattern underwent a radical change with the advent of EMANCIPATION. Up to that time, Jews had no way of opting out of the Jewish community (unless they abandoned their faith). Once the Jew was granted civil rights, however, he became a full member of the larger community and his membership in the Jewish communal organization was no longer compulsory but voluntary. A new type of Jewish organizational framework was imposed by Napoleon, who secured the agreement of a "Grand Sanhedrin" in Paris (1807) to far-reaching enactments that destroyed French Jewry's autonomous existence and made it a subservient "religious community." In return for the granting of civic rights and responsibilities, certain new Jewish bodies willingly confined themselves to religious functions which they — not the State — were often charged with maintaining (see CONSISTORY).

In the modern world, Jews adjusted their communal life to changing circumstances. In the United States, for example, new forms of association have emerged, but the bold attempt to establish a New York City "*Kehillah*" (1908-22) eventually failed. Many Jewish organizations, growing out of individual aspects of the traditional community, are structured on a nationwide basis and often display a zealous independence that makes them unwilling to cooperate effectively with other bodies. Thus, the functions of rabbis in the United States and Canada are supervised by national rabbinical associations, while synagogue "roof organizations" exist throughout the world (including Israel). Different bodies take charge of education and the modern equivalent of philanthropy. In some countries (e.g., Britain and Scandinavia), the welfare state has taken over many of the functions that were basic to the traditional community (e.g., care of the sick and the aged). The general pluralism of American life is also reflected in the pluralism of American Jewish life, where each synagogue or Jewish community center operates as a kind of mini-community.

The organized Jewish community or *kehillah* has undergone many changes and vicissitudes over the centuries, but its basic vitality and adaptability in the face of challenges — both external and internal — have been determining factors in the social and religious development of the Jewish people.

CONCLUDING SERVICE (DAY OF ATONEMENT)
See NE'ILAH

CONFESSION (Heb. *viddu'i*) The acknowledgement of SIN is a primary step in seeking forgiveness and ATONEMENT for any wrong committed. True confession involves several elements. The first is the act of confession itself which recognizes the act as a sin with the acknowledgment of guilt. The second step is the feeling of regret and REPENTANCE on the part of the sinner for having been guilty of the offense. The final element in true confession is the resolve not to repeat the sin. Without the third steps the confession is of no value from a religious viewpoint. Examples of confession abound in the Bible; the stories of Cain (Gen. 4:13), Judah (Gen. 38:36), Saul (I Sam. 15:24), and David (II Sam. 12:13) are a few of the more prominent. Further, at the time of bringing an offering in the Temple for unwitting sin the person bringing his SACRIFICE was required to confess his sin while placing his hands on the animal. Again, in the DAY OF ATONEMENT ritual (the AVODAH), the HIGH PRIEST confessed his sins, those of the priesthood, and the sins of the people.

Judaism does not posit the existence of any intermediary to whom the sinner must confess. The act of confession is made by a sinner directly to God, and in the case of a social sin, it must be made to the victim of the sinner's misdeed in an honest effort to repair the damage and to obtain the forgiveness of the person wronged. The sinner must repay a theft and compensate for damage, and suffer any penalties which the law imposes upon him, as an integral part of the process of true repentance.

All five Day of Atonement services contain a ritual of *viddu'i* or confession, the text of which was fixed before the year 1000 CE. There is a short confession, ASHAMNU and a long one, AL ḤET. Both are written in an alphabetic acrostic, not only as a medieval poetic form but as an aid to the majority of the worshipers who in the days before printing had no prayer books of their own. The alphabetic order helped them to remember the text or to follow the reader more easily.

The text of both confessions is in the first person plural, to emphasize the corporate responsibility which is the ideal in a sensitive community, according to the rabbinic teaching,

Kol Yisrael arevim zeh ba-zeh, "All Jews are responsible for each other" (*San.* 16 b.). Nevertheless, some old texts left a blank line after the ritual confession with a rubric suggesting to the worshiper that he could confess his own private sins.

In some rituals, the shorter confession, *Ashamnu*, is included in the service every Monday and Thursday morning on those days when the TAḤANUN propitiatory prayers are read. There is also a custom for a bridegroom to recite the confession of sins in the Afternoon Service before his wedding, since it is thought that bride and groom are forgiven past misdeeds as they start their new life together.

Confession is also said for or by a person considered to be near DEATH after a longer statement of faith and an acknowledgement that life and death is in the hands of God.

CONFIRMATION Public ceremony in which young people in their teens affirm their commitment to Judaism and the Jewish community; found primarily in non-Orthodox congregations in the English-speaking world. While the term "confirmation" is borrowed from the Church, the concept is very different as Jewishness is not a matter of declaration. Conservative Jews use the phrase *ben* or *bat Torah* (son, or daughter, of the Torah) to refer to confirmants.

The practice originated in the first decade of the 19th century, in the towns of the Kingdom of Westphalia (in present-day Germany) under the impetus of the Napoleonic conquest and the subsequent emancipation of the Jews there. The early reformers of Jewish religious life and ritual viewed confirmation as complementary and supplementary to BAR MITSVAH; the latter implied a technical change of status, unrequested and often unappreciated, whereas the former was intended to reflect knowledge, willingness and personal commitment.

In its common contemporary form, confirmation is a group ceremony for boys and girls, who have completed the course of study in a congregational, post bar/bat mitsvah religious school program, within the framework of a synagogue SHAVU'OT service, in which the confirmants take an active, creative part. This format evolved gradually and irregularly. Two fundamental issues in the development of the confirmation ceremony were whether it was meant to supplement or replace bar/bat mitsvah and what was the appropriate age. Additional ideological arguments emerged over whether the ceremony should be for individuals or a group; whether girls and boys should be confirmed together; whether the ceremony should be held in a public hall or school, or a synagogue, and if in a synagogue, within the regular service or at a special convocation. All such questions were ideologically argued, with each community adopting its own position. One of the main considerations in Diaspora Judaism has been to insure that the child will not cease his Jewish education upon reaching bar/bat mitsvah at the age of 12-13, as often happens, but will continue for at least a few more years up to the Confirmation ceremony, usually held at the age of 15.

CONGREGATION See KEHILLAH

CONSECRATION The act of making something or someone holy. Consecration may be performed by God, or it may require man's action; it may involve a time, a space, a person, or an object. The biblical account of Creation states that "God blessed the seventh day, and declared it holy" (Gen.2:3), indicating that the consecration of the SABBATH was a Divine act. As a copartner with God in creation, however, it is man who, by fixing the date of the New Moon, consecrates each of the festivals.

Various people or groups of people were also consecrated, notably the FIRSTBORN of Israel (Ex. 13:2). Later, following the Golden Calf transgression, the sanctity of the firstborn was transferred to the LEVITES. When installed as HIGH PRIEST of Israel, AARON was anointed with oil (Ex. 28:41), a form of consecration that marked the appointment of all subsequent High Priests until the destruction of the First Temple. ANOINTING was also used for the appointment of kings.

The different utensils in the SANCTUARY (Heb. *Mikdash*, a word derived from the term meaning "holy") were anointed with oil in order to consecrate them (Ex. ch. 40). The Sanctuary itself and all its utensils (v. 9), the altar of the burnt offerings and its utensils (v. 10), and the laver and its stand (v. 11) were all anointed with oil. Subsequently, the TEMPLE would also be consecrated, as were the animals used for sacrifice (see HEKDESH).

Once the Temple had been destroyed, however, only three forms of consecration became applicable in Jewish life: the consecration of a new SYNAGOGUE, of a new CEMETERY and of a new home. For none of these three acts of consecration is any specific ceremony laid down by Jewish law, and whatever practices are followed today stem from evolving religious CUSTOM.

The consecration of a synagogue, for example, frequently involves the arranging of a festive procession whereby the Scrolls of the Law are brought into the new house of worship. Seven circuits (HAKKAFOT) are then usually made around the synagogue with the scrolls. The officiating rabbi often wears festive clothes and recites the SHE-HEḤEYANU blessing in the course of the ceremony. Appropriate readings might include Psalms 122, 82, and 24.

At the consecration of a new cemetery, penitential prayers are added to the Morning Service on that particular day. Members of the *ḥevrah kaddisha* (BURIAL SOCIETY) also observe a fast. Various psalms are recited, and all present walk around the cemetery. As this circuit is made, "Let the favor of the Lord our God be upon us" (Ps. 90:17) is often recited. The ceremony then concludes with a prayer that no evil may befall anyone and that death will cease.

The consecration (or dedication) of a new home is known

in Hebrew as *ḥanukkat ha-bayit*, this custom being already indicated in the Pentateuch (Deut.20:5). It always includes — and usually begins with — the affixing of the MEZUZAH on the front doorpost of the house, together with the prescribed benedictions (which include *She-heḥeyanu*). Among Ashkenazim, it is customary for various psalms to be read on this occasion, e.g., Ps.30 ("A Song for the Dedication of the House"), Ps.15, and Ps. 127:1; prayers may also be recited for the welfare of the household and for the rebuilding of the Temple. Refreshments or a meal usually conclude the dedication ceremony. If one moves into a new home in the Land of Israel, the meal is considered to be an obligatory *se'udat mitsvah* after fulfilling a commandment; elsewhere, it is an optional *se'udat reshut*. During the Middle Ages, it was commonly believed that evil spirits inhabited a new house before the owners took possession. To guard against their malevolent influence, people would slaughter a rooster and a hen prior to moving into their new home, as if to show that they were not the first inhabitants. Such folk practices were denounced by rabbis of the time, who considered them un-Jewish and idolatrous.

CONSERVATIVE JUDAISM Religious movement of the post-Emancipation era which developed from the stand adopted by the "positive-historical" school of Zacharias FRANKEL, head of the Jewish Theological Seminary in Breslau (1854-75). Frankel, an eminent rabbinical scholar, found himself unable to identify either with "old-fashioned" ORTHODOXY or with REFORM JUDAISM. Orthodoxy rejected critical scholarship and scientific investigation of Judaism, while its approach in halakhic matters was seen as rigid; Reform championed a radical approach to religion, failing to distinguish between ritual *mitsvot* (precepts) of greater and lesser importance, largely abandoning Hebrew, and rejecting every aspect of Jewish nationalism and ethnicity. Frankel advocated a middle-of-the-road approach, whereby the Jewish people and its traditions would be central to Judaism, *halakhah* (Jewish law) would be observed but modified according to the needs of the day, and critical methodology would be accepted and utilized. His standpoint was historical, viewing Judaism as the outcome of historical processes; and positive, seeking to preserve the tradition and further its growth. This approach to Judaism as an evolving religious way of life for the Jewish people remained at the center of the movement throughout its subsequent developments. In addition, Frankel was strongly attached to Jewish national aspirations, advocating a return to Zion and a political reestablishment of Jewish nationhood long before political Zionism came into being.

In the United States, this philosophy was carried forward by the Jewish Theological Seminary of America, founded in 1886 by a group of traditionally-minded scholars and rabbis. Led by Sabato Morais of Philadelphia, they were opposed to the Reform movement's Pittsburgh Platform (1885), but did not feel part of East European Orthodoxy. Though as yet a minority group, they represented traditional congregations deeply rooted in American society. After the initial attempt to establish the Jewish Theological Seminary and unite all traditionalist elements had failed, the Seminary was reconstituted under the presidency of Solomon SCHECHTER in 1902; it succeeded in halting the growth of Reform and in offering a viable alternative to Orthodoxy. Schechter, who built upon Frankel's work while criticizing its lack of a specific theological basis, shouldered the task of creating institutions that would meet the needs of a rapidly expanding American Jewish community. In 1913, he founded the United Synagogue as the movement's lay organization. Schechter then hoped that "historical Judaism" would encompass the major segments of observant Jewry, including moderate Orthodox groups. His concern was for "catholic Israel," i.e., the general body and "collective conscience" of the Jewish people, and for the retention of Jewish unity. Though impractical and unattainable, this vision did facilitate a wide range of diversity within the Conservative movement, making it less doctrinaire and ideological than the other groups. By bringing such outstanding scholars as Louis GINZBERG to America, Schechter reinforced the Seminary, enabling it to become one of the leading centers of Jewish scholarship in the Western world and the "fountainhead" of the Conservative movement.

For Schechter, the challenges to Judaism lay in the discovery of natural law and in greater scientific knowledge of Jewish texts, both of which undermined simple belief. The intellectual basis for the Conservative movement and its rabbis lay in the scholarly, historical understanding of Judaism as an organic structure capable of absorbing modern knowledge without radically changing its own nature. Where halakhic innovations were contemplated, not only did Conservatism take account of the ways in which the *halakhah* overtly functioned, it also sought to grasp what had actually happened in halakhic development — making explicit what had always been implicit. Its approach to Judaism might be described as holistic, seeking to preserve and maintain ritual and ethics, law and lore, belief and practice, universalism and nationalism.

This proved most suitable for large numbers of Jewish immigrants from Eastern Europe who had abandoned Orthodoxy in the U.S. but who considered Reform Judaism to be alien and bereft of Jewish warmth. They accordingly felt at home in Conservative Judaism and transformed it into the largest American Jewish religious movement. What mattered to them was not so much this movement's intellectual base as its palpable authenticity, its aesthetic improvements and moderate approach to religious practice, allowing them to feel comfortable belonging to a Conservative synagogue, regardless of their level of personal observance. The peak of rapid growth was reached after World War II. With Louis FINKELSTEIN heading the Seminary (1940-72), the movement then proceeded to incorporate synagogues in the new suburban communities to which Jews were flocking, also opening a West Coast affiliate of the Seminary — the University of Judaism in Los Angeles (1947).

In this period, the Conservative Movement grew rapidly and became the largest trend in American Judaism. Its rabbinical body, the Rabbinical Assembly, by now had rabbis serving on all continents, reflecting the growing international character of the movement. Similar expansion was recorded by its synagogue body, the United Synagogue of America. Innovative programming included the movement's own camping organization, Ramah, its junior affiliate, the United Synagogue Youth, regular radio ("Eternal Light") and TV ("Frontiers of Faith") programs, the Solomon Schechter Day Schools, and New York's Jewish Museum.

Within the movement, various ideological trends could be discerned, ranging from traditional positions that were close to Orthodoxy to radical views that were scarcely distinguishable from Reform. The Rabbinical Assembly's Committee on Jewish Law and Standards grappled with problems of interpretation of Jewish law but their decisions often aroused controversy within the movement, and considerable leeway was left to the individual congregations.

Finkelstein was succeeded as chancellor by Gerson D. Cohen (1972-85) under whom the more liberal elements grew stronger and farreaching changes were introduced. Most noteworthy was the question of the role of WOMEN in public worship and ritual. Already from 1955, women could be called to the Reading of the Law and from 1973, counted in a prayer quorum (*minyan*). From 1983, women were admitted to rabbinical study and in 1985 the first woman rabbi was ordained. The issue threatened to split the movement and led to the organization of a minority right-wing group of rabbis and laymen. While separatist, they chose not to break away and remained active within the movement as the Union for Traditional Conservative Judaism.

The Rabbinical Assembly grew threefold in membership in the 30 years up to 1985 when it had 1,200 members, including many coming from Orthodox and Reform backgrounds. In an attempt to decentralize the synagogues, a proliferation of subgroups (e.g., the ḤAVURAH) emerged as an attempt to provide serious alternatives. A series of ambitious liturgical publications was issued including daily, Sabbath, and festival prayerbooks and a Haggadah (see PRAYER-BOOKS). By 1985, 830 congregations were affiliated to the United Synagogue of America with a total membership estimated at around 1,250,000 people. The international aspects were reflected in the growth of the movement's World Council of Synagogues.

By the mid-1980s, however, a certain concern was felt by the fact that the movement's growth pattern was being overtaken by the Orthodox on the one hand and the Reform on the other. This has led to a decline in the percentage of Conservative Jews in the organized synagogue community. Various contributory factors have been cited: Orthodoxy is no longer seen as an immigrant "Old World" manifestation and has adapted itself to the American scene, while the general swing towards fundamentalists has strengthened ultra-Orthodoxy. Major changes in Reform's ideology — its attitude to Zionism and nationhood, its reassessment of ethnic practices and the restoration of certain rituals and the use of Hebrew — have blurred the lines between it and Conservatism. Already in the 1930s, the RECONSTRUCTIONIST movement broke away from Conservatism over two questions of principle: its naturalistic approach to God and its liberal attitude towards *halakhah*. These issues are still the subject of conflict within Conservative Judaism. In addition to all these aspects, the present-day U.S. scene has been witnessing a falling-off in synagogue affiliation as well as a general decline in numbers. Conservative circles are engaged in a search for new creative expressions to attract the younger generation.

For the past century, Conservative Judaism has endeavored to reconcile tradition and change. This has set up a creative tension, and while the movement has sought to move with the times, it has also maintained a continuity of ideology, ritual, and practice.

The Conservative movement is the only trend in American Jewry that has maintained a consistently Zionist stand from its very inception. It was, however, slow in finding a place for itself in Israel, and its growth there did not keep pace with its development in the U.S. and Canada or in South America; the establishment by Marshall Meyer of a rabbinical school in Argentina, the Seminario Rabinico Latino-Americano (1962), gave new impetus to the movement's South American branch. Although a few Conservative synagogues and the American Student Center (Neveh Schechter) had existed in Israel prior to that time, it was not until the 1970s that efforts were made to create an actual movement in Israel and not until the 1980s were serious activities undertaken toward that goal. The Mesorati (i.e., Traditional) movement, as Conservatism is styled in Israel, has now established the basic institutions needed for growth, including the Seminary of Judaic Studies, a rabbinical school for Israelis opened in 1984; a youth movement (Noam), summer camps and schools; a kibbutz (Ḥanaton) and a moshav (Shorashim); and some 40 congregations. It was also responsible for the creation of a new traditional (but non-Orthodox) stream of education in Israel (Tali), which reflects the movement's basic ideology. However, despite these achievements, the movement in Israel remains comparatively small (see ISRAEL, STATE OF).

Conservative ideology may be summarized as follows:

1. Judaism is an amalgam of religion and ethnic nationhood which has evolved from biblical times down to the present day.

2. It is organized as a system of *mitsvot* embracing all human conduct and governing relationships between people and between ourselves and God, whether ethical or ritual.

3. The process through which the ideals of Judaism are interpreted and made relevant to life is known as *halakhah*.

4. *Halakhah* is flexible enough to meet the needs of modern human beings when interpreted creatively by knowledgeable, committed rabbinic authorities.

5. There is room within *halakhah* for change and for multiple opinions.

6. Scientific, historical study of Judaism is a positive development which helps us to understand ourselves and to make Judaism as creative today as it was in the past.

Its commitment to the halakhic process and to the importance of ritual distinguishes Conservative Judaism from Reform. Its commitment to the flexible, evolving nature of *halakhah*, to pluralism, and to open inquiry distinguishes it from Orthodoxy. The first official statement of Conservative principles was issued by the Mesorati movement in Israel (1986), various pamphlets having also been issued to explain the major points. Two years later, in 1988, the Rabbinical Assembly published a far more comprehensive statement on ideology, reflecting the concerns of the American movement and differing significantly from the Israeli document, especially in matters concerning the role of Israel in world Jewry.

CONSISTORY (French *Consistoire*). A type of state-controlled Jewish communal body first established by Napoleon in 1808 to convert the Jews of France into "useful citizens." In the previous year, he had convened a "Great Sanhedrin," patterned after the ancient SANHEDRIN of 71 members and intended to exercise similar authority. In obedience to the Emperor's wishes, it confirmed the "religious" precepts of Judaism as eternally binding, yet declared the Torah's "political" statutes to be no longer valid since the Jews could not be regarded as a nation. New regulations provided for the surrender of Jewish legal autonomy and for marriages and divorces to be performed only after a civil registration. "Mixed marriages" were recognized under civil law, but the traditionalists won the concession that no rabbi should have to officiate at such a union. In the short term, French Jews were humiliated by a series of discriminatory and economically ruinous laws; in the long term, these Napoleonic regulations also undermined traditional observance, promoting rampant assimilation and even apostasy. Jews lost their national status and henceforward were regarded solely as a religious community. Napoleon declared Judaism to be an "official religion of France."

The formerly independent rabbinate and communal structure now gave way to a nationwide organization of "consistories," a term borrowed from the assemblies of the Reformed (Calvinist) Church in France. Directed by a Central Consistory of *grands-rabbins* (chief rabbis) and laymen in Paris, local consistories were appointed to regulate congregational affairs in every French department. Their responsibilities included maintaining synagogues and public worship, the inculcation of patriotism, encouraging young Jews to serve in the army, and persuading traders to adopt "more useful" occupations such as agriculture. David Sinzheim, the traditionalist rabbi of Strasbourg who had presided over Napoleon's "Great Sanhedrin," became *grand-rabbin* of the Central Consistory.

A CHIEF RABBINATE of France was established in 1844 and a new regional consistory of Algeria was set up a year later. During the reign of Napoleon III (1852-70), more democratic elections to consistorial office were held. A compromising form of ORTHODOXY evolved, characterized by decorous, somewhat abbreviated services held within Ashkenazi and Sephardi "temples." After the separation of Church and State in France (1905), the Central Consistory and its affiliates became voluntary religious organizations, but the original system was maintained in Belgium and Luxembourg. While many strictly Orthodox (as well as a few Liberal) congregations developed alongside this elaborate structure, the *Consistoire Central Israélite de France et d'Algérie* shed much of its old formalism after World War II.

CONVERSION TO JUDAISM (*giyyur*). Conversion to Judaism is the decision of a non-Jew (traditionally defined as a person born to a non-Jewish mother) to adopt the Jewish faith with its religious way of life, and his/her experiencing the rites of conversion and being accepted as a full-fledged member of the Jewish people by a *bet din* (a religious court). Since Judaism recognizes non-Jews who follow the seven Noachide laws as meeting the essential general religious duties of man, it regards those who take the special step of changing their religious and ethnic identity to Jewish and accepting for themselves the laws of the Torah as *geré tsedek*, righteous converts. They are mentioned with the righteous and the pious in the daily prayers and particular sensitivity to their feelings is praised. Thus, it is specifically forbidden to mention their past in a derogatory manner. Morever, the Jew is commanded, "The stranger who resides with you shall be to you as one of your citizens; you shall love him as yourself" (Lev. 19:34).

The educational process preceding conversion varies with the time, place, and needs of the candidate for conversion. Its objective is to assure an informed and fullhearted lifelong commitment and integration in the Jewish community. "Some of the major and some of the lesser commandments" must be taught. The candidate must be warned of the persecutions and efforts to annihilate the Jewish people. He/she must also be told that by converting many things which were heretofore permitted will be forbidden, such as performing work on the Sabbath. In fact Jewish law specifically requires that at the beginning, an effort be made to dissuade the person from converting. This step is meant to screen out those whose motives are not sincere, such as those who may seek to convert for material benefit, to attain a desired position, or out of fear. Once the candidate for conversion shows a determination to convert, then he/she is encouraged.

The essential rites of conversion are, for the male, CIRCUMCISION as entry into the "covenant of Abraham" (or for the already circumcised, the taking of a drop of blood in a symbolic circumcision) and *tevilah*, i.e., complete immersion in a ritual bath or other authorized body of water. For the female, *tevilah* is the essential ritual. At the time of the Temple, the convert was also required to bring a sacrifice. Children who are converted at the behest of parents or legal guardians, may, when of age, opt out of their Judaism, but the adult convert who relapses remains technically Jewish and is still subject to Jewish law. He or she may thus return to the Jewish fold without a new conversion.

Conversion has a long history among Jews. According to midrashic tradition, ABRAHAM would proselytize the men and SARAH the women. The Bible referred to "the *ger* in your gates" as a special class of the population. *Ger* is usually translated as "stranger." In rabbinic law the "stranger" could be either the *ger tsedek*, the convert, or the *ger toshav*, a foreigner who lived in the land and accepted the Noachide laws.

In biblical times Ruth, who proclaimed "your people are my people and your God is my God," is the model proselyte and was the ancestor of King David. At the end of the second century BCE, John Hyrcanus forced the Edomites (Idumeans) to convert, and some of the valiant defenders of Jerusalem against the Romans came from the Edomite ranks. Another large-scale conversion occurred many centuries later, when the KHAZARS converted.

In the Greco-Roman era, large numbers of non-Jews associated themselves with the Jewish communities of the ever-growing Diaspora, finding in the Jewish faith an answer to their dissatisfaction with pagan polytheism. Some of the greatest of early rabbinic scholars like Shemayah, Avtalyon, and R. Akiva were said to be descendants of converts, and Onkelos, who translated the Pentateuch into Aramaic, was a convert.

A minority opinion among the talmudic sages offers some opposition to the policy of accepting converts. Thus, one of the *amoraim* expressed his opposition to conversion by claiming that "converts are as hard for Israel [to endure] as a sore" (*Yev.* 47b). This seems to have been a reflection of the external situation in which the Jewish community could be punished for attempts to proselytize. There are numerous expressions to the contrary, praising converts and their contribution to the Jewish people, and even recommending steps "not to close the door before potential proselytes." This latter view is the most prevalent in talmudic literature. It would appear that the different views on the subject were less a product of any particular philosophy than of the circumstances prevailing at any given time.

The teachers of CHRISTIANITY offered non-Jews on the periphery of the Jewish communities a competing faith which did not require circumcision and the acceptance of a stringent legal code. Nonetheless, Jewish proselytizing continued apace until Christianity became the official religion of the Roman Empire, after which proselytizing was forbidden under pain of death to the convert and the Jews who converted him. Several centuries later, ISLAM, as it conquered country after country, took a similar position. Jewish proselytizing went underground and became far less common.

Rabbinic literature found answers to many questions about the status of the convert. He is considered as if born afresh and not related to his previous family; is counted as a member of a *minyan*, the prayer quorum; may serve as prayer leader; may serve as judge in a rabbinic court dealing with civil cases; and in general is obligated by the same commandments as his fellow Jews. The scholars ruled that in prayer he too should pray, "our God and God of our fathers," "...for once having come under the wings of the Divine Presence, there is no difference between us; all the miracles done for us were done for him too!" There are nevertheless certain restrictions: a female proselyte is not permitted to marry a *Kohen* (priest), while a proselyte could not be anointed king.

In modern times many non-Jews have turned to the Jewish faith, some out of dissatisfaction with their faith of origin, some initially out of a wish to marry Jews and others, in Israel, out of a desire to be registered as Jews on state documents. Instruction of conversion candidates today is designed so that, no matter what the original motivation, the conversion is only granted when religious motivation is genuine.

Reform and Conservative rabbis have performed or officiated at the vast majority of conversions to Judaism throughout the world in recent decades, especially in the United States where thousands of non-Jews convert to Judaism annually, often as with many Orthodox conversions, within a marriage situation. Most Reform rabbis do not require circumcision or immersion in the ritual bath, but only a course of study and a ceremony that emphasizes the commitment to join faith with the people of Israel and to adopt the Jewish religion and culture. Reform Judaism encourages conversion to Judaism as a means of establishing the Jewish identity of families of mixed marriage, and of bolstering the population of the Jewish people that has been decimated in the present century by the Holocaust and mass assimilation. Reform Judaism considers converts to be of full Jewish status, without any restrictions, including marriage eligibility. Converts are often referred to in Reform literature by the more expressive term "Jews by choice."

The Orthodox rabbinate in most places refuses to recognize the validity of conversion under non-Orthodox auspices and denies the Jewishness of offspring of women so converted. When asked to conduct a religious service, e.g., a wedding for such converts, or in Israel to register them as Jews (see JEW, WHO IS A), Orthodox rabbis often require a new conversion under Orthodox auspices on the grounds that the non-Orthodox conversion was not according to *halakhah*, that the convert does not intend to lead an Orthodox life, that the rabbis concerned are not qualified to sit on a *bet din*, or that the convert was not adequately prepared.

Conservative rabbis counter that they do follow the *halakhah* of conversion meticulously, and that many current Orthodox rulings are new TAKKANOT, matters of policy rather than of basic Jewish law. Orthodox and non-Orthodox, each from their own perspective, warn against splintering the Jewish people over this issue.

CORDOVERO, MOSES (1522-1570). Kabbalist. Born to a family of Spanish origin, he was a disciple of R. Solomon ALKABETS in Safed. He worked with R. Joseph CARO, and may have briefly taught Isaac LURIA, who arrived in Safed in the year Cordovero died. He had several disciples in Safed, among them R. Elijah de Vidas, author of the important kabbalistic ethical work, *Reshit Ḫokhmah*.

Cordovero's most influential work is *Pardes Rimmonim*, one of the most profound works of the KABBALAH. Cordovero presents the Kabbalah as a theosophic system, and organizes its symbols and myths in a coherent sequence, beginning with the *En Sof*, the hidden Godhead, descending in stages through the emanated divine forces, and concluding with cosmic phenomena. Cordovero saw himself as a zoharic kabbalist, presenting in a systematic manner the teachings of the ZOHAR, but in most cases he combined the Zohar with the ideas of other Kabbalists and his original contribution is very meaningful throughout.

Cordovero de-emphasized the Zohar's mythological symbolism, especially the sexual elements and the myth of the powers of evil, the *Sitra Aḫra*, substituting for it a view that sees the Godhead as completely free of evil tendencies while the roots of evil are to be found within the cosmos and in man's ethical choices. Cordovero's concepts of the relationship between God and the world may have some pantheistic inclination, though mostly it can be described as panentheistic, the presence of God within everything.

Cordovero's greatest work is the multi-volume commentary on the Zohar, *Or Yakar*. He also wrote commentaries on the prayers and monographs on other kabbalistic subjects, among them a brief ethical treatise, *Tomer Devorah*, which was the first to combine kabbalistic symbolism with man's everyday ethical behavior. Cordovero's concept in this work is one of *imitatio dei* (IMITATION OF GOD) — man's deeds should reflect his adherence and imitation of the conduct of the Divine SEFIROT, and his whole life should reflect the inner structure of the Divine world. This idea had a profound impact on subsequent works of kabbalistic ethics.

CORPSE Body of a dead person. Attending to the dead is considered the most selfless of the commandments in the Torah. According to the rabbis, the respect and care given the newly deceased stems from the belief that man was created in the image of God; although the life is now gone, the human form must be respected for having once embodied a Divine spirit. The dead body renders the house in which it is situated and anyone coming in contact with the body ritually impure, *tamé met*. Even one who walks over a grave takes on this status. In Temple times, those who were *tamé met* were purified by a priest sprinkling upon them a special mixture of pure spring water and the ashes of the RED HEIFER (Num. 19:14-22). Today, since this ritual is no longer possible, everyone is considered *tamé met*. High Priests and NAZIRITES were absolutely forbidden to come in contact with a corpse. The relevant laws are given in the Misnaic tractate OHOLOT.

From the moment of DEATH until the BURIAL, the body is not to be left alone and the family must arrange for a "watcher" (*shomer*) to sit by the deceased and recite Psalms. If the person died at home, his body must remain there until the BURIAL SOCIETY (*ḫevrah kaddisha*) arrives to prepare it for burial. The eyes and mouth of the deceased are closed, he is covered by a sheet, and placed with his feet toward the door. A candle is lit and placed near his head. With few exceptions, the dead are buried according to Orthodox practice, within 24 hours of death; CREMATION is forbidden and no AUTOPSY may be performed.

Close to the time of burial, the *ḫevrah kaddisha* perform the TOHORAH (ritual washing of the body). Any person touching a corpse must wash his hands as soon as possible. The Burial Society then brings the shrouded body to the place where the FUNERAL SERVICE will be held. Persons of priestly descent (*kohanim*) must avoid all proximity to a corpse. The carcass of an animal also conveys ritual impurity and any person coming in contact with one must wash himself. It is considered particularly meritorious to see to the burial of an individual who has no relatives or acquaintances to do so, or of an unidentified corpse (*met mitsvah*).

COSTA, URIEL DA (1585-1640). Rationalist and freethinker. Originally named Gabriel da Costa (or Acosta), he was born in Oporto, his family being descended from Portuguese MARRANOS. Having studied canon law and taken a minor appointment in the Catholic church, Da Costa became alienated from Christian doctrine; through reading the Hebrew Bible, he finally decided that a formal return to Judaism was his most logical course. Around 1615, therefore, Da Costa sought refuge in Amsterdam, together with his mother and four brothers, all thankful for the opportunity to profess their Jewish faith openly. Within a year or two, however, Da Costa and the Sephardi rabbinate of Amsterdam were at loggerheads. His "biblical" concept of Judaism took no account of halakhic developments, nor did his approach endear him to the rabbis of the Dutch community, whom he derisively called "Pharisees." They, for their part, insisted on a rigid communal discipline and — fearing Dutch Protestant reaction to this nonconformist — regarded him as a troublemaker. Da Costa's critique of rabbinic doctrine and practice, attacking "ritualism" as well as questioning belief in the soul's immortality, outraged the Sephardi leadership and, once published in 1624, it was burned. A ban of excommunication imposed on the author remained in force until 1633, when he could no longer bear his isolation and submitted to the rabbinate.

Socially acceptable, though secretly unrepentant, Da Costa now proceeded from rejection of the Oral Law to a deistic view of the Bible which anticipated the philosophical approach of SPINOZA. As related in the moving Latin autobiography published many years after his death, "I began to ask myself whether the law of Moses should be considered the law of God, and I concluded that it was nothing more than human invention" (*Exemplar Humanae Vitae*, 1687). Such heretical opinions, added to Da Costa's abandonment of religious observance, renewed his conflict with the rabbinate and led to a second ban (1633-40). After another seven years of ostracism, which his own family also maintained, Da Costa again recanted; but the public humiliation to which he was subjected, notably 39 lashes in the Amsterdam synagogue, preyed on his mind and induced him to commit suicide. To many intellectuals ever since, Uriel da Costa has been an idealized "hero of conscience" and a pioneer in the struggle against bigotry.

COURT OF LAW See BET DIN

COVENANT (Heb. *berit*). An agreement or contract between two sides. The etymology of the Hebrew *berit* is unclear. Some have suggested that the word is related to the root meaning to cut, while others have suggested a connection to a root meaning to eat — based upon the common practice of marking a covenant with a ceremonial meal. The predominant view, however, relates *berit* to the Akkadian *biritu*, "fetter", conveying the sense of binding — a *berit* being an arrangement that binds two sides together.

The Bible records numerous covenants. In Genesis 6:18, God, after telling NOAH of His intent to destroy all life, informs Noah that he will be granted a covenant and be saved by means of the ark he has constructed. After the Flood, God again invokes a covenant (although it is not clear if this is the same covenant or a new one) in which He obligates Himself never again to destroy all of life by flood (Gen. 9:8). Covenants are also common between individuals in the Bible (e.g., Gen. 21:28; Josh. 9:15, etc.).

Establishment of a covenant was usually marked by a ceremonial act. For instance, Genesis 26:26-33 tells of a covenant being accompanied by a meal as well as an oath; Jeremiah 34:18 refers to passing between the "halves" of a calf cloven in two (see below). Another common feature of covenants in the Bible is the designation of an *ot* or symbol of the covenant, such as the rainbow of Genesis 9:13, or the monument of stones erected by Jacob and Laban (Gen. 31:51). The covenants of the Bible resemble other legal documents of the ancient Near East.

Three covenants recounted in the Bible have figured significantly in subsequent Jewish history. They are the covenant between the pieces, the covenant of CIRCUMCISION, and the Sinaitic covenant.

The covenant between the pieces (Gen. 15:7-21) In response to Abraham's query as to how he will know for certain that he is to inherit the Land of Canaan, God instructs him to take a number of animals and cut them in half. Abraham arranges the halves opposite one another. God promises Abraham the land between "the river of Egypt to the great river Euphrates," informing him that his right to the land will not be realized until his descendants have undergone an extended exile. A "flaming torch" (symbolically representing God) then passes between the animal parts.

Based upon this passage and Jeremiah 34:18 (see above), it seems clear that a common way of enacting a covenant was for both parties to pass through the halves of slaughtered animals. The meaning of this was probably something akin to a curse upon anyone violating the agreement — that he suffer the same fate as the animals between whose parts he has passed. This method of finalizing an agreement explains the Hebrew terminology "to cut a covenant" (*li-kherot berit*). Traditional sources view the covenant between the pieces as a legally binding commitment by God to grant perpetual ownership of the Land of Canaan, subsequently Erets Israel, to Abraham's progeny.

The covenant of circumcision (Gen. 17) The Bible recounts the appearance of God to Abraham, when the latter is 99 years old. God promises to grant Abraham a covenant and reiterates various other promises. He commands Abraham to circumcise all male descendants and slaves, explaining that this will be the *ot* — symbol — of the covenant. Abraham obeys, circumcising himself, his slaves, and his thirteen year old son Ishmael. Subsequently, every newborn male child is to be circumcised at the age of eight days.

The Sinaitic covenant (Ex. 19-24) This covenant is generally understood to be a renewal and expansion of Abraham's covenant with God. Some three months after the EXODUS from Egypt, the children of Israel arrive at Mount SINAI. MOSES ascends the mountain and returns with a decree from God to establish a covenant according to which the children of Israel will obey God and thus be considered unique among the peoples, a holy nation and a kingdom of priests. The people agree and there follows a great theophany during which the entire people experiences God. The content of this theophany is the Decalogue (the TEN COMMANDMENTS). With the conclusion of the Decalogue, the people, fearful and overwhelmed by the experience of the Deity, demand that Moses henceforth serve as mediator. There follows a large body of additional legislation, which Moses records and submits to the people for final confirmation. When the people declare their approval, Moses sprinkles the blood of sacrifices upon them: "Behold, this is the blood of the covenant, which the Lord hath made with you in agreement with all these words" (Ex. 24:8). Moses and the elders then partake of a ceremonial meal.

The Sinaitic covenant between man and Deity is the biblical covenant par excellence. It contains all the trappings of a legal act. The text emphasizes the voluntary nature of this covenant. Prior to the theophany and subsequent to the giving of legislation, the children of Israel are required to voice their consent. The covenant is marked by ceremonial acts — the bringing of sacrifices, the sprinkling of their blood upon the people, the meal consumed by Moses and the elders — evidently to finalize the agreement. After the covenant is finalized, Moses is invited to ascend the mountain to receive the "tablets of stone," subsequently known as the tablets of the covenant.

While recent research has shown significant parallels between ancient Near Eastern treaties and the Sinaitic covenant, the idea of a covenant or treaty between the Deity and an entire people is unique to the Israelite religion and central to its development. Fundamentals of the Israelite religion such as the liberation from myth, the personal relationship with God, revelation, and the kingship of God are all rooted in the notion of covenant. Throughout the Bible, the covenant functions as the legal basis of the relationship between God and the people with whom He has contracted. Thus the prophets reprove the people using the formulations of a law suit (see for example Hos. 4:1) in which God calls heaven and earth to witness (Is. 1:2 et. al).

The uniqueness of the covenant resides less in the content of its laws than in the revelation of those laws by the Deity. Law promulgated in the covenant is not the fiat of a particular ruler or the wisdom of sages but the command of God. The belief in God's revelation to an entire people rather than to one particular visionary or priest was also unprecedented. Since the laws of the Torah were given to the entire nation, the nation as a whole became responsible for their observance. The covenant related not only to cultic considerations, but to moral ones as well. Thus, not only worship and cult but morality and the functioning of society become expressions of the Divine will. Moral law is no longer secular but religious.

The notion of covenant remained central in all subsequent Jewish thought. If the Exodus was traditionally perceived as the central motif of Judaism, the covenant was viewed as its central mechanism. The Exodus was understood theologically to offer an alternate view of reality; one based not on the principle of power as expressed in Egyptian slavery, but rather on the premise of a concerned and benevolent creator who intervenes in history and guarantees its ultimate redemption. In the covenant, God is seen as calling upon the Jewish people to be loyal to Him and live according to the principles of the Exodus. Contemporary Jewish theologians continue to view the idea of a covenant between the Jewish people and God as a relevant and fundamental principle of Jewish doctrine. Thus, Joseph Dov SOLOVEICHIK distinguishes between two covenants: the covenant of "Egypt," or fate, which binds all Jews to their shared history, suffering, and responsibility; and the covenant of "Sinai," which is a covenant of destiny in which the Jew realizes his "historic being" through *halakhah* . The Reform thinker, Eugene Borowitz, allows for revisons of the covenant by each generation on condition that they are appropriate to the situation and remain true to the basic nature of the covenant.

COVERING THE HEAD (*kissu'i rosh*). Although no form of headgear is required by biblical law, the HIGH PRIEST wore a cloth miter or turban (Ex. 28:4, 29:6; Lev. 8:9, etc.), while ordinary priests wore a ceremonial cap (Ex. 28:40, 29:9; Lev. 8.13). In Temple times, only those of high rank appear to have covered their heads, as was the CUSTOM in Mesopotamia. Conflicting opinions are expressed in the Talmud. According to one view, headgear for Jewish males was only a matter of custom and therefore optional (*Ned.* 30b). Many of the sages regarded bareheadedness as objectionable in a scholar, and some would not walk four cubits (less than 2 yards) bareheaded in view of the Divine Presence (*Shekhinah*) above them (*Kid.* 31a; *Shab.* 118b). Others considered it praiseworthy to muffle the face as well as the head during worship (*RH.* 17b; *Ta'an* 20a); and others again made it a rule never to lead the congregation in prayer without covering the head (*Sof.* 14.15). The question of Jewish males praying bareheaded remained a hotly debated issue for centuries to come. However, the sages were unanimous in castigating any (married) woman who displayed the "crowning beauty" of her tresses.

Rabbinic codifiers and scholars of the medieval period were also divided over this issue. Covering the head during prayer and Torah study was not thought obligatory in France and Spain, although Isaac ALFASI and MAIMONIDES favored the stricter Babylonian tradition. While some later authorities, including even the 18th century ELIJAH GAON OF VILNA (*Be'ur Ha-Gra* to *Sh. Ar., OH* 8.2), continued to regard it as an optional "worthy" custom, most Ashkenazi and Sephardi rabbis from the Middle Ages onward associated the wearing of headgear with piety and bareheadedness with frivolity. In Christian Europe, moreover, Jews increasingly condemned bareheaded worship as a Gentile custom not to be followed. Synagogue and Passover *Seder* observances depicted in medieval Jewish illuminated manuscripts invariably show Jews with their heads covered, Spanish and Portuguese Jews wearing hoods and German Jews wearing the pointed "Jew's hat" (*Judenhut*). Before long, certain types of headgear became distinctively Jewish and (by Gentile legislation) obligatory: turbans and skullcaps throughout the Orient, the *Judenhut* followed by the round black *barrette* in Central Europe, wide-brimmed weekday hats, fur-trimmed Ḥasidic *shtraymels* and *spodiks* for Sabbaths and holy days in Poland and Russia. When praying, attending synagogue, engaging in Torah study, and reciting benedictions before and after meals, the Jewish male now covered his head. This practice also won recognition from civil authorities when Jews had to testify in courts of law.

Among Ashkenazim especially, the wearing of a skullcap (Heb. *kippah*; Yiddish *kappel* or *yarmulka*) throughout all working hours became prevalent from the early 18th century. It usually replaced any other form of male headgear indoors, and its constant use became an outward sign of Jewish piety. What started as a custom eventually assumed halakhic validity. REFORM JUDAISM tended to abandon the custom, however, even during prayer. German NEO-ORTHODOXY set the tone for other observant Jews in the West by not demanding that the 19th-century Jew cover his head at all times; CONSERVATIVE JUDAISM followed suit, limiting the obligation to synagogue, private worship, study of sacred texts, and all rituals. Many keep their heads covered during meals. Within the Reform movement itself, however, attitudes have never been uniform: while radical elements (chiefly in the USA) either banned hats and skullcaps from the temple or made their use optional, many European Liberal Jews and Hungarian NEOLOGY tended to favor the covering of head, at least at prayer. As a badge of loyalty to Jewish tradition, the wearing of a hat or skullcap has become widespread among Jews since World War II and crocheted skullcaps are sometimes worn more as a sign of Jewish identification than for any religious reason.

Whereas the covering of a man's head was long regarded as no more than a pious act, the covering of a (married) woman's hair was even in biblical times considered a defense of her modesty (*tseni'ut*). For a woman's head to be bared in public was a supreme humiliation (Isa. 3:17), justifiable only in the case of a SOTAH on trial for adultery (Num. 5:18). This standard, rigorously maintained in the talmudic period (*BK* 8.6; *Ned.* 30b), also had some impact on the early Christians (cf. I Corinthians, 4-15). It meant that a man could divorce his wife for the act of walking bareheaded outdoors, yet lose no part of her dowry (*Ket.* 7.6), and some even forbade a blessing to be recited indoors when a woman's uncovered hair was visible (*Ber.* 24a). Single girls were exempt, however, and rabbinic law showed less severity towards the unveiling of a woman's hair at home, although even this was eventually often frowned upon. From the Middle Ages onward, women's headgear became more elaborate, especially in Eastern Europe and Muslim countries. The Polish *shtern-tikhel*, for example, with its bejeweled or pearl-studded tiara, had weekday and Sabbath variations. Ḥasidic wives still have their hair shorn prior to the wedding ceremony and thereafter wear a headscarf (*tikhel*) covering all of their hair.

The use of a wig, already known in talmudic times (*Shab.* 6.5; *Naz.* 28b), first became fashionable among Ashkenazi women in the 18th century. Whether made of natural or artificial hair, the wig (Hebrew. *pe'ah nokhrit*; Yiddish *sheytel*) seemed too great a compromise to many rabbis — including Jonathan EYBESCHÜTZ and Moses SOFER — but their furious objections had little effect on Western Jewish society. Nowadays, while Orthodox, many Conservative, and some Reform Jewish women cover their heads in synagogue, all but the ultra-Orthodox maintain other standards of practice elsewhere. Often, Orthodox wives, who may not cover their heads at home, will wear a hat or a headscarf when going outdoors or attending social functions.

COVETOUSNESS Inability to master one's craving for wrongful possession, an uncontrollable longing to appropriate what rightfully belongs to someone else. Envy and greed are moral offenses prohibited by the last of the TEN COMMANDMENTS (Ex. 20:14, Deut. 5:18). The Bible repeatedly condemns insatiable longings (Prov. 14:30, 27:20; Eccl. 5:9), emphasizes their destructive effects (Prov. 28:22), and stigmatizes greed as a prime cause of social injustice (Isa. 5:8; Mic. 2:1-2). The same theme permeates rabbinic literature. "Envy, lust, and ambition drive a man out of the world" (*Avot* 4.21); and these in turn expose him to new forms of perversity and degeneration — the EVIL EYE, the evil inclination, and finally hatred of mankind (*Avot* 2.11). Nor can the average person anticipate the ruinous outcome of such failings: "Whoever fastens his eyes on what is not his will also lose what is his" (*Sot.* 9a); that thought is restated picturesquely in the talmudic aphorism, "Because the camel desired horns, his ears were cut off" (*San.* 106a). In particular, the rabbis observed that envy gives rise to other sins and that whoever transgresses the Tenth Commandment may be said to violate the entire Decalogue (*Pesikta Rabbati* 107a). Following Isaac ABOAB, who affirmed that "greed is the root of all sin" (*Menorat ha-Ma'or*, c. 1300), Jewish ethical writers down to the modern age have stressed the universal duty to help build a just and civilized world in which people will be content with what they have and will not envy or desire other lands, possessions, and human beings.

CREATION The origin of the universe described in the biblical narrative in the first two chapters of GENESIS, which developed conceptually as one of the ideological pillars of Judaism through rabbinic interpretation, mysticism, and philosophy.

The Bible The Hebrew Scriptures, apparently influenced by Mesopotamian epic prototypes, opens with two creation stories. In the first, God creates the universe in six days and rests on the seventh day (Gen. 1:1-2:4). The six days of creation are divided equally; three days in which light, day, night, sky, dry land, seas, and vegetation were created, and three days in which the celestial bodies and all the living creatures of the sea, sky, and land were created. "And God saw that it was good; and there was evening and there was morning..." is repeated at the conclusion of nearly every day's activity. The ultimate act of creation, the birth of humankind on the sixth day, is announced by an unidentified angelic court: "Let us make man in our image, after our likeness" (Gen. 1:26). God then created a man and a woman, blessed them and told them, "Be fertile and increase, fill the earth and master it; and rule the fish of the sea, the birds of the sky, and all the living things that creep on earth" (1:28). Having completed the creation, God ceased from work on the seventh day, which He blessed and declared holy (2:2-3).

In the second biblical account of creation (Gen. 2:4-24), the barren ground is watered by an underground flow, a man is formed from the earth and brought to life by a divine breath, a woman is created from the man's rib, and the two are placed in the Garden of EDEN "to till it and tend it" (Gen. 2:15). The two epic traditions differ in numerous ways: (1) the use of the names of God, (2) the order of plants, animals, and humankind in the creation narrative, (3) the way that man and woman are formed, and (4) the purpose of their existence (cf. 1:26,27,28 with 2:7,15,22) (see also EVOLUTION).

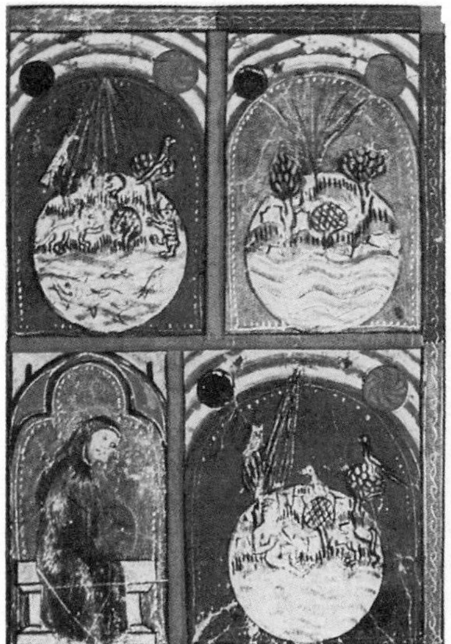

The creation of the world. Miniature from the Sarajevo Haggadah, *Spain, c. 1400.*

THE CREATION OF THE WORLD ACCORDING TO GENESIS 1

DAY ONE:	Light, Day, and Night
DAY TWO:	Sky
DAY THREE:	Land, Seas, and Vegetation
DAY FOUR:	Celestial Bodies
DAY FIVE:	Sea, Animals, and Birds
DAY SIX:	Land, Animals, and Humankind

Middle Eastern Parallels The biblical account contains parallels with some of the themes and terminology of ancient Near Eastern prototypes. In Egyptian cosmogony, for example, the first man was created in the image of his creator god; the Mesopotamian king is referred to as the "image" or "likeness" of his deity; and in the Babylonian epic, *Enuma Elish*, separating a watery abyss from the firmament brings about heaven and earth, with the same order of creation as exists in Genesis — firmament, land, celestial bodies, man, and divine rest. References to man being formed out of clay are found in the Babylonian Gilgamesh Epic, and the great sea monsters of Genesis 1:21 have been seen as demythologized remnants of the primeval war between them (as symbols of chaos) and the godhead of Mesopotamian cosmogonic literature. The comparative distinction of Genesis, however, lies in its rejection of polytheism in favor of a single, omnipotent Creator, and the preeminent role of humankind to rule the universe, not merely as an afterthought to serve the whim of the gods.

Rabbinic Literature In the rabbinic period, and especially during the time of the *tannaim*, *ma'aseh bereshit* ("the act of creation") was considered a systematic discipline, and a mystery not to be expounded publicly and not to be the subject of metaphysical speculation (*Ḫag.* 2:1). "Why does the story of creation begin with the letter *bet* [in *be-réshit*]?" the rabbis asked. "Just as the letter *bet* is closed on all sides and only open in the front, so you are not permitted to inquire into what is before or what is behind, but only from the actual time of creation" (TJ. *Ḫag.* 77c). In a discussion, R. AKIVA defended the position that creation was out of nothing (*creatio ex nihilo*), and refuted gnostic and dualist heresies claiming the eternal preexistence of physical matter and that angels, not God alone, created the world (Gen. R. 1:14). The Midrash teaches that "before the world was created, the Holy One, Blessed be He, with His name alone existed" (*Pirké de-Rabbi Eliezer* 10). R. ABBAHU and others believed in successive creations and that this world was one of many that God created (Gen. R. 3:7,9 and 9:2).

The sages offered differing opinions in response to the textual problem that light was the first act of creation but the sun appeared only on the fourth day. One theory posited that the celestial bodies were created on the first day, but displayed only on the fourth. Others maintained that the light of the first day was stored away for the righteous in anticipation of the evil generations of the flood and the Tower of Babel (*Ḫag.* 12a). Although God completed the work of creating the physical universe, with regard to "the work of the righteous and the wicked," God did not rest (Gen. R. 11), and depends upon humankind to complete the task as "partner with God in the work of creation" (*Shab.* 10). The rabbis included this belief in the ongoing nature of God's creative act in the daily morning liturgy, "...Who in His goodness renews each day continuously the act of creation" (see also Isa. 43:19). In the later amoraic period, a mythological influence is evident from the Hellenistic world, when the prohibitions against metaphysical speculation were relaxed and cosmological discussion was extended (*BB* 74b).

Kabbalah The Kabbalah, or Jewish mystical tradition, insists that there can be no knowledge of God without contemplating God's relationship to creation. Since God is the hidden, unknowable EN SOF ("Infinite"), creation represents the problem of God's transition from concealment to manifestation (or the first Divine "emanation") and therefore can only be described approximately or symbolically.

God's free decision to emerge into the world through creation remains a constant and impenetrable mystery. Was God's first creative step an outward venture at all, or rather an inward withdrawal of *En Sof* into the depths of itself? Did the Divine will to create always coexist with the *En Sof*, or did it originate at the moment of its emanation? Or does the entire creative process depend upon an intellectual act, "pure thought," and not on a volitional one? Does God's first step toward manifestation defy definition in qualitative terms and can it therefore only be described as "nothingness" (*ayin*)? Is the power of the *En Sof* identical with the ten SEFIROT, or stages of God's emanations, and if not, what is the difference between them?" Isaac LURIA's kabbalistic cosmology involves "the breaking of the vessels," whereby the sparks of the primeval light of creation spilled over onto the lower *Sefirot* and need to be restored to their proper places through a messianic healing of the cosmic order (TIKKUN).

The teachings and terminology of kabbalistic cosmology are largely borrowed from medieval Neoplatonic and Aristotelian philosophy. The Kabbalah's unique contribution was the new religious impulse it introduced to integrate this philosophy into traditional Jewish sources. (See MYSTICISM).

Philosophy As the first Jewish representative of theological philosophy, PHILO (c.25 BCE-40 CE) reconciled the Greek doctrine of creation, which depends upon eternal preexistent matter, with the scriptural account of *creatio ex nihilo* by introducing a mediating LOGOS as the agency that links a purely spiritual God with the created material world. In the tenth century, the same challenge was addressed by Saadiah Gaon, who maintained that the world was created in time, out of nothing, and completely separate from its Creator. The Neoplatonists of the next century, especially Isaac Israeli and Solomon IBN GABIROL, postulated a timeless "emanation" of primary matter from God's free creative power. None of the medieval Jewish philosophers was prepared to accept the Aristotelian teaching that matter is eternal. MAIMONIDES claimed that although the issue of *creatio ex nihilo* is not crucial for religious faith, it is the accepted Jewish position since Plato's theory of creation had not been successfully demonstrated. Acccording to his *Hilkhot Yesodé ha-Torah*, the earth is surrounded by concentric, incorporeal, and "intelligent" spheres and occupies a position at the center of the universe. At the outset of his code he stated that the First Being brought all things into being and that all things only enjoy existence by virtue of His True Being (*Yad, Yesodé ha-Torah*, 1:1-3). LEVI BEN GERSHOM and Ḥasdai CRESCAS dis agreed with Maimonides, the former believing that the doctrine of an eternal formless matter is indeed taught by the Torah (cf. Ps. 104; Job 38), and the latter exhibiting an ambivalence between the eternity of the universe and its temporal beginning.

Most modern Jewish thinkers reject a literalist and fundamentalist approach to the biblical cosmological account, although the 19th century German thinker Solomon Steinheim preferred the God of revelation to the God of reason because the latter cannot be a creator, only an organizer. For Franz ROSENZWEIG, belief in creation and revelation were mutually dependent. The experience of Divine love is rooted in the fact that God, whose love is made known to humanity, is also the Creator on whom man's existence depends. Martin BUBER envisioned creation as the "communication between Creator and creature," and humankind as God's partner, completing the creative act and thus initiating redemption. Creation in Jewish religious thought has been defended as the process of regenerating life, by overcoming its internal contradictions and composite nature and thereby rediscovering its divinely ordained unity.

CREED See BELIEF; SHEMA; PRINCIPLES OF FAITH

CREMATION The disposal of a CORPSE by burning it to ashes. In the traditional Jewish view, cremation of human bodies is totally abhorrent and it is prohibited by Jewish law. Since a human being's remains once housed a soul, they deserve to be treated with respect and cremating the BODY is therefore considered a mark of irreverence and dishonor. In biblical times, cremation was occasionally practiced by the Israelites (cf. I Sam. 31:12), but it was associated with human sacrifice (Deut. 12:31; Isa. 30:33) and chiefly reserved for criminals (Gen. 38:24; Lev. 20:14, 21:9). The cremation of pagan kings, as mentioned both in the Bible (Amos 2:1) and in the Mishnah (*Av.Zar* 1.3), was also linked with IDOLATRY. For Jews, BURIAL in the earth is a positive commandment which takes its authority from Genesis (3:19): "For dust you are, and to dust you shall return." The Talmud (*San.* 46b) additionally cites the verse referring to the affront which even the exposed body of an executed criminal offers in God's world: "You must not let his corpse remain all night on the tree, but must bury him the same day" (Deut. 21:23). Hence the laws encoded by Maimonides and the *Shulḥan Arukh* (*YD* 362.1).

Halakhic authorities have consistently forbidden cremation, ruling that even if a person's will specifically laid down that he be cremated after death, this wish must be ignored. A responsum by Solomon ADRET, one of the leading rabbis of medieval Spain, did allow the placing of lime on a corpse to hasten its decomposition, but this is not regarded as the same as cremation. While most Orthodox authorities stipulate that the ashes of anyone who was cremated must not be buried in a Jewish cemetery, more lenient opinions have sometimes been expressed. Two British chief rabbis, Nathan Marcus Adler and Hermann Adler, permitted such an interment, as did Chief Rabbi Zadoc Kahn in France. David Hoffmann, a leading Orthodox scholar in Germany, concluded that although there is no obligation to facilitate the burial of ashes in a cemetery, it is also not forbidden (*Melammed le-Ho'il, YD* 113). Orthodox BURIAL SOCIETY attitudes have likewise differed: that of London's United Synagogue is not opposed to traditional burial rites, provided the ashes of one already cremated are first laid in a coffin. Jewish law does not, however, allow a rabbi to officiate at the funeral of one who is about to be cremated, nor may any observant Jew accompany the body to the crematorium. The family of a person who was cremated by his own request does not observe the laws of MOURNING. Nevertheless, according to a responsum by Rabbi Elijah Bekhor Ḥazzan of Alexandria (*Ta'alumot Lev*, vol. 4, no.33), close relatives who opposed the cremation and who are distressed by it may observe those customs which reflect honor on the mourners (rather than the deceased), including the recitation of KADDISH.

Conservative practice is in general close to that of Orthodoxy. Reform Judaism, however, permits its rabbis to officiate at cremation ceremonies. The ashes of persons who have been cremated may also be buried in cemeteries under Reform jurisdiction.

CRESCAS, ḤASDAI (c.1340-c.1410). Spanish Jewish philosopher and communal leader (Crown Rabbi of Aragon). In 1383, he was one of several delegates of Catalonian Jewry who regained the renewal of Jewish rights from the king of Aragon. Despite his close association with the court of Aragon, his son suffered martyrdom in the 1391 anti-Jewish massacres in Barcelona.

Crescas' fame rests on his place in medieval Jewish philosophy. Of his two important works, the first, written in Spanish (1397), was translated into Hebrew by Joseph Ibn Shem Tov, under the title *Bittul Ikarei ha-Notzerim* (1451), "A Refutation of the Principles of the Christians," and is a strong criticism of Christian dogma, notably the dogma of the Trinity. Crescas' motives were to help maintain the strong loyalty of the Jews to Judaism and to attract back Jewish apostates at a time when the influence of the Church was becoming increasingly more powerful.

His other work, written in Hebrew, is *Or Adonai* ("The Light of the Lord," 1410) the primary aim of which is to present a systematic exposition of the Jewish faith, its principles, beliefs, and opinions. In much of his treatment, Crescas seeks to refute the philosophy of MAIMONIDES. He is critical of Maimonides' formulation of basic Jewish beliefs and formulates his own principles which he divides into a number of groups. First is the basic belief in the existence, unity, and incorporeality of God. Then he lists those fundamentals without which Judaism could not exist, including certain attributes of God, the nature of prophecy, and the Torah. Crescas then turns to what he calls "true opinions." Anyone who disbelieves them is a heretic, but it is nevertheless conceivable to be a Jew without holding to these opinions. These include Creation, Immortality and Resurrection, Reward and Punishment, the Messiah, and the efficacy of prayers. Finally, there are beliefs which are only "probabilities" and which, while Crescas holds them to be correct, are nevertheless of such a nature as to allow for different opinions. Anyone who does not believe in them is not to be censured, although he is in error. These "probabilities" relate to such things as the power of the stars and the existence of demons.

Crescas is the only medieval Jewish philosopher of note who seems to limit human freedom in order to preserve the belief in God's foreknowledge of events. He reconciled this qualified determinism with his belief in Reward and Punishment by making a clear distinction between determinism and fatalism; it is only the latter concept that has no room for human effort, with the resultant reward or punishment. Unlike Maimonides, Crescas rejected the idea that only the intellectual soul is immortal. Every soul, he argued, is an eternal substance and there is soul life, of one kind or another, for each individual soul. Crescas' *Or Adonai* influenced later philosophers, and Spinoza's treatment of freedom and necessity owes much to Crescas.

CULI (HULI), JACOB (c. 1685-1732). Rabbinic scholar and Judeo-Spanish author. Born and educated in Jerusalem, Culi later moved to Constantinople (1714), where he served as a rabbinic judge (*dayyan*). The heretical movement of SHABBETAI TSEVI had damaged the very foundations of Jewish life throughout the Ottoman Empire, and Culi realized the need for inspiring religious literature that would win back the Sephardi masses to Orthodox belief and observance. Furthermore, there was a need to publish popular religious texts in the JUDEO-SPANISH ("Ladino") vernacular. Culi's answer was to write an encyclopedic guide to Judaism and the Sephardi way of life entitled *Me-Am Lo'ez* ("From a People of Alien Speech," Ps. 114:1). Organized as a commentary on the Pentateuch, it was interlaced with rabbinic interpretations, material drawn from the Midrash and the mystical classic, the Zohar, Jewish laws and customs, ethical teachings and reproof. Culi added legends, parables, and folktales, which he wove into his exposition of the weekly Torah portion. The first volume, on Genesis, appeared in 1730 and was an immediate success, but only about half of Exodus was finished when Culi died. Utilizing his manuscripts, other writers completed the Pentateuch (1733-82) and later extended the project. *Me-Am Lo'ez* enjoyed wide popularity among Sephardi Jews and became the the classic religious work in Judeo-Spanish. Infused with a spirit of piety and trust in God, the author urges man to disdain earthly rewards and to be grateful for what he has. Culi attaches great importance to Torah study, recommending that his book be used as a guide to the coming Sabbath's portion of the Law. There has recently been an impressive revival of interest in *Me-Am Lo'ez*, among Ashkenazi Jews as well as Sephardim, prompting translations into Hebrew and English, and a transliteration into Latin letters in Spain.

CULTS The existence of destructive religious cults constitutes a serious problem for the Jewish communities in the United States, Europe, and Israel. In recent years, many cults have abandoned their previous bizarre dress and behavior in favor of a more "mainstream" approach to the general public. Nonetheless, deception, family separation, psychological and physical abuse, and coercive recruitment tactics still persist within the cults.

While Jews make up less than three percent of the total American population, the Jewish membership component in many of the cults is much higher. Indeed, some groups are estimated to have as many as 30 percent of their members who are Jews.

While such cults as the Unification Church, Hare Krishna, and Scientology, are among the best known, there are also some cult-like "human potential" groups that also attract a high Jewish membership. These include EST and Life Spring. Finally, one of the world's oldest cults, Satanism, has also appeared in the United States.

The American Jewish community has been in the forefront in opposing the destructive actions of the cults. Cult clinics and task forces have been established in New York City and Los Angeles. Other Jewish communities have also set up cult committees, and Jewish cult specialists have played a major role in organizing the Interreligious Committee of Concern about Cults (ICCC) whose headquarters are in Manhattan.

In addition to the religious and human potential cults, the "Hebrew Christian" missionaries are also active in both the United States and Israel. The best known of these groups is the "Jews for Jesus" who proclaim that one can be Jewish and Christian at the same time, and further declare that they, in fact, are "completed or fulfilled Jews." They have been sharply attacked by both Jewish and Christian leaders who have publicly charged that the missionary group engages in deceptive tactics of distortion and duplicity to recruit new members. The deliberate manipulation of sacred Jewish religious symbols like the unleavened bread (MATSAH) and the ḤANUKKAH candelabrum by the "Hebrew Christians" has been condemned, and the attempt by the "Jews for Jesus" to present themselves as authentically Jewish while at the same time engaging in traditional Christian missionary activities has also been criticized.

Because the "Jews for Jesus" often mask their true intentions with Jewish symbols, Hebrew language songs and prayers, support for the State of Israel, as well as the use of prayer shawls, head coverings, and other familiar forms of Jewish worship, many young Jews have been confused and sometimes become members of the group. In recent years "Jews for Jesus" have also sought new members among the Jewish elderly in hospitals or in nursing homes. Finally, the group is actively seeking allies and supporters within the organized Christian community, especially among Christian fundamentalists.

Just as with the destructive cults, the American Jewish community has mounted an intensive public educational campaign within synagogue schools and youth groups and on college campuses, to counter the "Hebrew Christian." The basic message of the Jewish community is that the "Jews for Jesus" and similar groups are in reality selling "old missionary wine in new bottles" that hide the true intention of the group. The act of accepting JESUS as the Messiah removes such a person from the Jewish community which, moreover, claims the right to define itself and the meaning of its own religious symbols and rituals.

The exact number of Jews who are members of the destructive cults or the "Hebrew Christians" is impossible to determine with any precision. However, the conversion campaigns of both groups that are aimed at Jews have increased.

Some knowledgeable observers believe that the proliferation of destructive cults and "Hebrew Christian" missionaries indicates a growing spiritual unease particularly among young people. They further assert that this phenomenon is global and not restricted to the United States.

CURSING See BLESSING AND CURSING

CUSTOM (Heb. *minhag*). A religious practice followed out of a spontaneous desire of the people, and not because of a specific biblical or rabbinic injunction. It invariably refers to a practice adopted only in a particular community or region, and is therefore known as *minhag ha-makom* ("local custom"). The sages of the Mishnah laid great stress on the obligation to comply with local custom (cf. *Suk.* 3.11, *Ket.* 6.4, *BM* 7.1), stating that "one should not deviate from the custom of the place in which one finds oneself in order to avoid controversy. Hence a person traveling from one place to another must observe the stringencies of both his home town and the place he is visiting" (*Pes.* 4.1). Nor should one follow in one's home town a ritual that is practiced only in another locality (*BB* 100b). Differences in custom usually arose when there was a dispute among the halakhic authorities as to whether a certain practice was or was not prohibited, one community deciding to follow the stringent opinion and another the more lenient one. Thus, the Mishnah lists a series of practices that were banned in one place but not in another, a situation to which the general rule applies.

Basically, the sages were opposed to communal disunity, some following one practice and others another. In case of doubt, the prevalent custom was to be followed (TJ *Pe'ah* 7.5). However, the many disputes among the sages made variations in custom inevitable, and they therefore warned against separatist tendencies. As the rabbis pointed out, BET SHAMMAI AND BET HILLEL had differed over fundamental issues, yet "they did not hesitate to intermarry — an indication that there was affection and friendship among them" (*Yev.* 13b-14b).

In the course of time, differences in ritual and observance arose between Palestinian and Babylonian Jewries, and in Babylonia itself between the two geonic ACADEMIES of Sura and Pumbedita. Later still, more differences emerged between ASHKENAZIM and SEPHARDIM, most of these being codified in the SHULḤAN ARUKH. Several originated in a ban pronounced by local (Ashkenazi) authorities, e.g., against polygamy or the consuming of legumes on Passover (see GEZERAH; TAKKANAH). Differences also arose with regard to the "*minhag*" observed by Ashkenazim and Sephardi-Eastern Jews in matters of prayer rite (see NUSAḤ). Such variations in custom were further accentuated in time as a result of the new practices introduced by Isaac LURIA (16th cent.) and, from the mid-18th century, by ḤASIDISM.

Some distinctive practices are attributable to the Gentile environment in which Jews lived, since they did not remain immune to the customs or life style of their non-Jewish neighbors. (For religiously objectionable customs, see ḤUKKAT HA-GOY.) This is evident from peculiarities of dress which Jews adopted and then endowed with religious significance. Thus, the *ge'onim* ruled that one should wrap oneself in one's *tallit* (prayer shawl) "as the Ishmaelites [Arabs] do" (*Tur, Oraḥ Ḥayyim* 8). Ḥasidic Jews, on Sabbaths and festivals, likewise wear the Polish-style fur hat known as a *shtraymel*. Additional evidence is provided by the many different *minhagim* followed by various Jewish communities at wedding ceremonies. Even the use of a ring for the act of BETROTHAL was not originally a Jewish custom: it is not once mentioned by such an outstanding legal authority as MAIMONIDES (12th cent.), yet was considered normative by the 16th-century codifier Moses ISSERLES. Significantly, too, numerous mourning customs of the talmudic era were declared obsolete in the Middle Ages because they were considered inappropriate in a different social milieu (*Tos.* to *MK* 21a)

At the same time, many practices dating back to the talmudic era, though no longer appropriate today , have been retained because of a general reluctance to abandon time-honored custom. The KETUBBAH (marriage contract) and the *get* (bill of DIVORCE), for example, are still written in the ancient Aramaic formulation. This tendency to retain the customs of other periods and localities — or even to revive talmudic customs fallen into desuetude — is maintained by contemporary Orthodox leadership as a reaction to the anti-traditional measures introduced by Reform Judaism. The motto of the traditionalists continues to be: "What is customary in Israel is Torah" (*Tos.* to *Men.* 20b).

A noticeable tendency has been for some local custom to spread to neighboring communities and eventually to be followed by more and more segments of the Jewish people. Where originally, in talmudic times, not every community accepted the rabbinic ban against mixing and eating fowl with milk (*Shab.* 130a), today it is observed universally. However, the period of time that must elapse after eating meat before one may eat dairy products varies to this day (from one to six hours); it is all a matter of local custom (cf. *Ḥul.* 105a).

The force of local custom is such that it is carried over from one generation to another; even if the situation is no longer the same, children have to observe "the custom of their fathers." A prominent example of this ruling is the observance of a SECOND DAY of Festivals by Jews in the Diaspora. Even though the reason for this extra day no longer applied, Jews outside Erets Israel were told to "retain the custom of your fathers" (*Bétsah* 4b). In economic affairs, local custom determined the hours a laborer had to work and the fringe benefits he should receive, to such an extent that one talmudic rabbi deduced the oft-quoted principle, "Custom nullifies law" (TJ. *Yev.* 12.3; *BM* 7.1). It also played an important role in commercial practice, agreements to buy and sell being fixed by local custom. Occasionally, popular custom would even decide the law: if the sages were in doubt concerning a particular ritual, they would say, "Go see what the people do," and that became authorized practice (*Ber.* 45a, 52a).

Custom becomes established law when it receives the sanction of the local rabbi or spiritual leader, and when he eventually includes it in a code of Jewish law written for public guidance. Typical of such codifications is the *Sefer Minhagé Maharil*, recording the customs observed by Jacob MÖLLN (c. 1360-1427), which serves as the basis for many Ashkenazi practices. The Talmud ruled that, in the event of a community adopting a certain practice under the mistaken impression that it is required by law, a scholar may advise the community of its error and it may then abandon the custom. Yet if such Jews are cognizant of the law and still wish to practice their custom, they should not be discouraged (*Pes.* 50b-51a).

D

DAF YOMI ("daily page"). A systematic approach to the daily study of the TALMUD, formulated by R. Meir Shapira of Lublin in 1928. The program was for students of the Talmud who would commit themselves to learning a *daf* (a double-sided page) of Talmud every day, the same *daf* to be studied simultaneously throughout the Jewish world. In this way, the participants would review the entire corpus of the Babylonian Talmud once every seven years.

The concept was received with enthusiasm, and the number of people committed to this self-imposed study regimen has risen steadily over the years. Today, many Jewish calendars record the *daf yomi*; in Israel, it is listed in some of the daily newspapers. The first cycle was completed in 1931, the seventh in 1988. The completion of each cycle is marked by a worldwide *siyyum* (conclusion) celebration.

In the wake of its success, other study cycles have been established, such as the daily study of MISHNAH, Maimonides' *Mishneh Torah* code, chapters of the Bible, and sections of the *halakhah*.

DAN See TRIBES, TWELVE

DANCE Dancing was an early component of Jewish ritual, ceremonial, festive, and commemorative occasions. Miriam and her maidens danced at the Red Sea (Ex. 15:20); the Israelites danced around the GOLDEN CALF (Ex. 32:19); and David danced before the Lord (II Sam. 6:14). It would appear that in biblical times, men and women danced separately but mostly on the same occasions. Some dances were circular, others in line, with one person leading. In Second Temple times, young maidens would dance in the vineyards on the 15th of Av when the young men would select their brides (*Ta'an* 4.8).

The tradition of dance remained among Jews through the ages. Talmudic rabbis danced at weddings (*Ket.* 17a) and dancing was part of the WATER-DRAWING FESTIVAL. In the ghettos of Europe, dance was so much part of life that some European communities had "dance houses," sometimes called "wedding houses." In Jewish homes in certain places, teachers came to give lessons not only in Torah and Talmud but also in music and dance, as there were specific dances for special occasions, such as Purim. The art of dance among Jews became so highly developed that in Renaissance Italy, Jews became dance masters for non-Jews, and on occasion participated in events outside their ghettos. In 1313, a Rabbi Hacen ben Salomo was forced to teach a choral dance to Christians for performance in a church at Tauste in Spain. In 1475, the Jews of Pesaro provided dances as part of the pageantry for the wedding of Camilla d'Aragona and Constanzo Sforza. On that occasion, one episode was symbolic of the Ten Commandments given to Moses, and another dealt with the Queen of Sheba and King Solomon.

Jews so maintained their love of dance that some rabbis frowned upon it. They forbade mixed dancing, which began to develop at the end of the 18th century. At that time, however, in Russia, a new form of religious Jewish dance came into being: the Ḥasidic dance. From the time of the BAAL SHEM TOV, dancing was approved as an expression of religious joy and fervor, but with men and women dancing separately. Some Ḥasidim conclude their daily prayer with dancing.

In the East, Jewish communities also evolved their own styles of dance, mostly, as in biblical times, for occasions such as weddings and religious festivals. When they arrived in modern Israel, communities such as the Yemenite, Kurdish, Bokharan, Ethiopian, and Indian Jews brought this heritage with them. The various strands have been absorbed into Israeli religious and secular dance. For all Jewish communities, the festival of SIMḤAT TORAH (Rejoicing of the Law) is focused on dancing in the synagogue with the Scrolls of the Law.

DANIEL, ADDITIONS TO See APOCRYPHA AND PSEUDEPIGRAPHA

DANIEL, BOOK OF Biblical book forming part of the HAGIOGRAPHA. It tells the story of Daniel, one of several talented young men belonging to the Judean nobility who were exiled to Babylon after Nebuchadnezzar's destruction of Jerusalem. They are handed over to the King's chief minister (or eunuch) to be trained for royal service, and he changes their Hebrew names to Babylonian ones. Daniel thus becomes Belteshazzar, and his friends Hananiah, Mishael, and Azariah, become Shadrach, Meshach, and Abed-Nego. Wise and Godfearing, these four young men refuse to eat the heathen food served to them; a vegetarian diet makes them healthier than the others. They also make a great

Daniel's three companions in the fiery furnace. From an illuminated Armenian Manuscript on Rituals, 1266.

impression on the king. Nebuchadnezzar has a frightening dream, which only Daniel can interpret to the satisfaction of the king, who then appoints Daniel and his companions to high positions. Hananiah, Mishael, and Azariah subsequently refuse to bow down to the golden idol which the king has set up; they are thrown into a fiery furnace, but the flames do not harm them and the king immediately restores them to office.

Later, Daniel interprets another disturbing dream for Nebuchadnezzar, forecasting his madness. At a feast held by the king's successor, Belshazzar, strange writing appears on the wall, but none of the Babylonian magicians and sages can decipher it. Daniel is able to do so, however, explaining that the words *Mené Mené, Tekel u-Farsin* (or *Peres*) forecast Belshazzar's overthrow, which indeed occurs that same night. Thanks to his personal qualities, Daniel retains high office under King Darius the Mede, but jealous rivals have a law passed laying down that no one but the king may be prayed to for 30 days. Daniel, who has continued to pray to God three times a day, is thrown into a lions' den, but emerges unscathed, to prosper in the reigns of Darius and Cyrus the Persian. The second part of the book (chaps. 7-12) consists of four apocalyptic visions.

Some portions of this book are written in Hebrew — (1:1-2:4; 8-12), the remainder (2:4-7:28) in Aramaic. Traditionally, the entire book was written by Daniel at the end of the Babylonian era (i.e., around 545-535 BCE). Most Bible scholars maintain, however, that the second half of the book dates from the period of the anti-Jewish decrees issued by the Syrian ruler, Antiochus IV Epiphanes (c. 168-165 BCE), whereas the first half of the book is more ancient and dates from around 300 BCE. This first part, they note, contains no allusions to Antiochus and his era. In the last vision of Daniel, scholars detect a veiled account of Jewish history from the time of Cyrus until the death of Antiochus Epiphanes (538-164 BCE). It seeks to work out the date of the end of the world and contains the first biblical reference to the partial resurrection of the dead.

The visions in Daniel are highly ambiguous and have often been used in attempts to calculate the End of Days, the coming of the Messiah, and the revival of the dead, but many Jewish authorities were violently opposed to such apocalyptic speculations. Despite discrepancies as well as historical problems, the spiritual message of the Book of Daniel is that the vicissitudes of world empires are determined by God and that His plan for the world will ultimately be fulfilled. In Jewish legend, Daniel was a descendant of King David. According to the Talmud (*Yoma* 77a), he was the wisest man of his time; God showed Daniel things which He never revealed to three prophets, Haggai, Zechariah, and Malachi (Gen.R. 98:3). According to later Jewish sources, it was thanks to Daniel that Cyrus issued his proclamation allowing the Jews to return to the Land of Israel and rebuild the Temple. Another Daniel is mentioned several times by the prophet Ezekiel. Later stories embellishing those of the Hagiographa are contained in the APOCRYPHA, the DEAD SEA SCROLLS, and Midrashic literature.

BOOK OF DANIEL

1:1 — 1:21	Daniel and his three friends at the court of Nebuchadnezzar
2:1 — 2:49	Daniel interprets Nebuchadnezzar's dream
3:1 — 3:33	Daniel's three friends are saved from the fiery furnace
4:1 — 4:34	Another dream by Nebuchadnezzar is interpreted by Daniel
5:1 — 5:30	Belshazzar's feast and the writing on the wall
6:1 — 6:29	Daniel in the lions' den
7:1 — 7:28	The vision of the four beasts
8:1 — 8:27	The vision of the ram and the he-goat
9:1 — 9:27	The 70 years
10:1 — 12:13	The vision of the End of Days

DAVID (c. 1040-c. 970 BCE). Israel's second and greatest king, founder of a dynasty that lasted four centuries. He was the son of Jesse, great-grandson of Boaz and Ruth, and was born in Bethlehem of the tribe of Judah. His early years were spent as a shepherd, but he joined the entourage of King Saul. The prophet Samuel, after rejecting Saul, clandestinely anointed David as Saul's successor (I Sam. 16:13). When Saul was dejected, one of his aides recommended David, an accomplished musician, to bring him solace, and thus began David's rapid rise at court — culminating in his victory over Goliath which made him a national hero. David's marriage with Saul's daughter, Michal, and his deep friendship with the masses convinced Saul that he represented a threat to the succession of Jonathan and Saul's attitude turned to envy and then to uncontrollable hatred. For most of the rest of Saul's life, David was a fugitive, evading the king's attempts to kill him. The tragic end came when Saul's army was routed by the Philistines in a battle on Mount Gilboa, Saul and Jonathan being among the slain.

David was now crowned king over Judah in Hebron (II Sam. 2:4). After he defeated in battle the forces of Saul's son, Ishbosheth, the other tribes accepted his leadership, and he ruled the entire country. He then proceeded to subdue Israel's hostile neighbors, destroying the power of the Philistines, Moab, Edom, Ammon, and Aram, and extending the country's borders. He stationed garrisons in Damascus and created the most far-flung empire in Israel's history.

Sensing the need to cement the people's unity and create a neutral center of administration not identified with any of the tribes, he captured the city of JERUSALEM (Jebus), establishing it as his capital ("the City of David"). He installed there the ARK OF THE COVENANT but his desire to build a TEMPLE was frustrated by the prophet Nathan, who told him that no man involved in wars could build a temple of peace (I Chron. 22:8); that task was to be accomplished by his son and successor, SOLOMON.

The Bible does not gloss over David's faults, notably his adultery with Bathsheba and his engineeering of the death of her husband. Unrest grew in his own household and his son, Absalom, led a revolt which, after initial success, was crushed and Absalom was killed. Even in his last years, his son Adonijah tried to engineer a palace coup to secure the succession; this was frustrated and Solomon was proclaimed David's heir.

David, "the sweet singer of Israel," became idealized in Jewish tradition. The PSALMS were ascribed to his authorship and the groundwork for music in the Temple was also attributed to him. On every occasion in the Jewish calendar, David is recalled in hope and prayer. The AMIDAH, GRACE AFTER MEALS, the blessings following the READING OF THE LAW, are regarded as invalid if the prayer for the restoration of the House of David is omitted from them. The blessing of the New Moon contains the declaration "David, King of Israel, lives on," while David is one of the seven guests (USHPIZIN) in the SUKKAH. His personality intrigued future generations and the Jewish national tradition invested his memory with a mystique and prestige, so that he became a symbol of messianic aspirations. The MESSIAH would emerge from the House of David (and in Christian tradition, JESUS' genealogy is traced back to David and his birthplace located at Bethlehem, where David was born). David was the subject of many stories in the *aggadah* and Jewish legend. A thousand-year-old tradition places his tomb on what is now called Mount Zion and, during the period between 1948 and 1967 when Jews were cut off from the Western Wall, this became a major site of pilgrimage, especially for Jews from eastern lands. David has also been a favorite subject of Western literature, music, painting, and sculpture.

David playing the harp, depicted on the mosaic floor of a 6th-century synagogue in Gaza.

DAVID BEN SAMUEL HA-LEVI (1586-1667). Rabbinical authority. He is generally known as *Taz*, the acronym of his *magnum opus* on the SHULḤAN ARUKH, *Turé Zahav* ("Rows of Gold"). Ha-Levi was born in Vladimir in the Ukraine and married the daughter of Joel SERKES (known as *Baḫ*). He held rabbinic positions in Putalicze and Posen, and after the death of his father-in-law in 1641 was invited to assume the position of rabbi of Ostrog. Following the Chmielnicki massacres of 1648-49, he fled to Germany. During this period of wandering, he was widely consulted on halakhic questions. A major controversy resulted at this time from a ruling which he issued, whereby a man was permitted to marry a second wife after witnesses had testified that his first wife, taken prisoner by non-Jews, had been forced to convert. He became rabbi of Lvow in 1654, holding the position until his death. *Turé Zahav* is one of the major commentaries on the *Shulhan Arukh*, incorporating a summary of the numerous commentaries which had been written on the *Shulhan Arukh* since its publication, and defending it against criticism. Ha-Levi was also the author of other works, including *Divré David*, on RASHI's commentary on the Pentateuch.

DAVNEN Yiddish term of uncertain origin meaning "to pray," widely used by Ashkenazim, particularly those of East European birth or descent. Nowadays, it is often modified to *davven*.

DAY OF ATONEMENT Holiest and most solemn day in the Jewish religious calendar; observed on 10 Tishri as the climax of the TEN DAYS OF PENITENCE which begin on the New Year, ROSH HA-SHANAH. It is kept as a strict 25-hour fast, from sunset when it commences until nightfall the next evening when it terminates. Like the other major FESTIVALS, its authority derives from the Pentateuch, where it is called *Yom (ha-) Kippurim*, "the Day of Atonement," and *Shabbat Shabbaton*, "the Sabbath of Sabbaths" or "a Sabbath of solemn rest" (Lev. 23:27,32; 25:9). Traditionally, it is also known as *Yom ha-Din*, the DAY OF JUDGMENT (cf. *RH* 1.2), and of all the Jewish fast days is the only one never postponed if it coincides with a Sabbath. Among Ashkenazim, the Day of Atonement is generally designated *Yom Kippur* ("Day of Atonement"), whereas Sephardim usually refer to it as "Kippur."

The importance of this day and the authority for its mode of observance rest upon specific biblical commandments "to make atonement before the Lord" and "afflict your soul" (Lev. 16:29-31, 23:27-32; Num. 29:7). Afflicting one's soul was interpreted by the sages to mean abstaining from food and drink; atoning was understood to mean three related acts that would relieve one from the burden of SIN — acknowledging the transgressions, declaring REPENTANCE through a process of CONFESSION, and then making ATONEMENT before God in order to obtain His FORGIVENESS. The fast, the penitential prayers (SELIHOT), the Bible readings, the formulas of confession (*viddu'i*), and every part of the Atonement Day ritual emphasize this single theme. All the basic laws are outlined in the Mishnaic tractate YOMA.

Every male over the age of 13 and every female over 12 is obligated to fast. Sick people may take medicine and small amounts of food and drink; on the advice of their doctor or rabbi, those who are ill may even be forbidden to fast altogether. Normal Sabbath prohibitions apply on the Day of Atonement together with the five statutory rules of mortification: abstention from food and drink, marital relations, wearing leather shoes, using cosmetics and lotions, and washing any part of the body other than the fingers and eyes.

The rabbis insisted that the Day of Atonement enables man to atone for sins against God, but not for those committed against his fellowman; unless forgiveness has been sought from the injured party, atonement will have no effect, nor should anyone transgress in the expectation that his sins will be pardoned on the Day of Atonement (*Yoma* 8.9). On the eve of the Day of Atonement, therefore, it has become customary for pious Jews to seek reconciliation with anyone whom they may have offended in the course of the year, so as to begin the religious exercises with a clear conscience and the hope of being inscribed in the BOOK OF LIFE. Symbolic *malkot* ("lashes") were once administered in the synagogue, to induce a feeling of contrition, but this custom has largely declined. Prior to the Day of Atonement, the KAPPAROT ritual is still maintained by Sephardi and eastern communities, and some Orthodox Ashkenazim. This entails the symbolic transfer of guilt from a person to a fowl, which is then slaughtered, and either eaten before the fast or sold for money that is given to charity. Many Jews nowadays substitute coins for the fowl, and in traditional congregations a number of charity boxes are available at the Morning and early Afternoon Services preceding the Day of Atonement.

Various traditional customs in the synagogue and home emphasize the day's distinctive message. If not held before Rosh ha-Shanah, an absolution of VOWS ceremony often takes place in Orthodox congregations on the eve of Atonement Day. Afternoon prayers are recited earlier than normal, the AMIDAH being extended by the two (ASHAMNU and AL HET) formulas of confession. Some Orthodox Jews customarily immerse themselves in a MIKVEH (ritual bath), as a sign of purification, before the fast commences. At home, a *se'udah mafseket* ("final meal") is eaten; prior to lighting the festival CANDLES, a special MEMORIAL LIGHT is kindled to burn throughout the day and leather shoes are replaced by non-leather shoes or slippers before worshipers leave for the synagogue. The TALLIT (prayer shawl) is worn continuously at all services, including those held after dark. Since the color white is a traditional symbol of purity and forgiveness, a white curtain (PAROKHET) adorns the synagogue Ark and the Scrolls of the Law; the reader's desk and other furnishings are also draped in white (as on Rosh ha-Shanah). In Ashkenazi congregations, the rabbi, cantor, and other officiants wear a white KITEL or gown, this practice often being followed by other male worshipers in Orthodox synagogues. Sephardim do not observe this custom, although they may dress in white.

Five services are held on the Day of Atonement, beginning with KOL NIDRÉ (the common name for the initial Evening Service, so-called after its introductory declarations) soon after the fast commences, proceeding with festive Morning, Additional, and Afternoon prayers, and ending with NE'ILAH (the Concluding Service). Apart from an extended *Amidah*, each service has its own special features and characteristic lit-

Silver buckle on a brocade belt worn by rabbis and cantors on the Day of Atonement. Eastern Europe, 19th century.

urgy. Common to all of them, however, is the *viddu'i* or confession of sins. Both the shorter confession and the longer one are written in the first person plural to emphasize collective responsibility for the individual, and the individual's responsibility for his community. In some liturgies, ancient and modern, room is also made for the confession of personal failings. Almost as frequent is the penitential AVINU MALKENU litany; when the Day of Atonement coincides with a Sabbath, however, Ashkenazim only recite this on Friday morning and at the end of *Ne'ilah*.

Except in a minority of Reform congregations in the United States, the *Kol Nidré* declaration of annulment of hasty vows made by man to God is recited universally on the eve of Yom Kippur (by Ashkenazim in Aramaic and by Sephardim in Hebrew). It was a custom (now only among the very Orthodox) to spend the night in synagogue reciting the entire Book of Psalms and other readings. Sephardi and Reform Jews recite MEMORIAL PRAYERS on *Kol Nidré* night.

In addition to penitential *Seliḇot* and other hymns, the Morning Service includes a prescribed Torah reading (Lev. 16) which sets forth the Day of Atonement ritual in the Sanctuary, a MAFTIR passage (Num. 29:7-11) on the various festival sacrifices, and a HAFTARAH prophetical reading (Isa. 57:14-58:14) which describes the kind of fast day that is truly acceptable to God. Ashkenazim (except Reform Jews) then recite *Yizkor* (memorial prayers), while Sephardi and Eastern communities repeat their *Hashkavah* service.

Prior to the Additional Service (*Musaf*) in traditional Ashkenazi congregations, a special prayer entitled HINENI HE-ANI MI-MA'AS is recited by the cantor or reader. Many liturgical hymns are included in the reader's repetition of the *Amidah*, notably the solemn U-NETANNEH TOKEF passage on the Day of Judgment theme. On a number of occasions during the repetition of the *Amidah*, Orthodox worshipers (or, at least, the reader) customarily prostrate themselves on the ground. A principal feature of the Additional Service is the AVODAH.

Interpolated in the penitential *Seliḇot* and confessions, toward the end of *Musaf*, is the *Elleh Ezkerah* martyrology. Based on a medieval Midrash of the same name, *Elleh Ezkerah* ("These Things I Remember") purports to be an account of the TEN MARTYRS who were tortured for defying the Roman Emperor Hadrian's ban on the study of Torah. There are numerous points of anachronism and inconsistency in this tale, however, which was more probably a reflection of the massacres and martyrdoms inflicted on Jewish communities in Northern Europe during the Crusades. In some non-Orthodox liturgies this has been expanded to include appropriate readings from Holocaust literature.

Special features of the Afternoon Service include the Pentateuchal reading (Lev. 18), which deals with prohibited marriages and sexual offenses that would imperil Israel's holiness, and a *haftarah*, the Book of JONAH, with its story of the repentance of the Ninevites.

Prior to the Concluding Service (*Ne'ilah*), the hymn EL NORA ALILAH is chanted in Sephardi synagogues. *Ne'ilah* is recited as twilight approaches and hymns such as *Petaḥ Lanu Sha'ar* ("Open the Gate for Us") are a reminder that the last opportunity for sincere repentance is at hand. In most Jewish communities the doors of the Ark remain open and worshipers stand throughout the service. The plea that God may "inscribe" each individual for a good life is now changed to one for Him to "seal" a favorable fate, and the GREETINGS exchanged at this time also express that wish. *Ne'ilah* ends with the chanting of *Avinu Malkenu*, followed by the SHEMA proclamation of God's Unity, a threefold recital of BARUKH SHEM KEVOD MALKHUTO, and a sevenfold acknowledgment that "the Lord, He is God!" (I Kings 18:39). The SHOFAR (ram's horn) is then sounded to indicate that the fast has come to an end, and congregants recite LA-SHANAH HA-BA'AH BI-YERUSHALAYIM ("Next Year in Jerusalem"); in Israel, the wording is changed to "Jerusalem Rebuilt." According to some, the blowing of the *shofar* at this point originally marked the proclamation of a 50th (JUBILEE) year of release when the appropriate Yom Kippur had ended.

A widespread custom is for construction of the SUKKAH to begin at home, once people have broken their fast. In Second Temple times, young folk danced in the vineyards, and this was also the "courting season" when young singles were invited to choose their marriage partners. Traces of this custom have remained among Yemenite and Ethiopian Jews.

In general, the Day of Atonement has always been the festival most widely observed by Jews, including those remote from traditional life during the rest of the year. Like Passover, it kept its hold on far-flung Jewish communities: Spanish and Portuguese MARRANOS defied the Inquisition by carefully recording the date of Yom Kippur ("*Dia Pura*") and fasting in secret, a practice which some of their descendants maintained down to recent times. A "Minor Day of Atonement" was also formerly observed by many pious Jews on the eve of the New Moon (see YOM KIPPUR KATAN).

In modern Israel, Yom Kippur is the one day in the year when restaurants, places of entertainment, stores, offices, factories, and even the radio and television close down for the space of more than 24 hours. It was on the Day of Atonement in 1973 that Egyptian and Syrian armies launched a sudden, premeditated attack on undermanned Israeli positions in the Sinai peninsula and on the Golan Heights. The events of the ensuing period became known in the West as the Yom Kippur War.

DAY OF ATONEMENT — YOM KIPPUR

Other Names:

Yom ha-Kippurim (Ashkenazim)
Kippur (Sephardim)
Yom ha-Din (Judgment Day)
Shabbat Shabbaton (Sabbath of Solemn Rest /Sabbath of Sabbaths)

Pentateuchal & Prophetical Readings:
Hebrew Date: 10 Tishri
Morning: Lev. 16:1-34; Num. 29:7-11 (*Maftir*); Isa. 57:14-58:14 (*Haftarah*)
Afternoon: Lev. 18:1-30; Book of Jonah, Micah 7:18-20 (*Haftarah*)
Yizkor: (Memorial prayers) recited:
morning only (Ashkenazim);
also Yom Kippur eve (Sephardim);
only Yom Kippur eve (Reform Jews)

Civil dates on which the holy day occurs, 1990-2010:

1990/5751	Sat.	29 September
1991/5752	Wed.	18 September
1992/5753	Wed.	7 October
1993/5754	Sat.	25 September
1994/5755	Thurs.	15 September
1995/5756	Wed.	4 October
1996/5757	Mon.	23 September
1997/5758	Sat.	11 October
1998/5759	Wed.	30 September
1999/5760	Mon.	20 September
2000/5761	Mon.	9 October
2001/5762	Thurs.	27 September
2002/5763	Mon.	16 September
2003/5764	Mon.	6 October
2004/5765	Sat.	25 September
2005/5766	Thurs.	13 October
2006/5767	Mon.	2 October
2007/5768	Sat.	22 September
2008/5769	Thurs.	9 October
2009/5770	Mon.	28 September
2010/5771	Sat.	18 September

Kol Nidré inaugurating the Day of Atonement, is on the previous evening.

DAY OF JUDGMENT Eschatological concept appearing frequently in the Prophets and referring to the final judgment of the world at the End of Days (*aharit ha-yamim*), when all of mankind will be judged. The prophets speak often of the Day of the Lord, implying the era in which God's sovereignty will be accepted by all. This idea was extended to include the final judgment which will take place at that time, hence "the Day of Judgment."

The Day of the Lord appears often in the prophetic literature: in Amos, Isaiah, Joel, Obadiah, Zephaniah, and Ezekiel. Other phrases, such as "on that day" and "the day of God's wrath," are considered synonyms for the Day of the Lord. All these phrases refer to a time in the future when God will manifest His Divine rule over all by a series of destructive judgments over the other nations and Israel. There will be frightening changes in the rules of nature: a day of darkness (Amos 5:20); a day when the lights of the heavenly bodies will be dimmed (Joel 2:10, 3:4); a "day of trouble and distress, a day of devastation and desolation" (Zeph. 1:15).

The Day of the Lord will bring about the destruction of God's enemies, who are the enemies of Israel (Isa. 13:6-11; Ezek. 30:1 ff.; Joel 3:1-8; Ob. v. 15). This will also mark the passing of idolatry (Isa. 2:18). Unlike the other prophets, who dwell on the punishment of the other nations on the Day of Judgment/the Lord, Amos extends the judgment to Israel as well: "Woe to you who desire the Day of the Lord! For what good is the Day of the Lord to you? It will be darkness, and not light" (Amos 5:18). If the wicked nations come to ruin, so will Israel (Isa. 2:12; Zeph. 1:7-16).

Ezekiel (13:5) regards the destruction of the Temple as the Day of the Lord. Certain prophecies of the Day of the Lord were directed against specific hostile nations: Babylonia (Isa. 13:6,9,13); Edom (Isa. 34:8; 63:4); and Egypt (Jer. 46:2-12).

On the other hand, the Day of the Lord is also regarded as a day of great salvation. Thus Isaiah (61:2-3) declares that God's vengeance will also bring consolation to the mourners of Zion. Ezekiel (34:12) affirms that God will deliver Israel. The day will bring purification and salvation to those who fear God (Mal. 3:2-3). For the wicked, however, it will be like a burning furnace which consumes straw. Before the coming of that "great and dreadful day," God will send the prophet Elijah, who will reconcile fathers and sons (Mal. 3:23-24).

Later eschatological literature extends the Day of Judgment even further. Before the advent of the day, all the dead will be revived, so that they too will be judged on that day. See ESCHATOLOGY, RESURRECTION.

According to the Mishnah (*RH* 1.1), God judges the world on four occasions during the year. In Jewish tradition ROSH HA-SHANAH, the New Year, is the annual day of judgment (*Yom ha-Din*) for mankind, with the Divine decrees being finally sealed on the DAY OF ATONEMENT.

DAY OF THE LORD See ESCHATOLOGY

DAYYAN ("judge"). Justice in a rabbinical court of law (BET DIN). The Talmud indicates that there were various courts, consisting of three, 23, or 71 judges, and that every community with 120 or more adult Jewish males was to have a *bet din* of 23 judges. The authority to impose monetary fines was granted to *dayyanim* by a process of ORDINATION traditionally believed to have originated with Moses (see Num. 11: 16-17, 24-25; 27: 22-23; Deut. 34:9). The chain of ordination having been broken some time in the early Middle Ages; however, such power no longer exists. Even during the talmudic period, judges residing in the Diaspora were technically not permitted to impose fines, since ordination was granted only in the Land of Israel. Nevertheless, they did in fact rule in cases brought before them, as they were considered to be acting as "messengers" (*shelihim*) for the rabbis who had been ordained.

Before EMANCIPATION, when Jews lived in their own relatively autonomous communities, the *bet din* would rule on all judicial questions, whether of a religious, personal status, or civil nature.

In Eastern Europe, those who sat on a local *bet din* were known as *dayyanim*. The town rabbi might or might not be a member of the local *bet din*. The title *dayyan* is still maintained in Great Britain, to connote a member of the *bet din*. These law courts, as in almost all countries except Israel, deal mainly with questions of divorce according to Jewish law. In Israel, the *dayyanim* are responsible for many other areas in the field of personal status, including CONVERSION.

DAYYÉNU ("It would have been enough for us"). Refrain and title of an old hymn of thanksgiving chanted in the Passover SEDER ritual. An introductory sentence ("How many favors we have to thank God for!") establishes the hymn's leitmotif — that the deliverance of the Israelites from Egyptian bondage "would have been sufficient" in itself, and that each subsequent manifestation of Divine providence only added to their gratitude for His initial redemption. Fifteen (in some rites, 16) instances of God's mercy and favor are listed, such as the parting of the Red Sea, the provision of manna in the wilderness, the gift of the Sabbath and the giving of the Torah, entering the Promised Land, and the building of the Temple. *Dayyénu* is sung or recited at the end of each stanza. Little is known about this hymn's origin or authorship. It first appears in the ninth century (prayer book of SAADIAH GAON) and may be post-talmudic.

DAYS OF AWE See HIGH HOLIDAYS

DEAD SEA SCROLLS Collection of ancient scrolls and fragments of scrolls found near the Dead Sea. One of the outstanding archeological discoveries of the 20th century, these findings constitute a major contribution toward the study of non-mainstream Judaism in the late Second Temple era.

The first finds occurred in 1947, when Bedouin chanced upon a Judean Desert cave containing a batch of seven scrolls wrapped in rags. These all eventually found their way to Jerusalem. Subsequent searches in the Judean Desert, including the specific area of Qumran along the Dead Sea shore, produced thousands of scroll remnants, in varying states of decipherability. Similar scrolls were discovered at Masada. These have all been connected with a sect living in Qumran in the last period of the Second Temple. The Damascus Covenant (or Zadokite) documents found at the end of the 19th century in the Cairo GENIZAH are now also assumed to have been the literary productions of the same sect. Pottery remains have assisted in dating both the documents and the community which authored many of them, to the first century BCE-first century CE.

The Qumran community is identified by many scholars with the ESSENES (or a group of them). Their origins in the area date to 140-130 BCE, and according to some even prior to the Maccabean uprising in 167 BCE. The founder of the sect, generally known by a title translated "Teacher of Righteousness" or "The Rightful Teacher" (the title is disputed), was apparently a priest.

The hierarchical organization of the community appears to have been an idealized arrangement along the tribal lines of ancient Israel. According to some, the supreme Qumran council appears to have consisted of twelve laymen and three priests. The latter occupied a position of preeminence in the sect, which also had a supreme lay leader, the *nasi* who, in the view of many, is to be identified with the MESSIAH (royal or priestly) of Israel.

A striking aspect of the Qumran sectaries was their belief in their special election as members of a "New Covenant." Other themes basic to their belief were the reality of Divine grace and individual salvation. Their lives centered around Divine worship (although there does appear to have been at least one offshoot whose members worked to earn their daily bread), with prayers held twice daily, at dawn and dusk. Unlike the rest of mainstream Jewry, the sect celebrated the traditional biblical festivals according to the 52-week solar calendar consisting of four 13-week seasons. The drastic consequence of this break with the traditional Jewish luni-solar calendar was that the Jewish festivals were celebrated by the sect on fixed days of the week and thus at times which, for the mass of Jewry, were ordinary working days.

A striking divergence from the predominant national PHARISEE-oriented outlook may be found in the sect's belief in predestination, despite the apparently contradictory stance in some parts of their writings that men would be judged by their deeds.

The sacred communal meals of the sect constituted one of its unique features, and may well have been intended as a substitute for the sacrificial meals at the TEMPLE in

Jerusalem. Here the Qumran sect struck out on perhaps its most divergent path in that it considered the Jerusalem Temple a place of abomination and pollution, although the biblically ordained Temple and service as such were held in deepest reverence by the Qumran community. According to the *War Rule*, the sacrificial cult would be properly resumed in the seventh year of the Great War before the onset of the messianic era, this war to be waged by the members of the Qumran sect — the Sons of Light — against the other nonsectaries — the Sons of Darkness. Ritual purity was another extremely important tenet of belief and practice.

Among the many writings of the Qumran community are portions of the so-called *pesharim* or commentaries on biblical texts, e.g., the commentaries on the prophets Nahum and Habakkuk and a *pesher* on Psalms. A sub-division of this category are the instructive compilations of biblical verses with or without accompanying commentary. Yet another sub-grouping consists of the scroll fragments of various non-canonical (apocryphal) works previously familiar from other non-sect sources.

Apocryphal compositions such as Enoch, Tobit, and Jubilees, seem to have been embraced by the sect. A type of apocryphal literature apparently originating with the Qumran community is to be found in such compositions as the Genesis Apocryphon, the Samuel Apocryphon, psalms not found in Jewish Scripture, and other writings of a similar nature. Of special interest in this respect are the minute scraps from the Hebrew *Ben Sira* (Ecclesiasticus) scroll. These, together with the fragmentary portions of two chapters found at Masada, and the substantial sections discovered in the Cairo Genizah almost a century ago, account for about two-thirds of the previously unknown original Hebrew text of this important non-canonical work.

A scroll category of prime interest is the numerous copies of the books of the Bible (with the sole exception of the Book of Esther), including the complete Book of Isaiah, and many fragments of the Hebrew Scriptures. Viewed in their entirety, the Qumran Bible fragments strongly resemble the traditional (Masoretic) Bible text. Nevertheless, careful scrutiny shows divergences, often indicating a close affinity with the SAMARITAN Bible and the SEPTUAGINT. The greater part of the Judean Desert sect's library is written in the literary Hebrew of the Second Temple era, the remainder in Aramaic, with an insignificant portion of tiny remnants comprising Greek translations of Scripture.

Members of the sect apparently participated in the Great Revolt against Rome (66-71 CE). In any case, the revolt's failure seems to have marked the end of the Qumran sect's existence.

The Qumran community is indicative of the sectarian diversity that prevailed among the Jewish people in the Land of Israel, certainly in the latter part of the Second Temple era. Unlike the Essenes, other sectarian offshoots are only hinted at here and there, whereas Qumran, through its literature and the depictions of others, has left behind a fairly well-limned portrayal of its life and beliefs and, most important, definite evidence of the existence of Jewish groupings other than the Pharisees and SADDUCEES.

Various scholars also regard the sect and its writings as an important contribution to the study of early Christianity, especially because of the sect's generally monastic or semi-monastic existence; its stress on man's innate sinfulness, Divine grace, and the concept of predestination.

MAIN WRITINGS OF THE QUMRAN COMMUNITY

1. Community Rule (Manual of Discipline) — Messianic hopes and the community's organization and practices.

2. Rule of the Congregation (Messianic Rule) — Rules and regulations concerning the "last days," education, and members' duties.

3. Thanksgiving Hymns — Communal or individual prayers of thanks.

4. Damascus Rule — Legal and moral precepts and sermonic material to strengthen the group's separatist way of life.

5. War Rule — Final battles and victory in the War of the Sons of Light against the Sons of Darkness.

6. Copper Scroll — Description (accurate or fictional?) of vast treasure hidden away in Jerusalem or elsewhere in the Land of Israel.

7. Genesis Apocryphon — Apocryphal recapitulation of the biblical account from Lamech to Abraham (Gen. 5:28-15:4).

8. Temple Scroll — Temple and other biblical laws, description of the Temple area, and purity of the cities of Israel.

DEAD, PRAYERS FOR THE

See MEMORIAL SERVICES

DEATH The end of human life. Concerning death, the Bible is primarily occupied with two questions: 1) Why must man die, and what is the force that deprives him of life? 2) What is man's fate after death? In Genesis 3:19, God informs man that he will return to the earth from which he was taken. On the other hand, after his temptation in the Garden of Eden, man was expelled lest he eat from the TREE OF LIFE and become immortal (Gen. 3:22-23), suggesting that death is the result of sin. Various attempts have been made to reconcile the contradiction.

Opposite page: The Day of Atonement. Painting by Maurycy Gottlieb. Poland (1856-1879).
Overleaf: Fragment of the Book of Isaiah, from one of the Dead Sea Scrolls.

לנשין׃ והות אחסנתהון על שבטא זרעית אבוהון׃ אלה המצות והמשפטים אשר צוה יהוה ביד משה אל בני ישראל בערבת מואב על ירדן ירחו׃ אלין פקודיא ודיניא דפקיד יי׳ ביד משה לבני ישראל במישריא דמואב על ירדנא דיריחו׃

חזק

[illegible]

אלה

הדברים אשר דבר משה אל כל ישראל בעבר הירדן במדבר בערבה מול סוף בין פארן ובין תפל ולבן וחצרת ודי זהב׃ אלין פתגמיא דמליל משה עם כל ישראל בעברא דירדנא אוכח יתהון על דחבו במדברא ועל דארגיזו במישרא לקבל ים סוף בפארן אתפלו על מנא ובחצרות ארגיזו על בסרא ועל דעבדו עגל דדהב׃

אלה הדברים׃ לפי שהן דברי תוכחות ומנה כאן כל המקומות [illegible]

[illegible]

Alongside the strict monotheism of the Bible, modern scholarship finds certain literary devices that may be remnants of a conception, existing in the ancient Near East, that death was a supernatural power independent of God (see, e.g., Isa. 25:8; Jer. 9:20; Hos. 13:14; Prov. 16:14; Job 18:13). Nevertheless, God remains the supreme arbiter of life and death.

Concerning man's fate after death, the pronouncement of Genesis 3:19, that man will return to the dust of the earth, negates the Egyptian conception that led to the embalming of the Pharaohs. BURIAL, particularly in the family tomb, is clearly of paramount concern to the Bible (Gen. 47:29-30, 49:29; I Kings 21:19). Sacrificing to the dead and communicating with them, although common in the ancient Near East, are forbidden in the Pentateuch (Deut. 26:14).

Many biblical passages indicate that all human beings descend to a region "inhabited" by the dead. This region is known by various names, most notably *sheol*, a name that appears in no other ancient language and is used as a proper noun — never appearing with the definite article (e.g., Gen. 37:35). Death, in this view, is the great equalizer; wealth and power are meaningless in *sheol* (Job 3:13-19). Nor does consciousness continue after death (Eccl. 9:4,5; Job 14:21; Ps. 88:12,13). On the other hand, a few passages indicate a different conception — that God may save man from *sheol* and take the individual to Himself, e.g., Enoch and Elijah (Gen. 5:24; II Kings 2:11; Ps. 49:16; I Sam. 2:6). Clear allusion to RESURRECTION of the dead appears in the later books of the Bible (e.g., Dan. 12:2). Thus the sources on the fate of man after death hardly present a unified picture (see AFTERLIFE).

The *halakhah* discusses the determination of the exact moment of death. The Talmud (*Yoma* 85a), in its discussion of Sabbath violation in order to save a life, rules that death occurs when respiration has ceased. With the development of modern medical technology, the halakhic definition of death has been subject to various refinements. It is now possible to detect respiration in individuals who previously would have been considered dead, or to resuscitate those whose breathing has stopped. Rabbi Mosheh SOFER (*Ḫatam* Sofer, YD 338) indicated that death is considered to have occurred when there has been both respiratory and cardiac arrest. Rabbi Mosheh Feinstein (*Iggerot Mosheh, YD* 3, 132) ruled that a person is considered to have died with the death of his brain stem, since he is then incapable of breathing on his own.

A critically ill person hovering between life and death (Heb. *goses*) is, in all respects, considered to be alive. The verbal instructions of a *goses* have the same legal force as a signed and witnessed document (*Git.* 13a), and thus a deathbed change of will and testament is recognized as binding. It is forbidden to hasten the death of a *goses* by any action to his body (*YD* 339). It is permitted, however, to remove some external obstacle which may be preventing his death. The example given is the case of a noise outside the window, such as the chopping of wood, which may be preventing the *goses* from dying. In such a case, the noise may be stopped (*ibid.*, gloss of the Rema). Rabbi Ḫayyim Palache ruled that it is permitted to pray for the death of a critically ill person who is suffering terribly and wishes to die (*Ḫikkekei Lev*, 1 *YD* 50).

The Jewish attitude towards death, as developed in rabbinic literature, is a combination of defiance and acceptance. Since Judaism does not negate the reality of the here and now, death is to be fought; LIFE is to be cherished and preserved. Death is an evil. Early death is viewed as a misfortune, and longevity as a blessing. God promises Abraham that he will live to "a ripe old age" (Gen. 15:15) and it is customary to wish one's acquaintances a life of 120 years' duration. Ritually, a CORPSE is the most intense source of impurity (see PURITY AND IMPURITY).

CONFESSION ON A DEATHBED

I admit before You, God, my God and God of my ancestors, that my cure and my death are in Your hands. May it be Your will that You heal me with a complete healing. And if I die, may my death be an atonement for the sins, transgressions, and violations which I have sinned, transgressed, and violated before You. And set my portion in the Garden of Eden, and let me merit the world to come reserved for the righteous. Hear, O Israel, the Lord our God, the Lord is One.

The *halakhah* takes for granted that no effort will be spared to save a dying patient (see MEDICAL ETHICS), and the Talmud (*RH* 16b) reports that a change of name may avert a harsh decree. The custom therefore developed of executing a formal name change on behalf of one seriously ill. Most commonly, a symbolic name such as Ḫayyim ("life") or Raphael ("God heals") is given.

Even after a death, the spirit of defiance is maintained. During the MOURNING period, it is customary to recite the verse from Isaiah (25:8) which states that "God will destroy death forever."

On the other hand, Judaism has a strong element of acceptance. The Midrash (Gen. R. 9.5) offers the opinion that when God declared the world He had created to be "very good," he was referring to death, implying that God created death to be a positive and necessary part of the universe. The *Tsidduk ha-Din* prayer, recited by mourners at the FUNERAL SERVICE, describes God as the righteous Judge and accepts the finality of His decrees.

As indicated in the text of the confession (see inset), the

Opening page of the Book of Deuteronomy. From the Castro Pentateuch. *Germany, 1344.*

individual's death is considered to be the most powerful possible atonement for his sins. Maimonides (*Yad, Teshuvah* 1.4) delineated the various means for ATONEMENT, but for sins involving the desecration of God's Name only death can bring full atonement. The sages of the Talmud believed, and this was accepted as fundamental Jewish doctrine, that the soul returns to God (see SOUL AND ITS IMMORTALITY).

Judaism lays down that the utmost regard be shown for both the dying and the body after the soul has departed. A dying person is not to be left alone, and it is considered meritorious to be present at the moment of death. When informing a dying patient of his responsibility to confess, every effort must be made to avoid frightening him or causing him to lose hope. The ill person should be told: "Many have confessed but have not died, and many who have not confessed have died. And many who are walking outside in the marketplace have confessed. By the merit of your confessing, you live. All who confess have a place in the world to come" (*YD* 338.1). (CONFESSION in Judaism does not have the status of a final sacrament as do the last rites of the Catholic Church.) All present at the moment of death recite the blessing, BARUKH DAYYAN HA-EMET ("Blessed be the True Judge"), and relatives recite the *Tsidduk ha-Din*. Arrangements made for care and burial of the body are known as *ḥesed shel emet* (true kindness), since they are made on behalf of one no longer capable of responding in kind. After death has been finally established, the eyes and mouth are closed and the mouth, if need be, tied shut. The body is placed on the floor, covered with a sheet, with a lighted candle close to the head. In the home of the deceased, mirrors are covered and any standing water poured out (*YD* 339.5). The origin of these last two customs is unclear; they may have been a method of announcing the death to those entering the house or they may be a relic of folklore and SUPERSTITION. Respect for the dead is basic: a dead body is not to be left alone; sitting with the body is considered a *mitsvah* and it is desirable to read Psalms in its presence. The watcher over the body is exempt from prayers and putting on TEFILLIN. Before burial, the body is cleansed (see TOHORAH) and clothed in shrouds (*takhrikhin*).

Mourners pray for God's mercy on the soul of the deceased. Some have the custom of visiting the graves of loved ones and saintly people, asking their souls to pray on behalf of the living. These two practices indicate the belief in an ongoing connection between the living and the dead.

DEATH ANNIVERSARY See YAHRZEIT

DEBORAH See JUDGES

DECALOGUE See TEN COMMANDMENTS

DEDICATION OF A HOUSE See CONSECRATION

DEMAI (lit. "a dubious object"). Produce of the land acquired from one who may not have separated the priestly and levitical dues according to biblical law. In ancient times, a farmer was obligated to set aside approximately one fiftieth part of his agricultural produce as a "heave-offering" or "gift" to the priests and one tenth of the remainder as the Levites' first tithe (see TITHES). The Levites, in turn, had to give one tenth of their first tithe to the priests. Finally, a second tithe was demanded of the farmer, to be eaten in Jerusalem or else given as a donation to the poor at two separate intervals between one SABBATICAL YEAR and the next. Farmers were scrupulous about the priestly "gift" as it amounted to a very small part of their crop, and neglecting it was punishable by death. Special measures proved necessary, however, to enforce the allocation of tithes which the average farmer thought unimportant. A ḤAVER (member of a highly pious group) of Second Temple times would therefore treat any crops bought from a farmer as suspect (*demai*), and only eat or make use of them after separating the levitical tithe and the second tithe. Halakhic regulations concerning doubtful produce are listed in the Mishnaic tractate DEMAI.

DEMAI ("produce suspected of not having been tithed"). Third tractate of Order ZERA'IM in the Mishnah. Its seven chapters deal with the requirement of tithing produce bought from an *am ha-arets* (common unlearned man), because it was assumed he had not tithed properly. The law against eating DEMAI is lenient in certain cases, most notably in permitting the suspect food to the poor or to Jewish soldiers. The subject matter is amplified in the Jerusalem Talmud and in the *Tosefta*.

DEMONS AND DEMONOLOGY Evil spirits inimical to men. The term *shedim* ("demons") occurs only twice in Scripture (Deut. 32:17; Ps 106:37). In both instances, Israel is accused of sacrificing to them. Demons, occasionally called satyrs (Heb. *se'irim*), are thought to dwell among ruins and in the wilderness. It is possible, though by no means certain, that AZAZEL, to whom the scapegoat was sent in the course of the DAY OF ATONEMENT ritual, was conceived of as a prince of the demons and the offering was meant to mollify his hostility to Israel. The Pseudepigrapha, Midrash, and Talmud contain a highly developed demonology, which may be traced to Babylonian and Persian influence.

According to one legend, fallen angels (Gen 6:1-4) begot a race of giants as a result of their sexual union with the daughters of men. Their offspring were the demons, beings who inflict physical injury upon men and entice them to sin. The Talmud and Midrash use, in addition to the biblical *shedim*, the term *mazzikin* ("the harmful ones"). These, it is said, resemble the ministering ANGELS in three respects, and in three respects they are similar to men. Like the former, they have wings and can fly from one end of the earth to another, they are invisible, and they know the future. Like men, they eat and drink, procreate, and die. Another characteristic is their ability to assume any guise they choose. In number, they far exceed the human race.

Convinced of the potential harmfulness of demons, some writers have much to say on how to avoid them. One should not venture out at night, particularly on Wednesdays and Fridays, for those are the times when demons await their prey. The Talmud records various incantations and adjurations against demons. Some of these are intended for use against specific demons who bear personal names and about whom whole cycles of legends are found in the sources. Such, for example, are the female demons LILITH, and Agrat, daughter of Maḫlat, and the king of the demons Samael or Azazel, and Ashmedai, the prince of the demons. Ashmedai (Asmodeus) is the subject of a series of legends in the Talmud, many connected with King Solomon (*Git.* 68a-b).

The Talmud describes the encounters of a number of sages with various demons and how, in each instance, the sage bested the demon. It is said that both HILLEL and JOHANAN BEN ZAKKAI understood the speech of demons.

In the Middle Ages, belief in the existence of demons and their potency for harm was commonly accepted among both Jews and Christians. *Sefer Ḫasidim* (the Book of the Pious) by JUDAH HE-ḪASID refers frequently to demons and recommends several methods to ward off the harm they can inflict. In this, the work reflects its environment as do other mystical-kabbalistic works of the period.

The kabbalistic classic, the Zohar, presents a doctrine of Divine EMANATION, one side of which is the aspect of holiness and good; this is counterbalanced by "the other side" (*sitra aḫra*), the aspect of impurity and evil whose minions are the demons. When the two sides of the Divine are held in balance, neither harm nor evil can befall. But when, through man's sins, they are torn asunder, the side of impurity and evil performed by the demons holds sway. While charms and AMULETS are already mentioned in the Talmud, under the influence of the Kabbalah, the practice of wearing such amulets, often inscribed with the names of mystical angels, became particularly widespread and continued up to the 20th century.

While belief in the existence of demons has persisted in some quarters to the present, as early as the Middle Ages a number of scholars, though by no means all, denied their existence. MAIMONIDES identified them with wild animals and in one of his responsa forbade the wearing of amulets. Abraham IBN EZRA denounced as sinners those who believed in the existence of demons. JUDAH HALEVI and NAḪMANIDES, however, argued for their existence. The SHULḪAN ARUKH contains a few laws (drawn from talmudic sources) that reflect a belief in demons, as do a number of the glosses of Moses ISSERLES.

DERASH (Heb. "exposition"). A homiletical method of interpreting Scripture. The rabbis devised rules and techniques for elucidating non-literal meanings in the biblical text that would point up its legal implication or ethical message. This approach to Scripture is known as *derash* (or *derush*) and constitutes one of the four traditional methods whereby the Bible may be interpreted (see PARDES). It gave rise to the *derashah* (i.e., "sermon"), the expository kernel of a rabbinic discourse, and *darshan* was one name for a preacher. See also MIDRASH and HOMILETICS.

DEREKH ERETS (literally: "the way of the world"). A mode of conduct which the rabbis interpreted to denote practices commendable in themselves, though not mandatory. According to the Mishnah, "he in whom other men are pleased, God also is pleased" (*Avot* 3.13), because he knows how to behave and creates a spirit of harmony around him. *Derekh erets* therefore signifies courtesy (*Ber.* 6b; *Ket.* 40a; *BK* 33a), cleanliness and attention to one's appearance (*Av. Zar.* 20b; *Shab.* 113a-114b), avoidance of coarse expressions (*Pes.* 3a), consideration for women (*Shab.* 10b), and the respect due to parents and teachers (*San.* 100b). Above all, it means good manners (*Yoma* 4b), for one possessing neither Torah nor *derekh erets* is an uncivilized boor (*Kid.* 1.10). The

SOME ADVICE FROM THE RABBIS ON DEREKH ERETS

A man should not weep among those enjoying themselves and should not enjoy himself among those weeping.

One guest does not invite another to be a guest.

When visiting, do not ask to eat until it is suggested to you.

Do not eat in company anything that causes an odor.

Do not drink at one gulp.

A sage with a stain on his clothes deserves to be punished.

Never speak a man's full praise in his presence — only in his absence.

Cleanliness brings holiness.

The servant who waits at the table should wear different clothes from those he uses for cooking.

Wear special clothes on the Sabbath.

Be zealous for the honor of your friend.

Never utter an unworthy thought.

Avoid whatever is ugly.

There are seven signs of a wise man: he does not speak before one who is wiser; he does not interrupt another's speech; he is not quick to reply; he asks according to the subject matter and answers to the point; he speaks about first things first, and last things last; he admits if he has not understood a subject; and he acknowledges the truth.

Mishnah also records a teaching of Rabban GAMALIEL, that "it is admirable to combine Torah study with *derekh erets*" (*Avot* 2.2); from the context, one sees that he was alluding to "a worldy occupation," such gainful employment as would enable a scholar or student to maintain his self-respect and prevent him becoming a burden on the community. This wider sense of *derekh erets* was extended still further by Samson Raphael HIRSCH, a founder of NEO-ORTHODOXY, when he advocated a life style combining traditional Judaism and secular culture through the principle of "Torah with *derekh erets*." Two minor tractates of the Talmud, *Derekh Erets Rabbah* and *Derekh Erets Zuta*, provide ethical guidance and rules of conduct; they normally appear at the end of the order NEZIKIN.

DESECRATION (Hebrew. *ḥillul*). Profanation of what is deemed holy. In general, the term *ḥillul* refers to those beings or objects possessing a certain degree of holiness, whose sanctity is diminished owing to an improper action or through contact with something ritually impure. Thus, a priest who marries a divorced woman violates a law of the Torah (Lev. 21:7) and, having been profaned by the action, is known as a *ḥalal* (see PRIESTS). Ritually pure objects and foods belonging to the Temple are also desecrated if brought into contact with objects considered as ritually impure, among them a CORPSE or one who has not undergone purification after touching a dead body. While some of these desecrated objects can be resanctified, others cannot and must be destroyed (see also PURITY AND IMPURITY).

Just as time can be sanctified, notably the SABBATH, so it can be profaned by any action forbidden during that time (*ḥillul Shabbat* — "desecration of the Sabbath"). God's Name can also be desecrated (ḤILLUL HA-SHEM — "profanation of the [Divine] Name") by someone whose actions are likely to cast opprobrium on Judaism or the Jewish people. The punishment for desecration is either KARET ("excision," i.e., premature death at the hand of God) or, as in the case of Sabbath desecration, sentence of death passed by a *bet din* (Jewish court of law) and executed by Divine intervention. Nevertheless, there are cases where it is permitted to divest persons or objects of their sanctity. Thus, for example, a person who has taken an oath to be a NAZIRITE for a fixed period brings a sacrifice at the end of that time, and then resumes his earlier profane state without incurring any penalty. The second TITHE, which should be brought to Jerusalem and consumed there, may likewise be profaned by converting it into money which is then brought to Jerusalem and used for purchasing food to be eaten in the city.

DESTINY AND DETERMINISM See FREE WILL

DEUTERONOMY, BOOK OF Fifth and last book of the PENTATEUCH, known in Hebrew as *Devarim*, "Words," from the opening phrase. The sages refer to it as *Mishneh Torah* (i.e., "the Repetition of the Torah" whence the Greek *Deuteronomion* — "Second Law"), as stated in 17:18, because most of this book is a review of the laws in the previous volumes: Exodus, Leviticus and Numbers. Following the Latin Vulgate, printed Hebrew Bibles divide Deuteronomy into 34 chapters and 955 verses. The Babylonian cycle of readings (which is followed today by all Jewish communities), divides the book into 11 pericopes (*sedarot*), but according to the Palestinian triennial cycle of Second Temple times, it contains 27 sections. Included in Deuteronomy are the TEN COMMANDMENTS (5:6-18) and the first two paragraphs of the SHEMA (6:4-9, 11:13-21).

Traditionally, its contents were spoken by MOSES during the last 37 days of his life, from 1 Shevat to 7 Adar, after which he died in the 40th year following the Exodus from Egypt.

Since Jewish tradition also maintains that Deuteronomy, like the other books of the Pentateuch, was dictated by God to Moses, this raises a well-known problem. Eight verses before the end of the book (34:5), it is stated that "Moses died there." How could Moses have written these words and the following verses? The Talmud gives two alternative answers: (a) the last eight verses were written by Joshua and not by Moses; (b) God dictated these last eight verses to Moses, in advance of his death, "and Moses wrote them down in tears."

The era in which Deuteronomy was written is a matter of dispute among scholars. Until a few decades ago, it was a commonly accepted view (as expounded by the 19th-century Bible critic Julius Wellhausen) that the volume written by priests of the Deuteronomistic group, a short time before King Josiah discovered the scroll in 621 BCE, is Source D. The priests would then have written this volume in order to persuade the king to concentrate worship in the Temple in Jerusalem, which had not been the situation up until then. Other researchers, however, associate Deuteronomy with the period after the Babylonian exile; others again place it earlier, in the time of King Hezekiah (725-697 BCE); while still others hold that it was written even earlier, at a time when there was strong opposition to pagan worship in the Canaanite temples. According to this last view, the book was written during the period of the Judges or at an early stage of the monarchy. Seventh century BCE seems to be the most likely date for the compilation and editing of Deuteronomy in its present form.

Yeḥezkel Kaufmann, a modern Israeli Bible scholar, claims that the narrative material, the sections dealing with admonition, and most of the statutes are very ancient, but that their influence was not great. Only during the period of Hezekiah and Josiah did these statutes become important.

The Jerusalem scholar, Mosheh Ḥayyim Cassuto, maintains that by far the greater part of Deuteronomy is extremely ancient, dating from even before David's time. Had the volume been written during the period of the monarchy, the author would certainly have attributed to Moses some hint that the ceremonial religious center of Israel would be Jerusalem, whereas Jerusalem is not mentioned at all.

In reply, defenders of the traditional view affirm that (a) the book's underlying theme is not the centralization of worship, but opposition to idolatry. The most intensive struggle against idolatry took place during the time of Moses, when the monotheistic character of the nation was established. This struggle was unusually appropriate to the time after Israel's sinful attachment to Baal-Peor (Num. 25), when Moses wished to stress the danger posed by Canaanite ritual. (b) Parallels to most of the laws in the Book of the Covenant (Ex.20:19-23:33), repeated in this volume, are to be found in other codes of the ancient Middle East (e.g., laws governing the monarchy and the appointment of judges), and these laws are therefore appropriate to that period. (c) The political background of Deuteronomy, such as the order to destroy the seven nations of Canaan, and Israel's relationship to the Edomites and to Egypt, is appropriate to the era of Moses and not to some other period. (d) Those passages dealing with contracts are appropriate to the laws of the ancient Middle East, and can be compared to the Hittite vassal law. (e) Linguistically, there is nothing to disprove the hypothesis that this volume was set down at the time of Moses. A number of ceremonial expressions have parallels in Ugaritic literature; furthermore, the use of parallelism in poetry and prose as well as the change of person are characteristic not only of the Bible but of all the literature of the ancient Middle East.

Scholars have tried to identify the circles from which the Book of Deuteronomy emanated. Some have pointed to the Levites, whose task it was to preach the Law; others have suggested political circles, notably court scribes.

BOOK OF DEUTERONOMY

1:1 — 1:5	Introduction
1:6 — 3:29	Moses' first speech: the lessons of the past
4:1 — 4:40	Moses' second speech: the uniqueness of God
4:41- 4:43	Three cities of refuge in Transjordan
4:44 — 11:32	Moses' third speech: the Giving of the Law and reasons for obeying God
12:1 — 26:19	Laws and statutes which Israel must obey in the land they are to inherit
27:1 — 28:69	The blessing in reward for observing the Torah and the punishment for disobeying it
29:1 — 31:30	Moses' final speech: preparing for the entry into Canaan
32:1 — 32:52	The Farewell Poem of Moses
33:1 — 33:29	Parting benediction to the tribes
34:1 — 34:12	Death of Moses

DEUTERONOMY RABBAH Homiletical MIDRASH (part of MIDRASH RABBAH) on the Book of DEUTERONOMY, known in Hebrew as *Devarim Rabbah* (see also MIDRASH AGGADAH). The printed version of this Midrash is divided into 11 sections, corresponding to the 11 sections of the (Babylonian) Torah reading cycle which Jews now follow. In fact, however, the work comprises 27 homilies, thus corresponding to the 27 sections of the TRIENNIAL CYCLE once common in Erets Israel. A major characteristic of this Midrash is its TANHUMA (*Yelammedenu*) style; each section is introduced by a simple halakhic question and answer formula: "What is the law for a man of Israel? — Our sages taught that it is such and such." Most of the homilies end with words of consolation and an expression of hope for speedy redemption.

Additional homilies on Deuteronomy, not found in standard printed editions of the Midrash, were published by Solomon Buber and later amplified by Saul LIEBERMAN. It appears that a number of different recensions of the Midrash were once available. These recensions, as well as the printed text, drew on the Jerusalem Talmud and on older amoraic Midrashim of Palestinian origin. Several of the sages quoted in Deuteronomy Rabbah lived after the fourth century CE, and polemical references to the KARAITES indicate that the text was edited in the ninth century CE or somewhat later.

DEVEKUT ("cleaving" or "clinging"). Term denoting a close attachment to God. In the Pentateuch, *davak* is a verb signifying wholehearted devotion to God and His commandments. Even at this early stage of Israel's religious history, *devekut* was presented as a culmination of loving God and obeying His laws (Deut. 30:20; cf. 4:4). Not until the Middle Ages, however, did the concept attain a new, mystical dimension in kabbalistic thought. It then came to mean the individual's total concentration on prayers, their wording and mystical significance, in order to reach "communion" with the Divine. Such was the aim of Abraham ABULAFIA's ecstatic kabbalism and of the *devekut* to which Isaac ben Samuel of Acre (c. 1250-1340) referred, an elevation of the mind leading one through the stages of equanimity and solitude to the *Ru'ah ha-Kodesh* (Holy Spirit) and prophecy. Most of the kabbalists interpreted *devekut* to mean the soul's ascent through prayer and meditation to the lowest rung of the Ten Spheres (SEFIROT), where it finally encountered the Divine Presence (*Shekhinah*). A new and important element was introduced, in 16th-century Safed, by Isaac Luria and his fellow kabbalists. Through prior concentration of the mind, aided by special meditations, each prayer recited or commandment performed could help one achieve *devekut* and thus attain religious perfection (see KAVVANAH). It remained for ḤASIDISM to give this concept a broader interpretation. According to Israel BA'AL SHEM TOV, *devekut* is the supreme goal and achievement of religious life, outweighing "mere" Torah scholarship; not reserved for a select few and not circumscribed by prayer or religious acts, it is an emotional state of mind that should accompany one through the day, enabling even the unlearned Jew to sanctify his existence and find redemption. Such "attachment to God" therefore implies no merging with the Divine, no *unio mystica*, but moving closer to God in order to realize one's true human potential.

DEVIL See SATAN

DEVOTION See KAVVANAH

DEW, PRAYER FOR (*Tefillat Tal*). Name given to various supplicatory hymns and prayers which form part of the AMIDAH during the dry season in the Land of Israel. There are many references in the Bible to the vital importance of dew (e.g., Gen. 27:28; Mic. 5:6; Ps. 133:3), often also in a symbolic context (cf. Deut. 32:2; Hos. 14:6; Zech. 8:12). The blessings of rain and dew are emphasized in the daily *Amidah*, which incorporates appreciative "references" (second benediction) as well as seasonal "requests" (ninth benediction), a liturgical development that gave rise to some controversy in the Mishnaic period (*Ta'an.* 1.1-2). According to an old tradition, the "heavenly stores of dew" are opened up at the beginning of PASSOVER. From the early Middle Ages, it became customary to recite special pleas for Divine intercession when the earth of the Holy Land needed moisture during the summer (prayers for dew on Passover) or else during the winter months (prayers for rain on SHEMINI ATSERET; see RAIN, PRAYERS FOR). These hymns and prayers have entered the liturgy of all Jewish rites, the Prayer for Dew being chanted in the Additional Service on the first day of Passover. Among Sephardim, these supplications are known as *Tikkun Tal* ("the Dew formula").

Few Orthodox congregations nowadays recite the whole series of alphabetical acrostic poems originally adopted by the Ashkenazi ritual. In most Diaspora communities, the Ark is opened and worshipers remain standing while the reader (dressed in his white robe or KITEL) chants the Prayer for Dew soon after commencing his repetition of the Additional Service *Amidah*. The opening words, *Tal ten li-retsot artsakh* ("Give dew to favor Your land"), introduce what chiefly remains of the older Ashkenazi ritual — a hymn in six rhyming stanzas with reversed acrostics, attributed to Eleazar KALLIR. A parallel is drawn between the revival of land and nature in springtime and Israel's own future restoration.

Part of the Prayer for Dew on a page from the Maḥzor of Worms *illustrated with the signs of the Zodiac, Germany, 1272.*

After the reader has proclaimed, *Mashiv ha-ru'aḥ u-Morid ha-tal* ("[For You are the Lord our God] who causes the wind to blow and the dew to fall"), he repeats the congregation's threefold prayer that dew may be granted "as a blessing, not as a curse; for life, not for death; for plenty, not for famine." Each wish is greeted by a congregational response of *amen*. This ritual is followed in Conservative synagogues, and an abbreviated version is used by Reform congregations.

In Israel, however, this (Diaspora) procedure is maintained only by Ḥasidic Jews; other Ashkenazi congregations recite *Tefillat Tal* immediately prior to the silent *Amidah*. Furthermore, all traditional rites in Israel have adopted the Sephardi practice of substituting *Morid ha-tal* ("Who causes the dew to fall"), in the second benediction of the *Amidah*, for the phrase *Mashiv ha-ru'aḥ u-Morid ha-geshem* ("Who causes the wind to blow and the rain to fall") used throughout the winter. "Grant blessing to the earth" — inserted in the ninth benediction of the weekday *Amidah* — is nevertheless a standard formula among Ashkenazim, voicing the hope for a prosperous year, which worshipers recite from the first intermediate day of Passover until the afternoon of 4 December (until 7 Ḥeshvan in Israel). Two quite different versions of this benediction (for summer and winter) are prescribed in the Sephardi and Eastern rites.

DIASPORA See GALUT

DIBBUK (or Dybbuk). A term which connotes the attachment to a soul of an evil spirit, or the soul of a wicked person who has died to the body of a living person. The dibbuk is thus the presence of a foreign entity inside a person, which speaks through his throat and causes the person distress and spiritual disturbance. The belief in dibbuks is a common folk view, but the term appears for the first time in 17th-century Eastern Europe, and is related to the kabbalistic theory of TRANSMIGRATION of souls.

The idea of evil spirits entering the human body was prevalent among Jews of the Second Temple era and the talmudic period. Stories about this are common in the Gospels of the NEW TESTAMENT. The belief that certain souls of the dead could not find rest and therefore attached themselves to living persons was common in both Judaism and Christianity in the Middle Ages.

According to the kabbalistic theory of the transmigration of souls, there is a phenomenon known as *ibbur*, the joining of the soul of a dead person to that of a person who is alive. According to the kabbalists, the soul of the righteous person joins the soul of another person in order to strengthen its good qualities and in order to aid the Jewish people as a whole. Only at a later period of time do the kabbalists speak of an "evil joining," the entry of the soul of an evil person into the body of a person who has allowed it entry through a sin which he committed.

The phenomenon of the evil *ibbur* is described at length in the writings of the kabbalists of Safed, primarily of R. Ḥayyim VITAL and of his son, R. Samuel Vital. The pupils of Isaac LURIA describe ceremonies for the exorcism of such dibbuks, and in many writings they give detailed instructions about how to chase away common ones.

Descriptions of dibbuks and ceremonies of exorcism are quite common from the 16th century on. They form the basis for a number of literary works, the most famous of these being *The Dibbuk*, a play written by S. An-Ski in 1916, which has been staged on numerous occasions and also filmed.

DIETARY LAWS A set of regulations that govern food permitted for consumption. The term KASHER or *kosher* associated with these laws means food that is ritually fit for consumption; the dietary laws are known in Hebrew as the laws of *kashrut* ("fitness"). The dietary laws do not concern fruit and vegetables. While there do exist regulations concerning their consumption (see AGRICULTURAL LAWS, MIXED SPECIES, TITHE, WINE), the source of such regulations is not in the dietary laws, according to which all fruits and vegetables are permitted.

The first dietary law in the Bible prohibits eating the limb of a living animal and the consumption of blood (Gen.9:4). The Bible (Deut.14:6) furnishes clear criteria for determining which quadrupeds are permitted or *tahor* ("clean"): "Every animal that has true hooves which are cleft in two, and brings up the cud, you may eat." All such animals, domestic or wild, are herbivorous. Animals that meet only one of these requirements, such as the pig, which has a wholly cloven hoof but does not bring up the cud, or the camel, which brings up the cud but does not have a split hoof, are forbidden (*tamé*, "unclean"). The Bible lists ten permitted animals: the ox, sheep, goat, deer, gazelle, roebuck, wild goat, ibex, antelope and mountain sheep (Deut. 14:4-5).

The Bible does not offer criteria for birds but, rather, enumerates the forbidden ones (Lev.11:13-19; Deut.14:12-18). From these two lists, the rabbis compiled a comprehensive list of 24 birds considered forbidden (*Ḥul.* 63b). Eggs of prohibited birds are likewise forbidden, as are fertilized eggs of permitted birds.

Among aquatic animals, only those that have at least one fin and at least one easily removable scale are permitted; thus crab, lobster, oysters, clams, etc. are forbidden. Caviar of forbidden fish is also prohibited (Lev.11:9-12).

In Leviticus (11:21-22), the Bible permits four types of locusts (although these are prohibited by rabbinic law because of the difficulty of identification). Otherwise, every sort of insect, arthropod, and worm (as well as all reptiles) is forbidden. A general rule of the dietary laws is that any product of a forbidden animal is forbidden (thus the prohibition of the eggs of forbidden birds and fish and the milk of forbidden mammals); the one exception is honey, for which the Talmud elicits special proof of permissibility (*Bekh.* 7b).

The dietary laws deal not only with the fitness of various species, but also with the manner of the animal's slaughter, its health at the time of death, and the manner of its preparation for consumption. The ritually specified method of slaughter is known in Hebrew as SHEḤITAH; one trained in this skill is known as a SHOḤET. An animal that has died in any but the prescribed way is not permitted for consumption. *Sheḥitah* consists of a rapid slitting of the esophagus and trachea with a razor-sharp knife; death is nearly instantaneous. The knife must be carefully inspected immediately prior to each use to ascertain that the blade has not even the tiniest blemish. Once the animal is slaughtered, it is suspended upside-down to insure that as much BLOOD as possible drains from the carcass. After slaughter, the *shoḥet* must perform an inspection (*bedikah*) of the animal. If the internal organs show any evidence of injury or disease that would have been likely to cause the animal's death within one year (*Ḥul.* 43a), the animal is classified as TEREFAH and is forbidden (in common Ashkenazi parlance, the word *tref* — usually used as the opposite of kasher — refers to food unfit for

Ritual slaughter of an ox. The inspector, on the right, makes sure that the dietary laws are observed. Italy, 1435.

any reason). Meat of any animal that has died of a natural cause (*nevelah*) is prohibited. Particularly meticulous observers of the dietary laws may demand a standard of *kashrut* known in Hebrew as *ḥalak* ("smooth") and in Yiddish as *glatt*. Meat that is "glatt kosher" comes from animals whose lungs, upon inspection, raised no question at all, since there was no evidence whatsoever of ill health. This classification is not relevant to poultry, for which inspection is required of the intestines only. Fish need not be ritually killed or inspected.

The Bible outlaws the consumption of blood (Lev. 7:26-27, 17: 10-14), and this prohibition results in a number of obligatory procedures in the preparation of food. Animals are hung after *sheḥitah* so as to maximize the amount of veinal blood drained. Beyond that, the *halakhah* prescribes one of two alternate procedures to extract as much blood as possible from muscle and organ tissues. The most common procedure is that of salting (*meliḥah*). Meat is first soaked in clean cold water for thirty minutes to open the pores. The meat is then covered on all surfaces with a medium-coarse SALT and placed on a grooved or perforated board for one hour. The board must be inclined to facilitate drainage. After the time has elapsed, the meat is rinsed several times in running water. An alternative method is to roast the meat over an open flame. This is considered more effective and is therefore required for certain tissues extremely rich in blood (e.g., liver) as well as meat that has not been salted within 72 hours of slaughter. Both roasting and salting are commonly known as koshering or kashering. Any blood remaining after a proper kashering is permitted. Today, most meat is salted prior to being sold. Roasting, however, remains a common household task in observant homes. The blood of fish is permitted.

Certain portions of permitted animals are also forbidden. The sciatic nerve (Heb. *gid ha-nasheh*) is not eaten (Gen. 32:33) and must be removed before meat may be taken from the hindquarter. In communities where the sciatic nerve is not removed, the hindquarter is not eaten but sold to non-Jewish packing houses. The fat attached to the stomach and intestines (Heb. *ḥelev*) was designated in sacrificial animals to be burned on the altar. In all animals, its consumption is forbidden. These two regulations do not concern fish or poultry.

The separation of milk and meat practiced in Jewish homes stems from the biblical prohibition, "You shall not cook a kid in its mother's milk," which appears three times in the Pentateuch (Ex. 23:19, 34:26; Deut. 14:21), probably as a measure against paganism, which prepared charms by seething kids in their mothers' milk. The laws deriving from this prohibition are known as the laws of *basar be-ḥalav* (meat in milk). The Talmud took the biblical prohibition to refer to the cooking of any domestic animal in the milk of any other domestic animal (*Ḥul.* 113b). The rabbis later added poultry to this prohibition. The threefold repetition of the same ban was interpreted as a prohibition not only of cooking but also of eating and deriving benefit from such a product (*Ḥul.* 115b). Milk for the purpose of this law is any dairy product. As is common in Jewish law, the rabbis greatly extended these rules in order to "erect a fence around the Torah." Thus, they prohibited eating milk together with meat at the same meal. Since utensils may absorb small quantities of hot foods with which they come in contact and later discharge what they have absorbed, completely separate sets of pots, pans, dishes, and cutlery are mandated, for fear that meat be contaminated by milk or vice versa. After eating meat, a specified period must pass before eating milk products. This period varies among different communities, some waiting six hours, some three, and a few waiting one hour only. It is permitted to eat meat after milk, however, if it is not part of the same meal and if the mouth has been rinsed or bread eaten. Fruit, vegetables, eggs, and fish may be eaten with milk or meat, and are commonly known as *stami* or *pareve* (neutral), although the rabbis felt that it was unhealthy to eat fish immediately after meat.

The Bible makes no attempt to explain the dietary laws, although it does on three separate occasions associate them with HOLINESS (Ex. 22:30, Lev.11:44-45, Deut.14:21). They are, however, classified as a *ḥok*, a regulation without explanation. Nor did the rabbis of the Talmud and Midrash go deeply into the rationale of these laws. In general, they felt that the observance of *kashrut* was an aid to the development of self-discipline and moral conduct (Gen.R. 44.1, *Sifra* on Lev. 20:26). Various other attempts have been made to explain the dietary laws, but these are not authoritative. Maimonides (*Guide* 3.48) wrote that the observance of the dietary laws teaches mastery of the appetites and restraint. He also felt that all the forbidden foods were unwholesome. The hygienic theme has been suggested by others as well. Some have claimed a humanitarian basis for the dietary laws: the revulsion to blood, the requirement of rapid painless slaughter, the consumption of only herbivorous animals, inculcate sensitivity to other living beings and an avoidance of violence.

Until the modern period, *kashrut* was one of the touchstones of Jewish observance and one of the unmistakable marks of Jewish identity. The 19th-century Reform movement in Germany decided that the dietary laws were connected with the Temple ritual and were to be regarded as a temporary regulation, not integral to the Jewish religion. American Reform Judaism rejected the dietary laws at its Pittsburgh Conference of 1885, declaring that "they fail to impress the modern Jew with a spirit of priestly holiness," and that "their observance in our days is apt rather to obstruct than to further modern spiritual elevation." Today, the dietary laws are disregarded by a large segment of the Jewish people. Conservative Judaism adheres to the laws of *kashrut*, although there is a tendency to select the more lenient opinions available in the *halakhah* over stricter rulings that may have previously gained acceptance. Observance of the dietary laws has recently enjoyed a certain revival in various Jewish communities with numerous kasher products widely available and new kasher restaurants opening. In the State of Israel, nearly all food products are produced under rabbinical supervision to insure conformity with the dietary laws. In the Israel Defense Forces and public institutions, the dietary laws are observed.

DINA DE-MALKHUTA DINA ("The law of the realm is the law"). Talmudic principle formulated (in Aramaic) by the Babylonian *amora* SAMUEL under the early Sassanid rulers of Persia (c. 242 CE). Cited in four different tractates (*Ned.* 28a, *Git.* 10b, *BK* 113a, *BB* 54b-55a), it accommodates Jewish law to the civil "law of the land," giving precedence to the latter where these conflict and endowing it with the force of *halakhah*. Biblical authority has been adduced in support of this classic ruling, but new political realities (i.e., the desirability of good relations with the non-Jewish government) lay behind its promulgation. Among the areas in which *dina de-malkhuta dina* applied were taxation and the payment of debts. Tax evasion was considered a form of robbery, while governmental decisions involving payment in coinage of the realm were to be obeyed, even if they might lead to infractions of Jewish law (e.g., where usury was concerned). *Dina de-malkhuta dina* could not, however, apply in matters of Jewish religious and ritual observance, nor where it involved any compromise with outright robbery, oppression, or manifest injustice. Similarly, any attempt to impose rabbis, judges, and other functionaries on the Jewish community might lawfully be resisted. According to many opinions, *dina de-malkhuta dina* nowadays applies to the civil law of a Jewish government, i.e., in the State of Israel.

DIN TORAH (literally "a judgment according to the Torah"). Term used for a court case held before judges (often DAYYANIM), who rule in accordance with rabbinic law. According to Jewish law, either party to the dispute may force the other to appear before a Jewish court (BET DIN) for a hearing; since Emancipation, however, the Jewish courts have had few powers to enforce this right. Today, except in Israel, where certain areas of personal status are legally assigned to the rabbinical courts, *diné Torah* (plur.) are generally held only where both parties have signed an agreement accepting the verdict of the *bet din* as binding.

A famous Yiddish folk song tells the legendary tale of how LEVI YITSHAK OF BERDICHEV had *"a din Torah with God,"* in which he, as it were, brought God to trial for allowing the Jewish people to suffer.

DISINTERMENT See BURIAL

DISPUTATIONS Term generally used to describe public debates between representatives of different faiths, with the aim of either persuading the representative of the other faith of the correctness of one's own, or of rebutting allegations. Josephus reports on two disputations before kings, one between Jews and SAMARITANS before Ptolemy VI in Alexandria, and the other before Caligula in Rome.

The best known disputations were held in the Middle Ages, when Jewish scholars were forced against their will to debate with Christian clerics and/or apostate Jews. Such disputations were meant to demonstrate the superiority of Christianity and were a source of great danger to the Jews who participated. The Jews were generally required to refrain from uttering anything which might be considered sacrilege in Christian eyes, thus greatly limiting the approach they might adopt.

The first major medieval Christian-Jewish disputation was staged in Paris before King Louis IX in 1240. The Jews were represented by R. Jehiel of Paris and three other rabbis, while the leader of the Catholics was Nicholas Donin, an apostate Jew who had become a Dominican monk. Donin, by distorting and deliberately misquoting the Talmud, represented it as violently anti-Christian. R. Jehiel answered all the arguments, showing where Donin had erred. Indeed, R. Jehiel may be said to have emerged victorious, but in 1242 all copies of the Talmud were ordered burned. Twenty-four cartloads of manuscripts were consigned to the flames — at a time when each copy of the Talmud was handwritten.

Probably the most famous of all disputations was that between NAHMANIDES and Pablo Christiani (an apostate Jew) in Barcelona in 1263, presided over by King James I of

Aragon. Pablo Christiani made four allegations, which Naḫmanides was challenged to disprove: a) that the Talmud agreed that the Messiah had come; b) that according to Scripture the Messiah was both mortal and Divine; c) that the Messiah had suffered and died in order to redeem mankind; d) that all the laws of the Torah were to be annulled once the Messiah arrived. Naḫmanides, risking his life, requested permission to give full answers to all the questions. After receiving permission to do so, Naḫmanides boldly proclaimed that what the Christians believed is accepted by them by their training from birth, but the idea of God assuming human form is not logical. Naḫmanides, writing of this disputation at a later time, mentions how the king listened attentively to his arguments and in the end gave him a purse with 300 gold coins. Yet Naḫmanides had made an enemy of the Church, and was forced to flee the country.

The longest disputation ever held was in Tortosa in Spain (1413-1415), between the apostate Jew Geronimo de Santa Fé and 22 learned rabbis, including Joseph ALBO. It extended for some 69 sessions and was held in the presence of the papal Curia. This disputation, which helped to undermine the position of Spanish Jewry, brought about a large number of conversions of Jews to Christianity. In 1757-59, two disputations were held in Poland when Jewish leaders were summoned to defend Judaism against charges brought by the FRANKISTS.

DIVINATION See WITCHCRAFT

DIVORCE The Bible contains no systematic legislation on divorce. Its two fundamental principles, however, derive from the verse: "When a man takes a wife and possesses her, if she fails to please him because he finds something obnoxious about her, then he writes her a bill of divorcement, hands it to her, and sends her away from his house" (see Deut. 24:1-4). From this verse, it is understood that the power of divorce rests exclusively with the husband; further, that the act of divorce must be in the form of a written document (*Git.* 20a). The precise meaning of "something obnoxious" is variously interpreted by the sages of the MISHNAH. According to the School of SHAMMAI, the reference is to unchastity. The School of HILLEL interprets the phrase to mean even if she displeased him by burning his meal. R. AKIVA goes even further and declares that a man may divorce his wife if he found someone prettier than she (*Git.*9:10).

In two instances, a man could never divorce his wife: if he charged that his wife had not been a virgin at the time of their marriage and the charge was proven false (Deut. 22:13-19); and if he raped a virgin whom he subsequently married (Deut. 22:28-29). Nor could a man remarry his divorced wife if in the interim she had married someone else and had been either divorced or widowed (Deut.24:2-4). A priest (*kohen*) may not marry a divorced woman (Lev. 21:7, 14), and this still holds today.

Divorce is frowned upon by both Prophetic and Wisdom literature. Malachi (2:14-16), apparently responding to the situation of his time, declares: "For I hate divorce, says the Lord, the God of Israel." In the same passage, the prophet describes divorce as an act of treachery, a betrayal of the covenant between husband and wife. Proverbs 5:15-19 urges conjugal fidelity.

While the Bible puts the right of divorce exclusively in the hands of the husband, documents found in the Jewish settlement of Elephantine, Egypt (fifth century BCE) indicate that the wife had the right to divorce her husband. This practice can be attributed to foreign influence.

According to the Talmud, "the altar sheds tears for the man who divorces his first wife" (*San.* 22a) and in the talmudic period, the law of divorce underwent a number of significant changes. Prominent among these was the establishment of a number of circumstances under which the court could compel a husband to grant his wife a divorce. These included: (1) if a wife remained barren after a period of ten years of marriage; (2) if a husband contracted a loathsome disease; (3) if a husband refused to support his wife or was in a position in which he could not support her; (4) if a husband denied his wife her conjugal rights; (5) if a husband continued to beat his wife, despite having been warned by the court to refrain.

These and similar provisos appear to run counter to the law that, while a wife may be divorced against her will, a husband in granting his wife a bill of divorcement (*get*) must act without constraint. The Talmud resolves the problem by declaring that he is to be coerced by the court, including the application of force, until he says: "I *want* to divorce my wife." The Talmud speaks of instances in which "a man should divorce his wife" and those in which it declares "a man is compelled to divorce his wife." On the basis of this difference, in Israel (where there is no civil divorce), rabbinical courts have been reluctant to use coercion in cases of the former category, even where a marriage appears to have lost all *raison d'être*. Occasionally, however, such courts declare a husband who refuses to grant his wife a divorce, in compliance with the court's decision, in contempt of court. He is then handed over to the secular authorities who remand him to jail until such time as he consents to comply with the decision of the rabbinical court. Usually, a couple about to seek a divorce, prior to applying to the rabbinical court, draw up a legal agreement stipulating who shall have custody of the children, a property settlement, and an agreement of support. Failing this, these matters fall under the jurisdiction of the rabbinical court. In countries which do not recognize religious divorce, rabbis often insist on the couple obtaining a civil divorce before they grant a *get*.

A man may not divorce a wife who is mentally deranged. If her condition is incurable, a document signed by 100 rabbis can permit him to remarry.

The *get* (bill of divorcement) is drawn up by a scribe (*sofer*)

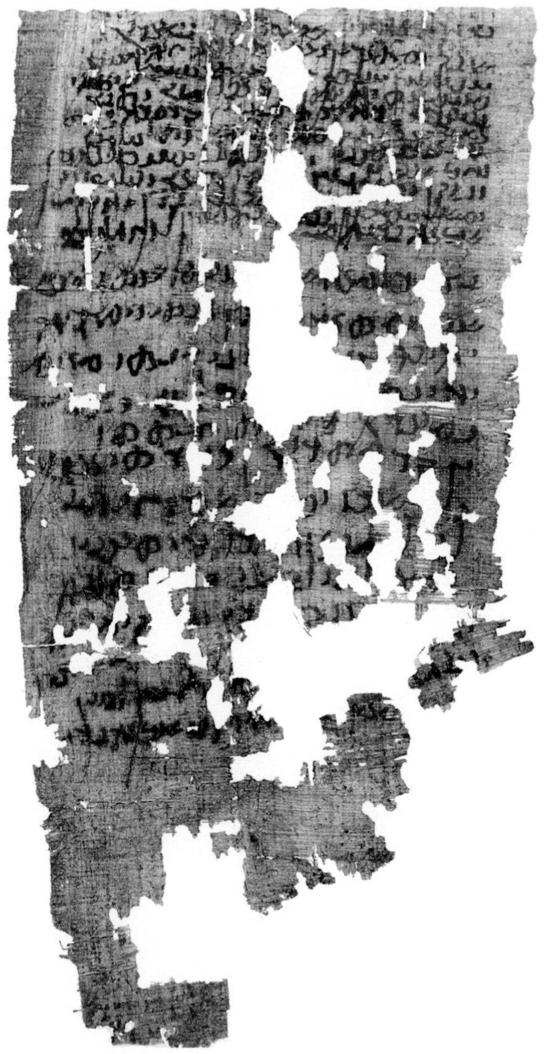

Bill of Divorce written in Aramaic on papyrus dated to 72 CE(?), found in a cave in the Judean Desert.

and follows a formula, part of which is found in the Mishnah. The document, written almost totally in Aramaic on parchment, must be witnessed and signed by two witnesses. The spelling and the form (12 lines) are enumerated in minute detail in halakhic literature. Once given to the wife, the *get* is retained by the rabbi who oversees the procedure. The latter cuts it in criss-cross fashion so that it cannot be used again. He then gives the wife a document (*petor*) attesting to the fact that she has been divorced and may remarry. The wife's remarriage is permitted only after 90 days. The purpose of the delay is to determine paternity in case she was pregnant at the time of her divorce.

A far-reaching enactment (TAKKANAH), promulgated by Rabbenu GERSHOM (approx. 960-1030), probably embodying what was already standard practice, effected a basic change in the law of divorce among ASHKENAZIM (also accepted in some SEPHARDI communities). The enactment provided that a husband may not divorce his wife without her consent. This made the rights of the wife nearly equal to those of the husband and henceforth divorce could only be by mutual consent. This enactment was further strengthened by later halakhists who declared that any writ of divorce issued in violation of the ruling was null and void. A century and a half later, R. Jacob TAM issued an ordinance decreeing that in certain emergencies the enactment requiring divorce by mutual consent could be set aside. An example of such an emergency would be if a woman apostasized and left the Jewish community, and was thus not amenable to a summons to appear before a Jewish court. In such case, the husband could deposit a *get* with the court.

Despite the very significant modifications undergone by the law of divorce over the centuries, certain problems remain. Since it is the husband who must give the *get* to his wife, a husband who cannot be located presents an insuperable problem. Similarly, outside Israel, rabbinic leaders have no authority to compel a husband to comply with their directives. In both instances, the wife remains an AGUNAH (a "tied" woman) and may not remarry in accordance with Jewish law. Halakhic authorities have wrestled with this problem for centuries and various solutions have been proposed.

This situation led to the adoption by the Rabbinical Assembly (Conservative) in 1953 of a *takkanah* proposed by Saul LIEBERMAN, calling for the insertion of a clause in the marriage contract (KETUBBAH) whereby both groom and bride, in case grave difficulties arise between them, agree to abide by the decision of the BET DIN (religious court) of the Conservative movement. In a test case before the Superior Court of the State of New York, the enforceability of the agreement was upheld. In cases where the husband is unavailable to appear before the *bet din*, the latter invokes the talmudic principle of retroactive annulment (*hafka'at kiddushin*), thereby obviating the necessity of a bill of divorcement. While the principle was invoked by the sages in a number of instances in the post-talmudic age, it was employed but rarely to dissolve a marriage and is currently not countenanced by Orthodox halakhic authorities. Reform Judaism has dropped the practice of the traditional bill of divorcement and accepts a civil divorce as sufficient for the purpose of remarriage.

The talmudic law of divorce is expounded in tractate GITTIN.

DÖNMEH See MESSIANIC MOVEMENTS; SHABBETAI TSEVI

DOV BAER OF MEZHIRECH (c.1710-1772). Leader of the main group of Ḥasidim after the death of Israel BA'AL SHEM TOV; organizer of the Ḥasidic movement and its principal theoretician (see ḤASIDISM). Dov Baer studied in his youth with the eminent talmudist, Jacob Joshua FALK, author of *Pené Yehoshu'a*. He served as the MAGGID (preacher) of Rovno and later of Mezhirech, Volhynia. In Ḥasidism he is known as "the Mezhirecher" or "the Great Maggid." It was only in his later years that Dov Baer came to know the Ba'al Shem Tov, whose life was already drawing to an end. Thus, for all the Ba'al Shem Tov's great influence on the Maggid, and despite the fact that Ḥasidim always refer to him as a disciple, Dov Baer was essentially an independent thinker within the movement, with his own interpretation of Ḥasidism. While the Maggid does quote the Ba'al Shem Tov, he never refers to him as his master nor does he ever mention his rival among the Ba'al Shem's disciples, JACOB JOSEPH OF POLONNOYE. There appears to have been a struggle for the succession when the Ba'al Shem Tov died; with few dissenting, however, the Maggid was accepted by the "holy company" as the Ba'al Shem Tov's legitimate successor. Dov Baer managed to create around him a circle of saintly disciples, a few of whom were, like LEVI YITSḤAK OF BERDICHEV and SHNEUR ZALMAN OF LYADY, learned rabbis. After the Maggid's death, his disciples also became Ḥasidic masters, each with his own following. Dov Baer can therefore be considered the real founder of Ḥasidism as a movement.

The Maggid left no writings of his own, but his doctrines are to be found in the works of his disciples, who frequently refer to his teachings. The most important collection of these was published in 1781 by Solomon of Lutsk, with the Maggid's approval. Solomon entitled it *Maggid Devarav le-Ya'akov* (cf. Psalm 147:19) and contributed an important introduction. In the Maggid's thought, the important thing for the Jew to know is that, in the language of the Zohar, "God fills all worlds and no space is unoccupied by Him." One must gaze beneath the cloak of the material world in order to perceive the Divine energy with which all things are infused. All human emotions have their Source on high: love, fear, and the other emotions should be traced back to their Source by dwelling on their origin, and in this way everything that happens to a man provides him with an opportunity of worshiping God. There is a strong element of asceticism in the Maggid's thought, although he never advocates protracted fasting or other physical mortifications. When a man gives up worldly pleasures, writes Dov Baer, he can really "serve God in truth."

The element of joy (SIMḤAH) in God's service is as essential to the Maggid's approach as to any other version of Ḥasidism. The philosopher Solomon Maimon (1753-1800) tells, in his autobiography, of a visit he paid to the "court" of the Maggid, where he found the Ḥasidim playing tricks on one another in the belief that this was conducive to the propagation of joy. Maimon also quotes a typical homily of the Maggid to the effect that, when a man regards himself solely as a musical instrument on which God plays, the spirit of the Lord will rest upon him. This suppression of man's ego — *bittul ha-yesh* or "the annihilation of selfhood" in the presence of God — is also an important element in the thought of the Maggid and his disciples.

APHORISMS OF DOV BAER OF MEZHIRECH

Man's energy and his soul are not his own. Even when he bestirs himself to worship God, it is God's doing — not his.

Overcoming one's pride demands a lifelong struggle.

Don't allow violent opposition to discourage you. Robbers hold up those owning precious jewels, not wagoners driving a load of manure, so be prepared to resist an attack!

What sin have I committed that I should be so popular?

A man should see to it that he spends time alone with God each day. Constant practice will make this second nature to him, and he will then have his mind on God even in the midst of a conversation.

Dov Baer's only son **Abraham** (1741-1776), known in Ḥasidic lore as *Ha-Malakh* ("the Angel"), followed and elaborated on his father's doctrines, but died young. Abraham's teachings, in the form of a Torah commentary, were published as a slender volume entitled *Ḥesed le-Avraham* (1851).

DOWRY The property, both movable and immovable, brought into a MARRIAGE by the bride. In Bible times, the custom was for the husband to pay a sum of money with which, in effect, he purchased his bride (Gen. 34:12). This payment of the *mohar* ("bride-price") is still to be found in the Arab world, and until recently it was also traditional among Jews of the Near East. However, the Bible also indicates circumstances in which the prospective husband must pay to get married, the relevant amount going to his future father-in-law. Thus, if a man had intercourse with an unmarried woman, he had to marry her and pay her father the bride-price involved (Ex. 22:15). From the context it would appear that the *mohar* was a penalty rather than a dowry payment. In other cases, the bride brought the dowry, as when Rebekah took maidservants on her journey to marry Isaac (Gen. 24:61).

By the talmudic period, it was customary for a bride to be endowed by her father, and a minimum sum was fixed. The term used for her marriage portion was *nadan* or *nedunyah* (*Ta'an.* 24a, *BM* 74b, etc.). Talmudic law mentions two distinct categories of property brought by the bride. The first, *Nikhsé tson barzel* (mortmain, lit. "the property of iron sheep"), comprises assets or property of which the husband has full use. He may invest these assets, and any gain is his, but he must recompense his wife for any loss.

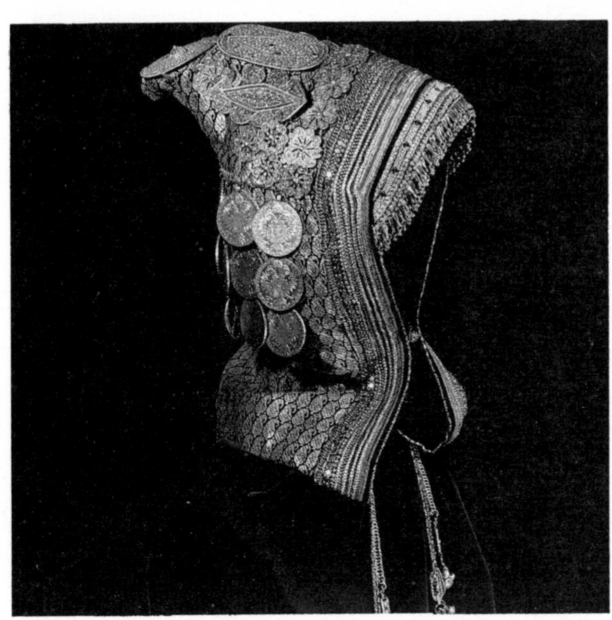

Head-covering with gold ornaments and coins worn by Yemenite brides which was part of their dowry ("bride-price").

Moreover, in the event of his divorcing her, the wife receives the full value of the property as calculated at the time of the wedding. The second type, *Nikhsé melog* (lit. "property which has been plucked"), comprises assets which remain in the wife's possession throughout, the husband being entitled to the usufruct, i.e., he may enjoy all the benefits accruing. In this case, he is not responsible for the property and any losses are absorbed by the wife. Israeli law decided against following these talmudic procedures, and the husband therefore has no rights concerning his wife's property.

The custom of "dowering the bride" was prevalent in Eastern Europe until modern times, and remains almost universal in the ultra-Orthodox community. The amount set aside by the bride's parents is often used to enable their new son-in-law to continue his studies in a *yeshivah* (talmudical academy) for a number of years. A form of dowry known in Yiddish as *kest* ("keep") provides for the bride's family to be responsible for the young couple's support while the husband remains at the *yeshivah*. Parents of the bride who cannot afford such a dowry often make application to various charitable societies and funds specifically created to help such young couples. "Dowering the bride" (HAKHNASAT KALLAH) was a permanent responsibility of Jewish communities down the ages. It was considered to be an especially meritorious good deed (*mitsvah*) and one of the highest precepts of Judaism (*Pe'ah* 1.1; *Shab.* 127a).

DREAMS The channel through which it was believed that revelations and prophetic insights were communicated from the supernatural world to man. Such experiences are frequently mentioned in the Bible as "visions" granted to chosen individuals or as words "spoken in a dream" (Gen. 15:1; Num. 22:20; Isa. 29:7; Job 33:14-16). True prophets mostly received their inspiration in this way, but Moses was the only one to whom God spoke face to face (Num. 12:6-8). While the seer could immediately grasp the message, kings and commoners who had a disturbing dream required the services of an expert interpreter. In ancient Egypt and Mesopotamia, therefore, special "dream books" were compiled for this purpose by trained experts. JOSEPH and DANIEL, the two outstanding biblical interpreters, regarded their ability as a gift from God (Gen. 41:16; Dan. 2:1-23).

Dreams in the Bible invariably point to future events, or they may serve as a warning (e.g., Gen. 20:3-7, 31:24; Num. 22:12,20). For the most part, they are symbolic and need to be interpreted; some notable examples are the dreams of Pharaoh's chief butler and chief baker (Gen. 40:5-19), of Pharaoh himself (Gen. 41:1-36), of the fearful Midianite (Judg. 7:13-15), and of Nebuchadnezzar (Dan. 2:1-45, 4:1-24). Only in rare instances, as with Jacob at Bethel (Gen. 28:12-16) or Joseph the young shepherd (Gen. 37:5-11), is the meaning obvious to the dreamer. A more skeptical attitude toward dreams becomes apparent in the later biblical books (Isa. 29:8, Job 20:8, Eccl. 5:6). From the Apocrypha it is clear that this view of dreams had become prevalent (Ecclus. 34.1-7) and that nightmares were regarded as a form of mental stress confounding the wicked (*Wisdom of Solomon* 17-18; Ecclus. 40.1-11).

In rabbinic sources there are often conflicting opinions about the significance of dreams. On the one hand, they were said to have no effect (*Git.* 52a; *Hor.* 13b), to reflect only the dreamer's own thoughts (*Ber.* 55b), and, of necessity to contain some nonsense (*Ber.* 55a). A more neutral view was that "a dream not interpreted is like an unread letter," never showing the impossible and always at least partially fulfilled (*Ber.* 55a-b). On the other hand, there were sages who took dreams very seriously. They maintained that if anyone heard a vow or ban of excommunication pronounced in a dream it had binding force and could be voided only by a quorum of ten (*Ned.* 8a). In particular, certain acts were prescribed to avert the possible effects of a bad dream. The Talmud also gave symbolic interpretations to a whole series of dream pictures: a well meant peace, a cockerel indicated the impending birth of a son, and entering a pool signified that the dreamer would head a rabbinical college; a white horse standing or galloping was a favorable omen, but a roan horse galloping was not; all animals dreamed about were a good sign, apart from an elephant, monkey, or porcupine (*Ber.* 56b-57b).

This trend continued throughout the Middle Ages, when the anonymous angel responsible for men's dreams (*Ber.* 10b) was personified as Gabriel in the ZOHAR. JACOB BEN ASHER proved exceptional when he warned against trusting in dreams or omens, and visiting fortune-tellers, because "such things reveal a lack of faith." Jacob ben Judah Ḥazzan of London, like ELEAZAR OF WORMS and many of the ḤASIDÉ ASHKENAZ, provided guidelines for the interpretation of dreams. Jacob Ha-Levi of Marvège, another 13th-century rabbi, even claimed that he was enabled to solve halakhic problems through the Divine revelations which came to him in dreams, and which he wrote down in a work entitled *She'elot u-Teshuvot min ha-Shamayim* ("Responsa from Heaven"). Three other halakhic authorities who made similar claims were MOSES BEN JACOB OF COUCY (*Semag*), MEIR (*Maharam*) OF ROTHENBURG, and ISAAC BEN MOSES OF VIENNA (*Or Zaru'a*).

MAIMONIDES devotes three chapters of his *Guide to the Perplexed* to an analysis of the relationship between dreams and prophecy (*Guide* 2.36-38). Elsewhere, he considers the practice of fasting after a bad dream to be an incentive for moral self-examination as well as psychologically therapeutic (*Yad, Ta'aniyyot* 1.12). In Jewish tradition, therefore, a skeptical or psychological approach to dreams has often given way to a mystical faith in their importance which gave rise to various SUPERSTITIONS. From rabbinic times, a number of techniques were prescribed to avert the possibly baleful effects of a nightmare. One might read certain biblical verses (e.g., Song 3:7-8), give to charity, or practice a ritual that transformed a frightening omen into a favorable one. Above all, however, an especially bad dream could be nullified by observing a private fast known as *ta'anit ḥalom* (Shab. 11a, *Ta'an.* 12b), even on a Sabbath, on Rosh ha-Shanah, or on the eve of the Day of Atonement. This was to ensure that the nightmare would not prey on the dreamer's mind, and the fast had to be observed within 24 hours. One lingering Ashkenazi custom, disfavored by many authorities but still followed by some Orthodox Jews, is the recitation of *Ribbono shel Olam* ("Master of the World"), a private prayer based on a formula in the Talmud (*Ber.* 55b). This is said twice in an undertone, when the *kohanim* prolong their chanting between clauses of the PRIESTLY BLESSING on festivals (but never on Sabbaths). Originally intended for anyone who had had an obscure or perplexing dream, it in time became a general supplication.

DUALISM The belief that there are two divine powers, one of which is good and the other evil. Zoroastrianism, the ancient religion of Persia, is based on this belief, and regards the entire universe as being marked by a constant struggle between the two. Another form of dualism was that propounded by GNOSTICISM. This held that the force creating evil, the "demiurge," is imperfect and is subservient to the greater, perfect deity. Judaism opposed dualism absolutely, as the prophet Isaiah (45:1,7) exclaims: "Thus says the Lord ... I form the light, and create darkness: I make weal and create darkness: I the Lord do all these things." The Talmud attacks those who believe in "two divine powers."

While certain dualistic notions seem to have crept into various Jewish mystical formulations, it is commonly acknowledged that the staunch and unequivocal refusal of various Jewish authorities, especially Maimonides, to brook any compromise with Judaism's strict monotheism prevented these works from deteriorating into dualism.

DUKHAN See PRIESTLY BLESSING

DURAN, SIMEON BEN TSEMAḤ (known by the acronym *Rashbats*; 1361-1444). Halakhic authority and philosopher. Born and raised in Majorca, Duran studied there under Ephraim Vidal and later under Jonah Desmaestre of Saragossa. He earned his livelihood as a physician and had acquired a knowledge of astronomy, mathematics, science, and philology. After the persecutions of 1391, Duran left Spain for Algiers, where he eventually succeeded Isaac bar Sheshet as rabbi. This post he accepted on condition that no government approval would be required, insisting that it was an internal Jewish matter and beyond the competence of secular authority. Opposing the view of Maimonides, he made it lawful for a rabbi to accept a salary so that he should be able to devote all his attention to communal affairs.

Duran wrote commentaries on several Mishnaic and talmudic tractates, also on Alfasi and the Passover *Haggadah*. His most famous work is the collection of his responsa (about 800) known as *Tashbets* (i.e., *Teshuvot Shimon ben Tsemaḥ*), many of which shed light on the condition of Spanish and North African Jewry at the time. The halakhic decisions in *Tashbets* were accepted as authoritative in North Africa. He worked hard to stem the decline in religious observance and was also one of the first to tackle the MARRANO problem.

Duran's chief philosophical work, *Magen Avot* ("Shield of the Fathers"), written as an introduction to tractate *Avot*, deals with theological concepts such as the nature of God, the eternity of the Torah, the coming of the Messiah, and the resurrection of the dead. He considered that Judaism has three dogmas only: the existence of God, the Torah's Divine origin, and reward and punishment; in this he was followed by Joseph ALBO. One section of *Magen Avot*, entitled *Keshet u-Magen* ("Bow and Shield"), is a polemic against Christianity and Islam. Duran also wrote a philosophical commentary on Job, novellae, and liturgical poems.

His three sons were also rabbinical authorities in Algiers. **Solomon ben Simeon Duran** (*Rashbash*; c.1400-1467) was the author of responsa and of *Milḥemet Mitsvah* ("Holy War"), a riposte to the anti-Jewish calumnies of a notorious apostate, Geronimo de Santa Fé (alias Joshua Lorki). Members of the Duran family were prominent religious and lay leaders in Algeria down to the early 19th century.

DYBBUK See DIBBUK

E

ECCLESIASTES, BOOK OF One of the Five Scrolls in the HAGIOGRAPHA section of the Bible. Ecclesiastes is read in the synagogue by Ashkenazi Jews on the Sabbath of Sukkot (or on SHEMINI ATSERET if there is no intermediate Sabbath). The Hebrew name of the book, *Kohelet*, is the name of the putative author mentioned in the first verse (traditionally mistranslated as "preacher").

The book, which has 12 chapters, has neither an organized structure, nor any logical progression of ideas. It is composed of between 15 to 20 units, each of which deals with a specific topic. It opens by depicting the monotonous cycle of nature. The book's motto is, "Vanity of vanities, all is vanity," a conclusion reached by observing nature, and from which it concludes that all are equal in death. Death wipes out all that man has achieved during his lifetime — wealth, wisdom, possessions, honor, pleasure, and labor. This being the case, *Kohelet* advises that one enjoy life to the extent possible. The book ends as it began, reflecting on the life cycle of man from youth to old age.

By tradition, the author is identified with King SOLOMON (Song R. 1:1). The author describes himself as having been king in Jerusalem (1:12), and the book begins with (1:1), "The words of Kohelet the son of David, king in Jerusalem." The editing of the work was later; according to *BB* 14a, "(King) Hezekiah and his cohorts wrote Ecclesiastes."

Opening page of the Book of Ecclesiastes. From the Duke of Sussex Pentateuch. Germany, 14th century.

BOOK OF ECCLESIASTES

1:1 — 3:15	All is vanity — life, wisdom and earthly pleasures
3:16 — 3:21	Man and the animals have the same fate
4:1 — 4:16	Man labors in vain
5:1 — 6:12	Man's wealth is meaningless
7:1 — 7:29	Various wise sayings
8:1 — 9:16	The righteous and the wicked share the same fate
9:17 — 10:20	Various wise sayings
11:1 — 11:8	The uncertainty of man's labors
11:9 — 12:8	The joy at birth, the weakness of old age
12:9 — 12:14	Conclusion

The pessimistic character of the book, as opposed to the Song of Songs (which is also attributed to Solomon), is explained, according to the Midrash, by the fact that Solomon wrote Ecclesiastes in his old age, while the Song of Songs was written in his youth (Song R. 1:1:10).

Many scholars regard this collection of words of wisdom without structure or plan as having been influenced by the ancient Near Eastern Wisdom Literature, particularly the Egyptian and Babylonian. Scholars date it to the late third century BCE.

In terms of language, the book represents a transitional stage between biblical Hebrew and the language of the sages. It has characteristics of the language of the MISHNAH as well as many ARAMAIC principles.

Among the sages, there was a dispute as to whether or not to include the book in the canon. In the Mishnah (*Yadayim* 3:5), the view of the School of Hillel that the book is holy and should therefore be included in the canon prevailed. Ben Sira, who composed his book (*Ecclesiasticus*) in the years 190-180 BCE, mentions Ecclesiastes as part of the Bible.

ECCLESIASTES RABBAH Homiletical Midrash on the Book of ECCLESIASTES, known in Hebrew as *Kohelet Rabbah* (see also MIDRASH AGGADAH). It is divided into four sections, according to the ancient Scriptural division, and portions may also be found in RUTH RABBAH. The editor's rabbinic sources included the Jerusalem Talmud and other early Palestinian works; he also utilized some Minor Tractates of the Talmud, a fact pointing to the geonic era (seventh-ninth centuries) as the time when Ecclesiastes Rabbah was redacted. It follows the biblical text, verse by verse, the editor borrowing proems from older Midrashim such as GENESIS RABBAH, LEVITICUS RABBAH, PESIKTA DE-RAV KAHANA, and SONG OF SONGS RABBAH.

In its homiletical exposition of the biblical text, this Midrash transforms the gratification of the senses, which Kohelet espoused, into religious ALLEGORY. Hence the declaration that "wherever eating and drinking are spoken of in this way [approvingly], the pleasures referred to are the study of Torah and the performance of good deeds." On the verse, "I searched in my heart how to pamper my flesh with wine..." (Eccl. 2:3), the Midrash likewise gives the allegorical sense: "to pamper my flesh with the wine of Torah, while my heart conducted itself with Torah wisdom." Similarly, the constant pessimistic statements of Ecclesiastes are elevated to religious optimism, as the following illustration shows. "What profit does a man have," asks Kohelet, "from all his labor under the sun?" (1:3). The Midrash, in the name of R. Judan, observes that "under the sun he has no profit, but above the sun [in the world to come] he does have."

ECCLESIASTICUS See APOCRYPHA

EDELS, SAMUEL ELIEZER BEN JUDAH HA-LEVI (known by the acronym *Maharsha*; 1555-1631). Talmudical scholar. Born in Cracow, where he studied under his father, Edels married the daughter of R. Moses Ashkenazi of Posen. There, for 20 years, he headed a *yeshivah* which his mother-in-law Edel maintained at her own expense. It was in gratitude to her that he adopted the surname Edels; after her death, he held rabbinical positions in Chelm, Lublin, and Ostrog.

An outstanding talmudist and a master of dialectics, Edels taught and influenced hundreds of students in Poland. His expositions, which display keen logical analysis and ingenuity, are incorporated in *Ḫiddushé Halakhot*, novellae on most talmudic tractates, and are printed in nearly all editions of the Talmud. He applies to his novellae the method employed by the Tosafists themselves: he tests the truth of statements by RASHI and TOSAFOT, raising objections to them and then refuting these objections by a deeper interpretation of the meaning of the statements. Occasionally, however, Edels is content simply to explain the difficult passages of the Gemara, Rashi, and *Tosafot*. In another work, *Ḫiddushé Aggadot*, he attempts to give a rational interpretation of the talmudic *aggadot*, sometimes understanding them as parables.

Edels had a thorough knowledge of the Jewish philosophers, was familiar with kabbalistic literature, and had delved into astronomy. He attacked the misuse of rabbinic authority and the attempt made by wealthy individuals to monopolize communal office. He took part in the session of the Council of the Four Lands which, in 1590, imposed a ban on those who used their money to acquire positions in the rabbinate. His other major work, *Zikhron Devarim* ("Recollection of Words"), contains novellae by scholars of Posen.

EDEN, GARDEN OF (*gan eden*). The garden where, according to Genesis 2, God placed ADAM immediately after creating him. Eden contained "every tree that is pleasant to the sight, and good for food," as well as "the TREE OF LIFE" and "the tree of knowledge of good and evil." From Eden sprang forth a river dividing into four branches: Pishon, Gihon, the Tigris, and the Euphrates. After Adam and Eve ate from the "tree of knowledge," they were banned from Eden, so they would not eat from the "tree of life" and live eternally. Angels with flaming swords barred their return.

The word Eden is either derived from the Hebrew root meaning "to be fruitful, plentiful," or from the Sumerian word meaning "steppe, flatland." Many scholars believe that in the light of the geographical information in Genesis 2:10-14, Eden is located near the Persian Gulf, possibly in Bahrain.

Throughout Jewish literature, Eden is considered to be the paradigm of perfection. Thus Ezekiel writes of "Eden, the garden of God," with every type of precious stone within it (Ezek. 28:13), and of the wondrous trees growing within the garden (Ezek. 31:8-10). Eden is also used to describe the reclamation of the land which had been laid waste, and which will eventually become like the Garden of Eden (Ezek. 36:35). Later rabbinic literature distinguishes between two different Gardens of Eden: the earthly one below and the heavenly one above. The heavenly Garden of Eden is Paradise ("paradise" is derived from the Greek word for garden). Thus *Avot* 5:20 says, "The brazen is doomed to Gehinnom while the modest will go to the Garden of Eden." The heavenly Garden of Eden is described in the most lyrical terms in YALKUT SHIMONI on Genesis as a place where four rivers flow: of milk, wine, balsam, and honey. In it 800,000 kinds of trees grow, the least of which is more fragrant than any tree found on earth. In each corner stand 600,000 angels singing praise of God in the sweetest of voices. God Himself sits in the Garden of Eden, explaining the Torah to the righteous of all the ages.

EDUCATION In a verse which has become part of the first paragraph of the SHEMA, recited in the daily morning and evening prayers, the Bible commands "You shall teach them diligently to your children" (Deut. 6:7) referring to the biblical laws. There are four references in the Bible to the father's responsibility to tell his children about the EXODUS from Egypt (Ex. 10:2; 13:8,14; Deut. 6:20-21). Indeed, in biblical times it was the father's duty to provide instruction, both in religious ritual and in practical training, to his children. To a large extent, this was undoubtedly informal. The Bible also assigns to the LEVITES the task of teaching the people: "They shall teach your laws to Jacob, and your instruction to Israel" (Deut. 33:10), but there is no indication as to what form this instruction took. From its earliest history Judaism has considered the study of TORAH of cardinal importance. Thus at the beginning of the Book of Joshua it says, "Let not this Book of the Teaching cease from your lips, but recite it day and night" (1:8). The Book of Proverbs contains various references to the way a child should be educated: "He that spares his rod hates his son" (13:24); "Train a child in the way he should go: and when he is old, he will not depart from it" (22:6). After the return from the Babylonian Exile, EZRA gathered the people together and read and expounded the Torah before them (Neh. 8). According to rabbinic tradition, it was Ezra who instituted the Bible reading every Monday and Thursday morning, on the days when people came to the local markets.

The MISHNAH provides a systematic directive by R. Judah ben Tema related to education: "Five years old [is the age] for [the study of] Bible, ten years old for the Mishnah, thirteen for [the obligation to keep] the commandments, fifteen years old for GEMARA" (*Avot* 5:25). Jewish law requires the parents to begin the child's religious education at the earliest possible age, and declares that as soon as a child begins to speak, he must be taught the verse, "Moses charged us with the Teaching as the heritage of the congregation of Jacob" (Deut. 33:4).

The Mishnah stresses the paramount importance of Torah study, when it lists various commandments, including honoring one's parents, charity, and bringing peace between individuals, and then concludes, "but the study of Torah is equivalent to them all" (*Pe'ah* 1:1, amplified in *Shab.* 127a). It was SIMEON BEN SHETAH̲ (first century BCE) who first established schools, and compelled parents to send their sons to them. Nevertheless, the person most credited with forging an educational system was R. Joshua ben Gamla (first century CE), who had been High Priest before the Temple was destroyed. He arranged for teachers to be appointed in every town, and the Talmud says of him: "May R. Joshua ben Gamla be remembered for the good, for had it not been for him, the Torah would have been forgotten from Israel" (*BB* 21a). Prior to R. Joshua ben Gamla's edict, the Talmud notes, those with fathers were taught by their fathers, while those without fathers received no instruction. Through this

A teacher and his pupils. Illustration from Tur Orah H̲ayyim *("The Path of Life") by Jacob ben Asher. Italy, 1497.*

edict, teachers had to be engaged in each community at the community's expense, and all children had to be given an education. The Talmud lays down the rules of class size. One teacher may handle up to 25 students. If there are between 25 and 40 students, an assistant must be hired to work alongside the teacher. More than 40 students require the hiring of two teachers.

Although it does not include any systematic program of education, the Talmud contains assorted aphorisms that convey a picture of education both as it was then and as it was envisioned in ideal terms. Emphasis is placed on the importance of a father teaching his son a gainful occupation, and "one who does not teach his son an occupation, (by default) teaches him to be a brigand" (*Kid.* 29a). In fact, among the various duties imposed on the father in regard to his son is the obligation to teach him the Torah, an occupation, and, according to some, to swim (*ibid.*).

The Talmud itself indicates that various sages were proficient in different fields, including the sciences of their day. Astronomy, for example, was indispensable for establishing the calendar of festivals, and the Talmud states that those who have the ability are obliged to study astronomy (*Shab.* 75a).

In Babylon, there were ACADEMIES where prominent scholars lectured but these were not aimed at the masses, and the subject matter was often beyond the ability of the common man. However, twice a year, during the months of Adar and Elul, special study sessions, known as *kallah*, were held in the study halls (see KALLAH MONTHS). The lectures given were deliberately geared for this lay audience.

It is likely that in the period between the completion of the Talmud (ca. 500 CE) and the EMANCIPATION of the Jews in modern times, the majority of male Jews received some sort of schooling, and most were literate. The studies themselves were generally limited to the sacred books. There were eras, however, when education also included secular studies.

This was, for example, the case among the Spanish Jews in the 12th and 13th centuries, who showed a much greater openness to the outside world. Thus, Joseph Ibn Aknin (1150-1220), who was born in Spain but later fled to Fez, Morocco, and who authored the work *Mevo ha-Talmud*, an introduction to the study of the Talmud, felt no contradiction between the necessity of studying the sacred works and his prescription that education should include the study of logic, rhetoric, arithmetic, geometry, astronomy, music, the sciences, and metaphysics. However, as the Jews came under growing persecution, the study of secular subjects was curtailed, and in many cases totally abolished.

The typical model of the educational structure immediately prior to the emancipation of the Jews (which occurred from the beginning of the 19th century onwards), was one of a single teacher with a number of students, with the subject matter being entirely religious. This was often known as the ḤEDER (Yid. and Heb. word for a room). This model was present almost universally, in both Ashkenazi and Sephardi communities. They were not schools in the modern sense, although a student might graduate from one teacher to another as he progressed in his studies. In certain communities there was an organized TALMUD TORAH, which had various classes, but here too the studies were largely or exclusively religious. Sometimes some secular subjects, such as mathematics and history, would be introduced, primarily to help in the understanding of the religious subjects. Most of the students would have a few years of schooling, but would then enter the labor market at a young age. Very few would have a really intensive education for a considerable number of years.

The 19th century was marked by the growth of organized *yeshivot* (talmudical colleges), primarily in Eastern Europe. Great talmudic study centers emerged, such as Tels, Ponevezh, and Slobodka, as well as different Ḥasidic centers. In these *yeshivot* there were official levels, with students progressing from one class to another. The *yeshivot* generally took students in their teens, and the better students might go on to a lifetime of Torah study. The subject matter was almost exclusively Talmud and *halakhah*, with students expected to learn the Bible and other sacred studies on their own. Secular studies were considered anathema.

With the Emancipation, Jews began once more to explore other fields of study: languages, mathematics, and the various sciences. This was the beginning of the HASKALAH ("Enlightenment") movement. At the outset, such studies were often carried out surreptitiously, especially in Eastern Europe, where some secular studies were regarded as heretical. In Western Europe, on the other hand, models began to develop of schools which combined both religious and secular studies. In the 19th century, R. Samson Raphael HIRSCH, of Frankfurt on Main, formulated the principles of *Torah im Derekh Erets*, a strong religious curriculum with secular studies, the basis for much of Jewish education to this day. The East European *yeshivot* also broadened their curriculum to study ethics under the influence of the MUSAR MOVEMENT. A pioneering role in the Muslim world was played by the French organization, *Alliance Isráelite Francaise*, which opened schools in North Africa and the Middle East in which the language of teaching was French and the pupils studied secular as well as religious subjects.

Once Jews were permitted to enter public schools and began doing so in increasing numbers, there was a need for Jewish education in addition to the secular studies offered during the school day. This supplementary education, which was generally known as *ḥeder* or *talmud torah* education, was in most instances offered under religious auspices, and was generally held on Sundays or in the afternoons, after public school. The hours might be as few as two per week or as many as 12. To a large extent, this was the model in Western Europe and in the English-speaking world during the first half of the 20th century. In certain areas, where the community felt that this education was insufficient, full-day schools were set up, where students would receive a full religious studies education, as well as instruction according to the State curriculum.

After World War II, the realization grew that supplementary education was not sufficient, and there was a tremendous growth in the day schools. Thus in the United States the number of day schools in the Orthodox *Torah U-Mesorah* day school network grew from under 100 schools immediately after the war, to approximately 600 schools today. The day school movement, at first an almost exclusively Orthodox domain, later embraced the Conservative Movement, with its Solomon Schechter schools. Even the Reform Movement, which formerly rejected the day school as serving to separate Jews from their fellow citizens, now sponsors day schools under its own auspices. In other countries, day schools have developed under the auspices of the Zionist movement, with a strong emphasis on the study of Modern Hebrew. A number of day schools were established in Yiddish circles; however, most of these schools have either closed down or merged with others. With the growth of the day school movement, there was a decline in the enrollment and vitality of the supplementary schools. As the day schools are generally able to offer a far superior Jewish education to that of even high-level supplementary schools, this development is generally regarded as a favorable one by Jewish educators.

The emancipation marked the development of new models of schools for higher Jewish studies (see RABBINICAL SEMINARIES), which sought to examine Judaism and Jewish practice with a modern approach. In the United States, the Reform and Conservative rabbinical seminaries, the Hebrew Union College and the Jewish Theological Seminary, founded in the last quarter of the 19th century, were modeled after their German predecessors in Berlin and Breslau. Orthodoxy, too, made changes, the most far-reaching being the founding of New York's Yeshiva University where a *yeshivah* curriculum was combined with a Liberal Arts education. These seminaries eventually developed graduate schools in all fields of Judaic Studies: Jewish Education, Jewish Communal Service, Sacred Music (Cantorial Studies), Biblical Archeology, and Ancient Near-Eastern Languages and Literature. Over the past century these seminaries have provided the American Jewish community not only with most of its rabbinic and cantorial leadership, but also with its cadre of trained community professionals.

Until as late as the 20th century, Jewish education was largely limited to the education of Jewish males. From the earliest times, women's education had been regarded as different from that of men, and R. Eliezer stated, "He who teaches his daughter Torah teaches her lewdness" (*Sot.* 3:4). While such extremism was not really representative, it guided normative *halakhah* for centuries, and resulted in women being taught only those laws of the Torah that pertained to them. The statement was interpreted to mean that women might be taught the Bible, but not the Oral Law. The Reform Movement, from its outset, rejected any differentiation in regard to sex.

In 1917, Sarah Schnirer, encouraged by leading Orthodox rabbis, started the Beth Jacob (*Beis Yakov*) Orthodox school system, which offered women an official educational framework, though these schools scrupulously refused to teach girls the Mishnah or Talmud. The Stern College for Women of Yeshiva University does offer intensive talmudic study for women, as do a number of Orthodox day schools. The Reform and Conservative theological seminaries both now ordain women as a matter of course.

A large-scale growth has occurred in classical *yeshivot* for post-high school students, especially in Israel and the United States. A relatively recent phenomenon is that of a large percentage of *yeshivah* graduates spending a number of years after their marriage studying in KOLELS, where they are supported by modest stipends, and often by the employment of their wives. Since World War II, there has been a remarkable growth of Judaic Studies departments in various universities throughout the world, where thousands of students, Jewish and non-Jewish, are able to take courses in Hebrew and in various other branches of Judaic Studies.

EDUYYOT ("Testimonies"). Seventh tractate of Order NEZIKIN in the MISHNAH. Unlike most other tractates, *Eduyyot* contains a great variety of laws on different subjects. The subjects include menstruation, the priest's share of the dough, the *mikveh* (ritual bath), the purity of the Levite, priestly dues, tithes, and marriage. Its title hints at the purpose of the collection, namely to record the "testimonies" of the later sages on the halakhic opinions of earlier authorities. Its eight chapters mention 30 laws in which the School of Hillel uncharacteristically adopts a stricter opinion than the School of Shammai (see BET SHAMMAI AND BET HILLEL). The fourth *mishnah* of the first chapter tells the purpose of recording opinions which are not adopted: "Why do they mention the words of Shammai and Hillel to no purpose? To teach the future generations that a man should not (stubbornly) stand on his opinions, for behold, the great teachers did not stubbornly maintain their opinions." The subject matter is amplified only in the *Tosefta*.

EGER, AKIVA BEN MOSES (1761-1837). Rabbinic authority. Known also as Akiva Gins. Eger was born in Eisenstadt. He studied at Breslau and Lissa.

In 1791, he moved to Märkisch-Friedland in Prussia where he became rabbi. Seven years later, Eger accepted the Chief Rabbinate of Posen, where he founded a noted *yeshivah* (rabbinical academy).

In 1818, he joined the battle against the REFORM MOVEMENT whose spiritual birthplace was Hamburg. He was a signatory to the statement entitled *Eleh Divré ha-Berit* ("These are the words of the Covenant"), published as a warning against those who sought to "modernize" Judaism by the abrogation of certain fundamental commandments.

Eger assisted those who were trying to popularize a knowledge of traditional Judaism through the use of German, and to meet government regulations, he allowed two hours a day of secular education in Jewish schools.

Eger wrote glosses to the Mishnah; short marginal notes to the Babylonian Talmud, entitled *Gilyon ha-Shas*, which had the distinction of being incorporated in the Vilna edition of the Talmud; novellae (*hiddushim*) to all four parts of the *Shulhan Arukh*; and responsa which reveal the problems of the time, while showing their author's humanity.

EHAD MI YODE'A ("Who knows One?"). Popular "table song" of unknown authorship, dating from the 15th century, which Ashkenazim chant near the end of the SEDER ritual on Passover eve. The song is in Hebrew, but a number of Aramaic words are included for the sake of the rhyme. Comprising brief questions and answers that explain the significance of numbers 1-13 in Jewish tradition, this song pro-

Detail from the page on which appears Ehad mi Yode'a. *From the* Vienna Haggadah, *Austria, 1752.*

gressively lengthens until the final (13th) stanza incorporates all of the preceding replies. It was probably designed as a response to the talmudic injunction that young children be encouraged to stay awake and ask questions throughout the *Seder* night (*Pes.* 109a). First included in Ashkenazi *Haggadot* of the 16th century, "Who knows One?" apparently derives from an old German song which monastic circles adapted to their own religious needs. The German-speaking Jews who borrowed it changed the wording, but retained "One is our God in heaven and on earth" as the *Eḫad Mi Yode'a* refrain. Similar compositions were written in other European lands throughout the Middle Ages, but all of the non-Jewish ditties end at 12, Christians holding 13 to be an "unlucky number." As a festive song for occasions other than Passover, *Eḫad Mi Yode'a* was later adopted by other Jewish communities (Avignon and even as far afield as India).

EḪAD MI YODE'A — WHO KNOWS ONE?
(last stanza)

Who knows Thirteen? I know Thirteen!
Thirteen are the attributes of God;
Twelve are the tribes of Israel;
Eleven are the stars [that Joseph saw in his dream];
Ten are the Commandments;
Nine are the months of pregnancy;
Eight are the days for circumcision;
Seven are the days of the week;
Six are the Orders of the Mishnah;
Five are the books of the Torah;
Four are the Matriarch mothers of Israel;
Three are the Patriarch fathers;
Two are the Tablets of the Law;
One is our God in heaven and on earth!

EINHORN, DAVID (1809-1879). American Reform rabbi. Born in Bavaria, Einhorn was one of the first German rabbis to supplement his *yeshivah* studies with university training. Early in life he espoused a radical Reform position, and in consequence found difficulty in obtaining a position in Germany. In 1852 he was appointed rabbi of the newly opened Liberal synagogue in Budapest, but shortly afterward this was closed by government order. Einhorn moved to the USA in 1855, becoming rabbi of the Har Sinai Congregation in Baltimore. Einhorn's vigorous support of the antislavery viewpoint compelled him to flee Baltimore in 1861. He served in Philadelphia until 1866, when he became rabbi of Adath Israel (later, Temple Beth El), New York.

Einhorn was embroiled in controversy from the moment of his arrival in America. A Reform rabbinical conference, meeting in Cleveland, endorsed a platform which required Biblical law to be expounded and practiced in accordance with the interpretation of the Talmud. Einhorn felt this formula betrayed Reform. In his view the "imperishable spirit" of Judaism was "the doctrinal and moral law of Scripture ...All other divine ordinances are only signs of the Covenant" which could not be dispensed with but must necessarily change with the times. Einhorn formulated his views liturgically in the prayer-book *Olat Tamid* (1856). Developing a following among the Reform rabbis on the eastern seaboard (as opposed to the mid-west base of Isaac Mayer WISE with whom he was in constant conflict), Einhorn was the moving spirit at the 1869 conference of Reform rabbis, held in Philadelphia. He was a thinker, not a builder, and his theological expositions were of little interest to the laity. Moreover, he remained an exile from Germany: he wrote and preached in German, and his farewell sermon contained a plea for the retention of German in American Reform Judaism.

In understanding the needs of American Jewish life he was far outshone by the untutored, energetic Isaac Mayer Wise. However, Einhorn's viewpoint became influential after his death. The Pittsburgh Platform (1885) was largely the work of Einhorn's son-in-law and disciple, Kaufman KOHLER, while the *Union Prayer Book* 1892, issued by the Central Conference of American Rabbis, drew largely on *Olat Tamid*.

EISENDRATH, MAURICE NATHAN (1902-1973). Rabbi and leader of American Reform Judaism. Born in Chicago, Eisendrath was educated at the University of Cincinnati and Hebrew Union College. From 1929 to 1943 he was rabbi of Holy Blossom Congregation, Toronto.

In 1943, Eisendrath returned to Cincinnati as director (later president) of the Union of American Hebrew Congregations, at a time when many of its supporters felt it to be unresponsive to recent developments in American Jewish life. Eisendrath quickly transformed the organization and transferred its headquarters from Cincinnati to New York.

At the same time, the Union began to articulate the viewpoint of REFORM JUDAISM in a number of matters outside the conventional range of synagogue activities. Eisendrath took a prominent part in the controversies surrounding the formation of an American Jewish Conference, support for the State of Israel, and later social action. The misgivings of the more conservative laity, who had previously dominated the Union, became vocal when he established a Social Action Center in Washington, which they feared would turn into a political lobbying organization.

In effect, Eisendrath was attuned to the outlook of a new generation of Reform Jews. East European Jews who did not share the anti-traditional bias of an earlier generation had begun to take part in the movement in the inter-war years. The Columbus Platform of 1937 had given recognition to their religious outlook; the Zionist movement and events in

Europe had deepened their sense of peoplehood; and the post-war mood encouraged the interest of institutional religion in social betterment. Eisendrath guided the movement in these directions and in shaping this phase of Reform Judaism Eisendrath was able both to take advantage of a strain prominent in the outlook of Isaac Mayer WISE and to leave his own stamp on the movement.

EL See GOD, NAMES OF

EL ADON ("God, the Lord [over all works]"). Alphabetical "Hymn of Creation" recited among the benedictions preceding the SHEMA in the Sabbath Morning Service. Probably composed in the geonic era (eighth-ninth centuries), it expands and replaces a briefer alphabetical poem entitled *El Barukh Gedol De'ah* ("The blessed God, great in knowledge") which is read at this point on weekdays. Metrical, but unrhymed, *El Adon* comprises 22 phrases of varying length; these give praise to God for creating the sun, moon, and planets, using imagery drawn from the Book of Ezekiel. As the Architect of universal harmony, exalted above the angelic host, God is portrayed fashioning the stars "with knowledge, insight, and discernment," endowing them with brightness and power to function only as He wishes. There are minor variations in the text, particularly between the Ashkenazi prayer book and its Sephardi, Oriental, and Ḥasidic counterparts.

ELDERS (*zekenim*). In biblical society, persons who acquired a special status of authority as a result of their age, wisdom, and social position. A relationship between eldership and leadership was recognized at a very early stage in Israel's history (Ex. 3:16). The first significant mention of elders is in Numbers (11:16,24) where God instructs Moses to gather 70 men already known as the elders of the people and its officers, who were to experience the Divine Presence, receive His inspiration, and share the responsibility of leadership with Moses. The concept of elders existed not only among the People of Israel but among their neighbors as well (Num. 22:7).

The Bible also refers to the "elders of the city" in connection with five laws appearing in Deuteronomy: blood redemption (Deut. 19:12), expiation of murder by an unknown assailant (Deut. 21:1-9), the rebellious son (*ibid.* 18-21), the defamation of a virgin (Deut. 22:13-21), and levirate marriage (Deut. 25:5-10). The apparent common denominator of all these laws is the proprietary involvement of the elders of the city in the interests of the family, clan, and community. The function of elder is distinguished in Deuteronomy from that of judge, who acts in cases of litigation and criminal prosecution (see, e.g., Deut. 17:8ff.; 19:17-18; 25:1-3). The Bible recognizes elders of the entire people, men whose communal function continued even after the establishment of the monarchy (II Sam. 3:17; 5:3; 17:4,15; I Kings 20:7). The Mishnah (*Avot* intro.) asserts that in the biblical period the elders (presumably of the entire people) were responsible for the continuity of religious tradition after the death of Joshua and that they ultimately passed this responsibility onto the prophets.

In the talmudic period, the title "elder" became identified with scholarship, the Talmud claiming the Hebrew *zaken* to be an acronym of the Hebrew words, "he has acquired wisdom" (*Kid.* 32b). The Talmud discusses the case of the ZAKEN MAMREH, the scholar who rules or acts in defiance of a final decision of the Great SANHEDRIN (see Deut. 17:8-12; *San.* 11:2) who, under certain circumstances might even incur the death penalty.

After the talmudic period, the title "elder" appears as both a communal leader and a scholar. From the middle of the 18th century, however, it disappears almost completely. On the other hand, modern anti-Semites have used the term in evoking the image of an aging Jewish leadership plotting political control of the entire planet, notably in the notorious late 19th century forgery, the "Protocols of the Learned Elders of Zion" (see ANTI-SEMITISM).

ELEAZAR BEN JUDAH BEN KALONYMUS OF WORMS (known as Eleazar Roke'aḥ; c.1165-c.1230). Kabbalist, halakhic scholar, and religious poet. The most prominent writer and chief spokesman of the ḤASIDÉ ASHKENAZ and the best-known disciple of its leader JUDAH HE-ḤASID. He and his family were victims of the Crusaders, probably during the third Crusade, when his wife and daughters were killed, and his son was wounded, dying some time later. Rabbi Eleazar described the persecutions and his family's tragedy in a memoir, and dedicated a poem to his wife and daughters. In the preface to his *Sefer ha-Ḥokhmah* ("The Book of Wisdom"), written in 1217, he describes his loneliness after the death of his teacher Judah he-Ḥasid in that year, when he was left without children, without a teacher, and he felt that the long line of his family as well as of the secret tradition which he inherited, were coming to an end.

Eleazar's works include a major halakhic treatise, the book *Roke'aḥ*, to which he added at its beginning two chapters dealing with ethics — one on the "Ways of Ḥasidism" and one on repentance. These chapters became very popular, and were copied and printed as separate treatises. Eleazar's major work, however, was his detailed commentary on the prayers, the first from the Middle Ages. Eleazar probably wrote it several times; three versions have survived in three manuscripts, and the differences between them seem to be the result of the author's own editing and adding to his work. The commentary includes many sections which deal with the theological meaning and the mystical significance of the prayers.

Rabbi Eleazar's major work in mysticism was *Sodé Razayya* ("The Secrets of Secrets"), written after his teacher's death and summarizing the esoteric traditions of the *Ḥasidé Ashkenaz*. It includes five treatises: *Sod Ma'aseh Bereshit* ("The Secret of Genesis"), *Sod ha-Merkavah* ("The Secret of the Chariot"), *Sefer ha-Shem* ("The Book of the Holy Name"), *Ḥokhmat ha-Nefesh* ("Psychology"), and the commentary on *Sefer* YETSIRAH. Eleazar made use of Judah he-Ḥasid's works in these treatises, copying and paraphrasing his teacher's ideas. He was strongly influenced by alphabetical and numerological speculation, contemplation of the Divine Names, the mysteries of the Divine Chariot, and other kabbalistic themes. Eleazar held that the Divine light or glory (Heb. *kavod*) once revealed to the prophets can still become visible to chosen mystics, thus bridging the void between God's transcendence in the realms above and mortal man here below. To attain this vision, one must continually seek God through a life of piety (*Ḥasidut*) demanding saintliness and humility, prayerful devotion and contemplation, altruism, religious example, and love of fellowman. According to Eleazar, the formulation of each blessing enables man to approach God as an intimate friend, while "no monument sheds such glory as an untarnished name." Many kabbalists in subsequent generations made use of Eleazar's works, and he was regarded by many of them as a sage, possessor of mystical secrets and powers.

ELECTION See CHOSEN PEOPLE

ELIEZER BEN HYRCANUS (c.40-c.120 CE). *Tanna* of the second generation, also known as R. Eliezer the Great, the outstanding pupil of JOHANAN BEN ZAKKAI (whom he helped to smuggle out of Jerusalem during the Roman siege). Because of his phenomenally retentive memory, R. Johanan compared him to "a plastered cistern that never loses a drop" and declared that this scholar outweighed all the other sages put together (*Avot* 2.8). Over 300 *halakhot* of his are recorded in the Mishnah and an equal number in the *Tosefta* and the *baraitot*. After the destruction of the Second Temple, R. Eliezer was among the sages who transferred their activities to the new Academy of Yavneh, but established one of his own in Lydda (Lod; see ACADEMIES). His wife, Imma Shalom, was the sister of the patriarch GAMALIEL II (Rabban Gamliel); and it was in an effort to alleviate the position of their community that these two great scholars led a delegation to Rome (c.95 CE).

Unyielding and conservative in his opinions, R. Eliezer tended to interpret Scripture with extreme literalness. Unlike all of his colleagues, for example, he insisted that biblical "eye for an eye" retribution (Ex. 21:23-24) (see RETALIATION) should be taken literally. This tendency brought him into sharp conflict with other sages, including his pupil R. AKIVA, who favored a broader view of the law. When the conflict led Eliezer to defy the unanimous opinion of his colleagues, who even ignored a *bat kol* (heavenly voice) in this particular issue, he was subjected to a partial ban of EXCOMMUNICATION (*BM* 59b). They dubbed him a *Shammuti*, one who obstinately followed the view of Shammai's school, even though the *halakhah* had been established in accordance with the opposing view of Hillel's disciples (see BET SHAMMAI AND BET HILLEL). Various midrashic works, notably the PIRKÉ DE-RABBI ELIEZER, are attributed to him. Despite the ban, R. Eliezer was universally esteemed. After his death, the ban was revoked and the sages mourned his passing.

APHORISMS OF ELIEZER BEN HYRCANUS

Great is work, for even Adam tasted nothing until he had labored to produce it (cf. Gen. 2:15).

One who brings no children into the world is like a murderer.

If two men appear in court before you, one wicked and the other pious, do not prejudice your decision against the wicked one.

Cherish your colleague's honor as your own; do not be easily provoked to anger; repent one day before your death [i.e., every day].

When you pray, know before Whom you stand!

When a man sincerely wishes to become a proselyte, draw him near rather than keep him at arm's length.

Do Your will, O God, in heaven above; grant a tranquil spirit to those who fear You below; and act as You see fit. Blessed are You, O Lord, who hears prayer.

ELIJAH (9th cent. BCE). Prophet who lived during the reign of Ahab, king of Israel and his son Ahaziah. His life is recounted in I Kings, 17-19, 21, and II Kings 1-2.

Elijah struggled to purify the belief in the one God and against the religious hypocrisy and the worship of BAAL which had spread among the Israelites under the influence of Jezebel, Ahab's wife from Sidon. The most striking instance of this clash was the encounter on Mount Carmel (I Kings 18:16ff.), where the priests of Baal had gathered. Elijah addressed the people, "How long will you waver between two opinions? If the Lord is God, follow Him; and if Baal, follow him!" The prophets of Baal could not bring down fire from heaven to burn their sacrifice which had been placed on the altar, while after Elijah's prayer, fire came down from heaven and consumed his offering. The people then exclaimed, "The Lord He is God." The prophets of Baal were seized and killed at the Kishon River.

Elijah was in constant conflict with Ahab also on moral grounds, most notably over Ahab's arranging the death of Naboth in order to inherit his vineyard. Ahab, upon hearing Elijah's bitter prophecy following the seizure of the vineyard, tore his clothes and dressed himself in sackcloth (I Kings 21).

Elijah on his part sought to undermine Ahab's status as king, but was forced to flee and wander from place to place. Various miracles are attributed to him in the course of his journeys.

A decisive episode in Elijah's life was the moment when God's word was revealed to him in the cave at Mount Horeb, traditionally identified with Mount SINAI. Here God commanded him regarding three acts that he was to perform in the future: to anoint Hazael as king of Aram, to anoint Jehu as king of Israel, and to anoint ELISHA son of Shafat to succeed him as a prophet (I Kings 19).

When the time came for Elijah to die, Elisha (whom Elijah had appointed as his successor) did not want to part from him. They walked to Jericho where Elisha requested, "Let a double portion of your spirit pass on to me." Elijah responded, "If you see me as I am being taken from you, this will be granted to you; if not, it will not." A fiery chariot with fiery horses suddenly appeared and separated one from the other, and Elijah ascended to heaven in a whirlwind (II Kings 2).

In rabbinic literature, Elijah occupies an important place, both in *halakhah* and in *aggadah*. He, it is believed, will give definitive rulings on questions which have remained undecided. Many of these unresolved questions in the Talmud conclude with the word *téku*, which means "it will stand, remain," in Aramaic, but is also understood to be an acronym of [Elijah] "the Tishbite will resolve queries." This is based on the belief that in the eschatological future Elijah will be revealed as the one who brings peace to the world and who reconciles parents and children (Mal. 3:24).

Since Elijah never died, many legends have been told of his reappearance, often to save Jews and Jewish communities at times of danger. In talmudic times, it was held that he taught some of the sages and that this is the origin of the books, *Midrash Eliyahu Rabbah* ("Great Midrash of Elijah") and *Midrash Eliyahu Zuta* ("Small Book of Elijah").

Because of his attribute of coming to the aid of those in need, references to his name are often followed by the phrase, "may he be remembered for the good," i.e., Elijah will be the herald of the good in the future. For this reason, the GRACE AFTER MEALS includes the statement, "The Merciful One (i.e., God), will send us Elijah the prophet, may he be remembered for the good, and he will herald to us good tidings, succor, and consolation." According to Jewish folk tradition, Elijah has also appeared to great Torah sages in later generations and to unknown righteous men. He has also appeared in synagogues when a tenth man for a prayer quorum was needed.

Elijah is known primarily in terms of heralding the REDEMPTION, as promised by the prophet Malachi (3:23), "Lo, I will send the prophet Elijah to you before the coming of the awesome, fearful day of the Lord." Longing for the redemption is included in the blessings of the reading of the prophetical portion in the synagogue on Sabbaths and festivals: "Let us rejoice, O Lord our God, with Elijah the prophet, Your servant." It is also shown in a concrete fashion in the placing of a fifth cup of wine on the Passover eve *seder* table, this being known as "Elijah's cup." This cup takes its name from a halakhic reason, for there is a dispute as to whether one is required to drink four or five cups of wine, and this will be resolved only with the coming of Elijah. In the hope that Elijah will arrive and bring redemption on Passover eve, the door to the street is opened in the course of the *seder* service so that he may enter. The longing for Elijah is reflected in the Sabbath ZEMIROT, in folk songs, and in the PIYYUTIM (religious poems). Many of these are sung after the Sabbath, when the longing for redemption and for a better future increases. Others are sung on festive and joyous occasions.

ELIJAH BEN SOLOMON ZALMAN (The Gaon of Vilna; also known by the acronym *ha-Gra*; 1720-1797). Outstanding talmudic scholar. Born at Selets (near Grodno) into a family of prominent rabbis, he received no formal education, studied with his father, and soon proved to be a prodigy, giving a learned discourse at the Great Synagogue of Vilna at the age of 6½. By the age of 13, he had mastered both talmudic and kabbalistic lore. Married at 18, he traveled extensively and at the age of 25, settled in Vilna already home to one of the most important learned communities in Europe. There he lived the life of a recluse at the outskirts of the town. Eventually, a special House of Study was built for him and he received a maintenance grant. By the age of 30 his fame as a scholar had spread throughout the Jewish world.

Elijah ben Solomon Zalman, the Gaon of Vilna.

He continued the austere life of a recluse-student to the age of 40, always clad in prayer-shawl and *tefillin*, seeing no one, sleeping no more than two hours a day, noting in his diary any wasted minutes, i.e., without Torah study. He never held an official position, nor did he correspond with other scholars or write responsa or approbations as was customary in the community of the learned. Following a talmudic tradition, he emerged from his seclusion at the age of 40, by which time he had written all his works. He then admitted to his presence a select band of disciples (perhaps 20 altogether) all of whom were experienced scholars in their own right.

In addition to studying the Bible, *halakhah*, and Kabbalah, Elijah strongly advocated the study of the natural sciences — mathematics, astronomy, zoology, botany, geography — which he considered indispensable for the understanding and application of talmudic law and lore. He encouraged his pupil Baruch Schick of Shklov, to translate Euclid into Hebrew (he himself knew only Hebrew and Yiddish). He was also very interested in the study of Hebrew grammar. However, he opposed the study of what he called the "accursed" philosophy, as referring specifically to Maimonides, whose *Guide to the Perplexed* he otherwise praised and quoted, and his mentor Aristotle. He also opposed the emerging HASKALAH movement, although its adherents were fully observant at the time.

The main target for his uncompromising hostility was ḤASIDISM, whose influence had begun to extend to Poland and Lithuania, and especially to Vilna. Elijah objected to this sectarianism, and to the popularization of KABBALAH, which was seen as superseding HALAKHAH. He considered the exaggerated *joie de vivre* of the Ḥasidim as levity and inimical to the serious study of Torah. With the memories of the disastrous SHABBETAI TSEVI movement still fresh, the cult of personality around the TSADDIK, the Ḥasidic leader, aroused fears of pseudo-messianism. Essentially, the clash was between an elitist spiritual and intellectual aristocracy and its conception of Judaism and a popular, grass-roots religious movement.

Elijah led a frontal attack against Ḥasidism which led to the closing of their conventicles, the burning of their books, and the repeated imposition of a *ḥerem* (EXCOMMUNICATION) against the new "sect." He refused to meet the Ḥasidic leaders Menahem Mendel of Vitebsk and SHNE'UR ZALMAN OF LYADY who wanted to explain to Elijah the true nature of their movement and saw the conflict as a huge misunderstanding. While the Gaon's opposition restricted the movement's spread in the short run and turned most Lithuanian Jews into MITNAGGEDIM (oppositionists), in the long run Ḥasidism could not be suppressed. It became a powerful component of Orthodox Judaism.

The Gaon's major achievement was the new impulse he gave to the study of the Bible and the Talmud and cognate literature. Opposing the sophistries of PILPUL, he stressed the close and critical study of the Talmud text in light of parallels and quotations by earlier authorities. This approach earned him the title of "father of Talmud criticism." He applied the dual methods of PESHAT (literal meaning) and DERASH (hermeneutics), normally associated with Bible interpretation, to his study of the Mishnah, and he devoted much attention to the rather neglected Palestinian Talmud (*Yerushalmi*). He considered both the Babylonian and the Palestinian Talmuds of equal importance; together with the Bible itself, they formed a divinely revealed whole. Kabbalah, to which he applied the same rigorous methodology as to Bible and Talmud, was a part of this holistic concept of Torah.

Toward the end of his life, he set out for the Land of Israel but for unexplained reasons he soon returned to Vilna. He encouraged his pupils to immigrate, which they did about a decade after his death.

The distinctive prayer customs and readings of the Gaon were collected by his pupil, Issachar Baer, in his compendium *Ma'aseh Rav*. These form the basis of the *Siddur ha-Gra*, a prayerbook associated with his name and tradition that is still in use.

He left 70 books and commentaries, 50 of which were published, posthumously. For the most part, his work took the form of annotations/commentaries on Bible, Mishnah, Tosefta, Talmud, halakhic Midrashim, early Kabbalistic works, and Joseph Caro's *Shulḥan Arukh*. In *Halakhah* he usually adopted a strict approach and tried to revive talmudic laws and customs which had fallen into disuse. His annotations are now to be found in standard editions of the Talmud.

SOME OF THE SAYINGS OF THE VILNA GAON

Desires must be purified and idealized, not eradicated.

Life is a series of vexations and pains, and sleepless nights are the common lot.

It is better to pray at home, for in the synagogue it is impossible to escape envy and hearing idle talk.

Like rain, the Torah nourishes useful plants and poisonous weeds.

The tongue's sin weighs as much as all other sins together.

Only things acquired by hard labor and great struggle are of any value.

ELIMELECH OF LYZHANSK (1717-1787). Early leader of ḤASIDISM who especially promoted the cult of the Ḥasidic *Rebbe* or TSADDIK. Together with his brother, Zusya of Annopol, Elimelech journeyed to DOV BAER OF MEZHIRECH, at that time the preacher of Rovno, and became one of Dov Baer's followers. After the death of Dov Baer, Elimelech assumed the role of a Hasidic master in Lyzhansk, Galicia, and fathered Galician and Polish Hasidism. Before joining the Hasidic movement, Elimelech had been a kabbalist who practiced asceticism and, despite the general Hasidic aversion to denial of the world, there are strong traces of his former attitude in Elimelech's thought. His work entitled *No'am Elimelekh*, first published in Lemberg (1787), soon became a manual for Hasidic Jews and has gone through many editions. Outwardly a running commentary on the Torah, *No'am Elimelekh* contains a great deal of material (including two letters) expounding the Hasidic ideology and way of life, laying particular stress on "Tsaddikism" — the *Rebbe's* function as a kind of religious superman who lives in a higher world and mediates between God and humanity. In most editions there is also a list of saintly practices (*hanhagot*) which devout Hasidim of every group endeavored to follow.

While Elimelech, like the other Hasidic masters, stressed joy in the service of God, there is a somber element in his thought which — as the writings about him suggest — also dominated his life. *Der Rebbe Elimelekh*, the Yiddish folksong in which he is portrayed as a Hasidic "Old King Cole," was almost certainly a typical piece of anti-Hasidic satire by a Lithuanian *Mitnagged* or HASKALAH writer. The two leading disciples of Elimelech were Jacob Isaac "the Seer" of Lublin (1745-1815), who broke with his master to found a rival Hasidic circle, and Kalonymus Kalman Epstein of Cracow (died 1823), author of *Ma'or va-Shemesh*, another classic work of Hasidism.

ELISHA Prophet, devoted disciple and successor of the prophet ELIJAH. After Elijah was commanded at Mount Horeb to anoint Elisha as a prophet, he cast his mantle over him (I Kings 19:19-21). Thereafter, Elisha followed Elijah and ministered to him, until Elijah's assumption to heaven.

A cycle of miracles were attributed to Elisha after the departure of Elijah. By striking the water of the Jordan with Elijah's fallen mantle, he caused it to divide so that he could cross over on dry land (II Kings 2:13). A widow's cruse of oil is miraculously refilled (II Kings 4:1-7); a son was born to a Shunammite woman after years of barrenness (II Kings 4:14-17); a child apparently dead was restored to life (II Kings 4:35); the leprosy of the Aramean captain Naaman was cured (II Kings 5). These and similar tales of miracles performed by Elisha emphasize his ethically sensitive nature. (See also II Kings 4:38-44; 6:1-7.)

Another cycle of stories about Elisha deals with his prophetic activity in relation to several kings of Israel. He continued Elijah's struggle against the House of Ahab, and against BAAL worship. He bid one of his disciples to anoint Jehu king and to instruct him to slay the House of Joram, the son of Ahab.

ELISHA BEN AVUYAH (c.70-c.140 CE). *Tanna* of the third generation, an outstanding scholar who nevertheless renounced the teachings and practices of the sages. Various reasons are given in the Talmud for his apostasy. One source (*Hag.* 14b) attributes it to his engagement in mystical speculation. Others suggest that he was affected by the Hadrianic persecutions which followed the collapse of the Bar Kokhba revolt (132-135 CE). Having lost his belief in Jewish fundamentals such as Divine providence and reward and punishment, Elisha ben Avuyah was evidently attracted to GNOSTICISM. So as to avoid mentioning him by name, the Talmud refers to him as *Aher* ("Another"). It is related that he once entered a classroom and told the pupils to give up their study of Torah in order to learn some more practical craft. Despite his apostasy and public violation of traditional law, Elisha was never abandoned by R. MEIR, who quoted the teachings of his old master ("Aherim"), frequently urging him to repent and return to the Jewish fold. Many of Elisha's sayings, which lay emphasis on ethical behavior and the performance of good deeds, appear in talmudic literature. Several Haskalah writers of the 19th century, empathizing with Elisha ben Avuyah, endeavored to "rehabilitate" him and maintained that he had been maligned by his contemporaries. *As a Driven Leaf* (1939), a historical novel by Milton Steinberg, portrays his life and career.

ELI TSIYYON VE-AREHA ("Let Zion and its cities lament"). Opening words of an elegy which, in the Ashkenazi rite, is chanted at the end of the Morning Service on the fast of TISHAH BE-AV. Though an anonymous composition of the Middle Ages, it is sometimes attributed to JUDAH HALEVI, either for stylistic reasons or because it concludes the final section of the elegies (KINOT) for the Ninth of Av headed by his celebrated "Ode to Zion." Structurally, *Eli Tsiyyon* is a monorhyme, the second word of each line beginning with a different Hebrew letter in alphabetical order (except for the 15th). The opening couplet serves as a refrain after each two-line stanza. Deliberately echoing a biblical verse (Joel 1:8), the couplet reads: "Let Zion and its cities lament like a woman crying out in her labor pains;/And like a maiden wrapped in sackcloth mourning for the husband of her youth." The elegy reflects the misery and horror that accompanied the destruction of the Second Temple. Before chanting *Eli Tsiyyon*, congregants rise to their feet. Whether responsively or in unison, the reader and congregation then sing the dirge to a traditional tune which Ashkenazim also employ for other elegies and for LEKHAH DODI during the Three Weeks of Mourning from 17 Tammuz.

EL MALÉ RAHAMIM ("God, full of compassion"). Prayer for the dead recited by Ashkenazim; it corresponds to the Sephardi *hashkavah* (see MEMORIAL PRAYERS). Although some maintain that *El Malé Rahamim* was originally composed to glorify Jews martyred in the era of the Crusades, it more probably dates from the Chmielnicki massacres in Eastern Europe (1648-49). Minor variations in the text have developed over the centuries in Eastern and Western Europe, and two more elaborate formulas have been composed recently (see below). One observing a YAHRZEIT anniversary for parents or other relatives is called to the Reading of the Law close to the date, and the *El Malé Rahamim* prayer is then recited in memory of the deceased person's soul. Frequently, in Orthodox practice, the mourner makes a donation to the synagogue or to charity and this is mentioned in the public recitation of the prayer. Reform Jews have abbreviated the text of *El Malé Rahamim*. The traditional plea is for "a perfect rest" to be granted to the souls of the departed "on the wings of the Divine Presence." This formula is recited during the *Yizkor* memorial prayers in synagogue on the three Pilgrim Festivals and on the Day of Atonement; at a funeral (except on days when the TAHANUN supplications are omitted); when visiting the graves of close relatives; and at the consecration of a tombstone.

Memorial services throughout the world now often include a special *El Malé Rahamim* for victims of the Nazi HOLOCAUST. This prayer recalls "our six million brethren, men, women, and children, the holy and the pure, who were murdered, gassed, burned to death, and buried alive for the sanctification of God's Name" (see KIDDUSH HA-SHEM). There is likewise an *azkarah* (requiem), said mainly in Israel, for those who lost their lives in the pre-State underground movements and in the Israel Defense Forces. The solemn melody to which *El Malé Rahamim* is chanted often attains great emotional and dramatic power.

EL MALÉ RAHAMIM

O God, full of compassion, Who dwells on high, grant a perfect rest on the wings of the Divine Presence — in the exalted places among the holy and the pure ones who shine like the brightness of the firmament — to the soul of ... who has gone to his (her) eternal repose [and for whose sake ... will make a contribution to charity in solemn remembrance]. May his (her) resting place be in the Garden of Eden. May the Compassionate One shelter him (her) forever in His protective wings and may his (her) soul be bound up in the bond of eternal life. The Lord is his (her) inheritance; may he (she) rest in peace, and let us say: Amen.

EL MELEKH NE'EMAN ("God is a faithful King"). Brief formula mainly recited by Ashkenazi (including Hasidic) Jews immediately before the SHEMA, when Morning or Evening Prayers are not said with a congregational quorum (*minyan*). A homiletic reason adduced for the addition of this phrase is that the number of words in the *Shema* must correspond to the 248 "limbs" which (according to the rabbis) make up the human body, and with the same number of positive commandments in the Torah. Since the *Shema* comprises 245 words only, three extra words need to be added. When public worship takes place these are supplied by the reader who recites aloud the last two words of the *Shema* with the initial word of the following paragraph — *Adonai Elohékhem emet*, "The Lord your God is true" (cf. Jer. 10:10). Those worshiping in private, however, recite *El Melekh Ne'eman* as a prefix to the opening verse of the *Shema*. From statements in the Talmud (*Shab.* 119b; *San.* 111a), it appears that this Hebrew phrase was not chosen at random. *El Melekh Ne'eman* was regarded both as a declaration of faith and (acrostically) as equivalent to AMEN.

EL NORA ALILAH ("God who does wondrous deeds"). Opening words and title of a liturgical hymn (*piyyut*), composed by Moses IBN EZRA, which both Sephardim and Yemenite Jews recite before the Concluding (NE'ILAH) Service on the Day of Atonement. It comprises eight stanzas, the initial Hebrew letters of which are an acronym of the author's name; the first stanza's fourth line is repeated throughout as a refrain. The text of this beautiful hymn conveys the worshiper's penitent trust in God "as the closing hour approaches," and the much-loved traditional melody sung by the entire congregation breathes a spirit of hope and optimism. Thanks to its emotive words and music, *El Nora Alilah* has recently been incorporated in the ritual of some Western Ashkenazi (Conservative) congregations for the Day of Atonement.

ELOHIM See GOD, NAMES OF

ELUL (Akkadian: *Elulu*) Sixth month of the Jewish religious CALENDAR; twelfth and last month of the Hebrew civil year counting from TISHRI. It has 29 days and normally coincides with August-September. Its sign of the zodiac is Virgo. There is only one mention of Elul in the Bible (Neh. 6:15) and another in the Apocrypha (I *Macc.* 14.27), its name being synonymous with "harvest." No festivals or fast days occur during Elul, which serves to prepare Jews for the High Holidays in Tishri. It is therefore known as "the month of repentance, Divine mercy, and forgiveness." In ancient times, messengers were dispatched from Jerusalem to announce the New Moon of Elul, thus making it easier to calculate subsequent important dates from Rosh ha-Shanah onward (*RH* 1.3). The *shofar* (ram's horn) is sounded after the Morning Service (except on Sabbath and the eve of the New Year) and Ps. 27 is recited each day from the first of Elul. Penitential SELIHOT calling for Israel's "return" to God are also read (by Sephardim from 1 or 15 Elul, by Ashkenazim during the last week of the month).

EMANATION (Heb. *atsilut*). A term which refers to the process whereby the absolute and transcendent One expands from within Himself and creates multiplicity. The concept of emanation is a major tenet of the neo-Platonic view of Plotinus and his disciples and in the writings of the neo-Platonic philosophers of medieval times. The first kabbalists were influenced by the neo-Platonic view, and described the expansion of the SEFIROT from the hidden God as a process of emanation.

Plotinus, the founder of the neo-Platonic school, described the creation of the multiplicity from the One as a process of flowing and expansion. According to the neo-Platonic ontology, the sequence of emanation begins with the One, the source of all existence, who allows a flow from Himself and creates all the other degrees of existence. The first entity which stems from the One is intelligence, which is identical with the Platonic world of ideas. Intelligence, in turn, emanates to the soul of the world, the link joining the spiritual world to the physical one, which is at the end of the sequence of emanation. Plotinus compares the process of emanation, which occurs outside the framework of time, to the spreading of a ray of light, which gets progressively weaker as it moves away from its source. Another common analogy is to compare the process of emanation to the flow of water from a spring.

Based on Plotinus' theory, the process of emanation is natural and unavoidable. Such a view is in opposition to the view of the CREATION of the universe as being based on the will of God of the monotheistic religions. At the same time, the neo-Platonic view affected the monotheistic philosophical views, and Muslim, Christian and Jewish thinkers in the Middle Ages adopted the view of emanation, while attempting to adapt it to the theological frameworks of the revealed religions. In the 10th century, Isaac Israeli was the first Jewish philosopher who described the process of creation *ex nihilo* as a process of emanation. The idea of emanation does not only exist among Jewish neo-Platonists, but also among Jewish philosophers who tended toward the Aristotelian view.

The concept of emanation occupies a major role in the literature of the KABBALAH. The kabbalists, like the neo-Platonic philosophers, stress that the process of emanation does not entail any decrease of any kind in the one who emanates. A common image used in the kabbalistic literature is the lighting of one flame from another, where the action does not diminish the first flame.

The kabbalists dispute whether the process of emanation takes place in the world of the Godhead or whether it continues outside the world of the Godhead as well.

EMANCIPATION The granting of civil rights to Jews. For many centuries, the Jews lived as second-class citizens in both the Christian and Muslim worlds. In the Western world, signs of new attitudes began to emerge in the late 17th century and became stronger with the growth of Enlightenment in the 18th century. New national states in the Protestant world now began to differentiate between Church and State. The Protestant adoption of the "Old Testament" (largely ignored in the Catholic world) also led to new understandings of Jews and Judaism. Debate raged between those who held that the Jews could not be assimilated and that their faith and practices prevented them from becoming part of the same society as Gentiles, and those who felt that given the chance Jews would become useful and productive citizens, contributing to the countries where they lived. Among Jews themselves, there were differences of opinion. The outstanding pioneer of Jewish emancipation was Moses MENDELSSOHN, who, emerging from a ghetto childhood, became one of Prussia's most respected intellectuals, while remaining an observant Jew. Others felt that emancipation would lead to ASSIMILATION and that isolation in the ghetto had in fact meant the preservation of Jewish tradition. They pointed to the fate of Mendelssohn's descendants, almost every one of whom converted to Christianity.

The first breakthrough came in the United States with the new State constitution of Virginia in 1776, which stated that "all men are entitled to the free exercise of religion according to the dictates of their conscience." The act establishing religious liberty in 1786 was phrased to include Jews, and the United States Constitution provided for religious freedom through Article VI and the First Amendment (1787).

At the time, however, this affected only a small number of Jews; more significant was the French Revolution and its consequences. Already in 1789 corporate autonomy was abolished for religious and other groups which meant that the Jews lost powers of self-government, and in 1791 they received the full rights of French citizenship. The Jews became loyal French patriots but this did not affect their religious feelings. Napoleon turned his attention to the position of the Jews in light of their new status, and in 1806 summoned an Assembly of Notables whom he confronted with difficult questions regarding possible contradictions between their loyalty to the State and their devotion to Judaism (e.g.,: Can Jews marry Christians? How does Jewish law regard French Christians?). The Notables found appropriate answers, emphasizing that rabbinical authority was only spiritual. Regarding mixed marriages, they replied that the ban applied to heathens in ancient times but not to France in their day. Napoleon then summoned a "Great Sanhedrin" in 1807, in which a majority of rabbis were included among the delegates, with a request to give official sanction to the decisions of the Notables. The Sanhedrin confirmed almost all the answers of the Notables. Napoleon received assurances on the basic issues — that rabbis no longer had jurisdiction in civil and judicial matters, and that Jews no longer regarded themselves as a separate nation, or hoped to leave their country of residence and return to Zion. He established

Lionel de Rothschild, the first Jew to be sworn into the House of Commons, in 1858. From a contemporary Germany newspaper.

a new structure of Jewish life on a purely religious basis (see CONSISTORY). The French Revolutionary and Napoleonic armies spread revolutionary ideals of equality and civil rights for all to other countries throughout Europe. In Italy, for example, the Napoleonic armies, together with the local population and the Jews, enthusiastically tore down the gates of the ghettos.

The process of Jewish emancipation was temporarily reversed with the defeat of Napoleon, but processes had been set in motion that were irreversible and by the 1870s, emancipation had reached virtually all the Jews of Central and Western Europe. The impact on Jewish life was tremendous. Jews now found themselves faced with new challenges, notably that of living between or synthesizing their Jewish culture and that of the environment. Inevitably, there was a process of acculturation, which often led to assimilation and estrangement from the Jewish community. Many cases were reported of conversion to CHRISTIANITY, although often — as in the case of the German Jewish poet, Heinrich Heine — this was manifestly for social betterment rather than out of religious conviction. Jewish religious life was also affected. REFORM JUDAISM was founded in response to the modernization of Jewish life, and to keep within the fold those Jews who regarded traditional Jewish life as anachronistic. Orthodoxy too was affected and certain elements adjusted themselves to the new realities, notably through the development of NEO-ORTHODOXY.

Emancipation did not reach the Jews of Eastern Europe until the March 1917 Revolution. Until then, Jews continued in their traditional framework. After the Bolshevik Revolution, Jewish equality was coupled with a bitter campaign against Judaism (and other religions) and religious education was outlawed. Although traces of Judaism remained (and in the Asiatic parts of the USSR Jewish religion continued to be openly practiced), the surge of Jewish identification after World War II was more nationally than religiously motivated.

In Muslim countries, emancipation was delayed. The colonial powers brought it to North Africa and in the wake of the breakup of the Ottoman Empire, Jews in those lands received rights in the first part of the 20th century. In the more distant Muslim lands, such as Yemen, Jews were never emancipated and only knew full civil rights when they left those countries and settled in Israel. Notwithstanding a certain secularization in some of the Muslim lands, the Jewish religious frameworks remained largely unaffected until the Jews left these lands after 1948.

EMDEN, JACOB (1697-1776). Talmudic scholar, rabbi and controversialist, son of "Ḥakham Tsevi" ASHKENAZI, also known by the acronym *Yavets* (Ya'akov ben Tsevi). Emden lived mainly in his native Altona and established his own press there, which he utilized to publish criticism of other German rabbis and of contemporary Jewish society. He wrote some 40 works on Jewish law (including responsa), as well as his *Siddur Bet Ya'akov* (1745-8), a prayer book with commentary. Like his father, Emden was influenced by Sephardi customs and vehemently opposed the heretical pseudo-messianic movement of SHABBETAI TSEVI, which he regarded as an insidious threat to Judaism. This motivated his hostile assessment of the kabbalistic classic, the ZOHAR, and his long campaign against Jonathan EYBESCHÜTZ, the rabbi of Altona, Hamburg, and Wandsbeck, whom he perhaps rightly suspected of Shabbatean sympathies. Emden's full-length autobiography, *Megillat Sefer* (first published in 1896), contains important religious and historical information about 18th-century German Jewry. Though given to polemics and heresy-hunting, Emden was on friendly terms with Moses MENDELSSOHN and showed remarkable broadmindedness in his scholarly interests.

EMET VE-EMUNAH ("True and faithful"). Blessing in praise of God's uniqueness and redemptive power, recited daily in the Evening Service, which forms a transition between the SHEMA and the AMIDAH. Mishnaic sources refer to it as the first (and longer) of two benedictions that follow the *Shema* (*Ber.* 1.4), the other being HASHKIVENU. Like its counterpart in the Morning Service, EMET VE-YATSIV, this prayer was evidently recited in the Temple (*Tam.* 5.1) and the general theme of deliverance gave rise to its designation as GE'ULAH, a "blessing of Redemption" (*Ber.* 4b, 9b). The origin of these two prayers has traditionally been linked with Ps. 92:3, which states that it is praiseworthy "to declare God's lovingkindness in the morning and His faithfulness every night." According to the rabbis, this constitutes an injunction to read *Emet ve-Yatsiv* after daybreak and *Emet ve-Emunah*, the declaration of God's "faithfulness," after nightfall (*Ber.* 12a). To affirm the truths contained in the *Shema*, and on the basis of a Scriptural declaration that "the Lord God is true" (Jer. 10:10), no interruption may be made between the last two words of the *Shema*'s third paragraph and the first word of *Emet ve-Emunah*. This governs both congregational worship and reading aloud by the prayer leader (*Ber.* 14 a-b). There are differences in content between the various liturgical rites.

EMET VE-YATSIV ("True and firm"). Opening words of the extended GE'ULAH ("Redemption") blessing, recited daily in the Morning Service, which forms a transition between the SHEMA and the AMIDAH. It is referred to in the Mishnah as the benediction that follows the *Shema* (*Ber.* 1.4) and was evidently recited in the Temple (*Tam.* 5.1; *Ber.* 2.2). In common with the parallel EMET VE-EMUNAH blessing recited in the Evening Service, this prayer derives its authority from a verse in Psalms (92:3), and there are similar rules forbidding any "interruption" when it is recited (*Ber.* 2.2, 9b, 14a-b). Despite certain textual variations, one central theme is emphasized in all the liturgical rites: Israel continues to proclaim its faith in the One God and in the eternal validity of His Torah.

EMISSARY See SHALI'AḤ

EN K(E)-ELOHÉNU ("There is none like our God"). Opening words and title of a hymn that has formed part of the liturgy since geonic times (ninth century). Ashkenazi congregations in the Diaspora sing it only on Sabbaths and festivals, at the end of the Additional Service, whereas those adhering to other rites also recite it at the end of the weekday Morning Service. This practice is followed by Israeli Ashkenazim. Structurally, the hymn comprises five sequences of four short phrases. In the Sephardi-Eastern rite, *En K(e)-Elohénu* ends with a biblical verse (Ps. 102:14), whereas the concluding line of the Ashkenazi version establishes a thematic connection with PITTUM HA-KETORET, the rabbinic passage on the Temple spices that follows. Ḥasidic Jews recite the Sephardi text on weekdays, but adhere to the Ashkenazi version on Sabbaths and festivals. Jewish mystics claimed that the four titles ("God," "Lord," "King," and "Savior") repeated in the hymn allude to four Divine powers involved in the process of creation.

ENOCH (Ḥanokh). Biblical figure. Enoch was the son of Jared (Gen. 5:18), the seventh generation after ADAM. In contrast to the other antediluvians, Enoch lived only 365 years (the number of days in the solar year). The Bible declares that he "walked with God; then he was no more, for God took him" (Gen. 5:23).

This unusual description of Enoch's death sparked the imaginations of the writers of pseudepigrapha and the rabbis of the later Midrash. Thus, two pseudepigraphic books are ascribed to him, while for the midrashic rabbis, Enoch's translation to heaven (interpreted as a bodily assumption) betokened his role there as heavenly scribe. According to these sources, Enoch was the inventor of all sciences and knowledge since he was privy to the secrets of God and could decipher the writing on the heavenly tablets. These and similar legends are to be found throughout the APOCRYPHA AND PSEUDEPIGRAPHA.

In sharp contrast, there is not a single reference to Enoch in the whole range of TANNAITIC LITERATURE. Early Christian sources, however (CHURCH FATHERS), contain many legends about Enoch. The silence of the early rabbis regarding Enoch is attributable to the New Testament's citation of Enoch and ELIJAH as two witnesses to the truth of the ascension of Jesus to heaven (Revelations 11:3). Perhaps in reflection of this, an early Midrash declares that Enoch vacillated between being a righteous man and a sinner. God, therefore, "took him" before he could relapse into sin.

It was only after the threat of early Christianity to the integrity of Judaism had come to an end, that Jewish authors began to weave legends about Enoch. A late Midrash asserts that Enoch ascended to heaven in a fiery chariot drawn by a fiery steed. Further, he was one of nine righteous men who did not suffer pangs of death and entered paradise alive. The ZOHAR, as well as earlier mystic literature, takes up many of the early legends centering on Enoch.

EN-SOF ("Infinite"). Term used as a designation for God in Jewish mystical literature, the Kabbalah, signifying the highest aspect of the Divinity, which is beyond human comprehension. The early kabbalists reserved this designation for the transcendental "hidden God," whereas the various SEFIROT denote those aspects of God which are revealed and active (see MYSTICISM). *En-Sof*, as an epithet for the hidden God, was used by the earliest kabbalists, Isaac the Blind and Azriel of Gerona, and in the ZOHAR. It originally described the infinite (i.e., *én-sof*) extension of God's thought, but later kabbalists used the term as a proper noun, speaking of God Himself as the "*En-Sof*" and the "*En-Sof*, Blessed be He." It signifies the total perfection of God, in which all contradictions and differentiations exist in a static harmony that defies human understanding. The existence of the *En-Sof* can only be recognized indirectly, as it is the Prime Cause of all that exists. In kabbalistic literature, the philosophical concepts relating to the God who is without attributes, the Prime Cause and the Cause of all causes, are viewed as referring to the *En-Sof*. The kabbalistic school of Gerona, Spain, designated the *En-Sof* as "that which is not conceivable by thought," the "Hidden Light," and the "Indistinguishable Unity" — all terms expressing the hidden nature of the Infinite and the unity of all contradictions within it. As the *En-Sof* is beyond man's comprehension, there is little kabbalistic discussion of this aspect of the Divine. *Ma'arekhet ha-Elohut* ("The Order of God"), a mystical treatise of the 13th-14th century, offered the radical conclusion that the *En-Sof* is so hidden that it is not even mentioned in the Bible. Some Jewish mystics identified the *En-Sof* with the primal will and with the highest of the *Sefirot, Keter Elyon* (the "Supreme Crown").

EN YA'AKOV An anthology comprising all the aggadic (or non-halakhic) sections of the Babylonian Talmud, as well as some from the Jerusalem Talmud. The work was compiled by Jacob ibn Ḫaviv (c.1445-1515), an exile from Spain who settled in Salonika where he was recognized as one of the great scholars of his day. Ibn Ḫaviv's emphasis in compiling *En Ya'akov* was chiefly didactic and religious. In his commentaries, which are based on the earlier classical commentators, he invariably stresses the plain meaning of the text and the importance of simple faith over the rationalizations of the philosophers. *En Ya'akov* gained immediate renown and was published in numerous editions. Although the text also attracted scholars, it was particularly popular among laymen, who found the rabbinic *aggadah* very appealing. Jacob ibn Ḫaviv finished only the orders ZERA'IM and MO'ED; the work was completed by his son Levi ibn Ḫaviv (c. 1480-1565).

EPHOD See PRIESTLY GARMENTS

EPHRAIM See TRIBES, TWELVE

EPIKOROS (or APIKOROS) A non-believer; a person lax in religious observance. The term was originally applied by rabbis to a follower of Epicurus, the fourth century BCE Greek philosopher who according to the Jewish tradition denied the immortality of the soul and considered hedonism to be the most important pursuit of this world. In talmudic literature, a person who denied the accepted faith of the tradition was labeled an *Epikoros*. Because of the similarity of this word to the Aramaic word *Apikruta*, which means irreverence, *Epikoros*, in Judaism, came to be applied to anyone who was irreverent vis-à-vis Torah and its teachers and students.

According to Maimonides in his Code (*Hilkhot Teshuvah* 3:8), three types of Jews are labeled *Epikoros*: (1) He who says there is no such thing as prophecy and that there is no knowledge that extends from the Creator to the heart of human beings; (2) He who denies the prophecy of Moses; (3) He who says that God does not know the ongoing daily deeds of humans.

An *Epikoros* was often considered as being outright evil and not enjoying a share in the Hereafter. This term has come to be applied among the rank-and-file to any Jew who is not faithful to the religious life-style of Judaism ("an *epikores*").

EPITAPHS See TOMBSTONES

ERETS ISRAEL See ISRAEL, LAND OF

EREV ("eve). In general usage, the day before a holy day. In this context Friday is referred to as *erev Shabbat* ("Sabbath eve") and the day before a festival is *erev yom tov*. Such days are distinguished by halakhic regulations. On the eve of Sabbaths and festivals, the TAḪANUN prayer is omitted in the Afternoon Service. The SHOFAR (ram's horn) is not blown on the eve of the New Year. The day preceding Passover is the Fast of the First-Born. The prohibition against eating leavened bread is applicable from Passover eve and some communities do not work on that day.

The Jewish concept of a day is a 24-hour period from sunset to sunset. Consequently, the Sabbath and all festivals begin at sunset of the previous day. The more precise meaning of *erev* therefore is the first evening of the holy day. In Temple times a *shofar* was sounded to signal the division between the pre-holiday non-sacred time, and the sacred time of the holiday itself. This has its modern parallel in the sirens which are sounded in certain localities in Israel to signal the commencement of the Sabbath or the festival.

ERUSIN See BETROTHAL

ERUV (lit. "mixing"). A legal device used to facilitate the observance of the Sabbath and festivals. As a device instituted by the rabbis, the *eruv* can be used to mitigate only the effects of rabbinic decrees. It may not be used to bypass or alleviate any Torah-mandated law. There are various types of *eruvin* (the plural of *eruv*):

Eruv Ḫatserot ("*eruv* of courtyards"). By Torah law, it is forbidden on the Sabbath to carry anything between a public and a private domain or for four cubits within a public domain. This law, however, does not prohibit carrying from one private domain to another. The rabbis forbade the latter as a preventive measure, lest one carry from a public to a private domain, or vice versa. If there are a number of private domains adjoining one another or with a commonly owned area linking them (as in a condominium), with Jewish inhabitants in all the different houses or apartments, they may arrange to have all the apartments and the communal area considered as one single domain, by means of an *eruv ḫatserot*. (Should there be non-Jews in some of the apartments, arrangements must be made to lease the joint property from them for the Sabbath.)

The ideal way to make an *eruv ḫatserot* is to have one of the occupants take a loaf of bread or other food before the Sabbath, and to hand it to an occupant of a different apartment with the clear understanding, expressed in words, that the latter is to acquire this as the joint property of all the occupants of the different apartments. After the second person has taken possession of the loaf or other food, by lifting it up at least a hand's-width (about 4"), the first one takes it back, pronounces a special blessing, and then announces that through this *eruv* all will be permitted to move and carry freely among apartments and between any apartment and the communal area. The food involved must be placed in an area accessible to all. This method is effective only if the common area is surrounded by some type of partition. Without a partition between the communal area and the public domain, it is forbidden to carry in the communal area, lest something be carried into the public domain, thereby violating a Torah commandment.

Eruv Reshuyyot ("*eruv* of domains" or simply *eruv*). This is the most commonly used meaning for the term. By surrounding an area — in Israel this may include an entire city — with a "partition" made of posts at least 10 handwidths (40") high, linked by string or wire going over the top of each post, the area is considered to be a single domain, and once an *eruv reshuyyot* has been made, it is permissible to carry within the entire area on the Sabbath. This is permitted because no street in the entire city in which the *eruv* is made has the status of a public domain by Torah law (only a street through which 600,000 people pass in a single 24-hour period is considered to be a public domain). Thus, carrying in the streets is prohibited only by rabbinic law. The *eruv* is the device that permits acts which would otherwise be forbidden by rabbinic law. As can be seen, few places would qualify as public domains according to the above definition. Not only in Israel, where every city has an *eruv*, but in many neighborhoods and cities, especially in North America, an *eruv* is erected, often utilizing telephone poles for this purpose.

Eruv Tavshilin ("*eruv* of prepared foods"). When a festival falls on a Friday, it is forbidden by rabbinic law to cook on the festival for the immediately following Sabbath, even though cooking on the festival for the festival itself is permitted. If, however, a person has already begun cooking on a weekday before the festival for the Sabbath, he may continue, as it were, to cook on the festival for the Sabbath. By making an *eruv tavshilin*, the food cooked before the festival allows one to "mix" the cooking done on the festival for both festival and Sabbath needs. An *eruv tavshilin* is made by taking a piece of bread and a cooked item, such as a boiled egg, on the day before the festival (i.e., on Wednesday or Thursday, as the case may be), and reciting the appropriate blessing and declaration that this *eruv* will permit the family to cook during the festival for the Sabbath. The two items must then be put away, to be eaten on the Sabbath.

Eruv Teḫumin ("*eruv* of boundaries"). The Bible specifies (Ex. 16:29), "Let no man go out of his place on the Sabbath day," which (as interpreted by the Oral Law) means that one is limited to an area within approximately 12 miles of wherever he or she was at the onset of the Sabbath. (The same law applies to the festivals.) For the purposes of this law, a city is considered a single location, and Torah law permits travel (by foot) within a 12 mile radius from the outskirts of the city. By rabbinic law, however, one is limited to 2,000 cubits (a cubit is about 18" or about 24", depending on different rulings) from the outskirts of the city, the outskirts beginning 70 2/3 cubits from the furthermost house of the city. If a person wishes to visit a place more than 2,000 cubits beyond the city on the Sabbath or festival, provided that it is within 4,000 cubits of the city, he may do so by the use of an *eruv teḫumin*. By going to a place outside the city, but within 2,000 cubits of it, before the Sabbath or festival, and leaving sufficient food at that place for two meals, one in essence defines that place as his "abode" for the Sabbath or festival. This allows him to walk 2,000 cubits in any direction from that place. Thus, if a person leaves an *eruv* 2,000 cubits to the east of city, he has the right to walk a total of 4,000 cubits to the east on the Sabbath or festival.

ERUVIN ("joining of Sabbath limits"). Second tractate of Order MO'ED in the Mishnah. It is a logical extension of the previous tractate (SHABBAT) because it concerns the limitations imposed on movement and carrying an object on the Sabbath (cf. Ex.16:29,30). Its ten chapters deal with the limits of the Sabbath boundary (see ERUV) and its extension, the joining together of several households in order to permit carrying in a courtyard or alley, and the activities permitted only in the Temple on the Sabbath.

The subject matter is amplified in both Talmuds and the Tosefta.

ESCHATOLOGY The concept of a perfected world which will arise by Divine design in the future at the end of days (Heb. *aḇarit ha-yamim*). Eschatology within Judaism deals primarily with the final destiny of the Jewish people and the world, with only minor emphasis on the future of the individual (see AFTERLIFE). The main thrust of Jewish eschatology revolves around Israel as God's people and the ultimate victory of God's truth and justice. When the eschatological era comes into being, there will be peace among human beings, between all peoples, and among all creatures in the universe. This has been a central aspect of Jewish thought from the biblical period to the modern age. During recent years, certain Ḥasidic groups, especially the Liubavich sect, have indicated that signs are present for the imminent coming of the MESSIAH. His advent is one of several elements in Jewish eschatology that also include the war between the forces of good and evil (GOG AND MAGOG), the return of the Jewish exiles to the original homeland, and the Day of the Lord or the DAY OF JUDGMENT.

In the ancient Middle East, where Judaism developed, there were other religions in the Canaanite, Mesopotamian, Egyptian, and Persian cultures containing eschatological concepts. These other religions primarily associated eschatological occurrences with what they viewed as the order of nature. Jewish eschatology, rooted in the Bible, is directed toward the unique relationship between God and His people. Therefore, while terms from other religious eschatologies may be used in Jewish thought, they have a completely different connotation. In general, eschatology in the biblical period focused on the entire nation, which was to carry forward the Divine promise (Isa. 60:21).

One of the key concepts in Jewish eschatology is the Day of the Lord which becomes the Day of Judgment. This special day has a twofold emphasis. First, it will be the time when God demonstrates His wrath against all those who have angered Him, and His people will have their revenge on their foes. Second, it will be the era when the righteous are vindicated. The prophets gave the concept moral content; punishment to the wicked and justification to the righteous. According to AMOS, the Day of the Lord will be one of great doom (Amos 5:18-20), and for the prophet ZEPHANIAH, a great era of destruction for all non-believers, followed by the establishment of the glory of the remnant of Israel (Zeph. 3:8-13). The great destruction that will occur will be succeeded, according to ISAIAH, by an era of solemnity and peace which will encompass both humankind and the animal world (Isa. 11:6). Then God alone will be King and all nations will come to serve Him.

The return of the Jewish people after the Babylonian EXILE was a turning point when it was assumed that the rebuilding of the TEMPLE would be the culmination of the people's hopes for restoration (Hag. 2:6-9, 21-23; Zech. 3:8; 4:6-14; 6:9-15; 8:2-13). When this did not occur, an apocalyptic strain in eschatological thinking emerged (see APOCALYPSE). This type of literature, to be found already in the prophecies of EZEKIEL and ZECHARIAH, was an uncovering of the future, with speculations on the nature of the end of the world. The apocalyptic messages had supposedly been hidden away centuries earlier, and only now were being revealed in response to the problems of the particular era. The latter part of the book of DANIEL contains apocalyptic visions unique to the Bible, with a greater emphasis on transcendence and the usage for the first time in Jewish thought of the concept of history divided into various eras. The Jewish rendering of this idea was a four-era history within the natural order, consisting of the Babylonian, Median, Persian, and Greek monarchies. This was to be followed by God's reign on earth, with the elevation of His CHOSEN PEOPLE, Israel. According to Daniel 3:33 this would be an "everlasting kingdom". Daniel also treats the term "one like the son of man" in symbolic fashion (chap. 7). In time, this "son of man" was transformed into the concept of the Messiah. The idea of the RESURRECTION of the dead now became prominent.

Many diverse concepts of eschatology arose in the wake of the Book of Daniel (second century BCE). The PHARISEES incorporated elements of eschatological thinking into their teachings but the SADDUCEES basically rejected the doctrine. Groups which brought both apocalyptic and eschatological categories strongly to the fore included the Dead Sea sect, the ESSENES, and early Christian groups. The DEAD SEA SCROLLS make clear that members of the sect believed that they were living at the end of the "era of wickedness" which was to be followed by "the era of Divine favor." They were convinced that they were living out "the last days" of this world, which would be followed by the coming of God's restored kingdom. One of the best known scrolls deals with the final battle between the "Sons of Light" and the "Sons of Darkness," in which God would ultimately triumph, upon which the messianic age would begin.

The destruction of the Second Temple in 70 CE brought to a close some aspects of eschatological speculation, but others survived and new ones emerged. Eschatology continued to be a leading force in the continuity of the Jewish faith and the Jewish people. Some ideas survived in the liturgy, others were incorporated into rabbinic literature. The Bar Kochba revolt (132-135 CE), with its initial successes against the Romans, was seen in an eschatological light, as was the persecution of the Jews in its wake.

In his formulation of the PRINCIPLES OF FAITH, MAIMONIDES included the belief in the world to come and in the coming of the Messiah, and although other philosophers challenged this listing of principles, these two were generally accepted.

In contemporary times, reinterpretation of the eschatological categories has called for the creation of a better world. Reform Judaism, which rejected belief in a personal Messiah, has adopted a vision of the world moving to an ultimate era in which peace and justice reign completely. A recent statement of principles by the Conservative Movement entitled *Emet ve-Emunah* states in the chapter on eschatology (p.29): "For the world community we dream of an age when warfare will be abolished, when justice and compassion will be the axioms of interpersonal and international relationships...for our people, we dream of the ingathering of all Jews to Zion where we can again be the masters of our destiny and express our distinctive genius in every area of national life...for the individual human being, we affirm that death does not mean extinction and oblivion."

ESHET ḤAYIL ("Woman of valor"). Alphabetical acrostic in praise of a virtuous wife recited by the husband before the Sabbath eve meal; it comprises verses from the last chapter of Proverbs (31:10-31). The poem describes an aristocratic woman, familiar with commerce and successful in management, responsible, industrious, charitable, and wise. She brings honor to her family, especially to her husband who, thanks to her support and behavior, is able to take his rightful place of leadership in the community. Midrash Proverbs, an eighth-century compilation, was the first of many commentaries to see in *Eshet Ḥayil* a parable for the Torah; according to this Midrash, each of the 22 verses echoes the deeds of a female character in the Bible. Under kabbalistic influence, *Eshet Ḥayil* was later reinterpreted as alluding to God (the SHEKHINAH). The *Tikkuné Shabbat*, a work published in Prague (1641), first recommended that *Eshet Ḥayil* be recited in the home prior to KIDDUSH on Sabbath eve. This custom became prevalent in most Jewish communities, sometimes out of reverence for the *Shekhinah*, but more usually as a man's tribute to his wife or mother. In keeping with its egalitarian approach, the American Reform movement's liturgy suggests the parallel reading of Ps. 112:1-9, "Happy is the man who fears the Lord...," for women to recite in tribute to their husbands or fathers.

ESHET ḤAYIL (opening)

A woman of valor who can find?
Her worth is far above rubies.
The heart of her husband safely trusts in her,
And he lacks nothing.
She does good to him, never evil,
All the days of her life.

ESNOGA Term used by Western Sephardim to denote a (Spanish or Portuguese) SYNAGOGUE. It is thought to be a composite of two Old Castilian or Judeo-Spanish words — *senoga* (derived from the late Latin *synagoga*) and *escola* (Lat. *schola*, "school"). The resulting hybrid, *esnoga* (often shortened to *snoga*), thus reflects the synagogue's dual function as a house of prayer and a house of study. For that reason, *esnoga* may be compared to the Ashkenazi (Yiddish) term SHUL.

View of remains at Qumran on the western shore of the Dead Sea where a community presumed to have been Essene lived.

ESSENES A Jewish semi-monastic sect active during the latter part of the Second Temple period (second century BCE to the first century CE) in various areas of the Land of Israel, with prominent concentrations along the western shore of the Dead Sea. The etymology and meaning of the name are unclear. PHILO, the first century Jewish thinker, regards the name as implying "holy ones", whereas modern views see the title as denoting "piety," and according to an even more recent approach, "healers."

Knowledge of the sect is mainly based on the following ancient sources: among the Jews, the historian Josephus and Philo; the Roman writer Pliny, and Eusebius, one of the church fathers. Recent discoveries in the Judean desert have added to knowledge of this group. The sect's historical origins are obscure, with Josephus first mentioning them in a mid-second century BCE context. There is a possibility that the group originated in the days of Antiochus IV's anti-Jewish persecutions in the years immediately preceding the Maccabean uprising in 167 BCE (*I Macc.* 2:29; *II Macc.* 5:27).

The Essenes numbered over 4,000 adherents in the early first century CE. The community was organized in the form of an order with superiors to whom members were bound in utter obedience. Potential members were required to undergo a three-year probationary period. Only on completion of this period, and after having sworn a formidable oath consisting of a vow of frankness towards the sect brethren and to keeping the teachings of the order secret from outsiders, could one be fully accepted into the order.

Only adult males were admitted, though children were allowed to enter in order to educate them in the principles of the community. Members engaged in agriculture and crafts. All property was held in common, as were wages, food supply, and clothing stocks. Elected officials supervised the apportionment of all these items. The order had no slaves. The sick were nursed at common expense. Philo, Josephus, and Pliny all mention that the community totally rejected marriage on the grounds that women were wanton and incapable of fidelity, yet Josephus also knew of a branch of the Essenes who permitted the marriage of their members (*War* 2:160-1).

Personal modesty was stressed by the order as were physical cleanliness and ritual purity and the wearing of white garments. Temperance was considered a virtue, common pleasures a vice. Meals were eaten in common and appear to have been imbued with some sort of sacral character. The Essenes, though excluding themselves from the Pharisaic and common pale, nevertheless sent votive offerings but no animal sacrifices to the Jerusalem Temple (Philo, *Every Good Man is Free* 7:5). In contrast to the Pharisees, the Essene sect, according to Josephus, believed in an unalterable destiny (*Jewish Antiquities* 13:127), which meant, in effect, eliminating the element of free will. They were severely strict in observance of the Sabbath, again in contradistinction to the more considerable Pharisaic *halakhah*.

Whoever blasphemed the name of Moses was punished by death, while conviction of other serious crimes was punishable by expulsion from the order. They studied ethics "with extreme care." The Torah was read and expounded among them as among other Jews, although they possessed sacred writings of their own. During the Great Revolt against Rome (66-70 CE) Essenes were to be found in the ranks of the Jewish fighters. With the destruction of the Temple in 70 CE the Essenes, like other non-mainstream sects, vanished from the stage of Jewish history.

The general consensus of opinion today favors the identification of the Essenes with the Qumran community of the DEAD SEA SCROLLS.

ESTHER, BOOK OF One of the five "scrolls" (*megillot*) in the HAGIOGRAPHA section of the Bible (in the SEPTUAGINT and Vulgate, it appears at the end of the historical books). It tells the story of how Esther and her uncle Mordecai foiled the plans of the chief minister, Haman, to destroy all the Jews in the kingdom of Ahasuerus (Xerxes I, King of Persia), to whom Esther was married. The book is almost unique in the Bible in that it does not mention God's name even once (the only other such book is the Song of Songs.) The story ends with the hanging of Haman and his replacement by Mordecai, and with the Jews avenging themselves on their enemies. When the Scriptures were being canonized, there was strong opposition to the inclusion of the Book of Esther.

The Book of Esther is read in the synagogue on the feast of PURIM the anniversary of the day when the situation was reversed (Est. 9:1), at both the evening and morning services. Rules for its reading are in tractate MEGILLAH. It must be read from a parchment scroll, and a blessing is pronounced before the reading. Women, too, are obligated to hear the reading for "they too were saved by the miracle."

No other source has verified the events described and indeed historical knowledge contradicts certain aspects. Scholars are divided as to its historical value and some have suggested that the book was either a work of fiction or contained some historical fact considerably altered to communicate a religious teaching — Divine providence and God's direction of all events on earth. It was a highly popular work among oppressed Jews in the Diaspora who took comfort in its message of the ultimate downfall of the enemies of the Jewish people.

The Scroll of Esther was a favorite object of Jewish folk art.

BOOK OF ESTHER

1:1 — 1:22	Ahasuerus' feast and the ousting of Vashti
2:1 — 2:23	Esther is chosen as queen
3:1 — 4:17	Haman's decree to destroy all the Jews
5:1 — 7:10	Esther reveals to the king at the second feast Haman's plan; he and his sons are hanged
8:1 — 10:4	Mordecai is appointed as second to the king. The Jews fight their enemies and the festival of Purim is established.

ESTHER, FAST OF See FASTING AND FAST DAYS

ESTHER RABBAH Homiletical Midrash on the Scroll of ESTHER (see also MIDRASH AGGADAH). In its earliest form, this work is divided into six sections; later versions divided the sixth and last of these into five, making ten sections in all, with an introductory poem (*petiḇta*). The editor's sources were both Talmuds, other Midrashim (initially GENESIS RABBAH and LEVITICUS RABBAH) and the two Aramaic (Targum) versions of the biblical book. Esther Rabbah's first half (sections 1-5) probably dates from the amoraic period (before 550 CE); its second half was written much later (11th-12th cent.) and contains a wealth of aggadic material borrowed from the TARGUM SHENI to Esther and from *Josippon*, a pseudo-historical work of the tenth century. These early medieval sources provided various passages and interpolations, e.g., the dreams of Mordecai and Esther together with the description of Esther's appearance before Ahasuerus. The date of Esther Rabbah's composition is indicated by the fact that quotations from it only began to appear in works of the later Middle Ages.

ETERNAL LIGHT (Heb. *ner tamid*). A perpetually burning lamp associated with Jewish worship. It originated with the biblical command to the Children of Israel "to bring ... clear oil of beaten olives for lighting, to maintain light regularly" (Ex. 27:20-21 and Lev. 24:2). During the desert wanderings, these lights were to be arranged on the lampstand, or MENORAH, which was placed within the Tent of Meeting, in the Sanctuary. Aaron and his sons were responsible for its care, "from evening to morning before the Lord regularly" (Lev. 24:3-4).

In remembrance of the *menorah*'s position in the Temple, the synagogue created a niche for the Eternal Light, on the western wall opposite the ark. Later it was transferred to the wall beside the ark, and finally as a suspended lamp above it where it usually hangs in synagogues today.

When the Eternal Light consisted of a wick burning in olive oil, it was considered a meritorious deed and an honor to give donations for its upkeep. Special mention of the benefactors was made in the MI SHE-BERAKH prayer recited after the reading of the Law in synagogues on Sabbath mornings. In the wooden synagogues of Eastern Europe, the Eternal Light was placed in specially vaulted stone niches, as a precaution against fire. In modern times, however, the Eternal Light is electrified with a bulb whose encasement and pendant chains are often made of precious metal.

ETHICAL LITERATURE Paradoxically, Judaism's concern with morality, so central in the primary sources, did not, in later eras, receive the same attention and development in Jewish thought as other aspects of Judaism.

While it is likely that there were talmudic discussions of the Mishnaic tractates AVOT, DEREKH ERETS, and KALLAH, which had ethical components, these have not been preserved. Many of the moral teachings, like the rest of aggadic literature, did not receive the systematic attention of the codifiers. Only those teachings with defined behavioral implications found their way into the halakhic process and received appropriate elaboration.

While some systematic philosophers of the Middle Ages, such as MAIMONIDES and SAADIAH GAON, included treatments of morality in their works, the first book devoted wholly to ETHICS was the 11th century work by BAḤYA IBN PAKUDA, *Ḥovot ha-Levavot* ("Duties of the Heart"); its title is meant to contrast with the "duties of the limbs." Baḥya criticizes the preoccupation of the scholars of his time with the external physical acts prescribed by Judaism and calls for greater attention to the internal — belief, love and fear of God, purity of motive, repentance, and humility.

Jonah ben Abraham Leon Gerondi's *Sha'aré Teshuvah* attempted to show how personal development and closeness to God are dependent upon attitudes and speech. In the 18th century, MOSES ḤAYYIM LUZZATTO's *Mesillat Yesharim* ("The Way of the Righteous"), which prescribed steps for reaching inner piety and holiness, became the most popular and widely studied work of its type.

None of these works deals with morality as such, or with the obligations between man and his fellow-man directly; they rather see personality traits, such as humility and purity, as rungs on the ladder of self-perfection and reverence for God. Such traits are, of course, central to morality. However, they are treated together with attitudes such as faith and trust in God, which may be characterized as specifically religious.

Another literary form in which moral instruction was given developed during the Middle Ages in Europe, known as ethical wills, letters in which parents, in rather brief form, conveyed their last teachings to their children, stressing the importance of moral behavior. These were particularly frequent in the Middle Ages and developed into a literary genre. It became a custom in some families for every generation to pass on an ethical testament.

In the 13th century, a group known as ḤASIDÉ ASHKENAZ produced an "ethical" literature including *Sefer ha-Roke'aḥ* by ELEAZAR OF WORMS and *Sefer Ḥasidim* by JUDAH HE-ḤASID. The kabbalists also produced a number of "ethical" works, such as *Reshit Ḥokhmah* by Elijah de Vidas and *Tomer Devorah* by Moses CORDOVERO.

Most of the literature produced in the 18th century by ḤASIDIM could be called "ethical." Among the better-known works are *Tanya* by SHNEUR ZALMAN OF LYADY and *Sefer ha-Middot* by NAḤMAN OF BRATSLAV.

The MUSAR MOVEMENT, founded in the 19th century by Israel SALANTER and continued by his disciple Isaac Blaser, stressed the ethical dimension of Judaism. The movement, an educational trend within the *yeshivot* of Lithuania, was a conscious reaction to what was believed to be an unfortunate distortion in the emphases of the religious community of the time. Although the rank and file of observant Jews had developed great sensitivity to the ritual precepts, the moral precepts such as the prohibition of gossip, respect for the privacy and property of others, readiness to extend kindness, and the avoidance of ostentation and vulgarity, were seen to be neglected.

The *Musar* Movement sought, by means of certain educational innovations in the curriculum of the *yeshivot*, to develop in the individual a greater sensitivity to the pietistic and ethical aspects of Judaism. Its founders and later exponents drew upon a keen intuitive understanding of human psychology in formulating their educational approach to character development.

ETHICS Ethics is the science of morality or the systematic study of moral rules and principles. The term "morality" refers to rules which prescribe the way people ought to behave and principles which reflect what is ultimately good or desirable for human beings. In classical Jewish sources there is no term which corresponds to "ethics" or "morality" in this sense. The modern Hebrew word *musar*, which is used today for this purpose, while found in the Bible (Prov. 1:8), means "rebuke" or "chastisement." However, the primary sources of Judaism, the Bible and rabbinic literature, undoubtedly contain an elaborate moral code and the rudiments of an ethical theory.

Morality in the Bible The teachings of proper behavior are found in the Bible in different literary forms. The historical narratives of Genesis and Exodus and the books of the early prophets contain implied approval of particular moral values such as gratitude (Gen. 4:3), hospitality (Gen. 18), righteousness (Gen. 18:19), self-restraint (Gen. 39:12), benevolence (Gen. 24:18-20), humility (Num. 12:3), and intercession on behalf of the exploited (Ex. 2:11-12) as well as disapproval of murder (Gen. 4:11), corruption (Gen. 6:11-12), jealousy (Gen. 37:4ff.), and deception (Gen. 27:5-11). Among the various lists of commandments (Ex. 21; Lev. 19,25; Deut. 21-25) are moral rules interspersed with ritual and theological statutes which address relations between family members, old and young, employers and employees, rich and poor, men and women, rulers and ruled. There are also imperatives referring to general moral principles such as: "You shall love your neighbor as yourself" (Lev. 19:18), "Righteousness, righteousness shall you pursue" (Deut. 16:20), and "You shall do what is right and good..." (Deut. 6:18).

Of particular importance are the moral attributes used to describe GOD. The actions of God in Creation and in judging the world are seen as good and just. God Himself is held to the principles of justice and righteousness (Gen. 18:25), and in a special revelation He is described as "...merciful and gracious, longsuffering and abundant in goodness and truth, keeping mercy unto the thousandth generation, forgiving iniquity..." (Ex. 34:6). Implicit in the Bible is the concept of *imitatio dei* (IMITATION OF GOD) which was to be fully articulated by the rabbis. For if man is "created in the image of God" (Gen. 1:27), then he is capable of being like God. If the "way of God is justice and righteousness" (Gen. 18:19), then it is proper for man to imitate God: "You shall walk in His ways" (Deut. 11:22).

The Pentateuch comprises the legislative core of Judaism and includes its essential moral teachings. In the books of the later prophets, these moral teachings are applied to the social problems of the time and are delivered in the contemporary context with passion and literary skill. While in the exhortations of Deuteronomy the moral element is absorbed in the overall religious demand, here the moral component is often emphasized as the single consideration upon which the destiny of Israel may depend (Jer. 9:23; Amos 2:6-14, 5:21-24; Mic. 6:7-8).

In the Hagiographa portion of the Bible, moral values figure in the narratives of Ruth and Esther and are frequently the Divine attributes praised by the Psalmist (Ps. 11:7, 97:2, 99:4). In the Book of Proverbs, these moral teachings are judged wise and useful by the standards of human experience. Morality is presented here as dispositional character traits associated with particular moral types such as *tsaddik* ("just"), *ḫakham* ("wise"), and *yashar* ("honest"), and such negative types as *rasha* ("evil"), *evil* ("empty-headed"), *kesil* ("foolish"), and *letz* ("scoffer"). While the literary prophets emphasized social morality (see SOCIAL ETHICS), the WISDOM LITERATURE (Proverbs, Job, Ecclesiastes) focused on personal morality, i.e., moral values which are internalized as character traits that become part of the individual's personality.

Already in the Bible the beginning of a reflective approach to morality can be found. The Book of Job deals with the theological problem of theodicy — of the apparently righteous person who is visited with suffering. The Book of Jonah is concerned with wicked people who are apparently permitted to escape punishment. In sections of the Psalms and the Prophets there are attempts to reduce the large number of Divine demands to a few essential moral requirements (Mic. 6:8; Ps. 15:1-2).

At first glance, the Bible seems to be unaware of morality as such, moral rules being presented simply as one of a variety of commandments with no distinction being made on the basis of content. All are equally important and equally obligatory. However, the use of special terms for different types of commandments (with moral rules falling into the category of *mishpatim*) the unusual concentration of moral rules in the Decalogue (Ex. 20:1-14), and the promise of special rewards for a certain type of commandment which calls for benevolence (Deut. 23:21, 22:7, 24:13, 15:10, 15:18) would seem to indicate that the Bible recognized the special nature of the moral commandments and accorded them special treatment and importance.

This is supported by the close identification of God with moral values. In pre-Sinaitic accounts, God Himself is associated with morality only in terms of His actions; He performs deeds of justice and kindness. However, in the special revelation granted to Moses (Ex. 34:6), God is described in dispositional moral attributes ("merciful," "kind") implying that, in some sense, moral qualities are essential attributes of God and by imitating God in this, man can come into close proximity with Him: "... to love the Lord your God, to walk in all of His ways and to cleave unto Him" (Deut. 11:22).

Morality in Rabbinic Literature The moral commandments with behavioral content were expounded by the rabbis using the same exegetical methods they employed in other areas of the *halakhah*. For example, a commandment such as: "When you build a new house, then you shall make a parapet for your roof so that you bring no blood upon your house if anyone falls from it" (Deut. 22:8) was regarded both as a particular law about houses and roofs and as a general principle about moral responsibility in the home for human safety. As the former, the rabbis reasonably limited its application to dwelling places of a certain minimum height (*BK* 51b); as the latter, they broadened it to apply to open cisterns and any other hazard on one's property, and by extension to concern for such things as unsafe drinking water and industrial dangers in places of employment (*Sif. ad loc.*; *Ket.* 41b).

In treating the moral content of the biblical narratives, the rabbis employed the methods of *aggadah* and were able to discover all sorts of additional moral insights. Thus, from Gen. 18:12,13 they learned that "one may bend the truth for the sake of domestic peace"; from Gen. 18:1-3 that "being kind to strangers is more important than receiving the Divine Presence," and from Gen. 38:25 that "one should prefer to be burned alive than to embarrass one's fellow-man in public." They also explicitly made role models out of such biblical heroes as Abraham, Moses, and Aaron (e.g., *Avot* 1:12). In the Mishnah AVOT there is a concentration of moral teachings which emphasize personal character traits in the style of the Book of Proverbs. Taking their lead from the Bible, the rabbis continued the search for the master principle or supreme values of the morality of Judaism (*Avot* 2:1, *Mak.* 23,24). Thus: "R. Akiva said of the command, 'You shall love your neighbor as yourself' that it is a great principle of the Torah. Ben Azzai said there is a principle that is even greater: 'This is the book of the generations of Adam... in the likeness of God made He him'" (Gen. 4:1; *Sif.ad loc.*). In seeking to define the highest reaches of religious experience, the rabbis suggested moral qualities such as *ḥasidut* ("kindliness") and *anavah* ("humility"), while the biblical concept of *kedushah* ("holiness") was seen to have primarily a moral content (*AZ.* 20).

The rabbis generally referred to morality by the phrase *bén adam le-ḥavero* ("norms between man and his fellow-man"), which was included in the term DEREKH ERETS ("ways of the world"). From various expressions by some of the most authoritative rabbis it could be inferred that morality was deemed one of the central components of Judaism: "Simon the Just said, 'The world stands on three things: Torah, *avodah* ("Divine service"), and acts of loving kindness'" (*Avot* 1:2). Hillel said, "What is hateful to yourself do not do to your fellow-man. This is the entire Torah, the rest is commentary. Go and study" (*Shab.* 31a).

In terms of the content of the morality of Judaism, the basic meaning of key moral terms such as *mishpat* ("justice"), *tsedakah* ("righteousness"), *ḥesed* ("kindness"), and *raḥamim* ("compassion") is much the same as what is understood by current philosophic analysis. Yet there are special qualities to the morality of Judaism, which, in turn, seem to be the result of distinctive approaches.

The involvement of God in the moral struggle imparts a quality of urgency and passion which is unique to Judaism. "For I know their sorrows," says God (Ex. 3:7) and "... it shall come to pass that when he cries out unto Me that I shall hear" (Ex. 22:26). Hence the "hysterical" tone of the prophets. Injustice cannot be tolerated. Cruelty and human suffering shake the foundations of society. Judaism did not introduce new definitions of moral terms but rather revealed the true source of morality: God rather than man, prophecy rather than wisdom. Therefore, man could no longer be complacent about the moral situation. "Righteousness was asleep until it was awakened by Abraham" (*Midrash Tehillim*, Ps. 110).

In Judaism, the realm of morality is not restricted to deed but rather includes man's inner world of consciousness: thoughts, emotions, intentions, attitudes, motives. All are to a degree subject to man's control and qualify for moral judgment. Thus the Bible warns against coveting (Ex. 20:14; Deut. 5:18), against hating one's brother (Lev. 19:17), against "hardening one's heart" (Deut. 15:9,10), while the rabbis inveighed against envy, desire, and anger (*Avot* 2:11) and noted that "thinking about transgression may be worse than transgression itself" (*Yoma* 29a).

Biblical sensitivity to the harm as well as the good that could be done by speech was unprecedented: "Death and life are in the power of the tongue" (Prov. 18:21). Man must be careful not to lie, curse or slander (Lev. 19:11,14,16), nor to receive a false report or speak evil (Ex. 23:1, Deut. 19:16-18). The rabbis also condemned the use of flattery, hypocrisy, and obscene speech and urged the practice of clean, pleasant, and non-abusive language. In terms of the good that could be achieved by speech, the rabbis encouraged proper greetings to all, the need to cheer people with good humor, rebuke properly, and comfort with words in times of bereavement (*BB* 9, *Ta'an.* 22a). The *halakhah* endowed the spoken word with legal force and in the area of vows and oaths applied the biblical teaching: "He shall not breach his word, he should do according to all that proceeds from his mouth" (Num. 30:3).

In the ancient world, animals were sometimes venerated as gods or exploited for work or sport with extreme cruelty. The morality of Judaism includes concern for man's relationship to all living creatures. They are seen as junior partners in the building of civilization and therefore entitled to rest on the Sabbath (Ex. 20:8-10). Since "the Lord is good to all and His tender mercies are over all His works" (Ps. 145:9), man must follow suit: "A righteous man regards the life of his beast" (Prov. 12:10). Man must provide for those animals he has domesticated and must not cause them any unnecessary pain (*BM* 32b). A number of biblical laws seem to aim at preventing "anguish" and "frustration" to animals, particularly in regard to their care for their young (Ex. 23:5; Lev. 22:27,28; Deut. 22:4,6,7,10, 25:4). The rabbis prohibited causing animals pain for the sake of sport or hunting when not for the sake of food, and permitted experimentation with living creatures only when it seemed likely to lead to practical advances in medical treatment.

Concern for the dignity of man is another distinctive feature of the morality of Judaism, expressing itself primarily as respecting each person's privacy and being careful not to cause anyone shame or embarrassment. The rabbis incorporated into the *halakhah* a special category of "shame" or "indignity" in awarding compensation for damages caused one's fellow (*BK* 8:1). In this area, they showed their awareness of the irreducible dignity or worth shared by every human being, as well as their sensitivity to the individual needs of people depending upon each one's self-image and standing in life.

Sources of Moral Knowledge Even before the Sinaitic revelation, man was considered a moral agent and held responsible for his deeds (Gen. 4:6-7, 9:5-6), as the Bible assumed some intuitive moral knowledge on his part. This was developed by the rabbis with their concept of the seven NOACHIDE LAWS (*Sanh.* 56 a-b). Evidently these moral intuitions or natural laws were not sufficient for man to know what is right in complex situations of conflicting moral principles or to provide adequate motivational force to do what is right. Hence the Torah became necessary first as a national constitution for the newly formed Jewish people, but ultimately as a means of transmitting a more elaborate and serviceable moral code to all men.

While the morality of Judaism is essentially theonomous, grounded in God, it has many features of moral autonomy. Morality is what man must do as man. Man, a creature formed in the likeness of God, is endowed with innate worth and freedom of will. This means that he deserves moral treatment and is capable of treating others morally. God commands man to be moral because He cannot do otherwise. It is in the nature of the good to do good to others. "You shall walk in His ways" (Deut. 28:9) teaches not only what God wants of man but what God Himself is. Once revealed by God, morality is seen to be independent of Him in the sense that God Himself is bound by it. Hence the religious Jew strives to be moral for the love of God, but since God is the absolute good, man may be said to be moral because it is moral.

The morality of Judaism is universal. Its principles of behavior apply to all men and obligate all men. In the Bible all men and women are created in the image of God and have equal opportunity to participate in man's ultimate destiny, be it immortality of the soul on the individual level or to experience the messianic redemption on the historical level. The Jew is called upon to love his fellow Jew as himself (Lev. 19:18), to love the stranger as himself (Lev. 19:33, 34), and indeed to love all of God's creatures (*Avot* 1:12).

The morality of Judaism constitutes a system in the sense that its parts are related to each other by common origin, common purpose, and logical connectives. Moral rules can be justified on the grounds that they are deducible from moral principles. Thus all deeds of lovingkindness such as visiting the sick, comforting the mourners, dowering the bride, are implied in the precept: "You shall love your neighbor as yourself." No moral code can possibly anticipate the ever-changing human condition by providing in advance particular rules to cover all possible situations. Man was, therefore, given moral principles so that the members of each generation can deduce from them rules for themselves. The presence of these principles enables the system to achieve comprehensiveness, which is the ability to provide correct moral decisions for all situations.

Consistency is another feature of a moral system, implying the ability to resolve incipient conflicts between moral principles. The rabbis used their exegetical methods to infer from the Bible a hierarchy of values. Thus, "a positive precept overrides a negative precept" (*Shab.*133a), all negative commandments may be suspended in order to save a human life (Lev. 18:5), love of God stands higher than fear of God (Naḫmanides on Ex. 20:8), and peace is higher than truth (*Sanh.* 10; *BM* 87a). Human life, however, is not the highest value in Judaism as the Jew must be prepared under certain conditions to sacrifice his life in defense of the Jewish people or in order to avoid desecrating the name of God.

In Judaism, moral norms which are of a behavioral nature are incorporated in the *halakhah*. However, morality and *halakhah* are not identical. There are areas in which the demands of morality may go beyond the requirements of the *halakhah*. These are called *li-fenim mi-shurat ha-din* ("inside the line of the law") and are deduced from a biblical source (Ex. 18:20; *BK* 99a). Thus, for example, there may be a situation where by the strict provisions of the law one is not required to return a certain lost object to its owner, yet the finder may be morally obligated to do so (*BM* 24b). Thus, there appears to be in Judaism a class of duties called supererogatory, i.e., actions for which one receives special credit if performed but for which one is not faulted if left undone. (See also ETHICAL LITERATURE).

Man's Choice In an all-embracing axiological system such as Judaism, moral teachings can be understood fully only in the context of the system's view of man and the universe. So, for instance, there may be found in the opening chapters of the Book of Genesis, which narrate the Creation, a particular existential stance in which morality becomes central. When the Bible records the creation of man in the image of God and God's granting him dominion over all the earth, the text hints that although other creatures attain full realization of their potential by merely being, for man this is not the case. It is up to man, by means of his actions, to become like God. The Bible never explains what is meant by the "image of God." However, various commentators have identified it with such characteristically human faculties as language, free will, self-consciousness, reason, moral deliberation, invention, and cultural creativity. Man is called to live and work for God's purposes in this world, and he is thus an ethical being, a creature with moral responsibility capable of "choosing life and the good."

When man chooses "the way of God," that is to say the moral life, he not only actualizes his human potential, he completes the work of creation. Since Judaism holds that man's nature remained essentially unaffected by his so-called Fall, it expected moral development leading to the Divine way of goodness to be initiated by man himself. Man, by fulfillment of God's commandments is capable, on his own, of fulfilling his God-granted potential.

Later Thinkers The medieval Jewish thinkers did not give sufficient recognition to the moral aspect of Judaism, more or less glossing over morality as part of the perfection of the soul and the attainment of immortality in the world to come. So, for example, MAIMONIDES felt that immortality of the soul depended chiefly upon intellectual attainments. The knowledge of God necessary for achieving the world to come does, of course, include knowledge of God's moral nature and activity. Nevertheless, moral perfection in Maimonides' system does not really touch man's essence. Most other Jewish thinkers of the Middle Ages, along with Maimonides, believed that morality was necessary to human perfection, but were aware chiefly of its social utility.

Among the medieval philosophers, JUDAH HALEVI and CRESCAS, unlike their rationalist predecessors, believed the essence of the God-idea to be goodness rather than thought. Refusing to accept that knowledge was the highest good, they taught that closeness to God and eternal happiness come from love of God and that this is achieved by keeping the commandments.

Only in the 16th century, however, did JUDAH LÖW OF PRAGUE make explicit that the religious and spiritual aspects of morality do not stem merely from its being commanded by God. The connection is actually more substantive, since the most that has ever been revealed to man of God is His moral nature. Thus, only by acting morally does man walk in the ways of God and imitate Him, thereby fulfilling his Divine image. Moral action is the most direct way of cleaving to God and entering into fellowship with Him. Cruelty and injustice distance man from God, while kindness, love, and concern for fellow-man draw man closer. Love and fear of God are themselves based upon such moral sentiments as gratitude, justice and responsibility. Samson Raphael HIRSCH taught that "justice is the sum total of life and is the sole concept which the Torah seeks to interpret. The Torah teaches us justice towards men, justice towards plants and animals and the earth, justice towards our own body and soul, and justice towards God who created us for love so that we may become a blessing for the world."

Later Jewish thinkers who accorded a central role to morality in their philosophy of Judaism included Samuel David Luzzatto, Hermann COHEN, and Martin BUBER. The latter taught that the love of man is connected to the love of God in yet another sense: "Every particular Thou is a glimpse through to the eternal Thou; by means of every particular Thou, the primary work addresses the eternal Thou."

According to Judaism, morality is the bridge by which man reaches out to God. Morality is what unites man with his fellow-man on the basis of values grounded in the Divine. It is the fabric out of which man weaves for himself an ethical self and society achieves its redemptive goal.

ETHICS OF THE FATHERS See AVOT

ETHIOPIAN JEWS Jews have lived in Ethiopia since ancient times. They were called by others "Falashas" (in Ge'ez: "strangers" or "outsiders") and by themselves "Beta Israel" (in Ge'ez: "House of Israel"). They were cut off from mainstream Judaism for many centuries and there are several theories concerning the community's origin: that Ethiopian Jews are descendants of King Solomon's union with the Queen of Sheba; that they are of Hamitic (Cushitic) origin who converted to Judaism; that they are a branch of Yemenite Jewry; that they migrated to Ethiopia from Egypt; or that they are descendants of the tribe of Dan.

The religion of the Ethiopian Jews is based upon the Bible in Ge'ez translation, and a number of apocryphal books such as Judith, Tobit, I & II Maccabees, Baruch, Ben Sira, and the Books of Enoch and Jubilees. They do not possess the ORAL LAW.

Religious life is led by a *kes* (priest) who is assisted by a *debtara* (a non-ordained musician who chants the liturgy). Prayer in Ge'ez takes place in the *mesgid* (synagogue), which is divided into an inner "holy of holies" and an outer hall.

Religion is observed as prescribed in the *Orit* (Torah). The Sabbath is strictly observed and no fire is lit. Beta Israel observe the laws of purity strictly. Menstruating women, as well as women in confinement, are secluded in a special hut outside the village. A woman is considered unclean 40 days after the birth of a son and 80 days after the birth of a daughter (cf. Lev. 12).

On Passover, a paschal lamb is sacrificed and unleavened bread eaten for seven days. On the Day of Atonement, Beta Israel fast but do not sound the SHOFAR. Many additional fast days, not commemorated by other Jews, are observed, as well as additional festivals, the most important of which is the *Segd*. On this day, portions of the *Orit* (Torah) are recited, a sacrifice is made, and the community fasts. Although the fast of Esther is observed, Purim is unknown.

Before the 1970s, few Ethiopian Jews went to live in Israel. In 1973, a responsum issued by the Sephardi Chief Rabbi Ovadiah Yosef ruled, on the basis of a 15th century precedent by David IBN ZIMRA (Radbaz), that the Jews of Ethiopia were descendants of the tribe of Dan. In 1975, the Ashkenazi Chief Rabbi, Shlomo Goren, concurred. An interministerial committee of the Israeli government decided that Ethiopian Jews were entitled to full immigrant rights as Jews. Prior to 1984, some 8,000 Ethiopian Jews, mainly from Tigray Province, immigrated to Israel. In 1984, an additional 7,000 Jews, mainly from the Gondar area, were airlifted to Israel from the Sudan. An estimated 15,000 Jews remain in Ethiopia.

Ethiopian Jews being addressed by their religious leader at the Western Wall, Jerusalem 1984.

In September 1985, several thousand Ethiopian Jews demonstrated in Israel near the Chief Rabbinate's offices in Jerusalem. They objected to the Rabbinate's policy of demanding symbolic conversion of Ethiopian Jews wishing to be married in Israel. Although the Rabbinate recognized the Beta Israel as Jews, they had halakhic doubts as to their divorce procedures and their personal status. Early in 1985, the Rabbinate waived its requirement of symbolic recircumcision, but it refused to forego ritual immersion. The demonstrations lasted over a month, but their conclusion was indeterminate. The Chief Rabbinate continues to demand ritual immersion, while the community continues to demand the cancellation of these directives.

ETIQUETTE See DEREKH ERETS

ETROG See FOUR SPECIES

ETTLINGER, JACOB (1798-1871). Rabbi and halakhic scholar, one of the pioneers of NEO-ORTHODOXY. Educated in Würzburg, where he studied under Rabbi Abraham Bing and at the local university, Ettlinger proceeded to found a *yeshivah* (rabbinical academy) in Mannheim while serving as rabbi there (1826-36). Subsequently, as chief rabbi of Altona from 1836, he headed Germany's last fully autonomous *bet din* (rabbinical court), established another important *yeshivah*, and was considered one of the preeminent talmudists of his generation. Like his colleague, *Ḫakham* Isaac BERNAYS in nearby Hamburg, Ettlinger vigorously opposed the spread of Reform Judaism. He adopted an enlightened traditional approach to religious issues. Through two of his many pupils, Samson Raphael HIRSCH and Azriel HILDESHEIMER, he exerted a far-reaching influence on the course of "modern" Orthodox Judaism in Western Europe.

EULOGY (*hesped*). Funeral oration, delivered at or after a BURIAL, honoring a deceased person's memory (see FUNERAL SERVICE). The Hebrew verb *li-spod* or *le-haspid* ("to mourn, lament, eulogize") is used recurrently throughout the Bible in the context of bewailing the dead: Abraham's grief for Sarah (Gen. 23:2), Egypt's state mourning for the patriarch Jacob (Gen. 50:10-11), Israel's lamentation for the prophet Samuel (I Sam. 25:1), David's for Saul and Jonathan (II Sam. 1:12). In the talmudic era, special eulogies were reserved for outstanding scholars and other persons of note (TJ *Ber.* 2.8; *MK* 21b), departed rabbis being mourned in this way at each KALLAH month session of the Babylonian ACADEMIES. It was presumably as a result of that custom, in later times, that Ashkenazim chose 7 Adar, the traditional anniversary of Moses' death, as the occasion for eulogizing men of distinction whose deaths had occurred in the course of the past year. Rules governing the delivery of a eulogy (*hesped*) were formulated in the Talmud: the virtues and pious acts of the deceased should be emphasized (though not excessively) as a last gesture of respect that will give comfort to the bereaved and encourage others to follow the departed one's example (*Ber.* 62a; *San.* 46b-47a). The initial week of MOURNING (*shiva*) is the most appropriate time for a eulogy (*MK* 27b), which should be delivered — in the first instance — either in a town square or at the cemetery prior to burial (*BB* 100b). According to the *Shulḫan Arukh* (*YD* 344-5), pronouncing a funeral oration is a religious duty for which the interment itself may even be delayed if the speaker has to come from another town, but no eulogy may be delivered for a suicide or a person who has been excommunicated.

Jewish law prescribes that no *hesped* be pronounced on Sabbaths, festivals, New Moons, the day before or after a festival, during the month of Nisan, or on days when the TAḪANUN supplication is omitted from prayer services. In most traditional rites, it is delivered in the cemetery's chapel (*ohel*) immediately before burial, or at the actual graveside. A widely observed practice (*YD* 344.20) is for eminent rabbis or communal leaders to be eulogized at a synagogue, where the funeral cortege halts en route to the burial ground. In Eastern Sephardi communities, another eulogy is delivered at the conclusion of the first week of mourning; Western (Spanish and Portuguese) Sephardim, however, delay it until after the 30-day *sheloshim* mourning period, when the *hesped* is incorporated in a talmudic address. Parallel to this custom is the Ashkenazi memorial tribute (*azkarah*). Both Ashkenazim and Western Sephardim normally arrange for a short eulogy to be delivered at the unveiling (or "setting") of TOMBSTONES. Eulogizing the dead became a veritable art among Jews; it gave rise to a class of specialist eulogizers and

Wall plaque illustrating the rabbinic enactment Eruv Tavshilin, *permitting cooking on the day of a festival if it precedes a Sabbath. Germany, 19th century.*

A eulogy of the deceased (hesped) *delivered before burial. From a serious of painting of the Burial Society of Prague, c. 1780.*

to collections of funeral orations published in book form, some notable examples having appeared in the USA after World War II. American funeral parlors often have rabbis on call to officiate at a burial; the latter make a point of meeting with the bereaved family prior to the funeral so as to glean appropriate information which can then be woven into the *hesped*.

EVAR MIN HA-ḤAI (lit. "a limb from a living animal"). Rabbinic expression denoting a fundamental law of Judaism derived from the Bible (Gen. 9:4; Lev. 17:10 ff.; Deut. 12:23-25), forbidding the consumption of any flesh cut from the body of an animal while it is still alive. Such abhorrent practices were evidently widespread in ancient polytheistic society. Biblical legislation sternly forbade this type of cruelty as an offense against God, prohibiting all "flesh with the life thereof" or consumption of an animal's lifeblood. The *évar min ha-ḥai* rule was also considered mandatory for non-Jews (*San.* 56a-57a, 59a-b), being incorporated in the seven NOACHIDE LAWS.

EVE See ADAM AND EVE

EVEN SHETIYYAH See TEMPLE MOUNT

EVENING SERVICE (*Ma'ariv*, "[God] Who brings on the dusk," from the initial benediction recited; or *Arvit*, also derived from *erev*, "evening"). Daily prayer service recited after nightfall; traditionally instituted by the patriarch Jacob (on the basis of Gen.28:11). Unlike the other two daily (Morning and Afternoon) services, *Ma'ariv* does not replace a sacrifice offered in the Temple, since no offerings were brought at night. Though referred to as a *reshut* or voluntary prayer, in the course of time it came to be recognized as obligatory, the suggestion being that it corresponded to the disposition of leftover parts of the various sacrifices which were burned up during the night in the Temple.

On weekdays, the service begins with Ps.78:38, 20:10 and BAREKHU, followed by two benedictions prior to the SHEMA (the second being AHAVAT OLAM) and two other blessings after it, EMET VE-EMUNAH and HASHKIVENU. Outside Israel, Ashkenazim add a third extended benediction. Originally (and until about the ninth century), this was the end of the Evening Service and no AMIDAH was recited, because the *Amidah* prayer was thought equivalent to a Temple sacrifice. However, as worshipers felt the need for an *Amidah* and its supplications, one was added to the service but read silently, with no repetition by the reader. Services usually conclude with the ALÉNU prayer, together with the mourner's KADDISH. On Friday night, the eve of Sabbath, services begin with KABBALAT SHABBAT and then proceed with *Barekhu* and the *Shema*; special prayers are added after the *Amidah* and the service concludes with KIDDUSH (in the Diaspora), *Alénu*, and either the YIGDAL hymn or ADON OLAM. On Saturday night, Psalms 144 and 67 are chanted at the beginning (except by Ḥasidic Jews) and the service ends with Ps. 91, other biblical verses, and the HAVDALAH ceremony. Parts of the service (*Barekhu* and the various recitations of *Kaddish*) are omitted when there is no prayer quorum. On the Pilgrim Festivals, many Ashkenazi congregations in the Diaspora recite special poems known as MA'ARAVOT, which are included in the blessings before and after the *Shema*. On the first night of Passover, in Israel, HALLEL is read after the Evening Service; on the eve of the Day of Atonement, services include an extensive range of liturgical poems after the *Amidah*.

The earliest time when one may recite the Evening Service is 1 1/4 "relative hours" before sunset, a "relative hour" being defined as one twelfth of the time between sunrise and sunset on that day. The Evening Service should take place no later than midnight, the midpoint between sunset and sunrise; if unavoidable, however, it may be recited until dawn. When saying the evening prayers before nightfall, all three paragraphs of the *Shema* must be repeated after nightfall, that being the earliest time when one may fulfill the obligation to recite the evening *Shema*. In order to make it easier for people to attend, many congregations arrange the Afternoon Service late in the day, so that only a short time will elapse before the Evening Service can begin. A study session often takes place between the two services.

EVEL RABBATI (Minor Tractate) See SEMAḤOT

EVIL The existence of evil, death, suffering, and injustice in the world presents major questions to monotheistic religious thought, which views God as good and responsible for

Iluminated Scroll of Esther. Ferrara, 1616.

everything which occurs in His world. Questions regarding the source of evil, its purpose, and its status vis-à-vis God's goodness have exercised Jewish thinkers since Bible times.

The biblical perception states unequivocally the responsibility of God for both good and evil. Lamentations 3:38 states: "Out of the mouth of the most High proceeds not evil and good?" As opposed to the dualistic Persian perception, which held that good and evil come from different sources, the Bible affirms that evil is part of the framework of God's creation, and God states (Isa. 45:7), "I form the light, and create darkness: I make peace, and create evil." Evil, as everything else made by the Creator, has a purpose which is part of God's plan — "The Lord has made all things for Himself: yea, even the wicked for the day of evil" (Prov. 16:4).

At the same time, the Bible recognizes the difficulty for man in understanding the existence of evil, and gives expression to man's protest against the suffering, pain, and injustice in the world.

Ecclesiastes expresses a pessimistic view of the insignificance of life and the deficiency in creation: "I have seen all the works that are done under the sun; and, behold, all is vanity and vexation of spirit. That which is crooked cannot be made straight: and that which is wanting cannot be numbered" (Eccl.1:14-15). The greatest difficulty is to understand the success of the wicked in the world and the suffering of the righteous. The prophet Jeremiah does not question God's justice, but he asks, "Wherefore does the way of the wicked prosper; wherefore are all they happy that deal very treacherously?" (Jer. 12:1). The strongest expression of man's cry in the face of the suffering of the good appears in the Book of JOB, the righteous man who suffers without cause. The Bible does not offer any solution which alleviates the problem presented in Job. Its answer is that the purpose of evil and the lack of justice which stem from God cannot be fathomed by man.

Following along the biblical thought, the sages adopted the view that God is responsible for both good and evil, and that evil is a part of the Divine plan. They stress the good aim behind all God's deeds — "Everything that God does, He does for the good" (*Ber.* 60b). They stress that in the end, all of creation, even death, is good. Evil in the world is not expressed only in the death and suffering which affect man, but even in his character. The aspect of evil found in the Evil Inclination, as expressed in the sexual urges of man, is also aimed at good — "for had it not been for the Evil Inclination, no man would build a house or marry a woman or procreate children" (Gen.R. 9:7).

On the question of why evil befalls the just and why wicked people receive good, the sages offer a number of answers. One answer is that the just are being punished for the sins of their fathers, while the wicked flourish because of the merits of their fathers. The Talmud questions this answer, and gives another one: "When evil befalls the just, it is because they are not completely just, while when good befalls the wicked, it is because they are not completely wicked" (*Ber.* 7a). Unlike the Bible, which does not recognize a reward in the World to Come, the sages use this idea as the major answer to the problem of the lack of justice in this world (see REWARD AND PUNISHMENT). The suffering that is the lot of the righteous, and the good which is the fate of the wicked are but a small part of the proper repayment of their deeds. The major payment is given to man in the World to Come.

The medieval thinkers continued to contend with the question of evil, using the answers given by the sages. Together with these answers, these thinkers also included concepts derived from Greek philosophy. The major innovation is the perception that evil is nothing but a positive term for something negative — the lack of good. Under the influence of the neo-Platonic philosophers, evil, which is related to matter and darkness, is regarded as a deficiency. Whereas the biblical perception and that of the sages recognized the existence of evil as such and stressed God's responsibility for it, the aim of medieval philosophy was to move God away from the responsibility for evil by a view which denies the existence of evil.

The influence of Greek philosophy is especially to be found in Maimonides' *Guide for the Perplexed*. In Chap. 12 of Part III, Maimonides notes three types of evil which befall man: a) evil related to man's material nature, such as bodily handicaps and injuries, which exists either from birth or as a result of injuries of nature; b) evil which is caused to people as a result of the actions of other people, such as theft, murder, or war; c) spiritual and physical evil that the person brings upon himself, by following his lusts or by not living his life in accordance with the dictates of common sense. The source of the first two types of evil is the matter of which the world and man are composed, and these are inescapable. The third and most common type of evil is man's responsibility. None of these kinds of evil contradicts the perfect goodness of God. One who truly cleaves to God is outside the power of evil. Man's suffering stems from his inability to continuously cleave intellectually to God (*Guide* III, 51).

The various mystical streams dealt at length with the question of evil. The kabbalists burst through the philosophical system of concepts and developed ideas which do not attempt to evade the problem of the reality of evil. The various kabbalistic schools have in common the definition of evil as a special ontological domain, often described as being subordinate to the world of the Godhead and sometimes even as part of it. Within the framework of the theory of the SEFIROT (spheres of emanation), the kabbalists see the root of evil, sometimes even the world of evil itself, as being rooted in the Godhead. The Book of BAHIR presents this view in the most extreme fashion, when it states that "God has an attribute called 'evil'." In certain kabbalistic streams, certain tendencies appear; the world of evil is depicted as a hierarchic system which parallels in its structure the system of Divine *sefirot.* The view of evil as a system of powers paralleling those of the Divine world and as being engaged in a struggle with it, is to be found in the ZOHAR.

The perception of man as responsible for evil was given new significance by the Kabbalah. Not only is he responsible for those troubles which befall him, but man's evil deeds influence the status of evil in the entire world. Evil, which is contained within the Godhead in potential, emerges in practice as a result of man's sins.

In the modern and post-modern periods, Jewish thinkers have continued to apply the guiding values of Judaism to the problems of evil in their generation. In the 19th century, the foremost Neo-Kantian philosopher, Hermann COHEN (1842-1918), denied the existence of evil as a metaphysical power, which, he wrote, "exists only in myth." Echoing an earlier kabbalistic voice, Cohen understood suffering in general, and Jewish suffering in particular, as God's way of chastening and challenging man to greater ethical heights. Israel, especially, is called upon to act in accordance with the high moral standards of God's covenant and therefore is destined to be the constantly beleaguered "suffering servant." A love of morality is expressed in an act of conscience and not in detached debate of the subject.

Missing the opportunity to enter into a relation with another, by omission or commission, is the source of evil for Martin BUBER (1878-1965). According to his existentialist approach, human potential becomes misdirected and then takes on a momentum of its own. Although evil is never capable of becoming an independent force, it acts within man to thwart the self-realization that comes through a redeeming encounter with the other.

Efforts to evolve a religious response to evil in this century have had to reevaluate the covenant theology of Hermann Cohen and the "Eternal Thou" of Buberian thought in light of the cataclystic extermination of European Jewry during World War II. Buber himself, after the HOLOCAUST, expressed doubt whether he could address God as "kind and merciful," but never surrendered his faith in humanity's potential to redeem evil and sanctify the world.

For Abraham Joshua HESCHEL, the Holocaust became possible out of modern man's callous and careless attitude towards brutalization and the blurring distinction between right and wrong. God is certainly concerned about man's distinguishing between good and evil, however, and so fortified him with MITSVOT as an antidote to evil. The ultimate human problem, then, is not evil, but man's relation with God. Only by raising his existence to the plane of the holy can man feel God's nearness, and knowing that he is not alone, make the world worthy of redemption.

Similarly, the contemporary thinkers Arthur A. Cohen and Eliezer Berkovits identify the Holocaust as a purely human product, utilizing the metaphor of students who have rejected the teachings of their Master. Emil Fackenheim rejects the literalist's punitive interpretation of the events of the Holocaust and reaffirms God's symbolic presence in history and His ongoing relation with Israel. Ignaz Maybaum insists upon the literal meaning of the covenant while identifying the Holocaust victims as vicarious sacrificial offerings for the world's redemption. Richard Rubenstein, among others, formulates the modern Jewish problem of evil as the choice between two theological statements: either the covenant between God and Israel is abiding and therefore God's omnipotent justice is maintained as it was in Jewish tradition's interpretation of the first and second destructions of Jerusalem, or God's action in Jewish history must be redefined according to a new metaphor in order to allow for the non-punitive character of the Holocaust.

EVIL EYE (*ayin ra'ah* or *én ha-ra*; popularly *ayin ha-ra*). Widespread belief that certain individuals have the ability to cause harm by directing their gaze at others. According to this ancient, deep-rooted preconception, anyone gifted with the evil eye may inflict bad luck, sickness, or even death, and the potential victim must therefore devise ways to safeguard his person or property against a harmful glance. Superstitions of this kind originated in an idolatrous fear of provoking the gods or of tempting jealous mortals and "familiars" to cast an evil spell on the unwary (see DEMONS AND DEMONOLOGY; WITCHCRAFT AND SORCERY).

Practical MAGIC was used by the ancient inhabitants of Canaan to neutralize the effects of human or demonic malevolence: at Gezer, for example, archeologists have unearthed eye-shaped talismans presumably designed for that purpose (see AMULET). Biblical law, however, sternly forbade the Israelites to adopt such heathen practices and the "evil eye" in both Bible and Mishnah simply denoted ill will, jealousy, or an envious, niggardly character, (e.g., Prov. 23:6-7, 28:22; *Avot* 2.9,11; 5.13).

A more sinister note begins to appear in the Talmud and Midrash, possibly as a result of foreign (Babylonian?) influences. The aggadic reinterpretation of biblical narrative portrays the evil eye at work, casting spells on Jacob and Joseph (*Ber.* 54b), inspiring the Golden Calf idolatry that led to the shattering of the first Mosaic tablets (Num. R. 12.4), and being responsible for the death of 99 persons out of 100 (*BM* 107b). Although some of the sages, notably R. SIMEON BAR YOḤAI, could use the power of the eye to good effect (*Shab.* 34a), their chief concern was to deflect the evil eye and biblical verses were ingeniously interpreted to demonstrate that Jews could not be affected by it (*Ber.* 20a). However, despite this assurance, various countermeasures were prescribed. The evil eye might be averted by such precautions as concealing a woman's beauty, not flaunting one's wealth, and giving another name to an infant. Protective charms and talismans might be worn, while red or blue colors and mirrors were used to ward off a malevolent glance. Amulets are often mentioned in early rabbinic sources.

Although roundly condemned by Maimonides (*Yad,*

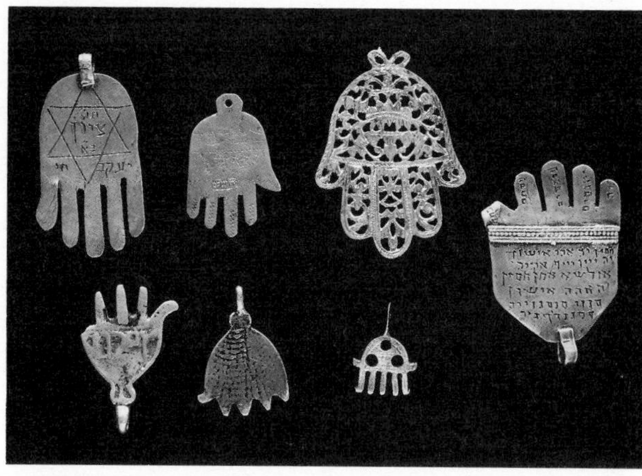

Amulets, in the form of hands with fingers spread, worn as pendants against the evil eye. North Africa, 19th century.

Akkum 11) and other authorities, popular faith in these superstitions never wavered. Among Jewish communities in both Christian and Islamic lands, various residual practices bear witness to a latent fear of the evil eye even today. It has been suggested as an explanation for the breaking of a glass at a wedding ceremony and for the rule whereby a father and son or two brothers are not called in succession to the Reading of the Law. Customs widely observed by Sephardi and Eastern Jews include the use of blue paint on a doorpost, displaying amulets inscribed with biblical or kabbalistic texts, and smearing a bride's hands with a reddish brown henna dye at the *ḥinna* ceremony arranged prior to the wedding. Eastern talismans often represent a hand with the fingers spread to "catch" or deflect the rays emitted by the evil eye. Parallel customs among Ashkenazim are the tying of a red ribbon or flannel strip to a newborn child and never giving the Hebrew name of a (living) father to his son. Ashkenazim often use the Yiddish expression, *Keyn ayn-hora* (shortened to *keynahora*, "May no one cast an evil eye"), to express the hope that a positive situation may continue.

EVOLUTION The theory propounded by the 19th century biologist, Charles Darwin, that all species of plants and animals developed over a period of millions of years from earlier forms by hereditary transmission of slight variations in successive generations. Jewish, as well as Christian, fundamentalists have considered evolution heretical since it is understood to contradict the biblical account of the six days of Creation during which all organisms were fully formed and after which no changes have occurred in them (cf. *Ḥul.* 60a). Menaḥem Mendel Shneerson, the rabbi of Liubavich, has repeatedly taught that a Jew must accept Genesis literally; God's creation was spontaneous, even if it created the seeds of gradual growth. Other Jewish religious thinkers point to aggadic and midrashic statements reflecting an evolutionary approach and warn against a literalistic interpretation of Genesis.

In talmudic times, R. Abbahu said that God created worlds and destroyed them before deciding on the existing world (Gen. R. 3:7), and in another rabbinic source, that Adam is not the first man, since "974 generations preceded the creation of the world and they were swept away because they were evil" (Midr. to Ps. 90:13; cf. *Shab.* 88b). According to R. Judah ben Simon there was "a succession of times (days and nights) before" the first day of creation (Gen. R. 3:7). Contrary to the biblical version, R. Nehemiah believed that "on the first day the entire world was created" (*Tanḥ.* B., Gen. 7). Moreover, R. Yosé held that hybridization, an adaptive agency in the evolution theory, represents one of humanity's most remarkable achievements since it enables the production of new organisms "like those formed by the Divine Creator" (*Pes.* 54a). Another rabbi suggested that God "changes his world every seven years," and cites certain creatures which are replaced by others (TJ. *Shab.* 1:3, 3b). R. Israel Lipschutz (1782-1860) in his *Tiferet Yisrael* quotes kabbalistic statements to back his theory that there were cycles of creation.

Although the literalists reject the idea that humankind has evolved from primates, rabbinic literature, in fact, alludes to this connection. R. Judah is quoted to have said "God made him (i.e., man) a tail like an animal and then removed it from him for his honor" (Gen. R. 14:12).

Jewish exponents of the evolution theory have also relied upon medieval sources for support. MAIMONIDES, for example, wrote: "Were we to accept Plato's teachings of the eternity of the universe, we should not be contradicting the basic principles of our faith... The biblical text could be explained in this manner" (*Guide*, 2:25). A statement from JUDAH HALEVI's *Kuzari* (1:67) is likewise brought in defense: "If one who believes in the Torah has to admit the existence of eternal matter and of other worlds prior to this one, his faith would not be affected." The British Chief Rabbi, Joseph Hermann Hertz, could affirm that "there is nothing inherently un-Jewish in the evolutionary conception of the origin and growth of forms of existence from the simple to the complex and from the lowest to the highest... Evolution, far from destroying the religious teaching of Genesis 1, is its profound confirmation" (*Pentateuch and Haftorahs*, 1938, p. 194).

The first Chief Rabbi of Palestine, Rabbi Abraham Isaac KOOK, endorsed the concept of evolution, holding that in any case the creation narrative is an esoteric teaching that must not be taken literally. He even applied the evolutionary concept to the upward trend in man's moral nature.

Other thinkers would see the Genesis story as the work of men with insight into moral truths but whose scientific knowledge was of their time. From this viewpoint, attempts to "reconcile" the Bible and the modern theory of evolution are irrelevant.

Many modern attempts to reconcile evolution and the

Bible have only homiletic value. Sermonic attempts in the 19th and 20th centuries to interpret the six days of Creation as a metaphor for geological epochs failed to respond to the philosophical problems inherent in the theory of evolution i.e., God's role in creation and in the moral direction and purpose of evolution. A comprehensive response to these crucial questions remains a major challenge to Jewish theologians today.

EXCOMMUNICATION Punishment decreed by a rabbinic court of law (BET DIN) upon those who gravely violate the commandments or fail to comply with decrees of the local rabbinate. At a time when the Jewish COMMUNITY was highly cohesive and its members were mutually dependent upon one another, the possibility of excommunication represented a serious deterrent. The first reference to the punishment of excommunication is to be found in Ezra 10:8, which states "Whosoever would not come within three days ... would be separated from the congregation." The Talmud (*BM* 59b) relates how, after R. Eliezer refused to acquiesce to the view of the majority of the sages, he was ultimately excommunicated.

At the time of the Talmud, there were, in practice, four different types of excommunication:

a) *nezifah* — a "rebuke" — which was the mildest form. In Erets Israel, this lasted for seven days and in Babylon for one. This device was used against those who showed disrespect to the exilarch (head of the Babylonian community), or against a student who showed disrespect for his teacher. The *nezifah* required the person to remain at home alone, and not come in contact with others.

b) *shamta* — a word of uncertain meaning, but possibly implying destruction. The exact punishment involved is a matter of debate. Some equate the *shamta* with *niddui* (below).

c) *niddui* — "separation." The standard term of *niddui* in Erets Israel was thirty days, and seven in the Diaspora, but the term could be renewed indefinitely if the person refused to change his ways. A person in *niddui* had to dress as a mourner and was permitted to enter the synagogue only by a side entrance to hear the Torah read.

d) *ḥerem* — "anathema." This was the most severe form. The person was forbidden to hear or teach Torah. Further, he had to observe all the laws of mourning, including not wearing leather shoes and not washing his entire body, although he did not have to tear his clothes. All except his immediate family had to shun him, and he could not be included in either a prayer quorum or a three person quorum for reciting the Grace After Meals. Should the person die in this state, a stone would be placed on his coffin, indicative of his being worthy of stoning. His close relatives were not to mourn for him.

The awe-inspring *ḥerem* ceremony was held in the synagogue. Black candles were lit, the Ark was opened, and the ram's horn (*shofar*) was sounded. A rabbinic court, consisting of three individuals, would then pronounce a curse, asking, *inter alia*, that the individual be struck by disease, that he lose his money, that he be cursed by all, that he not be buried as a Jew, and that his wife marry another. The *ḥerem* was open-ended and lasted until revoked.

After the talmudic era, the first three methods of excommunication fell into disuse. The *ḥerem*, used sparingly, was a powerful weapon. The restrictions listed above were the minimal *ḥerem*. Various courts added punishments as they saw fit. Sometimes, the person's children would be deprived of the right to be circumcised, educated in the local school, or even married. Even the MEZUZAH might be removed from the person's door.

A famous example of the use of the threat of excommunication was that of Rabbenu GERSHOM (960-1028 CE), for certain specified offenses. These included reading letters addressed to others, divorcing one's wife without her consent, and bigamy.

Two excommunications, which resounded throughout the Jewish world and beyond, took place in Amsterdam in the 17th century, where Uriel ACOSTA (who later committed suicide) was excommunicated, as was Baruch (Benedict) SPINOZA. The *ḥerem* was often utilized in religious disputes, one outstanding example being that imposed by Elijah, the Vilna Gaon, upon the ḤASIDIM. In Italy, it was used to enforce the payment of taxes.

OFFENSES PUNISHABLE BY TEMPORARY EXCOMMUNICATION (Niddui)

Continuing to work while a corpse lies unburied.

Trying to circumvent a court decision by appealing to the ruler.

Insulting a scholar.

Keeping dangerous dogs without proper precautions.

Referring to anyone as a slave.

Masturbation.

Working on the eve of Passover, and failing, in the Diaspora, to observe the second days of festivals.

Punishing anyone with temporary excommunication (*niddui*) without adequate grounds.

As the Jewish communities grew weaker, especially after Emancipation, the rabbinic courts resorted to ever more frequent use of the *ḥerem* in an attempt to maintain their power over the people. The result, though, was the opposite: the frequent use of *ḥerem* led to a general cheapening of its effect. Furthermore, the opening of the general society to Jews led to less dependence on the community, with the result that those in *ḥerem* were affected marginally or not at all.

In recent years, the *Edah Ḥaredit* — the extreme ultra-Orthodox community in Israel — has frequently invoked the *ḥerem* as a sign of its displeasure.

EXEGESIS See BIBLE COMMENTARIES

EXILARCH Head of the [Jewish communities in] Exile (Aramaic: *Rêsh Galuta*): A title borne by a distinguished Jew who represented the Jewish community of Babylonia to the non-Jewish rulesrs. The title was hereditary and traditionally its holders were descendants of the house of David. While the actual origins of the office are obscure, the first references to it in the Talmud date to the second century CE. The Talmud mentions 15-17 exilarchs, the most prominent being Mar Ukba, a noted scholar.

The exilarch was responsible for the collection of taxes from the Jewish community. He had the authority to impose fines on delinquents and to subject them to flagellation and imprisonment. His authority and influence varied in accordance with the attitude of the reigning king or caliph towards Judaism and Jews.

The relationship between the exilarch and the religious heads of the community, the *ge'onim* (see GAON) was frequently marked by conflict. Towards the end of the geonic period, the exilarch had to receive the approval of the *ge'onim* before his appointment by the caliph. As the Caliphate expanded geographically in the 12th-13th centuries, a number of exilarchs served simultaneously in various cities of the widespread Caliphate.

EXILE See GALUT

EXILE, BABYLONIAN The exile of part of the population of the kingdom of Judah by the Babylonian monarch, Nebuchadnezzar, in the early part of the 6th century BCE. The first deportation took place in 598 BCE, when King Jehoiachin of Judah surrendered to the armies of Nebuchadnezzar that had besieged Jerusalem. The king, his palace retinue, and 10,000 other captives were deported (II Kings 24:12-16) and Nebuchadnezzar set up Zedekiah, Jehoiachin's uncle, as king. Zedekiah, however, soon revolted and again Jerusalem was besieged. This time, in 586 BCE, the city was destroyed. The second deportation is described in II Kings 25:8-21. Only in 538 BCE were the exiles given permission by the Persian ruler, Cyrus, who had conquered Babylonia, to return to their homeland (Ezra 1:1-4).

Not all the exiles answered the call to return. Many remained behind in Babylonia, which became (along with Egypt) the first community of the Jewish Diaspora.

According to tradition, the Babylonian Exile lasted 70 years (Jer.29:10). It had a profound impact on Jewish religion, which for the first time, had no Temple focus. It is possible that under these circumstances, SYNAGOGUE worship emerged. The exiles would have held their own prayer services (the embryo of the LITURGY) with petitions to God for a return to Zion and the rebuilding of the Temple. The exiles would have been encouraged and inspired by the prophets of the exile, notably EZEKIEL and, according to modern scholars, the author of the second part of the book of ISAIAH. According to the rabbis, the period of the Babylonian Exile saw the change from Hebrew script to square script (see ALPHABET) and the introduction of Babylonian names for the months of the calendar. It also appears that Babylonian influence led to a more developed concept of ANGELS in Jewish tradition.

EXODUS, BOOK OF Second book of the PENTATEUCH, known in Hebrew as *Shemot* ("Names") from the second word of the opening sentence. In the Midrash it is referred to as *Sefer ha-Ge'ulah* ("the Book of Redemption"), because of its contents; the Greek Septuagint, however, calls it *Exodos*, "the Departure from Egypt".

BOOK OF EXODUS

1:1 — 2:25	Enslavement of the Israelites and early career of Moses
3:1 — 7:13	The call and mission of Moses
7:14 — 11:10	The first nine plagues visited upon Egypt
12:1 — 13:16	The paschal sacrifice and the tenth plague, — the slaying of the firstborn
13:17 — 15:21	The Exodus from Egypt and the Song at the Sea
15:22 — 17:16	The complaints of the Israelites and the battle with Amalek
18:1 — 18:27	Jethro's visit and advice
19:1 — 20:18	The Giving of the Law on Mount Sinai — the Ten Commandments
20:19 — 23:33	Statutes and laws
24:1 — 24:18	The ceremony of the covenant
25:1 — 31:18	The commandment to build the Sanctuary and its utensils
32:1 — 34:35	The Golden Calf, idolatry; replacement of the broken Tablets;
35:1 — 40:38	The building of the Sanctuary and its utensils.

Following the Latin Vulgate, printed Hebrew Bibles divide Exodus into 40 chapters and 1,209 verses. The Babylonian cycle of readings (which is followed today by all Jewish communities) divides the book into 11 sections (*sedarot*), but according to the Palestinian TRIENNIAL CYCLE of Second Temple times it contains 33 (or 29) sections. Traditionally, this volume encompasses a period of 129 years, from the death of Joseph to the building of the Sanctuary. Jewish tradition also maintains that Exodus, like the rest of the Pentateuch, was written by Moses with Divine inspiration.

In terms of form and content, this volume is a direct continuation of the Book of GENESIS, but constitutes a separate unit. Genesis describes the beginning of the Israelite people, first as individuals and later as a family; Exodus describes Israel's transformation into a nation. The Book of Genesis tells of God's assurance to the patriarchs that they will have descendants and a Promised Land, whereas Exodus demonstrates the gradual fulfillment of these promises in three stages: (1) The redemption of the Israelites from Egypt; (2) The covenant made by God with His people; and (3) The building of the Sanctuary.

The only hint concerning the historicity of events described in this book is the mention of two Egyptian cities, Pithom and Raamses (Ex. 1:11). Raamses was the capital of Egypt under the 19th dynasty, and was built by Ramses II (Usermare Ramses, 1294-1224 BCE). It is generally assumed that Ramses II was "the Pharaoh of the Oppression" and that the EXODUS from Egypt took place during the reign of his son and heir, Baenre Merneptah (1224-1204 BCE).

Among Bible critics, some hold Exodus to contain elements of three sources (J, E, and P) that were combined. The school of "form criticism" regards this volume as a narrative epic created to explain the festival of Passover. Chapters 1-15 constitute "the Passover legend," representing the *Sitz im Leben* of the book. According to this view, the sources which deal with the Giving of the Torah, the various laws (chapters 21-24), and the details of the Sanctuary (Tabernacle) are of later origin.

EXODUS Departure of Israelites from slavery in Egypt. According to the biblical account, the Israelites were slaves in Egypt for 430 years (Ex. 12:41) before being set free following the tenth plague — the killing of the Egyptian firstborn. Later, as the Israelites fled, the Red Sea miraculously parted for them and then closed over Pharaoh's hosts, who drowned in the sea (Ex. 14:15-14:30). The Exodus has symbolized the concept of freedom not only to Jews but to many other peoples. It was the Exodus from Egypt which led to the formation of the Jewish people as a single nation, and as such it is a pivotal event in Jewish history second only to the subsequent receiving of the Torah at Sinai. The Exodus also marks the direct intervention of God in history, and negates the conception of God as transcendent Creator Who, as it were, permits the world to run its course without Divine supervision.

The exact date of the Exodus is not indicated in the Pentateuch, but many scholars, basing themselves on external evidence, place the event as occurring approximately in 1280 BCE.

The Exodus has played a major role in Jewish life throughout the ages. The Pentateuch mentions the Exodus no fewer than 160 times, and the event is linked to many of the laws, such as: "I the Lord am He Who brought you up from the land of Egypt, to be your God; you shall be holy, for I am holy" (Lev. 11:45); "The stranger who resides with you shall be to you as one of your citizens ... for you were strangers in the land of Egypt" (Lev. 19:34); "You shall have an honest balance, honest weights... I the Lord am your God, Who freed you from the land of Egypt" (Lev. 19:36); "They (i.e., your fellow-Israelites) are My servants, whom I freed from the land of Egypt; they may not give themselves over into servitude" (Lev. 25:42); "For every first-born among the

The "dividing" of the Red Sea at the time of the Exodus from Egypt. Illustration from a Haggadah, *Trieste, 1864.*

Israelites, man as well as beast, is Mine; at the time that I smote every first-born in the land of Egypt I consecrated them for Myself" (Num. 8:17); "Remember that you were a slave in the land of Egypt, and the Lord your God freed you from there ... therefore the Lord your God has commanded you to observe the Sabbath day" (Deut. 5:15).

There is a specific commandment to remember the Exodus daily, as stated in the verse (Deut. 16:3): "You shall remember the day of your departure from the land of Egypt as long as you live." This requirement is fulfilled by reciting the third paragraph of the daily SHEMA, which states (Num. 15:41), "I am the Lord your God, Who brought you out of the land of Egypt, to be your God." There is a separate commandment to recall and discuss the Exodus on PASSOVER eve "You shall tell your son on that day, saying (Ex. 13:8) 'This is done because of that which the Lord did unto me when I came forth from Egypt,'" and the HAGGADAH recited at the Passover SEDER is devoted entirely to retelling the story. The KIDDUSH (sanctification) recited on Sabbath eve notes that the Sabbath "is a remembrance of the Exodus from Egypt."

EXODUS RABBAH Homiletical Midrash on the Book of EXODUS, apparently intended as a continuation of GENESIS RABBAH; in Hebrew, it is known as *Shemot Rabbah* (see also MIDRASH AGGADAH). Divided into 52 sections, it is a composite work of two unequal parts differing in style and terminology. Part 1 covers the first 14 sections and ends at the point (Ex. 12:2) where the MEKHILTA DE-RABBI ISHMAEL begins. In this first portion of the Midrash, each verse of the biblical text (and, at times, each word) is expounded homiletically. While the language employed is basically Mishnaic, traces of early medieval Hebrew can also be detected. The editor's rabbinic sources included the tannaitic and amoraic Midrashim, both Talmuds, and other Midrashim of the TANḤUMA (Yelammedenu) type. In dividing this work into sections, the editor followed the TRIENNIAL CYCLE of Torah readings once customary in Erets Israel.

The second half of Exodus Rabbah, a homiletical Midrash on chapters 12-40 of the biblical book, is also written in the style of *Tanḥuma* and the divisions are again based on the triennial cycle. Each section is introduced by a proem (*petiḥta*), sometimes in the name of R. Tanḥuma. As in DEUTERONOMY RABBAH, the homilies often conclude with words of consolation and an expression of hope for speedy redemption. The language employed is Mishnaic Hebrew with an admixture of Galilean Aramaic. While utilizing the tannaitic Midrashim, this editor only occasionally draws on the Babylonian Talmud. Since many of the homilies are found also in the *Midrash Tanḥuma*, Part 2 must have been redacted some time in the ninth century. A copyist, probably in the 11th century, combined the two parts into a single Midrash which NAḤMANIDES (in his commentary on the Pentateuch) was the first medieval author to quote.

EXORCISM See DIBBUK; WITCHCRAFT AND SORCERY

EYBESCHÜTZ, JONATHAN BEN NATHAN NATA (c. 1690-1764). Talmudist and kabbalist. Although Eybeschütz was born in Cracow, his father was a rabbi in Eibenschitz, Moravia, hence the family surname. After studying in *yeshivot*, Eybeschütz traveled to Vienna and then to Prague where he became a popular preacher. Hostility on the part of family and friends played a major role in an accusation that he was a follower of the false Messiah, SHABBETAI TSEVI. Eybeschütz swore that the accusation was untrue, and he was among the signatories of the rabbinic letter of *ḥerem* (EXCOMMUNICATION) written in Prague against adherents of Shabbetai Tsevi.

Realizing that his future was bleak in Prague, he became a candidate for the rabbinate of Metz (1733), but was chosen only eight years later. In Metz, he again had admirers and detractors. Eventually, in 1750, Eybeschütz became Chief Rabbi of the three neighboring German communities of Altona, Wandsbeck, and Hamburg. His rival had been Rabbi Jacob EMDEN. Rumors immediately spread that Eybeschütz had given amulets to ward off illness, in which the words "His anointed one Shabbetai Tsevi" had been found. The amulets were shown to Jacob Emden, then living in Altona, who stated that the writer was a Shabbatean. The greatest rabbis of Poland and Moravia, together with the leaders of his own community, defended Eybeschütz, and Emden was forced to take refuge in Amsterdam, where his brother-in-law was rabbi, until the controversy subsided (1752). Three years later, Eybeschütz published his *Luḥot Edut*, in which he countered the accusations against him.

In 1756, he was accorded royal and state recognition as Chief Rabbi of the Three Communities, by the Danish king and the Hamburg senate.

The last eight years of his life were the most peaceful, and when he died, even Eybeschütz's enemies admitted that the communities mourned a beloved and respected rabbi.

He was among the greatest preachers and talmudists of his age, and his writings include novellae (*ḥiddushim*) on the *Shulḥan Arukh* which show his keen intellect; volumes of sermons; and a kabbalistic work — *Shem Olam*.

Scholars still dispute whether Eybeschütz was a secret Shabbatean.

EYE FOR AN EYE See RETALIATION

EZEKIEL The third of the major prophets in the Prophetical section of the Bible, the other two being ISAIAH and JEREMIAH. From the scarce and scattered references to his life, embedded in his prophecies, it appears that he was the son of Buzi, probably from the priestly family of Zadok. In 597 BCE he was among those carried to Babylonia by Nebuchadnezzar, along with King Jehoiachin and the aristocracy of the kingdom of Judah. He settled in or near Tel

Abib, a Jewish colony by the Chebar canal, where he had a vision of the throne-chariot of God and was consecrated as a prophet. Ezekiel's prophetic activity began in the fifth year of Jehoiachin's exile and extended through 22 years (the latest date indicated in his book is 571 BCE). There is a Jewish tradition that Ezekiel is buried in Babylonia, his grave being located between the Euphrates river and the Chebar canal. See EZEKIEL, BOOK OF.

EZEKIEL, BOOK OF Third book in the Prophetical section of the Bible. Presented in the first person by the prophet EZEKIEL, it consists of 48 chapters, and is divided into 1,273 verses. According to Jewish tradition, the book was edited by the Men of the GREAT ASSEMBLY (*BB.* 15a). Notwithstanding the occasional interweaving of heterogenous prophetic utterances, it may be thematically divided into the following sections: a) Chapters 1-24: Denunciations addressed against Judah and Jerusalem. Ezekiel portrays a very gloomy picture of the entire history of Israel, as one of continuous sinfulness and rebellion against God. Consequently, his message is essentially of utter and inevitable doom. The dramatic representations and bizarre symbolic acts which often accompany his utterances give color and forcefulness to his message. Notable among the acts representing the impending doom are the eating of a scroll in which "lamentations and mourning and woe" are inscribed (chaps. 2:9-3:3); the drawing of the city of Jerusalem on a clay tablet and raising a siege against it as a symbol of its fate (4:1-4:8); baking barley loaves over human excrement, representing the unclean food the Israelites will eat in exile (4:12-4:13); shaving his head and beard with a sharp razor, and burning one third of the hair in fire, striking another third with a sword, and strewing the last in the wind. Even the death of the prophet's wife and his dramatic abstention from mourning serve as a powerful symbol of doom (24:15-24:23). Ezekiel's denunciation and his dramatic representations, though attracting a wide audience, were looked upon as a sort of entertainment (33:31-32). b) Chapters 25-32: Oracles of doom against foreign nations: Ammon, Moab, Edom, Philistia, Sidon, Tyre, and Egypt — all severely denounced for their attitude toward Judah, particularly after the destruction of Jerusalem in 586 BCE. Tyre and Egypt are the main targets of the oracles. The acts of chastisement against the foreign nations are intended to achieve a grand divine purpose: the sanctification of God's name and the magnification of His glory. Each of the oracles against the nations includes variations of the well-known Ezekelian recognition formula: "That they may know that I am the Lord God." c) Chapters 33-48: Oracles of consolation and restoration. These chapters include the celebrated vision relating to the revival of the dry bones, symbolizing the Israelites in exile (chap. 37) and the Gog and Magog oracles (chaps. 38-39). The last nine chapters of the book (40-48) provide visions of the new Jerusalem and a sketch of the constitution of the new Israel, centered around the newly restored sanctuary, to which the glory of God will return.

Ezekiel is noted for the introduction of unusual themes, some being unique to him, others the products of elaboration and forceful articulation of scattered biblical notions. They include: a) The restoration of Israel as a coercive act of God; b) a total rejection of corporate responsibility and a strong emphasis on the individual's responsibility for his own deeds; c) The Gog prophecy, in which he envisions a vast invasion by GOG and his hordes against the restored people of Israel which will be repelled. This victory will demonstrate God's superiority to the world.

The legal, ritual and theological teachings contained in the Book of Ezekiel conflict in a number of points with those of the Torah. The rabbis were troubled by the many divergences, and only admitted the book into the canon after long discussions. As the Talmud states it, the sages wished to exclude the book from the canon, until Hananiah son of Yehezkiah reconciled Ezekiel's rulings with Jewish law (*Shab.* 13b). Yet, because of the numerous rulings it contains and the prophecy concerning the rebuilding of the Temple, the book is considered by Jewish tradition to be the most sacrosanct of all books of the Bible after the Pentateuch. At the same time, the sages are adamant in asserting that there is no law originated by Ezekiel, for no prophet has the right to originate any new commandment. Instead, his work is seen as being based on the ORAL LAW which, by tradition, was handed down with the Pentateuch and explains it. Ezekiel is often used by the sages to expound on the meaning of laws in the Pentateuch. The Book of Ezekiel is also the source for laws pertaining to MOURNING, as deduced from chap. 24 (*MK* 15a-b, 27b).

BOOK OF EZEKIEL

1: 1- 3:21	Ezekiel's call
3: 22-24:27	Prophecies directed against Judah and Jerusalem prior to the destruction of Jerusalem
25: 1-32:32	Oracles of doom against seven foreign nations
33: 1-39:29	Prophecies of Israel's restoration
40: 1-43:12	Vision of the future Temple
43:13-46:24	The restored cult
47: 1-47:23	The river of holiness
48: 1-48:35	The holy land

Scholars over the last century have disputed the unity and authorship of the book with views ranging from a strictly traditional approach affirming its unity, to a highly critical view questioning its unity, authorship, and date. Recent studies tend to a basically conservative approach, adhering to the book's own assertions concerning the time and place of the prophet's proclamations while maintaining that portions of the text have been disfigured by corruptions and are therefore confused.

EZRA Priest, scribe and religious reformer who led a group of Babylonian exiles back to Jerusalem in 458 BCE. His known activity began in the seventh year of the reign of the Persian king, Artaxerxes I (Ezra 7:7). At first, he seems to have acted unassisted, but after he was joined by NEHEMIAH, the two worked together.

Ezra was a descendant of the High Priest at the time of the destruction of the Temple in 586 BCE. He is called "a scribe expert in the Teaching of Moses" (Ezra 7:6) and "a priest-scribe, a scholar in matters connected with the commandments of the Lord, and His Laws to Israel" (Ezra 7:11). When Ezra moved to Judah from Babylonia, the king permitted him to accept gifts for the Temple, to appoint judges and to teach the Torah. On the Feast of SUKKOT after his arrival in Jerusalem, he convened a great assembly, which, under his influence, resolved to make a covenant to evict all foreign wives taken by Jewish men who had not gone into Exile, as well as the children of these wives.

His second project was the convening of an assembly of the people on ROSH HA-SHANAH. Ezra read the Torah until midday, and influenced the people to observe its commandments. The people confessed their sins and made a covenant to observe the Torah and to divorce their foreign wives.

Rabbinical tradition holds Ezra in great respect. He is considered to have been on a level with Moses in his knowledge of the Torah (*San.* 21b). The Jews of Judah had forgotten the Torah during the Babylonian Exile, and Ezra taught it to them anew (*Suk.* 20a). He established the GREAT ASSEMBLY. Ezra ordained ten decrees, including the READING OF THE LAW at the Sabbath Afternoon Service and at the MONDAY AND THURSDAY Morning Services. He also ordained that courts be convened on market days (*San.* 43b). Ezra, say the rabbis, changed the script from the ancient Hebrew script to the Assyrian (square) script (see ALPHABET). Ezra was involved in the codification of the Pentateuch, in that he ordained that certain words be marked with dots above them in cases where there was doubt concerning how they should be written (*ARN* 34). According to Josephus, he was buried in Jerusalem; however, another tradition holds that his grave is on the Shatt-el-Arab by the banks of the River Tigris. (See EZRA AND NEHEMIAH, BOOKS OF).

EZRA AND NEHEMIAH, BOOKS OF Two books in the HAGIOGRAPHA section of the Bible. According to rabbinic tradition (*BB* 14b), they were originally a single book called Ezra, written by EZRA the Scribe and completed by NEHEMIAH. The Church Father, Origen, and following him the Vulgate (the Latin translation of the Bible), divided the book into two, labeling the second part the Book of Nehemiah. The sages also believed that the Book of Chronicles was written by Ezra. However, modern scholarship suggests that the three works are separate compositions. In the Hebrew Bible, Ezra-Nehemiah appears after the Book of Daniel, although according to the Talmud (*ibid.*) it belongs before Chronicles.

Ezra-Nehemiah is the main source of information for the period of the Return to Zion from the Babylonian EXILE and the rebuilding of Jerusalem and the Temple. It covers a century of history from Cyrus' decree (538 BCE) to the reign of Darius II (c. 420 BCE).

Ezra-Nehemiah is a compilation of various sources and documents. Parts of the Book of Ezra (4:8-6:18; 7:12-7:26) are in ARAMAIC which is used in quoting official documents as well as in telling the story.

BOOKS OF EZRA AND NEHEMIAH

	Ezra
1:1 — 1:11	Declaration by Cyrus and the first emigration from Babylonia
2:1 — 2:70	List of those who came to Zion under Zerubbabel's leadership
3:1 — 3:13	The building of the altar and the festivities at the laying of the foundations of the Temple
4:1 — 4:24	Disturbances to the building by the Samaritans
5:1 — 6:22	The completion of the building of the Temple after the receipt of permission from Darius
7:1 — 7:10	Ezra's lineage and his move to Jerusalem
7:11 — 7:22	Artaxerxes' letter to Ezra
8:1 — 8:14	List of those who traveled with Ezra and their lineage
8:15 — 8:30	The move by the Levites, the Nethinim (Temple servants), and the priests
8:31 — 8:36	The journey to Jerusalem and the offering of sacrifices
9:1 — 10:44	The sin of the inhabitants of Jerusalem — mixed marriages with foreign wives as well as a list of priests who had done so.
	Nehemiah
1:1 — 2:10	Nehemiah is concerned about the condition of his fellow Jews in Jerusalem, and receives permission from the king to go to Jerusalem

2:11 — 2:20	Nehemiah decides to rebuild the wall of Jerusalem
3:1 — 4:17	The building of the wall of Jerusalem, disturbed by members of neighboring nations
5:1 — 5:14	The freeing of the Hebrew slaves and the lowering of the tax burden
6:1 — 7:4	In spite of the disturbances, Nehemiah completes the building of the city wall
7:5 — 7:72A	A list of the lineage of those who returned from exile in Zerubbabel's time
7:72B — 8:12	The reading of the Torah by Ezra on Rosh ha-Shanah
8:12 — 8:18	The Sukkot festival
9:1 — 9:37	Isolation from the foreigners and the confession
11:3 — 11:36	List of the residents of Jerusalem and the cities of Judah
12:1 — 12:26	A list of priests and Levites who went into exile with Zerubbabel
12:27 — 12:43	The dedication of the Jerusalem wall
12:44 — 13:13	The appointing of officials in the Temple, Ezra's second trip to Jerusalem
13:14 — 13:31	Ezra's decrees about the Sabbath and the banishing of the foreign wives.

EZRAT NASHIM (lit. "women's court"). Separate prayer area for women. The original *ezrat nashim* was located in the eastern sector of the court of the Second Temple. Square in shape with no roof overhead, each side was 35 cubits long. In each corner there were square chambers. The chamber for NAZIRITES was in the southeastern corner; for the lepers in the northwest. A balcony circled around the entire court and during the celebration of the Water-Drawing festival, in order to prevent any licentiousness, the women ascended to the balcony.

The separate section for women in the Temple does not seem to have affected the early synagogues in Erets Israel and the Diaspora. Where such early synagogues have been found, there has been no evidence of a separate women's section. By medieval times, women were definitely separated from men in the SYNAGOGUE. Sometimes the women sat in a gallery (curtained from view) and sometimes in an annex to the main hall. In synagogues in southern France of the late Middle Ages, the women sat in a room under the main prayer hall with a grating in the ceiling that permitted them to hear the service. In Muslim lands, the women often sat

The women's gallery (Ezrat Nashim) *above the main hall, closed in by a wood divider* (meḫitsah) *in the Veneto Synagogue, Italy, 1702.*

outside the prayer hall and listened through the windows. In the wooden synagogues of Poland, women were generally consigned to a lean-to annex, to which there was a separate entrance so that men and women would not enter the synagogue by the same door.

The separation in the synagogue of men and women sitting on the same level or with the women on a slightly raised balcony, was made possible by the addition of a *meḫitsah*, a divider of wood, metal, or cloth. This division clearly delineated the men's and women's sections. While the original dimensions of the *meḫitsah* are unknown, various rabbinic responsa were promulgated detailing specific height, width, and other measurements.

The *meḫitsah*, when made of cloth, was never opened during the service. In Sephardi synagogues, the *meḫitsah*, as a curtain, was pulled back when the Scrolls of the Law were taken out of the ark and while they were being read. This practice is still in effect in most Sephardi congregations and frequently the rabbi speaks just after the Scrolls are returned to the ark while the *meḫitsah* is still open. The practice of opening the *meḫitsah* has reached certain Ashkenazi circles, and during the rabbi's sermon the *meḫitsah* is sometimes opened so that the women can see the rabbi and hear him better.

The Reform Movement, at its inception in 19th century Germany, called for family seating in the synagogue, removed the *meḫitsah*, and closed down the separate balconies. The Conservative Movement moved more slowly, in some instances having men and women sitting in separate sections of the sanctuary on the same level. Now almost all Conservative congregations have family seating.

F

FAITH Acceptance of a concept that cannot be proved beyond all doubt by human reasoning. The Hebrew words *emunah* and *bittaḥon* refer to different aspects of faith: *emunah* is the traditional meaning of 'faith' while *bittaḥon* is trust or faithfulness. The biblical use of the former means "faith in," which is the effective attitude of trust in God and confidence in the fulfillment of His promises. In the ancient sources, use of *emunah* does not signify belief that God exists, which was taken for granted. The term '*emunah*' is found in the Bible in various contexts whose basic meaning is "to be firm" (from which AMEN also derives): "They had faith in the Lord and in Moses, His servant" (Ex. 14:31) or "The righteous shall live by his faith" (Hab. 2.4).

Faith in God as "trust" is important in biblical religion since so much of man's encounter with God has to do with promises which are to be fulfilled in the distant future. Thus landless and barren PATRIARCHS are asked to envision their eventually developing into a numerous people, with a land of their own. With each of the biblical generations, the word of God is mainly directed toward the future. Therefore, in the formative period, the vital "faith" element is not so much whether God appeared at some point in the past or even whether He exists somewhere at the present time, but rather, "can we rely upon His promises for the future?" and this requires "trust," an abiding confidence in the essential goodness, steadfastness, and consistency of the Promisor.

Nowhere does the Bible speak unequivocally of the importance of "faith" in the cognitive sense of "belief that" something is the case, namely, that God exists. This is not because these cognitive beliefs played no role in Judaism. On the contrary, "belief *in*..." presupposes "belief *that*..." God cannot be trusted in if His existence is denied. "Belief that..." is not stressed in the Bible in connection with God because it was taken for granted. The sense of the presence of God as a living, palpable reality was strongly self-evident.

The prophets inveighed against those who, while acknowledging the existence of God, denied that He is aware of human affairs (Ps. 94:7) or that He governs justly (Ezek. 18:23; Mal. 2:17, 3:14). Most important for them is the question of the kind of God believed in and its implications. Belief that the Lord your God "took you out of the land of Egypt" (Ex. 20:2), means that He intervenes in human affairs. "The Lord our God is One" (Deut. 6:4) implies that IDOLATRY and polytheism are lies without power. Here, in the view of the rabbis, "He who denies idolatry is as if he acknowledged the entire Torah" (*Sif.*, Deut. 28). Rather than emphasize the importance of "belief" as such or the saving power of dogma, the rabbis stressed the disastrous consequences of denying the basic beliefs. They spoke of the *kofer ba-ikkar* ("he who denies the roots," i.e., belief in the one God) and ruled in the Mishnah (*San.* 11.1): These are the ones who are excluded from the World to Come: He who denies the Resurrection, that there is no Torah from Heaven [denies Divine revelation], and the EPIKOROS..." (who denies) belief in Providence and reward and punishment; see HERESY). Furthermore, the rabbis frequently traced specific transgressions to a lack of faith on the part of the sinner (e.g., *San.* 38b).

The entire structure of beliefs and practices called Judaism rests upon certain cognitive presuppositions, in the absence of which the entire structure collapses. However, absent from Judaism is the concept of catechism, that there is some special spiritual efficacy in the act of affirming the belief itself.

In the Middle Ages, Jews encountered atheism, and in expounding theism used the term *emunah* to affirm the belief in the existence of God. Now, a differentiation is made between *emunah* and *bittaḥon*, as proof of the existence of God precedes the concept of trust. Jewish philosophers now debated the question as to what are the basic principles of Judaism. Moses MAIMONIDES (1135-1204) was the first to formulate the creed of Judaism in thirteen PRINCIPLES OF FAITH. These were intended as criteria for membership in the community of Israel, thereby granting a share in the world to come.

The controversies precipitated by this formulation over the next three centuries affected the philosophical development of Judaism. They resulted in a clarification of the content of these fundamental beliefs themselves and helped to refine the concepts of rational analysis and to remove folk accretions. They also helped to define the position of Judaism vis-à-vis Christianity and Islam.

Few of those who disagreed with Maimonides actually denied that any of the Thirteen Principles were in some sense part of Judaism. The issues were rather: can any group of doctrines in Judaism be said to be more important than any other (Abravanel); can it be said that denial of any one of the Thirteen Principles bars one from a share in the world to come? (Ibn Daud); are all the Thirteen equally fundamental in the sense that denial of any one renders the entire structure of Judaism untenable? (Albo); and why were certain important principles, such as freedom of will, omitted?

The rabbis had already detected in the SHEMA (Deut. 6:4) and in the first statement of the Decalogue (Ex. 20:2) a call to accept "the yoke of the Kingdom of Heaven" (*Ber.* 2.1) which implied a total subjection of the individual to the authority of God. Maimonides saw in this a command to believe in the existence of God. On purely logical grounds, Ḥasdai CRESCAS argued that one could hardly speak of a "commandment" before one had accepted the notion of a "commander." Others raised the objection that since faith was a condition of the mind which came about in respect to evidence, how could one speak of a "command to believe"? Either there is adequate evidence, in which case a command is not necessary, or there is not adequate evidence, in which case a command to believe is futile. ABRAVANEL suggests that while the intellect cannot be commanded to assent to propositions, one could be ordered to do certain things that might possibly bring about belief, such as investigate certain questions, weigh possibilities, gather evidence, seek out the counsel of believers.

Grounds for Belief To those who lived in the biblical period, it seemed that evidence of God's presence and activity was so apparent that only willful blindness motivated by self-interest or being misled by a false prophet could explain disobedience. By the time of the rabbis, however, in the absence of direct encounters with God, the need to justify one's faith in the face of challenges by Greeks and Romans had become commonplace. By the tenth century CE, the rise of the KARAITE sect within Judaism, as well as claims by Christianity and Islam to valid religious revelations, resulted in critical reason being employed to determine the true faith (although faith was never actually identified with reason), as can be seen already in the works of SAADIAH GAON in the tenth century. While the content of Judaism is seen as uniquely religious, the reasons for faith are of a general epistemological nature. The religious Jew believes that the fundamentals of Judaism are true, because they are verified by a reliable tradition which is a valid source of historical knowledge according to general philosophical criteria. While simple unquestioning faith is acceptable, the demonstrable justified belief of the reflecting mind is preferred by God (BAḤYA IBN PAKUDA).

Maimonides went further. In his view, not only is religious faith justified by an appeal to rational deductive proofs for the existence of God, but it is possible to lay down an intellectual concept of faith in which religious certitude and proximity to God become identical with depth in philosophical knowledge.

Others thought differently. While acknowledging that the basis of Jewish religious belief is a form of historical knowledge, JUDAH HALEVI maintained that the religious relationship itself, which is communion with God, is higher than knowledge, not reachable by philosophy, and prompted by love of God.

By the end of the Middle Ages, the issue was joined as to the nature of the ultimate religious experience of Judaism. It could be seen as centering about the meaning of *emunah* in the verse, "The righteous shall live by his faith" (*emunato*). The intellectualist school of Saadiah, Baḥya, and Maimonides interpreted "faith" in the cognitive mode of "faith that...," a form of intellectual knowledge. The voluntarist school of Judah Halevi and Crescas interpreted *emunah* as "faith in...," a "trust" which is a total emotional commitment characterized by love and joy.

FALASHAS See ETHIOPIAN JEWS

FALK, JACOB JOSHUA BEN TSEVI HIRSCH (1680-1756). Rabbinic authority. Falk was born in Cracow, but after his marriage moved to Lvov. At first he devoted himself to business, and was very successful in his endeavors. In 1702, a cataclysmic event occurred which changed his life. A gunpowder storehouse exploded, killing his wife, daughter, and mother-in-law, and he himself was only saved by a miracle. As a result, he resolved to devote all his time to study. In the following years, Falk served as rabbi in various small towns, before being invited back to Lvov in 1727, this time as the town rabbi. Following major disagreements in the community, Falk served in Buczacz, eventually moving to Berlin, then to Metz and later to Frankfurt. Falk was in the vanguard of those who fought against R. Jonathan EYBESCHÜTZ, one of the greatest scholars of his day, who had been accused by R. Jacob Emden of being a follower of SHABBETAI TSEVI, the false messiah. Falk's *magnum opus, Pené Yehoshu'a*, written to defend RASHI against questions posed by the TOSAFOT, is still considered a mainstay of talmudic study, offering incisive comments on the Talmud.

FAMILY The Book of Genesis, which contains stories of the PATRIARCHS, the MATRIARCHS, and their children, is the original source for forming images and deriving values of Jewish family life in the classical tradition. It is a book about diverse families, barren wives, sibling rivalries, and constant threats to the process of transmission and continuity. Families are the scene of spiritual struggle, the paradigms of intimate connection and intense ambivalence. Biblical heroes do not attain identity and glory away from their families; their problems are deeply domestic.

In the Bible, the division between men and women is sharply drawn. The men are dominant in the political domain, as leaders in the public sphere, while the women dominate the domestic scene, the private sphere. The matriarchs are not docile women who are subservient to their husbands' authority. They argue (Gen. 30:1), give orders (Gen.

16:2), and even deceive their husbands (Gen. 27:5-17) not for the purpose of domination, but in order to play a central role in the formation of a nation. Biblical families fought and made up. Strong feelings were expressed, and hurtful as well as caring actions were taken. Their awareness of their historic destiny (Gen. 12:7; 26:2-4), and the values they espoused, sustained them and were transmitted to future generations.

The family in the Bible was called *bét av*, "house of father" (Gen. 24:38; 46:31). In founding a family, one was "building a house" (Deut. 25:10). The *bayit* — house — was a subdivision of the *mishpaḇah* — clan, large family (Josh. 7:14). The criteria for membership in a family were blood relationship, legal ties such as marriage, or geographic proximity. It was also the framework for the execution of justice, for example, in avenging the murder of a kinsman (see BLOOD AVENGER).

Each family had its own religious traditions and its own burial ground (Gen. 23:1-20). If one of the family members became indigent and had to sell his land, the other members had the right and duty to redeem it (Lev. 25:25). In the JUBILEE YEAR, land that had been sold reverted to the family. LEVIRATE MARRIAGE (Deut. 24:5-10) was another practice that reflected family interdependence — "To establish a name in Israel...by building up his brother's house" (Deut. 25:7,9).

The head of the biblical family was the patriarch who exercised authority over his wife and children. The wife enjoyed a high status in the family, but not as high as the husband's. He could force her to submit to a test of infidelity (Num. 5:11-31) and if found guilty, she was executed. Women could participate in religious festivals, were permitted to possess property and trade it even when married, and could inherit from their fathers when there were no sons (Num. 27:1-11). The wife went along with her husband into servitude if he could not repay his debts (Ex. 21:2,3). MARRIAGE could be dissolved by death or by the husband's giving his wife a bill of DIVORCE (Deut. 24:1-4). The motive for divorce was childlessness or finding "something obnoxious about her" (Deut. 24:2; *Git* 90a).

The functions of a father and mother can be deduced from various passages scattered throughout the Bible. As the head of the family, the father's authority over his children was almost supreme. Abraham was ready to sacrifice his son Isaac (Gen. 22); Jephthah sacrificed his daughter (Judg. 11:39); Judah ordered his daughter-in-law Tamar burned for breaking the marriage vow (Gen. 38:24). Children were regarded as the father's property and could be seized for debt (II Kings 4:1). The father could sell his daughter into marriage (Ex. 21:7-11) but not into prostitution (Lev. 19:29). He could annul her vows (Num. 30:4-6). His rights over her extended only until she attained 12 1/2, the age of puberty. Children who smote or cursed their parents could be put to death (Ex. 21:15, 17). The rebellious son was to be stoned to death (Deut. 21:18-21). Though the Talmud says that this never occurred, it still served as a deterrent.

The mother occupied a place of honor in the family despite her subordination to the father. She loved her children (Gen. 25:28) and was more directly involved in their early training (Prov. 1:8). Motherhood was a blessing and barrenness a misfortune (Gen. 30:23; I Sam. 1). Children were a blessing from God (Gen. 22:17) and assured the continuity of the family name. If a woman was childless, she could employ another woman in order to have children vicariously (Gen. 16:1,2; 30:3).

The pattern of Jewish family life set down in the Talmud was the model and practice until modern times. The age of marriage was set at 18 (*Avot* 5.24) although some sages encouraged marriage earlier (*Kid.* 29b). CELIBACY was discouraged and rare. Marriages were usually arranged by the parents of both families. The BETROTHAL (*erusin*) was considered a formal MARRIAGE that could only be dissolved through divorce or death, with ADULTERY punishable by death. The marriage ceremony (*nissu'in*) was usually held a year later for maidens and 30 days for widows. The time span of a year allowed for wedding and home preparations to proceed. While polygamy was technically permitted by the Bible, monogamy was formally decreed by R. GERSHON ME'OR HA-GOLAH for Ashkenazi Jews in the year 1000. Sexual life was regulated and great importance was attached to ritual aspects, known as FAMILY PURITY (*tohorat ha-mishpaḇah*).

Divorce was permitted in the Bible (Deut. 24:1-4) but was frowned upon by the sages (*Git.* 90b). However, they laid down grounds for divorce by the husband and the wife. They required the husband to give the *get* (bill of divorce) to the wife, but the wife could not divorce her husband. Divorce tended to be rare in Jewish communities and was considered a stigma.

Children were expected to "honor" (Ex. 20:12) and "revere" (Lev. 19:3) their parents, i.e., to obey them. "Honor," according to the Talmud, referred to providing food and drink, clothing, and transportation. "Reverence" required that the child not sit in his parents' seat, not interrupt them, nor take the side of the other in a dispute. Honor implied providing service and reverence implied preserving dignity. The former obtains particularly when the parents become old and need services because of their relative incapacity. Addressed primarily to adult children, though younger children were not exempt, this commandment promises long life to those who minister to their elderly parents. Reverence, however, pertains to children of all ages. Throughout history and up to modern times, children refrained from sitting in their fathers' seats. The Talmud exalted the honor that children bestow on their parents. "There are three partners in man, the Holy One, blessed be He, the father, and the mother. When a man honors his father and his mother, the Holy One, blessed be He, says, 'I ascribe (merit) to them as though I had dwelt among them and they had honored Me'" (*Kid.* 30b).

The father is duty bound to circumcise his son, redeem

A Moroccan family at the turn of the 20th century. The mother wears the traditional dress reserved for festive occasions.

An Ashkenazi family from Jerusalem at the turn of the 20th century. The father of the family wears the traditional "streimel".

him if he is the first-born, teach him Torah, marry him off, and teach him a craft. The duties of CIRCUMCISION and REDEMPTION OF THE FIRST-BORN require the father to introduce the son to the covenant entered into between Abraham and God, and to the Jews' historical memory that began with the Exodus from Egypt. The father is required to serve as a teacher and role model for the transmission of Jewish values and moral behavior to his children.

Teaching a trade requires parents to help their children to become economically self-sufficient. Daughters were taught about Judaism and the domestic responsibilities of a Jewish woman at home by their mothers.

Historically, children were viewed as extensions of their parents. Children's joy and pain as well as successes and failures were felt by parents. Children felt the pressure of the parent's expectations; a son was expected to grow up into a scholar.

Domestic harmony was an ideal toward which Jewish families strove. The guidelines were made very explicit. "A man should spend less than his means on food, up to his means on clothes, beyond his means in honoring wife and children because they are dependent on him" (*Ḥul.* 84b). Harmony was not only achieved through the give and take of interpersonal relationships but also through the experience of ritual and holy events. The rituals of the Jewish year and life-cycle served to unify the family and elevate the mundane to the level of the holy.

The portrait of the traditional Jewish family becomes less idyllic in modern times. Trends in the larger society that have brought changes and breakdown in family structure in Western society have had a serious impact on the Jewish family. Low fertility, high incidence of divorce, mixed marriage, singlehood by choice, homosexuality, alchoholism and drugs, child and wife abuse, homelessness, women in the work force — these social and demographic trends have brought strain on marriage and family life and have altered the family structure. There is an increasing number of single-parent families headed by women who struggle to become economically self-sufficient, children who have been negatively affected by divorce, blended families that require new modes of relationships among stepchildren and stepparents, nuclear families separated geographically from extended families, mixed families where the children are often not raised as Jews. However, there are counterforces and the organized Jewish community has mobilized itself to combat the disintegration of the family via educational programs and social services. In non-Orthodox circles, synagogue services have become more family centered, with seating in family pews. Family life has remained especially strong among Jews in and from Moslem lands. The older generations are accorded great respect and many occasions bring together both immediate and extended families. Where members are sick and disabled or have other misfortunes, the family participates in the responsibility. The Jewish home remains the most vital factor in contributing to Jewish survival, and the preservation of a Jewish consciousness and the Jewish ways of life. See also FATHER; HOME; HUSBAND AND WIFE; MOTHER; PARENT AND CHILD.

FAMILY PURITY (Heb. *Tohorat ha-mishpaḥah*). Laws regulating sexual relations between husband and wife. According to these, couples may not engage in relations during the wife's menstrual period and for seven "clean days" thereafter. During this time, it is customary for observant couples to abstain from any physical contact including sleeping in the same bed. When the period of abstention ends, the wife immerses herself in the ritual bath (MIKVEH), and it is presumed that she will reunite sexually with her husband that same night. The laws of family purity are based upon Lev. 20:18, "If a man shall lie with a woman having

A man in bed waiting for his wife to return from the ritual bath (mikveh). *From a Hebrew manuscript, Germany, 15th century.*

her period, and shall uncover her nakedness, he has laid bare her flow, and she has exposed her blood flow; both of them shall be cut off from among their people." An entire tractate of the Talmud, NIDDAH (i.e. menstruation), is devoted to family purity.

In modern times, it has been noted that women are usually most fertile at the time of the cycle when relations may be resumed. It has further been suggested that periodic enforced abstinence helps husband and wife to strengthen the bond between them and brings freshness to their sexual relationship when contact is renewed each month. The Talmud was also aware of this aspect: "The husband becomes over-familiar with his wife and tired of her, thus the Torah prohibited her to him (each month) so that she may remain as beloved to him as she was on her wedding day" (*Nid.* 31b). Traditionally, observance of the laws of family purity was one of the foundations of Jewish family life, but today broad sectors of the Jewish community disregard or are ignorant of these laws, although the practicing Orthodox still consider them fundamental.

The halakhic authorities of the Conservative Movement have always maintained the importance and validity of the laws of family purity. However, all indications are that in spite of the official view of the rabbinic leadership, the laws of family purity are not generally observed by Conservative Jews. Reform Jews do not accept the halakhic requirements concerning family purity.

FASTING AND FAST DAYS Fasting in Jewish tradition is a religious discipline involving the abstention from food, drink, and physical pleasures, for the purpose of intensifying spiritual experience in atonement for sin, in commemoration of national tragedies, or as part of a personal petition to God in seeking His help.

The best-known example of fasting for the first of the above reasons is the biblical fast of the DAY OF ATONEMENT which is commanded to atone for sin. While fasting is not explicitly mentioned, the Bible ordains for this day "You shall afflict your souls" (Lev. 16:31), and from early times the rabbis interpreted this to mean fasting (*Yoma* 11a; 73b ff). Part of the "affliction of the soul" also involves a prohibition against bathing, anointing, wearing leather footwear, and engaging in conjugal relations. The gratification of such bodily appetites is seen as a prime source of sin. In biblical times, rending one's garments and putting on sackcloth and ashes were further signs of distress, accompanying abstention from food (Jonah 3:6ff; Ezek. 9:5). In other cases the fasting is clearly implied (Josh. 7:5-13; Jer. 6:26; Lam. 2:10).

The second category of fasts commemorates tragic events in Jewish history. These are the four fasts mentioned in the Bible: 10 Tevet (see ASARAH BE-TEVET), 17 Tammuz (see SHIVAH ASAR BE-TAMMUZ), 9 Av (see TISHAH BE-AV), and 3 Tishri (the Fast of Gedaliah). All of them are connected with the sieges of Jerusalem and the destruction of the First and Second Temples. The post-exilic prophet Zechariah proclaimed that in the future period of national redemption these four historical fasts would be changed to days of gladness and joy (Zech. 8:19).

With the exception of Tishah be-Av these historical fasts are usually described as "minor." Two halakhic stipulations emphasize this distinction. First, the fast begins at dawn on the day itself and not at sunset on the previous evening as is the case with the Day of Atonement and Tishah be-Av. Secondly, the additional four prohibitions (bathing, anointing, leather shoes, and sexual relations) are not added to the prohibition against eating and drinking as on the Day of Atonement and Tishah be-Av.

The Bible records other instances of fasting with sackcloth and ashes at times of national crises. Thus, after the defeat at Ai (Josh. 7:5-13) and in the tribal war against Benjamin (Judg. 20:23-26), the leaders of the time proclaimed a fast.

The third category of fasting, the fast of petition, is illustrated by Esther's call to her fellow Jews to observe a three-day fast as she prepared to plead with the king for her people (Est. 4:16-17). The fast of petition is represented in enactments by the rabbis proclaiming fasts in times of national danger. Just as in Bible times the leaders called the people to a fast and a special assembly (Joel 2:14), so in the rabbinic

Illustration of the "Four Questions", traditionally asked at the Passover Seder. *From* Erna Michael Haggadah. *Germany, 1400.*

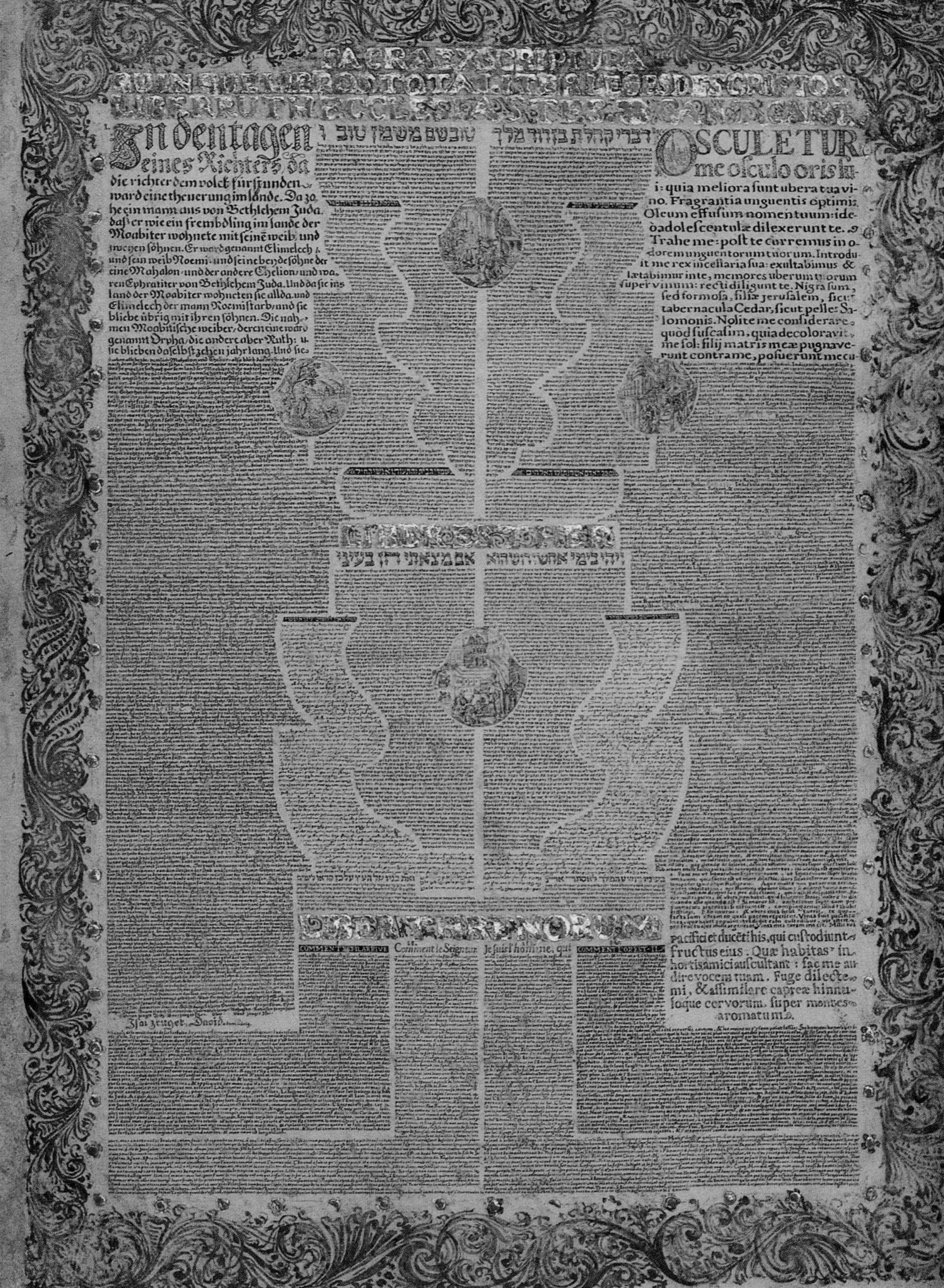

In den tagen Eines Richters, da die richter dem volck fürstunden, ward eine theuerung im lande. Da zohe ein mann aus von Bethlehem Juda, daß er wie ein frembdling im lande der Moabiter wohnete mit seinē weib, und zweyen söhnen. Er ward genannt Elimelech, und sein weib Noemi, und seine beyde söhne der eine Mahalon, und der andere Chelion, und waren Ephratiter von Bethlehem Juda. Und da sie ins land der Moabiter wohneten sie allda. und Elimelech der mann Noemi starb, und sie bliebe übrig mit ihren söhnen. Die nahmen Moabitische weiber, deren eine ward genannt Orpha, die andere aber Ruth: u. sie blieben daselbst zehen jahr lang. Und sie

טוב שם משמן טוב

דברי קהלת בן דוד מלך

OSCULETUR me osculo oris sui: quia meliora sunt ubera tua vino. Fragrantia unguentis optimis: Oleum effusum nomen tuum: ideò adolescentulæ dilexerunt te. Trahe me: post te curremus in odorem unguentorum tuorum. Introduxit me rex in cellaria sua: exultabimus & lætabimur in te, memores uberum tuorum super vinum: recti diligunt te. Nigra sum, sed formosa, filiæ Jerusalem, sicut tabernacula Cedar, sicut pelles Salomonis. Nolite me considerare, quòd fusca sim, quia decoloravit me sol: filij matris meæ pugnaverunt contra me, posuerunt me cu-

ויהי בימי אחשורוש הוא

אם מצאתי חן בעיני

Isai zeuget David

pacifici et ducenti his, qui custodiunt fructus eius. Quæ habitas in hortis amici auscultant: fac me audire vocem tuam. Fuge dilecte mi, & assimilare capreæ hinnuloque cervorum super montes aromatum.

tradition fast days were called by the rabbis when the people were exhorted to fast and pray for God's help in times of severe drought or plague (*Ta'an.* 3.5-8). An entire tractate of the Talmud, viz., TA'ANIT (Fast) is devoted to the subject.

Various rabbinic laws are associated with fasting. The obligatory fasts have to be observed by all males over the age of 13 and females over the age of 12. In order to train the religious loyalty and self-discipline of younger people, the rabbis encouraged youngsters below those ages to observe partial fasts. Sick people and women in an advanced stage of pregnancy, as well as nursing mothers who have recently given birth, are not required to fast. Where there is a danger to health, the rabbis ruled that fasting is not only excused but prohibited.

With the exception of the Day of Atonement, any fast which falls on the Sabbath is postponed to Sunday. The Fast of Esther cannot be postponed to the next day since that day is the Festival of Purim, and as it cannot be predated to Friday because fasting on the day before the Sabbath is not permitted, the fast is put back to Thursday.

Laws and customs also laid down additional penitential prayers, such as AVINU MALKENU and Torah readings for certain fast days, the story of the intercession of Moses when he prayed for God's forgiveness of the people after they had sinned with the Golden Calf (Ex. 32, 34). The same passage is read both during the Morning and Afternoon services. The prophetical reading for the Afternoon Service is Isa. 55:6-56:8 which tells of God's forgiveness to the sinner who repents.

The Bible also records cases of individuals undertaking a private fast, usually a fast of petition. David fasted when his first child by Bathsheba was near to death (II Sam. 12:16) and the Book of Psalms testifies to individually imposed fasting (Ps. 35:13; 69:11-12). In much later periods individual fasts were undertaken or traditionally observed for one of a variety of reasons, such as to break the feared effect of a bad dream. Some mourners would fast on the day of the burial of a parent, or on the observance of a *yahrzeit* (anniversary) of the death. More widely observed is the custom for a bride and bridegroom to fast on the day of their wedding before the ceremony. This is in token of their desire for forgiveness for any sins as they are about to start a new life.

Various other non-obligatory fasts were observed mainly by extremely pious individuals rather than by the wide community.

For example, in the months following the festivals of Passover and Sukkot, i.e., in Iyyar and Ḫeshvan, it became a special mark of piety to fast on the Monday, Thursday, and the following Monday after the conclusion of the festival (known as *Ta'anit BeHaB*). The observance is not known before the 13th century and the reason generally given is that it was a special gesture seeking atonement for any superfluous jollifications indulged in during the festival period. The same class of pietistic fasts includes *Yom Kippur Katan*, the "little Yom Kippur" observed on the day before New Moons. This was introduced by the 16th century kabbalist, Moses CORDOVERO of Safed, as a penitential fast for any sins committed in the previous month. Also of kabbalistic origin is the period of fasting in the winter months of January and February known as *SHoVeVVIM TaT* from the initial letters of the first eight weekly Bible portions of the Book of Exodus, read during this period. Some very pious Jews fast every Monday and Thursday throughout the year.

FAST DAYS OF THE JEWISH CALENDAR

Date	Name	Reason	How Observed
3 Tishri	Fast of Gedaliah	Commemorates assassination of Gedaliah (II Kings 25:25)	Dawn to dusk
10 Tishri	Day of Atonement	Atonement for sins (Lev. 26-32 etc.)	Dusk to dusk
10 Tevet	Asarah be-Tevet	Nebuchadnezzar besieges Jerusalem (II Kings 25:1)	Dawn to dusk
13 Adar	Fast of Esther	Traditionally connected with fast-day decreed by Esther (Est. 4:16)	Dawn to dusk
14 Nisan	Fast of the First-born	Commemorates last of the ten plagues (Ex. 12:29)	Dawn to dusk*
17 Tammuz	Shivah Asar be-Tammuz	Associated with breaches of walls of Jerusalem by Nebuchadnezzar (Jer. 39:2)	Dawn to dusk
9 Av	Tishah be-Av	Associated with Destruction of Temple (II Kings 25:8-9)	Dusk to dusk

*(usually cancelled by participation in joyful conclusion of study of Talmudic Tractate).

The Five Scrolls written in micrography: Ruth in German; Song of Songs in Latin; Ecclesiastes and Esther in Hebrew, and Lamentations in French. Vienna, 1748.

The Fast of the First-born on 14 Nisan, the day before Passover, is the only fast which is neither an atonement for sin nor a fast of petition. It is in a class on its own and is placed in the calendar as a reminder of the death of the Egyptian firstborn and the miraculous escape of the Israelite firstborn. However, it is observed only symbolically by firstborn male Jews, with provision made to avoid the obligation of fasting by participating in a *siyyum* — the study of a concluding passage of a Talmud tractate, which permits the participants to eat and drink.

In spite of, or perhaps because of, the accumulation of many additional kinds of private or communal fast days for various reasons, some outstanding rabbinic leaders opposed self-inflicted fasts and strongly criticized them. They taught that the spirituality of Judaism is not necessarily best experienced through the exercise of self-mortification, but rather through the practice of charity and good deeds.

The prophet Isaiah castigated fasting without an inner religious and charitable spirit. Isaiah 58, part of the prophetical reading for the Day of Atonement, teaches that great moral good can be derived from a fast; but only if it is sincerely observed, when it can remake man's character by arousing his sympathy for the plight of the needy and his fellowman.

FATHER The male parent. When a married woman gives birth, Jewish law presumes her husband to be the father; the presumption applies even in the presence of rumored unfaithfulness by the mother. An unmarried woman's claim that a particular man fathered her child, however, does not establish paternity since the law presumes that she may have had relations with other men as well (*Hul.* 11b). If a man says "this is my child," his paternity is accepted. In cases of marriage between Jew and non-Jew, family lineage follows the status of the mother. In marriage between two Jews, however, family lineage is determined by the father (*Kid.* 3.12). Thus, if a PRIEST (*kohen*) marries a non-priestly (Levite or Israelite) woman, the children are priests. Similarly, if an Israelite man marries a woman of priestly descent, the children are Israelites.

In biblical times the father was under a moral but not a legal obligation to support his children during their minority. The rabbis legalized this duty at the Synod of Usha (2nd. century). The father owns all income of his minor children. This right was awarded him in recognition of his obligation to support and maintain them. However, the father has no right to the income of a son over the age of six who is not dependent upon him for support (perhaps by virtue of inheritance). The father has the right to annul vows taken by his daughter while still a minor. According to the Talmud, the father had the biblical right to "marry off" daughters (i.e., to choose their husbands and receive any consideration granted by the groom) who had not reached the age of twelve years and six months. The rabbis, however, advised against the exercise of this right until after the daughter had reached the age of majority (twelve; see ADULT) when she could give her consent (*Kid.* 41a, *Ket.* 46a).

The father is required to give his children an appropriate Jewish education, to teach them right from wrong, and to prepare them to perform the Commandments upon attaining their majority. The father is obligated to have his son circumcised and redeem him if he is the first-born (see FIRST-BORN, REDEMPTION OF), to take a wife for him, and teach him a craft (*Kid.* 29a). One opinion in the Talmud obligates the father to teach his son to swim (*ibid.*). When the son becomes BAR MITSVAH, the father recites a special blessing on being relieved of legal responsibility (BARUKH SHE-PETARANI). The father must provide his daughter with the proper clothes and amenities to prepare her for MARRIAGE.

Traditionally, it was considered natural that the father show compassion to his children and not be envious of their accomplishments. He was to be generous with his time, money, and feelings, and was expected to give of himself to help his children grow and develop. The father was also expected to discipline his children as required, and was thus the chief authority figure of the family.

In the East European *shtetl*, the father's activity within the home was mostly spiritual and intellectual, and his authority was largely unquestioned. As a matter of course, other FAMILY members would not interrupt his conversation or sit in his chair. His position was more remote than that of the MOTHER, and, when home, his time was often dominated by his own affairs rather than by active participation in the family circle. Among immigrant families in the Western world and in Eastern communities in Israel the father's traditional authority was greatly eroded, representing, as he did, the culture of the past.

In contemporary Jewish homes in the West and in Israel, parent-child relationships are based less on authority and more upon egalitarian principles than in the past. Modern theories of child-rearing are more influential than Jewish tradition in the majority of homes. As in many cases mothers have become important breadwinners for the family, the father takes a greater share in child-rearing and other domestic tasks than ever before. Even in the various Orthodox communities, where Jewish tradition remains authoritative, there is a greater degree of role flexibility and egalitarianism than in previous generations. (See also HUSBAND-WIFE RELATIONSHIP, PARENT-CHILD RELATIONSHIP).

FATHERHOOD OF GOD "God as Father" is one of several ways in which Jewish tradition relates to the Divine. Fatherhood may have various connotations, including the generative activity of producing offspring, the assumption of responsibility for their care, and provision for their correction and discipline.

Ancient religions took the generative aspect literally: the Egyptian Pharaoh was regarded as the actual progeny of the god Ra. This belief is echoed in Psalms (2:7): "The Lord has said to me [David the King], 'You are My son; This day I have begotten you.'" A number of biblical names also embody this belief, e.g., Abijah, literally "Yah [The Lord] is my father." However, the implication in the Hebrew Bible is one of creation and relationship rather than of procreation. God is considered to be the Father of the people of Israel, and the caring and nurturing parent is described by HOSEA: "When Israel was still a child, I loved him, and ever since Egypt I have called My son... It was I who taught Ephraim to walk, taking them up in My arms; I drew them with bands of love..." (Chap. 11:1-4).

Discipline and chastisement are a significant part of the relationship: "Bear in mind that the Lord your God disciplines you [the entire people], just as a man disciplines his son" (Deut. 8:5). God's fatherhood extends not only to Israel, however, but to all mankind, which is one of the original concepts of Judaism. Its corollary is the brotherhood of all mankind.

God's fatherhood is inseparable from His compassion, as expressed liturgically in the oft-repeated phrase "Our Father, the merciful Father" (see AHAVAH RABBAH). Many prayers address God in this way, sometimes using the phrase AVINU SHE-BA-SHAMAYIM ("Our Father in heaven"; *Sot.* 9.15) or AVINU MALKENU ("Our Father, our King"; ascribed to R. Akiva *Ta'an.* 25b). The latter formula has become the core of Jewish penitential prayers.

The contemporary Jewish feminist movement, concerned with the exclusively masculine conception of God in early Judaism, has pointed to images such as giving birth, nuturing, and feeding which are primarily maternal images and metaphors. Some Jewish feminists now seek to redress the balance by avoiding solely male terminology in prayer and by introducing female imagery, often kabbalistic.

FEAR OF GOD (*yirat Elohim*; in rabbinic literature "fear of heaven," *yirat shamayim*). An attitude of reverence and awe toward God. Fear of God is a positive commandment derived from the verse, "Fear only the Lord your God, and worship Him alone..." (Deut. 6:13). This injunction is repeated many times in the Bible: "and the man who fears God speaks truth in his heart" (Ps. 15:2). Fear of God is the beginning of wisdom (Prov. 9:10). According to the medieval commentator RASHI, it relates especially to those commandments which are "known to the heart," i.e., those sins that no man sees being committed. In the Talmud, JOHANAN BEN ZAKKAI told his disciples before his death, "Let the fear of heaven be upon you as the fear of flesh and blood." When they replied "Is that all?" he answered them, "If only you could attain this! For when a man wants to commit a sin, he says, 'I hope no man will see me'" (*Ber.* 28b). R. Antigonus of Sokho's best-known maxim was that in serving God one should "be like servants who do not seek a reward — but let the fear of heaven be upon you" (*Avot* 1.3).

Fear of God lies in the province of man's FREE WILL because there are no social pressures to enforce it. Moreover, the sages stated that Divine Providence rules over much of a man's life (i.e., wealth, poverty, health, sickness, children, etc.), but whether he will be righteous or wicked is left to him. The Talmud states, "Everything is in the hands of heaven except the fear of heaven" (*Ber.* 33b). MAIMONIDES writes that in order to attain fear of heaven, a person should contemplate God's wondrous creation and thereby obtain a glimpse of His incomparable and infinite wisdom. Considering God's greatness, he will be afraid and realize that he is a "small, lowly creature, endowed with a meager intelligence, standing in the presence of Him who is perfect in knowledge" (*Yad. Yesodé ha-Torah* 2.2) (See also LOVE OF GOD).

FEINSTEIN, MOSHEH (1895-1986). Rabbinical authority and leader of Orthodox Judaism in the US. Feinstein was born near Minsk, White Russia, and studied in the *yeshivot* of Slutsk and Shklov. In 1921, he became rabbi of Luban, near Minsk, where he served until his emigration to the United States in 1937. Feinstein was then appointed *rosh yeshivah* (head of the talmudical academy) of Mesivtha Tifereth Jerusalem on Manhattan's Lower East Side, where he remained until his death. It was on the basis of his halakhic RESPONSA that Feinstein achieved the greatest renown, and his rulings were accepted as authoritative throughout the Jewish world. His responsa were published in seven volumes entitled *Iggerot Mosheh* (1959-85), arranged according to the order of the SHULḤAN ARUKH code. Feinstein's decisions covered many areas of scientific and medical advancement in the light of *halakhah*, including ABORTION, BIRTH CONTROL, ARTIFICIAL INSEMINATION, and transplants. Others dealt with personal status in the areas of CONVERSION TO JUDAISM, marriage, and divorce resulting from the breakdown of religious life in Europe and the United States. He also reviewed the status of the *agunah* (a woman whose husband's fate is unknown) following the Holocaust and as a result of air disasters. Feinstein was elected to leading positions in the Orthodox Jewish world, serving as president of the Union of Orthodox Rabbis and chairman of the American branch of Agudat Israel's Council of Torah Sages.

FESTIVALS (*yom tov* [lit. "a good day"]). Biblical law ordains seven festival days upon which work is forbidden, namely ROSH HA-SHANAH, (the New Year, 1 Tishri), the DAY OF ATONEMENT (Yom Kippur, 10 Tishri), which although a FAST day is reckoned among the festivals, SUKKOT, (the first day of Tabernacles, 15 Tishri), SHEMINI ATSERET, (the Eighth Day of Solemn Assembly, 23 Tishri), the first and last days of PASSOVER (*Pesaḥ*, 15 and 22 Nisan), and SHAVU'OT, (the Feast of Weeks, 6 Sivan). Due to doubts as to the date upon which the New Moon appeared, it was subsequently laid down that those living outside the Land of Israel would keep two days rather than one for each of the festivals, with the

Details from a silver engraved festival cup representing Rosh ha-Shanah and Shavu'ot. Narva, Estonia, 17th-18th century.

exception of the Day of Atonement. Even those living in Israel kept two days of Rosh ha-Shanah for the same reason. Once the CALENDAR was formulated during talmudic times, there was theoretically no need to keep the extra days, but the Talmud (*Bétsah* 4b) nevertheless required the previous customs to be maintained (see SECOND DAY OF FESTIVALS).

As with the Sabbath, all types of work are forbidden on the Day of Atonement (called the Sabbath of Sabbaths). On the other festivals, categories of work related to the preparation of food are permitted. Thus, cooking is allowed on these festivals (unless they fall on the Sabbath). Fire may be transferred, but not created. Carrying from one domain to another is permitted.

The three PILGRIM FESTIVALS, Passover, Shavu'ot, and Sukkot, all have both agricultural and national significance. Thus Passover celebrates the EXODUS from Egypt and is "the festival of the spring," and on the second night of this festival an OMER — a specific measure — of barley was harvested and taken to the Temple. Shavu'ot is the day upon which traditionally the Torah was given at Mount Sinai, and is also the "harvest festival," which marks the end of the barley harvest and the beginning of the wheat harvest. Finally, Sukkot commemorates the forty years during which the Israelites wandered in the desert but is also "the festival of ingathering," when the grain is brought from the fields into the barns. The other two festivals, Rosh ha-Shanah and the Day of Atonement, have neither a national nor an agricultural element, but are days of introspection at a time when the entire world is being judged for the coming year.

Generally, whenever a festival is celebrated for two days, the ceremonial aspects of the two are identical, except for some minor changes in PIYYUTIM (liturgical poems). The exception is Shemini Atseret, on which, outside Israel, the different ceremonial aspects of the day are divided between the two days of Shemini Atseret and SIMḤAT TORAH. Thus, in the Diaspora, the completion of the yearly cycle of the Pentateuchal readings was moved from Shemini Atseret to Simḥat Torah. The intermediate days of Passover and Sukkot (ḤOL HA-MO'ED) are semi-holidays when work is permitted, although the rabbis encouraged these days too to be observed as a holiday if possible.

In addition to these seven festival days, the Bible singles out each New Moon as being a special day, and in ancient times it was celebrated as such. These observances have since lapsed (except for liturgical additions) and there is no prohibition against working on the New Moon.

Various festivals are rabbinically ordained, the two major ones being PURIM and ḤANUKKAH. Other semi-festive days include the NEW YEAR FOR TREES (Tu bi-Shevat), Purim Katan (the 14th and 15th days of Adar I in leap years, see PURIM), Second Passover (the 14th day of Iyyar, see PASSOVER), LAG BA-OMER, and the Fifteenth of AV. While there are specific liturgical additions to the service on Purim and Ḥanukkah, the only difference in the liturgy of the semi-festive days is the omission of the TAḤANUN prayer.

Modern-day Israel has seen the development of two new festivals, Israel INDEPENDENCE DAY (Yom ha-Atsma'ut, 5 Iyyar), and JERUSALEM DAY (Yom Yerushalayim, 28 Iyyar). These festivals are still too new to have been adopted universally in the Diaspora, or to have a universally accepted ritual.

Festival Liturgy On all the days of the biblically ordained festivals, a special AMIDAH is said in the evening, morning, and afternoon services, consisting of seven blessings. The central blessing relates to the special nature of the day itself. On all of these days (except Rosh ha-Shanah and the Day of Atonement), HALLEL is added to the Morning Service and an ADDITIONAL SERVICE is read. On the non-biblical festivals of Ḥanukkah and Purim, there is no Additional Service but there is a Reading of the Law and, on Ḥanukkah, *Hallel* is recited. On all days except Rosh ha-Shanah, the *Amidah* of the Additional Service also consists of seven blessings, with the middle blessing asking God to return the Jewish people to its land and quoting the biblical text ordaining the additional sacrifices which were offered on that particular day. On Rosh ha-Shanah, the Additional Service *Amidah* contains nine blessings, the three middle ones being devoted respectively to the acceptance of God as King over the entire world, beseeching God to remember the pious deeds of the forefathers, and references to the *shofar*.

On the Day of Atonement, a fifth service is added just prior to the conclusion of the fast day, this being called the *Ne'ilah*. The text of each Day of Atonement *Amidah* (except in the *Ne'ilah*) is followed by a lengthy CONFESSION of Israel's sins, and a fervent request for God to forgive them.

The Rosh ha-Shanah and Day of Atonement liturgy is much more extensive than that of the other festivals, both in the silent recitation of the *Amidah* and in the cantor's repetition. During this repetition, various poems (*piyyutim*) are added, some glorifying God's deeds in the world, others dwelling on the solemnity of the day as one of judgment. In modern times, the number of these *piyyutim* is often considerably reduced.

The prayers of certain biblically ordained festivals include the use of specific ritual objects. Thus the *shofar* must be blown on Rosh ha-Shanah, while the FOUR SPECIES must be taken and waved on Sukkot (except when these fall on the Sabbath).

Two special prayers are recited for the benefit of the Land of Israel: the prayer for RAIN on Shemini Atseret and the prayer for DEW on the first day of Passover. This coincides with the needs of the climate of the Land of Israel.

The FIVE SCROLLS (*megillot*) are read during the course of the year: the SONG OF SONGS on the Sabbath day of Passover, RUTH on Shavu'ot, LAMENTATIONS on Tishah be-Av, ECCLESIASTES on the Sabbath day of Sukkot, and ESTHER on Purim.

The two new festivals of Israel Independence Day and Jerusalem Day are generally marked, in religious Zionist communities, by the reciting of *Hallel.*

FIFTEENTH OF SHEVAT See NEW YEAR FOR TREES

FINKELSTEIN, LOUIS (1895-). Rabbinic scholar and leader of CONSERVATIVE JUDAISM; president (1940-51) and chancellor (1951-72) of the Jewish Theological Seminary of America. Finkelstein was born in Cincinnati, studied at City College, New York, and received his doctorate from Columbia University (1918). In the following year he was ordained at the Seminary. While serving as a congregational rabbi, he joined the Seminary's teaching staff and quickly rose to prominence both in the faculty and in the world of scholarship. He wrote on Jewish social and religious history and on rabbinic texts and concepts. Finkelstein published the first critical edition of *Sifré* on Deuteronomy (1939), and the first volumes of his edition and commentary on the *Sifra* have also appeared. His works on the PHARISEES stressed the economic and social basis of Pharisaic Judaism. His exhaustive studies of rabbinic classics and liturgical texts proved controversial because of the early dating which he attributed to many of them. Finkelstein attempted to trace basic theological positions of the schools of Shammai and Hillel, showing the influence of these schools on the legal and non-legal documents of classical Judaism.

As head of the Jewish Theological Seminary, he not only continued the scholarly and religious policies and activities of his predecessors, but also placed great emphasis on contacts with the non-Jewish community and on the moral and ethical aspects of Jewish teaching. He thus founded the Institute for Religious and Social Studies, which brings together theologians of all religions and leading thinkers in various fields to consider moral problems of the day. Finkelstein was also instrumental in developing the Seminary's radio and television programs, outstanding among which has been *The Eternal Light*. Under his leadership, Conservative Judaism expanded and became the largest organized religious movement in American Jewry.

FIRST-BORN, REDEMPTION OF (Heb. *pidyon ha-ben*). The practice of redeeming the first-born male child from a priest. In biblical times, preeminence and authority attached to the first-born son (Gen. 49:3). The first-born sons were consecrated to Divine service and were the original priests in the Sanctuary until they were replaced by the Levites (Num. 3:12). Just as the FIRST FRUITS and the first-born of animals (Num. 18:15-18; Deut. 15:19-23) had to be given to the priests (Deut. 26:1-10), so the male first-born belonged to God.

The obligation to redeem a first-born son is first mentioned in connection with the slaying of the first-born of the Egyptians (Ex. 13:13, 22:28, 34:20; Num. 3:13). "For every first-born among the Israelites, man as well as beast, is Mine; I consecrated them to Myself at the time that I smote every first-born in the land of Egypt" (Num. 8:17). The dim background of this connection may echo the Canaanite practice of sacrificing first-born sons, a practice sharply denounced in the Bible.

The Book of Exodus speaks of the obligation to redeem the first-born son, and in Numbers (3:44-51) it is mentioned that this redemption is to be effected by payment of five shekels to a priest. The passage in Numbers describes how Moses required such payment from the first-born Israelites who were more numerous than the number of Levites supplanting them as priests assigned to service in the Sanctuary. Moses gave the money collected in this manner to Aaron and his sons.

The detailed laws of the Redemption of the First-born are to be found in the eighth chapter of the Mishnah tractate

Salver used for the ceremony of the Redemption of the First-born, engraved with the sacrifice of Isaac. Poland, early 19th century.

BEKHOROT, and are expanded in the GEMARA of that chapter. These laws state that the sons of priests and Levites are exempt from redemption as are first-born sons whose mother is the daughter of either a priest or Levite. If a mother has had a previous miscarriage or stillbirth, the child is not regarded as first-born.

Aside from the statutory requirement of the payment of five shekels to a priest, the Talmud does not indicate any fixed form in which such payment was to take place. In the geonic period, a ceremony was formalized. In it, the father of the child — on the 31st day after its birth (unless this falls on a Sabbath or festival, in which case it is held on the evening after the end of the Sabbath or festival) — declares to the priest that this is the first-born son of his mother and that the father is obligated to redeem him — and here the father quotes Num. 18:16 and Ex. 13:1. The priest turns to the father and asks whether he prefers to give his son to the priest or to redeem him for five shekels. The father replies that he wants to redeem his son and thereupon hands the priest the five shekels. The father then recites two blessings, one on fulfilling the commandment (of *pidyon ha-ben*) and one expressing gratitude to God (SHE-HEḤEYANU). This ceremony is found in the sources both in a Hebrew and an Aramaic version. It is the latter version that has been in use ever since the late Middle Ages.

FIRST FRUITS (Heb. *bikkurim*). The earliest ripening fruits and grains of certain species, brought in offering each year to the Temple in Jerusalem in accordance with biblical legislation. Exodus 23:19 commands: "the choice first fruits of your soil, you shall bring to the house of the Lord your God..." (see also Ex. 34:26). The traditional interpretation of this injunction restricts it to fruits and grains of the seven species (wheat, barley, grapes, figs, pomegranates, olives, dates) considered native to Erets Israel (*Bik.* 1.3). Thus farmers in the Holy Land were required, early in the season, to mark those specimens of the fruits and grains designated that were most advanced in their maturation. Upon marking them, the farmer would declare them to be first fruits (*ibid.* 3.1). The marked specimens were subsequently taken to the Temple in Jerusalem as an offering to God. Although the Mishnah (*Pe'ah* 1.1) establishes that no particular quantity was stipulated for first fruits, later Rabbinic legislation set a minimum of one sixtieth of the harvest of each species brought.

The bringing of first fruits was accompanied by the liturgical recitation detailing Israelite origins, the move to Egypt, and the Exodus, as specified in Deuteronomy 26:1-11. The passage in Deuteronomy concludes (*ibid.* verse 10) with the prescription that the first fruits be "set before the Lord," and according to Numbers 18:12-13 they became the property of the priests, part of their cultic income.

The season during which the first fruits were brought opened on the festival of Shavu'ot (which was known as *Ḥag ha-Bikkurim*, Festival of the First Fruits) and closed with Ḥanukkah, although it was considered advisable to bring them prior to Sukkot.

An imaginary representation of the First Fruits festival showing a procession carrying produce to the Temple, preceded by a flute player.

The Hebrew root of *bikkurim* (first fruits) is the same as that of *bekhor* (first-born), and the obligation to dedicate the first fruits to God is part of an overall biblical belief that the first of everything, including the first-born of man and beast, belongs to God (see FIRST-BORN, REDEMPTION OF). After the destruction of the Temple, the rabbis suggested charity be given to replace the first fruits.

A first fruits ceremony in various forms has been revived in agricultural settlements of contemporary Israel. Celebrations replete with colorful costumes, folk dancing, and the active participation of young children are widely held on or about the festival of Shavu'ot.

THE BRINGING OF THE FIRST FRUITS

When you enter the land that the Lord your God is giving you as a heritage, and you possess it and settle in it, you shall take some of every first fruit of the soil, which you harvest from the land that the Lord your God is giving you, put it in a basket, and go to the place where the Lord your God will choose to establish His name. You shall go to the priest in charge at that time and say to him, "I acknowledge this day before the Lord your God that I have entered the land that the Lord swore to our fathers to assign us". The priest shall take the basket from your hand and set it down in front of the altar of the Lord your God. (Deut. 26:1-3)

FIVE BOOKS OF MOSES See PENTATEUCH

FIVE SCROLLS (*Hamesh Megillot*). The biblical books entitled SONG OF SONGS (Canticles), RUTH, LAMENTATIONS, ECCLESIASTES, and ESTHER. They appear together in this order in the Hagiographa section, in printed Hebrew Bibles and in Ashkenazi manuscripts, following the biblical calendar. Song of Songs is read in synagogue on Passover, in the month of Nisan; Ruth on Shavu'ot; Lamentations on Tishah be-Av; Ecclesiastes on Sukkot; and Esther on Purim. In Sephardi manuscripts and in the oldest known masoretic Bibles, the Aleppo and Leningrad codices, the order is chronological: Ruth (period of the Judges); Song of Songs and Ecclesiastes (Solomonic authorship); Lamentations (commemorating the destruction of the First Temple); and Esther (the Persian or Hellenistic era). The order in the Talmud (*BB* 14b), which has them interspersed among the other books of the Hagiographa, is: Ruth, Ecclesiastes, Song of Songs, Lamentations, and Esther; except for Esther, the Talmud does not mention their public reading. It follows that they were grouped together according to their liturgical use, first cited in the minor tractate *Soferim* (c. seventh century). Not all of the scrolls are read by all communities: some traditions divide Ruth over both days of Shavu'ot in the Diaspora and *Soferim* mentions a similar practice with regard to the Song of Songs on the last days of Passover. It is obligatory to read the Book of Esther ("the *Megillah*") from a parchment scroll upon which the text is handwritten with pen (a quill) and ink. Generally speaking, the other scrolls are read today from printed texts. However, certain Ashkenazi congregations in Jerusalem read all but Lamentations from a handwritten parchment scroll.

FIVE SPECIES Varieties of cereal, grain, or "corn" (*dagan*), indigenous to the Land of Israel, which are subject to the biblical and rabbinic laws governing its agricultural produce (*Ned.* 7.2). When flour ground from any of these five "species" or "kinds" of cereal is kneaded into dough, a portion of HALLAH must be separated and thrown into the fire, since they constitute the "bread of the land" (Num. 15:19). According to the Mishnah (*Hal.* 1.1), these cereals are wheat (*hittim*), barley (*se'orim*), emmer (*kusmin*), oats (*shibbolet shu'al*), and spelt (*shifon*; now translated as "rye"). All five are also listed as the grains from which unleavened bread (MATSAH) can lawfully be prepared (*Pes.* 2.5), as they are subject to fermentation.

Apart from the separation of *hallah* and the preparation of unleavened bread, these five cereals are also subject to other halakhic regulations: when used for baking BREAD, a benediction must be recited before they are eaten (see GRACE BEFORE MEALS) and other blessings must follow (GRACE AFTER MEALS). Their flour is categorized as leaven (HAMETS) on Passover, and anything prepared from it may neither be used nor stored over the festival. In the talmudic period, Babylonian Jews made rice part of their staple diet and there were evidently some who believed that rice fell under the biblical *hallah* law (*Pes.* 50b-51a). Unlike most Sephardim, Ashkenazi Jews prohibit the use of rice on Passover, as well as any other cereals, apart from potato flour, that have not been specially supervised for Passover cooking. Nowadays, in practice, only wheat flour is used for making unleavened bread; since KARAITES regard it as "poor man's bread" (*lehem oni*), they persist in baking unleavened bread from barley.

FLOOD Deluge which, according to the biblical narrative (Gen. 6:9-9:17), covered the earth and destroyed mankind as a Divine punishment for its wickedness. The sole righteous person on earth, NOAH, is forewarned by God and builds an ark that provides a refuge for his family and for representatives of every species of terrestrial creature. The deluge lasts for 40 days and, after five months, the ark comes to rest on Mount Ararat. Noah makes four probes to see if the land is dry — once with a raven and three times with a dove, which the second time brings back an olive leaf and the third time does not return, showing that there is dry land. A year after the onset of the flood, when the occupants leave the ark, Noah builds an altar and offers a sacrifice to God in thankfulness for his deliverance. God vows never again to doom the world on man's account, in token of which He sets the rainbow in the sky and makes a covenant with Noah.

A parallel story of the flood, in many versions, is to be found in ancient Mesopotamian literature (most notably in the Gilgamesh Epic, where the Babylonian "Noah" is called Ut-Napishtim). The many similarities leave little doubt of a close relationship, but the differences are also striking. The Babylonian stories are polytheistic and the details mythological. After the flood, Noah's Babylonian counterpart is himself elevated into a god. Whereas in the Bible God condemns man for his immoral conduct, in the Babylonian version the gods bring on the flood because mankind is making so much noise that their sleep is disturbed. It has been suggested that those responsible for the biblical account (and Bible critics detect two original sources that have been welded into one) took the raw material of the Babylonian myths and transformed this into a paradigm of the moral principles governing God's relationship to man.

FOOD, SABBATH AND FESTIVAL The DIETARY LAWS (*kashrut*) and the observances associated with the Sabbath, Pilgrim Festivals, and other holidays were the factors that made Jewish cuisine different from that of other peoples. The basis of the *kashrut* laws is stated in a biblical verse: "You shall be holy to Me; for I the Lord am holy, and I have set you apart from other peoples to be Mine" (Lev. 20:26). Holiness is accordingly the fundamental reason for Judaism's dietary regulations. The dining table is considered to be an altar of God and the proper offering to be placed on it is victuals for the less fortunate: "He who does not leave some food for the poor deprives himself of God's blessing" (*San.* 92b). Despite the restrictions that faced observant Jews, including separate meat and dairy meals and utensils, they learned to use the available foods and the styles of cooking prevalent in every land of their dispersion. Jewish culinary art was often molded by the non-Jewish environment, hence the substantial differences between Ashkenazi and Sephardi-Eastern cuisine. Sephardim in North Africa and the Middle East used an abundance of herbs, spices, olive oil, vegetables, and lamb to prepare foods not generally popular among Ashkenazim. Furthermore, the names of most Sephardi dishes are of Judeo-Spanish, Arabic, or Persian origin, while Ashkenazi dishes usually bear Yiddish names.

Some foods have been traditional among Jews from time immemorial. When the Israelites were in the wilderness, they complained about their monotonous diet, saying, "We remember the fish that we used to eat freely in Egypt" (Num. 11:5). Fish has long been eaten by Jews on Friday nights. Its attractiveness stemmed from the fact that it was inexpensive, did not call for ritual slaughtering, and could be eaten with dairy or meat meals.

The three meals prescribed for the Sabbath — Friday evening, Saturday midday and late afternoon — are a significant element in the Day of Rest. Sabbath meals open with the KIDDUSH (sanctification) over a cup of wine, followed by the *Ha-Motsi* blessing recited over two *hallot* (twisted loaves of bread). A typical Ashkenazi menu includes chopped herring or *gefilte fish* (fishballs), chicken soup with noodles, roasted chicken or meat, *tsimmes* (side dish of carrots and prunes), and a fruit compote. The highlight of the Sabbath midday meal is usually a steaming hot *tcholent* (called *hammin* by Sephardi Jews), which consists of potatoes, beans, barley, groats, and meat placed in a heated oven before the Sabbath and allowed to stew and thicken. A dish of chopped eggs and onions or chopped liver serves as an appetizer, often with a savory noodle or potato *kugel* (pudding) as a side dish. Stuffed derma is another favorite in many communities. Hasidic Jews consider the third meal (*se'udah shelishit*) most important as they eat it in the presence of their *Rebbe* (rabbi). After dark, they and other Orthodox folk may enjoy a fourth repast known as MELAVVEH MALKAH ("Escorting the [Sabbath] Queen").

Rosh ha-Shanah, the Jewish New Year, has its own culinary practices. The *hallah* loaves are usually baked round or in different shapes, each with a symbolic meaning. Following *Kiddush* at the evening meal, a piece of *hallah* is dipped in honey (instead of salt) and eaten. On the second night, the blessing for fruit is recited over a slice of apple dipped in honey, followed by a traditional formula: "May it be Your will...to renew unto us a good and sweet year." Carrot *tsimmes* and *leykakh* honey cake are other Ashkenazi favorites. Eating the head of a fish symbolizes the hope that one may become "the head [a leader] and not the tail [a follower]" (Deut. 28:1,43-44). Sour or bitter foods are not eaten on Rosh ha-Shanah, nor are nuts since in Hebrew the numerical value of "nut" (*egoz*) is 17, the same as for "sin" (*het*) when the silent *aleph* is dropped from the latter.

Another festive meal is served before the Day of Atonement. "If a man eats and drinks on the ninth [of Tishri], Scripture considers it as if he fasted on both the ninth and tenth [Yom Kippur] days" (*Yoma* 81b). The *hallot* placed on the table for this meal are round and braided; accompanying the soup are ravioli-like *kreplakh* (dough filled with meat). Salty fish or spiced dishes are traditional appetizers after the fast.

Culinary practices for the Sukkot (Tabernacles) festival varied from country to country. In Yemen, a number of families would join together in buying a sheep or an ox, so as to be assured of sufficient meat for this lengthy festival. In Poland and Russia, a favorite dish was *holishkes*, cabbage leaves stuffed with chopped meat, while cabbage or beetroot *borsht* often replaced the usual meat soup. German Jews were accustomed to eat a type of cabbage, known as *Wasserkohl*, on Hoshana Rabbah because on this day the *Kol Mevasser* hymn is recited. *Kreplakh* are also eaten on Hoshana Rabbah. *Teyglakh*, a confection made with honey, is the typical Sukkot delicacy.

Latkes, pancakes made of grated potatoes and fried in oil, have long been the distinctive Hanukkah food among Ashkenazim. In Eastern lands fried pastries are served and sugar and sesame seeds are added to other pancakes. The various traditions have latterly combined in Israel to produce *levivot* (pancakes) and *sufganiyyot* (doughnuts), both commemorating the miracle of the oil which Hanukkah commemorates. Dairy dishes are likewise characteristic of this festival, commemorating the heroism of Judith who, according to a late legend, was of the Maccabean family, and who slew the enemy general Holofernes after feeding him milk, cheese, and wine until he fell into a stupor. On the Sabbath of Hanukkah, East European Jews ate two different types of *kugel* — one in honor of the Sabbath and the other to mark the festival.

The Purim tradition of *mishlo'ah manot* ("sending portions," i.e., gifts) to one's friends gave the Jewish housewife an opportunity to create baked delicacies. The most popular of these dishes are the three-cornered poppyseed buns known as *hamantashen* (traditionally the shape of Haman's hat), which in Israel are called *ozné Haman* ("Haman's ears") and are filled with dates or prunes. Almond and marzipan cakes are baked by Sephardi-Eastern Jews, while *bob un arbes* (salted peas and beans) have remained popular among East European Ashkenazim. The place of honor on the table set for the Purim SE'UDAH ("meal") is reserved for the *keylitsh*, an outsized braided *hallah* decorated with raisins.

Passover laws require abstention from HAMETS (leaven) and the eating of MATSAH (unleavened bread). "Seven days you shall eat unleavened bread; on the very first day you shall remove leaven from your homes" (Ex. 12:15). *Hamets* includes the fermented products of the FIVE SPECIES of grain — wheat, barley, oats, rye, and spelt — as well as all foods containing yeast or leaven. The table setting for the Passover eve *Seder* service comprises three *matsot* in a specially designed cover, wine cups, and a large platter displaying salt water and a roasted egg symbolizing the festival offering; a roasted shankbone, in lieu of the paschal lamb sacrificed in the Temple; bitter herbs (MAROR), recalling the privations of the enslaved Israelites in Egypt; a green vegetable; and *ḇaroset*, a sweet paste made of apples, nuts, cinnamon, and wine, symbolizing the mortar out of which the Israelites made bricks for the Egyptians. During the *Seder*, each participant drinks four cups of wine to recall the four expressions of redemption (Ex. 6:6-7). It is customary to begin the meal with an hors d'oeuvre of hard-boiled eggs in salt water.

Among the favorite Passover dishes are beetroot *borsht* and various drinks; cakes made of *matsah* meal or potato flour; almond and coconut macaroons; *khreyn*, a horseradish or beetroot relish; *ayngemakhtz*, a jam made of radish or beetroot with ginger and nuts; *matsah* puddings; crumbled *matsah* fried with eggs; and *matsah* meal fritters (*khremzlakh*) and dumplings (*kneydlakh*).

ON FOOD

You shall serve the Lord your God, and He will bless your bread and your water.

The generous man shall be blessed, for he gives of his bread to the poor.

When Rav Huna had a meal, he would open wide the door and say: "Let all who are hungry, come and eat."

No sage should live in a town where vegetables are hard to obtain.

If three men have eaten at the same table and have spoken over it words of Torah, it is considered as if they had eaten at the table of God.

Food must not be treated disrespectfully

The wise man eats to live; the fool lives to eat.

Dairy dishes typify the meals served on Shavu'ot. Various reasons have been advanced for this tradition, notably the fact that the Torah, received on the date of this festival, is compared to milk and honey (Song 4:11). The special dishes associated with Shavu'ot include *blintzes* (rolled pancakes filled with sweetened cream cheese), cheese *knishes* (filled and baked dough), fruit *strudels*, cheesecake, and cheese *kreplakh*. Jewish housewives in Eastern countries bake a seven-layer cake called *Siete Cielos* ("Seven Heavens"), recalling the number of heavenly spheres which God broke asunder to present the Torah to Moses on Mount Sinai. Others make *baklava*, a sweet pastry comprising many layers of thin dough stuffed with nuts, sugar, and honey.

Throughout the year, doughnut-shaped hard bread rolls know as *beygelakh* ("bagels") have become a Sunday morning favorite, together with yeast dough *kukhen* of different types. Several other traditional Jewish dishes — *blintzes*, *borsht*, chicken soup with noodles or *kreplakh*, and even *gefilte fish* — have become widely popular in the United States and now form part of a more international cuisine.

FORGIVENESS (Heb. *meḇilah, seliḇah*). Forgiving sin and transgression is one of the thirteen Divine Attributes (Ex. 34:6-7); in the sixth blessing of the AMIDAH prayer, God is addressed three times daily as "the One who forgives abundantly." Throughout the Bible, God's compassion, and readiness to forgive His sinning people, is repeatedly attested. Even in the most extreme case, when the Israelites abandoned Him and worshiped the GOLDEN CALF, God acceded to the plea of Moses and renounced his anger (Ex. 32:11-14). The central feature of the prophetic writings is the call for REPENTANCE and for a return to God's ways (*teshuvah*), an act made possible by this Divine capacity for forgiveness.

MAIMONIDES teaches that in order to secure God's forgiveness, the individual must confess to having sinned, then repent, and finally resolve not to sin again. The process of sinning, repentance, and forgiveness is the central theme of the DAY OF ATONEMENT liturgy and of the preceding SELIḆOT period; the key phrases are Moses' plea for Israel (Num. 14:19-20) and "God of forgiveness, forgive us, pardon us, grant us atonement."

In the Jewish tradition, great emphasis is placed upon the responsibility of the individual to seek forgiveness not only from God but from his fellowman as well. God is viewed as being eager to forgive at the very first sign of repentance (Ḫag.5a); human beings are enjoined to "walk in His ways," by imitating Him, and to espouse this quality. The sages quote the example of Abraham, who not only forgave Abimelech but even prayed to God on his behalf (Gen. 20:17). In the rabbinic view, a readiness to forgive is a virtue of great importance; one who thrice rejects a plea for forgiveness is himself considered a sinner.

It is understood, however, that human beings are not easily placated. In addition to making restitution for the offense, the offender must personally seek the injured party's forgiveness (cf. *RH.* 17b). On the eve of the Day of Atonement, it is customary to approach those whom one may have wronged in order to beg their forgiveness and offer to make amends. Here again, the sages require the injured party to be "soft as a reed and not hard as a cedar" (*Ta'an* 20b), and to display that same readiness to forgive which is attributed to God Himself.

As important as forgiveness may be, tradition is aware that it may conflict with other equally important Divine attributes, particularly the requirement to do JUSTICE. The relative positions of these values in rabbinic thought are made quite clear in the legend where God is shown praying that His qualities of mercy and forgiveness may override His demand for strict justice.

FORGIVENESS

To him who is compassionate toward his fellow creatures, and forgives wrongs done to him, compassion is shown from heaven.
Let a man forgive the disgrace to which he has been subjected: let him seek no honor through the disgrace of his neighbor.
If your fellow has done you some good, let it be great in your eyes; but if he has done you a great wrong, let it be small in your eyes.
Even though a man pays another compensation for having insulted him, he is not forgiven by God until he seeks forgiveness from the man he has insulted. That man, if he does not forgive the other, is called merciless.
If a man has sinned all his life, yet repents on the day of his death, all his sins are forgiven him.
Imitate God by being compassionate and forgiving. He, in turn, will have compassion on you and pardon your offense.

FOUR QUESTIONS (*Arba kushiyot*). Traditional formula recited during the Passover SEDER. These Four Questions, usually asked by the youngest child or participant, have acquired a popular, alternative designation from the opening words: *Mah Nishtannah*, "How different [this night is from all other nights!]" The inquiries deal with the eating of unleavened bread (MATSAH) and a bitter herb (MAROR), and with the ceremonies of dipping two vegetables and reclining at the *Seder* table. The purpose is to enable the father to fulfill the Biblical injunctions to tell his son about Israel's deliverance from Egyptian bondage (Ex. 13:8, 14-15), and the answer comes in a lengthy exposition that concludes just before the meal. This procedure has evolved from the more spontaneous table talk of the Second Temple period when the *Seder* ceremony took shape. At that time, no set formula had as yet been devised: questions were then asked at a later point in the ceremony to elicit fuller discussion of the *Seder* customs. Since children often began to fall asleep at that stage, the questions and answers were transferred to a point in the *Seder* shortly after its commencement.

Three specific questions first became popular within the family circle: one related to the eating of unleavened bread exclusively on Passover, another to seasoning food not once (as was the custom) but twice, a third to the practice of eating only roasted (not stewed or cooked) meat at the *Seder* table. This last inquiry, about the paschal lamb, became superfluous following the Temple's destruction and was subsequently replaced by an allusion to the custom of reclining which had gone out of fashion at the time. A fourth question, about eating the bitter herb, expanded the original text.

The present-day text of the Four Questions, varying in some particulars from that of the Talmud (*Pes.* 116a), dates from the geonic era, when a different order was introduced. This places the reference to dipping first, followed by the unleavened bread, bitter herb, and reclining; the Sephardi and Eastern rituals follow that order, while Ashkenazim retain the talmudic sequence. From Mishnaic times until the later Middle Ages, the father — or some adult — posed the Four Questions, but in recent centuries this privilege has again been given to a youngster. When a man and his wife are the sole participants, she asks the questions; but in the absence of both children and women, even scholarly men have to ask each other. In some Israeli kibbutzim, new answers were introduced, e.g., "This night is different from all other nights because parents and children eat separately during the year, but on Passover night they eat together."

THE FOUR QUESTIONS

How different this night is from all other nights!
On all other nights we can eat leavened or unleavened bread; why, on this night, only unleavened?
On all other nights we can eat any kind of herbs; why, on this night, bitter herbs?
On all other nights we do not dip herbs even once; why, on this night, do we dip twice?
On all other nights we may eat either sitting up or reclining; why, on this night, do we all recline?

FOUR SPECIES (*arba'ah minim*). Four different plants used as part of the SUKKOT ritual. The Bible commands, "You shall take on the first day [of Sukkot] the fruit of goodly trees, branches of palm trees, and boughs of thick trees, and willows of the brook, and you shall rejoice before the Lord your God seven days" (Lev. 23:40). While the identity of two of the species, "branches of palm trees," and "willows of the brook" is clear from the text, the identity of the other two is known only by oral tradition. The accepted interpretation identifies the "fruit of goodly trees" as the *etrog* (citron), and the "boughs of thick trees" as branches of myrtle (*hadas*; *Suk.* 32b-33a). A complete set of four species thus consists of the *lulav* — a closed frond of a date palm, an *etrog*, two branches of willow (*aravot*), and three sprigs of myrtle. The *lulav*, myrtle, and willows are bound together with strips of palm leaves, the myrtle on the right side of the *lulav* and the willows on the left. In the ritual taking of the four species, the *etrog* is held in the left hand and the three other species of the *lulav* are in the right (*Suk.* 37b). The appropriate blessing is recited and then all the species are brought together, to be waved in six different directions: forward (east), right, backward, left, up, and down, apparently in a symbolic acknowledgement of God's omnipresence. The order of this waving varies according to local custom.

When the TEMPLE stood, the main focus of the ceremonies of the four species was the Temple itself. There, they were taken and waved on each of the seven days of Sukkot. In all other locales, the species were taken on the first day only (*Suk*. 3.12). In the Temple, the taking of the species accompanied the chanting of HALLEL. After the offering of the *Musaf* sacrifice (see ADDITIONAL SERVICE), the species were taken up again and a procession was held around the altar, this time accompanied by the reading of Psalms 118:25. On the first six days of Sukkot, one circuit was made around the altar each day; on the seventh day (HOSHANA RABBAH), seven circuits (HAKKAFOT) were made. With the Temple's destruction, R. JOHANAN BEN ZAKKAI proclaimed that in remembrance of the Temple, the species would henceforth be taken on all seven days of the festival in all locales and that the practices of the Temple ceremony would be transferred to the local synagogues (*Suk*. 3.12). Nowadays (except on a Sabbath), the four species are taken throughout Sukkot and waved during *Hallel* and the subsequent *Hakkafot* (see also HOSHANOT).

The Bible gives no explanation of the commandment of the four species, although various interpretations have been offered by other sources. The best-known of these turns upon the characteristics of each species: the *etrog* that has both taste and fragrance symbolizes the "model" Jew who has both knowledge of the Torah and good deeds to his credit, taste symbolizing knowledge of the Torah and fragrance good deeds. The myrtle has only fragrance, the date palm only taste, and the willow neither. Thus each species symbolizes a different type of Jew, but the Jewish people is regarded as one unified entity (the species must be held together, and the commandment may not be fulfilled if one of the species is damaged or missing), and when united each makes up for the shortcomings of the other (Lev. R. 30.12).

A man holding the Four Species besides the word Hosha-na, *the prayer recited when carrying the Four Species around the synagogue.*

FRANKEL, ZACHARIAS (1801-1875). Founder of the "positive-historical" school, later to be known as CONSERVATIVE JUDAISM; rabbinic scholar and leader of German Jewry. Born in Prague, Frankel received a traditional Jewish education and later studied philosophy and philology in Budapest. Having served from 1836 as the rabbi of Dresden, he was appointed director of the Jüdisch-Theologisches Seminar in Breslau (1854), a post which he retained until his death. Among his outstanding scholarly publications were an introduction to the Mishnah (*Darkhé ha-Mishnah*, 1859) and *Ahavat Tsiyyon*, a commentary on sections of the Jerusalem Talmud (1874-5). The former work proved especially controversial in traditionalist circles because of its historical approach to the Mishnah and the *halakhah*. In accordance with modern scholarship, Frankel interpreted each text in the light of historical knowledge and avoided a dogmatic stand on the Sinaitic origins of the ORAL LAW. At the Breslau seminary, he set the standards for modern rabbinic education, combining critical, historical analysis and secular knowledge with reverence and loyalty to religious observance. His institution and its philosophy represented an attempt to synthesize modern knowledge and scholarly methods with traditional Jewish belief and practice. In 1851, he founded (and edited until 1868) the outstanding Jewish scholarly journal of that time, the *Monatsschrift für Geschichte und Wissenschaft des Judentums*.

Frankel became involved in the controversies of his day between NEO-ORTHODOXY and REFORM JUDAISM (whether radical or moderate). At the Frankfurt rabbinical conference of 1845, he endeavored to influence the non-Orthodox rabbis, with a view to their adopting firm guidelines in regard to proposed changes. Frankel considered the post-biblical development of Judaism to be an organic growth stemming from biblical principles, as interpreted by human authorities. The conference, however, was in no mood to accept the implicit restrictions of this approach. When it called for the abolition of Hebrew as the language of prayer, Frankel left in protest, splitting the non-Orthodox into two different camps — the Reform and the Positive-Historical. On the one hand, Frankel condemned Reform's abandonment of *halakhah* and the national element in Judaism; on the other hand, he rejected Orthodoxy's opposition to scientific research and minor ritual changes. Frankel emphasized the role of the people in developing the *halakhah*, and in following its spirit and intent, to preserve "historical" Judaism. A passionate advocate of Jewish settlement in Erets Israel, he anticipated Herzl in essays outlining a political Zionism.

FRANKISTS Followers of the pseudo-MESSIAH, Jacob Frank. They formed a Shabbatean sect, many members of which formally embraced Catholicism in 1759, although continuing to maintain various Jewish practices in secret. Among themselves, the Frankists were known as "believers" or "Zoharites." Although no scholar, Jacob Frank

(1726-1791), the movement's leader, was an ambitious and charismatic personality. He was influenced by the doctrines of SHABBETAI TSEVI, first in his native Podolia and later in Turkey, where he established contact with the Dönmeh and began to regard himself as a reincarnation of Shabbetai Tsevi, the 17th-century false messiah. Declaring that he would complete Shabbetai Tsevi's mission, Frank developed a kabbalistic theology that was an amalgam of Jewish and Christian beliefs. Frank's theology, however, was much simpler than that of Shabbetai Tsevi. According to his system, which closely paralleled the Christian trinity, God's nature consisted of three separate incarnations: the "First One" (Shabbetai Tsevi), the "Holy Lord" (Jacob Frank), and "the Lady," a female Messiah (or, as Frank referred to her, "the Virgin," namely, a combination of the SHEKHINAH and the Virgin Mary).

Frank demanded of his followers an ironclad commitment to religious nihilism. The true "believer" had to be prepared for "descent into the abyss," which meant not only abandoning all religious and moral codes, but indulging in orgiastic sexual rites as well (see ANTINOMIANISM). To pursue these goals successfully, adherents had to assume the "burden of silence." They were expected to pass from one religion to another, their ultimate goal being the attainment of "secret knowledge." Conversion to Christianity was simply one means of attaining that objective.

After a ban of excommunication had been pronounced against them at Brody in 1756, the "Zoharites" enlisted the support of Nicholas Dembowski, the Catholic bishop of Kamieniec-Podolski, who ordered the excommunicating rabbis to defend the Talmud at a public disputation in the following year. When the rabbis were judged to have lost the debate, thousands of copies of the Talmud were seized and burned. Two years later, in 1759, another disputation was held and this time the rabbinical spokesmen outwitted their opponents. Shortly afterwards, thousands of Frankists converted to Catholicism, Jacob Frank himself arranging to be baptized a second time in Warsaw Cathedral. However, when the Polish clergy learned that his trinitarian doctrine was not identical with that of Christianity and that he was still regarded by his followers as the Messiah, Frank was arrested and spent 13 years in prison (1760-1773). As had been the case with Shabbetai Tsevi, imprisonment enhanced Frank's messianic role among the "believers." Upon his release, he moved to Brno and later to Offenbach (near Frankfurt), where the sect was reorganized under the "Holy Lord" (who now styled himself "Baron von Frank"). Subsequently, from 1791 until 1817, it degenerated still further under "the Queen" (Frank's daughter Eva-Emunah) and then ceased to exist. Many well-to-do Frankists intermarried with the Polish aristocracy; their descendants included Adam Mickiewicz, Poland's national poet. Others, in Bohemia and elsewhere, reverted to Judaism. See also MESSIANIC MOVEMENTS.

FREE WILL God's first utterance to man in the Bible is a command which he disobeys and for which he is punished. This implies that man is a responsible being, possessing freedom of choice to obey or disobey. Man's actions, emanating from his will, are his own for which he is, therefore, accountable.

God tells Cain that although he is subject to powerful emotions and sin "couches at the door; its urge is toward you, yet you can be its master." (Gen. 4:7) After reviewing their history, Moses tells the people of Israel that the key to their national destiny is ultimately in their own hands: "I have set before you life and death, the blessing and the curse, therefore choose life.." (Deut. 30:19).

This principle of man's freedom of will has been described as "a great principle and pillar of the Torah and the MITSVOT" (Maim., *Yad, Teshuvah* 5.3). The entire concept of repentance, TESHUVAH, which is taught in the Pentateuch (Deut. 4:30, 31, 30:11-14), emphasized by the prophets (e.g. Hos. 14:2-3), and is the heart of the Day of Atonement service, presumes freedom of the will. This constant call to man to return to God with the promise of Divine forgiveness assumes that man has the power to free himself from his past, from his set ways, and change completely. Indeed, God wishes man to come to Him voluntarily, out of free choice. God does not overwhelm but waits for man's response (Ex. 19:8)

Biblical law clearly distinguishes between intentional and unintentional acts (Num. 35:1-34). Jewish law treats at length the limits of legal and moral responsibility and the effects of various degrees of compulsion upon the individual (*BK.* 8.4).

Not all Jews accepted human free will. The ESSENES believed in predestination and held that everything was predetermined by the Divine will, while the SADDUCEES denied Divine Providence and felt that everything occurred by chance. The rabbis reiterate the biblical concept of man's freedom: "All is in the hand of heaven except the fear of heaven" (*Ber.* 33b). "The angel appointed over conception takes a seminal drop, sets it before the Holy One, Blessed be He and asks, 'Sovereign of the universe, what is to become of this drop? Is it to develop into a person strong or weak, wise or foolish, rich or poor?' But no mention is made of its becoming wicked or righteous." This is left to the person himself (*Nid.* 16b).

The first challenge to the concept of free will came from the sphere of theology itself, from the concept of God's omniscience or foreknowledge. If God knows everything in advance, how could man have freedom of choice? The talmudic rabbis simply affirmed both principles without attempting any solution: "Everything is foreseen yet permission (freedom) is given" (*Avot* 3.15). Maimonides (*Yad, ibid.* 5,5) discusses the problem and suggests that God's "knowledge" is completely different from man's knowledge. This has been interpreted to mean that since God is above time, His is not strictly a "foreknowledge." God knows the future intuitively in that He sees the future as part of an eternal present. Hence, His knowledge does not conflict with man's freedom of choice. Even when God providentially intervenes in history, He does not interfere with the inner workings of man's volition and the integrity of man's selfhood (Maim. *ibid.* 5.4). The "hardening of the heart of Pharaoh" (Ex. 4:21) is construed as a restoration of Pharaoh's own free will in face of the coercive effects of the plagues (Naḥmanides).

Judaism's insistence upon the existence of human freedom would seem to conflict with the implications of much of contemporary psychology which sees the mind of man, like the rest of nature, locked into a tight causal nexus. This implies that were enough known about the character, background, and circumstances of any individual all of his decisions could be predicted. The biblical-rabbinic concept of moral responsibility, on the other hand, seems to be compatible only with a libertarian concept of contra-causal freedom and incompatible with any sort of deterministic theory.

Modern Jewish thinkers have suggested, in reply to this challenge, that if man, alone of all creatures, possesses categorical freedom in which the self can originate changes, then this provides a dramatic manifestation of man's having been created "in the image of God" (Gen. 1:26). Even as God, the Prime Mover, created the world "out of nothing," so does man, each time he makes a moral decision, act as a self-originating creative power.

These thinkers hold that with each moral decision man experiences his selfhood, his ability to feel and act as an "I". Furthermore, with each such decision, he builds and extends his own character and personality. In short, in making moral choices in freedom, man works his *tselem* ("image of God") into *demut* (likeness of God) (*ibid.*) and thus fulfills his humanity (see also ETHICS).

FREEWILL OFFERING See SACRIFICES AND OFFERINGS

FRINGES See TSITSIT

FUNERAL SERVICE While the texts prescribed for the BURIAL service and the order in which they are recited vary even within the major (Ashkenazi and Sephardi) prayer rites, certain features are common to all. Thus, *keri'ah* — the RENDING OF GARMENTS — is performed on mourners, biblical and liturgical verses are chanted by the rabbi as he leads the funeral procession into the cemetery, stops may be made en route to the gravesite, and often a EULOGY is pronounced either in the funeral chapel (*ohel*) or when the coffin is lowered into the grave, which male participants help to fill with earth. MEMORIAL PRAYERS and a special mourner's KADDISH bring the funeral to a close, after which those present offer words of comfort to the bereaved family and wash their hands before leaving the cemetery.

A standard designation for the burial service is *Tsidduk ha-Din* (lit. "Justification of [the Divine] Judgement"), i.e., man's acknowledgment of and submission to God's will. This actually refers to one central portion of the service, a collection of verses in which the mourners are called upon to accept the inevitable and, while giving vent to their sorrow, reaffirm their trust in God.

In general, Ashkenazi funerals conform to a basic pattern. Distinguished rabbis and scholars who are being conveyed to the cemetery may be honored with a short stop at their synagogue en route to the burial ground. There, relatives and friends of the deceased gather in the prayer hall (chapel), mourners recite the BARUKH DAYYAN HA-EMET formula as their outer garments are rent, and a prescribed benediction is recited by anyone who has not visited a cemetery for the previous 30 days. In Israel especially, the deceased is eulogized in the chapel before the bier or coffin is taken by pallbearers into the graveyard. A special trolley is used to wheel the coffin in some Diaspora communities. *Attah Gibbor* ("Your might is boundless"), the second blessing of the daily AMIDAH, is then read by the officiating rabbi. It is followed by *Tsidduk ha-Din*, commencing with *Ha-Tsur Tamim Po'olo* (Deut. 32:4) and a sequence of other biblical verses which conclude with Jer. 32:19, Ps. 92:16, Job 1:21, and *Ve-Hu Raḥum* ("He, the Merciful One," Ps. 78:38). On days when the TAḤANUN supplication is not read in synagogue (e.g., the eve of Sabbaths and festivals), the verses after *Attah Gibbor* are replaced by *Mikhtam le-David* (Ps. 16) or simply omitted.

As he leads the funeral procession to the grave site, the rabbi often chants Ps. 91 and may stop three times on the way, allowing the mourners to express their grief. In certain Diaspora communities, it is not unusual for portions of the burial service to be read or repeated in the vernacular. As the coffin or shrouded body is lowered into the grave, "May he [she] come to his [her] rest in peace" is said by the officiant. A eulogy may then be given. Adult males, headed by the mourners, cast three shovelfuls of earth into the grave until the mortal remains have been covered, taking care not to pass the spade from hand to hand (it should first be replaced in the ground). Next, either at the grave site or after returning to the chapel, an amplified version of the *Kaddish* (alluding to God's revival of the dead and praying for Jerusalem's restoration) is said by the mourners, after which an *azkarah* memorial prayer including EL MALÉ RAḤAMIM may be recited. Those present form two rows between which the mourners pass and are offered traditional words of consolation: "May the Almighty comfort you among the other mourners of Zion and Jerusalem" (see GREETINGS). In Britain and some other English-speaking countries, they are wished a "long life." Before leaving the cemetery, many Jews pluck a few blades of grass and recite one of two biblical verses (Ps. 72:16 or 103:14); all wash their hands and sometimes recite Isa. 25:8.

A funeral. From a series of paintings of the Burial Society (Ḥevrah Kaddisha) *of Prague, c. 1780.*

The traditional Sephardi burial service differs in a number of ways from that of Ashkenazim, although various Sephardi rituals have been adopted by some Ashkenazi communities in Israel. The custom of making seven circuits (HAKKAFOT) around the bier, while a prayer for God's mercy on the deceased is chanted, thus found its way into Israeli Ḥasidic practice; and the kabbalistic tradition prohibiting sons from accompanying their father's body to the grave is now honored by some *Mitnaggedim* (particularly in Jerusalem). In some places forgiveness is asked from the dead for any sins that may unwittingly have been committed against them. Placing a stone on the grave of a relative is a widely observed custom in Israel.

Sephardim often begin the funeral service in synagogue rather than in the chapel of the cemetery, and women may refrain from attending the actual interment. If the deceased man left children, Syrian Jews blow a ram's horn (*shofar*) after *Kaddish* has been recited at the synagogue service prior to the burial. They recite Ps. 91 for a man and Prov. 31 for a woman, but Moroccan Jews omit Ps. 91 on days when *Taḇanun* is read. The funeral procession makes up to seven stops en route to the grave, where Ps. 78:38 is recited three times as the body is lowered. In contrast to Ashkenazi practice, *Tsidduk ha-Din* follows the burial; thereafter, mourners rend their garments, recite *Kaddish*, and hear the memorial prayer (*hashkavah*) intoned. Western Sephardim (Spanish and Portuguese Jews), however, begin and end their services in the burial ground's chapel, where the rending of garments takes place before the cortege leaves for the grave site. When the deceased is a woman, Ps. 16 is substituted for Ps.91. In certain communities, *Tsidduk ha-Din* is first chanted in the house of mourning and again after the funeral. Consoling the mourners, washing the hands before leaving the cemetery, and similar burial rites are observed by Sephardim and Ashkenazim alike.

G

GAD See TRIBES, TWELVE

GALUT Hebrew term used in the Bible to denote "exile" or "captivity" (II Kings 25:27; Jer. 29:22; Ezek. 33:21; Lam. 1:2); a synonym is *Golah* (II Kings 24:15-16; Jer. 24:5; Est. 2:6; I Chr. 5:22). Both *Galut* and *Golah* refer only to the particular group of Jewish exiles in Babylon, or to the fact of their having been "taken into captivity" there. Nowhere in the Bible is the word *Galut* used as an abstract term signifying exile, wandering, enslavement, or alienation either as an objective condition or as a state of consciousness. Its association with these concepts is rabbinic, postdating the destruction of the Second Temple. In time, also, *Golah* became synonymous with the Greek term *diaspora* ("dispersion"), i.e., any land outside of Erets Israel where Jews live, regardless of how they came to be there (*RH* 1.4).

The concept of exile or of the Jewish people living outside of their land is found early in the Bible. The Israelites' enslavement in Egypt, "the house of bondage," dominates the second book of the Pentateuch; and the EXODUS from Egypt at God's hand constitutes one of the momentous events in Israel's relationship to God. Moreover, it is this "prenatal" Egyptian servitude which becomes the paradigm of *Galut* in the rabbinic mind. God's words to Abraham already contain a hint of future alienation ("strangers in a land not theirs," Gen. 15:13).

After the Israelites entered into the covenant and received the Torah, they were repeatedly warned to keep God's commandments. Obedience will guarantee blessings, while transgression will bring dire punishments climaxing in expulsion from the land for "the Lord will scatter you among all peoples, from one end of the earth to the other..." (Deut. 28:64).

Exile and dispersion are not irreversible, however, since God also promises that if Israel return to Him, "the Lord your God will turn your captivity...and gather you from all the peoples...and bring you into the land which your fathers possessed" (Deut. 30:3-5).

In the historical outlook of the literary prophets, expulsion and exile are the punishments visited on a sinful Israel. National repentance can avert the severe decree; even if exile should come, this does not mean that the covenant between Israel and God has been abrogated. The causal link between sin and expulsion is underlined by Amos (3:3 ff., 6:3-8). Hosea, who had already witnessed the exile of some of the northern tribes to Assyria, refers to it (6:6ff.; 9:3). Similarly, for Isaiah (5:11-13) and Micah (1:5-7, 3:9-12), exile had become a historical fact, and its origin in the nation's waywardness had become self-evident. It remained for Jeremiah (3:19-20, 5:19, 7:9ff.) to apply the experience of the Northern Kingdom to Judah in the south. However, the exile of the inhabitants of the Kingdom of Judah to Babylonia could still be averted if they would only return to God (25:3-9; 36:1-7).

To the Jewish exiles in Babylonia, Ezekiel later brought a message of encouragement. God had not deserted them and could be a "minor sanctuary" even far from the Land of Israel (11:16). Furthermore, with His help, the Jewish people would revive and be restored to its heritage (11:17-20, 37:21ff.). In the sense of (returning) "captives," *Galut* is twice used by Obadiah (v.20) with reference to the promised national redemption.

While the rabbis castigated the Babylonian Jewish community for not returning en masse to the Land of Israel when Cyrus gave them permission to do so (*Yoma* 9b), they also warned the Jews to obey a lawful Gentile ruler. God, said the rabbis, had compelled the Jewish people and the nations of the world to swear three oaths: "...that Israel would not escape from the *Galut* by force of arms, nor rebel against their host nations; and that the nations, in their turn, would not rule Israel oppressively" (*Ket.* 111a).

In rabbinic terminology, *Galut* came to mean the whole tragic state of exile and alienation, both physical and psychological, in which Jews found themselves after 70 CE. The rabbis, nevertheless, differentiated between living in Erets Israel under foreign rulers and actual expulsion from their land, between a Diaspora existence in areas close to Erets Israel and in areas far away, between dispersal in large centers of Jewish population and — far worse — in tiny scattered communities.

Galut, for the rabbis, was a dire and harrowing punishment rightly thrust upon Israel by Divine Providence (*Avot* 5.9; *Sif.* to Deut. 11:17). It meant homelessness, encountering hostility and discrimination, and an all-pervasive sense of alienation. Exile, however, was an unnatural condition and would not last forever. Through the liturgy and various halakhic practices, the rabbis kept the Jew mindful of the lapsed religious institutions which he might hope to see restored. Thus, in a sense, the rabbis never accepted the *Galut*. While understanding it as a just punishment, they hastened to plead Israel's cause before God; and, in midrashic works, they credited the patriarchs and prophets with various moving entreaties that Israel be released from the suffering and indignity of exile. At the same time, however, they were aware that hatred of the Jew often had the effect of inhibiting ASSIMILATION and rekindling a sense of Jewish identity. Given a modicum of acceptance and an enlightened cultural environment, Jews might well succumb to the dangers of acculturation. Two different rabbinic approaches to *Galut* existence are discernible. On the one hand, "the seal-ring of Haman" legalizing the genocidal edict against Persian Jewry did more to bring Jews back to Judaism than all the preaching of the Hebrew prophets (*Meg.* 14a). On the other hand, it was claimed, "God scattered Israel among the nations only in order that proselytes should be numerous among them" (*Pes.* 87b).

It was the Egyptian paradigm that enabled the sages to view Israel's exile in such broad perspective. Just as they compared the first redeemer (Moses) to the final redeemer (Messiah of the house of David), and the first redemption to the final redemption, so they considered the first *Galut* to be the model for all future exiles. God's promise to Jacob was thus interpreted by the rabbis as applying to every *Galut* experience: "Fear not to go down into Egypt, for I will...go down with you into Egypt and surely bring you up again" (Gen. 46:3-4). The rabbis understand this literally to mean that God Himself, as it were, accompanies His people into exile. A new concept was thus born, known as *Shekhinta be-Galuta*, "the Divine Presence [is] in exile" (*Meg.* 29a), which would later become potent in the Kabbalah. It suggested that just as the Jew undergoes humiliation in *Galut*, so God also "descends" with His exiled people into some kind of "diminishment." On a formal level, the sages lamented Israel's inability to perform the many *mitsvot* connected with the Land of Israel and the Temple, to the point where they actually declared that: "Whoever lives outside of the land is regarded like one who has no God" (*Ket.* 110b; cf. *Tosef. AZ.* 4.5). Yet this mystical doctrine of *Shekhinta be-Galuta* was borne out by the actual experience of the people: their religious devotion found satisfying expression in the other commandments, in the study of the Torah which had been made accessible by the work of commentators and codifiers, and in the expanding role of prayer and the synagogue.

This doctrine of "God's Presence in Exile" may also be seen as a promise of continued Torah creativity on the part of the people. The Jewish soul and intellect respond to the proximity of God, just as the study of Torah evokes His presence (*Avot* 3.6). Development of the Oral Law, which started in the period of the Second Temple, developed in Babylonia and would be maintained in the other exiles as well. Thus, the *Galut* would not simply endeavor to preserve what already existed, but could be expected to produce an effulgence of new cultural and religious forms: *Shekhinta be-Galuta*.

After the First Temple's destruction, the prophets had confidently assured those in captivity that their exile would not be of long duration. Earlier, in God's revelation to Abraham that his seed would be enslaved and oppressed "in a land that is not theirs," the 400-year length of that servitude was made clear (Gen. 15:13). For the rabbis, however, the age of prophecy had passed. While their faith remained strong that Israel's redemption was sure to come, no one knew for certain when that would be.

Each successive exilic community, from Babylonia to Spain and Poland, bore the title of a *Galut*. The Babylonian EXILARCH was styled *Resh Galuta* ("Head of the Captivity"), and, when R. GERSHOM BEN JUDAH's brilliant scholarship pierced through the darkness of medieval Germany, he won lasting renown as *Me'or ha-Golah* ("Light of the Exile"). Among the great Hebrew poets of Spanish Jewry's Golden Age, JUDAH HALEVI gave the most powerful expression to his people's feeling of estrangement. "As long as the *Golus*" became the proverbial Yiddish phrase, while the notion of *Shekhinta be-Galuta* was given a Ḫasidic imprint by LEVI YITSḪAK OF BERDICHEV: "Here in exile, God Himself is in exile."

From the mid-19th century, deteriorating conditions in eastern Europe coupled with the rise of various European national movements helped to reawaken the age-old Jewish hope for *kibbutz galuyyot*, the INGATHERING OF THE EXILES. Moses Hess, a German socialist, was one of the first to reappraise the historical experience and lessons of *Galut* from a Zionist viewpoint: "In exile", he wrote, "the Jewish people cannot be regenerated" (*Rome and Jerusalem*, 1862). Since the State of Israel's establishment in 1948, there has been an ongoing controversy over the role of Diaspora Zionism and the continued application of *Galut* to such important, free and self-assertive Jewish communities as that of the USA. The classical Zionist position was affirmed by Hayim Greenberg: "Wherever Jews live as a minority [i.e., outside Israel] is *Galut*." The terms *Golah*, *Artsot ha-Pezurah* (lands of the dispersion), and *Tefutsot* (Diaspora) are used interchangeably in Israel when referring to Diaspora Jewry. *Galut* has acquired pejorative overtones, the adjective *galuti* signifying a timorous "ghetto" attitude or mentality. Long before the Jewish State came into being, Shemaryahu Levin (a Russian Zionist leader) indicated this pejorative sense in his aphorism: "It is easier to take the Jew out of *Galut* than to take *Galut* out of the Jew."

GAMALIEL Rabbinical dynasty.

Gamaliel I Known as "The Elder" (1st century CE), president-patriarch (*Nasi*) of the SANHEDRIN, grandson of

HILLEL. He and his descendants-successors were distinguished by the honorific title *Rabban* ("our master") in the place of the usual Rabbi ("my master") applied to talmudic sages.

As a contemporary of King Agrippa I, he was consulted by him (and his queen) on halakhic problems. As the supreme halakhic authority, he issued from the Temple precincts proclamations to the communities in Erets Israel and in the Diaspora concerning tithing problems and a leap year (*Sanh.* 11b). The privilege of the Sanhedrin to regulate the Jewish CALENDAR was at the heart of its authority, and Gamaliel issued a number of regulations (see TAKKANAH) to assure the examination of witnesses who had seen the New Moon, thus enabling the court to proclaim the beginning of another month.

Of particular importance are his regulations affecting marriage (divorce) law (*Git.* 4.2-3). To protect the divorcee, he introduced a number of restrictions into the issue of a letter of divorce (*get*). The biblical rules of evidence were relaxed to prove the death of the husband and to free the wife from the shackled status of an AGUNAH (*Yev.* 16,7).

Gamaliel adopted a humane attitude to Gentiles who were to be given equal charitable treatment with Jews: in material support, visiting their sick, eulogizing and burying their dead and comforting their mourners. They should not be discriminated against when gathering their dues in the fields (Lev. 23:22).

Even in his attitude to the emerging Judeo-Christian sect he showed tolerance and adopted a "wait and see" policy when Peter and other apostles were brought before the Sanhedrin. The NEW TESTAMENT calls him, "a teacher of the Law held in high regard by all the people" (Acts 5:34).

Rabban Gamaliel and his disciples. From the Sassoon Haggadah, *France or Spain, 14th century.*

No aggadic-midrashic statements are reported in his name, but he gave some sound advice to his students: provide yourself with a teacher; rid yourself of doubt; and when giving tithe do not do so by approximation (*Avot* 1,16).

Simeon ben Gamaliel I succeeded his father Gamaliel I as *Nasi* of the Sanhedrin and was active during the last few decades before 70 CE (*Shab.* 15a). Like his father, he issued proclamations to the Jewish communities inside and outside Erets Israel informing them of the Sanhedrin's decision to intercalate a month in leap years and instruct them about their tithing duties (*Sanh.* 11a).

Simeon's modesty is evident in his saying: "All my days I have grown up among the sages, and I have found no better way than silence; not learning but doing is the chief thing; and too many words cause sin" (*Avot* 1,18). When ecstatically rejoicing at the WATER-DRAWING FESTIVAL at the Temple, he could juggle with eight lighted torches.

Josephus refers in glowing terms to the role played by Simeon in the rebellion against Roman rule (66 CE). Simeon joined the revolutionary council directing the war against Rome. When the Zealots progressively established their disastrous dictatorship over Jerusalem and the Temple, he spoke out forcefully (though in vain) against them.

Gamaliel II (of Yavneh, mid-1st century CE — d. before 132 CE), a son of Simeon ben Gamaliel I, was also *Nasi* of the Sanhedrin. He presided over the national-religious restoration after the destruction of the Temple and Jerusalem by the Romans in 70 CE, a work begun by JOHANAN BEN ZAKKAI. He maintained the authority of the Sanhedrin-Academy of Yavneh by making it the rallying point for a galaxy of scholars. Under his guidance, the community of sages, often at variance with each other, produced a body of theological, legal, ritual, and ethical teachings which, under his grandson JUDAH HA-NASI, formed the basis of the MISHNAH. Gamaliel's opinions are quoted in this code about 70 times. Only a man of strong character, besides great intellectual powers, and a deeply religious, saintly spirit could have accomplished such a task. However, it involved him in many conflicts. In one clash with Joshua ben Ḫananyah, Gamaliel overstepped the line by humiliating the elderly scholar. This led to a revolt in which it was decided to depose the authoritarian president and to replace him, but he was eventually reinstated. There remained a tension between him and the Sanhedrin as to their respective authority, but he succeeded in assuring the primacy of his office in such matters as leap years and the ordination of rabbis (*Sanh.* 11a; TJ *Sanh.* 1,19a).

In addition to his duties as President of the High Court and Academy, Gamaliel was the leader of the nation. His frequent hazardous sea journeys to Rome at the head of delegations reveal him as the political spokesman of his nation, approaching the Roman government, particularly Emperor

Domitian. Tradition reports many disputations between Gamaliel and highly placed Romans, "philosophers," and heretics on theological, biblical, and rabbinical problems.

There was hardly an area of Jewish practice and faith in which Gamaliel did not intervene. He standardized the AMIDAH and made its recital obligatory (*Ber.* 4,3; 28b), and included in it a blessing (or rather curse) against heretics (MINIM), probably Judeo-Christians, who thus would be prevented from leading or joining public prayer, together with other "enemies of the people" such as informers or apostates. He also declared the Evening Prayer obligatory. He sought to strengthen the observance of festivals, and tried to assure the continued observance of offerings and tithes to priests and Levites and the laws of ritual purity, originally connected to the Temple and Jerusalem. The final Bible canon may also be due to the work of Gamaliel and his Sanhedrin at Yavneh.

Simeon ben Gamaliel II (2nd century CE), son of Gamaliel II, head of the Sanhedrin. When he became *Nasi*, the Sanhedrin had moved to Usha (*RH* 32a). His opinions are quoted frequently in tannaitic texts — one hundred times in the Mishnah, where they are accepted, with three exceptions, as authoritative (*Ket.* 78a). He warned against imposing restrictions which the public would find hard to bear (*AZ* 36a) and that local customs had to be respected (*Ket.* 6,4 a.e.).

Simeon's dicta are very much concerned with peace. The world, he said, rests on three pillars: Law, Truth, and Peace (*Avot* 1:18). Law has to serve peace, and arbitration is therefore preferable to apodictic judgment (*Sanh.* 5b). Peace begins in the home and ends in the nation.

GAON (pl. *ge'onim*). Honorific title borne by the heads of the ACADEMIES of Sura and Pumbedita in Babylonia in the post-talmudic period from the seventh to 11th centuries; it alludes to the phrase, "For the Lord has restored the pride [*ge'on*] of Jacob" (Nah. 2:3). The office bestowed power and authority far beyond that enjoyed by the heads of the Academies in the preceding talmudic period.

The *ge'onim*'s influence extended far beyond the confines of Babylonia, then the religious and cultural center of Diaspora Jewry, and they were a major factor in the maintenance of Jewish unity. From Egypt, North Africa, Christian and Muslim Spain, questions on all aspects of Judaism were sent to the Academies, and the *ge'onim* possessed the exclusive right to respond to them.

These RESPONSA constitute an invaluable source for the religious, economic, and social history of the time, to which the discovery of the Cairo GENIZAH, where numerous geonic Responsa were found, added immeasurably.

The unquestioned authority of the *ge'onim* is reflected in the almost stereotyped conclusion of their Responsa: for example, "This is the law and it is forbidden to deviate from it to the right or to the left."

In Babylonia itself, the authority of the *gaonate* rested primarily on the semi-official recognition by the Caliphate. The *ge'onim* were appointed by the head of the Jewish community, the EXILARCH; however, the office was quasi-hereditary, and came to be looked upon as the prescriptive right of a few influential families. In Sura, for example, over almost two hundred years, the *gaonate* was the almost exclusive possession of three families.

A *gaon* received a fixed salary, as well as a share of the donations sent to the Academies by individuals and communities, both local and foreign. For both fiscal and administrative purposes, Babylonia was divided into three districts, two of which were under the jurisdiction of the *ge'onim* of the two Academies, and one under the Exilarch. In the district assigned to him, the *gaon* or Exilarch had the exclusive right of appointing judges and other communal officers. The judges had the right (approved by the Muslim authorities) to either publicly flog a violator of the *halakhah* or to excommunicate him.

The *gaon* was installed into his office with great pomp. His primary emphasis was on learning, and in this, in most instances, he far surpassed the Exilarch. Hence, the decisions of the latter's court had to receive the approval of the *ge'onim*. There were periods of sharp controversy between the two parties, the most famous of which was between SAADIAH GAON and the Exilarch David ben Zakkai, who at one stage deposed him as *gaon* of Sura. Saadiah, in turn, deposed the Exilarch and, as a result, was compelled to go into hiding. After some time, he was restored to his post.

Saadiah Gaon, appointed in 928, was the greatest figure connected with Sura, excelling in *halakhah*, biblical exegesis, and philosophy. Following his death, the Academy closed for 45 years, becoming prominent again under his successor Samuel ben Hofni (1003-13).

The Pumbedita Academy's greatest period was under the leadership of SHERIRA GAON (968-98) and his son HAI GAON (998-1038). The former, author of a letter which is the only source for the history of the geonic period, restored for a time the prestige of the Babylonian center which was being supplanted by the new settlements in the West. Under Hai, Pumbedita continued as the foremost world center of Jewish scholarship. After his death, the two Academies, by then both in Baghdad, joined together and continued for another 150 years. Erets Israel too evolved its own gaonate, beginning at the end of the ninth century and lasting until 1109. However, the *ge'onim* there were less learned than their Babylonian counterparts, their main achievement being in maintaining the tradition of the Academies in the Land of Israel under difficult political circumstances.

The *ge'onim* made a lasting contribution to literature, especially talmudic literature; in their time they succeeded in giving the TALMUD a key role in national life. In this regard, the *ge'onim* of Sura, with a few exceptions, far outshone those of Pumbedita. The responsa of the *ge'onim* of Sura were four times more numerous than those by the Pumbedita *ge'onim*. The *ge'onim* provided numerous explanations of passages in the Talmud in response to inquiries by correspondents. Their unique value derives from the fact that in that time there was an oral tradition of talmudic interpretation dating back to the times of the SAVORAIM (who preceded the *ge'onim*). Of special importance is the *ge'onim*'s pioneering work in the CODIFICATION of the *halakhah*. Since the Talmud is highly discursive, to determine the final *halakhah* in a specific matter would require reviewing its three thousand folio pages. The pioneering work in this area of codification is HALAKHOT GEDOLOT by R. Yehudai Gaon of Sura (approx. 757-761), later supplemented by R. Simeon Kayyara. In this area, the collections and classifications of specific halakhic topics by Saadiah Gaon are models of logical and systematic arrangement, which inspired Hai to compile similar collections.

The *ge'onim* also pioneered in the field of liturgy. Rav AMRAM GAON of Sura (853-856) compiled the first complete Order of Prayers (see PRAYER BOOK). Particularly valuable are the halakhic annotations that accompany the prayers. A somewhat similar Order of Prayers, based on Egyptian liturgical practice, was compiled by Saadiah.

The term *gaon*, in later usage in other countries, came to mean an outstanding scholar; the great eastern European scholar and spiritual leader, ELIJAH BEN SOLOMON ZALMAN (1720-1797) for example, was known as the Vilna Gaon.

GARDEN OF EDEN See EDEN, GARDEN OF

GEDALIAH, FAST OF (*Tsom Gedalyah*). A minor FAST, observed on the third of Tishri in remembrance of the tragic fate of Gedaliah, the governor of Judah. His story is mainly told in the book of JEREMIAH, (40:5-41:3; cf.II Kings 25:22-26). After the destruction of the First Temple, the downfall of the Judean kingdom in 586 BCE, and the exile to Babylonia of most of Judah's population, the victorious Babylonian king, Nebuchadnezzar, appointed an able Jewish governor named Gedaliah ben Ahikam to administer affairs in the conquered territory. Gedaliah was a realist who achieved much for the people who had remained in the country, but his governorship was brief. The neighboring Ammonites, fearing the revival of a prosperous Judah, hired a certain Ishmael ben Nethaniah, an officer of royal descent, to kill Gedaliah. Despite advance warnings of the conspiracy, Gedaliah chose to entertain Ishmael and his men at his own home in Mizpah, where they treacherously murdered him and his bodyguards. The surviving Jewish loyalists, believing that Nebuchadnezzar would interpret the assassination of his governor as an act of rebellion, ignored Jeremiah's advice and fled to Egypt. The Babylonian king did view their departure as a confession of guilt and he therefore carried more of the surviving population away to exile in Babylonia. These calamitous events left Judah defenseless and shattered the last Jewish hopes for a peaceful restoration of the land. The murder of Gedaliah was accordingly associated with Judah's final collapse.

The Bible gives Tishri as the month in which it occurred and later tradition (*RH* 18b) records the actual date, 3 Tishri, which was subsequently observed as the "fast of the seventh [month]" (Zech. 7:5; 8:19). Although this day immediately follows ROSH HA-SHANAH, the Jewish New Year, all the laws and rituals of minor fast days apply to *Tsom Gedalyah*. Fasting is from dawn to dusk and SELIḤOT are read in the Morning Service. Should it fall on a Sabbath, the fast is observed the next day.

GEHENNA See AFTERLIFE

GEIGER, ABRAHAM (1810-1874). Reform rabbi and theologian, chief protagonist of REFORM JUDAISM in 19th-century Germany. Having received a traditional Jewish education in his native Frankfurt, Geiger attended university in Bonn, where a fellow student was Samson Raphael HIRSCH, later to become his most outspoken ideological opponent. As rabbi in Wiesbaden (1832-8), Geiger introduced various liturgical reforms and organized the first of several conferences (or SYNODS) of German Reform rabbis. It was, however, in Breslau (1838-63) that he assumed leadership of the Reform camp. Championing a denationalized religion, Geiger proclaimed Judaism's "universal mission" and termed circumcision "a barbaric and bloody rite." The revised prayer book which he issued in 1854 omitted mention of angels and the resurrection of the dead, as well as all prayers for the Ingathering of the Exiles, the Return to Zion, and the rebuilding of the Temple, which he regarded as outmoded ideas conflicting with the "spirit of the age." He also introduced choral singing and sermons in the (German) vernacular into the Reform prayer service. After serving as rabbi in Frankfurt (1863-70), Geiger moved to Berlin, where he became director of the new *Hochschule für die Wissenschaft des Judentums* (see RABBINICAL SEMINARIES) in 1872.

Geiger believed that German Jewry should be reformed gradually, from within the existing communal structure, and utilized his scholarly research work in the "Science of Judaism" (WISSENSCHAFT DES JUDENTUMS) to justify his reformist program and opinions. His works covered many topics, from biblical scholarship, the Second Temple period and Jewish religious history to studies and translations of medieval Spanish Hebrew poets. Despite his retention of Hebrew in worship and his professed adherence to biblical and talmudic tradition, Geiger did not believe in the Divine origin of the Pentateuch and cared little for hallowed practices which he considered no longer obligatory for Jews. He retreated from his more extreme positions in later years, restoring some of the prayers and practices which he had earlier abandoned, but this was largely a tactical response to the growing spirit of moderation within German non-Orthodox Jewry. Through such doctrines as "progressive revelation" and

Judaism's "world mission," as well as through his ritual and liturgical reforms, Geiger had a major impact on later rabbis and preachers of Central European origin in the USA.

GELILAH See READING OF THE LAW

GEMARA See TALMUD

GEMATRIA (*gimatriyya*,"numerology"; from the Greek *geometria*). A device to reveal a deeper, alternative, or hidden meaning in words or phrases. Each letter of the Hebrew alphabet possesses a numerical value (see table under NUMBERS), as does any word if one adds up the value of its letters. Thus, when JACOB tells his sons to "*go down*" (Heb. *redu* = 210) and purchase grain in Egypt to stave off the famine (Gen. 42:2), this is interpreted to mean that Israel's sojourn there will last 210 years (Gen. R. 91.2). *Gematria* is one of the 32 hermeneutical rules used for interpreting the Torah (see HERMENEUTICS), a system found throughout midrashic literature and the Babylonian Talmud (e.g. *Shab.* 149b; *Sanh.* 22a; *Mak.* 23b-24a). Abraham's faithful servant, Eliezer (= 318), was thus as valuable to him as all his 318 retainers (*Ned.* 32a). Kabbalistic literature is replete with *gematria*, which was the basis for AMULETS. However, some authorities, (NAḪMANIDES, for example), tended to discourage its exaggerated use.

Gematria has also been exploited in less serious ways. Both *yayin* ("wine") and *sod* ("mystery") have the numerical value of 70, hence the saying, "when wine goes in, the secret will out" (*Er.* 65a). Jews often disburse charity in multiples of 18 (= *ḫai*, "alive, life"), and at weddings many a toast to the bride and groom will contain a *gematria* of their names, promising a happy future. Other Jews specialize in finding omens in the *gematria* of the forthcoming Jewish year. A lengthy inscription to do with the building of Solomon's Temple, worked into the floor of the historic synagogue at Worms, was ignored until the 20th century: only then did a scholar notice that the numerical value of the inscription's text — 4935 — gave the date of that synagogue's rebuilding (1174/5 CE).

As the term itself implies, *gematria* is not a Jewish invention; the technique was first used by the Greeks, Assyrians, and Babylonians. One ancient example can be found in an inscription of Sargon II (722-705 BCE), who built the Khorsabad Wall 16,283 cubits long so as to correspond to the numerical value of his name. During the Hellenistic period, *gematria* was likewise used by magi and dream interpreters. Currently some experts on the subject are endeavoring to prove its value scientifically, computerization revealing some logical pattern as a key to understanding the Bible.

GEMILUT ḪASADIM ("Deeds of lovingkindness"). Benevolent and kindly acts that traditionally constitute one

Visiting the sick: a "deed of lovingkindness" (Gemilut Ḫasidim). *From the* Rothschild Miscellany Manuscript, *Italy, c. 1470.*

of the three foundations of the world, along with Torah and worship (*Avot* 1.2). According to the rabbis, *gemilut ḫasadim* and *raḫmanut* (consideration or "tender-heartedness") are distinguishing characteristics of the Jewish people (Deut. R. 3.6). The practice of "kindly deeds" brings a double reward, since it is a precept "yielding fruit in this world while retaining its stock in the afterlife" (*Shab.* 127a). Both charity and *gemilut ḫasadim* are equal to all the commandments in the Torah, but the former is outweighed by the latter. In the first benediction of the daily *Amidah*, God is called *Gomel ḫasadim tovim* ("Bestower of lovingkindness"), an idea which the Talmud explains on the basis of His exemplary acts (*Sot.* 14a).

The sages regarded *gemilut ḫasadim* as a social virtue embracing humane and philanthropic activities of every kind: providing HOSPITALITY, dowering a bride (HAKHNASAT KALLAH), visiting the SICK, feeding the POOR, comforting a mourner, or attending a funeral. According to the rabbis, "lending without interest is preferable to giving charity, and investing money in a poor man's business is more laudable still" (*Shab.* 63a). The term *gemilut ḫesed* came to be used in the sense of granting an interest-free loan, for which purpose special *gemilut ḫesed* charitable societies were administered by most Jewish communities and continue to function in some parts of the world.

GENESIS, BOOK OF First book of the Bible and of the PENTATEUCH, known in Hebrew as *Be-Réshit* ("In the Beginning") from its opening word. The traditional Jewish designations for this book include *Sefer Beri'at ha-Olam* and *Sefer Ma'aseh Be-Réshit* ("The Book of Creation"). Its familiar name, in English and other modern languages, derives from the Greek (Septuagint) translation of Gen. 2:4 — "This is the book of the origin [*genesis*] of heaven and earth." Following the Latin Vulgate, printed Hebrew Bibles divide Genesis into 50 chapters and 1,534 verses. The Babylonian cycle of weekly readings (which is followed today by all Jewish communities) divides the book into 12 pericopes (*sedarot*), but according to the Palestinian triennial cycle of Second Temple times it consists of 43 sections.

The Book of Genesis contains three segments: (1) a history of the universe and of early mankind, together with an account of God's relation to the universe and man (chapters 1-11); (2) the history of the Patriarchs, ABRAHAM, ISAAC, and JACOB (12-36); (3) the story of JOSEPH (37-50). Its salient religious teachings include the oneness of God, the nature of creation as ordered by God, and man's superior role in creation; the origin of evil, the moral law emanating from the one God, and the unity of mankind; God's election of Israel and His promise that the Land of Canaan will belong to the descendants of the Patriarchs, who are bound by the covenant "to do justice and righteousness"; and the notion of a God directing the course of history.

In Jewish tradition, the PENTATEUCH (which this Book introduces) was in its entirety of Mosaic authorship, written under Divine inspiration. Modern critical scholars, basing themselves on anachronisms within the text, on duplications, and on the differing names of God, have asserted that Genesis (like the rest of the Pentateuch) is a composite work drawn from a number of sources. Striking parallels with the early chapters (notably the stories of Creation and the Flood) have been found in other ancient Near Eastern cultures, but the monotheistic and moral emphases of the Hebrew Bible are unique.

Opening of Genesis. From the Castro Pentateuch, *Germany, 1344.*

BOOK OF GENESIS

1: 1 — 2:7	Creation of the world
2: 8 — 3:24	The Garden of Eden
4: 1 — 26	Cain and Abel
5: 1 — 32	From Adam to Noah
6: 1 — 9:29	The Flood and Noah
10: 1 — 32	The Table of Nations
11: 1 — 32	The Tower of Babel and the genealogy of Abraham
12: 1 — 25:18	The story of Abraham and the early years of Isaac
25:19 — 35:29	The latter years of Isaac and the story of Jacob
36: 1 — 43	Esau and his Edomite descendants
37: 1 — 47:31	The story of Joseph
48: 1 — 50:13	Final blessing and death of Jacob
50:14 — 26	The latter years and death of Joseph

GENESIS RABBAH Homiletical Midrash on the Book of GENESIS, known in Hebrew as *Be-Réshit Rabbah* (see also MIDRASH AGGADAH). Traditionally ascribed to Hoshaya Rabbah ("the great"), a Palestinian AMORA, it was probably written somewhat later than his time. This Midrash expounds Genesis homiletically, chapter by chapter and verse by verse, in a text divided into 101 sections. These sections are determined either by the Masoretic tradition or by the TRIENNIAL CYCLE of Torah readings once followed in Erets Israel. With few exceptions, each homily is introduced by a proem (*petiḇta*), most of these having their origin in verses from the Hagiographa (chiefly Psalms and Proverbs) and given in the name of Palestinian *amoraim*. The language employed in this Midrash is generally Hebrew, but some portions closely resemble that of the Jerusalem Talmud, Galilean Aramaic containing a strong admixture of Greek and Latin. This dialect is mainly used for the telling of stories and parables.

According to contemporary scholars, Genesis Rabbah, while closely paralleling the Jerusalem Talmud in its language and other features, did not draw directly on the latter but rather on an ancient source common to both. Like the Jerusalem Talmud, it was redacted in Erets Israel some time in the fifth century CE. The anonymous editor utilized early Greek and Aramaic translations of the Pentateuch. In the case of the former, he referred to the translation of Aquila; in the latter case, he relied on the TARGUM of Pseudo-Jonathan but not on Onkelos. Although this editor does cite the Mishnah, he was probably unacquainted with the

Tosefta since it goes unquoted. Nor are there any citations from the MIDRASH HALAKHAH or from AVOT DE-RABBI NATAN, whereas the apocryphal Book of Ecclesiasticus (Ben Sira) is quoted four times. An unusual feature of Genesis Rabbah is its relatively large content of legends that have parallels in the APOCRYPHA and Pseudepigrapha, PHILO, and Josephus. Together with LEVITICUS RABBAH and LAMENTATIONS RABBAH, it is the earliest amoraic Midrash extant.

GENESIS RABBATI A "major" Midrash on the Book of GENESIS, traditionally ascribed to R. Moses ha-Darshan (11th cent.), and known in Hebrew as *Bereshit Rabbati* (see also MIDRASH AGGADAH). Numerous quotations from this work may be found in the *Pugio Fidei* (c. 1280), an anti-Jewish polemic by Raymond Martini. The exact relationship of these quotations to the present text of Genesis Rabbati is debatable. According to modern scholarly opinion, it is an abridgment of GENESIS RABBAH made by some anonymous anthologist who included in it quotations from Moses ha-Darshan's writings. A comparison of the work with NUMBERS RABBAH (chaps. 1-15) shows that the latter is to a great extent based on Genesis Rabbati. The latter's editor drew widely on classical halakhic sources and on the whole of midrashic literature. His citations from the Midrash include significant variant readings.

Genesis Rabbati is unique in its frequent exploitation of GEMATRIA and in its many references to the APOCRYPHA AND PSEUDEPIGRAPHA, quoting these sources either directly or at second hand (from MIDRASH TADSHE). In so doing, the editor-anthologist paraphrases the texts rather than quoting them verbatim.

GENIZAH A storeroom for worn-out and damaged holy manuscripts and books, as well as ritual objects such as TEFILLIN or MEZUZOT. By Jewish law, such items cannot be thrown out but must be disposed of in a reverential manner. Generally, this has meant burying the items involved in the local Jewish cemetery. To facilitate the disposal of such items, many synagogues put aside a special area such as a room or chest as a *genizah* (literally "storage"), where congregants could leave items for later burial.

Nowadays, the term "The Genizah" is used to refer to the storeroom of the ancient Ben Ezra synagogue in Fostat, a suburb of Cairo. In 1896, two scholarly Scottish ladies, on a visit to Cairo, bought a bundle of fragments of Hebrew manuscripts. The following year, Solomon SCHECHTER, then reader in Rabbinics at Cambridge University, identified one of the pages as part of the Hebrew original of *Ecclesiasticus* (the *Wisdom of Ben Sira*) which had only survived in translation. Journeying to the synagogue in 1897, Schechter acquired most of the contents of the Genizah on behalf of Cambridge University. He took back 140,000 fragments, while another 60,000, sold off before his arrival, reached other libraries around the world (especially Leningrad).

Reconstruction of old manuscripts being placed in the Cairo Genizah *in the Ezra Synagogue of Fostat.*

Throughout the 20th century, the process of identifying these fragments has continued. As a result, new light has been shed on a variety of aspects of Jewish history hitherto either unknown or completely vague. The diversity of material of both Palestinian and Babylonian origin is explained by the fact that for centuries Cairo served as the point of transmission from these countries to the Jewish communities of North Africa and the West. Before being forwarded, the material was copied and stored in the Genizah.

Among the material recovered are significant fragments from an ancient text of the Palestinian Talmud; parts of hitherto unknown Midrashim; numerous geonic RESPONSA; KARAITE writings; liturgy and poetry of the post-talmudic age; large fragments of a halakhic work emanating from the ACADEMY of Tiberias in the sixth or seventh century; manuscript letters by MAIMONIDES; and the earliest written examples of YIDDISH.

GENTILE A non-Jew, i.e., any person not either born of a Jewish mother or converted to Judaism. Various Hebrew terms are employed for the gentile, bearing different connotations. The term *goy*, although used frequently, is strictly speaking a misnomer, for it means "a nation," and there are numerous biblical references to the Jewish people as a *goy* in this sense (see Ex. 19:6, for example). A more correct term is *nokhri*, implying a foreigner or stranger. Ancient Judaism differentiates between two overall categories of gentiles, the *ger toshav* (literally "resident alien") and the *akum*, the latter being an acronym for a Hebrew phrase meaning "worshipers of stars and planets." To be considered a *ger toshav*, a non-Jew must live by the seven NOACHIDE LAWS. These laws require belief in the One God, forbid blasphemy, murder, theft, sexual immorality and the eating of a limb from a living creature, and mandate the setting up of courts of law. One who does not accept the Noachide laws is considered an *akum*, or pagan. The status of gentiles of the Christian and Muslim faiths is generally considered to be that of *ger toshav*. While Maimonides demurs in regard to Christians, seeing the belief in the Trinity as violating the first Noachide law, most other commentators (among them the Tosafists [see TOSAFOT] and Joseph CARO) are of the opinion that non-Jews (but not Jews) may hold a belief in the Trinity within the framework of the Noachide laws. Jewish law requires any non-Jew wishing to live in the Land of Israel to accept upon himself the laws of the *ger toshav*. The Bible mentions a further sub-category of gentiles, the "seven nations" dwelling in Canaan, whom the Israelites were commanded to kill because of their depravity. The Talmud states that Sennacherib, King of Assyria, merged the populations of all the different nations that he conquered, and that since his time no person can be considered to be a member of the "seven nations."

Judaism sees itself as a universal religion, with the seven Noachide laws applying to gentiles just as the 613 COMMANDMENTS apply to Jews. Those gentiles who are righteous and observe the Noachide laws out of conviction that these are God-given are by Jewish tradition vouchsafed a place in the World to Come.

Various laws are mentioned in the Talmud, reflecting the tension between the Jews and non-Jews at the time. Thus, for example, a Jew was not to walk on the left side of a non-Jew who wore a sword, evidently for fear of being stabbed. Yet here too the Talmud differentiates between those nations which respected human life, such as the Greeks, and those which did not, such as the Persians (*BK* 117a). Another law along these lines forbade a Jew from selling distinctively Jewish clothing, such as TSITSIT, to a non-Jew, for fear that the latter might dress up as a Jew and thus approach unsuspecting Jews with impunity and harm them. Other laws governing contacts with non-Jews were meant to prevent the Jew from violating specific Jewish laws. An example of this was the prohibition against drinking wine handled by non-Jews at any stage. This was an extension of the biblical prohibition against drinking wine used as a libation as part of the gentiles' religious rituals. Nor were Jews permitted to buy milk from a gentile, for fear of adulteration with pig milk or other forbidden substances. Recent rulings by leading halakhic authorities have relaxed this provision in those countries where government control of milk production and distribution serves as a deterrent against adulteration. Certain laws were meant to minimize, if not eliminate, social intermingling, for this was regarded as endangering the Jews' spiritual life, in accordance with the biblical warning (Deut. 20:18), "lest they lead you into doing abhorrent things."

However, there were also other understandings. The Palestinian Talmud (*Git.* 5.9), for example, says, "In a city in which both Jews and gentiles live, we appoint Jewish and gentile overseers and we support gentile poor together with the Jewish poor, visit their sick, and console their mourners." While *Tanna de-vé Eliyahu*, 9, contains the statement "I will call heaven and earth to witness whether Jews or gentiles, whether man or woman, whether slave or freeman, all is according to one's deeds in that the Holy Spirit rests upon one."

Although some of the rabbinic statements in regard to gentiles are quite harsh, they must be seen against the historical context of the time. Suffering frequent persecutions in both the Christian and Muslim worlds, the Jews inevitably developed negative "stereotypes" of non-Jews which was reflected in particularistic laws, attitudes, writings, and practices. At the same time, the 13th century halakhist R. Menahem Ha-Meiri writes repeatedly in his *Bet ha-Beḇirah* that the laws in the Talmud relating to relations between Jews and gentiles apply only to pagans but not to the nations among whom Jews currently live since they do observe the basic laws of morality.

The fall of the ghetto walls after the emancipation of the Jews has served to remove most of the barriers between Jews and non-Jews. This has changed the traditional relationship between Jews and gentiles, with both positive and negative consequences. The intermingling has served to remove certain stereotypes on both sides, and led to firsthand contact with greater mutual understanding.

Certain residues, prejudices, and suspicions remain from previous periods. Many Jews continue to believe that Christians — all or some — have missionary objectives or hopes vis-à-vis the Jews. Others are wary of close contacts for fear of ASSIMILATION and INTERMARRIAGE. However, once the Jew received equal rights and became part of the general society, universalist elements in Judaism — which had been minimized in ghetto society — again became prominent (see UNIVERSALISM AND PARTICULARISM) and led in a world of pluralism and open society to the lowering or disappearance of barriers. In the western world, in particular, the Jewish attitude to non-Jews is generally one of fellowship, without all or most of the historical tensions. However, in certain circles, including some in Israel, mistrust has not disappeared.

GER See CONVERSION TO JUDAISM

GERIZIM, MOUNT Mountain located within the biblical inheritance of the tribe of Ephraim. The biblical Mount Gerizim is identified as the mountain bearing the same name today (Arab. Jebel al-Tur), located directly opposite

Mount Ebal to its north. Mount Gerizim rises to an altitude of approximately 2,600 feet (881 m.); Mount Ebal to approximately 2,800 feet (940 m.); and between these two mountains lies the city of Shechem (Nablus).

In the Bible the Children of Israel are commanded, upon entrance into the promised land, to conduct a ceremony in the presence of the entire people in which tribes standing upon Mount Gerizim are to invoke God's blessings upon those who observe the commandments, and tribes standing upon Mount Ebal are to curse those who do not (Deut. 11:29ff.). The account of the actual ceremony is contained in the Book of Joshua (8:30ff.).

Mount Gerizim is the chief holy place of the SAMARITANS, who believe that here, and not Jerusalem, is the site chosen by God for His spirit to dwell (Deut. 12:11; 14:23; *et al.*). It is therefore known to them as the "chosen mountain," one of 13 different Samaritan names for the place. Josephus (*Ant.* 11:310-11) records that the Samaritans received permission from Alexander the Great to erect a Temple there. Many scholars, however, believe that this account reflects events that occurred earlier, in the time of NEHEMIAH (Neh. Chap.13). According to Samaritan tradition, most of the events in the lives of the Patriarchs recorded in the Bible occurred at various sites on Mount Gerizim.

Samaritans always face Mount Gerizim when praying, and the Samaritan community, that numbers today no more than 600, still celebrates all of its holy events on Mount Gerizim, including various prayer ceremonies, pilgrimage festivals, and the offering of the Passover sacrifice. The entire community takes up residence there from the tenth of Nisan until after Passover. Remains of structures holy to the Samaritans (Khirbat al-Luza; al-Sakhra — the rock; the place of twelve stones) are still extant on the mountain, while it has been conjectured that an altar found on Mount Ebal goes back to the assembly in the time of Joshua.

GERSHOM BEN JUDAH Known as *Me'or ha-Golah* ("Light of the Exile"; 960-1028). Rabbinic authority. Born in Metz, he established his academy in Mainz where he continued to teach for the remainder of his life. He exercised great rabbinic authority over European Jewry due both to his scholarship and his leadership ability. His TAKKANOT (new ordinances) promulgated at rabbinical assemblies upon his initiative were accepted as binding by all Ashkenazi communities. Two of the most important regulations associated with his name dealt with the status of women in Jewish law: the first outlawed bigamy for Jews; the second modified the practical aspect of the biblical laws of divorce. According to biblical law, it is only the husband who can take the initiative in a divorce proceeding. He has the bill of divorce (*get*) written and delivered to his wife, with or without her consent. Rabbenu Gershom ruled that the divorce can be effected only with the consent of both parties. The husband must agree to have the bill of divorce written and the wife must be willing to accept it. Another regulation was the prohibition against reading letters addressed to others.

One of his greatest achievements was the collation of a complete and authentic text of the Talmud. Before the invention of printing, texts of the Talmud, and even of the Bible, were very rare and extremely expensive. Most of the teaching was therefore conducted orally, usually with only the teacher possessing a copy of the text he was expounding. Students, scholars, and scribes copied out the texts for themselves. Errors resulting from faulty transcription, or from the deliberate emendation of a text thought to be incorrect, were frequent. This resulted in variant readings of the same passage, with the concomitant problem of deciding which text was authentic. Rabbenu Gershom compiled a complete Talmud manuscript bearing his signature, which became, more or less, the accepted text of the Talmud. He also prepared a complete Bible text which was correct to the last detail of the MASORAH.

Few of his comments on the Talmud have survived, but some are quoted by RASHI. He also wrote several SELIḤOT (penitential prayers) and PIYYUTIM (liturgical poems), some of which are still to be found in the prayer book.

Gershom's eminence as a scholar and his acknowledged authority gained him the title *Me'or ha-Golah* — the Light of the Exile. This apparently derives from a reference to him in a responsum of RASHI who said "Rabbenu Gershom has enlightened the eyes of the Exile, for all live by his instruction. All the Jews of these [European] countries call themselves disciples of his disciples."

GET See DIVORCE

GE'ULAH ("Redemption"). Term applied to several forms of liturgical composition which invoke God's merciful deliverance of His people Israel; for the theological concept, see REDEMPTION. In talmudic literature, *Ge'ulah* normally designates the two lengthy passages recited each day between the *Shema* and the *Amidah* — EMET VE-YATSIV in the Morning Service and EMET VE-EMUNAH in the Evening Service. Both conclude with the blessing, "He who redeemed Israel." Closely associated with these benedictions are numerous liturgical poems (*piyyutim*) of medieval origin, chiefly recited on special Sabbaths and the three Pilgrim Festivals. They include the BERAḤ DODI poems inserted in Morning Services for Passover (each of which is also entitled *Ge'ulah*) and the various MA'ARAVOT read in the Evening Service for Passover, Shavu'ot and Sukkot. All of these poems are confined to the Ashkenazi rite, and their present-day use is mainly limited to Orthodox congregations in the Diaspora. The term *Ge'ulah* also denotes a benediction recited after Psalms 113-114 during the Passover SEDER. Immediately preceding the second cup of wine drunk by all the participants, it constitutes a festive "toast to Redemption." *Ge'ulah* likewise connotes the seventh benediction of the weekday *Amidah*, imploring Israel's "mighty Redeemer" to "behold our affliction and plead our cause."

GEZERAH (lit. "Decree, edict"; plur. *gezerot*). Hebrew term with several meanings that is used in different contexts. Some major instances are: (1) A Divine command for which no reason is given, such as the RED HEIFER (Num. 19), concerning which the Midrash quotes God as saying, "I have decreed a *gezerah*, and you have no right to question it" (Num. R. 19.4). Similarly, when God refuses to reveal the time appointed for someone's death (*Shab*. 30a), or does not explain why righteous people suffer martyrdom, He is said to declare: "It is a *gezerah* issued by Me" (*ibid.*). (2) An edict promulgated by a foreign ruler banning the observance of Jewish law. Such decrees were issued by Antiochus IV Epiphanes in the Hasmonean era, and by the Roman Emperor Hadrian in the days of Rabbi Akiva. (3) A synonym for organized forced conversion, religious persecutions, massacres, and pogroms. Two notable examples of this usage are *gezerot tatnu* (lit. decrees of the year 4856=1096 CE), referring to the annihilation of Jewish communities (particularly in the Rhineland) during the First Crusade; and *gezerot taḇ ve-tat* (decrees of 5048-9 = 1648-9), the wholesale massacre of Jews in Poland and the Ukraine during the Cossack uprising led by Bogdan Chmielnicki. (4) A restrictive or preventive measure enacted by the rabbinical authorities with the aim of safeguarding the observance of Scriptural law, in keeping with the admonition of the Men of the GREAT ASSEMBLY to "make a fence [Heb. *seyag*] around the Torah" (*Avot* 1.1). Among the early ordinances of this type are the "18 *gezerot*" adopted by the disciples of Hillel and Shammai at the beginning of the first century CE (TB *Shab*. 11a-17b; TJ *Shab*. 1.4, 3c). These were designed to strengthen the barriers between Jews and non-Jews, particularly in regard to sexual morality, and to uphold the laws of ritual cleanness. Other restrictive measures were devised to safeguard observance of the Sabbath and festivals.

The sages did think it necessary to limit such restrictions. For example, they laid down that "no *gezerah* should be imposed on the community unless the majority is able to comply with it" (*Av. Zar*. 36a). However, once a *gezerah* is decreed by the proper authorities and widely accepted by Jews, no subsequent authority can rescind it (*ibid.*). Furthermore, even if the reason prompting an earlier authority to adopt a *gezerah* no longer applies, the decree may not be canceled without a specific proclamation of annulment by a later authority (*Bétsah* 5a-b). Some halakhic authorities nevertheless maintain that if it is clear that the *gezerah* would not have been enacted under present circumstances, such a decree becomes null and void of itself (Menahem Ha-Meiri, *Bet ha-Beḇirah* to *Bétsah* 5a). Thus, many of the restrictions imposed by the sages against commerce with non-Jews only applied to the ancient idolators, and not to Christians and Muslims who do not worship idols (*Tos.* to *Av. Zar.* 2a).

Restrictions added to Jewish law by post-talmudic authorities are usually styled *ḥerem* (lit. "excommunication") and include the Ashkenazi regulation banning polygamy which is known as *ḥerem de-Rabbenu Gershom* (see GERSHOM ME'OR HA-GOLAH; TAKKANAH). Other post-talmudic measures, such as the Ashkenazi rule prohibiting the consumption of legumes (*kitniyyot*) on Passover, fall under the category of *minhag* (local CUSTOM) and are not observed by all Jewish communities.

GILGUL See TRANSMIGRATION OF SOULS

GINZBERG, LOUIS (1873-1953). Rabbinic scholar. Born in Kovno, Ginzberg studied in Lithuanian *yeshivot* and moved to Germany. In 1899 he went to the United States and headed the rabbinics department of the *Jewish Encyclopaedia*. On Solomon SCHECHTER's invitation, he became Professor of Talmud at the Jewish Theological Seminary.

In addition to numerous essays in many learned journals, he published fragments of manuscripts of the Jerusalem Talmud found in the Cairo GENIZAH; *Geonica* (two volumes); and the seven-volume *Legends of the Jews*, which weaves into a continuous narrative the rabbinic legends (*aggadah*) relating to the biblical period and its events and characters.

Two volumes, entitled *Ginzei Schechter*, deal with hitherto unpublished geonic material. In this work, as well as in his monumental commentary on the Jerusalem Talmud's tractate BERAKHOT (five volumes covering the first five chapters of the tractate), Ginzberg illuminates the talmudic text by reference to its historical background. While previous commentators had sought to reconcile the differences between the Jerusalem and Babylonian Talmuds, Ginzberg frequently explains these differences as resulting from the differing historical and economic situations prevailing in the two countries. On a more popular level, he published a series of biographical essays, *Students, Scholars and Saints*, and a volume entitled *On Jewish Law and Lore*.

GITTIN ("Bills of divorce"). Sixth tractate of Order NASHIM in the Mishnah. Its nine chapters explain the laws regarding the annulment of marriage by DIVORCE (Deut.24:1-4). According to Jewish law, a *get* (letter of divorce) is the only means of separating a husband and wife. The rabbinic court cannot issue a *get*; it must be given by the husband himself to his wife. The Mishnah discusses the exact wording of the *get*, the necessity for witnesses, the cancellation of a *get* before its delivery, the payment of alimony, divorcing a minor, and the issuing of a *get* by a man not of sound mind. The subject matter is amplified in both Talmuds and the Tosefta.

GIYYUR See CONVERSION TO JUDAISM

GLEANINGS See LEKET SHIKHḤAH VE-PE'AH

GOD The Supreme Being; creator of the world, Lord of the universe. In biblical and rabbinic sources, knowledge of God comes not as the product of philosophic speculation or mystical insight but as inferences gleaned from His actions and self-revelation.

In the Bible God is supreme over all and possesses absolute sovereignty: "For the Lord your God is God supreme and Lord supreme, the great, the mighty and the awesome God" (Deut. 10:17). He is utterly distinct from the world, subject to no laws or limitations, omnipotent and omniscient.

God is One (Deut. 4:35; 6:4), which also means unique and incomparable (see MONOTHEISM). He is the source of everything in the world, including evil (Isa. 45:7). God is above time (Ps. 90:2) and outside of space (Is. 66:1; Jer. 23:24). He is infinite, without beginning and end, and unchanging (Mal. 3:6).

The word *kadosh* ("holy") applied to God means metaphysical transcendence, while the word *kavod* ("glory") refers to the indwelling experienced presence of God. Thus the hymn, "Holy, Holy, Holy is the Lord of Hosts, the whole world is full of His glory" (Isa. 6:3), expresses the paradoxical nature of God's utter transcendence coupled with His constant immanence. God is beyond the world, far removed from it ontologically and conceptually (Ps. 97:9), yet He is very much the ground of all being (Ex. 3:12-15), the "soul of our soul," accessible to man at all times (Ps. 145:18). He is God who reveals Himself to man, yet often appears to be a "hidden God" (Isa. 45:15).

The biblical concept of God is personalistic, i.e., He is portrayed in terms of personality. He appears as a moral will who engages in dialogue with men, demanding and commanding, judging, punishing and rewarding. God contemplates and plans, decides and chooses, and acts purposefully. He is aware of the human condition (Ex. 2:24) and reaches out to man in love.

God is the creator of the universe which of itself has no divine quality. He brought all into existence, out of nothing, as a divine act of will (Ps. 33:9). This implies that the entire universe from subatomic particles to meteor galaxies constitutes a unity, with the same laws of nature holding uniformly throughout the cosmos. However, the universe has no independent existence outside of God who constantly infuses it with life. If it could be imagined that God should cease to exist, the universe would collapse into nothingness.

God is the Lord of universal history Who manifests Himself in the affairs of nations and particularly in the history of Israel. After completing the creation of the world of nature, God continues to guide the course of history (Deut. 32:8). Though in fashioning the physical world God had no opposition, in history He must contend with man's freedom, which often turns to rebelliousness. The prophets affirm however, that ultimately in the "end of days," God's Will will be done.

Having given man freedom, God does not overwhelm him, either in personal relationship or in His direction of history. In creating man, God, as it were, accepts a certain self-limitation in order to preserve man's freedom. God relates to man more as a loving father, that is to say, as an educator rather than as a king.

In spite of the theological problem it creates, the Bible describes God in terms of emotions: He is angry (Ex. 22:23), pleased (Gen. 1:31), sad and disappointed (Gen. 6:6), has pity (Jonah 4:11), loves (Deut. 23:6), and hates (Amos 5:21). In reference to these ANTHROPOMORPHISMS, the rabbis explained that "the Bible speaks in human language" (*Ber.* 31b) in order to render intelligible God's actions. However, it is not assumed that God experiences the psychic state that man calls emotions.

On the general question of the propriety of describing God in corporeal terms, the evidence of the Bible is ambiguous (Ex. 33:23, 24:10, 15:6). Later philosophical analysis of the type presented by MAIMONIDES and others shows that this has implications that are inconsistent with other fundamental principles, such as God's unity and eternity. Therefore, the incorporeality of God is established in such passages as, "The Lord spoke to you out of the fire, you heard the sound of words but perceived no shape, only a voice"; and, "For you saw no shape when the Lord your God spoke to you at Horeb... lest you act wickedly and make for yourselves a sculptured image..." (Deut. 4:12,15-16).

God and Morality The two major theophanies of the Bible take place at Mount SINAI. The first is witnessed by all of Israel and results in the giving of the TABLETS OF THE COVENANT which contain the DECALOGUE (Ex. 20). The second is experienced by MOSES alone, prior to receiving the second set of Tablets, and consists of the response of God to Moses' request: "Teach me Your ways" and "Show me Your presence" (Ex. 33:13,18). The essential message of both revelations, however, is a self-disclosure of the moral nature of God.

Six of the nine imperatives contained in the Decalogue are of a moral nature and cover deeds, speech, and thought. God demands of man moral character and behavior, which is the essence of His covenant with Israel. God's disclosure to Moses is not given in terms of a promise of certain kinds of actions, but in terms of resident character traits: "...God, compassionate and gracious, slow to anger, abounding in kindness and faithfulness, extending kindness unto the thousandth generation, forgiving iniquity...yet by no means clearing the guilty" (Ex. 34:6).

While the social morality within the Decalogue is contained in a framework that is national, the moral qualities ascribed to God in the encounter of Moses imply universality. Indeed, the account in Genesis suggests that morality was already known to and expected from earliest man. Morality is willed by God because it is in some sense constitutive of Himself. God could not have willed otherwise.

Thus morality has intrinsic though not independent value; although grounded in God and although by being moral man fulfills his humanity and Divine image, it may be said to be valued for its own sake. For, while the Jew may view morality — the good — as a means of reaching God, once he has reached Him, he has once again reached the good. It is because of this special relationship between God and morality that the problem of theodicy (see REWARD AND PUNISHMENT), which challenges God's goodness and justice, takes on such importance and is treated at length in the Book of Job.

Divine Attributes While God is unique, transcendent, and completely other than anything in human experience, there is no alternative, in speaking of Him, but to use concepts drawn from human experience. Thus, any qualities ascribed to God must not be interpreted literally. The most appropriate way to speak of God is to attribute to Him certain works or actions. It is perfectly legitimate, according to Maimonides, to say: "God is the creator of the world, the giver of the Torah, the liberator of Israel from Egypt, the healer of the sick, etc.," because this does not imply how these acts are produced or what element must be contained in the agent in order to produce the act. Similarly, emotional qualities ascribed to God, such as love, mercy, anger, and jealousy can be analyzed in terms of action predicates. Thus, to say that "God was angry with the people of Sodom" is to assert that the city could expect from God actions associated with anger in human beings.

However, to predicate of God certain actions, such as creation of the world and redemption of the Children of Israel from slavery, implies in the context of the larger story of the Bible that God is in some sense alive, possessing tremendous power and intelligence, and capable of purposive planning. This leads to the positing of what Maimonides calls "God's essential attributes," i.e., qualities which define His primary nature; that which makes a thing what it is: life, wisdom, power. However, the principle of God's unity states that God's essence and His existence are one. Therefore, while man knows his own life, power, will, and understanding to be different things, in God He and His wisdom, His life, His will, and His power are one. But God's essence is unknowable and beyond human comprehension.

Is there anything man can know about God? Since there is no similarity between God and man, the term "know" does not mean the same when predicated of God as it does when predicated of man. Christian theology, following Thomas Aquinas, generally favors the theory of analogical predication. This maintains that the human term when used in reference to God retains some similarity to its original meaning, only allowing for modifications emanating from the divine context. Thus, it could be said, for example, that God possesses something which does for Him what "knowledge" does for man.

Maimonides, however, preferred the theory of double privative attributes which employs a complex logical analysis. The statement, "God is wise," is to be translated into, "God is not not-wise," which means that whatever knowledge man may exclude from being predicated about God, man must be able to say that He is wise. In short, the assertion removes the possibility of eliminating wisdom from God.

While Maimonides had logical difficulties in applying the quality of relation to God, modern theologians insist that the richness of religious experience, particularly as it is described in the Bible, necessitates the positing of real relationship between man and God in its fullest existential sense. Indeed, from the perspective of Judaism, what is important is not whether human God-talk is translatable into well-formed logical expressions, but the belief that God has acted in nature and history, which brings Him into relationship with man in ways in which man feels obliged to respond.

In Talmudic Literature The rabbis reinforced the centrality of the concept of God in Judaism and characterized one who denies the existence of God or His awareness of man as *kofar be-ikkar*, "a denier of the root" (*Ar.*15b). They also carried on the prophetic struggle against IDOLATRY and polytheism, which was an elaboration of the biblical concept: "You shalt have no other gods before Me... for I, the Lord thy God, am an impassioned God" (Ex. 20:3-5), even in the difficult and often dangerous circumstances of the pagan Persian and Roman rule. So strong was their conviction of the imperative of eliminating polytheism that they taught: "Whosoever denies idolatry is as if he acknowledges the entire Torah" (*Sif.*, Deut. 28). The rabbis saw as one of the permanent achievements of history the fact that the strong attraction of paganism for the people of the civilized world had faded by the Second Temple period (*Yoma* 69b).

Among the moral attributes of God are the traits of mercy and kindness, as well as justice which is reward for obedience and punishment for transgression (Ex. 34:5-6). Both mercy and justice are positive moral qualities. However, each is not absolute nor is each complete by itself. Often in the social context they must qualify each other. Justice must sometimes be softened by mercy, while mercy must sometimes be restrained by the requirements of retributive justice. The rabbis developed these two concepts as major aspects of God's behavior, calling them *middat ha-din*, "His measure of strict justice," and *middat ha-raḥamim*, "His measure of mercy." In rabbinic usage the word *middah*, which means "measure," was often applied to the "measure" of reward or punishment that was meted out by the judge. However, these two terms soon became hypostatized as resident attributes of God Himself.

The rabbis found no general formula to determine what proportion of mercy and justice should be applied to a given situation. They therefore pushed this question back into the recesses of the divine mystery of God's moral self. Sometimes the attribute of justice was seen as an abstract moral ideal or even as an angel external to God, while the attribute of mercy was identified with God Himself (*Sanh.* 97b). The rabbis actually depicted God as praying to Himself that His compassion should overcome His wrath (*Ber.* 7a).

In Medieval Jewish Philosophy Under the stimulus of Arabic and Greek philosophy, Jewish thought in the Middle Ages turned reflective and developed a theology. Its first fruit was the principle enunciated by SAADIAH GAON that human reason given by God is a valid source of truth equal to that of Revelation. It is therefore a religious duty to seek to understand by rational means the concepts given in Scripture. Indeed, many medieval Jewish thinkers held that religious convictions based upon rational demonstration were more acceptable before God than those based on faith alone. Thus, they resorted to familiar deductive arguments such as the cosmological (argument from the fact of a contingent world), the teleological (argument from design), and the argument from notion favored by Maimonides.

The biblical concept of God's unity was the subject of intense philosophic scrutiny. It was taken to mean not simply that there is only one God and not two, but that the essence of God could in no way be conceived of as possessing any multiplicity. This logically excluded any attribution of corporeal features to God, which led Maimonides to a systematic reinterpretation of all anthropomorphic passages in the Bible (in the first part of his *Guide*). This rigorous interpretation of God's unity influenced their understanding of the Divine Attributes, as well as the entire question of God's relation to the world and particularly the notion of Divine Providence. How could the eternal, unchanging, wholly-other God be in contact with a universe that is contingent and constantly changing? Maimonides' solution is that God alone knows His own unchanging essence and thus has a knowledge of all that results from any of His acts.

There is a vast difference between merely engaging in rational reflection on the existence and nature of God and claiming that the rational reflection itself is the ultimate form of religious experience. JUDAH HALEVI denied the latter and argued that genuine religious relationship is immediate communication between man and God which goes beyond the exercise of the intellect. Only a God-given REVELATION can teach man how to achieve that communion. Halevi contended that the God discovered in the conclusion of the deductive proofs was not yet the God of Abraham.

In Kabbalah In the mystical tradition of Judaism as in all MYSTICISM, there is an emphasis on the direct and intimate consciousness of the Divine Presence. In face of the philosophic insistence upon the complete transcendence of God, His unknowableness, and His utter unity, how is one to account for the vibrant, rich, and variegated multiplicity which the mystic experiences?

The Kabbalah contains the distinction between "God in Himself, hidden in the depth of His being," generally called the EN SOF ("the infinite"), about whom nothing can be said except that He exists, and the revealed God who manifests Himself in His creation. It is the latter whom the religious personality encounters in his mystical experiences. The ten SEFIROT ("emanations") represent a sort of theosophy of the revealed God or SHEKHINAH ("Indwelling Presence"). These can be viewed as successive stages in the process of creation or as instruments, powers, or attributes of the revealing God. To avoid suggestions of DUALISM, Kabbalah insists on the complete unity of both aspects of God, the *En Sof* as well as the *Sefirot*.

In Kabbalah, and Ḥasidic thought based upon it, there is a strong measure of immanence (which sometimes borders on PANTHEISM), in which elements of the Divine extend into all of creation including man. Thus the Torah is not merely the historic law of the Jewish people but the living incarnation of the divine wisdom which eternally sends out new rays of light.

The Kabbalah of Isaac LURIA contributed the doctrine of *Tsimtsum* ("concentration" or "contraction") as answer to the question: How can there be a world if God is everywhere? This doctrine states that God the infinite (*En Sof*), Who as plenum fills all space, withdrew into Himself leaving a primordial space into which He sends His rays of creation (*Sefirot*). According to Gershom SCHOLEM, this daring and profoundly seminal concept not only elucidated the concept of "creation out of nothing," but was able to explain how there is a touch of the divine in all beings which nevertheless possesses a reality of its own.

Modern Period Moses MENDELSSOHN (1729-1786), committed to the ideals of the German Enlightenment, found no difficulty in presenting the biblical God idea of a Supreme Being who unites within Himself the highest wisdom, righteousness, goodness, and power, who is the creator of the world, and guarantees the immortality of the human soul.

Although Hume and Kant had sought to refute the traditional proofs for the existence of God, and thereby demonstrated the inability of metaphysics to prove the basic truths of religion, a new basis for belief in God was found. Theologies now turned to practical reason or to the religious presuppositions of ethical idealism. Thus Solomon Formstecher (1808-1889) could speak of a divine world-soul, identified with God, who is the ideal ethical being to be emulated by man. Similarly Samson Raphael HIRSCH (1808-1888) conceived God as the free and omnipotent spirit who in Judaism teaches man to find self-fulfillment in ethical self-consciousness and concrete freedom.

Mordecai KAPLAN (1881-1983) departs completely from the biblical-rabbinic concept of a transcendent super-creatural God. Committed to the tenets of scientific naturalism, Kaplan speaks of God as the sum total of forces in nature working for human fulfillment.

Franz ROSENZWEIG (1886-1929), on the basis of his "new thinking," which takes into account the existential condition of the individual and his personal experience, validates and upholds the biblical-rabbinic view of God and the world. Man meets God in direct personal encounter. This revelation is a manifestation of God's love which turns towards the individual and commands him to love God in return. According to Rosenzweig this love relation between man and God redeems the ego from its isolation and its crippling form of death.

Martin BUBER (1878-1965) similarly reinstates the biblical categories in which God is discussed. He speaks of a transcendent reality whose Presence can be encountered in the present as the Eternal Thou. Buber and Rosenzweig disagree on the question of whether an encounter with God yields "commandments" or only a sense of Presence.

Abraham Joshua HESCHEL (1907-1972) develops what he calls "depth-theology," in which the starting point is the human situation and the question is: What are the grounds for man's believing in the realness of the living God? Heschel replies that there are moments when man experiences awe, wonder, and a sense of "radical amazement" at the grandeur and sublimity of the world, at the "immense preciousness" of being, at the fact that there are facts at all. This can lead to intimations of God's Presence and allusions to His concern. The special thrust of biblical thought is caught by Heschel when he emphasizes that it is God who is pursuing man and that faith comes out of an awareness of man being called upon. (See THEOLOGY).

GOD, NAMES OF The various names of God which are found in the Bible and in the Talmud are a way of comprehending His essence. Therefore, in the story of the burning bush (Ex. 3), Moses is hesitant to accept God's commission because he will be asked by the Egyptians "What is His (God's) name?" Hence God answers him using the name of YHWH, the Tetragrammaton.

The significance of God's name relates to the reality of His being. Since the name of God discloses aspects of God's nature, that name carries with it the elements of authority, power, and holiness, and this is why the name is treated with such deference. In the Ten Commandments (Ex. 20:7 and Deut. 5:11) it is clearly stated that God's name YHWH must not be taken in vain. When the priests pronounced their benediction (Num. 6:24-26) they utilized the name of YHWH to bless the people of Israel.

The power of God's name is carried even further when it is stated that people will fear Israel because it is called by God's name YHWH (Deut. 28:10). His name is glorious in all the earth (Ps. 8:1; 48:11) is another way of expressing it. Hence, those who know God's name (Ps. 9:11; 91:14) are aware of His identity and the elements of His nature. There are a variety of Hebrew names by which God is known, each of which has its own essential meaning in terms of defining the characteristics of God.

El *El* is the generic Semitic name for God. In Akkadian it appears as *Ilu* and is found in other Semitic languages. The term probably derives from the root *yl* or *wl* meaning "to be powerful"; however, the meaning may just be "power." The name *El* is not used as a personal name of God. It is found primarily in the poetic literature in the Bible reflecting an ancient form of usage. The name *El* is also used as a beginning element in names such as Elijah, Elisha and Elihu; it may also be employed as a suffix in names such as Israel, Ishmael, and Samuel.

Various Divine names are a combination beginning with *El*, and each has its own specific significance. *El Elyon* is the "exalted *El*." An early use of this name is in Genesis 14:18-20 where Melchizedek is designated as the priest of "*El elyon*," who actually blesses ABRAHAM in the name of the One who "possesses heaven and earth." This name of God, from the Israelite perspective, came to refer to the transcendence of the nature of the one God as opposed to a god reigning supreme over a group of gods. *El Olam* was "*El* the everlasting." This name of God seems to have been specifically related to the sanctuary at Beersheba (Gen. 21:33). *El Shaddai* may mean "God, the one of the mountains," or "God the omnipotent". The term *El Shaddai* is identified with God who "appeared to Abraham, Isaac, and Jacob" (Ex. 6:3). The name *Shaddai* has roots in antiquity and is found in the personal names Zurishaddai and Ammishaddai (Num. 1:6,12). The word *Shaddai* is also mentioned in the prophecies of Balaam (Num. 24:4). Outside the books of Genesis and Exodus, the term *El Shaddai* occurs 35 times in the Bible, 31 of which are in the Book of Job. *El Berit*, the "God of the covenant," appears only in Judges 9:46, referring to the temple of *El Berit* at Shechem, a locale which has been excavated and identified with the sanctuary there.

Elohim Two other well-known names of God are *Eloha* and *Elohim*. *Eloha* occurs in the Book of Job in this singular form and refers to the God of Israel. *Elohim* (translated "God") is the name of God which appears most frequently in the Bible. For the most part it refers to the God of Israel, but it can be used to connote a pagan deity and even a "goddess." Although the word is in a plural form, it is treated as if it were a singular noun, although it can refer to pagan "gods."

The term *Adonai* is derived from the word *adon*, best

Tiled lintel of a Persian synagogue where one of the names of God, Elohim, *is substituted by* Elokim.

translated as "Lord." Since in the Bible, God is the "Lord of all the earth," he is referred to as *Adonai*, "my Lord."

YHWH The most important name for God, YHWH, is the one which is only written but never pronounced. This specific name is known as the Tetragrammaton (i.e., four-lettered). According to ancient sources, during the First Temple period, the pronunciation of this name was in use, but from the third century BCE, the name YHWH started to be read as *Adonai*. In the Middle Ages the Christian scholars, who learned Hebrew and read the Bible in the original, transformed the word YHWH with the voweling for the word "Adonai" into Jehovah, and this became the basic name of God in the Christian tradition.

Regarding the development of the name YHWH, God reveals Himself as YHWH to Moses at the burning bush, and it is as YHWH that God frees His people from Egyptian bondage (Ex. 20:2; Hos. 11:1, 12:10). This name provided for a new type of relationship with God whose essence was designated as *Ehyeh Asher Ehyeh*, with "I am what I am" (Ex. 3:14).

The basic question which arose in the talmudic period was which names of God may be written, which may be intoned, and which may be removed from documents after they had been written. Seven names of God may be written but "not erased." These are *El*, *Elohim*, *Ehyeh Asher Ehyeh*, *Adonai*, YHWH, *Tseva'ot* ("hosts"), and *Shaddai* (*Shevu.* 35a-b). The Talmud states there that all other names of God may be written freely without any restraints. Orthodox Jews, however have substituted various names such as *Elokim* for *Elohim* and *Ha-Shem* ("the Name") or *Adoshem* for *Adonai* because they believe that there are restrictions on the pronunciation of all of God's names.

In the Talmud restrictions are mentioned concerning the intoning of the name YHWH by the High Priest; it could only be done by him on the DAY OF ATONEMENT and in the Holy of Holies. The impact of that experience in ancient times is recalled each year in the Day of Atonement liturgy, when during the recitation of the description of ancient Temple worship in the Additional Service AMIDAH the congregation in the synagogue falls prostrate (or bows) at the point when the text describes the High Priest intoning the "YHWH." There also references in the Talmud (*Kid.* 71a) to God's name consisting of "12 letters," and "42 letters." There were probably a number of traditions of names of God of varying lengths, but these are the only two which have survived. The medieval poets and the mystics also coined various names of God.

The Hebrew texts containing the name of God are not to be destroyed when they are damaged or worn out but must be buried or placed in an appropriate place, similar to the ancient *genizot* established to serve as final resting places for such documents (see GENIZAH). A recent tendency in Orthodox circles is not to write the name of God in full even in translation, and in English they use the form G-d.

SOME NAMES OF GOD IN JEWISH TRADITION

YHWH (The Tetragrammaton) —	The Lord (also, *Adonai, Yah)*
El, Eloha, Elohim —	God
Shaddai —	Almighty
Ha-Kadosh Barukh Hu —	The Holy One, Blessed be He
Ribono Shel Olam —	Master of the Universe
Ha-Makom —	The Place
Ha-Rahman —	The Merciful
Shekhinah —	Divine Presence
En Soph —	The Infinite
Gevurah —	The All-Strong
Tsur Yisrael —	Rock of Israel
Shomer Yisrael —	Guardian of Israel
Melekh Malkhé Melakhim —	The Supreme King of Kings

GOG AND MAGOG King (Gog) and country (Magog, ruled by Gog) mentioned in Ezekiel 38-39. Gog, it was believed, would lead an alliance of the forces of evil in an invasion of Israel after the latter's restoration to its land. The subsequent defeat of Gog and the survival of Israel would lead to the recognition by all peoples that Israel's previous suffering was the result not of God having abandoned Israel but of His punishing Israel for its transgressions. The terminology of these chapters of Ezekiel, as well as the supernatural, disastrous punishment to be visited on the invaders, mark this prophecy as apocalyptic. Further, the prolixity of these two chapters as well as their inconsistency in detail are highly characteristic of apocalyptic writings.

Opinion is divided as to what historical figure or episode, if any, Ezekiel had in mind when he wrote these chapters. In any case, the catastrophic events described in the prophet's vision would serve as the prelude for the acknowledgment by the nations of the world that only the God of Israel is the true God.

These two chapters are echoed in Apocalyptic literature (Book of Enoch), in the DEAD SEA SCROLLS, in the New Testament (Revelation), and in Talmud and Midrash which view the wars of Gog and Magog (in post-Ezekiel literature, the latter also is conceived as a person) as a sign of the imminent coming of the MESSIAH. Consequently, in the course of Jewish history, great armed conflicts between the nations stirred expectations of the imminent arrival of the Messiah. The struggle between Christendom and Islam also aroused such hopes.

GOLDEN CALF Israelite object of worship. The golden calf was the representation of a young bull made of wood and overlaid with a plaiting of gold. The Bible relates two episodes of a golden calf: one in the wilderness when Moses was on Mount Sinai (Ex. 32), and the second by King Jeroboam I (I Kings 12:28,29). In the former narrative, the golden calf was made by AARON in response to the request of the Israelites for a god to lead them as they awaited the delayed return of MOSES from the top of Mount Sinai (Ex. 32:1-4). This calf was made of golden ornaments collected from the people, melted and molded, and then worshiped amidst dancing, feasting, and playing. When Moses returned after 40 days, he broke the tablets bearing the Ten Commandments, destroyed the calf, and forced the people to drink its remains mixed with water. The Levites then slew 3,000 of the worshipers and the Lord sent a plague upon the people for their sin. This episode has received a number of different interpretations. It was held that this golden calf was an imitation of the idolatrous bull worship in Egypt which the Israelites had just left. NAHMANIDES, followed by a number of traditional Bible commentators, declared that the golden calf was intended as a substitute for Moses whom the people feared would not return from Mount Sinai having been there for 40 days.

Recently, scholars have proposed that, in line with ancient Semitic practice, the golden calf was meant to represent the seat of the invisible God of Israel. Moses' destruction of the golden calf and his orders to execute those who had worshiped it were based on the fear that it would be deemed a god. The MIDRASH seeks to exculpate Aaron for his role in the episode.

The Israelites dancing around the Golden Calf. Engraving by Peter van der Borcht, 1584.

The motivation behind King Jeroboam's making of two golden calves, one at Beth El and one at Dan, is spelled out in I Kings 12:28. It was to provide an alternative to the Temple in Jerusalem and deter the people from going to Jerusalem and thus accepting the rule of King Rehoboam, against whom Jeroboam had revolted. The prophet Hosea (8:5-6; 13:2) denounced the worship of these calves as idolatry.

GOLDEN RULE The generally used appellation for the statement in the New Testament (Matt. 7:12; Luke 6:31), "As you would that men should do to you, do you also to them likewise." This is no more than a rephrasing of (Lev. 19:18), "Love your fellow as yourself." HILLEL (1st century BCE), when asked by a gentile to teach him the entire Torah "on one foot," gave an operative rewording of this same idea, "Whatever is hateful unto you, do not do to your fellow" (*Shab.* 31a). Hillel also phrased this positively (*Avot* 1:12): "Love all creatures."

GOLEM ("shapeless matter"). Term used once only in the Bible to describe an "unformed substance" or embryo (Ps. 139:16) and, in the Mishnah, to denote a stupid, uncultured person (*Avot* 5.9). This Hebrew term covers a wide range of meanings: a stupid person, a tactless individual, one easily led and unable to think for himself, and even a robot. In the Talmud, *golem* designates an early stage of Adam's creation (*Sanh.* 38b); in the Kabbalah, it denotes primordial matter lacking shape or form. The concept of man-created creatures is found in a talmudic passage where two *amoraim* create a calf to be eaten at their Sabbath meal and RAVA produces a manlike creature which Zera indignantly returns to the dust (*Sanh.* 65b). Such ideas, including magical use of the word *emet* ("truth") and of the Tetragrammaton (see GOD, NAMES OF), were based on the creative power of Hebrew letters expounded in Jewish mysticism (*Sefer Yetsirah*; cf. *Ber.* 55a). They took a more practical direction in medieval Germany, when the HASIDÉ ASHKENAZ converted the legendary *golem* into a useful servant who could be brought to life and rendered inanimate. In the 16th century, Jewish folklore began attributing such wondrous powers to Elijah of Chelm, whose grandson R. Tsevi Hirsch ASHKENAZI considered the question of whether a *golem* could be numbered in a prayer quorum. The powers of creating a *golem* were eventually attributed to R. JUDAH LÖW (*Maharal*) of Prague. According to these tales, R. Judah and two chosen disciples fashioned a *Golem* out of clay and breathed life (though not speech) into it by means of certain incantations. Stationed in Prague's Altneuschul synagogue, this automaton became R. Judah's trusty aide and often saved the Jews from anti-Semitic plots. One Sabbath eve, however, it got out of control and R. Judah had to bring its career to an end. Hidden in the Altneuschul's attic, say some legends, the *Golem* still awaits resurrection by a new Jewish master.

GOMEL BLESSING Benediction recited as an expression of gratitude to God by anyone who has just lived through a perilous experience. In Temple times, such an individual brought a thanksgiving offering; on the basis of Ps. 107:4-32, however, the rabbis stipulated that praise for God who "bestows favors" (Heb. *ha-Gomel*) must be expressed by those who return safely from a voyage on the high seas, who complete a journey through the desert, who have recovered from a serious illness, or who are newly released from captivity (*Ber.* 54b). A short formula is mentioned in the Talmud and other requirements — that the *Gomel* blessing should be recited in the presence of a prayer quorum (*minyan*) and, if possible, within three days of the event — are stipulated by later authorities. In traditional congregations, on the first available opportunity when the READING OF THE LAW takes place (a Monday, Thursday, or Sabbath), any worshiper needing to pronounce the benediction is called to the Torah Reading, after which he recites the blessing (to which there is a congregational response). All prayer rites use the same wording for this benediction. Women, particularly after childbirth, customarily recite the blessing in synagogue either after the Torah reading (Israeli practice) or at the end of public worship.

In the Reform liturgy, this blessing is retained but frequently it is recited on Friday evening, when the Torah is read in a number of Reform synagogues. Today, in both the Conservative and the Reform movements, a woman may recite the *Gomel* blessing after being called to the Reading of the Law.

> **GOMEL BLESSING**
>
> Blessed are You, O Lord our God, King of the universe, who bestows favors on the undeserving and who has also bestowed favors on me.

GOOD See EVIL; RIGHTEOUSNESS

GOVERNMENT, PRAYER FOR THE Benediction recited in many congregations on Sabbaths and festivals, after the Reading of the Law, which invokes God's blessing on the sovereign or president and government of the state. Sephardim also recite it after *Kol Nidré* on the eve of the Day of Atonement. This custom is rooted in Biblical injunctions to "fear the Lord and the king" through submission to lawful authority (Prov. 24:21), and to "seek the peace of the city" where Jews live "and pray unto the Lord for it," since the welfare of all its inhabitants is involved (Jer. 29:7). According to a later biblical record, Darius king of Persia authorized the offering of sacrifices and prayers for the monarchy in the rebuilt Temple at Jerusalem (Ezra 6:10). Prayers for the welfare of the Roman emperor were a standard feature of Jewish worship in Second Temple times. R. Ḥanina, the deputy High Priest, urged that one "pray for the welfare of the regime — since, but for the fear of it, men would swallow each other alive" (*Avot* 3.2). After the Temple's destruction, this was still stressed by the rabbis, who counseled obedience to the government or "ruling power" (*Zev.* 102a).

Prayer invoking God's blessing on the Sultan Abdul Hamid, in Hebrew and in Arabic. Jerusalem, c. 1900.

The oldest surviving prayer for the welfare of the monarchy was composed in the Rhineland (11th century), but others were current in medieval Spain. From there, refugee Sephardim brought with them to other lands a formula known as *Ha-Noten teshu'ah* ("He who gives salvation unto kings"; Ps. 144:10) that gained widespread acceptance. Biblical citations and echoes (Ps. 145:13; Isa. 43:16; Ps. 47:4; Jer. 23:6; Isa. 59:20; etc.) dominate the text, a modified version of which is recited in British Commonwealth synagogues. There are variations of custom within American Jewry. Orthodox congregations retain *Ha-Noten teshu'ah*, but pray that God may "bless and protect the President and the Vice-President, together with all the officers of this country..." Non-Orthodox trends have abandoned the old text; Conservative Jews recite a prayer for the United States, "its government, leader, and advisors," composed by Louis GINZBERG.

Following Israel's establishment in 1948, *Ha-Noten teshu'ah* was replaced there by a new Prayer for the Welfare of Israel (*Tefillah li-shelom ha-Medinah*). Introduced by the AVINU SHE-BE-SHAMAYIM formula, this prayer contains a sequence of verses from the Pentateuch (Deut. 30:3-5) and many biblical echoes. It terms the restoration of Jewish independence in Israel "the first dawning of our Redemption" and includes petitions for the welfare of Diaspora Jewry and for the INGATHERING OF THE EXILES. When recited in Israeli synagogues, this prayer is often coupled with a special prayer (*Mi she-Berakh*) for the soldiers of Israel's Defense Forces. Abbreviated forms of the standard Prayer for the Welfare of Israel are recited, after the Prayer for the Government, in many congregations throughout the Diaspora.

PRAYER FOR THE WELFARE OF THE SOVEREIGN AND GOVERNMENT
(Excerpt)

He who gives salvation unto kings and dominion unto princes, whose kingdom is an everlasting kingdom, who delivered His servant David from the destructive sword, who makes a way in the sea and a path in the mighty waters: may He bless, preserve, guard and assist, exalt, magnify, and highly aggrandize our Sovereign... whose glory be ever exalted!

PRAYER FOR THE WELFARE OF THE STATE OF ISRAEL
(Excerpt)

Our Father in heaven, Rock and Redeemer of Israel, bless the State of Israel, the first dawning of our Redemption. Shelter it under the wings of Your lovingkindness and spread over it the tabernacle of Your peace. Grant Your light and Your truth to its leaders, ministers, and advisors, and inspire them with good counsel.

Strengthen the defenders of our Holy Land: grant them deliverance, O Lord, and crown them with victory. Bestow peace on the Land and everlasting joy on its inhabitants.

GRACE AFTER MEALS (*Birkat ha-Mazon*). A series of blessings and prayers recited after any meal which includes the eating of BREAD. Saying Grace takes its authority from a verse in the Pentateuch: "When you have eaten and are satisfied, you shall bless the Lord your God for the good land which He has given you" (Deut. 8:10). This is the source quoted by the rabbis (*Ber.* 3.4; 21a, 44a), who determined the basic formulation of Grace and laid down that it may be recited in any language (*Sot.* 7.1). A specified minimal quantity of food ("the size of an olive") must have been eaten, diners retain their places, and while Grace is said it is customary to remove knives from the table on which, however, some bread is left. Certain Jews also maintain the ancient practice of dipping their fingers in water (MAYIM AḆARONIM) beforehand.

When at least three males above 13 have eaten together, an "invitation" to say Grace known as *Birkat ha-Zimmun* is first recited by one of them (*Ber.* 7.1-5; 49b-50a). Slightly differing forms of summons and response have been preserved in the various rites, but all give praise to "the One of whose bounty we have partaken." If a quorum (MINYAN) of at least ten males is present, the word *Elohénu* ("our God") is included in the summons and response; and if *kohanim* (priests) or rabbis are among the diners, their presence is verbally acknowledged. Ashkenazim still occasionally recite the opening invitation in Yiddish, the saying of Grace then being called BENTSHEN. Although the Mishnah (*Ber.* 7.2) disallowed the inclusion of women and minors among those counted, three or more women who have eaten together have the Talmud's permission to form a *zimmun* of their own (*Ber.* 45b). Sephardim also allow a boy of at least six to be included if he can recite Grace and understand its meaning. Originally, the rabbis laid down that "the householder breaks bread and the guest says Grace...in order to bless the host" (*Ber.* 46a), but nowadays anyone at the table may be honored with leading the Grace after Meals.

On Sabbaths, festivals, and other happy occasions, Psalm 126 (SHIR HA-MA'ALOT) is usually sung prior to the full Grace by Ashkenazim, who sometimes add four other verses from Psalms (145:2, 115:18, 118:1, and 106:2). Sephardi and Italian Jews often substitute Psalm 67. The practice of chanting Psalm 137 on weekdays has latterly fallen into abeyance.

Structurally, Grace after Meals consists of four benedictions, three ancient and one mishnaic, interspersed with various prayers of a seasonal nature and sundry personal and national petitions. The first blessing, traditionally ascribed to Moses (*Ber.* 48b), is of a universal character, praising God for sustaining all His creatures with food. The second, attributed to Joshua, is a national expression of thanks for the deliverance from Egypt, God's covenant with Israel, and the land which He gave to His people; on Ḥanukkah and Purim, the AL HA-NISSIM prayer is introduced here. The third of these older blessings, ascribed jointly to David and Solomon, begs God to provide Israel with relief from want and humiliation, and to vindicate His people by restoring Jerusalem. An extra prayer is inserted here on the Sabbath, while YA'ALEH VE-YAVO is recited on the New Moon, Pilgrim Festivals, and the New Year.

Traditionally composed after 135 CE by the sages of Yavneh, the fourth and last blessing acknowledges all the benefits for which God has to be thanked. This is followed by a series of petitions, each invoking "the All-Merciful" or "Compassionate One" (*Ha-Raḇaman*). Only four such petitions are recited by Yemenite Jews and nine by Ashkenazim, whereas the number increases to 18 in the Sephardi rite and to 22 in the Italian ("Roman") liturgy. Common to most,

Part of Grace After Meals, with an illustration of six men at table. From a manuscript. Germany, 1738.

however, are prayers for Israel's speedy redemption from "the yoke of exile" and for the household in which the meal has taken place, as well as appropriate insertions for special occasions. Whenever the Additional Service is recited on that particular day, Grace concludes with *Migdol Yeshu'ot* ("A tower of salvation," II Sam. 22:51), *Oseh Shalom* (a prayer for peace), and other verses; otherwise, *Magdil Yeshu'ot* ("Great salvation," Ps. 18:51) replaces the first verse. On certain festive occasions, when three or more have said Grace together, a blessing is recited over a glass of wine drunk at the end. Sephardim may also chant the *Bendigamos* hymn in Judeo-Spanish.

Special introductory formulas and other passages are added to Grace after Meals in a house of MOURNING and at the meal following a CIRCUMCISION or at a wedding feast (see MARRIAGE). On the basis of talmudic law (*Ber.* 16a, 44a, etc.), various shorter forms of Grace are prescribed for workers, children, soldiers, and other persons whose time is limited; while Grace may also be abbreviated to one "final benediction" (*berakhah aharonah*), summarizing the first three paragraphs. Reform Judaism in English-speaking countries has substituted a brief English text for the traditional Grace, retaining only the end of the first benediction in Hebrew. Conservative Judaism preserves the traditional text, adding special *Ha-Rahaman* prayers for the State of Israel, Jews suffering persecution, and a bar mitsvah or bat mitsvah. The tendency in non-Orthodox communities is for women to be counted with men in the *zimmun* "invitation" to say Grace.

GRACE AFTER MEALS
THE FIRST BLESSING

Blessed are You, O Lord our God, King of the universe, who feeds the whole world with Your goodness, grace, kindness, and mercy. You give food to all flesh, for Your kindness is for ever. Through Your great goodness, food has never failed us: may it never fail us, for the sake of Your great Name, for You nourish and sustain all beings, and do good to all, and provide food for all Your creatures whom You have created. Blessed are You, O Lord, who gives food to all.

GRACE BEFORE MEALS Benediction recited over BREAD, a practice traditionally instituted by the Men of the GREAT ASSEMBLY. In Hebrew, this blessing is popularly known as *ha-motsi* since the text reads: "Blessed are You, O Lord... who brings forth [*ha-motsi*] bread from the earth." Based on Ps. 104:14, the wording used was fixed by the sages (*Ber.* 6.1, 38a). Pronouncing this benediction accords with the rabbinic view that "it is forbidden and sacrilegious for anyone to enjoy [the good things] of this world without a blessing" (*Ber.* 35a), and that failure to recite a benediction over food is tantamount to "defrauding the Almighty" (*Tosef. Ber.* 4.1). After the performance of ABLUTIONS (*mayim rishonim*) through washing and drying the hands, *ha-motsi* is recited over bread made from any of the FIVE SPECIES of grain indigenous to the Land of Israel. On weekdays, it is preferable to use a whole loaf; on Sabbaths, after KIDDUSH, Grace is said over two special Sabbath loaves (*hallot*, see HALLAH); on festivals, only one *hallah* is mandatory (except when the festival coincides with the Sabbath). The same blessing is recited over unleavened bread (MATSAH) on Passover, although a second benediction is added at the *Seder* for the precept of eating unleavened bread.

When several people join together in a meal, the householder or oldest male present recites the Grace and then distributes portions of the loaf to everyone else. In non-Orthodox circles, this function may be performed by a woman. The act of saying Grace before a meal automatically exempts one from having to recite any other benedictions at table, apart from the statutory blessings over WINE and fruit. When the piece of bread eaten is equivalent to the size of an olive, the recitation of GRACE AFTER MEALS becomes obligatory. Except during the New Year season, it is general practice for bread to be sprinkled with a little SALT; this custom links the modern Jewish table with the ancient offerings made on the Temple altar (Lev. 2:13).

GREAT ASSEMBLY, THE (also known as Great Synagogue, Heb. *Keneset Gedolah*). An institution in Jerusalem from the Persian period about which little is known. In the opening paragraph of Mishnah AVOT, the Torah (Oral Law) is said to have been handed down by the prophets directly to "the men of the Great Assembly." In a parallel passage (AVOT DE R. NATAN), HAGGAI, ZECHARIAH, and MALACHI form an intermediary stage between the prophets and the men of the Great Assembly.

The precursor of the Great Assembly, according to some scholars, is to be found in the assembly convened by EZRA AND NEHEMIAH in 444 BCE, in which a compact was signed by 83 leaders of the community, priests, Levites, and Israelites. This compact included a number of significant enactments (Neh. 10). They included an agreement not to buy or sell on the Sabbath; to observe the Sabbatical year; a pledge not to intermarry with neighboring nations; to pay an annual tax of a third of a shekel for the sacrifices brought to the TEMPLE; and wood offerings for its altar to be brought by the various priestly watches (see MISHMAROT and MA'AMADOT).

Three sayings are attributed in *Avot* to the men of the Great Assembly, and are seen as a reflection of its activities: "Be deliberate in judgment, raise up many disciples, and erect a fence around the Torah" (*Avot*. 1:1). The first of these reflects the judicial function of that body; the second, the fact that SCRIBES (*soferim*), whose task it was to interpret and teach the Torah, were members of the Great Assembly; the last is an expression of the Great Assembly's legislative function. On the basis of these conclusions, some scholars view the Great Assembly as the institution which in time developed into the SANHEDRIN.

Sources offer conflicting reports regarding its number of members, one refers to 85 members including 30 prophets; another speaks of 120 elders, also including some prophets. It has been conjectured that out of the Great Assembly evolved a body originally known by the Greek name *Gerousia* ("governing council"). It was in this body that learned laymen for the first time joined with priests and Levites in interpreting the Law. Subsequently, the Greek name of this council was dropped in favor of the Hebrew name *Bet Din ha-Gadol* ("the High Court").

The legislative function of the Great Assembly took the form of ordinances (TAKKANOT) and enactments (*gezerot*). The former introduced new procedures to be followed in the practice of Judaism, among which the Talmud mentions: the practice of the public reading of the Pentateuch on Mondays and Thursdays (market days in ancient Erets Israel); the fixing of PURIM; a preliminary determination of the canon of Scripture so as to include the books of Ezekiel, Daniel, and the twelve Minor Prophets; fixing the content and number of benedictions in the AMIDAH; the formation of the KIDDUSH (prayer of sanctification recited over wine on Sabbaths and festivals); and the HAVDALAH prayer (recited at the end of Sabbaths and festivals). It was probably during the days of the Great Assembly that the square Hebrew script replaced the script that was in use during the First Temple period (see ALPHABET).

Only one enactment (GEZERAH) in the Talmud is ascribed to the period of the Great Assembly, viz., the prohibition of handling vessels on the Sabbath not actually required for use. However, some of the prohibitions enacted by later sages may well have originated with the Great Assembly.

GREETINGS, CONGRATULATIONS, AND GOOD WISHES As the Bible indicates, many forms of salutation and well-wishing were current in ancient Israel, often consisting of merely two or three words (Gen. 24:31; Deut. 31:23; Ruth 2:4). By rabbinic times, such Hebrew greetings had been extended occasionally with new phrases in ARAMAIC; and, from the Middle Ages, these were sometimes given YIDDISH equivalents among the Ashkenazim of Central and Eastern Europe. The Hebrew term which most commonly figures in such expressions is *shalom* (PEACE), since it is closely associated with man's health, well-being, and natural state of mind. According to the sages, a person's character may be gauged from his walk, dress, and way of greeting others; if possible, one should "be the first to greet" (*Avot*. 4.15) and "he who fails to return a greeting is considered a robber" (*Ber.* 6b). There are appropriate formulas covering every occasion in Jewish life, and a biblical, talmudic, or liturgical source can often be located for them. Where alternatives occur, these usually reflect Ashkenazi or Sephardi custom and expression. Jewish law prohibits any exchange of greetings on TISHA BE-AV or in a house of MOURNING.

GREETINGS, CONGRATULATIONS AND GOOD WISHES

...l Salutations	Source	When used
'Shalom lekha* (...lo" or "goodbye")	Gen. 43:27 Ex. 18:7; Judg. 6:23	Daily
...rav (...nuch peace")	Ps. 119:165	Daily in the same sense
...u-verakhah (...eace and blessing")		
...alekhem (...e to You")	TJShev.35.2	Also to someone coming from a distance whom one has not met for a long time
...shalom (...e to you also")		Response to the above

General Salutations	Source	When used
Barukh ha-ba ("Blessed be the one who comes," i.e., "Welcome!")	Ps.118:26	At circumcisions and weddings; also as a general expression of welcome to guests
Barukh ha-nimtsa ("Blessed be the one [already] present")		Standard response to *barukh ha-ba*
Berukhim ha-yoshevim ("Blessed be the one [already] seated")		When the host or others are at the table, etc. (alternative response)
Lekh le-shalom/be-shalom ("Go in Peace")	Ex:. 4:18; II Sam. 15:9	To a departing friend or guest
Bo' akha le-shalom ("Welcome")	Liturgy (*Zemirot*)	Phrases usually addressed to those coming from a distance
Tsetekha le-shalom ("Bon voyage")	Liturgy (*Zemirot*)	Phrases usually addressed to those coming from a distance

General Salutations	Source	When used
Derekh tselaḥah	cf. Jer. 12:1	As "bon voyage"
Ad me'ah ve-esrim [shana] ("[May you live] until 120")	Gen. 6:3	Good wishes for a long life
Biz hundert un tzvantzik		(Yiddish equivalent)
Le-veri'ut (pop. *La-beri'ut*) ("Good health")		When someone sneezes also "Bon appetit!"
Asuta (lit."healing) i.e., "God bless you")	*BM* 113b	(Aramaic equivalent)
Tzu gezunt		(Yiddish equivalent)
Li-yeshu'atekha kivviti Ha-Shem ("For Your salvation I wait, O Lord")	Gen. 49:18	Said by North African Jews when they sneeze
Refu'ah ve-ḥayyim ("Healing and life")		Response to the above
Li-refu'ah ("May it cure you")		To a person taking medicine
Refu'ah shelemah ("[May you be granted] a complete recovery")	Liturgy (Prayer for the New moon	To a sick person
Haḥamahh mehirah ("A speedy convalescence")		Similar to the above
Barukh Rofe holim ("Blessed be the Healer of the sick")	cf.*Ber. 60b*	To someone who has recovered from an illness
Titḥadesh (lit. "Renew yourself, i.e., "Wear it in good health")	cf.Ps.103:5	To someone wearing a new outfit
Beli ayin ha-ra/ra'ah ("[May there be] no evil eye")		Expression qualifying words of praise, etc., to show there is no envy
Keyn ayn hora		(Yiddish equivalent)
Beli neder (lit. "Without taking a vow"; i.e., "All being well")		When referring to future plans or events

Congratulations on the Fulfillment of *Mitsvot*	Source	When used
Yishar koḥakha ("May your strength increase") or *Yeyasher ko'aḥ* ("May [the Lord] the strengthen you")	*Shab.* 87a	Among Ashkenazim, on successful endeavors, esp. to someone who has been called to Reading of the Law etc.
Ḥazak (u-) barukh ("Be strong and blessed")		As above, in Sephardi congregations; *kohen* after he has recited the Priestly Blessing
Barukh tiheyeh ("May you be blessed")		Ashkenazi response to congratulations; also used by Western Sephardim
Hazak ve-emats ("Be strong and of good courage")	Deut. 31:23 Josh. 1:9, etc.	Usual Sephardi response to such congratulations; also, among Ashkenazim, to a bar mitsvah boy when he completes his haftarah
Be-khavod or *be-khabod* ("With honor")		Salutation to a rabbi or scholar when he is called to the Torah Reading in a Sephardi congregation
Ha-Shem (Adonai) immakhem ("The Lord be with you")	Ruth 2:4	Salutations extended and reciprocated by Sephardim when ascending the *tevah* for the Reading of the Law (see Liturgical RESPONSES)
Ḥazak ḥazak ve-nithazzek ("Be strong and encouraged")	cf.II Sam. 10:12	Congratulations exchanged when the reading of any Pentateuchal book has been completed in synagogue

Sabbath and Holiday Greetings	Source	When used
Shabbat shalom ("A peaceful Sabbath")		Traditional greetings
Shabbat shalom u-mevorah ("A peaceful and blessed Sabbath")		Traditional response
Gut Shabbes ("Good Sabbath")		Yiddish greeting
Shavu'a tov		On Saturday night
A gute vokh ("a good week")		(Yiddish equivalent)
Ḥodesh tov		On the New Moon
Ḥag same'aḥ ("a happy holiday")		On festivals
Mo'adim le-simḥah ("Festivals for Gladness")	Liturgy (*Amidah* and *Kiddush*)	On Pilgrim Festivals
Ḥaggim u-zemannim le-sason ("Joyous holidays")		Response to either of the a
Gut yontef ("a good holiday")		Yiddish greeting on festiva
Ve-hayita akh same'aḥ ("You shall have nothing but joy")	Deut. 16:15	When visiting a person in sukkah ("booth") on Suk
Shanah Tovah ("A happy New Year")	Liturgy (*Avinu Malkenu; Amidah* etc.)	On Rosh ha-Shanah
Le-shanah tovah tikatev(u) ve-teḥatem(u) ("May you be inscribed and sealed for a good year")	Liturgy (*Avinu Malkenu; Amidah* etc.)	From before Rosh ha-Shan the Day of Atonement; also in correspondence and Year cards
Ketivah va-ḥatimah tovah ("A good inscription and sealing [in the Book of Life")		Until Rosh ha-Shanah; als correspondence and New cards
(Gemar) ḥatimah tovah ("A propitious final sealing [in the Book of Life]")		From immediately after Ro ha-Shanah until the Day Atonement; often extend Hoshana Rabba
Gemar tov ("A good conclusion")		
Le-altar le-ḥayyim tovim ("Immediately, for a good life")	cf.*RH 16b*	On Rosh ha-Shanah
Le-altar li-ge'ulah shelemah ("Speedily, for a complete redemption")		On Israel's Independence D
Le-shanah ha-ba'ah bi-Yerushalayin (ha-benuyah) ("Next year in [rebuilt] Jerusalem")		Near the conclusion of the Passover Seder; on Israel's Independence Day; and a conclusion of the Day of Atonement
Be-siman tov (u-ve-mazzal tov) ("Good luck," "Every happiness")	Liturgy (*Kiddush Lavanah*) prayer for the New Moon	Among Sephardim, on the a son, the occasion of a marriage, a bar mitsvah, (also used as the heading invitation)
Mazzal tov		Among Ashkenazim, at eve happy event; the shorter *tov* formula is used by Sephardim only for the b a daughter
Barukh tiheyeh ("May you be blessed")		Response to the above
Le-ḥayyim! ("To life," i.e., "Good health, Cheers")	Cf.*Shab* 67b	The traditional Jewish toast
Le-ḥayyim tovim u-le-shalom	Midrash	As above
Tizkeh le-shanim rabbot ("Long life to you," i.e., "Happy Birthday")		On the occasion of an anniv birthday, etc.

n and Holiday Greetings	Source	When used
-gaddelo le-Torah le-ḥuppah u-le-ma'asim tovim you live to raise him for Torah, marriage, ood deeds")	*Shab.* Eccl.R. 3.4.	To the parents at a circumcision or bar mitsvah ceremony
-gaddelah le-ḥuppah u-le-ma'asim tovim		To the parents of a newborn daughter; also on the occasion of her bat mitsvah

escence and Similar Expression	Source	When used
on yenaḥem etkhem be-tokh (she'ar) avele n vi-Yerushalayim the Almighty comfort you among the] mourners of Zion and Jerusalem")	Liturgy (Burial Service)	To mourners after a funeral and during the week of *shivah*
shamayim tenuḥamu ven grant you comfort")	Cf. *Av.Zar* 18a	As above, among Eastern Jews
you long life"		As above, among British Jews
a yeraḥem Lord will be merciful")		Traditional words of comfort that "all will be well"
/Lo alekhem t not befall us/you," i.e., we/you be spared")	Lam. 1:12; *San.* 104b	When describing a tragic event, esp. in Ashkenazi usage
nan (Aram. from him")		(Sephardi equivalent)
halom forbid")	*Shab.* 13b, 13b; *Kid.* 31b; *Av.* Zar. 18b	Common expression
halilah or h ve-ḥas		As above
yishmerenu ven preserve us," "God forbid")		As above
na li-tslan . "Heaven forfend")	*Shab.* 84b; *Ta'an.* 9b	As above

Abbreviated Phrases	Source	Including Acronyms
Ad me'ah shanah ("Until 100 years")		Heading a private letter after the addresse's name
Be-Ezrat ha-Shem ("With God's help")		As above
Derishat shalom ("Kindest regards")		At the end of a letter and in conversation (sometimes as "*Dash*")
Alav ha-shalom/aleha ha'shalom ("Peace be upon him/her")	*Avot* 5.3	After naming a deceased person; also in speech
Zikhrono li-verakhah ("Of blessed memory")	*Kid.* 31b	As above (often as "Zal")
Zekher tsaddik li-verakhah ("May the memory of the rightenous be for a blessing")	Prov. 10:7	After naming a deceased rabbi or other saintly individual; also in speech (often as *Zatsal*)
Zekhuto yagen alenu ("May his merit protect us/stand us in good stead")		As above
Ha-Shem yikkom damo ("May the Lord avenge his blood")		After naming a martyr or fallen soldier of Israel, esp. on inscriptions
She-yiḥyeh le-orekh tovim amen ("May he [also you] have as good long life, Amen!")		When speaking of eminent rabbis or addressing them in a letter (often as "*Shelita*")
Tehi nishmato/nafsho tserurah bi-tseror ha-ḥayyim ("May his soul be bound up in the bond of ever-lasting life")	I. Sam. 25:29	Final inscription on a tombstone (for women as well as men)

GRODZENSKI, ḤAYYIM OZER (1863-1940), rabbinical scholar and spiritual leader of Lithuanian Orthodox Jewry. Born in Ivia, a small town near Vilna, Grodzenski studied at the Volozhin Yeshivah. In 1887 he became one of Vilna's three *dayyanim* (rabbinic judges), and gradually became recognized as the unofficial Chief Rabbi. Later the community decided to elect him officially to the post but Grodzenski refused in deference to the Vilna tradition of not designating a Chief Rabbi. Grodzenski established a *yeshivah* for advanced rabbinical studies which became known as the "Kibbutz of Rav Ḥayyim Ozer." In 1912 he participated in the organizational meeting of the ultra-Orthodox religious organization, Agudat Israel. After the war, Grodzenski spread the ideals of the nascent movement throughout Europe. As president of Agudat Israel's supreme body, the *Mo'etzet Gedolei ha-Torah*, he was the spiritual leader of the organization. In 1924 Grodzenski was instrumental in organizing the *Va'ad ha-Yeshivot* (Council of Talmudic Academies) which later sustained the East European *yeshivot.*

Grodzenski's responsa were published in three volumes under the title of *Aḥi'ezer* (1922, 1925, 1939). These volumes consisted of pertinent responsa on all four divisions of the SHULḤAN ARUKH code. Among the topics covered were conversion, contraception, AGUNOT, the status of Sabbath desecrators, and the ritual permissability of gelatin.

Following Hitler's takeover of Poland in 1939, many *yeshivot* were transferred to Vilna in the expectation that Grodzenski would enable them to survive. The aged spiritual leader intensified his activities during this desperate period despite his failing health.

H

H̱ABAD Movement in H̱ASIDISM founded by SHNEUR ZALMAN OF LYADY (1745-1813). Shneur Zalman claimed that he obtained his basic ideas from DOV BAER, the Maggid of Mezhirech, and from the latter's son, Abraham "the Angel," but he gave systematic form to the original ideas and drew out their full implications in a manner unprecedented in H̱asidism. H̱abad is virtually a new movement within H̱asidism, and so it is regarded by itself as well as by H̱asidim of other groups, who tend to dub the H̱abad approach "philosophy," i.e., mere intellectual playing with concepts and thus almost a betrayal of the warm, intimate, and emotional approach of Israel BA'AL SHEM TOV. H̱abad theory is expounded in Shneur Zalman's *Tanya* and *Likkuté Torah*; in the works of his son, Dov Baer (1773-1827), and of his disciple, Aaron ben Moses of Starosielce (1766-1828); and in the many writings of successive H̱abad thinkers. Although there were a number of H̱abad branches, the central dynasty was that of Dov Baer's descendants, who settled in Lubavich, with the result that "H̱abad" and "Lubavich" are nowadays interchangeable terms.

The term *H̱abad* is an acronym of *H̱okhmah, Binah, Da'at* — "Wisdom," "Understanding," and "Knowledge." These are kabbalistic designations for the higher SEFIROT (emanations) in the Godhead, representing the operations of the Divine mind, as it were, in contradistinction to the lower *Sefirot* which represent the Divine emotional processes in creation. Since man is created in God's image, the emanative or "Sefirotic" processes are, as in a mirror, in his own being. Just as, in the realm of emanation, the emotional processes come after (and as a result of) the intellectual processes, so man's religious emotions should stem from his profound contemplation of the Divine. If he tries to reverse the process, putting his religious feelings in the center, the result will be a distortion of true worship. Dov Baer, when he succeeded his father in the H̱abad leadership, wrote his followers the *Kuntres ha-Hitpa'alut* ("Tract on Ecstasy"), in which he advised them how to distinguish between genuine ecstasy in worship, the fruit of severe contemplation, and the spurious ecstasy that is no more than an artificial whipping up of emotionalism.

H̱abad thought seeks also to deepen the panentheistic or acosmic tendencies in H̱asidism. Drawing on the kabbalistic doctrine of TSIMTSUM ("withdrawal"), according to which the ÉN SOF or Infinite withdraws "from Itself into Itself" in order to leave a primordial "space" into which the finite universe can eventually emerge, Shneur Zalman developed the idea that, from the viewpoint of ultimate reality, no *tsimtsum* actually takes place. All that happens is a screening of the Divine light, so that the finite universe appears to enjoy an existence apart from God. Through contemplation of the whole chain of being (as taught in the Kabbalah), the worshiper restores it all in his mind to its source in the *Én Sof*, performing the "unification from below." On his deathbed, Shneur Zalman is said to have remarked that he now saw no room and no furniture in it, only the Divine energy that is the true reality. In another saying, Shneur Zalman observed: "What is God? — That which is apprehended [*vos man derhert*]. What is the world? — That in which one apprehends [*vu man derhert*]. And what is the soul? — That with which one apprehends [*mit vos man derhert*]."

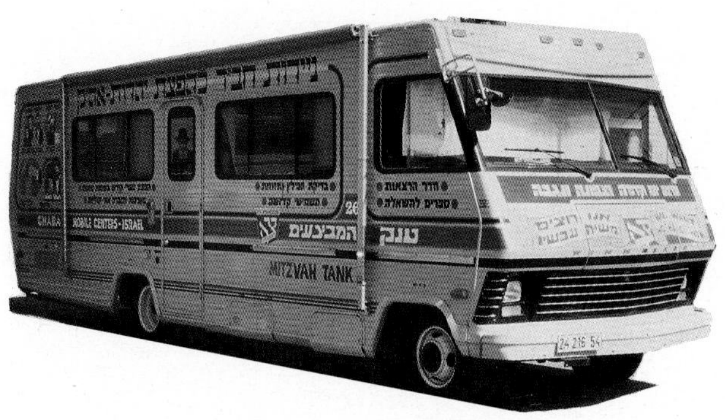

A traveling "Mitsvah Tank" of the H̱abad movement in Israel, for the distribution of phylacteries and other ritual articles to non-observant Jews.

For H̱abad, the H̱asidic idea of *bittul ha-yesh* — negation of existence or "annihilation of that which is" — means two things. Firstly, the reference is to the material universe which, from the human point of view, is substantial ("that which is") but which, from the Divine point of view, is as nothing. The chorus of the seraphim proclaiming, "The whole earth is full of His glory" (Isa. 6:5), is taken literally by H̱abad to mean that ultimately there is no world at all, only the Divine vitality. ELIJAH GAON OF VILNA and his fellow MITNAGGEDIM understood the verse as an allusion only to Divine providence. To say, as the H̱abad thinkers did, that God is actually present in the material was, for the Gaon and his followers, rank heresy.

Secondly, *bittul ha-yesh* refers to the loss of individual selfhood in God, the transcendence of man's grasping ego. A further radical extension of this in Ḥabad thought involves the idea that deep in the recesses of the Jewish psyche there is literally a portion of the *Én Sof*, so that — through transcendence of the ego — the true self, the Divine spark in the soul, is awakened, and like meets like. This is one of the very few instances in Jewish mystical thought of the *unio mystica*. To this day, some "Ḥabadniks" spend an hour or more reciting the SHEMA, singing softly to themselves, lost and totally absorbed in the Divine, to which they restore in their minds all the upper and lower worlds.

HABAKKUK One of the MINOR PROPHETS, whose book is included in the Prophets' section of the Bible. He lived in Judah, possibly at the time when the Chaldeans became a great power (612 BCE). Nothing is known of his life. The book of his prophecies is the eighth among the Minor Prophets, has three chapters and 56 verses, and is traditionally divided into a narrative (chaps. 1 and 2) and a psalm (chap. 3). The narrative consists of five prophetic utterances and deals at length with the problem of injustice in the world. The prophet asks how God can allow the wicked to devour the righteous. The psalm contains the recollection of God's deeds and a prayer; some scholars see it as a response to the question posed by the prophet in the earlier chapters; others, however, see it as an independent unit.

THE BOOK OF HABAKKUK

1:1 — 1:4	Complaint against violence and oppression
1:5 — 1:11	The Chaldeans as instruments of God
1:12 — 1:17	The prophet protests concerning the oppressor
2:1 — 2:5	The righteous shall live by his faith and the wicked shall perish
2:6 — 2:20	Five woes against oppressors
3:1 — 3:19	God will come to save His people.

Some rabbinic commentators regard the psalm in the last chapter as evidence that Habakkuk was a Levite, and among those who sang in the Temple. His statement that "the just shall live by his faith" (2:4) was described by the rabbis as the kernel of Judaism (*Mak.* 24a). The Talmud (*Sot.* 49a) states that had it not been for the prayers of Habakkuk, there would have been such poverty in the land that two scholars would have had to share the same garment. A midrashic commentary (*pesher*) on the book was found among the DEAD SEA SCROLLS.

ḤAD GADYA ("Only one kid"). Title of a popular folksong, written in Aramaic, which is chanted at the end of the Passover SEDER. Its authorship and date of composition are uncertain, but it probably had a medieval German prototype which derived from an old French nursery rhyme. Structurally, *Ḥad Gadya* comprises ten stanzas with a constant refrain, each stanza incorporating all of the previous lines (this structure has been compared with that of an 18th-century English nursery rhyme, *The House that Jack Built*). By the later Middle Ages, *Ḥad Gadya* had become popular among Ashkenazi Jews, the text appearing (with a Yiddish translation) in an Italian *Haggadah* of the 15th century. Until recently, it was unknown to Sephardi and Eastern Jewry as a "table song" for Passover.

Primarily intended to amuse young children and keep them awake until the *Seder's* conclusion, *Ḥad Gadya* has lent itself to many interpretations. Beneath the outward trappings of a secular ballad, it has been suggested, lie a historical allegory and a religious message. The "only kid that father bought for two zuzim" is thus assumed to represent the Jewish people, acquired by God at Sinai with the two tablets of the Law (or, alternatively, through the agency of Moses and Aaron). The remaining figures in this story would then personify nations that successively oppressed Israel, each being overthrown in its turn by a new tyranny. Assyria or Babylon (the cat) fell to Persia (the dog), which succumbed to Greece (the stick), which was swallowed up in the Roman Empire (the fire); Rome fell to the Barbarians (the water), who were vanquished by the armies of Islam (the ox), which yielded to the Crusaders (the slaughterer). Finally, in the ANGEL OF DEATH, one is intended to see the latest conqueror or persecutors whom the God of history will bring to account. Concealed within this allegory, therefore, would be the Jewish concept of retributive justice. A religious message proposed is that all men will be held accountable for their deeds, while the people of Israel may take comfort in the knowledge that their survival and ultimate vindication will

FINAL STANZA OF ḤAD GADYA

Then came the Holy One, Blessed be He,
And smote the Angel of Death
Who slew the slaughterer
Who slaughtered the ox
That drank the water
That quenched the fire
That burned the stick
That beat the dog
That bit the cat
That ate the kid
That father bought for two zuzim,
An only kid, an only kid!

be assured under Divine providence. *Ḥad Gadya* is sung to a wide variety of melodies in a rapid tempo; some of these melodies are traditional, others (in Israel especially) are still being composed.

ḤAFETS ḤAYYIM (Israel Meir Ha-Kohen Kagan; 1838-1933). Rabbi and author. After studying in Vilna, Lithuania, he settled in Radun, Poland, which was to remain his home for the rest of his life. He refused to enter the rabbinate, and was supported by a small grocery store which his wife managed and for which he did the bookkeeping.

In Radun, a group gathered around him which became known as the Ḥafets Ḥayyim *yeshivah* of Radun. Over the years, its student body increased and an official head of the *yeshivah* (*rosh yeshivah*), Rabbi Moshe Landinsky, was appointed in 1900. In 1904 the *yeshivah* acquired its own building and became a leading European Orthodox institution.

His first volume, entitled *Ḥafets Ḥayyim*, was published anonymously in 1873. The work was devoted to an exposition of the importance of the laws of slander, gossip, and talebearing, and the author became universally known by the title of his volume. Subsequent publications included *Shemirat ha-Lashon* on the importance of righteous speech, *Ahavat Ḥesed* on acts of "lovingkindness," *Maḥaneh Yisra'el* — special halakhic guidance for Jewish soldiers, and *Niddeḥé Yisra'el* — to inspire Jews who had emigrated to the West. The Ḥafets Ḥayyim's most famous and widely studied work is his six-volume comprehensive commentary on the SHULḤAN ARUKH: *Oraḥ Ḥayyim* code entitled *Mishnah Berurah* (1884-1907). This treatise gained acceptance as a practical guide and reference book for daily halakhic matters. The Ḥafets Ḥayyim also encouraged the study of the talmudic tractate of KODASHIM since he stressed that the Messiah could come at any moment and rebuild the Temple. To facilitate this study, he penned his five-volume *Likkuté Halakhot* (1900-1925).

The Ḥafets Ḥayyim was active in the organization of the ultra-Orthodox organization, Agudat Israel, in 1912 and was revered as its spiritual mentor. He also aided in the formation of the *Va'ad ha-Yeshivot* (Council of Talmudic Academies) in 1924 to sustain the East European *yeshivot*. Many *yeshivot* and religious institutions throughout the world perpetuated his memory by naming themselves after the Ḥafets Ḥayyim.

HAFTARAH ("conclusion"). Section from the prophetical books recited in synagogue after the READING OF THE LAW at Morning Service on Sabbaths and festivals, during the Afternoon Service on fast days, and at both services on Tishah be-Av. From talmudic references it would appear that reading from the prophetical books had become a well-established custom long before the destruction of the Second Temple. There are also early Christian allusions to the "reading of the Law and the Prophets" (Luke 4:17; Acts 13:15). In ancient times, a *haftarah* was read at the Sabbath Afternoon Service (*Shab.* 24a, 116b; and 84a), but nowadays a *haftarah* is read in the afternoon only on a fast day.

Historians of the liturgy trace the origin of the *haftarah* to the anti-Jewish persecutions launched by the Syrian tyrant Antiochus Epiphanes in 165 BCE, when he banned the study or public reading of the Torah (Pentateuch). The sages are then thought to have substituted a passage from the Prophets which had some thematic link with the Torah portion for that week. This theory is supported by the fact that there invariably is some connection, however slight, between the reading from the Pentateuch and its prescribed *haftarah*. Likewise, there is always some relationship between the festival *haftarah* and the day on which it is read, a similarity visible also in the *haftarot* scheduled for the five Sabbaths before Passover, the three preceding Tishah be-Av, and the seven after that fast day (see SABBATHS, SPECIAL). The second group consists of appropriate "chapters of rebuke," while the third (all from Isaiah) forms "chapters of consolation." Another theory, accounting for the origin of the *haftarah*, maintains that the rabbis instituted this practice in opposition to the SAMARITANS, who denied the canonicity and Divine inspiration of the prophetical books.

It is not known when the *haftarah* for each week was designated or by whom. The Talmud specifies the *haftarot* for special Sabbaths and the Sabbath of Ḥanukkah, for Tishah be-Av, the Intermediate Sabbath of the festivals, the Sabbath coinciding with the New Moon, and for the Sabbath which falls on the eve of the New Moon, as well as the *haftarah* for each major festival (*Meg.* 4.1, 31a). It is thus likely that the *haftarah* for the regular Sabbaths was not fixed until after the talmudic era, and that a variety of customs prevailed until then. In any case, the Erets Israel community adhered to the TRIENNIAL CYCLE, reading the Pentateuch over a three-year period, and this would have necessitated an entirely different selection of *haftarot* from that of the Babylonian community with its annual Torah reading cycle. To this day, there are differences between Ashkenazi and Sephardi-Eastern usage, and even between various groups within the latter.

The length of the *haftarah* was generally regulated by custom, which suggested a minimum of 21 verses. In the talmudic period, the reading of each verse of the Pentateuch was followed by a translation into the Aramaic vernacular, but for the *haftarah* this was done after each group of three verses. However, the suggested minimum length of the *haftarah* has not been preserved throughout, and there are some instances where the *haftarah* contains less than 21 verses.

Within the selection of weekly and festival *haftarot*, all the prophetic books of the Bible are represented, apart from Nahum, Zephaniah, and Haggai.

Among the Sephardi and Eastern communities, a minor

Opposite Page: Illustration of Ḥad Gadya *("Only one kid"), a popular folksong chanted at the end of the Passover* Seder. *Lithograph by E. Lissitzky (1890-1941).*

Overleaf: The passage Matsah zu *("this unleavened bread") on a double page from the* Second Nuremberg Haggadah, *15th century.*

זו שאנו אוכלים על שו
ם מה על שום שלא הספיק
בצקת של אבותינו להחמיץ
עד שנגלה עליהם מלך
מלכי המלכים הקב"ה וגאלם
שנאמר ויאפו את הבצק אשר
הוציאו ממצרים עוגות

הן פסח מצה ומרור ׃

פסח שהיו אבותינו
אוכלין בזמן
שבית המקדש קיים ׃ על
שום מה על שום שפסח
הקדוש על בתי אבותינו ׃
במצרים שנ׳ ואמרתם זבח
פסח הוא ליי׳ אשר פסח על
בתי בני ישר׳ בנגפו את
מצרים ואת בתינו הציל
ויקוד העם וישתחוו ׃

may be given the privilege of reading the *haftarah*, and it is a universal practice for the BAR MITSVAH boy to receive this honor. In Conservative and Reform congregations, it is often given to a BAT MITSVAH girl. Orthodox and Conservative Jews chant the *haftarah* to a special melody; on *Shabbat Naḫamu* (the Sabbath before Tishah be-Av) the melody is that of the Book of Lamentations. Separate melodic traditions are preserved by Ashkenazim and Sephardim, but even within these two major communities there are regional differences: Ashkenazim, for example, have separate "German" and "Lithuanian" traditions, the latter predominating in Israel and America. Reform Jews normally declaim (rather than chant) the *haftarah*. There are now few communities where the *haftarah* is read from a handwritten scroll; the standard practice today is for it to be chanted from a printed Bible, Pentateuch, or festival prayer book.

The person who chants the *haftarah* is normally the worshiper who has been "called up" for MAFTIR, the last few verses of the weekly (or special) Torah portion. After the scroll has been raised, he stays on the platform to chant the *haftarah*. Even when another congregant does so in his place, however, one honored with *maftir* chants the introductory benediction and, after the *haftarah*, he concludes with four blessings which emphasize faith in the truth of Scripture, hope for the restoration of Jewish sovereignty in the Land of Israel, and an affirmation of the holiness of that Sabbath or festival.

For a full list of the *haftarot*, see READING OF THE LAW.

HAGBAHAH See READING OF THE LAW

HAGGADAH (lit. "narration, recital"). A Hebrew term, equivalent to AGGADAH, specifically denoting the text prescribed for the home service on Passover and the book containing this ritual (see SEDER). Both the term *haggadah* and the Jew's obligation to relate on Passover the miraculous events accompanying the EXODUS from Egypt have their basis in Scripture: "You shall tell your son on that day: it is because of what the Lord did for me when I came forth out of Egypt..." (Ex. 13:8). Three similar Pentateuchal injunctions (Ex. 12:26-27, 13:14; Deut. 6:20ff.) stress this duty to educate the young, by bringing an ancient historical experience to life in the *Seder*, year after year. Apart from eating MATSAH (unleavened bread), the chief essential of Passover is reading the *haggadah* on the first two nights in Diaspora communities, but only on the first night in Israel (and according to Reform practice).

The most ancient portions of the *haggadah* are the many biblical verses and psalms incorporated, but some other passages may well date from early Second Temple times (fifth cent. BCE). A framework and much of the content had already been standardized by the *tannaim* in the MISHNAH (*Pes.* 10), which includes the traditional FOUR QUESTIONS, but "reciting the *haggadah*" is only mentioned later in the Talmud (*Pes.* 116b). Amplified and embroidered with midrashic commentaries, blessings, prayers, hymns, explanations of the *Seder* ritual, and (in the Ashkenazi rite) with a concluding group of songs, the *haggadah* became a unique anthology of literature drawn from many periods and cultures. Thus, while both were written in ARAMAIC, HA LAḪMA ANYA probably originated in Babylonia, whereas ḪAD GADYA was first chanted in 15th-century Germany. Among the lessons which the *haggadah* imparts are God's shaping of history, the value of Jewish nationhood, the covenantal relationship between God and Israel, and the idea that liberty cannot be taken for granted.

Because of its ancient roots, inspiring content, and ongoing relevance, the *haggadah* is an especially beloved Jewish ritual. Since the days of AMRAM BEN SHESHNA GAON and RASHI, it has attracted a vast number of commentaries and supercommentaries, as well as translations into many languages. Moreover, the fact that each participant in the *Seder* must have his or her own copy led to artistic embellishment of the *haggadah* on a grand scale, often for the participating women and children. Richly illuminated *haggadot* were commissioned by wealthy Jews of the Middle Ages, great care being lavished on both the illustrations and the text (an entire page sometimes being devoted to one theme or word). Separate artistic traditions developed in Muslim Spain and Christian Germany or Italy; and a growing number of the finest illuminated manuscripts are now available in facsimile editions. The first printed *haggadot* came from Spain (c. 1482) and Italy (1505), but the oldest surviving illustrated edition was that printed by Gershom Cohen in Prague (1526). Since then, it is estimated, more than 2,000 editions of the *haggadah* have appeared in print, and new ones are still being published.

Modern Reform and Reconstructionist *haggadot* include numerous departures from the traditional text; this was true also of the special kibbutz editions, published in Palestine from the 1920s, which suppressed all prayers and religious allusions, replacing them with "appropriate" socialist messages. In recent years, however, there has been a return to more hallowed norms. From 1917, special army *haggadot* appeared in the United States, and one based on a "unified rite" (*nusaḫ aḫid*), designed for all sections of the Jewish community, was first published by the Chaplaincy Corps of the Israel Defense Forces in 1956.

HAGGAI One of the MINOR PROPHETS, whose book is included in the Prophets' section of the Bible and consists of two chapters and 38 verses. It is built on four prophetic revelations experienced by Haggai during the second regnal year of Darius I of Persia, i.e., 520 BCE. Haggai concerns himself with the construction of the Second TEMPLE, criticizing the delay in its rebuilding, and assuring the people that even though this Temple is not as magnificent as that of Solomon, it will eventually be so. He also cautions that the Temple cannot confer holiness on a people whose deeds are

Engraved silver Ḫanukkah lamp from Poland, 18th century.

impure. The final prophecy foretells the imminent toppling of the Persian empire in a civil war.

By rabbinic tradition, Haggai was the first of three prophets (Haggai, Zechariah, Malachi) who prophesied in the time of Ezra. When these three died, "the Divine Spirit departed from Israel" (*Yoma* 9b). Haggai is quoted in the Talmud as the source of various laws (see, for example, *Yev.* 16a, *Kid.* 43a, *RH* 9a). The rabbis wrote that the Book of Haggai was edited by the men of the GREAT ASSEMBLY (*BB* 21a).

BOOK OF HAGGAI

1:1 — 1:11	Exhortation to build the Temple
1:12 — 1:15	Historical account of beginning of work
2:1 — 2:9	Encouragement to the builders
2:10 — 2:19	Promise of prosperity to accompany work of restoration
2:20 — 2:23	Messianic promise to Zerubbabel.

ḪAGIGAH ("Sacrifice" brought on the first day of the PILGRIM FESTIVALS). Twelfth tractate of Order MO'ED in the Mishnah. Its three chapters deal with two principal subjects: 1) the obligation of every male to appear in Jerusalem for the three Pilgrim Festivals (Passover, Shavu'ot, and Sukkot) and to bring a "free-will" offering on the first day; 2) the laws of purity and impurity with regard to tithes, sacrifices, and the vessels that contain them (cf. Ex. 23:14-17; 34:18-23; Deut. 16:16,17). The connection is that all who entered the Temple to eat of the sacrifices were required to be in a state of ritual purity. The subject matter is amplified in both Talmuds and the *Tosefta*.

HAGIOGRAPHA (lit. "Holy Writings"). The third and last section of the Hebrew Bible, known in Hebrew as *Ketuvim*, "the Writings." The Hagiographa include the Books of Psalms, Proverbs, Job, the Five Scrolls (*megillot*: Song of Songs, Ruth, Lamentations, Ecclesiastes, Esther), Daniel, Ezra, Nehemiah and Chronicles. The Hagiographa was the last part of the Hebrew Bible to be canonized, and the Talmud records debates about the inclusion or exclusion of various books, such as the Song of Songs and the Book of Esther.

HAI GAON (939-1038). Last GAON of the Academy in Pumbedita (see ACADEMIES). Hai belonged to a distinguished family and married the daughter of Samuel ben Hophni, *gaon* of Sura; he succeeded his father, SHERIRA GAON, in 998, and occupied the gaonate for the next 40 years. His fame throughout the Diaspora can be gauged from the fact that almost 1,000 of his RESPONSA have been preserved, covering a wide range of subjects which include both theological and philosophical questions. Although none of his commentaries on various tractates of the Talmud has survived intact, quotations from these commentaries may be found in the writings of medieval authorities. Some of his works are known only by their title, although fragments of some have been discovered in the Cairo GENIZAH. Hai's chief importance lies in the field of halakhic CODIFICATION. His code on legal documents (*shetarot*) and parts of two other codes on oaths and sales have survived. These were originally written in Arabic and then translated into Hebrew. Their systematic arrangement and exposition show Hai Gaon to have been a preeminent halakhist who, like his father, Sherira, was influenced by SAADIAH GAON. Hai Gaon formulated the rule that the Babylonian Talmud must take precedence over the Jerusalem Talmud when their authorities clash.

ḪAKHAM ("wise man") A sage. In biblical times, it was a general term, but in mishnaic times, there was a formal post of *ḥakham*, this being the third rank after the NASI and the *av bet din* (*Hor.* 13b), although his duties are unknown. The title was found in both Erets Israel and Babylonia. Sephardi Jews refer to an ordained rabbi in the community as a *ḥakham* and sometimes expand the title to *ḥakham mushlam*. In England, the chief Sephardi rabbi has the title of *Haham*.

ḪAKHAM BASHI Title given to the Chief Rabbi in the countries of the Ottoman Empire in the 19th century. The term is made up of the Hebrew *ḥakham* (wise man) and the Turkish word *bashi* (chief). The *Ḥakham Bashi* was officially recognized by the Turkish authorities as the leader of the Jewish communities and the title was also applied to leading provincial rabbis. It remained in use in Turkey and Egypt, and to designate the Sephardi Chief Rabbi of Palestine up to 1918.

HAKHEL Religious ceremony performed in the biblical period in the year following the SABBATICAL YEAR. The Bible (Deut. 31:12) states, "Gather (*hakhel*) the people together, men, and women, and children, and your stranger that is within your gates, that they may hear, and that they may learn, and fear the Lord your God, and observe to do all the words of this law." Under the provisions of the *hakhel* law, all men, women and even children (of an age where they would at least be curious as to what was taking place) were to gather in the Temple courtyard in Jerusalem on the Sukkot holiday of the year following the Sabbatical Year, to hear the king read aloud various portions of Deuteronomy. While there is a dispute as to whether the biblical commandment refers to the first or second day of Sukkot, there is a consensus that the ceremony was held on the second day. The portions read aloud included, among others, the two paragraphs of the SHEMA, the laws regarding the king, and the blessings for observing the Torah and curses for failing to do so. In the absence of a king, a priest or Torah sage was to read the passages. The reader stood on a specially constructed wooden platform in the women's courtyard in the Temple. As the Talmud explains it, the men were to come and learn, the women to listen, and the children to reward those who brought them. Although the *hakhel* ceremony lapsed with the destruction of the Temple, there have been modern attempts by the Chief Rabbinate in Israel and rabbinates elsewhere to revive the ceremony. At the *hakhel* commemoration of 5748 (1987), at the Western Wall in Jerusalem, the Ashkenazi and Sephardi Chief Rabbis read from the Torah, as did the President of the State of Israel.

HAKHNASAT KALLAH (lit. "bringing in the bride," i.e., enabling the bride to enter into marriage). Fund devoted to provide needy brides with a dowry to buy the basic necessities of married life. In the Morning Prayer, it is said that *hakhnasat kallah* is among those precepts "whose fruit is eaten in this world, while the principal remains for the World to Come" — implying its particular importance. In the historical Jewish COMMUNITY, special societies were organized to raise and dispense funds for *hakhnasat kallah*.

The *Shulḥan Arukh* states that no charitable cause is greater than that of enabling a poor young girl to marry. Where only limited funds are available, priority is given to a poor young woman over a poor young man, "for it is more embarrassing for a woman to be unmarried than it is for a man" (*Sh. Ar., YD* 251.8). Great stress is placed in rabbinic literature on insuring that the aid offered for *hakhnasat kallah* be given secretly.

The commandment of *hakhnasat kallah* also includes making the bride rejoice at her wedding. So important is this that according to some halakhic works it is even permitted to use the Torah ornaments of the SCROLLS OF THE LAW to dress up the bride, although customarily these may not be used for any other purpose than their original one.

HAKKAFOT (lit. "circuits"). The circular processions made in synagogue or elsewhere on various occasions, both festive and solemn. A classic paradigm for these in the Bible was the Israelite circumambulation of Jericho resulting in the collapse of its walls (Josh. 6:3-20). Symbolically, however, *hakkafot* also imply completeness, as does their link with the number 7 (see NUMBERS). Orthodox Ashkenazi brides sometimes make three or seven *hakkafot* around the bridegroom under the wedding canopy prior to the wedding ceremony (see MARRIAGE); seven circuits are made around the synagogue with Torah scrolls when it is dedicated; the same number is made around a new CEMETERY at its consecration; and Sephardi and Ḥasidic Jews make seven circuits around the coffin or bier (usually in honor of a scholarly or pious man) immediately prior to BURIAL. These processions, known in Judeo-Spanish as *rodeamentos* ("rounds"), are often accompanied by the chanting of psalms.

Toral Scrolls carried in procession in seven circuits (hakkafot) *in the synagogue on the Simḥat Torah festival.*

Best known, however, are the festive processions held in synagogue during the SUKKOT (Tabernacles) holiday. On the first six days, in Temple times, pilgrims made one circuit of the altar holding willow branches and chanting Psalm 118:25 ("O Lord, deliver us; O Lord, let us prosper"). On the seventh day, the number of circuits was increased to seven. That ancient practice is reflected each morning of Sukkot, when the Ark is opened and a Scroll of the Law is carried to the reader's platform. Congregants make one circuit around the synagogue, holding the FOUR SPECIES and chanting prescribed HOSHANOT hymns with the cantor. On the seventh day, HOSHANA RABBAH, seven processions take place and the seven *hoshanot* are augmented by psalms and a biblical passage (I Chron. 29:11) alluding to seven of the Divine attributes. These also have a mystical link with the seven ancestral "holy guests" (USHPIZIN) welcomed on Sukkot, and with seven of the Divine emanations or SEFIROT. Sephardim often blow the *shofar* (ram's horn) during the Hoshana Rabbah circuits. No *hakkafot* take place on a Sabbath.

In accordance with the practice introduced by Safed kabbalists in the 16th century, *hakkafot* also mark the observance of SIMḤAT TORAH, the Rejoicing of the Law. After Evening and Morning Services, all the Torah scrolls are removed from the Ark and carried around the synagogue in seven successive processions. Short acrostic verses headed by Psalm 118:25 are chanted each time around, children bearing lighted candles or miniature Torah scrolls are encouraged to join the processions as a symbolic "army of the Lord," and after each *hakkafah* there is an interlude of joyous dancing and singing.

Ḥasidic Jews in the Diaspora follow Israeli practice by holding their Torah scroll processions on the eighth night

(SHEMINI ATSERET), but also do so again on the evening and morning of 23 Tishri (when Diaspora communities observe Simḥat Torah). Reform Jews arrange *hakkafot* on the eighth night only, whether in Israel or the Diaspora. Sephardi practice varies. Some have elaborate choral processions after Evening Service and the Morning or Additional Service on the following day; Western Sephardi (Spanish and Portuguese) congregations, however, never adopted this custom until recently, and even today *hakkafot* on Simḥat Torah are intended primarily for children. Syrian and Moroccan Jews often have another round of processions on *Shabbat ha-Gadol* (see SABBATHS, SPECIAL). In Israel "second *hakkafot*" are held throughout the country, usually in the open air, on the night after Simḥat Torah, with the participation of bands, singers, and enthusiastic crowds.

HA LAḤMA ANYA ("This is the bread of affliction"). Opening words of an Aramaic declaration recited prior to the FOUR QUESTIONS during the Passover SEDER. The term "bread of affliction" is used in a dual sense, referring both to the poor man's daily fare and to the unleavened bread which the Israelites baked hurriedly when they were expelled from Egypt (Ex. 21:39). Owing to apparent contradictions in the text, it is not clear where and when this paragraph of the HAGGADAH was composed. Thus, the invitation to join those present in celebrating the Passover (i.e., to take part in eating the paschal lamb) would indicate that *Ha Laḥma Anya* dates from the era of the Second Temple. The wording of the next sentence, however, points to a later Diaspora origin (in Babylonia perhaps) after the Second Exile (70 CE). Before *Ha Laḥma Anya* is recited, the three ritual *matsot* are uncovered, raised, and displayed; some families also open the door at this point to welcome a potential guest. Among both Ashkenazim and Sephardim, the declaration is usually chanted (and often sung) to a traditional melody.

> This is the bread of affliction which our forefathers ate in the land of Egypt. Let all who are hungry come and eat; let all who are in need come and celebrate the Passover. This year (we are) here; next year (may we be) in the Land of Israel. This year (we are) slaves; next year (may we be) free men!

HALAKHAH (rabbinic jurisprudence). The branch of rabbinic literature which deals with the religious obligations of members of the Jewish faith, both in their interpersonal relationships ("between man and his neighbor") and in their ritual performances ("between man and his Maker"), all equally binding. It encompasses practically all aspects of human behavior: birth and marriage, joy and grief, agriculture and commerce, ethics and theology.

The term *halakhah* is derived from the Hebrew *halakh*, "to walk," for it is the legal system which points out the way of life for the Jewish people, following the statement, "Enjoin upon them the laws and the teachings, and make known to them the way they are to go and the practices they are to follow" (Ex. 18:20). In a more restricted sense, as first employed by the *tannaim*, a *halakhah* (plur. *halakhot*) referred to an oral ruling handed down by the religious authorities. Later, *halakhah* came to mean the accepted or authorized opinion when a ruling was in dispute. The term is also used generically to denote the legal parts of Jewish tradition in contradistinction to AGGADAH, the homilies of the sages, though they naturally influenced each other.

The Commandments. *Halakhah* is rooted in the Bible, specifically the Five Books of Moses, and is almost synonymous with TORAH. The Torah is said to contain 613 COMMANDMENTS (*Taryag Mitsvot*), 248 positive and 365 negative prescriptions (*Mak.* 23b). *Halakhah*, in the first instance, is the formal declaration of the manner in which these commandments are to be performed and the penalty incurred for transgressing them.

The commandments are regarded by the *halakhah* as having been revealed by God to Moses at Sinai (*Torah min ha-Shamayim*; lit. Torah from heaven). (Later, the sages prescribed a few additional commandments, such as lighting candles in honor of the Sabbath and festivals, and the reading of the Scroll of Esther on Purim. These are recognized as *mitsvot de-rabbanan*, i.e., commandments of rabbinic origin).

The Oral Law. The sages of the Talmud, who laid down the basic rulings of the *halakhah*, postulated the existence of two Laws, the WRITTEN LAW as recorded in the Pentateuch (*Torah she-bi-khetav*), and the ORAL LAW (*Torah she-be'al peh*), which was to be transmitted by word of mouth from master to disciple. It was asserted as a principle of faith that the Oral Law was communicated to Moses simultaneously with the Written Law. This was a logical necessity, for no written text can simply be handed over without the addition of some explanatory clarification. For example, the Written Law prescribes: You shall not do any work on the Sabbath"; the Oral Law defines exactly which acts of labor constitute a violation of this injunction (*Shab.* 73a).

The existence of the Oral Law has brought about two basic features of Jewish life: the chain of TRADITION linking the generations, and the extraordinary emphasis upon the study and teaching of Torah (TALMUD TORAH). According to the Mishnah, "Moses received the Torah from Sinai and handed it to Joshua; Joshua to the Elders; the Elders to the Prophets; and the Prophets to the Men of the Great Assembly" (*Avot* 1.1). The Men of the GREAT ASSEMBLY were led by EZRA the Scribe (*sofer*, Ezra 7:6), and his colleagues are known as the *soferim*; so called — according to the Talmud — "Because they would count [*sofer* also means "to count"] all the letters of the Torah." They flourished a half-century after the return to Judah from the Babylonian Exile (c. 450 BCE), and their major task was "to return the Torah to Israel" (cf. Ezra 7:10).

The sages interpreted Scripture by a method called MIDRASH. This took the form of *Midrash Halakhah*, the expounding of Scripture in order to substantiate halakhic rulings, and *Midrash Aggadah*, which records the homilies of the sages. (Ordinarily, the term Midrash by itself denotes *Midrash Aggadah*.) Many of the early halakhic rulings are therefore called *divré Soferim* ("words of the scribes") and the sages attributed to them the force of biblical law, according them even greater importance. "More precious than the words of the Torah are the words of the scribes; the penalty for disregarding them is greater than that for disregarding the words of Torah" (TJ. *Sanh.* 11.4). Eventually, *divré Soferim* referred to rulings of rabbinic, rather than Scriptural, origin. As time went on, the midrashic method became more involved, allowing for the derivation of more and more halakhic rulings from Scriptural exegesis or HERMENEUTICS. Thus HILLEL employed seven methods of Midrash, the best known being *kal va-ḥomer*, an *a fortiori* inference from a less stringent to a more stringent case, and *gezerah shavah*, an inference from a similarity of phraseology. A generation or two later, two *tannaim*, Nehuniah ben ha-Kanah and Nahum Ish Gimzo, introduced two different methods of expounding passages that begin with a general statement (*kelal*) and continue with a series of particulars (*perat*). One of their disciples, ISHMAEL BEN ELISHA, elaborated the hermeneutic principles to thirteen. His colleague AKIVA reached a high point of midrashic exposition by deriving additional rulings from the Torah's use of the word *et*, which has no intrinsic meaning, and in turn collated the halakhic midrashim, to wit: MEKHILTA on Exodus, SIFRA on Leviticus, SIFRÉ on Numbers and Deuteronomy.

Much of this Midrash was not taught in order to create new *halakhah*, but rather to substantiate *halakhah* which had been transmitted as part of the Oral Law. Many *halakhot* had little support from Scripture. Thus the Mishnah states, "The law which provides that a sage may absolve a person from his vow hovers in the air and has nothing (in Scripture) to support it" (*Ḥag.* 18a). Rabbinic exegesis invariably went beyond the simple meaning of the biblical text, and in several instances "detoured" from its meaning in order to lay down a law. Some *halakhot* were transmitted without any reference to Scripture, and they were designated HALAKHAH LE-MOSHEH MI-SINAI ("a ruling received by Moses on Mount Sinai"). (Later commentators point out that some rulings designated as such in the Talmud are not literally from Sinai, but were said to be so because of their widespread acceptance.)

Authority of the sages. It was held that in certain areas the Torah did not prescribe any specific legislation, but left the matter to the sages to lay down the rules. Thus, concerning work on the intermediate days of festivals (ḤOL HA-MO'ED) it is said, "Scripture gave it over to the sages to decide which type of work is forbidden and which is permitted" (*Ḥag.* 18a). In fact, the decision in all questions of Jewish law was given over to the sages. "'The Torah is not in heaven' (Deut. 30:12); it has already been given over from Sinai, and in the Torah it is written, 'Bend the law after the majority' [interpreted as 'of the sages' Ex. 23:2]" (*BM* 59b). Their decisions constitute the *halakhah*, the norm and practice in Jewish life.

The authority of the sages was practically unlimited. They did not hesitate to assert their right to abrogate a law of the Torah if they deemed it necessary for the general upholding of the law. It was their conviction that their interpretation of Scripture was part of the Divine revelation even when opinions were divided, saying, "Both opinions are words of the living God" (*Eruv.* 13a).

Nevertheless, the sages were anxious that the distinction between the Written Law and the Oral Law be scrupulously maintained. They ruled, "Teachings which were given orally may not be committed to writing; teachings given in writing [i.e., Scripture] may not be transmitted orally" (*Git.* 60b). It was only later, due to the exigencies of Jewish life and the tremendous volume of *halakhot* that had accumulated during the period of the *tannaim*, that JUDAH HA-NASI (c. 170-220) decided to collect the *halakhot*, organize them according to subject matter, and create a second text for the study of Torah: the MISHNAH.

The rationale behind this ruling was twofold: no commentary, exegetical or otherwise, can ever be added to the sacred text, for the text is Divine and all commentary is human. Secondly, it is essential to preserve the original text and the fluidity of all commentary; for Revelation of the Torah is the dialogue between God who is eternal and Man who is subject to the accidents of time. From the very beginning, there is imbedded in the words of the Torah an "eternal contemporaneity," a relevance to contemporary life in every circumstance. "The Torah," say the sages, "speaks in contemporary language, in the language of man" (*BK* 5.7, *Ket.* 67b). It is this feature of the *halakhah* that enabled it to serve in the past, and to continue to serve in a radically changed world, as the guiding line for traditional Jewry.

Ordination. The "judge of the time" is the biblical *shofet* (judge), the rabbinic *ḥakham* (sage) or *dayyan* (judge). The original source of his authority is MOSES, who laid the foundation for the vesting of authority to decide questions of Jewish law when he "handed over the Torah to Joshua" by the laying on of hands (*semikhah*, Num. 27:18). This ORDINATION also empowered the recipient to transfer authority to another, usually by a teacher to his disciple, thus creating a chain of halakhic tradition that passed on from generation to generation. By the time of the Talmud, ordination was not conveyed by the physical laying on of hands, but by conferring the title "Ḥakham" or "Rabbi." Candidates for ordination had to possess, besides knowledge of the law, certain moral qualities summed up by Maimonides as follows:

"Each judge must possess seven qualities: wisdom, humility, awe (of God), spurning wealth, love of truth, beloved by the people, and a good reputation; all these are specified in the Torah" (*Yad, Sanh.* 2.7).

The sages ruled that ordination could be conferred only in the Land of Israel. This did not mean that communities in the Diaspora were to be deprived of recognized halakhic authorities. To insure the proper administration of Jewish law with officially authorized sages — and for centuries most communities in the Diaspora were autonomous in this respect — a corresponding form of ordination was instituted, although it did not confer the major prerogatives of the original ordination. It was the recognition by a superior authority that the conferee "*higi'a le-hora'ah*," i.e., his knowledge of talmudic law was sufficient to allow him to render halakhic decisions.

The Sanhedrin. With the exception of Moses, no individual, regardless of his erudition, could make decisions binding upon all Israel. For such comprehensive authority a duly constituted body comprising individuals who had received ordination was necessary. Such a body was first constituted when Moses gathered 70 ELDERS to share with him the burden of leading the Children of Israel (Num. 11:16-17). In the days of Ezra the supreme governing body is said to have been the 120-member Great Assembly. Subsequently, as the body was reconstituted in the days of the Hasmoneans (2nd century BCE), it consisted of seventy members and was known as "the Great SANHEDRIN," a term of Greek origin meaning "Council." It is also referred to in rabbinic literature as *Bet ha-Din ha-Gadol*, the "Great Court of Law."

The Sanhedrin was much more than a court of law. Its chief function in fact was to expound and interpret the Torah's teachings for all Israel, and Maimonides called it the root of the Oral Law (*Yad, Mam.* 1.1). Once it proclaimed the law, any scholar who defied its ruling was liable to punishment by death (Deut. 17:12; in talmudic parlance, ZAKEN MAMREH).

Anti-Halakhah Movements. In the early days of the Sanhedrin, some questioned the validity of the whole concept of the Oral Law, halakhic rulings based upon hermeneutic interpretation. These opponents of the sages were the SADDUCEES, who questioned the principle of REWARD AND PUNISHMENT and denied the *Olam ha-Ba* (AFTERLIFE) as formulated by the rabbis. The latter, troubled by the contradiction in real life to this principle, postulated that the ultimate reward and punishment for man's deeds upon earth is rendered in the *Olam ha-Ba* ("world to come"), the abode of the soul after death.

After the destruction of the Temple (70 CE), the Sadducees ceased to exist as a force in Jewish life. In the eighth century, during the period of the *ge'onim*, there emerged a new group opposed to rabbinic Judaism, the KARAITES, so called because they asserted that Jewish law is inferred only from a literal interpretation of Scripture (*Mikra*). Indeed, they repudiated the whole concept of the Oral Law. The rabbis, Saadiah Gaon in particular, waged a fierce polemic against them, and by the 12th century, with the exception of a few communities, they ceased to attract Jews to their ideology. A moot question among the halakhists was the status of the Karaites; whether they were to be regarded as Jews despite their heresy, or not.

The heirs of the anti-halakhists in modern times were the founders of REFORM JUDAISM in the early 19th century. Again controversy raged as rabbinic leaders warned against any deviation from the halakhic tradition. The reaction against Reform led to a rigidity in halakhic interpretation, manifested today in the reinforcement of many stringencies in religious observance among the Orthodox.

Gezerot. The Men of the Great Assembly laid down another principle for the sages to implement: "Make a hedge around the Torah" (*Avot* 1.1), i.e., institute new restrictions in addition to those of the Torah in order to insure against violation of the commandments. Thus, to the *halakhah* were added in successive generations various rulings of rabbinic origin which have become integrated into the corpus of Jewish law.

These added restrictions are called *gezerot* (sing. GEZERAH). They are considered so important as even to override a positive commandment of the Torah. For example, if the only available *shofar* (ram's horn) on Rosh ha-Shanah is on a tree, the tree may not be climbed to obtain the *shofar* even though it means not being able to perform the commandment of sounding the *shofar* (*RH* 4.8). Furthermore, once a *gezerah* is decreed by the competent authorities and has been accepted by Jewry at large, it cannot be rescinded by later authorities.

Hierarchy of authority. The assumption of the *halakhah* is that every later group of scholars is inferior to an earlier one and is therefore bound by the decrees of its predecessors. Nevertheless, the rule is that where the earlier authorities differ, the *halakhah* (the accepted ruling) is according to the later authority. The latter has no doubt examined the opinions of the former, and "like a dwarf upon the shoulders of a giant" sees further and reasons more correctly. Since the redaction of the Babylonian TALMUD was later than that of the Jerusalem Talmud, the *halakhah* invariably follows the former whenever the two differ. (As a consequence, halakhic studies were largely confined to the Babylonian Talmud.)

The authority of the Talmud is supreme. Maimonides states emphatically, "All Israel is obliged to follow all the statements in the Babylonian Talmud. Every city and every province is compelled to conduct itself in accord with the customs, decrees and regulations instituted by the sages of the GEMARA, since all Israel agreed to accept them" (Introduction to *Mishneh Torah*). As a result, many of the "liberties" taken by the sages of the Talmud in applying the *halakhah* were deemed by post-talmudic authorities as beyond their competence. (A prime example is the power to annul marriages *ab initio.*) However, significant restrictions were added by later authorities by proclaiming a *ḥerem* (EXCOMMUNICATION) against those who would defy them. Thus, Rabbenu GERSHOM ME'OR HA-GOLAH (tenth century) banned, *inter alia*, the practice of polygamy. This ban was accepted by Ashkenazi, but not by Sephardi, Jewry.

Takkanot. The sages understood that no basic code of law can anticipate all social and economic situations that may arise, and therefore there has to be included in the basic code a provision for the ongoing issuing of regulations to insure law and order in society. In the *halakhah* these regulations are called *takkanot* (sing. TAKKANAH). The regions covered by them varied according to the scope of the authority proclaiming them. Many attributed by the Talmud to Moses, Joshua, and King Solomon, and others instituted by the sages themselves, devolved upon all Jews. Thus liturgy of the daily prayers and benedictions (*berakhot*) are ascribed to the Men of the Great Assembly (*Meg.* 17b). Hillel introduced the PROSBUL, a document promoting the extension of loans beyond the SABBATICAL YEAR (*Git.* 4.3). JOHANAN BEN ZAKKAI instituted many *takkanot* after the destruction of the Temple in order to insure the continuity of religious practice despite the absence of the Temple (*RH* 4.1-4). His successor Rabban GAMALIEL II instituted an additional benediction in the daily AMIDAH to invoke the wrath of God against heretics (MINIM, probably the early Christians). Other important *takkanot* included the regulation of marriage contracts (*ketubbot*) and the distribution of inherited estates.

The *halakhah* also empowered municipalities and economic groups to regulate the affairs of their respective constituents. In 18th-century Poland the Jewish representative body, the Council of Four Lands, adopted many *takkanot* for the Jewish communities of Eastern Europe. About the same time, Rabbi Jacob ben Tsur edited a *Sefer ha-Takkanot* ("Book of Ordinances") listing the many regulations adopted by the communities in Muslim lands. With the establishment of the Chief Rabbinate in Israel, Rabbi Abraham Isaac KOOK and his successor Rabbi Isaac Halevi HERZOG called for the adoption of *takkanot* in domestic affairs, but other rabbis refused to cooperate.

Minhag. Another division of rabbinic law incorporated in the halakhah is *minhag* (CUSTOM), a practice which came about not as a specific ruling or *takkanah*, but as a result of the spontaneous desire of a community to adopt a certain ritual that received the sanction of the local sage. Thus *minhag* invariably refers to a local custom, though many such customs spread from their original locale to a much wider region. The sages laid great stress upon the obligation to conform to local custom so as to avoid divisiveness and conflict. A traveler is obliged to follow both the stringencies of his home-town and those of the community he is visiting (*Pes.* 4.1). Local custom also became the norm in fixing employer-employee relations. From talmudic times differences in prayer rite (NUSAḤ) between Jews in Erets Israel and Babylonia led to many more differences between Ashkenazi-European Jews and Sephardi Jews of Muslim lands.

According to many halakhists the practices of rabbinic origin, *gezerot*, *takkanot*, and *minhagim*, once incorporated in the *halakhah* remain obligatory, even if the original rationale for their adoption no longer exists. Thus, even after the CALENDAR was fixed and the Jews outside Erets Israel were no longer in doubt as to which day the festival occurs, they were advised "Keep the custom of your fathers and continue to observe two days of festivals" (*Bétsah* 4b). Nevertheless, post-talmudic authorities recognized that many practices in force by talmudic law were not meant to apply to a changed situation. Many restrictions imposed by the Talmud against dealing with non-Jews are no longer considered applicable; they were designed against idol-worshipers and not the Christian or Muslim of today.

Codification. The Talmud is discursive, it deals with many theoretical questions and many of its discussions are non-conclusive. It therefore could not serve as a practical guide for the layman. To fill this need, digests of the *halakhah*, concise and arranged systematically, were composed, beginning with the period of the *ge'onim* (see CODIFICATION). Among them are the *She'iltot* of AḤAI OF SHABḤA (a series of sermons outlining pertinent commandments), *Halakhot Pesukot* of Yehudai Gaon, and *Halakhot Gedolot* of Simeon Kayyara (8th century). Saadiah Gaon (882-942) composed a whole series of halakhic digests, the most popular being his *Siddur* (prayer book), containing not only the text of the prayers but also the relevant laws. Even before him, AMRAM GAON wrote a prayer book in response to a request from the Barcelona community. The last of the *ge'onim*, HAI (939-1038), also composed a series of halakhic treatises for specific subjects.

The first of the RISHONIM, Isaac ALFASI (1013-1103), employed another method. His major work, *Hilkhot ha-Rif*, is an abridgment of those sections of the Talmud that have practical significance and a statement of the *halakhah*. This method was later followed by ASHER BEN JEHIEL (the *Rosh*; 1250-1327), whose *halakhot* appear in many editions of the Talmud. The most comprehensive and systematic code of Jewish law, including laws rendered obsolete by history but which hopefully will be restored in the Messianic era, is the *Mishneh Torah* of MAIMONIDES (1135-1204). Most authoritative in modern times is the SHULḤAN ARUKH of Joseph Caro (1488-1575), a Sephardi, with the glosses of Moses ISSERLES (1525-1572) for Ashkenazi practice. All these codes are surrounded by commentators who brought the rulings up-to-date. For Ashkenazi Jewry, most authoritative today is the *Mishnah Berurah* of Israel Meir Kagan, the ḤAFETS ḤAYYIM (1838-1933). Sephardim generally follow *Sefer Ben Ish Ḥai* of Joseph Ḥayyim of Baghdad and *Kaf ha-Ḥayyim* of Ḥayyim Palaggi of Izmir.

Responsa. Another branch of rabbinic literature which serves as a halakhic guide comprises the many thousands of RESPONSA (*teshuvot*) spanning the centuries from the talmudic period to this very day. These are responses by halakhic authorities to practical questions addressed to them by laymen or by colleagues, though some responsa in latter days expatiate in discussion of talmudic statements. Their halakhic authority is largely measured by the reputation of the author, as well as by his persuasive reasoning.

The voluminous material amassed through the ages has led to the production in recent times of several talmudic encyclopedias, with subjects arranged alphabetically. The *Encyclopedia Talmudit* now being published in Jerusalem is most comprehensive. In contrast to the codes mentioned above, the encyclopedias do not render decisive halakhic judgments; their purpose is to provide the scholar with all the available material from which he can draw his own conclusion. It is a principle of the *halakhah* that "a judge can decide only upon the basis of his own judgment."

Contemporary Issues. The application of this principle can be seen in the host of questions being answered by today's halakhist. Modern technology and its devices, undreamed of in previous generations, pose problems for which there is little precedent in traditional *halakhah* (see HALAKHAH AND TECHNOLOGY). What is the nature of electricity; is it the *ésh* (fire) which Scripture prohibits on the Sabbath, or not? What about telecommunication; does one fulfil the commandment of listening to the *shofar* on Rosh ha-Shanah by hearing it broadcast? The halakhist is faced with more crucial problems by advances in medical practice. At what point can we say that death has occurred and a vital organ may be removed for transplant? What about artificial insemination, surrogate mothers, in vitro fertilization? (see MEDICAL ETHICS).

Current events also call for the halakhist to exercise ingenuity in jugment. What is the relation of *halakhah* to the State of Israel? How does it react to the feminist demand for greater participation of women in ritual?

Thanks to the continuous vitality of the *halakhah*, rabbis today are responding to these questions, arguing not only by analogy with traditional sources, but — more importantly — moved by the basic nature of the *halakhah*. Though a legal system, it is by no means the harsh legalism which its denigrators depict. "The ways of the entire Torah," say the sages, "are ways of pleasantness" (*Git.* 59b). Justice is to be tempered with mercy, truth with kindness, the law with compassion. The *halakhah* advises that a man should act *lifnim mi-shurat ha-din* (beyond the "strict letter of the law") and yield rights in favor of the needy (*BM* 30b). Because of the *halakhah*, *tsedakah*/righteousness/ is construed to mean charity. Since "all its paths are peace" it urges good-neighborly relations with all, including the non-Jew.

The Conservative Approach. While recognizing the central importance of *halakhah*, CONSERVATIVE JUDAISM insists that it is a developing concept which permits ordered change. Throughout history many factors have influenced such changes, including the forces of sociology, ethics, intercommunal relationships, politics, and above all in modern times technological, scientific, and economic realities.

With regard to the source of *halakhah*, Conservative scholars generally reject the belief that the Written Law is the literal work of God and that the Oral Law is an extension of Divine revelation. In Conservative teaching the Written Law contains a revealed Divine teaching but the actual words were written down and transmitted by man. It is still authoritative revelation, but not in its literal form. The Oral Law is also an authoritative source for *halakhah* because it represents the ongoing search to discover the meaning and relevance of the Written Law with its Divinely inspired message. That process of search is continuous so that each generation is challenged to find the contemporary relevance of the *halakhah*. It is bound to involve some development and even change from age to age, as is the case, for example, with the Conservative approach to the status of the woman in Jewish law. This is so because *halakhah* is the law which guides every aspect of life. Since life itself is dynamic, each age will call for new interpretation and application of the received laws. Conservative Judaism bases its thesis on the conviction that this approach has been recognized by the rabbis throughout history and that accordingly the *halakhah* has in fact been subject to change. It also emphasizes that the Torah itself requires such judicial activity.

This does not mean that the law may be arbitrarily changed or that every rabbi has the mandate to bring about such changes. Conservative theologians recognize the importance of the past and the authority of earlier rabbinic legislators. They differ from some Orthodox schools of thought in also giving due weight to the present. Against this tension between the past and the present, the Conservative scholar seeks the balance which respects that past with its decisions and the need to bring modern relevance to the *halakhah*.

Such changes as are found necessary are decided only after extensive scholarly debate and then by final decision of the Law Committee of the Conservative Rabbinical Assembly.

The Reform Approach. REFORM JUDAISM, which is pluralistic by nature, has given rise to many differing theoretical and practical views on *halakhah*. In the early stages, in Germany, the two major positions were represented by Abraham GEIGER and Samuel HOLDHEIM. The former put the emphasis on reforming *halakhah* and invoking tradition, in a scientific and critical way, to justify changes. This was done through gradual and organic development while accepting the concept of *halakhah* as vital and holding that both biblical and post-biblical Judaism are necessary to guide the contemporary Jew. The latter accepted the authority of biblical law, though in an eclectic way, but attributed very little weight to later formulations of the Jewish tradition, seeing the need to release progress from the "rigid hand of the Talmud."

In the U.S. a similar diversity exists. Isaac Mayer WISE and David EINHORN represented the differing approaches, the moderate and the radical, in the early days of Reform in the U.S. The development that Reform has undergone as a movement can best be seen in the nature of its platforms. The Pittsburgh Platform of 1885 stated: "We accept as binding only the moral laws and maintain only such ceremonies as elevate and sanctify our lives, but reject all such as are not adapted to the views and habits of modern civilization. We hold that all such Mosaic and rabbinical laws as regulate diet, priestly purity, and dress originated in ages and under the influence of ideas altogether foreign to our present mental and spiritual state." The Columbus Platform of 1937 spoke of the continuous process of revelation and declared that both Written and Oral Law "preserve the historical precedents, patterns of goodness and holiness... Torah remains the dynamic source of the life of Israel... Judaism as a way of life requires, in addition to its moral and spiritual demands, the preservation of the Sabbath, festivals, and holy days, the retention and development of such customs, symbols and ceremonies as possess inspirational value." In the 1976 Centenary Perspective, the Reform position was stated as follows: "Judaism emphasizes action rather than creed as the primary expression of a religious life, the means by which we strive to achieve universal justice and peace. Reform Judaism shares this emphasis on duty and obligation... the past century has taught us that the claims made upon us may begin with our ethical obligations but they extend to many other aspects of Jewish living... Within each area of Jewish observance Reform Jews are called upon to confront the claims of Jewish tradition, however differently perceived, and to exercise their individual autonomy, choosing and creating on the basis of commitment and knowledge."

This trend has been influenced by the growing notion of peoplehood in Reform ideology, large influxes of East European Jews into the ranks of Reform, the rise of Zionism, and the establishment of the State of Israel. With the growing calls to set norms for present-day Jewish life, a series of guides have been published by the Central Conference of American Rabbis for home and communal observance, the festivals, Sabbath and daily use.

In Israel, the Movement for Progressive Judaism has developed a set of criteria for applying and acceptance of the *mitsvot* (commandments): 1. The purpose of a *mitsvah* and its historical development; 2. The possibility of sanctifying life with its observance; 3. The feasibility of fulfilling it in contemporary conditions; 4. The impact of the *mitsvah* on KELAL YISRAEL (the total Jewish people); and 5. There being no conflict between the *mitsvah* and the dictates of conscience.

HALAKHAH AND TECHNOLOGY The development of the different branches of technology, which gained increased impetus in the 20th century, and the obligation to observe the HALAKHAH as formulated thousands of years ago, have created a special relationship between the terms *halakhah* and "technology." This relationship is expressed in two areas: in halakhic decisions on questions posed by modern technology in areas not faced by earlier generations; and in the availability of technological advances to facilitate the observance of the *halakhah*. Both areas require extensive knowledge of *halakhah* as well as technology, in order to enable each to avail itself of the other. As a result, few modern rabbis have acquired the prerequisite qualifications to make halakhic decisions in this area. On occasion, ignorance in one of these areas may result in an incorrect halakhic decision. At the same time, a number of institutions have been established in Israel to deal with this specific problem. These include the Scientific-Technological Institute for the Solution of Halakhic Problems; *Tomet* (Teams of Science and Torah); the Institute for the Investigation of Agriculture in Accordance with the Torah, and others.

Technological advances have profoundly changed the world of the observant Jew and broadened the scope of his everyday life within the boundaries laid down by *halakhah*. The discovery of electricity and related inventions resulted in a number of complex halakhic questions. In regard to the SABBATH and festivals, the question arose as to whether it was permissible to use electric energy produced on the Sabbath, or to utilize electrical appliances. The categories of forbidden work which may be violated by use of electricity on the Sabbath include: producing a flame, burning, cooking and building. Most halakhic authorities rule that electrical appliances may not be operated or electric light turned on or off on the Sabbath or festivals, even if the action itself does not produce either heat or light. Based on the rules of the *halakhah* governing a product obtained through the desecration of the Sabbath, there is a dispute concerning the utilization of electricity produced on the Sabbath, even if the appliance is made operational beforehand (e.g., by having it turned on by a time clock).

The rabbinic authorities also considered to what extent an action carried out by means of electricity may be considered to be the direct action of the operator. Thus, for example, is MATSAH (unleavened bread) baked in an electric oven or are TSITSIT produced on an electric spinning wheel considered man-made? Has a deaf person who hears the reading of the Scroll of Esther by means of a hearing aid fulfilled the obligation to hear the reading? Given that a ritual bath (MIKVEH) is acceptable only if the water in it was not drawn by hand, is a person who operates an electric pump considered to have manually drawn the water into the bath?

Even when the action is completely automatic, halakhic questions remain concerning the extent to which the action is to be attributed to man. Thus, for example, there is a dispute whether one may operate a factory automatically on the Sabbath, or whether a mourner, who is forbidden to work during the seven days of mourning, may do so.

Many positive and negative commandments involve fire: the Sabbath and Ḥanukkah CANDLES, HAVDALAH, the search for LEAVEN, and the prohibitions against combustion and cooking on the Sabbath, of cooking meat and milk together, etc. Is "fire" produced in an electrical element considered halakhically equivalent to the fire involved in all the above?

Halakhah distinguished clearly between life and death when all the vital organs (heart, brain, lungs, etc.) ceased to function at more or less the same time. Rabbinic authorities have had to deal with new definitions of the exact dividing line between life and death ever since medicine learned how to separate the functioning of different vital organs (e.g., the heart may beat even though the brain has ceased functioning). The determination of parenthood (both paternity and maternity) was relatively simple as long as pregnancy was the result of sexual intercourse between a man and woman. It became a major question once birth became the product of ARTIFICIAL INSEMINATION or of the implanting of ova (see MEDICAL ETHICS).

Hundreds of years ago, many bodily defects were considered incurable. *Halakhah* regards those with certain bodily defects as *terèfah*, i.e., with a presumption that death will occur in a relatively short time. What is the status of such people if they are cured through recent medical advances? In former times, the deaf were not considered to have legal capacity, due to their inability to communicate with the outside world. Today, many deaf people are equipped with hearing aids that enable them to function almost as well as those without hearing problems. Are the laws regarding the deaf still operative?

Halakhah demands that the blood be removed from meat either by soaking and salting, or by roasting over a fire. Are chemical substances with properties similar to those of salt acceptable for this purpose? Can the same end be realized through other physical means (heat, radiation)?

Man's vision has improved since telescopes and microscopes were invented. Through television, one can see items located far away from him. One can hear voices from afar by telephone. Where the *halakhah* demands actual seeing (e.g., the new MOON, eyewitness testimony, etc.) or hearing (the sounding of the SHOFAR, the reading of the Scroll of Esther, etc.), does this include seeing or hearing by technological means? According to oral tradition TEFILLIN boxes must be square. What appears to be square may be found to be somewhat different when one employs the more refined measuring instruments now available. In previous times, decisions as to whether a stain was menstrual blood or not depended on visual inspection. May chemical and physical analysis now be used to make this determination?

Modern technology has expanded the concept of writing. Today, one can "write" on magnetic tape and computer diskettes. Is it forbidden to erase God's Name if it is "written" in one of these forms, just as it is forbidden to do so when the name appears on paper?

In earlier times, a person's reliability could be determined only by the testimony of a disinterested third party. Since the polygraph was invented, rabbinic authorities have debated how much such a device may be relied upon.

Previously, the date and the time in which a person found himself seemed to be absolute. It was impossible to be in two different time zones simultaneously. Modern technology has blurred this distinction. It enables a person to act from one time zone to another, so that, for example, he can send a facsimile during daylight hours to a place where night has already fallen. In previous times, "travel" was either by land or sea. Today it encompasses air and space travel as well. Do these new forms of travel require the recitation of the PRAYER BEFORE A JOURNEY? Space travel involves many potential challenges to the observant Jew.

The systems of measurement have also changed. *Halakhah* often measures time by distance, as, for example, in regard to the length of a journey that would obligate one to recite the Prayer before a Journey. The same is true of the distance a person may travel from his home on the Sabbath. Today, such distances can be traversed in a very short time. Does that mean that the halakhic requirements have also changed?

Modern man uses substances not available to his ancestors. Do the laws applied to glass apply also to modern materials such as Duralex, Pyrex, etc.? The laws of ritual PURITY AND IMPURITY acquired new dimensions once man began using synthetic fibers. In each of these questions debates have been based on the comparisons to be drawn between the new situations produced by technology and the principles of *halakhah*.

Electricity also plays a role in the question of assistance by technological means. The time clock, for example, is used for lighting, cooking (preserving the heat of hot foods), etc. on the Sabbath. Various technological means (electricity and pneumatics) aid in the milking of cows on the Sabbath, thus enabling religious farmers in Israel to enter the dairy industry. The possibility of recording things in different fashions has also enabled places where such notation is essential, such as hospitals or police stations, to find ways of recording crucial information on the Sabbath. In many cases, it is possible to isolate the involvement of the individual from the electrical action which he performs, so that in halakhic terms he will not be considered to have performed that action. A number of devices have been developed to take advantage of this isolation.

The mass production of items has greatly aided the observant population in such areas as the baking of unleavened bread or the weaving of *tsitsit*, etc. The ease with which merchandise can be shipped has also been of great assistance, enabling far-flung communities to obtain items, such as citrons (*etrogim*), that were hitherto unobtainable. Improved transport has also aided in making *kasher* food available. Bills of DIVORCE are transferred across oceans.

Technology has made it possible to avoid the need to violate *halakhah*. The electric shaver permitted many to shave without violating the prohibitions involved in using a razor. The developments in medical science have aided greatly in combating infertility. Women who in former eras would have been unable to conceive because their fertile period was during the time when they were required to abstain from sexual relations may find a solution through the use of hormones which alter the menstrual cycle. The manufacture of plastic dishes has eliminated the need for immersion in a ritual bath before use, as must be done with dishes and pots of metal, glass, or pottery manufactured by non-Jews.

The technology of X-ray and of portable pumps has made it easier to determine whether an animal or fowl is *terefah*. Sifting machines and crop dusting keep insects and rodents out of food. Crops which were once annuals have now been made perennials through artificial means, thus aiding in the observance of the SABBATICAL YEAR. The computerized optical reader helps to identify errors in Torah scrolls.

The development of printing in general and of the offset press especially has made it easier for the masses to study Torah. The various forms of communication have also helped to bring the word of Torah to places where it was never heard before. Computerized systems now make it easier to find relevant halakhic texts on any topic.

HALAKHAH LE-MOSHEH MI-SINAI ("A law [given] to Moses at Sinai"). Various laws and ordinances which, though not found in the Pentateuch or directly derived from it, have a reputed Mosaic origin and authority. The term occurs three times in the Mishnah and is used frequently in talmudic sources. The sages understood it literally to mean that such regulations were communicated by God to Moses at the Sinaitic revelation; Moses was then instructed to transmit them orally (see ORAL LAW) and not to incorporate them in the WRITTEN LAW. Many of these ordinances supplement biblical commandments. For example, a large number have to do with the design and making of phylacteries (TEFILLIN; see *Er.* 97a, *Men.* 35a); others indicate the defects which render a slaughtered beast TEREFAH (*Ḥul.* 42a) or discuss observances connected with the WATER-DRAWING FESTIVAL (*Suk.* 34a). There was no general agreement among the sages, however, as to which particular laws fell under this category. According to the Talmud, any legal innovation by a diligent scholar had already been "given to Moses at Sinai" and this also applied to laws whose Scriptural basis was questionable. MAIMONIDES (*Yad, Tefillin* 1.6-8) later declared that the types of parchment used in preparing *mezuzot, tefillin*, and Torah scrolls had a *halakhah le-Mosheh mi-Sinai* authorization. Despite ambiguities and discrepancies, any law so described is usually not subject to further dispute. In the opinion of some medieval authorities, the term *halakhah le-Mosheh mi-Sinai* was not meant to be taken literally but used to describe a time-honored Jewish rule or custom.

HALAKHOT GEDOLOT AND HALAKHOT PESUKOT The first two major codes of rabbinic law, written in Babylonia during the geonic period and containing the earliest systematic digest of the HALAKHAH. Attributed to Yehudai Gaon, the *Halakhot Pesukot* ("Decided Laws," c. 760) dealt with practical rules and observances governing the Sabbath, festivals, etc., its concise presentation of the talmudic *halakhot* being especially useful to remote Jewish communities. The original Aramaic text was soon translated into Hebrew under the title of *Hilkhot Re'u*, as its starting point was tractate ERUVIN and its opening sentence a verse from Exodus (16:29): "See [*Re'u*], the Lord has given you the Sabbath..." On the basis of this pioneering work, other summaries of talmudic legislation were compiled, notably the *Halakhot Gedolot* ("Great [Code of] Laws," c. 825). Its precise date and authorship are still disputed, although the *Halakhot Gedolot* may well have been compiled by Simeon Kayyara in the Babylonian academy of Sura. While chiefly based on the Talmud of Babylon, it also quoted the Jerusalem Talmud and other sources (e.g., geonic responsa), dealing with both practical *halakhah* and laws that had ceased to be applicable after the Temple's destruction. Evidently aimed against the KARAITES, this was the first work of its type to contain introductory aggadic material and a detailed list of the 613 COMMANDMENTS. There are two recensions of the *Halakhot Gedolot*: one transmitted from Babylonia to France and Germany, which was later printed in Venice (1584); and another, much amplified, which spread to North Africa, Spain, and Italy. A third work, entitled *Halakhot Ketsuvot* ("Accepted Laws," c. 860), was an abridgment of the *Halakhot Pesukot* written in southern Italy. Unlike the other two codes, this was written in Hebrew; known to the pupils of RASHI, it has the distinction of being the earliest European work on *halakhah*, reflecting the customs and everyday life of Italian Jewry. See also CODIFICATION.

ḤALITSAH See LEVIRATE MARRIAGE

ḤALLAH (1) Portion of dough which, in accordance with biblical law, had to be set aside as a gift to the priests (Num. 15:18-21); (2) Sabbath loaf of bread. Though decreed for all time, the law of "the first yield of your baking" was regarded by the sages as applying to the Jewish community in the Land of Israel and not binding on Jews in the Diaspora (*Ket.* 25a). Since ancient times, however, the practice of "separating the dough" has been maintained by observant Jews throughout the world in order to keep alive its import and remembrance. The term *ḥallah* denotes a loaf or "cake" of baked BREAD in various Scriptural passages (e.g., Ex. 29:23, Lev. 24:5, II Sam. 6:19). Traditionally, it is also the name given to the special loaves, made from white flour and usually plaited, for Sabbaths and festivals.

The *ḥallah* regulations apply only to dough prepared from

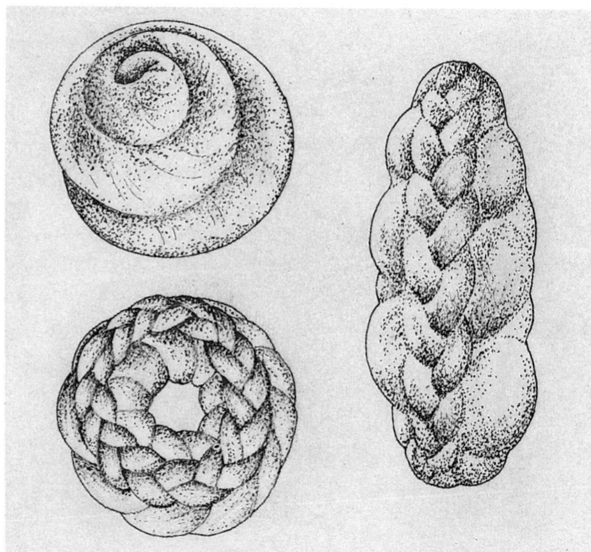

Special loaves of bread (ḥallot), *for Sabbaths and festivals.*

one of the FIVE SPECIES of grain — wheat, barley, spelt, oats, or rye; other grains (e.g., maize) and rice or potato flour are therefore exempt from this law. Separation of the dough should take place immediately after it is kneaded, failing which it may be taken from the newly baked bread. The precise volume of dough subject to the laws of *ḥallah* cannot be determined from the Bible and was only indicated by the rabbis. They laid down that a baker must set aside 1/48th part of his dough, while the housewife (who prepares a smaller amount) must separate 1/24th. From the calculations made by later authorities it appears that dough weighing 1.25 kg. (about 2 lb 12 oz) and upward requires the *ḥallah* separation.

For reasons connected with the laws of PURITY AND IMPURITY, *ḥallah* is no longer given to Jews of priestly descent. Instead, a piece the size of an olive is separated from any portion of dough to be baked, boiled, or fried, and that small piece is then thrown into the fire. "Taking the *ḥallah*" has long been a prerogative of the Jewish housewife. Should the quantity of dough for baking only amount to 1.75 kg (about 3 lb 12 oz), a prescribed benediction must also be recited: "Blessed are You, Lord our God, King of the universe, who has sanctified us with His commandments and commanded us to separate *ḥallah* from the dough." Before burning it, some add: "Behold, this is *ḥallah*." All applicable laws are contained in tractate ḤALLAH.

ḤALLAH ("Portion of dough"). Ninth tractate of Order ZERA'IM in the Mishnah (cf. Num. 15:17-21). Its four chapters deal with the laws of separating the priest's share from one's dough, whether bread is baked privately or commercially (see ḤALLEL above). The Mishnah discusses the FIVE SPECIES of grain which are subject to *ḥallel*, the minimum quantity of dough from which the priest's share must be separated, the use of imported grain, and the consumption of *ḥallel* by the priest in a state of ritual purity. The subject matter is amplified in the Jerusalem Talmud and in the *Tosefta*.

HALLEL ("Praise"). Term denoting those hymns of thanksgiving and praise to God, taken from the Book of PSALMS, which form part of the liturgy on festive occasions. Three varieties of *Hallel* have been recited since ancient times:

1. **Hallel ha-Gadol** ("The Great *Hallel*"), which according to the Talmud (*Pes.* 118a) comprises the 136th chapter of Psalms. Its 26 verses are said to parallel the 26 generations of mankind from the Creation to the Giving of the Law on Mount Sinai, and each verse ends with the refrain, "His steadfast love is eternal" (*ki le-olam ḥasdo*; see below). This "Great *Hallel*" is recited in the "Passages of Song" (PESUKÉ DE-ZIMRA), at the beginning of Morning Service, on Sabbaths and festivals; as an additional psalm for the last day of Passover; and as part of the *Haggadah* on the first "*Seder*" night(s) of Passover. In Mishnaic times, it was also recited when supplicatory prayers for rain had been answered.

2. **Hallel** proper, also known as "full *Hallel*" and on Passover eve as *Hallel ha-Mitsri* ("The Egyptian *Hallel*," since Ps. 114 refers to the Exodus), consisting of Ps. 113-118. From early rabbinic times, this has been the standard version of *Hallel*.

3. **Ḥatsi Hallel** ("Half-*Hallel*"), a shortened form of the above, omitting the first 11 verses of Ps. 115 and 116. The Yemenite "half-*Hallel*" also omits the two verses of Ps. 117, a practice based on Maimonides (*Yad, Ḥanukkah* 3.8).

Religious Significance: Although there is no certainty as to why tradition chose these particular psalms for *Hallel*, their theological content as well as their literary structure make them especially appropriate for recitation on festive occasions and at times of deliverance from crisis. The major ideas contained in the sequence are as follows:

Psalm 113: God's Name should be praised forever and everywhere. While enthroned on high, God displays His concern for the lowly, the childless, for each individual.

Psalm 114: God acts for His people and nature responds. The (Reed) Sea parted at the Exodus from Egypt and the Jordan also responded at the entrance into Canaan. Mountains "skipped" and trembled at His presence. It was He who turned solid rock into pools of water.

Psalm 115: Our God is all-powerful, whereas the gods of the nations are lifeless idols. All Israel should trust in the Lord; He, in turn, will bless them. The dead cannot praise the Lord, but we the living can.

Psalm 116: God is compassionate, hearing the prayers of the simple and lowly, delivering those afflicted by death, trouble, and sorrow. How can individuals respond to God's goodness? — By invoking His Name, by bringing sacrificial offerings, by doing so in the presence of all His people, in Jerusalem.

Psalm 117: The steadfast love of God for His people should motivate all nations to praise and extol Him.

Psalm 118: All Israel should proclaim God's steadfast love. When the Lord is with me, I have nothing to fear. My enemies test me, so does God, but my faith does not waver. Open the Temple gates for me, since this is the day that the Lord has made. I will enter and praise the Lord for He is good, and His steadfast love is eternal.

Origin of Hallel: Rabbinic tradition credits King David with having written almost all of the Psalms, including those which now make up *Hallel*. R. Eleazar ben Yosé, however, ascribed *Hallel* to Moses and the Israelites; while R. Judah taught that the prophets had decreed that these psalms be recited to mark national events and deliverance from peril. Other sages maintained that *Hallel* was recited by various leaders of Israel throughout the biblical period — by Joshua, Deborah, and Hezekiah, by Hananiah, Mishael, and Azariah, by Mordecai and Esther (*Pes.* 117a-118a).

In Second Temple times, *Hallel* was recited while the paschal sacrifices were taking place and during the Passover *Seder* ritual (*Pes.* 5.7, 10.5-7).

Prescribed Occasions: Neither "full *Hallel*" nor "half-*Hallel*" is recited on:

a. A regular Sabbath: the Sabbath is not considered a festival.

b. Rosh ha-Shanah and the Day of Atonement: "When the King sits on His throne on the Day of Judgment, and the Books of Life and Death are open before Him, is it appropriate for Israel to sing joyous songs?" (*Ar.* 10b).

c. Purim: (1) The Scroll of Esther replaces *Hallel*; (2) The Jewish people, though saved from immediate danger, remained in subjugation to Persia; (3) The miraculous deliverance took place outside of Erets Israel (*Meg.* 14a).

d. New Moon or during Ḫanukkah in a house of mourning: Hymns of praise and thanksgiving are inappropriate on such occasions.

"Full *Hallel*" is recited, according to the Babylonian Talmud (*Ta'an.* 28b), on 18 days each year in the Land of Israel: on the eight days of Sukkot (including Shemini Atseret), the eight days of Ḫanukkah, on Shavu'ot, and on the first day of Passover. It is recited on 21 days each year in the Diaspora: on the nine days of Sukkot (including Shemini Atseret-Simḫat Torah), on the eight days of Ḫanukkah, on both days of Shavu'ot, and on the first two days of Passover. "Full Hallel" is also recited during the *Seder* on Passover and (according to Sephardi and Israeli Ashkenazi practice) at the conclusion of the Evening Service preceding the *Seder*. The biblical verse, "For you, there shall be singing as on a night when a festival is hallowed" (Isa. 30:29), is applied to Passover eve, the only "night when a festival is hallowed" in the religious calendar.

"Half-*Hallel*" is recited, in accordance with a Babylonian practice that was later generally accepted (*Ta'an.* 28b), on days when the New Moon is celebrated. "Half-*Hallel*" is also said on the latter days of Passover, even though "full *Hallel*" is recited on the latter days of Sukkot-Shemini Atseret. Two reasons are given: (1) The Torah prescribes a different sacrifice for each day of Sukkot; each day therefore merits its own *Hallel*. Each day of Passover has the same sacrifice, however, so one *Hallel* is sufficient (*Ar.* 10b). (2) After the Exodus, when the Egyptians were perishing in the Reed Sea, God prevented the angels from rejoicing with words of rebuke (*Meg.* 10b); also, "if your enemy falls, do not exult" (Prov. 24:17).

Briefly stated, the general rule is as follows:

No *Hallel* is recited on days when there is no pilgrimage to Jerusalem: Sabbath, Rosh ha-Shanah, Day of Atonement, and Purim.

"Full *Hallel*" is recited on festivals associated with a pilgrimage to Jerusalem and/or dedication of the Temple: the first day(s) of Passover and all the days of Sukkot, Shavu'ot, and Ḫanukkah.

"Half-*Hallel*" is recited on the latter days of Passover, because the people left Jerusalem after the first day and observed the last days at home (see Deut. 16:7). It is also recited on the New Moon in accordance with Babylonian practice.

Israel's Chief Rabbinate has ruled that "full *Hallel*," with the appropriate benedictions, should be recited on Israel's Independence Day (5 Iyyar) and on the anniversary of the Reunification of Jerusalem (28 Iyyar). This practice is followed by most Orthodox, as well as Conservative and Reform congregations. Some Orthodox congregations (both Ashkenazi and Sephardi-Eastern) recite *Hallel*, but omit the benedictions; anti-Zionist congregations do not recite *Hallel* on either date.

Hallel, whether "full" or abbreviated, may be said at any time during the festive day, but the general custom is to recite it between the Morning Service *Amidah* and the Reading of the Law. One may do so, however, without attending a *minyan* for public worship. Those Ashkenazim who wear *tefillin* on the intermediate days of Passover and Sukkot (chiefly in the Diaspora) remove them before reciting *Hallel*. According to Orthodox practice, women are obligated to say *Hallel* at the Passover *Seder*, but not otherwise. Most authorities agree, however, that a woman who accepts the obligation of this *mitsvah* can recite *Hallel* with its prescribed

The word Hallel *decorated with stylized foliage. From the* Saul Raskin Haggadah.

benedictions. This is also the position of the Conservative movement. Reform Judaism makes no distinction between men and women in regard to saying *Hallel.*

Mode of Recitation: There is good reason to believe that, in Temple times, a levitical choir sang *Hallel* responsively (*Tosef. Sot.* 6.2; cf. *Tos.* to *Pes.* 95b). Later traditions differed, Yemenite Jews having retained the ancient practice whereby the congregation repeats each verse after the reader and then responds "Hallelujah" (*Suk.* 3.10). In other (Sephardi and Ashkenazi) congregations, verse sequences from Ps. 118 are repeated by the worshipers. Many Ashkenazi synagogues throughout the world favor congregational singing of various passages, as well as solo renditions by the cantor or set pieces by the choir. Psalm 118:1 traditionally serves as a congregational response to each of the following three verses, and Ps. 118:25 is extended to four lines chanted responsively. On Sukkot, the *lulav* and *etrog* (FOUR SPECIES) are waved when Ps. 118:1-4, 25, and 29 are recited.

It is customary to stand during *Hallel,* except when it forms part of the *Seder* home service. Ashkenazi Jews pronounce a benediction before and after *Hallel* whenever it is recited, the first benediction concluding with the words *li-kro et ha-Hallel* ("to read the *Hallel*"). According to general Sephardi-Eastern practice, however, this wording is changed to *li-gmor et ha-Hallel* ("to complete the *Hallel*") and neither benediction may be recited when "half-*Hallel*" only is read.

HALLELUJAH Biblical expression found only in the Book of PSALMS and meaning "Praise the Lord!" (*halelu-Yah*). An exclamation of joy, praise, or thanksgiving, it occurs in 13 psalms either as the opening word (111, 112), or the closing word (104, 105, 115-117), or both (106, 113, 135, 146-150). Its original purpose, in Temple times, was to signal that a congregational response should be given to the levitical choir. Each verse of the HALLEL psalms was likewise answered by *halelu-Yah* (*Suk.* 3.10), and this may also have characterized the sequence culminating in the "Grand Hallelujah" (Ps. 150). Like AMEN, the Hebrew term entered the Jewish prayer book and also became part of the Christian tradition, finding its way into many languages.

ḤALUKKAH ("distribution"). Financial assistance given to Jews in the Holy Land by their fellow-Jews in the Diaspora, especially from the end of the 18th century following the Ḥasidic immigration.

The practise of sending support to Jews in Erets Israel dates back to the early Second Temple period (Ezra 1:6, 8:33), and continued through all periods of Jewish settlement in the Land. Leading rabbis left their homes in Erets Israel to travel all over the Jewish world to seek support for the Torah scholars in the Holy Land. Thus *ḥalukkah* played a major role in the maintenance of a living relationship between Erets Israel and the Diaspora.

From the 16th century, organized methods were instituted to collect contributions from various communities in central Europe which were transferred to Erets Israel through major commercial centers. Money was often collected by means of charity boxes named for R. MEIR BA'AL HA-NES ("Meir the Miracle Worker").

From the late 18th century *ḥalukkah* was a major factor in maintaining the new Ḥasidic immigrants as well as the *Perushim* settlers (followers of R. ELIJAH GAON OF VILNA) from the early 19th century. The donations were distributed in the four HOLY CITIES of Jerusalem, Tiberias, Safed, and Hebron. The Ashkenazi community divided itself into small organizations, or KOLELIM, based on places of origin, primarily out of economic considerations. By 1913 there were 26 *kolelim* in Jerusalem.

The importance of *ḥalukkah* diminished with the growth of the modern Zionist movement and support became limited to the circles of the old-time settlers. Today Orthodox Jews still send considerable funds to *kolelim* to maintain rabbinical scholars and academies, especially among the non-Zionist elements.

HA-MAVDIL See HAVDALAH

ḤAMETS Leaven, which Jews are forbidden to have in their homes or possession from the end of the first third of the day preceding PASSOVER until the conclusion of the festival. The prohibition is explained as a commemoration of the night of the EXODUS from Egypt when the Children of Israel left in haste and no time remained for the dough they were baking to rise (Ex. 12:39). The Bible establishes that any person eating leaven during the period of the Passover festival "shall be cut off from his people" (Ex. 12:15). Technically speaking, there are two separate substances which are forbidden: *se'or* — leavening agents (sour dough starter); and *ḥamets* — any product containing flour which has been permitted to ferment. *Ḥamets* includes not only bread but cakes and other baked goods, as well as pasta in all its forms. The prohibition also includes products which contain any of the above as ingredients. The ban refers to all dough made from the FIVE SPECIES of grain: wheat, barley, rye, spelt and oats. According to most views, whiskey is also regarded as *ḥamets,* for it is made by fermenting grain. Before Passover, *ḥamets* in the home is gradually removed, and on the night before Passover, the head of the household searches for any remaining *ḥamets* (see LEAVEN, SEARCH FOR). Any *ḥamets* remaining in the home is burned on the morning before Passover. For those to whom the disposal of *ḥamets* would entail a considerable hardship, provisions are available whereby the *ḥamets* is sold to a non-Jew for the duration of the prohibited time. If any amount of *ḥamets* whatsoever falls into Passover food, the entire dish becomes forbidden on Passover. Leaven was also forbidden in meal-offerings in the Temple.

HA-MOTSI See BREAD; GRACE BEFORE MEALS

HANNAH AND HER SEVEN SONS See APOCRYPHA

ḤANUKKAH ("Dedication"). Festival celebrated for eight days commencing on 25 Kislev, commemorating the victory of the traditionalist Maccabees (see HASMONEANS) over the Hellenistic Syrians who attempted to eradicate the Jewish religion as part of their plan to hellenize their entire kingdom. The main events associated with Ḥanukkah took place between 165 and 163 BCE, although the Maccabees continued a military struggle with the Syrians for many years until the Jews of Erets Israel had gained *de facto* independence. Ḥanukkah is thus a post-biblical festival, and the historical events it commemorates are described in the apocryphal First Book of the Maccabees (see APOCRYPHA AND PSEUDEPIGRAPHA). It is not a full festival and there are no restrictions on work or other activities.

The Greeks took various steps to achieve their goal, among them the desecration of the TEMPLE in Jerusalem. I Maccabees (4.36-59) reports that the altar had been defiled, the Syrian ruler, Antiochus Epiphanes, having commanded that sacrifices to pagan gods be offered on it. After a three-year struggle, the Maccabees under Judah Maccabee conquered Jerusalem, and demolished and rebuilt the defiled altar. They also produced new vessels for the Temple service, including a candelabrum, an altar for incense, a table, and curtains. According to a talmudic tradition, a small quantity of consecrated oil, for use in the candelabrum (MENORAH), was found within the Temple precincts (*Shab.* 21b). Although it was only enough to burn for one day, the oil lasted for eight days, and the festival was established for this length of time to commemorate the miracle. The Books of Maccabees do not record this tradition. In the Second Book of the Maccabees, it is noted that the eight-day festival was instituted by Judah upon his rededicating the Temple, according to the precedent of SOLOMON's eight-day dedication of the First Temple. Some scholars have advanced the theory that the festival was established for eight days owing to the Jews' inability to observe the eight-day festival of SUKKOT during the fighting. With the Maccabean victory, this omission was rectified, and a celebration was held that

Kindling of Lights. *Painting by Moritz Oppenheim, showing a family lighting a Ḥanukkah lamp at the window of their home.*

combined Sukkot with thanksgiving for the victory and the rededication of the Temple.

The main observance of Ḥanukkah is the kindling of the festival lamp (*ḥanukkiyyah*) each night of the holiday. This practice gave the festival the additional name of *Ḥag ha-Urim*, "the festival of lights." The Talmud explains the lighting as publicizing the miracle (*pirsumé nissa*; *Shab.* 23b) and in ancient times the lamp was put in the doorway or even in the street outside the house for this purpose. The lighting takes place immediately after dark except on Friday evenings, when it must be done before the kindling of the Sabbath lights, i.e., approximately half an hour before sunset. The CANDLES are meant to burn for at least one half hour and must be kindled in a conspicuous place. They may be lit any time during the night as long as someone other than the lighter will see them. The practice of kindling the lights appears not to have been instituted until many years after the events which it commemorates.

The accepted procedure for kindling the Ḥanukkah lights is to light one candle (or oil lamp) on the first night and one additional candle each night (going from left to right), until the last night when eight candles are lit (kindling them from left to right). An alternate tradition is recorded whereby eight candles are lit on the first night, seven on the second, and so forth, until only one candle is lit on the eighth night. An additional candle called the *shammash* ("serving light") is used to kindle the other lights. The practice is essentially a home ceremony, but candles are lit also in the synagogue. Children are usually given a gift of money (*hanukkah gelt*) for the festival.

Hanukkah is expressed in the liturgy in a number of ways, the most important being the introduction of the AL HA-NISSIM prayer in the AMIDAH and GRACE AFTER MEALS. HALLEL is recited at the Morning Service, and there is a special READING OF THE LAW each day of the festival. A Hanukkah hymn, MA'OZ TSUR, written in the 13th century, is very popular in the home and synagogue, and is sung in Ashkenazi communities after the kindling of the lights. The Sephardi practice is to read Psalm 30.

HANUKKAH
FESTIVAL OF DEDICATION

Other Names: *Hag ha-Urim* (Festival of Lights)

Hebrew Dates: 25 Kislev — 3 Tevet

Torah & Prophetical Readings:

Weekday portions from: Num. 7:1-8:4
1st Sabbath: prescribed Torah reading and *Maftir*, Zech. 2:14-4:7 (*Haftarah*)
2nd Sabbath (if relevant): prescribed Torah reading and *Maftir*, I Kings 7:40-50 (*Haftarah*)
Hallel: recited daily (in full); Hanukkah lights kindled each evening

Civil dates on which the festival occurs, 1990-2010:

1990/5751	12-19 December
1991/5752	2-9 December
1992/5753	20-27 December
1993/5754	9-16 December
1994/5755	28 November-5 December
1995/5756	18-25 December
1996/5757	6-13 December
1997/5758	24-31 December
1999/5759	14-21 December
1999/5760	4-11 December
2000/5761	22-29 December
2001/5762	10-17 December
2002/5763	30 November-7 December
2003/5764	20-27 December
2004/5765	8-15 December
2005/5766	26 December-1 January
2006/5767	16-23 December
2007/5768	5-12 December
2008/5769	22-29 December
2009/5770	12-19 December
2010/5771	2-9 December

It has become customary to hold Hanukkah parties with songs and games, especially for children. The best-known of the Hanukkah games is the *dreydel*, a spinning top used for a kind of "put and take" game. The *dreydel* is inscribed for this purpose on its four sides with the Hebrew letters, *nun, gimmel, hé, shin*, an acrostic for the words *nes gadol hayah sham* ("a great miracle happened there"). Presumably because of the association with oil, it has become popular to eat *latkes* (potato pancakes) and *sufganiyyot* (doughnuts).

In modern Israel Hanukkah has become an occasion when the theme of national courage is underlined, since it was this quality which gained the Jews of the Maccabean period their independence. In recognition of the heroism and battlefield prowess of the Maccabees, a torch is carried from their traditional burial site at Modi'in, located between Jerusalem and Tel Aviv, to various points throughout the country. In many Diaspora countries, especially the US, Hanukkah has received a previously unknown emphasis, largely to compensate the Jewish child for the overwhelming impact of Christmas in his surroundings.

HANUKKAH LAMP (*hanukkiyyah*, also known as the Hanukkah MENORAH). Eight-branched candlelabrum ritually lit in celebration of HANUKKAH. According to the Talmud and artefacts from the Greco-Roman period, it originally took the form of either clay, ceramic, or metal oil lamps mounted on an elongated vertical base, or one circular lamp with eight apertures in the shape of a pointed star. The lights of the Hanukkah lamp are not permitted to burn into a single flame, but must be distinguishable one from the other (*Shab.* 23b). The Hanukkah lamp was originally placed outside the entrance of the house, to the left of the door, in order to proclaim publicly the miracle of the holiday (*Shab.* 23b, *Sof.* 20.3). Glass lanterns, in Mishnaic, talmudic and apostolic sources, protected the lamp from the winter winds and rains, in ancient Israel and Babylonia.

As a result of the prohibition against using old clay lamps for Hanukkah (*Sof.* 20.3), an Ashkenazi eight-spout metal Hanukkah lamp and a Sephardi glazed ceramic one developed during the Middle Ages (*Tur, OH* 673). In Spain, the tradition began of introducing a back-wall, from which the lamp was hung, sometimes with an extra one, the *shammash* or "server," standing in the middle or to the left. If danger was involved in placing the lamp outside, the rabbis permitted its lighting inside the home where it was hung at the entrance on the doorpost opposite the MEZUZAH. For this reason, many Hanukkah lamps have been found with the inscription "Blessed shall you be in your coming and blessed shall you be in your going" (Deut. 28:6). In Germany, the custom arose of constructing a lamp in the form of a star and hanging it near the door for Hanukkah and using it as a Sabbath lamp during the rest of the year. The German Jews were also the first to use an eight-branched standing candelabrum, especially in synagogues, inspired by the Temple *menorah*; a ninth socket was added for the *shammash* from which the other lights were lit. The Polish custom was to place the lamp on the windowsill or on a table during the lighting ceremony. Throughout the Jewish world, the Ḫanukkah lamp became an object of rich embellishment, artistic creativity, and fine craftsmanship.

Since CANDLES have been used, they are put in from right to left — one on the first night, two on the second, etc. (following the view of the School of Hillel as against the followers of Shammai who put in eight on the first night and decreased by one every successive evening). The candles themselves are lit from left to right.

ḪAROSET See SEDER

HASHKAVAH See MEMORIAL SERVICES

HASHKIVENU ("Cause us to lie down [in peace]"). Opening word of the second benediction after the *Shema* in the daily Evening Service. According to the Talmud (*Ber.* 4b), it serves to extend the preceding Redemption prayer, EMET VE-EMUNAH. However, whereas the previous blessing concentrates on the past and future salvation of Israel, *Hashkivenu* emphasizes man's helplessness (particularly while asleep) and begs for Divine protection to ward off physical or spiritual danger. Two versions of *Hashkivenu* found a place in the liturgy: a Babylonian text that concludes with the benediction "Who guards His people Israel forever," and a slightly longer Palestinian formula concluding "Who spreads the shelter of peace over us, over all His people Israel, and over Jerusalem" (TJ *Ber.* 4.5). Since geonic times, the first has been recited on weekdays and the second on Sabbaths and festivals. Minor differences, concerning both the text and the word order, have emerged in the various rites. There are several musical settings of *Hashkivenu*; the outstanding example is Louis Lewandowski's *Ve-Hagen ba'adenu* ("Be our shield"), a 19th-century composition for cantor and choir.

> Enable us, O Lord our God, to lie down peacefully [in sleep] and awaken us again, our King, to life. Spread over us the shelter of Your peace; set us aright with Your good counsel; and save us for Your Name's sake...

ḪASIDÉ ASHKENAZ ("the pious men of Franco-Germany" or ASHKENAZI Ḫasidim"). The term "Ashkenazi Ḫasidism" denotes several groups of Jewish scholars who flourished in Germany in the second half of the 12th century and the first half of the 13th, and created new concepts in Jewish thought, mysticism, and ethics. This was not a movement, there was no organized effort, nor a clear concept of spiritual leadership, and often one group was not aware of the existence of the others. Yet, together, they changed the character of Jewish culture in Germany and comprise one of the most important original contributions of Ashkenazi Jewry in these fields in the Middle Ages. They wrote their work under the traumatic impact of the repeated massacres of Ashkenazi Jewry by the Crusaders, which started in 1096 and continued throughout the 12th century. The reaction to these persecutions is recognizable in many of their ideas.

From a historical point of view, the most important contribution of the Ashkenazi Ḫasidim to Jewish culture was in the field of ETHICS, but THEOLOGY was their main concern and their efforts were directed at solving some of the most complex theosophical problems facing Judaism at that time. They were the first in the Jewish Middle Ages to present a concept of the Divine world in which several powers together comprise the Divine unity; separate Divine powers fulfill different functions, according to their various theological systems. Thus they preceded the kabbalists in presenting Judaism with a multi-faceted concept of the Divine realm.

Ashkenazi Ḫasidim saw themselves (like the KABBALAH) as continuing and commenting on ancient traditions, rather than as innovators. For several generations before the end of the 12th century, theological and mystical matters were discussed orally in the schools of Ashkenazi rabbis, secrets being transmitted from rabbi to disciple. Their main source of influence was the literature of the ancient Jewish mystics of the talmudic period, the HEKHALOT AND MERKAVAH MYSTICISM, which they preserved, paraphrased, and commented upon. They also sought more direct sources, claiming, for instance, that many of their secrets were received from R. Aaron ben Samuel of Baghdad, also known as Abu Aharon, who visited the Kalonymus family in southern Italy probably in the eighth century, and brought Babylonian traditions to this school; when the Kalonymus family migrated to Mainz in the ninth century, the secrets continued to be transmitted from generation to generation.

The first writer of this school was R. Samuel ben Kalonymus he-Ḫasid (the Pious), in the mid-12th century, who was followed by his son, JUDAH HE-ḪASID. The most important writer of this group was the latter's disciple, ELEAZAR OF WORMS. These last two scholars were the first to write detailed commentaries on the Jewish prayer book.

Besides this central school of the Kalonymus family, other groups produced theological and mystical treatises. Around 1200 an anonymous writer composed *Sefer ha-Ḫayyim* ("The Book of Life"), an original theological work relying on the work of Abraham IBN EZRA, and combining mysticism, science, and a system of ethics. Another anonymous work unrelated to any school is the *Sefer ha-Navon*, a commentary on the SHEMA, which also includes a commentary on the *Shi'ur Komah*, the ancient work of mysticism describing the parts of the Divine supreme figure anthropomorphically. Another school which produced theological works for two or three generations relied on a pseudepigraphic treatise called "*Mishnat Yosef ben Uzziel*" ("The Teaching of Joseph, son of Uzziel"). This work is based on the ancient *Sefer* YETSIRAH, describing the creation in a combination of scientific and mystical terms. The work is attributed to Joseph ben Uzziel, who is described as the great-grandson of Ben Sira, who was, according to medieval literary traditions, the son of the prophet Jeremiah. Thus this school could base its speculations on a tradition claiming to go back to biblical times. A prominent writer of this school was R. Elhanan ben Yakar, who wrote two commentaries on the *Sefer Yetsirah* and a work called *Sod ha-Sodot* ("The Secret of Secrets"), in London in the 13th century.

These theologians and mystics were interested mainly in the two basic phenomena of Divine revelation: prophecy and prayer. The most perplexing problem facing their theology was the impossibility that a supreme God, eternal and unchanging, could reveal Himself to prophets or make decisions when listening to prayers. Their solution was to describe secondary Divine powers, especially the Divine Glory, which were revealed to the prophets and heard and answered individual prayers.

The Hasidé Ashkenaz fiercely opposed philosophy, and probably participated in the conflict between rationalists and traditionalists in the 13th century on the side of the traditionalists. Nevertheless they accepted some philosophical notions, and relied heavily on SAADIAH GAON's *Emunot ve-De' ot* in its ancient, poetic paraphrase.

The most important work of ethics to emerge from the schools of the Ashkenazi Hasidim is the *Sefer Hasidim* ("The Book of the Pious"), written mainly by R. Judah he-Hasid (d. 1217). This is the most detailed work of ethics written in Judaism in the Middle Ages, and covers every aspect of man's life — family relationships, education, the attitude toward non-Jews, prayer, study, social relationships, and every aspect of religious worship. The main message of the work is that religious life, dedicated to a spiritual God, should be spiritual and that man is judged by his spiritual efforts, not by his material deeds. The commandments of the Torah and the ethical demands placed before man are tests: can he overcome his human nature and endure every hardship in order to fulfill God's commands? The more effort required to perform a precept, the more meaningful it is. Every sin includes an element of pleasure, which has to be atoned for by self-inflicted suffering, described in the detailed Ashkenazi-Hasidic literature dedicated to repentance. Every ethical and religious deed, on the other hand, includes an element of suffering and sacrifice. Thus, the supreme sacrifice, that of KIDDUSH HA-SHEM, giving one's body and soul to God, is also the supreme religious-ethical achievement; but every ethical act is, in miniature, a *Kiddush Ha-Shem*. Thus, Ashkenazi Hasidic ethics may be viewed as a literature intended to educate and prepare every Jew for the trial of *Kiddush Ha-Shem*.

HASIDÉ UMMOT HA-OLAM ("Righteous Gentiles"). Term of rabbinic origin applied to God-fearing non-Jews; it has acquired a special meaning in recent times as a designation for Gentiles who saved Jews during the HOLOCAUST. There are references in the Bible to certain pious Gentiles who observed the Sabbath, honored the Torah, and came from distant lands to worship in the Temple (I Kings 8:41; Isa. 56:6), which was therefore designated "a house of prayer for all peoples." The rabbis called such non-Jews *hasidé ummot ha-olam* — "the pious ones among the nations" who will have a share in the world to come (*Tosef. San.* 13.2; see AFTERLIFE). Allusions to righteous Gentiles can be found throughout rabbinic literature, as well as in the Zohar and Jewish writings of the Middle Ages. Maimonides included among the *hasidé ummot ha-olam* every Gentile embracing the seven NOACHIDE LAWS (*Yad, Melakhim* 8.11). By the medieval period, however, any Christian, Muslim, or other believer who displayed goodwill toward Jews would have been considered a righteous Gentile. This presumably accounts for the grateful mention of those "righteous people of the world" (*tsaddiké ha-olam*) which found its way into the AV HA-RAHAMIM martyrs'dirge recited by Ashkenazim on most Sabbaths.

The Avenue of the Righteous at the Holocaust memorial, Jerusalem, where hasidé ummot ha-olam *are invited to plant trees.*

During the Nazi period, those non-Jews who unhesitatingly risked their own lives in order to save Jews from deportation and mass murder were designated *hasidé ummot ha-olam* and, in the State of Israel, both collective and individual honors have been bestowed on hundreds of deserving recipients by Yad Vashem, the national Martyrs' and Heroes' Remembrance Authority. Within Yad Vashem, a special department investigates non-Jewish rescue activities during the Holocaust and invites such *ḥasidé ummot ha-olam* (translated as "Righteous of the Nations") to plant a tree on the "Avenue of the Righteous" overlooking the western suburbs of Jerusalem. Those honored receive a silver medal, which displays the talmudic adage: "Whoever saves even one life is regarded as having saved the whole world" (*Sanh.* 4.5).

ḤASIDIM RISHONIM ("the pious men of former generations"). Term used in early rabbinic literature to refer to individuals noted for their piety and scrupulous observance of the commandments. The Talmud and Midrash contain numerous references to individuals described as *ḥasidim*. The word *ḥasid* derives from the Hebrew *ḥesed*, "lovingkindness," one of the attributes of God which man is commanded to practice (Ex. 34:6-7). The title seems to refer to the highest possible level of personal piety and *imitatio dei* (see IMITATION OF GOD). One Mishnaic sage declared that the piety of the *ḥasid* leads to Divine inspiration and ultimately to redemption (*Sot.* 9.15), and the *Sifré* to Deut. 11:22 stated that just as God is a *ḥasid*, always doing more than is required, so is man commanded to be a *ḥasid*. The various definitions and accounts relating to such individuals indicate that there was never one universally held definition of the term for all periods. All passages, however, point to behavior that went beyond the letter of the law in at least one area of observance.

It is not known precisely what is meant by "former generations" when referring to *ḥasidim*, although the period seems to have ended by the time of HILLEL (late first cent. BCE). The accounts of the *ḥasidim rishonim* create a picture of complete dedication to the observance of the commandments without regard to danger or expense; avoidance of all acts, even those permitted, that could possibly result in sin; and extreme concern for the welfare of their fellow men. Thus, the Mishnah says that the pious men of former generations always took an hour in preparing for prayer (*Ber.* 5.1). They also gave charity beyond their means; some would cohabit with their wives only on those days that would preclude their wives from giving birth on the Sabbath (even though it is permitted to desecrate the Sabbath for a woman in labor). The pious men were known to bury thorns and broken glass deep in their fields for fear that they would be exposed by plowing and constitute a danger to passersby (*Tosef. BK* 32b).

Early rabbinic literature also refers to *ḥasidim ve-anshé ma'aseh* ("pious men and men of action"). These include Ḥoni the circle-maker, and Ḥanina ben Dosa who lived at the end of the Second Temple period and was the last of the "men of action" (*Sot.* 9.15). The term *ḥasid* continued to be used throughout the talmudic period to describe individuals who displayed exemplary behavior in one or more areas of life.

Despite attempts by various scholars to identify the *ḥasidim rishonim* with the ESSENES or to ascribe to them various roles in the transmission and redaction of the ORAL LAW, they seem to have been exemplary individuals, active only in their own vicinity, who lived extremely modest lives and formed no sect or institutional framework. No *halakhot* are reported in their name.

ḤASIDISM (*Ḥasidut*). Popular revivalist movement founded by Israel ben Eliezer BA'AL SHEM TOV (known generally by his acronym *Besht*) in 18th-century Podolia. Small groups of religio-mystical pneumatics were then active in his part of the Jewish world, pursuing the ideal of *ḥasidut* ("saintliness"), namely, an acute sensitivity to the demands of the religious life. The group that looked upon Israel Ba'al Shem Tov as its spiritual guide was thus one of several, but eventually the rest either vanished from the scene or became submerged in his *ḥavurah kaddisha* ("holy company"). In older Jewish sources, the *ḥasid* is a pietist on a higher level than the TSADDIK, the latter being simply a good and righteous man. In the Ḥasidism of the Ba'al Shem Tov, however, where all the group's members were known as Ḥasidim, the designation *Tsaddik* was used for the saintly mentor, and the roles were reversed. According to a widespread misconception, the doctrine of the *Tsaddik* was a later development in Ḥasidism, but from the Ba'al Shem Tov's lifetime onward Ḥasidism became inseparable from the concept of the holy man who acts as a spiritual mentor to his followers and who prays to God on their behalf.

Two of the Ba'al Shem Tov's disciples, in particular, were responsible for the astonishing successes which this new movement achieved after the master's death in 1760. The first, JACOB JOSEPH OF POLONNOYE, was also the first Ḥasidic author; his work, *Toledot Ya'akov Yosef* (1780), quoted the maxims of the Ba'al Shem Tov and served as the model for a host of later writings in the spirit of Ḥasidism. The second disciple, DOV BAER, the "Maggid" of Mezhirech, deserves to be considered the real founder of the movement. He gathered around him a remarkable group of disciples who were themselves to become Ḥasidic masters in Volhynia, Poland, Russia, and Lithuania. Despite — perhaps even because of — the opposition of the MITNAGGEDIM, traditionalist rabbis and communal leaders who branded Ḥasidic doctrine as rank heresy, the movement expanded so rapidly that by the beginning of the 19th century it had won over perhaps half the Jewish population of Eastern Europe.

"A river flowed out of Eden to water the garden; it then divided and became four branches" (Gen. 2:10). This verse was applied to the spread of Ḥasidism to Poland. "Eden" was the Ba'al Shem Tov; the "river" stood for the Maggid of Mezhirech; the "garden" represented ELIMELECH OF LYZHANSK; and the "four branches" were Menaḥem Mendel of Rymanow, Israel of Kozienice, Meir of Apta (Opatow), and Jacob Isaac, the "Seer" of Lublin. Other preeminent Ḥasidic leaders of this period included LEVI YITSḤAK OF BERDICHEV, NAḤMAN OF BRATSLAV, SHNEUR ZALMAN OF LYADY, and MENAḤEM

MENDEL OF KOTSK. Each *Tsaddik* or *Rebbe* (the title distinguishing this new type of leader from the traditional *Rav*; see also ADMOR) had his own "court," the center to which his own devoted followers journeyed so as to be near him, especially on the festivals. At the earliest stage, a prominent disciple succeeded to the leadership when the *Rebbe* died; later on, however, the sons or near relatives of the *Rebbe* took over the succession, with the result that dynastic *Tsaddikim* became the norm. There were often fierce rivalries between the various Ḥasidic dynasties, and struggles within them over the succession. When Mordecai of Chernobyl died in 1837, each of his eight sons founded a new dynasty, as did his sons-in-law.

For all the novelty of its approach, Ḥasidism is less an entirely new philosophy of Judaism than a number of fresh emphases on certain ideas found in the Bible, talmudic literature, and especially in the Zohar and Kabbalah. The movement has been described as "mysticism for the masses." While there is some truth in this description — Ḥasidism was initially a revolt against dry intellectualism and it did succeed in bringing prayerful joy (SIMḤAH) and intense religious enthusiasm (*hitlahavut*) to ordinary Jews — it conveys only half the picture. There was an elitist side to Ḥasidism from its very inception. Ḥasidism was not only a popular movement; it appealed also, in some versions especially, to the earnest God-seekers willing to be guided by the *Tsaddik* to saintly heights. Considerable tension between these two aims is frequently to be observed in the literature of the movement. On the one hand, it was frequently emphasized that all God demands of the Ḥasid is simple faith; on the other hand, the demands of high, saintly conduct could only have been intended for the few.

Two ideas in particular are common to every version of Ḥasidism: the doctrine of the *Tsaddik* and that of DEVEKUT. Ḥasidism maintains that the *Tsaddik* is the channel through which Divine grace flows. Only through close association with the *Tsaddik* can the Ḥasid approach God. By observing the *Tsaddik*'s conduct, the Ḥasid learns how God is to be worshiped — not only through Torah study and prayer, but also in everyday behavior and worldly affairs. A typical Ḥasidic story tells of a disciple of the Maggid of Mezhirech who confessed that he did not go to the Maggid to study Torah but to witness how he tied his shoes. *Devekut*, "attachment," means having God constantly in mind whatever one does. This very exacting ideal (which Maimonides thought beyond the reach of most human beings) is attainable only by the *Tsaddik*, but the Ḥasid can approach it by being close to his *Rebbe*. In Ḥasidism the concept of *devekut* rests upon another idea, that God is immanent in the universe, that (as the Zohar phrases it) "no space is void of Him." This notion has been called "pantheism" ("all is God"), but it would be more accurately described as "panentheism" ("all is *in* God"). At every step, the true Ḥasid sees the Divine energy pervading the material universe. Provided he uses the world in a spirit of holiness, he worships his Creator even when eating, drinking, and attending to his other physical needs. This is what Ḥasidism refers to when it speaks of *avodah be-gashmiyyut*, "worship in the material."

The *Mitnaggedim* attacked Ḥasidism on various grounds, social as well as theological. On social grounds, they objected to the adoption of a new prayer rite and to the fact that Ḥasidim separated themselves from the general community, forming their own conventicles. This posed a challenge to the hegemony of the *Kahal* (communal council) — the rabbis and lay leaders forming the "Establishment." A particular scandal involved young married men who forsook their wives and families to spend many months at the court of the *Rebbe*, despite the communal rabbi's ruling that such action was contrary to Jewish law. The real issue here was a conflict of authority between the Ḥasidic *Rebbe* and the local rabbi. At a later period, the *Rebbe* became sufficiently influential to have a decisive say in the town rabbi's appointment. Furthermore, the early Ḥasidim adopted the practice of slaughtering animals with honed knives, which the *Mitnaggedim* declared halakhically impermissible. As a result, the Ḥasidim organized their own SHEḤITAH (ritual slaughter) and contributed nothing to the sizable revenues which the *Kahal* derived from *sheḥitah* fees and taxes. In short, Ḥasidism was seen as a rebellion against the community.

Opposition to the theological views of the Ḥasidim was manifold. Firstly, they were suspected of Shabbateanism, of secretly believing in the heretical false messiah SHABBETAI TSEVI, and the charge of sectarianism was leveled against them. Ḥasidic Jews were often derided by the *Mitnaggedim* as a *kat* ("sect") or else as *shepselekh* ("sheep"), a punning Yiddish allusion to the Shabbateans. Secondly, the doctrine of the *Tsaddik* as an intermediary was also offensive to the *Mitnaggedim*, who declared such a notion to be un-Jewish and extreme veneration of the *Tsaddik* to border on the idolatrous. Great opposition was also expressed to the panentheistic doctrines of Ḥasidism. The notion that all things are in God, it was claimed, must inevitably result in a complete blurring of the distinction between right and wrong, the pure and the impure, the sacred and the profane. As the *Mitnaggedim* put it, such a doctrine leads to "thinking on the words of Torah in unclean places" since, if "all is *in* God," there are ultimately *no* unclean places.

The Ḥasidic emphasis on *devekut* was also a serious cause of offense. To Ḥasidim, the rabbinic ideal of *Torah li-shmah* — "learning for its own sake" — means that Torah study should be engaged in more as a devotional than as an intellectual exercise. Thus, one who studied in order to win fame, or even because he enjoyed the intellectual challenge, was far removed from the ideal, whereas the comparatively ignorant Ḥasid whose mind was attuned to God while he studied Torah came much closer to the ideal. Moreover, Ḥasidism taught that *devekut* could be attained more readily in fervent prayer than in study, bringing about a complete reversal of the traditional rabbinic scale of values in which Torah study is the supreme religious act. For the *Mitnaggedim*, it was axiomatic that (as the talmudic rabbis say) the study of Torah should be pursued irrespective of one's motives and that it is impossible, while studying, to concentrate one's mind on God. The Ḥasidim were therefore charged with denigrating scholars and scholarship and with pandering to the ignorant masses.

During the late 18th century, several bans of EXCOMMUNICATION (*ḥerem*) were proclaimed against the Ḥasidim in major centers of East European Jewish life such as Brody and Vilna. The Lithuanian opposition was spearheaded by ELIJAH BEN SOLOMON ZALMAN, the Gaon of Vilna, who sternly rejected an attempt at reconciliation made by two Ḥasidic leaders, Menaḥem Mendel of Vitebsk and Shneur Zalman of Lyady. The height of acrimony was reached after the Vilna Gaon's death, when each side appealed to the Russian government against its opponents. Nor was it rare among the *Mitnaggedim* for parents to "sit *shivah*" in mourning when a son of theirs became a Ḥasid.

Opposition to Ḥasidism was also voiced from another quarter. Devotees of the HASKALAH (Jewish Enlightenment) movement in 19th-century Russia vehemently attacked and satirized what they considered to be the obscurantism of the Ḥasidim and their *Rebbes*. Maskilim accused the latter of encouraging their adherents to reject all secular learning and to rely on the prayers of the *Tsaddik*, instead of taking practical measures to alleviate the poverty and suffering of the Jewish masses. However, since the more radical Maskilim abandoned religious observance and opposed the traditional rabbis as well, both Ḥasidim and *Mitnaggedim* soon viewed the Haskalah as a common foe, leading them to unite in defense of tradition. This, above all, prevented Ḥasidism from degenerating into a real sectarian movement, and so what had begun as a revolt against socioreligious norms eventually became ultra-conservative in its theory and practice.

Ḥasidism produced a vast literature, both narrative-hagiological and didactic. First, there are the numerous tales of the *Tsaddikim*. At some early stage, the belief took root that it was highly meritorious to relate stories about the Ḥasidic saints, their miraculous powers, and the manner in which they worshiped God. There was a semi-magical element, too, in the relating of these tales because of a popular belief that the saints' miraculous powers were reawakened as the story unfolded, and that fresh miracles could then be wrought on behalf of the narrators and their audience. Many collections of these stories have been published, especially in the past 100 years: some are no more than fairy tales, others display an acute literary and imaginative skill. Not a few of the Ḥasidim took a skeptical view of the miracle tales. A Ḥasidic saying states, "Whoever believes all these tales is a fool, but anyone who cannot believe them is a heretic."

The second and more important type of Ḥasidic literature comprises halakhic, kabbalistic, and ideological writings, as well as the Ḥasidic "Torah," namely, the ideas of the *Tsaddikim*, which generally take the form of homiletical commentaries on the weekly Torah portion. A few of these works were actually written by the *Rebbes* themselves, but the more usual practice was for a disciple to make notes of the *Rebbe's* discourse, once the Sabbath had terminated, especially the one he delivered in the highly charged atmosphere of the third meal (*se'udah shelishit*). Ḥasidic Jews believed that on such occasions the *Rebbe* was inspired ("the *Shekhinah* speaking from his throat"), and indeed the *Rebbe* would later often admit to being unaware of what he had said.

While Ḥasidim first reached Erets Israel in 1777, and others later settled in Western Europe and America, the vast majority remained in Eastern Europe. There, prior to World War II, hundreds of Ḥasidic dynasties flourished, each with its own faithful adherents. After the Holocaust and the destruction of the great European communities, most of the surviving *Rebbes* created a new home for themselves in the State of Israel and in the USA, taking care to preserve the names of the towns in which their ancestors had held court. Among the best-known groups active today are the Belz, Bobova, Gur ("Gerer"), Klausenburg-Zanz, Lubavich (ḤABAD), Satmar, and Vizhnits Ḥasidim.

Although each dynasty preserves its own traditions, Yiddish is spoken widely and certain practices are common to most versions of Ḥasidism. The familiar Ḥasidic garb is really the type of dress worn by Polish noblemen in the 18th century, but Ḥasidism has read into it various mystical ideas. The wide fur hat known as a *shtraymel*, for example, with its 13 sable tails, is said to represent the 13 qualities of Divine mercy. Gur Ḥasidim wear a tall fur *spodik*, however, while members of the Lubavich movement wear neither. Some Ḥasidim wear white socks on the Sabbath as a symbol of purity. All male Ḥasidim don a *gartel* (girdle) for prayer, in order to separate the upper and lower parts of the body.

Another universal practice among Ḥasidim is the distribution of *shirayim* ("leftovers") from the *Rebbe's* table. When presiding over his *tish* (literally "table"), the sacred meal reserved for Sabbaths and festivals, the *Rebbe* tastes a little of each course and then distributes the remainder among his Ḥasidim, who believe that eating food that the *Tsaddik* has already tasted is conducive to holiness. Around the *tish*, the Ḥasidim listen with bated breath to the *Rebbe's* "Torah," then sing and dance in fulfillment of the call to "serve the Lord with gladness" (Ps. 100:2). Singing for joy and raising one's feet heavenward in dance is a high mode of worship in Ḥasidism. Some *Rebbes* composed their own melodies (see NIGGUN), and recordings of these and other Ḥasidic tunes have become extremely popular even in circles otherwise far removed from Ḥasidism.

To eat in a spirit of holiness is also an important religious

Ḫasidim expressing their religious fervor in an ecstatic dance. Watercolor by Chaim Gross, 1941.

obligation for the Ḫasid, who thereby rescues the "holy sparks" imprisoned in the *kelipot* (demonic powers). For the same reason, many of the *Rebbes* smoked a pipe or cigars. Tobacco was discovered so late in the history of the West, Ḫasidim claim, because the Messiah's advent will not take place until the subtle sparks inherent in the weed are rescued by those smoking while engaged in mystical contemplation (*devekut*).

In addition to the mass audiences given by the *Rebbe*, he may receive any of his followers in private. A standard practice is for the Ḫasid to bring a written petition (*kvitl*), outlining his individual needs and problems, so that the *Rebbe* can pray to God on his behalf. The theory is that the *Rebbe* must have some material association with his followers, if these prayers are to be answered. Consequently, together with his petition, the Ḫasid hands over a sum of money known as the *pidyon* ("redemption") for the upkeep of the *Rebbe's* court.

Several modern writers have helped to popularize — and often idealize — the Ḫasidic movement, its leaders, aspirations, and now vanished milieu. The Neo-Ḫasidism of Martin BUBER is, in reality, an adaptation of Buber's "I and Thou" philosophy. Though valuable in itself, no doubt, this philosophy is basically different from Ḫasidism proper in that it is not mystical, has no room for a particular *Rebbe*, and derives its inspiration from Ḫasidic tales rather than from the essential Ḫasidic "Torah." Nevertheless, through Buber's writings, especially free versions of Ḫasidic stories and legends, the Western world has become better acquainted with this movement of spiritual striving within Judaism.

HASKALAH (lit. "enlightenment"). The Haskalah movement is directly related to the EMANCIPATION of the Jews from the late 18th century onward and to the growing trends toward acculturation and ASSIMILATION among Jews as a result.

Essentially, Haskalah was the expression of a more sympathetic attitude among Jews towards the secular world of their Gentile neighbors. During the centuries of persecution in medieval Europe, Jews were forced to live in isolation in ghettos. Even when they were tolerated, they needed the protection of the crown in whatever country they happened to find themselves. This atmosphere changed dramatically when revolutionary changes swept through France in the latter part of the 18th century and when Gentile intellectuals began to champion the cause of Jewish liberty on the basis of a fundamental "bill of rights" of all human beings. As the trend toward emancipation began to gain momentum, not only in France but in the surrounding countries captured by Napoleon's victorious armies, the Jews adopted an increasingly sympathetic attitude toward the secular culture of their champions. Furthermore, as the restrictions against Jewish participation in the social, economic, and cultural spheres of Gentile society diminished, the urge on the part of the Jews to play a more active role in these fields increased.

The Haskalah movement comprised several concepts, some of which conflicted with one another:

1. Secular studies should be an integral part of the education of the Jewish child. This concept was usually adopted eagerly by Haskalah-minded Jews, although, in some countries (such as those of the Austro-Hungarian Empire), secularization was made a *sine qua non* condition in the curriculum to be followed by Jewish children.

2. Jews must be thoroughly educated in the language of the general society. At times, this idea led to an abandonment of, and even a hostility toward YIDDISH, which was seen as the language of exile and of Jewish self-deprecation.

3. Judaism and Jewish history should be studied at length. The growing interest in the secularized study of Jewish history aroused a growing interest in Jewish roots and thus led to increased sympathy for the language of lost Jewish sovereignty, namely, HEBREW.

4. The study of Hebrew must be promoted. In view of the sympathetic approach to Jewish history, ancient (but not Mishnaic) Hebrew became increasingly attractive and also played an important role in the revival of Jewish national consciousness.

5. The Jewish religion must adapt itself to the changing conditions of the modern world. Now that the Jews were a part of that world and were no longer confined to physical and spiritual ghettos, there was a growing feeling that Judaism must be modernized. In its more extreme forms, this tendency expressed itself in the development of REFORM JUDAISM, which sought to establish a bridge between Judaism and the secular environment, and declared that Zion existed not in the Land of Israel but primarily in the lands of Jewish dispersion. In its less extreme form, it expressed itself in the modern Orthodox movement (NEO-ORTHODOXY), one of whose leaders was Samson Raphael HIRSCH and which sought a moderate adaptation of some of Judaism's outward trappings (the integration of secular and Jewish studies, the concept of decorum in the synagogue, limited utilization of Gentile scholarship in the study of the Bible, etc.).

6. Like other nations of the world, the Jews must have their own homeland and must conduct a national struggle in order to obtain it. At this point, a number of the previous points coalesce: an appreciation of secular values (as expressed in philosophy, history, and the sciences), a growing fascination with Jewish history, the increased attractiveness of Hebrew and the concomitant trend toward abandoning the language of exile and segregation (Yiddish). On the one hand, the adoption by the Jews of the ideological notion of modern, secular nationalism was a rejection of the traditionalist reliance on a Messianic deliverance of the Jewish people, a rejection that acquired strength from the profound failure of the Shabbatean (see SHABBETAI TSEVI) and FRANKIST pseudo-messianic movements. On the other hand, the growth of modern Jewish nationalism, which was expressed first in the *Ḥoveṿé Zion* ("Lovers of Zion") movement and later in the more pragmatically minded political Zionist movement under Theodor Herzl, was a secularized version of a basic tenet of Judaism, namely that the Land of Israel is the eternal homeland of the Jewish people.

7. Jewish society, like others, must become more productive and stress more "concrete" occupations, such as agriculture and manual labor, while eschewing "traditional" Jewish ones, such as moneylending and petty artisanship. On the one hand, this tendency was an acceptance of anti-Semitic charges of alleged exploitation of Christians. On the other hand, the desire to become more "productive" reflected a growing Jewish identification with the more balanced structure of Gentile society and can be linked with the "return to the land" motif in modern political Zionist thought, particularly of the socialist variety. In light of this tendency, programs were set up to teach Jewish youth more practical occupations. The spirit behind these movements inspired the philosophy of the world network of ORT schools and that of pioneering ("*ḥalutsic*") Zionism.

Haskalah combined both assimilatory and counter-assimilatory tendencies. There were Jews who drifted from Haskalah thought to a total identification with non-Jewish society; however, there were also those whose identity as Jews was strengthened through the bonding of Judaism and secular approaches.

HASKAMAH ("approval"). The rabbinical equivalent of an imprimatur; permission to publish a book. When the early presses began to print Hebrew works, many of the books had been transmitted for centuries in manuscript form. Different manuscripts of the same volume might show extensive variations, and the first printer might have to put in considerable effort to insure that the text was correct. In order to protect the printer's work, it was customary for a prominent rabbi to offer his *haskamah*, which was printed at the front of the volume. The *haskamah* often forbade any other printer from reprinting the work within a given period of time, usually ten years, thus allowing the original printer the opportunity to recoup his investment. This was thus a type of copyright. Some *haskamot* even invoked all types of dire troubles upon anyone who might dare to reprint the work within the specified time limit. In addition, the fact that many of the printers were non-Jews or unlearned Jews caused concern that they might print works which were objectionable in terms of Jewish belief. The *haskamah* thus certified that the work was commendable and worthy of study. It was also a precaution ensuring that nothing would be printed to which the local Christian authorities might object.

The *haskamah* is still used in the printing of new rabbinic works or in the re-issue of older works which have been revised for errors that might have crept in over the years. Often an author seeks a *haskamah* (from a rabbinic authority) to endorse his Orthodoxy and scholarship. On occasion, several *haskamot* from various rabbis are published.

The same term (usually written *Ascama*) is used by Western Sephardim to indicate the rules governing their community.

HASMONEANS Title applied (together with the name "Maccabees") to the Jewish family and later dynasty in Erets Israel which raised the standard of revolt against the religious oppresssion of the Syrian Seleucid ruler, Antiochus IV (Epiphanes), in 167 BCE.

In the year 168/167 BCE, Antiochus promulgated a series of anti-Jewish decrees coincident with the profanation of the Jerusalem TEMPLE and the transformation of its precincts into a pagan stronghold. Mattathias, the aged head of a distinguished priestly family, realized that the decrees, if unchecked, would mean the extirpation of the Jewish faith. He initiated the armed struggle against the pagan authors of the oppression and their Jewish collaborators. His son, Judah (surnamed the "Maccabee"), was appointed shortly thereafter by his dying father to carry on the battle. Under his brilliant generalship and astute political leadership, the Jewish people witnessed the rededication of their Temple in

164 BCE (the origin of the HANUKKAH festival), and the end of the threat to their very existence and to the monotheistic idea. Judah's brothers, Jonathan and Simon, took over the leadership in 160 BCE and 142 BCE respectively. Jonathan was the first of the Hasmoneans to don the High Priestly robes, thereby abrogating the prerogative of the House of Zadok which had lasted since the days of King SOLOMON some 800 years before. Astute diplomatic maneuvers led to pacts with Rome and Sparta.

The severe PHARISEE-SADDUCEE split occurred during the reign of Simon's son, John Hyrcanus (134-104 BCE), according to Josephus, the ancient Jewish historian (*Ant.* 13.288-297). In the years that followed, under Aristobulus I and especially under Alexander Yannai (Jannaeus), Jewish political-geographical sway over the Land of Israel reached an extent unsurpassed even during the Golden Age of David and Solomon. Yannai's wife and successor, Shlomzion (Salome), enjoyed what appears to have been a tranquil though short reign (76-67 BCE). The Pharisee (rabbinical) leadership which had been out of favor, again came into Hasmonean esteem at this time (and perhaps already in the time of Alexander Yannai).

Coin of Mattathias Antigonus, the last Hasmonean king (40-37 BCE) with the menorah *appearing for the first time in Jewish art.*

Erets Israel became the Roman province of Judea in 63 BCE, thereby spelling the end of Hasmonean rule, although bitter fighting by the Hasmonean family continued — this time against Rome and its vassal, Herod — until the latter was firmly established on his throne in 37 BCE with the aid of Roman military support.

The Hasmonean revolt and its aftermath were more in the nature of a revolution, drastically affecting both Jewish and world history. For the Jews it meant their reemergence on the world political scene as a sovereign nation to be reckoned with by local and global powers. The Hasmonean century (167-67 BCE) witnessed the reestablishment of a Jewish presence throughout the length and breadth of the Land of Israel, with its cultural and physical imprint on the face of the land. The most far-reaching consequence of the revolt was the perpetuation of the monotheistic idea, which was threatened by the HELLENISM that Antiochus would have imposed by force and that certain Jewish circles would have accepted voluntarily.

HATRED See VIOLENCE

HAVDALAH ("separation"). Blessing recited at the end of the SABBATH and FESTIVALS marking the passage from a consecrated day to a routine weekday. A *havdalah* paragraph, *Attah ḥonantanu* ("You have favored us"), is inserted in the fourth benediction of the Evening Service *Amidah* on Saturday nights. Although generally a home ceremony, in many synagogues *havdalah* is also made at the conclusion of the Saturday Evening Service.

The *havdalah* ceremony comprises four blessings: three over WINE, spices, and lights, and the *havdalah* blessing. In the various rites, (Ashkenazi, Sephardi, and Yemenite), the blessings themselves are almost identical, the lead phrase being *kos yeshu'ot essa* ("I will lift the cup of salvation"), but the introductory sentences preceding it are different: the Ashkenazi recites biblical phrases containing the term *yeshu'ah* ("salvation"), the Sephardi asks for the granting of general bountifulness and success, and the Yemenite prays for a successful week.

Although wine is the preferred beverage for the blessing, if none is available, other liquids, except water, may be used.

It is now customary to use aromatic SPICES for the second blessing, but until the 12th century plants such as myrtle (*hadas*) were used. In some Sephardi and Eastern communities sweet-smelling plants are still used. They recite the alternate benedictions on *atsé vesamim* ("fragrant trees" or "plants") alongside the more common phrase, used by both Sephardim and Ashkenazim, *miné vesamim* ("kinds of aromatics"). The origin for this blessing is unknown. Some explain it as lifting sadness at the end of Sabbath as one's "extra Sabbath soul" is departing. Others attribute it to the ancient custom, predating Mishnaic times, of burning aromatic plants at the end of a meal to give a pleasant fragrance to the dining room. As this could not be done on the Sabbath, a blessing over spices was instituted.

The *havdalah* spices are often kept in a special container called a *besamim* box or *hadas*. These containers, first noted in a literary source in the 15th century, come in a wide variety of shapes, such as towers, fish and flowers, and are made of silver, wood, and other materials (see SPICE BOX).

The *havdalah* candle has more than one wick, as there has to be a combination of at least two flames, stemming from the plural term "lights" used in the blessing (*Boré me'oré ha-esh*, "Who creates the lights of the fire"). The candle often has six wicks and is made of interwoven strands in colorful combinations. The blessing signifies that kindling, traditionally prohibited on the Sabbath, is once again permitted on the weekday.

The final blessing, the *havdalah* itself, opens with the phrase, "Blessed are You, O Lord our God, King of the universe, who distinguishes...," and is followed by a series of contrasts, most commonly "...between the holy and the profane, between light and darkness, between Israel and the nations, between the seventh day and the six days of labor," a text already found in the Talmud (*Pes.* 104a).

The hymn *Ha-Mavdil* ("He who distinguishes") following the *havdalah* ceremony asks for forgiveness of sins and for the granting of a large number of offspring. Another virtually universal hymn sung at the end of *havdalah* is *Eliyyahu ha-Navi* ("Elijah the Prophet"), for traditionally Elijah is to herald the redemption.

The *havdalah* for a festival ending on a weekday consists only of the blessing over wine and the benediction, without the candle or the spices.

When a Sabbath is followed immediately by a festival, *havdalah* is said in combination with the KIDDUSH, in a series

Left: Havdalah *candlestick from Frankfurt. Right: Lighting the* ḥavdalah *candle (with two wicks). Germany, 18th century.*

known by the mnemonic-acrostic *Yaknehaz (Yayin* [wine], *Kiddush, Ner* [candle], *Havdalah, Zeman* [season]), indicating the order of recitation of the blessings: wine, *Kiddush*, light, *havdalah*, and SHE-HEḤEYANU.

On Ḥanukkah, in the synagogue Ḥanukkah candles are lit prior to the *havdalah* ceremony, while at home the opposite order prevails.

A variety of customs are associated with *havdalah*, from filling the cup to overflowing and extinguishing the candle in wine poured from the cup to dipping one's fingers in the wine and putting drops on the forehead or in the pockets. It is customary to extend one's fingers or look at one's nails with the blessing over the light. In Germany a special plate, with *Ha-Mavdil* written on it, was used to hold the appurtenances of the ceremony. Each community has its own rules regarding the drinking of the wine, the holding of the wine cup, the inhaling of the aroma of the spices, whether the *havdalah* is recited sitting or standing, and so on.

REFORM JUDAISM has an alternate *havdalah* service incorporating additional readings with the traditional blessings, and it also uses the occasion for various expressions of religious creativity, such as song, dance, etc.

ḤAVER (lit. "colleague," "companion"). During the Second Temple period, title bestowed upon those who were considered trustworthy in observing the laws of the separation of TITHES and the laws of ritual PURITY. As the laws of tithing are complex and the ignorant might not observe them properly, the bestowal of the title implied that the person could be trusted to have tithed whatever needed tithing. Talmudic sages were automatically considered to be in the category of *ḥaver*, as were those less learned people who accepted all the provisions involved, including tithing all produce which they ate or sold. Acceptance as a *ḥaver* could only be made by three talmudic sages sitting for the purpose. The Talmud (*Sanh.* 9b) also mentions a female *ḥaverah* who met these criteria.

The title was revived in Germany in the late Middle Ages, and bestowed upon individuals who were considered to be both learned and God-fearing, although they were not sufficiently learned to receive rabbinic ORDINATION. In modern Israel, the term *ḥaver* may be used to denote a member of a cooperative organization, such as a bus cooperative, a sick fund or a kibbutz.

ḤAVURAH ("fellowship"). A small group of individuals who seek fellowship and an enriched Jewish communal life. The concept originated in antiquity in the ESSENE and PHARISEE communities. Modern *ḥavurot* were initiated in the USA in response to disillusionment with large, impersonal synagogues which, some felt, were not serving congregants' spiritual and communal needs.

Most *ḥavurot* fall into one of three categories. The first type is that of a small, fervent, and Jewishly educated congregation, such as the one founded in Denver in 1967 and another, Fabrangen, founded in Washington DC, in 1971. Another kind of *ḥavurah* is much like a commune. Ḥavurat Shalom, the first of this type, was founded by university students and graduates in Somerville, Massachusetts, in 1968. While living together, the members studied, observed holidays, and worked daily to improve the quality of their Jewish experience. Similar *ḥavurot* thrived on college campuses during the 1960s and 1970s.

The third type of *ḥavurah*, which exists within a larger synagogue, was suggested by Rabbi Harold M. Schulweis of

Encino, California, as an answer to the alienation and lack of communal feeling of many congregants. In this framework, members study, celebrate holidays and the Sabbath together, and act as a support network for each other. Rabbi Schulweis believed that a synagogue's *ẖavurah* would provide its members with an extended family and invest the entire synagogue with a greater sense of purpose and unity.

Professor Jacob Neusner of Brown University has explained that *ẖavurah* members share concern for each other as well as for their common goals. Unlike Schulweis, however, he sees a *ẖavurah* as providing an improved experience for the individual, but not as a means for transforming the entire synagogue. Neusner indicates five areas of communal activity necessary for a fulfilling *ẖavurah* experience: prayer, celebrating the Sabbath, performing acts of kindness, study, and keeping a written record of the *ẖavurah*'s communal life.

H̱avurot affiliated with synagogues are usually autonomous in determining the structure and purpose of the group. Most *ẖavurot* study Torah, Jewish history, and Jewish culture through discussions and individual presentations. Conversations often turn to practical concerns, such as how to raise Jewish children in a non-Jewish environment. *H̱avurot* are also often involved in community projects, such as visiting the sick or elderly.

According to two studies done at the UCLA School of Social Welfare in the 1970s, the eight observed *ẖavurot* served as peer support groups by creating a safe atmosphere in which to discuss general problems as well as Jewish issues. The studies also found that after approximately two years a crisis arose over the *ẖavurah*'s direction and emphasis on study versus social activities. *H̱avurot* which stressed study tended to become more emotionally cohesive as time passed, with members helping each other in illness and death, and celebrating each other's happy occasions. However, *ẖavurot* which initially emphasized social interaction sometimes found it difficult to introduce study at a later time.

As more and more people pursue religious activity invested with warmth and closeness, the number of *ẖavurot* continues to grow. Since modern *ẖavurot* are a recent phenomenon, it is difficult to assess their long-term impact on the larger Jewish community.

H̱AZON ISH See KARELITZ, AVRAHAM

H̱AZZAN See CANTOR

HEAVEN See AFTERLIFE; ESCHATOLOGY

HEAVE OFFERING See SACRIFICES AND OFFERINGS

HEBREW A Semitic language (*Ivrit*) traditionally described as "the Holy Tongue" (*leshon ha-kodesh*). The oldest Semitic languages known are Eblaite in northern Syria and Akkadian (Babylonian and Assyrian) in Mesopotamia, attested in writing from the third millennium BCE. Closer to Hebrew is Ugaritic, the language of Ugarit, a coastal city in northern Syria, with literary and other texts from the mid-14th century. The language of CANAAN, the earlier name of Erets Israel, is known from Canaanite words and forms in the Akkadian (then a lingua franca) of letters written to the Egyptian governor of Canaan in the 14th century BCE. This Canaanite resembles Hebrew closely, and some scholars held that biblical Hebrew was Canaanite with an admixture of the language the Israelites spoke before entering Canaan.

Children's Hebrew primer of the 11th century from the Cairo Genizah; the first letters of the alphabet are repeated several times.

One of the earliest texts in Hebrew is the Song of Deborah (Judg. 5); there are some archaic forms in other early poems, as well as instances of dialect (e.g., Judg. 12:6). The classical literary Hebrew of the Bible was probably created in the era of King Solomon, when a regular administration was established and people from all parts of the country came on festivals to the Temple in Jerusalem, where they were addressed by priests and "wise men." This is the language in which the prose texts of the pre-exilic era are cast. Poetry, as exemplified by the Psalms, had its own style and vocabulary, and the speeches of the prophets represent a rhetorical style; both are marked by "parallelism," the repetition of a statement in different words.

The latest books of the Bible, such as Ecclesiastes, Ezra, Nehemiah, Esther, and probably Chronicles, display a later form of biblical Hebrew, based perhaps on the official language of royal administration. After the Babylonian Exile, the language of the educated class (most of whom had been exiled) was strongly influenced by ARAMAIC, then the common spoken language of Babylonia and one also used internationally for contracts, etc. Any changes that may have affected the pronunciation of Hebrew words are not visible in the late texts, however, because the spelling gave only incomplete information about the vowels.

During the Second Temple period, the teaching of religion was assumed by the *tannaim* who used the spoken language of the time. It differed in grammar, syntax, and vocabulary from biblical Hebrew, and was called "the language of the wise men." At this period, when local synagogues came into being, prayers such as the AMIDAH were composed in a Hebrew close to the spoken language. This stage is called Mishnaic Hebrew after the MISHNAH, which consists largely of statements and discussions by individual rabbis.

In Eastern Jewish communities a traditional way of pronouncing the text of the Mishnah and other halakhic (legal) collections of that period has been preserved, with some regional differences. Mishnaic Hebrew was used for religious texts throughout the Middle Ages and it was influenced by the various languages which Jews spoke in different areas (e.g., Judeo-Arabic). The Mishnaic language became an important element in modern Hebrew, because it provided words and phrases for everyday life.

The traditional attitude to the early beginnings of Hebrew emerges from a Midrash (Gen. R. 18.6) on Gen. 2:23: "She shall be called Woman (*ishah*), because she was taken out of the Man (*ish*). From this one learns that the Torah was given in the Holy Tongue. Because only in Hebrew (*ish, ishah*) do the words correspond." The Holy Tongue was the usual designation for Hebrew, and it was even seen as the language of the angels (*Ḫag.* 16a). Furthermore, according to the rabbis, one who made it his practice to speak Hebrew would have a share in the afterlife (TJ *Shab.* 1.2, *Shek.* 3.4).

In the Middle Ages, Jewish scholars thought that Aramaic and Arabic, two other Semitic languages, were corrupt Hebrew. They claimed that Hebrew was the original Semitic tongue and that historical changes in a language are not, as is now recognized, developments caused by social and cultural innovations and influences. On the other hand, Jewish scholars in Morocco and Muslim Spain used Aramaic and Arabic words in order to establish the meaning of difficult biblical terms.

Although Hebrew ceased to be an everyday language, Jews speaking other vernaculars, it did not disappear from Jewish life. The prayer services continued to be mainly in Hebrew and, in the course of time, many special prayers, liturgical poems (*piyyutim*), and songs were added, again mostly in Hebrew. A Jew was obliged to study the weekly Torah portion twice in Hebrew and once in the TARGUM. Study of the Mishnah was widespread, and other halakhic and moral books written over the centuries were widely read. Most of the commentaries to the Bible, from the Middle Ages, were in Hebrew, so that adult Bible study meant a double occupation with the meaning of Hebrew texts: the biblical wording and the commentaries.

As was the case in other oriental civilizations, learning to write and to handle the written language was restricted to males. At the same time, the languages which all Jews spoke (see JEWISH LANGUAGES) were absorbing large quantities of Hebrew words. As for boys, to quote the saying in *Sifré* (*Ekev* 46), "If a father does not speak to his son in the Holy Tongue, it is as if he had buried him" (*Tos. Ḫag.*1.2). In accordance with this principle, Jewish communities however small or isolated invested in engaging a teacher, and boys of three years and upward were kept for long hours every weekday, learning to read and to translate word for word. There was no teaching of grammar, which was rejected by Orthodox Ashkenazi Jews until modern times, and the select few who wrote books in Hebrew did so in a form taken mainly from Mishnaic Hebrew, but with a syntax that was influenced by the language of their country, often with literal translation of words from that language. Such is the case with RASHI, although he wrote a more elegant Hebrew than other Ashkenazim of his time and developed a grammatical system of his own for the analysis of biblical sentences. Yet when explaining words in the Bible and in the Talmud, he frequently supplies an Old French equivalent in Hebrew transliteration instead of attempting to define the sense in Hebrew.

The Jewish scholars of the later Middle Ages lived among nations that had not yet begun to analyze their own languages or to use them for scientific writing, medieval Latin being utilized instead. There was little that Jewish writers could learn from their host nations. One exceptional influence can be seen in the medieval German chivalrous narrative poems, some of which were transcribed into Hebrew letters.

The situation was quite different in those areas of Spain occupied at that time by the Muslims. In Arabic there was then — as still today — a sharp differentiation between the written language, identical in all Arabic-speaking areas and regulated by grammarians, and the spoken language, which differed from region to region. This differentiation was taken up by the Jews, who wrote poetry only in biblical Hebrew and regulated this poetical idiom through the compiling of detailed grammars. Syntax found no place in these grammars, however, because the Arabic language's syntax was based upon the cases of nouns and moods of verbs, while biblical Hebrew had neither cases nor moods.

Nor could biblical Hebrew be used for scientific writing in the way that written Arabic could, since its vocabulary was too limited. The alternative — to use Mishnaic Hebrew — was not acceptable, because this "language of our forefathers" was assumed to have been a spoken tongue which, by Arab standards, could therefore not be written or used for serious purposes. It was thus customary among Spanish Jews to write scientific prose in Arabic only.

This situation changed completely after 1148, when many Jews in Muslim Spain escaped persecution by moving to southern France, where they encountered a positive attitude to Mishnaic Hebrew and so produced writings in it. Not only were works written in Arabic now translated into Hebrew: original works were also written in Hebrew which, like the translations, devised new technical terms on the basis of Arabic models. Some features of Arabic syntax were likewise adopted, thus laying the ideological foundation for an enlargement of the Hebrew vocabulary. The ensuing flow of translations and original scientific writings made Hebrew the oustanding scientific language of the later Middle Ages.

Hebrew was thus never a dead language. Apart from writing letters, there is evidence that Jewish men could speak Hebrew to Jews with whom they had no other language in common. The kabbalists also endowed the Hebrew language and ALPHABET with mystical significance. In the latter half of the 18th century, adherents of HASKALAH (Jewish Enlightenment) began to publish Hebrew articles on social and cultural problems, which involved new ways of argumentation and new terminology. Modern Hebrew is associated with Eliezer Ben-Yehuda, who in the late 19th century stressed the connection between language and nationalism, on the one hand, and on the other, the importance of speaking Hebrew at home and in all situations, to the exclusion of those Jewish or other languages which the immigrants to Erets Israel had brought with them.

Modern Hebrew was not, as is often stated, an *ad hoc* fusion of biblical and Mishnaic Hebrew. This fusion had already taken place in the Middle Ages and gave rise both to learned writing and popular literature on religious topics. After an era of pure biblical Hebrew in the late 18th and 19th centuries, modern Hebrew was reinstated and artistically developed from 1886 by the writer Mendelé Mokher Seforim (Shalom Ya'akov Abramovitch). Its use was further promoted by the establishment of all-Hebrew schools in Erets Israel during the 1880s, which were soon followed by others in Eastern Europe. As the everyday language in Erets Israel, Hebrew facilitated communication among immigrants speaking many different languages and gave birth to a modern-style literature. With the establishment of the State of Israel in 1948, it was declared the national language; at that time also, the Sephardi pronunciation of Hebrew became normative.

In ultra-Orthodox Ashkenazi circles, modern Hebrew was for long not accepted as a language of communication except with outsiders. YIDDISH was the everyday language and the traditional Ashkenazi pronunciation remained obligatory for prayer and religious study in these circles. Lately, however, ever-increasing numbers of the ultra-Orthodox in Israel have begun speaking and conducting their business in Hebrew. The modern Conservative and Reform movements both introduced the vernacular into their prayer services, and some Reform congregations virtually abandoned Hebrew altogether. However, in recent decades, this trend has been reversed and Hebrew can now be heard, to a lesser or greater extent, in every type of Jewish service.

ḤEDER (lit. "room"). A type of schooling institution widespread especially in eastern Europe until World War II, and still to be found in more Orthodox communities. The *ḥeder* generally consisted of a small group of young boys, their ages varying from five to 13, who met at the home of the "*rebbe*" (rabbi). The parents would pay a pittance, and that would be the *rebbe*'s income. The *rebbe* generally had no pedagogical training or background, and anyone with some knowledge of the sacred texts could open his own *ḥeder* as a means to support his family. The *rebbe* would often divide the students into three age groups, working with each in rotation. The youngest students learned how to read, the emphasis being on learning to pray from a prayer book. The middle group generally studied the Pentateuch with RASHI's commentary, while the older group studied the Talmud. Exceptional students might go on to YESHIVOT, but the vast majority entered the labor market after completing their *ḥeder* studies. The *ḥeder* teacher used corporal punishment to impose iron discipline. He was often assisted by a *belfer* (a corruption of the Yiddish *behelfer* — assistant), whose duties would include bringing the children to the *ḥeder* and taking them home at the end of the day. The course of studies was exclusively sacred literature, and the hours were long, even for the youngest children. From the 19th century, following the HASKALAH ("Enlightenment"), an attempt was made by some instructors to modify the *ḥeder* by introducing Hebrew language, and other Haskalah studies. This was referred to as the *ḥeder metukkan* ("reformed *ḥeder*"), but the experiment did not succeed and it was soon discontinued. Attempts to transplant the *ḥeder* to the USA as a supplement to public school studies were also unsuccessful.

A ḥeder *in the small Jewish community of Tiznit, south Morocco, where children are taught Hebrew, prayers and the Bible.*

In North Africa, children started *ḥeder* at the age of two or three. After learning to read Hebrew, they studied the prayer book and the Bible. In Britain, the (Orthodox) congregational Hebrew school was also known as a *ḥeder*.

HEKDESH ("consecrated"). Term used in the Talmud to denote those objects which were consecrated for TEMPLE use, including the Temple utensils and animals to be used for SACRIFICES AND OFFERINGS. Later, the term was expanded to mean anything consecrated for synagogue or other charitable purposes, or for the performance of Jewish ritual.

A person who wished to donate something to the Temple could give it for the Temple upkeep (*hekdesh bedek ha-bayit*) or, if suitable, to be used for the sacrificial service (*hekdesh mizbe'aḥ*). The donation might take one of two forms: *neder* — a pledge to give a certain sum or a certain type of object (e.g., a bull) to the Temple; or *nedavah* — a pledge to give a specific object (e.g., a specific bull which one owned) to the Temple. In the former case, should the object be lost before being transferred to the Temple's possession, it would have to be replaced. In the latter, it would not be replaced.

Unlike general business transactions, which require an action of some kind before they are made binding, an oral pledge to *hekdesh* is binding and obligatory. Halakhically, the same is true today of pledges made to charitable organizations.

No benefit may be derived from an item belonging to *hekdesh*, such illicit benefit being termed *me'ilah* or misappropriation. One guilty of *me'ilah* brought a *me'ilah* sacrifice and paid the Temple for the value of benefit received, plus an additional fifth of that value. After the Temple was destroyed, the rabbis decreed that no one was to consecrate anything for Temple use. In general, according to later rulings, if one consecrates any object or money without specific designation, the object or money is donated to a charitable cause.

In the late Middle Ages, many Jewish communities, including almost all the major ones, developed a shelter for those who were ill, poor, or in transit from one place to another. This structure was known as a *hekdesh*, as it was supported by community funds. While the funding came from the local community, the administration was left to the local *bikkur ḥolim* ("visiting the sick") society. Such forerunners of modern hospitals existed in some cities as late as the 19th century. They were often neglected and squalid, thus "*hekdesh*" in Yiddish came to mean a slovenly, disordered place.

HÉKHALOT AND MERKAVAH MYSTICISM The earliest phase in the development of Jewish mysticism is to be found in about 20 brief treatises, originating from the talmudic and early geonic period (third-seventh centuries CE), collectively called *Hékhalot* (Palaces) and *Merkavah* (Chariot) literature. Their focus is an ascension through the celestial palaces to the vision of God's chariot or throne. Not all of these texts are mystical. Some deal mainly with magic, like *Ḥarba de-Mosheh* ("The Sword of Moses"); *The Havdalah of Rabbi Akiva*, and part of *Sefer ha-Razim* ("The Book of Mysteries"); others deal mainly with homiletical interpretation, in an esoteric manner, of Ezekiel's vision, reflecting the tradition known in the Mishnah by the term *Ma'aseh Merkavah* ("The Work of the Chariot," from Ezekiel's vision of the Divine Chariot in the Book of EZEKIEL). This term, and the surviving material relating to it, does not include active mysticism but rather homiletical speculations concerning the structure of the celestial realm.

Five treatises comprise the heart of ancient Jewish mysticism, describing the activities and speculations of the early mystics. The first is *Hékhalot Zutarté* ("The Smaller Book of Celestial Palaces"), in which the ascension of AKIVA to the Divine Chariot is described. Next is *Hékhalot Rabbati* ("The Greater Book of Celestial Palaces"); here the ascension of R. Ishmael, who is described as a "high priest," is central to the work, which is about the legendary TEN MARTYRS. The third treatise is *Ma'aseh Merkavah*, an anthology of hymns heard or recited by the mystics during their ascension to the seven Divine palaces. The fourth is *Sefer Hékhalot*, better known as the Third Book of Enoch or the Hebrew Book of Enoch, in which R. Ishmael describes his ascension to heaven and his meeting with Metatron, the *Sar ha-Panim* ("Prince of the Countenance"). In the first part of this work Metatron relates his biography to P.abbi Ishmael, starting with his being born as ENOCH, son of Jared, who was taken by God to heaven to serve as a witness for the sins which brought about the Flood. Enoch was transformed, stage by stage, into the Divine power Metatron, second only to God himself. The second part of the work is a detailed description of the celestial realm and the hierarchy of Divine powers around God (see also ANGELS). The fifth treatise is *Shi'ur Komah* ("The Measurement of the Height"), the first Hebrew mystical work dedicated to a description of God Himself, using extreme anthropomorphic images (based on Song 5: 10-16); the figure of the *Shi'ur Komah* was the target of the ancient mystics when they ascended from heaven to heaven and palace to palace until they reached the seventh palace in the seventh heaven, where the great King, the Creator, sat on His throne of glory, surrounded by hosts of angels and a plethora of Divine powers. In most of these works hymns occupy an important part: those sung by the angels and recorded by the mystics, and those composed by the mystics themselves to express their wonder at facing these visions. Some of the hymns were later introduced into the Jewish prayer book.

The ancient mystics, paradoxically, described themselves as the "Descenders to the Chariot" (*Yordé ha-Merkavah*), and not only the "Ascenders." This may have been derived from Song of Songs 6:11, like many other elements in *Hékhalot* mysticism which were based on the mystical interpretation of this book. In fact, two texts were basic for

Hékhalot mysticism: the vision of Ezekiel, as interpreted in the homiletical *Ma'aseh Merkavah* tradition, and the new understanding of the Song of Songs as the holiest work in the Bible (as R. Akiva states in the Mishnah), regarded as having been given by God Himself to Israel during the Mount Sinai theophany.

The origin of this mystical group seems to be within tannaitic traditions (see TANNA), but it developed as a separate, distinct religious phenomenon, linked but not identical with the rabbinic-midrashic cultural world. These mystics derived some of their symbols from apocalyptic and apocryphal literature of the Second Temple period, and there may be some parallels in the DEAD SEA SCROLLS sect, in early Christian works, and in ancient gnostic symbolism (the Gnostics, most probably, derived some of their symbols from the same source as did the *Hékhalot* mystics). They presented in their works a new attitude toward the relationship between man and God, a new vigor in human endeavor to approach God by mystical means, and their literature and symbols served all later Jewish mystics, especially the medieval ḤASIDÉ ASHKENAZ as well as the KABBALAH.

HEKHSHER (lit. "making ritually fit"). Certificate of "attestation" by a rabbinical court (*bet din*) or individual qualified rabbi with reference to foodstuffs and other commodities. The *hekhsher*, covering meat, wines and spirits, mass-produced foods, and (especially) Passover provisions, guarantees that such items have been supervised or approved by the rabbinate for observant Jewish households, and that they meet all requirements of the DIETARY LAWS. A similar *hekhsher* is granted to approved "kosher" butchers, bakers, hotels, and restaurants. Business premises display this certificate, while a recognized symbol is usually incorporated in the packaging of foodstuffs. Occasionally, as in Israel, separate *hekhsherim* may be issued for the same product or establishment by the Chief Rabbinate and an ultra-Orthodox *bet din*.

HELL See AFTERLIFE; ESCHATOLOGY

HELLENISM Term denoting the social, political, economic, and mainly cultural/religious influences on Europe and the Near and Middle East beginning with the final decades of the fourth century BCE. The new dominant features of the era were basically an amalgam of the culture of classical Greece (with its architectural forms as perhaps Hellenism's most immediately distinguishing hallmark), and the societal and cultural features of the peoples to the east, conquered by Alexander the Great.

The Jews in Erets Israel and, to a greater extent, those in the far-flung Diaspora, could not remain immune to these tremendous changes. Yet, while the Jews and Judaism absorbed much of what Hellenism had to offer (from synagogal structure to literary forms and philosophical speculation), they were conspicuous for their virtually unending battle against this very Hellenism. Its pagan world outlook was perceived as no different from that of the rest of its polytheistic forerunners in the threat which it posed to the essence of Jewish existence. This attitude is indirectly yet indubitably reflected in the impressively large output of Jewish "apologetic" literature of the age, constituting, in effect, Jewry's ideological confrontation with the surrounding, generally hostile, pagan society.

Scores of extant Jewish non-rabbinical and non-canonical literary works of the Greco-Roman period — written almost exclusively in the Greek tongue — extending down to the second century CE, were undoubtedly directed as much toward the outside world as toward the communities of the Jewish dispersion. These works may be broadly categorized as follows: apocryphal literature (the bulk of the output, see APOCRYPHA AND PSEUDEPIGRAPHA); biblical exegesis (e.g., Demetrius the Chronographer and Aristobulus, "teacher of Ptolemy," two of the better known figures in this category); and historical or pseudo-historical compositions (for example, *The Exodus from Egypt* by Ezekiel the Tragedian, and the Third Book of Maccabees). Towering above these and the many other books and authors, are the figures and works of PHILO of Alexandria and Josephus Flavius, one of the outstanding historians of antiquity.

A cursory glance at two literary works, the Letter of ARISTEAS and the Fourth Book of Maccabees, reveals the polemical nature of much of the Jewish writing of the period. The former work, purporting to recount the origins of the SEPTUAGINT (translation of the Bible into Greek), employs the framework of the Greek symposium to extol the glories of Judaism as against the inanity of pagan polytheism. The Fourth Book of Maccabees depicts the supposed confrontation between the wicked monarch Antiochus Epiphanes and the soon-to-be-martyred mother and her seven sons and the aged Eleazar. In this composition as well, the beliefs and practices of Judaism are elevated to sublime heights and the pagan religious outlook refuted — all in the course of a typically Greek philosophical (strongly Stoic-oriented) encounter between the Jewish protagonists and the pagan sovereign.

Nevertheless, the Jewish communities (from Italy in the west to the borders of Babylonia and Persia in the east) were strongly affected by the political, social, and cultural currents eddying about them. Certain upper-class segments of Jewish society, even in the Land of Israel, learned increasingly to swim with the Hellenistic tide, until matters came to a head in the reconstitution of Jerusalem as a Greek *polis* and the establishment of Greek-style *gymnasia* in the Holy City. The HASMONEAN revolution put an end to this blatant antithesis of Judaism but not to other less radical influences. Thus the selfsame Hasmonean rulers, while making strenuous efforts to eradicate pagan practices in newly conquered Jewish areas, were themselves prone to Hellenistic influences, at least in their outward form. Even during the early days of the Hasmonean uprising, some of Judah the Maccabee's diplomatic envoys had decidedly Greek names, while later Hasmonean rulers bore names such as Hyrcanus and Aristobulus.

Talmudic literature testifies to the subtle yet strong infiltration of Greek and Latin loan words (two of the more commonly known being SANHEDRIN and PROSBUL), phrases, and concepts into the Aramaic and Hebrew texts. Much of the HERMENEUTIC basis of talmudic legal reasoning, such as the Seven Rules of Hillel, is regarded as having a Greek-Hellenistic grounding. Herod's crowning achievement, certainly in Jewish eyes, namely, the vastly enlarged and enhanced Jerusalem TEMPLE, was a masterpiece of Greco-Roman architecture and perhaps even the primary reason for the illustriousness of Jerusalem in pagan eyes (cf. the elder Pliny and Tacitus). Inscriptions, ancient literature, and other archeological evidence, indicate that Jewish communal structures, though intrinsically Jewish, nevertheless did not remain unaffected by the societies around them. Terms such as *gerousia, boulei* and ARCHISYNAGOGOS, denoting the various autonomous Jewish governing communal bodies and their officialdom, speak for themselves in this respect.

It is apparent, therefore, that Hellenism left a strong imprint on Jewish outward forms (literary, architectural, and otherwise), and, to some extent, practice. Where essential content was concerned, however, the Jews refused to accept the Hellenistic order of the day. Unlike many other pagan authors of that age who, though of Semitic stock (e.g. Philo of Byblos and Berossus the Babylonian), strove to prove how really Greek their cultural heritage was, the Jews not only stressed the uniqueness of Jewish culture, but addressed themselves to what they perceived as the basic vapidity of paganism. Finally, having emerged triumphant from their encounter with Hellenism, the Jews could apply the talmudic dictum, "Let the beauty of [the Greek language of] Japheth stay within the tents of Shem [i.e., Israel]" in its broadest sense; i.e., maintain what was valid and essential in Hellenistic culture, while placing it within a Jewish context and framework.

HELLER, YOM TOV LIPMANN (1579-1654). Rabbinic scholar and commentator on the MISHNAH. Heller left his native Bavaria to study under JUDAH LÖW BEN BEZALEL in Prague, where he was appointed *dayyan* (rabbinical judge) as a youth of 18. In 1625, he became *av bet din* (head of the rabbinical court) in Vienna, but two years later was elected chief rabbi of Prague.

From 1631, he officiated in various Polish communities, and was rabbi of Cracow from 1643 and head of its *yeshivah* (talmudic academy). His last years were embittered by the Chmielnicki massacres of 1648-9, to which he devoted some of his penitential SELIḤOT.

Heller's fame rests on his commentary on the Mishnah, known as *Tosefot Yom Tov* ("The Additions of Yom Tov"). His purpose in this work was to supply "additions" to the Mishnaic commentary of Obadiah di BERTINORO with the object of determining the legal decision, *halakhah*; he provided linguistic clarifications, established accurate readings, reconciled contradictions in the Mishnaic text, indicated Bertinoro's sources, and explained the latter's own comments. The authoritative nature and lucid Hebrew style of *Tosefot Yom Tov* made it very popular, and it is now included in most editions of the Mishnah together with Bertinoro's commentary.

Among Heller's many other works are three volumes of responsa and commentaries on the code of ASHER BEN JEHIEL, entitled *Ma'adané Melekh* and *Leḥem Ḥamudot*. His autobiography, *Megillat Évah*, sheds important light on Jewish communal life and history in his time. Heller was well versed in Kabbalah, mathematics, and astronomy.

ḤEREM See EXCOMMUNICATION

HERESY A belief contrary to authoritative religious teaching. Although neither the Bible nor the Talmud presents a systematic formulation of dogmas which followers of the Torah must believe, certain beliefs are integral to Judaism. These include, for example, belief in God, revelation, reward and punishment.

It was not until MAIMONIDES (12th century) drew up 13 PRINCIPLES OF FAITH that Judaism had a clearly formulated list of dogmas. Denial of any of these principles, according to Maimonides, meant that the heretic had forfeited his portion in the world to come (AFTERLIFE). Simeon ben Tsemaḥ DURAN (1361-1444), while generally agreeing with Maimonides' formulation, argued that a person did not lose his portion in the world to come if he denied any of the principles erroneously. If he were taught incorrectly, or came to incorrect conclusions based on his own faulty reasoning, he was not a true heretic. Various writers after Maimonides offered different formulations of basic Jewish beliefs. Most of them viewed the lists of principles as effective teaching devices or as important (but not the only) statements of Jewish faith. Isaac ABRAVANEL and David IBN ZIMRA, writing in the generation of the expulsion of Jews from Spain, argued that each and every detail of the Torah must be maintained. The denial of any point, however small, was heresy. Ibn Zimra stated in a responsum (Vol.1, no. 344): "My mind does not agree to designate any essential principle of our perfect Torah, because it is all essential."

The Mishnah (*Sanh.* 10.1) does classify certain heresies which cause a man to lose his portion in the world to come. These include denial that resurrection of the dead is taught by the Torah; denial that the Torah is from heaven; holding beliefs which make one an EPIKOROS. Maimonides (*Yad, Teshuvah* 3.8) defines an *epikoros* as a person who denies that God communicates with humans through prophecy; who denies the prophecy of Moses; or who denies God's knowledge of the affairs of humans. The Talmud (*Sanh.* 99b) defines an *epikoros* as one who scorns rabbinic sages or who scorns others in the presence of rabbinic sages. The *Shulḥan Arukh* (*YD* 243.6) rules that it is a great sin to humiliate or hate rabbinic scholars. One who holds the sages in contempt has no portion in the world to come. Denigration of sages leads to the mocking of rabbinic authority — and of the *halakhah* which depends on rabbinic authority.

Maimonides (*Yad, Teshuvah* 3) defines other terms which refer to individuals who hold incorrect beliefs. A MIN ("sectary") is one who denies the existence of God; or believes in more than one God; or that God is corporeal; or that God is not alone eternal; or worships stars or other objects as mediators between himself and God (cf. *Sanh.* 38b-39a). A *mumar* is one who consistently and intentionally does not observe a Torah commandment, acting as though it does not exist. A broader category of *mumar* includes one who abandons the Jewish religion under duress, stating that it is better to join the stronger group than to remain part of the oppressed Jewish people. A *kofer* is one who denies the Torah, resurrection of the dead, and the future coming of the Messiah.

In rabbinic literature, a person guilty of heresy is frequently referred to as *kofer ba-ikkar*, a denier of a basic principle. The term is often used generically to designate an individual whose beliefs or actions reflect disregard for the Divine origin of the Torah and for the *halakhah*. It is incorrectly used to denigrate someone whose opinion differs from that of the defining group — even though that person's opinion has ample support in tradition. For example, in some fundamentalist Jewish circles, the term *epikoros* is used for a student of secular wisdom — even though he accepts the 13 Principles of Maimonides and the other basic Jewish beliefs.

HERMENEUTICS Rules of biblical exegesis developed by the *tannaim* (see TANNA). The roots of such rabbinic interpretation of Scripture, deducing halakhic rulings not immediately apparent from the text itself, may be found in the process known as MIDRASH, i.e., expounding Scripture, traditionally first employed by EZRA (mid-fifth century BCE; Ezra 7:10). Thus, at Ezra's instigation, the Pentateuch was read in public assembly and then "the Levites explained the Pentateuch to the people...They read from the scroll of the teaching of God, translating it and giving the sense; so they understood the reading" (Neh. 8:7-8).

As time went on, principles of Midrash, known as *middot* or "measures," were formulated to derive from Scripture the increasing number of *halakhot* (rulings) being taught by the sages. HILLEL the Elder (end of first century BCE) "expounded [*darash*] seven methods of interpretation" (*Tosef. Sanh.* end of chap. 7). These included: 1. *Kal va-Ḥomer*: Deduction from a minor to a major case; 2. *Gezerah Shavah*: Drawing a conclusion by word analogy (when two biblical passages contain the same word, both laws may receive the same application); 3. *Binyan Av mi-Katuv Eḥad*: Application of a principle derived from a single verse to a wider range of cases; 4. *Binyan Av mi-Shené Ketuvim*: Application of a principle, that may be derived only from two particular verses taken together, to a wider range of cases; 5. *Kelal u-Ferat u-Ferat u-Khelal*:A restriction on a general principle, derived from a specific case; or expanded application of specific cases by a subsequent general principle; 6. *Ka-Yotsé Bo be-Makom Aḥer*: Drawing conclusions on the basis of similarity between passages (some commentators count rule five as two rules and do not include six as a rule at all); 7. *Davar ha-Lamed mi-Inyano*: Drawing a conclusion from the context.

Subsequently, two early *tannaim*, Nehuniah ben ha-Kanah and Nahum of Gimzo, applied respectively the methods of *Kelal u-Ferat* (see point 5 above), and *Ribu'i u-Mi'ut* (the general statement implying the inclusion of all similar particulars and the stated particular excluding only the least similar; cf. Rashi on *Sanh.* 46a). Two outstanding disciples developed the methods of their respective teachers even further, AKIVA following the method of R, Nehuniah and ISHMAEL that of R. Nahum (*Shevu.* 26a). R. Ishmael formulated 13 rules by which the Bible is expounded (Introduction to *Sifra*) and details of their application are discussed in tractate *Zevaḥim* (50a-51a; they are included in the daily Morning Service, after the Mish. *Zev.* chap. 5). The two best-known rules are *kal va-ḥomer* and *gezerah shavah* (points one and two, above). There is, however, a significant difference between these. A scholar may infer a ruling by means of a *kal va-ḥomer* on his own, since it is a purely logical principle. He may not, however, expound a *gezerah shavah* on his own, but may only transmit an exposition already taught by his master (*Nid.* 19b). Apparently, some curb had to be placed upon the use of these methods of biblical exegesis. According to post-talmudic literature, R. Eliezer ben Yosé ha-Gelili expanded R. Ishmael's 13 rules to 32. Most of the additional ones, however, were meant to be used for aggadic exegesis.

The height of midrashic exposition was reached by R. Akiva, who inferred additional rulings from prefixes, suffixes, and superfluous words, and even from the word *et*, which has no meaning by itself but rather indicates the following noun to be the object of a transitive verb (*Pes.* 22b; cf. *Men.* 29b). R. Ishmael opposed R. Akiva's methods, holding that "the Bible speaks in the language of men." According to this principle, the possibility of legal deduction was limited by the Bible's need to be written in common parlance. It was, therefore, impossible to draw sweeping conclusions, as R. Akiva did, from the subtleties of the written text. In later years, R. Ishmael's opinion gained ascendance, with subsequent generations ruling that nothing can override the plain meaning of the text (*Shab.* 63a).

These exegetical measures were utilized by the sages not necessarily to introduce new rulings; rather they were meant to substantiate traditional rulings which were part of the

ORAL LAW (*Torah she-be'al-Peh*). Thus, the sages were able to ascribe to the oral tradition the force of biblical law. There were, however, instances where the sages would acknowledge that a ruling based on exegetical exposition was of rabbinic origin; its attachment to the biblical verse in such a case was known as an *asmakhta*, a handy reference.

HERZOG, ISAAC HA-LEVI (1888-1959). Rabbinic scholar and second Ashkenazi Chief Rabbi of modern Israel. Born in Lomza, Poland, he later lived in Leeds, England, and Paris, France, where his father served in rabbinical positions. He pursued rabbinical studies on his own, and by the age of 16 had completed study of the entire Talmud. Herzog also devoted himself to secular studies, and received a doctorate in literature from London University for his thesis on "The Dyeing of Purple in Ancient Israel." He served as rabbi in Belfast (1916-19) and in Dublin, the capital of Ireland (1919-36). He was appointed Chief Rabbi of the Irish Free State, and forged excellent relations with its political and ecclesiastical leaders.

In 1936, Herzog was elected to succeed Abraham Isaac KOOK as Ashkenazi Chief Rabbi of Palestine. Settling in Jerusalem in 1937, Herzog was soon caught up with the difficult problems that beset the country's Jewish community. He made numerous journeys to Europe both during and after the Holocaust to return Jewish children who had been placed for safekeeping in Christian homes and institutions to their people.

Herzog worked incessantly to guide the Orthodox community after the establishment of the State of Israel in 1948. He had to deal with a host of halakhic problems which had been purely academic since the fall of the Second Commonwealth. Among these was the observance of the Sabbath and dietary laws within the framework of a modern state and society. Above all, he struggled to secure recognition for halakhic standards in the spheres of marital and personal status.

Endowed with a brilliant analytical mind and a phenomenal memory, Herzog was recognized as one of the leading rabbinical scholars of his time. He published the first two volumes of his planned five-volume work, *Main Institutions of Jewish Law* (1936, 1939). Three volumes of his extensive responsa, entitled *Hékhal Yitsḫak*, appeared posthumously (1960-72). These are a valuable source of rabbinic guidance for contemporary issues. His son **Chaim Herzog** (1918-), a former general and diplomat, was elected sixth President of the State of Israel in 1983.

HESCHEL, ABRAHAM JOSHUA (1907-1972). Scholar and philosopher of religion. Born in Poland into a distinguished line of Ḥasidic rabbis, he received a thorough talmudic training, to which he added a deep study of ḤASIDISM and Kabbalah. He went to Berlin where he was a student of philosophy at the university, going on to teach Talmud in the Hochschule für die Wissenschaft des Judentums. Martin BUBER appointed him as his successor at the central organization for adult Jewish education, but the Nazis deported him to Poland in 1938. He remained there for less than a year, teaching at the Warsaw Institute for Jewish Studies, before moving to London. Finally, he emigrated to the United States, where he served first as associate professor of philosophy and rabbinics at the Hebrew Union College of Cincinnati and then at the Jewish Theological Seminary in New York, where he was professor of Jewish ethics and mysticism from 1945 until his death.

Heschel's books cover almost every aspect of classical Jewish thought. His first major work was on the biblical prophets. This was followed by writings on medieval Jewish philosophers, including SAADIAH GAON, IBN GABIROL and MAIMONIDES. He also wrote extensively on Kabbalah and Ḥasidism, while one of his last works, *Torah min ha-Shamayim*, examines in depth the different schools in rabbinic methodology, exegesis and philosophy. His other important books include *The Sabbath* (1951), *Man is not Alone* (1951), *Man's Quest for God* (1954), *God in Search of Man* (1956), *Who is Man?* (1962), and *Israel: an Echo of Eternity* (1969).

Heschel taught that Judaism is not a religion of reason only, for this would describe it as a philosophy. Nor is it only a culture of religious experience, which would make it a psychological system. He sought to explain Judaism as a combination of both elements — philosophical and experimental. Above all, Judaism is a teaching with a living relationship between God and man. On God's side there is a Divine concern and a Divine passion for His creatures, while the nature of true religion is man's response to God's bond with him. The root of Jewish observance is found when this human response is expressed with love and devotion. When man rises to the holy dimension of his meeting with God through the acceptance of the Divine will, he also shows the true character of human freedom. Jewish history is the record of Israel's successes and failures to respond to God's call, and the Bible is the book containing that record.

Heschel attempted to examine the classic sources of Judaism to show their relevance to modern problems. He insisted that Jewish ethics must guide Jewish behavior in all aspects of social concern. His enthusiasm for the relevance of Judaism brought him to a position of leadership in the United States in the Civil Rights Movement and in other humanistic causes. Heschel was also active in Jewish-Christian dialogue and was involved in the high-level discussions which led to the Vatican II statement introducing a more theologically liberal Catholic attitude toward Judaism and the Jews.

His views on the central question of REVELATION place him in a position which is neither fundamentalist nor extreme liberal. On the one hand, he taught that the assumption that every iota of the Law is of Mosaic origin revealed at Sinai is a misreading of the rabbinic concept of Revelation. On the other hand, he emphasized that Judaism is built on the certainty that God made His will known to His people. This approach to Revelation did not diminish for him the basic importance of *halakhah*, the laws of rabbinic Judaism. He argued that these are like the musical notes without which the great symphony of Judaism in all its holy dimensions could not be played.

A special emphasis in Heschel's writings is seen in his description of the holiness of time. Judaism has not given to the world any holy places — temples or cathedrals. Judaism created, instead, palaces in time, the Sabbath and the festivals.

Heschel's last book was a work on the Hasidic master MENAHEM MENDEL of Kotzk (the Kotzker *Rebbe*) and in a way this biography reveals something about Heschel the man. Whereas the founder of Hasidism, Israel BAAL SHEM TOV, had upheld the value of joy, Menahem Mendel lived a life filled with near pessimism and despair. Heschel himself wrote that he was "at home with the Baal Shem but driven by the Kotzker *Rebbe*... living both in fervor and horror, with my conscience on mercy and my eyes on Auschwitz...My heart was in Medzibezh (the center of the Baal Shem's activity); my mind in Kotzk."

From seminary lectern, lecture platform, and through his numerous writings Heschel influenced generations of rabbis and teachers, thousands of people, Jews and non-Jews, and left a lasting impression on students of Judaism all over the world.

HESHVAN Eighth month of the Jewish religious CALENDAR; second month of the Hebrew civil year counting from TISHRI. It is a variable month of either 29 or 30 days and normally coincides with October-November. Its sign of the zodiac, Scorpio, was associated by the rabbis with the earth's thirst for water in the autumn. Heshvan is a popular abbreviation of Marheshvan, which derives from the Babylonian term signifying "eighth month." Its shortened form came into use because of a widespread but mistaken belief that *Mar* possessed the Hebrew sense of "bitter." There is no mention of Heshvan in the Bible, where the eighth month is called Bul (I Kings 6:38). An extra (30th) day is periodically added to this month so as to prevent the next DAY OF ATONEMENT falling on a Friday or Sunday. Traditional significant dates include 6 Heshvan, when the Judean king Zedekiah had his eyes put out by the Babylonians (II Kings 25:7); 11 Heshvan, when Rachel was interred near Bethlehem (Gen. 35:19); and 17 Heshvan, the anniversary of the Flood, which also marks the Balfour Declaration (2 November 1917) inaugurating a Jewish National Home in Palestine.

HESPED See EULOGY

HEVRAH KADDISHA See BURIAL SOCIETY

HIBBUT HA-KEVER See DEATH

HIDDUSHIM See NOVELLAE

HIGH HOLIDAYS Name given to ROSH HA-SHANAH and the DAY OF ATONEMENT which occur on 1 and 2 TISHRI and 10 Tishri respectively. These two FESTIVALS mark the most solemn time of the Jewish year, Rosh ha-Shanah being the day when, traditionally, all are judged for the coming year and the Day of Atonement the day when the final sealing of the verdict takes place. The ten days from the beginning of Rosh ha-Shanah to the conclusion of the Day of Atonement are known as the TEN DAYS OF PENITENCE (or of Repentance). The Hebrew phrase, *Yamim Nora'im* (literally "Days of Awe") is first found in a 14th-century work; it is used either for the Ten Days of Penitence or for the period from 1 Elul to the Day of Atonement, all of which is regarded as a penitential season. Some even extend this period to HOSHANA RABBAH, seen as the final sealing of the Divine decree.

HIGH PLACES See IDOLATRY

HIGH PRIEST (Heb. *kohen gadol*). The chief among the PRIESTS; the first was AARON (Ex. 28:1), and all later Priests (and other priests) were required to be descended from him. The High Priest was distinguished from the ordinary priest in several ways. In addition to the four garments worn by all priests (coat, girdle, turban, breeches), the High Priest also wore the apron (*ephod*) made of wool and linen, the breastplate (*hoshen*) which contained the 12 precious stones inscribed with the names of the 12 tribes, a robe made of blue wool, and a gold headplate on which were inscribed the words "Holy to the Lord" (see PRIESTLY GARMENTS). These garments were worn during the High Priest's service in the Temple. Although all priests were anointed with holy oil, only the High Priest had the oil poured over his head. In his garments of gold, blue, and purple, the gold plate worn on his head, and the anointing with oil, the High Priest resembled royalty, sharing these features with the Jewish monarch.

The outstanding garment worn by the High Priest was the breastplate, which contained the oracle, the URIM AND THUMMIM (Divine Names which could not be erased). If a king or the head of the Sanhedrin wished to inquire of God about embarking on a war or other issues of community importance, he went to the High Priest while he wore the breastplate. The High Priest faced the Divine Presence as the question was asked, and when the letters inscribed on the stones lit up, he would read the answer (*Yoma* 73a).

The High Priest's service in the Temple was distinguished by the permission he received to make sin-offerings on the inner altar and to enter the HOLY OF HOLIES. The offerings were made to atone for his personal sins, for sins in judgment made by the Sanhedrin, and for communal sins. The High

Priest's most solemn (AVODAH) service was performed on the DAY OF ATONEMENT. To prepare for this day, he separated from his family one week earlier and lived in the Temple in order to purify himself and review the laws of his service. After staying up all night on the Day of Atonement itself, the High Priest offered up personal and communal sacrifices, changed his clothes, and immersed in a ritual bath (*mikveh*) five different times, then entered the Holy of Holies and offered special incense before the Ark of the Covenant. This incense offering required both spiritual purity and physical dexterity, and if any part of this ritual was flawed, the High Priest, it was believed, would not return from the Holy of Holies alive. When carried out properly, the service atoned for the sins of the entire Jewish nation.

According to Jewish law, the High Priest was more restricted than an ordinary priest. Not only was he forbidden to defile himself by proximity to the dead, as were all priests, but he was not even allowed to mourn for his closest relatives. In addition to the restrictions placed on all priests regarding the choice of a spouse, the High Priest had to marry a virgin.

Coin bearing the inscription: "Yehoḇanan the High Priest and head of the ḥever *[ethnarch?] of the Jews". Minted in c. 47 BCE.*

During the Second Temple period, the office of High Priest took on more administrative responsibilities. The High Priest was often the NASI (President) of the SANHEDRIN. The Hasmonean rulers, after Judah the Maccabee, took over the office of High Priest, against the stipulations of Jewish law. After the Roman conquest (63 BCE) and especially during Herod's rule (37-4 BCE), the position of High Priest degenerated and became a political tool in the hands of the Romans. During the war with Rome (66-70 CE), the office was filled by lot. High Priests were often chosen from among the SADDUCEES, who did not accept the Oral Law, and subsequently the title of High Priest was belittled by the sages. The office of the High Priest ended with the destruction of the Second Temple. Traditionally there were 18 High Priests in the First Temple period and about 60 in Second Temple times.

HILDESHEIMER, AZRIEL (1820-1899). Rabbinical scholar and leader of German NEO-ORTHODOXY. Having first received a traditional rabbinic education, he gained his doctorate at the University of Halle, and then turned to Jewish communal work in his native Halberstadt. Following his appointment as rabbi of Eisenstadt in the Austro-Hungarian Empire (1851), Hildesheimer devoted himself to combating the Reform movement. On the one hand, he believed in harmonizing traditional Judaism and modern culture; on the other hand, he demanded "unconditional steadfastness in the faith and traditions of Judaism." A modernized rabbinical training program (which included secular studies) proved vastly successful at Hildesheimer's new rabbinical academy, but exposed him to attacks from both religious extremes, ultra-Orthodox zealots even placing him under a ban of excommunication. The onslaught by extremists made it impossible for him to remain in Eisenstadt and in 1869 he accepted a post as rabbi of the newly established Adass Yisroel congregation in Berlin, where he spent the remainder of his life.

A champion of the Neo-Orthodox cause, he devised a plan for the training of rabbis as well as pious laymen, implemented in the Berlin Rabbinical Seminary, established in 1873 (see RABBINICAL SEMINARIES). As its founder and first principal, Hildesheimer gave it leadership and prestige, recruited its teachers, and determined its high standard of Jewish scholarship. An edition of the HALAKHOT GEDOLOT (1888-90), based on a Vatican manuscript, was Hildesheimer's own major achievement in the field of Jewish scholarship. He was an exceptionally powerful advocate of "practical" Zionism and Jewish settlement in Erets Israel.

HILLEL (c.70 BCE-c.10 CE). A leader of the PHARISEES during the reign of King Herod and greatest sage of the Second Temple period; known as Hillel the Elder (or "the Babylonian"). Born into a family that claimed Davidic descent, Hillel first studied Torah in his native Babylonia, then in Jerusalem under SHEMAYAH AND AVTALYON. While perfecting his Torah scholarship in Jerusalem, he was forced to maintain his family and himself on whatever he could earn from manual labor, half of which went to the porter at the house of study. Once on a Friday, at the height of winter, Hillel lacked the fee and was unable to gain admission; he therefore crawled onto the roof so as to hear the lesson through a skylight. At daybreak, Shemayah and Avtalyon caught sight of his figure blocking the light and had him brought down, nearly frozen to death under a blanket of snow. Although it was a Sabbath, they had a fire lit to revive him, declaring that he was worthy of the Sabbath being profaned for his sake (*Yoma* 35b). After his masters' death, Hillel apparently spent some time either in Babylonia or Alexandria, or else with a sectarian group in the wilderness.

His emergence as an authoritative teacher of *halakhah* is described in a talmudic passage (*Pes.* 66a) indicating the way in which he found a solution to the problem as to whether the paschal offering might be made if Passover eve coincided with the Sabbath. Hillel used his canon of HERMENEUTICS, seven rules of Bible interpretation (later expanded to 13 by Ishmael ben Elisha) which appear to have been previously unknown and which were only accepted after he appealed to the authority of his teachers, Shemayah and Avtalyon. Though at first treated with disdain on account of his Babylonian origin, Hillel was eventually appointed NASI (president or patriarch), an office which remained hereditary among his descendants for several centuries. Like his predecessors, he shared authority with a vice-president of the Sanhedrin or a "father of the court" (*av bet din*) — first with a certain Menaẖem who resigned, taking with him many of his students, then with SHAMMAI, who became Hillel's colleague and lifelong controversialist. In the face of Herod's reign of terror, Hillel seems to have adopted a quietist policy, but he did not hesitate to criticize the opulent life style of rich and powerful families in the Jerusalem of his time (*Avot* 2.7).

As head of the Sanhedrin, Hillel presided over the Jewish people's supreme religious and legal authority. Once his hermeneutical canon (MIDRASH) had been accepted, it provided greater adaptability, allowing both extensive and restrictive interpretation of Scripture. Oral tradition, received from his teachers, played an important part. Inter-rabbinic controversies, which later multiplied between the schools of Hillel and Shammai (see BET HILLEL AND BET SHAMMAI), were as yet few. In the legal sphere, Hillel introduced certain reforms (*takkanot*) motivated by social concern — notably the PROSBUL, an institution of Greek law, which virtually abolished the Scriptural law cancelling debts in the SABBATICAL YEAR of release (*shemittah*; Deut. 15:1-18).

Above all, however, Hillel was a teacher of Torah. As one source puts it (*Suk.* 20a), Hillel — like Ezra before him — came from Babylon to restore the Torah when it had been forgotten in Israel, and he endeavored to bring it closer to his fellowmen. There was a tendency in his day (exemplified by Shammai) to discriminate in the choice of pupils, with good breeding and wealth as preconditions. Hillel rejected this kind of procedure emphatically, and he is described as teaching Torah to laborers on their way to work and receiving questioners at his home. He set high standards for his pupils. Torah should be studied unselfishly for its own sake and not for ulterior motives (*Avot* 1.12-13). Although a life of Torah study might involve hardship, as Hillel knew to his cost, the heavenly reward would be commensurate (cf. *Avot* 5.22). Learning, and learning alone, could refine the student's character and religious personality, endow him with the fear of God, and raise him to the level of a *ẖasid*, a genuinely pious man (*ibid.*, 2.5).

Hillel's teaching methods were Socratic and peripatetic, most likely showing a Hellenistic influence: question and answer, enigmatic statements provoking a response and sharpening the student's mind. The teacher must be patient (*ibid.*) and teaching must be practical, through personal example; the concept of "serving scholars" (*shimmush*) has been rabbinic pedagogics ever since. As for the teaching's

One of Hillel's sayings: "If I am not for myself, who is for me?" illustrated by US artist Ben Shahn (1898-1969).

content, it was Scripture — both the Written and the Oral Torah — whose equal Sinaitic origin Hillel was the first to formulate (*Shab.* 31a). The Oral Torah consisted of immemorial traditions (HALAKHAH LE-MOSHEH MI-SINAI), CUSTOMS (*minhagim*), and, increasingly since Hillel, Midrash (see above). Popular wisdom, the result of cumulative human experience, was also taught by him, and supported by quotations from Scripture.

It was preeminently as a *ẖasid*, a man of pious action, that Hillel made his mark on his and all future generations. Every action of his was "for the sake of heaven," motivated by the desire only to serve God and do His will. Hillel believed in Divine justice and, on seeing a skull floating in the water, he remarked: "Because you drowned others, they have drowned you; and, in the end, those who drowned you will also be drowned" (*Avot* 2.6).

On Sukkot, at the WATER DRAWING FESTIVAL, however, he would joyfully exclaim: "If I [meaning God] am here, everyone is here; but if I am not here, then who is?" (*Suk.* 53a).

The piety which Hillel evinced was bound up with a great measure of forbearance toward others. Asked by a would-be proselyte to teach him the whole Torah while standing on one foot, Shammai had angrily driven the man away; but Hillel accepted him with the instruction: "What is hateful to you, don't do to your fellowman; this is the whole Torah, all the rest is its explanation. Now go and learn!" (*Shab.* 31a). Hillel considered this "golden rule" not only the best introduction to Judaism for a neophyte, but also its sum total.

Of Hillel's pupils, traditionally 80 in number, 30 were said to be worthy of the "holy spirit" (prophecy); the youngest of his disciples was Rabban JOHANAN BEN ZAKKAI (*Suk.* 28a). A heavenly voice is reported to have declared that Hillel himself would have merited the "holy spirit," had his generation also been worthy. When he died (at the age of 120 according to *Sif.* Deut. 357.7), he was mourned for his humility and piety. Hillel played a decisive role in the history of Judaism. His hermeneutical rules expanded and revolutionized the Jewish tradition; his stress on the primacy of ethical conduct, his tolerance and humanity, deeply influenced the character and image of Judaism as well as the thought of Christianity's founders a generation or two after him. In modern times, movements of Jewish dissent have sought justification in his teachings. Hillel was the patron of what has been termed "classical Judaism": to the worship of power and the State he opposed the ideal of a community of the learned — Jews who love God and their fellowman.

FROM THE SAYINGS OF HILLEL

Be a disciple of Aaron, loving peace and pursuing peace, loving your fellow creatures and attracting them to the [study of] Torah.

He who seeks fame will lose his name; knowledge not increased is knowledge decreased; one who does not study deserves to die; and one who exploits the crown [of Torah] will perish.

If I am not [concerned] for myself, who will be for me? But if I am for myself alone, what [good] am I? and if [the time to act is] not now, when [will it be]? (*Avot* 1.14).

Do not withdraw from the community; do not be sure of yourself until the day you die; do not judge your fellowman until you have stood in his place; and do not say "When I have time, I will study." You may never find time.

HILLULA Aramaic word meaning "festivity," originally used to designate a marriage party. Among Jews in Muslim lands, the *hillula* generally commemorates the death of a sage, whose soul is regarded as having been reunited with its Creator. The classic instance of the *hillula* is that marking the traditional anniversary of the death of SIMEON BAR YOHAI on Lag ba-Omer, which is celebrated at his putative burial place and that of his son Eleazar in Meron, in northern Israel. Crowds as large as 100,000 people attend the festivities and large bonfires are lit and burn throughout the night. Another *hillula* is that of MEIR BA'AL HA-NES, on 14 Iyyar (Second Passover) in Tiberias. Since the death of R. Israel Abuhatzera, known as the Baba Sali, in 1983, his grave in Netivot has become the venue for an annual *hillula* on 3 Shevat.

Outside Israel, one of the largest *hillulot* is the Lag ba-Omer celebration in the courtyard of the El-Ghriba synagogue in Djerba, Tunisia.

HILLUL HA-SHEM See KIDDUSH HA-SHEM

HIRSCH, SAMSON RAPHAEL (1808-1888). German rabbi and a founder of the School of NEO-ORTHODOXY. He taught that Orthodox Judaism should accept and become involved in Western culture — expressed in the slogan *Torah im derekh erets*, "Torah together with worldly involvement" — while forcefully articulating and defending a traditional approach to Judaism against the nascent REFORM movement. A dynamic and charismatic speaker, teacher, and leader, Hirsch succeeded in bringing a substantial portion of the relatively assimilated community of Frankfurt am Main to return to strict traditional observance. He was a strong advocate of Orthodox separatism on an operational level, and broke with the established Jewish communal institutions to set up a separatist framework based upon Orthodox principles.

His basic outlook is presented in *The Nineteen Letters on Judaism*, published under the pseudonym Ben Uzziel, in which he presents a polemic on behalf of traditional Judaism oriented toward the ethical and humanistic values of 19th-century Europe. One of the central thrusts of his argument is that the *mitsvot* (COMMANDMENTS) bring the Jew to the highest stage of perfection in general human terms. His ideal type, the *Jissroel-Mensch*, or "Jewish human-being," is at once a humanistic and a spiritual ideal type. *The Nineteen Letters* may be seen as a model for the contemporary genre of Orthodox literature presenting the case for Judaism to the acculturated, Western-educated Jew.

Hirsch's other writings include *Choreb*, a systematic exposition and classification of the *mitsvot*; German translations and commentary on the Pentateuch, the Psalms, the prayer book; and numerous articles in the journal *Jeschurun*, which he founded and edited. These works reflect a highly original exegetical approach: in *Choreb*, he develops a systematic, largely symbolic, understanding of the reasons for the commandments, while in the *Commentary to the Pentateuch* he develops a method of biblical exegesis based upon the symbolic understanding of the words of the Hebrew language, and their component roots and letters.

HISTORIOGRAPHY The term *history* is of Greek origin and means an investigation or inquiry, namely, of the actions of human beings in the past. The word is used nowadays to refer either to those past events themselves or to what is known of them. In the latter sense, it was the Greeks who invented the concept of "scientific" history concerned with the evidential grounds of historical knowledge. However, it is to the Hebrew Bible and Judaism that one should attribute the notion that the entire course of history is endowed with a goal or purpose which transcends the actual events themselves, that history or particular events within it are charged with great significance. Such is the case only when one brings to bear some nonempirical, transcendent point of view in which the entire historical process can be seen as a teleological development. The biblical God, who is the Lord of history, brings nations into existence, has plans for them, and is watchful and judgmental as their careers stretch out into time. History can likewise have significance for the Bible because of its "this-worldly" orientation, which consistently upholds the reality of events occurring in time.

While the Bible contains many different types of literary expression, such as poetry, laws, narratives, and exhortations, all of this is held together in a framework of history, albeit theocentric or sacred history. The Hebrew Bible exhibits the continuity of an unraveling plot, the realization of a purposive process in time; it is the story of the origins, formation, and subsequent career of a nation-people called Israel told against a universal backdrop.

Yet despite the centrality of Israel, the moral God of Scripture is — indeed, has to be — the Lord of universal history. The biblical narrator's perspective is universal; it reaches back to the origins of men, nations, and empires, to creation itself; and it reaches into the far-distant future, to the ultimate realization of God's kingdom at the end of days.

However, it is with the people of Israel that God makes His covenant, demonstrating the Bible's inner connection with history. For the story of a nation whose career spans millennia and brings it into collision with world empires, whose migrations span continents, can only be understood within the framework of history. Hence the genealogical data, the allusions to pagan kingdoms and (lost) Israelite records, and the historical documents interspersed in the biblical Prophets and Writings. While proclaiming the fact that God reveals Himself in nature (Ps. 19), the Bible emphasizes His manifestations in historical events such as the Exodus and the Revelation at Mount Sinai. These "mighty events" testify not only to His existence but also to His attributes of mercy and justice, as well as to His overall plan for Israel and mankind. In order to know God, therefore, it is essential to relive these events and understand the history of this people.

The literary prophets display an awareness of history that is much more explicit and distinctive. Jeremiah, who is called "a prophet to the nations" (Jer. 1:5), like Isaiah, Ezekiel, and Amos, makes detailed prophecies concerning foreign nations such as Edom, Moab, Egypt, Babylon, Philistia, Elam, and Phoenicia (Sidon). Although the prophets address these peoples by name, their message in the first instance is for Israel. Sometimes they condemn the nations for their mistreatment of Israel; at other times they judge them for their neglect of basic moral values in their dealings with each other and for their practice of idolatry (Isa. 13-24; Jer. 46-51; Ezek. 25-28; Amos 1-2). Israel is urged to learn from history the disastrous fate of those nations that have proved morally incorrigible.

The prophet's view of history does not include a succession of recognizable eras. He sees essentially a present that he decries, a near future that will be destructive, and a redemptive distant future. Each of these time sequences is presented in monochromatic form. Only in the Book of Daniel is there the first glimpse of an idea (the vision of Four Kingdoms) suggesting that the long stretch of events prior to the final Redemption exhibits a historical pattern.

Despite the tradition of history-writing which the Jews developed — including, after the Bible, the Books of the Maccabees and the works of Josephus (*Antiquities of the Jews* and *The Jewish War*) — the rabbis felt no need to write a systematic history of their times, although some of their works (e.g., MEGILLAT TA'ANIT and the *Seder Olam Rabbah* chronology ascribed to YOSÉ BEN ḤALAFTA) contain much historical material.

In aggadic literature, the rabbis continued to discuss and develop many basic elements of the historiography found in Scripture: the concept of Israel as God's CHOSEN PEOPLE and Israel's relationship to the other nations; the role of Providence in human affairs; the function of Jewish leaders within the context of their times; exile, the Messiah, and Redemption. A favourite theme of the rabbis was that of the Four Kingdoms (Babylon, Persia-Media, Greece, and Rome) to which Israel would be subject before the advent of God's messianic kingdom. This provided an overall schema within which to place the events of the recent past as well as to anticipate the future. Another influential schema can be found in the teaching that "the world will exist for 6,000 years: the first 2,000 will be chaos, followed by 2,000 years of Torah and 2,000 years of the messianic era" (*Sanh.* 97a). This seems to have derived its inspiration from the Genesis story portraying six days of Divine creative activity followed by a seventh day of rest. The implication here is that the six millennia of ongoing events will be followed by the Sabbath of history. These two schemata offer a perspective in which the various ages are related to each other both causally and sequentially.

The Book of Josippon, an anonymous Hebrew work of the mid-tenth century, written in Italy, bridges the gap between Near Eastern and European Jewish historiography. Though not in itself authoritative, relying on Josephus and the Apocrypha, *Josippon*'s account of the Second Temple period was much quoted throughout the Middle Ages. Apart from

Seder Olam Rabbah, the only chronological "histories" to appear before the 16th century form part of the genre known as "chain of tradition" literature. Such works, describing the way in which rabbinic law was transmitted down the ages, include the *Epistle (Iggeret)* of SHERIRA GAON (987) and the *Sefer ha-Kabbalah* of Abraham IBN DAUD (c. 1160). A new and different genre of history writing, pioneeered by Ashkenazim, was the martyrology: here, drawing upon the most recent accounts of massacre and persecution during the Crusades, medieval chroniclers such as Eliezer ben Nathan of Mainz and Ephraim ben Jacob of Bonn established a pattern that would be followed by Sephardim as well for centuries to come.

After 1492, the need to grapple with the meaning of virtually unprecedented disasters — first and foremost the Spanish Expulsion — promoted a more intensive and scholarly analysis of the Jewish fate, often in the context of general history. Thus, Elijah Capsali's work on the Ottoman Empire, *Seder Eliyyahu Zuta* (written in 1523), became a major source of information regarding the Jewish communities in Spain and Portugal; while *Shevet Yehudah* ("The Scepter of Judah," 1554), an impressively detailed account of anti-Jewish persecution throughout the ages, served as the vehicle for Solomon Ibn Verga's bold defiance of traditional assumptions, pointing to life in exile as the real cause of Jewish misery.

Other 16th-century writers adhered to the older approach of tracing the development of religious tradition. In his *Sefer ha-Yuḫasin* ("Book of Genealogies," 1566), Abraham ben Samuel Zacuto updated the history of the Oral Law with many original touches, whereas Gedaliah ben Joseph Ibn Yaḫya injected much anecdotal, scientific, and legendary material into his popular *Shalshelet ha-Kabbalah* ("The Chain of Tradition," 1587).

Only when the Science of Judaism (WISSENSCHAFT DES JUDENTUMS) made its appearance in the early 19th century did Jews begin writing systematic histories of their people. The pioneers in this field regarded the Jewish historical experience as centered around the evolving concept of Divine unity, no less valid in the modern age than it had been in the past. Among the German Reformers, Abraham GEIGER defined that experience as the history of ethical monotheism. Isaac Marcus Jost, a more moderate Reformer, led the field with his voluminous and "scientific" history of the Jews from Maccabean to modern times (1820-47), but then proceeded to concentrate on Jewish religious history. Nachman KROCHMAL expounded a major philosophy of Jewish history, maintaining that only Jewish national existence is eternal and contrasting the uniquely religious spirit of the Jews — a full manifestation of the Absolute Spirit — with its no more than partial manifestation in other national cultures. Krochmal saw Israel's "mission" as bringing this Absolute Spirit to the rest of mankind.

For Heinrich Graetz, the best-known Jewish historian of the 19th century, Judaism's originality lay in its concept of God. Both the religious ideal and the political concept (including the Jewish people's institutions and devotion to the Land of Israel) are the warp and woof of Judaism, which is further distinguished by its messianic orientation to the future. A decidedly rationalist spirit pervades Graetz's much-translated *History of the Jews* (11 vols., 1853-76); this made him (unlike the Orthodox Ze'ev Jawitz, for example) neglect certain traditional factors and prejudiced him against everything connected with mysticism. Yet for all its manifestly scientific foundations, his work is permeated by the conviction that history in general — and Jewish history in particular — is Divinely ordained and conducted, with the Jewish people functioning as the instrument of God's will. Nations, like individuals, are free agents, but it is the Jewish people's commitment to a higher ethic that has determined its history.

Simon Dubnow, the foremost 20th-century Jewish historian, brought the social sciences to bear in his *World History of the Jewish People* (11 vols., 1923-40). Dubnow's viewpoint was a secular one, attributing Jewry's survival to its crystallization as a "spiritual people." He rejected the idea that any single concept represented the totality of Jewish history; in his view, the central determining factor was the Jewish people itself. Judaism, in the religious sense, had fulfilled its role in the past; Zionism, however interpreted, was a pseudo-messianic delusion; "Diaspora nationalism" alone guaranteed the Jewish future.

More recently, Zionist historians such as Benzion Dinur have emphasized the nationalist impulse and age-old links with Erets Israel as the two key factors in Jewish history. Others, including Salo W. Baron in the US (*A Social and Religious History of the Jews*, 18 vols., 1952-83), believe that Israel and the Diaspora each has a vital role to play, and insist on the basic religious motivation that has ensured Jewish continuity.

In recent decades, Jewish historians have been faced with the challenges of the Holocaust and of the State of Israel. Religious Jews seek to reconcile the omnipotence of a benevolent God with the realities of Auschwitz (see HOLOCAUST), while secular Jews wrestle with the nature of man and human morality. The establishment of the State has divided the Jewish world between Israel and the Diaspora, and the question of their interrelation, both in their commonalty and their separateness, is already exercising the Jewish historian.

HOLDHEIM, SAMUEL (1806-1860). Protagonist of REFORM JUDAISM in Germany. Having received both a talmudic and a secular (university) education, Holdheim displayed his liberal approach by implementing reforms in the liturgy and advocating a wholesale revision of the ORAL LAW. He called for a separation between the religio-ethical and the national elements in Judaism, only the former, in his view, still requiring the allegiance of a true patriot and good citizen. If the Talmud was right in its day, Holdheim insisted, "I voice the convictions of my time, and from that standpoint I am right." Paradoxically, however, this anti-halakhic radicalism was based squarely on the talmudic principle of DINA DE-MALKHUTA DINA, that Jews must uphold "the law of the land." As rabbi of the new Berlin temple *Reformgemeinde*) from 1847, Holdheim speedily jettisoned almost everything that savored of "exclusiveness and particularism." Services were conducted entirely in German, male worshipers came bareheaded, the Sabbath was transferred to Sunday morning for convenience, and even marriages between Jews and Gentiles had the rabbi's blessing. Such extremism, in the cause of a denationalized "higher religion," proved unacceptable to other European reformers, including Abraham GEIGER, although Holdheim was not always consistent. Holdheim's radical Reform had a much greater impact in the US, determining the outlook of David EINHORN, Kaufmann KOHLER, and the Pittsburgh Platform (1885).

ḤOL HA-MO'ED The intermediate days of the PASSOVER and SUKKOT festivals. Unlike the first and last days of the festivals themselves, when all work save the types related to the preparation of food is forbidden, it is generally permitted to perform such work on *ḥol ha-mo'ed*, with certain limitations. In Israel, *ḥol ha-mo'ed* lasts five days during Passover and six days during Sukkot, whereas in the Diaspora the numbers are four and five days respectively (because of the observance of SECOND DAYS OF FESTIVALS in the Diaspora).

The phrase *ḥol ha-mo'ed*, translated literally, means "the weekdays of the festival," thus indicating a combination of the ordinary weekday and the festival. While various activities, such as lighting a fire, driving, cutting, etc., are permissible, it is forbidden to perform any such action in order to make a profit. On the other hand, it is allowed to undertake such actions to prevent a loss; for example, watering plants in a nursery. Many rabbinic authorities forbid writing on *ḥol ha-mo'ed* except to avoid a monetary loss. Even when one does write or perform another such action to prevent a monetary loss, it must be in a manner different than the usual.

Praying with TEFILLIN on *ḥol ha-mo'ed* is a matter of custom. In the Ashkenazi community outside Israel, it is customary to put on the *tefillin* but without reciting the usual blessing, and to wear them until the cantor's repetition of the AMIDAH prayer, during which time they are removed. The custom of Sephardim, Ḥasidim, and Ashkenazi Jews living in Israel is not to put on *tefillin* at all during *ḥol ha-mo'ed*. It is generally forbidden to shave or have a haircut on *ḥol ha-mo'ed*, although there have been recent rulings permitting a person who shaves on a regular basis throughout the year to do so on *ḥol ha-mo'ed* as well.

During the *Amidah* prayer and in GRACE AFTER MEALS, a special passage, YA'ALEH VE-YAVO, is added. In the Morning Service, full HALLEL is recited during Sukkot, but only "half-*Hallel*" during Passover. *Hallel* is followed by a READING OF THE LAW each day and by the distinctive *Musaf* (ADDITIONAL SERVICE) for the festival. Weddings may not be held during *ḥol ha-mo'ed*, because of the prohibition of mingling two causes for joy, that of the festival and the joy of the wedding. One does not sit *Shivah* in MOURNING on *ḥol ha-mo'ed*, nor are eulogies delivered during that time. In Israel, the days of *ḥol ha-mo'ed* are generally treated as "half-festivals," and stores and government offices are open only in the morning hours.

A tractate of the Talmud, MO'ED KATAN (lit. "minor festival"), is devoted to the laws of *ḥol ha-mo'ed* (see also FESTIVALS).

HOLINESS (*kedushah*). A religious quality or value invested in special objects, places, times, and persons. The root meaning of *kedushah* and its derivatives is "to be set apart" or "distinguished." The source of all holiness is the holiness of GOD, the "Holy One, blessed be He." Several times in the Bible, the people of Israel is exhorted to be holy because God is holy (e.g., Lev. 19:2). To describe God as holy in this context means to say that He is totally transcendent. He is the great Other, over and above the universe and all things in it. When the attribute of holiness is ascribed to God, it also embraces His awesomeness. Thus, the liturgy for the HIGH HOLIDAYS celebrates God as *Kadosh ve-Nora*, "holy and awesome."

The Bible describes the SANCTUARY, its furnishings and utensils as holy [Ex. 26:33; 28:2-4; 29:1; 30:29ff., 37]. In Jewish teaching, JERUSALEM is the Holy City and Erets Israel is the Holy Land (*Kelim* 1,6; *Ta'an*. 5a). The special days of the calendar, starting with the Sabbath and including all the biblical festivals, are holy days (Ex. 31:12ff.; Lev. 23; Num. 28-29). While there is a certain reluctance in Judaism to identify holy men, there is a special degree of holiness attached to the PRIESTS (Lev. 21).

Some identification of the awesome with the holy seems to apply, at least in the Bible, to the Temple, its sacred objects, and service. Thus no one other than the High Priest could enter the HOLY OF HOLIES in the Sanctuary; and at that time he pronounced the otherwise unspoken, ineffable Name of God. Further, no layman could touch an object of the Temple ritual; to handle such an object was a grave sin (Ex. 30:33, 38; Num. 1:51; 3:10, 38; 18:7). When David attempted to bring the ARK OF THE COVENANT into Jerusalem, Uzzah was killed in a fatal accident because he handled it (II Sam. 6:1ff).

When, however, the concept of holiness is applied to the people of Israel and held up to its members as the ultimate religious ideal, only the idea of separateness is invoked. Thus, just as God is holy, i.e., separate and distinguished from all other existences, so Israel should be separate and distinguished from all other peoples (Ex. 19:6; Lev. 19:2; 20:7). Holiness as a quality of life for the people of Israel is not an abstract concept. The rabbis maintained that Israel's holiness, experienced in its separateness from other peoples, is to be translated in practice into a distinctive pattern of behavior. In the Pentateuch, the call to holiness is first and foremost a call for *imitatio Dei* (see IMITATION OF GOD): "You shall be holy; for I the Lord your God am holy" (Lev. 19:2). The Talmud states that holiness is attained by modeling individual and communal life upon the attributes of God: "As He is merciful, you be merciful; as He is gracious, you be gracious" (*Shab.* 133b). Leviticus 19:2 (see above) is explained not in philosophical but in practical terms by the 11th-century commentator RASHI (*ad loc.*): "You shall distance yourselves from sexual immoralities." It is the pure, moral, and ideal behavior of the individual man which can bring him to a state of holiness. So the Talmud asserts, "Purity leads to holiness, holiness leads to humility," and elsewhere: "The fear of sin leads to holiness, holiness leads to the spirit of God" (TJ *Shek.* 3.3; *Av. Zar.* 20b).

The rabbis also relate the achievement of holiness by the Jewish people to the observance of the DIETARY LAWS, since the Pentateuch itself draws this connection (Lev. 11:45; 20:26). The Jewish ideal of holiness, however, requires neither asceticism nor withdrawal from the world. It is rather a call to separate from that which contaminates without sacrificing involvement in the world. The prophets emphasized that the ceremonial holiness of the festivals and Temple service was meaningless in the absence of moral excellence and SOCIAL ETHICS.

The rabbis taught that holiness was to be achieved through the sanctification of the most mundane affairs. This ideal received its greatest articulation in ḤASIDISM. Martin Buber (*The Way of Man*) wrote: "Man, according to Ḥasidism, contributes to the unity of the sacred and profane by holy living in relationship to the world in which he has been set, at the place on which he stands."

HOLOCAUST: Religious Responses among the Victims, and Subsequent Religious Thinking Six million Jews perished in the Holocaust of European Jewry in World War II. Religious responses to the Holocaust as experienced by its victims were expressed in an abundance of reactions, which have still been inadequately stated and studied. To make some simple, general statements:

1. Jews and non-Jews entered the camps and other sections of the Kingdom of Hell. They lived and died there. Some lived again, often in an incomplete manner, after surviving the ordeal.

2. Each of the six million Jews who died was an individual, was unique, and made the response of uniqueness. There were believers who became unbelievers, and unbelievers who became believers. Certainties became doubt, doubt could become a certainty. Many did not understand and waited for an understanding which never came.

3. Some of the responses at those moments were written down in the shadow of the death camps. Some were recorded in diaries, in letters, in remembered or forgotten conversations. Nothing was the definitive answer, even when it was declared to be so.

4. Religious responses were not confined to the rabbis. Musicians, poets, children, and many others spoke out.

5. Religious resistance to evil took on many forms: active and passive, silent and unspoken, violent and non-violent.

Accepting this, a beginning can be made in charting various religious responses. Starting in the heart of the tradition, one recalls the many *yeshivot* (talmudic academies) which were destroyed, according to the injunction of Rabbi Nahum Yanchiker of the Slobodka MUSAR movement *yeshivah*, enjoining his disciples to remember those who died and the institutions which died. That response was clear: one surrounded oneself with the Law, and tried to live by it. When one rabbinical student wanted to take the place of a brilliant colleague, his rabbi refused to let him commit suicide. Pious Jews could not comprehend the evil any more than the others. They lived within the traditional answers: *Mi-pené ḥata'énu* ("Because of our sins we suffer exile and death") they continued to pray, and spoke of *yissurim shel ahavah* (God inflicting tribulations upon those He loves in order to test them).

Psychologists have concluded that those who believed anything strongly had a better chance of survival; in part, because they had a support group (Zionists, Communists, *landsmanshaft*), and in part because they could set an inner reality against the surrounding evil. It can be argued that the post-camp teachings of Victor Frankl or of Eugene Heimler were in the realm of religion as much as in that of psychology. Any human response, any awareness of the other, of the tradition, shines with a special light: a child watching his father save fat to make a Ḥanukkah candle; workers finding water in the forest and sharing it; a father comforting his child on the way into the gas chamber — these are religious responses, acts of spiritual resistance, affirmations. Every religious response imaginable took place inside the camps.

The post-Holocaust response within the Jewish community took on many forms. It was partly dictated by the language used. The term *ḥurban* ("destruction") was mainly employed by the traditionalists who linked it with the First and Second *Ḥurban* (destruction of the two Temples); they saw its difference only in terms of intensity, and therefore did not see it as unique. The Holocaust was viewed as the third *ḥurban*, to be understood as part of God's plan which man cannot fully understand. A Reform rabbi, Ignaz Maybaum, clearly formulated the concept that God used the Jewish people as sacrificial victims in an act of creative destruction. The old feudal world of Europe had to be ended, and Hitler was God's tool in reshaping the world. The Jews became God's suffering servants, who will bring the rule of God through their anguish, with a "righteous remnant" surviving as God's witnesses. It was a "crucifixion," "Auschwitz as analogue to Golgotha," which instructs the world.

The traditionalist position is clearly expounded by Menahem Immanuel Hartom, who developed the *mi-pené ḥata'énu* (punishment for sin) concept within history, showing that living in the dispersion (GALUT), suborned by the freedom of living outside the Torah, made the Jews deserving of God's long-delayed punishment. Jewry has not yet repented, and can only hope for God's mercy; a new *Sho'ah* (Holocaust) would therefore not be unjust punishment.

Rabbi Isaac Hutner rejects the term *Sho'ah* (lit. "calamity") as a historical limitation. *Ḥurban* remains the proper term for him, harking back to the notion that Jews carry the burden of the CHOSEN PEOPLE, and that the truth of Jewish existence can only be approached when "we turn to the Torah as the only sign-post leading us through the interwoven pathways of history to find the truth all of us seek."

The most creative traditional thinkers have written largely in North America. Eliezer Berkovits sees Judaism as a developing faith, and rejects the disillusioned thinkers who often stood outside the anguish itself. God was in the camps, and many found him, and Berkovits does not hesitate to set the faith of the suffering Jew against the complacency of the guilty Christian whose religion contributed to the Holocaust. "After Auschwitz, leave us alone!" is Berkovits' response to missionary Christianity and modern skepticism. In his view, Jews have earned the right to go their own way.

Irving Greenberg reaches out to Progressive Jews through Orthodoxy. He subsumes Auschwitz under Sinai, challenging Richard Rubenstein's and Emil Fackenheim's notion of the uniqueness of the Holocaust. Using Buber's concept of a God who is in hiding, he urges the Jewish community to reestablish its links with God by reentering the Covenant as a new existential reality. He also calls on Jews to abandon modernity and follow Job in searching for God. Jews must witness to God even when He is in hiding, and to life itself.

Emil Fackenheim's concept of the "Commanding Voice of Auschwitz" as formulating the 614th Commandment, "The Jew must survive," is a major statement on the Holocaust. There must be no final victory for Hitler. Jews and Judaism must survive; and, for Fackenheim, this means a full loyalty to the State of Israel since the Diaspora has proven a false haven. Israel's victory in the Six-Day War was, for him, a Divine revelation: "Israel is collectively what every survivor is individually, a 'No' to Auschwitz, a 'Yes' to Jewish survival."

Richard Rubenstein remains a challenging American thinker, having moved from a "God-is-dead" stance in his *After Auschwitz*, which rejected the theological premise and promise with a humanistic stance (but left the mystic *Én Sof*, the Ultimate Nothingness, within its framework). Rubenstein moved from the problematics of traditional belief toward Lurianic premises and new insights of Far Eastern thought. His philosophy of history places the Holocaust within the framework of the abandonment of the human being as inviolable, which commenced centuries ago (see his *Triage*). Affirmation of the State of Israel is also basic to Rubenstein's thought.

The philosopher Hans Jonas rewrote his Ingersoll Lecture on "Immortality" as a German text on "The Concept of God after Auschwitz." The original had contained a "Platonic" myth in which God surrenders part of Himself to the finite world, letting it pass through the changes of time and space, and enduring suffering with the anguish of human lives etched upon His countenance. Now, God is defined as a limited God who must accept the freedom granted to humanity, and suffers with every evil act. God cares, and needs the world He has created.

Jonas taught in New York, as did Arthur A. Cohen, a deeply believing writer, editor, and novelist who challenged most of the above-mentioned positions. Cohen uses the term *tremendum* (derived from Rudolf Otto's *mysterium tremendum* describing the holy) to define the Holocaust as that absolute evil beyond comprehension, calling the death camps the *tremendum*, as "the monument of a meaningless inversion of life to an orgiastic celebration of death, to a psychosexual and pathological degeneracy unparalleled and unfathomable to any person bonded to life." Cohen also turned to Lurianic mysticism in an effort to believe in God after Auschwitz, and set three criteria for post-Auschwitz theology: (1) God must abide in a universe in which neither evil nor God's presence is accounted unreal; (2) God must be related to all of creation, including the evil, in a meaningful way; (3) the reality of God is linked to a real involvement in the life of creation. Unless these criteria are accepted and sustained, the word "God" can best be used as a metaphor for the inexplicable. God gave man freedom, but not full rationality; the result was the Holocaust. Past and present are therefore dark; but God as Teacher gave Jews the *halakhah* to find their way into a future where God awaits them. In a sense, Cohen links up with Fackenheim here, in that the return to God is the beginning of TIKKUN, the rebuilding of the world according to God's teachings. However, Cohen's vision is darker; he sees the ultimate evil, the abyss to which he can point but which he cannot cross. Yet he joins Eliezer Berkovits in placing this darkness and the cause of the *tremendum* in humanity: it is not God's punishment but the obscene use of freedom which brought this ultimate crime into the world.

This theological discussion continues in the United States, where Holocaust studies are prominent (although the theological dimension is often ignored). Teachers continue their search, including Michael Wyschogrod, as the devout traditionalist awaiting God's redemption, Eugene Borowitz, as the questioning scholarly Reform theologian with a Covenant theology stressing personal responsibility, and a younger generation of rabbis, in every type of pulpit, continue to confront the tragedy in a variety of responses. The issue is kept especially alive within the INTERFAITH dialogue.

The Holocaust has led to upheaval and doctrinal changes

Woodcut print from a Passover Haggadah *supplement prepared for Holocaust survivors and US army Jewish soldiers in 1946. The words of the text were illustrated with depictions of Nazi atrocities.*

within Christianity. Anti-Judaism and anti-Semitism have not been eliminated, but the evil of anti-Semitism and the responsibility of Christian teachings in creating an atmosphere in which a Holocaust became possible are increasingly understood. Some Christian theologians have been saying that Christianity had to change after Auschwitz. In the USA, Roy and Alice Eckardt, and Franklin H. Littell have created a whole body of work which particularly challenges Christian notions of mission and triumphalism after Auschwitz. Father John Pawlikowski and Paul Van Buren have made advances within Catholic and Protestant thinking which draw far more strongly upon the Jewish roots of the Christian faith.

In Germany, the discussion has been intense and painful. Synods have made declarations in which Christianity admits its guilt, recognizes the validity of the Jewish faith which Christians may no longer attack, and in various other ways intimidates the Christian traditionalists who prefer to forget the past. Once Johann-Baptist Metz proclaimed that "the Christian living after Auschwitz must change his faith fundamentally," the battle lines were drawn. Radical theologians like Dorothee Soelle (her book *Suffering* builds a new theology upon Elie Wiesel's book *Night*) work alongside traditionalists such as Jürgen Moltmann (who has altered greatly his first approaches, which linked Calvary and Auschwitz in an unacceptable way), Eberhard Bethge Dietrich (Bonhoeffer's amanuensis and biographer), Martin Stoehr (a Luther specialist who carefully examines the bad and good side of that tradition), and Peter von der Osten-Sacken, whose book on R. Akiva shows that Jewish teachings must enter Christian awareness after the Holocaust. Hans Hermann Hendrix's Catholic academy has brought Christian thinkers to a confrontation on these issues with Jewish teachers, including Emmanuel Levinas, Lord Jakobovits, Jakob Petuchowski, and Albert H. Friedlander.

The theologians after the Holocaust cannot be understood without discerning the Israel dimension contained inside them. The State of Israel itself, born out of the travail of Auschwitz, cannot think, hope, express anguish or despair without including a dimension of that darkness. All gradations of religious thought after Auschwitz can be found in Israel: in Jerusalem, at the Holocaust Memorial Center, Yad Vashem, and at Yad Mordekhai, the kibbutz established by Ghetto fighters. A creative dialogue exists between Israel and the Diaspora: between Fackenheim who has moved to Jerusalem, George Steiner who is in Cambridge and Geneva (a remembrancer and teacher who brought Freudian insights to the Holocaust, and whose *A Season in Hell* remains a clear and disturbing text), and Elie Wiesel, who is in New York, among others. The unique contribution of the State of Israel to religious thought after the Holocaust can be summed up very simply: Israel is there, it exists. It is one answer, no more than that, since it cannot provide solace or a solution to the ultimate anguish of Auschwitz.

Central to Jewish religious thinking after the Holocaust is the emphasis on Jewish life, no matter how dark the environment may be. Theology is not a formal area of Jewish thought. Judaism is to be lived. The people of Israel have come through a time of darkness which has maimed them, but they still exist as witness to God and for God. One of the oustanding modern Jewish teachers, Leo BAECK, refused to leave his congregation in Berlin and entered the world of the concentration camp. There he drafted his last book: *This People Israel: The Meaning of Jewish Existence*. Baeck envisioned renewal and rebirth for Israel, after the time of darkness, which he lived to see.

HOLY CITIES Term applied to the Erets Israel towns of JERUSALEM, Hebron, Safed and Tiberias. These were the four main centers of Jewish life after the Ottoman conquest of 1516. The concept of the holy cities dates only from the 1640s, when the Jewish communities of Jerusalem, Hebron, and Safed organized an association to improve the system of fundraising in the Diaspora. Previously, such fundraising had been undertaken by individual institutions; now it was agreed that the emissaries would be sent on behalf of each urban Jewish community as a whole, with not more than one emissary per town. After Tiberias was refounded in 1740, it also joined the association. This arrangement did not last long, however, and by the mid-19th century there was no authority strong enough to enforce a centralized collection of HALUKKAH funds. The term "Four Holy Cities" became a convenient designation by historians rather than the title of an actual functioning body. In Jewish tradition, going back to ancient times, the only city regarded as holy is Jerusalem (see HOLY PLACES).

HOLY LAND See ISRAEL, LAND OF

HOLY OF HOLIES The most sacred place in the SANCTUARY, and later the TEMPLE, which only the HIGH PRIEST was permitted to enter. Following a pattern generally prevalent in the ancient world, the Temple structure was composed of a series of rooms or spaces within or behind other rooms, the level of holiness increasing as one progressed from front/outermost to back/innermost.

In the Temple of Jerusalem, constructed in the tenth century BCE by King Solomon, the outermost area was the vestibule (*ulam*). The main hall or nave (*hékhal*), inside, was the largest room of the building. Behind it, in the rear of the Temple building, was the Holy of Holies (*devir*), which measured 20 by 20 by 20 cubits.

The ARK OF THE COVENANT and two CHERUBIM were housed in this innermost room (I Kings 6:19, 23-28). These objects disappeared when the Temple was destroyed by the Babylonians in 586 BCE. Subsequent reconstruction of building and precincts, half a century later, by those who returned from exile in Babylonia, followed the plan and measurements of Solomon's Temple. Throughout the Second Temple period the Holy of Holies was an empty room.

The Holy of Holies had no windows and if repairs or maintenance were required, a workman was lowered by rope from the roof, since it was forbidden for anyone other than the High Priest to touch the floor. The original Holy of Holies was part of the portable Sanctuary (*Mishkan*) which the Jews set up in the wilderness at God's command. A cloth partition separated it from the rest of the Sanctuary (Ex. 26:33-34).

Imaginary representation of the Holy of Holies. Lithography, Holland, 18th century.

Only on the DAY OF ATONEMENT, when he was required to atone for the sins of the entire nation, did the High Priest enter the Holy of Holies. He prepared for this moment by separating from his family a week in advance and remaining inside the Temple. He purified himself physically and spiritually and reviewed all the laws pertaining to his service. On the Day of Atonement, as part of a day of fasting, offering sacrifices, and confession of sins, the High Priest entered the Holy of Holies. He placed two handfuls of incense on a pan of burning coals, and as the smoke filled the chamber, the Divine Presence was revealed and the nation of Israel forgiven for its sins (*Yoma* 5.1). Because of the supreme sanctity of the Holy of Holies, if any part of this service was performed incorrectly, the High Priest would incur the death penalty by the hand of heaven.

HOLY PLACES Term which, in a Jewish source, is used in various contexts: for shrines in the Land of Israel associated with biblical events and personalities; for places of pilgrimage associated with revered sites; and for graves (real or traditional) in Israel and the Diaspora of famous rabbis and wonderworkers. The Hebrew word for holy, *kadosh*, carries with it the sense of separate and designated (see HOLINESS). The classic Jewish source on holy places appears in the Mishnah (*Kelim* 1.6ff.): "There are ten degrees of holiness. The Land of Israel is holier than any other..." The holiness of the "Holy Land," it is explained, is expressed in the particular commandments that may be performed only there. The Mishnah explores further levels of holiness, moving through the holiness of JERUSALEM and concluding with that of the HOLY OF HOLIES, the inner sanctum of the TEMPLE deemed to be the holiest place on earth. It lists a system of restrictions and commands that applies to each place/level of holiness. Thus the separation and designation of Jewish holy places is always accomplished through a set of restrictions and commandments. Although the holy places enumerated in the Mishnah may have some unique ontological essence, early Jewish sources show little or no concern with this. It is a moot question whether there exists any form of (earthly) holiness in the absence of legal implications. Historical events such as miracles, theophanies, etc., do not seem to leave any residue of holiness where they occur, and so Jewish law shows no particular reverence for the Red Sea or Mount Sinai. This classic view contrasts with the Christian approach, according to which historical events (e.g., events in the life of JESUS) do generate holy places.

The Jewish holy place *par excellence* was the Temple in Jerusalem. The Mishnah (*ibid.*) catalogues a different level

homiletics a new lease of life and a new role. Reformers such as Abraham GEIGER emphasized the preaching of sermons in the vernacular during synagogue worship, whereas Orthodox Jews mostly opposed this at first, particularly where the older type of rabbi-preacher was unfamiliar with modern idiom. The French (Napoleonic) CONSISTORY, however, made sermons in the vernacular compulsory; from 1808, Tobias Goodman pioneered the English sermon in traditional British synagogues; and, within the framework of NEO-ORTHODOXY, rabbis such as Isaac BERNAYS, Jacob ETTLINGER, and Samson Raphael HIRSCH preached effectively in German. Leopold ZUNZ's pioneering work on the Jewish sermon (*Gottesdienstliche Vorträge, 1832*) was intended to demonstrate its rootedness in an ancient tradition.

While these modern sermons were still based on quotations from the Bible and Midrash, their form and subject matter changed radically from admonition to edification. Preachers could no longer assume basic Jewish knowledge among their hearers. Now theology and ethics had to share a place with actualities in politics, literature, and social life — sermons turned into lectures. The flourishing of the sermon and homiletical literature in Protestant Europe had a considerable influence on its Jewish counterparts, though a later reaction demanded more Jewishness and solid instruction, and less rhetoric and edification.

In Germany, some of the first modern preachers were scholarly reformers (Zunz, Geiger, Samuel HOLDHEIM); but in Austria-Hungary they tended to be more conservative (Adolf Jellinek, Adolf Schwarz, Moritz Güdemann, David Kaufmann, Tsevi Perets Chajes). Vernacular sermons in the USA were first delivered by German-educated preachers such as David EINHORN before German-speaking immigrant congregations that had begun to abandon Orthodoxy. Prominent American preachers in English later included Stephen S. Wise, Abba Hillel Silver, and Solomon Freehof (Reform); Israel H. Levinthal, Solomon Goldman, and Israel Goldstein (Conservative); and Joseph H. Lookstein (Orthodox). Some outstanding British preachers also came from the Reform camp (Morris Joseph, Israel Abrahams, Claude Montefiore), but Abraham Cohen, Ephraim Levine, and Chief Rabbis Nathan Marcus and Hermann Adler, Joseph H. Hertz, and Sir Israel Brodie, were eminent exponents of Orthodoxy. In Eastern Europe, a new type of *Maggid* often attacked the HASKALAH and political Zionism, but some who moved to the West preached in favor of the Hebrew and Jewish national revival; an outstanding example in the US was the Zionist *Maggid*-orator Tsevi Hirsch Masliansky. The Lithuanian MUSAR movement also produced its own school of homiletics and preaching.

Many preachers published their sermons, thus creating a vast literature, while others prepared collections of sermons by various authors and sermonic material for the use of rabbis in the synagogue. Jewish weekly journals usually included a sermon for the current Sabbath. Sermons are now recorded and made available on tapes. Jewish homiletics has become a separate discipline to which Sigmund Maybaum, Ludwig Philippson, and Joseph Wohlgemuth have devoted works (in German), Michel Weill (in French), Simeon Singer, Abraham Cohen, Solomon Freehof; and others (in English) and S.Y. Glicksberg (in Hebrew). Modern RABBINICAL SEMINARIES include courses in homiletics in their teaching programs.

HOMOSEXUALITY In modern usage, homosexuality is defined as sexual relations between individuals of the same sex. In the Bible it refers to illicit relations between males (Lev. 18:22); the sages extend the prohibition, though not the penalty, to lesbianism (*Yev.* 76a). Intimacies between men and between women are in the category of the abhorrent practices of the Egyptians and the Canaanites (*Sif.* 9.8) which are to be avoided. Homosexual relations between males are considered an abomination punishable by death (Lev. 20:13).

Another term for homosexuality, sodomy, is named after the immoral practices of the people of Sodom. In ancient times, the Sodomites practiced homosexual rape, as when the entire population surrounded the home of Lot, Abraham's nephew, and demanded that he release his guests (the two angels) to them "that we may know them" (Gen. 19:5). Judges 19 records the decimation of the tribe of Benjamin as a result of the desire of some of its members to commit homosexual rape.

The incidence of homosexuality was practically nonexistent among Jews. For this reason the sages permitted two bachelors to sleep in the same bed, though R. Judah prohibited it (*Kid.* 4.14). Maimonides followed the opinion of the sages and explained that "Jews are not suspected of practicing homosexuality" (*Yad, Issuré Bi'ah* 22.2).

Various reasons are advanced for the ban on homosexuality. Since this sexual act cannot result in procreation, it denies one of the major functions of sexuality (Gen. 1:28). Secondly, the married man with homosexual tendencies may abandon his wife and family in order to indulge his perversion. He would thereby destroy the unity of the family whose preservation is a supreme value in Judaism. Transcending these explanations is the Bible's designation of homosexuality as an "abomination." This indicates that the act is repulsive, no matter how it may be accepted in other cultures.

Jewish law rejects the view that homosexuality is a disease, morally neutral, or an alternate life style. It is condemned even though the two adults mutually consent to live together in a love relationship. Orthodox Judaism opposes the modern tendency to legitimize homosexual behavior, but distinguishes between the homosexual act and the homosexual person. It is the homosexual act that is condemned as an abomination, not the individuals involved. Judaism encourages compassion for the individuals and efforts at changing their sexual habits.

In recent years, "gay" congregations have been established in the United States by homosexuals, male and female, who have felt themselves rejected within the general Jewish community. The validity of such congregations has been accepted by the Reform movement which has taken them under its auspices.

HORA'AT SHA'AH ("temporary provision"). Legal ruling adopted by Jewish religious authorities in face of an emergency situation, and not meant to have permanent validity. A notable biblical precedent was the prophet Elijah's offering of a sacrifice on Mount Carmel at a time when this ritual was to be performed only in the Temple; though conflicting with Torah law, his action was viewed as a justifiable departure from the norm — aimed at discrediting the prophets of Baal — in accordance with "the need of the hour" (I Kings 18:31-39; cf. *Yev.* 90b). A Mishnaic source affirms that there is a time limit on such regulations (*Parah* 7.6), but the Talmud records an opinion that occasions do arise "when the [*pro tem*] cancellation of Torah precepts may serve to reestablish the Law" (*Men.* 99b). The *hora'at sha'ah* rule (or "directive for the hour") is still, though only occasionally, invoked when traditional Jewish authorities are faced with a crisis. At the outbreak of World War II, for example, Britain's Chief Rabbi J.H. Hertz issued an emergency regulation for Jewish youngsters evacuated to parts of the country where supplies of *kasher* food were not readily available. Similar measures were also adopted by rabbis in Nazi-occupied Europe.

HORAYOT ("Legal Decisions"). Tenth tractate of Order NEZIKIN in the Mishnah. Its three chapters deal with the laws of unintentional sins perpetrated either by the individual or by the community, e.g., one who was unknowingly "unclean" and ate sanctified food (Lev. 4:1-35). The Mishnah also discusses erroneous decisions passed by the court, special offerings by the *Nasi* (President of the Sanhedrin), sin-offerings of the High Priest, and the precedence of certain classes (priests, Levites) in being called to the Reading of the Law. Maimonides states that *Horayot* follows tractate *Avot* in the Mishnah to teach that even after all the moral and ethical instruction to perfect oneself (as in *Avot*), it is in the nature of human beings to make mistakes, and no one, even the High Priest, is exempt from this. The subject matter is amplified in both Talmuds and the *Tosefta*.

HOROWITZ, ISAIAH BEN ABRAHAM HA-LEVI (1570-1630). Talmudist and kabbalist, known as *Shelah ha-Kadosh* ("the holy Shelah") after the initials of his main work. Born in Prague, Horowitz moved to Poland, where his teachers were Solomon ben Judah of Cracow, Meir of Lublin (the *Maharam*), and Joshua Falk. He was *av bet din* (head of the rabbinical court) in Dubno, Ostraha, and then in Frankfurt am Main, Germany. He returned in 1614 to Prague where he became rabbi. In 1621, he left Prague for Erets Israel, stopping for a month in Aleppo where he gave discourses in Hebrew. Invited to become the rabbi of both Safed and Jerusalem, he chose the latter because of its greater sanctity. There in 1625 he was imprisoned by the pasha and held for ransom. Upon his release he settled in Safed and then in Tiberias where he died, and — as a mark of the special honor paid him — was buried close to the grave of Maimonides.

Horowitz' fame rests on his encyclopedic work *Shené Luḇot ha-Berit* ("The Two Tablets of the Covenant," cf. Deut. 9:15), edited by his son Shabbetai Sheftel. Known by the acronym *Shelah*, it consists of two parts, the first, *Derekh Ḥayyim*, containing laws according to the order of the festivals, the second, *Luḇot ha-Berit*, the 613 COMMANDMENTS arranged in the order in which they are found in the Bible. The book is also divided into three sections: *Ner Mitsvah*, the body of the work; *Torah Or*, a mystical commentary on the commandments; and *Tokhaḇat Musar*, dealing with the ethical aspects of each commandment. Interwoven with homilies and explanations, the work left its mark upon several generations of Jews.

The most important of Horowitz' other works is *Sha'ar ha-Shamayim*, a commentary on the prayer book, edited by his great-grandson. A number of kabbalistic prayers were incorporated into the prayer book through Horowitz' influence.

HOSEA One of the twelve MINOR PROPHETS, whose book is included in the Prophets' section of the Bible. According to the Book of Hosea, he experienced his revelations during the reigns of Uzziah (769-733 BCE), Jotham, Ahaz, and Hezekiah (727-698 BCE), kings of Judah, and during the reigns of Jeroboam II and Menahem, kings of Israel (784-737 BCE). The only information on his personal life is contained at the beginning of the book where he is commanded in a vision to marry a harlot and thereby symbolize Israel's disloyalty to God. He thereupon marries Gomer, who bears him three children. It is not clear, however, whether these details are historical or symbolic.

The Book of Hosea is the first and one of the longest books of the Minor Prophets, and is composed of 14 chapters and 197 verses. The first three chapters compare Israel's flirtation with the Phoenician god BAAL to an adulterous wife's flirtation with her paramours. These transgressions are to be punished by the cessation of the land's fertility and the abolition of all joyous festivals. However, this is linked to a prophecy of consolation. Hosea 4-14 (which some modern scholars suggest emanate from a different hand from the first three chapters) contains oracles addressed to the Northern Kingdom during the reign of King Menahem (746-737 BCE). The prophet regards Israel's alliances with foreign powers as disloyalty to God, and condemns Israel for not "knowing the Lord." He stresses that immoral acts are not mitigated by the culprits' performance of religious rituals; on the contrary, their immorality makes such religiosity an abomination. He is the first prophet to declare that the worship of God at a number of altars is an abomination (Hos. 4:13; 8:11). Hosea prophesied to the Kingdom of Israel, although some of his prophecy was directed toward the Kingdom of Judah as well. The Talmud (*Pes.* 87a) states that Hosea, Isaiah, Amos, and Micah all prophesied at the same time, and that the greatest of the four was Hosea.

BOOK OF HOSEA

1: 1- 9	Hosea's marriage to an unfaithful wife
2: 1- 3	The restoration of Israel
2: 4-25	God the spouse of Israel
3: 1- 5	Hosea's marriage
4: 1- 5:7	Reproaches aimed at corrupt priests, superstitious people, and idolatry
5: 8- 6:6	Rebuke of Israel and Judah
6: 7- 9:10	Rebuke of Israel for various sins including idolatry, civil strife, and lack of trust in God
9:11-10:15	Oracles based on historical sins of Israel
11:1-12:1	God's love for Israel
12:2-14:10	Divine judgment and call for repentance

HOSHANA RABBAH The seventh day of the SUKKOT festival. During each of the preceding days of the festival, a single stanza of the HOSHANOT litany is said, and during the recital (except on Sabbath), the congregation makes a circuit around the reader's platform carrying the FOUR SPECIES. On Hoshana Rabbah — literally "the Great Hoshana" — seven circuits (HAKKAFOT) are made, with a different stanza of the *hoshanot* recited each time, and they commemorate the circuits around the ALTAR made in the Temple. After the circuits are completed, the Four Species are laid down and a bunch of five willow branches is taken up, which, during the recital of the rest of the *hoshanot* liturgy, is beaten on the ground three times until some of the leaves have been detached, to indicate man's dependence on RAIN. While the sages viewed the beating of the willow branches as part of the oral tradition of the Torah, the SADDUCEES were violently opposed to it, for there is no reference to such a law in the Bible. In order to ensure that no year would go by without the willow branches being beaten, Hillel II (c. 360 CE) so arranged the calendar that Hoshana Rabbah cannot occur on the Sabbath, for on that day it would be forbidden to carry the willow branches.

Since the Middle Ages, Hoshana Rabbah has been considered the last possible day on which one can seek and obtain forgiveness for the sins of the previous year. As a result, the Morning Service is extremely solemn and contains an element of the High Holiday prayers. The Sephardi rite stresses this aspect more than the Ashkenazi one. According to Jewish mystical tradition, Hoshana Rabbah is an extension of the DAY OF ATONEMENT when the Divine judgment receives its final seal. The folk belief was that notes fell from Heaven on which the fate of each individual was recorded. The traditional Yiddish greeting was "*a gute kvitl*" ("[May you receive] a good note"), while the Day of Atonement greeting "May you be sealed [in the Book of Life]" is also used. The kabbalists spent the night in prayer and study for which a special TIKKUN service was devised. A popular superstition is that if a man does not see his shadow on this night, it is a sign that he is fated to die in the coming year.

According to Ashkenazi custom, the cantor wears a white *kitel* or robe, and the preliminary prayers (until BAREKHU) are recited according to the solemn High Holiday melody. Similarly, those called to the Reading of the Law use the High Holiday melody when reciting the blessings before and after the reading, although the reading itself uses the normal melody. The PESUKÉ DE-ZIMRA — "Chapters of Song" which precede *Barekhu* — are expanded to include the extra section recited on the Sabbath and festivals (except for the omission of NISHMAT KOL ḤAI).

HOSHANOT The prayers beginning with the word *hosha-na* ("please save"), which are recited as congregants make circuits (HAKKAFOT)in the synagogue while holding the FOUR SPECIES on the SUKKOT festival. The name *hoshana* for the willow branches which the worshiper holds and beats against the ground, on the seventh day of Sukkot (HOSHANA RABBAH), was derived from this.

The Mishnah (*Suk.*4.5) states that during Sukkot in Temple times, large willow branches would be set up on each side of the altar, with their tops bent toward it. After four blasts on a SHOFAR (ram's horn), pilgrims would make a circuit of the altar each day, chanting: "O Lord, deliver us: O Lord, let us prosper!" (Ps. 118:25). In talmudic times, the Four Species were referred to as *hoshanot*.

The daily circuit was accompanied by prayers and liturgical poems (*piyyutim*). In the course of time a fixed text developed for each day, the common factor of all the *piyyutim* being the *ḥosha-na* refrain. Even on a Sabbath, when the Four Species are not taken and no circuit is made, the *ḥosha-na* passage for the Sabbath is recited. Most of the *piyyutim* were composed by Eleazar KALLIR, or by his teacher, R. Yannai, and by later poets. The *ḥosha-na piyyutim* express the feelings of those praying, contain praises of God's attributes, and affirm the longing for redemption.

HOSPITALITY (Heb. *hakhnasat oreḥim*). The patriarch ABRAHAM typifies the virtue of hospitality on the basis of the

The patriarch Abraham gives hospitality to the three angels. Miniature from the Rothschild Miscellany Manuscript, *Italy, 1470.*

story of his generous welcome to three wayfarers (who proved to be angels) as recounted in Genesis 18. The importance of hospitality, especially to those in need, was expressed by Yosé ben Johanan, when he stated (*Avot* 1.5): "Let your home be wide open, and treat poor people as the members of your household." The Talmud (*Shab.* 127a) lists hospitality among those precepts "whose fruit is eaten in this world, while the principal remains for the World to Come." The statement at the beginning of the Passover SEDER, "Let all who are hungry come and eat," was originally recited by R. Huna before every meal throughout the year (*Ta'an.* 20b).

The rabbis advise how to make guests feel comfortable. Upon their arrival, they should be treated with the utmost courtesy, no matter how boorish they may be. Food should be brought to them as soon as possible because if they are poor they may be too embarrassed to ask for it, even if they are hungry. Although the host may be troubled by his own personal problems, he must appear to be cheerful and in good spirits, nor may he boast of his wealth and possessions, because this would make the guests feel inferior. Furthermore, like Abraham, the host should attend to the guests himself, and not rely on his servants to take care of them.

The guests, for their part, should express their appreciation to the host. A special insertion is added to the GRACE AFTER MEALS in which guests ask for God's blessing on the host and his family (*Ber.* 58a).

In the Middle Ages and thereafter, when many Jews were forced to wander from town to town, special *Hakhnasat Orehim* societies were founded in Jewish communities, to feed and shelter visitors, often on the premises of the synagogue or in a special hostel constructed for the purpose.

ABRAHAM AND THE TRAVELERS

He lifted up his eyes and looked, and three men were standing by him. When he saw them, he ran from the tent entrance to greet them, and bowed to the ground, saying, "My lords, if it please you, do not go on past your servant. Let a little water be brought and bathe your feet, and rest under the tree. Let me fetch a morsel of bread that you may refresh yourselves: after that you shall go on" (Gen. 18. 2-5).

HOZER BI-TESHUVAH See BA'AL TESHUVAH

HUKKAT HA-GOY ("Law of the Gentile"). Term denoting various alien practices which Jews are forbidden to imitate. This prohibition is based on the Scriptural injunctions not to "copy the practices" of heathen neighbors or to "follow their laws" (Lev. 18:3), which are denounced as abhorrent (Lev. 20:23); to "beware of being lured into their ways" (Deut. 12:30); to keep away from their IDOLATRY and SUPERSTITIONS (Jer. 10:2ff.); and to obey God's commandments rather than "the ordinances of the nations around you" (Ezek. 11:12). In the Talmud, such pagan customs are known as *darkhé ha-Emori* ("the ways of the Amorites") and numerous examples, ranging from alien beliefs to non-Jewish dress, are provided (*Shab.* 67a-b; *Sanh.* 74a-b). However, whereas the rabbis condemned all practices and superstitions that were unmistakably idolatrous or that might foster immorality, they were more lenient with regard to prevalent social customs and folkways which had no obvious roots in idol worship. Thus, Gentile practices linked with healing the sick were excluded from the general ban (*Shab.* 67a).

The concept of *darkhé ha-Emori* was reinterpreted in the Middle Ages, owing to new social realities in Christian and Muslim lands. RASHI, commenting on Lev. 18:3, saw it as applying to non-Jewish forms of public entertainment ("theaters and horse races"); MAIMONIDES, however, extended it to include not only WITCHCRAFT and sorcery, ASTROLOGY, and the creation of hybrids (*Guide* 3.37), but the copying of Gentile dress and hairstyles as well (*Yad, Akkum* 11.1-3). Halakhic authorities reemphasized the prohibitions against CREMATION and embalming, the mutilation or castration of animals, use of consecrated "libation" WINE, the wearing of SHA'ATNEZ (wool and linen mixtures), etc., not only because these had a biblical mandate but also to preserve Jewish distinctiveness. Even the practice of KAPPAROT on the eve of Atonement Day was denounced as un-Jewish by Solomon Adret, Nahmanides, and Joseph Caro.

In modern times, any custom which rabbis think observant Jews should avoid is termed *hukkat ha-Goy*. Traditionalists therefore consider the innovations of Reform Judaism (bareheaded worship, the abolition of separate seating for men and women, the playing of an organ, and vernacular prayers in the synagogue) to come under this heading. Even within Orthodoxy, however, attitudes have differed. By the 19th century, Jews in Western Europe had adopted modern forms of dress and were often clean-shaven; in Eastern Europe, such changes were fiercely opposed by Hasidic Jews (who still cling to an outmoded garb inherited, in fact, from the Polish gentry), but gradually accepted by non-Hasidic *Mitnaggedim*. Furthermore, local CUSTOM, "traditional" Jewish FOOD, liturgical MUSIC, and even synagogue architecture throughout the world have been influenced by the Gentile environment. Currently, hunting for sport and having a Christmas tree in the home would be regarded as examples of *hukkat ha-Goy*, but the laying of wreaths or flowers on a grave (though avoided by observant Jews in the Diaspora) is widely accepted in Israel. Apart from a section of the ultra-Orthodox, therefore, most Jews adopt a pragmatic attitude toward Gentile customs and fashions.

HULLIN ("Unhallowed Things"). Third tractate of Order KODASHIM in the Mishnah (cf. Deut. 12:20-24; Lev. 17:13-14). Its 12 chapters deal mostly with two related topics: the laws governing SHEHITAH, the ritual slaughter of permitted beasts and fowl that are not meant for sacrifice bur for normal ("profane") consumption; and all aspects of the Jewish DIETARY LAWS, e.g., the prohibition of blood, forbidden meats (TEREFAH AND NEVELAH), meat and dairy mixtures, etc. The subject matter is amplified in the Babylonian Talmud and in the *Tosefta*.

HUMANISTIC JUDAISM (or Secular Humanistic Judaism). A tendency that sees in Judaism the civilization of the Jewish people rather than a solely or mainly religious concept. Jewish secularism claims that the theocentric foundations of Judaism were questioned even in ancient times (cf. ELISHA BEN AVUYAH who reached the conclusion that there is "no Law and no Judge"). Since the Emancipation period, increasing numbers of Jews identified with the Jewish people while declining to observe religious traditions, and many embraced an agnostic or atheistic philosophy. Today, many Jews both in Israel and the Diaspora have no contact at all with any kind of organized religious life. In the USA, the proportion of the religiously non-affiliated (that is, those who do not belong to any type of synagogue and do not visit one at any time) has been estimated at over 50%, but in Israel the number is lower. Modern Zionism emerged as a mainly secular movement, and many of the founders of Israel (such as David Ben-Gurion and Vladimir Jabotinsky) were people who identified with the history and culture of the Jewish people, but were non-observant. A prime role in the creation of a non-religious Jewish culture in Israel was and is the kibbutz movement. In the Diaspora, mass movements such as the Bund in Eastern Europe supported a non-religious, Yiddish-language Jewish autonomous culture in the framework of a progressive gentile environment.

Secular humanistic Judaism contends that the belief in an omnipotent and omnipresent God who presides over history, such as is posited by religious Judaism, presents insuperable problems. The Bible and the writings of the sages were the product of a developing civilization and of a people that tried to adapt itself to changing conditions. Judaism contains philosophy, literature and folklore, and its religious and moral teachings, for all their great importance, are far from being consistent — just like those of any other civilization. Secular Jewish humanists deny that there are any specific Jewish values, but they affirm that general human moral values received the special coloring of the Jewish culture and that, in many cases, the Jewish people preceded others in its moral teachings. Humanism puts the individual autonomous human and not a Supreme Being squarely in the center of the human world.

In 1985, an International Federation of Secular Humanistic Jews was founded. In the US, the Society of Humanistic Jews and the Congress of Secular Jewish Organizations are affiliated to it, as are the Centre du Judaïsme Laïc in Brussels and the Israeli Association for Secular Humanistic Judaism.

HUMILITY One of the virtues most admired and held up as an example among Jews since biblical times. Moses is described as "a very humble man, more so than any other man on earth" (Num. 12:3), and precisely for that reason, the rabbis said, he was deemed worthy of receiving the Torah. Jeremiah likewise revealed this inner quality when he proved hesitant about undertaking his Divine mission. "The humble," it is said, "shall inherit the land" (Ps. 37:11); the Lord gives them courage (Ps. 147:6); and "wisdom is with the unassuming" (Prov. 11:2). A pithy ethical message is conveyed in the prophet's famous statement that man is required "to do justice, and to love goodness, and to walk modestly with God" (Mic. 6:8); according to the rabbis (*Mak.* 24a), this verse epitomizes the whole Torah and "walking modestly with God" is the highest Jewish ideal. The talmudic sages regarded humility as an essential attribute of the scholar, Hillel declaring that "one who seeks fame will lose his name" (*Avot* 1.13). "The greater the man, the humbler he is" (Lev. R. 36.2) and "one who does not exalt himself will be exalted by others" (*MK* 28b). "Take your seat

RABBINIC TEACHINGS ABOUT HUMILITY

Why are the words of the Torah likened to water, wine, and milk (Isa. 55:1)? The answer is: Just as these liquids are kept only in the simplest of vessels, so those holy words are preserved only in the men of humble spirit.

Holiness leads to humility and humility to the fear of sin.

Man's prayers are only effective when he regards himself as dust.

Let a man be ever humble in learning Torah and performing good deeds, humble with his parents, teacher, and wife, with his children, with his household, with his kinfolk near and far, humble even with the heathen in the street, so that he may become lovingly regarded on high and deservedly respected on earth.

Good deeds performed modestly are more enduring than those performed with a fanfare of publicity.

Humility displayed for the sake of approval is the worst form of arrogance.

a little below the one due to you," R. Akiva advised, "for it is better to be told 'Come up!' than 'Go down!'" (Lev. R. 1.5). There are, however, times when humility is out of place: "Disciples of the wise should be proud enough to stand up in defense of the Law" (*Sot.* 5a). Meekness provides a key to the afterlife (*Sanh.* 88b) and this virtue is also attributed to God Himself. "Wherever in Scripture you find the power of God mentioned, there too you will find a reference to His humility" (*Meg.* 31a). Similarly, "God revealed Himself in a bush, to teach us that the loftiest may be found in the lowliest" (*Mekhilta de-Rabbi Shimon bar Yoḇai*; cf. *Shab.* 67a).

ḤUMMASH See PENTATEUCH

HUNA (c. 216-c. 297) Second-generation Babylonian AMORA and outstanding student of RAV, whom he succeeded as head of the ACADEMY of Sura. Under his aegis, the Academy flourished and is reported to have had 800 regular students besides the hundreds who came to study during the KALLAH months. So numerous were the students that Rav Huna used the services of 13 *amoraim* (spokesmen) to convey his discourses to his listeners. For 40 years, he was a leader of Babylonian Jewry and his views were highly regarded also by the scholars of Erets Israel.

In his early years, Huna lived in poverty and engaged in agricultural labor. His highly ethical character is portrayed in a whole series of anecdotes. Despite his renown as a scholar and his high office, he would refuse to permit his students to perform any service for him that he considered demeaning. In the areas of both HALAKHAH and AGGADAH, his statements run into the hundreds. He died at an advanced age and his coffin was brought from Babylonia to Erets Israel for interment.

HUSBAND-WIFE RELATIONSHIP See FAMILY; FAMILY PURITY

HYMN OF GLORY See AN'IM ZEMIROT

I

IBN DAUD, ABRAHAM BEN DAVID HA-LEVI (known by the acronym *Rabad*; c.1110 — c.1180). Spanish historian and philosopher. Born in Cordoba, he acquired a broad Jewish and secular education. As a result of the Almohad invasion in 1146, Ibn Daud fled to Castile and settled in Toledo, where he died a martyr. His two major works, both dating from 1161, were a chronicle entitled *Sefer ha-Kabbalah* ("The Book of Tradition") and a philosophical treatise originally written in Arabic and translated into Hebrew as *Ha-Emunah ha-Ramah* ("The Exalted Faith"). In the former work, Ibn Daud traced the development of rabbinic Judaism from Moses to his own time. His purpose was less historical than polemical, the book answering KARAITES who maintained that the rabbinic tradition had been shattered through exile and persecution.

In *Ha-Emunah ha-Ramah*, Ibn Daud investigated the principles of Judaism and sought to harmonize them with Aristotelian rationalist philosophy. The first section deals with metaphysics and general philosophical questions. The second discusses particularly Jewish concerns: The existence and incorporeality of God; the nature of His unity; His attributes, judged to be essentially negative; the existence of intermediate forces between God and the world, as well as the soul's immortality; creation, prophecy, the Sinaitic revelation and its immutability; Divine omniscience, the problem of evil, and man's free will; and ethics and virtue as "medicine of the soul" which religious observance activates.

In discussing the first and penultimate questions, Ibn Daud brings original thought to bear on these problems. A coldly precise thinker, he "solves" the problem of determinism and free will by analyzing the various types of knowledge possible and then boldly declares that God cannot foretell the "objectively undetermined" event.

Ibn Daud was familiar with earlier Jewish and Arabic philosophy, utilized it for his own ends, and through his own work influenced MAIMONIDES. Later Jewish philosophers, Ḥasdai Crescas and Joseph Albo, knew little of his writings, not only because most of them were lost or poorly translated, but also (and primarily) because they were superseded by the classical works of Maimonides.

IBN EZRA, ABRAHAM (c. 1092-1167). Bible commentator, poet, grammarian, philosopher, scientific writer, and physician. When about 50, Ibn Ezra left his native Spain and became a roving scholar. Dogged by poverty and misfortune, he once alluded to these hardships in characteristically tragicomic verse: "Were I to deal in candles,/The sun would never set;/Were selling shrouds my business,/No one would ever die!" A contributory factor in Ibn Ezra's wanderings may well have been his son Isaac's conversion to Islam, which prompted an initial journey to the Orient (Egypt, Erets Israel, and Iraq) in the hope of winning this only surviving son back to Judaism. Over the next 25 years or more, Ibn Ezra lived in Rome (1140-45), visited Lucca, Pisa, and Mantua, then moved to Verona (1147-48), and eventually spent a decade in France (1148-58). From there he went to England and stayed in London (1158-60) before making his way back to France and Spain.

His scholarship amazed people wherever he roved and left an enduring impression, but Ibn Ezra always had a bitter sense of exile: he often made touching references to his native land and proudly called himself *ha-Sefaradi*, "the Spaniard." Although such a wandering existence was not conducive to literary work, he managed to write prolifically short treatises — in Hebrew — so as to bring the learning and enlightenment of Spain to Jews unfamiliar with Arabic in Christian Europe.

Apart from a number of books on Hebrew grammar, secular poetry (including satiric verse, poems on friendship, love, nature and wine), and liturgical poems (e.g., the Sabbath eve hymn *Ki Eshmerah Shabbat*), Ibn Ezra composed two short religio- philosophical works: *Sefer ha-Shem*, a treatise on the Divine Names, written in France (1155), and *Yesod Mora* ("The Foundation of Fear"), dealing with the Torah precepts and their significance, which he wrote in London (1158). His philosophical views are mainly scattered through his commentaries on the Pentateuch and other biblical books; from them it appears that his outlook was Neo-Platonic — allegorical, symbolic, and much influenced by Solomon IBN GABIROL. The Garden of Eden, the Tree of Knowledge, and the Tree of Life are thus endowed with cosmological and ethical importance. Cryptic phrases are often resorted to so as to avoid shocking the religious sensibilities of Jews in Christian Europe, and "the intelligent will understand" is a recurring hint. For Ibn Ezra, the most important duty of man is to pursue the knowledge of God.

It is, however, as a Bible commentator whose popularity was exceeded only by RASHI's that Ibn Ezra enjoys enduring fame. His style is curt, strictly to the point, often playful or characterized by a mordant wit. In the introduction to his commentary on the Pentateuch, Ibn Ezra alludes to the methods employed by his major forerunners, but rejects them. He condemns the over-abundance of secular, foreign learning displayed by the *ge'onim* (particularly SAADIAH GAON): this type of exegesis is notable only for its prolixity and "those who would devote themselves to external wisdom should learn it [directly] from the source books." He then attacks the Karaites, insisting on an unqualified acceptance of both the Oral and the Written Law; criticizes those who favor the allegorical method of exegesis, as well as Christian scholars who looked for a "spiritualized" interpretation of the biblical text; and finally admonishes the Jewish commentators in Christian Europe who underrated the importance of Hebrew grammar. For his own part, Ibn Ezra sought to reveal the *peshat* — the "plain," natural, and reasonable interpretation — as Rashi had done half a century earlier, though more tersely and without midrashic embellishments. Combining a respect for tradition with a bold, independent approach, he made statements that earned him the reputation of being the first Jewish Bible critic. He thus hinted that the passage relating the death of Moses (Deut. 34) was set down by Joshua and, in guarded references, concluded that the last 26 chapters of Isaiah had been written by a "second Isaiah" who lived and taught in the Babylonian exile.

The last few years of his life are clouded with mystery. He appears to have made the return journey to his native land, dying at Calahorra on the borders of Navarre and Aragon (January 23, 1167).

IBN EZRA, MOSES (c. 1055-after 1135). Spanish Hebrew poet. Born and raised in Granada into a wealthy and cultured family, he formed a lasting friendship there with JUDAH HALEVI. After the conquest of Granada by the fanatical Muslim Almoravides, he fled to Christian Spain. For the rest of his life, he was a wanderer, suffering many misfortunes.

Master of both sacred and secular poetry, Ibn Ezra composed 220 PIYYUTIM (liturgical poems). Excelling in *seliḇot* (penitential poems) in which he expresses his longing for his Maker, he is known as Ha-Salaḥ (writer of *seliḇot*). Many of his poems are recited in the High Holidays service in Sephardi congregations and in other rites. His poetic paraphrase of the Book of Jonah for the Day of Atonement was adopted in the Avignon festival prayer book. His secular poetry is largely found in his *Sefer ha-Anak* ("Necklace"), the themes being mainly love, wine, and nature. Ibn Ezra wrote a treatise in Arabic on rhetoric, translated into Hebrew under the title *Shirat Yisrael*. He also wrote a philosophical work in Arabic, known in its Hebrew translation as *Arugat ha-Bosem*, dealing with the relationship between God and the universe.

IBN GABIROL, SOLOMON (c.1020-c.1057). Poet and philosopher. Little is known about his life, the main biographical source of information being his poetic works. He indicates that he was born in Malaga, Spain, and was raised in Saragossa. He began to write poetry while still young and became known for both his secular and sacred poems. The former include moving love lyrics, drinking poems, nature poetry, and ethical verse. Ibn Gabirol is best known for his sacred poetry and is recognized as one of the most prominent and seminal of the medieval Spanish-Jewish religious poets. His mastery of the Hebrew language, his deep and austere religious feeling, and his familiarity with Arabic prosody combined to produce a body of sacred verse that entered the Jewish liturgy in all rites — Sephardi, Ashkenazi, and Karaite. His works are characterized by a deep reverence for God and identification with the tribulations of the Jewish people in exile as well as hope and confidence in the redemption. His most famous poem is the philosophical meditation *Keter Malkhut* ("Royal Crown"), which is also a prayer written from an awareness of the triviality of man as compared with the greatness of God, Who is called upon for His mercy and forgiveness. It entered the Sephardi ritual for the Day of Atonement.

His major philosophical work, written in Arabic, was *Mekor Ḥayyim* ("Source of Life"). It is a Neo-Platonic metaphysical work, devoted to the relationship of matter and form, which are united in the world by the will of God. The book influenced Jewish thinkers of the time, whose orientation remained Neo-Platonic for the next century. However, it had no recognizable Jewish content, and after its translation into Latin (*Fons Vitae*), its authorship was forgotten. It was attributed to a Christian author believed to have been called Avicebron, and was studied by the Christian scholastics. Only when quotations of the original were discovered in the mid-19th century was the author identified.

Ibn Gabirol's ethical work *Tikkun Midot ha-Nefesh* ("On the Improvement of the Moral Qualities"), also written in Arabic, was translated into Hebrew by Judah Ibn Tibbon. It is a popular work, discussing what benefits and what harms the human soul, bringing citations from the Bible and from Arabic writers.

IBN ZIMRA, DAVID BEN SOLOMON (known by the acronym *Radbaz*; 1479-1573). Halakhic scholar and kabbalist. Born in Spain, Ibn Zimra reached Safed as a boy of 13, arriving with the first victims of the 1492 expulsion, and later moved to Jerusalem. From 1512 he spent 40 years in Egypt, at first in Alexandria and then in Cairo. He joined the rabbinical court of the last *nagid*, Isaac Sholal, and later served as chief rabbi of Egypt. Ibn Zimra settled disputes and brought about important changes in the community; they included his attempt to reintroduce the silent congregational reading of the *Amidah*, which had been abolished by Maimonides. In 1552, he returned to Jerusalem. Being taxed heavily by the local governor and otherwise dissatisfied, however, he moved to Safed and served as *dayyan* there for the remainder of his life.

Ibn Zimra was considered the leading rabbi of his day, questions being addressed to him by scholars in Safed, Jerusalem, and Salonika, as well as by distant communities in Africa and Italy. He wrote over 3,000 responsa; those dealing with polygamy, the emancipation of slaves, and the status of black Jews in India reflect contemporary Jewish life in eastern lands. As a *posek* (decisor), Ibn Zimra was lenient in his interpretation of the *halakhah*. Though a kabbalist, he always upheld the supremacy of *halakhah* when it ran counter to mystical teachings. He would not allow his own pupils to study philosophy, but defended personalities such as Ibn Gabirol and Maimonides who had done so. Isaac LURIA (the "Ari") was one of his pupils.

Many of Ibn Zimra's responsa have been published as *Teshuvot ha-Radbaz* (1852). His other works include a commentary on part of Maimonides' *Mishneh Torah*; a kabbalistic commentary on the Song of Songs; a work on talmudic methodology; an exposition of the 613 Commandments; and a liturgical poem for the Day of Atonement, *Keter Malkhut* ("The Royal Crown").

IDOLATRY (*Avodah Zarah*, lit. "foreign worship"). The practice of worshiping "graven images" made of wood, stone, metal, etc., as was the universal form of religion in the ancient world, outside of Judaism. Idolatry is repeatedly forbidden by biblical law, notably in the second of the Ten Commandments: "you shall have no other gods besides Me... you shall not make for yourself a graven image or any likeness of anything that is in the heaven above or on the earth below...you shall not bow down to them or serve them" (Ex. 20:3-5). The basic SHEMA prayer warns "Beware lest your heart be seduced and you go astray and worship alien gods and bow down to them" (Deut. 11:16). Further prohibitions concerning idolatry include the laws against planting an *asherah* (tree used for worship by the Canaanites) near the altar or setting up a pillar for worshiping God. There were, however, legitimate uses of images and figures in religious life. Above the Holy Ark, which rested in the HOLY OF HOLIES, was a pair of CHERUBIM, which were also embroidered on the PAROKHET (curtain of the Holy of Holies). These two instances were constructed at specific Divine command (Ex. 25:18).

Idolatry is considered one of the three cardinal sins which, along with incest and murder, must not be transgressed even if one's life has to be forfeited. An entire tractate of the Talmud, AVODAH ZARAH, deals with the details of this prohibition, which cover not only worshiping idols, but also making idols for someone else's use. It is even forbidden for a Jew to do any business with an idolater three days prior to the gentile's festival because with the profit earned he might purchase an offering for his idol (*Av. Zar.* 1:1). A Jew is also

Idolatry as depicted in an engraving, with inscription (in French): "Hebrews and Jews worshiping gods of Egypt, Syria, Babylonia, and Samaria." France, 18th century.

prohibited from drinking the wine of a gentile because it might have been made for a libation offering to an idol. Jews are forbidden to sell land in Erets Israel to an idolater.

Despite the seriousness of the prohibition of idolatry, the Israelites transgressed it many times in their early history. The worship of the GOLDEN CALF in the wilderness was the first instance of the young nation's loss of faith and lapse into idolatry. Later, upon entering the Land of Canaan, they encountered a proliferation of idolatrous practices and repeatedly fell prey to the temptation (especially to the worship of BAAL and Astarte) being recalled to the path of MONOTHEISM by the rebukes of the Judges and Prophets. Idolatry was a frequent phenomenon in the northern kingdom of Israel where King Jeroboam set up idols of bulls at the sanctuary.

The Talmud states that the weakness for idolatry was finally quashed by the Men of the Great Assembly after the destruction of the First Temple and added that whoever rejected idolatry is as though he accepted the entire Torah (*Yoma* 69b).

One of the favorite stories in the Midrash relates that ABRAHAM smashed the idols of his father, Terah, in protest against the practice of idolatry.

Muslims were not regarded as idolaters in view of their rejection of idols and the pure monotheism of their faith. Christians were also usually not regarded as idolaters but attitudes were ambiguous in the light of their use of images and certain doctrines seen as compromising pure monotheism.

ILLEGITIMACY The Hebrew term usually translated as "illegitimate child" is *mamzer* but the meaning is very different from the English term "bastard." Scripture provides that "a *mamzer* shall not be admitted into the congregation of the Lord" (Deut. 23:3) and while the sages understood this to mean that a *mamzer* may not marry an Israelite "even to the tenth generation," they disagreed as to who is included in the term *mamzer*. R. AKIVA maintained that it includes the offspring, male or female, of any union forbidden by the Torah because of family relationship. R. Simeon of Timna held that only the offspring of a union for which the Bible provides the penalty of KARET (excision or premature death) or execution is included; i.e., an adulterous or incestuous union. This would mean that one born from intercourse with a menstruating woman would be excepted. R. Joshua's view was that a *mamzer* is only the issue of a union for which there is the death penalty (see Lev. 18:16-20; 20:10-21). The law as finally accepted follows the opinion of R. Simeon (*Yev.* 4:12-13). The offspring of any union between a *mamzer* and one of legitimate birth is also a *mamzer* (*ibid.*) The sages disagreed as to whether a child born from a union between a non-Jew and a Jewess is a *mamzer* (Maimonides, *Yad, Hilkhot Issurei Bi'ah*; Sh. Ar. *EH* 4:19). A *mamzer*, then, is a child born of an adulterous or incestuous union. However, in Jewish law, the child of an unmarried mother is not a *mamzer* and bears no stigma.

The sages were mindful of the apparent injustice in branding a child illegitimate because of the sin of his/her parents. Commenting on the passage in Ecclesiastes (4:1), "I observed...the tears of the oppressed, with none to comfort them from the power of their oppressors," they said, "This verse refers to *mamzerim*, whose fathers sinned yet they are condemned to exclusion from the congregation by the Great Sanhedrin of Israel who act by authority of the Torah. Therefore, the Holy One, blessed be He, says, 'I will comfort them in future life'" (Lev. R. 32:7). In keeping with this sentiment, the Sages suggested a way in which this stain of illegitimacy can be removed from their offspring. "R. Tarfon says, '*Mamzerim* can purify themselves by marrying a female slave (non-Jewish); the child born to them has the status of a male slave, who upon being freed from servitude by his master, becomes legitimate'" (*Kid.* 3:13). The sages also ruled that a proselyte (*ger*) may marry an illegitimate woman (*Kid.* 72b, bottom), while a *mamzer* may marry another *mamzer*. Furthermore, the bar to marriage is in effect only if the illegitimacy is proven; a mere suspicion of illegitimacy does not bar the suspect from marriage (*ibid.* 73a); and even the parents' claim that their son is illegitimate is not accepted (*ibid.* 78b).

Most cases of *mamzerut* nowadays occur when a woman remarries without having received an halakhically valid divorce (*get*) from her first husband. In the eyes of Jewish law she remains married to the first husband, hence her second marriage is an adulterous union and any children born therefrom are considered *mamzerim*. This does not apply among Reform Jews who do not require a *get* before remarriage. However, if the first marriage was to a non-Jew, or was performed in a civil but not in a religious ceremony, then it is not recognized as a valid marriage and the second marriage, as well as the children born therefrom, are legitimate.

Except for the bar to marriage, a *mamzer* is a Jew in all respects and is obligated to observe all the commandments. Therefore he celebrates his bar mitsvah and may be called up to the Reading of the Law. The Mishnah even asserts, "A *mamzer* who is a Torah scholar takes precedence over an ignorant High Priest" (*Hor* 3:5). He is also recognized as a son, and shares with his legitimate brothers in any inheritance left by his parents. If his brother died childless, he is required to perform the ceremony of LEVIRATE MARRIAGE with the widow (*Yev.* 2:5).

Other types of illegitimacy are cases of "doubtful illegitimacy" — the *shetuki* (where the mother is unmarried and does not know the identity of the father) and the *asufi* (foundling, where neither parent is known). Because of the uncertainty involved, these are restricted in marriage regulations and may only marry among themselves. The *ḥallal* is the offspring of a priest and a woman whom he is forbidden to marry by virtue of his priesthood; the only restrictions on such a child concern his right to be considered a priest.

In the Conservative Movement there is a consensus of opinion that in view of the unknown number of children born of second marriages where there was no Jewish religious divorce (*get*) from the first marriage, the laws of *mamzerut* are today inoperative. In accordance with this general attitude, inquiries of couples about to be wed stop short of the kind of investigation which could uncover a status of *mamzerut* in one of the parties to a marriage.

Talmudic warrant is cited for a refusal to investigate too closely, and the rule of probability that the couple wishing to marry are not *mamzerim* can be relied upon.

IMITATION OF GOD (Lat. *imitatio Dei*). A theological doctrine positing an obligation for man to emulate God's (moral) behavior. Central to Jewish thought, the doctrine receives its fullest development in rabbinic and subsequent literature, but its roots are clearly biblical, presuming man's creation in the image of God (Gen. 1:26,27). The notion of imitation of God is suggested also in the narrative of Abraham: "For I have known him in order that he may command his children and his household after him, that they may keep the way of the Lord to do righteousness and justice" (Gen. 18:19). Here, "the way of the Lord" is identified with moral behavior, and the "way" prescribed for man is not only that in which God wishes him to walk but the way in which God Himself, as it were, walks.

Subsequently, the Pentateuch commands man to "be holy, for I the Lord your God am holy" (Lev. 19:2), and "...to walk in His ways" (Deut. 11:22; 28:9). The latter was taken by the medieval codifiers to mean that man is required to "emulate God and His beneficent and righteous ways to the best of his ability," and this was reckoned by them as one of the 613 COMMANDMENTS. The codification of such a commandment is based upon a number of rabbinic statements: "It is written, 'After the Lord your God shall you walk' (Deut. 13:5). How shall man be able to walk in the footsteps of the Divine Presence? Is it not written, 'The Lord your God is a devouring fire' (Deut. 4:24)? Rather follow His attributes: as He clothed the naked [Adam and Eve] (Gen. 3:21), so shall you clothe the naked, as he visited the sick [Abraham] (Gen. 18:1) so do you visit the sick; as He comforts mourners [Aaron] (Lev. 16:1) so shall you comfort those who mourn; as He buried the dead [Moses] (Deut. 34:6) so shall you bury the dead" (*Sot.* 14a).

The doctrine of *imitatio Dei* has occupied Jewish thinkers in all generations. It was elaborated on in the writings of the 16th-century kabbalists, and in more recent generations in Ḥasidic writings and those of the MUSAR movement. The rabbis of the Talmud, as well as subsequent writers, saw the ability and the obligation to emulate God as a unique privilege; "Beloved is man who was created in the image of God, but it was a special act of love that made it known to him" (*Avot* 3:14). The contemporary thinker Martin BUBER (*Israel and the World*) has remarked regarding this passage: "The fact that it has been revealed to us that we are made in His image gives us the incentive to unfold the image and in so doing to imitate God," indicating his belief in the relevance of *imitatio Dei* for modern man (see also ETHICS and HOLINESS).

IMMORTALITY OF THE SOUL See SOUL

IMPURITY See PURITY AND IMPURITY

IM YIRTSEH HA-SHEM ("God willing"). Popular Hebrew phrase expressing the hope or promise that something will take place as foreseen or planned. As a pious expression, it first appears in *Tsava'at Rabbi Eliezer ha-Gadol*, an ethical work attributed to R. Eliezer of Worms (c.1050): "In all that you propose, add the proviso 'if the Lord so wills'..." Observant Jews make use of a standard abbreviation in Hebrew when writing the phrase.

INCENSE The Hebrew for "incense," *ketoret*, derives from a verb, *k-t-r*, meaning "to cause to smoke," and is used to designate the smoke from a sacrifice burned on the altar (I Sam. 2:15). There were two types of incense. One consisted entirely of frankincense (Lev. 2:1), and was used in conjunction with certain meal offerings. The other was compounded of eleven ingredients, as outlined in the Talmud (*Ker.* 6a), which gives a description of the quantity used to make up a full year's supply: 70 *manehs* (a *maneh* is somewhat less than 13 oz.) each of stacte, onycha, galbanum, and frankincense; 16 *manehs* each of myrrh, cassia, spikenard, and saffron; 12 *manehs* of costus; three of aromatic bark; and nine of cinnamon. In addition, various quantities of Carshina lye and wine (preferably Cyprus wine, but if neces-

Incense burners from Tel Zafit and Tel Amal, two excavation sites in Israel, dating from the 11th-10th century BCE.

sary old white wine) and Sodom salt were added, as was a minute quantity of *ma'aleh ashan* — an ingredient which produced smoke. Only the first four of these ingredients are mentioned by name in the Pentateuch (Ex. 30:34). All the ingredients had to be pounded into the finest of powders. This incense was brought twice daily, once in the morning and once toward the evening, and was burned on a special "incense ALTAR" which was overlaid with gold, and which measured one cubit square and was two cubits high. This offering also constituted part of the HIGH PRIEST's ritual prescribed for the DAY OF ATONEMENT, when he entered the HOLY OF HOLIES. The incense was either burned on the altar or was brought in a special fire pan and sprinkled on live coals (Lev. 16:12-13). Only the priests were permitted to offer incense (Num. 17:5).

The special efficacy of the incense offering as well as the ban on its being brought by an unauthorized person are reflected in two episodes. Numbers 17:11-15 relates how, at Moses' command, Aaron used incense to stay a plague caused by Divine wrath, that had broken out among Korah's rebels. The other (Lev. 10:1-3) tells how Nadab and Abihu, the two sons of Aaron, were consumed by fire when they brought an incense offering of "strange fire." Later, King Uzziah (II Chr. 26:16) was struck by leprosy for having in his arrogance presumed to bring incense in the Temple. Jeremiah (41:5) mentions that even after the destruction of the Temple, men came from Samaria bearing a meal offering and incense. Twelve incense vessels, each weighing ten shekels of gold, are mentioned in Numbers 7:84-86 and elsewhere. These were taken by the Babylonians as plunder when they destroyed the Temple in 586 BCE (II Kings 25:14).

Incense was also used in private homes, although Jewish

law (Ex. 30:37) specifically forbids copying the formula used for the incense burned in the Temple. Guests were welcomed by the burning of incense in their honor (Ezek. 6:13; 23:41; Dan. 2:46). The Talmud also refers to *mugmar*, a process in which incense was burned in order to impart a pleasant odor to clothing.

INCEST Sexual intercourse between persons too closely related to marry legally, the "near of kin" (Lev. 18:6). These include: parents (18:7); step-mother (18:8); sister (18:9); grand-daughter (18:10); aunt (18:12-14); daughter-in-law (18:15); sister-in-law (18:16); step-daughter and step-grand-daughter (18:17); and wife's sister during the former's lifetime (18:18). This listing is complete and does not include any other relations.

Maimonides explains that the female relatives whom a man may not marry are, as a rule, constantly together with him in the house and he would have no difficulty in procuring them. "If we were allowed to marry any of them, and were only precluded from sexual intercourse with them without marriage, most people would constantly have become guilty of misconduct with them. But as they are entirely forbidden to us...there is reason to expect that people will not seek intercourse and will not think of it" (*Guide* III, 49).

Punishment for incest varies. In some instances, it consists of death by stoning, in others, death by burning, and in still others, KARET, (a form of Divine punishment), or flogging by the court.

The act of incest, to be considered a capital offense, must consist of sexual intercourse (*Shab.* 13a), although complete penetration was not required (*Maim. Yad, Issuré Bi'ah* 1:10). However, since the Torah used the term "near of kin," the sages also prohibited bodily proximity that provided physical pleasure (*Yad. Issuré Bi'ah* 21:1). Kissing and hugging such close relatives as a sister and an aunt is to be avoided, but a mother and a son and a father and a daughter are permissible when the children are minors (21:6,7). Females, as well as males, are forbidden to commit incest (*Yev.* 84b).

Incest is condemned by such terms as "depravity" (Lev. 20:14); "corruption" (Lev. 20:12); "reproach" (Lev. 20:17); "indecency" (Lev. 20:21). It is one of the three cardinal sins, along with idolatry and murder, which call for martyrdom rather than their performance. Incest may not be committed to save another person's life (*Tosef. Shab.* 15:17) nor on medical grounds (*Pes.* 25a).

INDEPENDENCE DAY OF ISRAEL (*Yom ha-Atsma'ut*). Israel's national day, the anniversary of the proclamation of its independence on 5 Iyyar, 1948 (5708). It was declared a religious holiday by the Israel Chief Rabbinate which formulated a special order of service for the evening and morning service now incorporated in many standard editions of Israeli and Diaspora prayer books. The service included the HALLEL, and a prophetical reading (Isa. 10:32-11:12) to be said without the accompanying benedictions. The Rabbinate also suspended any fast falling on that day, recitation of the TAHANUN prayer, and the suspension of mourning restrictions of the OMER period. By Knesset statute, Independence Day is moved to the preceding Thursday if it falls on Friday or Saturday to avoid desecration of the Sabbath. Many worshipers with the support of Rabbi Shlomo GOREN and the religious kibbutz movement felt that the Rabbinate's response was inadequate. They recite the accompanying benedictions and the SHE-HEHEYANU blessing. Reactions of the ultra-Orthodox have ranged from the *de facto* acceptance by the Agudat Israel Movement of the secular character of the day as a national holiday, carefully refraining from giving it any religious expression, to proclaiming it a day of mourning and lamentation as do the anti-Zionist Neturé Karta.

The normative halakhic opinion on the liturgical prescriptions for Independence Day is expressed in a responsum issued by R. Meshullam Rath, a leading halakhic authority at the time. He wrote: "There is not the slightest shadow of a doubt that it is a religious duty to celebrate this day which commemorates the miracle of our deliverance and liberation... all authorities concur that for a miracle which affects the whole Jewish people, which this event certainly did, the *Hallel* should be recited complete with its benediction, with eulogies for the dead and fasting forbidden...nevertheless concerning the pronouncing of the *Hallel* benediction I cannot render a decision binding future generations since this would be an innovation after a lapse of 2,000 years. For this I need the prior assent of the leading rabbinic authorities. Similarly the recital of the *She-Heheyanu* is halakhically justified but cannot be imposed. Whoever wishes to is certainly authorized to pronounce it...the person for whom the anniversary of the state constitutes an occasion of genuine happiness and joy is not only permitted to pronounce the blessing, but he is obliged to!" (*Kol Mevasser* no. 21 p.68).

In Israel, the previous day (4 Iyyar) is set aside as a day of remembrance (*Yom ha-Zikkaron*) for remembering Israeli soldiers who fell in battle.

Yizkor (Memorial) prayers, including the *Kaddish*, are recited on that day, and next-of-kin visit the military cemeteries. In the home, memorial candles are lit and in many congregations Psalm 9, "Over the death of the son", is also read.

INGATHERING OF THE EXILES (*kibbuts galuyyot*). Prophetic concept expressed in the Pentateuch (Deut. 30:3-5) as the "gathering together" of Israel's scattered remnants, and their restoration to prosperity in the ancestral homeland, by an act of Divine intervention. From the era of the Babylonian EXILE (sixth cent. BCE), this concept was developed and intensified, equating exile (GALUT) with homelessness and the Land of Israel with spiritual as well as

The Ingathering of the Exiles: the theme chosen to illustrate a leather case for the Book of Ezra. Sketch by Meir Gur-Arie, 1925.

physical restoration. Prophetic literature is imbued with such hopes and beliefs, which also make their appearance in Jewish eschatology. According to Isaiah, the banished captives of Israel and the dispersed exiles of Judah will be assembled "from the four corners of the earth" (11:11-12; cf. 43:5-6, 56:7-8). Jeremiah likewise foretells this process of national restoration (16:14-15, 23:7-8), when the exiles will be gathered from all their lands of banishment (29:14, 31:8ff., 32:37). He even calls upon "Rachel" to cease weeping for her lost children: "There is hope for your future, declares the Lord, your children shall return to their country" (Jer. 31:15-17). Ezekiel similarly reiterates these promises (20:41, 34:13, 37:21), specifically linking them to the Jewish people's religious obligations (11:17-20).

In the talmudic era, this "Ingathering of the Exiles" became a full-fledged Jewish concept, "equal in significance to the day on which heaven and earth were created" (*Pes.* 88a). After the Second Temple's destruction and the exile of the Jews, it was apparent that the dream of an "Ingathering" would be far harder to realize. That dream therefore became associated in rabbinic thought with prayers for the Return to Zion, faith in the coming of the Messiah, and an unshaken belief in Israel's final Redemption.

The notion of *kibbuts galuyyot* remained a deeply cherished hope which found expression throughout the Jewish liturgy. "Bring us in peace from the four corners of the earth and lead us proudly to our land" is a phrase in the AHAVAH RABBAH prayer, while the tenth benediction of the weekday AMIDAH implores God to "sound the great ram's horn for our freedom, raise the banner to assemble our exiles, and gather us together from the four corners of the earth." Similar statements can be found in many other portions of the liturgy.

Kibbuts galuyyot became a central Zionist concept, enshrined in Israel's Declaration of Independence, and the mass immigration (*aliyah*) of Jews from over 100 lands of exile, which began in 1948, was regarded by some as the first stage of this prophecy's fulfillment.

INHERITANCE The laws of inheritance were first laid down in the Bible. Scripture provides as follows: The first-born son (*bekhor*) shall receive a double portion of the inheritance (Deut. 21:17). If a man dies without leaving a son, his property shall be transferred to his daughter. If he has no daughter, his property goes to his brothers. If he has no brothers, to his nearest relative from his own family. On the basis of this, the rabbis ruled: "This is the order of inheritance: The son precedes the daughter (i.e., if the inheritor leaves both a son and a daughter, only the son inherits), and all the son's offspring (i.e., if he died before the inheritor and left children) precede the daughter. The daughter precedes the brothers (of the inheritor), and the daughter's offspring precede the brothers. The brothers precede the father's brothers, and the brothers' offspring precede the father's brothers. But the father (who survives his son) precedes all his offspring (i.e., the brothers of the deceased or their heirs)" (*BB* 8:2). Furthermore, "When a man leaves both sons and daughters, if the estate is large the sons inherit and the daughters are maintained from the estate (until they marry), but if the estate is small the daughters are maintained and the sons go begging" (*ibid.* 9:1). In addition, any expenses incurred when the daughter marries are covered by the estate. A further talmudic regulation awarded a daughter, in addition to her maintenance, ten percent of the estate (*Ket.* 68a).

Notwithstanding the above, a person has the power to circumvent the biblical laws of inheritance by distributing his property as gifts to others. This distribution has to be confirmed in a written document properly witnessed, called a *tsava'ah* (a will). In the case of a seriously ill person, the rabbis ruled that the distribution is valid even if made orally. Furthermore, if he distributed all his property, probably assuming that he will not recover, he may in the event of recovery retract the distribution (*BB.* 151b). The rabbis expressed their disapproval of the person who disinherits his sons, but R. Simeon b. Gamaliel holds that if his sons had not behaved properly, this is commendable (*ibid.* 8:5). Provision was made that a person could transfer his property to his son in his lifetime on condition that he enjoy the income therefrom as long as he lives (*ibid.* 8:7).

The rabbis ruled that a husband inherits his wife, but a wife does not inherit her husband (*ibid.* 8:1). However, by the provisions of the KETUBBAH (marriage contract), upon the death of the husband the widow either collects the sum stipulated in the *ketubbah*, or may continue to live in her husband's house and be maintained from the estate as long as she remains a widow (*Ket.* 4:13).

In the Middle Ages, regulations (*takkanot*) were adopted in order to remove some of the discriminatory features of the biblical and talmudic laws of inheritance. For example, if a woman died within a year of her marriage and left no child, then her husband has to return to her family the entire dowry and trousseau which she brought with her upon her marriage. In a Sephardi community a regulation provided that a husband would inherit only half of his wife's property, the other half going to her other heirs. In some communities daughters shared equally with sons in their parent's estate. These regulations were based upon the power of the court to expropriate property and on the principle that in money matters a person may make a condition contrary to that which is written in the Torah (*Kid.* 19b).

In the Diaspora today, the distribution of an estate is governed by the law of the state, following the talmudic principle that "the law of the kingdom is law" (BK 113a; cf. *Sh. Ar.*, *EE* 108). In Israel, the law of the Knesset grants daughters equal rights with sons in the estate of their parents. A wife is entitled to half her husband's estate, including the assets of a business which the husband conducted, in addition to the domicile and its furnishings which they shared. A controversial amendment granted a common-law wife the same rights of inheritance as a lawfully-wedded wife.

INSANITY In Jewish law, an insane person (*shoteh*) is regarded as incompetent and irresponsible in all respects. He is exempt from the performance of all commandments; his testimony is not accepted in court; his contractual obligations — such as sale of property or entering into marriage or granting his wife a divorce (if he married her while sane) — are null and void; he is not liable for any damage or assault that he caused, although others who assaulted him must compensate him (*BK* 87a.) It is assumed that he has no sense of shame, and one who shames him is not liable (*ibid.* 86b). Moreover, if someone sends a *shoteh* with a flame to set fire to someone's property, the sender is liable (*ibid.* 59b). An insane person may not marry, since he/she cannot give the consent legally required for marriage. If a man's wife becomes insane, he may not divorce her for fear she may be sexually abused (*Git.* 71b). Since he cannot maintain normal conjugal relations with her, he may marry another woman despite the ban against bigamy, on condition that one hundred rabbis sign a release and he makes arrangements for the proper maintenance of his insane wife (*EH*, 1:10).

The Talmud lists as symptoms of a person's mental incompetence: going out alone at night; remaining overnight in a cemetery; tearing his garment (provided there is no rational explanation for such acts; *Ḥag.* 3b). Maimonides adds: "A *shoteh* is not only one who walks about naked or breaks vessels or throws stones, but also one whose mind is deranged and is always confused about matters; even though he speaks and asks pertinent questions, he is included among the mentally incompetent" (*Hilkhot Edut* 9:9).

Some persons are subject to temporary spells of insanity; when sane they are regarded as normal in all respects, and when insane they are regarded as insane in all respects (*RH* 28a; *Ket.* 20a).

INSPIRATION See REVELATION

INTERFAITH RELATIONS For Jews, interfaith activity has been conducted primarily with Christians. Dialogue with Islam — or trialogue among the three — has been very limited, partly because of the nature of Islam, which does not encourage such relations, and partly because of the issue of the State of Israel, which is basic to both sides and on which compromise has not been found. On the other hand, the dialogue between Judaism and Christianity has become a significant feature of Jewish and Christian life in the Western world since World War II.

Prior to that war, there was virtually no interfaith activity. Western Jewish thinkers from the time of the Emancipation, starting with Moses MENDELSSOHN, had shown an openness to Christianity, culminating in the teachings of Franz ROSENZWEIG and Martin BUBER who saw both Judaism and Christianity as valid roads to God. There was no parallel movement on the Christian side where the churches continued to maintain their anti-Jewish teachings and prayers.

Christian thinking changed only as a result of the impact of the HOLOCAUST. It was realized that centuries of Christian anti-Jewish indoctrination had contributed to an atmosphere in which the Holocaust became possible. This led, over the following decades, to basic revisions in Christian thinking on the subject, especially in the Catholic and mainline Protestant churches (the Eastern Orthodox churches ignored the subject, set in their traditional ways).

For the Catholic Church, the turning point began with the adoption of the *Nostra Aetate* (Declaration on the Relation of the Church to Non-Christian Religions) by the Second Vatican Council in 1965. Abandoning the long-held Church doctrine of the continuing responsibility of the entire Jewish people for the death of Jesus, it inaugurated a process in which it removed anti-Jewish teachings from Catholic prayers and textbooks, ceased its missions to convert Jews, condemned anti-Semitism, and fostered Christian-Jewish relations throughout the world. The Protestant Churches moved in a similar direction, although due to the lack of monolithic structure of the Catholic Church, there have been variations among them. So, for example, not all have abandoned missions to the Jews, and certain Protestant circles continue to maintain the displacement of the Jews and the discontinuity of the Jewish role in the Divine scheme as a result of the rejection of the messiahship of Jesus.

The new Christian thinking has evoked various Jewish responses. In general, Jews have welcomed the new openness and have entered into dialogue and interfaith activities. Abraham Joshua HESCHEL pointed out that common concern for the world has replaced the mutual isolation of the respective faith communities. Heschel stressed the interdependence of all men of faith in view of the challenges of atheism and nihilism. Reservations have been expressed to interfaith activities in Orthodox circles, notably by Joseph Dov SOLOVEICHIK who opposed any faith dialogue on the grounds that the inner life of faith must not be exposed to interreligious encounters. However, he approved dialogue directed to humanitarian and common cultural concern. An extreme viewpoint has been offered by Eliezer Berkovits who finds dialogue futile in the light of the Christian historical record, culminating in the Holocaust. Other Jews have expressed their suspicions of dialogue for what they believe is the hidden agenda of Christians who continue — by the nature of Christianity — to hope for the eventual conversion of the Jews.

A frequently recurring obstacle in the Jewish-Christian dialogue is the State of Israel. Jews believe an appreciation of the position of Israel in Jewish self-determination to be paramount. The Catholic attitude (including the continuing refusal of the Holy See to establish diplomatic relations with Israel) is officially based on political and pragmatic considerations, but Jewish suspicions of the residues of the theological objection to the Jews' return to Zion have not been fully allayed. Many of the Protestant Churches tend to be highly critical of Israeli policies, while traces of the doctrine of discontinuity also affect their attitudes. Evangelical Churches have been highly supportive of Israel because the return of the Jews to the Promised Land accords with their own eschatological expectations, which also include strong hopes of Jewish conversion to Christianity.

While theological issues prevail in the dialogue of elites, the main progress of interfaith relations is to be seen at grassroots level. Rabbi, priest and minister frequently work together on social issues and in promoting mutual understanding, with joint Christian-Jewish activities, visits to the other's house of worship, etc. An important role in breaking stereotypes has been played by the media, which have brought Jews, Jewish history and Jewish religious life into the homes of millions who would otherwise never have encountered a Jew and whose concept of Judaism had been fashioned by anti-Jewish teaching, especially of a religious nature.

Theologically, one of the most encouraging developments is that the two sides no longer look upon each other as objects. There is an awareness that the dialogue has limits with ultimate barriers on either side that cannot be overcome. There is also an assymetry between the Jewish and the Christian approach. For Christians, the relationship to Judaism has elements of dependency and causality absent from the Jewish relationship to Christianity. Jews for their part have special expectations, often motivated more by history than by theology.

A basic premise for Jewish participants in the dialogue is that the new understanding be founded on the self-definition of the other, which each side seeks to comprehend but not to change, and that the dialogue is entered into with the acceptance of the principle of equality by the two sides.

INTERMARRIAGE Marriage between a Jew and a non-Jew; historically has been anathema to the Jewish community. The Pentateuch, referring to marriage between Israelites and members of the seven indigenous Canaanite tribes, states, "You shall not intermarry with them; do not give your daughters to their sons, nor take their daughters for your sons. For they will turn your children from following Me to worship other gods" (Deut. 7:3-4). The motive was fear of the attraction of idolatry; the end result was a cohesive and tight-knit community. However, despite this specific injunction, biblical examples of marriage to pagans abound, from Moses onward. Many were political matches, as kings took wives from among the neighboring peoples. One of the most notorious was Ahab's union with Jezebel, the Baal-worshiping Phoenician princess whose influence enhanced the practice of the Baal cult in the Northern Kingdom.

A particularly flagrant example of widespread intermarriage on all levels of society occurred in the period of the Return from the Babylonian Exile (sixth-fifth century BCE), which elicited a most extreme response, as recorded in the Book of EZRA (9-10). Upon discovering that the returning Israelites were marrying local pagan women, Ezra extracted a solemn agreement from the people to banish the "foreign" wives and their children. Since that time, marriage to any non-Jew is invalid according to the HALAKHAH; a rabbi could not officiate nor is a *get* (bill of divorce) required when such a marriage is dissolved. As Jewish law determines that the child follows the religion of the mother, offspring of such a union are Jewish if the woman is Jewish and no halakhic stigma attaches to the children. In the reverse situation, the children are not Jewish.

Marrying "out of the fold" has had difficult implications throughout Jewish history, variously representing a lack of commitment to the religion and the community; a response to persecution; political expediency; in modern times, a response to the Enlightenment and the granting of equal rights to Jews; escape from the community and a consequence of the blurring of ethnic lines and the entrance of Jews into mass higher education.

Until recent times "marrying out" was condemned throughout the Jewish community and parents would often observe mourning rites for a child who had intermarried. Emancipation in the West as well as the rise of non-Orthodox movements in Judaism over the past 150 years loosened rabbinic control over most of the Jewish community and introduced an element of individual choice. One of the main areas of Jewish life affected is intermarriage. Today, the widespread incidence of intermarriage in both the free countries and the communist world, and the degree of social acceptance it now receives, are a matter of grave concern to religious leaders, and are the subject of innumerable studies and learned papers. Responses and opinions vary. The majority of rabbis still do not officiate at such marriages; a significant percentage of Reform rabbis in the United States will do so if convinced that the non-Jewish partner is genuinely interested in the possibility of future conversion, and in order not to totally alienate the Jewish partner. Reconstructionist rabbis will officiate at a secular ceremony. The Reform Movement's Outreach Program in the US addresses itself to mixed families in an attempt to bring them into the community. In many non-Orthodox congregations throughout the world, both partners in a mixed marriage are active in the synagogue and in the Jewish community, and their children attend the Jewish school; some congregations draw the line at actual membership.

Many REFORM leaders presently accept the decision of PATRILINEAL DESCENT, by which they recognize the child of a mixed marriage as Jewish, regardless of which parent is Jewish, provided the child is raised as a Jew, given a Jewish education, and upon achieving adulthood continues to personally identify himself with the Jewish community. This is in contrast to the traditional halakhic view by which the child's religion follows that of his mother.

The designation "intermarriage" does not relate to a union between a born Jew and a converted Jew, which is a Jewish marriage in every sense of the word.

INTERMEDIATE DAYS OF FESTIVALS See ḤOL HA-MO'ED

ISAAC The second of the three PATRIARCHS, son of ABRAHAM, born when his father was 100 and his mother Sarah 90 years old (Gen. 21:5). The name (*Yitsḥak*) is derived from the fact that Sarah laughed (*tsaḥaka*) when told that she would bear a child at her age (Gen. 18:12). Isaac is the least colorful of the Patriarchs and only a few minor incidents are related of his life. After his older half-brother, Ishmael, attempted to mock Isaac, Ishmael and his mother, Hagar, were banished from Abraham's household (Gen. 21:9ff.), although later, when Abraham died, his sons came together to bury him (Gen. 25:9).

When Isaac was a young man, God instructed Abraham to offer him as a sacrifice (Gen. 19:1-19). Isaac's readiness to permit this is praised by the sages, and his readiness to die for God was the model for countless Jews who preferred martyrdom to violation of Jewish law (see AKEDAH). Contrary to common portrayals of Isaac as a child, the rabbis reckoned that Isaac was 37 years old at the time of the binding (Gen.R. 56.8). They also taught that the news about the potential sacrifice caused Sarah's death (*Pirké de-Rabbi Eliezer* 32).

When Isaac was forty years old, Abraham sent his servant, Eliezer, to his family in Mesopotamia, where Eliezer found REBEKAH, whom he brought back to marry Isaac (Gen. 24). After Rebekah had difficulty conceiving, both Isaac and Rebekah prayed to God, who granted them twins, JACOB and Esau. Isaac was 60 years old when his sons were born (Gen. 25:19-26).

In his later years, Isaac's eyesight failed him. It was then that Jacob, at the urging of Rebekah, posed as Esau and received Isaac's blessing as the firstborn (Gen. 27). Isaac died at the age of 180 and was buried by Jacob and Esau in the Cave of MACHPELAH, where his parents had been buried (Gen. 35: 27-29).

Isaac was the only one of the Patriarchs not to leave Canaan, and on the one occasion when he tried, he was instructed by God not to do so (Gen. 26:2). Rabbinic tradition gives as the reason for this the fact that he had almost been sacrificed, and anything or anyone dedicated as a sacrifice may not leave the Land of Israel (Gen. R. 64.3).

According to tradition (based on Gen. 24:63 — " Isaac went out to meditate in the field at the eventide"), Isaac instituted the afternoon prayer (*Ber.* 26b).

ISAAC BEN MOSES OF VIENNA (also known as Isaac Or Zaru'a; c.1180-c.1260). Halakhic authority and codifier. Much of Isaac's youth was spent wandering through Germany and France in search of talmudic knowledge, studying under distinguished scholars at the great *yeshivot* of his day. His teachers included Abraham ben Azriel (the author of *Arugat ha-Bosem*), Eliezer ben Joel Ha-Levi (known as *Ravyah*), Judah ben Isaac Sir Leon of Paris, and Samson of Coucy. He was also taught Kabbalah by Judah he-Ḥasid of Regensburg (see ḤASIDÉ ASHKENAZ) and one of his pupils was MEIR OF ROTHENBURG.

Isaac's fame rests upon the huge code entitled *Or Zaru'a* ("Light is Sown," from Ps. 97:11), which deals mainly with the religious laws practiced in the Ashkenazi world of his time. Although this work is arranged according to the talmudic tractates, the various laws are nevertheless grouped together. *Or Zaru'a* comprises two sections: the first sets forth the laws governing prayer, benedictions, dietary regulations, family purity, marriage and divorce, while the second covers the Sabbath and festivals. An outstanding medieval talmudist, Isaac of Vienna favored a strict interpretation of the *halakhah*. He quotes the responsa, codes, and commentaries of the *ge'onim*, together with those of the Franco-German school, also referring to the Jerusalem Talmud, and he repeats long sections from these works verbatim. Though not widely circulated, *Or Zaru'a* was often quoted (from secondary sources) by later scholars, but the first printed edition appeared only in 1862. An abridgment of the work was made by the author's son, Ḥayyim Eliezer.

ISAIAH (*Yeshayahu*). One of the major biblical prophets. He prophesied in the late eighth century BCE in Judah, during the reign of four kings of Judah: Uzziah, Jotham, Ahaz and Hezekiah, at a time when the southern kingdom was under great external pressure from the alliance of Syria and the northern kingdom of Israel (735 BCE), and from the expansion of Assyria (701 BCE).

Isaiah's two sons, through their names, play a symbolic role in his prophecies. The first son was Shear-jashub (Isa. 7:3), which means "a remnant shall return." The name was given to convey hope to King Ahaz that Judah would survive the attack of Syria and the northern kingdom. The second son, Maher-shalal-hash-baz (Isa. 8:1-4), means "the spoil speeds, the prey hastens," and probably refers to the coming destruction of Syria and the Kingdom of Israel by the Assyrians.

There is only limited information regarding the background of Isaiah. According to Isaiah 6:1, he began prophesying in the year that King Uzziah died (733 BCE). Some scholars suggest that he must have been a priest, in view of his knowledge of Temple functions. He may have been of a noble family, judging by his easy access to court circles.

According to later Jewish tradition, Isaiah was killed by King Manasseh (698-642 BCE). There is, however, no evidence of any activity on his part after the Assyrian king Sennacherib's attack on Jerusalem in 701 BCE. Isaiah is one of the few prophets who is said to have had disciples (Isa. 8:16).

Isaiah bitterly criticized the moral shortcomings of the people and warned them that sacrifices were meaningless without morality. Politically, he urged them to put their trust solely in God and not to rely on alliances with other states. The people of God will be punished for its sins, he said, but the covenant with God will be fulfilled through a remnant. The prophet's vision of the ultimate reign of God, when the lion shall lie down with the lamb and the sword will be beaten into a plowshare, has inspired many in the western world. His messages of comfort are read as the prophetical portions in the synagogue in the weeks following the fast of TISHAH BE-AV.

Modern scholarship tends to the view that the Book of Isaiah represents the prophecies of more than one person and the historical Isaiah was responsible only for the first part. See also ISAIAH, BOOK OF.

ISAIAH, BOOK OF First book in the prophetical section of the Bible; traditionally the record of the prophecies of ISAIAH son of Amoz (Isa. 1:1). The book has 66 chapters, and 1,295 verses. Many modern scholars maintain that the Book of Isaiah is a composite work written by more than one prophet, and that only chapters 1-39 are the words of Isaiah the son of Amoz. However, attempts have been made, with varying degrees of success, to prove that the entire book was the work of a single author.

According to the "two Isaiahs" theory, the first Isaiah lived in the late eighth century, and his prophecies (chapters 1-39) focused on the oracles of "woe" to Judah. The second Isaiah (Deutero-Isaiah), on the other hand, author of Isaiah chapters 40-66, dates from the early post-exilic period, and in contrast to Isaiah chapters 1-39, presents prophecies of hope and consolation. There are also scholars who maintain that Deutero-Isaiah prophesied in the BABYLONIAN EXILE and that there was a third Isaiah (Trito-Isaiah), author of chapters 56-66, who was a prophet of the post-exilic period.

The first Isaiah is identified as Isaiah, son of Amoz (Isa. 1:1), who had a wife (8:3), children (7:3; 8:3), and disciples (8:16). Beyond this, little is known of him. The historical period of his prophecy spans three significant events. The earliest (735 BCE) was the war between Aram and Israel, followed later by both countries falling into Assyria's hands (the former in 734 BCE and the latter in 722 BCE). Eventually, Jerusalem was besieged by Assyria and nearly captured. On all three occasions, Isaiah voiced prophecies proclaiming the proper path to be followed. He claimed that Jerusalem had not gone the way of the others only because King Hezekiah had repented and turned to reliance upon the God of Israel.

Like many other prophets, Isaiah condemned the moral malpractices of the people (1:4; 10:1-3), calling upon them to repent and mend their ways (1:18-20). However, his pleas seem to have fallen on deaf ears (5:8-23). He also talked about a coming "Day of the Lord" (2:6-22), not in a definitive eschatological sense, but in the firm belief that sinfulness would not go unpunished (3:1-17).

The middle portion of Isaiah chapters 1-39 is composed of oracles against the different nations, and anticipates the turning of God's hand against the enemies of Judah. The later oracles, on the other hand, concern the kingdoms of Judah and Israel. Finally, chapters 36-39 deal with the siege of Jerusalem by Sennacherib of Assyria and the miraculous delivery of the city after King Hezekiah repented.

Historical background, prophecies and theological perspective would seem to point to a different author of Chapters 40-66, but if this is the case, nothing is known of him. This section contains references to the victorious Chaldeans (Babylonians), who did not rise to power until 605 BCE, and to their demise, which took place in 538 BCE. There are two references to Cyrus, king of Persia (44:28; 45:1), who defeated the Babylonians in 539 BCE, and allowed the Israelite exiles in Babylonia to return to Jerusalem and rebuild their Temple.

Unlike the harsh invective against the people in the first chapters, there is here a stress on hope, consolation and reconciliation. It is time for a new beginning. The people need to be reassured by the knowledge that their sufferings were not by chance, but were brought about by God as punishment for their former sins. God is hailed as the only God, and is a direct challenge to the viability of other gods.

A key role is played by the SERVANT OF GOD who will proclaim truth and justice to the world. The identity of this "servant" has been much disputed, and there is disagreement among scholars as to whether these sections are even integral to the work.

Chapters 55-66 are usually dated slightly later than Isaiah chapters 40-55, relying on references to the rebuilding of the Temple (56:5,7; 60:7,10). An eloquent plea for deliverance (63:7-64:12) anticipates the glorious intervention of God, which will come to Zion and the faithful people (chaps. 60-61). This glorious future will include all nations together at last; Jews and Gentile will both worship and serve God (56:3-8; 66:18-23).

According to the sages, Isaiah was the son of a prophet (*Meg.* 15a) and was of the tribe of Judah (*Sotah* 10b). He encapsulated all of Jewish belief in two terse statements: "Observe what is right and do what is just" (56:1) (*Mak.* 24a).

Isaiah's message has always impressed the Jewish people, and no less than 15 of the 54 yearly Sabbath prophetical readings (*haftarot*) are taken from it, including all seven of the "*haftarot* of consolation" which follow the fast of Tishah be-Av.

BOOK OF ISAIAH

1:1 — 6:13	Denunciation of the sins of Israel
7:1 — 11:16	Encouragement to look to God as savior from Assyrian armies
12:1 — 12:6	Hymn of thanksgiving
13:1 — 23:18	Prophecies against Babylon, Philistia, Moab, Syria, Egypt, Arabia and Tyre
24:1 — 27:13	Universal prophecies
28:1 — 35:10	Prophecies of consolation and rebuke
36:1 — 39: 8	Historical section on Sennacherib's siege of Jerusalem
40:1 — 41:29	Prophecies of comfort and salvation
42:1 — 44:28	The Servant of the Lord passages
45:1 — 48:22	God's power demonstrated through Cyrus and fall of Babylon
49:1 — 55:13	Hymns of Jerusalem and Zion
56:1 — 59:21	The cultic concerns of the restored community
60:1 — 60:22	Glory of the new Jerusalem
61:1 — 62:12	Consolation of Zion
63:1 — 64:11	God's vengeance and hymn of lamentation
65:1 — 66:24	God destroys idol-worshipers but saves the faithful.

ISHMAEL BEN ELISHA (flourished 100-130 CE). *Tanna* of the third generation who helped to consolidate rabbinic Judaism in the years following the Temple's destruction (70 CE). Ishmael was a *kohen* (of priestly descent) and, as a child captive in Rome, had been ransomed by Joshua ben Hananiah. His teachers were R. Joshua, ELIEZER BEN HYRCANUS, and Neḫunyah ben ha-Kanah. In contrast to R. AKIVA, with whom he engaged in many halakhic and aggadic controversies, Ishmael stayed fairly close to the plain meaning (PESHAT) in his interpretation of Scripture. On that basis, he enunciated the oft-quoted principle that the Torah employs human idiom or "speaks the language of men" (*Ker.* 11a, etc.). While Akiva emphasized reward in the afterlife, Ishmael stressed the reward accruing to man in this life for his observance of the commandments and performance of good deeds. From the School of Ishmael came important halakhic (or tannaitic) midrashim — notably the MEKHILTA on Exodus and the SIFRÉ on Numbers and Deuteronomy. He believed that the commandments had been given so that one might "live by them" rather than die in their performance (*Sanh.* 74a). Though one of the legendary TEN MARTYRS, Ishmael probably died before the last (Bar Kokhba) revolt against Rome. In the sphere of HERMENEUTICS, he expanded the seven rules of HILLEL to 13. These were, at an early date, incorporated in the daily Morning Service and (as the "*baraita* of R. Ishmael") now conclude its opening section.

ISLAM System of beliefs and rituals based on the Koran. It is a monotheistic religion, founded by Muhammad in the seventh century. The term *Islam* is derived from the Arabic verb *aslama* ("submit"), and *muslim* means "one who has submitted," in the sense of acknowledging or admitting the truthfulness and/or the existence of something — in this case, the one God and the mission of Muhammad. In its barest outline, the creed consists of the declaration: "There is no god but God (*Allah*) and Muhammad is His prophet." Islam is a religion both of faith and works, faith being but one of the five pillars which comprise Islam and which a believer should observe. In addition to faith, *iman*, which is expressed in recital of the creed, a Muslim is required to observe *salat*, divine worship, five times a day; *zakat*, payment of the legal alms; *sawm*, the month-long fast of Ramadan; and *hajj*, pilgrimage to Mecca.

Like Judaism, Islam stresses the unity of God; the Koran specifically rejects the Christian concept of Trinity. God has revealed Himself to man through prophets, starting with Adam and including Noah, Abraham, and others; but He has given books only to three of them — the Law (*tawrat*) to Moses, the Gospel (*injil*) to Jesus, and the Koran to Muhammad. Muhammad, however, is the last of the prophets, the chosen instrument by which God sent the eternal message in its last and definitive form.

The Jewish and Christian presence in Arabia, where Muhammad was born and grew up, and his travels are gen-

Mohammad's tomb at Medina (left) and the Kaaba at Mecca. From a collection of Prayers to the Prophet. Turkey, 18th century.

erally considered the most crucial influences on Muhammad's life and on his mission. According to the Koran, at the age of about 40, in the year 610, Muhammad received a Divine call through the archangel Gabriel commanding him to assume the role of prophet bearing a new message embodied in an Arabic Scripture. In 622, following years of persistent opposition on the part of the notables of Mecca — where he resided — Muhammad accepted an invitation to go to Yathrib (later known as Medina). The event was to prove to be the turning point in his mission. Arriving in Yathrib with a number of faithful followers, Muhammad established himself there as a political as well as spiritual leader, and soon became master of the situation, extending his control to Mecca itself, which he purged of idols and "infidels." Jewish and Christian tribes in and around Medina were brought under tribute and delegations from Arab tribes came to declare allegiance and pay *zakat*. At the time of his death in 632, Muhammad was the undisputed ruler of all Arabia, and the year of his and his followers' migration (*hijra*) to Yathrib came to mark the beginning of the Islamic era and the first in the Muslim calendar.

At the time of Muhammad's appearance many Jews lived in Arabia; large-scale commercial relations between Arabia and Erets Israel had existed already in the days of Solomon. The Hebrew Bible has a number of references to the close relationship between Arabs and Jews, and the Books of Job and Proverbs contain many Arabic words. In addition, some paragraphs in the Mishnah refer to the Jews of the Arabian Peninsula.

Although proclaiming himself the Messenger of God and "the Seal of the Prophets," Muhammad did not intend to establish Islam as a new religion. Rather, he regarded himself as having been sent by Allah to confirm the Scriptures. His basic contention was that God could not have omitted the Arabs from the revelations with which he had favored the Jews and the Christians, and subsequently he accused the Jews of deliberately deleting from the Bible predictions of his advent.

Judaic influences in Islam abound, and there is a wealth of evidence to show the extent to which they have been deep-rooted and lasting. The very name for Islam's Scripture, Koran, while it may be a genuine Arabic word meaning "reading" or "reciting," is thought to be borrowed from the Hebrew or Aramaic *mikra*, used by the rabbis to designate the Scripture or Torah. Muhammad's principal Jewish source, however, was not the Bible but the later AGGADAH, which was communicated to him by word of mouth. This is especially apparent in the numerous references in the Koran to "prophets" preceding Moses. Noteworthy among these is the exceptional position allotted to Abraham. Abraham is the "friend (of God)" — *Ibrahim al-khalil*; he is neither Jew nor Christian but, as a true believer in one God, is considered the first Muslim, the first to have submitted unquestioningly to the will of Allah.

While Judaism is a religion of *halakhah*, Islam is a religion of *shari'a*, both words denoting the same thing, namely a God-given law minutely regulating all aspects of a believer's life: law, worship, ethics, social behavior. *Halakhah* and *shari'a* are both grounded upon oral tradition, called *hadith* in Arabic and *torah she-be-al peh* (Oral Law) in Hebrew. In both Jewish and Muslim literatures the oral tradition falls into two parts, one legal and the other moral, and in both cases they assume the same form of loosely connected maxims and short anecdotes. Again, the logical reasoning applied to the development of religious law is largely identical in Islam and Judaism, which has been seen not as mere coincidence inherent in the nature of things but, as the similar terms used in both traditions show, the result of direct contact. Finally, in both religions the study of even purely legal matters is regarded as worship, the holy men of Islam and Judaism being not priests or monks but students of the Divinely-revealed law. Scholars have also remarked on the fact that Muslim religious law developed mainly in Iraq (Babylonia), which at the time was the leading center of rabbinic learning.

Another manifestation of this close interaction between Islam and Judaism is the laws governing *taharah*, ritual purity and cleanliness, which are the same in both religions, as is the term itself. These laws concern forbidden food and drink, touching the sexual organs, bodily discharge, and contact with a corpse or a carcass — all of which cause ritual impurity and bar the affected from fulfilling religious duties such as prayer, presence in a place of worship, and recitation of Scripture.

Prayer is another shared feature of the two faiths. In Islam, the first essential of prayer is *niyya*, intent, literally corresponding to the Jewish *kavvanah*, without which prayer is incomplete. As far as Jewish dietary laws are concerned, while Muhammad came to reject most of them (which he considered a punishment for the Jews), he retained the prohibition against eating pig, blood, and carcasses, and decreed ritual slaughtering of all animals permitted for human consumption. Of social obligations and duties — which in both Islam and Judaism are considered religious duties incumbent upon every believer — *zakat* in Islam corresponds to *tsedakah* (the giving of charity) in Judaism. The care of widows and orphans is also a religious obligation in both Islam and Judaism, while visiting the sick is commended in Islam in terms identical to aggadic recommendations.

Strictly speaking, as "People of the Book" Jews are not regarded as nonbelievers, since they share with Muslims the belief in the one and only God. However, Jews are not regarded as true believers because they have failed to believe in the Koran and the mission of Muhammad. Consequently these "scripturaries", (*ahl al-kitab*), while allowed to live in the Islamic domain unmolested, were granted this right on condition that they pay a poll tax, *jizya*, and accept the status defined in treaties and charters concluded with the Muslim community. As a protected minority, however, the Jews, along with the Christians and other "People of the Covenant" (*ahl al-dhimma*), were exempted from payment of *zakat*, the alms tax imposed on Muslims as a religious precept. In this way the imposition of the *jizya* has been seen, not as a penalty for religious nonconformity but as a kind of substitute for *zakat*. Equally important is the fact that the tolerated non-Muslims were supposed to pay this special tax also as a compensation for their exemption from taking part in the wars of the Muslims.

ISRAEL The name given to JACOB after he wrestled with an angel until dawn (Gen. 32:29). Jacob, alone at the ford of Jabbok, discovered that the antagonist with whom he had struggled all night was no man but an angel, who begged to be released at daybreak. Jacob insisted on first receiving a blessing, and the angel then renamed him *Yisra'el* (Israel) "for you have striven [*sarita*] with beings Divine and human." Later, Jacob's twelve sons were known as *Bené Yisra'el*, the "Children of Israel," or more simply, as ISRAELITES. The Land of CANAAN also became known as *Erets Yisra'el*, the Land of Israel (see ISRAEL, LAND OF).

After the death of King SOLOMON, when the ten tribes under Jeroboam seceded and formed their own state (the northern kingdom), that state became known as Israel while the southern kingdom populated by the remaining two tribes was called Judah (see TRIBES, THE TWELVE).

In May, 1948, on the eve of the establishment of the new Jewish state, there was much discussion as to what name it should receive. One obvious suggestion was "Judah," but in the end it was decided to call it "Israel" (see ISRAEL, STATE OF). All citizens of Israel are called Israelis, regardless of their religion.

ISRAEL, LAND OF (*Erets Yisrael*). The land which the ISRAELITES would eventually occupy was previously known as Canaan, and it was to this land that ABRAHAM was sent by God from Mesopotamia (Gen. 12:1). This was also the land promised by God to Abraham for his descendants (Gen 12:7), and it therefore became known as the Promised Land.

The biblical account tells how the descendants of JACOB (ISRAEL) after four centuries of bondage in Egypt made their way back to Canaan, where, under JOSHUA, they conquered much of the land from its Canaanite rulers. The land became known as the Land of Israel, indicative of the occupation by the 12 Israelite tribes. There the Israelites remained uninterruptedly until exiled — the northern kingdom of Israel until 722 BCE and the elite of the southern kingdom of Judah until 586 BCE. Some 50 years after the exile from the southern kingdom, the Israelites were permitted to return to the Land of Israel, and many went back, although a considerable number remained in Babylonia in what was now a voluntary diaspora. For the next six centuries, Jews lived in the Land of Israel under Persian, Syrian, independent and Roman rule. In 70 CE, they lost the last vestiges of independence and many were sent into exile by the Romans, who even changed the name of the country from Judea to Palestine, in order to eradicate the Jewish connection from the country, the new name being taken from the ancient Philistine people of the region. Jews continued to live there, in the first centuries CE mainly in Galilee. However, under Christian persecutions and economic pressures most of them left and the numbers remaining by the 7th-8th century were not large. Nevertheless, Jewish settlement was uninterrupted and whenever possible groups and individual Jews made their way there both for PILGRIMAGE and settlement. Those who settled (see ZION, RETURN TO) often devoted themselves to study and prayer, and were supported by Jews in the Diaspora. At the end of the 19th century, the organized Zionist movement was founded and led to the 1917 Balfour Declaration recognizing a Jewish national home in the country and to the proclamation of the State of Israel in 1948.

The boundaries of the biblical Land of Israel have shifted over the course of the centuries, and different biblical accounts even list different frontiers. Some of these descriptions of the boundaries are maximalist, from the "Euphrates to the Nile" (Gen. 15:18), while others are far more modest, as, for example, "Dan to Beersheba" (Judg. 20:1) and the boundaries listed in Numbers 34:2-12. The actual boundaries have also varied. The greatest expansion of the country under Israelite rule came under DAVID and SOLOMON, but there were times during the Second Temple era when the part under Jewish control was little more than an enclave surrounding Jerusalem.

Jewish law discusses at length the holiness of the land. The consensus is that the land was first sanctified by Joshua's conquest, and subsequently lost its sanctity when the Babylonian ruler, Nebuchadnezzar, in turn conquered the land. Later, the land was sanctified for a second time following the return from Babylonian exile. This sanctification was brought about by the Israelites' residing in the land, and the rabbis generally agree that all the land sanctified at that time has retained its sanctity until the present. Where the exact borders of this lie is a matter of considerable debate. The border, for example, went through the ancient city of Acre (which was no doubt close to the present Acre), but there is a dispute as to where exactly the border lay. The question of where the border lay during Second Temple times is of halakhic significance to this day, for those areas not included in these original boundaries are not required to observe the laws relating to the Land of Israel, such as tithing and the sabbatical year.

The holiness of the Land of Israel has always been part of Jewish tradition, and the Mishnah (*Kel.* 1:2) declares that the Land of Israel is more holy than all other countries. Thus, throughout the ages Jews have been drawn to the country or even to anything originating in it. Jews would travel great distances, often at peril to their very lives, to live in the Land of Israel or at least to die in it. Those living abroad would seek a little bag of soil from the Land of Israel, to be placed with them in their graves. Stories abound of how even an envelope of a letter sent from the land would be treasured, almost as a sacred relic.

Within Jewish law there are numerous provisions which relate to the Land of Israel specifically, primarily the AGRICULTURAL LAWS (tithing produce, Sabbatical year, etc.) and laws concerned with the TEMPLE (sacrifices, pilgrimages to Jerusalem, etc.). As the land of the SEVEN SPECIES — wheat, barley, grapes, pomegranates, figs, olives and dates — various laws apply to the blessings to be recited over these species, and the concluding blessing recited after eating of the five fruits mentioned is different, for example, from that recited after eating other fruits. Other laws, while not governing the Land of Israel as such, differentiate between it and other lands, such as whether to observe one day or two of the different FESTIVALS.

The Midrash, later quoted by Naḫmanides, goes so far as to state that the commandments were given primarily for those who live in the Land of Israel, while all those living outside it must observe them primarily in order not to forget the proper observance for the time when they will return to the land.

The importance of the Land of Israel is also seen in various other laws. For example, a person has the right to demand that his/her spouse move with him/her to the Land of Israel, and failure to comply with this is considered to be sufficient grounds for divorce. In such a case, the person who refuses to accede to the move loses all attendant rights. By the same token, a spouse who wishes to leave the Land of Israel loses whatever attendant rights there would be as a result of divorce. Jewish law forbids the export of essential foodstuffs — wine, oil and flour — from the country, in order to keep the prices of such commodities in check (*BB* 90). In order to preserve the productivity of the land (*Tam.* 2:3), it was forbidden to burn either olive wood or grape vines on the altar in the Temple. Other examples also exist of laws aimed at preserving the ecology of the country, such as the provision that it is not permitted to raise small animals inside the country (*BK* 79b), for their close grazing affects the land adversely.

The Land of Israel is central in Jewish life and prayer. The three pilgrim festivals are celebrated throughout the world in accordance with the agricultural seasons in the Land, and the prayers for RAIN or DEW are recited worldwide in accordance with the climatic conditions in the Land of Israel.

LAND OF ISRAEL: SAYINGS

A land flowing with milk and honey.

To effect the purchase of a house in the Land of Israel, the deed may even be written on the Sabbath.

Only in the Holy Land can the Jewish spirit develop and be a light for the world.

The air of the Land of Israel makes a man wise.

God took the measure of all the lands and found that only the Land of Israel was suitable for the Jewish people.

One who lives in the Land of Israel is considered to worship the One God; one who lives outside the Land of Israel is considered as though he has no God.

Living in the Land of Israel is equal to all the other commandments.

The first thing to do when you enter the Land of Israel is to cultivate the land.

The dead of the Land of Israel will be the first to be resurrected [at the end of days].

The synagogues of the Diaspora will [at the end of days] be transported to the Land of Israel.

Even the everyday conversation of those who live in the Land of Israel is Torah.

A three week period between 17 Tammuz and 9 Av is set aside annually in mourning for the destruction of the Temple and for the Jews' exile from their land. Various other laws and customs also commemorate the destruction, such as the law that one leave an area measuring a cubit of one's home unpainted, and perhaps the custom of the groom's breaking a glass at his wedding as a sign of mourning.

Whether one is duty-bound to live in the Land of Israel is a matter of dispute among different commentators, but it is generally accepted that a person living in the country is not permitted to emigrate from it unless the prices of basic commodities have doubled. Even if there is no obligation to move to the Land of Israel, the sages note, among numerous sayings in praise of the land, that "Whoever lives in the Land of Israel is as if he worshiped God, while one who lives outside it is as if he worshiped idolatry" (*Ket* 110b). The sages even suggest that it is better to live in the Land of Israel in a city full of non-Jews than to live outside it in a city full of Jews. Another example of the special nature of the land is the talmudic assertion that prophecy can only exist in the land, not outside it. Similarly, it is ruled that the poor of the Land of Israel take precedence over others in the allocation of charity funds.

The general consensus of the importance of the Land of Israel was broken by the 19th century REFORM MOVEMENT, which removed the land from its scale of values, excising all references to it in the prayers. This stand was eventually overthrown, and the present day Reform movement is enthusiastically Zionist. Conservative Judaism has always regarded the Land of Israel as one of the mainstays of its beliefs and has associated throughout with the Zionist movement. Orthodoxy, while divided between those who are avowed Zionists and those who are non- or even anti-Zionists, is completely committed to the return of the Jews to their land, the point at issue being whether or not to await Divine intervention for this to occur.

ISRAEL, RELIGION IN THE STATE OF Ever since the Roman period, the restoration of Jewish sovereignty in Erets Israel (see ISRAEL, LAND OF) and the INGATHERING OF THE EXILES have formed part of the messianic vision of Judaism and found expression in the daily liturgy dating from the first to second centuries. This teaching was formulated by MAIMONIDES in his Code (*Melakhim* 11-12) and Mishnah Commentary (*Sanh.* 10): "The days of the Messiah will be the period when sovereignty is restored to Israel and the Jewish people return to Erets Israel." The actual realization of this dream in the emergence of the State of Israel on 14 May, 1948 qualified it in the eyes of the Israel Chief Rabbinate at the time to be described as "the beginning of the flowering of our redemption" (*reshit tsemiḫat ge'ulatenu*) in the Prayer for the GOVERNMENT, which they formulated to be recited in the synagogue on Sabbaths, festivals, and ceremonial occasions. The actual phrase *Medinat Yisra'el* (State of Israel) occurs in the writings of Rabbi Abraham Isaac KOOK, referring to the ideal Jewish state dedicated to spiritual perfection which he envisaged as the goal of the Zionist enterprise, 30 years before the phrase came into daily use.

The attitudes of interpreters of Judaism to a state-in-fact after 2,000 years of homelessness have ranged from disownment of its significance as a redemptive phenomenon to varying degrees of acceptance, all finding appropriate supporting texts in the corpus of Jewish tradition. A number of factors underlay the reservations with which the non-Zionist rabbis regarded the state: (1) their belief that the messianic redemption would be an entirely miraculous occurrence and could not occur under human auspices; (2) the talmudic tradition that God had extracted a solemn promise from Israel that they would not rebel, i.e., not regain the Holy Land by force of arms (*Ket.* 11a); and (3) the fact that the state was a secular one led by non-observant and even anti-religious Jews. The most extreme exponent of this view was the Satmar rabbi, Yoel Mosheh Teitelbaum, leader of the Neturé Karta, for whom the "heretical" state was the work of the devil and a trial for the faithful. A more pragmatic attitude prevailed among the vast majority of the ultra-Orthodox world, represented by the Agudat Israel organization (later, party), whose delegate, Rabbi Yitsḫak Meir Levin, penned his signature to Israel's Declaration of Independence. In deference to Jewish tradition, the declaration ended — not without murmurs of dissent from secular Zionist leaders — with the epilogue beginning: "With trust in the Rock of Israel" (in the official English version: "Almighty God"). Among non-Orthodox Jews, the Conservatives, who had always had a Zionist orientation, welcomed the new state unreservedly. So did the Reform movement, which rejected its earlier anti-Zionism and (with the exception of a tiny minority, concentrated in the American Council for Judaism) enthusiastically backed the state and, like the Conservatives, entered the Zionist movement and began activities in Israel.

The first basic law of the State of Israel, the Law of Return, recognized all Jews as potential citizens of the state, acquiring automatic citizenship upon immigration — a measure reflecting an ancient Jewish tradition that "every Jew has a portion in Erets Israel" (*Otsar ha-Ge'onim, Kid.* 60-63). Once the Jewish state was established, identifiably religious Jews were, and have remained, in a minority. This minority element, at the time almost all Orthodox Jews, presented certain demands, many of which were accepted — partly for political reasons (the religious parties were needed to establish a ruling coalition government), partly out of the wish of the leader of the infant state, David Ben-Gurion, not to add a *kulturkampf* (a struggle between secular and religious) to the many problems with which he was faced, and partly out of a determination to give the Jewish state a Jewish complexion. As a result, laws were enacted guaranteeing the observance in all areas of public life of the DIETARY LAWS, the SABBATH, and the FESTIVALS. On the Sabbath and on festivals work can continue only in factories, industries, and utilities connected with health and security, and then only with a special permit from a government committee on which the rabbinate has a representative.

Rabbinical courts exercise exclusive jurisdiction in matters of the personal status of Jews — marriage and divorce being in accordance with HALAKHAH for the Jewish population, administered by Orthodox religious judges (*dayyanim*), presided over by the two (Sephardi and Ashkenazi) Chief Rabbis. The definition of a Jew for both civil and religious purposes and for the Law of Return is basically, though not unequivocally, halakhic — i.e., one born of a Jewish mother or converted to Judaism (see JEW, WHO IS A?). At the municipal level, religious councils cater to religious needs. Their services include the provision of ritual baths, burial facilities, registration of marriages, care of synagogues, and the promotion of religious study circles, all under the supervision and administration of the appropriate departments of the Ministry of Religion. A state religious school system run on Orthodox lines exists alongside the state school system, the latter also providing hours of Bible and post-biblical Judaic studies. In recent years a stream of classes and even complete schools, known as *Tali* schools (from the Hebrew letters standing for "Increased Religious Education"), have developed as part of the state system. These schools provide a religious non-Orthodox education along historical or Conservative lines. Generous state aid is provided for the private ultra-Orthodox schools, which opt for a more intensive and fundamentalist Torah syllabus and a minimum of secular subjects. The traditional houses of rabbinical study, the *yeshivot*, flourish as never before in Jewish history, attracting scores of thousands of students from all over the world, benefiting from state grants and, often, from the postponement of compulsory military service for those continuing their studies there. Direct religious legislation includes the prohibition of pig-rearing and the sale of *ḥamets* (leaven) during PASSOVER in Jewish areas. Much state legislation owes a great deal to *halakhah* in its spirit and wording — as, for example, those laws relating to the withholding of wages (after Lev. 19,13; Deut. 24:15) or to the responsibility of bailees (after *BM* 8).

In the first Knesset elections, a united religious bloc obtained 16 of the 120 Knesset seats. Since that time, religious parties representing both the religious Zionists and the non-Zionist Agudah camps have generally won from 15 to 18 seats (out of 120) in the Knesset. As neither the left nor the right bloc has ever won an absolute majority, it has been necessary to form government coalitions, in which religious parties have formed a constant element. Up to 1967, the dominant religious faction was the Zionist party (*Mizrachi-Ha-Poel-ha-Mizrachi*, later the National Religious Party). Prior to 1967 it was generally content to vote with the ruling Labor party in questions such as foreign policy and defense, in return for concessions on the religious and educational fronts. After the Six-Day War, many religious Zionists decided that they wanted to enter the political fray. They played a leading part in the Greater Erets Israel movement, founding settlements in the "administered areas" and opposing proposals to return territory to Arab control, on the grounds that Jews should never relinquish any part of the Holy Land Divinely promised to them. (This was not accepted by some rabbinical authorities, who ruled that the "holiness of human life," endangered by remaining in the territories, outweighed the holiness of the Land itself). The 1980s saw a marked change in the internal composition of the religious representation. The non-Zionist ultra-Orthodox religious groups received considerable encouragement from the Likud party, which had come to power for the first time in 1977, in return for their support of a Likud government. Whereas up to the 1980s the Zionist religious faction had generally secured two-thirds of the religious vote, in 1988 it received only five of the 18 seats obtained by all Orthodox parties. The other seats went to the ultra-Orthodox (*ḥaredi*) parties, whose influence had grown rapidly over the previous decade and who had obtained considerable financial support from the government for their institutions and educational system. The ultra-Orthodox parties were themselves fragmented because of internal rivalries between Ashkenazim and Sephardim and between the various schools that were successors of Eastern European disputes (between MITNAGGEDIM and ḤASIDIM and among various Ḥasidic groups). The religious establishment has remained in the hands of the Orthodox, dating back to the arrangements determined by the British during the period of the Mandate. This establishment has bitterly opposed the growth of non-Orthodox Judaism, which became notable in the early 1960s. Although hampered by this establishment, and its control of all procedures of domestic law (marriage, divorce, personal status), the non-Orthodox religious groups — CONSERVATIVE and REFORM — have sought to gain recognition for their rabbis and synagogues and introduce Jewish religious pluralism in the state. So far these efforts have failed to produce any significant changes in the system, despite the extension of the non-Orthodox religious programs to education, settlement, social action, etc.

ISRAELITE The earliest name for a member of the nation formed by the twelve sons of JACOB, the "Children of ISRAEL." The earliest recorded collective name applied to the Jewish forefathers, used in connection with Abraham and later by the Egyptians with reference to the descendants of Jacob, was *Ivri* ("Hebrew"), from a root meaning "across," since Abraham had come from "across" the river. By the time Jacob's descendants left Egypt, they were known as *Bené Yisra'el*, the Children of Israel or Israelites. It is this name, or sometimes just "Israel," by which the Jewish people is generally known in the Bible and throughout the biblical era. After the division of the tribes between the kingdoms of Judah and Israel, the word *Yehudi* ("Judahite") appears to have been used for inhabitants of the southern kingdom, while only those of the northern kingdom were known as Israelites. Later, after the fall of the northern kingdom in 721 BCE, those of the southern kingdom were also known as Israelites.

Yehudi (Heb. term from which JEW originated) became the common name for descendants of the ancient Israelites.

The term *Yisra'el* ("Israelite") continued to distinguish the majority of Jews, who were called to the READING OF THE LAW only after priests and Levites. In Western and Central Europe, at the time of EMANCIPATION, acculturated Jews began referring to themselves as "Israelites" or "Hebrews" rather than "Jews," believing the latter to have acquired a pejorative connotation. The term "Israelite" is still current as a synonym for "Jew" in certain languages (French, German, Italian).

ISRAEL MEIR HA-KOHEN See ḤAFETS ḤAYYIM

ISRU ḤAG (lit. "bind the festival offering," cf. Ps. 118:27; used to mean "day after the feast"). The day following each of the three PILGRIM FESTIVALS, observed as a minor holiday in liturgical practice. While the TEMPLE stood, pilgrims who had visited it would make their way home on the day after Passover, Shavu'ot, or Sukkot, still in a holiday mood, and the Talmud says that "one who makes an addition to the festival [lit. "observes *isru ḥag*"] by eating and drinking is considered to have offered a sacrifice on the altar" (*Suk.* 45b). Another explanation is that since there was no opportunity for individual offerings during the sacrificial rite, the following day was set apart for this purpose, observed with feasting and drinking. According to traditional practice, penitential prayers and the *Taḥanun* supplications are omitted at Morning and Afternoon Services on *isru ḥag*, while fasting and funeral eulogies are prohibited. Because of calendar differences, *isru ḥag* in the Diaspora is observed a day later than in Israel.

ISSACHAR See TRIBES, TWELVE

ISSERLEIN, ISRAEL BEN PETAḤYAH (1390-1460). Halakhic authority in Central Europe, known also as Rabbenu Isserlein. Born in the German city of Regensburg, Isserlein lost his father while still a child and was raised in Wiener-Neustadt by his maternal uncle, Aaron Blümlein, a leading Austrian rabbi. His mother and uncle were among the large group of Jews burned at the stake in Vienna on 12 March 1421 — a tragedy known as "the *Wiener Gezerah*." Thereafter, Isserlein led a wandering life (1421-45), first in Italy and then in the Austro-Slovenian town of Marburg, before returning to Wiener-Neustadt, where he headed both the rabbinical court and the *yeshivah*. From that time onward, Isserlein achieved wide renown as a *posek* (halakhic authority), many questions being referred to him by contemporaries in the rabbinate.

Isserlein's greatest work, *Terumat ha-Deshen* ("The Offering of Ashes," first printed in 1519), consists of two parts: *She'elot u-Teshuvot*, 354 responsa (*deshen* having the numerical value of 354 in Hebrew), and *Pesakim u-Khetavim* ("Decisions and Letters"), 267 replies to his correspondents. The overall title of this work, *Terumat ha-Deshen*, could not have been more appropriate, since much of the content deals with perils and tragic events that overwhelmed Ashkenazi Jews in the 15th century. This may be seen not only from the "Decisions and Letters," but also from the responsa of the first part, which Isserlein himself composed in order to anticipate every possible contingency. Forced conversion, apostasy, traveling disguised as a non-Jew, relations with Gentiles, and emigration to Erets Israel are among the many topics discussed. Other halakhists of his day tended to rely almost exclusively on standard codifications, such as the *Mishneh Torah* of Maimonides and the *Arba'ah Turim* of Jacob ben Asher. Isserlein, however, wished to trace each law back to its talmudic source, while emphasizing the decisions of the Babylonian *ge'onim* and of German authorities such as Meir (*Maharam*) of Rothenburg.

Personal glimpses of Isserlein, by one of his pupils, were later compiled in a work entitled *Leket Yosher*. His rulings in the sphere of *halakhah*, together with those of Jacob MÖLLN, influenced the development of the Ashkenazi *minhag* (see CUSTOMS). Moses ISSERLES, in his glosses to the *Shulḥan Arukh*, quotes Isserlein as one of his principal sources.

ISSERLES, MOSES BEN ISRAEL (known by the acronym *Rema*; c.1525-1572). Halakhic authority and codifier. Isserles studied in Lublin under the famous scholar Shalom Shakhna, whose daughter he then married. Isserles' father built a synagogue in Cracow in honor of his son; known as the *Rema* Synagogue, it survived the Nazi occupation of Poland and still functions in Cracow. Isserles founded a *yeshiva* (rabbinical college) in Cracow, maintaining its students at his own expense. He eventually headed Cracow's rabbinical court and became renowned as a *posek* (halakhic authority), corresponding with the great scholars of his day. They included Joseph CARO, author of the SHULḤAN ARUKH, who became his friend.

Isserles was Polish Jewry's first great literary figure. His *Darkhé Mosheh* ("Ways of Moses") had been intended as a commentary on the *Arba'ah Turim* of JACOB BEN ASHER, but when Caro's *Bet Yosef* appeared in 1565, he utilized his own work to counterbalance Caro's Sephardi rulings and to uphold the decisions of the Ashkenazi codifiers. An abridgment of *Darké Mosheh*, written by Isserles himself and called *Darké Mosheh ha-Katsar*, was later published on the *Tur*. His detailed glosses on and annotations (*Haggahot*) to the *Shulḥan Arukh*, based on *Darké Mosheh*, appeared in 1569-71 under the title of *Ha-Mappah* ("The Tablecloth"). Wherever Caro had failed to take account of Polish customs or of rulings made by Ashkenazi halakhic authorities since the time of Asher ben Jehiel, these were incorporated in Isserles's supplement. By "covering" the *Shulḥan Arukh* ("Prepared Table") with his own *Mappah* ("tablecloth"), as it were, Isserles made Caro's work acceptable to all Jewish communities. Ashkenazim now understand the term "*Shulḥan Arukh*" to include Isserles's supplementary notes;

Moses ben Israel Isserles (known as Rema) *depicted on a New Year (Rosh ha-Shanah) greetings card.*

when there is a difference of opinion between the two, they accept Isserles's view as authoritative. He paid special attention to matters of CUSTOM (*minhag*), asserting in his *Darkhé Mosheh* that "the *minhag* of our fathers is the law." Moreover, he made every effort to reach a lenient decision in cases where a substantial material loss was involved.

Isserles also wrote many other halakhic works, some of which were published years after his death. Outstanding among them are *Torat ha-Ḥattat* (1569), on the laws of forbidden and permitted foods; a volume of responsa (1640); and glosses to various works by Maimonides, Elijah Mizraḥi, Mordecai ben Hillel, and other scholars. His *Meḥir Yayin* (1559) provided a homiletical exposition of the Scroll of Esther, while *Torat ha-Olah* (1570) was a philosophical work dealing with the symbolic meaning of the Temple and its service. Isserles had a knowledge of Aristotelian philosophy, gained from the works of Maimonides, and of Kabbalah, history, and astronomy. He had an unusually broad cultural outlook, and was able to synthesize philosophy and Jewish mysticism and then to combine them with the *halakhah*. Isserles was revered by Polish Jewry and had many eminent pupils and descendants.

Inscribed upon his tombstone which still stands in the courtyard of the *Rema* Synagogue, is this tribute: "From Moses [Maimonides] to Moses [Isserles] there has arisen no one like Moses."

ISSUR VE-HETTER (lit. "forbidden and permitted"). Genre of halakhic works which deal with the laws and customs of forbidden and permitted foods. As Jewish communities spread throughout Germany, each developed its own customs. Much of the material in these books related to the customs in effect in various locales, in addition to the halakhic aspects involved. Books of this nature began to appear in Germany in the late Middle Ages. Evidently the first book of this kind to be published appeared in 1534, and is known as *Sha'aré Dura* or *Sefer ha-She'arim* of R. Isaac ben Meir of Dura. Noteworthy is also the *Issur ve-Hetter he-Arokh*, published in Ferrara in 1555. Many such books were published anonymously, and some of these works were emended by later writers, who wished to include their own local customs, without any indication as to which was part of the original work and which was added later. As a result, detailed study of these works has been seriously hampered.

IYYAR (Akkadian: *Ayaru*) Second month of the Jewish religious CALENDAR; eighth month of the Hebrew civil year counting from TISHRI. It has 29 days and normally coincides with April-May. Its sign of the zodiac, Taurus the Bull, was associated by the rabbis with the pasturing of cattle. In the Bible (I Kings 6:1, 37), this month is called Ziv ("glory" or "splendor"), a term appropriate for the height of spring; its Babylonian name, Iyyar, has a similar connotation. *Pesaḥ Sheni*, the Second PASSOVER, was in ancient times observed on 14 Iyyar, by Jews who had found it impossible to celebrate Passover a month earlier on the proper date (*RH* 1.3). According to the Bible (II Chron. 3:2), Solomon began the Temple's construction on the second day of this month. The minor festival of LAG BA-OMER, which falls on 18 Iyyar, heralds a break in the religious stringencies of the OMER period. Two modern anniversaries falling in this month are Israel's INDEPENDENCE DAY (5 Iyyar) and, the anniversary of Jerusalem's liberation (28 Iyyar) and subsequent reunification in 1967.

J

JACOB (*Ya'akov*; later also called Israel). The third of the PATRIARCHS, son of ISAAC and REBEKAH. At the age of 130 Jacob himself testified before Pharaoh: "few and evil have been the days of the years of my life" (Gen. 47:9).

Jacob's life is the most documented of the lives of the Patriarchs, with the Bible covering events from his birth to his death. From the outset, evidence is given of friction with his twin brother Esau; Jacob is born with his hand clinging to Esau's heel (*ekev*, hence the name *Ya'akov* = Jacob) (Gen. 25:25-26). The brothers' early development was noticeably divergent, Esau being a hunter and Jacob a husbandman, preferring to remain in tents (Gen. 25:27; the rabbis interpreted this as the "tents of Torah" [see Rashi *ad loc.*]).

Twice Jacob acquired from Esau what by rights should have belonged to the older brother; Esau sold his birthright (the preferred share of the inheritance) for a "mess of pottage" (Gen. 25:29-34) while Jacob obtained the blessing of the firstborn with a ruse devised by his mother (Gen. 27). Fearing Esau's vengeance, Rebekah persuaded Isaac to send Jacob to the home of her brother, Laban, in Mesopotamia, and Jacob left his own home with nothing but the staff in his hand (Gen. 32:10).

It was on this trip that he dreamed of a ladder reaching to the heavens and angels ascending and descending the ladder. God stood beside him and promised to grant him and his descendants possession of the country. When Jacob awoke, he consecrated the stone on which his head had lain and so founded the sanctuary of Bethel (Gen. 28:10ff.). Arriving penniless in Aram Naharaim, Jacob was put to work by Laban, who by deceit gave him LEAH as a wife instead of RACHEL, whom Jacob had wished to marry, thus insuring that Jacob would work an additional seven years to obtain Rachel (Gen. 29:16-30). Only after he had worked 14 years for his two wives did Jacob receive any pay for his labor, and he soon acquired considerable possessions. This aroused the envy of Laban's sons and Jacob fled back to Canaan (Gen. 31)

As Jacob's entourage approached Esau's territory, Jacob divided his camp into two, hoping that, in the eventuality of a battle, at least one group would be saved. On the night before the reunion of the brothers Jacob struggled with an angel, who, at dawn, sought to escape. Before releasing him, Jacob demanded a blessing, and the angel renamed him Israel, "for you have contended (*sarita*) with man and God, and you have emerged victorious" (Gen. 32:25-30). Jacob's meeting with Esau passed peacefully. Nevertheless, Jacob insisted that Esau accept the considerable gifts he had sent him (Gen. 33: 1-15).

Jacob dreaming of a ladder with angels ascending and descending. Detail from a prayer book binding. Austria, 18th century.

Jacob had 12 sons and a daughter from his two wives and his concubines, Bilhah and Zilpah, all but the youngest, Benjamin, born outside Canaan. These were the eponymous progenitors of the Twelve TRIBES. Benjamin, son of Jacob's beloved Rachel, was born near Bethlehem, but Rachel died in childbirth (Gen. 35:16-22).

Jacob was not to know peace. As a result of his favoritism for his son JOSEPH, Joseph's brothers sold him to passing traders who eventually took him to Egypt. Jacob was shown Joseph's coat stained with the blood of an animal the brothers had slaughtered, and the impression was given that Joseph had been killed. Jacob could not be comforted (Gen. 37).

Jacob was tried even further, when his sons were forced by Joseph to bring Benjamin, the youngest, down with them to Egypt. Only afterwards did Jacob learn that Joseph was still alive, and that he ruled Egypt.

The last 17 years of Jacob's life (he died at the age of 147) were spent in Egypt, but before his death, he left instructions to be buried in the Cave of Machpelah (see HOLY PLACES).

Jacob died after blessing his sons who brought his body back to Canaan as he had wished (Gen. 49:29- 50:13).

According to the Talmud, Jacob established the evening prayer service (*Ber*. 26b).

JACOB BEN ASHER (known also as *Ba'al ha-Turim*; c.1270-1340). Codifier and Bible commentator. He was the son of ASHER BEN JEHIEL, who taught him *halakhah* while they were still in Germany. After their flight to Spain in 1303, Jacob lived first in Barcelona and then in Toledo. Preferring study to communal honors, he never accepted a rabbinical position and lived in great poverty. His first important work, *Kitsur Piské ha-Rosh* ("Abridgment of the Decisions of Rabbi Asher"), was a digest of his father's Talmud commentary, giving only the halakhic decision and omitting the discussion.

The name of Jacob ben Asher is chiefly associated, however, with the great code entitled *Arba'ah Turim* ("Four Rows," cf. Ex. 28:17), popularly known as "the *Tur*." Based largely on the *Mishneh Torah* of MAIMONIDES, but omitting all laws that do not apply while no Temple is in existence, it is divided into four parts ("rows") comprising some 1,700 chapters in all and embracing the whole of Jewish law. Written in a clear and simple style, and taking account of both the Franco-German and the Spanish rabbinic traditions, this code became widely authoritative. It provided Joseph CARO with the substructure for his *Bet Yosef* and *Shulḫan Arukh*, while commentaries on the *Tur* were written by Jacob Ibn Ḫabib, Moses ISSERLES, Joel SERKES, and DAVID BEN SAMUEL HA-LEVI.

Page from the section Orah Ḫayyim *("The Path of Life") from Jacob ben Asher's* Arba'ah Turim *("Four Rows"). Italy, 1435.*

Earlier Bible scholarship was utilized in Jacob ben Asher's Torah commentary. The prefaces to each section, containing fanciful explanations based on GEMATRIA and *notarikon* (interpreting a word by using each letter as the initial of other words), soon became the most popular feature of this work and they are printed in most editions of the Pentateuch under the title *Ba'al ha-Turim*.

THE FOUR PARTS OF THE "TUR"

1. *Oraḫ Ḫayyim* ("The Path of Life," see Ps.16:11) on the laws of Jewish religious conduct from waking up in the morning until going to sleep at night — blessings, prayers, and synagogue ritual; observance of the Sabbath, festivals, and fast days.
2. *Yoreh De'ah* ("The Teaching of Knowledge," see Isa. 28:9) on forbidden and permitted things (*issur ve-hetter*), including dietary laws, family purity, oaths, charging interest, and mourning.
3. *Even ha-Ezer* ("The Stone of Help," see I Sam. 5:1) on laws concerning women, notably marriage and divorce.
4. *Ḫoshen Mishpat* ("The Breastplate of Judgment," see Ex. 28:15) on civil jurisprudence and legal procedure.

JACOB JOSEPH OF POLONNOYE (c.1710-c.1784). Disciple of Israel BA'AL SHEM TOV and the first Ḫasidic author to be published (see ḪASIDISM). Jacob Joseph was already a prominent Volhynian rabbi when he met and was influenced by the Ba'al Shem Tov; once his Ḫasidic leanings became known (around 1748), he was forced to abandon his rabbinical post in Shargorod. Jacob Joseph then conducted Ḫasidic propaganda in Nemirov, but eventually succeeded Aryeh Leib of Polonnoye as that town's *maggid* (preacher). A somewhat aloof figure in Ḫasidism, Jacob Joseph founded no dynasty and appears to have clashed with DOV BAER, the Maggid of Mezhirech (whom he never mentions in his writings), over the right to succeed the Ba'al Shem Tov. All Ḫasidim show great respect for Jacob Joseph, however, as one who transmitted the Ba'al Shem Tov's teachings directly and as the Ḫasidic movement's first leading theoretician.

His works, mingling biblical commentary and homiletics with Ḫasidic doctrine, include *Toledot Ya'akov Yosef* (1780), *Ben Porat Yosef* (1781), and *Tsafenat Pane'aḫ* (1782). In the first of these, he attacked the traditional rabbinate and its concept of Torah study, glorifying the TSADDIK as "the channel through which God's influence flows to the common people." This infuriated the MITNAGGEDIM (opponents of Ḫasidism) and induced ELIJAH GAON OF VILNA to renew his ban against the Ḫasidim.

JACOBSON, ISRAEL (1768-1828). Pioneer of REFORM JUDAISM. A financier traditionally educated in his native Halberstadt, he was inspired both by Moses MENDELSSOHN and the French Revolution. Seeking to integrate Jews within Christian society, Jacobson established a vocational school for boys at Seesen (1801), the first of several, and later published a book flattering Napoleon as "the Great Emancipator." The Westphalian consistory that Jacobson headed in 1808-13 built new "temples" and schools in which Lutheran-style CONFIRMATION ceremonies were held, prayers were recited partly in Hebrew and partly in German, and German hymns were sung by a choir, periodically with ORGAN accompaniment. The temple which he built in Seesen (1810) was dedicated with great ceremony in the presence of non-Jewish clergymen and government officials. A Westphalian law of 1811 banned prayer quorums (*minyanim*) and silenced Jacobson's traditionalist opponents. After the overthrow of Napoleon, Jacobson moved to Berlin, where he organized private chapels on similar lines until the Prussian authorities closed them in 1823. Jacobson claimed to work within the Oral Law and never meant to cause a rift in German Jewry. Motivated by the growing indifference of cultured German-speaking Jews to their religion, he sought to counter the prevailing lifeless formalism of synagogue worship, partly by making the service and its setting more aesthetic.

JEREMIAH (7th-6th centuries BCE). Second of the three major prophets in the Prophetical section of the Bible. He was born in Anathoth, a small village of priests northeast of Jerusalem. He lived in Jerusalem and his long career, spanning more than four decades, coincided with the fall of the Assyrian Empire and with the rise of Babylonia to supremacy in the ancient Near East, Judah's alliance with Egypt which Jeremiah denounced, Babylonia's defeat of Egypt, and the destruction by the Babylonians of the Temple and the Kingdom of Judah. His prophetic call came in 626 BCE, while he was a young man, and covered the reigns of the last kings of Judah.

His political message was to submit to Babylonia and make the most of captivity. This message of submission and doom, graphically conveyed also by symbolic actions, earned him the wrath of the rulers, notably Jehoiakim and Zedekiah, and of the masses who regarded the prophet as a traitor. He suffered persecution, almost losing his life in one instance. His religious message was also greeted with hostility. He denounced the Temple and the general wickedness of the people, even accusing the spiritual leaders, including the other prophets, of falsehood and hypocrisy. His basic teaching was "not to glory in wisdom, might, and wealth but only in the service of God who is just" (Jer. 9:23-24). He also foretells a new covenant with God, which will be written in the hearts of the Israelites (31:31-34). His insistence on the futility of opposition to the Babylonians made him a *persona grata* with them after they had conquered Jerusalem. He was not exiled to Babylonia (see EXILE, BABYLONIAN) with the rest of the elite and was left in Judah where they expected him to act as a pacifying element. However, after the assassination of the Babylonian-appointed governor, Gedaliah, the other leading Jews who had remained, fearing Babylonian reprisals, fled to Egypt, forcing the prophet to go along with them. He is last heard of denouncing the idolatry of the Jews of Egypt.

In Jewish tradition, Jeremiah is regarded as the author of the Book of LAMENTATIONS and (less probably) of the Books of KINGS. See also JEREMIAH, BOOK OF.

Jeremiah mourning the destruction of Jerusalem. From an illustrated manuscript of the Book of Lamentations. Germany, 12th century.

JEREMIAH, BOOK OF Second book in the Prophetical section of the Bible, a collection of 52 chapters and 1,365 verses incorporating the biography and prophecies of JEREMIAH, whose activity covered over four decades during momentous events in the Near East (c. 626-580 BCE). The book contains four distinct kinds of materials: a) poetic oracles of judgment; b) sermons in prose; c) biographical narratives; and d) poetic oracles against foreign nations. The prophetic utterances were initially oral, and remained such for over two decades. The actual decision to write them down came about because Jeremiah had incurred royal anger. As a result of King Jehoiakim's hostility toward him, the prophet dictated his oracles of the last 20 years to his scribe, Baruch, who wrote them on a scroll, which he read before some chief officials and subsequently before the king. Jehoiakim showed his contempt for Jeremiah by cutting up the scroll and burning it. Thereupon, Jeremiah dictated the oracles once more, adding further words of similar content (see chap. 36).

The book contains five poignant laments (11:18-12:6; 15:10-15:21; 17:14-17:18; 18:18-18:23; 20:7-20:18) that have been frequently mined for personal information about Jeremiah and a section of consolation (chaps. 30-31) which includes the promise that God will institute a new covenant, replacing the heart of stone of the people with one of flesh. Another major literary complex within the book is the prose narrative about Jeremiah's suffering.

The major themes of the book are not readily perceived. One message that stands out is that the nation of Judah had rejected God who was therefore determined to punish them by sending Babylon against them. Unimpressed by the nationalistic sentiments of his compatriots, Jeremiah urged capitulation to avoid a disastrous siege. The book has several extensive accounts of prophecy dramatized in the presence of the onlookers: the burial of a linen waistcloth and its retrieval; refusal to marry; breaking a potter's vessel; purchasing a field during a siege of the city; offering wine to Rechabites who were opposed to the fruit of the vine.

BOOK OF JEREMIAH

1:1 — 1:19	Introduction
2:1 — 6:30	Reaction to current events, mostly in the reign of Josiah
7:1 — 20:18	Reaction to current events, mostly from the reign of Jehoiakim
21:1 — 25:38	Shorter prophecies, against the kings of Judah and the false prophets
26:1 — 29:32	Biography of Jeremiah
30:1 — 31:40	Consolation for the Exile
32:1 — 44:30	Biography of Jeremiah, continued
45:1 — 45:5	Oracle promising deliverance to Baruch
46:1 — 51:64	Oracle against foreign nations
52::1 — 52:34	Appendix on the fall of Jerusalem

JERUSALEM (*Yerushalayim*). Capital of Israel and holy city of the Jewish people. The first known mention of Jerusalem is in the so-called Egyptian Execration Texts of the 19th-18th centuries BCE. During King David's time (c. 1000 BCE), the city was called Jebus, for the Jebusites who lived there at the time. Although the name Jerusalem does not appear in the Pentateuch, it is probable that the traditional identification of Salem in Genesis (14:18) with Jerusalem is correct (Gen. R. 56, 10). Tradition also identifies the Land of Moriah associated with the AKEDAH (binding of Isaac) (Gen. 22:2) as Jerusalem.

The centrality of Jerusalem to Judaism is the result of religious and political decisions made by King DAVID. Prior to his time, Jerusalem was a relatively insignificant settlement located far from the main thoroughfares of the period and lacking the natural resources to grow into a settlement of importance. David conquered Jerusalem and moved his capital there after reigning in Hebron for over six years (II Sam. 5:1-13). His choice was probably based on Jerusalem's proximity to the geographic center of his kingdom and to its neutrality: hitherto unconquered, the city belonged to no particular tribe and was located approximately on the border between the northern and southern confederations. After David's conquest, Jerusalem is occasionally referred to in the Bible as the City of David (e.g., II Sam. 6:12).

David soon transferred the ARK OF THE COVENANT to Jerusalem (II Sam. 6), his new capital. He was later instructed by the prophet Gad to erect an altar on land adjacent to the city. David purchased the site from Araunah the Jebusite, although Araunah wished to give the plot to David as a gift (II Sam. 24:18-15). This site is believed to be the TEMPLE MOUNT. Jerusalem became the religious as well as the political center of the Israelite nation. The eternity of Jerusalem as a capital of the Jewish people is related to God's promise to David of an eternal dynasty (II Sam. 7). However, it was SOLOMON, David's son, who built the first Temple in Jerusalem and cemented the association of the city and God (I Kings 7).

Once recognized as the place chosen by God (see also II Kings 21:4; Psalms 132), the Jerusalem Temple became not only the exclusive site permitted for sacrifice, but also the object of the PILGRIMAGES undertaken in accord with the biblical injunction that "three times a year all males shall appear before the Lord God" (on the PASSOVER, SHAVU'OT, and SUKKOT holidays) to offer the obligatory SACRIFICES of these festivals (Ex. 23:17; Deut. 16:16-17). Pilgrimage, and the concomitant extended stay in Jerusalem, became a unique feature of national cultural life during the First and Second Temple periods; in the Second Temple era, pilgrims came from the Diaspora as well. Pilgrimages continued even after the destruction of Jerusalem and the Temple by the Romans in 70 CE (*Ned.* 23a), although these pilgrimages now served primarily as occasions for mourning and prayer for the redemption. It was customary to rend one's garment in mourning for the destruction of the Temple upon first seeing the Western Wall or the Temple Mount. The Jews continued to visit Jerusalem whenever it was permitted (see also HOLY PLACES).

As the city chosen by God, Jerusalem came to symbolize Judaism's most sublime values and aspirations. It was amply celebrated in prophecy and in psalms. Isaiah calls Jerusalem "the city of righteousness," and asserts that "from Zion will go forth teaching and the word of God from Jerusalem" (Isa. 1:26, 2:3). Jeremiah prophecies that in the future, "Jerusalem shall be called 'Throne of the Lord' and all the nations shall assemble there" (Jer. 3:17). Biblical tradition also reveals a great admiration for Jerusalem's beauty. In the Song of Songs (6:4), the beloved is compared to the holy city, and its great beauty and nobility are extolled in numerous passages (see, e.g., Ps. 48:3; 50:2; Lam. 1:1). The *aggadah* carried on this tradition. The Talmud (*Suk.* 51b) asserts that one who has not seen Jerusalem in her glory has not seen a beautiful city in his life. The Midrash (Gen. R. 14:8) tells that Adam was created from the earth of the site of Jerusalem's altar, and various ancients were said to have sacrificed there (*Pirké de Rabbi Eliezer* chap. 31). This uniqueness was due, according to the Midrash, to the city's becoming the focus of Israel's atonement through the sacrifices offered in the Temple. Another source (*Yoma* 54b) claims that the entire world was created from Zion (originally the Temple Mount, later a synonym for all Jerusalem).

The *halakhah* declared the entire Land of Israel to be holy and the city of Jerusalem to be holier still. The holiest place on earth, the Temple's inner sanctum (see HOLY OF HOLIES) was in Jerusalem. The implications of this holiness are spelled out in a system of restrictions and commands that applies solely to Jerusalem (*Kelim* 1,6ff; *BK* 82b; *et al.*).

After its destruction in 70 CE, Jerusalem's role in national life diminished. It remained, however, an embodiment of religious faith, a symbol of spiritual glory. The *halakhah* required that a small area near the entrance of every home be left unfinished or a portion of a wall unpainted, in memory of Jerusalem (*Sh. Ar. OH̱* 560:1). The popular longing and affection for Jerusalem was expressed in the liturgy. Whenever and wherever Jews prayed, they faced in the direction of Jerusalem. The text of the GRACE AFTER MEALS included a prayer for the rebuilding of Jerusalem, and the introductory Psalm appended to the Grace on weekdays includes the vow, "If I forget thee, O Jerusalem, let my right hand forget her cunning" (Ps. 137:5). The AMIDAH recited three times daily, is said facing toward Jerusalem, and contains an entire paragraph beseeching God to return to Jersualem, rebuild the city, and reestablish the Davidic dynasty. Three FASTS are observed each year to mourn different stages of the destruction of Jerusalem, the chief among them being on the Ninth of Av (TISHAH BE-AV).

Placard: "If I forget you, O Jerusalem" with depictions of holy shrines in Jerusalem. Drawing, Erets Israel, 1926.

Jerusalem's importance in liturgy and ritual is predicated upon the belief in the messianic restoration of the Jewish commonwealth in Erets Israel (see ESCHATOLOGY; MESSIAH), for which the rebuilding of Jerusalem and its Temple have always been the symbol. Based upon Isaiah's vision of a heavenly Temple, the *aggadah* developed the idea of a heavenly Jerusalem (*Yerushalayim shel Ma'alah*) (Isa. 6). In the Talmud, God declares His solidarity with the exiled Jewish people by swearing that He will not enter the heavenly Jerusalem until He can enter the earthly one (*Ta'an.* 5a). The sages asserted that God would rebuild Jerusalem and never destroy it (*Tanẖ. Noaẖ* 11), and some sources in the apocalyptic literature (Enoch 90:28-29; IV Esdras 7:26; 10:54) claim that the heavenly Jerusalem will ultimately descend and take the place of the earthly one. At all times, Jews have wished to be buried on the Mount of Olives, believing that its proximity to the Temple Mount would save them time and travail when Jerusalem would be restored and the dead resurrected. As a result of this belief, many elderly Jews made the arduous trip from the most distant Diaspora communities to spend their final years in Jerusalem and be buried there. The Passover SEDER and the Day of Atonement Service both conclude with the words "Next year in Jerusalem."

Since David's conquest, control of Jerusalem has changed hands numerous times. Little is known of the city's fate during the period immediately after its first destruction in 586 BCE, although it is believed that it lay unpopulated and in ruin until the Return to Zion some 40 years later. From the time of EZRA, until the second destruction in 70 CE, when Jews were again excluded from the city, Jerusalem remained the capital of Judah/Judea. The Romans burned the Temple, but left the retaining walls intact. Since the *halakhah* did not permit entry to the actual Temple site, a portion of the western retaining wall became, in later years, the most tangible remembrance of the Temple and a favored site of prayer and mourning. The site known to Jews as the WESTERN WALL (*Kotel Ma'aravi*) was referred to by non-Jews as the Wailing Wall. Between the destruction and the Bar Kokhba revolt against the Romans in 132 CE, Jews apparently visited Jerusalem's ruins and prayed there. After the revolt, they were not permitted even this contact. Subsequently, Jewish access was dependent upon the good will of whoever controlled the city. Because of its association with the last days of JESUS, Jerusalem became CHRISTIANITY's holy city and from the fourth century, a focus of Christian pilgrimage. Byzantine (324-638 CE) rulers were generally hostile to Jews, while the Arab rulers who controlled Jerusalem from 638 until the Crusader conquest in 1099 permitted Jews to resettle in the city. The Muslims associated Jerusalem with a crucial event in the life of Muhammad and it became their third holy city, after Mecca (its Arab. name is *El-Quds*, "the holy one"). Those Jews who did not flee Jerusalem in 1099 were massacred by the invading Crusaders. In 1187, the city was reconquered by the Muslims and Jews were permitted to return. In 1267, NAH̱MANIDES went to Jerusalem and reported finding only two Jewish families. He encouraged more Jews to settle in Jerusalem and Jewish settlement

Jerusalem as seen from the Mount of Olives. Fragment of a pictorial map of the Holy Land. Germany, 1483.

seems to have continued uninterrupted since then. From the fall of the Crusaders until 1917, Jerusalem was controlled by various Muslim rulers, whose attitudes toward Jerusalem's Jewish residents varied widely.

In 1917, Erets Israel was conquered by the British who established a mandatory government with Jerusalem as its capital. By this time the city had expanded beyond the walls of the Old City. During Israel's 1948 War of Independence, the Old City fell to the Jordanian Arab Legion, and its Jewish inhabitants were expelled. Most of them took up residence in the Jewish controlled western portion of the city, and Jerusalem remained divided for the next 19 years. During this period, despite agreements to the contrary, the Jordanian government denied the Jews access to the Western Wall and to the synagogues within the Old City (which they destroyed).

The newly formed government of the State of Israel declared Jerusalem its capital, establishing there its parliament (the Knesset), and government offices. On 7 June 1967 (28 Iyyar 5727), the city was reunited in the course of the Six-Day War (see JERUSALEM DAY). A large plaza was cleared adjacent to the Western Wall. Extensive archeological excavations, undertaken at the southern corner of the Temple Mount, in the Jewish Quarter, in the City of David, and at other sites have contributed greatly to the knowledge of Jerusalem's history in all periods. With the conclusion of excavations there, the Jewish Quarter was restored as a residential neighborhood. The State of Israel guarantees access to people of all religions to Jerusalem's holy places.

SAYINGS ABOUT JERUSALEM

If I forget you, O Jerusalem, let my right hand wither.

Pray for the well-being of Jerusalem; may those who love you be at peace.

Fair-crested, joy of all the earth.

Ten measures of beauty descended on the world; Jerusalem took nine and the rest of the world, one.

A city that joins all Jews together because they are all partners in her.

All who pray in Jerusalem are as though they pray before the Divine throne.

When Jerusalem was destroyed even God went into mourning and there will be no joy before Him until it is rebuilt and Israel returns into its midst.

When a Jew prays, he must mention Jerusalem.

Jerusalem has 70 names including City of David (II Sam. 5:9); Lion of God (Isa. 29:1); City of God (Ps. 87:2); City of Truth (Zech. 8:3); Joyful City (Isa. 22:2); Faithful City (Isa. 1:26); and Paragon of Beauty (Lam. 2:15).

JERUSALEM DAY (*Yom Yerushalayim*). Annual celebration in Israel and in some Diaspora communities of the reunification of JERUSALEM that occurred in the course of the Six-Day War on 28 Iyyar, 5727 (7 June, 1967). On that day, the Israel Defense Forces reunited the "Old City" of Jerusalem (which had been under Jordanian rule) with the "New City," and all Jerusalem came under Jewish sovereignty for the first time since the Second Temple period.

28 Iyyar was proclaimed in Israel as an official day of celebration. In most congregations the entire HALLEL Service is recited (including the blessing for *Hallel*).

The official prayer book of the Conservative Movement includes the recitation of the *Hallel* and other special prayers.

JERUSALEM TALMUD See TALMUD

JEW ("WHO IS A JEW?") Controversy concerning the definition of who is a member of the Jewish people. Historically, the definition of a Jew has been according to *halakhah*, namely a person born of a halakhically Jewish mother, or who was converted according to *halakhah*. Halakhic conversion requires CIRCUMCISION for males and immersion in a MIKVEH (ritual bath) for both males and females, as well as the acceptance of the dictates of *halakhah*. With the advent of the REFORM movement in the first half of the 19th century, Orthodox circles questioned those conversions which dispensed with the ritual aspects (i.e., circumcision and immersion), and which were satisfied with a pledge by the new converts to be faithful Jews. A relatively recent decision of the Reform movement, whereby a child of a Jewish father (and a non-Jewish mother) is also to be considered Jewish (the so-called PATRILINEAL DESCENT ruling), evoked strong opposition by both the Orthodox and Conservative movements, who accept only the halakhic guidelines as to who is a Jew. The Orthodox, however, also dispute whether the members of the Conservative rabbinate are following halakhic guidelines.

While the various religious denominations debate the legalities of "who is a Jew?," a secular approach regards being Jewish as more of a national than a religious definition, whereby anyone voluntarily associating with the Jewish people's lot is to be considered Jewish. This view regards the Jewish religion as but one of the components of being Jewish, and not necessarily an essential one. Others, including Jean-Paul Sartre, have suggested simply that a Jew is anyone considered by non-Jews to be a Jew.

While the debates in the Diaspora have been to a large extent theoretical, the question of "who is a Jew?" has had practical and political repercussions in Israel. The problem stems from the Law of Return, which entitles any Jew to immigrate to Israel and to automatically receive Israeli citizenship without having to be naturalized. In the law, as originally formulated, there was no qualification whatsoever as to who was a Jew, and anyone who declared himself a Jew was registered as such. Under pressure to change this definition, the then Prime Minister, David Ben-Gurion, sent a questionnaire to 50 leading thinkers throughout the world, as to whom they considered a Jew. The majority replied in halakhic terms. Two court cases then defined the issue more precisely. The first, known as that of Brother Daniel (Oswald Rufeisen) concerned a Polish Jew who had converted to Catholicism and became a monk. He then moved to Israel, but refused to apply for citizenship as a resident in the country. Instead, basing himself on the Law of Return, he demanded the right as a Jew to receive Israeli citizenship. When the case reached the High Court of Israel in 1966, it ruled — although this was not stated as such in the law itself — that any person opting out of the history and destiny of the Jewish people, although halakhically being Jewish, is not eligible for citizenship under the Law of Return. A second case eventually led to a change in the wording of the law. Benjamin Shalit, who had married a non-Jewish woman, demanded that his children be registered as Jews on their identity cards under the category of nationality, and as having no religion whatsoever. As the law did not specify differently, the High Court ruled that the children had to be registered as Jews. Under pressure of the religious political parties, the Knesset then modified the law to apply to Jews, now defined as those born of a Jewish mother or who have converted.

The latter phrase has been a bone of contention ever since the law was passed. As it stands, any convert to Judaism, regardless of whether the rabbi performing the conversion was Orthodox, Conservative, or Reform, is eligible to immigrate to Israel under the Law of Return. Ever since the law was passed, there have been efforts by various Orthodox religious groups to modify the law to specify "conversion in accordance with the *halakhah*." Those pressing for this change hope thus to limit the right to immigrate to Israel to only those born Jewish or those that have converted under Orthodox auspices, thereby excluding Conservative and Reform converts under the law. Since the Law of Return was passed, demands for such a change have been a standard request by various religious parties as part of the coalition negotiations with whichever party was asked by the Israeli president to form a new government. While a bill to modify the law has been submitted numerous times, it has never won the required majority.

In view of their failure to change the Law of Return, the religious parties in Israel have also sought to introduce a new law, which would serve to differentiate between Orthodox and other conversions. Under this proposal, all converts entering Israel under the Law of Return would be required to have their conversions validated by the Israeli Chief Rabbinate, an Orthodox body.

In reality, the provisions of the Law of Return affect only a handful of individuals each year. Many see the attempts to modify the law as aimed at delegitimizing Conservative and Reform Judaism and their rabbis by invalidating their conversions. This is perhaps especially the case with the Conservative movement which, in spite of some Orthodox claims to the contrary, insists that its conversion procedures are in accordance with halakhic requirements. As such, these attempts have been vehemently opposed by non-Orthodox Jews in the Diaspora (especially in the US, where the great majority of synagogue-affiliated Jews belong to the Reform and Conservative movements), who have warned that the acceptance of such legislation could lead to a schism between Israel and the Diaspora.

JEWISH LANGUAGES Those forms of national speech, vernacular, or dialect which Jews have employed in the course of their history. As the language of Divine revelation, of the Bible, MISHNAH, and rabbinic scholarship, HEBREW is Judaism's sacred tongue; as the language of the TARGUM and TALMUD, of portions of the MIDRASH, and of the ZOHAR, ARAMAIC enjoys a somewhat lesser degree of holiness. Both were living, spoken languages prior to the Second Exile and, following its modern revival, Hebrew is once more the national language of Israel, the Jewish state. Even before the Temple's final destruction in 70 CE, however, Jews in the Diaspora spoke a variety of other languages. With the expansion of these communities and the creation of others, down to the late medieval period, Jews adapted each language to their own specific needs: in particular, Hebrew and Aramaic terminology was often absorbed while religious considerations motivated the use of Hebrew characters (in preference to the Roman, Greek, or other alphabets) in writing. New Jewish languages thus emerged, and from them several important literatures were to develop. The assumption that these were merely Jewish dialects or jargons is incorrect.

With one possible exception, the Jewish languages of North Africa and the Near East all predate the rise of Islam in the seventh century CE. Judeo-Arabic (*Arvic*) became widely used after the Muslim conquest of Western Asia, but its origins can be traced to warlike Jewish tribes in sixth-century Hejaz. The Hebrew alphabet was invariably used for writing Judeo-Arabic and this language developed regional forms in Asia and North Africa, from where Jews carried it to Muslim Spain. Little or nothing of Spanish Judeo-Arabic survived the 1492 expulsion from Spain, but elsewhere the language flourished, serving rabbis, preachers, educators, and all the requirements of daily life. Bible translations and commentaries, religious and secular verse, philosophical and mystical writings — from Spain to the Yemen — were composed in a scholarly form of the tongue. Major figures who wrote in Judeo-Arabic included SAADIAH GAON, BAḤYA IBN PAKUDA, Solomon IBN GABIROL, JUDAH HALEVI, and MAIMONIDES. Judeo-Berber, a language restricted to Morocco, Algeria, and Tunisia, was also current among some Judeo-Arabic-speaking communities. Its most ancient and important literary product was a translation of the Passover *Haggadah*.

Judeo-Persian (*Parsic*) was one of the oldest of these Jewish languages. It had regional dialects in Daghestan (Judeo-Tat) and Bukhara (Judeo-Tajik). Until the 1917 Revolution, Judeo-Tat used the Hebrew alphabet; since 1939, however, as one of Daghestan's official languages, it has been printed in Cyrillic to conform with Soviet russification. A flourishing and creative Judeo-Persian literature developed under the tolerant rulers of 13th-century Persia. Bible translators utilized both Western and Oriental Jewish scholarship, while others either enabled Jews to read the great Persian classics in Hebrew script or wrote outstanding paraphrases of the Bible in verse. Although this process continued on a smaller scale in Bukhara, anti-Jewish repression from the 17th century onward in Persia brought the literary "Golden Age" to an end. Thereafter, martyrologies and chronicles occupied the Jewish writer. Until the late 19th century, Judeo-Persian culture (being preserved in the Hebrew alphabet) was virtually unknown to both Iranians and outsiders alike. Its revival, within Jerusalem's Bukharan colony and in modern Iran, stemmed from the religious and national upsurge which this ancient community experienced after 1900.

The finding of Moses in the Nile. From a Judeo-Persian commentary on the Book of Exodus. Iran, 1686.

Two minor Jewish languages were spoken by peripheral groups long settled in the Crimea. Judeo-Tatar developed among the KARAITES, while Krimtchak was the native language of their Rabbanite opponents. Both groups, however, laid claim to an old Judeo-Tatar Bible translation, new versions of which appeared in the 19th century.

The origins of Judeo-Greek (*Yevanic*) probably go back to Second Temple times, when Ezekiel the Poet, a Hellenistic Jew of Alexandria, wrote *Exagogé* ("The Exodus") and other Greek dramas on biblical themes. Discriminatory laws may have promoted this language's development in the Byzantine Empire. Liturgical hymns with brief Hebrew refrains, Bible commentaries, and a 14th-century Pentateuch were some of its literary monuments. As a spoken and written language, Judeo-Greek remained vital until the Nazi Holocaust.

No less than six Jewish languages eventually sprang from an orally transmitted Latin version of the Bible, current among the Jews of Rome and southern Italy. Their Hebrew-Aramaic content was slender, however, and (apart from the fact that they were written in Hebrew) there was little to distinguish these Romance tongues from parallel Christian vernaculars in the same areas of Western Europe. Judeo-Italian (*Italkic, Latino*, or *Volgare*) was perhaps exceptional in its readiness to assimilate Hebrew roots; from the Middle Ages onward, its use spread throughout Italy and as far afield as Corfu. Rabbis of the 13th century deemed their old version of the Bible to be on a par with the Targum, and this explains the development of a flourishing Judeo-Italian literature over the next 500 years. It produced religious hymns and secular verse, as well as translations of biblical and rabbinic texts, the Italian rite prayer book, the Passover *Haggadah*, and Maimonides' *Guide to the Perplexed*. The *Arukh*, a lexicon of the Talmud and Midrash compiled by R. Nathan ben Jehiel of Rome (c. 1100), includes 600 Judeo-Italian *le'azim* — foreign-language glosses in Hebrew transliteration. Jewish poets of the Renaissance later displayed much ingenuity in writing verse that could be read either in Hebrew or in Italian. This Jewish language still survives, mainly within the old "ghetto" of Rome.

Judeo-Spanish (*Giudezmo*, "Ladino," or "Spaniolish") and Judeo-Portuguese achieved real significance after 1492-97 as *linguae francae* of the Sephardi Diaspora. Until the early 19th century, Judeo-Portuguese was used for official purposes and announcements in the Sephardi congregations of Amsterdam and London. Judeo-Spanish gave birth to a flourishing culture that is still very much alive (see JUDEO-SPANISH; SEPHARDIM). Glossaries and *le'azim* in Judeo-Catalan give a strong indication that the language had served the purposes of Bible translation prior to the 14th century.

Judeo-Provençal, spoken throughout the provinces of southern France, was more generally known as *Shuadit* (*Yehudit*, "Jewish"). Its earliest written form occurs in 12th-century *le'azim* by R. Isaac ben Abba Mari of Marseilles; literature included an Esther scroll meant for women who could read the Hebrew alphabet and a prayer book of the Provençal rite, both dating from the 14th century. As a spoken language, Judeo-Provençal flourished much later (until after the French Revolution), but its small Hebrew component underwent drastic phonetic changes and it never amounted to more than the regional tongue in Hebraic dress. Purim songs (*Obras*) and a drama entitled *La Tragediou de la Reine Esther* shed light on social and religious conditions in the 17th century.

For all practical purposes, Judeo-French was simply the Old French language spoken by ASHKENAZIM living in northern France and the Rhineland until their expulsion from the realm in 1394. As both Jewish and Christian documents of that period indicate, the Jews of France and England were culturally part of their environment, spoke French at home, in synagogue, and in the marketplace, and even gallicized their names. *Le'azim* by the tens of thousands — in the commentaries of RASHI and SAMUEL BEN MEIR (*Rashbam*), in prayer books, codes of law, responsa, and other medieval works — bear witness to this short-lived process of integration. Six 13th-century glossaries and at least two complete biblical lexicons not only embrace many of the *le'azim* but also prove that the Hebrew Bible must have been familiar to these Ashkenazi communities in Judeo-French. With their departure from Valois lands at the end of the 14th century, this Jewish language died out and was replaced by Judeo-German (see YIDDISH).

JEWISH LAW See HALAKHAH

JOB, BOOK OF The third book of the Hagiographa, divided by the Masoretic tradition into 42 chapters and 1,070 verses.

The book itself is a poetic dialogue (3:1-42:6), enclosed within a prose framework (1-2, 42:7-42:17), which probes the mystery of disinterested righteousness and explores the question of correct responses to suffering.

The opening introduces Job, a man of exemplary character, who is wealthy and has a large family. A member of God's heavenly council, who is identified here as the "Adversary" (the SATAN), suggests that piety will not stand up to adversity, prompting God to suggest Job as a test case. Soon Job loses all his possessions and family, but his faith is unshakable: "Naked I came from my mother's womb, and naked shall I return there; the Lord gave, and the Lord has taken away; blessed be the name of the Lord" (Job 1:21). The Satan, though, is not satisfied. He claims that all the afflictions he has suffered involved only Job's possessions; if Job himself were afflicted bodily, he would indeed curse God. Job is then covered with boils "from the sole of his foot to his crown" (2:7). His wife calls upon him to curse God and put an end to his misery, but he spurns her advice. In the epilogue, Job is restored to his former glory, his wealth doubles, and he is granted a new family whom he lives to see to the fourth generation (chaps. 4-42).

The mainstay of the poetic dialogues is as follows: First, there is the dispute between Job and his three friends, Eliphaz the Temanite, Bildad the Shuhite, and Zophar, the Naamathite, each of whom offers his own explanation of Job's trials, maintaining that suffering is a result of sin and Job's misfortunes are the result of misconduct. Job indignantly denies the accusation and in chap.31, he pronounces an oath of innocence. Then the youngest of Job's friends,

Opening page of the Book of Job, showing Job with his wife and friends. From an illuminated manuscript, Italy, 15th century.

angry at Job because he holds to his righteousness, and with the friends because they had not really answered Job but only condemned him, embarks on a monologue (chap. 32-37) in the same spirit as the three friends. Finally God, too, enters the dispute, speaking out of the whirlwind and rebuking Job for presuming to understand the ways of the Almighty. He explains to Job in terms of His Omnipotence rather than of His justice, and evokes repentant words from him (38:1-40:5). Then God rebukes Job a second time, and once more Job submits (40:6-42:6).

The Book of Job plays a large role in midrashic literature, especially in questions dealing with God's justice (see, for example, *Midrash Shoḥar Tov* to Ps. 101, Deut. R. 1:17). The rabbis themselves are divided on the issue of Job's suffering. A common view regards Job's punishment as a test, unrelated to any action or inaction on his part.

Whether Job actually existed is a question posed by the rabbis of the Talmud (*BB* 15a-b). According to one view, Job lived at the time of Abraham, and the book itself was written by Moses. Other views (the most prevalent) see him as living in the time of Moses, or as returning from the Babylonian EXILE, or as living at the period of the Judges or of Ahasuerus. Finally, one view claims that Job never existed, and that the entire book is a parable of good and EVIL, REWARD AND PUNISHMENT. There is also rabbinic discussion on whether Job was a Jew or not, and in a similar vein, whether he was a truly righteous man or not. The majority of the sages regarded him as righteous, some say even more righteous than Abraham.

Scholars differ on the date of the composition of the work, and some suggest a non-Jewish origin, possibly containing Edomite elements (it is set in the "Land of Uz," which is in the territory of Edom). Some say that the speeches of Elihu are a later addition. There is general agreement that it belongs to the genre known as WISDOM LITERATURE. Internal evidence seems to date it as no earlier than the sixth century BCE, though it is possible that it is of considerably later origin.

According to the Talmud, the HIGH PRIEST read the Book of Job before the Day of Atonement, the day he had to atone for all of Israel. The Ashkenazi ritual does not include the reading of the book on any occasion, but according to the Sephardi ritual it is read on TISHAH BE-AV, the fast commemorating the destruction of both Temples. With its somber message, the Book of Job is one of the few books the rabbis permitted those in mourning to study.

THE BOOK OF JOB

1:1 — 1:5	The prosperity of Job
1:6 — 1:12	Satan's challenge
1:13 — 2:13	The trials of Job; the arrival of the friends
3:1 — 3:26	Job's lament
4:1 — 14:22	First cycle of dialogue between the three friends and Job
15:1 — 21:34	Second cycle
22:1 — 27:23	Third cycle
28:1 — 28:28	In praise of wisdom
29:1 — 31:40	Job's final speech
32:1 — 37:24	The speeches of Elihu
38:1 — 42:6	Speeches of God and the submission of Job
42:7 — 42:17	Job's prosperity is restored

JOEL One of the MINOR PROPHETS whose book is included in the Prophetical section of the Bible. No biographical data is known about the prophet. As his prophecies mention Judah and Jerusalem, but carry no reference to the kingdom of Israel, it would seem that he preached in Judah. The Book of Joel is divided into four chapters (the Septuagint and Vulgate combine Chapters 2 and 3) and include a total of 73 verses. Chapters 1-2 depict a plague of locusts that is seen as the Day of the Lord and a promise of deliverance. In 1:8-18, the prophet calls upon the priests and the people to appeal to God for help by mourning, fasting, and prayer. The following verses contain the prophet's own prayer of supplication over the calamity. Chapters 3 and 4 are an apocalyptic poem. God promises the repentant — both Jew and Gentile — deliverance from disaster, and warns of punishment against the nations who have wronged the Jews. Those Jews who remain unrepentant will also be punished. Jewish sources (*Seder Olam*) regard Joel as having lived at the time of King Manasseh of Judah, and consider him to have been a contemporary of the prophets NAHUM and HABAKKUK. Further evidence for this dating is adduced from the purity of the Hebrew language used, a purity which was allegedly corrupted during the Second Temple era. Modern scholars, on the other hand, see various references in the book as tending to indicate that it was composed after the rebuilding of the Second Temple (515 BCE), but prior to the conquest of Sidon by the Persians (348 BCE). Some of them question the unity of the authorship. The portrayal of the Jerusalem Temple as the sole sanctuary, and the references to "elders" and "priests," combined with the absence of any mention of a king of Judah, support the dating of the book's composition to the Persian era.

THE BOOK OF JOEL

1:1 — 2:17	The plague of the locusts, description, lamentations, calls to repentance
2:18 — 2:27	Oracle of deliverance
3:1 — 4:15	The Day of the Lord, portents, judgment of the nations
4:16 — 4:21	Deliverance of Israel.

JOHANAN BAR NAPPAḤA (c. 185-279 CE). Palestinian *amora* and the chief authority in compiling the Jerusalem Talmud, where he is mentioned more often than any other amoraic teacher. Born in Sepphoris, R. Johanan studied under Ḥanina ben Ḥama, Hoshaya Rabbah, and other members of the transitional generation between the *tannaim* and the *amoraim*. His most prominent colleague (and brother-in-law) was SIMEON BEN LAKISH. The Academy which Johanan established in Tiberias was attended by a host of gifted disciples, including ABBAHU, Ḥiyya bar Abba, Yosé ben Ḥanina, and Eleazar ben Pedat (who frequently quoted his master). A number of these students came from Babylonia, bringing with them lessons taught by RAV and SAMUEL (Mar), the only non-Palestinian authorities to whom Johanan himself deferred. Thanks to his mastery of earlier tannaitic sources, Johanan bar Nappaḥa was able to identify the authors of anonymous sayings in the Mishnah; he also taught that the author of any text quoted should be named. He formulated the rules for determining the *halakhah* whenever conflicts of opinion arose in the Mishnah.

R. Johanan often refers to the joys and griefs of family life, observing that "one whose first wife dies is grieved as much as if the Temple had been destroyed in his day" (*Sanh.* 22a). Though blessed with several daughters, he apparently lost ten sons during his own lifetime. His aversion to the Roman oppressors led him to warn Jewish elected officials against serving as tax gatherers. The duty of a scholar was to serve as a model for others, and one who appeared with even a stain on his clothing was guilty of a capital offense (*Shab.* 114a). Humanity and modesty were the hallmarks of a Jew, R. Johanan affirmed, since "wherever God's power is mentioned in Scripture, reference is also made to His humility" (*Meg.* 31a).

SAYINGS OF JOHANAN BAR NAPPAḤA

As long as there is life, there is hope.

"Charity delivers from death" (Prov. 11:4) only when the giver and the recipient are unknown to each other.

Whoever walks four cubits in the Land of Israel has a share in the afterlife.

There are three crowns: of priesthood, royalty, and Torah. Aaron took the first and David the second; the third is available to anyone worthy of it.

The Holy One offered the Torah to every nation, but Israel alone accepted it.

To smile at your neighbor is more important than treating him to a drink.

When the angels were about to sing a hymn at the Red Sea, the Almighty rebuked them: "My children [the Egyptians] lie drowned, and you would sing!"

Since the Temple's destruction, prophecy has been given to fools and children.

Each word spoken by God at the Revelation on Sinai was transposed into the 70 languages of mankind.

As long as the Temple was in existence, the altar used to atone for Israel; now a man's table serves as his altar.

In time to come God will make Jerusalem the metropolis of the whole world.

JOHANAN BEN ZAKKAI (first century CE). Sage and leader of the PHARISEES in Jerusalem. Little is known about his family and ancestry or his birthplace. He was a pupil of HILLEL, who foretold a brilliant future for him.

He spent 18 years in the town of Arav in Lower Galilee but was not happy there because during these years he was only twice asked to give a halakhic opinion, a fact which made him forcefully express his disapproval of the Galilean's neglect of Torah (*TJ Shab.* 16.15d). From about 30 CE he lived in Jerusalem. Here he abolished the ordeal of the wife suspected of adultery (Num. 5) as adultery had become too common, and it was probably he who also discontinued the rite of the "beheaded heifer," which atoned for an unresolved murder (Deut. 21:1-9) as murder multiplied, particularly during the siege of Jerusalem (67-69 CE; *Sot.* 9.9). Tradition accorded him the honorific title *Rabban* (our master), which was a higher title than *Rabbi* (my master), and was usually reserved for the *Nasi*.

Johanan's considerable authority as head of the Pharisaic party can be gauged from his confrontations with the priests and the Sadducees, these two groups largely overlapping.

These controversies mainly concerned the regulations of the Temple service and the laws of purity and impurity, but also civil and criminal law as well. Johanan tried to curtail the privileges and arbitrary powers of the priesthood, such as their claim to be exempt from the annual Temple tax (*Shek.* 1.4).

The Temple and Temple Mount were at the center of religious and communal life. Johanan's task was to supervise the Temple services, and to see that they were carried out in accordance with Pharisaic tradition. Sitting in the shadow of the Temple, he would expound the law all day long before a large assembly of pilgrims who came in their thousands from all over, particularly for the Passover (*Pes.* 26a).

When the revolt against the Romans broke out (66 CE), Johanan kept clear of politics. He, like many others, probably opposed the revolt and did not believe it could succeed. As in besieged Jerusalem, things went from bad to worse, Johanan decided to escape from the city by feigning illness and death, and by having himself carried out in a coffin with the help of his pupils, ELIEZER BEN HYRCANUS and JOSHUA BEN HANANIAH. Outside the city, he was taken to the Roman camp and, according to a talmudic story, was received by Vespasian, the general commanding the besieging legions whom Johanan greeted as King-Emperor. Rebuked by Vespasian for giving him an undeserved title, Johanan quoted Scripture that Jerusalem, and the Temple, would not fall except through the hands of a king. While they were talking, a message arrived from Rome that the Emperor Nero was dead and that Vespasian had been chosen as his successor. Before Vespasian returned to Rome, he permitted Johanan to make a request, upon which he asked: "Give me Yavneh and its sages" (*Git.*56a-b).

Scholars have cast doubt on the historical value of this story, which appears to be a mixture of fact and fiction. However, it became engrained in Jewish tradition.

The Temple, Jerusalem, and much else were now doomed. Johanan, watching the fire from a distance, "tore his clothes, took off his phylacteries, and sat there weeping and his pupils did likewise." But when once his pupil, Joshua ben Hananiah, lamented the destruction which had deprived Israel of atonement for their sins, Johanan comforted him by quoting Hosea 6:6, "Do not fear, we now have charity as a substitute." He saw the national-religious disaster as punishment for Israel's failure to observe God's Torah.

By asking for Yavneh (which was the center of learning even before the destruction of Jerusalem) and its sages, Johanan secured a substitute for what was lost in the disastrous war against the Romans: a new seat for the SANHEDRIN and the preservation of its leadership. Johanan successfully transferred to the academy of Yavneh some of the important functions of the Temple Sanhedrin, in particular the sanctification of the new MOON and the decision on determining leap years, on both of which the universal Jewish festival CALENDAR depended.

Johanan himself was the head of the Court in Yavneh as he had been in Jerusalem, and various crucial regulations are ascribed to him (*RH* 31b). He was joined by senior colleagues from the Temple times, and together they clarified and settled halakhic controversies. He lived in Beror Ḫayil, not far from Yavneh (*Sanh.* 32b). Torah study was supreme in his scale of values. He used Hillel's HERMENEUTIC rules to establish the finer points of law, but also tried to discover the underlying ethical ideas of apparently neutral rules of the biblical codes.

JONAH One of the 12 Minor Prophets. Jonah was commanded by God to go east to preach to Nineveh, that unless all repented, the town would be destroyed within 40 days. As Nineveh was an enemy of the Israelites, Jonah was loath to undertake the mission. Instead, he went to Jaffa and took a ship bound for Tarshish, hoping to escape his mission. On the trip, a storm threatened to engulf the ship, and when the travelers drew lots as to who was to blame, the lot fell on Jonah. Jonah, who had been sleeping peacefully, was hauled up and questioned. All the queries to him were answered by but one comment: "I am a Hebrew, and I fear the Lord, God of heaven ..." Finally, the men threw Jonah overboard and the storm subsided.

At that point Jonah was swallowed by a "great fish" (no where in the Bible is there mention of a whale), and he remained there inside the fish for three days and three nights, praying to God. Finally, the fish cast him up on the shore.

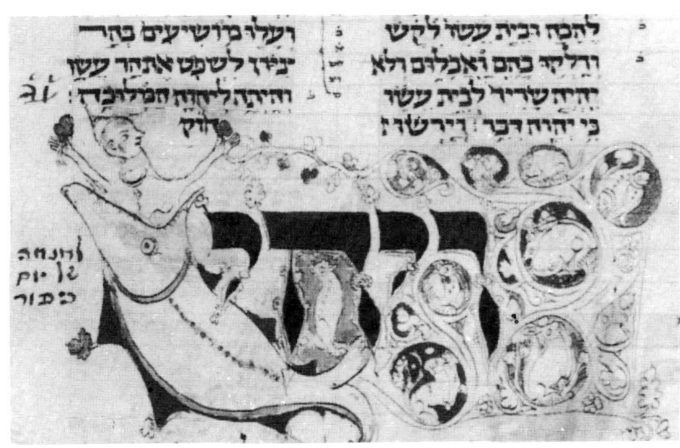

Jonah swallowed by a great fish. Opening page of the Book of Jonah. From the Xanten Bible, *Germany, 1294.*

Realizing that there was no alternative, Jonah went to Nineveh, where he preached of the imminent destruction. The king and the people took his preaching to heart, and all repented and fasted. The city was saved, but Jonah was distressed. God then made a gourd grow up, under which Jonah took shelter from the sun. When God had the gourd shrivel up and Jonah grieved, He used that as an object lesson to Jonah, for if Jonah cared about a humble gourd which he had not even planted, how could God neglect a city of 40,000 people whom He had created?

The Book of Jonah, which has four chapters, has various unusual features among the prophetical books of the Bible. It is a short story rather than a collection of prophecies. The main lesson is taught to the prophet, not by the prophet, and Jonah is more the object than the subject, in modern literary terms, an anti-hero. Apart from his message to the people of Nineveh that they repent, Jonah utters no prophecies or moral teachings. The story has a strong universalistic message in that God calls on a heathen city, and not His own people, to repent, and is deeply concerned over the inhabitants' fate and just survival.

The entire book is read as the prophetical portion (HAFTARAH) at the afternoon service on the DAY OF ATONEMENT as a reminder of the power of repentance.

BOOK OF JONAH

1:1-3	Jonah flees from his mission and embarks for Tarshish.
1:3-16	Jonah is blamed for the storm and thrown into the sea.
1:17-2:10	He is swallowed by a fish, prays to the Lord from its belly and is vomited forth on dry land.
3:1-4	Jonah goes to Nineveh, foretells its destruction.
3:5-10	The people of Nineveh repent and the Lord relents.
4:1-5	Jonah calls on the Lord to fulfill His original intention.
4:6-11	The Lord explains to Jonah why He relented.

JOSEPH Elder son of the patriarch JACOB and his beloved wife RACHEL. The Bible relates that Jacob's preferential treatment for Joseph angered his ten elder brothers. Further incensed by Joseph's two prophetic dreams, where metaphorically his brothers, father, and mother bow down to him, they conspire to kill him but are convinced by one of the brothers, Judah, to sell him as a slave. Ultimately he is taken to Egypt and sold to Potiphar, the captain of the Pharaoh's guard, who makes him overseer of his house. Joseph's charm arouses the desire of his master's wife; but finding her advances rejected, she in turn accuses him of trying to rape her, for which his master puts him in prison. There he acquires the reputation of an interpreter of dreams for which he is recommended to Pharaoh. Successfully interpreting Pharaoh's dreams as forecasting a period of famine, he is freed and made viceroy, charged with the task of preparing for the famine period — which he accomplishes impressively. When the famine materializes, it also affects Canaan and his brothers come to Egypt to seek food and there they bow down to Joseph, not knowing his identity. Eventually they show repentance for their mistreatment of him, and he reveals himself to them. He then tells them to bring their aged father Jacob to Egypt to join them and he settles them in the land of Goshen. Before his death, at the age of 110, Joseph makes his family swear that his bones will be buried in Canaan. At the time of the Exodus from Egypt (traditionally 400 years later), Moses fulfills Joseph's last wish by taking along his bones. Joseph was finally buried by Joshua near Shechem (Josh. 24:32). The story of Joseph is told in Genesis 37-50.

According to the rabbis, Joseph possessed two distinct qualities: His trust in Divine Providence, and his ability to live as a Jew in a Gentile land and culture. The sages, who called him Joseph the Righteous, relate many legends about his life. Scholars have suggested that the story should be dated to the period of the Hyksos, a Semitic people who ruled Egypt in the 18th-16th centuries BCE. They are divided as to the historicity of the story, as many of the details are not corroborated in any other source.

JOSHUA The son of Nun of the tribe of Ephraim. MOSES' successor and leader of the Israelite tribes in their conquest of Canaan. His original name was Hoshea, and Moses changed it to Joshua (*Yehoshu'a*). In the early stages of the Israelites' wanderings in the desert, he led the people in their war against Amalek (Ex. 17:8-16) and is described as Moses' assistant (Ex. 24:12). Joshua was one of the 12 spies sent by Moses to Canaan, and later only he and Caleb were privileged to enter it because they did not bring back a bad report about the land (Num. 13:6,8; 14:6-8,30,38; 26:65). He succeeded Moses after the latter's death within sight of the Promised Land and led Israel in the conquest of Canaan and its division among the tribes. As depicted in the Bible, Joshua was a combination of prophet, judge, and military leader. He made use of various military devices, such as spies in the conquest of Jericho (Josh. 2), and capturing cities without bloodshed by ambush, as in the conquest of Ai (Josh. 8). Joshua is also depicted as continuing in Moses' path, and he crossed the Jordan (3:9-17) just as Moses did for the Red Sea. He set up an altar on Mount Ebal where he uttered the blessings and the curses, as commanded by Moses (Josh. 8:30-35 cf. Deut 11:29; 27:11-13). During the conquest of Canaan, Joshua vanquished 31 kings (Josh. 12), including the allied kings of the north led by the king of Hazor (11:1-14). Joshua died at the age of 110.

Assuming that the Exodus from Egypt took place in c. 1230 BCE, Joshua became leader in c. 1190 BCE. Modern scholars dispute whether Joshua was a historical figure. Some hold that he was the eponym of a family of the tribe of Ephraim. Others claim that Joshua was indeed a historical figure, but that he only led the two tribes of Joseph and conquered a small number of places in Canaan. As opposed to this, the biblical scholar Yehezkel Kaufman claims that Joshua led a pact of the 12 tribes, which had already been organized at Sinai, and the conquest was a military one.

In the AGGADAH Joshua is considered to be Moses' spiritual successor; "Moses received the Torah from Sinai and transmitted it to Joshua" (*Avot* 1:1). According to one tradition (*Yalkut Shimoni*) Joshua was Israel's leader for 35 years, whereas according to another tradition (*Seder Olam Rabbah*) for 28 years. See JOSHUA, BOOK OF.

JOSHUA, BOOK OF First book of the Former Prophets section of the Bible, and a direct continuation of DEUTERONOMY. It relates how MOSES' designated successor, JOSHUA, leads the twelve Israelite tribes to conquer the land of Canaan and settle there. The book begins with the preparations for entering Canaan and relates the crossing of the Jordan, the conquest of Jericho and Ai, the building of an altar at Shechem, the conquest of the southern areas (from Bethel to Hebron), and the northern areas (from Hazor to Shechem) of the country, and the division of the land, including Transjordan, among the tribes. It describes the borders of the territories of the tribes, the remaining land not conquered by the Israelites, the cities of refuge and of the Levites, the building of the altar in Transjordan by the tribes of Reuben and Gad and half the tribe of Manasseh, and Joshua's death and burial. The conquest was a much more lengthy process than the biblical account suggests and possibly some of the later battles were credited to Joshua only in retrospect.

The real hero of the account of the conquest is the God of the Israelites, who throughout demonstrates awesome power. His eagerness to eradicate the Canaanites is described as resulting from His determination that their paganism should be eliminated and not serve as a temptation to the Israelites.

According to Jewish tradition (*BB.* 14b), Joshua wrote the work himself, but it was completed after his death by Eleazar the High Priest, and after the death of Eleazar, by his son Phineas. Some traditional commentators state that the volume contains verses composed after Joshua's death. Many modern scholars feel that the Book of Joshua is a continuation of the PENTATEUCH, based on the same sources, and refer to the entire unit as the Hexateuch — the "Six Books." Some claim that the volume was only edited a short time before the destruction of the First Temple. As opposed to this, the Bible scholar Yekezkel Kaufman concludes that the book is a single unit, composed a short time after the events it describes.

Joshua leading the Israelites. Opening page of the Book of Joshua. From a 13th-century manuscript.

BOOK OF JOSHUA

1:1 — 5:12	Crossing of the Jordan, preparations for conquest of the land
5:13 — 8:35	The conquest of the south (Jericho, Ai)
9:1 — 10:27	The conquest of the center of the country
11:1 — 12:24	The conquest of the north of the country
13:1 — 19:51	The division of the land among the tribes
20:1 — 21:4	The cities of the Levites and the cities of refuge
22:1 — 22:34	Two and a half tribes receive an inheritance in Transjordan.

JOSHUA BEN HANANIAH Tanna who lived at the time of the destruction of the Second Temple (70 CE), and was still living when Emperor Hadrian arrived in Erets Israel (130 CE). Whenever the Talmud mentions "Rabbi Joshua" with no further specification, the reference is to Joshua ben Hananiah. One of the five students of R. JOHANAN BEN ZAKKAI, he was a Levite who served as chorister in the Temple before its destruction. He preached to the people not to rebel against Rome, after the Roman emperor reneged on his undertaking to rebuild the Temple (Gen. R. 64). To prevent the people from lapsing into total depression following the Temple's destruction, he advocated moderation in their expression of grief (*BB* 60b). He was also against excessive stringency in the application of the law (*Shab.* 153b). R. Joshua established an academy at Peki'in, a small town between Yavneh and Lydda. Humble and peace-loving, he lived in poverty, making needles to earn a living. A famous Mishnah tells how R. Joshua argued that ROSH HA-SHANAH (the New Year) should have been proclaimed on a specific day, whereas R. GAMALIEL, the exilarch, differed. R. Gamaliel then ordered R. Joshua to appear before him, carrying his staff and his moneybelt, on the day that, according to Joshua's calculations, was to be the Day of Atonement. R.

Joshua acceded, and arrived on the appointed day, although it meant desecrating the date he thought should be sanctified. R. Gamaliel greeted him with the words, "Shalom to you, my teacher and my disciple: my teacher, for you are superior in wisdom; and my disciple, for obeying me" (*RH* 25a). In another dispute between the two, R. Gamaliel had R. Joshua stand rather than sit. As the people all supported R. Joshua and were disturbed by the treatment meted out to him, R. Gamaliel was removed from his post. As his successor, R. Joshua showed leniency in permitting Jews to marry Ammonites, against the specific biblical prohibition against this, explaining that the Assyrian ruler Sennacherib had mixed up all nations, and therefore the prohibition did not necessarily apply to the Ammonites of his day.

JUBILEE (*yovel*, from which the word "jubilee" is derived). An institution of biblical law providing every 50 years for the release of Hebrew slaves and the restoration of family property. The jubilee was observed after every seven cycles of SABBATICAL YEARS, each cycle being seven years. The Talmud records a dispute whether the jubilee was a separate year, in addition to the seven sabbatical years in the cycle, or whether the jubilee was observed the first year of the next sabbatical cycle, so that there were only 49 years in each jubilee cycle. The jubilee year began on ROSH HA-SHANAH, and when the SHOFAR (ram's horn) was blown on the DAY OF ATONEMENT that year "you shall proclaim release throughout the land for all its inhabitants" (Lev. 25:9-10).

The laws of the jubilee year were such as to enable each Jew to begin life again on an equal basis. Thus, all land sold since the previous jubilee had to revert to the original owner, this ultimately meaning the original families to whom the land had been assigned after Joshua's conquest of the land. All Jewish slaves, including those who had voluntarily accepted a continuation of their slavery after their term had expired, had to be released and given a grant to enable them to begin life anew. If applied perfectly, these provisions would insure that no individual amassed excessive wealth, nor would any Jew be reduced to perpetual poverty and servitude.

All the agricultural laws of the sabbatical year, such as leaving the land fallow, were also in effect in the jubilee year. As the laws of the jubilee year depended on all the 12 tribes living in their own land, the Jews who returned to the Land of Israel after the Babylonian exile no longer kept these laws.

JUDAH See TRIBES, TWELVE

JUDAH BAR ILAI (usually known just as R. Judah; c.100-c.180 CE) Palestinian *tanna* of the fourth generation; pupil of R. AKIVA and R. Tarfon. Ordained by R. Judah ben Bava, he was a founder of the ACADEMY in his native Usha and taught R. JUDAH HA-NASI, redactor of the MISHNAH. Both in Usha and in Yavneh, Judah bar Ilai figured prominently in the reestablishment of the SANHEDRIN. Following the exegetical methods of his teacher Akiva, Judah bar Ilai laid the foundations of the halakhic Midrash on Leviticus (SIFRA). Over 600 of his legal decisions are quoted in the Mishnah, approximately 3,000 of his sayings are on record, and in the *Sifra* and the TOSEFTA his name appears more often than that of any other *tanna*. Wherever he became involved in a legal dispute with R. MEIR or R. SIMEON BAR YOḤAI, the *halakhah* was ultimately decided in accordance with Judah's opinion (*Er.* 46b). Because of his many statements, both halakhic and aggadic, he is described in the Talmud as *rosh ha-medabberim*, "the chief spokesman on all topics and occasions" (*Ber.* 63b; *Shab.* 33b). It was from his Mishnah collection that Judah ha-Nasi derived a considerable portion of his own standard Mishnah.

Like many other sages, he was content to earn his livelihood by manual work — as reflected in two of his sayings: "Great is work, for it honors the one who performs it" (*Ned.* 49b) and "Whoever does not teach his son a handicraft virtually makes him become a robber" (*Kid.* 29a). Unlike most other sages, however, Judah maintained that good deeds take precedence over study: he would interrupt his own studies in order to attend a funeral or help celebrate a wedding.

JUDAH HALEVI (c. 1075-1141). Poet and philosopher. Born in Spain, he lived most of his life there, and studied medicine, philosophy, Hebrew and Arabic. He lived in various places, including Toledo and Cordova, practicing medicine and engaging in commerce. He was successful in his chosen fields and enjoyed a comfortable life, surrounded by many friends, including Moses IBN EZRA and Abraham IBN EZRA. This was a time of upheaval — the period of the First Crusade — when many, including Jews, were convinced that the final redemption was at hand. This may explain why, at the age of 60, Judah decided to leave his home, his wife, and his children, to move to Erets Israel. He was convinced that a Jew living outside the Holy Land, by definition, lived an incomplete life, and that only in Erets Israel could he realize his full potential. This acute longing is reflected in many of his poems.

Judah remained in Egypt for a time and recent discoveries have shown that he died there before being able to proceed to his destination. This disproves a popular legend according to which he was killed by an Arab horseman in sight of Jerusalem, while reciting one of his famous laments for Zion.

Judah Halevi's poetry is adapted to Hebrew from the prevalent Arabic patterns, and is noted for its remarkable rhyme, meter, and symbolism. His 800 known poems may be divided into various categories: songs in praise of friends; songs of nature; PIYYUTIM (religious poems), many of which are included in the liturgy; KINOT or lamentations, both on Erets Israel and on individual friends who had died; and poems about Erets Israel. The last may be divided into three subcategories: poems of longing for the Land of Israel (the

Sukkah: *The wooden walls are painted with traditional Jewish themes including a depiction of Jerusalem.*

17
19
20

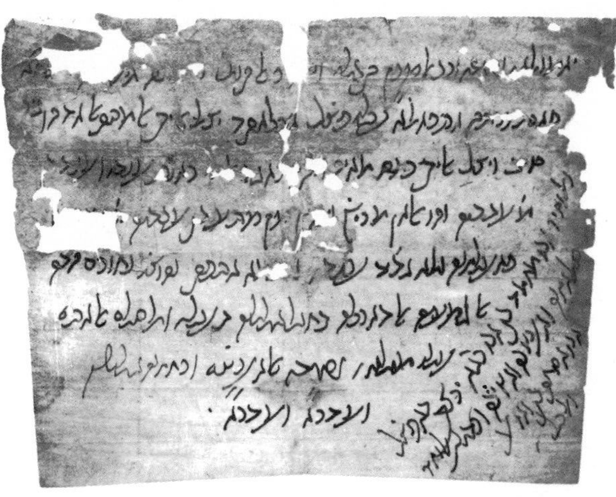

Letter written by Judah Halevi in Arabic (before 1075), addressed to a friend, while both were in Spain. From the Cairo Genizah.

Zionides); poems in which he disputes with his friends about the wisdom of traveling to Israel; and poems describing his travels on his way to the Land of Israel.

It has been suggested that at a certain point in Judah's life he underwent a crisis which deeply affected him. This would explain the seeming incongruous combination of love poems, some with clearly erotic overtones, and his later, deeply religious poetry. Already during his lifetime, his poems were known beyond the borders of Spain. They have been included in collections of *piyyutim* and poetry, in prayer books, and in collections of *kinot* and SELIḤOT.

Judah Halevi's religious philosophy is contained in a single book, written in Arabic and commonly known as *Sefer ha-Kuzari*, ("The Book of the KHAZARS"). The book uses the dramatic background of a dialogue between a Jewish scholar and the king of the Khazar tribe who subsequently converted to Judaism. Judah is concerned with the conflict between philosophy and religious faith. Jewish scholars in his time were exposed to classical Greek thought, through the abridged translations of the Greek philosophers by Arab scholars, with the obvious challenge to religion. He tries to show that Aristotelianism is valid only in the sciences of mathematics and logic but defective in psychology and metaphysics. In any case, it is only religious faith which can give real satisfaction to man and bring him close to God. Judaism does this the most effectively because it is a Divinely revealed religion, and the Torah with its commandments is God's prescription and laws for human happiness.

The *Kuzari* is not a systematic exploration of Judaism and yet it is more than mere apologetics. It expounds a number of key themes, particularly the concepts of prophecy, revelation, the place of the law, and the uniqueness of the Jewish people. It is also the first serious attempt to confront the challenges of Christianity and Islam for supremacy over Judaism. Prophecy is dealt with at length. For the philosopher, prophecy is a natural outflow of the perfect man's imaginative faculty. For Judah Halevi, prophecy is primarily the intervention of God in choosing a messenger to transmit his will. The patriarchs were prophets, and they were followed by the great biblical prophets who instilled a prophetic seed in the hearts of the Jewish people. Because of their devotion to God and the Torah, the Jews alone are the people of prophecy, and the Land of Israel is the land of the prophetic word. These concepts are the core of what seems to be Halevi's particularism.

In another part of the book, he examines the Divine Names *Elohim* and *YHWH*. The first describes God in His transcendent power — almost identifiable with the impersonal First Cause of Greek philosophy. But it is as *YHWH* that God relates to the individual and illustrates the deep significance of religious faith for the believer. The role of the Jews as the true prophetic people with this close experience of God is to spread a knowledge of God to all mankind to be ultimately transformed by submission to God's will.

The *Kuzari* had a great influence in its time, when Jews needed answers to challenges which came from many directions. Its influence continued throughout the ages and provided an important point of comparison and contrast with the writings of MAIMONIDES.

FROM THE PROSE AND POETRY OF JUDAH HALEVI

My heart is in the East,
But I am in the furthermost West.
How can I then taste what I eat
And how can food be sweet to me?

.Israel is the heart of mankind.
.For Your songs, O God, my heart is a harp.
.The Sabbath and festivals are the main reasons for Jewish continuity and glory.

(On Jerusalem). Beautiful of elevation,
Joy of the world,
City of the Great King!
For you my soul is longing.
O that I might fly to you on eagles' wings.

JUDAH HA-NASI ("Judah the patriarch"; (c. 138-c.217 CE). Spiritual and political leader of Jewry in Erets Israel; son of Simeon ben GAMALIEL II whom he succeeded in the patriarchate, c.170. His teachers were, apart from his father, JUDAH BAR ILAI, YOSÉ BEN ḤALAFTA, SIMEON BAR YOḤAI, and Eleazar ben Shammu'a.

As patriarch (NASI) and head of the SANHEDRIN, Judah

*Engraved, partly gilt silver Torah crown (*keter Torah*). Poland,* wielded almost unlimited authority. He reserved for himself the right to appoint judges and teachers throughout the land. Much of his legislative activity was devoted to the application of the laws of the SABBATICAL year and of the levitical TITHES: both weighed heavily on the overwhelmingly agricultural community, plagued as they were by extortionate taxes imposed by the Roman administration and natural disasters like famine.

Judah's authority was strengthened by his great wealth. He was able to increase the large tracts of land, hereditary in his family, which he farmed intensively, producing corn, wine, and vegetables; he also bred cattle, manufactured wool and linen, and exported and imported these commodities in his own ships. Managing personally his widespread affairs, he combined learning, wealth, and high political status.

As the effective leader and spokesman of the Jewish community, Judah was recognized as such by the Roman authorities. The intimate relationship between them is reflected in the numerous accounts about the friendship between "Rabbi Judah" and the Roman ruler "Antoninus," which constitute one of the great riddles of talmudic and midrashic literature. Not only is there no certainty as to which member of the Antonine dynasty they refer to, but the Rabbi mentioned may be Judah I or his grandson Judah II. The tales describe personal meetings, correspondence, common business ventures, and even conviviality between these two representative figures.

Judah assured his historic importance in the field of Torah learning and the preservation and ordering of the vast store of traditions through his MISHNAH. There had been previous attempts at arranging the ORAL LAW and its teachings, the latest having been made in the school of R. AKIVA and his pupils. Now Judah made a supreme effort, in cooperation with the leading teachers of his time, each of whom contributed his own store of tradition to compile what was to become the authoritative canon of the Law which contained not only law but also theology, ethics, and historical recollections. The material was classified and organized; there was much editing and cutting, but the excluded materials were collected by Judah's colleagues and pupils, into parallel collections such as the TOSEFTA (Addenda), or were scattered in the form of *Beraitot* (external Mishnah material). The Mishnah formed the foundation on which the monumental TALMUDS, the Jerusalem and the Babylonian, were built.

Judah's opinions are quoted innumerable times, not only in his own Mishnah but in the rest of halakhic literature, in the name of Rabbi, "The Master," for short. No less numerous are his aggadic sayings, usually based on the interpretation of biblical verses. The themes of his *Aggadah* include the dualism of the good and the evil inclination in man, of the body and the soul, of this world and the hereafter, of the relative importance of the Righteous and the World.

Judah's deep religiosity found expression in a number of prayers, some of which have been received into daily liturgy, such as the prayer for protection against arrogance, against bad company, and against a hard law case or litigant (Jewish or gentile) (*Ber.* 16b). His personality was most complex. Though posterity praised his humility (*Sot.* 9.15), he could be extremely authoritarian as patriarch and head of the Academy. He was very touchy when the dignity of his office was in question, and showed jealousy towards his rival, the Exilarch in Babylon, who had stronger claims than he to Davidic descent (TJ *Kil.* 9.4. 32b). For the last 17 years of his life he lived in Sepphoris. In his last will he appointed his son Gamaliel to succeed him in the patriarchate. In his dying hour he lifted both his hands to Heaven, swearing that he had labored in the study of Torah with all his strength but had not benefited from it even with his small finger. Judah was laid to rest in the necropolis of Bet She'arim.

SAYINGS OF JUDAH HA-NASI

What is the virtuous path which a man should follow? Whatever brings honor to his Maker and honor from his fellow-man.

Be as punctilious in observing a light as a weighty commandment, for you do not know their relative reward.

Contemplate three things and you will avoid transgressions: above you [in Heaven] is an eye that sees, an ear that hears, and all your deeds are faithfully recorded.

Fulfill God's precepts joyfully, just as Israel accepted the Torah at Sinai with joy.

I have learned much from my teachers, more from my colleagues, but most from my pupils.

Do not be deceived by the outward appearance of age or youth; a new pitcher might be full of good, old wine while an old one might be empty altogether.

A man should revere his father and mother as he reveres God, for all three are partners in him.

JUDAH HE-ḤASID (Judah ben Samuel ben Kalonymus He-Ḥasid, "the Pious"; c.1150-1217). The most important thinker in the main school of ḤASIDÉ ASHKENAZ, that of the Kalonymus family, which was headed in the middle of the 12th century by Judah's father, R. Samuel. Judah lived for many years in the Rhineland, probably at Speyer, but the later part of his life was spent at Regensburg.

Judah insisted that a writer should never acknowledge the authorship of his works, so as to prevent him and his descendants from taking pride in them. All his works, therefore, do not bear his name, a fact which poses difficult bibliographical problems. Apparently he was the author of a collection of mystical treatises (preserved at Oxford, Mss. 1566 and 1567), and wrote another lost theological work

tify. Eating, for example, requires BENEDICTIONS both before and after the consumption of food, making, as the sages put it, "the table equivalent to the ALTAR." Judaism has numerous laws which regulate the minutiae of human life, the object of which is to transform man's actions into service of God.

Along these same lines, Judaism regards the Torah's myriad restrictions upon the Jew's conduct as serving to elevate him. It sees the unbridled attainment of all man's lusts and desires as being animal-like behavior, and the restraints imposed upon him as serving to raise him to a higher level. Thus, the Jew must first consider whether the particular food he wishes to eat has met the requirements of the DIETARY LAWS, TITHES, etc.

At the same time, Judaism does not regard ASCETICISM as a virtue, and the Midrash states that when each person gives an accounting after his death, he must account for those permitted pleasures on earth which he refrained from enjoying.

Jewish law encompasses all aspects of life. A concept such as "rendering unto Caesar that which is Caesar's and to God, that which is God's" would thus be alien to the Jewish view of the world. Conduct toward one's fellow-man is governed by the same Jewish law which mandates the observance of the Sabbath and the keeping of the dietary laws. Judaism actually considers a violation of the law against a fellow-man as worse than a violation of ritual law, for the former encompasses a transgression against God's law as well.

Except for the hereditary monarchy and priesthood (see PRIESTS), the former having lapsed and the latter having been reduced to a mere token of its former place in Jewish life with the destruction of the Second Temple, Judaism is very much a meritocracy, based on scholarship in Jewish law. The dominant role is played by the RABBI. Originally an honorary title, since the Middle Ages the rabbi's position has been that of the salaried leader of the congregation, who educates the congregants, decides issues of Jewish law, and guides in matters of morality.

Various attempts have been made at categorizing Jewish law and belief (see CODIFICATION). One of the earliest of these is the talmudic statement that the Pentateuch contains 613 commandments, 248 positive and 365 negative (*Mak.* 24a). The Talmud then goes on to say that David condensed all the requirements made upon the Jew into 11 principles, ISAIAH into six, MICAH into three ("to do justly, to love mercy, and to walk humbly with your God" *Mic.* 6:8), and Amos and Habakkuk into one ("Seek me and live," Amos 5:4; "The righteous shall live by his faith," Hab. 2:4). The medieval scholar, Moses MAIMONIDES, listed Thirteen PRINCIPLES OF FAITH in which the Jew must believe or be considered a heretic, which include the belief in the One God and in the coming of the MESSIAH.

Rabbinic Judaism, of which modern-day Orthodox Judaism is the direct lineal heir, takes as a fundamental principle that, alongside the Torah (PENTATEUCH) which was given at Sinai, an ORAL LAW was given to Moses, to be passed on by word of mouth from one generation to the next. This Oral Law was eventually transcribed in the MISHNAH and expounded in the TALMUD and in later TALMUDIC COMMENTARIES.

It was this principle of the Oral Law as accompanying the WRITTEN LAW which marked the great divide between Judaism and various sects which broke off from the mainstream, including the SAMARITANS, the SADDUCEES, and later the KARAITES. All three of these groups denied the authority of the Oral Law, and relied purely on the Written Law, with their own interpretations of it.

Mainstream Judaism, which developed from the PHARISEES, has also had various movements, but until modern times, all began with an acceptance of the fundamental belief in the Divine origin of both the written and the oral laws. Thus, in the Middle Ages, in Europe and especially later in Safed in Erets Israel, school of MYSTICISM developed, based on an earlier mystical tradition, which was preoccupied with the study of the Kabbalah; in the 18th century, ḤASIDISM emerged to extend the concept of the truly righteous man from the learned to the less lettered man who achieves religious heights through prayer and purity of intention.

With Jewish Emancipation from the late 18th century onward, various Jewish movements arose, some along religious lines, others along national or political lines. (It was now possible for Jews to express their Jewish identification while not accepting a religious belief.) Among the religious movements which arose, the REFORM movement, which began in Germany in the 18th century, spread to other countries, eventually taking solid root in the United States.

Reform Judaism does not recognize the absolute and literal Divine origin of either the written or the oral law. Rather, it views them both as a composite of divinely inspired eternal values and ephemeral human elements.

Reform Judaism emphasizes the ethical and moral teachings of the prophets and the rabbis, as taking precedence over many ritual practices. Reform liturgy, which is largely in the vernacular, has excluded traditional prayers for the restoration of the sacrificial cult and modified references to resurrection of the dead, a personal Messiah, and the chosenness of Israel. Reform Judaism has instituted full equality of the sexes in religious life. It encourages conversion to Judaism (though it does not "missionize"); and many Reform leaders recognize as Jewish the children of mixed marriages, provided they are raised as Jews and continue to identify with the Jewish people after achieving adulthood.

Whereas Reform Judaism views the totality of Jewish tradition as the heritage of the Jewish people, when applying it to contemporary Jewish life, it scrutinizes the tradition in a critical-historical way, and measures particular beliefs and rituals against modern universal values. It rejects any fundamentalist interpretation of the Bible or of any other classical Jewish source.

The Reform movement believes in individual responsibility and autonomy, and as such delegates to each rabbi and community the right to determine which practices it regards as worthwhile and as enhancing Jewish life.

CONSERVATIVE JUDAISM, which began as a movement in America at the beginning of the 20th century, is sometimes known as historical Judaism because its founders and leaders wished to stress the character of Judaism as a civilization which has developed as a result of historical factors. The philosophy of the movement maintains therefore, firstly, that the *halakhah* of Judaism is dynamic: it grows, it changes, since life itself, which is dynamic, demands that the *halakhah* be made relevant. Secondly, Conservative Judaism emphasizes the ethical dimension of Judaism above all other values. Thirdly, its leaders have taught that reason is an important and even central feature of Jewish philosophy so that there is little or no place for any practice regarded as anti-rational. Conservative Judaism became the largest Jewish religious group in the United States.

The RECONSTRUCTIONIST movement applies naturalism to Judaism, stressing it as an evolving religious civilization and spiritual nationalism, and believes the basis of Judaism to be the life of the group rather than a God-given set of doctrines and practices. The recent and small movement for HUMANISTIC JUDAISM has developed a non-theistic Judaism.

The most prominent example of a Jewish movement along national lines was the Zionist movement, which regarded the conversion of the Land of ISRAEL into a Jewish state as the solution to what was then known throughout the world as "the Jewish problem." Other movements sought other solutions to the "Jewish problem." Thus, for example, the pre-war Bund in Eastern Europe was a socialist party, which argued that Jews should remain in their countries and should be granted autonomy.

The main institutions within Jewish life have developed over the ages. At first, worship consisted of offering sacrifices at various HIGH PLACES. Later, such worship was centralized in the Temple in Jerusalem. After the destruction of the Second Temple, its place was taken by the SYNAGOGUE (which had emerged as an institution a couple of centuries earlier), which served as the focus for Jewish PRAYER. In addition to the synagogue, the BET MIDRASH (the study hall for Torah studies) has been a staple in Jewish communities throughout the world, in which EDUCATION has always played a prime role. In order to fulfill the laws of ritual purity, the ritual bath (the MIKVEH), was considered an essential facility in the traditional Jewish community, its construction taking precedence over that of a synagogue.

Just as certain elements of space (the Temple, Jerusalem, the Land of Israel, the synagogue) were considered as endowed with an special holiness, so elements of time were consecrated. First and foremost was the SABBATH, in commemoration of God's day of rest after creating the world. In the annual cycle of the Jewish year, the three PILGRIM FESTIVALS of PASSOVER, SHAVU'OT, and SUKKOT, as well as the penitential season centering around ROSH HA-SHANAH and the DAY OF ATONEMENT were regarded as holy days. In the course of time, further FESTIVALS and FASTS were added to the Jewish CALENDAR.

The commandments prescribed to the Jew had to be observed in every situation, but their main focus was in the synagogue and in the home. The Jewish home and family life have been fundamentally integrated into Jewish practice and have constituted a basic Jewish value.

The basic religious statement in Judaism, known from its first Hebrew word as the SHEMA, is the verse from Deuteronomy: "Hear, O Israel, the Lord is our God, the Lord is One" (6:4).

JUDEO-SPANISH A language spoken by SEPHARDI Jews, primarily in Turkey and the Balkan countries. The Judeo-Spanish language of the Sephardim of Northern Morocco is called *Haketia*. In printed form, Judeo-Spanish is often called Ladino; in cursive form, it is called *Solitreo*. The language is also sometimes referred to as *Espanyol*, *Judezmo*, and *Judeo-espanyol*.

When the Jews were expelled from Spain in 1492, many settled in the lands of the Ottoman Empire. They brought with them the Spanish of the day, whether Castilian or that of northern Spain, interspersed with Hebrew words and phrases, which they continued to speak over the centuries, in isolation from the Spanish which developed in Spain. Consequently, their language retained certain medieval features and vocabulary. It also incorporated many words from the new languages with which they came in contact, e.g., Turkish, Greek, French, Arabic, and English.

Judeo-Spanish was the mother tongue and the communal language of many Sephardim until the mid-20th century, irrespective of where they lived and of the languages spoken around them. Despite the slight variations in pronunciation among the different Sephardi communities, this basic language was understood by all and was an important unifying element in the maintenance of a distinctive Sephardi culture. In it they created a vast literature including translations of classic Hebrew works, original rabbinic works, textbooks for schools, novels, poetry, newspapers, dramatic works, and folkloric materials. The language was generally printed in Hebrew (Rashi) letters. In the 20th century, it has sometimes been published in Latin letters.

A major classic of Judeo-Spanish literature is the ME'AM LO'EZ, an expansive rabbinic work by Jacob CULI in the form of a biblical commentary, which appeared in Istanbul in 1730. It went into many editions and was a major agent of religious education.

The mid-20th century saw a steep decline in the use of Judeo-Spanish. Due to migrations from Turkey and the Balkans, as well as the breakdown of the old social and political systems of those lands, Sephardim began to speak the lan-

Illustrated page from a Passover Haggadah *in Judeo-Spanish showing women preparing unleavened bread. Italy, 18th century.*

guages of the lands in which they lived. The younger generation no longer related to Judeo-Spanish as its mother tongue. In present times the language is spoken primarily by the elder generation of Sephardim. While various songs, proverbs, and prayers in Judeo-Spanish remain popular among younger Sephardim (many of them in Israel), little original literature is being produced in Judeo-Spanish and very few use it as their primary language.

JUDGES, BOOK OF The second volume in the Prophetical section of the Bible, named after the judges who judged Israel after the death of Joshua until the prophet Samuel. The major function of the judges was to lead the nation (or a number of tribes) in war. Only in the case of Deborah is there a hint of a judge having a judicial function. The judges did not bequeath their positions to their children (except in the case of Abimelech), or even to another member of their tribe.

The book opens with an account of the conquest and settlement of Canaan. This parallels the story in Joshua 1-11 and according to many modern scholars, is a different and more authentic description. In Judges, the conquest was a series of independent battles conducted by the individual tribes for their own regions of land in contrast to the unified conquest of the Book of Joshua. Next come the stories of the various judges, in which there is a basic formula: Israel sins, God sends enemies who torment them, the Israelites pray to God, God sends them a judge-savior, and afterward, the land remains quiet, the Israelites return to their wickedness, and so on. The judges can be divided into two categories: the major (or charismatic) judges — these are the judges who save the people (or a number of tribes) from the enemy; and the minor judges, who did not carry out any noteworthy actions.

The Book of Judges is of great historical value and provides information on a period of Israelite history otherwise unknown. According to the rabbis (*BB* 14b), the prophet Samuel was the author of this book. Modern scholars hold that the material was assembled early in the period of the monarchy, edited about the seventh century BCE, and received its final form after the destruction of Jerusalem in 586 BCE.

BOOK OF JUDGES

1:1 — 2:5	The completion of the conquest of the land of Canaan
2:6 — 3:6	Introduction to the era of the judges
3:7 — 3:11	Othniel
3:12 — 3:30	Ehud
3:31	Shamgar
4:1 — 5:31	Deborah and the Song of Deborah
6:1 — 8:35	Gideon
9:1 — 9:57	Abimelech
10:1 — 10:5	Tola and Jair
10:6 — 10:11	Preface to the latter judges
10:17 -12:7	Jephthah
12:8 — 12:15	Ibzan, Elon, Abdon
13:1 — 16:31	Samson
17:1 — 18:31	The statue of Micah and the settling of the tribe of Dan in the north
19:1 — 21:25	The concubine of Gibeah and the war against Benjamin

JUSTICE According to Judaism, justice is an attribute of GOD, which is tempered with His attribute of MERCY. God, in creating the world, is depicted in Genesis as exercising both justice and mercy in His role as Creator of the Universe. According to the rabbinic interpretation, the Bible refers to God by the name of *elohim*, which connotes His role as the ultimate Judge, while, on the other hand, it uses the Tetragrammaton, which connotes God's mercy (see GOD, NAMES OF). Thus, while God commands strict adherence to the laws He has given to humanity, He takes into account human weakness and therefore does not judge merely by the letter of the law, otherwise all individuals would be doomed. The merging of justice and mercy is a constant theme in the Bible and is presented in dramatic form in the dialogues between God and Abraham and between God and Moses. In arguing for the salvation of the inhabitants of the cities of Sodom and Gemorrah (Gen. 18:16-32), Abraham pleads with God to go beyond the letter of the law and to commute the sentence of death and destruction about to be imposed on all the inhabitants of the cities, for the sake of a handful, purely hypothetical as it turns out, of righteous people. Midrash Rabbah, discussing this encounter, notes that absolute justice cannot be applied to the imperfect human world.

Similarly, when God wishes to destroy the Jewish people for the sin of the GOLDEN CALF (Ex. 32), Moses prays for Divine mercy and his prayer is answered both explicitly — in God's expressly stated tone of forgiveness — and implicitly, in God's declaration of His attributes.

Jewish liturgy makes frequent references to God's role as ultimate Judge. On weekdays, within the context of the AMIDAH, which occupies a central position in the prayer book, God is addressed in terms of justice merged with mercy as "the King Who loves charity and justice". Even on the death of close relatives, Jews bless God as the "true Judge." During the High Holy Days (Rosh ha-Shanah, the Day of Atonement, and the intervening Days of Penitence), when, according to Jewish tradition, God sits in judgment over the people of Israel, His role as judge is even further reinforced and the liturgy is filled with references to God as both King and Judge.

The issue of the nature of Divine justice is essential in Jewish theodicy. As in Psalms 92, Judaism has always asked the question, "Why do the innocent suffer and the wicked prosper?" The traditional Jewish response has been to affirm God's wisdom and fairness, even if the human individual is unable to comprehend the infinite depths of that wisdom. When Job is confronted by misery and sorrow, he questions God's judgment. The Bible does not condemn Job for doing so; rather, he is informed that his human power of reasoning is far too limited to comprehend the intricacies of God's plan (see REWARD AND PUNISHMENT).

At various times in Jewish history, specifically during periods of great distress — such as the destruction of the First and Second Temples, the Inquisition and the expulsion from Spain and Portugal, the massacres in the Ukraine in 1648-49 — serious questions have been raised about Divine justice. The issue of theodicy has been perhaps most painful in recent Jewish history, occasioned by the Holocaust, with the death of six million Jews. For the varied religious responses, see HOLOCAUST.

By virtue of the principle of the IMITATION OF GOD, it is axiomatic that mankind in general, and the Jew in particular, is expected to live within a framework of justice — tempered by mercy. Moses commanded the people "Justice, justice shall you pursue" (Deut. 16:20) and this directive is a leitmotif of the prophets and of the rabbis in formulating Jewish law. The same Hebrew root is used for "justice" and "RIGHTEOUSNESS" and the thought and practices of the Jewish people have been strongly molded by this concept and the conviction that the world is preserved "by truth, justice, and peace" (*Avot* 1.18).

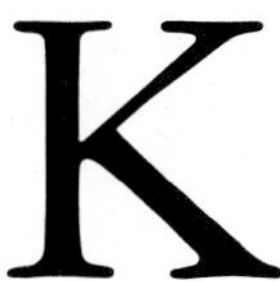

KABBALAH See MYSTICISM, JEWISH

KABBALAT SHABBAT See SABBATH

KADDISH ("Sanctification"). Aramaic prayer of praise to God. It may have been originally a brief prayer, recited at the conclusion of a lesson in the ancient synagogues or houses of study. These study sessions based on biblical and rabbinic passages usually concluded with a message of hope. The use of the *Kaddish* was expanded and was inserted in the service. An additional function of the *Kaddish* was its recitation as a mourner's prayer. Currently there are four basic forms of the *Kaddish*: the half *Kaddish*, the whole *Kaddish*, the rabbis' *Kaddish* (*Kaddish de-rabbanan*), and the mourner's *Kaddish*.

The half *Kaddish*, comprising only the first two major paragraphs of the full prayer, is said at the conclusion of certain sections of the service, including at the end of the reading of the weekly portion of the Pentateuch prior to the reading of the MAFTIR portion.

The whole *Kaddish* is recited by the person leading the service at the conclusion of his repetition of the silent devotion prayer (AMIDAH) and on one other occasion in the Morning Service.

The *Kaddish de-rabbanan* contains the whole Kaddish, with the following paragraph recited after the regular first two paragraphs: "We pray for Israel, for our teachers and their disciples, and for all who study the Torah, here and everywhere. May they have abundant peace, loving kindness, ample sustenance, and salvation from their Father who is in heaven." This *Kaddish* is recited after study sessions, and is read in the synagogue after certain passages in the service which are taken from rabbinic literature.

The mourner's *Kaddish* contains the entire *Kaddish* with the exception of the third paragraph. It is recited by mourners at the grave of parents or close relatives, and also during the three daily services in the presence of a prayer quorum (MINYAN) during 11 months following the death of a parent or close relative, and on the anniversary of the death. There is no reference to the dead or mourning in this *Kaddish*. In the special burial *Kaddish* an additional prayer does refer to the resurrection of the dead.

The *Kaddish* prayer is always recited standing and facing in the direction of Jerusalem. In the REFORM movement the custom is for the mourner's *Kaddish* to be recited by the whole congregation in unison. In the early Reform prayer books the text of the *Kaddish* was changed, but in all recent Reform prayer books the original text has been restored. Ḫasidim and the Sephardi and Eastern Jewish communities add the words: "May He make His salvation closer and bring His Messiah near," in the initial paragraph.

The *Kaddish* prayer is basically a doxology praising God and calling for the speedy establishment of God's kingdom on earth. A key line is the congregational response, "May his great name be blessed forever and to all eternity" (see BARUKH SHEM KEVODO). The prayer does not seem to have been originally a part of the synagogue service, and was said by a preacher at the end of a sermon or after the study of AGGADAH (*Sota* 49a). The first references to the *Kaddish* as a part of the synagogue service are in the minor talmudic tractate *Soferim*, where the name *kaddish* first appears (10:7), and where it states that if less than ten adult males are present the *Kaddish* cannot be recited.

FROM THE KADDISH

Glorified and sanctified be God's great Name throughout the world which He has created according to His will. May He establish His kingdom in your lifetime and during your days and within the life of the entire house of Israel, speedily and soon. Blessed and praised, glorified and exalted, extolled and honored, adored and lauded be the Name of the Holy One blessed be He, beyond all the blessing and hymns, praises and consolations that are ever spoken in the world, and let us say Amen.

The mourner's *Kaddish* appears to have become accepted practice in the 13th century, and is associated with the calamities of the Crusades, while its recitation on the anniversary of a death dates from the 15th century. It was originally recited for the deceased for 12 months, but in view of the belief that sinners are punished for 12 months after their death, this was shortened to 11 months to avoid any implication that the prayers were for the sake of a sinner. Traditionally, *Kaddish* was only recited by male relatives, but Reform and Conservative practice includes women also. In certain Orthodox circles today there is a growing tendency for recitation of *Kaddish* by female relatives as well. The recitation of *Kaddish* has often been observed by mourners who otherwise have ceased to keep many other aspects of Judaism, and in many synagogues the daily prayer quorum is filled only because of the presence of mourners attending the service for the purpose of reciting *Kaddish*.

Special melodies characterize the *Kaddish* on ROSH HA-SHANAH, the DAY OF ATONEMENT, and the three PILGRIM FESTIVALS.

KALLAH (MINOR TRACTATE) See NEZIKIN

KALLAH MONTHS (*yarḥé kallah*, "months of assembly"). Name (of uncertain origin) given in Babylonia to month-long "extension courses" in which Jews from near and far joined regular students in the ACADEMIES for the intensive study of a talmudic tractate. The custom lasted throughout the amoraic and geonic periods (third to 11th centuries). Courses were held twice a year, in Adar and Elul, since these were not busy agricultural months and were therefore a convenient time for the working population to set aside for a period of study.

Relief showing Rav Ashi (right) at the Sura Academy where students convened during the kallah *months for intensive study.*

At these gatherings the head of the Academy took his place in front of seven rows of sages, ten to a row, seated according to rank and seniority. Behind them sat the regular students, about 400 in number, and around them gathered thousands of listeners. One of the sages in the first rows would raise an issue from the tractate selected, this would be debated by his colleagues, and the head of the Academy would then provide his own comments and answers. Study leaders were appointed to work with the students in smaller groups. During the last week of the month, the head of the Academy would examine the students and those whose knowledge proved unsatisfactory would have their stipends reduced. Finally, the head of the Academy would announce the tractate to be discussed at the next course, in six months' time, until when the students and the listeners would have a chance to prepare themselves.

The *kallah* month tradition has been revived by the rabbinical academies (YESHIVOT) of modern Israel; the courses, held in the month of Elul prior to the New Year, last for three or four days.

KALLIR, ELEAZAR (ha-Kallir; flourished c. 600-630). One of the earliest Jewish liturgical poets, reputedly the greatest and certainly the most prolific. Details as to when and where he lived are still unclear, hence the various legends woven around his personality. There is, however, reason to suppose that he was the foremost cantor and *paytan* (liturgical poet) of Tiberias shortly before the Muslim conquest in 636. Kallir's works abound in midrashic references and allegorical expression; they are also steeped in Jewish mysticism. He specialized in a type of PIYYUT (liturgical poetry), widely imitated by his successors, which laid emphasis on rhyme, linguistic compression, and the use of alphabetical acrostics (sometimes reversed) sometimes incorporating his name. Such features, together with the writer's predilection for an archaic Palestinian Hebrew, tend to make his poetry rather abstruse and even aroused criticism in the Middle Ages. A large proportion of the 200 or more poems attributed to Kallir nevertheless found their way into the Ashkenazi rite. Others came to light in the Cairo GENIZAH. Notable examples include hymns (e.g., YOTSEROT) for the Morning Service and other occasions; High Holiday prayers such as *Addiré Ayummah* and the *Teki'ata* sequences read on the New Year; penitential SELIḤOT; and KINOT (elegies) for the fast of *Tishah be-Av*. Best known of all, perhaps, are the Prayer for DEW (*Tal*) recited on Passover and the Prayer for RAIN (*Geshem*) chanted on *Shemini Atseret*.

KAPLAN, MORDECAI MENAHEM (1881-1983). Rabbi and educator in the United States; founder and leader of Jewish RECONSTRUCTIONISM. The author of many significant books, Kaplan was at the center of Jewish intellectual leadership in America for nearly 80 years and contributed to almost every aspect of Jewish life and thought. His Socratic method of teaching challenged people to question the past and the nature of its relevance for the present. While respecting the past and its traditions, he insisted on the primacy of contemporary needs, saying that "the past has a vote but not a veto."

Born in Lithuania, Kaplan was taken to the United States

when he was nine years old. He studied at the Jewish Theological Seminary and, after graduating at the early age of 21, was appointed rabbi of the (Orthodox) Kehillath Jeshurun congregation in New York. Despite his personal standards of religious piety, standards which he maintained throughout his long life, Kaplan began to entertain doubts about Orthodox Jewish belief. These doubts were increased by his studies of the sociology of Durkheim, the biological sciences of Spencer and Darwin, the Bible criticism of Wellhausen, the psychology of religion of William James, and the writings of Freud and Marx. Kaplan left his pulpit and was appointed to head the newly formed Teachers' Training Institute at the Jewish Theological Seminary. There he remained for half a century, lecturing in homiletics, Midrash, and Jewish philosophy to several generations of rabbis. His radical views eventually led him to break with the normative Conservative thinking of the time and, in 1922, he founded the Jewish Reconstructionist movement so as to provide a platform for the discussion and dissemination of his teachings. The movement established its own press, which issued prayer books (one of which was formally burned by a group of Orthodox zealots), a new *Haggadah*, and the *Reconstructionist Magazine*.

Foremost in Mordecai M. Kaplan's teaching was his concept of God, which represented a serious departure from classical Jewish belief. He wrote that "the traditional conception of God is challenged by history, anthropology, and psychology." Kaplan describes God as an impersonal "Power that makes for righteousness," as the force that "makes for salvation," or as a "cosmic process that makes for life's abundance or salvation." All supernaturalism is omitted and he argues that "supernatural religion is the astrology and alchemy stage of Religion."

The fact that Kaplan did not believe that the commandments were revealed or ordained by God does not necessarily mean that he discounted them as unimportant. He insists that the rituals — the *mitsvot* — have a very special place: they are what he calls the "sancta" of Judaism, conveying the greatest ideal and the spiritual concepts of the Jewish people. More than most teachers of his time, Kaplan emphasized the social values of organized religion. "To have a religion in common, people must have other things in common besides religion." In line with this approach, Kaplan developed the idea of the synagogue as a center for communal activity which would house all the varied programs of an organized community.

In his Zionist philosophy, Mordecai M. Kaplan reflects the influence of Aḫad ha-Am. The Diaspora is not rejected, but Israel is the spiritual center of world Jewry. His approach to Israel-Diaspora relationships may be illustrated by a wheel: its hub represents the Jewish community in Erets Israel, its spokes are the various Diaspora communities, while the rim which holds everything together is the culture of the Jewish people.

Kaplan wrote several important works, the most influential of which was *Judaism as a Civilization* (1934). The title itself proclaims one of his chief ideas. A "civilization" is a people's total way of life, comprising several elements that have gone through many stages of growth and development. In Judaism these include art, music, language, literature, and philosophy. Since Judaism, however, is a religious civilization, it is the Jewish religion which is focal and which, in a significant way, influences all other aspects of Jewish civilization.

KAPPAROT ("expiation"). The custom whereby, during the night or early morning of the day before the DAY OF ATONEMENT, an adult Jew takes a live fowl (male for male, female for a female) and, holding it by the neck, swings it around his/her head three times, saying, "This is my atonement, this is my ransom, this is my substitute. This cock (hen) shall meet its death but I shall find a long and pleasant life." The fowl is then slaughtered and either given to the poor directly or its monetary value donated to charity; the innards are thrown to the birds, also deemed an act of charity. The sins of the penitent person (an adult may also make separate expiation for his children) are thus symbolically transferred to the fowl, rescuing the individual from a possible negative judgment on the Day of Atonement. In modern times, 18 coins are often substituted for the fowl. Prior to the ceremony it is customary to recite verses from Psalms 107 (10, 14, 17-21) and Job 33 (23-24) which relate to God's readiness to forgive those who sit in gloom and darkness.

Woodcut showing the custom of kapparot *performed with two fowls. Woodcut from the "Book of Customs", Venice 1593.*

The ceremony of *kapparot* is not mentioned in the Talmud and the earliest reference apparently originated in Babylonia in the geonic period (9th century), but the first description of the entire procedure appears in the *Maḇzor Vitry*, the liturgical compendium produced by a pupil of RASHI. The details are similar but not identical to those of the present-day practice.

While the custom of *kapparot* is still observed in certain Orthodox circles, historically it has been opposed by numerous authorities, including NAḤMANIDES and Joseph CARO who viewed it as both pagan and superstitious. Other authorities, however, gave their approval and the kabbalists gave it a mystic interpretation. The mainstream of rabbinic thought maintained that, rather than atoning for sins directly, the ceremony provides an opportunity to reflect upon one's sins and to make true repentance for them.

KARAISM (lit. "Scripturalism"). Sectarian form of Judaism. Karaism is distinguished first and foremost from Rabbanite (i.e., of the rabbis) Judaism by its rejection of the ORAL LAW as embodied in the Talmud. This rejection has resulted in an alternate form of Jewish ritual practice which separated Karaites from other Jews.

Most historians place the origin of the Karaite schism in the eighth-century CE revolt of Anan ben David, while Karaites (and some historians) claim that identifiable proto-Karaite elements are discernible in various Second Temple groups (e.g., the Dead Sea Scrolls Covenanters, Alexandrian Judaism, and other non-Pharisaic and non-Sadducean parties). According to the traditional Rabbanite account Anan, passed over for exilarch in preference for his younger brother, set up his own rival exilarchate for which he was jailed by the Caliph. Anan escaped the death penalty, however, by claiming to be the head of a different religion, closer to ISLAM than to rabbinic Judaism. His rebellion against rabbinic leadership was, then, a combination of personal pique and simple prudence. While the details of this story, reported a few hundred years after Anan's death, are not universally accepted, most scholars believe that Anan did play a major role in the development of what is now known as Karaism (a term first used in the ninth century by Benjamin al-Nahawendi).

Karaism began in Babylonia (Iraq), but it had its golden age in Erets Israel (10th-11th centuries). The Karaite community there was founded by Daniel al-Qumisi, who called upon Karaite communities of the Diaspora to send five representatives each to Erets Israel along with their own means of livelihood. Other important figures of the Karaite golden age were Sahl ben Matsliaḥ, Salmon ben Yeruḥim, Yefet ben Eli and his son Levi, Joseph al-Basir, and Yeshu'a ben Judah. Later Karaite communities of note were in Egypt, Byzantium, Crimea and Lithuania.

Whereas the Karaite calendar was originally based on observation of the moon and agricultural phenomena, it is now calculated, rarely differing by more than a day or so from the Rabbanite one. There are variations in the holiday observances: no second day of the holidays, even on ROSH HA-SHANAH; SHAVU'OT always on Sunday; no ḤANUKKAH; different fast days; PURIM in First Adar; no blowing the SHOFAR on Rosh ha-Shanah; and no FOUR SPECIES on SUKKOT. Karaites observe ritual slaughter and prohibit the biblically proscribed animals; they allow the eating of meat and milk together if they are of different species, e.g., cow milk with mutton. Karaite synagogues are without chairs, and worshipers remove their shoes before entering them; TEFILLIN are not worn; full genuflection is practiced at various times in the service, the order of which is entirely different from the Rabbanite pattern. Originally, Karaites proscribed the lighting of candles or fire before the Sabbath, but they now allow it (without a blessing); food may not be warmed, and sexual relations are forbidden on the Sabbath and holidays.

Prayer at the Karaite Synagogue in Cairo. Men and women pray together and kneel during prayer.

A very significant difference between Rabbanite and Karaite Judaism is in the area of personal status. As a result of different laws of marriage, divorce, and forbidden relations, each group suspects the other of being possible *mamzerim* (see ILLEGITIMACY) and, thus, being unfit for intermarriage. Sephardi rabbinates generally follow a more liberal halakhic view and allow intermarriage under certain circumstances; the major Karaite objection today to intermarriage is the danger of assimilation to Rabbanism.

At present, there are approximately 20,000 Karaites in Israel, a few thousand in Russia (contact with them having more or less been cut off), 1,500 in the United States (generally in the Bay Area, California), 100 families in Istanbul, and a handful in Cairo maintaining the synagogue and Karaite treasures there. The spiritual leader of Karaites today is Haim Hallevi of Ashdod, Chief Rabbi of the Karaite Jews in Israel.

THE TEN PRINCIPLES OF KARAISM

1. Creation of the world.
2. The existence of an eternal Creator.
3. Unity and incorporeality of the Creator.
4. Superiority of Mosaic prophecy.
5. Perfection of the Torah.
6. The obligation to understand Hebrew.
7. The mission of non-Mosiac prophets.
8. Resurrection of the dead.
9. Divine providence.
10. The coming of the Messiah.

(From Elijah Bashyatchi [d. 1490], *Adderet Eliyyahu*).

KARELITZ, AVRAHAM YESHAYAHU (1878-1953). Talmudic scholar popularly known as *Ḫazon Ish* after the title of his published writings. Born in Kossovo, a town in the Russian province of Grodno, Karelitz soon displayed his outstanding ability as a student of Torah and *halakhah*. After living for some time in Kedainiai, he went to Minsk, then to Stolbtsy during World War I, and in 1920 moved to Vilna. There he published novellae on *Oraḫ Ḫayyim* and other sections of the SHULḪAN ARUKH, which appeared anonymously under the title *Ḫazon Ish* ("Vision of Man," 1911). The word *Ish* was an acronym of his first names, and 23 of the works that he later wrote on the Talmud and halakhic codes were all entitled *Ḫazon Ish*. His depth of knowledge and saintly, unassuming character made a great impression on Ḫayyim Ozer Grodzinski, one of the rabbinical heads of Lithuanian Jewry and a leader of Agudat Israel's "Council of Sages." The two men remained in close touch over the next 20 years.

In 1933, Ḫazon Ish emigrated to Erets Israel and settled in Bené Berak. His presence there greatly influenced that community's development as a citadel of Orthodoxy and Torah learning. Although he occupied no formal rabbinic or communal positions, Ḫazon Ish became a venerated figure in Israel's religious life and an acknowledged world authority on all aspects of Jewish law. Thousands of rabbis, communal leaders, and *yeshivah* students visited his modest home in Bené Berak to obtain advice and halakhic decisions. Though never identified as a Zionist, he was keenly aware of the problems facing Israel and even David Ben-Gurion — Israel's first prime minister — visited him on one occasion to discuss the vexed issue of conscripting *yeshivah* students for military service. The halakhic rulings of Ḫazon Ish were of decisive importance to the Po'alé Agudat Israel (Orthodox workers) movement and its agricultural settlements, whether through the devising of permissible techniques for milking on the Sabbath or through the use of hydroponics to avoid infringing SABBATICAL YEAR (*shemittah*) laws. Of his 40 or more scholarly works, those dealing with the precepts governing everyday life in Erets Israel became practical guides for the strictly observant Jew.

KARET (lit. "cutting off.") Punishment prescribed in the Bible for various offenses, such as violating the laws of the DAY OF ATONEMENT or eating bread on PASSOVER. The Bible commands that for such a sin, the guilty person "shall be cut off (in Hebrew, *ve-nikhreta*) from the people." While various explanations have been given, it is accepted that it means a punishment imposed by God, not by man. Among interpretations of the punishments are dying prematurely and dying childless. Unlike those offenses for which punishment is to be meted out by man, offenses for which the penalty is *karet* can be atoned for. The Mishnah (*Ker.* 1:1) lists 36 sins for which the punishment is *karet*, more than half of which deal with illicit sexual unions. Further, the Mishnah (1:2) lays down the rule that where the punishment for deliberate violation is *karet*, the punishment for a violation committed inadvertently or through negligence is the offering of a sacrifice.

KASHER (or "kosher," lit. "fit"). Hebrew term denoting those foods which are judged "fit" or "proper" for consumption in accordance with the biblical and rabbinic DIETARY LAWS (*kashrut*). The word *kasher* does not occur in the Pentateuch, where animals that the Israelites are permitted to eat are described as *tahor* ("clean"), while those prohibited by Mosaic law are called *tamé* ("unclean"), *shekets* ("an abomination"), or *to'evah* ("abhorrent"; see Lev. 11, Deut. 14: 3-20). Use of the term *kasher*, in its present sense, originates in the Talmud.

A growing practice in recent years is for terms such as *li-mehadderin* or *mehadderin min ha-mehadderin* ("superfine") to accompany the word *kasher*, so as to indicate that the supervision of a particular food is meticulous and strictly Orthodox. Similarly, *ḫalak* (literally "smooth") or "*glatt* kosher" are terms reserved for meat products to which the highest degree of *kashrut* is attached. Here, the procedure requires that certain internal organs be examined — and the entire carcass rejected — if they appear to contain any defect, even if a rabbinical authority concludes that the blemish does not render the meat TEREFAH (ritually unfit).

A certificate guaranteeing rabbinical supervision can now be found on thousands of mass-produced foods, especially in Israel and the United States. This takes the form of an easily recognized symbol, although it may also be the full name of the rabbi, authority, or organization providing the supervision (see HEKHSHER). Airlines, hotels, restaurants, and catering firms throughout the world supply *kasher* food on a regular basis. The symbol is legally protected. Both in Israel and in certain major Diaspora communities, ultra-Orthodox

A modern advertisement from Atlanta, Georgia, indicating that the drink is kasher *for Passover.*

groups (occasionally more than one) refuse to accept the *kashrut* of the chief rabbinate or central authority. They provide their own "attestation" of approved foodstuffs, often involving rivalry.

"Kosher" is also a term used to describe ethnic dishes such as "kosher dill pickles" or other European Jewish delicacies. Use of the expression "kosher-style" thus indicates a particular type of cuisine, not the ritual fitness of a dish from the standpoint of Jewish law. *Kasher*, in its original sense, may also be employed to describe the fitness of a particular individual to officiate or participate in Jewish religious observances. The term is similarly applied to ritual objects, which are regarded as *kasher* when suitably produced and maintained in proper condition.

KAVVANAH ("intention," or "direction"). State of wholehearted concentration and spiritual directedness which Judaism deems essential for praying to God. The term is given explicit formulation by the rabbis, although it is implicit in biblical thought, most notably in the fundamental commandment to "love the Lord your God with all your heart and with all your soul and with all your might" (Deut. 6:5). "Prayer needs *kavvanah*," stated the rabbis (TJ *Ber.* 4.1). It is necessary for reading the SHEMA (*Ber.* 16a) and "one must not stand up to recite the *Tefillah* [AMIDAH] except in a serious frame of mind" (*Ber.* 5.1). Any person whose mind is unsettled and who finds himself unable to concentrate should not try to pray; indeed, the ḤASIDIM RISHONIM "used to wait an hour before the *Tefillah* so as to attune their hearts to the Almighty" (*ibid.*) and down the ages this custom was widespread. The admonition of ELIEZER BEN HYRCANUS to his disciples was especially applicable: "When you pray, know before Whom you stand!" (*Ber.* 28b).

It is in regard to saying the *Shema* and the *Amidah* that MAIMONIDES gives the classic definition of praying with *kavvanah*: "The first thing you must do is turn your thoughts away from everything else while you recite the *Shema* or *Tefillah*... When you have mastered this, accustom yourself to relieving your mind of all other thoughts when you say any benediction... When engaged in the performance of religious duties, have your mind concentrated entirely on what you are doing" (*Guide* 3.51). The implication of *kavvanah* is that praying in a routine fashion is not equivalent to true prayer. As R. Simeon (second cent. CE) taught: "Be careful in reciting the *Shema* and *Tefillah*; and when you pray, do not treat your prayer as a mechanical obligation but as a plea for mercy and grace before God" (*Avot* 2.18). Thus prayer without *kavvanah* is for the sages no prayer at all, and elsewhere Maimonides even states that "if one has prayed without *kavvanah*, he must pray again with it" (*Yad, Tefillah* 4.15).

The role of *kavvanah* in fulfilling commandments other than those of prayer is more controversial. While all the sages agree that it is a desirable element in ritual observance, there is much discussion as to whether, for example, a person who hears the blowing of the SHOFAR on Rosh ha-Shanah or the reading of the Esther Scroll on PURIM, without directing his heart to the performance of the commandment, has in fact fulfilled his religious obligation.

The concept of *kavvanah* has had great significance throughout the long history of Jewish thought, and is central to medieval devotional works such as BAḤYA IBN PAKUDA's *Duties of the Heart*. It attained especially intense development in Jewish mystical thought, where *kavvanah* is regarded not only as a means of uplifting the soul of the individual toward closer attachment to the Divine Source of life, but also as a means of transforming the higher spiritual realm itself. In kabbalistic practice, *kavvanah* relates to a special concentration in prayer on certain words and letters so as to release their hidden meaning. Even in everyday observance, a pious Jew closes or covers his eyes as an aid to concentration when reciting the first verse of the *Shema*. For ḤASIDISM, *kavvanah* has special meaning not only in prayer but also as a preliminary to and preparation for it. Certain Ḥasidic formulas of this type — notably "Behold, I am prepared and ready to perform the commandment" before counting the OMER — have found their way into standard Jewish practice.

KAZYONNY RAVVIN (Rus. "government rabbi"). Title given in the 19th century to Jewish officials whose task was to regulate communal life and secure compliance with Tsarist directives. The enforced assimilation of Russian Jewry became state policy under Nicholas I, an imperial decree of 1835 establishing the post of "government rabbi" and prescribing his duties. The major qualification for such an appointment was not rabbinical ORDINATION, but a working knowledge of Russian. As opposed to the traditional kind of spiritual leader, whom the Tsarist authorities continued to recognize unofficially, the "government" or "crown" rabbi was no more than a low-grade civil servant. His tasks included registering Jewish births, marriages, and deaths; promoting military conscription; delivering patriotic sermons; and acting as the community's representative before tsarist officialdom. When specifically religious duties had to be performed, he often sought the aid of a genuine rabbi. A nominal salary was paid to each *kazyonny ravvin* by the community which he supervised, but Jews tended to regard him as a "walking caricature" of a rabbi and as a government stooge; they dubbed him *Rabbiner* or (in Hebrew) *rav mi-ta' am* — "officially appointed rabbi." In practice, anyone with a few years of secular education (and little or no Jewish knowledge) could have himself elected to such a post. With Tsarism's downfall in 1917, the unpopular and discredited office of *kazyonny ravvin* ceased to exist.

KEDUSHAH ("sanctification"). Hebrew term applied to various components of the liturgy (see KADDISH and KIDDUSH). Liturgically, *Kedushah* denotes three forms of doxology quoting expressions of praise for God in the visions of Isaiah (6:3) and Ezekiel (3:12). Their underlying significance is that the angelic chorus on high is echoed on earth by the congregation of Israel hallowing God's Name. One version, the *Kedushah de-Amidah* (*Kedushah* of the AMIDAH, i.e., standing prayer), is chanted responsively whenever the *Amidah* blessings are repeated with a prayer quorum (*minyan*). A second version, the *Kedushah di-Yeshivah* ("sitting *Kedushah*") or *Kedushah de-Yotser*, forms part of the YOTSEROT section of the MORNING SERVICE. The third version, the *Kedushah de-Sidra* (*Kedushah* recited at the end of study), occurs in the prayer entitled *U-Va le-Tsiyyon Go'el* ("May a redeemer come to Zion") which is recited at the end of the weekday Morning Service and at the commencement of the Sabbath Afternoon Service. All three forms are ancient, the first and second having traditionally been composed by the Men of the GREAT ASSEMBLY (*Ber.* 33a). The third enables those coming late, and who missed the reciting of *Kedushah* twice in the morning, to say it in an undertone at the end of the service.

The *Kedushah de-Amidah* is recited while standing, as part of the third benediction, during the reader's repetition of the *Amidah*. Originally, this *Kedushah* was only included in the Erets Israel (Palestinian) rite on Sabbaths and festivals; from about the eighth century, however, the influence of Babylonian practice led to its incorporation in the daily synagogue prayers. By geonic times, different liturgical rites based either on the Palestinian or the Babylonian tradition had emerged, and these shaped the various forms of *Kedushah* in use today.

The most frequent and shortest of these, recited (*inter alia*) at Morning and Afternoon Services on weekdays and at the Afternoon Service on Sabbaths and festivals, commences with *Nekaddesh et Shimkha ba-olam* ("We will sanctify Your Name on earth") in the Ashkenazi rite and concludes with *Le-dor va-dor* ("Unto all generations..."), the standard ending. On Sabbath and festival mornings, this is expanded to include a plea for the Temple's restoration. In the Sephardi-Eastern rites, however, one form only is recited on these occasions, introduced by *Nakdishakh ve-na' aritsakh* ("We will sanctify and revere You"). The Additional Service *Kedushah* for Sabbaths and festivals, which is the lengthiest form recited, is known as *Kedushah Rabbah* ("the Great Sanctification"). It incorporates the first and last phrases of the *Shema* ("Hear, O Israel... I am the Lord your God"). Owing to religious persecution under the Byzantine Christians (or the Persian Zoroastrians), Jews were forbidden to proclaim the monotheistic *Shema* in synagogue; to outwit government watchdogs, the rabbis decreed that it be recited in an abbreviated form (as part of the Additional Service *Kedushah*) after the agents had left, and this temporary measure became a widely observed practice. A later ruling by MAIMONIDES, which canceled this insertion of the *Shema*, affected only the Persian and Yemenite rituals. In both Ashkenazi and Sephardi congregations, the reader and worshipers sometimes recite the *Amidah* together until the end of *Kedushah*, after which the remainder is concluded in silent prayer without the usual repetition. Reform Jews recite abbreviated versions of the text. On the High Holidays, modifications are introduced in the Additional Service *Kedushah* through an overlapping *piyyut* (liturgical poem) at the beginning; on the Day of Atonement, the longer Additional Service version is also recited during morning and afternoon prayers. In all rites, *Kedushah* is chanted to special prayer modes on Sabbaths and festivals (particularly the High Holidays).

KEHILLAH ("congregation"). One of the Hebrew terms which, in a broad sense, was applied to a Jewish COMMUNITY (the others were *edah* and *kahal*); from the later Middle Ages it also acquired the more restricted religious meaning of a Jewish congregation, i.e., the membership of a specific SYNAGOGUE. Western Sephardi congregations often incorporate "K.K." (*Kahal Kadosh*, "Holy Congregation") in their official titles — K.K. Talmud Torah (Amsterdam), K.K. Sha'ar ha-Shamayim (London), and K.K. Shearith Israel (New York).

KELAL ISRAEL (literally, "the entire community of Israel"). Term applied to the Jewish people as a single unit in terms of its common destiny and responsibility. Jewish belief holds all Jews responsible for one another spiritually, and the sin of one Jew is considered to be the sin of the totality (which is why the CONFESSIONS on the DAY OF ATONEMENT are recited in the plural form). The rule of collective responsibility has also halakhic ramifications: a Jew must not act in any way that may aid another Jew to violate Jewish law. The classic example in the Talmud is that one may not offer wine to a NAZIRITE (who is forbidden to ingest anything derived from grapes). By the same token, the Torah law commands that a Jew who sees another Jew violating the law must rebuke him, and attempt to make him cease his forbidden activity. The concept of *Kelal Israel* encompasses all Jews, virtuous and sinner alike. In fact there are various aggadic passages which imply that sinners are as necessary as the righteous to the Jewish people.

KELIM ("Vessels"). First tractate of Order TOHOROT in the Mishnah. Its 30 chapters deal with the susceptibility of vessels, domestic utensils, and clothing to acquire ritual uncleanness (cf. Lev. 11:29-35). Some of the subjects covered are: the primary sources of uncleanness, the grades of uncleanness, the utensils which are susceptible to uncleanness, how ovens and fireplaces can become unclean, contracting uncleanness through touching, sitting, or lying upon unclean things, and intention and liability to uncleanness. Since the destruction of the Temple and the unavailability of the ashes of the RED HEIFER, it is not longer possible for anyone to purify himself from the primary form of *tumah* (impurity), which is contact with a dead body. For this reason, everyone is considered unclean (*tamé met*), and most of these laws have had no practical application since the destruction of the Second Temple. The subject matter is amplified in the *Tosefta* but in neither Talmud.

KENESET ISRAEL (lit. "the Assembly of Israel" or "the Community of Israel"). Term sometimes used in the MIDRASH as a synonym for the Jewish people. The context is often that of *Keneset Israel* holding a dialogue with God. The term is common in kabbalistic literature. The general use refers to the Jewish people in the spiritual, rather than the physical, sense. This name was also used by the organized Jewish community in Palestine, when it was officially incorporated in 1927. *Keneset Israel*, translated into English as "Catholic Israel," was used as a concept by Solomon SCHECHTER to indicate the adoption of certain practices as a result of the consensus of the Jewish people.

KENESET GEDOLAH See GREAT ASSEMBLY

KERI'AH See RENDING OF GARMENTS

KERITOT ("Excommunications"). Seventh tractate of Order KODASHIM in the Mishnah. Its six chapters deal with the transgressions subject to the penalty of KARET and their atonement by sacrifices. In this case, *karet* means premature death at the "hand of heaven". The Mishnah lists the 36 transgressions which are punishable by *karet*, the offerings of women after childbirth, sin offerings for various transgressions, guilt offerings for transgressing dietary laws, Sabbath restrictions, and forbidden sexual relations. Maimonides states that *karet* means that a person is "cut off" not only from this world, but that his soul is separated in the "world to come" as well. The subject matter is amplified in the Babylonian Talmud and the *Tosefta*.

KETER ("a crown") In the Bible the term is found only in the Book of Esther where it denotes royalty: "He set the royal crown upon her head and made her queen" (Est. 2:17). The Talmud depicts the "crowning" of the Almighty by angels and man, as a way of expressing their praise of Him (*Keter Malkhut*, "crown of royalty"). The archangel Sandalphon is described as standing behind the Divine chariot wreathing crowns for his Maker (*Ḫag.* 13b). According to the Midrash, an angel takes all the prayers said by Israel in synagogues all over and makes a wreath out of them with which he crowns the supreme King of Kings (Ex. R. 21:4).

The term is also used as a metaphor for learning (*Keter Torah*, "crown of Torah"). According to the Mishnah, "R. SIMEON BAR YOḪAI [second century CE] said: 'There are three crowns: the crown of Torah, the crown of priesthood, and the crown of royalty; but the crown of a good name excels them all'" (*Avot* 4:17).

The term *Keter Torah* also refers to the ornament used to crown the SCROLL OF THE LAW in synagogues (see also TORAH ORNAMENTS). Eastern Jews also referred to valuable Bible manuscripts as *Keter*. The best-known is the *Keter Aram Tsova* (Aleppo manuscript) which was rescued from a burning synagogue during a 1947 pogrom, smuggled into Israel, and today serves as the basis of a standard critical edition of the Hebrew text of the Bible.

KETUBBAH Marriage contract, a legal document prepared prior to the MARRIAGE and handed to the bride during the wedding ceremony. In it are set forth the husband's obligations (largely financial) towards his wife. These obligations include those specified in the Bible (cf. Ex. 21:10) and many added by the sages of the Talmud. The standard text of the *ketubbah* is written according to regulations found in Tractate KETUBBOT and the codes of Jewish law such as the *Mishneh Torah* of MAIMONIDES and the SHULKḪAN ARUKH, *Even ha-Ezer*. The obligations set forth in the *ketubbah* are statutory and hence binding, even though they may not have been specified. Beyond the traditional text, the *ketubbah* may also list other conditions to the marriage which have been agreed upon by the couple before the wedding. In countries where polygamy was permitted, a clause was often added pledging the groom not to take another wife; in Syria, a further clause released the groom from that promise after ten years if his bride proved to be barren. Another provision appearing in many *ketubbot* in the past committed the couple to making their home in the Land of Israel.

The development of the *ketubbah* since ancient times may be traced back to a statement in the Talmud (*Ket.* 82b). In biblical times marriage was a contractual arrangement in which a man acquired a wife through payment of a sum of

Ketubbah *(marriage contract) from Casale Monferrato, Italy, 1671.*

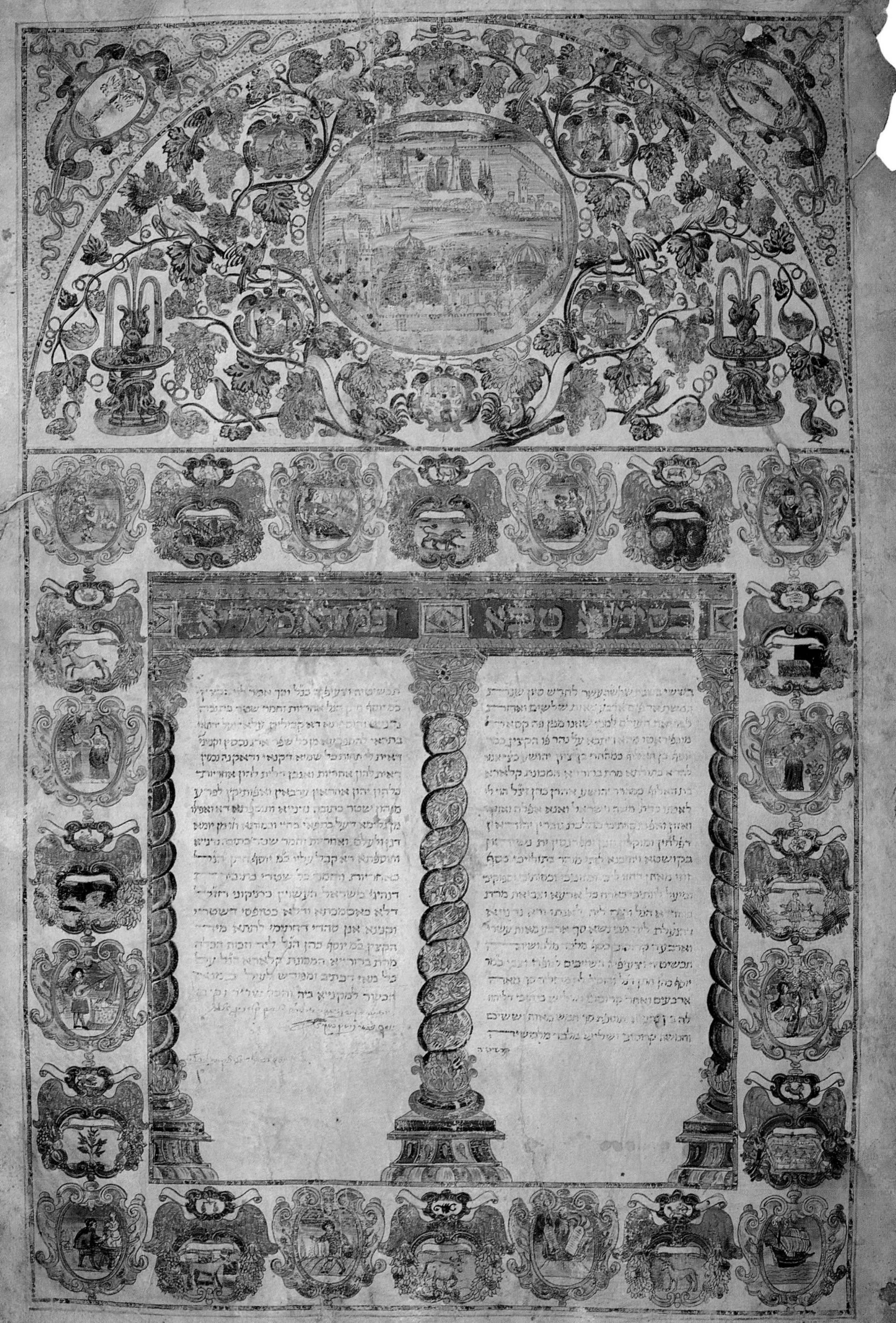
בסימנא טבא ובמזלא מעליא

ISRAEL
ARIE
OFIR
STERLING

money called *mohar* (cf. Gen. 34:12), or bride-price, paid by the groom's father to the bride's father. Because of economic hardship in the early Second Temple era, families could not afford the bridal payment and men could not marry at the customary early age. It was therefore instituted that, in lieu of an actual payment, the groom would pledge in writing to make the payment at some future date. To retain the custom of an actual payment, the groom would give the bride an object of minimal value as a token of marriage (*Kid.* 1:1). A minimum sum for the marriage contract was fixed: 200 *zuz* (dinar) for a virgin, corresponding to the 50 silver coins (shekels) established by the Bible (Deut. 22:29; cf. Ex. 22:16), and 100 *zuz* for a widow or a divorcee. The groom, however, was not limited to this amount and, if he were so inclined, could add on any amount he wished.

Since postponing the actual payment of the bride-price was not welcomed by the bride's family, it became mandatory for the groom to deposit as surety some household utensil or trinket equivalent in value to the sum stipulated in the marriage contract. Even this did not provide satisfactory security for the wife, for in a fit of anger the husband could effectively divorce her merely by saying: "Take the surety and get thee hence." In the first century BCE this problem was mitigated by SIMEON BEN SHETAḤ, head of the Sanhedrin, who ruled for all time that all the husband's property, both that which was already in his possession and that which he might acquire in the future, would be security for the marriage contract. The full payment became due either upon divorce or the death of the husband; a claim upon the husband's estate had to be satisfied prior to any other claims which originated after the marriage. It thus appears that the *ketubbah's* ultimate goal was "that it should not be easy for a husband to divorce his wife" (*Yev.* 89a).

The contract also included a statement of the value of the household goods (*nedunyah*) which the bride brought as a dowry from her father's house. The groom accepted financial responsibility for the dowry, enlarging it with a sum of his own. Since the *ketubbah* served as a contractual obligation, it called for a symbolic gesture affirming it. This was the *kinyan* (meaning, literally, an acquisition of goods): in the presence of two witnesses, a member of the bride's family handed a kerchief over to the groom. The witnesses would then sign the contract, attesting to all its provisions. The custom arose among Ashkenazim for the groom to sign the document as well, the witnesses signing on the right-hand side and the groom on the left — a custom generally followed today in Israel.

Throughout the centuries, the text of the *ketubbah* has been written in Aramaic, the daily language of the Jews in the days of the MISHNAH (2nd-century Palestine). At times a translation also appeared: in some Sephardi communities, for example, Ladino was used alongside the Aramaic. Special provisions could be written in phraseology and language determined by the families themselves, unrestricted by any stipulations of the sages (*BM.* 104a). Although it has been suggested that the contemporary *ketubbah* be written in Hebrew, Israel's Chief Rabbinate has yet to approve the idea. However, after reading the Aramaic text aloud, many officiants at contemporary wedding ceremonies then read an extract from the text in the language of the bride and groom.

In the Talmud, there is a difference of opinion among the sages whether the *ketubbah* is a requirement of biblical law, or only a requirement of the rabbis. Where the former opinion is followed (generally by the Ashkenazi authorities) after the words "200 silver *zuzim* due you" the word *mi-de-orataita* (by the Torah) is added; where the second opinion holds sway (now generally in Israel) this word is omitted.

Today the financial provisions of the marriage contract are not enforced in most countries. In the event of the death of the husband, the wife in any case inherits a portion of his estate (see INHERITANCE); in the event of DIVORCE, alimony and distribution of property is generally settled by a suit in the civil courts. Nevertheless, the writing of a *ketubbah* is to this day an absolute requirement of Jewish law and an indispensable component of a religious wedding ceremony.

The oldest known *ketubbah*, dating from the fifth century BCE, comes from Yeb (Elephantine) in southern Egypt, where there was a Jewish settlement. Although written in ancient Aramaic, its language is very similar to that in use today. Another ancient marriage document, from about 120 CE, was found in a cave near the Dead Sea. The first specific reference to the *ketubbah* is in the Apocryphal Book of Tobit, dating from Second Temple times. Most of the subsequent laws and practices regarding the *ketubbah* were related to its wording; they prescribed no set form or format for its visual aspects. Thus the scribes had the rare freedom to arrange the text and draw its letters as they wished, and could let their imaginations reign when they turned to illustrate or design a *ketubbah*.

One of the oldest known illustrated *ketubbot* comes from Fostat (Egypt) and dates from the 10th-11th century. The oldest such Ashkenazi *ketubbah*, from Krems, Austria, was designed in 1392. From the Middle Ages onward, many *ketubbot* were artistically illustrated and decorated with relevant verses, such as "Who finds a wife has found happiness" (Prov. 18:22).

The illumination of *ketubbot* reflected the art of the countries in which they were made, and their decorative elements — such as flags, portals, and flora and fauna — were often identical to those seen in other ritual works. In Italy, hand-painted *ketubbot* became fashionable in the 17th century and were clearly the products of Renaissance taste. In 19th century Persia, each major city had its own distinctive *ketubbah* style, derived largely from local decorative modes and at times closely resembling Muslim ritual texts. In the Muslim world in general, *ketubbah* artists usually followed Muslim custom and refrained from depicting human figures.

The changes in Jewish life in the 20th century have been

Modern Kiddush *(benediction) cup in silver and anodized titanium. Arié Ofir, 1983.*

reflected in the *ketubbah*. The Conservative Movement introduced an English-language *ketubbah* with a clause in which both husband and wife agree to accept the decision of the rabbinical court in the event of divorce, thereby avoiding the halakhic problem of the recalcitrant husband who refuses to grant his wife a *get* (bill of divorce according to Jewish law).

The Reform Movement does not use the traditional *ketubbah*. Some Reform Jews prefer a simple marriage certificate attesting to the fact that the marriage ceremony has taken place. Others use a modern "egalitarian *ketubbah*" calling on the bride and groom to found their relationship upon mutual spiritual obligations, openness, and sensitivity to each other's needs. These *ketubbot*, composed by rabbis of the Reform Movement, are written in the vernacular, with or without a parallel Hebrew text, and usually omit the financial and legalistic elements which were the basis of the traditional *ketubbah*.

The late 1960s saw a renaissance of the hand-illuminated *ketubbah*, starting in the USA and eventually spreading to Israel and other countries. The artists ranged from amateurs — sometimes the newlyweds themselves — to highly professional calligraphers and graphic designers specializing in this art form. While most of the contemporary *ketubbot* derived their general formal style and symbolism from older European or Oriental models, a notable few were boldly innovative, combining both traditional and contemporary techniques with late-20th century aesthetic sensibilities. The popularity of the original painted *ketubbah* also bred a new generation of more popular-priced printed *ketubbot*; a number of them were hand-tinted to satisfy the demand for "hand-made" works of art.

KETUBBOT ("marriage contracts"). Second tractate of Order NASHIM in the Mishnah. Its 13 chapters deal with the laws of the marriage contract (KETUBBAH), the document which contains the written obligations of the husband towards his wife (cf. Ex. 22:15,16; Deut. 22:13-29). Included in the *ketubbah* is the amount of the dowry which the wife brings into the marriage and the monetary settlement paid to her in the event of divorce or the death of the husband. The Mishnah also discusses the marriage ceremony, the penalties for seduction and rape, grounds for divorce, and the laws of inheritance. The last Mishnah speaks of the greatness of Erets Israel and of Jerusalem in particular, stating that a husband may force his wife and children to move there, but neither can be forced to move away from the Holy Land or the Holy City. The subject matter is amplified in both Talmuds and the *Tosefta*.

KEVER AVOT (literally "grave of the fathers"). The practice of visiting the graves of parents or close relatives, either to pray for the souls of the departed or to pray to God to aid the living through the deeds of the departed.

Judaism generally downplays excessive visits to graves, regarding these as detrimental. Thus there are prescribed fixed times for such visits, which include the anniversary of the person's death, the day before each New Moon, the month of Elul and the Ten Days of Penitence, and, according to some, the fast days throughout the year. One should not visit a grave on the days regarded by Jewish law as joyful, including the intermediate days of Passover and Sukkot, or on Purim. It is also customary to visit a grave at the end of *shivah* (the week of mourning following the person's death), and at the end of *sheloshim* (30 days after the person's death). Some visit the grave before a major event or a family rejoicing or during a critical stage in one's life.

ḤASIDISM laid great stress on visiting the graves of its leaders, even considering the soil in which the leaders were buried to be as holy as that of the Land of Israel. Their opponents, the MITNAGGEDIM, objected to such practices, and some of their leaders made a point of never visiting the graves of even close relatives.

KHAZARS Turkic people of south-central Russia who converted to Judaism. The Khazarian kingdom flourished in Caucasia in the seventh to tenth centuries CE. According to letters written two centuries after the fact, the Khazar king Bulan (786-809), together with many of his nobles, converted to a form of Judaism in the middle of the eighth century, as a result of a debate held by representatives of Judaism, Christianity, and Islam. Although there was once doubt about both the extent and the sincerity of Khazarian Judaism, recent research indicates that conversion to Judaism (apparently the Rabbanite variety) was widespread and that the Khazarians themselves as well as their contemporaries considered them to be Jews. Jewish tradition, medieval Islamic historiography, and GENIZAH documents testify to the Jewish nature of the Khazarian kingdom.

The conversion of the Khazars, and the subsequent existence of a powerful, if remote, Jewish state, served as an encouragement to medieval Jews who were called upon to face and explain Jewish powerlessness vis-à-vis Christian and Muslim temporal successes. This is one major reason that JUDAH HALEVI chose the story of the conversion as the literary framework for his exposition of Judaism (*Sefer ha-Kuzari*). This work, a fictionalized account of the discussions between the king of the Khazars and a Jewish scholar, is the main lasting monument to the Khazars in Jewish history.

The Khazar kingdom was destroyed by the 11th century, though scattered references to Khazars persist for a few more centuries. The notion that Ashkenazi Jewry is descended from the Khazars has absolutely no basis in fact.

KIBBUTZ FESTIVALS In the Israeli kibbutz, FESTIVALS of the Jewish year and life cycle rites of passage are practiced without synagogues, rabbis, and cantors, or the declamation of prayer (this excludes the Orthodox kibbutzim, which follow traditional patterns). A form of holiday practice totally at variance with the theological movements of modern Judaism arose in Erets Israel in the 1930s and has taken its place as a Jewish ceremonial and cultural option.

The founders of the kibbutz visualized themselves as creators of a revolutionary communal society that would accept responsibility for its members' total needs. Included within the spectrum of human concerns was to be culture, which the community obligated itself to provide, along with the satisfaction of material wants. Only in the 1930s, when the kibbutz became a settled community, were energy and thought invested in the process of firmly securing the holiday as part of the developing kibbutz way of life. Once families grew and children began to ask questions, the place of holidays in the kibbutz could not be ignored.

With the task now laid out before them, kibbutz members of the cultural avant-garde drew up a series of questions for guidance in the serious preparation of ceremony for the emerging kibbutz festival: (1) How to balance liberation from the rejected Diaspora religious past with the wish to connect with a "healthy" tradition of the fathers? (2) How to create new ceremonies, appealing to the mind and heart, derived from historical memories of the periods when the Jewish people lived on its land and practiced natural agricultural festivals? (3) How to integrate biblical texts with emerging Hebrew literature, and familiar Diaspora melodies with new tunes from Erets Israel? (4) How to bridge the gap between the holiday as practiced within the nuclear family and as practiced jointly within the kibbutz community? (5) How to interpret traditional sources in a secular-national manner when they are predominantly religious in character? (6) Should all the holidays be celebrated or only the ones fitting members' secular outlook? Agreement prevailed on the agricultural-national holidays such as Passover, Shavu'ot, Sukkot, Purim, Tu be-Shevat, and Lag ba-Omer. Later, Rosh Ha-Shanah joined this group; but the Day of Atonement remains outside the accepted festivals. (7) How to integrate the new holidays produced by historical events and circumstance? (8) How to merge individual rites of passage, such as bar/bat mitsvah and marriage, into communal patterns of celebration? (9) What to emphasize in preparing festivals — textual content or "presentations" in song, dance, and drama? Considering the limited time span since initiation of holidays on the kibbutz, no definitive answers are yet forthcoming. Although bearing similarities to the ceremonies originating in the 1930s, kibbutz holiday practice has developed in unanticipated directions. Only of Passover can it be said that a "tradition" exists; the remainder of the holidays are still in transition.

Page from a Passover Haggadah *of Kibbutz ha-Artzi of the Ha-Shomer ha-Tsa'ir movement. It reads:* "The Third Cup: *We raise a cup of consolation for peace of Israel and the peace of the world; may there be peace in our homes; tranquillity in our tents. To life and peace!"*

Young girls bearing trays with greenery, performing at a Passover kibbutz festival (at harvest time).

PASSOVER is the main holiday. The first kibbutz HAGGADAH appeared in 1935 in Én Harod, initiating an outflow of local productions by numerous kibbutzim. This can be attributed to the stock of warm memories many members brought with them from the Diaspora. Passover escaped the rejection reflex against traditional Jewish life because, as an eminently family festival, it could be experienced in the home without recourse to the synagogue. Despite their affection for the traditional SEDER, the founders' enactment departed radically from accepted custom. After a creative eruption of hundreds of locally produced *Haggadot*, the kibbutz movements began, over the years, to draw up versions of a unified *Haggadah* that became the accepted text for most kibbutz communities. The earlier simple handwritten or mimeographed *Haggadot* gave way to artistic productions. The conceptual message of the kibbutz *Haggadah* is that freedom from Egyptian domination was achieved by natural means and not through supernatural intervention. Other traditional Passover themes were transplanted into kibbutz society and easily absorbed, such as the INGATHERING OF THE EXILES, spring, and the EXODUS.

Significant events in the Jewish world, whether in the kibbutz, Erets Israel, or the Diaspora, were noted in kibbutz *Haggadot*. Passover acted as a ceremonial outlet whereby kibbutz members identified with the struggle for freedom of the Jewish people.

With the founding of the State of Israel, many of the pre-state themes found a place in newly established civil days of observance; ISRAEL INDEPENDENCE DAY, Holocaust Memorial Day, Memorial Day for soldiers and civilians who fell in the struggle for independence — these additions to the calendar year emptied the kibbutz Passover of its topical commentary and content. The editors of the kibbutz *Haggadot* were now confronted with the problem of restoring Passover's timelessness without recourse to the traditional *Haggadah*. This led to affirmation of certain traditional themes but dissent from others. With the denial of God's supernatural attributes or His intervention in history, entire sections of the *Haggadah* offering praise to God, as well as the GRACE AFTER MEALS, were omitted. However, not all references to God were struck out. Psalms and well-loved table songs from the traditional *Haggadah*, such as EḤAD MI YODE'A ("Who knows one?") are read and sung in the dining room at the kibbutz communal celebration. Biblical selections, particularly from the Book of Exodus, are woven together to form a narrative outline of the Exodus from Egypt. Mention of God in the kibbutz *Haggadah* is inevitable, but at no point is He praised or offered thanks.

The major aim of the *Haggadah* — of whatever persuasion — is to relate the story of the Exodus from Egypt. The kibbutz version of this event is descriptively plentiful, for the retelling of the Exodus has become the kibbutz focus. The result is a *seder* with an enlarged biblical content. The omission of any mention of MOSES in the traditional *Haggadah* has been rectified by including narratively connected biblical verses portraying Moses in his role as shepherd, representative of his people confronting Pharaoh, and leader of the "mixed multitude" departing from Egypt.

The coming of spring, only hinted at in the traditional *Haggadah*, acts as an opening motif. Portions from the SONG OF SONGS interweave with medieval Hebrew poetry on the cessation of the winter rains and the beginning of dew. The use of time-honored classical sources in place of the modern Hebrew writers whose works on spring appeared in earlier *Haggadot* testifies to the vigor of traditional material.

A final theme is the ingathering of the exiles. The concluding cry of the *seder* — "next year in Jerusalem" — has been enlarged by interposing poems by JUDAH HALEVI and selections from AMOS and ISAIAH, all centering on the return of the Jewish people to their ancestral land. The 1985 *Haggadah* of the United Kibbutz Movement remains close to Jewish sources, adhering to the central historical theme of deliverance from slavery, while introducing motifs based on a solid underpinning of traditional materials.

The early years of kibbutz holiday ceremony were characterized by radical departures. Attempts to renew ancient agricultural festivals tied into Zionist values of tilling the soil and of settling the land through working it. Appropriate ceremonies were soon forthcoming that evoked an emotional receptiveness to the earth by identifying with the biblical and post-biblical past when Jewish farmers tilled the soil. The OMER of Passover and the FIRST FRUITS of SHAVU'OT illustrate the interaction between the kibbutz, the land, and the Jewish heritage.

Today, community attitudes towards nature festivals have undergone modifications and reinterpretations. This is especially noticeable on Shavu'ot, a holiday dedicated in the Diaspora primarily to the commemoration of the Torah's revelation on Sinai; Shavu'ot as Festival of the First Fruits was underplayed. As the festival emerged from the secular kibbutzim, agriculture acted as its foundation stone, and the Giving of the Law was absent.

The contemporary return by a handful of kibbutzim to a historical focus is often attributed to the increased mechanization of agriculture, but this view overlooks a basic revision in the kibbutz community's relationship to agriculture. Shavu'ot retains its former significance with difficulty as kibbutz industry moves forward to the position of major employer and provider. Another explanation is the temperamental unsuitability of the native-born generation for a nature festival. Nature festivals demand of their practitioners a romantic sensibility toward the land and its soil. The new kibbutz generations are more sober and pragmatic than their parents, which tends to dampen the emotional impressions and sensations a nature festival elicits from its participants.

Kibbutz festivals act to reinforce the social web of communal life. Engagement of the community in ordinary acts that bear special significance binds people together in rare moments of togetherness (*yaḇad*). Not all holidays can be absorbed into the kibbutz way of life by skillful reinterpretation. The HIGH HOLIDAYS lack the historical and national perspective of the PILGRIM FESTIVALS or of ḤANNUKAH and PURIM. As eminently religious holidays, the New Year and Day of Atonement seemed inflexible. Indeed, some kibbutzim made a point of either ignoring the Day of Atonement or using it for special work projects. The tacit decision to consign the High Holidays to spiritual exile is now open to debate. The entire Jewish calendar is being progressively included in the kibbutz festival cycle as questions of Jewish identity increasingly turn up on the kibbutz agenda. In addition, the kibbutz movement is experiencing a severe crisis of self-confidence, making the average member more conscious of failings in kibbutz life. Awareness of human limitations is a precondition for the reappearance of days devoted in part to an evaluation of the human condition.

Like Passover, ROSH HA-SHANAH takes place around a festive table in the kibbutz dining room. Apples and honey are the only special foods prepared. Outward resemblances to Passover are there — a booklet of readings, community singing, and large quantities of food heaped on the tables; but Rosh ha-Shanah as a "Day of Awe" is absent on the kibbutz. The themes within the ceremonial material remain broadly traditional: the return from exile, the New Year as a day for assessment of the relationship between man and man, man and society, man and his environment. A distinct kibbutz motif is the dignity of humanity, an outlook deriving from an optimistic ideology that holds humans to be progressively developing toward a greater and fuller spirituality. Belief in the human being is an existential kibbutz necessity, for faith and mutual trust in one's fellows are pragmatic requirements of a cooperative society.

The DAY OF ATONEMENT on the kibbutz differs from other holidays by reason of the absence of full community participation. With no communal meal or active participation of children, the day focuses on content. Only a small minority support Yom Kippur, for many members experience holidays as social events, ignoring any message. A recurrent Yom Kippur theme is the necessity for a collective *ḥeshbon nefesh*, a self-examination and evaluation, and a joint stock-taking of the community collective conscience. In the kibbutz, the interdependence of the collective and the individual requires periodic renewal.

The experimental mood of some of the cultural pacesetters led them to "restore" some of the minor holidays mentioned in Jewish sources that could be linked to special agricultural sectors. Attempts to celebrate a vineyard festival, a shearing festival, and a love festival on *Tu be-Av* (see AV, FIFTEENTH OF), proved abortive. Experience has taught that only traditional holidays with a continuous history of practice can be reconstituted.

The future of kibbutz-style holidays is uncertain. Native-born generations have yet to reveal the creativity that distinguished their parents and grandparents. It is still premature to hand down a verdict on the future of these unique cultural forms born out of the kibbutz.

KIDDUSH ("Sanctification") Prayer recited on SABBATHS and FESTIVALS, usually over a cup of WINE, to consecrate the day. The principal *Kiddush*, recited in the evening at the beginning of the holy day, was instituted on the basis of Exodus 20:8, "Remember the Sabbath day and keep it holy" (*le-kaddesho*). The sages of the Talmud interpreted this to mean "remember it, over wine" (*Pes.* 106a). The choice of wine as the object of this blessing was perhaps the normalization of an established custom. It was also determined that this blessing should be recited close to the beginning of the Sabbath or festival and that "There is no *Kiddush* except at the place of a meal" (*Pes.* 101a), i.e., the prayer was to be said at home rather than in the synagogue. If wine is not available, the benediction of the day may be made over two loaves of bread following the blessing over bread.

From the difference of opinion between the Schools of Hillel and Shammai (*Ber.* 8:1) as to whether the blessing over wine should precede the benediction of the day, it can be seen that the practice of *Kiddush* is ancient. Although there is some discussion in the sources, it cannot be determined whether it was originally recited before or after the meal.

On the Sabbath and festival mornings, a *Kiddush* is also recited prior to the first meal of the day; this practice was instituted by the rabbis, and although it is basically only the prayer over wine it is called euphemistically *Kiddusha rabba*, "the great *Kiddush*." If wine is not at hand, any strong drink may be used and the appropriate blessing recited.

According to the Talmud (*Ber.* 20b), women are obligated to hear or recite the *Kiddush*, even though it is a time-bound positive commandment from which they were normally exempted. The reason given is that since women are commanded to "Observe the Sabbath day and keep it holy," and the obligation to "observe" includes to "remember," it follows that women are also obligated concerning *Kiddush*.

The custom early developed of reciting the evening *Kiddush* in the synagogue also at the end of the Friday night services. In the Talmud this is explained as being for the benefit of guests who were housed in a room next to the synagogue (*Pes.* 101a). Another source cites the fact that in certain areas of Babylonia wine was scarce and this public prayer was for those who could not obtain it. Since the rabbis had determined that *Kiddush* should be said "near the meal," this public recitation was never fully accepted. Sephardi communities stopped it in medieval times, it did not take root in Erets Israel, while in Ashkenazi synagogues in the Diaspora the wine over which the blessing is recited is given to children under bar mitsvah age.

Today, in many congregations, on Sabbath mornings, after services, a public *Kiddush* is recited and other refreshments eaten as a means of socializing.

The *Kiddush* today consists of two sections: the blessing over wine and the benediction of the day. The latter was initially a simple phrase, whose precise formulation is unknown, although one example is the prayer in *Tosef. Ber.* 3:7, "Blessed be [He Who] sanctified the Sabbath day."

The introductory biblical phrases which precede the *Kiddush* on Sabbath eve are Genesis 1:31 and 2:1-3. The blessing for wine is next recited, followed by that for the sanctification of the day. A number of ideas are included in the lengthy blessing; that Israel was itself made holy by God's commandments, that it was favored by having been given the Sabbath as an inheritance in remembrance of Creation, that the Sabbath is the first of the holy convocations mentioned in the list of "sacred occasions" (Lev. 23:3) and is in commemoration of the Exodus from Egypt (Deut. 5:12-15). This is followed by a sentence whose form is reminiscent of the festival *Kiddush*. The final phrase, "Blessed are You, O Lord, who hallows the Sabbath" was in earlier times "hallows Israel and the Sabbath day" (TJ, *Ber.* 8:1, *Pes.* 10:2).

On Sabbath morning, it is sufficient to recite only the prayer over wine. However, opening sentences (Ex. 31: 16-17 or 20: 8-11 or both), which call upon Israel to observe the Sabbath "throughout the generations as a covenant for all time," are often added.

The festival *Kiddush* also consists of the blessing over the wine and a blessing over the day. Should the beginning of a festival coincide with Sabbath, interpolated into the festival *Kiddush* are appropriate phrases noting the Sabbath. The festival *Kiddush* is followed, except on the concluding days of Passover, by the recitation of the SHE-HEḤEYANU prayer. On a Sabbath occurring during the intermediate days of a festival, the regular Sabbath *Kiddush* is recited.

Wine goblets reserved for the prayer over wine are a common item in the Jewish home; they are often made of silver and bear an inscription, such as the blessing over wine or "Observe the Sabbath day and keep it holy."

In general it is customary to stand for the evening *Kiddush*, either for all of it or for the introductory phrases from Genesis; some who stand for the evening *Kiddush*, prefer to sit for the morning recitation. In some families each person has his own cup of wine and the blessing is recited in unison. The most common procedure is that following the *Kiddush*, the participants in the meal wash hands in preparation for the blessing over bread.

Kiddush *cups. From left to right: one from Bohemia, in red glass; two from Poland and one from Germany, in silver. 19th century.*

While the Hebrew text among Orthodox, Conservative, and Reform Jews is the same, the English translation appearing in the Reform *Gates of Prayer* (New York, 1975) is not a literal one and reflects an additional interpretation of the aim of the *Kiddush*, namely, thanksgiving. ("The seventh day is consecrated to the Lord our God. With wine, our symbol of joy, we celebrate this day and its holiness. We give thanks for all our blessings, for life and health, for work and rest, for home and love and friendship, on Sabbath, eternal sign of Creation. We remember that we are created in the Divine image. We therefore raise the cup in thanksgiving.")

SABBATH KIDDUSH

Blessed are You, O Lord our God, King of the universe, Who has sanctified us by Your commandments and has taken pleasure in us, and in love and favor has given us Your holy Sabbath as an inheritance, a memorial of the Creation, that day being the first of the holy convocations, in remembrance of the Exodus from Egypt. For You have chosen us and hallowed us above all nations, and in love and favor have given us Your holy Sabbath as an inheritance. Blessed are You O Lord, Who sanctifies the Sabbath.

KIDDUSH HA-SHEM AND ḤILLUL HA-SHEM (literally, "the sanctification of the [Divine] Name" and "the desecration of the [Divine] Name"). Two opposing concepts defining actions which directly or by implication tend to reflect either glory or dishonor on the Jewish people and hence God. The terms were formulated by the rabbis who saw the concepts as rooted in the Bible, particularly in the commandment, "You shall not profane My holy name, but I will be sanctified among the Children of Israel" (Lev. 22:32). The rabbis suggested that for the violation of this law MOSES and AARON were not allowed to enter the Holy Land: "Because you did not believe in Me, to sanctify me in the eyes of the Children of Israel, therefore you shall not bring this congregation into the land which I have given them" (Num. 20:12). The obligation to sanctify God's name is codified by Maimonides in his *Sefer ha-Mitsvot* (Positive Commandments 297).

Kiddush ha-Shem includes the obligation to remain steadfast in one's religious belief and actions, even at the cost of one's life. If a Jew is faced with the choice between death or committing an act of idolatry, murder or sexual immorality, he must choose to die rather than commit the sin involved. Should he indeed die in these circumstances, his action is considered to be a *kiddush ha-Shem*, while if he commits any of these sins it is considered a *ḥillul ha-Shem*. At times of persecution against the Jews, the law requires the Jew to resist violating any law, even at the peril of his life. It was this law which led thousands of Jews throughout the ages to prefer martyrdom — which is identified with dying for the sake of *kiddush ha-Shem* — to forced conversion.

Another category of laws related to *kiddush ha-Shem* applies where a Jew is commanded to violate any law other than the three above-mentioned, where the motivation of the person commanding the action is for his own benefit rather than as a display of anti-Jewish persecution. In such a case, the Jew is duty-bound to save his life by carrying out the prohibited action. In fact if he is killed because of his resistance, some rabbinic authorities regard this as akin to suicide. The exception to this rule is when the Jew is commanded to commit a sin in the presence of ten other adult Jews. The presence of a quorum of Jewish witnesses makes this a question of *kiddush ha-Shem ba-rabbim* — sanctifying God's name in public — and Jewish law requires the person to forfeit his life rather than submit.

Sometimes, *kiddush ha-Shem* and *ḥillul ha-Shem* are relative concepts, depending on the individual involved. This is expressed in the Talmud, and was later codified by Maimonides, who rules (*Hil. Yesodei ha-Torah* 5:11) that a great Torah sage can be guilty of *ḥillul ha-Shem* if he acts in an untoward manner, even if his actions are strictly in accordance with the letter of the law. Thus a Torah sage is forbidden to take an item on credit, if he gives the impression that he is receiving the item without payment. Nor may such a person carouse with others, nor treat others in a peremptory fashion. All such behavior is considered *ḥillul ha-Shem*.

Another usage of the terms *kiddush ha-Shem* and *ḥillul ha-Shem* relates to how the actions of a Jew will be regarded in the non-Jewish world. Thus actions by a Jew which may lead non-Jews to praise the Jewish religion are considered to be a *kiddush ha-Shem*, whereas actions which reflect negatively on the Jewish people — such as illicit financial transactions — are regarded as *ḥillul ha-Shem*.

It is also considered to be *ḥillul ha-Shem* to erase God's name wherever it may appear, in accordance with the verses (Deut. 12:3-4), "You shall hew down the graven images of their gods ... You shall not do so unto the Lord your God."

KIDDUSHIN ("Sanctification"). Seventh tractate of Order NASHIM in the Mishnah. Its four chapters deal with the procedure for acquiring a wife through two acts: (1) *Erusin* (BETROTHAL) — twelve months prior to formal marriage; (2) *Nissu'in* — the conclusion of legal MARRIAGE by giving of a token (*shaveh prutah*) and cohabitation (Deut. 24:1). The Mishnah discusses the laws of marriage by proxy, the denial of the marriage ceremony, and the permissibility of certain classes within the Jewish people to intermarry. Also mentioned are some general moral precepts referring to social behavior between men and women. The subject matter is amplified in both Talmuds and the *Tosefta*.

KILAYIM ("mixed species"). Fourth tractate of Order ZERA'IM. Its nine chapters cover the laws concerning three main categories of forbidden mixtures: (1) Mixed seeds, *kilay zera'im*, i.e., one may not plant the seeds of two different species (e.g., wheat and barley) in one's field or vineyard (cf. Lev. 19:19; Deut. 22:9-11) (see AGRICULTURAL LAWS); (2) Mixed animals, *kilay behemah*: (a) one may not harness two different kinds of animal (e.g., an ox and a donkey) together for work; (b) one may not cross-breed two different types of animals; and (3) Mixed garments, *kilay begadim*, the prohibition of wearing a garment woven from wool and flax together (called SHA'ATNEZ). The subject matter is amplified in the Jerusalem Talmud and the *Tosefta*.

KI LO NA'EH See ADDIR BI-MELUKHAH

KIMḤI Twelfth-century family of Bible commentators and Hebrew grammarians of Spanish origin, living in Provence.

Joseph Kimḥi (1105-1170; known as *Rikam*, the acronym of Rabbi Joseph Kimḥi), was born in southern Spain; to escape persecution, he moved to Narbonne, Provence, where he died. He was a contemporary of Abraham IBN EZRA who quoted him in his commentaries. Both devoted themselves to making Arabic-Jewish works available to the Jews in Europe through Hebrew translation. Among Kimḥi's translations is BAḤYA IBN PAKUDA's ethical work *Ḥovot ha-Levavot* ("Duties of the Heart"). His contribution to Hebrew grammar was significant. He was not afraid of polemics and wrote one of the earliest Jewish anti-Christian polemical treatises in Europe, the *Sefer ha-Berit*, in which he rejected a number of Christian interpretations of Scriptural concepts, such as original sin, the relative morality of Jews and Christians, and the attitude towards usury. The treatise is written in the form of a discussion between a 'believer' (*ma'amin*) and an apostate or heretic (*min*). In his commentaries he preferred a terse style, giving the *peshat*, or plain sense, and avoiding the aggadic, or homiletic approach, common in the Provencal schools. He wrote a commentary on the Pentateuch called *Sefer ha-Torah*.

Moses Kimḥi, (died c.1190; known as *Remak*, the acronym of Rabbi Moses Kimḥi), was Joseph's eldest son. He was a pupil of his father, and he too adopted a "plain" style and wrote commentaries on the Books of Proverbs, Ezra and Nehemiah, and Job. His principle work was a pioneer Hebrew grammar, *Mahalakh Shevilé ha-Da'at*, in which he presented an innovative order and arrangement of the verb conjugations, followed to this day. Translated into Latin, the

Mahalakh was widely used by Christian Hebraists in the 16th century.

David Kimhi (c. 1160-1235; known as *Radak*, the acronym of Rabbi David Kimhi) was born in Narbonne. He was the youngest son of the Kimhi family and its most illustrious member. His biblical commentaries are published in most rabbinic editions of the Bible. His commentaries were translated into Latin and widely studied by Christian Hebraists during the Renaissance, despite the fact that they contained polemical material, especially in his commentary on the Psalms. (For a time these polemical passages were omitted by order of the censor; eventually they were published separately under the title *Teshuvot la-Notserim*, "Answers to the Christians").

Due to the popularity of his commentaries, he may be said to have profoundly if indirectly influenced the first English version of the Bible, the King James Bible, Authorised Version, published in 1611, and other European translations. In his commentaries, he makes frequent reference to contemporary events. For example, on the verse, "Pray for the peace of Jerusalem" (Ps. 122:6), he refers to the Crusades: "For until now Jerusalem had no peace, for the uncircumcised (i.e., the Christians) and the Ishmaelites were fighting for her possession." He quotes prolifically from the works of his predecessors. He draws extensively on talmudic and midrashic literature and refers to such authorities as SAADIAH GAON, Samuel ha-Nagid, and IBN GABIROL, whose literary works were known to him in Arabic.

Page from the Sefer Mikhlol, *the Hebrew grammar compendium by David Kimhi. Spain, 1476.*

The major issue of the day among Jewish scholars was the controversy over the rationalist writings of MAIMONIDES. Kimhi took a vigorous stand in defense of Maimonides against the rabbis of northern France who had pronounced a ban against the *Guide* and the philosophic portions of the *Mishneh Torah*, and journeyed to Spain to persuade the scholars there to join with the men of Provence on the side of tolerance.

In the area of Hebrew grammar, David Kimhi's *Mikhlol*, which primarily compiled and systematized earlier works, is a significant contribution due to its lucidity and to the vast knowledge of its author. He enjoyed great popularity as a preacher and teacher, and took pains to make the text understood by his listeners, which made him somewhat prolix and repetitious. Playing on the words of *Avot* (3,21), "If there is no *kemah* (lit. "flour," i.e., bread, but here referred to *Kimhi*) there is no Torah," it was said of him that one cannot understand Scripture without Kimhi's interpretations.

KING, KINGSHIP The supreme king in Jewish tradition is God, who is called King of Kings and Lord King of the World. When a Jew takes on the obligation of the commandments upon entering adulthood, this is referred to as "undertaking the yoke of the kingdom of heaven." The Rosh ha-Shanah Additional Service AMIDAH incorporates a series of biblical verses concerning God as King (MALKHUYYOT) (see KINGSHIP OF GOD).

Moses commanded the children of Israel to appoint a king after entering the Land of Canaan (Deut. 17:14ff.), although the concept of royal authority is foreign to the rest of the laws and customs of the Pentateuch. The choice of king and his conduct were subject to restrictions and he was to have a copy of the Law of God from which to read at all times.

The Israelites did not institute a monarchy until after the period of the Judges and then only at a time of crisis when in danger of Philistine domination. Samuel bowed to the people's will and anointed Saul as the first king (I Sam. 10:17ff.) but the institution was subject to religious and social obligations from the very outset. However, the Jewish king was also considered as an expression of God's grace.

The kings had the power to impose taxes, conscript men for the army or for labor service, and declare war (though in later times, they were required to consult the SANHEDRIN). They had the power to decree execution and to confiscate the property of a rebellious subject. The people were instructed to honor the king, but he was cautioned to be inwardly humble, merciful, and kind. He was at all times subservient to the laws of the Torah; should he sin, retribution would be severe.

Saul's successor was DAVID whose success in battle and humility before God resulted in the Divine promise conveyed through the prophet Nathan: "Your house and your kingdom shall be confirmed forever before you; your throne shall be established forever" (II Sam. 7:16). As a result, the belief in the hereditary monarchy of the House of David became engrained in Jewish thought to the extent that it was held that the Messiah would be of the House of David. After the split in the kingdom, a king of the ten tribes was regarded as legitimate if appointed by a prophet, but only a king of the House of David could be anointed with olive oil.

Kingship was an ideal, and many Psalms laud the king as the Divinely-appointed savior (Ps. 2:2-11), conqueror (Ps. 2:6-9), and upholder of justice (Ps. 45:7-8). The Psalms also express the concept of the covenant of kingship (Ps. 132:11-12).

After the destruction of Jewish sovereignty in the first century CE, the question of kingship appeared academic — at least until the messianic age — and little systematic attention was paid to the subject in the Talmud and codes. Only Maimonides in the 12th century, in his comprehensive codification, expounded the relevant laws. Kingship, he wrote, was a positive command and any king must be of the house of David. The traditional liturgy contains frequent references to God as King and prays for the restoration of the House of David.

KINGSHIP OF GOD (also referred to as the Kingship of Heaven). Eschatological reference to the End of Days, when the existing world will be replaced with a new and better one (see ESCHATOLOGY). The prophets often speak of that era, when, according to Isaiah (11:6), "The wolf shall dwell with the lamb, and the leopard shall lie down with the kid." The Talmud does not offer a single view as to the anticipated nature of the Kingdom of Heaven. According to one opinion, it refers to the era of the MESSIAH, while according to another it alludes to the World to Come (see AFTERLIFE). In both cases, it is seen as a time when mankind will acknowledge God as Ruler of the universe.

The longing for the advent of the era of the Kingship of God is a common theme in Jewish prayer. Thus the ALÉNU LE-SHABBE'AH prayer, which concludes each daily service, prays for the day that "all will accept the yoke of Your kingship, and You will soon rule over all of them eternally."

On the other hand, the frequent references in Judaism to "the acceptance of the yoke of God's Kingship" are related to this world, and imply the individual's acceptance and fulfillment of the commandments of the Torah. Thus, the recitation of the first verse of the SHEMA, in which God is acknowledged as Ruler of all, is regarded as "the acceptance of the yoke of God's Kingship."

KINGS, BOOK OF The fourth book of the Former Prophets section of the Bible. In Jewish tradition, Kings is a single book. The division into two books, I Kings and II Kings, comes from the SEPTUAGINT and the Vulgate, according to which the Books of Samuel and Kings are a single unit divided into four books of Kings.

The name of the book is derived from its content, which deals with Kings DAVID and SOLOMON, and the subsequent kings of Judah and of Israel.

The Books deal with the period from the time that Solomon assumed the throne (approximately 970 BCE) until the release from imprisonment in Babylonia of King Jehoiachin (561 BCE). In terms of content, the volume is divided into two parts: 1) the story of Solomon's reign (I Kings 1-11), 2) the story of the kingdoms of Judah and Israel (I Kings 12-II Kings 25). The latter can be subdivided further: a) From the ascent of Rehoboam to the throne (I Kings 12) to the destruction of the kingdom of Israel (II Kings 17:6); b) From the accession of Samaria to the conquest of Jerusalem and the Babylonian EXILE (II Kings 25:1).

BOOK OF KINGS

I Kings	
1:1 — 2:46	The last days of David and Solomon's ascension to the throne
3:1 — 11:43	Solomon's reign
12:1 — 12:24	The division of the united kingdom
12:25 — 14:20	The reign of Jeroboam
14:21 — 16:34	Combined history of Judah and Israel
17:1 — II Kings 10:31	The reign of Ahab and the fall of the house of Omri
II Kings	
10:32 — 17:41	Combined history of Judah and Israel until the fall of Samaria
18:1 — 20:21	Reign of Hezekiah
21:1 — 21:26	Reign of Manasseh and Amon
22:1 — 23:30	Reign of Josiah and the religious reform
23:31 — 23:35	Reign of Jehoahaz
23:36 — 25:30	Last days of Judah and the destruction of Jerusalem.

The history of Solomon's reign is described at length, and includes an account of the building of the TEMPLE. This is followed by a description of the division of the kingdom at the time of Rehoboam. The northern and larger kingdom, that of Israel, comprises ten tribes, while the smaller kingdom, Judah, comprises the two tribes of Judah and Benjamin. The volume continues with a combined account of the history of the two kingdoms. The political history and biographical information are seen in a religious light, and the rulers are assessed according to their faithfulness to God. An important role is played by PROPHETS, notably ELIJAH and ELISHA, who serve as the conscience of the rulers, guiding them along the right path and castigating them when they or the people go astray. A recurrent theme is the centralization of worship, as prescribed in DEUTERONOMY and effected by the seventh century king of Judah, Josiah.

In addition to various archives, the volume notes three sources: the book of Solomon; the book of the Chronicles of the Kings of Judah; and the Book of the Chronicles of the Kings of Israel.

According to Jewish tradition (*BB.* 14b), the book was written by the prophet JEREMIAH.

KINNIM ("Bird Offerings"). Eleventh and last tractate of Order KODASHIM in the Mishnah. Its three chapters deal with the laws governing the bird offerings, sacrificed either voluntarily or as a legal obligation (cf. Lev. 1:14-17; 15:13-15). This offering consisted of either two pigeons or two turtledoves. The Mishnah discusses sprinkling the blood of the bird-offerings, the confusion of two different kinds of offerings (free-will, sin offering, etc.), and cases where one or both of the birds flies off. There is no Talmud or *Tosefta* to this tractate.

KINOT (sing. *kinah*). Elegaic poems which express mourning, pain and suffering; one of the most ancient types of liturgical poetry (PIYYUT).

The Bible mentions various laments: ABRAHAM for Sarah (Gen. 23:2), JACOB's sons for their father (Gen. 50:10), the Israelites for the prophet Samuel (I Sam. 25:1), David's famous lament over Saul and Jonathan: "The beauty of Israel is slain upon your high places: how are the mighty fallen..." (II Sam. 3:33-34).

Apparently different *kinot* were collected in a separate volume: "Behold, they are written in the lamentations" (II Chron. 35:25). The entire Book of LAMENTATIONS is a *kinah* and the sages called it "kinot" (JT *Shab.* 15, Lev. R. 15:4).

The *kinot* could be recited by women keeners: "Consider, and call for the mourning women... Let them make haste, and take up a wailing for us... Teach your daughters wailing, and every one her neighbor lamentation" (Jer. 9:16, 19-25).

The Book of Lamentations is read on the night of 9 Av (TISHAH BE-AV) and, according to certain customs, on the following morning as well. In the SEPTUAGINT, the book begins with "It came to pass after the exile of Judah and the destruction of Jerusalem, that Jeremiah sat and wept and lamented this *kinah* for Jerusalem." Over the course of time, many other *kinot* were written to be recited on 9 Av.

As a type, the *kinot* are a product of Erets Israel. Eliezer KALLIR wrote many laments that occupy a prominent place in the books of laments used by Ashkenazi Jews. Using these books as a base, other *kinot* were added in the Middle Ages in Europe and in eastern countries, following the Crusades and other persecutions of the Jews.

Numerous *kinot* are known as "Zions," as they begin with the word "Zion." Expressing mourning for destroyed Zion and longing for its revival, they all followed the precedent of the lament of JUDAH HALEVI which begins, "Zion, shall you not ask..." A noteworthy *kinah* was that composed by R. MEIR OF ROTHENBURG, "*Sha'ali serufah...*" to commemorate the burning of the Talmud which he witnessed in Paris in 1242.

The first book of *kinot* according to the Ashkenazi rite was printed in Cracow in 1585. Among Eastern Jewish communities, the *kinot* were printed in *Seder Arba Ta'aniyyot* (Venice, 1590), in the prayer book according to the Yemenite ritual (*Tiklal*), and in many others.

KISLEV (Akkadian: *Kislimu*). Ninth month of the Jewish religious CALENDAR; third month of the Hebrew civil year counting from TISHRI. It is a variable month of either 29 or 30 days and normally coincides with November-December. Kislev's sign of the zodiac is Sagittarius the Archer. It is referred to in the Bible (Zech. 7:1; Neh. 1:1) as well as in the Apocrypha and rabbinic sources. The 15th of Kislev, according to some, marked the onset of winter (*BM* 106b) and the biblical account of an assembly held in Jerusalem on 20 Kislev mentions that it took place in pouring rain (Ezra 10:9-13). If no rain had fallen by the New Moon of Kislev, and the land was threatened by a drought, fast days and special prayers were customary in Judea (*Ta'an.* 1.5). The eight-day festival of ḤANUKKAH, recalling the Maccabean victory over the Syrian invaders and the Temple's restoration, begins on the eve of 25 Kislev (when the first Ḥanukkah light is kindled) and lasts until the second or third of Tevet (depending on whether Kislev has 29 or 30 days). In ancient times, messengers were dispatched in advance by the Sanhedrin in Jerusalem to announce the precise date of the festival (*RH* 1.3).

KITEL Yiddish term (cf. German *Kittel*, "smock") denoting the loose white vestment or surplice worn by ASHKENAZIM on solemn occasions in the Jewish calendar. It was originally worn every Sabbath, but now is used by officiants and pious worshipers on the HIGH HOLY DAYS; also by the cantor during the Additional Service, when the Prayer for RAIN is recited on Shemini Atseret, the Prayer for DEW on the first day of Passover, and on Hoshana Rabbah. Some Ashkenazi Jews likewise favor its use by the person conducting the Passover *Seder* service, and by the bridegroom under the marriage canopy. Jewish tradition closely associates the color white with atonement and purity and with life's transience, for which reason some Jews are also buried in their *kitel*.

KLAUS See SYNAGOGUE

KODASHIM ("Holy Things"). Fifth Order of the Mishnah. Its eleven tractates (ZEVAHIM, MENAHOT, HULLIN, BEKHOROT, ARAKHIM, TEMURAH, KERITOT, ME'ILAH, TAMID, MIDDOT, and KINNIM) deal almost entirely with the laws and regulations of offering SACRIFICES. The Order also includes a tractate dealing with the sins which incur excision (*Keritot*), and one which records the dimensions of the Temple (*Middot*). The tractate *Hullin* is of great practical importance as it deals with the methods of ritual slaughter (*shehitah*). Since the destruction of the Second Temple, however, the other tractates are useful only in terms of study, but are not applicable in Jewish life. All the tractates except for *Middot* and *Kinnim* are expanded upon in the Babylonian Talmud.

KOHANIM See PRIESTS

KOHELET See ECCLESIASTES

KOHLER, KAUFMANN (1843-1926). Reform rabbi and theologian, an architect of REFORM JUDAISM in the USA. Born in Fürth, Bavaria, he received an Orthodox rabbinical education, one of his teachers being Samson Raphael HIRSCH. The thesis for which Kohler was awarded his doctorate (1867) betrayed radical tendencies that precluded any rabbinical appointment in Germany; he therefore emigrated to the United States, becoming rabbi of Congregation Beth El, Detroit, in 1869. Two years later, he moved to Chicago, then married the daughter of David EINHORN and succeeded his father-in-law as rabbi of Temple Beth El, New York, in 1879.

Kohler promoted the type of radical reforms which Einhorn had favored in Germany, introducing Sunday services and elevating the "unwritten moral law" above Torah law as well as the *halakhah*. He also opposed the attempts made by Isaac Mayer WISE to create a unified *"Minhag America"* at the expense of Reform ideology. Kohler's national position as the champion of Reform was established in 1885, when Alexander Kohut began a vigorous campaign against radicalism from the pulpit of Congregation Ahabath Chesed, New York. Week by week, Kohler answered Kohut in his sermons. This controversy led him to summon a conference of Reform rabbis in Pittsburgh, on 16-18 November 1885, at which Kohler's "Declaration of Principles" was adopted with little change. Known as the "Pittsburgh Platform," it had a decisive influence on the American Reform movement for over half a century.

Throughout his ministry, Kohler engaged in scholarly research. Having succeeded Wise as president of Hebrew Union College (1903-21), he set a far more clearly defined Reform stamp on HUC and found himself in conflict with some other members of the faculty because of his vehement anti-Zionism. Kohler's most notable work, *Jewish Theology*, appeared in 1918 (English edition). He was one of the editors of the *Jewish Encyclopedia* (1901-6) and a member of the editorial board that produced the JPSA translation of *The Holy Scriptures* (1917). Combining deep religious convictions with a rational, scientific outlook, Kohler was the chief exponent of "classical" Reform, which dominated American Reform Judaism until the late 1930s.

KOLEL (lit. "comprehensive," "all-inclusive"). Term most commonly used today to describe YESHIVOT — institutions of higher Talmudic study — specifically for married students, who receive a monthly stipend that enables them to maintain their families, and to devote themselves entirely to Torah studies. The development of this form of institution has been one of the striking features of the *yeshivah* world in Israel since the late 1960s.

R. Israel SALANTER coined the term *kolel*. In 1878, he found a wealthy man in Berlin who set aside a considerable sum of money for the purpose of establishing in Kovno a Great *Yeshivah* for young married men who left home and family to devote themselves to Torah study.

The term was also used to describe various groups of Ashkenazi Jews in pre-state Erets Israel, all of whom came from the same country or the same district of a country, and who were supported by the monies raised for them by their fellow-countrymen.

KOL NIDRÉ ("All vows"). Opening words and title of an Aramaic declaration that forms a prelude to the synagogue service on the eve of the DAY OF ATONEMENT. It solemnly remits "all vows, obligations, oaths, promises, and undertakings" of a religious nature, made by each worshiper in the course of the year, if he or she has done so unintentionally, on the spur of the moment, or under duress. Though not a prayer, this dry legal formula and its ceremonial accompaniment have been charged with emotional undertones since the medieval period, creating a dramatic introduction to the Day of Atonement on what is often dubbed "*Kol Nidré* night." Judaism discourages the taking of vows and makes no provision for the annulment of public or communal undertakings between man and man. *Kol Nidré* may therefore be considered another form of the ceremony often held by Orthodox congregations on the eve of the ROSH HA-SHANAH (New Year) festival, when undischarged religious bonds are canceled by an *ad hoc* three-man court. Over 1,000 years ago, however, leading sages opposed the whole idea of *Kol Nidré*, AMRAM Gaon (ninth century) dismissing it as a "foolish custom." The formula was accordingly not accepted by some Jewish communities, yet in time all found a place for it in their Day of Atonement ritual. The older version, adopted by Sephardim and Eastern communities, retrospectively cancels vows made "from the past Day of Atonement to this" which could not be fulfilled owing to events beyond the control of the one making the vow. A later form, introduced by

Part of an East European version of Kol Nidré.

Rabbenu TAM in 12th-century France and recited by Ashkenazim, speaks of vows due to be fulfilled in the coming year, "from this Day of Atonement to the next Day of Atonement," which may be beyond the vower's ability to discharge. Apart from that phrase, Ashkenazim chant the text in Aramaic, whereas Sephardim read the entire passage in Hebrew. Some Eastern communities have amalgamated these slightly differing versions of the formula.

Since Jewish law prohibits the convening of any rabbinical court (BET DIN) on Sabbaths and holidays, *Kol Nidré* must be recited before twilight. Congregants therefore wear their prayer shawl (*tallit*) from the point when they enter the synagogue until after the Evening Service is concluded. On no other occasion in the Jewish year is this practice followed, and it enhances the solemnity of "*Kol Nidré* night." Two officiants or wardens bearing Torah scrolls position themselves on either side of the cantor, to form a *bet din* of three, as the congregation stands and hears him first chant the words of *Bi-yeshivah shel ma'lah*: "By the authority of the tribunal on high and of the court below... we declare it lawful for prayers to be said with transgressors." This brief passage, traditionally introduced by Rabbi MEIR OF ROTHENBURG in the 13th century, once enabled repentant sinners who had been under a ban of excommunication to confess their misdeeds on the Day of Atonement and so find their way back to the communal fold. Some have identified these "transgressors" with rueful apostates or Jews converted by force in various lands throughout the Middle Ages, now secretly joining their brethren for the Day of Atonement services, but this theory is rejected by most authorities. The reader then pronounces *Kol Nidré* three times, in conformance with Jewish legal usage, the emphasis and pathos of his declaration increasing each successive time. This threefold repetition allows latecomers to hear at least part of *Kol Nidré* and also prolongs the introductory chants until nightfall, before which the Evening Service cannot begin.

From medieval times until the late 19th century, Christian anti-Semites repeatedly alleged that a Jew's word could not be trusted, producing as evidence a maliciously distorted interpretation of *Kol Nidré*. Reform Judaism excised *Kol Nidré* from its prayer book during the years 1844-1961, substituting for it Psalm 103 or Psalm 130, or the hymn *O Tag des Herrn* ("O Day of the Lord") composed by a German rabbi, Leopold Stein. Alternatively, Reform rabbis composed Hebrew prayers to fit the traditional *Kol Nidré* melody. However, this hallowed passage's authority and appeal never waned. Its psychological and emotional hold on the Jewish masses no doubt owes much to the soul-stirring, plaintive melody chanted by the Ashkenazi cantor, originating in the 16th century. Perhaps the most famous musical setting of the traditional melody was written by a non-Jewish composer, Max Bruch, in 1880.

The "*Kol Nidré* night" ceremonial, emphasizing Jewish fellowship and the sense of human inadequacy, is a psychological preparation for the soul-cleansing experience of the Day of Atonement, when Jews acknowledge their failings and undertake the kind of self-improvement that will give a new spiritual vitality to their lives in the coming year.

KOOK, ABRAHAM ISAAC (1865-1935). Rabbinical scholar and philosopher; first Ashkenazi Chief Rabbi of modern Erets Israel. Born in Greiva, a small Latvian hamlet, he received his earliest education from his father. At the age of 16 he entered the Volozhin *yeshivah* where he came under the influence of its head, R. Naphtali Tzevi Yehudah BERLIN. In 1888 Kook was appointed rabbi of Zaumel and in 1895 of Bausk.

Kook immigrated to Erets Israel in 1904 to become the Chief Rabbi of Jaffa and rapidly became involved in the developing Jewish community. He visited new agricultural settlements both to encourage and praise their pioneering efforts and to seek to influence their returning to a religious lifestyle. Kook's identification with the Zionist movement alienated some of the country's oldtime rabbinical leaders. With the approach of the SABBATICAL YEAR of 5670 (1909/1910), which posed a problem for the agricultural pioneers, Kook issued a lenient ruling permitting the nominal sale of the land to Muslims, in which he was opposed by R. Jacob David Willowsky of Safed. Since then the Chief Rabbinate in Israel has continued to abide by this lenient ruling. In 1914 Kook traveled to Europe to participate in the planned conference of the recently organized ultra-orthodox Agudat Israel which he hoped to influence towards Zionism. With the outbreak of World War I, Kook was stranded in Europe, making his home first in St. Gallen, Switzerland

Rabbi Abraham Isaac Kook, in the center, speaking at the laying of the cornerstone of a new quarter in Jerusalem, 1925.

and in 1916 becoming the rabbi of London's Maḫzikei ha-Dat synagogue.

He returned to Palestine in 1919 to assume the post of Ashkenazi Chief Rabbi of Jerusalem. With the organization of the Chief Rabbinate in 1921, Kook was elected Ashkenazi chief rabbi for Palestine. He became the guiding spirit of the new institution, viewing it as a major stage towards Jewish self-government and ultimately the restoration of the SANHEDRIN. This innovation antagonized the old rabbinical leaders and they intensified their efforts to preserve the traditional patterns of rabbinical authority. In 1921, Kook founded a *yeshivah* (talmudic academy) in Jerusalem which was to be positive towards Zionism and universal in its outlook and curriculum of studies. This *yeshivah* became known as Merkaz ha-Rav ("the Center of the Rabbi"), in honor of its founder.

Kook's uniqueness lay in his ability to synthesize many different perspectives within his own outlook. He was a Lithuanian-trained rabbinic scholar of the old school, a deeply religious mystic who took an active interest in human affairs, an advocate of the study of secular sciences to complement Torah study, and an active Zionist who bridged the worlds of both its religious and secular elements. Kook was also a prolific author; while not constructing a comprehensive system of his thought and philosophy, his writings nevertheless reflect his personal insights, mystical reflections, and manifold interests. Among his speculative and philosophic writings are *Orot, Orot ha-Kodesh*, and *Orot ha-Teshuvah*. His correspondence was published under the title of *Iggeret ha-Re'ayah*, and his novellae and responsa were published on the four divisions of the SHULḪAN ARUKH code. Kook also wrote *Halakhah Berurah*, a commentary on the Talmud which stressed its interrelationship with Jewish law, and attempted to bridge Talmudic theory with halakhic practice.

Kook, Tzevi Yehudah (1891-1982), *yeshivah* head and spiritual father of the religious nationalist organization *Gush Emunim* ("Bloc of the Faithful") which spearheaded Jewish settlement in the Administered Areas after the 1967 Six-Day War. The only son of Abraham Isaac Kook, he moved to Erets Israel with his parents in 1904. He assisted his father in the administration of the Merkaz ha-Rav *yeshivah*, succeeding him as co-head of the institution after his father's death. Viewed as the heir to his father's outlook and method in education, Kook succeeded in influencing hundreds of students from all segments of the Israel population. His stress on Zionism and the spiritual dimensions of the State of Israel made his *yeshivah* unique among such institutions.

Kook published numerous articles dealing with halakhic and philosophic attitudes towards contemporary events. He also devoted himself to editing and publishing many of his father's manuscripts.

KORBANOT See SACRIFICES AND OFFERINGS

KRANZ, JACOB BEN ZE'EV WOLF (known as the Maggid of Dubno; 1741-1804). Preacher (MAGGID) and rabbinical scholar. Born in the Lithuanian town of Zhetel (Dyatlovo), he became the community's preacher at the age of 20. Before long, however, his growing reputation led to journeys throughout Eastern Europe, where the eloquence and homespun wisdom of his sermons drew vast and admiring crowds. He spent 18 years in the city of Dubno (1768-1786) and served as preacher in Zamosc from 1789 until the end of his life. Kranz was a gifted storyteller. In the course of his travels, he collected hundreds of anecdotes and parables which he used to point his teachings. Once asked how he always managed to find the right parable for every situation, he characteristically replied with another parable. An army cadet was amazed to discover a whole series of targets drawn on a wall, each pierced with a bull's-eye through the very center. He naturally questioned the amateur marksman about his expertise. "First I shoot at the wall," came the reply, "then I chalk a circle around the bullet hole." In exactly the same way, Jacob of Dubno kept each good story in his mind, knowing that he would sooner or later find use for it. Hearing the Dubno Maggid preach in Berlin, Moses MENDELSSOHN styled him "the Jewish Aesop," although none of Kranz's parables and fables drew their characters from the animal world. His admirers included ELIJAH BEN SOLOMON ZALMAN, the Vilna Gaon, who invited him to Vilna in 1790, when he had fallen ill, to "entertain and revive" him.

Relying on Kranz's notes and their own recollections, his followers published several volumes of his works years after he died. Among them are anthologies of Kranz's parables in English and Yiddish as well as Hebrew.

SAYINGS OF THE MAGGID OF DUBNO

In Dubno, Jews tell the truth in the marketplace and tell lies in the synagogue, whereas the situation is reversed in Berlin. How so? Our Polish Jews are loyal to the Torah, fearing God at all times and checking their scales, yet on the Day of Atonement they beat their breasts and cry *Ashamnu, bagadnu...* ("We have sinned, we have been faithless!"). In Berlin, however, Jews want to get rich quickly and find an excuse for every misdemeanor, so when they recite *Ashamnu*, they are telling the plain, unvarnished truth!

At a bar mitsvah celebration, the Vilna Gaon happened to notice some guests eyeing the food laid out rather than listening to the youngster's talmudic discourse. "Gentlemen," he chided, "I see that you prefer the *Shulkhan Arukh* ('Prepared Table') to the Gemara."

KROCHMAL, NACHMAN (1785-1840). Historian, philosopher, and leader of the *Haskalah* (Movement for Enlightenment) and of the WISSENSCHAFT DES JUDENTUMS (Science of Judaism). Born in Galicia, his scholarship attracted the leading figures of the Jewish Enlightenment to Zolkiew, where he lived for most of his life.

Krochmal's interests were philosophy and history, but his chief aim was to explain Judaism against the background of its developing history throughout the ages. Somewhat reluctant to commit his teachings and ideas to writing, he was finally persuaded by his friends to do so and his great work, *Moreh Nevukhé ha-Zeman* ("Guide for the Perplexed of the Time") is the result.

Krochmal's philosophy expounds the idea of God and creation. In this he approaches several central kabbalistic ideas. God is the Absolute Being and nothing exists without Him. The transition from this Absolute Being, without Whom nothing exists, is explained as a process of Divine self-confinement. The conclusion is that God created the world out of Himself. It was this thought which led some critics of Krochmal to the belief that his philosophy approaches pure pantheism.

In his philosophy of history, he explains that in the record of every nation three stages are to be discerned: birth, vigor, and decline. Every nation's history is influenced by countless social and cultural factors, but they can all be examined and explained in the light of these three stages. Krochmal believed that Jewish history also follows these three stages, but that Jewish history is different from the histories of all other nations because Israel's decline in its third stage is followed by a rebirth and renewal to continue in a new process of birth, vigor, and decline. Israel's constant renewal derives from its special relationship with God and from its intense spiritual life. These factors in Jewish history make the Jews an eternal people.

Krochmal also made significant contributions in the study of *halakhah* (Jewish law), which he explains as an organic unity which developed naturally from the Mosaic laws through various stages of growth, calling for timely rabbinic interpretations, new ordinances, restrictions, and customs. Krochmal's work in the study of *halakhah* as an evolutionary system had a great influence on many later talmudic scholars.

L

LABOR AND LABOR LAWS Judaism stresses the intrinsic value of physical labor in countless laws and aphorisms. Adam is first placed in the Garden of Eden "to work it and guard it" (Gen. 2:15), although subsequently the hard toil involved in agriculture is seen as a punishment for Adam's disobedience (Gen. 3:17-19). Some of the early rabbis interpreted the verse "Six days shall you labor" (Ex. 20:9) as a positive commandment, and R. Judah the Exilarch stated, "Just as Israel was commanded to rest on the Sabbath, so were they commanded to work on the other six days" (*Mekhilta* on Ex. 20:9-10). R. Judah ben Betéra ruled that a person with no work to do should busy himself with a barren field, rather than sit idle (*Avot de-Rabbi Natan* 11). Abraham, Jacob, Moses, and David were all shepherds, and the prophet Amos described himself as a "herdsman and a gatherer of sycamore fruit" (Amos 7:14).

The Talmud records the occupations of many outstanding scholars. HILLEL, for example, was a woodcutter, R. Judah a baker, R. Johanan a shoemaker, R. HUNA a farmer, and R. Isaac a blacksmith. A classic dispute in the Talmud is that between R. SIMEON BAR YOḤAI and R. Ishmael. R. Simeon claimed that a person should ideally spend all his time studying the Torah, and if he were worthy, others would do all his work for him. R. Ishmael insisted that Torah study must be accompanied by an occupation. The Talmud relates that there were those who attempted to emulate R. Simeon and failed, while those who attempted to emulate R. Ishmael succeeded. Along the same lines as R. Ishmael, R. GAMALIEL said: "Great is the study of Torah together with an occupation, for laboring over both makes a man forget sin" (*Avot* 2:2). The same *mishnah* continues: "Any [study of the] Torah which is not combined with a [worldly] occupation will eventually cease and will draw sin in its wake."

MAIMONIDES castigated the practice of having Torah scholars supported by funds collected on their behalf in his commentary on Tractate *Avot* (ch. 4), where he stated that a Torah scholar should support himself by a gainful occupation. In fact, he added, a scholar whose study was supported was exploiting the Torah. Maimonides went on to show that nowhere in the Talmud were there records of Torah scholars who were sustained by donations. Some scholars were wealthy, some poor, but their income was based on what they earned from their occupations. He cites the talmudic saying, "One who does not teach his son an occupation, teaches him [by default] to be a brigand" (*Kid.* 29a).

However, not all scholars accepted Maimonides' view. In a responsum to a young man who felt that it was improper to study in a KOLEL because of Maimonides' dictum, R. Mosheh FEINSTEIN rejected this view as "the work of the evil inclination" (*YD* II, 190).

Jewish law also shows clear concern for the worker. A worker employed by the day must be paid his wages before sunrise of the following day (Lev. 19:13), while one employed by the night must be paid by the following sunset (Deut. 24:15). The Talmud goes so far as to state that an employer who withholds his workers' wages is like a person who takes the life of another (*BM*, 112a); furthermore, payment was to be made in money, not in goods (*BM*, 10:5). In his commentary on Deuteronomy 20, NAḤMANIDES notes that prisoners of war taken by Israel may be assigned to chop wood and draw water, but must be paid fair wages. Whereas an employer cannot terminate a worker's employment without cause in the middle of an agreed contract, the worker may resign at any time, even in the middle of the day (*BM*, 77a); this, in essence, gives the worker the right to strike. However, if an employer incurs a loss as a result of the worker having taken such an action, the latter may be forced to compensate him for the loss. An employer may not impose work on his workers beyond their physical capacity. He must feed his workers, and they were allowed to partake of any edible produce on which they were laboring.

The talmudic sages even bypassed biblical law in their concern to protect the worker. Whereas a person who claims that another owes him money can force the other person to swear as to his allegation, an employer sued for back wages does not have to take an oath but it is enough that the worker swears that he is owed the wages (*BM* 9:13). The sages explain this ruling by noting that an employer dealing with a number of workers may forget whether he paid one of them; the worker, on the other hand, will know very well if he has been paid or not. Although there are rules protecting the worker, the rabbinic view was not completely one-sided: the workers must work diligently and to the best of their ability, not wasting time during the working day (Maimonides, *Mishneh Torah, Hilkhut Sekhirut*, "Laws of Employment" 13:7). So careful were the sages of the worker's responsibility to his employer, that they ruled that if he recites the GRACE AFTER MEALS during working hours, he should omit the last blessing (a later addition to the Grace) in order not to deprive his employer of his services unnecessarily.

Members of a given profession may assemble and determine their working hours by a majority vote, thereby preventing any of them from working except at those times specified (*Sh.Ar.*, *ḺM* 231:28).

> **LABOR**
>
> When you eat the fruit of your own labors, you shall be happy and contented.
>
> Sweet is the sleep of the laborer.
>
> Great is labor, for it gives a man dignity.
>
> The man who lives from the labor of his hands is greater than the one who fears heaven.
>
> Better to skin a carcass for a fee in the market than to be supported by charity.
>
> Hebrew has only one word, *avodah*, for "work" and for "worship."
>
> Only manual labor can make you blessed.
>
> Man dies when he stops working.
>
> The rights of the workman always take precedence over those of his employer.

LADINO See JUDEO-SPANISH

LAG BA-OMER ("Thirty-third [day] of the OMER"). Minor festival in the Jewish calendar; its name incorporates the Hebrew letters *lamed* and *gimmel*, which have the combined numerical value of 33 (spelled "*lag*"). This festival has been observed since geonic times on 18 Iyyar, during the counting of the OMER between Passover and Shavu'ot, but its origin is uncertain. It is popularly thought to commemorate the end of a devastating plague which killed many thousands of the students of R. AKIVA during Bar Kokhba's war against Rome (132-135 CE). The additional name of "Scholars Festival" given to *Lag ba-Omer* may well reflect such a historical event.

Various theories have been proposed as to the significance of this date. One suggests that Bar Kokhba's army suffered defeats over an extended period; then, on the 33rd day of the *Omer*, his forces scored a momentary victory. This so fortified national morale that its remembrance was kept alive by an annual commemorative festivity on *Lag ba-Omer*. Another theory with a military background, though of earlier date, is presented by Josephus (*War*, 2, 16-17). He describes the outbreak of the first Jewish revolt againt Rome in 66 CE. Jewish nationalist groups which had been preparing an insurrection against the Roman oppressor decided to take up arms on 18 Iyyar, corresponding to the 33rd day of the *Omer*. In order to distract Roman attention, the scheduled date of the uprising was concealed in the term "*Lag ba-Omer*," thus disguising the actual calendar date.

Accordingly, for one reason or another, this day acquired

Left: Part of a text in pen and ink on parchment, on the "counting of the Omer" (the seven-week period between Passover and Shavu'ot); Germany, 1772. Center: Lag ba-Omer *celebrated with bonfires at Meron. Right: During the celebration three-year old boys of ultra-Orthodox families get their first haircut.*

significance in the history of Jewish nationalism. Even after their defeat, the Jews made a point of observing *Lag ba-Omer* to remind future generations of their desperate struggle for freedom. The new political circumstances resulting from the destruction of the Second Jewish Commonwealth made it impossible, however, for celebrations to be held publicly. *Lag ba-Omer* was therefore observed in secret over a period of many years, during which time its real motivation was apparently forgotten.

There are no special laws governing *Lag ba-Omer*'s observance, but the restrictions of the *Omer* period are set aside on that day by Ashkenazim. Thus, marriages may be performed, festivities (whether public or private), musical entertainment, and haircuts are permitted, and the TAḤANUN supplication is omitted in Morning and Afternoon Services. For Sephardi and Eastern Jews, *Lag ba-Omer* marks the conclusion of the mourning period, but the restrictions are only waived on the following day; thereafter, marriages can take place throughout the remaining fortnight of the *Omer* period. Sephardim call the festival *Lag la-Omer*; among their Western (Spanish and Portuguese) communities, however, no special festivities are held.

In Israel especially, some additional *Lag ba-Omer* customs emphasize the connection of this "Scholars' Festival" with the ancient war against Rome. Children enjoy a break from their normal school routine, bonfires are lit after dark, Students' Day is observed on university campuses, family picnics are arranged, and youngsters often play games with toy bows and arrows (possibly indicating a link with the Jewish-Roman War).

Other Israeli customs derive from *Lag ba-Omer*'s association with the second-century *tanna*, SIMEON BAR YOḤAI, legendary author of the ZOHAR, who, according to tradition, died on 18 Iyyar. Simeon was buried in Meron, near Safed, and to this day thousands of Sephardi and Ḥasidic Jews from all over Israel make a *Lag ba-Omer* pilgrimage to the traditional site of his grave. This mass celebration, held after nightfall in Meron, is known as *Hillula de-Rabbi Shimon bar Yoḥai* ("Festivity of R. Simeon": see HILLULA). Pious Jews visit the reputed burial places of many sages in the vicinity; they study the Zohar, sing hymns, light memorial candles, and (according to ultra-Orthodox practice) give three-year-old boys their first haircut.

LAMED VAV TSADDIKIM The "36 righteous individuals" who are to be found in each generation, according to the Babylonian Talmud, upon whom the SHEKHINAH (Divine Presence) rests, and whose very existence in the world prevents its destruction (*Sanh.* 97a-b; *Suk.* 45b). Later legend describes them as usually humble, unassuming Jews who make their living by the sweat of their brow. They are unaware of each other's existence and live in anonymity, denying their special status lest it be accidentally discovered. At times of great peril, particularly anti-Semitic violence, they emerge to rescue their fellow-Jews from danger, after which they immediately return to their previous unobtrusive lives, usually in a place where they are not known.

While the number 36 has special significance in GEMATRIA (numerology), various traditions cite different figures; one states that the presence of one single righteous person insures the world's continuing existence (*Yoma* 38b). Many legends were woven around the "36 righteous men."

In Yiddish, the *Lamed Vav tsaddikim* are referred to as *lamedvavnikim*. A considerable body of kabbalistic (16th-17th centuries) and ḥasidic (18th century) lore relates to their merit. In one set of legends, the Messiah himself is said to be one of them. It has been suggested, particularly by Gershom Scholem, the Kabbalah scholar, that these legendary figures, as well as the number 36, are related or parallel to certain non-Jewish sources.

LAMENTATIONS, BOOK OF (Heb. *Ékhah* after its first word; in the Talmud, *Kinot*, "elegies"). Book in the HAGIOGRAPHA section of the Bible consisting of five elegies; one of the FIVE SCROLLS. Its overall theological themes are: the destruction of Jerusalem and the Temple (586 BCE) and the subsequent exile of the Israelites are direct results of Judah's grievous sins and are not an accident of history; the prophets did not call Judah's faults to its attention, and the misdeeds of the prophets and priests contributed to the sinful atmosphere; and the people can blame only themselves for the destruction.

BOOK OF LAMENTATIONS

1:1-1:22	Desolation of Jerusalem
2:1-2:22	God's wrath and Zion's ruin
3:1-3:66	Man's yoke of suffering
4:1-4:22	The agony of the holy city
5:1-5:22	O Lord, remember and save us

Chapters 1, 2, and 4 are alphabetic acrostics, containing a single verse beginning with each letter of the Hebrew alphabet, while chapter 3 has three verses for each letter of the alphabet. Thus chapters 1, 2, and 4 have 22 verses each, while chapter 3 consists of 66 verses. Chapter 5, while not an acrostic, also contains 22 verses. The traditional view attributing the authorship of Lamentations to JEREMIAH may possibly be wrong on this point, but it is at least approximately right about the period of composition as being the first exilic period (586-538 BCE), when all the horrors of the destruction and the upheaval were still fresh, and the Temple was not yet rebuilt. Some critics have suggested it is the work of more than one hand. Lamentations shows no knowledge of the rise of Cyrus, king of Persia, or of any subsequent history.

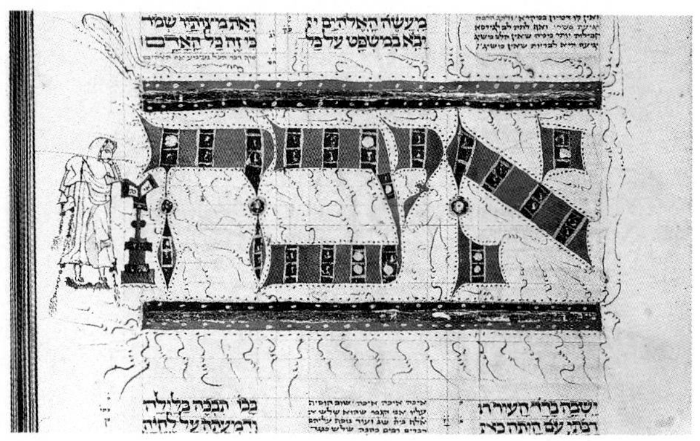

Opening page of the Book of Lamentations. From the Castro Pentateuch. *Germany, 14th century.*

In Jewish tradition, the Book of Lamentations is read on the evening of TISHAH BE-AV, the fast day commemorating the fall of the Temple. In some Ashkenazi communities, the book is read from a scroll, and the appropriate blessings are recited before the reading. Some also reread the book during the day.

LAMENTATIONS RABBAH (*Ékhah Rabbah*). Homiletical MIDRASH to the Book of LAMENTATIONS. One of the oldest Midrashim in Erets Israel (edited early in the sixth century CE), it opens with an introduction that contains no less than 36 proems (the numerical value of the Hebrew word *Ékhah* with which the Book of Lamentations begins). Then follows a homiletical commentary on Lamentations verse by verse. Noteworthy in this Midrash are ten stories about the cleverness of the people of Jerusalem; the description of the persecution of the Jews by the Romans; and the mocking of Jews in plays performed in Roman amphitheaters.

While much of the material of the Midrash is found in the Jerusalem Talmud, recent scholars feel that it did not draw directly on it, but rather on an aggadic collection which also served as a source for GENESIS RABBAH, PESIKTA DE-RAV KAHANA, and the Jerusalem Talmud.

LANDAU, EZEKIEL (1713-1793). Talmudic scholar, generally known after his book of responsa as *Noda bi-Yehudah*. Landau was also the author of a number of other works, including novellae on various talmudic tractates. His works are studied regularly in talmudic academies (*yeshivot*) and are frequently reprinted. Although born in Poland, Landau is known best as the rabbi of Prague, where he served from 1755 until his death. In that city, he founded a *yeshivah* that attracted hundreds of students from throughout the Jewish world, drawn by his legendary mastery of the talmudic literature and his intellectual acumen. As a contemporary of Jacob EMDEN, whose accusations against R. Jonathan Eybeschütz as a secret follower of SHABBETAI TSEVI had rocked the entire Jewish world, Landau attempted to mediate in the controversy. Although he was not convinced of Eybeschütz' innocence, he felt that the damage being done by the controversy required that the bitter dispute be brought to an end. Landau was a strong opponent of the Sabbateans and Frankists, as well as of the then budding Ḥasidic movement, which he was afraid might lapse into messianism. He was also a strong opponent of Enlightenment. His tremendous moral stature enabled him to offer lenient rulings on various questions of Jewish law, such as permitting shaving during the intermediate days of the festivals. This ruling, though, was overturned by the following generation of rabbis. Landau also enacted various decrees within his community aimed at avoiding ostentatious luxury.

LANDESRABBINER See RABBI

LA-SHANAH HA-BA'AH BI-YERUSHALAYIM ("Next Year in Jerusalem!"). Traditional Hebrew phrase recited especially toward the end of the Passover SEDER service and after the *shofar* (ram's horn) is sounded at the conclusion of the DAY OF ATONEMENT. The dual use of this formula, an expression of the Jew's hope and longing for the messianic Redemption, stems from a scholarly dispute recorded in the Talmud. R. Joshua held that Israel's future deliverance will take place in the month of Nisan, when the Exodus from Egypt occurred; but R. Eliezer insisted that it will take place in the month of Tishri, when the Day of Atonement occurs (*RH* 11a). As a compromise, therefore, it became the standard practice to anticipate the coming Redemption on both these occasions. "Next Year [may we be] in Jerusalem" is recited as a kind of toast after the fourth cup of wine has been drunk at the *Seder*, but in Ashkenazi congregations it is often sung to a merry traditional tune as the fast ends on Yom Kippur. On the basis of Psalm 122:3, the concluding words in Israel are *bi-Yerushalayim ha-Benuyah* ("in rebuilt Jerusalem").

LAW See HALAKHAH

LAW COURTS See BET DIN

LEAH Elder daughter of Laban, whom the patriarch JACOB married through her father's trickery, after he substituted her for her sister RACHEL, who had been promised to Jacob (Gen. 29-31). Of Jacob's thirteen children, Leah had seven — six of his twelve sons, and his only daughter, Dinah. Another two of his sons he begot from Leah's concubine, Zilpah. Although there is no reference to Leah's death, she is said to be buried beside Jacob in the Cave of MACHPELAH (Gen. 49:30-31). Both the tribe of LEVI, which also included the priests and the high priesthood, and the tribe of JUDAH, from which the Davidic dynasty issued, were descendants of

Leah. Leah is considered the third of the four MATRIARCHS.

LEAP YEAR See CALENDAR

LEAVEN, SEARCH FOR (*bedikat ḥamets*). Ceremony performed in accordance with biblical law on the night before PASSOVER eve (i.e., the night of 13-14 Nisan); when the first day of Passover falls on a Sunday, however, the search is conducted on the previous Thursday night (12-13 Nisan). The Bible's injunction (Ex. 12:15ff.) concerning the Passover festival declares: "Seven days you shall eat unleavened bread [MATSAH], but on the previous [lit. first] day you shall eliminate leaven [ḤAMETS] from your houses." Expounding this precept, the Mishnah of tractate *Pesaḥim* opens with the directive, "At (twi)light of the 14th day (of Nisan) we search for *ḥamets* by the light of the lamp."

The Talmud (*Pes.* 7b-8a) explains that this is the time when everyone is at home and the light of a lamp is "good" for searching in the dark. It also quotes a series of biblical texts which relate this external search to an inner search of man's soul (relieving it of pollution).

The laws governing *bedikat ḥamets* may be summarized as follows: (1) After Evening Service on the night before Passover eve, no work should be done or food eaten until the search for leaven has been undertaken. The householder first recites the benediction, "Who has sanctified us with His commandments and commanded us to remove the leaven." (2) He then conducts a thorough search of the house (or premises), checking every place (especially holes and crevices) where *ḥamets* may have been left in the course of the year. Should the husband be absent, his wife or another adult member of the family performs this task. (3) The search is conducted in silence. As an aid to concentration, it is customary to switch off electric lights, only an oil lamp or candle being used. (4) Since pre-Passover "spring-cleaning" will already have disposed of most leaven, small pieces of bread and crumbs are left around the house in advance (usually on paper) for the searcher to find, so that his benediction should not have been recited in vain. Certain pious Jews have ten such scraps of bread ready in accordance with the mystical practice of R. Isaac LURIA (*Ari*). (5) All unleavened bread discovered is carefully placed in a bag or other combustible container with the aid of feathers (some also use a disposable wooden spoon), tied up with the candle and feathers, and put to one side for burning the next day. (6) Once the search has been completed, a formula renouncing any leaven that remains is pronounced in Aramaic. (7) Before 10 a.m. the next morning (or as specified by the local rabbinate), the parcel of unleavened bread is burned outdoors (*bi'ur ḥamets*) and a modified version of the previous formula is then recited. (8) The first of these legal declarations is worded so as not to include unleavened items reserved for breakfast (within the time permitted) on the following morning (14 Nisan). Jewish law also permits either formula to be recited in a language (e.g., Hebrew or English) more readily understood than Aramaic.

Searching for leaven. From Bernard Picart's Cérémonies et Coutumes de tous les Juifs du Monde. *Amsterdam, 1723-43.*

LEKAḤ TOV ("Good Doctrine"). A 12th-century MIDRASH on the Pentateuch and Five Scrolls by Tobiah ben Eliezer, a resident of one of the Balkan countries, probably Greece. Its name comes from the opening verse with which the Midrash begins (Prov. 4:2). Similarly, the exposition of each weekly portion of the Pentateuch opens with a verse that contains the word "*tov*" (good), an allusion to the author's name. For his sources, the editor drew on the Jerusalem TALMUD, the halakhic and early aggadic Midrashim (some of which are no longer extant), and also on early mystical works. In his quotations from the above-mentioned sources, the author, where necessary, translates the original Aramaic into Hebrew as he does any Greek words they contain. Longer quotations are given in abridged form. The work is markedly anti-KARAITE in its polemic. The 12th-century dating is based on the author's reference to the martyrs of the First Crusades.

LEKET, SHIKHEḤAH, PE'AH (known collectively as *mattanot aniyyim*, "the gifts to the poor"). Those portions of the produce which a farmer must leave for the poor.

a) *Leket*, "gleaning." If the reapers drop wheat stalks, they may not retrieve them, but must leave them for the poor. Three or more stalks may be retrieved. By the same token, individual grapes dropped on the ground must be left for the poor. Furthermore, small clusters of grapes, which are passed over during the harvest, cannot be retrieved at a later time, and must also be left for the poor (Lev. 19:9-10). The classic example of this law being observed is the case of RUTH the Moabite, who was sent to glean in the fields of Boaz.

b) *Shikheḥah*, "forgotten." If, when bringing the harvest to the storage area, the workers leave a quantity in the field, they may not go back to pick it (Deut. 24:19). By rabbinic law, all grain or fruit not harvested must also be left.

c) *Pe'ah*, "corner." When harvesting his field, the farmer is required to leave one corner unharvested for the poor (Lev. 23:22). By Torah law, there are no minimum or maximum quantities involved, one stalk being sufficient to fulfill the obligation, but the rabbis imposed a minimum of 1/60 of the crop to be left as *Pe'ah*. Similarly, while the Torah law applies only to grain, the rabbis extended it to include vineyards and orchards.

Taken together with the poor man's TITHE that the farmer must give, these are all aspects of the social legislation of the Pentateuch, meant to aid the needy. The Pentateuch singles out widows and orphans in this regard. These laws are obligatory only in the Land of Israel, although the rabbis imposed it on other lands as well. Furthermore, while the Pentateuch only enjoins leaving these gifts for the Jewish poor, the rabbis extended the law to the non-Jewish poor as well, "in the interest of peace." See also AGRICULTURAL LAWS.

LEKHAH DODI ("Come, my Beloved"). Opening words and title of a Sabbath eve hymn written by the mystic and poet Solomon ben Moses Ha-Levi ALKABETS. His Hebrew name, Shelomoh Ha-Levi, appears as an acrostic in the first eight stanzas. He spent most of his life in Safed, where the 16th-century Lurianic Kabbalah developed. Inspired by the midrashic concept of the SABBATH as Israel's bride (Gen. R. 11.9), Alkabets and his fellow mystics adopted the practice of leading a joyful procession through the countryside around Safed each week, chanting psalms and verses from the Song of Songs to welcome the Sabbath Queen and Bride. That personification also derived from the rabbis (*Shab.* 119a), and the customs associated with the Day of Rest's inauguration in Safed eventually gained permanence in the Sabbath eve service. *Lekhah Dodi*, composed around 1540, ranks first among all the hymns written in Safed and quickly won a place in most liturgical rites, German Ashkenazim having recited it since the early 17th century. A direct quotation from the Song of Songs (7:12) may be found in the two opening words, which allude to the Safed practice of "going out into the field" as the Sabbath drew near. Stylistically, this hymn is a patchwork of biblical phrases and echoes, enhanced by puns, alliteration, and multiple rhyme.

From LEKHAH DODI

Come, my Beloved, with chorus of praise;
Welcome Sabbath the Bride, Queen of our days.

Come, let us all greet Queen Sabbath sublime,
Fountain of blessings in every clime.
Anointed and regal since earliest time,
In thought she preceded Creation's six days.

Recited toward the end of *Kabbalat* SHABBAT, which forms a prelude to the Friday evening service, *Lekhah Dodi* may be sung responsively or else by the entire congregation. In many communities, mourners remain outside while the hymn is recited and then enter the synagogue to be greeted with the traditional words of comfort. Before singing the final stanza, worshipers turn to face west, toward the entrance of the synagogue, and bow in symbolic homage to the Sabbath Queen as she makes her appearance. Some of the stanzas are omitted in Reform temples. No less than 2,000 different melodies have been used for *Lekhah Dodi* over the past 350 years, and others are still being composed.

LÉL SHIMMURIM ("night of vigil"). Term for the first night (outside Israel, first two nights) of PASSOVER. The Bible says of the night of the EXODUS from Egypt (Ex. 12:42), "It is a night of vigil for the Lord to bring them out from the land of Egypt; that same night is the Lord's, one of vigil for all the children of Israel throughout the ages." The sages interpreted the word *shimmurim* as meaning "being protected"; thus *lél shimmurim* implies that on the first night of Passover all of Israel are protected. This idea underlies the custom of opening the front door in the midst of the Passover eve SEDER service, as a sign that one has no fear of harm that night. For the same reason, the lengthy prayer said before retiring, which is a prayer against harm during the night, is omitted, and only the first paragraph of the SHEMA is recited.

LESHON HA-RA (evil speech). Talebearing, slander, considered in both biblical and talmudic writings, a most serious offense. The negative biblical commandment is found in Leviticus 19:16: "You shall not spread slanderous tales among your people." *Leshon ha-ra* includes all forms of talebearing, the mildest of which is gossip (Heb. *reḇilut*). Even a "trace of evil speech" is prohibited. The worst offense is deliberately speaking falsely, with the intention of injuring the other party, the most extreme example of which is accusations made to the ruling authorities with the intention of endangering a fellow Jew's livelihood, or even his life. Perpetrators of such an offense are designated as *malshinim* (informers) of whom the AMIDAH prayer is highly condemnatory.

The gravity of *leshon ha-ra* within the biblical context is indicated by the severity of the punishment dealt out to offenders. Miriam was stricken with leprosy for having spoken ill of her brother Moses, even though what she said about him was true (Num. 12). The talmudic sages even went so far as to assert that slander is worse than the capital sins of murder, idolatry, and incest. This in part derives from their belief in the great power inherent in speech, derived from the biblical saying "Death and life are in the power of the tongue" (Prov. 15:2). They frequently compare the slanderer to the thief and the adulterer, and deny him a portion in the world to come. Four categories of people will not be received into the Divine Presence: flatterers, liars, slanderers, and scorners (*Sot.* 42a). The slanderer is regarded as killing three persons: himself, the one who listens, and the person being slandered.

The most comprehensive discussion of all the issues pertaining to *leshon ha-Ra* is found in the work of the modern halakhic scholar ḤAFETZ ḤAYYIM.

LESHON HA-RA

There are three sins that men encounter daily and cannot avoid: impure thoughts, lack of devotion in prayer, and slander.

Keep your mouth from evil talk and live a life of peace.

What is spoken in Rome may kill in Syria.

Silence is good for the wise. How much more so for the foolish.

The punishment of the liar is that he is not believed even when he speaks the truth.

LEVIATHAN (*livyatan*). Name applied to various types of sea monster in biblical and rabbinic literature. From some references it would appear that *livyatan* meant a whale (Ps. 104:26) or a crocodile (Job 40:25-41:26). Elsewhere, the allusions are to mythological monsters armed with seven heads, at war with the Creator, and doomed to destruction (Ps. 74:14, Job 3:8, Isa. 27:1). The concept of Leviathan has a parallel in the monstrous Lotan of Ugaritic mythology. Associated with Leviathan is the mighty Behemoth (Job 40:15-24), and in the Apocrypha (II Esdras 6.49-52) these two creatures are said to have existed since the fifth day of Creation. According to aggadic sources, they are the "great sea monsters" of Genesis (1:21) which will provide a banquet for the righteous in the afterlife (Lev. R. 13.3; *BB* 74b-75a). God will then slaughter both Leviathan and Behemoth or the Wild Ox (*shor ha-bar*), serve their meat at the "eschatological feast," make a tent from Leviathan's skin, and supply the righteous banqueters with "wine stored since Creation."

The Leviathan, shown here as a large fish, and the Behemoth, as a wild ox. From a page of the Leipzig Maḥzor *(prayer book).*

LEVI BEN GERSHOM (1288-1344, known by his acronym *Ralbag* or as Gersonides). Philosopher, talmudist, mathematician, astronomer, and exegete. He wrote a monumental commentary on the Pentateuch and on most of the rest of the Bible. As a philosopher, he followed in the Aristotelian thinking of MAIMONIDES. Gersonides was born and lived in Provence, France, throughout his life. He was on close terms with leading Church figures of his time, and lectured on astronomy at the papal university and medical school.

Gersonides wrote a commentary on the first tractate of the Babylonian Talmud, *Berakhot*. He was also the author of a lengthy work on astronomy. His major work, though, which he wrote between 1317 and 1329, was *Sefer Milḥamot Adonai* ("The Book of the Wars of the Lord"), a philosophical treatise which the author saw as complementing those areas not sufficiently dealt with by earlier philosophers, especially Maimonides. In this volume, he deals with six major topics, including the nature of the soul, Divine Providence, and the eternity of matter. After giving the views of the philosophers who preceded him, Gersonides then proceeds to express his own views rationally. He also shows how his position is in keeping with the Torah. Nevertheless, Gersonides' views were attacked by later rabbinic authorities, in particular by Ḥasdai CRESCAS, who felt that some of his unorthodox views were heretical and should not be studied. Gersonides is quoted extensively in rabbinic literature.

LEVI YITSḆAK OF BERDICHEV (c.1740-1810). Rabbi and Ḥasidic leader. Perhaps the most greatly loved figure in ḤASIDISM after Israel BA'AL SHEM TOV, he is known within the movement as "the Berdichever *Rov*," since unlike most Ḥasidic masters he was both a TSADDIK and a communal rabbi (in Berdichev). To achieve this was difficult at a time when the traditional rabbinate in Eastern Europe bitterly opposed the Ḥasidic movement. In 1766, Levi Yitsḥak became a disciple of DOV BAER, the Maggid of Mezhirech, and he is considered to be a leading exponent of the Maggid's teachings.

A few years after his appointment as rabbi of Zhelechow in Poland, Levi Yitsḥak had to resign because of the community's strong opposition to his Ḥasidic views. The story was repeated when he became rabbi of Pinsk in Belorussia. Reliable reports indicate that, as a result of the persecution to which he was subjected by the MITNAGGEDIM, Levi Yitsḥak suffered a nervous breakdown; he recovered, however, and eventually found peace in the rabbinate of Berdichev, where he remained from 1785 until his death.

Levi Yitsḥak's role in Ḥasidic lore is that of an untiring advocate of the Jewish people before the throne of God. "You always make demands of Your people Israel," he is said to have protested. "Why not help them in their troubles?" When Levi Yitsḥak noticed a Jew decked in *tallit* and *tefillin* interrupting his prayers to grease the wheels of his cart, he turned his eyes heavenward and declared: "Lord, what a wonderful people You have! Even when they grease their cartwheels, they do not forget to wear their *tallit* and *tefillin*."

His two-part work, *Kedushat Levi*, was published in Slavuta (1798) and Berdichev (1811), since when it has gone through many editions. Though not strikingly original, this is a very readable account of Ḥasidic doctrine in the form of a running commentary on the Torah and the rabbinic *Aggadah*. HUMILITY, a special theme of the book, is for Levi Yitsḥak a religious value. The humble man need not be unaware of his attainments and worth, but he must realize that all he has achieved and is capable of achieving means nothing when humanity's insignificance before the majesty of God is taken into account. One cannot strive to be humble for that would be mere pretense. It is only as a result of profound reflection on God filling all the worlds, upper and lower, that humility penetrates man's heart in an effortless way.

APHORISMS OF LEVI YITSḤAK OF BERDICHEV

I don't wish to know why I suffer, only whether it is for Your sake.

Here in Exile, God Himself is in Exile.

Whether a man really loves God can be determined by the love he displays for his fellowman.

A tailor informed Levi Yitsḥak of the way he had argued with God on the Day of Atonement, saying: "I may have kept leftover cloth or eaten without first performing an ablution, but are these offenses so terrible? You, Lord, have committed far greater transgressions, snatching infants from their mothers and mothers from their babies. So let's call it quits — if You will forgive me, I'll forgive You." Said Levi Yitsḥak to the tailor: "Why did you let God off so lightly? Had you really pressed the Almighty, He would have been compelled to forgive the entire Jewish people!"

When a man believes he is distant from his Creator, it is then that he is especially near.

LEVIRATE MARRIAGE (*yibbum*). Marriage contracted between a widow (*yevamah*) whose husband has died childless, and the brother of her deceased husband (*yavem* or *levir*). The intent of the commandment requiring such a marriage is that "the first son that she bears shall be accounted to the dead brother, that his name may not be blotted out in Israel" (Deut. 25:5-6). In Genesis 38, the episode of Judah and Tamar shows that levirate marriage was an ancient custom among the Israelites as well as among neighboring peoples. One of the basic differences between the Genesis story and the laws in Deuteronomy is that the former has no stated provision for the release via *ḥalitsah*, the ceremony required when the *levir* refuses to marry his brother's widow. In the latter case, Deuteronomy provides for a ceremony so that the widow and her brother-in-law can be absolved from marriage. The widow summons the *levir* before the elders, and if he insists in his refusal, "she pulls the shoe off his foot, spits in his face (the sages interpret this as 'spits in front of him') and declares, 'Thus shall be done to the man who will not build up his brother's house'" (Deut. 25:7-9). This ceremony is called *ḥalitsah* from the Hebrew *ḥalats*, to pull off the shoe. Until the widow undergoes either levirate marriage or *ḥalitsah*, she is forbidden to marry another man.

The exposition of the laws relating to levirate marriage is to be found in the talmudic tractate, YEVAMOT. First, to clarify that it applies only to the widow who has had no offspring at all, the word *ben* (son) in Deuteronomy 25:5 has been interpreted as including a daughter. Therefore, the commandment for levirate marriage applies only when the deceased has had no issue at all, either from the widow, or from another wife. This includes a child conceived while the husband was still alive but not born until after his death, even if that child did not survive (*Yev.* 2:5, 22b; *Nid.* 5:3).

The Mishnah also explains that the obligation of levirate marriage applies only to brothers of the deceased who were alive at the time of his death. This includes an infant brother born any time prior to the husband's death, in which case the widow is obligated to wait until the younger brother (assuming there are no others) reaches the age of 13 and one day, when he is considered an adult by Jewish law. Then he can either marry her or give *ḥalitsah* (*Nid.* 5:3; *Yev.* 105b).

The obligation applies only if the widow is still capable of having children. Once the husband is dead, his widow and his brother are linked together, *zikkah* ("tied") being the official term. Her status becomes that of a *shomeret yavam*, waiting for the levirate marriage to take place. The waiting period between the death and the levirate marriage or *ḥalitsah* is three months after the husband's death (*Yev.* 4:10).

Technically, the biblical commandment does not obligate the widow and her brother-in-law to have an official wedding ceremony because there exists, by law, this *zikkah* which binds them as if they were wife and husband. The talmudic sages felt something was needed and required a marriage ceremony which is called *ma'amar* (declaration) and not *kiddushin*, the name applied to the regular ceremony (*Tosef. Yev.* 7:2, *Yev.* 52a).

In the post-talmudic age there was considerable debate over whether levirate marriage or *ḥalitsah* was to be preferred. At the Academy of Sura in Babylonia, levirate marriage was the choice; at Pumbedita, it was *ḥalitsah*. The major Sephardi authorities were in favor of levirate marriage, arguing that there had to be a reason for the entire process, else the Bible and Talmud would not have spelled it out. The Ashkenazi scholars in Europe, on the other hand, stressed that *ḥalitsah* should be practiced.

In Palestine in 1944 the Chief Rabbinate made a *takkanah* (enactment) requiring the levir to maintain the widow until he released her by *ḥalitsah*. A later *takkanah* of the Israeli rabbinate in 1950 made it obligatory upon the levir to grant *ḥalitsah*, thus freeing the woman for remarriage to someone else. The levir was not permitted to marry her even if he so desired. This *takkanah* was made applicable to Sephardim and Eastern Jewish communities because until then they practiced polygamy and upheld the commandment of the levirate marriage when necessary. In 1953 Israel's parliament codified the marriage and divorce laws giving the rabbinical courts complete authority over the act of *ḥalitsah*. If the levir is ordered by the courts to give *ḥalitsah*, and he has not done so after three months, the authorities can order his imprisonment.

Engraving showing the ceremony performed by a widow exempting her from a levirate marriage. Nuremberg, 1724.

Reform Judaism has eliminated levirate marriage as an operative commandment and thus has ruled out *ḥalitsah* as well. Conservative Judaism has also invalidated levirate marriage, but there is still some discussion as to whether the ceremony of *ḥalitsah* is required. Orthodox Judaism still follows the rabbinic ruling that a woman who has undergone the ceremony of *ḥalitsah* is put in the same category as a divorcee, and thus a *kohen* (priest) is forbidden to marry her. Since the Reform and Conservative do not follow the priest-divorcee ruling in general, this ruling is not applicable for them.

The ceremony of *ḥalitsah* is performed before a rabbinical court of five. The widow reads the biblical passage dealing with levirate marriage and *ḥalitsah* (Deut. 25:7-10), unlaces and pulls off the levir's right shoe (which has to be of leather with no metal component), and spits on the ground in front of him.

LEVITES The tribe descended from Levi, third son of the patriarch JACOB. The *kohanim* — PRIESTS — are a sub-group of the Levites, representing the direct male descendants of AARON, the High Priest, who belonged to the tribe of Levi.

According to the Bible, the roles eventually assigned to this tribe were originally reserved for the first-born. After the sin of the GOLDEN CALF, in which the first-born participated but the Levites abstained, the Levites were chosen for the special mission of serving in the SANCTUARY and later in the TEMPLE. The Pentateuch describes how the Levites and the first-born were counted. As the number of first-born exceeded the number of Levites, the excess number of first-born had to be redeemed by giving five shekels per head to the priests. By this process, the sanctity was transferred from the first-born to the Levites (Num. 3:11-13). The ceremony of *pidyon ha-ben* — the redeeming of the first-born — relates back to the original sanctity of the first-born (see FIRST-BORN, REDEMPTION OF).

Unlike the other tribes, for which the census in the desert included all males who were 20 years or more, the members of the tribe of Levi were numbered from the age of one month, and came to a total of about 22,000. The Midrash explains that unlike the other tribes, among which all those who were 20 years or older died before the Israelites entered Canaan, the members of the tribe of Levi did not die.

The Levites were responsible for carrying the different parts of the Sanctuary and its vessels as the Israelites moved from one location to another in the wilderness. Each of the three clans within the Levite tribe — Gershon, Kehat and Merari — was each assigned to carry specific items. When the tribes camped around the Sanctuary, the Levites were in the inner perimeter, while the other tribes camped in the outer perimeter.

The Levites were charged with teaching the people the Torah (Deut. 33:10). As their calling precluded them from agricultural pursuits, they were not given land, as were the other tribes. Instead, those who were not connected with the Temple lived in 48 cities spread throughout Canaan (Josh. 21). In lieu of the agricultural produce raised by the other tribes, the Levites were granted a TITHE of all produce, of which they had in turn to give a tithe to the priests.

The Levites assisted the priests in the Temple, and were the Temple singers and musicians (see MUSIC). They also served in the Temple administration and as gatekeepers. The Mishnah (*Tam.* 7:4) records the different psalms recited by the Levites on each day of the week. The only relic of this service in the Temple to have survived is the law that the Levites wash the hands of the priests prior to the priestly blessing in the synagogue. The Levites are also called up second, after the priests, to the READING OF THE LAW.

LEVITICAL CITIES See ASYLUM

LEVITICUS, BOOK OF The third book of the PENTATEUCH known in Hebrew as *Va-Yikra* ("And He called") from the opening word. The sages referred to it as *Torat Kohanim* ("The Priests' Manual"), in view of the book's content. This was given the translation of *Levitikos* in the (Greek) Septuagint, as the word "Levites" also connoted priests in the Hellenistic era.

According to the Masoretic tradition, Leviticus has 27 chapters and 859 verses. The Babylonian cycle of readings (which is followed today by all Jewish communities) divides the book into ten pericopes (*sedarot*), but according to the Palestinian triennial cycle of Second Temple times, it contains 25 sections. Jewish tradition maintains that Leviticus, in common with the other books of the Pentateuch, was dictated by God to Moses.

Opening page of the Book of Leviticus decorated with micrographic writing. Germany, 1290.

BOOK OF LEVITICUS

1:1 — 7:38	Laws of the sacrifices
8:1 — 10:20	Consecration of the priests to work in the tabernacle
11:1 — 15:33	Forbidden foods and laws of ritual impurity
16:1 — 16:34	The Day of Atonement
17:1 — 17:16	Laws of ritual slaughter
18:1 — 20:27	Laws of holiness
21 — 22:33	Ritual impurity of priests
23:1 — 23:44	The festivals
24:1 — 24:23	Laws concerning the *menorah*, the showbread, and the blasphemer
25:1 — 25:55	The Sabbatical and jubilee years
26:1 — 26:46	The Blessing and the Admonition
27:1 — 27:34	Pledges to the Sanctuary.

From the standpoint of Bible criticism, Leviticus derives from a single priestly source (known as Source P), although some term Lev. 17-26 "the Holiness Code" and assign it to another source (H). While Jewish tradition regards the book as an integral part of the Torah given by God on Mount Sinai, critical scholarship has different views concerning the era in which it was composed. For example, it has been suggested that Leviticus was the last volume of the Pentateuch to have been edited, and that the editing was only completed after the Return to Zion from Babylonia. On the other hand, Yeḫezkel Kaufmann, the modern Israeli Bible scholar, considered Leviticus to be the most ancient source, a remnant of the laws governing sacrifices on the high places. The Jerusalem scholar, Mosheh David Cassuto, declared that the book is actually a collection of traditions which were handed down to Moses and from one generation to the next, all of them beginning: "The Lord spoke to Moses, saying." Thus, according to Cassuto, there is no reason to claim that the volume is much later than the time of Moses.

LEVITICUS RABBAH MIDRASH on the Book of LEVITICUS. It is a collection of 37 expositions arranged according to the sections of the (Palestinian) triennial READING OF THE LAW. Each exposition is an independent unit with a specific theme, starts with one or more introductions, generally based on a number of verses drawn from the Hagiographa, and concludes with a verse that links up with the midrashic sermon that follows. The purpose of the introduction, which is sometimes more extensive than the sermon which follows, is to demonstrate the inner unity of Scripture. The sermon concludes with a brief blessing and some words of consolation.

The sages cited in Leviticus Rabbah are exclusively third and fourth century Palestinian *amoraim*. The language is a mixture of Hebrew and Galilean Aramaic with an admixture of Greek. Its origin in Erets Israel is evidenced not only by its language and by the authorities it cites, but also by the numerous locales it mentions. Moreover, the occasional *halakhah* or custom quoted correspond with those found in the Jerusalem Talmud. It was edited some time in the fifth century, probably in Tiberias.

LEX TALIONIS See RETALIATION

LIBERAL JUDAISM See REFORM JUDAISM

LIEBERMAN, SAUL (1898-1984) Talmudic scholar. Born in Russia, his early training was at the Mir and Slobodka *yeshivot*. After studying in France, Lieberman moved in 1929 to Palestine, where he studied philology and classical literature at the Hebrew University. For a few years he was an instructor at the university and then became dean of the Harry Fischel Institute in Jerusalem. In 1940 he moved to the Jewish Theological Seminary of America in New York, where he was professor of Talmud and later rector of the Rabbinical School.

His early interest was in the Jerusalem Talmud. In the 1930s he published a commentary on that work and a brief commentary on the TOSEFTA. Subsequently, he began to issue a critical edition of the *Tosefta* on the entire Talmud, which he entitled *Tosefta Ki-Feshuta*. Over half this work appeared before his death, and further volumes were produced posthumously by his students.

Lieberman's expertise in the classical world made it possible for him to identify many of the influences of Greek and Latin culture and language in rabbinic literature. His two volumes, *Greek in Jewish Palestine* and *Hellenism in Jewish Palestine*, are important contributions in their field.

Lieberman's many essays, books, and critical editions of rabbinic texts provided new directions for understanding the life, institutions, beliefs, and literary products of Jewish Palestine in the talmudic period. The Lieberman Institute, established in Jerusalem by the Jewish Theological Seminary in his memory, is placing on computer all manuscripts of the Babylonian Talmud in order to produce a definitive text.

LIFE The sanctity of life is a supreme Jewish value, as life is a gift of God. After creating the natural phenomena and the earth's plant life and animals, God "breathed into man's nostrils the breath of life" (Gen. 2:7). Thus, human life is different from the rest of creation, for it embodies the image of God and demands the IMITATION OF GOD.

In biblical thought the COMMANDMENTS of God to man form a "tree of life" (Prov. 3:18) and through loving God and heeding His commandments, the Jew "shall have life and shall long endure" (Deut. 30:20). God also presents the human being with the choice between life and good on the one hand, death and evil on the other, and enjoins him to "choose life that you and your seed shall live" (Deut. 30:15-19).

The words in Leviticus 18:5 "to live by them [i.e., the commandments]" are interpreted in rabbinic teaching to mean that God's commandments are to be a means of life, not destruction, for His children. Therefore, with the exception of three prohibitions (idolatry, bloodshed, and sexual license), all commandments of the law may be violated if life is endangered.

While one is alive, every effort must be made to enhance life, both in its physical and spiritual dimension. The destruction of a single life (*Sanh.* 4.5) is considered tantamount to the destruction of the whole world, just as the saving of a life is the saving of an entire world. Although the Bible defines the desecration of the Sabbath as a capital crime, *pikku'aḥ nefesh* (the endangerment of life) supersedes the Sabbath commandments. In the same spirit, insuring the health of the mother and infant during childbirth or feeding a sick person on the Day of Atonement is more important than the observance of any of the commandments. These acts are not merely desirable, they are required by Jewish law.

Thanksgiving for the beauty and sanctity of life is expressed in BENEDICTIONS to be recited on various occasions. RAV's comment on the last verse of Psalms, "Let everything that breathes praise the Lord" is that "we must thank God for every fragrant breath that we breathe."

See also DEATH; RESURRECTION; SOUL, IMMORTALITY OF.

LILITH The main female character in Jewish DEMONOLOGY, from biblical times through the Middle Ages and the modern period. Originally Lilith referred to a certain type of evil spirit; only in the Middle Ages was she identified as a specific demon, the first wife of Adam and consort of Samael.

Lilith's origins lie in Babylonian demonology, which mentions male and female evil spirits named Lilu and Lilithu. The actions of these spirits include the seduction of men and endangering of women in childbirth. Lilin and Lilith are names for types of evil spirits in the Talmud and in midrashic literature. Lilith is mentioned once in the Bible: "Wildcats shall meet hyenas, goat-demons shall greet each other; There too the lilith shall repose and find herself a resting place" (Isa. 34:14).

Lilith is described in the Talmud as a winged creature with long hair (*Er.* 100b, *Nid.* 24b) who haunts people sleeping alone in their homes (*Shab.* 151b). The Talmud recounts that during the time that Adam lived separated from Eve, he gave birth to spirits, demons, and liliths (*Er.* 18b). According to later traditions, it was Lilith who seduced Adam and bore from him spirits and demons.

According to Jewish folklore, Lilith is particularly threatening to newborn babies. Already in ancient times, it was customary to write AMULETS for protection against her.

Amulet for the protection of a newborn child against Lilith.

The geonic text *Alphabet of Ben Sira* views Lilith as a specific demon, as does kabbalistic literature. In the writing of 13th-century kabbalists, especially in the ZOHAR, Lilith is described as the wife of Samael and mother of the demons. In kabbalistic literature, too, Lilith retains her role as strangler of babies and seductress of sleeping men for the purpose of conceiving demons.

LITURGY In First Temple times, PRAYER was individual and a formulated ritual of public worship was still unknown. An exception was the prescribed biblical ceremony for the tithing of the FIRST FRUITS, *Viddu'i Bikkurim*. With a basket of choice harvest, the ancient Israelite approached the priest and declared, "I acknowledge this day before the Lord your God that I have entered the land which the Lord swore to our fathers to give us" (Deut. 26:3). The priest set the basket down in front of the altar as the pilgrim uttered a prayer praising God, who had freed His people from Egyptian slavery and brought them to a land of milk and honey (Deut. 26:5-10). The confessions of the High Priest found in the Book of Leviticus (16:21) were probably formalized as well, although their texts are extant only in later talmudic sources (*Yoma* 3:8). References to praying three times daily are found in Daniel (6:10) and Psalms (55:17), but without mention of a defined ritual. The priests of the First Temple were expected "to stand every morning to thank and praise the Lord and likewise at evening" according to I Chronicles 23:30. Although selections from the Psalms were chanted by levitical choirs in the course of theses daily services, there is no evidence of lay participation.

The MISHNAH states that priests serving in the Second Temple shared in a short liturgy consisting of the SHEMA (Deut 6:4), the TEN COMMANDMENTS (Ex. 20:3-17), and the PRIESTLY BLESSING (Num. 6:24-26). The first public prayer responses probably began in this setting, when those present with sacrifices would bow and praise God aloud after the officiating priests (*Tam.* 5:1, 7:3; *Ber.* 11b). It was during this era that the whole congregation began to pray at fixed times and according to an order of prayers attributed to the Men of the GREAT ASSEMBLY (*Ber.* 33a; *Meg.* 17b, 25a). Regular weekday services were held four times daily by the *ma'amadot*, the delegations of representatives from 24 districts of the country, part of whom were present at the Temple sacrifices, and the rest assembled concurrently in their hometowns. These liturgies were given the names *Shaḇarit* (morning), *Musaf* (additional), *Minḇah* (afternoon), and *Ne'ilat She'arim* (evening, literally "closing of the [Temple] gates").

Several orders of prayers coexisted until GAMALIEL II forged an accepted standard after the destruction of the Second Temple in 70 CE (*Ber.* 28b), when prayer services officially replaced the sacrifices that could no longer be offered (*Ber.* 26b). The new ritual, *avodah she-ba-lev* (service of the heart), was conducted in synagogues wherever Jews lived by individuals distinguished by learning and not by their priestly lineage alone. The obligatory core of the liturgy, which has remained unchanged in its fundamental form from that time, includes the prayer formula "*Barukh attah Adonai...*" ("Blessed are You, O God..."), the requirement for reciting the *Shema* twice daily with its attendant blessings (three in the morning and four in the evening), and the daily AMIDAH, also known as the *Tefillah*, of 19 benedictions and recited twice daily in lieu of the morning and afternoon Temple sacrifices. On special occasions, such as the Sabbath and festivals, when the additional sacrifice had been offered in the Temple, an additional *Amidah* was included, which became distinguished in time by special prayers for the restoration of the sacrificial service and pilgrimages to Jerusalem. Ideally, prayers were recited by a quorum of ten adult male worshipers (MINYAN). They could also be recited by the individual, in which case certain parts of the liturgy, including the KADDISH, KEDUSHAH, and READING OF THE LAW, were omitted. It was not long before the *ma'ariv* or *arevit* (evening) *amidah* came to be regarded as a daily requirement as well (*Ber.* 27b). The ALÉNU prayer, originally from the New Year's liturgy, and the *Kaddish*, constitute the concluding prayers of every service.

In an attempt to guard against mechanical repetition of the same formulas, and also to spark the worshiper's personal meditation, Jewish liturgy encouraged private prayers and petitions, once the prescribed service had been completed (*Ber.* 29b; TJ.*Ber.* 4:3). Talmudic examples of these devotions, known variously as *devarim*, *teḇinnot* (see TEḴINNAH and *taḇanunim* (see TAḴANUN) have been preserved in tractate *Berakhot* (16b-17a) and found a permanent place in PRAYER BOOKS through the ages. Psalms also served for personal meditation and became obligatory in the form of the HALLEL for festivals (*RH 4:7; Ta'an.* 3:9).

Reflecting the Judaic attitude that study is a form of worship, portions of the Pentateuch and the Prophets were read publicly during the prayer service. This was already considered a venerated practice in the time of the Mishnah, when specific texts and the ceremonial calling of individuals to bless the readings were fixed (*Meg.* 3:4ff).

By the end of the talmudic period and especially in Erets Israel, the prayer service had become supplemented by PIYYUTIM, liturgical hymns and whole prayers rendered poetically.

Piyyutim distinguished the liturgical rite of Erets Israel from that of Babylonia from early geonic times and flourished until the 12th century. The Erets Israel rite is also characterized by a triennial cycle of the reading of the Pentateuch, its particular recension of the benedictions of the *Amidah*, and an introductory blessing before the recitation of the *Shema*. The Babylonian rite is initially recorded in *Seder Rav* AMRAM GAON (9th cent.), which serves as the first ordering of prayer texts with their halakhic requirements. This liturgical arrangement signaled the end of a ban against committing the prayers to writing but was meant exclusively for communal prayer leaders. The first authoritative *siddur* (prayer book) for the ordinary worshiper was edited by SAADIAH GAON (10th cent.), who produced a logical and economical order of the prayers with a commentary in the Arabic vernacular of the people.

From these two ancient liturgical traditions, Erets Israel and Babylonia, various rites developed throughout the Jewish world (see NUSAḴ). The former gave rise to the Romanian (Greek) rite of the Byzantine Empire, the Roman rite (*minhag ha-Lo'azim*) of Italian Jewry, and the northern French and Ashkenazi rite of Western and central Europe. The last of these gave birth to the Sephardi rite (which beginning on the Iberian peninsula spread to Western Europe, North Africa and the Middle East, and the New World after the Expulsion), the Provencal rite of Southern France, and the Yemenite rite (*minhag Teman*). The Ḥasidic rite of the 18th century, although borrowing aspects of the Sephardi tradition and hence known as *Nosaḥ Sefarad*, utilized liturgical poems (*piyyutim*) that are generally Ashkenazi. In addition to the *piyyutim*, SELIḤOT (penitential prayers), and KEROVOT (hymns inserted after each *Amidah* benediction on festivals) distinguish all the rites one from the other, since the liturgical structure uniformly follows that set down by Rav Amram. The Ashkenazi and Sephardi rites are the two most widely in use today. Among Ashkenazim, it became customary to produce the liturgy for the festivals in a separate volume known as the MAḤZOR. Wherever Jews lived, the language of liturgy was Hebrew (with some prayers in Aramaic).

The synagogue service was a prime focus of innovation in response to the Emancipation and Enlightenment from the early 19th century. In an attempt to stem the tide of assimilation and conversion, the reformers of Central Europe introduced new prayer forms intended to conform with the cultural, spiritual, and intellectual style of a new generation of modern Jews. Modeled after the popular Protestant worship of the day, the service was now conducted in the vernacular as well as in Hebrew, included a sermon, and was considerably shortened by altering and/or eliminating prayers, *piyyutim*, and study portions. New Western melodies to the accompaniment of a choir and organ were introduced (see MUSIC), as well as the reading of the Pentateuch and prophetical portions without the traditional chant. Prayers that were seen as representing anachronisms were abandoned, such as the Aramaic YEKUM PURKAN (asking blessing upon the Babylonian exilarch), the Priestly Blessing (the blessing of the congregation by the *kohanim* [priests]), and even the KOL NIDRÉ in the liturgy for the Day of Atonement, although the last was reinstated (after rephrasing) by popular demand. In addition, this universalistic attitude dictated various changes, such as alteration of the prayers in which men thank God for not having been made a woman or a non-Jew, and the deletion of references to Zion and its rebuilding and to reinstating the Temple's sacrificial service (and also to resurrection).

The Conservative movement has also produced prayer books suited to its particular theological position. For the past half-century it has published several editions for daily use, for Sabbath and festivals, and for the HIGH HOLIDAYS as well as special prayer booklets for TISHAH BE-AV and for *Seliḥot* (penitential prayers) and its own editions of the Passover HAGGADAH. In general, the Conservative liturgy follows the accepted traditional Ashkenazi prayer book, with the following main differences: (1) References to the hope for the restoration of sacrifices are either omitted or changed to the historical past tense. (2) The early morning benediction to be recited by a male worshiper thanking God "Who has not made me a woman," is amended to a perhaps earlier text: "Who has made me in His image" — to be read by women as well as men. The next two blessings are couched in the positive, "Who has made me a Jew" and "Who has made me free." (3) There is a more explicit reference to universal peace by adding the word *ba-olam* (in the world) in the daily prayers for peace, *Sim Shalom*. (4) The *Yekum Purkan* prayer for the schools and the sages of the ancient academies of Babylon has been omitted. On the other hand, several new prayers, meditations, and readings have been added as supplementary passages for contemplation, study, or responsive reading. (5) In most Conservative synagogues the *kohanim* (priests) do not ascend to the ark to chant the priestly benediction. (6) There is a reluctance to repeat the *Amidah*. This certainly applies to the Additional Service *Amidah*, which is not repeated by the reader following the silent prayer of the congregation. However, on the High Holidays, the usual traditional practice is followed.

As Judaism in all its denominational manifestations spread to North America, Jewish liturgical development progressed in far-reaching directions, especially during the last half-century. Pioneers in creative liturgy have provided the worshiper with an entire spectrum of prayerful compositions, from the most avant-garde innovation and adaptation to the most faithful preservation of the traditional forms. Historical events inspire new liturgies, as in those that commemorate Holocaust Remembrance Day, Israel INDEPENDENCE DAY, and Jerusalem Reunification Day. Prayer books have been edited and issued by every major Jewish denomination, each illustrating a distinct interpretation of Judaism through its weaving of classical, medieval, and contemporary texts. A plethora of occasional liturgies exists for camps, youth groups, ḤAVUROT, and other informal settings, as well as for the highly choreographed synagogue service. Vital issues facing the Jewish community find themselves translated liturgically, making for a renewed emphasis on Israel and Hebrew in the Reform liturgy, a growing sensitivity to egalitarian, gender-free language, and a more democratic sense of responsibility, with less reliance on traditional figures of authority.

LOGOS See PHILO

LOVE OF GOD Israel is commanded to "love the Lord your God with all your heart and with all your soul and with all your might" (Deut. 6:5). Elsewhere (*Deut.* 6:13), the Pentateuch commands, "You shall fear the Lord your God...." (see FEAR OF GOD). Commentators have interpreted fear and love as two different aspects of the manner in which man relates to God (Maimonides, *Sefer ha-Mitsvot*, positive commandments 3,4). In the Bible, both these terms seem to be commended, not as a desired emotional state but rather as a motivation for doing God's will. From the contexts in which love of God appears in the Bible, it would appear to represent the highest form of religious relationship — a relationship in which man communes with and comes close to God: "to love the Lord your God, to walk in all His ways and to cleave unto Him" (Deut. 11:22; 13:4,5). In the Bible, the object of Divine love is almost always the people of Israel. God's love for Israel demands a corresponding love. In the talmudic period, the differentiation between love and fear of God was taken for granted, with love clearly the preferred mode of relating. The *Sifré* to Deuteronomy 32 states: "Act out of love, for the Torah makes a distinction between one who acts out of love and one who acts out of fear.... In the former case his reward is doubled and redoubled." MAIMONIDES saw fear as a stage in the development of love of God and wrote that those whose religious capabilities are limited might not advance beyond this level. Love of God was, in any case, the level to which one should aspire (*Yad Teshuvah* 10).

Maimonides, as well as other thinkers, was not unaware of the difficulties posed by the commandment to love God. He therefore detailed how this might be achieved: "What is the way that will lead to love of God and fear of Him? When a person contemplates His great and wondrous works and creatures and from them perceives His wisdom which is incomparable and infinite he will straightaway love Him, praise Him, glorify Him, and long to know His great name" (*Yesodé Torah* 1:1,2). God Himself can be known only by His works, contemplation of which, to Maimonides, reveals God's wisdom, kindness, and love for man and Israel. More than naked power or cold intelligence, Maimonides would argue, man may perceive in the universe the good, the true, and the beautiful, which reflect a loving God. Man's love of God in its most sublime form is disinterested, not for the sake of any practical need. While this love, in Maimonides' conception, could indeed give pleasure, it arises from the contemplation of intrinsic value. It is essentially an intellectual, cognitive process. Maimonides retained, out of the range of emotions normally associated with the word "love," its exclusivity and comprehensive relation to its object.

Others, however, equated love of God with the ecstatic joyful state of the mystic. In the words of Joseph ALBO, "Love is the union and complete mental identification of love and the loved." According to BAḤYA IBN-PAKUDA, "It is the inclination of man's divine spiritual substance to its Maker, to adhere to Him aglow with His sublime light." A natural consequence of such intense and obsessive mystical longing is the withdrawal from all worldliness and its pleasures and disdain of the material world and all other interests. The rabbis, however, while appreciating the powerful nature of love of God, saw it as the highest value among a hierarchy of values and denied that the service of God requires a total withdrawal from all else.

A third approach may be discerned in the words of the *Sifré* on Deuteronomy 6:5: "'These words, which I command you this day, shall be upon your heart; and you shall teach them diligently to your children, and shall talk of them when you sit in your house, and when you rise up.' Take these words of the Torah to your heart, and in this way learn to acknowledge Him at whose word the world came into being and cleave to His paths." Unlike Maimonides' approach or that of the mystics, this approach does not suggest that the study of the Torah and the performance of the commandments lead to the love of God, but rather that these actions in and of themselves are the love of God.

Jewish thinkers in modern times hardly relate to the notion of fear of God, in that it seems to represent man as a passive and abject creature. The modern emphasis on the reciprocal love between man and God to the exclusion of fear continues a trend that may be traced from the Bible's apparent preference of love through the Talmud and the medieval thinkers. Since, however, such trends may ultimately minimize or dispose entirely of the distance between man and God, as in certain humanist systems, some thinkers have begun to consider the possibility that fear of God is a necessary consequence of His transcendence and not altogether incompatible with the dignity of man.

LOVE OF ISRAEL (*Ahavat Yisra'el*). Term designating both love of one's fellow Jew and a loving regard for the Jewish people as a natural (and national) virtue. Judaism inculcates an all-encompassing love of neighbor, but at the same time, the concept of Israel's election as God's CHOSEN PEOPLE led to a parallel emphasis of Divine love for Israel which finds expression in rabbinic literature, allegorical interpretation of Scripture, and the liturgy (see AHAVAH RABBAH and AHAVAT OLAM).

As a virtue demonstrated through relations between Jew and Jew, *ahavat Yisra'el* was stressed by Israel BA'AL SHEM TOV, who preached "the love of God, of Israel, and of Torah" as a central doctrine of ḤASIDISM. The term entered standard Hebrew no earlier than the 19th century. It is given a specific formulation by Avraham Yitsḥak KOOK. As opposed to the "groundless hatred" (*Sinat Ḥinnam*) which led to the Second Temple's destruction (*Yoma* 9b), Kook maintained that Israel's redemption and the building of the Third Temple would only come about through *ahavat ḥinnam*, i.e., groundless love of fellow Jews. *Ohev Yisra'el* ("lover of Israel"), a closely related term, less often describes a Jew than a Gentile philo-Semite.

LOVE OF NEIGHBOR The command to love one's neighbor as oneself is found in Leviticus 19:18 and reads: "You shall not take vengeance nor bear any grudge against the children of your people, but you shall love your neighbor as yourself: I am the Lord." HILLEL (first cent. CE), at the request of a non-Jew, summarized the message of Judaism as: "That which is hateful to you, do not do unto others" (*Shab.* 31a). This formulation later appeared as an Aramaic translation of Leviticus 19:18 (Targum Jonathan).

MAIMONIDES, following the lead of the rabbis, interpreted this command as "Be loving to your fellowman," stressing behavior rather than emotions: "...to speak of him positively and to have compassion upon his possessions" (*Yad, De'ot* 6.3).

R. AKIVA noted that this verse was a "great principle of the Torah" (*Sif.* on Lev. 19:18), implying that this imperative would be seen not only as a particular moral rule with specific behavioral prescriptions (such as not to marry a woman without seeing her first lest one learn to despise her, or to choose for criminals the least painful form of death) but also as a general principle from which could be generated any number of obligations of benevolence such as visiting the sick, consoling the bereaved, dowering the bride, etc. (*Yad, Avél* 14.1).

NAḪMANIDES considered whether "... as yourself" suggests that the love of the other should be equal to the love of self and concluded that this would be inconsistent with the accepted ruling of R. Akiva that "your own life takes precedence" (*BM.* 62a), i.e., one is not required to sacrifice one's life for the sake of another. Nevertheless, says Naḫmanides, all envy must be removed from one's heart, to the extent that a man is able to wish all sorts of blessings far greater than his own on his neighbor.

In the New Testament, Hillel's statement of this law of love is given a positive formulation and in this form has come to be known as the GOLDEN RULE: "Do unto others as you would have others do unto you" (Matt. 7:12). Apparently the New Testament author understood the biblical passage to say: "Love your neighbor as you naturally love yourself." Since the love of self is naturally supreme and all-consuming, so in this manner love your neighbor, i.e., be prepared to sacrifice all for him. The rabbis, on the other hand, read the passage as, "Love your neighbor as you ought to love yourself." Since morality requires that love of self must be qualified and tempered by love of the other, so must love of the other be qualified by legitimate concern for oneself. One's own life is also a human life.

Some believe that aside from terminology there is no real difference between the positive and negative formulation of the Golden Rule. Others, such as the Zionist thinker Aḫad Ha-Am and certain rabbinic scholars (e.g., R. Samuel EDELS on *Shab.* 31a), argue that the negative formulation is more precise and effective as a moral principle than the positive version, which could lead to certain dilemmas.

It is not clear whether the word usually translated as "neighbor" ("fellow" in the new translation of the Jewish Publication Society of America) in Leviticus 19:18 refers to all men or to fellow Jews only. Internal biblical evidence favors the more restrictive interpretation. On the other hand, love of the stranger is enjoined elsewhere: "If a stranger sojourns with you in your land, you shall not do him wrong... and you shall love him as yourself... for you were strangers in the Land of Egypt" (Lev. 19:33, 34). Rabbinic interpretation clearly excluded the possibility that the love of neighbor might include idolators, idolatry being the classic evil. (See also ETHICS.)

The concept of the brotherhood of man is built into Judaism as a natural corollary of the fatherhood of God extending to all mankind. The idea comes out in the Bible especially in the prophetic utterances: "Have we not all one father? Has not one God created us?" (Mal. 2:10). In practice, while accepting the theological concept as fundamental, Jewish attitudes have been shaped by the exigencies of history (see GENTILE; UNIVERSALISM AND PARTICULARISM).

LURIA, ISAAC AND LURIANIC KABBALAH Isaac Luria (1534-1572, (known as the *Ari*, acronym of the Hebrew for "The Divine Rabbi Isaac," was the founder of Lurianic KABBALAH. Very little is known about his life before he went to Safed in 1570. He was raised in Egypt, and probably was a scholar and merchant. The Safed mystics later attributed to him many legends, and the first extensive Hebrew hagiographic cycle of stories was composed around his personality. In Safed he had a small group of disciples, the most prominent of whom was R. Ḫayyim VITAL, who later wrote the main books of Lurianic Kabbalah. Luria and Vital tried to keep the new revelations a secret, and had no intention of publishing them. After Luria's death, Vital collected the notes written by the other disciples, and forbade them to write anything or to study this Kabbalah except in his presence. Two of them did not comply with this command, and so there are two other versions of Luria's teachings which can be compared with Vital's books.

Legend has it that when Vital was ill his manuscripts were stolen from his house and were copied, and in this way Luria's ideas began to spread in the last decade of the 16th century. Luria himself wrote almost nothing; he explained this by saying that when he held a pen visions appeared before him like a great river, and he could not channel this river through the slender pen in his hand. Luria's mysticism is based on vast, dynamic pictures, which cannot be translated into sentences and paragraphs. The works of his disciples are, therefore, only remnants and glimpses of his mystical vision.

Luria was unique among Jewish mystics because he did not rely on the traditions of a particular school of Kabbalah as did other kabbalists whose views were supported by the tradition received from their teachers. For his disciples, the truth of his revelations was attested by his personality, and not by the reputation of his teacher or teacher's teacher. In this sense, Luria was the first charismatic kabbalistic visionary, to be followed later by Nathan of Gaza, the prophet of SHABBETAI TSEVI, and the BA'AL SHEM TOV, the founder of ḤASIDISM.

Luria's early death in a plague at the age of 38, presented a religious problem to his disciples: Judaism usually believed early death to be a Divine punishment for a very grave sin. Was Luria a sinner? One answer suggested that Luria had indeed committed a sin by revealing to his students the great Divine secrets which should have remained only in his heart.

Luria and his circle should be regarded as a part of the intense messianic expectations which prevailed in Safed from the beginning of the 16th century. His contribution, however, was in his weaving these messianic elements into a vast cosmic mystical myth, which encompassed the whole past, present, and future of Divine and earthly realms.

Luria introduced into the Kabbalah three basic terms, which comprise the three main elements of the mythology presented by his mystical visions: *tsimtsum* (contraction), *shevirah* (breaking [of the vessels]), and *tikkun* (mending or correcting).

Early Kabbalah and the ZOHAR begin their account of the emergence of Divine and earthly existence with the appearance, within the eternal Godhead, of the first idea, or will to create something outside Himself. Luria, however, starts his myth one step before that. He asks the seemingly logical question: how could God contemplate creation of something outside Himself when there was nothing, no place or space, outside Himself? Before such a wish could be contemplated, the Godhead had to create a certain space which is not filled with the pure Divine essence.

The process of the emergence of the empty space is called by Luria the *tsimtsum*, i.e., the contraction of the Godhead into Himself, contracting away from a certain space in His "middle." This term was used in ancient Midrash to denote the contraction of God into the Holy of Holies in the Temple in Jerusalem, but Luria utilized it in an opposite way: the Godhead contracted Himself away from the empty space into Himself. To some extent the process of *tsimtsum* can be regarded as an exile: the first act in the history of existence is God's exile.

After this stage, the process of emanation and CREATION could progress: a straight line of Divine light emanated from God, ÉN-SOF, entering the primordial space, the *tehiru*, and began to take the form of the huge anthropomorphic figure of the Divine emanations, the SEFIROT. Here, however, a catastrophe occurred: the attempt was not successful, the Divine emanated powers disintegrated, and destruction

Emanation of the Sephirot *depicted as vessels, as described in Lurianic Kabbalah. Manuscript, Lithuania, 1749.*

replaced creation. This catastrophe was called by Luria the *shevirah* (or *shevirat ha-kelim*), the breaking of the Divine vessels. The vessels, failing to contain within them the Divine light which flowed into them, broke down, their shards spreading, and the Divine light inside rose back to the Godhead.

The most important element in Lurianic Kabbalah is the explanation given to this catastrophe. It is unimaginable that the Godhead could not create vessels strong enough for their purpose. Why was the Divine plan interrupted and destroyed? The works of Vital and other disciples of Luria contain several explanations, but the true one seems to be that the vessels contained some different, potentially evil, powers which refused to take part in the positive process of Creation. The *shevirah* is thus the result of a rebellion which occurred within the Divine realm and caused the destruction of the attempt to emanate the *Sefirot*.

This rebellion gives a new explanation for the previous stage, that of the *tsimtsum*. This was not just a technical stage which was intended to create an empty space in which Creation could proceed. It was a necessary Divine process of purification, for deep within the Godhead, before the *tsimtsum* began, there was not complete unity, but only some Divine elements which, potentially, were different from the others. The *tsimtsum* was intended to separate these two varieties of potential Divine essence. Lurianic Kabbalah describes this by depicting the *tsimtsum* as emptying a bucket of water: the walls of the bucket remain wet, some water clings to the sides. This "remnant" of Divine light after the *tsimtsum* is the "impression" which remained following the *tsimtsum*. The different Divine elements within the Godhead were separated and remained in the "impression." Thus, the *tsimtsum* achieved its purpose: the Godhead was now "clean" of the different elements, which were concentrated on the "walls" of the empty space.

The process which culminated in the *shevirah* was intended by the Godhead to achieve a more ambitious goal than the separation between the different elements within Him. It was an attempt to annihilate the difference, to make the two separate Divine essences work together toward a common goal, and thus to unite them into one entity.

In the Divine realm there can be no differentiation between essence and function: if two Divine powers fulfill the same function, they are one and the same. If the Godhead had succeeded in causing the powers now residing within the *reshimu* (an inchoate mixture which will provide the future universe with matter) to participate in the process of emanation of the world of the *Sefirot*, and later in the Creation of heaven and earth, then the differences would have been erased and the true unity of the Divine realm established.

From a theological point of view, the *shevirah* in Lurianic Kabbalah expresses the emergence of the inherent DUALISM of good and evil, which existed potentially within the Godhead, into actual existence. Luria's mythological daring is revealed in this system, which does not hesitate to stipulate the existence of at least some sort of dualism within the Godhead before Creation or emanation ever began. The source of EVIL is as Divine as the source of good; both existed within the eternal Godhead and came into actual being in the *tsimtsum* and the *shevirah*.

The most meaningful concept that Lurianic Kabbalah introduced into Jewish mysticism, and into Jewish culture as a whole, is that of the *tikkun*, the mending or correcting of the catastrophe of the *shevirah*. This concept revolutionized the Kabbalah not only because it contained all the elements of messianic redemption, but more than that, because it turned the face of the Kabbalah toward historical activity, and transformed kabbalistic mystical symbols into historical forces. This happened because Lurianic Kabbalah was the first Jewish theology which stipulated that true Divine unity cannot be found in the past, in the beginning; it will only emerge at the end, when the duality of existence will be "mended," when the process of the *tikkun* will be complete. Now the mystic could look only toward the future when searching for spiritual perfection. Looking into the future enables the mystic to participate in historical activity, to work towards the achievement of that desired unity.

According to the unfolding Lurianic myth, after the *shevirah* the Godhead again emanated a line of light which gave shape to the world of the Divine powers, this time without the participation of the *reshimu* elements. The Divine world thus emanated was in conflict with the independent realm of evil which was below it. A struggle began, in which the evil powers derived their strength from the many "sparks" of Divine light which fell together with them into the abyss in the *shevirah*. According to Lurianic Kabbalah (following ancient Neo-Platonic concepts), existence is derived only from good Divine light; without its sustenance, nothing can exist for even a moment. Evil, therefore, does not have an independent source of being; it must rely on Divine light captured from the good powers. These captive "sparks" of Divine light, which crave to return to their original position within the realm of good, are the reason for the struggle between good and evil, and as long as they are kept in captivity by the forces of Satan, evil can exist and prosper.

History, according to Luria, is the story of the repeated attempts by the Godhead to bring about the *tikkun* and to free the captured sparks. The world was created, and ADAM was put in the GARDEN OF EDEN, in order to carry on this struggle. Adam represented, symbolically, the cosmic duality: he had a Divine spirit but a material body governed by evil desires. The task of achieving the *tikkun* was placed on his shoulders: if he were to obey God's commands, and thus subjugate his material body to his Divine soul, then good would triumph all over the world, the sparks would be freed, and evil would cease to exist. Adam, however, committed the "original sin," and caused a repetition of the *shevirah*. Sparks of his Divine soul fell into the realm of evil and strengthened it, while the good powers within the created world became weaker; the task of achieving the *tikkun* became more difficult.

God then chose a people as his tool to bring about the *tikkun* — he chose ABRAHAM and the people of Israel. After the Jews were delivered from the captivity in Egypt and assembled near Mount Sinai, a great opportunity to achieve the *tikkun* was reached; everything was ready, most of the sparks in evil captivity had been freed, and when the Torah was given to Moses the victory of the good powers was imminent. Then the Jews committed the sin of the GOLDEN CALF, and again a fierce *shevirah* occurred, many new sparks fell into the abyss, and the forces of evil increased their hold over the created world. In a similar way all history is interpreted by Lurianic Kabbalah as chapters and episodes in this constant mythological struggle.

The task of the *tikkun* has been given, since the creation of the world, to Man, and especially to the people of Israel. Lurianic Kabbalah is anthropocentric, giving Man a key role not only in deciding his own fate, but at the same time in deciding the fate of the world, the cosmos, and, indeed, that of the Divine realm itself. The true unity of God can be achieved only by the works of Man; God, in this sense, is dependent on Man's deeds.

Religious life as a whole is the main tool or weapon in Man's struggle to bring about his own and God's redemption. Every commandment, every ethical deed, even every good thought or intention, is related to this struggle. When a Jew pronounces a blessing, or helps his poor brother, or prays with a pure heart, or eats a ceremonial meal, a spark is set free from the captivity of evil. The opposite is also true. When a man commits a sin, or transgresses one of the ritualistic or ethical commandments, or has an evil thought, another good spark (from his Divine soul) is captured by the evil powers, sustains them, and strengthens them. Every moment in Man's life is a part of this constant, unending struggle. No one and nothing can be neutral, because everything one does or does not do has a meaning in the framework of this mythical war. It does not matter whether a person is a mystic or not, what he does always counts and always influences the fate of the captured sparks and the future of the cosmos. One cannot resign from this task; a Jew is born into it, and even if he converts to another religion he is still a part of this struggle.

Lurianic Kabbalah thus places a very heavy burden on its believers. Luria and his disciples, like many others at that time, believed that REDEMPTION was imminent, and that the MESSIAH might appear in their lifetime. This means that every single deed and thought could be the last decisive one in the history of the *tikkun*. One small sin of every individual can delay the redemption, while every ethical deed may be the last, freeing the last spark from captivity and bringing forth the complete *tikkun*. The resultant sense of responsibility is enormous. At every moment each Jew is responsible not only to himself, but to the people as a whole, the world, the cosmos, and even to God's fate. Evil cannot be attributed to any external, ungovernable force; Man can and should overcome it by the power of religious adherence, and if it continues to exist, he alone is to blame. In this sense Luria's system is the first Jewish nationalistic ideology in early modern times. It gives the people of Israel a distinct, unique purpose, with the tool to carry it out, the Torah, and communal responsibility for achieving it.

Lurianic Kabbalah is clearly messianic, in the sense that it puts the redemption at the center of its message. Luria's disciples believed in the messianic role of Luria himself. However, in the Lurianic system there is no place for the individual Messiah; he has no specific role to play. The *tikkun* will be achieved by the combined efforts of all Jews, and the coming of the Messiah will be the result, not the cause, of this effort.

Luria's extreme mythological system was revolutionary in nature. It is, therefore, paradoxical that its main message to the Jewish people is a conservative, Orthodox one. The belief in Lurianic Kabbalah, when translated into everyday behavior, is anything but revolutionary. In order to participate successfully in the mythological struggle between good and evil and bring about the true unity within the Godhead a Jew has to follow the traditional laws of Jewish *halakhah* and ethics. Luria and his disciples did innovate some customs and rituals, and developed a whole system of mystical intentions during prayers, which assist in the process of the *tikkun*. These innovated rituals are not normative; the *tikkun* can and will be achieved by following the traditional demands of the Torah and Talmud. In this sense Lurianic Kabbalah is revolutionary in its ideas and terminology, but conservative in its actual, behavioral message. It does not preach a new way of life, but gives renewed meaning and a novel sense of purpose to those continuing in the old way.

This strong element of Orthodoxy in Lurianic Kabbalah can explain the fact that even though Luria's terminology and mythological expressions were foreign to many Jews, no controversy arose around his teachings, and in the first half of the 17th century Lurianism spread rapidly throughout the Jewish world, reaching almost every community from Yemen to Amsterdam, from Poland to Morocco. The deep sense of exile which prevailed in 16th and 17th century Judaism, especially as a result of the tragedy of the expulsion from Spain, made doubly attractive and appealing a system which placed the exile of Divinity in its center and gave everyday life a new meaning as a struggle towards deliverance from that exile.

LURIA, SOLOMON (BEN JEHIEL) (known by the acronym *Maharshal*; 1510-1573). Luria was born in Brest-Litovsk (Brisk), Lithuania, and died in Lublin. He was rabbi of Brest-Litovsk and founded a *yeshivah* there. Later, he served in Ostraha, and in 1555 he became the rabbi of Lublin.

His approach to the study of the Talmud was rational, and he criticized those who relied on the commentators and codifiers rather than on the actual text. He stressed the importance of ascertaining the correct textual rendition of each passage of the Talmud and its major commentators (RASHI and TOSAFOT). Unlike Rabbenu TAM, who attempted to show that every textual variant might be correct in the context, Luria was always interested in finding the accurate reading. While emphasizing the importance of using the Talmud as the basic source for decisions, he made a point

Initial-word panel from a festival prayer book, the Worms Maḥzor. *Germany, 1272.*

מתנשא

לכל לראש בחר באום דלת ראש׳ כבכורה בתאנה בראש׳ ביטח

ואותה דרוש מכל אום לפרוש ׳לנשאה על כל ראש׳ גועלה תשיה

למעוד ראש׳ והיא תרים ראש׳ בכסא כבוד מראש״

הלכות ק״ש
מה אהבתי תורתך כל היום
היא שיחתי״
ספר שני
והוא ספר
אהבה
הלכותיו שש וזהו סדורן
הלכות קרית שמע
הלכות תפלה וברכת כהנים
הלכות תפלין ומזוזה
וספר תורה
הלכות ציצית
הלכות ברכות״

of exhaustively studying every possible work with a bearing on the subject before issuing his own decision on questions of *halakhah*. Luria wrote *Yam shel Shelomo* (Solomon's Sea) of which only part has been published. On the other hand, his *Ḫokhmat Shelomo* (Solomon's Wisdom), which is a short work on the different tractates of the Talmud, has been published in almost every edition of the Talmud ever printed since.

LUZZATTO, MOSES ḆAYYIM (known by the acronym *Ramḫal*; 1707-1747). Poet and kabbalist. Luzzatto was born in Padua, Italy. His father was a wealthy merchant. Already in his youth he began to study Kabbalah, a practice that he continued for the rest of his life. He was so carried away with this study that he attempted to take concrete steps to hasten the advent of the Messiah, and attracted a circle of followers to whom he hinted he might himself be the Messiah. He passed on to them heavenly revelations that he believed reached him from the spirits of the great figures of the Bible. He often went into a trance, in which he believed he received messages from God. As a result of his actions, he was hounded and forced to flee, settling in Amsterdam, where he was employed as a diamond polisher. In Amsterdam, too, he encountered opposition to his views, and he was forbidden, under pain of excommunication, from studying Kabbalah. Yet, in spite of being harassed, it was in Amsterdam that he wrote his *Mesillat Yesharim* (The Path of the Upright), one of the most widely studied of all Jewish ethical works (see ETHICS). In 1743, overcome with a longing to live in Erets Israel, he traveled there and settled in Safed. Following a plague in 1746, in which his wife and son died, he fled to Acre, where he died a year later. He was buried in Tiberias.

Traditional tomb of Moses Ḫayyim Luzzatto at Tiberias, overlooking the Sea of Galilee.

Luzzatto's entire life was marked by a struggle between his strong kabbalistic leanings and his desire to devote himself to the traditional study of the Talmud. From his earliest youth, he gave evidence of his ability as a poet, and fragments of a poem he wrote at the age of 12 have come down to us. Luzzatto also wrote a number of dramas in honor of the weddings of close friends. He has been described as one of the fathers of modern Hebrew literature and greatly influenced subsequent Hebrew poetry.

Opening page of Ahavah *(Love), one of the fourteen books of Maimonides'* Mishneh Torah. *Italy, c.1400.*

M

MA'AMAD (MAHAMAD) (lit. "stand"). Sephardi equivalent of the Ashkenazi *kahal*, or community leadership. The *ma'amad* ruled over all community matters, and its decisions were binding. Members of the *ma'amad* were not elected, but each *ma'amad* appointed its successors. Those designated to serve had no choice but to accept the assignment.

MA'ARAVOT (sing. *ma'aravit*). A series of liturgical poems (PIYYUTIM) added to the EVENING SERVICE (*ma'ariv*). The *ma'aravot* correspond to the YOTSEROT recited in the morning. The *ma'aravot* are meant to embellish the evening services of festivals and special Sabbaths. The form was created in Erets Israel but spread primarily among the poets (*Paytanim*) of France and Germany. Each series consists of six poems, which are recited before the four blessings (two before and two after the recital of the SHEMA) and before the two verses of *Mi-Khamokhah* (Who is like You) and *Adonai Yimlokh* (The Lord will reign). A *ma'aravit* consists of six stanzas, each of four lines in length, based on simple alphabetic ACROSTICS together with verses setting the framework and biblical openings. The third section is larger than the others; this *piyyut* is independent and sometimes contains an acrostic of the entire alphabet. The subjects relate to the individual festivals, and each section ends with a hint at the blessing that is to follow. Originally, these *piyyutim* were meant to replace the standard text of the prayers, but over the course of time they were added to it instead. In Germany, the *piyyutim* were written at the outset to be incorporated into the existing text.

The German *paytanim* added a seventh section (First Fruits), which is added after the sixth, and leads into the blessing before the AMIDAH prayer.

MA'ARIV See EVENING SERVICE

MA'ASEH (lit. "an event"). A factual circumstance used to bolster a position in *halakhah*. The *ma'aseh* may be either an actual decision taken by a sage in a particular case, akin somewhat to a legal precedent (although precedent is not binding in *halakhah*), or the behavior of a specific sage under specific circumstances, from which attempts are made to derive the *halakhah*. The Talmud (*BB* 130b) limits the applicability of *ma'aseh* to actual *halakhah* by specifying that one may only use a *ma'aseh* as proof where it was clearly ascertained that the case was meant to be declarative in practice, and not merely theoretical. *Ma'aseh* is particularly relevant to the vast body of responsa literature, where the rulings on thousands of specific cases serve as an important source of halakhic decision-making. The word is used in Hebrew and Yiddish for a story.

MA'ASEROT ("Tithes"). Seventh tractate of Order ZERA'IM in the Mishnah. Its five chapters discuss the kinds of produce subject to tithes, when the tithes must be separated, doubtfully tithed produce, the eating of produce by laborers before tithing, and the Sabbatical year with regards to tithes (cf. Lev. 27:30-33; Num. 18:21-28). The laws in this tractate include all categories of tithes: the heave-offering, first tithe, second tithe, and poor man's tithe (see TITHE). The subject matter is amplified in the Jerusalem Talmud and the *Tosefta*.

MA'ASER SHENI ("Second Tithe"). Eighth tractate of Order ZERA'IM in the Mishnah. Its five chapters deal with the laws governing the separation and consumption of the second TITHE (one-tenth of the remaining produce after the first tithe) (cf. Deut. 14:22-29; 26:12-15). The Mishnah discusses uses to which the second tithe may be put, the "redemption" of second tithe produce for money, the mixture of second tithe coins with ordinary coins, the marking of all orchards and vineyards in the fourth year to indicate its fruits were forbidden for consumption (*orlah*), and the declaration made after separation of the second tithe. In the last chapter is the statement that Johanan the High Priest abolished the declaration following the taking of tithes because of the decree of EZRA, which deprived the Levites from receiving the first tithe.

The subject-matter is amplified in the Jerusalem Talmud and the *Tosefta*. See also TITHE.

MACCABEES See HASMONEANS

MACCABEES, BOOK OF See APOCRYPHA

MACHPELAH, CAVE OF See HOLY PLACES

MAFTIR ("One who concludes"). Honor reserved for the last worshiper summoned to the READING OF THE LAW in the synagogue; it comprises the final verses (never less than three) of the portion read from the Torah scroll on that particular Sabbath, festival, or fast day. On a regular Sabbath, after the statutory number of seven worshipers have been called to the Torah and "half-*Kaddish*" has been recited, the last few verses are repeated for *maftir*. On a Sabbath coinciding with the New MOON, HIGH HOLIDAYS, and the PILGRIM FESTIVALS, a special *maftir* is read from a second scroll to recall the Temple offerings made on that particular day. These passages are taken from Num. 28-29. Other sections of the Pentateuch are reserved for *maftir* on special SABBATHS, the Sabbath of HANUKKAH, and the afternoon of fast days. The person called as *maftir* recites the TORAH blessings before and after this section and he usually chants the prophetical reading (HAFTARAH).

A boy celebrating his BAR MITSVAH customarily recites both *maftir* and *haftarah*; if capable, he may read the complete Torah portion for that Sabbath. Most congregations reserve the *maftir* of the Sabbaths before PASSOVER and the DAY OF ATONEMENT for the rabbi or some learned and pious layman.

Magen David *("Shield of David") carved on a stone frieze of the synagogue of Capernaum, 2nd-3rd century CE.*

MAGEN DAVID (lit. "shield of David"). Hexagram or six-pointed star formed by two superimposed equilateral triangles, which in recent centuries has become a distinctive Jewish symbol. This figure was often used in Europe and the Middle East for decoration, possibly with magical connotation, as early as the Bronze Age. It first appeared on a Jewish seal found at Sidon from the seventh century BCE. Although the hexagram is commonly displayed on artefacts and buildings from the Second Temple period by Jews and non-Jews alike (including the third century CE Capernaum synagogue where it is found next to a pentagram and a swastika), it had no particular Jewish significance and is completely absent as a Jewish symbol during Hellenistic times. It appeared on some synagogues in Germany during the 13th and 14th centuries, and in medieval Hebrew manuscripts, but without indication of a particular name or meaning. It was also widespread on amulets and *mezuzot* and in magical Hebrew texts of the later Middle Ages.

The term *magen david* can be traced back to the geonic period where it is associated with a popular magical alphabet; it reappeared in the 12th century in a Karaitic work by Judah Hadassi and among the HASIDÉ ASHKENAZ. It also occurs as a designation of God in the third benediction after the prophetical reading (HAFTARAH) in the synagogue. The hexagram is first identified as the "shield of David" in a 14th century kabbalistic work written by the grandson of Nahmanides. An alternative tradition links the term with the seven-branched candelabrum (MENORAH) which became a powerful talisman in the 16th century.

Between the 14th and the 18th centuries, the symbol was widely used by Jewish and non-Jewish printers and found its way into some coats-of-arms. It appeared on the flag of the Jewish community of Prague and on their official seal. Other Jewish communities, including Vienna (1655) and Amsterdam (1671), began to put the symbol on their seals. In Eastern Europe it was found as an ornamentation on ritual objects from 1643 onwards.

Within kabbalistic circles, the "shield of David" became the "shield of the son of David," the Messiah, and was popular among the followers of SHABBETAI TSEVI as their esoteric symbol of the vision of redemption.

As Jews of the ENLIGHTENMENT entered the mainstream of society in the 19th century, they chose the *magen david* as their identifying symbol in contradistinction to the Christian use of the cross. From Central and Western Europe, the "Jewish star" traversed the entire Jewish world to become a unifying symbol, appearing on synagogues and Jewish communal institutions, seals and letterheads, ritual objects and personal items.

The *magen david* was adopted by the Zionist movement during its first Zionist Congress (1897) and appeared that year on the first issue of *Die Welt*, Theodor Herzl's Zionist journal. Subsequently, it was chosen as the central figure on the blue and white flag of the State of Israel, although the older, more authentic Jewish emblem of the *menorah* appears on the state seal. For Franz ROSENZWEIG, the symbol represented his philosophy of Judaism as articulated in *The Star of Redemption* (1921) in which each point of the star represents an essential element of his thought: Creation, Redemption, Revelation, Humanity, World, and God.

The Nazis used the Jewish star on a yellow "badge of shame" to accompany millions on their way to being murdered. A red *magen david* in Israel corresponds to the Red Cross in Western countries.

MAGGID (lit. "narrator"). Hebrew term denoting "one who brings a message" (II Sam. 15:13). To the kabbalists, a *maggid* was a mysterious voice or agency that communicated secret knowledge to the privileged through DREAMS or daytime revelations. Thus, Joseph CARO affirmed that his own *maggid* had inspired his journey to the Land of Israel and the composition of his outstanding halakhic works. Similar claims were made by followers of SHABBETAI TSEVI and, at an early stage of his career, by Moses Ḥayyim LUZZATTO. Most of these strange experiences might today be ascribed to telepathy, extrasensory perception, and kindred factors.

From Mishnaic times, however, the term *maggid* was synonymous with preacher (see also DERASH; PREACHING). He delivered three-part sermons comprising (1) a biblical verse usually chosen from the weekly Pentateuch reading; (2) an exposition of this verse based on HOMILETICS, ALLEGORY, parables, and topical comments; (3) a final message of encouragement ending with Isaiah 59:20 and the recital of KADDISH. The role of the *maggid mésharim* (lit. "one who proclaims what is true," Isa. 45:19) became especially important in the Ashkenazi communities of medieval Europe, where wandering preachers often had to revitalize Jewish morale. From the late 17th century onward, these itinerant *maggidim* were joined by salaried preachers who shared religious leadership with the communal rabbis. Instead of dwelling on ritual failings, the *maggid* was now called upon to influence public opinion with outspoken criticism of social evils and religious hypocrisy. The preacher should "raise his voice in protest against the malpractices of eminent men," urged Jonathan EYBESCHÜTZ (*Ya'arot Devash*, 1782). By his time, ḤASIDISM was spreading through Eastern Europe thanks to the activity of Ḥasidic *maggidim* such as DOV BAER OF MEZHIRECH; heading their traditionalist opponents, the MITNAGGEDIM, were Jacob KRANZ (the famous *Maggid* of Dubno) and scores of other preachers. Utilizing admonition, dramatic touches, and a characteristic singsong delivery, they and their successors were capable of moving a rapt audience to tears. This tradition accompanied East European Jews when they settled in other parts of the world, both the ethical MUSAR movement and Zionism finding eloquent exponents. Ḥayyim Zundel Maccoby (1858-1916), for example, the *Maggid* of Kamenets, transferred his Zionist activity to Britain; Tsevi Hirsch Masliansky (1856-1943) also left tsarist Russia, to become an outstanding Yiddish orator and Zionist *maggid* in the USA.

MAGIC The Bible demonstrates considerable interest in magic. The list of persons who practice magic is given in Deuteronomy 18:10-11; it mentions three types of magicians: those who predict the future by means of various signs (soothsayers, augurers, and diviners); those who engage in actual magic (sorcerers and casters of spells) and those who make predictions and perform actual magic, using the spirits of the dead as a source of information.

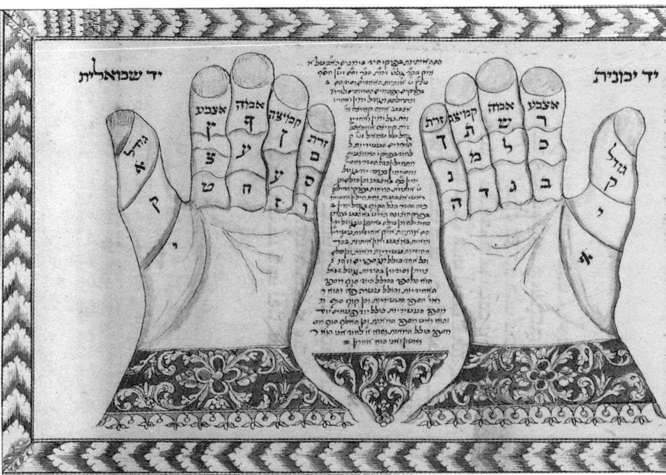

Use of the letters of the Hebrew alphabet in the context of chiromantic mysteries. Manuscript, Lithuania, 1754.

Since the ancient Israelites lived in a civilization in which magic was a commonplace, many biblical provisions are directed to opposing sorcery of any type. Any belief in the abilities of magic to obtain certain ends is seen to contradict the omnipotence of God, who cannot be influenced by any human device. Even the death penalty is required by the Bible for certain types of individuals who practice magic (Ex. 22:17; Lev. 20:27). Witchcraft and divination by the *teraphim* (household idols) are identified with rebellion (I Sam. 15:23). Sorcerers and astrologers are the personification of delusion (Isa. 47:12-15; Jer. 10:2-3).

Nevertheless, all the legislation forbidding the practice of magic did not eradicate sorcery, astrology, and other forms of divination from the Israelites, as is clear from the testimony of the prophets, who speak out against all forms of magic. However, some elements of magic were adapted and accepted, as is seen in Saul's visit to the witch of En-Dor (I Sam. 28:7-25).

The Mishnah (*Sanh.* 7:7) equates magic with idolatry. The biblical commandment to execute witches (Ex. 22:17) is widened to include male sorcerers as well (*Sanh.* 67a). According to the Talmud, the practitioner of magic was to be put to death only when a magical act was performed, not when there was mere illusion.

Magic emerges in the Middle Ages in new forms, such as in the use of Divine names in *segullot* (remedies or charms), *kame'ot* (amulets), etc. (see SUPERSTITION). By introducing such concepts, the medieval writers and the Jewish public in general were able to circumvent the biblical injunction against magic. Much of this developed under the influence of the Kabbalah. Among those who did not hesitate to deal with the concept of magic in their works were NAḤMANIDES, Moses Ḥayyim LUZZATTO, and Manasseh Ben Israel.

The ceremony of excommunication (*ḥerem*) appears to have been an occasion when a type of magic actually received a certain legitimization. The edicts of excommunication and the ceremony itself incorporated magical undertones. Furthermore, in the 17th and 18th centuries in Eastern European communities, the *ba'alé shem*, wonderworkers, began to appear, practicing magic and popular medicine, and using amulets to drive away demons. Reputedly, from their knowledge of secret names, they were able to activate certain powers to unmask thieves, find lost articles and purify houses from evil spirits. A magical ceremony was also used to exorcise the spirits of the dead believed to be lodged in the bodies of the living (see DIBBUK). Another form of magic was the creation of robot-like creatures (see GOLEM).

Still, in general magic played no major role in Jewish life. The Jewish people had their "magicians," just like every other people, but their role was minor. This is in direct contradiction to the magical powers imputed to the Jews by the Christians in medieval times. Jews were thought to be the devil's people and as such to have access to great supernatural secrets. Such beliefs were a major cause of persecution of Jews.

The biblical scholar Yehezkel Kaufman suggested that the Israelites could condemn magic so vigorously because it was not an ingrained part of society. Magic was practiced on a superficial level by some Jews, but the core community either frowned upon such practices or ultimately integrated them in some form into the mainstream. Thus, certain standard Jewish practices may have had a magical origin, but their nature was completely transformed and their source forgotten.

MAH NISHTANNAH See FOUR QUESTIONS

MAH TOVU ("How lovely"). Opening words of a prayer recited by Ashkenazim on entering the synagogue, immediately prior to the MORNING BENEDICTIONS. It comprises a sequence of five biblical verses (Num. 24:5; Ps. 5:8, 26:8, 95:6, 69:14), with the wording of Ps. 95:6 changed from the first person plural to singular. In Sephardi and other rites one verse only (Ps. 5:8) is said on entering the synagogue and another verse (Ps. 5:9) on departing. According to the Talmud (*Sanh.* 105b), the "tents" and "dwellings" mentioned by the heathen prophet Balaam in Numbers 24:5 denote Israel's synagogues and houses of study. Liturgically, this prayer expresses the Jew's love and reverence for the synagogue, his delight in attending services there, and his confident belief that the prayers recited in an atmosphere untouched by worldly cares will obtain God's favorable acceptance. On Sabbaths and festivals, it is occasionally sung by a choir, before the Reading of the Law, in Western Orthodox congregations.

MAH TOVU

How lovely are your tents, O Jacob, your dwelling places, O Israel! As for me, through Your abundant kindness I will enter Your house, and filled with awe for You I will bow down toward Your holy Temple. O Lord, I love the house of Your abode, the dwelling place of Your glory.

MAḤZOR (pl. *maḥzorim*, "cycle"). Prayer book for FESTIVALS. The *maḥzor* has undergone fundamental changes since the term was first used in the Middle Ages. As its Hebrew meaning reveals, the word originally referred to the "cycle" of the liturgy chronologically arranged for the entire year and was therefore synonymous with the term *siddur* (PRAYER BOOK). *Maḥzor Vitry*, an 11th-century Ashkenazi prayer book from northern France, chronicles the accepted liturgical formulas for weekdays, Sabbaths, and festivals throughout the year. A Passover HAGGADAH, prayers for SIMḤAT TORAH, and liturgical poems (PIYYUTIM) are appended to this comprehensive work, together with the relevant halakhic rulings and aggadic commentaries of the Talmud, the *ge'onim*, and RASHI. Laws regarding the Sabbath, marriage, and ritual slaughter were also included. Another early festival prayer book was the *Maḥzor Romania* containing the festival prayers as recited in the area of influence of the Byzantine Empire.

In the 13th century, Ashkenazi Jews began to make the distinction between the *siddur* as the prayer book of daily and Sabbath devotion and the *maḥzor* which contained the communal prayers for the festivals and the seven special Sabbaths of the year. Primarily intended for use by the *ḥazzan* (prayer leader), these *maḥzorim*, some of them beautifully illuminated, offered a variety of *piyyutim* from which to choose for each festival. Most of the examples from the 13th and 14th centuries begin in a first volume with prayers for the four special Sabbaths before Passover (see SABBATHS, SPECIAL) and continue with prayers for all the major holy days which follow, i.e., Passover, Shavu'ot, the New Year, the Day of Atonement, and Sukkot. Four of the "Scrolls" (*Megillot*) found in the biblical writings and read publicly in the synagogue during the festivals, namely, Song of Songs, Ruth, Lamentations, and Ecclesiastes, are usually included as well. The second volume of the medieval Ashkenazi *maḥzor* contains the complete liturgies for the New Year and the Day of Atonement. The former is sometimes illustrated by the Binding of Isaac (AKEDAH) and the latter illuminated within full page-arches symbolic of the Gates of Mercy open to accept petitions of forgiveness. Although many of the illustrated *maḥzorim* are elaborately enhanced with depictions of biblical scenes appropriate to the festival, some are decorated merely with scrolls and geometric designs.

Piyyut *(liturgical poem) associated with the Torah portion* Shekalim *(Ex. 30:11-16). From a* Maẖzor. Germany, 13th-14th century.

Two Ashkenazi *maẖzorim* of this period are of particular interest. The Leipzig *maẖzor* is the most richly and extensively illuminated of all the southern German examples. The Worms *maẖzor*, the first volume of which was completed in 1272, serves as one of the earliest dated Hebrew manuscripts illustrated from this time.

Following the resettlement of many Ashkenazim in Italy, the 15th century witnessed a major change in the development of the *maẖzor*, as the large illuminated form came to be replaced by a smaller-sized, personal volume. The indigenous Italian rite, however, retained the older, traditional definition of the *maẖzor* as the daily, Sabbath, and festival prayer book for the entire year, and usually contained a *Haggadah* for home use. This rite is preserved in the very first printed *maẖzor* of 1485-1486, *Maẖzor Roma*, which marks the beginning of the prayer book's popular accessibility to the individual Jew.

In contrast to the Ashkenazi tradition which produced *Ha-Maẖzor ha-Gadol* with Sabbath and festival prayers for the year and another *Maẖzor* for the festival prayers only, Sephardim refer to their prayer book for the three pilgrimage festivals as *Mo'adim*, and provide separate volumes for the New Year and the Day of Atonement. The H̱asidim modified their Ashkenazi *maẖzor* to include Sephardi *piyyutim*, following their adoption of Isaac LURIA's version of the liturgy. The Arabic-speaking Jews of Yemen worship from their all-inclusive *Tikhlal*, which remained hand-written until published in Jerusalem at the end of the 19th century.

As a result of EMANCIPATION, prayer book reform in Europe and subsequently in the United States transformed the *maẖzor*. The Union Prayer Book II (1925, 1945, and 1962) represents one of the earliest attempts by American Reform to revise traditional High Holidays liturgical texts. It was replaced in 1978 with *Sha'aré Teshuvah: The Gates of Repentance*, which anthologizes from Jewish and non-Jewish sources and speaks in a modern idiom of the social, moral, and spiritual issues facing Reform Jews in the second half of the 20th century.

Conservative Judaism also departed from the traditional *maẖzor*, although adhering more faithfully to the classical structure. Its first publication in 1927, *Maẖzor le-Shalosh Regalim: The Festival Prayer Book* reveals a marked kinship with the enlightened Orthodoxy of its day. The volume currently in use in most Conservative congregations is the *Maẖzor le-Yamim Nora'im: Maẖzor for Rosh Hashanah and Yom Kippur* (1972) which preserves much of the traditional liturgy in interpretive translation with evocative readings and a decidedly Zionist emphasis.

Reconstructionist Judaism published its *Maẖzor leYamim Nora'im: High Holy Day Prayer Book* in 1948 and a *Festival Prayer Book* in 1958 which made extensive use of auxiliary material to enhance the traditionally-oriented Conservative style service.

In the American Orthodox community, the *maẖzor* in use by most congregations is P. Birnbaum's *High Holiday Prayer Book* (1951), based upon S. Singer's work of the last century. Creative *maẖzorim* for individual congregations, camp and retreat settings, *ẖavurot* and schools are also found in abundance.

MAIMONIDES, MOSES (widely known as *Rambam* from the acronym of Rabbi Moses Ben Maimon; 1135 or 1138-1204). Halakhist and philosopher, the leading intellectual figure of medieval Judaism. A physician by profession, Maimonides made major contributions to Jewish religious literature and thought in the areas of both *halakhah* and philosophy. His major halakhic work, *Mishneh Torah* ("The Second Torah"), is universally accepted as one of the most important compendia of Jewish law of all ages. His philosophic work, *Moreh Nevukhim* (*Guide for the Perplexed*), is the highpoint of medieval Jewish Aristotelianism and the most important work of medieval Jewish philosophy. His philosophical concerns also find expression in his halakhic and epistolary works, which he composed as one of the major rabbinic authorities of his time.

Moses ben Maimon was born in Cordoba, Spain, to a distinguished rabbinical family. As the result of the ascent to power of the fanatical Muslim Almohad dynasty, the family was forced to flee in 1148 and, following a period of wanderings, settled around 1160 in the North African city of Fez, where Maimonides received his professional training as a physician. In 1165, the family journeyed to Erets Israel and to Egypt, first to Alexandria and then to Fostat, the Old City of Cairo. Maimonides' brother, David, a prosperous merchant, supported him financially (until the latter died in the Indian Ocean in 1169). This enabled Maimonides to devote himself exclusively to his scholarly work. He began to practice medicine and in 1185 was appointed court physician to Saladin's vizier, al-Fadil. He had already been appointed head of the Jewish community of Fostat in 1177. He continued to hold both of these positions until his death in 1204. His two major works, the *Mishneh Torah* and the *Guide to the Perplexed*, as well as several important epistles and other writings, were written during this Cairo period. He was buried in Tiberias, where his grave is still visited today.

Halakhic Writings Maimonides' halakhic writings are marked by clarity of style and systematic arrangement, both serving his didactic intent which tends to emphasize and build upon first principles of both a formal-legal and a theological nature. His writings include:

The Commentary to the MISHNAH (the *Siraj*) written in Arabic while Maimonides was a relatively young man, intended for both popular and learned audiences. This work includes several essays which are important in their own right: a) *Hakdamah le-Seder Zera'im* ("Introduction to the Order 'Seeds'"), the introduction to the work as a whole, which expounds the nature of *halakhah*, of the ORAL LAW and of the centrality of the authority of the rabbinic tradition within Judaism; b) *Shemonah Perakim* ("Eight Chapters"), the introduction to tractate AVOT, in which Maimonides outlines his ethical philosophy; c) *Hakdamah le-Perek Ḫelek* ("introduction to the tenth chapter of tractate *Sanhedrin*"), which presents Maimonides' approach to the problematics of the *aggadah*, his interpretation of rabbinic teaching concerning ESCHATOLOGY and the RESURRECTION OF THE DEAD and his famous Thirteen PRINCIPLES OF FAITH.

Pastoral Letters or Epistles: Maimonides was regarded as spiritual leader and guide by many Jewish communities of the Mediterranean region. His pastoral letters, responsa, and epistles are among the most humanly sensitive and religiously serious of Jewish theology. The most important of these are: (a) *Iggeret ha-Shemad* ("Epistle on Forced Conversion") or *Ma'amar Kiddush ha-Shem* ("Article on Martyrdom"), addressed to the Jewish community of Morocco, many of whose members had been forcibly converted to Islam by the Almohad regime. In this epistle he comforts these Jews and encourages them to continue living as Jews, despite their forced apostasy; (b) *Iggeret Téman* ("Epistle to Yemen"), addressed to the Jewish community of Yemen during a period of difficulty marked by a series of Messianic pretenders, in which he addresses himself to a broad discussion of the nature of the Messiah; (c) *Ma'amar Teḫiyyat ha-Metim* ("Article on Resurrection"), in which he defends himself against the accusation of having denied the doctrine of the resurrection of the dead.

Responsum by Maimonides on a dispute between two mohalim *(officials performing circumcision). From the Cairo Genizah.*

Sefer ha-Mitsvot ("The Book of the Commandments"), the introductory volume to the *Mishneh Torah*, contains an enumeration of the 613 COMMANDMENTS around which his code is structured, together with a scholarly preface analyzing the principles for determining which commandments are included in that number.

The *Mishneh Torah* or *Yad ha-Ḫazakah* ("Mighty Hand," so-called because the numerical value of *yad* is 14, which corresponds to the number of divisions of the work; see inset), completed about 1185, was his major halakhic work; it is a monumental synthesis and codification of all Jewish law, organized in a clear and logical system of classification. The work is unusual on several counts. It is written in a clear, lucid, classical mishnaic Hebrew. It is organized in such a way that the basic principles underlying each group of laws are presented, the whole being arranged within a framework reflecting the underlying structure of *halakhah* rather than being based on the exegetical, text-oriented, or chronological principles found in other codes. Another innovation consists in the author's refraining from citing sources for his rulings, for which reason it is not written in the dialectical, often dense style of traditional rabbinic texts (although these omissions became a subject of criticism). Most significant is its comprehensive character: unlike other works of this genre, such as Isaac ALFASI's *Hilkhot ha-Rif* or JACOB BEN ASHER's *Arba'ah Turim*, Maimonides' code encompasses the full gamut of classical rabbinic law, including those laws that were outdated or inoperative in his own day, such as the laws of the Temple, sacrifices, ritual purity and impurity, and laws concerning the government of a theocratic Jewish monarchy as it existed in the biblical and Second Temple period. The work is strongly marked by the desire for wholeness and a perception of the *halakhah* as a totality, as well as by what

Gershom SCHOLEM has called "restorative Messianism" — i.e., the longing for the restoration of Jewish society on the basis of the sanctified models of the past.

Important and characteristic is the inclusion within this code of philosophical, religious and ethical discussions. These topics are so ubiquitous that they may justly be described as expressive of a central concern of the work as a whole. The first of the 14 books — *Sefer Ha-Mada* (the "Book of Knowledge") — is devoted entirely to discussion of the fundaments of Judaism: the nature of God; the problem of the Divine attributes and the nature of religious language; physics and metaphysics; prophecy; ethics; Torah study (as at once a cognitive and devotional act); the rejection of paganism and all that it involves, which in Maimonides acquires central importance as the counter-thesis to monotheism; the issues of repentance, free will and Divine Providence and Maimonides' eschatology.

THE FOURTEEN BOOKS OF THE MISHNEH TORAH

Mada	Knowledge
Ahavah	Love
Zemanim	Seasons
Nashim	Women
Kedushah	Holiness
Hafla'ah	Vowing
Zera'im	Seeds
Avodah	Service (i.e., of Temple)
Korbanot	Sacrifices
Toharah	Purity
Kinyan	Acquisition
Nezikin	Damages
Mishpatin	Law (Torts)
Shofetim	Judges

Philosophical Positions The issues raised in his major philosophic work, *The Guide for the Perplexed*, set the tone for Jewish philosophic discussion and controversy for hundreds of years thereafter. *Dalilat al-Hariain*, or *The Guide for the Perplexed*, written in Arabic and completed in 1190, is seen as a response to the spiritual and theological perplexity of the contemporary Jew, disturbed by the contradictions between the doctrines of the then-dominant Aristotelian philosophy and a literal reading of rabbinic Judaism. It opens with a lengthy discussion of the problem with the anthropomorphic terms used to describe God or His actions in the Bible: very briefly, Maimonides' solution was to describe these as terms used metaphorically, invoking the ancient principle, "The Torah speaks in the language of man." The book continues with philosophical proofs of the existence of God and of His unity; discussions of prophecy, the nature of good and evil, and Divine Providence and concludes with his interpretation of the commandments and their reasons and with a picture of the ideal man.

Maimonides' ideal is that of a theocentric spirituality fully integrated with the rational faculty — the medieval ideal of the love of God through reason. This is expressed, both in the advocacy of the use of reason itself as the proper means to attain religious, spiritual goals and in the severe critique and vigorous, uncompromising struggle against those religious beliefs or doctrines which do not stand up before the bar of reason — implying a critical attitude towards emotional or mystical religion. In many passages in his writings, Maimonides strongly rejects knowledge of God acquired through the faculty of the imagination, stating in one place that the object of such knowledge or belief is not the true God, but essentially a projection or creation of the human imagination. He goes as far as to view those doctrines which smack of superstition or which violate his pristine understanding of monotheism as akin to idolatry. The ideal spiritual state, by contrast, is marked by calmness, intense discipline and mental alertness and clarity.

Thus, the esoteric teaching of Judaism, referred to in the Talmud as "The Account of the Creation" and "The Account of the Chariot," which was identified in Kabbalah with esoteric mystical doctrine, Maimonides equates with physics and metaphysics. The path towards the love and fear of God entails the acquisition of true and philosophically rigorous knowledge of the cosmos and of theology (*Mishneh Torah, Yesodé ha-Torah* 2:2ff., 4:12ff.; *Teshuvah* 10:5-6). One of the essential aims of the *Guide* was to foster this enterprise.

His insistence upon the purity of the monotheistic conception also underlies his so-called "negative theology" of the Divine attributes. According to this conception — which owes not a little to the concepts of Aristotelian metaphysics, according to which any changes or "accidents" occurring to a body indicate its imperfection — it is impossible to speak of God's actions or attributes, and certainly not of His essence, save in negative terms. For example, the Divine attribute of wisdom is the absence of ignorance or defect of knowledge, but is itself not an attribute. This principle is consistently applied to the anthropomorphisms and anthropopathisms appearing in the Bible and in much of the rabbinic *aggadah*; the metaphorical reinterpretation of those passages in which God is described either as possessing physical organs, feeling human emotions, or acting in human ways constitutes the primary theme of Book I of the *Guide*.

A similar rational, philosophical attitude to dogma marks Maimonides' approach to other theological issues. For the most part he accepts the reign of natural law in the universe and plays down the role of miracle and direct Divine intervention. He thus deemphasizes involvement with the details of the messianic age and discourages speculation upon either the date of the coming of the Messiah or the exact character of the messianic age, stating that it is enough to believe in these things in general terms. His own portrayal of the messianic age places the stress squarely upon the spiritual, intellectual pleasures which it shall facilitate.

He views Divine Providence as rather limited and he rejects the nearly all-encompassing determinism sometimes suggested by other Jewish sources. He strongly emphasizes the role of human free will and ethical choice, so much so that he finds considerable difficulty in reconciling it with Divine foreknowledge.

His discussion of the commandments (*mitsvot*) is again rationalistic: the commandments are the product of Divine wisdom, intended for man's well-being, both spiritual (i.e., intellectual, through correct beliefs) and physical (i.e., concerning man's personal and social morality); they may be understood by man through deep reflection, albeit their observance is not dependent upon their being understood. Some of the ritual laws which seem senseless and archaic are explained by Maimonides in the *Guide* in terms of the context of the ancient world and the struggle of Judaism with ancient paganism.

Because the ideal of Maimonidean spirituality is the love of God through the intellect, there is thus a strong emphasis upon study and the pursuit of knowledge, coupled with philosophical reflection upon the cosmos and upon the correct religious doctrine. The prophet is seen as the ideal religious type, combining human ethical and intellectual perfection with Divine illumination.

One of the major issues in Maimonidean scholarship is the integration of the divergent sides of his work — the philosophic and the talmudic-religious — and the resolution of apparent contradictions among various passages in his writings, particularly between the *Guide* and the *Mishneh Torah*. Various opinions have been expressed by Maimonidean scholars regarding this problem. Some have a dichotomous view of Maimonides' work, i.e., they believe that the *Guide* contains an esoteric teaching intended for the elite and reflecting Maimonides' true theological position, whereas the *Yad* was written in a more political-communal vein with the aim of retaining the loyalty and communal integrity of the Jewish masses. Alternatively, some maintain that the *Guide* was written as an apologia addressed to those semi-assimilated Jews who were influenced by "Greek wisdom" and needed to be shown that Judaism and neo-Aristotelianism were reconcilable, whereas Maimonides' "real" inner concerns were with the *halakhah*, as found in the *Yad* (a common Orthodox interpretation of Maimonides). Then again, some have an integrative view of Maimonides' writings, i.e., they contend that both works are equally authentic expressions of Maimonides' "true" position and represent one, holistic attempt to reconcile the truths of received religious tradition with those of rational philosophy.

Many of Maimonides' views were contested by his contemporaries and were the focus of a series of controversies both during his lifetime and thereafter. Traditionalists saw his symbolic reinterpretations of anthropomorphic expressions in the Bible and Talmud, as well as his rationalistic approach to such doctrines as individual providence and bodily resurrection, as being tantamount to heresy. The Maimonidean controversy continued in one form or another throughout the Middle Ages.

MAIMUNA A joyous celebration held by the Jews of North Africa and some Eastern communities to mark the end of PASSOVER. Its origins are obscure. The name stems from the Arabic word meaning "good fortune." After sunset, on the last day of Passover, the *Maimuna* table is laid out in every home with dairy foods and decorated with wild flowers, wheat stalks, and other greenery. On the table there is also a dish of flour with gold coins or gold trinkets in it (for prosperity) and a bowl of yeast (for making the first loaf of bread the next day after a whole week of unleavened bread). An uncooked fish is also set on the table, symbolizing fertility. During the whole evening, the house is open for relatives and friends who visit until late into the night. The host gives each newcomer a leaf of lettuce dipped in honey, the green lettuce representing crops, i.e., prosperity, and the honey symbolizing sweetness. The next morning, the *Maimuna* day, families go on picnics to the countryside.

Dish of flour with stalks of wheat, dates, green broad beans, gold coins, for the Maimouna table.

These were frowned upon and condemned by the rabbis, when what was originally meant to be family gatherings turned into large, rowdy outdoor parties. In modern Israel, *Maimuna* day is celebrated by organized communal picnics with a central gathering held in Jerusalem. Similar celebrations are held in some other Sephardi and Eastern communities.

MAJOR PROPHETS See ISAIAH; JEREMIAH; EZEKIEL

MAKHSHIRIN ("liquids that render food susceptible to impurity"). Eighth tractate of Order TOHOROT in the Mishnah. Its six chapters deal with the laws of liquids which, when they come in contact with food, render it liable to uncleanness (cf. Lev. 11:34,38). The tractate discusses the conditions in which liquids render food unclean, public baths, produce of Gentiles with regard to uncleanness, persons rendered unclean through contact with water, transferring liquids from vessel to vessel, and some of the liquids which do not impart uncleanness. The subject matter is amplified in the *Tosefta* but not in the Talmuds.

MAKKOT ("lashes"). Fifth tractate of Order NEZIKIN in the Mishnah. Its three chapters deal with the trial and punishment of false witnesses, cases of manslaughter, flight to a City of Refuge (see ASYLUM), and the 59 offenses which are punishable by lashes (cf. Num. 35:9-34; Deut. 19:1-13, 15-21). It has been suggested that this tractate was originally combined with the previous one, SANHEDRIN, because both deal with criminal cases. The name is derived from the verse "He may be given up to 40 lashes, but not more, lest being flogged further to excess, your brother be degraded before your eyes" (Deut. 25:3). The subject matter is amplified in both Talmuds and the *Tosefta*.

MALACHI Last book of the MINOR PROPHETS in the Prophetical section of the Bible. Malachi may be the personal name of the prophetic author; on the other hand the term may be derived from the Hebrew *malakhi* (my messenger) referring to the poet's Divine mission (cf. Mal. 3:1) and his given name is unknown. The Book of Malachi supplies no biographical details concerning the prophet. Some talmudic rabbis identified this last of the prophets with EZRA, maintaining, for example, that the evils against which Malachi preached are similar to those encountered by Ezra and Nehemiah. According to the Talmud (*Meg.* 15a), Malachi was a contemporary of HAGGAI and ZECHARIAH, and all prophesied in the second year of the reign of King Darius of Persia. Once these three died, the Talmud states, prophecy came to an end.

The Book of Malachi is divided into three chapters and contains 55 verses. (The second-last verse is repeated at the end, in order not to have the book — and the entire prophetical section — end on a negative note.) According to modern scholars, the contents indicate that the book was written in the post-exilic period after the rebuilding of the Temple, probably in the time preceding the reforms that were finally instituted by Ezra and Nehemiah. Worthy of note is the book's universalism: "For from where the sun rises to where it sets, My name is honored among the nations, and everywhere incense and pure oblation are offered to My name; for My name is honored among the nations — says the Lord of Hosts" (1:11). Malachi was the first to suggest an eschatological role for ELIJAH (4:5). The last verses of Malachi (4:4-6) have been interpreted as being not only the end of the book but also the culmination of the entire prophetical section of the Bible.

THE BOOK OF MALACHI

1:1 — 1:5	Preamble
1:6 — 2:9	Priests rebuked as responsible for spiritual backsliding
2:10 — 2:16	Denunciation of mixed marriages and of divorces
2:17 — 3:5	The approach of the Day of the Lord
3:6 — 3:12	Denunciation of the Jews for failing to pay tithes to the Temple
3:13 — 3:21	Condemnation of those who lack belief in Divine justice
3:22 — 3:24	The coming of Elijah before the Day of the Lord

MALBIM, MEIR LEIB BEN JEḤIEL MICHAEL (1809-1879). Volhynian-born rabbi and Bible commentator. An uncompromising champion of Orthodoxy, Malbim was appointed chief rabbi of Romania in 1858, but his stand on religious fundamentals (such as the dietary laws) and his strenuous opposition to Reform antagonized the Bucharest Jewish community leaders, who favored acculturation. Their slanderous charges, which he tried vainly to rebut, induced the Romanian government to side with his enemies; following a term of imprisonment, he was released through the personal intervention of the English Jewish leader, Sir Moses Montefiore, and then had to leave the country in 1864. Ḥasidim and radical advocates of Enlightenment joined Malbim's persecutors, further embittering his last years. He wrote halakhic works, sermons, and an autobiography, but it was his commentary on the Hebrew Bible (1845-76) that achieved lasting renown. Its popular title, based on the acronym of the author's name, is "The Malbim." This commentary's purpose was ideological as well as expository — to show that the Written and Oral Law are both of Divine origin, to elucidate the plain meaning (PESHAT) of the biblical text, and thereby to undermine the Reform movement's prestige in the sphere of exegesis.

MALKHUYYOT ("kingships"). The first of the three middle blessings of the AMIDAH prayer of the Additional Service of ROSH HA-SHANAH (the New Year). This section combines mention of the additional SACRIFICES in the TEMPLE on Rosh ha-Shanah, and ten verses relating to the acceptance of God as king. The latter accords with the talmudic dictum, where God, as it were, exclaims, "Recite *Malkhuyyot* before Me so as to accept Me as King over you" (*RH* 16a). While the number of verses is specified in the Mishnah (*RH* 4.6), their choice is not. The Talmud only demands a rubric of three verses from the Pentateuch, three from the Hagiographa, and three from the Prophets, with the final verse again from the Pentateuch. Over the years, specific verses were chosen, and these are incorporated in the MAHZOR (festival prayer book) for Rosh ha-Shanah. The *Malkhuyyot* section includes the ALÉNU LE-SHABBEAH prayer, a suuplication for a time when all the people of the earth will accept God as their King.

MAMZER See ILLEGITIMACY

MAN According to the biblical narrative, man was created by God as part of the world. However, he is set apart from the rest of nature and constitutes the climax and purpose of the entire CREATION. Abraham Joshua HESCHEL commented that the BIBLE is not a book about God, but a book about man. Indeed, once the world is created its entire focus becomes man and his history. When after a series of disappointments God decides to develop a special people called Israel, the human focus is not abandoned. The COVENANT with the patriarchs and with Israel is simply the means to bring "blessing to all the families of the earth" (Gen. 12:3). Man is created last, after the rest of creation is brought into existence in an orderly graduated process, and is blessed to have dominion over all that preceded him (Gen. 1:28, 29). Previously, God announced His intention: "Let us make man in our image, after our likeness..." (Gen. 1:26). Man's creation is described not in terms of God's word, as had previously been the case (e.g., "God said: Let the earth put forth grass..." [Gen. 1:11] "God said:...Let the waters swarm..." [Gen. 1:20]) but in terms of a direct act of God: "God created man..." [Gen. 1:27]. The second chapter of Genesis, which goes into greater detail about the creation of man, states: "And the Lord God formed man of the dust of the ground and breathed into his nostrils the breath of life and man became a living soul" (Gen. 2:7). This figure of speech has been interpreted as implying that in man alone is a direct import from God Himself, the vivifying principle.

After the creation of man, it is not said — as in regard to other orders of creation — "And the Lord saw that it was good" (Gen. 1:10,12,18,21,25). This, say the rabbis, indicates that unlike other creatures, man is not complete until he develops his own personality and becomes a moral "self." The "image of God" in man has been variously associated with his possession of freedom of choice; his ability to invent and to learn and use conceptual language; his ability to employ intelligence in creative ways; his ability to experience his "self" as a unique, individual person; his ability to be self-reflective and become aware that he bears the "image of God" (*Avot* 3:4). Most significant of all is "freedom of choice," which makes of man a moral agent, responsive to moral obligation yet with the power to disobey, and confers upon him responsibility for his actions (see FREE WILL).

> "When I behold Your heavens, the work of Your fingers, The moon and the stars which You have established; What is man that You are mindful of him? And the son of man that You think of him? Yet You have made him but little lower than the angels, And have crowned him with glory and honor; You have made him to have dominion over the works of Your hands; You have put all things under his feet." (Psalms 8:4-7)

The rabbis insisted that the "image of God" confers special dignity even upon the human body, requiring that it be kept in a state of cleanliness (*Sanh.* 46b) and entitled to special treatment after death (*Rashi* on Deut. 21:23). The origin of all men from a common human ancestor reinforces the concept of the essential equality of all people and at the same time declares the infinite worth of every individual qua individual. Men and women share equally in the distinction of being created in the "image of God" (Gen. 1:27). Man was created first and was not introduced to his "helpmate" until he himself realized that "it was not good for man to be alone" (Gen. 2:20).

According to Judaism, the effect of the first sin of Adam and Eve in eating of the fruit of the tree of knowledge of good and EVIL, whatever else it might have done, did not affect man's freedom to obey or disobey. While certain expressions in the Bible point to a deeply rooted propensity in man toward evil (Gen. 8:21), the steady appearance of some good people suggests that even before man receives additional help from God in the form of special revelations, he is able to "choose life and the good." The rabbis taught that each man possesses a *yetser ha-tov* (good inclination) and a *yetser ha-ra* (evil inclination) but that he "himself" can decide to serve God with both inclinations (*Sifré* on Deut. 6:5). According to Martin BUBER, the rabbinic notion of the natural evil in man can best be understood as a "directionless passion," an unchallenged brute energy rather than any demonic or satanic power.

The Bible speaks of man as a psychosomatic unity. The words *nefesh* (soul) and *ru'ah* (spirit) in the Bible generally denote the total living reality that is man rather than any separate or disembodied part of man. The rabbis, however, developed the biblical suggestion of man's composite origin into an explicit dualism without perceiving in the body the source of all evil: "All creatures from heaven have their bodies and souls from heaven. All creatures created from earth have their bodies and souls from the earth. Man alone has the body from the earth and the soul from heaven. Thus, if he does the will of his Father in heaven, he becomes like a heavenly creature. If he does not he becomes totally an earthly creature" (*Sif.* 30b).

This explicit dualism raised questions as to how proper retribution and reward were to be accorded man for his actions in the afterworld (see REWARD AND PUNISHMENT). The rabbis also saw man as a microcosm of the entire universe ("All that God created in the world He created in man") and as ultimately experiencing a palpable yearning for God (Midrash on Eccl. 6:7). Created by a benevolent God and placed in a world that He pronounced "very good," man can be expected to see his life in optimistic terms. However, when man contemplates his history, both as a Jew and as human being, he has cause for anxiety and even pessimism. Because of this ambiguity and because of Judaism's respect for individual differences, there is an acceptance of various temperaments and combinations of character traits as possible versions of the ideal pious personality. In terms of social morality, a rigorous standard of justice, righteousness, and compassion is insisted upon. However, in the area of personal morality the rabbis were satisfied to urge the acquisition of certain key traits, such as *kedushah* (holiness) or *yirat ha-Shem* (fear of God) or *lev tov* (a good heart). However, once one of these is mastered, the individual is free to structure his personality in any variety of combinations: inner- or outer-directed, cheerful or worried, puritanical or pleasure-oriented.

Since the Bible deals primarily with Israel as a nation, it does not discuss the ultimate destiny of man as an individual. The rabbis, however, made it clear that the career of man does not end with physical death. They spoke of a "world to come," of a spiritual existence, and of a "RESURRECTION of the dead" as realms in which man attains fulfillment in accordance with his deserts (see AFTERLIFE).

MANASSEH See TRIBES, TWELVE

MANNA The food miraculously supplied to the Israelites during their wanderings in the wilderness, as described in Exodus 16:14-35. According to Joshua 5:12, the Israelites ate it until the day after the first Passover in Canaan (although Exodus 16:35 says they ate it until reaching the border of Canaan). It is called "bread" and is described as a "fine, flaky substance" or akin to "coriander seed, white, and [tasting] like wafers in honey" (Ex 16:31). It was gathered, ground or pounded, boiled and made into cakes (Num. 11:8). When the manna first appeared, MOSES instructed the people to gather an *omer* (dry measure) for every person in their household. They were further instructed not to leave any over for the next day; those who did so found that it contained "maggots and stank." On Fridays, each Israelite gathered two *omers* to provide for the Sabbath, when no manna fell (Ex. 16:22-25). Moses charged AARON to take a jarful of manna and place it before the Lord in the SANCTUARY, where it was to be permanently preserved. The Midrash ascribes remarkable qualities to the manna. To young children it tasted like milk, to the youth it had the taste of bread, to old men it had the taste of honey. A talmudic sage declared that it was the food of angels. Exploration in the Sinai peninsula has revealed in fairly recent times a food that strongly resembles the biblical manna. Myriads of insects that cover the trees, particularly the tamarisk, secrete liquid drops up to the size of a pea that crystallize and have a sweetish taste. Roaming Beduin use it as food. It must be gathered early in the morning before the ants devour it. These characteristics accord with the biblical description of manna.

Manna and quails fall from heaven. Illustration from the Birds' Head Haggadah. *Germany, 14th century.*

MANNHEIMER, ISAAC NOAH (1793-1865). Rabbi and preacher who fostered a "middle-of-the-road" tradition between Orthodoxy and Reform. Mannheimer was born and educated in Copenhagen, where he instituted a CONFIRMATION ceremony for children (1817) and weekday services of a non-traditional character. In Berlin and Hamburg, he was subsequently identified with the early innovations of REFORM JUDAISM. Mannheimer adopted an increasingly different religious line from 1826, however, when he became spiritual leader of Vienna's elegant new synagogue, the *Stadt-Tempel*. Though in favor of moderate changes (e.g., suppressing references to animal sacrifices), he demanded the retention of Hebrew and of the traditional liturgy (including prayers for Israel's national restoration), criticized the decline of religious observance, opposed the use of an ORGAN in synagogue, and (together with Leopold ZUNZ) defended CIRCUMCISION against attempts in some Reform circles to have it banned. In collaboration with Solomon Sulzer, the eminent cantor-composer, he also improved the services and decorum of his "City Temple." This conservative form of public worship, known as the "Viennese" or "Mannheimer" rite, maintained communal unity and served as a model for other Austrian and German congregations. Mannheimer was an inspiring preacher and a stanch defender of Jewish rights. He published sermons in Danish and German, but his outstanding work was his prayer book (with German translation) which from 1840 went through numerous editions.

MANSLAUGHTER Judaism differentiates between culpable and inculpable manslaughter, the first involving cases in which a person, through an act of negligence, causes the death of another (see MURDER), the second referring to cases in which a person caused death, but without any negligence on his part. In the latter situation, the person is absolved from any crime and is not punished. The rabbis still require him to do penance for the rest of his life, for he was the cause of another human being's loss of life.

When a person killed someone through negligence (the example in the Bible is of a man who was chopping wood and the head of the ax flew off and killed someone, the implication being that he was negligent in chopping when there were other people in the vicinity) he was forced to take ASYLUM in one of the cities of refuge set up throughout Canaan, and had to remain there until the death of the HIGH PRIEST, at which time he became free. If he ventured outside the city of refuge before that time, the immediate relatives of the person he killed had the right to kill him (see BLOOD AVENGER).

Where the killing was an act of criminal negligence or homicide, the culprit was denied entry to the cities of refuge, and would thus effectively have to remain a fugitive from the immediate relatives of the person whom he had killed.

The rabbis of the Talmud debated on how to distinguish between manslaughter and homicide, and offered two basic guidelines: a) the instrument which caused the death should be examined to ascertain if it was liable to cause death; and b) the relations between the victim and the one who killed him should be investigated. Should the instrument be one that could reasonably be assumed to cause death, as, for example, a knife, this would indicate that there was premeditation rather than manslaughter, especially if the victim had been hit in a vital organ. Similarly, if there was known enmity between the two, the presumption would be that it was a case of homicide rather than manslaughter (Maim., *Hilkhot Rotse'aḫ*, 3).

In the past few centuries, various responsa have discussed the question of how a person who has committed manslaughter must atone. It is suggested that the person must do penance, give charity, and attempt to help the family of the victim.

MA'OT ḪITTIM (lit. "funds for grain"). The annual collection of money to supply those in need with the means to purchase their PASSOVER supplies. The practice of donations to the poor for their Passover needs is mentioned in the Talmud, where it is referred to as *kimḫa de-piskha* ("flour for Passover"). The Jerusalem Talmud (*BB* 1:6) rules that anyone who has lived in a city for 12 months is both obligated to pay this tax and entitled to receive his needs from it if necessary. In the Middle Ages, where the Jewish community was highly organized, the payment of the *ma'ot ḫittim* tax was compulsory for all. Various *ma'ot ḫittim* funds exist to this day. Most donate money to the poor to enable them to buy their Passover needs, while some give them the various Passover foods.

MA'OZ TSUR ("O Fortress, Rock [of my salvation]"; cf. Isa. 17:10). Opening words and popular title of a hymn sung by Ashkenazim on the ḪANUKKAH festival, both at home and in synagogue, after the lights have been kindled and the prescribed benedictions recited. Written in 13th-century Germany, this hymn comprises six stanzas, the initial letters of the first five being an acrostic of the author's name, Mordecai, who is otherwise unknown. Stanza 1 is a prayer for the Temple's restoration and for the deliverance of Israel; stanzas 2-4 gratefully recall successive rescues from Egyptian bondage, exile in Babylonia, and Haman's bid to annihilate Persian Jewry; stanza 5 then concludes with a summary of the events that are celebrated on Ḫanukkah. A sixth stanza, rarely sung, alludes either to the Holy Roman Emperor Frederick I (Barbarossa), who protected the Jews to some extent, or to the armies of the Crusaders who massacred Jewish communities. Other stanzas were written subsequently in the course of time, but have been forgotten.

Of the traditional tunes to which *Ma'oz Tsur* is sung, one current among the Ashkenazi communities of northern Italy has spread to Israel and the USA. Though less Jewishly authentic, another and older melody (15th cent., Germany) has become popular throughout the world and is now regarded as the standard motif. Several versified English translations of *Ma'oz Tsur* have been written, notably the *Rock of Ages* paraphrase by two American Zionist rabbis, Gustav Gottheil and Marcus Jastrow. This often replaces the Hebrew text in US Reform worship. *Ma'oz Tsur* never entered the Sephardi, Yemenite, and other non-Ashkenazi rituals, but, in Israel especially, the practice of singing this hymn on Ḫanukkah has been adopted by many Sephardi-Eastern communities.

MA'OZ TSUR

Rock of Ages, let our song Praise Your saving power;
You amid the raging throng, were our sheltering tower.
Furious they assailed us; but Your help availed us;
And Your word broke their sword when our own strength failed us.

MARḪESHVAN See ḪESHVAN

MAROR The "bitter herb" eaten with unleavened bread (MATSAH) and the paschal sacrifice (*pesaḫ*) as part of the original meal prior to the Children of Israel's exodus from Egypt (Ex. 12:8). The commandment was expanded to be observed by Jews "throughout the ages" (Ex. 12:7; Num. 9:10-11) and thus became a part of the PASSOVER eve SEDER ritual. In the Bible the word appears only in the plural form,

A man holding horseradish roots used by Ashkenazim as maror *("bitter herb") at the Passover* Seder. *From the* Copenhagen Haggadah.

merorim, but in the Talmud the singular form is noted and appears in the HAGGADAH. The bitter herbs are explained as symbolizing the bitterness of the Israelites' slavery in Egypt.

The Talmud (*Pes.* 39a) discusses the characteristics of the plants which can be used for the bitter herbs, defined as those containing an "acrid [pungent] sap and faded leaves." The Mishnah (*Pes.* 2:5) enumerates five types of plants which can be used. They are: "lettuce (*ḫazeret*), chevril (*tamka*), a plant, Cichorium itybus, succory (*ḫarḫavina*), endives (*olshin*), and maror." Many biologists today link the *maror* with a plant that grows wild in Israel and is known by the Arabic name *murar*. In Eastern Europe it became customary to use the horseradish root for the bitter herb.

During the *Seder* service itself the *maror* is eaten twice: once with the *ḫaroset* (the nut-apple mixture) to temper its bitterness and, immediately following, with the *matsah* in a sandwich form when the full strength of the bitterness is experienced.

MARRANOS (Span. for "swine"). A deliberately offensive and contemptuous term applied in Spain and Portugal to baptized Jews and their descendants from about the early 15th century onward. In the island of Majorca a kindred term — *Chueta* — still designates pious Catholics of remote Jewish origin. Since ancient times, all Jews compelled to embrace another faith have been known in Hebrew as *anusim* (forced converts), the assumption being that they would revert to Judaism once they were free to do so. Instances of forced APOSTASY, when the only alternative was death, always met with understanding on the part of rabbinic authorities.

Following widespread outbreaks of mob violence in 1391, some 50,000 Jews were massacred in Aragon and Castile. Rather than face slaughter or exile, perhaps as many as 100,000 Spanish Jews submitted to baptism at the time. This process continued over the next few decades, either because of anti-Jewish preachers such as Vicente Ferrer or because of further bloody riots. Meanwhile, through social acceptance or intermarriage, a number of wealthy converted Jews (*conversos*) had begun to assume influential positions in the Church, the nobility, and the government. A typical and early example was the apostate rabbi of Burgos, Solomon Ha-Levi, who (as Pablo de Santa Maria) became that city's bishop and a notorious anti-Jewish propagandist. The prominence that these *conversos* now enjoyed gave rise to much popular resentment; but it was chiefly a growing suspicion that many of them were only nominal Christians which led to the establishment of the Spanish Inquisition in 1480. Henceforth, as "New Christians," all Spaniards of Jewish descent might have to face long and searching investigation. The first Marranos convicting of Judaizing (i.e., "relapsing" into Jewish practices) were burned at the stake in 1481 in Seville. Unconverted Jews, whom inquisitors of the Holy Office could not touch, nevertheless posed a threat: their very presence in Spain was bound to encourage and facilitate crypto-Judaism among those ostensibly Catholic. Despite economic and other considerations, this reasoning motivated the royal decree expelling what remained of Spanish Jewry by no later than 31 July 1492. A minority of the Jews, about 150,000, chose exile — most crossing into Portugal, but others laying the foundations of a Sephardi diaspora in Turkey and North Africa; the rest chose to swell the existing Marrano population, either as sincere "New Christians" or as an underground Jewish community. Less than

Marranos condemned to be burned at the stake for relapsing into Jewish practices. Engraving by Maurice Picart, 1722.

five years later, a brutal forced conversion of Portuguese Jewry (allowing no immediate possibility of emigration) gave rise to vast numbers of genuine *anusim*. By contrast with the Spanish Marranos, they made little secret of their true religious loyalty, but from 1540 the newly introduced Portuguese Inquisition began to eliminate these Judaizers.

Although some festivals and observances, as well as knowledge of Hebrew and the prayer book, inevitably grew dim in time, the Marrano practice of Judaism always combined monotheistic faith with basic rituals. Strenuous efforts were made to avoid forbidden food, to make only a pretence of Christian worship and to kindle Sabbath lights, observe Passover, and fast on the Day of Atonement — secret gatherings being held within the family circle or in an underground synagogue. Leading this kind of double life was obviously fraught with danger: one might be betrayed by servants or vindictive relatives. Inquisitional spies learned how to detect crypto-Judaism, and informers were richly rewarded. Those apprehended by the Inquisition were usually tortured to make them reveal the names of other "heretics"; first offenders were given penances; the obstinate were burned at a subsequent *auto-da-fé*.

Whenever escape was possible, Marranos fled to more hospitable and tolerant lands, establishing settlements (and later open Jewish communities) in places as far afield as Salonika, Venice, Amsterdam, London, and the New World. For many ex-Marranos, Amsterdam became the "Dutch Jerusalem," where entire families accompanied by their *converso* servants and priestly confessors reverted to Judaism.

Crypto-Judaism had been largely eradicated in Spain by 1700, although the Spanish Inquisition was abolished only in 1834. According to reliable estimates, some 350,000 Spanish Marranos fell victim to the Inquisition between 1480 and 1808; of these, nearly 32,000 were burned in person and about 18,000 in effigy. Between 1540 and 1771 in Portugal and its overseas dominions, the total number of convicted Marranos was more than 37,000; of these, over 1,400 were burned in person and about half that number in effigy. Until 1917, it was assumed that all trace of Iberian crypto-Judaism had long disappeared. Since then, however, various groups practicing semi-Jewish rites have been discovered in Portugal and in Mexico, some individuals of Marrano descent have immigrated to Israel, and a number of secret Marrano prayer houses have been unearthed in Spain.

MARRIAGE **The Concept.** From the time of creation, marriage has been integral to the Divine plan, exemplified in the story of ADAM AND EVE. Marriage is viewed as a Divine command, a sacred bond, and a means of personal fulfillment. Judaism legitimates marriage as a social institution by bestowing upon it an ontological status, by locating it within a cosmic frame of reference, and it is never questioned that marriage is the natural and desirable state of every adult. Monogamous marriage between a man and a woman has its analogue in the marriage between God and the Jewish people (Hos. 2:21-22; Song of Songs) and between the Sabbath and the Jewish people (see LEKHAH DODI). Thus, by entering marriage, men and women participate in the Divine cosmos. According to the Zohar, the soul descending from heaven is composed of two parts — one male, one female — which become separated and enter different bodies. If they prove worthy, they will be reunited in marriage.

Marriage is the norm and the ideal way of life. The High Priest could not perform the Day of Atonement rituals unless he was married. In the talmudic age an unmarried sage was rare (see CELIBACY). Among the duties of a father towards his son, the Talmud lists that of finding him a wife.

Marriage is more than a contract entered into between a man and a woman. It is a sacrament, an institution with cosmic significance legitimated by religious motifs. Marriage is called *kiddushin* (sanctification). Judaism invests the marriage union with sanctity by giving it Divine authority.

The concept of *kiddushin* means that the wife is no longer available to anyone else for marriage purposes (*Kid.* 2b). It implies exclusivity and thus leads to intimacy. Marriage is elevated from the plane of private contract to that of morality. The primary purpose of marriage is to build a home, an independent unit (Gen. 2:18, 24), and FAMILY and thereby perpetuate society (Gen. 1:28). In biblical law, the groom was excused military service for a year "for the sake of his household, to give happiness to the woman he has married" (Deut. 24:5). According to biblical law a man may take a second wife. However, this was banned in Ashkenazi communities with the decree of Rabbenu GERSHOM ME'OR HA-GOLAH in the year 1000. Today almost all Jewish communities, Sephardi as well as Ashkenazi, follow the ban. A married woman was never allowed to take a second husband (see MONOGAMY AND POLYGAMY).

Little is known from the Bible of the marriage ceremony. However, the negotiations regarding the arrangements for a marriage are seen through various examples. Marriages of both sons and daughters were arranged by their fathers. Thus, ABRAHAM sends his servant to find a wife for Isaac (Gen. 24:35-53), and Judah arranges the marriage of his first-born son (Gen. 38:6). Once the proposal of marriage was accepted by the girl's father or, in his absence, by her elder brother, the amount and nature of the *mohar* (payment by the groom) was agreed upon (see DOWRY). In ancient times, the husband "purchased" his wife (or wives) and she became his property. Jewish law enshrines the concept that the husband marries the wife, and not vice-versa. By Second Temple times, there was an element of choice, as twice a year (AV, FIFTEENTH OF and the DAY OF ATONEMENT) young unmarried men would select their brides from among the girls dancing in the vineyards. The Talmud lays down: "A man is forbidden to accept betrothal for his daughter while she is a minor. He must wait until she is of age and says, 'This is the man I choose'" (*Kid.* 41a).

The marriage ceremony itself was originally a civil contract between groom and bride, although later books of the Bible call it a covenant (Mal. 2:4; Prov. 2:17). It was preceded by a period of engagement (I Sam. 18:17-19). The ceremony, whatever its nature, was an occasion of rejoicing during which love songs in praise of bride and groom were sung (Song 4:1-7) and it was followed by a great feast (Gen. 29:27; Judg. 14:10) that normally lasted seven days (Gen. 29:27; Judg. 14:4).

Marriage in the talmudic age shows both continuity with marriage in the biblical period as well as significant new developments. A major development occurred in the custom of *mohar*. Since it could be used up by the father of the bride, as indeed happened in the case of Rachel and Leah (Gen. 31:13), a wife could remain penniless if her husband divorced her or predeceased her. It thus became necessary to provide for a widow. As a result, the practice of *mohar* evolved through a number of stages into a KETUBBAH (marriage document).

One of the far-reaching developments in the talmudic age was the conversion of the act of marriage from a personal civil procedure to a public religious ceremony that required the presence of a quorum (*minyan*) and the recitation of a number of fixed benedictions. The legal basis of the act of marriage, however, remained unchanged.

Eligibility for Marriage. A person has to be chronologically, physically, and mentally fit for marriage. The determinant criterion is the ability to make a contract and express one's will. This excludes the deaf and dumb, and minors, and those who are psychologically impaired or mentally ill. The deaf and dumb, however, may marry if they can demonstrate their competence to make such a decision.

In order for a childless widow to be eligible to remarry at will, rather than marry her husband's brother as prescribed in the Bible, the *ḥalitsah* ceremony must be performed, according to Jewish law (see LEVIRATE MARRIAGE).

Great emphasis is traditionally placed on the bride's VIRGINITY which symbolizes the moral purity of marriage. A virgin stands to gain double that of a non-virgin from her *ketubbah*.

With regard to age, since a 13-year-old male and a 12.5-year-old female are regarded as adults, their marriage would be perfectly valid. The biblical practice of a father marrying off a minor daughter continued for some time in the talmudic period until the *amora* RAV declared such practice forbidden. The Mishnah declares the age of 18 to be the proper age for marriage for a male, but marriages at an earlier age were not uncommon. Today, Ḥasidic communities have their children marry at close to 18; among Western communities non-Jewish sociological factors have led to Jews marrying at significantly later ages. Child brides were to be found among the North African and Kurdish Jewish communities until recently. For forbidden relations, see MARRIAGES, PROHIBITED. In Israel, the legal minimum age is 18 for men, 17 for women.

Days and Periods when Weddings are not Celebrated. No weddings are to be held on the Sabbath or festivals, including the intermediate days (ḤOL HA-MO'ED) of Passover and Sukkot (because of the rabbinical injunction not to mix one joy with another). By custom, weddings generally do not take place on the day before a festival, nor on Purim if at all possible (weddings are permissible on Ḥanukkah). Friday morning or early Friday afternoon weddings are permissible.

In the period of the counting of the OMER, from Passover through Shavu'ot, weddings are not conducted, except for the New Moon, Lag ba-Omer (18 Iyyar), and 3-5 Sivan (among Sephardim, they are permitted from Lag ba-Omer onward). Likewise, during the THREE WEEKS preceding TISHAH BE-AV marriages are forbidden. It is also a custom to avoid holding weddings during the TEN DAYS OF PENITENCE from Rosh Ha-Shanah to Yom Kippur. It became popular to hold weddings on Tuesdays, regarded as a lucky day because on that day God twice said, "It was good" (Gen. 1:10,12).

The Marriage Process. In biblical and talmudic times, marriage was a two-stage process. It began with the betrothal — *kiddushin* (or *erusin*) — and concluded with *nissu'in* — marriage.

Betrothal. The English term "betrothal" has various Hebrew meanings in relation to the Jewish marriage: (1) *Shiddukhin*: the commitment by a couple to marry at some date in the future and the terms of financial and other obligations undertaken. (2) *Kiddushin* (or *erusin*): a ceremony establishing a nuptial relationship prior to and separate from the wedding ceremony which alone allows the consummation of the marriage by cohabitation. It is the prescribed ceremony which gives the participants the status of a married

Betrothal ceremony. Engraving from Johann Bodenschatz's Book on Jewish Customs in Germany, 1748.

Menorah *(candelabrum), carved on a stone slab found in the synagogue of Eshtemoa, 4th-5th century CE.*

ד ע לפני מי אתה עומד ולפני מי אתה בא
להתפרד
ולפני מי אתה עתיד ליתן
אנכי יי
לא יהיה
לא תשא
זכור את
כבד את
לא תרצח
לא תנאף
לא תגנב
לא תענה
לא תחמ"
כתר תורה
הר ציון
הר ציון
מזרח
שויתי יהוה לנגדי תמיד
הוי קל כנשר רץ כצבי וגבור
אל מול פני המנורה יאירו שבעת הנרות
כארי לעשות רצון אביך ש"
שמן כתית
זית זך למאור
והעלה את נרתיה שבעה
ועשית מנרת זהב טהור
נר תמיד
עמוד ימיני
עמוד שמאלי
סמוט
אטלס
לשנת
תרפב
כשהמלאך המות יבוא ליטול את הנשמה ובידו
התער אז אינו שואל אם הוא זקן או נער
למתנה להחבירה אהבת רעים

couple, and in biblical and talmudic times was the first stage of the marriage process, taking place up to 12 months before the formal marriage ceremony. (3) The common term "engagement" referring to a preliminary contractual agreement between two parties to marry; it has no legal application.

Shiddukhin. An ancient example of preliminary negotiations towards marriage is found in Genesis 34 where the term for the sum of money the father of the groom would pay to the father of the bride is called *mohar*. By talmudic times the term was in disuse, with the Talmud phrasing the negotiations between the respective parents as "How much are you giving to your son?... How much are you giving to your daughter?" (*Kid.* 9b), and the term for them being *shiddukhin*, an Aramaic term meaning "tranquillity." (The common Hebrew term for engagement is *erusin*, which actually has a different legal meaning; see below.) The terms agreed upon were committed to writing in a document called *shetar pesikta*; the sum given to the son was called *nedunyah* (dowry), which later on in common parlance referred to the sum given to the daughter.

From the late medieval period until the present, the prenuptial agreement was divided into two stages: first a verbal understanding (called *vort*: Yid., "a word" among Ashkenazim). A ceremony, *kinyan*, signifying the acceptance of the obligation to marry, is generally made at a meal arranging the *vort*. The act of acceptance is done by taking an object, usually the corner of a handkerchief, which the officiant is holding; this is an act of biblical practice (Ruth 4:7). Secondly, the commitment undertaken was later put in writing in a document called *tena'im* ("terms" of the agreement). In addition to the financial stipulations the *tena'im* would stipulate the date and place of the nuptial ceremony. Breaching the *tena'im* is extremely undesirable. The ceremony of the *tena'im* is concluded with the mothers of the bride and groom breaking a dish or pottery, indicating that "just as a broken shard cannot be repaired, so it is preferable to proceed with the nuptials and then dissolve them by divorce than break a pre-nuptial agreement." The breaking of the dish also carries the same significance as the crushing of the glass under the *ḫuppah* (see below).

This betrothal ceremony is often celebrated with a dinner and during the following period the bride and groom exchange gifts, called *sivlonot*.

Kiddushin or erusin. The Bible designates the betrothal or nuptial ceremony held prior to the wedding and cohabitation of the bride and groom as *erusin* (see Deut. 20:7), and it is so designated in the Talmud from its legal aspects. However, the sages, who codified the manner in which the ceremony is to be performed, called it *kiddushin*, or consecration, indicating that the woman becomes forbidden (inviolate) to all men except her husband just as an object consecrated to the Temple (*hekdesh*) becomes forbidden to all for profane use (*Kid.* 2b).

Referring to this stage of the marriage process the Mishnah states: "A woman is acquired (in marriage) in three ways: by money, by deed, or by intercourse." In talmudic times the sages had already begun to frown on men who used intercourse as the means for contracting marriage. Over the centuries the traditional method became the placing of an unadorned ring on the bride's finger. This stage of the marriage ceremony began with the groom saying, "Behold, you are consecrated (*mekuddeshet*) unto me with this ring according to the law of Moses and of Israel." This was followed by the blessing over wine and "Blessed are You, O Lord our God, King of the Universe, who has hallowed us by Your commandments, and has commanded us concerning forbidden marriages; who has forbidden unto us those who are betrothed, but has sanctioned unto us such as are wedded unto us by the rite of the nuptial canopy and the sacred covenant of wedlock..."

Following this ceremony, the bride continued to reside in her father's house until the *nissu'in*.

Nissu'in. This second stage of the marriage process, when the bride moved into the groom's home, was accompanied by the recitation of seven blessings (*sheva berakhot*).

An important element of this stage of the wedding is that two valid witnesses must be present and follow the proceedings.

In the Middle Ages, due to the precarious situation of many Jewish communities so frequently subject to expulsion, it became customary among Ashkenazi Jews to postpone the betrothal ceremony until immediately prior to the *nissu'in* wedding ceremony itself; this is the custom today also followed by Sephardi Jews. In Ḫasidic circles, however, the traditional *tena'im* ceremony is still common.

From the 13th century, marriages were often arranged by a matchmaker, who was paid a fee for his services (see SHADKHAN).

The Contemporary Wedding Ceremony. Even Orthodox ceremonies are uniform but customs vary. The following is a description of one such ceremony: The groom signs the *ketubbah*. If it is before evening, the Afternoon Service is held and the groom, who is fasting, recites the Day of Atonement confession. The groom is led to the bride and covers her face with her veil. The couple is led to the marriage canopy, ḪUPPAH, with the respective parents walking with groom and bride or the fathers accompanying the groom and the mothers the bride. There is a custom for those leading the couple to carry lit candles.

Once under the canopy the rabbi conducting the ceremony recites the blessing over wine and the *erusin* blessing. The bride and groom drink from the cup. The groom then recites the appropriate phrase (see above, "Behold, you are consecrated...") and places the ring on the bride's right index finger.

To indicate that the marriage act consists of two ceremonies, each with its own standardized blessings, the *ketubbah*

Mizraḫ *(East) plaque, hung in the synagogue to show direction for prayer. Paper-cut and watercolor, by Reicher, Brooklyn, NY, 1922.*

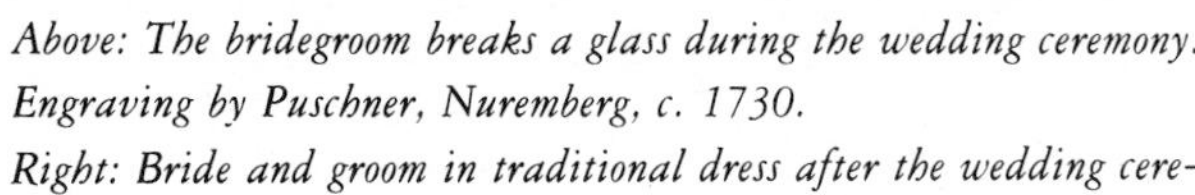

Above: The bridegroom breaks a glass during the wedding ceremony. Engraving by Puschner, Nuremberg, c. 1730.
Right: Bride and groom in traditional dress after the wedding ceremony. Yemen, in the 1930s.

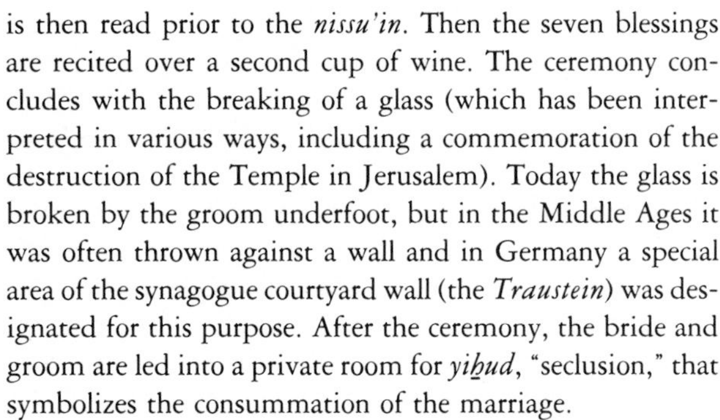

is then read prior to the *nissu'in*. Then the seven blessings are recited over a second cup of wine. The ceremony concludes with the breaking of a glass (which has been interpreted in various ways, including a commemoration of the destruction of the Temple in Jerusalem). Today the glass is broken by the groom underfoot, but in the Middle Ages it was often thrown against a wall and in Germany a special area of the synagogue courtyard wall (the *Traustein*) was designated for this purpose. After the ceremony, the bride and groom are led into a private room for *yiḥud*, "seclusion," that symbolizes the consummation of the marriage.

At the conclusion of the joyous wedding meal, the Grace after Meals is followed by another recitation of the Seven Blessings.

Conservative and Reform weddings follow the traditional pattern, with varying of nuances. However, in many cases, the custom of the groom covering the face of the bride before the ceremony, the procession to the *ḥuppah* with candles, and the *yiḥud* arrangement are observances which are omitted (as is also the case in many modern Orthodox ceremonies, outside Israel). Conservative and Reform ceremonies have introduced the double ring ceremony in which the bride puts a ring on the groom's finger, with or without a blessing or biblical verse. The Reform service is often suppplemented with poetry, prose and song of the rabbi's and the couple's choosing. The etiquette of the procession and other organizational issues follow local customs. Jewish communities the world over often adopted some of the customs or styles of weddings from their environment.

THE SEVEN WEDDING BLESSINGS

Blessed are You, O Lord our God, King of the universe, who creates the fruit of the vine.

... who has created all things to Your glory.

... Creator of man.

... who has made man in Your image, after Your likeness...

... may she who was barren (Zion) be glad and exult when her children are gathered within her in joy. Blessed are You, O Lord, who makes Zion joyful through her children. O make these loved companions greatly to rejoice, even as of old You did gladden Your creatures in the Garden of Eden. Blessed are You, O Lord, who makes bridegroom and bride to rejoice.

... who has created joy and gladness, bridegroom and bride, mirth and exultation, pleasure and delight, love, brotherhood, peace and fellowship. Soon may there be heard in the cities of Judah and in the streets of Jerusalem, the voice of joy and gladness, the voice of the bridegroom and the voice of the bride, the happy sound of bridegrooms from their canopies, and of youths from their feasts of song.

... Blessed are You, O Lord, who makes the bridegroom to rejoice with the bride.

In the Bible it is related that weddings were an occasion of rejoicing during which love songs in praise of bride and groom were sung (Song 4:1-7). The ceremony was followed by a great feast (Gen. 29:27; Judg. 14:4). In the Talmud to gladden a bride and groom at their marriage by joining in the singing and dancing is regarded as fulfillment of a commandment. It records how various sages participated in wedding festivities, and came with lighted candles, myrtle branches, dancing, and entertainments.

In time each community developed individual styles for expressing joy at weddings through music and musicians specializing in weddings (*klezmer* in Yiddish), singing, acrobatics, and the "*mitsvah* dance," in which the bride dances with selected male guests with the man holding one end of a handkerchief and the bride the other. A regular feature at wedding feasts, especially among Ashkenazi Jews, was the jester (the *badhan* or *marshalik*).

Preparations and Customs. Traditionally, the bride must immerse herself in a *mikveh* (ritual bath) prior to the wedding, customarily the evening before the ceremony, and if not then as close to the wedding as possible. The wedding date is carefully fixed so that it does not fall during the period of menstruation or the following week (see NIDDAH). In some Sephardi and Eastern communities, the visit to the *mikveh* was a public celebration.

Most Sephardi communities hold a special celebration for the bride on the eve of the wedding, called the *hinnah*. The women friends and family come to the home of the bride whose hands are painted with red henna. In Yemen, for instance, women who specialized in this dressed the brides in colorful clothes and jewelry to the accompaniment of singing, and then applied the henna. The purpose of the ceremony is to avoid the EVIL EYE.

On the Sabbath prior to the wedding, among Ashkenazi communities, the groom is called to the READING OF THE LAW (the *oyfrufn*) and is showered with candies upon recitation of the blessings. In Sephardi and Eastern communities it is the Sabbath after the wedding which is *Shabbat hatan*, the groom's Sabbath, on which he is called to the Reading.

In Muslim lands, the dressing of the bride is a major ceremony, compared to the robing of a queen for her coronation.

During the procession to the *huppah* it is customary to shower the couple with rice, confetti, and so forth. There is a widespread custom that the couple fast prior to the ceremony.

In some Ashkenazi circles, the bride upon reaching the *huppah* is led around the groom a number of times, often seven, illustrating Jeremiah 32:21.

The ceremony could be held anywhere but from the Middle Ages, the synagogue or synagogue courtyard was a favorite venue. Many insisted on holding it in the open air, connecting this with God's promise to Abraham to make his progeny as numerous as the stars. As time went on, it became popular to hold it in a hall.

According to Jewish religious law, no religious functionary is required to perform the ceremony but from the 15th century, weddings were customarily conducted by a rabbi. With Emancipation, the rabbi in many countries was recognized as a state official and gave the marriage its civil legitimacy.

During the week following the wedding, and in some communities for longer periods, festivities continued. Today many couples, during that week, attend special meals which are concluded with the Seven Blessings.

SAYINGS ABOUT MARRIAGE

Any man who has no wife is not a complete human being.

The sins of man are forgiven at marriage.

Marriage takes precedence over the study of Torah.

Whoever spends his days without a wife has no joy, no blessing and no good in his life.

God's occupation is sitting and arranging marriages.

Forty days before a child is created, it is proclaimed in heaven, "This man's daughter shall marry that man's son."

When an old man marries a young wife, the man becomes young and the woman old.

A man is not even called a man until united with a woman.

A groom may not enter the bridal chamber until the bride gives him permission.

MARRIAGE CONTRACT

See KETUBBAH

MARRIAGES, PROHIBITED

A marriage is prohibited if it may not be contracted under biblical or rabbinic law. Prohibited marriages can be divided into two categories: permanent and temporary.

Permanent Prohibitions Marriages between relatives as detailed in Leviticus 18 and 20, including a man's parents, stepmother, sister, granddaughter, aunt, daughter-in-law, sister-in-law, stepdaughter, and step-granddaughter, and wife's sister during the wife's lifetime. The Bible offers no reason for these prohibited marriages except to call them "depravity," "reproach," and "indecency." Maimonides explained that their purpose was to preserve chastity and morality within the family (*Guide* III,49). In addition:

a. If a husband divorced his wife and she remarried and was subsequently set free either by divorce or her second husband's death, her first husband may not remarry her.

b. A wife who had willingly committed adultery becomes prohibited to her husband, and to the adulterer even after a divorce from her husband (*Sot.* 27b). If she was raped, she is prohibited to her husband only if he is a priest (*kohen*).

c. A woman is not permitted to marry anyone who represented her in her divorce case or who witnessed her husband's death, to avoid the suspicion of collusion (*Sh. Ar. EH* 12:1).

d. A priest may not marry a divorcee (Lev. 21:14), even his own wife if he had divorced her, nor may he marry a widow. He may also not marry a harlot because of his sanctity (Lev. 21:7; *Guide* III,49).

e. A *mamzer* (offspring of an adulterous or incestuous relationship; see ILLEGITIMACY) may not marry a Jewish man or woman. Maimonides explains that this prohibition creates "a horror of illicit marriages...the adulterer and adultress were thus taught that by their act they bring upon their seed irreparable injury" (*Guide* III,49).

f. Mixed marriage is forbidden. The Bible forbade the Israelites to marry the Canaanites because of the fear of idolatry and assimilation: "For they will turn your children away from Me to worship other gods" (Deut. 7:3-4). This prohibition was later extended to all non-Jews. INTERMARRIAGE, however, where the non-Jewish partner converts to Judaism prior to marriage, is permitted.

g. A man may not take another wife while still married to his first wife, according to the decree of Rabbenu GERSHOM in the year 1000. Although the second marriage is valid, the parties will be compelled to divorce. This ban applied to Ashkenazi Jewry, and was also accepted in many parts of the non-Ashkenazi world.

Temporary Prohibitions Certain marriages are prohibited only for certain periods, after which they are permitted:

a. A widow or divorcee may not remarry within 90 days after the death of her husband or after receiving the *get* (bill of divorce). The purpose of this law was to avoid confusion over the paternity of any child.

b. An individual may not marry within the 30-day period of mourning prescribed by Jewish law, and a widower must wait until three festivals have passed. However, if he has no children or has young children who need a mother's care, he need not wait that long to remarry (*Sh. Ar. YD* 392.2).

c. It is forbidden to marry a pregnant woman, or a nursing mother until the child has reached the age of 24 months, which was the prevailing length of time for nursing (*Yev.* 42a).

d. If a woman's two successive husbands died not due to accidents, she may not marry a third time because the fate of her former husbands may bring bad luck to the third marriage (*Yev.* 64b). In post-talmudic times this prohibition was not viewed as compulsory.

e. A married woman may not take a second husband. In order for a divorce to be valid, the husband must give his wife the *get* as decreed by the Bible (Deut. 24:1). If he refuses, or if he is missing and cannot be found, as in times of war, the wife is left in a distressing situation. Since she does not have a *get*, nor is there definite proof of her husband's death, she is in the status of an AGUNAH — a chained woman, still attached to her husband and not free to remarry. The rabbis throughout the centuries have in many instances successfully resolved *agunah* situations involving missing husbands. In the case of husbands refusing to give a *get*, various pressures are brought to bear upon husbands (including imprisonment, in the State of Israel), though not always successfully.

MARTYRDOM

See KIDDUSH HA-SHEM

MASHGI'AH̱

("supervisor"). a) The spiritual mentor in a rabbinical academy (*yeshivah*); the person who directs the students in proper behavior both inside and outside the *yeshivah*. It is his responsibility to supervise the scholastic activities of the students and their progress as well as their behavior toward their fellow-students. Ideally, the *mashgi'aẖ*'s influence over his students is such that they feel his counsel even when he is not physically present. He is also the ethical presence in the *yeshivah*, who at fixed times, and on special occasions, gives lectures on proper moral behavior. These are generally referred to as *siẖot* ("conversations") and play a prominent role in *yeshivot* of the Lithuanian tradition.

b) A person empowered by a rabbi to supervise the application of the DIETARY LAWS in a factory, restaurant, or any other place where food is prepared. He insures that the preparation of the food is in accordance with Jewish law, both with regard to the ingredients used and methods of preparation. He makes sure that the food is not cooked on the Sabbath or prepared in any other way which would render it unfit in terms of Jewish law. The *mashgi'aẖ* must report back to the rabbi who appointed him, and issue a warning if he notices any violation. When the *mashgi'aẖ*'s report is satisfactory, the supervising rabbi endorses the product as being "*kosher.*"

MASORAH AND MASORETIC ACCENTS

The system of rules, principles, and tradition devised to preserve the authentic biblical text (see BIBLE). Various opinions have been offered as to the meaning of the word. Some say that it is related to the verb *m-s-r*, implying transmission, i.e., the handing down of a TRADITION. Others believe that the word relates to "counting," for those involved in the Masorah, the Masoretes, would count each letter of each book, to insure that no letters were added or left out. Based on Ezekiel 20:37, the connotation of fencing off has also been suggested, in that the Masoretes "fenced off" the text from those who might change it.

Originally, the biblical books were written as continuous strings of letters, without breaks between words. This led to great confusion in understanding the text. To insure the accuracy of the text, there arose a number of scholars, known collectively as the Masoretes in the sixth century CE, and continuing into the tenth century.

The Masoretes divided the text into words and sentences, as well as into segments, either major (indicated in the Torah scroll by the balance of the line remaining blank), or minor (indicated by a gap equivalent of at least nine letters in the midst of a line). They added the vowel signs (see HEBREW), and the CANTILLATION marks (although these were added primarily as a punctuation aid to proper reading of the text, they are also used to indicate the melody for public recitation). The Masoretes also indicated those cases where the written form of the word (*ketiv*) differs from the way it is read (*keri*), as well as correct spellings. They also established cases in which a particular letter is to be written larger than the rest, or smaller, and set out the pattern for the writing of the verses within the text.

Originally, there were two separate systems of vowelization: the Babylonian, where the vowels were primarily above the letters, and the Tiberian (i.e., from Tiberias), where they were below. Eventually, the Tiberian system was accepted universally, and is used to this day.

The work of the Masoretes is printed in the various Hebrew editions of the biblical books. In the margins are the minor notes, known as the *masorah ketannah* (the "minor *masorah*"), while above and below the text are major notes regarding the text, known as the *masorah gedolah* (the "major *masorah*"). Further extensive notes are printed at the end of each volume.

The accepted text of the Bible is that determined by Aaron ben Asher (930 CE) of the Tiberias school of Masoretes, which was accepted as the authorized text, at the recommendation of Moses MAIMONIDES. The oldest extant copy of this, dating back to the first half of the tenth century CE, was to be found in the synagogue in Aleppo, Syria, and was known as the KETER *Aram Zovah*. While parts of this manuscript were destroyed in the riots against the Syrian Jews in 1947, the majority of the work survived, and was brought to Israel, where it is now part of the library collection of the Ben Zvi Institute.

The importance of the work of the Masoretes is attested by R. Solomon Jedidiah, 16th-century author of *Minḥat Shai*, who writes in the introduction to this work: "Had it not been for the Masoretes who established the correct version of the Torah, almost nobody would have been able to come to any clear decision in disputes. The entire Torah would then have been forgotten by Israel, and the one Torah would have become many different Torahs, Heaven forbid, and we would not have found two scrolls of the same book which were identical to one another, as is the case with other books by various authors."

MASSEKHET (lit. "web of loom" or "woven fabric"). A tractate of the MISHNAH or TALMUD, more commonly called *Masekhta* (Aram.). The term *Massekhet* is particularly apt for designating a talmudic tract, with its complex web of themes and ideas. The six Orders of the Mishnah edited by R. JUDAH HA-NASI were originally divided into 60 tractates of the Talmud, but the subsequent sub-division of *Nezikin* into three, and the separation of *Makkot* from *Sanhedrin*, brought the number to 63. Each tractate deals with a specific subject or area of law. After a person completes the study of a *Massekhet*, it is customary to hold a SIYYUM ("conclusion"), a celebration at which he gives an exposition of the final few lines or final idea of the tractate.

MATRIARCHS (*immahot*). SARAH, REBEKAH, RACHEL, and LEAH, the "full" wives of the PATRIARCHS and ancestors of the Jewish people. Each of these figures played a role at the dawn of Israel's history. Just as Abraham, Isaac, and Jacob were chosen by God to participate in the covenant, so the matriarchs were the "chosen" rather than the accidental wives and mothers. With the exception of Sarah, the biblical narrative describes in great detail how and why each was chosen. A close reading of the text reveals the personality of each matriarch with her struggles, successes, and failures, all seeking to insure their sons' position in the Divine plan. Deception, intrigue, and manipulation, as well as love and support, were accepted weapons. Details missing in the biblical descriptions were supplied, by the rabbis, in the Midrash.

The four matriarchs (Sarah, Rebekah, Rachel, and Leah). From the Amsterdam Haggadah, *1743.*

The matriarchs have an honored place in Jewish folk perception. Their names are invoked in the MI SHE-BERAKH prayer recited after the birth of a child and (in some rites) on behalf of a sick female, as well as in the PARENTAL BLESSING of daughters by the father on Sabbath eve. However, they are not mentioned in the liturgy, where God is referred to solely as the "God of our Fathers," and the "God of Abraham...Isaac and...Jacob." In recent years, under the impact of Jewish feminism, a conscious effort has been made by certain groups to redress what is seen as a masculine bias in the liturgy. The verbal addition of "and mothers" to the fathers, or of "and Sarah, Rebekah, Rachel and Leah" to the names of the patriarchs wherever thought appropriate (as in the opening passage of the AMIDAH), is not uncommon in many Reform, Conservative, and Reconstructionist congregations, particularly in North America. Written changes, however, are less widespread. The latest Reform prayer books published in the US (*Gates of Prayer*, 1975) and Israel (*Ha-Avodah she-ba-Lev*, 1981; *Maḥzor Kavvanat ha-Lev* 1988), as well as the American Conservative prayer book (*Siddur Sim Shalom*, 1985), introduce the matriarchs by name in additional, alternative versions of the *Amidah*.

MATSAH Unleavened bread made from dough which is completely free of yeast or leavening and which is baked before the onset of fermentation. The opposite of *matsah* is ḤAMETS (regular leavened bread, cakes, etc.). Both are made of one of the five species of grain: wheat, rye, barley, oats, and spelt. The *halakhah* determined that once any of these grains comes into contact with water, a process of fermentation begins 18 minutes later. Dough is made by kneading flour and water together; to qualify as *matsah*, it must be baked before fermentation can begin, i.e., before 18 minutes have elapsed.

The Bible prohibits the consumption and possession of *ḥamets* for the seven days (eight outside Israel) of PASSOVER, and obligates the consumption of at least an olive's weight (*ka-zayit*) of *matsah* on the SEDER night (Ex. 12:15-20, 13:7; see also *Pes.* 28b, 120a). *Matsah* is associated with the sacrificial cult (Lev. 2:4-5), being the only type of dough permitted to be offered upon the altar as part of the meal offering.

Flour for *matsah* is generally ground from wheat, but any of the five species of grain may be used (*Pes.* 35a). The process of baking *matsah* begins with the guarding of the grain against any contact with water. Although the *halakhah* mandates such guarding from the time the grain is ground into flour, many strictly observant Jews will use only *matsah* where the grain has been guarded from its harvesting. Such *matsah* is known as *matsah shemurah* ("guarded *matsah*") and is usually kneaded by hand, although machine-made *matsah shemurah* is also available. Many observant Jews, while not requiring *matsah shemurah* during all of Passover, are careful to use it for the *Seder*. Water used in unleavened bread is called *mayim she-lannu* ("water that has rested overnight"). It is drawn from a well or river at dusk and left to "cool" until morning (*Pes.* 94b); the water is mixed with the guarded flour, after which the dough is kneaded, rolled flat, and pierced with a pin roller to prevent it from rising. It is then baked at a high temperature before 18 minutes have elapsed.

Baking matsah *(the unleavened bread eaten at Passover) in the ghetto of Roman in the 20th century.*

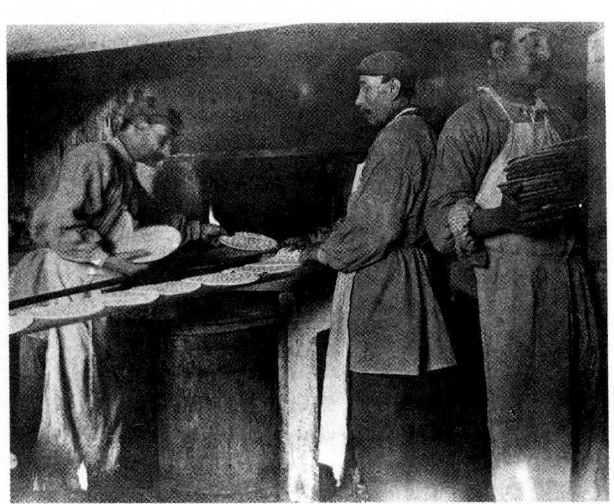

At the *Seder*, in addition to the normal blessing over bread, a special benediction is said before partaking of the unleavened bread: "Blessed are You, Eternal our God, Ruler of the universe, Who has sanctified us with Your commandments and commanded us concerning the eating of *matsah*." To dramatize the moment when unleavened bread is eaten at the *Seder*, the custom has arisen of refraining from eating *matsah* from Purim (approximately four weeks prior to Passover), or from the first of the month of Nisan (two weeks before Passover).

The symbolic association of *matsah* is twofold and dialectical. On the one hand, *matsah* is a symbol of freedom based upon Exodus 12:39, "They baked unleavened cakes of dough which they brought forth from Egypt, for it was not leavened; because they had been driven out of Egypt, and could not delay..." The Passover HAGGADAH explains, "It is because there was not time for the dough of our ancestors to rise, before the Ruler of All revealed Himself and redeemed them." On the other hand, *matsah* is a symbol of the Egyptian slavery. Deuteronomy 16:3 refers to it as the bread of affliction (*leḥem oni*), and the *Haggadah* declares, "This is the bread of affliction that our ancestors ate in the Land of Egypt." Thus *matsah* recalls both slavery and redemption.

MATTAN TORAH See REVELATION

MAYIM AḤARONIM ("Latter waters"). Symbolic rinsing of the fingers prior to the recitation of GRACE AFTER MEALS. This practice evidently derives from ancient table manners: since only a knife and the fingers were used at meals, no Grace could be recited until each diner had cleansed his hands (*Ber.* 53b). According to the rabbis (*Ber.* 46b), both forms of ritual ablution must be performed by everyone at table in order of seniority. One explanation given was that the condiment known as "salt of Sodom" included an admixture of Dead Sea potassium chloride and, unless the hands were thoroughly washed, it might be rubbed into the eyes and lead to blindness (*Er.* 17b; *Ḥul.* 105a-106a). However, new hygienic conditions in the West, coupled with the fact that no "salt of Sodom" was used by medieval French Jewry, led Rabbenu TAM to declare *mayim aḥaronim* superfluous (*Tos. to Ḥul.* 105a). While no benediction is prescribed for this ritual, the *Shulḥan Arukh* nevertheless insisted on its continued validity (*OḤ* 181.7,10), a stand adopted by later authorities such as ELIJAH GAON OF VILNA and the ḤAFETS ḤAYYIM. Those Orthodox Jews who follow their ruling use cold water and rinse each hand in turn, up to the second joint of the fingers, allowing the water to drip into a vessel. Some make use of a finger bowl, others prefer a specially designed unit comprising a miniature bowl and pitcher.

MEAL OFFERINGS See SACRIFICES AND OFFERINGS

MEAT AND MILK See DIETARY LAWS

MEDICAL ETHICS, JEWISH Guiding principles and standards of conduct in the practice of medicine which are based on the traditional religious and moral norms of Judaism. The subject became a distinct discipline only recently, and it is now beginning to have its own experts, literature, and specialized research institutes. Directives on medical matters are found in all sources of Jewish law — from the Bible to the latest rabbinic RESPONSA. These responsa constitute an appreciable part of the corpus of Jewish legal and ethical literature.

The belated "recognition" of Jewish medical ethics is strikingly illustrated by a comparison between the old *Jewish Encyclopedia* (1901-6), which included no articles on the subject at all, and the more recent *Encyclopaedia Judaica* (1972), which contains fairly extensive entries under abortion, artificial insemination, autopsies, birth control, castration, euthanasia, homosexuality, and transplants. Yet it still had no comprehensive article on medical ethics generally, and there were also other notable omissions (e.g., eugenics, experimentation, and faith healing).

Publications: The relatively sudden proliferation of writings on the subject was generated partly by the contemporary quest for "relevance" in the search for Jewish values, and partly by the popular concern with medico-moral problems — stimulated by the spectacular advances in modern medicine and its ever-increasing incursions into the moral sphere. Related also was the revolutionary shift in the climate of public opinion, commonly characterized by the "permissive society," which has created a vacuum previously filled by legislation and traditional mores. Indeed, the widespread demand for authoritative guidance has spawned an entirely new genre of Jewish literature. It includes a growing array of textbooks and manuals, as well as articles in virtually every journal of Jewish thought.

These books and articles are, however, only collections and discussions of the secondary sources. The primary source material chiefly derives from the massive output of responsa by great contemporary masters of rabbinic law such as Mosheh FEINSTEIN, Eliezer Waldenberg, and Isaac Jacob Weiss. These multivolume works reproduce the answers given by the authors to questions submitted to them for rabbinic decision. Their verdicts are invariably based on principles enshrined as relevant precedents in the Talmud, the Codes, and earlier responsa within the constantly evolving process of Jewish lawmaking.

Among the many hundreds of individual responsa now published annually, a considerable proportion is devoted to questions on medical ethics. Opinions will often differ quite significantly, owing to divergent interpretations or even conflicting assessments of the medical data — on the definition of death, for example, or the status of the embryo. As a consensus gradually emerges, however, that becomes the norm of Jewish law, it will generally be accepted as authentic among those committed to the sovereignty of religious imperatives in their lives and to rabbinical mentors as the exponents of Jewish ethical values and standards.

Institutes: This burgeoning literature is also academically promoted by several institutes specifically dedicated to the study, teaching, and literary advancement of Jewish medical ethics. Such institutes are now associated with leading universities and religious hospitals in Israel, and with Yeshiva University in New York. They engage in research as well as in the instruction of medical students, nurses, and hospital staffs, especially through periodical seminars and symposia. Within the past few years, international conferences on Jewish medical ethics have been held in Israel, Europe, and America — another indication of the significant rise of professional interest in the subject, with a corresponding growth in research and literary output. The first theses for postgraduate degrees in Jewish medical ethics are currently being prepared at Israeli universities.

Scope: Most moral problems encountered in medicine arise at or before the inception of life (e.g., contraception, ABORTION, ARTIFICIAL INSEMINATION and fertilization, genetic engineering, sex determination, etc.), or else at its terminal stage prior to or immediately following death (e.g., resuscitation, suspension of treatment, definition of death, removal of donor organs, AUTOPSIES, etc.). To a lesser extent, though likewise increasingly acute, there are also ethical dilemmas in the intermediate stages of life, notably issues such as confidentiality, experimentation on human beings as well as on animals, allocation of resources, informing patients, and doctor-patient relationships generally. Specifically Jewish issues further include Sabbath observance, food or medication containing religiously prohibited substances, and fasting on the Day of Atonement, together with visiting and praying for the sick, reliance on irrational cures, or exposure to health hazards such as smoking or dietary risks.

The enormously ramified decisions in all these areas are binding on doctors and patients alike. In most cases, particularly where they affect life-and-death decisions (such as pregnancy termination or transplant operations), the principles involved would be regarded as of universal validity, although Jewish practitioners treating Gentile patients would be expected to pay due respect to the teachings of their own faith as well.

Trends: Naturally, ethical principles and guidelines rooted in a traditional code of laws, which in turn derive their authenticity from antecedents relying on earlier authority (whether Divine or human), are bound to be conservative in character. More often than not, therefore, the conclusions reached are restrictive rather than permissive. The area of personal choice by individual preference or conscience is frequently limited. Purely utilitarian motives are rarely sanctioned or encouraged.

The attitude reflected in traditional Jewish rulings is nevertheless often remarkably liberal, especially when contrasted with some other religiously inspired systems of medical ethics. For instance, in Jewish law, there is no absolute ban on BIRTH CONTROL or abortion, and the avoidance or mitigation of suffering features high among the considerations to be weighed where conflicting ethical interests require careful assessment to determine the verdict. Thus, where informing a patient of a fatal prognosis might cause a physical or mental setback, one should rather forgo the opportunity for confession — or even violate the truth by outright denial — because the patient's welfare and peace of mind should enjoy priority over purely spiritual concerns.

Where some shift of opinion is discernible, particularly in relation to modern advances, it has usually been in the direction of greater leniency. Thus, while previously there was a fairly clear line of demarcation between abortions permitted to save the mother's life and all others which could not be sanctioned, quite a few judgments have lately veered toward permitting abortions even where the risk is only to the mother's health, or even where fears of grave abnormalities in the child are suspected or ascertained. A similar move toward greater permissiveness, albeit under carefully defined conditions, is apparent in regard to organic heart transplants. The former virtually unanimous opposition to heart transplants, condemned as "double murder" (of the donor and the recipient) by some, has thus lately given way to cautious endorsement, notably by a conditional agreement between the Israel Chief Rabbinate and the Hadassah Hospital in Jerusalem. Other leading rabbis, however, continue to challenge this ruling; they insist on heart stoppage, not mere brain-stem death, before a vital organ can be removed from the donor.

Some Major Principles: Jewish medical ethics are governed by several fundamental principles. These are usually of biblical origin and further elaborated in the Talmud, being then applied by rabbinic exegesis and interpretation to contemporary situations.

(1) *The sanctity of life* or, more precisely, the infinite value of every innocent human life. Stemming from this cardinal rule are decisions concerning euthanasia, experimentation on human beings, the suspension of religious laws when these conflict with life, and the recourse to doubtful or unproven cures in any attempt to save life.

(2) *The religious precept to preserve life and health.* To apply medical skills by those who possess them for those who need them is never optional but always mandatory. Accordingly, a doctor must not refuse his services, nor is the patient's consent required for lifesaving operations, except where needed to secure his cooperation.

(3) *The duty to procreate.* This naturally affects in particular the attitude to abortion and contraception as well as sterilization, sanctioned only for urgent medical reasons and never on purely social or economic grounds, except when these may relate to the mother's health.

(4) *Sanctity of the marriage bond.* This precludes the generation of human life outside MARRIAGE, including by donor insemination or fertilization. Pre-marital and extramarital liaisons are also strictly proscribed, in order to secure the uniqueness and stability of the marital relationship (see SEX).

To the same category belong the laws on sexual morality in general, including the prohibitions of INCEST (by consanguinity and affinity), active homosexuality, and conjugal relations for about 12 days covering the menstrual period. All these laws have some medical ramifications — for instance, the need for certainty in establishing a person's paternity as well as maternity, by accurate records of biological origins, particularly in cases of ADOPTION, artificial insemination, and in vitro fertilization (the latter two being restricted to husband and wife only).

(5) *The duty to alleviate pain and suffering.* Jewish law provides many exemptions from religious observances otherwise mandatory in order to secure relief from physical pain or distress. Conversely, the infliction of pain or injury, even on oneself, is an offense. A person does not own his body, but is merely its custodian, charged to preserve it from all hurt. Accordingly, purely cosmetic operations would be sanctioned only if intended to promote some legitimate ends or superior value, such as marriage or employment prospects.

(6) *Respect for the dead.* This biblical principle, based on the human body's having once borne the incomparable imprint of God's image, governs the Orthodox Jewish insistence on speedy BURIAL, opposition to CREMATION, and restriction of autopsies to cases in which the findings might help to save the life of a patient at hand — by tracing a hereditary cause of death which may affect other family members, for example, or by establishing the effect of new drugs or treatments given to other patients as well. Since the saving of life invariably overrides other religious precepts (see PIKKU'AḤ NEFESH), there is also no objection to using cadaver organs for transplant purposes (including corneal transplants to preserve or restore sight, since blindness is deemed a potential life hazard), provided that the postmortem operation is limited to a minimum and all unused parts of the dead are eventually interred.

Gray Areas and Some Summary Conclusions: There are, of course, numerous situations in which no clear-cut "yes-or-no" answers can be given. In other areas, the conclusions reached can only be stated in very general terms. Only a few examples can be listed here.

The inception of life. The infinite value of human life sets in only from the moment of birth. All authorities are thus agreed that the mother's life enjoys priority over that of her unborn child if it threatens her, as they are also agreed on the non-admissibility of any but medical indications. However, where the threat is to the mother's health rather than her life, or where the child is suspected or known to suffer from some grave abnormality, rabbinic opinions continue to differ on terminating the pregnancy. This argument would, of course, also extend to amniocentesis with a view to an abortion, if a genetic defect is discovered (see also "Trends" above). Any genetic intervention is sanctioned only for therapeutic ends, never for eugenic manipulation or sex determination.

Also still moot, however, is the establishment of maternity in cases of surrogate motherhood; some authorities would favor the genetic mother (the ovum or egg donor), although most would regard the host who carried the child for nine months — and gave birth to it — as the legal mother. Few responsa have so far appeared about experiments on embryos, but it would be necessary to limit embryonic substances for such use to "spares" only, and breeding them for experimental purposes would be excluded.

The terminal stage of life. Patients should be advised that they suffer from a terminal condition only if such knowledge is not likely to aggravate their condition. It is never permitted to purchase relief from suffering at the cost of life itself, by deliberately hastening death. Several authorities are inclined to sanction the suspension of "heroic methods" to sustain a lingering life, provided no direct action is taken to this end (e.g., by "pulling the plug") through not applying or reapplying resuscitation machinery or other artificial means to prolong the dying process. The onus of decision-making in such cases, or in the choice of alternative lifesaving procedures (e.g., cancer treatment by surgery, chemotherapy, or radiation), rests on expert medical practitioners — where applicable, in consultation with competent rabbinical opinion — and not on the patient or his family.

Miscellaneous. Possibly hazardous experiments on human beings can only be carried out on subjects who themselves would be the first beneficiaries of successful tests. Experimental or doubtful cures or medications could then be applied in efforts to save the subjects where no known treatments exist, and, if successful, can then be applied to others. Healthy persons must not be set at risk, however, even if they volunteer, since no life may ever be jeopardized — even if there is a subsequent possibility of saving millions of others.

Nevertheless, there is no objection to medical experiments on animals, provided every effort is made to reduce all pain to a minimum. In principle, the promotion of human health is expressly excluded from the biblical commandment to protect animals from suffering (*tsa'ar ba'alé ḫayyim*).

Alternative medicine and irrational cures, including faith healing, are generally frowned upon. However, even practices normally forbidden as superstitious may be admitted for patients who believe in them, so as not to disturb their peace of mind, provided that rational cures are not thereby displaced where necessary.

In various areas, Reform Judaism takes a more lenient position than some of the above-mentioned Orthodox attitudes, based on the *halakhah*.

MEGILLAH (scroll). Tenth tractate of Order MO'ED in the Mishnah. Its four chapters deal principally with the times, places, and manner of reading the Scroll of ESTHER on PURIM. Also included are laws regarding the four special Sabbaths (see SABBATHS, SPECIAL), the manner of reading from a SCROLL OF THE LAW and the prophetical portion (HAFTARAH), and general synagogue procedure. In the time of the Mishnah, all books were written on a *megillah* (scroll), but later "the *Megillah*" came to mean the Scroll of Esther. The subject matter is amplified in both Talmuds and the *Tosefta*.

MEGILLAT TA'ANIT (Fast Scroll). Ancient Aramaic text that with extreme brevity lists the days on which fasting is not permitted, since on these days joyful historical events took place. It follows the CALENDAR beginning with Nisan and ending with Adar. The Talmud ascribes the work to Hananiah ben Hezekiah ben Goren, who lived in the first part of the first century. Some scholars date its composition to the early stages of the war against Rome; others view it as having been composed at the time of the outbreak of the Bar Kokhba Revolt (132 CE). In either event, its purpose seems to have been to inspire Jewish soldiers in their struggle by holding up to them the example of Jewish victories over the Seleucids in the period of the HASMONEANS. Of the historic events recorded, 33 fall in the Maccabean period and only one in the Roman period — namely, the cancellation of the decree by Gaius Caligula ordering the Jews to worship the emperor. There is a commentary on the work written in tannaitic and amoraic times. This interprets most of the days recorded in the scroll as marking the victories of the PHARISEES over the SADDUCEES in their halakhic disputes. In the course of time, the significance of the dates recorded was no longer relevant, and the days listed became indistinguishable from normal days. The Scroll is an important source for the history of the Second Temple period, since it precedes the redaction of the MISHNAH.

MEḪITSAH See EZRAT NASHIM

ME'ILAH ("unlawful use of sacred property"). Eighth tractate of Order KODASHIM in the Mishnah. Its six chapters deal with the transgression of unintentionally enjoying benefit from sacred things, and the atonement for this through payment of money and/or receiving lashes (Lev. 5:15-16). The law of *me'ilah* applies to sacrifices designated for the altar, and to anything else which has been dedicated to the

Temple. Anyone who makes use of such property must make full restitution for any damage, and add an additional fifth of the sum. The Mishnah discusses which sacrifices are included in this prohibition, how *me'ilah* applies to forbidden things (e.g., blood), the minimum benefit necessary to obligate one to pay restitution, and the law of sacrilege by proxy. The subject matter is amplified in the Babylonian Talmud and the *Tosefta.*

MEIR (c.110-c.175 CE). *Tanna* of the fourth generation, an outstanding scholar and master of dialectics, whose teachers included R. AKIVA, R. ISHMAEL BEN ELISHA, and ELISHA BEN AVUYAH. During the persecutions instigated by Emperor Hadrian, Meir was one of the few secretly ordained by R. Judah ben Bava, the last of the TEN MARTYRS. The main period of R. Meir's activity followed the death of Hadrian (138 CE), when the Yavneh Academy moved to Usha in Galilee where the Sanhedrin was reestablished. A traditional scribe (*sofer*) by profession, he once wrote an Esther scroll from memory and often set down brief interpretive comments on the edges of Torah scrolls that he penned. His attempt, with R. Nathan, to depose the *nasi* (patriarch), Simeon ben GAMALIEL, led to disciplinary measures against him, and he died in exile.

FROM THE SAYINGS OF RABBI MEIR

When addressing the Holy One, blessed be He, a man should keep his words to a minimum.

Reduce your business engagements and study Torah.

Whoever lives permanently in the Land of Israel, eats its fruits in ritual purity, speaks Hebrew, and recites the *Shema* each morning and evening is assured of a place in the afterlife.

For the sake of one true penitent the whole world is forgiven.

The dust used for creating Adam was gathered from every part of the world.

All mankind are judged on Rosh ha-Shanah and the verdict is sealed on the Day of Atonement.

Don't look at the flask, but rather at its contents; a new flask may be filled with old wine, yet there may not even be new wine in an old container.

A man should recite 100 benedictions daily.

As God returns good for evil, so should you.

The chief importance of R. Meir lies in his role as an architect of the MISHNAH, where he figures in many halakhic controversies, and it was largely on the basis of his formulation that JUDAH HA-NASI edited the Mishnah's definitive text. Meir's name appears upward of 330 times in the Mishnah and 452 times in the TOSEFTA; most of the anonymous (nonascribed) Mishnaic statements are attributed either to Meir or to R. Nathan, whose names were traditionally removed from such passages in consequence of their abortive attempt to depose the *nasi*. As a preacher, R. Meir drew women as well as men to the Academy whenever he gave a public discourse. His method was to devote one third of his talk to *halakhah*, one third to *aggadah*, and the remaining third to fables and parables. Meir's political realism, after the failure of the Bar Kokhba revolt (132-135 CE), led him to adopt a conciliatory approach toward the Romans and to display a generally liberal attitude toward Gentiles such as the Cynic philosopher Oenomaus (Abnimos) of Gadara (*Hag.* 15b). For Meir, Torah study was the supreme religious value. Thus, when asked how he continued to respect and learn from a heretic (Elisha ben Avuyah), he declared that "a Gentile who observes the Torah [i.e., leads a righteous life] is equal to a High Priest" (*BK* 38a).

A number of stories about Meir in the Talmud and Midrash point to his saintliness and deep humility. While frequently differing with his colleagues in halakhic matters, R. Meir had regard for their views. Other details, concerning his wife and tragic family life, may be found under BERURYAH.

MEIR BA'AL HA-NES ("Meir the miracle worker"). Name applied to R. Meir who had the reputation in aggadic literature of performing miracles. Traditionally his tomb is in Tiberias but there are various views as to which R. Meir lies buried there. Some say it is the *tanna*, R. MEIR (second century CE); some a R. Meir ben Jacob, who went to the Land of Israel in the 13th century, and there are other views. The tomb is the site of an annual pilgrimage on *Pesaḥ Sheni* (14 Iyyar) each year (see PASSOVER, SECOND). From the 18th

Traditional tomb of Meir Ba'al ha-Nes at Tiberias, the site of an annual pilgrimage where thousands of people flock each year.

century on, emissaries from the Land of Israel would distribute charity boxes of R. Meir Ba'al ha-Nes, and almost all Jewish homes would have such a box, where coins were deposited before the Sabbath candles were lit. A folk belief maintained that contributions to this cause would avert various types of calamities. Many rabbis were opposed to the annual pilgrimage and the use of these charity boxes, as they regarded these practices as groundless superstition, but this opposition, however, has still not abolished the practice in many homes. To this day numerous charity boxes contain the words "R. Meir Ba'al ha-Nes," and various religious organizations invoke this name in their fund-raising efforts.

MEIR (BEN BARUCH) OF ROTHENBURG (known by the acronym of *Maharam*; c. 1215-1293). Leading German Tosafist (see TOSAFOT) and author of PIYYUTIM (liturgical poems). His teachers included his father in Worms, R. Jehiel of Paris, and R. ISAAC BEN MOSES of Vienna. Meir was a prolific correspondent on halakhic matters, and approximately 1,000 of his responsa have survived. He was regarded as the leading talmudic scholar of his day, and his rulings, as handed down by his students, were accepted by Ashkenazi Jews as authoritative. Meir, who witnessed the burning of the Talmud in Paris in 1242, subsequently wrote an elegy, *Sha'ali Serufah ba-Esh* (Ask, more burned by fire), which is recited by Ashkenazi Jews on the fast of TISHAH BE-AV. As one of the Tosafists, his opinion is brought in numerous places in the *Tosafot*. He was also the author of a commentary on 18 of the tractates of the Talmud. Meir's life ended tragically. In 1286 he was incarcerated by Emperor Rudolf I in a prison tower in Alsace on trumped-up charges. The emperor was willing to release Meir for a very large ransom, but the rabbi refused to allow the community to pay the ransom, fearing that it would set a precedent for the future seizure of Jews. Meir died in 1293, but only in 1306 was his body returned to the Jews, after a high ransom price had been paid. It was buried in the cemetery in Worms, where the tombstone can still be seen. Meir profoundly influenced the determination of law and ritual among Ashkenazi Jews, both through his own writings and through the legacy he passed on to his students, notably R. ASHER BEN JEHIEL.

MEIRI, MENAHEM BEN SOLOMON (also known as Don Vidal Shlomo; 1249-1316). French talmudic commentator. Meiri was a rationalist and rejected the existence of DEMONS (even though the Talmud has numerous references to such creatures) or the efficacy of AMULETS, ASTROLOGY, and SUPERSTITIONS. He argued that the existence of any of the above would deprive man of his free will. When, following the major controversy about the philosophical works of MAIMONIDES, he was asked to sign a declaration forbidding the study of philosophy under penalty of excommunication, he refused, although he was willing to forbid the study of philosophy to those who did not first gain a solid grounding in talmudic studies. On the other hand, he was opposed to the use of philosophy to interpret the Torah not in accordance with the literal meaning of the text. His classic work is *Bet ha-Beḥirah*, a massive commentary on 36 tractates of the Talmud explaining the text in a lucid and logical manner. Many of these volumes have been printed for the first time only in the past few decades. Meiri is also the author of *Ḥibbur ha-Teshuvah*, on repentance, and a commentary on the Bible, of which only two volumes were printed.

MEKHILTA DE-RABBI ISHMAEL Tannaitic MIDRASH on Exodus, beginning with an exposition of Exodus 12:2. The term *Mekhilta* ("measure" or "method") is found for the first time in the literature of the *ge'onim*. Although classed with the halakhic *midrashim*, slightly more than half the work is aggadic in character. It is divided into nine tractates. Most of the sages quoted were pupils of R. ISHMAEL, although some of the interpretations emanated from the School of R. Akiva and a fairly large number of Babylonian sages are cited. A number of statements quoted in the Talmud in the name of R. JOHANAN BEN NAPPAḤA are found as anonymous statements in the *Mekhilta*. This points to R. Johanan ben Nappaḥa as having been one of the last editors of the work.

The method of interpretation is distinguished by its exceptional simplicity, with a strong preference for using an argument *a fortiori* rather than a forced interpretation of a verse or a word. Also characteristic is its tentative suggestion of an interpretation, followed by its rejection in favor of another interpretation. The rejected opinions are largely those of other contemporary academies.

The *Mekhilta* is distinguished by its broad universalistic spirit. It preserves a number of ancient legends not found elsewhere, a fact that reflects the antiquity of its original version.

MEKHILTA DE-RABBI SIMEON BAR YOḤAI (*Mekhilta* ("method") of Rabbi Simeon). Tannaitic MIDRASH on EXODUS, ascribed to the school of R. AKIVA. Until the 17th century, it was known in its entirety and was frequently cited by medieval authorities. However, it was then apparently lost and was known only from quotations in the works of medieval authors, principally in MIDRASH HA-GADOL. On the basis of these quotations, a partial reconstruction of the text was published. Subsequently, on the basis of a number of Cairo GENIZAH fragments, a more complete version was made possible.

Its name may derive from the fact that many of its anonymous statements tally with those cited in the Talmud in the name of R. SIMEON BAR YOḤAI, a pupil of R. Akiva. Moreover, most of the sages quoted are known to have belonged to the school of R. Akiva. Some scholars have suggested that its name derives from its opening statement which quotes R. Simeon.

The midrashic exposition begins with Exodus 3:1, and

proceeds to expound the book verse by verse. Its hermeneutical method is characteristic of that of R. Akiva and his school. Most of its aggadic passages have parallels in MEKHILTA DE-RABBI ISHMAEL. Its language is Hebrew with a strong admixture of Greek and Latin, a sign of its Palestinian origin. It contains a number of comparatively late features, particularly in its language. Since the book in its present form is unknown to the Talmuds, it is conjectured that it was redacted late in the fifth century.

MELAVVEH MALKAH ("Escorting the [Sabbath] Queen"). Festive gathering and meal arranged by many congregations on Saturday night after HAVDALAH has been recited at the SABBATH's termination. This practice was evidently instituted in talmudic times, when the sages differed over the number of meals to be eaten on the Sabbath (*Shab.* 117b), one opinion being that after the Sabbath a light meal should be served (*Shab* 119b; see also SE'UDAH). An obvious parallel exists between the *Kabbalat Shabbat* service welcoming the Sabbath on Friday evening and the *Melavveh Malkah* ceremony prolonging its departure, as it were, on Saturday night. Another name for this gathering is *Se'udat David* ("[King] David's banquet"), which recalls the tradition that David learned from God that he would die on a Sabbath but was never given the precise date (*Shab.* 30a). Each new Sabbath's conclusion therefore provided grounds for rejoicing.

The gathering is sometimes also known as "Rabbi Ḥidka's meal," being named for a talmudic sage who laid down that one should eat four (not three) meals on the Sabbath (*Shab.* 117b). Its mystical importance was particularly emphasized by the 16th-century kabbalists of Safed and by ḤASIDISM. Unlike the three Sabbath meals, however, no halakhic obligation is attached to the *Melavveh Malkah* and it is merely regarded as a praiseworthy custom.

The standard practice nowadays is for this gathering to take place in a synagogue or communal hall. Light refreshments are normally served (although Ḥasidic Jews may prepare a fish meal), the rabbi or some guest speaker gives an appropriate talk, and in Ashkenazi communities the cantor sings traditional Hebrew and Yiddish melodies. Since, according to an old legend, the prophet Elijah will bring tidings of the messianic Redemption shortly after the Sabbath terminates, *Eliyyahu ha-Navi* ("Elijah the Prophet") is one of the songs (ZEMIROT) most often chanted.

MEMORIAL LIGHT (*ner neshamah* or *ner zikkaron*). A special lamp or light kindled in memory of a departed relative. Based on the scriptural idea that "the soul of man is a lamp for the Lord" (Prov. 20:27), this tradition seems to have originated in medieval Germany but soon spread to other Jewish communities (see also YAHRZEIT). A memorial light is prescribed on three specific occasions: during the first seven days of MOURNING (*Shivah*) in the home of a bereaved family; on the (Hebrew calendar) anniversary or *yahrzeit* of a parent's or other close relative's death; and on the eve of the DAY OF ATONEMENT. Since the memorial light (known in Yiddish as a *yahrzeit-licht*) must burn for at least 24 hours, normal wax CANDLES are unserviceable and specially designed lights (fitted into a glass or metal receptacle) are used instead. It is sometimes customary for a memorial light to be kindled on those festivals when *Yizkor* MEMORIAL PRAYERS are read in synagogue.

An old woman praying before memorial lights in an old people's home in Canada. The lights are electrically powered to prevent fire.

Currently, in synagogues and homes for the aged, electrically powered memorial lights are often installed by bereaved families, a donation also being made for the recitation of KADDISH on the appropriate date. In Israel, Yom Ha-Sho'ah (HOLOCAUST Memorial Day) and Yom Ha-Zikkaron (Remembrance Day for Israel's fallen) are additional occasions for the kindling of memorial lights.

MEMORIAL PRAYERS AND SERVICES (*hazkarat neshamot*, "commemorating souls"; often abbreviated as *hazkarah, azkarah,* or *mazkir*). Traditional prayers memorializing the dead and expressing the hope that their souls may be granted eternal repose. This practice is clearly ancient, since there is a reference in the APOCRYPHA to Judah Maccabee's dispatch of contributions to Jerusalem, after his victory over Gorgias, "to pray for the dead and make atonement for them, so that they might be cleared of their sin" (II Maccabees 12.43ff.). By the talmudic period, as various Midrashic statements indicate, prayers in memory of the dead had become an accepted custom. In the Ashkenazi world, memorializing the departed was restricted to certain specified occasions.

A common practice in all rites is for memorial prayers to be said at a FUNERAL, during the week of MOURNING after burial, at the consecration of a TOMBSTONE, and on a YAHRZEIT, the anniversary of a close relative's death. A short version of these prayers is also intoned on the DAY OF ATONEMENT and (among Ashkenazim) on each of the PILGRIM FESTIVALS (PASSOVER, SHAVU'OT, SUKKOT). In general, the prayers express reverence for the departed and call for God's merciful treatment of their souls, the assumption being that the heartfelt prayers of living descendants will benefit the deceased.

The best-known memorial prayer is the KADDISH, recited during the mourning period and on a *yahrzeit*. In fact this is not a memorial prayer but a doxology hallowing God's name that Jews recited after hearing an aggadic sermon or discourse. The general practice is to recite it for 11 months.

For deceased relatives other than parents, *Kaddish* is said only for the first 30 days in most rites. Western Sephardim maintain the original custom whereby mourners do not recite *Kaddish* on the Sabbath and festivals.

Among Sephardi, Italian, and Eastern Jews, the standard memorial prayer is known as *hashkavah* (also spelled *hashkabah* or *ashcava*), which means "laying to rest." Whoever wishes to memorialize a deceased relative is called to the READING OF THE LAW and, after his portion has been read, the *ḫazzan* chants the *hashkavah*, including in it the name(s) of the deceased. Separate texts are used for men and women, and special introductory verses honor a deceased rabbi or president of the community. The *hashkavah* is read on the Sabbath either before or after a death anniversary, according to local custom, and on such occasions a contribution is often pledged to the synagogue in memory of the deceased.

In many Sephardi congregations, an additional *hashkavah* is recited each Sabbath morning (or afternoon) for those members who died within the past 11 months. A special *hashkavah* is recited on the Day of Atonement, both at the KOL NIDRÉ service and the next morning, in memory of the community's former rabbis. Spanish and Portuguese congregations retain a book of "perpetual *hashkavot*" with the names of members who left bequests to the congregation or who distinguished themselves in leadership, all of these names being mentioned in a *hashkavah* for the Day of Atonement.

Ashkenazi practice differs from the above in several important respects. First, the *hashkavah* is replaced by a formula known as *hazkarat neshamot*, its central feature being the EL MALÉ RAḪAMIM prayer. This is recited after the Torah reading on weekdays (and never on a regular Sabbath), either when that Monday or Thursday coincides with the *yahrzeit* or when it immediately precedes the appropriate date. From the *Maḫzor Vitry*, compiled in 11th-century France, it appears that charitable offerings and prayers for the dead were then customary on the Day of Atonement only. As a result of the massacres accompanying the First Crusade, however, a special prayer for martyrs and destroyed Jewish communities entered the Franco-German ritual. This memorial prayer, entitled AV HA-RAḪAMIM ("Father of mercy"), is recited by Ashkenazim on most Sabbath mornings throughout the year.

Also unique to the Ashkenazi tradition is the elaborate memorial service held after the Reading of the Law on four annual occasions: the last day of Passover, Shavu'ot, the Day of Atonement, and Shemini Atseret. Until as late as the 18th century, it took place on the Day of Atonement only. From the first word of the opening prayer, this memorial service is known as *Yizkor* ("May [God] remember"), and it comprises special prayers in memory of parents and other close relatives, as well as *El Malé Raḫamim* prayers for individuals, the six million HOLOCAUST martyrs, and those who fell in defense of the State of Israel. A custom widely observed (though not obligatory) is for those with two living parents to leave the synagogue while *Yizkor* is recited; one reason for this may originally have been a wish to avert the EVIL EYE. A vestige of the *Yizkor* formula has been preserved in the Italian rite, and some non-Ashkenazim have latterly introduced a comparable memorial service in their own festival liturgy.

Various memorial services of a more general nature have been introduced in recent decades, a precedent having been set by the Remembrance Day services held in various countries for the fallen of both World Wars. Yom Ha-Sho'ah (Holocaust Memorial Day) is now observed throughout the Jewish world (on 27 Nisan in Israel; on 19 April in the Diaspora), and some communities also hold a special memorial service for the martyrs of the 1943 Warsaw Ghetto uprising against the Nazis. In Israel, Yom Ha-Zikkaron (Remembrance Day) is observed on 4 Iyyar in tribute to these who fell in defense of the State of Israel. MEMORIAL LIGHTS are kindled on each of these solemn occasions.

MENAHEM MENDEL OF KOTSK (known as "the Kotsker"; 1787-1859). Polish Ḫasidic leader whose teachings marked a radical departure from the mainstream of ḪASIDISM. A renowned talmudic scholar, he was a man of fiery temperament who devoted his life and all his gifts to challenging the lack of sincerity apparent even among the religious. In his quest for *emet* ("truth" or sincerity), not even the Ḫasidic masters were spared his scathing rebukes, and those Ḫasidim who came hoping that he would bless them with worldly success were generally ignored. He once declared that all he sought was a company of 200 young devotees prepared to shout from the rooftops: "The Lord, He is God!"

As a youth, Menahem Mendel came under the influence of Jacob Isaac, "the Seer" of Lublin, but followed the latter's disciple, Jacob Isaac, "the Holy Jew" of Przysucha (1766-1814), in his break with "the Seer." After the death of "the Holy Jew," the Przysucha school was headed by Simḫah Bunem, of whom Menahem Mendel was the outstanding disciple. This branch of Ḫasidism emphasized inwardness as the vital aspect of religious life. Hypocrisy in religious matters was anathema to followers of the Przysucha school: they prided themselves on doing good by stealth and, when they sinned, did so openly.

The mantle of Przysucha fell on Menahem Mendel after Simḥah Bunem's death in 1827. By then, a singular devotion to Torah (especially talmudic) study had divided him from other Ḥasidic masters, bringing him closer to traditionalist MITNAGGEDIM. For reasons that have never been explained satisfactorily, he spent his last 20 years as a recluse: shut away in his room, he refused to see the Ḥasidim who still flocked to Kotsk in the hope of gaining inspiration from their master. Although the *Rebbe*'s son David was appointed his successor, the majority of his Ḥasidim preferred to follow the Kotsker's brother-in-law, Yitsḥak Meir Alter (1789-1866); he founded the new dynasty of Gur (Gora Kalwaria) in the spirit of Kotsk learning, but displayed less vehement zeal and more tolerance of the spiritually weak. Menahem Mendel's disciple, Mordecai Joseph Leiner of Izbica (died 1854), broke with his master during the Kotsker's lifetime and founded the Radzyn dynasty.

Menahem Mendel of Kotsk left no writings, but his ideas can be found in the works of his followers and in a number of anthologies published after his death. Like Israel Ba'al Shem Tov and several other Ḥasidic leaders, the Kotsker made use of the aphorism to convey his teachings.

APHORISMS OF MENAHEM MENDEL "THE KOTSKER"

Everything in this world can be imitated except truth — for truth once imitated is no longer truth.

Whoever has no place anywhere has a place everywhere.

Take care of your own soul and of another man's body, not of your own body and of another man's soul.

God dwells wherever man lets Him in.

The whole world is not worth sighing over; not even a single sigh.

The preparations involved in being ready to perform a *mitsvah* are more important than the *mitsvah* itself.

MENAḤOT ("meal offerings"). Second tractate of Order KODASHIM in the Mishnah. Its 13 chapters deal principally with the laws of the nine categories of meal offerings made from wheat or barley flour brought to the Temple (cf. Lev. 2:5-16, 6:7-11, 23:13-17). The Mishnah includes all the procedural details in bringing the meal offering, how this was carried out in the Sanctuary, the validity or invalidity of these offerings if performed incorrectly, the manner of reaping, threshing, and transporting the grain, and the preparation of the showbread and the two loaves used for the Festival of Shavu'ot. Also included are the laws pertaining to drink offerings. The *minḥah* (lit. a gift or present) was also referred to as the poor man's offering, because those too poor to bring an animal sacrifice were allowed to bring a meal offering instead (see SACRIFICES AND OFFERINGS). The subject matter is amplified in the Babylonian Talmud and the *Tosefta*.

MENDELSSOHN, MOSES (1729-86). German-Jewish pioneer of EMANCIPATION and communal leader, philosopher and literary critic, Bible scholar and translator. Born in Dessau, son of a Torah scribe, he received a traditional Jewish education and was a pupil of the local rabbi, David Fränkel. When Fränkel became chief rabbi in Berlin (1743), Mendelssohn followed him there, earning a meager living as a copyist and private tutor. Only 20 years after his arrival in Berlin did he obtain a limited residence permit.

Mendelssohn taught himself High German and, with the help of friends, Latin, Greek, French, and English, as well as philosophy and mathematics. He was befriended by the writer and dramatist G.E. Lessing. Mendelssohn had been an ardent student of MAIMONIDES' *Guide for the Perplexed* in his boyhood, and early in his career wrote a commentary on Maimonides' treatise on logic. He wrote metaphysical-psychological-aesthetic treatises, such as *Phaedon* on immortality (1776) and *Morning Hours* on the existence of God and theodicy (1785), which won him a place as a leading philosopher of European Enlightenment. His *Jerusalem*, with a more Jewish angle, postulated the separation of State and Religion, freedom of worship and conscience, and explained post-exilic Judaism as non-dogmatic, non-coercive revealed legislation in contrast to self-evident philosophical truths. As a literary critic he wrote review articles for a scientific-artistic journal, making him, with his pure and elegant style, a leader in German literature.

Mendelssohn was publicly challenged by the Swiss pastor J.C. Lavater either to disprove the truth of Christianity or to convert. This forced him to publish a dignified reply, proudly proclaiming his Jewishness and his loyalty to Judaism. This incident was a crisis in his life, and he now turned to more specifically Jewish concerns. He had always been a loyal and honored member of the Berlin Jewish community, for which he composed prayers, hymns, and sermons for various patriotic occasions. Communities and individuals turned to him for help in their distress, as did harassed Alsatian Jewry, and Mendelssohn prevailed on C.W. Dohm to write a memorandum for submission to the French government, "On the civil improvement of the Jews" (1781), which proved a major event in the fight for emancipation of European Jews. For the use of the Prussian courts, Mendelssohn wrote *Ritualgesetze der Juden* (1778), a precis of Jewish laws and customs. Again at government request, he reformulated the infamous OATH *More Judaico* into a milder version, not daring to demand its abolition.

Though always maintaining tradition, Mendelssohn realized the need for an inner religious emancipation as much

Moses Mendelssohn, on the left, playing chess with the Lutheran theologian J.C. Lavater. Looking on, Gotthold Lessing. 1866.

as a civil one. To this end he published in 1783 a translation of the Pentateuch into German (in Hebrew characters), accompanied by a commentary (*Bi'ur*) written in part by himself. This project had a revolutionary impact on German Jewry, whom it taught High German and gave a rational explanation of their Torah, based on the main classical commentaries. Many contemporary rabbis welcomed the work, but some remained fiercely antagonistic. Mendelssohn also translated the Psalms and the Song of Songs. He supported attempts for the reform of Jewish education by modern schools and textbooks and at his initiative, a Jewish Free School was opened in Berlin in 1781, an example followed in other communities, particularly in the Austro-Hungarian Empire.

The new cultural tendencies included the revival of classical Hebrew. Mendelssohn himself wrote an excellent Hebrew, and as early as 1758 published (anonymously) with the help of a friend a Hebrew journal (*Kohelet Musar*) of which only two issues appeared. He supported, and contributed to, *Ha-Me'assef*, the periodical of Berlin Enlightenment. When approached about plans to settle Jews in their own land and state, he considered this premature but prophetically thought that such a project would have to await a major European war. He was also a pioneer of understanding between Judaism and Christianity, writing: "What a world of bliss we would live in if all men adopted the true principles which the best of the Christians and the best of the Jews hold in common."

Mendelssohn broke through the barriers of prejudice to become the most widely admired Jew of his time (he inspired Lessing's "Nathan the Wise"). He guided the Jews of Germany out of the ghetto and into the environment of Emancipation and Enlightenment.

MENORAH Candelabrum, especially with seven branches like the one which was a central feature in the SANCTUARY and TEMPLE, and became the prime Jewish symbol. It is described for the first time in Exodus 25:31-38, where God gives Moses detailed directions for its construction. "You shall make a candelabrum of pure gold... Its base and its shaft, its branches, bowls, its knops, and its flowers, shall be of one piece. Six branches shall come out of its sides; three branches out of either side..."

A similar description appears in Exodus 37:17-24. The *Menorah* was to be placed in the Sanctuary and presumably the candelabra which stood in the Temple were similar. It is known that there were ten gold candelabra in Solomon's Temple. Legend has it that one of these was taken with the exiles to Babylon in the sixth century BCE, was returned to Jerusalem by those Jews who came back from that exile and was placed in the Second Temple. The latter Temple certainly contained a gold *menorah* that was looted by the Syrian ruler army of Antiochus Epiphanes in the second century BCE. After the Hasmoneans defeated the Syrians, Judah the Maccabee constructed a new seven-branched *menorah*. Talmudic sources indicate three stages in the installation of this *menorah*. At first it was made of simple and inexpensive materials, afterwards of silver, and finally of pure gold.

After the Roman conquest and the destruction of Jerusalem in the year 70 CE, all traces of the *menorah* vanished. The Romans displayed it in their victory procession in Rome, as depicted to this day in a stone relief on the Arch of Titus. The top portion of the *menorah* shown there accords with the literal description of the *menorah* of the Sanctuary and the Temple. However, the base is not in keeping with the Jewish tradition, both in terms of design and structure. Archeological findings depicting the *menorah* show a different base from that depicted on the Arch of Titus.

The fate of the *menorah* after being seized by the Romans was the subject of many legends.

The *menorah* became a central motif in the consciousness of the Jewish people. Already in ancient times, it was commonly used as a symbol and is found in decorations that have been discovered on mosaic floors, walls, door lintels, and latticework in synagogues. It was carved and painted in Jewish cemeteries and was used to decorate utensils made of glass, ceramics, or metal. Schematic drawings of the *menorah* symbol were also found in the caves and hiding places of Jewish rebels and zealots.

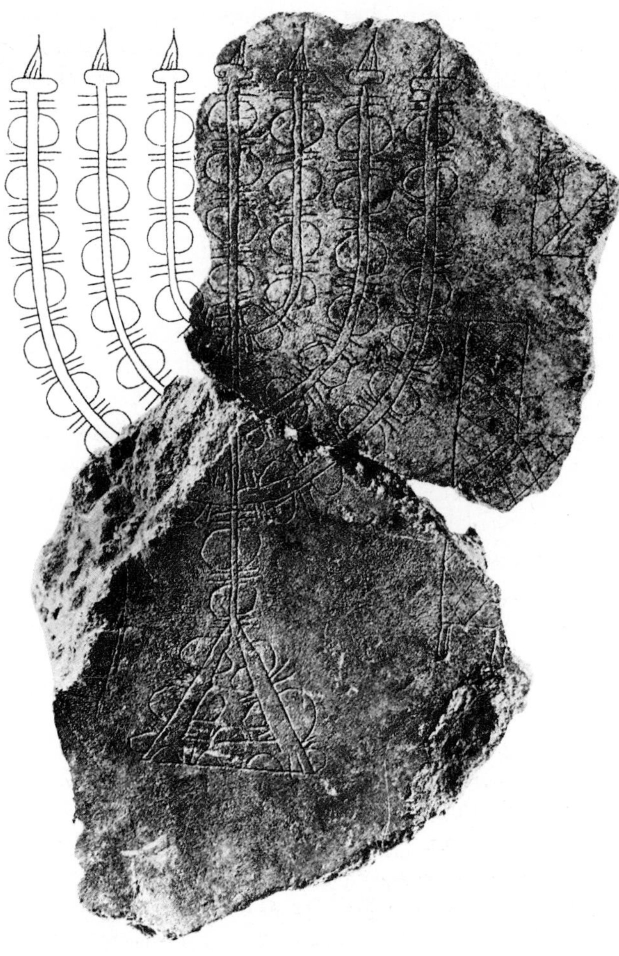

Earliest known representation of the Temple menorah, *found in Jerusalem, dating from the reign of Herod (c.37 BCE — 4 CE).*

Over the generations, the seven-branched *menorah* has been given different and varied interpretations. It was accepted by the Jewish people as a central and continuous symbol, which expressed the great myth of the exile and the hope for redemption. It was incorporated in synagogues of various eras, on ritual objects, in illuminated manuscripts, and on amulets. It has been fashioned using various techniques, including embroidery, metal work, paper cuts, glass tablets and engraving.

The candelabrum in art is sometimes in accordance with the detailed description in the Bible, where all the different elements are stressed, while at other times it assumes a different form, symbolical and metaphorical, intertwined with a tree, with birds at its side, with its base spread out. Various mystical streams which developed among the Jews influenced the shape and style of the *menorah* in art and the images found in the Kabbalah extended its symbolic significance.

In spite of its wide use as a symbol, the *menorah* has seldom been fashioned in three dimensions. This is derived from the prohibition imposed by the sages of the Talmud against forming a *menorah* which would be identical to the one which stood in the Temple. This prohibition included making a *menorah* of gold.

The last few centuries have seen fluctuations in the popularity of the *menorah* as a symbol. The Jewish communities in Central and Western Europe, which had gradually attained emancipation and sought for a suitable expression of their new status, limited the use of the *menorah* as a symbol because of the mystical and metaphorical images it had evoked in the Middle Ages and because it was associated with worship in the Temple which they felt contradicted their own tendencies to universalism. In the 19th century, the Jews preferred to use the Shield of David (*Magen David*), which became the most distinctive Jewish symbol, or the Two Tablets of the Decalogue which accorded better with the desire to present Judaism as a message for all mankind.

The beginning of the 20th century, with the development of the Zionist movement and as a result of archeological findings in Erets Israel, saw a reawakening of interest in and increased use of the *menorah* as a central Jewish symbol. It was chosen to represent Jewish organizations and the artists who identified with Zionism tended to include various forms of the candelabrum in their works. The Bezalel Academy for fine arts, founded in Jerusalem in 1906 and noted for its Zionist-cultural orientation, fostered the integration of traditional Jewish symbols, including the *menorah*. The teachers and students of Bezalel included the *menorah* in decorative compositions, tapestry, ritual objects, jewelry etc.

After the establishment of the State of Israel, the official symbol of the State centered around the seven-branched *menorah*. The design corresponded with the one engraved on the Arch of Titus in Rome. This choice, in spite of the availability of a large number of other forms known from archeological findings, expressed the desire to symbolize the national revival as the antithesis of the destruction and exile of the past.

MENSTRUATION See NIDDAH

MERCY An attribute of GOD which is to inspire man in general and the Jews in particular. The Hebrew word for mercy or compassion, *raḇamim*, is derived from the same root as *reḇem*, "womb," and mercy is related to the mother's feeling for her child. Judaism lays great stress on the importance of mercy, and ideally, the three distinguishing characteristics of the Jewish people are that they be "merciful, modest, and perform deeds of lovingkindness" (*Yev.* 79a). Since God is merciful, as in Psalm 145:9, "His mercy extends to all His creatures," man, too, must adopt this quality: "Just as God is merciful, so must you, too, be merciful" (*Sifré Ekev* 89; see IMITATION OF GOD). One of the NAMES OF

GOD is *ha-Rahaman* — the Merciful One. However, God weighs His attribute of mercy against His attribute of JUSTICE and a similar tension poses a continual challenge to man.

Numerous laws of the Pentateuch are based on the quality of mercy. Thus, a lender who takes a poor man's cloak as a pledge against his loan is required to return the cloak at night, so that the poor man may be able to sleep in it (Ex. 22:26-27). Mercy extends to other creatures as well as man and various laws are directed at the merciful treatment of ANIMALS.

Unlimited mercy is considered to be inappropriate and "He that spares his rod hates his son" (Prov. 13:24). In the prayer following the blowing of the SHOFAR (ram's horn) in the cantor's repetition of the additional AMIDAH on ROSH HA-SHANAH, the Jew appeals to God to "have mercy on us as a father has mercy on his children," the implication being that the father's mercy is tempered by a broader consideration for what is best for the child.

On verse Deuteronomy 13:18, "He will show you mercy, and have compassion," Rabban Gamaliel elaborated: "He who shows mercy to his fellow-creatures will be dealt with in a merciful fashion from Heaven, whereas he who is not merciful to his fellow-creatures will not be dealt with in a merciful fashion from Heaven."

MERKAVAH MYSTICISM See HÉKHALOT

MERIT (*zekhut*). A virtue which, in Jewish thought, is attainable through freely choosing to obey God's commandments and to perform other good deeds or "acts of lovingkindness" (see GEMILUT HASADIM). The term *zekhut* is also used in the sense of giving someone the benefit of the doubt: "Judge every man in the scale of merit [i.e., favorably]," the rabbis urged (*Avot.* 1.6), since "one who judges his fellowman in the scale of merit is likewise judged favorably by others" (*Shab.* 127b).

Doctrinally, this concept gave birth to the notion of *zekhut avot* (ancestral virtue or "the merits of one's fathers"), according to which the merit acquired by past generations — including the PATRIARCHS of Israel — may not only be stored up, but can actually benefit their descendants. This explains why "the pious deeds of our ancestors" are so frequently mentioned throughout the Jewish liturgy (in the first paragraph of the AMIDAH, for example), and why "showing kindness to the thousandth generation of those who love Me and keep My commandments" in the Decalogue (Ex. 20:6) has been described as Judaism's doctrine of Original Virtue. The "merits of the fathers" are one of the five things that will hasten Israel's redemption (Midr. *Tehillim* on Ps. 106:44); by virtue of Abraham's trust in God the Israelites were privileged to sing the Song of the Red Sea, and in time to come they will likewise "sing a new song" to the Lord (Ex. R. 23.6); but ancestral merits are no substitute for religious discipline, they do not outweigh the sin of abandoning the Land of Israel to reside elsewhere, and they can never excuse a person's failure to do good on his own account in this life (Midr. *Tehillim* on Ps. 146:3; cf. *Shab.* 55a). However, they can be a source of ALTRUISM and inspiring example: "All who engage in communal affairs should do so for the sake of heaven; their work will prosper thanks to the merit of predecessors whose good deeds are everlasting" (*Avot* 2.2). This concept of meritorious living fortified Jewish solidarity, prompted tales of "hidden saints" (e.g., the LAMED VAV TSADDIKIM), and led the rabbis to claim that "for the sake of even one righteous man the world would have been created... and for the sake of only one it will endure" (*Yoma* 38b). Similarly, through the observance of one precept, "a man can tip the scales in favor of himself and of the entire world" (*Kid.* 40b).

MESSIAH (from the Heb. *mashi'ah*, "anointed"). The savior and redeemer at the End of Days. First encountered in Leviticus 4:3-5 as the "anointed priest," the term was originally used for anyone with a Divine mission, such as priests, prophets, and kings — even Cyrus of Persia, who was seen as fulfilling a Divine mission (Isa. 45:1). After the promise made to DAVID (II Sam. 7:12-13), the Davidic dynasty was regarded as specially chosen (II Sam. 22:51; Ps. 89:35), and later, when the kingdom was threatened by external powers, ISAIAH and JEREMIAH prophesied the appearance of a king of the house of David, whose rule would be glorious. In the First Temple period, Judaism was not a messianic religion and the term *mashi'ah* did not have its later connotation. The concept strengthened from the time of the Babylonian EXILE, when the idea became associated with the "end of days."

Messianism and Messianic era. Messianism contains both restorative and utopian elements. According to the former, the Messianic era will restore the throne of the Jewish kingdom to the House of David and, in the post-exilic conception, will bring back all Jewish exiles to the land of Israel. The latter posits that this era will also usher in a perfect society in which humanity will live in peace and harmony and will worship one God.

Interwoven with the concept of the Messianic era are such ideas as the RESURRECTION of the dead, REWARD AND PUNISHMENT (both individual and national), the Last Judgment, Paradise and Hell. The Book of Isaiah depicts the Messianic era as possessed of two aspects, catastrophic and utopian, comprising both the DAY OF THE LORD, a day of utter chaos and upheaval, and the End of Days, when the House of the Lord will be established on a mountaintop and the peoples of earth will stream up to that place of spiritual fulfillment. Both Jews and Christians have interpreted the Book of Daniel's apocalyptic vision of the four evil beasts as a reference to a messianic era that would be ushered in by the rise and fall of four successive empires.

Messianism was a major element in the literature of the Second Temple, when it acquired its eschatological significance (see ESCHATOLOGY), and as the situation of the Jews under the Romans grew more difficult, their messianic enthusiasm and speculation flourished. The doctrines of the imminent arrival of the Messiah and the resurrection of the dead were key elements in the belief of the PHARISEES (although rejected by the SADDUCEES). Messianism is a major theme of the literature of the APOCRYPHA AND PSEUDEPIGRAPHA. During this entire period the Messiah was seen not as a Divine figure but as an ideal human individual who would save the Jewish people. This would not be a miraculous event nor would man's nature be changed. God's sovereignty would be accepted by all, and justice would flourish. This hope was fixed on many men, ranging from Zerubbabel at the time of the return from Babylonia to Bar Kokhba, leader of the second century CE anti-Roman revolt, who was acclaimed as Messiah by R. AKIVA.

Messianism was a major feature of the DEAD SEA SECT, an extremist Jewish apocalyptic group active during the Second Temple period. Here, however, the concept received a strong other-worldly emphasis. The sect, which regarded itself as the nucleus of the future society of the post-apocalyptic world, believed that there would be a final and decisive battle between the Prince of Light (a Messiah-figure) and the Angel of Darkness. An expression of their messianic longings can be seen in their ritualistic meals, which were called messianic banquets, in anticipation of the great messianic banquet referred to in other contemporary apocalyptic writings, such as the New Testament. They stressed not national redemption but the Day of Divine Judgment. The concept of a supernatural redeemer known as the Son of Man developed in some circles, including the early Christian sect. However, these ideas were outside the Jewish mainstream.

Messianic belief has played a crucial role in Jewish history. Following the destruction of the Second Temple and the Roman conquest of Judea, the belief in a Messiah helped the Jews to make the transition from a condition of national sovereignty to a condition of political powerlessness in the Diaspora. Throughout the periods of persecution, the messianic hope helped sustain the spirit of the Jewish people and insured that the dream of a return to the Land of Israel, as expressed in the liturgy, would one day be realized.

According to Jewish tradition, the coming of the Messiah will be preceded by a period referred to as the "birth pangs of the Messiah" (*hevlé mashi'aḫ*), which came to be identified with exile from the Holy Land. Judaism does not, however, specify the precise nature of the conditions necessary for the arrival of the Messiah. The talmudic tractate *Sanhedrin*, for example, states that the Messiah will come when the world is either all evil or all good.

The arrival of the Messiah, who will be a descendant of King David, will be heralded by the appearance of a pre-Messianic figure, who will be a descendant of Joseph and who will do battle with the forces of evil in order to bring about the redemption of the people of Israel. Following the inevitable defeat of the Josephic Messiah, the stage will be

The Messiah on a donkey entering Jerusalem, preceded by the prophet Elijah blowing the shofar. *From the* Venice Haggadah, *18th century.*

set for the triumphant entry of the Davidic Messiah. Traditional Jewish sources do not dwell on the personality of the Messiah; moreover, they differ in their conception of the powers with which he will be endowed.

The longing for the Messiah invaded all aspects of Jewish life, notably the LITURGY, which is permeated with prayers for the coming of the Messiah. Every service contains such a prayer, and the daily AMIDAH has no less than five benedictions expressing the messianic hope.

MAIMONIDES indicates the importance of the messianic hope in Judaism by including it as one of the 13 PRINCIPLES OF FAITH incumbent on every Jew. According to him, the flesh and blood Messiah King would be a "very eminent prophet" with extraordinary intellectual prowess, who would be totally devoted to the spirit and letter of Judaism, thereby serving as a model for all Jews. As a mortal, the Messiah would found a dynasty to rule after him.

Maimonides envisaged the messianic era as a "natural" time in which nearly all the physical laws of the universe would be maintained; nonetheless, it would not be totally devoid of supernatural occurrences. Thus, there would be a resurrection of the dead, whose bodies and souls would be reunited for a limited period of time. Essentially, however, the messianic era would witness an end to Israel's subjugation by other nations, a view shared by SAADIAH GAON in a previous era, and would introduce a period of complete social justice. The Messiah would concern himself not only with the INGATHERING OF THE EXILES from the four corners of the earth to the Holy Land, but also with international harmony and peace, and with the promotion of humanity's acceptance of God as sole ruler of the universe.

As depicted in the Kabbalah, the Messiah is essentially

personal and human. According to the major kabbalistic work, the 13th-century ZOHAR, the Messiah's first earthly appearance in Upper Galilee will be preceded by a period of residence in a palace (*Ken Tsippor*, "Bird's Nest") in the Garden of Eden. Some kabbalists argued that the Messiah's soul is that of ADAM KADMON (primeval man), which had transmigrated to King David before its transmigration to the Messiah. As evidence, the three Hebrew letters of the name *Adam — alef, dalet, mem* — were interpreted as referring to Adam, David, and Messiah. The Messiah, who would be endowed with supernatural abilities, would usher in a thousand-year period in which the passage of time would be slower than in the pre-messianic era, and in which the very nature of the universe would undergo basic change.

In the Kabbalah of Isaac LURIA, emphasis is placed on the restorative aspect of the messianic era, which would be a period of TIKKUN or reparation, bringing about a renascence of the world's harmony.

During times of catastrophe, such as the Expulsion from Spain in 1492, devout Jewish scholars made calculations, based on the numerical value of words and passages in the Bible, to determine the precise date of the Messiah's arrival. The messianic hope has also expressed itself in the various false MESSIANIC MOVEMENTS that have arisen throughout Jewish history.

Modern Orthodox Jewish tradition essentially sees the messianic era as one in which Jews, finally gathered together in their ancestral homeland in the dramatic process of the Ingathering of the Exiles, will be able to fulfill all their religious obligations, particularly those connected with the Land of Israel. According to Orthodox thinkers, even the ritual sacrifices in the Temple in Jerusalem will be reintroduced.

In contrast to the Orthodox outlook, classical 19th-century REFORM JUDAISM rejected the concept of a personal Messiah and sought to transform the messianic idea into a notion of progress towards a state of intellectual and moral human perfection. In its 1885 Pittsburgh Platform, Reform Judaism interpreted Jewish messianism as a movement for universal progress and justice, as distinct from a movement aimed at the renewal of Jewish national life in Erets Israel or the restoration in the ancestral Jewish homeland of a community bound by religious observance and cultic sacrifices in the Temple of Jerusalem. This belief in progress and human perfectability was shattered with the rise of Nazism, and the 1937 Pittsburgh Platform defined its messianic goal as aiding the building of a Jewish homeland and cooperating with all men in the establishment of the Kingdom of God, universal brotherhood, justice, truth, and peace on earth.

CONSERVATIVE teachers in general have also translated the belief in the Messiah as a belief in a messianic period. Such a period will be characterized by a state of universal peace, social justice, and the solution of the problems of disease and all forms of evil. There will be nothing supernatural in this, and the world will be redeemed by the efforts of all good people. In the vanguard of all those working for a messianic period, the Jew is to make his stand. In a socio-religious sense this is the eternal challenge of the Jew, viz., to bring nearer the age of the Messiah. Although this emphasis is found in most Conservative writings, in fact it is seen as an interpretation of the classical messianic texts in Isaiah 2:2-4 and Micah 4:1-6 as well as in the second paragraph of the *Alénu* prayer. This emphasis on the Jew's responsibility to live and work for a messianic age is thought to add greater social relevance to modern Judaism.

Reconstructionism rejected the notion of a personal Messiah, references to which were deleted from the movement's prayer book.

In its modern post-Enlightenment western reinterpretation, messianism has been secularized. According to Martin Buber, the extensive involvement of Jews in modern revolutionary movements can be attributed to the strong element of messianism in Jewish tradition.

Zionism can be viewed as a secularization of the messianic idea, with the Jewish people itself initiating a fundamental change rather than waiting for the arrival of the Messiah. Zionism's assumption of the mantle of traditional messianism helps explain the bitter antagonism of ultra-Orthodox groups toward Zionism and toward the very idea of a Jewish state established under natural and secular auspices. However, in the view of R. Abraham Isaac KOOK, the first Ashkenazi Chief Rabbi of Palestine, the modern-day Jewish resettlement of the Holy Land represented the first stage in the process of Divine redemption (*at<u>h</u>alta de-ge'ulah*) that would ultimately usher in the messianic era.

The power of the messianic hope was most vividly displayed during the Holocaust when Jews who were taken to the gas chambers sang the words of Maimonides' Principle of Faith: "I believe completely that the Messiah will come, and even though he delays, I continue to believe." See also ESCHATOLOGY.

MESSIANIC MOVEMENTS Organized attempts by various charismatic leaders to present themselves as the MESSIAH and to restore the Davidic kingdom and Jewish independence in Erets Israel. From the period of the Babylonian EXILE down to the 18th century, such movements were galvanized by interrelated factors: age-old yearning for the promised Messiah, Jewish homelessness and the acute sense of exile in GALUT, religious persecution, and a burning desire for revived sovereignty as a means of vindicating God's justice in the eyes of the world. So long as Jewish life in exile could be maintained peacefully, the messianic impulse was restricted to prayer; once Jews faced expulsion, massacre, or other threats to their existence, it could be harnessed by pseudo-messianic "prophets" and militants who won varying degrees of popular support, only to be discredited when their claims proved false.

In the Bible, messianic roles are suggested for Hezekiah

(Isa. 11), and later for Zerubbabel (Hag. 2:21-23; Zech. 4:6-10). Though not of Davidic ancestry, a qualification attributed to the Messiah, the HASMONEANS also appear to have aroused messianic expectations in their time. A growing belief that God's salvation would be preceded by *Ḥevlé Mashi'aḥ*, "the birth pangs of the Messiah," fostered the notion that this might be synonymous with political turmoil. "When you see great empires at war with each other," said the rabbis, "look for the Messiah's advent" (Gen. R. 42.7). Similarly, because of the belief that "the redeemer will come when men despair of the REDEMPTION" (*Sanh.* 97a), outbursts of anti-Jewish persecution invariably gave rise to new messianic movements.

Some of those pledged to end Roman domination claimed supernatural powers. A certain "prophet" named Theudas, for example, announced that he would part the waters of the Jordan (in 45 CE), but was arrested and beheaded before making the attempt. Judah the Galilean (d. 6 CE), a leader of the Sicarii Zealots, proved more troublesome to the Romans. Amidst the political and moral upheaval that characterized the period of the Roman government of Judea, various pseudo-messianic leaders emerged, the most famous of whom was Jesus of Nazareth. The DEAD SEA SCROLLS also refer to powerful messianic feelings that motivated the Dead Sea Sect. During the period of the first revolt, which led to the Temple's destruction, both Simeon bar Giora and Eleazar ben Jair (who held the fortress of Masada until 73 CE) evidently cast themselves in messianic roles. Far more influential, however, was Simeon Bar Kokhba ("Son of the Star"), who headed the second ill-fated revolt in 132-135 CE and died fighting the Roman legions at Betar. R. AKIVA, who had saluted him as "King Messiah," and whose pupils are said to have perished in that war, was later faced with the reproach that "grass will grow through your cheeks long before the Messiah's advent" (TJ *Ta'an.* 4.8).

An isolated phenomenon, in the early centuries of dispersion, was the appearance of a Cretan "prophet" who (believing himself to be a new Moses) led Jews into suicidal madness or apostasy in 431.

The rise of Islam, and the atmosphere of armed struggle which it engendered, had a major impact on the Jewish messianic movements, which became increasingly militant throughout the Near East. Those headed by Abu Isa al-Isfahani and Yudghan in eighth-century Persia to combat the Muslims were both sectarian and revolutionary in nature. Another, founded by David Alroy in Kurdistan, derived its strength from the turbulence produced by the conflict between Islam and Christendom during the period of the Second Crusade (c. 1146-7). Through skillful propaganda, Alroy gained many followers, particularly among the warlike mountain Jews, with the object of defeating their Muslim oppressors and preparing for the messianic kingdom in Jerusalem. After some initial successes, this campaign was foiled by David Alroy's murder. Loyal followers who continued to believe in this pseudo-messiah were styled "Menahemites."

At about the same time (1172), the Jews of Yemen also underwent severe persecution and many were therefore inclined to place their trust in a self-proclaimed redeemer who interpreted their hardships as the "birth pangs of the Messiah" heralding the Redemption. When asked for his advice, however, MAIMONIDES responded with the famous "Yemenite Epistle" (*Iggeret Téman*), in which he urged his fellow Jews not to be deceived by revolutionary, pseudo-messianic preachings.

Despite the horrors inflicted on them during the Crusades, Ashkenazim remained generally passive and did not involve themselves in messianic activity. This was not the case among the Sephardi communities of Spain and Portugal, where kabbalistic doctrines made a strong impression from the 13th century. Abraham ABULAFIA gained notoriety as the first of many Sephardi "prophets" bent on hastening the Redemption through mystical devices or appeals to Popes and Emperors. Two other factors, however, gave rise to an upsurge of messianic speculation over the next 300 years: travelers' tales concerning the River SAMBATYON and the Ten Lost TRIBES of Israel who were rumored to live beyond it; and the appearance of the ZOHAR (c.1300), the outstanding kabbalistic work, which had an especially powerful impact on the Jews of Christian Spain.

Thanks to the messianic teachings of the Zohar, events such as the forced conversions in Spain of 1391, the fall of Constantinople to the Turks in 1453, and the expulsion of the Jews from Spain in 1492 were regarded in turn as signs pointing to the imminent arrival of the Messiah. In the 16th century, Ashkenazi Jews were also swept up by these currents. Among the Spanish exiles, the campaigns of persecution launched against Spanish and Portuguese MARRANOS, the kabbalistic doctrine of *tikkun* propagated by the mystics of Safed (see Isaac LURIA), and the sudden appearance of David Reuveni in Europe (1524) heightened messianic expectations.

Reuveni, a mysterious adventurer, claimed to be the son of a King Solomon and brother of a King Joseph who ruled the lost tribes of Reuben, Gad, and Manasseh in the Arabian province of Khaibar. Like David Alroy, he sought to wrest Jerusalem from the Muslims, but his mission was to gain Christian backing for this grand enterprise. Reuveni's princely appearance and story at first impressed Jew and non-Jew alike, including Pope Clement VII. Great enthusiasm was also aroused among the Portuguese Marranos, one of whom, a certain Diego Pines, reverted to Judaism under the name of Solomon Molkho, later escaping from Portugal to become a kabbalist and also a pseudo-messiah. He and Reuveni joined forces in an unsuccessful appeal to the Holy Roman Emperor; Molkho was burned at the stake as a relapsed Catholic in 1532, while Reuveni died in prison. Before his death, Molkho had attracted many followers in

Spain, Portugal, Italy, and even Poland, thus preparing the way for the most celebrated false messiah, SHABBETAI TSEVI.

Just as a cataclysm had sparked one messianic movement after another in the past, so did the Thirty Years' War (1618-48) and the Chmielnicki Massacres of 1648-9 create an atmosphere favorable to the spread of Shabbateanism. Kabbalists believed that 1648 was the ordained "messianic year," whereas Christian mystics reckoned that it would be 1666. Shabbetai Tsevi first antagonized the Smyrna rabbinate with his messianic claims in the early 1650s. He found a powerful advocate in Nathan of Gaza, the visionary who proclaimed that the Messiah had arrived and would overthrow the sultan of Turkey in 1666. With Nathan casting himself in the role of Elijah, "harbinger of the Messiah,"

Letter from Nathan of Gaza to Jews throughout Europe, with an illustration showing him anointing Shabbetai Tsevi. Jerusalem, 1665.

Shabbetai Tsevi rapidly established himself as the most charismatic and revered messianic pretender of all time. His antinomian revolution produced great numbers of "believers" everywhere, imperiling the skeptical minority and shaking the very foundations of normative Judaism. Even after the apostasy and obscure death of this false messiah, vast numbers continued to believe in him. One Shabbatean sect, the Dönmeh, remained active and survived until recent times in Turkey and the Balkans; another, the FRANKISTS, headed by a Podolian adventurer named Jacob Frank, exerted a nefarious influence in Central Europe until about 1830.

METURGEMAN (also *turgeman*; lit. "translator"). Person who stood beside the reader of the Torah in the ancient synagogue and recited the TARGUM (Aramaic translation of the Bible) verse by verse for the Pentateuch, and three verses at a time for the Prophets.

Rules governing the *meturgeman* are set forth in the Talmud and in related rabbinic literature. He was to stand upright next to the reader, reciting orally (not from a written text), and not raising his voice louder than that of the reader. These rules were invoked in order to preserve the primacy of the original Hebrew text. The blind and minors are explicitly qualified to serve in this function.

The terms *meturgeman, turgeman* and AMORA are also applied to an assistant in the ancient talmudic academy, who stood alongside the rabbinic scholar and served as his public mouthpiece or amplifier. The rabbi would deliver his lesson or homily in a low voice, and the *meturgeman* would repeat it loudly for the audience to hear. In this case, the repetition was in the same language, and, with few exceptions, without alteration or elaboration (*Kid.* 31b; *Sot.* 40a).

MEZUMMAN See GRACE AFTER MEALS

MEZUZAH ("doorpost"). The small scroll of parchment containing selected biblical passages, which is traditionally affixed to the doorposts of the Jewish home. The custom is derived from the biblical commandment to "write them upon the doorposts of your house and in your gates" (Deut. 6:9. 11:20). The term *mezuzah*, whose literal meaning in Hebrew is "doorpost," was later taken to mean the scroll of parchment itself upon which the biblical passages are written. The first passage (Deut. 6:4-9) contains the opening paragraph of the basic Jewish confession of faith, the SHEMA. It includes the commandments to: 1) love God; 2) study the Torah; 3) read the *Shema* prayer, expressing the unity of God, twice daily; 4) wear TEFILLIN; 5) affix a *mezuzah*. The second passage (Deut. 11:13-21), which is also part of the daily *Shema* reading, associates prosperity and well-being with proper observance of the commandments, and recapitulates the commandments of the first paragraph.

The *mezuzah* must be written by a qualified SCRIBE on parchment made from the skin of a clean animal. The scroll is rolled and placed into a case with a small opening through which the word *Shaddai* ("Almighty"), written on the back of the parchment, is visible. The *mezuzah* is attached to the upper part of the doorpost at the entrance of each room in a slanting position. This position is a compromise resulting from the dispute between RASHI, who favored a vertical position, and his grandson R. Jacob ben Meir (TAM), who argued that the *mezuzah* should be attached horizontally.

In earlier periods, it was common to place the *mezuzah* parchment directly into a small compartment hollowed out of the doorpost.

A *mezuzah* must be placed on every right-hand doorpost which fulfills the following conditions:

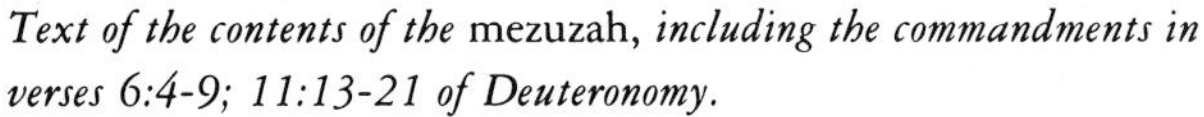
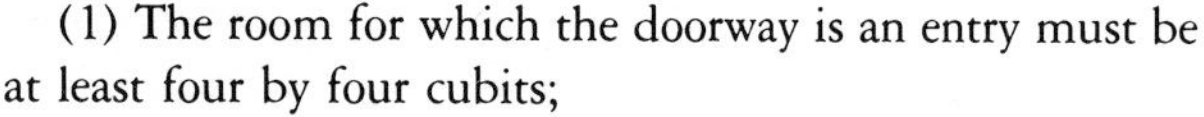

שמע ישראל יהוה אלהינו יהוה אחד ואהבת את
יהוה אלהיך בכל לבבך ובכל נפשך ובכל מאדך והיו
הדברים האלה אשר אנכי מצוך היום על לבבך ושננתם
לבניך ודברת בם בשבתך בביתך ובלכתך בדרך
ובשכבך ובקומך וקשרתם לאות על ידך והיו לטטפת
בין עיניך וכתבתם על מזזות ביתך ובשעריך
והיה אם שמע תשמעו אל מצותי אשר אנכי
מצוה אתכם היום לאהבה את יהוה אלהיכם ולעבדו
בכל לבבכם ובכל נפשכם ונתתי מטר ארצכם בעתו
יורה ומלקוש ואספת דגנך ותירשך ויצהרך ונתתי
עשב בשדך לבהמתך ואכלת ושבעת השמרו לכם
פן יפתה לבבכם וסרתם ועבדתם אלהים אחרים
והשתחויתם להם וחרה אף יהוה בכם ועצר את
השמים ולא יהיה מטר והאדמה לא תתן את יבולה
ואבדתם מהרה מעל הארץ הטבה אשר יהוה נתן לכם
ושמתם את דברי אלה על לבבכם ועל נפשכם וקשרתם
אתם לאות על ידכם והיו לטוטפת בין עיניכם ולמדתם
אתם את בניכם לדבר בם בשבתך בביתך ובלכתך
בדרך ובשכבך ובקומך וכתבתם על מזוזות ביתך
ובשעריך למען ירבו ימיכם וימי בניכם על האדמה
אשר נשבע יהוה לאבתיכם לתת להם כימי השמים
על הארץ

Text of the contents of the mezuzah, *including the commandments in verses 6:4-9; 11:13-21 of Deuteronomy.*

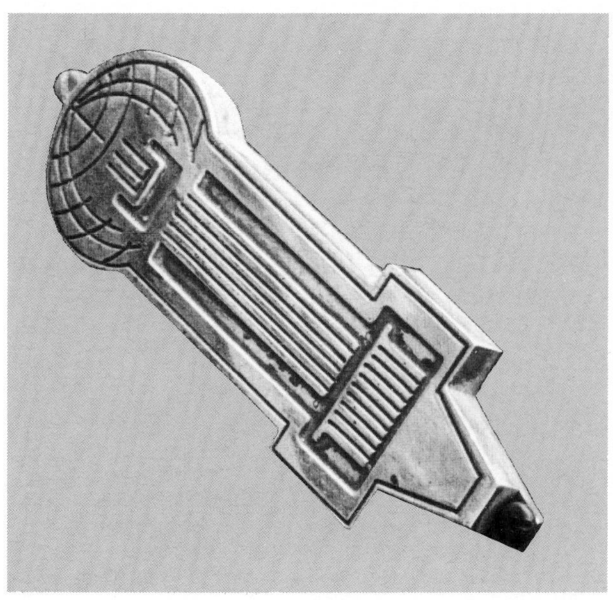

Engraved silver mezuzah *affixed to the doorpost of the Great Synagogue in Jerusalem.*

(1) The room for which the doorway is an entry must be at least four by four cubits;

(2) The doorway must have doorposts on either side;

(3) The doorway must have a lintel;

(4) The doorway must be an entry into a room with a ceiling (although this is disputed);

(5) The doorway must have doors that open and close (also disputed);

(6) The doorway must be a minimum of 40 inches high and 16 inches wide;

(7) The room must be for ordinary dwelling;

(8) The room must be for human, not animal, dwelling;

(9) The room must be for dignified dwelling or usage (thus toilets and bathrooms are exempt);

(10) The room must be for continued or permanent-like dwelling (thus a tent and a SUKKAH are exempt).

Although synagogues and public dwellings are exempt from the commandment, as they are not ordinary dwellings, it has become customary to attach *mezuzot* to their entrances.

When the *mezuzah* is affixed, the benediction, "Who has commanded us to affix the *mezuzah* is recited. In the Diaspora, affixing the *mezuzah* may be deferred for 30 days after entering a rented dwelling, while in the Land of Israel the custom is to attach it immediately. *Mezuzot* should be checked twice every seven years by a qualified expert to make certain they are still valid.

It became customary among traditional Jews to touch the *mezuzah* with their hand upon leaving or entering the house to express awareness of the fulfillment of the commandment, and to show reliance upon God's protection.

MICAH One of the twelve MINOR PROPHETS in the Prophetical section of the Bible. He is said to have received his revelations during the reigns of Jotham, Ahaz, and Hezekiah (c.745-700 BCE), kings of Judah (Jer. 26:18; Mic. 1:1). According to both these references Micah came from Moresheth, probably identical with the town near Gath called Moresheth-Gath. Like his contemporary AMOS, Micah was a native of the southern kingdom of Judah, but he addressed his prophetic message both to the northern kingdom of Israel and to Judah.

According to the Talmud (*BB* 14b), he was also a contemporary of HOSEA and ISAIAH. He was the first prophet to foretell Jerusalem's destruction as a punishment for the city's sins against God. As a result of Micah's prophecy, King Hezekiah prayed to God, thereby procuring a reprieve from the Divine punishment. Micah's declaration that God requires man "only to do justice, to love mercy, and to walk humbly with your God" (Micah 6:8) became a universally famous quotation.

The Book of Micah is the sixth of the 12 Minor Prophets. Its seven chapters consist of 105 verses which are divided into three major parts. The first part (chapters 1-3) predicts the destruction of both Samaria and Jerusalem for their sins. The second (chapters 4-5) anticipates the destruction of the state of Judah and speaks of its restoration to an existence more glorious than before. In the final part (chapters 6-7), Micah denounces dishonesty in the marketplace and corruption in the government in Samaria, and Samaria's response to the charges leveled against it follows. Micah was so filled with the word of God that he dedicated his life to delivering

His message, "But I, I am filled with strength by the spirit of the Lord, And with judgment and courage, To declare to Jacob his transgressions And to Israel his sin" (Micah 3:8).

BOOK OF MICAH

1:1 — 3:12	Threatening prophecies: sins of Israel and Judah; condemnation of rich oppressors, tyrannical rulers, false prophets
4:1 — 5:15	Promise of restoration of Zion, rebuilding of the Temple, in-gathering of the Jewish exiles and advent of the Messiah
6:1 — 6:16	God's charges against Israel; the city threatened
7:1 — 7:20	Conquest of enemies and restoration of the exiles.

MIDDOT ("Measurements"). Tenth tractate of Order KODASHIM in the Mishnah. Its five chapters describe the Second TEMPLE and give the dimensions of each of its parts. The Mishnah begins by enumerating all the places where the priests stood watch, the location of all the Temple gates, followed by the dimensions of the TEMPLE MOUNT, the walls, railing, steps, gates, doors, Inner Court, Altar, and Chambers of the SANCTUARY. The tractate concludes with a description of the meeting hall of the Great SANHEDRIN and the determination of the fitness of priests for service (according to the accuracy of their descent from AARON). MAIMONIDES wrote that the dimensions of the Temple were included in the Mishnah as a reminder of the preciousness of the Temple and of its glory. There is no Talmud on this tractate.

MIDRASH (exposition). Rabbinic commentary on the Bible, clarifying legal points or bringing out lessons by literary devices: story, parable, legends. The word Midrash is also applied to the vast literature to which this gave rise. It derives from a Hebrew root meaning "to inquire, study, investigate," and (by extension) "to preach." Thus, in the days of Ezra those who endeavored "to seek God's Law" (Ezra 7:10) were already developing the ORAL LAW through interpretive methods that would explain it fully to the people (see DERASH). The early sages probably expounded biblical texts in a particular "house of study" (the first BET MIDRASH). Wherever guidance could not be found in the WRITTEN LAW, they delved beyond the literal meaning so as to elucidate the essential, underlying one. Attending the "house of study" was commendable (Ecclus. 51.23), but the rabbis taught that "practice, rather than study [*midrash*] is what matters" (*Avot* 1.17).

During the tannaitic era, Midrash began to serve two distinct purposes and evolved into separate literary genres. The first, based on teaching in the ACADEMIES, helped to clarify legal issues and to extract Jewish law from Scriptural texts (see MIDRASH HALAKHAH). The second, based on preaching in the synagogues, was not legalistic but far more extensive, HOMILETICS and instructive tales (see AGGADAH) woven around biblical or rabbinic figures being used to derive lessons from the Bible (see MIDRASH AGGADAH).

Extending in time from the Mishnaic period to the 13th century, the aggadic type of Midrash incorporated a wealth of maxims, ethical teachings, homilies, anecdotes, and folklore in its running commentary on various biblical books. It has been a constant source of inspiration for Jewish preachers and laymen, and has also influenced Christians and Muslims (through the Koran which contains biblical stories derived from the Midrash).

MIDRASH AGGADAH Homiletical MIDRASH bringing lessons through stories, parables, and other illustrations, often linked with biblical figures. In a limited sense, the practice of interpreting the past in the light of current ideologized tendencies is already apparent in the Book of CHRONICLES. With the sages of the Midrash, this tendentiousness becomes sharper and is motivated by a variety of ideological concerns. The sages viewed the Bible not only as a record of Divine revelation in the past, but as a book that speaks to the present in its problems and concerns. This interpretation of the biblical text is rendered possible by the midrashic method, which seeks to uncover and derive meanings from the mere juxtaposition of certain events and commandments in Scripture.

For the modern exegete, the context of a phrase or word determines its meaning; not so for the authors of Midrash. Each word or phrase of the biblical text can be interpreted independently regardless of the immediate context. For example, it is clear that in Psalms 22:7 ("But I am a worm, less than human, scorned by men, despised by people"), the Psalmist is referring to his own personal experience. The Midrash, however, takes it as a reference to Israel's despised position among the nations: "Just as the worm is the most despised of all creatures, so Israel is the most despised among the nations. But just as the only [visible] organ of the worm is its mouth, so by its mouth [through prayers and pleas to God] does Israel annul the evil decrees planned against them by the nations" (Midr. Ps. 22.18). Sometimes a biblical phrase is interpreted to yield a meaning diametrically opposed to its original intent. Thus, for example, the first verse of LAMENTATIONS ("Jerusalem has become like a widow") is turned into an expression of optimistic hope: "Like a widow, but not actually a widow. Rather as a woman whose husband has gone abroad but who intends to return to her" (*MK* 20a). The Midrash inverts the pessimism of Ecclesiastes into an expression of hope. Ecclesiastes 7:1 declares that "the day of death is better than the day of birth"; this general sentiment is illustrated with the lives of a number of biblical figures: Miriam, Aaron, David, and Samuel (Eccl. R. *ad loc.*) When they were born, they attracted little attention, but on their death, they were universally mourned. Even the stern warnings in Scripture of the fearful fate that will overtake Israel should it fail to observe the Torah are turned by the midrashic method into promises of succor and salvation. Deuteronomy 1:44 ("They [the Amorites] chased after you as the bees and crushed you") is explained: "Just as the bee dies as soon as it has bitten someone, so will the enemy collapse the moment he strikes one of you."

Biblical narrative is marked by a certain repetitiveness, a style found in ancient Semitic literature. For the sages of the Midrash these seemingly superfluous repetitions offered a challenge and an opportunity to create aggadic interpretations that would explain why these were necessary. Generally, the Midrash accepts the principle enunciated by R. Akiva: "The juxtaposition of two sections of the Torah is meant to teach some lesson" (*Sif.* Num. *Balak* 139). Thus the Midrash asks why the account of the death of AARON follows that of the breaking of the two Tablets of the Covenant (Deut. 10:6-7). It answers: "The order is meant to teach that the death of the righteous is as grievous in the sight of God as the breaking of the two tablets" (Lev. R. 20.7).

Scripture rarely states the reason or the background of the commandments, events, or emotional states of its characters, but only records them. The Midrash frequently supplies reasons and motives. Thus, following the account of ABRAHAM's successful battle against the five kings (Gen. 14), the Bible says that the Divine word came to Abraham in a vision saying: "Do not fear, Abraham..." (Gen. 15:1). Why, the Midrash asks, was Abraham afraid? And it answers: "Abraham feared and said to himself 'Perhaps there was a righteous man among those whom I slew'" (Gen. R. 44.4).

Innumerable details in Scripture serve the Midrash as a resource for providing them with a wider symbolic meaning. Judah gives Tamar his seal, cord, and staff (Gen. 38:18); the Midrash asserts that these are symbolic omens of the future kingdom, the SANHEDRIN, and the MESSIAH (Gen. R. 85). From the injunction "You shall not remove the boundary stone of your neighbor" (Deut. 19:14), the Midrash claims that it is forbidden to sell an ancestral grave site (Midr. *Tannaim* 19.14).

The Midrash utilizes metaphor and allegory in interpreting the biblical text. The wanton woman, against whose wiles the author of Proverbs repeatedly warns, is equated either with idolatry or sectarianism (e.g., Prov. 2:11-22). The sages of the Midrash often reject the plain meaning (*peshat*) of the biblical text, for a variety of reasons: it may contradict common knowledge or experience; or they may wish to explain away anthropomorphisms. The plain meaning of the sensuousness of the Song of Songs and the cynical pessimism of Ecclesiastes offended the sages' sense of modesty, in the former instance, and their sense of religious faith in the latter. They interpreted the Song of Songs as an allegorical dialogue between God the lover and Israel His beloved, while to Ecclesiastes' repeated counsel to enjoy the material pleasures life offers, they applied his own final judgment: "Behold it is all futile and a pursuit of wind" (Eccl. 2:11). These midrashic interpretations had an influence when some sages proposed to exclude both books from the biblical Canon.

Nowhere is the concern to replace the plain meaning of the biblical text by a more acceptable midrashic meaning more perceptible than in the treatment of certain discreditable episodes in the lives of biblical figures. Thus, DAVID's affair with Bathsheba is explained away with the theory that she had already been divorced by her husband Uriah, since before going into battle David's soldiers granted a conditional divorce to their wives (*Shab.* 56a). In the Midrash, David even emerges as a talmudic rabbi engaged in deciding ritual law (*Ber.* 3b).

A further characteristic of the midrashic method is its repeated use of plays on words to derive some moral or religious message. Deuteronomy 23:14 says: "With your gear (*azenekha*) you shall have a spike." The Midrash reads *azenekha* as *oznekha* ("your ear"), and explains that the Bible intends to state that when you hear malicious gossip, put a finger to your ear and thus shut out the words (*Ket.* 5a).

Midrashic literature may to a considerable extent consist of fragments of sermons delivered in the synagogue on Friday evenings or on Sabbath afternoons. In addition to these, there is at least one Midrash (Lev. R.) in which each homily consists of a single consistent theme, virtually an entire sermon.

The final type of *Aggadah* is the legend either unrelated to a Scriptural verse or only tangentially so. Frequently, the motifs of these legends are to be found in general folk tales. The legend of King Solomon and Ashmedai (Asmodeus), prince of the demons, is a typical example (*Git.* 68a). However, almost invariably, some specifically Jewish cast is given to such legends.

The Talmud (TJ *Pe'ah* 2.8) says that halakhic conclusions are not to be drawn from the *Aggadah*. Nevertheless, later halakhists did so repeatedly in the RESPONSA literature.

See also: MIDRASH RABBAH; GENESIS RABBAH; EXODUS RABBAH; LEVITICUS RABBAH; NUMBERS RABBAH; DEUTERONOMY RABBAH; LAMENTATIONS RABBAH; ESTHER RABBAH; SONG OF SONGS RABBAH; RUTH RABBAH; ECCLESIASTES RABBAH ("Rabbati"); PESIKTA DE-RAV KAHANA; TANNA DE-VÉ ELIYYAHU; PIRKÉ DE-RABBI ELIEZER; MIDRASH VA-YISSA'U; MIDRASH TADSHÉ; TARGUM SHENI; MIDRASH PROVERBS; MIDRASH SAMUEL; TANHUMA; PESIKTA RABBATI; MIDRASH TEHILLIM (PSALMS); AGGADAT BERESHIT; LEKAH TOV; YALKUT SHIMONI; MIDRASH HA-GADOL; YALKUT MAKHIRI; ÉN YA'AKOV.

MIDRASH HA-GADOL ("The Great Midrash"). 13th-century anthology of *midrashim* drawn from the entire range of rabbinic literature compiled by R. David ben Aaron of Aden, Yemen. It expounds the five books of the Pentateuch according to their weekly readings. Each weekly reading is preceded by a rhymed introduction written by the editor. He utilized not only the generally known ancient sources but also many works that are now lost or available only in fragmentary form. Thus, he quotes frequently from SAADIAH GAON'S Arabic translation of the Pentateuch (*Tafsir*), otherwise almost unknown. Several important rabbinic texts lost during the course of the centuries have been reconstructed on the basis of quotations in *Midrash ha-Gadol* (supplemented and corroborated by Cairo GENIZAH fragments); for example, MEKHILTA DE-RABBI SIMEON and *Mishmar Rabbi Eliezer.* The importance of *Midrash ha-Gadol* for studies of MAIMONIDES lies in the breadth of the literature on which the author draws including otherwise unknown sources employed by Maimonides in composing the *Mishneh Torah.*

The compiler rarely indicates his sources. At times he quotes talmudic statements not directly from the Talmud but from the medieval lexicon, *Arukh*, of R. Nathan of Rome. He weaves together statements from disparate talmudic sources with quotations from Maimonides' *Mishneh Torah.* Despite the singularity of the compiler-editor's method, *Midrash ha-Gadol* remains of importance for the recovery of lost ancient Jewish literature.

MIDRASH HALAKHAH MIDRASH primarily directed to the clarification of legal issues. This term is usually used to designate the tannaitic *midrashim* on the last four books of the Pentateuch, which also contain varying proportions of MIDRASH AGGADAH. Thus the SIFRA is almost exclusively halakhic (legal), while MEKHILTA DE-RABBI ISHMAEL is slightly more than half aggadic.

A number of indications point to an ancient common source from which the editors drew their material. The identical exposition (*derash*) appears in a number of the tannaitic *midrashim.* Since this common ancient source was taught in the various schools, each one left the mark of its own terminology and method on the material. The *midrashim* that come from the School of R. ISHMAEL favor deriving legal decisions by HERMENEUTICS. Those that stem from the school of R. AKIVA prefer to derive the law by expounding the biblical text.

Current scholarly opinion maintains that there is no positive evidence that the sages of the Talmud drew directly on *Midrash Halakhah*, though some scholars maintain that the Talmud does quote the tannaitic midrashim directly. The TOSEFTA quotes extensively from the halakhic *midrashim.*

Midreshé Halakhah from the school of R. Ishmael are: *Mekhilta de-Rabbi Ishmael* on Exodus; fragments on Leviticus; SIFRÉ-NUMBERS on Numbers; and SIFRÉ-DEUTERONOMY on Deuteronomy. The corresponding works from the school of R. Akiva are MEKHILTA DE-RABBI SIMEON; Sifra; *Sifré Zuta*; and *Midrash Tanna'im.*

MIDRASH PROVERBS MIDRASH on the Book of PROVERBS. The unknown editor based his work on selected passages from the Babylonian Talmud and the amoraic *midrashim* that expounded individual verses in the Book of Proverbs. He chose expositions that are for the most part close to the plain meaning of the biblical text, and paraphrased these sources. Likewise, he drew freely on HÉKHALOT mystical literature. No quotations are found in this Midrash from the Palestinian TALMUD, a fact which points to its Babylonian origin. The first quotations from the Midrash are found in geonic literature. Solomon Buber, the editor of the text, dates it in eighth-century Babylonia.

MIDRASH SAMUEL MIDRASH consisting of 32 chapters, of which 24 are based on I Samuel and eight on II Samuel. The compilation is based on such early works as the MISHNAH, TOSEFTA, and halakhic as well as later *midrashim*, with the editor's own interpretations. The editor joins homiletical with exegetical material, a method unknown in early *midrashim.* The sources on which he draws are exclusively from Erets Israel, quoting as he does only the AMORAIM of that country. The work was edited in Erets Israel not earlier than the 11th century. Its late date is evidenced by the artificial character of the 14 proems it contains. It is quoted by RASHI (11th cent.), but its editor, Solomon Buber, maintained that it is based on an original text from a much earlier period.

MIDRASH TADSHÉ Medieval MIDRASH. The name derives from the first verse in it, "Let the earth sprout vegetation (*tadshé*)" (Gen. 1:11), which the author expounds.

A substantial part of the Midrash is devoted to a detailed symbolic interpretation of the Sanctuary and its various implements, a method the author also applies to the description of the Solomonic TEMPLE found in I Kings 7 and II Chr. 3 and 4.

The entire work is divided into 22 sections (corresponding to the number of letters in the Hebrew alphabet).

MIDRASH TANHUMA See TANHUMA

MIDRASH TEHILLIM A homiletical MIDRASH on the Book of PSALMS (except Psalms 123 and 133). The work is also known as *Midrash Shoher Tov* because the verse with which it opens (Prov. 11:27) begins with this phrase ("He who earnestly seeks what is good"). The Midrash on Psalms 119-150 is later than the original composition. The Midrash on many psalms was copied from YALKHUT SHIMONI. The editor of the text, Solomon Buber, argued for its early Palestinian origin, but his theory is rejected today by most scholars. According to ZUNZ, it was edited in Italy during the last centuries of the geonic period. The lateness of the date of composition is evidenced by various internal indications. It contains many lofty ethical sentiments and abounds in stories and parables.

MIDRASH VA-YISSA'U A medieval MIDRASH on the wars of JACOB and his sons. Its title derives from the first word in Genesis 35:5 ("As they set out"). It is quoted by Naḥmanides (on Gen. 34:13) under the name of "The Book of the Wars of the Sons of Jacob," probably its original name. The Midrash consists of three chapters, each of which deals with one of the legendary wars of Jacob and his sons. With the exception of the first chapter, it is a free translation from a Greek text which in turn was based on an Aramaic text dating from Second Temple times. Some scholars see chapters 2 and 3 (the war against the Amorites and the war against Esau) as projections into the biblical past of the wars of John Hyrcanus against the Samaritans and against the Edomites: the latter, according to biblical genealogy, are the descendants of Esau. The book was rewritten and used by the author of the medieval work, *Sefer ha-Yashar*.

MIKRA See BIBLE

MIKVA'OT ("Ritual Baths"). Sixth tractate of Order TOHOROT in the Mishnah. Its ten chapters deal with the laws of building and immersing in a ritual bath (*mikveh*; cf. Lev. 11:36, 15:16). Included are the dimensions of a ritual bath, proper immersion, the invalidity of a *mikveh*, the use of springs, rivers, and seas as ritual baths, and the vessels that require immersion in a *mikveh*. According to Jewish law, contact with all forms of impurity, from the most severe to the lightest, requires immersion (see MIKVEH). The subject is amplified in the *Tosefta*.

MIKVEH (pl. *mikva'ot*; lit. a "collection" or "gathering together" of water). Ritual bath. Together with the synagogue and religious school, the *mikveh* was from ancient times a basic institution of Jewish community life. It is first mentioned in the Pentateuch (Lev. 11:36) as the exclusive medium for purifying individuals or utensils from the numerous sources of impurity listed there: "Only a spring, cistern, or collection (*mikveh*) of waters shall be cleansing." Among the sources of impurity were contact with a corpse, childbirth, menstruation, venereal disease, and seminal issue. Without resort to the *mikveh*, the Jew in Temple times could not participate in any religious ceremony, for which he had to be ritually pure. Remains of some of the numerous baths used by pilgrims have been unearthed in Jerusalem. Even after most of the laws of defilement fell into abeyance with the destruction of the Temple, the ritual bath remained an essential component of family life for observant Jews, since a wife has to immerse herself in it after her menstrual period before cohabitation (see FAMILY PURITY). Immersion in a ritual bath is similarly required for initiating proselytes and to purify metal cooking utensils and glassware manufactured by non-Jews. In all these cases, a prescribed benediction must be recited. It is also customary, though not strictly a ritual requirement, for very pious Jews to visit the ritual bath

Immersion of a woman in a mikveh *(ritual bath) assisted by two other women. Engraving, Amsterdam, 1792.*

before the Day of Atonement, and adherents of Ḥasidic groups do so before the Sabbath.

A whole tractate of the Mishnah (MIKVA'OT) is devoted to the halakhic requirements for constructing a *mikveh*, and archeological excavations have uncovered *mikva'ot* conforming to these regulations at Masada, in ancient synagogues, and even in private homes. The *mikveh* is always linked to public bathing facilities, since the immersion is only valid if the person concerned has previously scrubbed away every possible speck of dirt. Such dirt constitutes a barrier (*ḥatsitsah*) to the cleansing power of the ritual bath, physical and spiritual cleanliness being interdependent in Judaism.

However, the rabbis insisted that no bath was to be taken immediately after immersion in the *mikveh* but only before, to stress the latter's exclusively spiritual power. No scholar was to reside in a community which had no public baths, and even a synagogue could be sold to defray the costs of a *mikveh*.

The basic requirements for the ritual bath include the source and quantity of the water, the materials from which it is built, and the mode of construction. The source must either be underground water (such as a spring) or rainwater, melted snow or ice. The ice may have been artificially frozen. Spring water — seas and rivers included — purifies when flowing or moving, but rainwater does so only when stationary in a bath or pool. For this reason, the exit plug must be tightly fitting or, alternatively, the water must be changed by pumping it out of the bath. The water itself must on no account be tapped by human agency through collection in a vessel, but must fall into a built-in or hewn-out (not prefabricated) pool or bath. The pipes, viaduct, or gutter through which the water passes on its way to the bath must have no cavities where the water can collect and must not be made of materials that attract biblical uncleanness (Num. 31:22), but rather of earthenware, stone, concrete, cement, asbestos, or plastic. This requirement can be waived if the water flows across an absorptive material (such as cement) for a length of about 12 inches before entering the bath.

The minimum amount of water collected in the ritually approved manner is 40 *se'ah*, which the rabbis calculated was needed to facilitate a person's complete immersion. They arrived at this measurement by basing it on the three dimensions of 1 x 1 cubits square by 3 cubits height (*Er.* 14b). The equivalent volume in present-day terms might be anything from 292 liters (77 gallons) to 532 liters (140.5 gallons); in most communities, however, 762 liters (201 gallons) is the standard minimum. Once the bath contains this minimum amount, it can purify any volume of ordinary water. In this way, hot and cold water can be added and one or more baths or pools can be joined to the original pure source by opening an aperture between them of at least 1.5 inches in diameter at a minimum height of 32 inches. Medieval European ritual baths chiefly derived their water from springs, but the most frequently used model today is based on rainwater collected on the roof and flowing down from a gutter into a built-in cistern; this cistern constitutes the original store through which all the other pools in the complex are made ritually fit by the approved means. Since both the construction and the regular functioning of the bath are subject to complicated halakhic regulations, expert rabbinical supervision is needed.

In Israel, the Ministry of Religious Affairs supervises and sponsors the construction of ritual baths. A number of standardized models have thus been developed, ranging from small basic utilities catering for 100-family villages to sophisticated urban complexes provided with the most up-to-date facilities, including a beauty parlor. During the first decade of the State, nearly 500 ritual baths were constructed, mostly in new settlements; today, there are over 1,200 ritual baths in Israel, few communities now lacking one. Outside of Israel, the ritual bath is almost exclusively confined to Orthodox communities. Conservative Judaism, upholds the main traditional laws and insists on *tevilah* (immersion) for proselytes. Despite some suggestions that lakes, oceans, rivers, and certain types of swimming pools are halakhically fit for immersion, the majority view of all Law Committees of the Conservative movement has upheld the traditional *mikveh* — for its historical, symbolic, and deep spiritual meaning. Reform Judaism in the United States considers the *mikveh* superfluous in the modern age, but outside the USA most Reform congregations insist on immersion for their proselytes. See also ABLUTIONS.

MILAH See CIRCUMCISION

MINHAG See CUSTOM

MINHAGIM, BOOKS OF Books listings Jewish customs (*minhagim*) of a certain time and place. A *minhag* by definition is a prevalent religious practice which is not specifically enjoined by Torah law (see CUSTOM). The earliest known book of Jewish customs, dating from the eighth century CE, records differences in customs between the Jews living in Babylonia and the Jews of Erets Israel. A later book, *Ḫillu Minhagim*, records the variations in custom between Sura and Pumbedita, the two great centers of Jewish learning in Babylon. As the Jewish Diaspora spread into Europe, new customs developed. The book *Sefer ha-Minhagot* by Asher ben Saul of Lunel, chronicles the customs of southern France, while Abraham ben Nathan ha-Yarḫi recorded the various customs he discovered while traveling through 12th-century Spain, Provence, France, and Germany in his book, *Ha-Minhag*.

Many collections of *minhagim* books appeared in medieval Germany in the 15th century. This was a time of terrible persecution and the rabbis strove, through the transmission of Jewish practices, to strengthen their communities. They sought to gather and examine the customs that had developed, cancel many that were no longer relevant, and provide guidance to the people. R. Jacob Mölln (*Maharil*), one of the foremost leaders of German Jewry, wrote a book entitled *Minhagé Maharil*, noting many of the customs of the

TABLE OF RITUAL BATH *(MIKVEH)* REGULATION

SOURCE	QUANTITY	MODE	MATERIALS	VOIDED BY	PURIFIES
Spring (sea or river)	minimal	flowing	stone, cement, asbestos, or earthenware, but not metal	change of color, other liquids, water collected by human agency in a vessel before the pool is filled with the minimum amount	bride, post-menstruant, mother of a newborn child, proselyte to Judaism, worshiper on eve of Day of Atonement or Sabbath
rainwater, ice, snow	40 *seah* 24×24×75.5ins. or 332 liters	stationary in built-in watertight pool			Other waters permissible by mingling or contact.

Ashkenazi countries. Many of these customs were later codified by R. Moses ISSERLES in his *Mappah* which added Ashkenazi practice to Joseph CARO's Sephardi-oriented SHULHAN ARUKH. Works appeared giving guidance to the customs of particular communities (e.g., Egypt, Algiers, Jerusalem). Compilations and studies continue to be published.

MINHAH See AFTERNOON SERVICE

MINIM ("sectarians"; sing. *min*). Term used widely by the rabbis to denote various Jewish sectarian groups: the SADDUCEES and Boethusians, SAMARITANS, and Nazarenes (Judeo-Christians). In rabbinic literature, *min* is often closely associated with EPIKOROS or *kofer* — one who derides the sages and their teachings, rejects their authority, and openly flouts the ORAL LAW. "Apostates [*minim*], informers and *epikorsim* who repudiate the Torah, deny that there will be a resurrection of the dead, and separate themselves from the ways of the community" are doomed to perdition (*RH* 17a). No less than two dozen sects could be identified in 70 CE, when the Temple was destroyed (TJ *Sanh.* 10.6), and their presence within the Jewish camp, undermining nationale morale, was increasingly regarded as a threat to Judaism. The practice of reciting the TEN COMMANDMENTS each morning in the synagogue was discontinued in response to assertions by the *minim* (Judeo-Christians) that the Decalogue alone had binding religious force (*Ber.* 12a). Finally, around 80-90 CE, an imprecation against apostates and heretics whose slanders had become intolerable was added to the weekday AMIDAH (see BIRKAT HA-MINIM). This chiefly had the effect of removing Judeo-Christians from the synagogue and of converting them from a heterodox Jewish fellowship into a sect persecuted and ultimately destroyed by the Gentile church. Subsequently, during the early talmudic period, *min* invariably designated pagan philosophers, Gnostics, or (Gentile) Christians. By the Middle Ages, it had become synonymous with atheism or idolatry. See also APOSTASY and HERESY.

MINOR PROPHETS (known in Aramaic as *Terei Asar*, or "Twelve"). The works of the 12 prophets contained in the prophetical section of the Bible. They are called "minor" in comparison with the much larger works of the three "major" prophets — Isaiah, Jeremiah, and Ezekiel. The Minor Prophets are HOSEA, JOEL, AMOS, OBADIAH, JONAH, MICAH, NAHUM, HABAKKUK, ZEPHANIAH, HAGGAI, ZECHARIAH and MALACHI. The Talmud (*BB* 14b) states that the 12 were gathered together because otherwise, "as they are small, they might be lost." Of the 12, nine prophesied during the First Temple era, while Haggai, Zechariah and Malachi prophesied during the Second Temple era.

MINYAN (Heb. "number", pl., *minyanim*). Traditional prayer quorum of at least ten males above the age of 13 who assemble for public worship and various other religious observances. A biblical phrase, "God stands in the Divine assembly" (Ps. 82:1), was interpreted by the rabbis to mean that if ten men pray together, the *Shekhinah* — God's Presence — hovers over them (*Avot* 3.6; *Ber.* 6a). The statutory minimum of ten worshipers is variously explained, on the basis of Abraham's last plea in favor of Sodom (Gen. 18:32); as a number deduced from the word *edah* ("assembly, congregation") used with reference to the ten spies (Num. 14:27; *Sanh.* 1.6, *Meg.* 23b); or likewise, with reference to Korah and his fellow rebels (Num. 16:21; *Ber.* 21b, *Meg.* 23b). No rabbi or professional "reader" is needed for a *minyan*, which may conduct services in any suitable place, including a member's home or even outdoors. The rabbis constantly emphasized the importance of praying with a *minyan* (*tefillah be-tsibbur*). Thus, according to the Talmud (*Ber.* 6b), "When the Holy One enters a synagogue and does not find ten worshipers there, His wrath is immediately kindled, as stated in the Bible: 'Why, when I came, was no one there; why, when I called, was there no answer?'" (Isa. 50:2). Consequently, "one should always rise early to attend synagogue and thus acquire the merit of making up the first prayer quorum" (*Ber.* 47b). Even one who, by force of circumstances, has to pray alone should do so when other Jews are attending synagogue. The concept of the *minyan* reflects Judaism's stress on the religious COMMUNITY. Where the need arose, in smaller congregations, paid "*minyan* men" insured the mustering of a quorum (see BATLANIM), for in the words of an old Yiddish proverb, "Nine rabbis do not constitute a *minyan*, but ten cobblers can." Reform Judaism, with its egalitarian approach, has adopted the practice of counting women as well as men in the prayer quorum. Since 1973, following a majority responsum of the Law Committee of the Conservative movement, an increasing number of Conservative congregations have accepted women in the *minyan*.

A *minyan* is required for:

Recitation of the BAREKHU invocation and the SHEMA (with accompanying blessings) in public worship.

Repetition of the AMIDAH with the KEDUSHAH prayer included.

Chanting of the PRIESTLY BLESSING by those of priestly descent.

Congregational READING OF THE LAW of the Law and prescribed section from the Prophets (HAFTARAH) with accompanying benedictions.

Recitation of the KADDISH in public worship (both by the reader and by individual mourners), at a funeral, or in a house of mourning.

The Seven Benedictions (*Sheva Berakhot*) recited under the HUPPAH (marriage canopy) at a wedding and for seven days thereafter.

Recitation of GRACE AFTER MEALS following a CIRCUMCISION, a Redemption of the FIRSTBORN (*pidyon ha-ben*) ceremony, or a banquet in honor of a newly married couple.

MIRACLES Extraordinary events which appear to violate the known laws of nature, the cause of which is ascribed to God. The Bible describes many events which appear to fit into this category; these include the parting of the Red Sea, the falling of the MANNA and the ascension of ELIJAH to heaven. However, it has no word which is the equivalent of "miracle." Rabbinic literature uses the word *"nes"* with the same semantic range as "miracle" (*"nes"* occurs in the Bible, but with a different meaning). Certain extraordinary events, however, are selected by the Bible for special emphasis and are variously called *gedolot*, "great things" (II Kings 8:4; Deut. 10:21) or *nifla'ot*, "marvels" (Ex. 34:10,11), or *otot u-mofetim*, "sign and wonders" (Jer. 32:21).

To the author of the Bible, the activity of God, as such, is nothing unusual and the recording of His "mighty deeds" is seen as precisely the essential subject-matter of the Bible. God destroys the cities of Sodom and Gomorrah, enables Sarah to give birth in old age, brings plagues upon Pharaoh for abducting Sarah (Gen:17), and causes a well of water to appear for Hagar in the wilderness (Gen. 21:29). Such actions are not referred to as "miraculous," although to the modern reader they are hardly compatible with his understanding of natural law. For the author of the Bible, the sufficient condition for a certain event to be designated as wondrous was not that it was caused by God and violated natural law, but that it had a certain psychological impact upon its witnesses and certain practical consequences. Thus, the classic "sign and wonder," which Israel was urged never to forget, was the EXODUS FROM EGYPT which involved the TEN PLAGUES and the Parting of the Red Sea. Those who experienced those events saw them as "the hand of God" (Ex. 14:31) primarily because of their prophetic context; the spokesman for God had predicted what was going to happen and the purpose of the events. For the Israelites, these events signified that God had liberated them from bondage so that they might become a covenanted people dedicated to His service (Ex. 6:6-8). In terms of Israel, these "signs and wonders" were performed not to prove the existence or power of God, but to reveal His intentions for and relationship to Israel.

Similarly, the significance of the blocking of the waters of the Jordan (Josh. 3:16,17) and the collapse of the walls of Jericho (Josh. 6:20) lies not in their being supernatural events, but in the fact that they constituted the fulfillment of God's promise to bring Israel into the Promised Land.

A pattern concerning "miracles" can be discerned in the Bible. Until the appearance of Moses, "miracles" occur to people but no individual is described as performing miracles. From Moses until Elijah, miracles are performed by individuals but only for a multitude. In the period of Elijah and Elisha miracles are performed for individuals by individuals.

According to MAIMONIDES (*Yesodé ha-Torah* 7), the miracles recorded in the Bible were performed in order to achieve particular concrete results: to save the Israelites, to provide food and drink in the wilderness, to break the rebellion of Korah. They were not intended to provide the evidential basis for belief in the Divine authority of Moses' mission. This basic tenet of the Jews was grounded in the direct encounter with God experienced by all Israel at Sinai. Subsequent to that event, the necessary qualifications of a prophet were that he uphold the teachings of the Torah. Should he fail to do so, even the performance of miracles could not give him credibility (Deut. 13:2-4). The talmudic rabbis ruled that the ability to perform miracles is no proof of the correctness of one's halakhic views (*BM* 29b). Maimonides held that the future Messiah will not be asked to validate his claims by the performance of miracles.

Since the world is seen as God's creation, the need to intervene with miracles would appear to raise questions about the effectiveness of His handiwork. The rabbis proposed a reconciliation between natural law and miracles. "At the time of creation, God made a condition with the sea that it should part before the Children of Israel upon their leaving Egypt... and so with all the other parts of creation... that the fire should not harm Hananiah, Mishael, and Azariah in the furnace, and with the fish that it should cast up Jonah" (Gen. R. 5.45). In this way, the "miracle" is part of preordained "natural" processes.

Nahmanides wrote that the purpose of overt miracles is to draw attention to the "hidden miracles" which are all round us daily. The greatest miracle of all is life itself. In fact, says Nahmanides, there is no such thing as "nature." It is all miracle!

While the talmudic rabbis believed that miracles continued to happen in their time (and the "miraculous" intervention of Honi ha-Me'aggel and Hanina ben Dosa are described in the Talmud) and were performed by their own colleagues, they ruled that a person must not rely on miracles (*Pes.* 64b). In the *halakhah* it is stated that a Jew visiting a place where miracles occurred to the Jewish people, must recite a special blessing (*Ber.* 9.1). (See also MAGIC; SUPERSTITION.)

MI SHE-BERAKH ("He who blessed [our fathers]"). Opening words and popular title of various invocations for blessings recited in connection with the READING OF THE LAW. On Sabbaths and festivals, in most rites, a *Mi she-Berakh* prayer is offered by the reader on behalf of each individual called to the Reading of the Law; in Orthodox congregations this may be followed by another such prayer, blessing the individual's family and anyone else whom he wishes to honor, a donation to the synagogue or to charity also being mentioned. According to Western Sephardi (Spanish and Portuguese) custom, each honor allocated in connection with the Torah reading is preceded by a separate *Mi she-Berakh*. On a Monday or Thursday coinciding with or preceding a death anniversary (YAHRZEIT), Ashkenazim may ask for a memorial prayer to be recited as well (in other rites this is not restricted to weekdays). After the usual *Mi she-Berakh*, additional prayers may be recited for a sick person, the mother of a newborn child (a daughter but not a son then being named in the synagogue), for a bar mitsvah boy, or for a bridegroom prior to his wedding. Conservative practice allows for such a *Mi she-Berakh* to be recited for a woman or bat mitsvah called to the Torah. Some traditional congregations substitute one general *Mi she-Berakh* after the Reading of the Law for the various individual prayers.

A separate and longer formula, dating from geonic times, is the Prayer for the Community recited on Sabbaths (and festivals coinciding with the Sabbath) after the Reading of the Law. In the Ashkenazi rite, this follows YEKUM PURKAN; it invokes God's blessing on the congregation, on all other synagogue worshipers in every land, and on all who perform communal tasks. The Italian rite preserves a similar wording, but a different text is used by Sephardi and Eastern congregations. In Israeli (and some Diaspora) synagogues, a third *Mi she-Berakh* is read calling for God's protection to be extended over all serving in the Israel Defense Forces.

MISHKAN See SANCTUARY

MISHMAROT AND MA'AMADOT (lit. "watches and stands"). Division of PRIESTS and LEVITES. At the time of the Second TEMPLE, all priests, Levites and Israelites were divided into 24 groups, each group serving in the Temple for one week each half year. During the remaining four weeks of the year, when the festivals occurred, all were divided into seven sections, each section serving for a day. The duty roster of the priests and Levites was known as the *mishmar*, and that of the Israelites as the *ma'amad*. As only a limited number of Israelites could be used in the Temple at any given time, those in that particular *ma'amad* that remained at home devoted their time to praying that the sacrifices of those in Jerusalem would be acceptable, and fasting for four consecutive days, from Monday to Thursday.

After the Temple was destroyed, the rabbis equated the recitation of verses relating to the sacrifices with the offering of the sacrifices. Thus the custom grew of reciting special prayers called *ma'amadot* after the morning prayers, in place of the *ma'amad* at the time of the Temple. The text of the *ma'amad* is to be found in *Mishnah Ta'anit* 4. This text, with additional sections, appears in the prayer book of R. AMRAM GAON (ninth century). The *ma'amadot* are not part of the prayers, and are only recited by those individuals who wish to do so.

Part of a marble plaque bearing a list of mishmarot *(watches) of priests of the Temple. Caesarea, 3rd-4th centuries CE.*

MISHNAH First authoritative compilation of the ORAL LAW, reflecting nearly five centuries of Jewish legal traditions, from the era of the SCRIBES to that of the *tannaim* (c. 300-200 CE). The Mishnah (lit. "teaching" or "instruction" handed down by word of mouth) is the most important Jewish religious document after the Bible itself, the WRITTEN LAW, and by virtue of its further interpretation and discussion in amoraic times it constituted the basis of the TALMUD (see also TANNA and AMORA). Although it includes some non-legal AGGADAH, the Mishnah chiefly represents the earliest comprehensive assemblage of the HALAKHAH, as collated and edited by R. JUDAH HA-NASI in Erets Israel between the years 200-220 CE. Its purpose was to supply judges and teachers of religion with an authoritative guide to Jewish law. Since problems arose with the oral transmission of laws, a halakhic CODIFICATION in writing became an urgent necessity. Hence this Mishnah, a record of legal debates and decisions by the tannaitic sages, which remains substantially as Judah ha-Nasi and his colleagues arranged it.

Collections of *halakhot* antedated Judah ha-Nasi by several generations. Preeminent among them was the collection of R. AKIVA, as recorded and arranged by his disciple, R. MEIR. Since these legal traditions were taught orally in the various Palestinian ACADEMIES, the material was arranged not topically, according to subject matter, but according to external criteria. Various unrelated *halakhot* might thus be grouped together, following the name of the *tanna* who enunciated them, or the arrangement might follow a certain pattern of phraseology. While these techniques served as an aid to memorization, they impeded the study and discussion of a single topic in all its aspects.

The achievement of Judah ha-Nasi and his collaborators lay in arranging the accumulated mass of legal opinions according to their subject matter. In doing so, however, R. Judah frequently incorporated into his Mishnah whole blocs of material, exactly as they appeared in older sources, despite his basic methodology. Thus, for example, chapter 13 of tractate KETUBBOT includes a miscellany of *halakhot* grouped together according to author. Similarly, the various TAKKANOT (enactments) of R. JOHANAN BEN ZAKKAI are grouped together (*RH.* 4.1-9) as are the *takkanot* ordained "for the betterment of society" (*Git.* 4.2-9).

Nearly 150 different sages are named in the Mishnah, from HILLEL and SHAMMAI to the compiler himself. Wherever a difference of opinion arises, the dissenting or minority view is recorded first to indicate that it had been taken into consideration (though finally rejected). The accepted, authoritative view, which determined the *halakhah*, is placed last and may be expressed in a standard formula: "R. Judah says..." or "but the sages declare..."

There are six "Orders" of the Mishnah, as indicated by the Hebrew term *Shishah Sidré Mishnah* ("six Orders of the Mishnah," often abbreviated to SHAS, a synonym for the Talmud in general). These Orders are divided into *massekhot* or tractates (see MASSEKHET), of which there are 63, and each tractate comprises a number of chapters (*perakim*), which are further subdivided into paragraphs. Each of these paragraphs of *halakhah* is known as a *mishnah* (pl. *mishnayyot*) and, excluding the sixth chapter of tractate AVOT (which was a later addition), there are altogether 523 chapters in the Mishnah. Briefly described, its six Orders are:

(1) ZERA'IM ("Seeds"), dealing first with BENEDICTIONS and daily prayers, then mostly with AGRICULTURAL LAWS;

(2) MO'ED ("Appointed Season"), on laws governing observance of the SABBATH, FESTIVALS, and FAST DAYS;

(3) NASHIM ("Women"), dealing with MARRIAGE and DIVORCE, etc., as well as with VOWS and other issues;

(4) NEZIKIN ("Damages"), on civil and criminal law, PUNISHMENTS, IDOLATRY, and the ethical teachings incorporated in *Avot*;

(5) KODASHIM ("Holy Things"), which discusses ritual slaughter, SACRIFICES AND OFFERINGS, the TEMPLE and its services;

(6) TOHOROT ("Cleanliness"), on the laws of ritual PURITY and impurity.

(For a general outline, see Table. See also entries on each tractate.)

Scholarly opinion is divided as to whether Judah ha-Nasi intended the Mishnah to serve as a final code on the basis of which the law could be decided. A prevailing view is that, essentially, the editor wished to systematize the *halakhah*. There are, in any case, very few of R. Judah's own opinions stated in the Mishnah, and he normally contented himself with transmitting an ancient *halakhah* found in other sources. Some of these opinions were inserted into the Mishnah by one of his disciples.

With the exception of a few statements by early sages, the Mishnah is written in a concise HEBREW differing significantly from biblical Hebrew in both grammar and vocabulary. Mishnaic Hebrew was a natural development from that spoken by the last prophets, and in the days of Ezra and Nehemiah. It contains about 200 words borrowed from Greek and Latin.

An extraneous halakhic statement, not included in the Mishnah but quoted later in the Talmud, is known as a BARAITA. Supplementary compilations, parallel to the Mishnah, are styled TOSEFTA.

In the Talmud, successive Mishnaic passages are followed by the relevant (amoraic) discussion, which appears under the heading of GEMARA. The first printed edition of the Mishnah appeared in Spain (c.1485), but the oldest surviving printed text was published in Italy (Naples, 1492).

There have been innumerable commentaries on the Mishnah, notably those of MAIMONIDES (first written in Arabic), Obadiah di BERTINORO, and Yom Tov Lipmann HELLER (*Tosafot Yom Tov*). The Mishnah is often printed as a separate work, for the use of students, and in standard editions one usually finds an introduction to the Oral Law by Maimonides, Bertinoro's commentary, and a digest of Heller's (*Ikkar Tosefot Yom Tov*) compiled by Meshulam ben Joel Katz. There are also two outstanding modern commentaries in Hebrew, by Ḥanokh Albeck and Pinḥas Kehati (the second of which is now being published in English translation). Herbert Danby's English version (1933) is regarded as a classic; Philip Blackman's dual langauge edition (1951-56) includes an English commentary.

Detail from the title page of a Hebrew-Latin Mishnah. Illustration by Michael Richey, Amsterdam 1700-1704.

TRACTATES OF THE MISHNAH AND TALMUD

Order	Number of Mishnaic chapters	Babylonian Talmud	Jerusalem Talmud	Tosefta
Order ZERA'IM				
Berakhot	9		●	●
Pe'ah	8		●	●
Demai	7		●	●
Kilayim	9		●	●
Shevi'it	10		●	●
Terumot	11		●	●
Ma'aserot	5		●	●
Ma'aser Sheni	5		●	●
Ḥallah	4		●	●
Orlah	3		●	●
Bikkurim	3		●	●
Order MO'ED				
Shabbat	24	●	●	●
Eruvin	10	●	●	●
Pesaḥim	10	●	●	●
Shekalim	8		●	●
Yoma	8	●	●	●
Sukkah	5	●	●	●
Bétsah	5	●	●	●
Rosh Ha-Shanah	4	●	●	●
Ta'anit	4	●	●	●
Megillah	4	●	●	●
Mo'ed Katan	3	●	●	●
Ḥagigah	3	●	●	●
Order NASHIM				
Yevamot	16	●	●	●
Ketubbot	13	●	●	●
Nedarim	11	●	●	●
Nazir	9	●	●	●
Sotah	9	●	●	●
Gittin	9	●	●	●
Kiddushin	4	●	●	●

Order	Number of Mishnaic chapters	Babylonian Talmud	Jerusalem Talmud	Tose
Order NEZIKIN				
Bava Kamma	10	●	●	●
Bava Metsi'a	10	●	●	●
Bava Batra	10	●	●	●
Sanhedrin	11	●	●	●
Makkot	3	●	●	●
Shevu'ot	8	●	●	●
Eduyyot	8			●
Avodah Zarah	5	●	●	●
Avot	5			
Horayot	3	●	●	●
Order KODASHIM				
Zevaḥim	14	●		●
Menaḥot	13	●		●
Ḥullin	12	●		●
Bekhorot	9	●		●
Arakhin	9	●		●
Temurah	7	●		●
Keritot	6	●		●
Me'ilah	6	●		●
Tamid	7	●		
Middot	5			
Kinnim	3			
Order TOHOROT				
Kelim	30			●
Oholot	18			●
Nega'im	14			●
Parah	12			●
Tohorot	10			●
Mikva'ot	10			●
Niddah	10	●	●	●
Makhshirin	6			●
Zavim	5			●
Tevul Yom	4			●
Yadayim	4			●
Uktsin	3			●

MISSION The Bible teaches that the ultimate concern of God is to bring REDEMPTION to all mankind. Abraham is told: "You will be for a blessing and in you will be blessed all the families of the earth" (Gen. 12:2,3). In some unspecified way, Abraham's seed is to bring blessing upon all men. This is made more explicit by the prophet: "I have kept you and set you for a covenant of the people, for a light unto the nations" (Is. 42:6). The concept that Israel as a nation has a task and a responsibility that reaches beyond itself and encompasses all mankind is referred to by the modern term "Mission of Israel." This task or mission is somehow to bring the word of God to the nations of the world. It was never spelled out how precisely this was to be done. In certain periods, this was understood to mean active discrediting of the false gods of paganism and aggressive programs of proselytization in which the Jewish people literally act as teachers. At other times it was construed primarily in terms of teaching by example. By observing the Torah, each Jewish community could become a living and inspiring embodiment of the highest principles of morality and sanctity. Also by persisting in their faith and loyalty to God to the point of martyrdom, Jewish survival becomes an impressive manifestation of God's miraculous Providence.

This notion of mission is related to the concept of Israel

as "witness" who "testifies" to the greatness and goodness of God (Is. 43:10). It is also related to the concept of the sanctification of the name of God (KIDDUSH HA-SHEM) attesting to the standing of God's reputation in the world. The aim and goal of Israel's mission, to "testify as witness," or to be a "blessing" or to "sanctify the name" is always the same, namely, to bring all men to acknowledge the sovereignty of God.

The rabbis saw the "mission" as one of the purposes of the Exile and dispersion: "The Almighty dispersed Israel among the nations in order that they may gather to themselves proselytes, as it is written: 'And I have sown her unto me in the land' (Hosea 2:25). Would a man sow a measure of grain unless it was to reap manyfold?" A connection between dispersion and mission is also alluded to in Genesis 28:14, in the words of God to Jacob: "Your seed shall be as the dust of the earth and you shall spread abroad to the west, and to the east, and to the south and to the north. And in you and in your seed shall all the families of the earth be blessed."

The mission concept became a central tenet of the theology of the REFORM movement receiving expression in the theology of Kaufmann KOHLER and incorporated in the Pittsburg Platform of 1885. Judaism was almost completely universalized with only the moral law in the Bible regarded as binding. The goal of Judaism was the establishment, together with other progressive religions, of the Kingdom of truth, justice, and peace among all men. Jews were no longer to be considered a nation but a religious community with the mission of being a priest for the dissemination of monotheism. The messianic concept of a return to Zion was rejected and the dispersed condition of the Jew affirmed as enabling the Priest-People to be in direct contact with the nations he was directed to influence and inspire. This approach was bitterly attacked by the Zionist philosopher, Aḥad Ha-Am, as a romantic rationalization of the emancipation in Western Europe which he termed "Slavery in Freedom." The Mission concept had become a cover for transforming Zionism and the Jewish National ideal into a vapid universalistic concept and a justification for rendering the GALUT permanent. Since the 1930s, Reform Judaism modified its concept of mission, especially in the aftermath of the Holocaust, and incorporated a strong Zionism in its theology and practice. At the same time, it maintained its broad UNIVERSALISM and in the 1980s adopted an outreach program seeking to attract non-Jews to Judaism, initially non-Jewish partners in mixed marriages.

MITNAGGEDIM ("Opponents"). An originally derisive Hebrew epithet which Ḥasidic Jews applied to their traditionalist adversaries in Eastern Europe (see ḤASIDISM). Resolutely upholding time-honored practices and a "way of life" that Ashkenazim had thought unchangeable, the *Mitnaggedim* tended to ignore the doctrinal aspects of Ḥasidism, concentrating their attack on the new and growing movement's deviations from the religious norm. They feared the spread of another heresy, in the wake of SHABBETAI TSEVI and the contemporary FRANKISTS. Accordingly, they mounted a vehement campaign against Ḥasidism during the last decades of the 18th century, protesting its adoption of the Sephardi prayer rite, breakaway houses of worship, minimal regard for Torah and Talmud study, and disparagement of traditional scholars. Their indignation was especially aroused by the Ḥasidic "cult" of the *Rebbe* or TSADDIK, a new kind of spiritual leader.

When the northward advance of Ḥasidism brought it to the gates of Vilna, the stronghold of the *Mitnaggedim*, conflict broke out in earnest. Headed by the outstanding religious authority, ELIJAH BEN SOLOMON ZALMAN, GAON OF VILNA, the *Mitnaggedim* launched their counterattack. The first ban of excommunication (*ḥerem*) was pronounced in 1772, outlawing the Ḥasidic movement, its advocates, synagogues and innovations. After the Vilna Gaon's death in 1797, hostility between the two camps descended to the level of economic sanctions, invective, and satire, accompanied by the imprisonment of some leaders on either side who had been denounced to the tsarist authorities. This state of affairs persisted well into the 19th century, before the bitterness died down, notably in face of common "menaces" — Emancipation and Enlightenment.

Paradoxically, the unyielding opposition of the Vilna Gaon and his disciples compelled Ḥasidism to abandon its earlier excesses and ultimately become as traditionalist as many of its arch-critics. New realities, such as a general decline in Torah learning and observance, also confronted the *Mitnaggedim* and forced them to change. Elijah Gaon's teachings and example gave rise to an educational philosophy that provided Lithuanian Jewry with a network of YESHIVOT; and from these, generations of scholars as well as the ethical MUSAR movement were to arise. A richly endowed Jewish culture flourished in Lithuania and neighboring Belorussia, to which students were attracted from all parts of the world. That culture produced a distinctive life style and a particular kind of Jew — the *Litvak* (Lithuanian), who spoke Hebrew and Yiddish with a special intonation and who proudly identified himself as a "*Misnagged*" (the Ashkenazi pronunciation of *Mitnagged*). Adherence to the Eastern Ashkenazi prayer rite, a profound contempt for Ḥasidic superstition, devotion to learning for its own sake, and a wry sense of humor became hallmarks of these "*Misnagdim*."

Broadly speaking, however, Ḥasidic Jews have always regarded any Ashkenazi who does not share their customs and ritual as a *Mitnagged*, whatever his origin. From 1770 onward, disciples of the Vilna Gaon migrated to the Land of Israel, where they eventually formed the largest Ashkenazi community in Jerusalem. Descendants of *Mitnaggedim* also constitute the overwhelming majority of Jews in English-speaking countries such as the United States and the British Commonwealth, as well as in Latin America.

MITSVAH (pl. *mitsvot*; lit. "commandment"). A religious duty commanded by the Torah and defined by talmudic law as being of biblical origin (*de-oraita*), although there are also *mitsvot* of rabbinic origin (*de-rabbanan*; see COMMANDMENTS, THE 613). Jewish teachers have suggested a rationale for the *mitsvot* of the Torah. RAV (early third cent.) asserted that "the *mitsvot* were given only in order to refine humanity" (Gen. R. 44.1). Some have interpreted this statement to imply that they were given to instill in man unquestioning obedience to God's commands, and that it is idle to inquire after any further purpose. MAIMONIDES rejects this interpretation, maintaining that the *mitsvot* are not arbitrary commands but were given for man's benefit. He says, "The general object of the commandments is twofold: the well-being of the soul and the well-being of the body." The former consists in teaching the people the correct opinions, the latter in promoting proper social relations (*Guide*, III, 27). Jewish teachers in all ages have been similarly divided between the rationalists who seek the reasons for the commandments (*ta'amé ha-mitsvot*), and the non-rationalists who decry the search for reasons. The *tannaim* disagreed as to whether a ruling may be inferred from the apparent reason for a biblical commandment (*Sanh.* 21a). Those who oppose such inference fear that once the rationale for a *mitsvah* is provided, people might rationalize that they can achieve the purpose of the *mitsvah* without necessarily complying with its prescriptions.

SAADIAH GAON (ninth cent.) offers another explanation for the *mitsvot*, arguing that they are a God-given gift to man "enabling him to attain constant bliss; for the person who achieves the good life as a reward for compliance with His commandments obtains double the benefit gained by one who is not called upon to comply but receives the good life only as a result of God's kindness" (*Emunot ve-De'ot*). A modern Jewish philosopher, Joseph D. SOLOVEICHIK, suggests that by giving commandments to man God has raised him to a higher level than that of the rest of His creatures, enabling him to act not only through natural instinct but through conscious choice (*The Lonely Man of Faith*).

The prophet Isaiah (29:13) decried the perfunctory fulfillment of the *mitsvot*, devoid of an awareness of their purpose, saying: "Because that people has approached Me with its mouth and honored Me with its lips; but it has kept its heart far from Me, and its worship of Me has been a commandment of men learned by rote." In keeping with this chastisement, the sages insisted that performance of a *mitsvah* is meaningful only if accompanied by an awareness — called KAVVANAH — that it is God who has commanded the ritual and it is in obedience to His word that man fulfills it. To insure such awareness, the sages instituted that the performance of a positive *mitsvah* be preceded by the recitation of a benediction praising God "Who has sanctified us with His commandments and has commanded us to perform [this particular *mitsvah*]" (*Pes.* 7b). (There are several exceptions to this rule. For example, a benediction is not recited before the giving of alms, or before reciting the HAGGADAH on the night of Passover.) There is a discussion in the Talmud as to whether *kavvanah* is an absolute requirement in the performance of a *mitsvah*, lacking which the *mitsvah* is invalid (*Ber.* 13a). However, the sages did not discount completely a *mitsvah* performed without *kavvanah*; better to act imperfectly than not to act at all. The greatest *mitsvah* is the study of Torah, yet the sages advised, "At all times a person should engage in Torah and *mitsvot* even if not for their own sake [i.e., if performed for some ulterior motive]; for from acting not for their own sake he will ultimately arrive at performing them for their own sake" (*Pes.* 50b). Thus the rabbis state, "Who says, 'I give this coin for charity on condition that my son [who is ill] should live,' is completely righteous" (*RH* 4b).

Teachers of Kabbalah attributed mystical powers to the *mitsvot*, and introduced into the liturgy certain prayers to be recited prior to the performance of a *mitsvah* to verbalize these esoteric intentions. Typical is the one recited before the benediction over the FOUR SPECIES held aloft and waved on Sukkot, which reads, "May it be Your will...that with the fruit of the goodly tree, branches of the palm, boughs of thick trees, and willows of the brook, the letters of Your singular Name (the Tetragrammaton) will approach each other and become as one in my hand." Even though many halakhists objected to these supplementary prayers, they are printed in most prayer books and their recitation became common practice.

The sages ruled that a girl is obliged to observe the *mitsvot* (BAT MITSVAH) from the age of 12, and a boy (BAR MITSVAH) from the age of 13. However, a father is obliged to train his children in the performance of *mitsvot* when they are younger, so they will be able to observe them properly when they come of age (*Suk.* 42a).

The sages urged that a *mitsvah* be performed aesthetically (*hiddur mitsvah*). "Make a beautiful SUKKAH, a beautiful SHOFAR, a beautiful SCROLL OF THE LAW" (*Shab.* 133b). However, they ruled that one should not expend over a third more than the normal cost for the sake of beauty (*BK* 9b). They also ruled that a *mitsvah* performed through committing a transgression is invalid (*Suk.* 30a). They asserted that the *mitsvot* were not given for pleasure (*RH* 28a), which was interpreted by RASHI to imply that they were given "as a yoke, to make known that we are His servants and the keepers of His commandments" (*Meg.* 32a). On the other hand, the sages speak of *simhah shel mitsvah*; that a *mitsvah* be performed with joy (Lev. R. 34:9).

Another ruling of the sages provides that one who is occupied with peforming a *mitsvah* is exempt from performing another occurring at the same time (*Ber.* 11a, 17b). Thus one who is occupied with making arrangements for the burial of a relative is exempt from all other religious duties. Furthermore, a *mitsvah* that is at hand may not be bypassed in favor of another (*Yoma* 33a). Indeed, if a *mitsvah* is at hand, there must be no delay in fulfilling it (*Mekhilta* to Ex. 12:17).

The Torah promises the blessings of peace and prosperity as a reward for keeping the *mitsvot*. The *tannaim* affirmed this by stating, "He who performs one *mitsvah* receives good things — his days are lengthened and he inherits the Land" (*Kid.* 1:9). They also exhort, "Be as eager to perform an easy *mitsvah* as a difficult one, for you do not know their [respective] rewards; and calculate any loss incurred in performing a *mitsvah* against its [overriding] gain" (*Avot* 2:1). On the other hand, one *amora* asserts categorically, "there is no reward for a *mitsvah* in this world" (*Kid.* 39b), and another, interpreting the passage, "You shall keep the commandment...which I command you today to do them" (Deut. 7:11), says, "Today [in this world] is for the doing; tomorrow [in the world to come] is for the receiving of the reward" (*Er.* 22a). (See REWARD AND PUNISHMENT.) *Mitsvah* has a redeeming power in this world; "When one is busy performing a *mitsvah*, it shields him [from pain] and protects him [from transgression]" (*Sot.* 21a), and when in pursuit of a *mitsvah* one is shielded from injury (*Pes.* 8a). The *mitsvot* a person does are credited to him, balanced against the transgressions he commits; one additional *mitsvah* can tip the scales in his favor so that he is considered a *tsaddik*, a righteous person (*Kid.* 39b; *RH* 17b).

The term *mitsvah* was extended in rabbinic parlance to refer to any religious obligation even though not biblically commanded. Thus, to explain why washing the hands before eating non-sacred food is called a *mitsvah*, though not required by biblical law, the Talmud says, "Because it is a *mitsvah* to hearken to the words of the sages" (*Ḫul.* 106a). Any meritorious deed was considered a *mitsvah*. Thus when Hillel the Elder went to the bath-house he told his disciples that he was going to perform a *mitsvah*; for cleansing the body created in the image of God is a meritorious deed (*Lev.R.* 34:3). The term was especially used to denote the giving of alms. In Eastern Europe the selling of the right to read in the synagogue a specific portion of the Pentateuch was called "the selling of *mitsvot*."

MIXED SPECIES See AGRICULTURAL LAWS

MIZMOR LE-TODAH ("A Psalm of Thanksgiving"). The text of Ps. 100, one of the best-known chapters of the Book of PSALMS incorporated in the Jewish liturgy. Calling upon the whole world to acknowledge and serve the true God, it stresses His loving fatherhood of all mankind. On days when the thanksgiving sacrifice (*korban todah*) was offered in the TEMPLE, this psalm was performed by the levitical choir and orchestra. An allusion to that practice, by the prophet Jeremiah (33:11), lays emphasis on the refrain (in verse 5): "For His kindness is everlasting" (*ki le-olam ḫasdo*). On Sabbaths and festivals, the eve of the Day of Atonement, and on the eve and intermediate days of Passover, no thanksgiving sacrifices were brought to the Temple; public offerings (see SACRIFICES) were substituted on holy days. In Temple times, a thanksgiving sacrifice was brought by anyone whose life had been endangered by sickness, captivity, or a perilous journey, an obligation transferred to the GOMEL blessing after the Temple was destroyed. The rabbis nevertheless considered the thanksgiving sacrifice to possess eternal validity, declaring that even when all other sacrifices are abolished with the Messiah's coming and the Temple's restoration, the *korban todah* will remain in force (Lev. R. 9.7). Accordingly, they laid down that Ps. 100 should be recited in the daily Morning Service, except on those occasions when it was omitted in the Sanctuary. It is now included in the "Psalms and Passages of Song" (PESUKÉ DE-ZIMRA) for weekdays.

MIZRAḪ ("east"). Point of the horizon where the sun rises, a fact emphasized in the expression *mizraḫ-shemesh*, "rising of the sun" (Deut. 4:47; Mal. 1:11; Ps. 113:3). From ancient times, *mizraḫ* (for Jews living west of the Land of Israel) became synonymous with the synagogue's "orientation" toward Jerusalem and the Temple Mount, and with the congregation's facing east in worship (see PRAYER). This term was therefore also used to denote the eastern wall of the synagogue, where the Ark housing the Torah scrolls was placed and near which the synagogue wardens as well as the rabbi had their seats. *Mizraḫ* is also the name given to ornamental plaques, usually displaying the Hebrew term in bold letters and often incorporating some appropriate biblical text (e.g., Ps. 113:3), which are placed on the eastern wall of the synagogue and BET MIDRASH. Observant Jews likewise hang a *mizraḫ* on the wall of their living room or study that faces Jerusalem. Such plaques may contain decorative papercuts or micrography, or they may be adorned with traditional motifs such as the seven-branched candelabrum (*menorah*), the Ten Commandments, lions of Judah, etc. This ornamental *mizraḫ* is intended to show any worshiper the direction to be faced in prayer, although it may not in fact be eastward in many parts of the world.

MODEH ANI ("I give thanks"). A brief prayer, expressing thankfulness for God's protection, which observant Jews recite when they awake in the morning. It is usually said before leaving the bedroom and, since it contains no specific mention of the Divine Name, may even be recited prior to washing the hands. The earliest known text of this prayer dates from the 17th century, and it may be an abstract of one on a similar theme (*Elohai neshamah*) now read in synagogue at the commencement of the MORNING BENEDICTIONS. Owing to its succinctness, *Modeh ani* has formed part of the youngster's religious training; boys and girls are taught to recite it each morning until they are old enough to attend (or read) the full prayer service.

THE MODEH ANI PRAYER

I give thanks to You, living and eternal King, for having mercifully restored my soul within me; great is Your faithfulness.

MO'ED ("Appointed Time"). Second Order of the MISHNAH dealing with the laws of the major and minor Jewish festivals. Its 12 tractates (SHABBAT, ERUVIN, PESAḤIM, SHEKALIM, YOMA, SUKKAH, BÉTSAH, ROSH HA-SHANAH, TA'ANIT, MEGILLAH, MO'ED KATAN, and ḤAGIGAH) are arranged in descending order according to number of chapters. The tractates *Shekalim* and *Ta'anit* are not concerned with festivals, but because they too deal with events that occur at fixed times, they are included in this Order. MAIMONIDES states that the tractate *Shabbat* begins the Order because it is the most frequent festival, occurring once every seven days. Every tractate in this Order is expanded upon in both the Babylonian and the Jerusalem Talmud (except for *Shekalim*, which is covered only in the Jerusalem Talmud) and the *Tosefta*.

MO'ED KATAN ("Minor Festival"). Eleventh tractate of Order MO'ED in the Mishnah. It comprises three chapters dealing mainly with the types of work permitted or forbidden on the intermediate days (ḤOL HA-MO'ED) of Passover and Sukkot (cf. Lev. 23:37). Also discussed are the rules of MOURNING on Sabbaths and festivals. This tractate, like the Mishnaic Order of which it forms part, was originally called *Mo'ed*; to avoid confusion, scholars also called it *Mashkin* ("one may irrigate") after the opening word. The subject matter is amplified in both Talmuds and in the *Tosefta*.

MOHEL See CIRCUMCISION

MOLCHO, SOLOMON See MESSIANIC MOVEMENTS

MÖLLN, JACOB BEN MOSES HA-LEVI (known by the acronym *Maharil*; c.1360-1427). Halakhic authority and spiritual leader of the Jewish communities in Germany, Austria, and Bohemia. Born in Mainz, he first studied under his father, then traveled to Vienna, where his teachers were Aaron Blümlein, Meir ben Baruch Ha-Levi (*Maharam*) of Vienna, and Shalom ben Isaac of Neustadt. Meir ben Baruch ordained Mölln with the new title *Morenu*, which was intended to distinguish rabbinical scholars from unauthorized persons who earned a livelihood from performing marriages and granting divorces. After succeeding his father as rabbi of Mainz, the Maharil founded a *yeshivah* there which attracted many students, some of whom were to become distinguished rabbis in Central Europe. When anti-Hussite crusaders devastated the Jewish communities of Austria, those in Bavaria and the Rhineland begged Mölln to intercede on their behalf. He proclaimed a three-day fast and used his influence with the ruling circles to avert a massacre.

Halakhic questions were sent to him from many parts of Europe. In weighing up any decision, Mölln took local conditions into account and insisted that rulings should not depend merely on what had been summarized in halakhic compendiums. He also wrote liturgical verse (*piyyutim*), excelled as a *ḥazzan* (cantor), and influenced the Ashkenazi prayer rite's development. His rulings helped to stabilize traditional life among the Ashkenazim. Together with his sermons, explanations of religious customs, and observations on liturgical music, these halakhic decisions were noted down by a pupil, Zalman of St. Goar, and later published as *Minhagé Maharil* (1556). A formative influence on the German-Polish rite, this work was consulted by Moses ISSERLES and quoted in his Ashkenazi glosses (*Mappah*) to the *Shulḥan Arukh*.

MONDAYS AND THURSDAYS Weekdays characterized by liturgical additions to the MORNING SERVICE. Since talmudic times, at least, these two weekdays have been singled out because on these days the local markets of each district convened; thus all the people of the area, most of them farmers, would gather together at the market venue. This was also the day when the courts convened. The Talmud ascribes to EZRA (fifth century BCE) the institution of special Torah teaching on those days. Later, the READING OF THE LAW was introduced in the synagogue every Monday and Thursday. The reading, to which three people are called, divides the first section of the following Sabbath reading into three parts. The Morning Service is also extended by the addition of an extensive penitential prayer, which precedes the Reading of the Law. Extremely pious Jews often observed these days as fast days. Among Ashkenazi Jews, the custom arose of fasting and reciting *seliḥot* (penitential prayers) on the Monday, Thursday, and second Monday following the festivals of Sukkot and Passover. This was meant to atone for any untoward behavior that might have come about in the general rejoicing on the festivals. Many congregations still recite penitential prayers on these days, but very few people fast on them.

MONOGAMY AND POLYGAMY From the very outset of biblical history, MARRIAGE is portrayed as monogamous. Cain's descendant, Lamech, is the first to contravene this norm by marrying two wives (Gen. 4:19). It is only when Sarah proves barren that Abraham — at her behest — takes Hagar also to wife (Gen. 16:1-3). Esau has three wives and Jacob marries two sisters, Leah and Rachel, who give him their respective handmaids as concubines. The Book of Deuteronomy (21:15-17) acknowledges the legality of a bigamous marriage (bigamy — or polygamy — being the prevalent custom in the ancient Near East).

During the era of the Judges, plural marriages were not uncommon, but thereafter (except for Elkanah, the father of Samuel) monogamy seems to have become the norm once again, only kings maintaining polygamous families. At Hebron, David already had six wives and he added considerably to that number once he moved to Jerusalem. Rehoboam had 18 wives, a number which the Talmud was later to declare the maximum for a king. Solomon maintained the most famous of these royal harems, which reportedly contained no less than 700 wives and 300 concubines (I Kings 11:3). A stern warning against such "multiplication of wives" and its foreseeable consequences had nevertheless appeared centuries earlier in the Pentateuch (Deut. 17:17).

Wisdom literature, when referring to marriage, always has the monogamous family in mind (cf. Prov. 5:15-19, 31:10-31; Eccl. 9:9) and this is true also of the Apocrypha (Ecclus. 26:1-4; Tobit). It is this concept of a man and his wife that underlies the prophetic metaphor describing the bond between God and Israel — God as the husband and Israel as the often disloyal wife (Hos. 2:4ff.; Isa. 50:1; Jer. 3:1).

Differing attitudes toward plural marriage came to the fore in Hellenistic and rabbinic times. Thus, while the Babylonian *amora* RAVA saw no legal objection to polygamy, always supposing that the husband could provide for each of his wives, a third-generation Palestinian *amora*, R. Ammi, formulated the rule whereby a man is not allowed to take a second wife unless his first spouse expressly consents to this arrangement (*Yev.* 65a). All such marriages could only be terminated by DIVORCE or the wife's death. Two other relevant factors were the duty to contract a LEVIRATE marriage and a woman's prolonged infertility. Some rabbis considered it obligatory for a man to perform *yibbum* (levirate marriage) with the widow of a brother who had died childless; others recommended the ceremony of *ḫalitsah* (levirate divorce), which relieved both the dead man's widow and surviving brother(s) of this duty. There was general agreement, however, that a man could take a second wife if the first had remained barren after ten years of marriage. Jewish law eventually insisted that the first (barren) wife be divorced and not retained by her husband.

Though increasingly rare, plural marriage is still halakhically permissible in the Sephardi-Eastern world, no doubt as a result of Muslim custom and influence. In the (Roman and medieval Christian) West, however, where monogamy was the rule, levirate marriage had been abolished and polygamy among Jews had virtually disappeared by the 13th century. A decisive factor here was the special *takkanah* (regulation) attributed to Rabbenu GERSHOM ME'OR HA-GOLAH, which outlawed the practice of bigamy throughout the Ashkenazi world and threatened to place offenders under a ban of EXCOMMUNICATION (*ḫerem*). This *Ḫerem de-Rabbenu Gershom*, as the law against plural marriage is known, also prohibited a man from divorcing his wife without her consent. In exceptional cases (e.g., on the grounds of a wife's insanity), the husband may obtain a "release" from 100 rabbis permitting him to marry a second wife.

In the State of Israel, both rabbinic and civil law have grappled with problems arising from a multiplicity of communal religious traditions. While new immigrants with more than one wife remained exempt, the chief rabbinate substituted *ḫalitsah* for levirate marriage in 1950 and bigamy was prohibited by the State in 1959. Israeli courts nevertheless make allowance for decisions of the rabbinical authorities permitting an additional marriage when the first wife has been committed to a mental institution or has refused to accept a rabbinically approved bill of divorce.

MONOTHEISM The belief in one GOD. Together with the belief in the existence of God, this is a basic principle of the Jewish faith and is listed second in MAIMONIDES' 13 PRINCIPLES OF FAITH. The uncompromising affirmation of monotheism is expressed in the most famous declaration of Judaism, SHEMA *Yisrael Adonai Elohenu Adonai Eḫad*, "Hear O Israel, the Lord is our God, the Lord is One" (Deut. 6:4).

Scholars are divided in their views about the origins of the monotheism of the Hebrews. The Bible is full of references to the belief in and the worship of many gods (polytheism); to the belief in and worship of the God of Israel together with a belief in the gods of the Canaanites (syncretism); and to the belief in a separate god for every people and country (monolatry). The history of Israel in the biblical period offers ample evidence of Israel's assimilation to such non-monotheistic cultures, which was the most constant target of prophetic denunciation from Elijah in the ninth century BCE to the post-exilic prophets at the end of the sixth century BCE. This has led some scholars to conclude that pure Hebrew monotheism did not spring up all at one time, but was the result of a long and difficult process of preaching, admonition and exhortation by MOSES and the PROPHETS until a pure monotheistic faith became the norm of Israelite religion in the post-exilic period.

Other scholars, notably Yehezkel Kaufman and W.F. Albright, emphasize the revolutionary impact of Hebrew monotheism. While acknowledging the frequent backsliding of the people into idolatrous beliefs and practices, they see the origins of monotheism as significantly lying with the fathers of the early Hebrew people. ABRAHAM is the first Hebrew because he was the founder of the monotheistic Faith. The tradition was maintained by his tribe and was central in the life of the Children of Israel, despite their lapses.

The theology of monotheism has two main doctrines. First, that the universe and all things in it owe their existence to the one God, the Creator of heaven and earth. The one Ultimate Being is a personal God who is close to each individual and is the Lord of History, that is, He is involved in the world that He created. In Jewish teaching, monotheism is closely connected with ethical values which are aspects of God's unity. Secondly, since the one God is the Creator of all mankind, all men and women in the world are ideally brothers and sisters in relation to one other. Thus, the belief in monotheism establishes not only that there is one God, but also that mankind is a unity in a unified world.

MONTHS OF THE YEAR See CALENDAR

MOON The Jewish months begin with the New Moon (*Rosh Hodesh*). The Jewish CALENDAR is a lunar calendar, each month lasting a little more than 29 days. Since it was impossible to arrange the calendar with months of alternate length, it was left to the SANHEDRIN to declare whether a month had 29 or 30 days. If the outgoing month had 29 days then the next day was *Rosh Hodesh*, i.e., the first day of the new month. When a month had 30 days, then the last day of the outgoing month and the first day of the new month were both declared *Rosh Hodesh*.

In early rabbinic times, the day of the New Moon was established by the Sanhedrin in Jerusalem, after accepting the evidence of eye witnesses who had claimed to see the new moon. Sometimes the rabbis would deliberately postpone *Rosh Hodesh* so as to prevent the DAY OF ATONEMENT from falling on a Friday or a Sunday. The permanent calendar was fixed by Hillel II in 325 CE and this provided the exact date of each *Rosh Hodesh* based on astronomical and mathematical calculations.

In the period of the First Temple, the New Moon was observed with the offering of special sacrifices, the blowing of trumpets, joyous feasting and a holiday from work. The Bible even refers to the New Moon in the same context as other FESTIVALS of the calendar (cf. II Kings 4:23; Isa. 1:13-14; 20:18 ff.; 66:23; Amos 8:5). Even in pre-Temple days it was already an established feast day (see I Sam. 20).

It is not clear when or how the New Moon lost its festive character. This had happened by the time the Jews returned from exile (see EXILE, BABYLONIAN) at the end of the sixth century BCE. It was then no longer a full holiday, but a semi-holiday, like *Hol ha-Mo'ed* (the intermediate, working days of PASSOVER and SUKKOT) when the rabbis discouraged all but necessary work and women were to have a holiday from their sewing and weaving. More stringent economic conditions were probably the reason for downgrading the New Moon, particularly since there were no religious or historical reasons for stopping work on that day. In the course of time, even this minor holiday status disappeared and it became a normal working day like any other, except for certain liturgical variations.

The distinctive liturgy for *Rosh Hodesh* includes a special

The moon, showing its different phases (when turned), on a pedestal bearing the benediction for the New Moon. Sculpture by Menahem Berman, 1984.

prayer, YA'ALEH VE-YAVO, which is read in the AMIDAH and in the GRACE AFTER MEALS and petitions God to remember His people for the good, for blessing and for life. Further, the (half) HALLEL psalms of praise are read in the Morning Service. The Bible reading from Numbers 28 describes the Temple service of sacrifice for the New Moon. Finally, as on Sabbath and on all festivals, an Additional Service is included, corresponding to the additional sacrifice which was offered on these occasions. Fasting and mourning are forbidden on the New Moon.

On the Sabbath before *Rosh Hodesh*, the new month is announced in the synagogue, giving the day in the coming week on which it will fall. In some synagogues this was combined with an announcement of the exact minute of the "birth" — or *molad* — of the new month. In the course of time, the simple proclamation of the month was made more elaborate by the inclusion of a prayer that the coming month be blessed with all desirable physical and spiritual goods, health, material prosperity, and religious strength. The prayer is an ancient text composed by RAV (*Ber.* 16b). When the text was adopted as a prayer for the new month — perhaps little more than 200 years ago — an introductory phrase was added beseeching God "to renew unto us this coming month for good and for blessing..." The Sabbath before the New Moon when the prayer is recited is called *Shabbat Mevarekhim*, i.e., the Sabbath on which God is asked to bless the new month. This blessing is not recited on the Sabbath preceding Rosh ha-Shanah because the inauguration of a New Year outshines the approach of a new month.

The beginning of a new month was regarded as an appropriate time for personal spiritual renewal. The Additional Service for the New Moon in fact refers to the day as a time of atonement. In this spirit the 16th-century kabbalists introduced a fast on the eve of the New Moon which expresses the theme of penitence. In time, the custom spread far beyond the circle of the mystics. The fast itself was never more than a minor exercise which lasted only until the Afternoon Service and even then it was never observed on any month which held a festival. This minor observance is called YOM KIPPUR KATAN ("the Little Day of Atonement"). Its observance has all but disappeared from Jewish religious life, although there are still pious individuals who observe it and a few congregations even recite special penitential prayers in the morning service.

There is a custom known as *Kiddush Levanah* which dates from the talmudic period, and has undergone changes during the centuries. It is the custom of sanctifying the new moon. While it is by no means widely observed it still retains a place in some very traditional prayer books and the actual text differs in various communities. When the moon is at least three days old, and before the 15th day when it begins to wane, the custom prescribes that the New Moon be "sanctified" with rejoicing and prayer. Because the ceremony is carried out with joyous optimism, it is never performed on the eve of TISHAH BE-AV or before the solemn DAY OF ATONEMENT. Ideally, it should be performed on a Saturday night before the atmosphere of the Sabbath has worn off and is usually recited by a prayer quorum in the courtyard of the synagogue.

MORIAH A place, originally unidentified, to which God sent Abraham: "Take your son, your favored one, Isaac, whom you love, and go to the Land of Moriah, and offer him there as a burnt offering" (Gen. 22:2). Moriah was identified as a mountain in Jerusalem, the site of the TEMPLE, by the Book of Chronicles: "Then Solomon began to build the house of the Lord in Jerusalem on Mount Moriah" (II Chr. 3:1). Henceforth it became synonymous with the Temple precinct and, from the first century BCE, more specifically with the platform Herod built around the Temple, also called the TEMPLE MOUNT.

MORNING BENEDICTIONS (*Birkhot ha-Shaḇar*). Blessings pronounced upon arising in the morning. Originally, each blessing was pronounced at the time of a given action, as for example, the blessing "who gives sight to the blind" upon first opening one's eyes. The custom now is not to recite the blessings upon first awakening but to say them all as part of the preliminary section of the Morning Service. The blessings include thanks to God for not having been created a Gentile or a slave and (by men) for not having been created a woman. A 13th-century addition for women thanks God for "having created me according to His will." The male blessing has been the subject of a great deal of debate and, together with the other negative blessings, has been reformulated in non-Orthodox Judaism in a positive form praising God "who made me a Jew, who made me free" (Conservative *Sim Shalom* Prayer Book). Further blessings relate, among other things, to seeing, getting dressed, standing up, walking, and being provided with daily needs. The morning benedictions are followed by extensive passages from the Bible and the Talmud, relating primarily to the SACRIFICES that were brought in the TEMPLE, in fulfillment of the verse: "Instead of bulls we will pay [the offerings] of our lips" (Hos. 14:2), which, after the destruction of the Temple, was seen as authorizing the recitation of the laws as equivalent to having actually brought the sacrifices.

MORNING SERVICE (Heb. *Shaḇarit*; from *shaḇar*, "dawn"). The most extensive of the three daily prayer services. Traditionally instituted by the patriarch Abraham (on the basis of Gen. 19:27), it replaces the morning sacrifice (*tamid*) which was brought daily in Temple times. Ideally, the AMIDAH portion of the service should not be recited before sunrise, the latest time for its recitation being at the conclusion of one third of the day (calculated from sunrise to sunset). The SHEMA, however, must be recited within the first quarter of the day.

The Morning Service invariably consists of (1) the MORNING BENEDICTIONS (*Birkhot ha-Shaḇar*), in which God is thanked for allowing the worshiper to arise once again; (2) PESUKÉ DE-ZIMRA ("Verses of song"), including BARUKH SHE-AMAR and drawn primarily from Psalms, although the SONG OF MOSES has a prominent place. This section is enlarged considerably on Sabbath and festival mornings; (3)BAREKHU, the reader's summons to prayer; (4) the *Shema* and its benedictions — two before (of which AHAVAH RABBAH is the second) and one afterwards (EMET VE-YATSIV), leading directly to (5) the *Amidah* and its repetition by the reader (which includes the KEDUSHAH). On weekdays, the repetition of the *Amidah* is followed by TAḴANUN, confessional and supplicatory prayers (but on days possessing any festive nature, e.g., New Moon, Ḥanukkah or Purim, this section is omitted).

On New Moon, Ḥanukkah, the Pilgrim Festivals (including their intermediate days), and, in many communities, on Israel's Independence Day, the *Amidah* is followed by HALLEL, after which the READING OF THE LAW takes place. On regular Sabbaths, as well as the High Holidays, only the prescribed Torah portion (no *Hallel*) is read. This is also the case on non-festive MONDAYS AND THURSDAYS, when the passage chanted is the first section of the following Sabbath's Torah reading, to which three worshipers only (a priest, a Levite, and an Israelite) are called. The weekday service then concludes (apart from minor variations between the different rites) with ASHRÉ, *U-Va le-Tsiyyon* (a sequence of mainly biblical verses headed by Isa. 59:20-21), ALÉNU, and the daily psalm (Sunday, Ps. 24; Monday, Ps. 48; Tuesday, Ps. 82; Wednesday, Ps. 94:1-95:3; Thursday, Ps. 81; Friday Ps.

93). The mourner's KADDISH is recited after the latter two sections. Ps. 92, for the Sabbath, may be read at an earlier point in the Morning Service; and other psalms are recited on various occasions (see PSALMS in the Liturgy).

On Sabbaths and festivals, when the ADDITIONAL (*Musaf*) SERVICE is recited following the Morning Service, the congregation may be addressed by the rabbi either before or immediately after the Torah reading.

As with all other services, the ideal is to pray with a MINYAN — the traditional quorum of ten adult males above the age of 13. As certain portions of the Morning Service can only be recited when a *minyan* is present (e.g., the *Kaddish*, *Barekhu*, and the reader's repetition of the *Amidah* together with the *Kedushah*), Jewish law places great emphasis on the importance of praying with a *minyan*, if this is at all possible.

At every Morning Service, except on Tishah be-Av, the TALLIT (prayer shawl) is worn. On all days apart from Sabbaths, the Pilgrim Festivals, High Holidays, and Tishah be-Av, men wear TEFILLIN (phylacteries) during the morning prayers, removing them before the Additional Service on those days when *Musaf* is recited. Customs differ with regard to *ḫol ha-mo'ed*, the intermediate days of Passover and Sukkot. Most Jews in the Diaspora wear *tefillin* on these days; Ḫasidism, Sephardim, and Israeli Ashkenazim do not.

MOSES Prophet, lawgiver, leader of his people out of Egypt and to the borders of the Promised Land, and the outstanding figure in the emergence and formulation of the Jewish religion. According to the Bible, the name Moses (*Mosheh* in Hebrew) is derived from the phrase "From the water I drew him" (*meshitihu*) (Ex. 2:10). However, this is generally regarded as ancient homiletic name derivation, and various other suggestions have been propounded.

Moses was born in Egypt, the son of Amram and Jochebed, both of the tribe of Levi. At the time of his birth, Pharaoh had issued the decree: "Every boy that is born you shall throw into the river" (Ex. 1:22). For the first three months of his life, the infant was hidden in his parents' home. Then Jochebed placed him in a wicker basket on the Nile River, where he was discovered by Pharaoh's daughter, who adopted him as her son. Moses grew up as an Egyptian prince; but when he killed an Egyptian taskmaster who was persecuting the Israelite slaves, Moses was forced to flee from Egypt and reached Midian. There he married Zipporah, the daughter of Jethro, the priest of Midian. Moses tended Jethro's sheep and arrived at Mount Horeb, where God appeared to him from the midst of a BURNING BUSH that was not burned up. God commanded him to return to Egypt in order to redeem his brothers from Egyptian slavery. After much hesitation, Moses accepted this mission, provided that his brother AARON would be the spokesman, because he himself had a speech impediment. At the age of 80, Moses appeared before Pharaoh, but Pharaoh refused to release the Israelites, even for a brief period. God then afflicted Pharaoh and Egypt with ten plagues. Only the last and the most severe, in which all the Egyptian first-born were killed, persuaded Pharaoh to release the Israelites (see EXODUS FROM EGYPT). When the Israelites arrived at the shore of the Sea of Reeds (Red Sea), with the Egyptians in pursuit, Moses raised his staff and the sea divided so that the Jews crossed it in the middle on dry land. Pharaoh and the Egyptians who were following drowned when the sea came crashing down on them. Moses and the Israelites then sang a song of praise and thanks to God. After a short period of wandering in the Sinai desert, the Israelites reached Mount SINAI (also known as the Mountain of God and traditionally identified with Mount Horeb). Here God appeared to them and gave them, through Moses, the TEN COMMANDMENTS (Ex. 20:1-17). Moses went up to Mount Sinai, where he remained for 40 days and nights without eating or drinking, in order to receive the TABLETS OF THE COVENANT. While Moses was on the mountain, the people forced Aaron to build a GOLDEN CALF to serve them as a god. When Moses came down, he broke the tablets in his anger, burned the calf, ground the gold to powder and scattered it on water, which he then forced the sinners to drink. However, he pleaded with God not to destroy His nation as a result of the sin, and God consented not to wipe them out. Moses then went up to the mountain a second time, and remained an additional 40 days and 40 nights in order to receive the second set of tablets. He also received the entire legal code laid out in the Pentateuch (WRITTEN LAW). According to Jewish tradition, he also received on this occasion an oral tradition (*Shab.* 93b); see ORAL LAW. Moses was ordered by God to build the Sanctuary and its vessels, and he appointed Bezalel to implement this command. When he came down from the mountain, Moses' face shone; to enable the Israelites to speak to him, he put on a veil. Moses was punished, along with Aaron, for disobeying God's command at Marah and smiting a rock to obtain water instead of speaking to it as he had been commanded. His punishment was that he was forbidden to enter the Promised Land. Moses pleaded unsuccessfully with God to annul the decree; when he and the people reached the borders of the Promised Land, he went up to Mount Nebo to die, and from there God showed him the entire land. Moses died at the age of 120 "and his eyes were undimmed and his vigor unabated." Prior to that, Moses gathered the people to hear a summary of the Sinaitic legislation and his farewell address (see DEUTERONOMY). His burial place remains unknown to this day. The Bible depicts him as the greatest prophet the Jewish people have ever had (Deut. 34:10): "Never again did there arise in Israel a prophet like Moses, whom the Lord singled out, face to face."

As a leader, Moses faced frequent problems. At first, he assumed all the judicial duties for the entire nation. Later, on his father-in-law's suggestion, he appointed other judges to help him (Ex. 18:13-23). The Israelites in the wilderness turned to him with their problems, frequently demanding that he take them back to Egypt. There was an attempted rebellion against him within his own tribe of Levi, when Korah, his cousin, gathered 250 prominent members of the nation in order to revolt against their leader (Num. 16: 1-19). His brother and sister, Aaron and Miriam, claimed that they were equal to Moses in prophecy, and criticized him for marrying a Cushite woman (Num. 12:1-15). Moses was also revealed as a military leader in the battles against Amalek (Ex. 17: 8-13), against Sihon, the Amorite king of Heshbon (Deut. 2:31-33), and against Og, king of Bashan (Deut. 3:1-4). Before he died, Moses blessed the tribes of Israel (Deut. 33), without criticizing or vexing them. Moses is referred to as "the servant of God" (Deut. 34:5) and as "a very humble man, more so than any other man on the face of the earth" (Num. 12:3).

According to the rabbis, the entire Pentateuch was dictated by God and written down by Moses. The usual epithet applied by the sages to Moses is *Moshe Rabbenu* — "Moses our Master." A certain tension emerges in the sayings of the sages between the depiction of Moses as the most choice individual of all mankind, the only one whom God addressed "face to face," and the fear of having the people ascribe any divinity to Moses. According to Jewish tradition, he was born on 7 Adar and died on his 120th birthday. Later, this day was set aside as a general memorial day for people who have died and whose place of burial is unknown, just as Moses' burial place is unknown.

The sages describe Moses' status as that of a king, or absolute ruler, although his sons did not inherit this position from their father. Moses' life is divided into three parts: 40 years in Egypt, 40 years in Midian, and 40 years when he led the Israelites. His wisdom is described as being close to the maximum possible: "50 levels of wisdom were created in the world, and all but one were given to Moses" (Zohar). There was a substantive difference between Moses' prophecy and that of the other prophets: "All the prophets saw through a murky glass, but Moses saw through a clear glass" (Lev. R. 1:14), namely, while the other prophets had visions that were blurred and unclear, Moses had clear and precise visions. Moses' greatness finds expression in the statement, "The heavens and the earth were only created because of the merit of Moses" (Lev. R. 36:4). Moses, as a true leader, wanted to participate in the distress of his people. In Israel's war against Amalek, Moses stood and raised up his hands and when he became tired, a rock was brought, upon which he sat down. "Didn't Moses then have a cushion that he could sit on? Rather, [he said], 'As Israel are in distress, I will be in distress with them'" (*Ta'an.* 11b). According to legend, Moses' holiness was already expressed at the time of his birth. He was born circumcised, began to speak at birth, and began to prophesy at the age of three months. He also refused to suckle from the breasts of an Egyptian woman, because he did not want to defile the lips with which he would ultimately speak to God. Moses was chosen as a leader of the Israelites after God saw how Moses the shepherd treated his flock with compassion (Ex. R. 2:12). He received the Torah from Sinai and transmitted it to Joshua, thereby initiating the "chains of tradition" (*Avot* 1:1).

The fundamental Jewish belief in Moses as the supreme prophet was encapsulated by MAIMONIDES in the seventh of his 13 PRINCIPLES OF FAITH, which states: "I believe with perfect faith that the prophecy of Moses our master was true, and that he was the chief of all the prophets — both those who preceded him and those who followed."

MOSES BEN JACOB OF COUCY (13th cent.). French tosafist (see TOSAFOT). Born in Coucy, Moses settled in Paris. An itinerant preacher, from 1236 he traveled in Provence and Spain, rebuking the Jewish masses for their laxity in the observance of the *mitsvot*, especially those of TEFILLIN, TSITSIT, and MEZUZAH. Through his powerful sermons he succeeded in making many Spanish Jews divorce their Gentile wives. In his preaching he emphasized the virtues of humility and of probity in business dealings with non-Jews. In Paris in 1240, he was one of four rabbis who defended the Talmud in a public disputation against the charges of the apostate Nicholas Donin.

Moses of Coucy's fame rests on his CODIFICATION, *Sefer ha-Mitsvot*, known as *Sefer Mitsvot Gadol* (*SeMaG*), to distinguish it from the abridgment by Isaac of Corbeil, the *Sefer Mitsvot Katan* (*SeMaK*). Divided into two parts, according to the 365 negative and 248 positive commandments, it summarizes the ORAL LAW and is greatly influenced by Maimonides' *Mishneh Torah*. Many commentaries on it were written. The work is quoted by numerous later authorities. Moses of Coucy also wrote *tosafot* to tractate *Yoma* and a commentary on the Pentateuch.

MOSES BEN SHEM TOV DE LEON (c. 1240-1305). Main author of the ZOHAR and one of the greatest Jewish mystics. Born in Leon, Castile, he studied both KABBALAH and Jewish philosophy (especially MAIMONIDES' *Guide to the Perplexed*). His main sources of influence were the teachings of the circle of R. Jacob and R. Isaac, sons of R. Jacob ha-Cohen, in Castile in the second half of the 13th century. He was closely associated with R. Joseph Gikatilla, a great kabbalist who had been a follower of the teachings of Abraham ABULAFIA but later joined Moses de Leon in expounding the teachings of his version of theosophical Kabbalah.

The works of Moses de Leon can be divided into four groups: (1) Hebrew works written before the Zohar, such as *Or Zaru'ah* ("Spreading Light"); (2) pre-zoharic works that were later woven into the Zohar, especially the partly Hebrew and partly Aramaic *Midrash ha-Ne'elam* (The Esoteric Midrash); (3) the body of the Zohar, by far his major and most influential work; and (4) Hebrew works composed after the writing of at least most of the Zohar — such as

Shekel ha-Kodesh (The Holy Shekel) and *Ha-Nefesh ha-Ḫakhamah* (The Wise Soul), which expound major zoharic ideas in a moderate and selective manner. The most important of these are his *Mishkan ha-Edut*, on the fate of the soul, and *Sefer ha-Rimmon*, on the mystical meaning of the *mitsvot*. In addition, he wrote many short treatises and responsa.

Moses de León died in Arevalo in 1305, by which time several portions of the Zohar were already circulating among the kabbalists of the time. R. Isaac of Acre met Moses shortly before his death and later set out in search of the original manuscript of the Zohar, from which, presumably, Moses had been copying (as the work was ascribed to the second-century R. SIMEON BAR YOḤAI). Moses' widow denied the existence of such a manuscript, and claimed that her husband wrote the Zohar as an original work. Since then, controversy has raged concerning the origin of the Zohar and Moses' role in its composition, the kabbalists adhering more and more strongly to the belief in its antiquity and tannaitic authorship, and modern scholarship (notably by Gershom Scholem) affirming that the work was written by Moses de León, utilizing earlier writings.

The symbolism used by Moses de León in the Zohar, although often derived from earlier sources, was presented in a forceful, vivid, and imaginative manner, systematizing kabbalistic mythical concepts of the Divine world, cosmic events, and powers of evil, and serving as a basis for the Kabbalah throughout its subsequent history.

MOTHER The female parent. In cases of marriage between Jew and non-Jew, family lineage follows the status of the mother. In marriage between two Jews, however, FAMILY lineage is determined by the father (*Kid.* 3:12). A woman who claims to be the mother of a child is believed if the child clings to her. She is not believed when she would invalidate her child's lineage, as when she claims him to have been conceived from an incestuous or adulterous union, thereby rendering him a *mamzer* (*Kid.*. 78b; see ILLEGITIMACY).

In the event of DIVORCE, a mother may claim custody of her sons until they reach the age of six. Daughters remain with their mother until they marry, even if the mother has herself remarried, and their natural father must continue to provide for their upkeep in all cases (*Even ha-Ezer* 82:7). If, however, the court deems it more beneficial for a daughter to live with her father it may award him custody (Rema, *ibid.*).

Although in Jewish law the father takes precedence over the mother (*Kid.* 28a), in practice both parents were seen as equally responsible for the upbringing of the child. The child, for his part, is instructed to accord equal honor and respect to both parents (*Kid.* 30b-31a; see PARENT-CHILD RELATIONS).

The mother is obligated to breast-feed her child unless the father can afford a wet nurse (Maim. *Yad, Ishut* 21:5, 13).

The word Imma *("Mother") inscribed on a stone ossuary found in the Kidron Valley, Jerusalem. 1st century BCE-1st century CE.*

She is exempt from various responsibilities toward the children that devolve upon the father such as the obligation to circumcise a son, educate the CHILDREN, and provide sons with wives. Various other nurturing behaviors were never specified as obligatory, since the sages believed that the mother was, by her nature, emotionally involved with her children and concerned for their welfare.

In spite of her legal exemption from involvement in the education of the children, the mother was traditionally the dominant presence in the Jewish household, leaving her imprint upon her children by her constant contact with them. The father's position vis-à-vis the family was often somewhat more remote.

The traditional Jewish respect for the mother is echoed in R. Joseph's remark when he heard his mother approaching: "I must stand up, for the Divine Presence is entering," and in the Jewish proverb "God could not be everywhere, so he created mothers." (See also HUSBAND-WIFE RELATIONSHIP).

MOURNERS OF ZION See AVELÉ ZION

MOURNING The act of grieving over the death of a loved one. Jewish law and traditions provide a specific framework to guide mourners through their grief. The laws of mourning apply to a male over the age of 13 or a female over the age of 12 who has lost a father or mother, husband or wife, son or daughter, brother or sister. Elements of the laws of mourning are also applicable when a great Torah sage has died and when one's main teacher of Torah has passed away.

Biblical and rabbinic literature contain numerous references to mourning the loss of family members, leaders and sages. Grief often manifested itself in the rending of garments, crying, ululating and expressing words of EULOGY.

Judaism has a strong element of the acceptance of death.

Biblical heroes and religious personalities throughout the generations accepted death as the natural end of life in this world and were not afraid of it. The Midrash (Gen. R. 1.31) states that death was a positive feature incorporated by God in His creation of the universe. Philosophically, then, death should not be mourned but accepted wisely.

The Jewish laws of mourning balance emotionalism and philosophic wisdom. Mourners are expected to cry, tear their garments and participate in the BURIAL ceremony. On the other hand, they are not allowed to mourn too much nor for too long a time. The emphasis of the mourning period is to recover from the loss and to focus on the business of living.

The classic Jewish attitude towards death is reflected in a talmudic discussion (*Ber.* 46b) which considers the blessing to be recited at the house of mourning. The sages rule that one should say *Barukh ha-tov ve-ha-métiv*, blessing God Who is good and Who does good. R. AKIVA proposes the blessing, *Barukh dayyan ha-emet*, blessing God Who is the true Judge. The sages are suggesting that death should be accepted as a positive good; R. Akiva, perhaps more realistically, suggests a blessing which reflects resignation. In fact, Jewish tradition incorporates both opinions. Both blessings are included in the benediction following the mourners' meal after a funeral.

The mourning process has a number of stages. From the moment that death occurs until the burial takes place, the mourners are in the category of ANINUT, when their main responsibility is to arrange the FUNERAL. During this period, the mourner is exempt from positive commandments, e.g., praying, reciting GRACE AFTER MEALS, wearing TEFILLIN. The commandments of prohibition, though, remain in effect. If a mourner cannot attend the funeral due to illness, distance, or another valid reason, and others are making the burial arrangements, the laws of *aninut* do not apply to him. An *onen* (person in *aninut*) may not participate in a festive meal nor engage in pleasurable activities.

A mourner must rend a garment (*keri'ah*: see RENDING OF GARMENTS). According to various customs, this is done on receiving the news of the death, just prior to the funeral, or after the funeral.

After the burial, the mourners return to the home of the deceased (or to the home where the mourning period will be observed) and eat a meal consisting of bread and a hard-boiled egg. This meal should be provided by others, as a sign of compassion and communal concern.

The mourning period, known popularly as SHIVA (seven), continues for seven days, starting with the day of burial. Mourners sit on the floor or on low cushions or benches. They are generally forbidden to shave, bathe, go to work, study Torah (except topics relating to mourning), engage in marital relations, wear leather shoes, extend greetings, have their hair cut, wash clothes, or wear freshly laundered clothes. Some have the custom of covering mirrors in the house of mourning.

During the *shiva*, it is customary for people to visit the mourners and offer them consolation. In some communities, the practice is for people to bring or prepare food for the mourners, while in other communities this is considered improper. Visitors do not greet the mourners, but speak to them quietly, offering words of consolation.

On the Sabbath during the *shiva*, public display of mourning is generally not allowed, although the relevant mourning laws are observed privately. In some communities, mourners do not sit in their regular seats in synagogue on Sabbath. In a number of Sephardi communities, members of the congregation leave their own seats to sit near the mourners for part of the service, as a sign of respect and compassion.

The *shiva* ends on the morning of the seventh day. Mourning of lesser intensity continues through the 30th day, a period known as SHELOSHIM (30). During this time mourners should not have their hair cut, shave, wear new clothes, or attend parties. While the *sheloshim* constitutes the full mourning period for relatives other than parents according to some traditions, other traditions continue the period of mourning for one year for all relatives. Mourning for parents lasts almost a year and the mourners are not supposed to shave or have their hair cut until their friends urge them to do so. Mourners of other relatives may shave or have their hair cut after the *sheloshim*. Those who are observing mourning for the year should not attend public celebrations and parties during that time. Mourners recite KADDISH daily throughout the period of mourning. In the case of those whose mourning continues for a year, it is sometimes customary to cease reciting *kaddish* one month or one week prior to the anniversary of the death.

The *shiva* is terminated if the holy days and festivals of Rosh Ha-Shanah, Day of Atonement, Sukkot, Passover, and Shavu'ot intervene. If a burial takes place during the middle days (*Ḥol ha-Moed*) of Sukkot or Passover, the laws of *shiva* take effect after the festival ends.

Under certain circumstances, if one receives news of the death of a relative while other mourners are sitting *shiva*, he may end his *shiva* period with the other mourners. If the news arrived within 30 days of the death, *shiva* must be observed in full from the time the news arrives. If the news arrives after 30 days, the mourner observes only a brief period of mourning, i.e., he removes his shoes and sits on the floor or on a low bench for about an hour. Whenever news arrives of the death of a parent, the mourner must rend his garment; but if he learns of the death of another relative after 30 days, he need not rend his garment although he should recite the blessing of God as true Judge.

The laws of mourning do not apply if the deceased was a notorious transgressor of Torah law. In the case of a suicide, the laws of mourning are not observed unless there is any reason to believe that it was the result of insanity (even temporary insanity).

It is customary to mark the anniversary of the death of relatives each year by the recitation of *kaddish*, a memorial prayer, a session of Torah study, chanting a *haftarah*, lighting memorial lights, and other observances (see YAHRZEIT).

MUKTSEH ("set apart," "excluded"). Hebrew term for objects which may not be handled or moved on Sabbaths and festivals. The reason is that touching these articles may lead a person to desecrate the Sabbath, either by proceeding to use them for some prohibited labor or by moving them contrary to the Sabbath law.

The *muktseh* rules set forth in the Babylonian Talmud (*Shab.* 124a) are elaborated by Maimonides, the *Shulḥan Arukh*, and later codifications. Among the items which it is forbidden to handle are (1) wood, earth, rocks, etc., which serve no purpose on a holy day; (2) tools, money, pens, and appliances such as calculators and typewriters, the use of which is prohibited on Sabbaths and festivals; (3) edibles which were inaccessible or did not yet exist before the Sabbath, e.g., freshly caught fish, new-laid eggs, newly fallen fruit; (4) objects which, though not themselves *muktseh*, are used as a base for something that is, e.g., a tray bearing candlesticks. This is only a general guide, however, and two important exceptions should be noted: kitchen tools such as a nutcracker or can opener may be used to obtain food that will be eaten on the Sabbath; and items such as candles and matches which are *muktseh* on the Sabbath and Day of Atonement may be utilized on festivals, when cooking is permitted.

Apart from the prohibition against handling objects "excluded because they are forbidden" (*muktseh me-ḥamat issur*), there is a ban on objects regarded as "loathsome" (*muktseh me-ḥamat mi'us*).

MURDER "You shall not murder" is the sixth of the TEN COMMANDMENTS although it was already forbidden under the NOACHIDE LAWS: "Whoever sheds man's blood, by man shall his blood be shed" (Gen. 9:6). Even before this, when CAIN killed Abel, the act was considered reprehensible and punishable. The Bible decrees death for anyone guilty of willful murder. However, the Oral Law posits so many restrictions as to make the death penalty almost academic. Two reliable witnesses have to observe the person who is about to murder another and must caution him that the act is forbidden. They must also indicate to him the precise punishment for the act. The person must then affirm that he is aware of these facts. The witnesses must see the actual killing; circumstantial evidence, no matter how damning, is not admissible. The trial of a murderer must be before a tribunal of 23 judges and can be held only when the Temple is in existence. A majority of one leads to acquittal, whereas a majority of two is needed for conviction. Should all the judges without exception vote for conviction, the person still cannot be executed; given the fact that the judges serve in place of both prosecuting and defense attorneys, the implication is that there is no judge really pleading on behalf of the defendant, and he is accordingly not punished. It is not surprising that the Mishnah (*Avot* 1:10) declared that a court that put a man to death every seven years (or according to R. Eleazar ben Azaryah, every 70 years) was to be considered bloodthirsty. R. Akiva and R. Tarfon went further and stated that had they been in a court deciding such questions, no person would ever be put to death. Although the courts were not often able to execute a person, given all the restrictions, they nevertheless had the power to imprison for a lengthy term a person who was undoubtedly guilty.

Whenever a person was found murdered and there was no evidence of the perpetrator, the elders of the city in which the body was found, or the city closest to where it was found, had to take responsibility, and a heifer had to be beheaded (*eglah arufah*: see Deut. 21:1-9). The elders then had to declare that they were not to blame. The ceremony served to convey to all the severity of the crime. However, once murders increased, the laws of *eglah arufah* lapsed as the law had lost its deterrent value.

Under various circumstances it is permitted to kill another person: for example, in self-defense or to prevent a person in hot pursuit of another (*rodef*) from killing that other person or to prevent a sexual crime such as rape. In all of the above, though, killing is permitted only if there is no alternative way to stop the other person. In Israel, murder is not punishable by death.

MUSAF See ADDITIONAL SERVICE

MUSAR MOVEMENT Movement centered primarily in the rabbinical academies (*yeshivot*) of Lithuania, dedicated to ethical teaching (*musar*) and the development of ethical behavior in the spirit of *halakhah*. The movement was founded in the 19th century by Israel Lipkin (SALANTER; 1810-1883); its influence is felt today mainly in the curricula of non-Ḥasidic *yeshivot*.

In the second half of the 19th century, the quality of religious life in the non-Ḥasidic circles of Eastern Europe was increasingly eroded under the impact of impoverished conditions on the one hand and the HASKALAH (Enlightenment) on the other. The community was faced with the difficulty of maintaining traditional observance, according to both the letter and the spirit of the law, based — unlike the Ḥasidic approach — mainly on learning and intellectuality. Salanter, possessed of an unusually keen intellect and known from his youth as an outstanding talmudic scholar, was troubled by this situation and by the tendency of many to devote more attention to the ritual than to the moral precepts of Judaism. Seeking to address the problem through community action, he proposed the establishment in Vilna of a *musar shtibl*, a room for moral reflection, where the city's busy tradesmen might meet on the Sabbath to work together on their ethical betterment. When it became apparent that this effort would not meet with success, Salanter together with two followers, Isaac Blaser and Simḥah Zissel Broida, redirected their focus to the *yeshivah* world, believing it would be easier to develop moral habits in the young and that the *yeshivah* world would ultimately influence the general population. In its early years the movement met with criticism in certain quarters, but it later succeeded in penetrating the curriculum of most rabbinic academies. The *Musar* movement sought to reinforce traditional values and stressed that Judaism makes no distinction between ethical and ritual law. Learning was not merely an intellectual exercise but was meant to lead to proper character traits and behavior. Salanter and his disciples taught strict observance of Jewish law, a life-long process of self-improvement, and service to man within the context of service of God.

As practiced in the majority of *yeshivot*, the movement focused largely on supplementing the traditional *yeshivah* curriculum of Talmud and codes with the study of religio-ethical texts, such as the writings of Moses Ḥayyim LUZZATTO, Jonah ben Abraham of Gerondi, and others — for a half-hour each day. In order to evoke a mood of serious reflection, these ethical texts were usually studied during twilight hours or in subdued light and read aloud to a particular tune. The other chief element of *Musar* was the MASHGI'AḤ or supervisor. The *mashgi'aḥ* gave regular talks on morals and character development and took a personal interest in the ethical and intellectual growth of the students. Students might also be asked to keep notebooks in which they recorded aspects of their personalities that required work as well as their progress on various projects of self-improvement. *Yeshivot* known for the development of this approach included Slobodka, Telshe, and Mir. A more maximalist approach with even greater attention applied to character development is associated with the *yeshivah* of Novardok (Novogrudok) led by Joseph Josel Hurwitz. In this school of *Musar*, students were given projects in order to uproot pride and vanity and implant humility. At present, *Musar*, in one form or another, constitutes an integral part of the curriculum of nearly every *yeshivah* of the Lithuanian type.

MUSIC AND SONG Musical idioms and genres, both original and borrowed, which have been used in Jewish functions or as means to express one or more aspects of Jewish life.

In the Bible. The Bible is concerned mainly with sacred music and deals little with secular song; the latter is sometimes mentioned only to be severely criticized. Descriptions of music are scanty and many of the musical terms are obscure. Nevertheless, information about the music of the ancient Israelites can be gleaned from Scripture and through comparative studies of other relevant cultures.

Jubal, the mythical father of music, is said to have invented the *kinnor* (probably an ancient type of lyre) and the *ugav* (perhaps an ancient *aulos*) (Gen. 4:21). Another instrument mentioned in Genesis (31:27) is the *tof* (probably a tambourine). The latter is associated with women's dance songs such as Miriam's song at the Red Sea (Ex. 15:20). The silver trumpets of the SANCTUARY may have been similar to those found in Egyptian tombs, and other instruments were also imported from Egypt, especially during the reign of King SOLOMON.

Some of the biblical poems were probably sung or chanted, as was the custom in the ancient world. Women welcomed victorious leaders with song and dance (Judg. Chap.5. 11:34, I Sam. 18:6). A "company of prophets" descending from the sacred shrine prophesied to the accompaniment of a *nevel, tof, ḥalil*, and *kinnor*. DAVID played the *kinnor* before King Saul to relieve him of his melancholy (I Sam. 16:23).

The few passages in the Bible referring to secular music are mostly reproachful. However, even the scanty references show that the people, especially the higher classes, had an active musical culture. The prophets see music as part of the general corruption of the rich; Isaiah even associates music with harlotry (ch. 23:15-16). Instrumental music is also associated with mourning. Sacred music began to play an important role with King David. The story of the transfer of the ARK to Jerusalem (II Sam. 6, I Chron. 13, 15-16) provides the first description of music as an integral part of the worship. Some discrepancy exists between the two versions of the story, yet both indicate clearly the use of string, wind and percussion instruments, singing, and dancing.

Although King David was prevented from building God's house, he was traditionally the founder of the music of the First TEMPLE. According to I Chronicles 25, he established 24 wards of musicians, each consisting of 12 singers and instrumentalists. All the wards were governed by chief musicians who are named. David was also considered an inventor of musical instruments (e.g., Amos 6:5).

The instruments played in the Temple were the *kinnor*, *nevel* (perhaps a cythara), *metsiltayim* (cymbals). No wind instruments (other than SHOFAR and trumpet) appear in Chronicles, but some mentioned in the Book of Psalms (especially Ps. 150) were probably of the flute or oboe types.

The LITURGY of the First Temple consisted mainly of psalms, many of which were attributed to David and his chief musicians. These were probably sung either antiphonally, between two groups of singers, or responsorially between the soloist and the congregation. Some psalms (e.g., Ps. 136) were sung as litanies with a recurring short response repeated by the lay people after varying phrases sung by a soloist or group of LEVITES. The music of the psalms is lost, yet remnants may have been preserved in some of the so- called "psalmodies" of the synagogue and the church. Sacred music was also used outside the Temple, in coronation ceremonies and in wars.

In the Second Temple. According to the mishnaic tractate *Arakhin* (2.3-3) the choir in the Second Temple consisted of at least 12 Levites. The orchestra contained two to six *nevalim*, *kinnorot*, two to 12 *ḫalilim* (pipes, perhaps shawms), and one cymbal. The priest blew at least two trumpets and used an unidentified loud instrument called *magrefah* to signal the beginning of the worship which was part of the morning sacrifice. Little is known about the secular music of the time. The most frequently mentioned musical instrument is the *ḫalil*, used at weddings and funerals.

By the first century BCE, synagogues were active in various towns throughout the country and in the Diaspora. The worship there centered on the reading of Scripture and chanting prayers. No musical instruments were used. A precentor nominated by the congregation led the services. The music consisted of three genres of chant, namely psalmody, cantillation of Scripture, and the liturgical recitative. Psalmody, borrowed from the Temple, was a manner of chanting psalm verses to a fixed yet elastic melodic formula. This was performed responsively by the precentor and congregation, or antiphonally by two groups of congregants (*Suk.* 38b). For the Torah cantillation, see CANTILLATION; READING OF THE LAW

The liturgical recitative was, and still is, the special art of the precentor. It utilized traditional melodic patterns, some of which were fixed while others were flexible or modular, so as to express the form and contents of the prayer and the function or the occasion of the service.

After 70 CE. After the destruction of the Second Temple, halakhic literature abounds with statements prohibiting playing or singing under certain circumstances. The sources of the prohibitions are three: (a) rules of Sabbath observance; (b) attempts to prevent promiscuity; and (c) mourning the destruction of the Temple. Later other injunctions were added in order to prevent the imitation of Gentile practices.

The talmudic dictum "A woman's voice is indecency" (*Ber.* 24a) was perhaps an ancient belief. In the Temple, and later in the synagogue, men and women were separated and only men sang. Antiphonal singing of men and women was unacceptable in Jewish worship (*Sot.* 48a).

The mourning over the destruction of the Second Temple and the subsequent calamities led the rabbis to ban all secular songs and instrumental music. It was later agreed that music, even instrumental, could be performed for the sake of a *mitsvah*, such as rejoicing with groom and bride. No musical instruments were played during the synagogue services; only the *shofar* was heard on Rosh ha-Shanah and other selected occasions.

With the standardization of the synagogue service after the fourth century CE, the need was felt to create new, poetic prayers (PIYYUTIM) to serve as artistic additions to the fixed prayers, or sometimes as substitutes for them. These were sung by the poet-singers (*paytanim*) who were in great demand. Some of the poems had short refrains for congregational singing, others had more complicated responsive texts which were probably sung by a small choir.

In Muslim Lands. Arabic culture had a deep influence on Jewish poetry and music. This was first felt in theoretical treatises on music (e.g., by SAADIAH GAON). After the expulsion from Spain, in 1492, the Jews remained faithful to some features of Andalusian music and poetry. Hebrew poetry and music constructed according the the Andalusian *nuba* are still sung at Friday night BAKKASHOT services and new poems are still created by the Jews of Morocco. A resurgence of Arabic influence was felt in the last decades of the 16th century when poets such as Menahem of Lonzano and Israel Najara influenced by the kabbalistic ideas of the Lurianic school of Safed (see LURIA, ISAAC), sought to revive and modernize Hebrew poetry according to medieval Spanish concepts. They built their sacred Hebrew poems after popular Arabic and Turkish songs so that the new poems could be sung to the original Arabic or Turkish tunes.

Arabic instrumental music was also highly esteemed by the Jews of the Muslim countries, and in spite of rabbinic injunctions against playing or even listening to such music, many Jews became connoiseurs of Arabic art music and some were excellent musicians. In some countries of the East, musicianship became a Jewish trade. The Arabic modal system of the *maqam* penetrated every musical activity of the Jews in the Muslim countries.

The co-existence of Jews and Gentiles in medieval Spain helped to created a treasure of songs in the JUDEO-SPANISH ("Ladino") language. These songs, many of Gentile origin, were preserved by the Jews, mostly by Jewish women, in the various countries where they lived after their expulsion from Spain. Many more songs were created in the new countries, especially in the Balkans and in Morocco. The main forms were: (a) the romances, narrative, sometimes epic, ballads based on medieval chivalry tales and sung to repeated four-line musical stanzas; (b) *complas*, songs in celebration of the Jewish holidays, or important life-cycle events; (c) *canticas*, life-cycle songs in simple, popular style. Many melodies of all three forms were adapted to sacred texts and are sung in synagogue services and para-liturgical functions, such as the SABBATH meals.

Ashkenazi Liturgical Chants. Ashkenazi Jews formulated their own synagogue songs, based partially on cantillation formulae mingled with non-Jewish melodic patterns. The Ashkenazi communities of Germany and northern France strove to unify the melodies of the prayers (*nusaḫ ha-tefillah*). Special melodies were singled out as *niggunim mi-sinai* (tunes from Sinai) and were held in great reverence. The most famous among these is the KOL NIDRÉ melody.

The Ashkenazi chants and *mi-sinai* melodies were transferred to eastern Europe during the various Jewish immigrations of the Middle Ages. There they assumed a new melodic guise and flourished in variants influenced by Slavic musical patterns.

It is not clear when polyphony was introduced into the synagogue. It is quite possible that small groups of singers improvised simple polyphony in some Ashkenazi (Tedeschi) synagogues of northern Italy at the end of the 16th century and that the later common trio of cantor, boy-singer, and bass-singer began at the same time in Germany. The first printed collection of polyphonic music for the synagogue was *Ha-Shirim asher li-Shelemoh* (Venice, 1622) by Salomone di Rossi of Mantua. The compositions, in the polyphonic styles of the Renaissance, were unique and did not have an immediate following; but 50 years later, Jews began to perform baroque-style Hebrew cantatas in special synagogue or family celebrations. The use of cantatas was fashionable in northern Italy, southern France, and in Amsterdam until the end of the 18th century. In Germany, the fashion tended towards cantorial compostitions in the style of rococo *gallanteries*. Marches, minuets and horn-calls were inserted in the services betwen old *nusaḥ* chants. Synagogues, such as the famous Altneuschul in Prague used the ORGAN and other instruments on Friday afternoons to welcome the Sabbath. *Klezmer* (Jewish instrumental musicians) played dance music at weddings, and participated in community processions.

New ideas of incorporating European polyphony into the synagogue services emerged with the rise of the REFORM movement in the 19th century. Early reformers introduced Protestant chorales with organ accompaniment into the newly shaped services; later musicians of the German Reform movement composed new part music for old Hebrew hymns in a popular German style. A different approach was taken by Solomon Sulzer of Vienna. He strove to preserve the ancient synagogue services and the general characteristics of the Ashkenazi cantorial music and at the same time to modernize the music by reshaping the recitatives to meet the standards of European art music and to introduce new choral pieces in the current style (see CANTORS and CANTORIAL MUSIC).

Kabbalah and Ḥasidism. Only in the Lurianic Kabbalah did music gain the theoretical support and encouragement that helped Jews overcome the medieval notion equating music with promiscuity. According to this Kabbalah, all music is divinely inspired, yet because of the ancient sin and the sins of mankind, many melodies are caught in the defiled *kelippot*. Righteous men must find a TIKKUN, a means of purification for the defiled melodies by singing them to sacred texts or on sacred occasions such as prayer, study of Torah, or the Sabbath meal.

Another kabbalistic idea that inspired music-making was the need to help the reunion of *sefirat malkhut*, the feminine Divine emanation, with the other SEFIROT on the Sabbath eve. The *Kabbalat Shabbat* ceremonies, welcoming Queen Sabbath and the Friday night meal became occasions of much music making. The kabbalistic poem LEKHAH DODI has been set to innumerable tunes. Singing ZEMIROT at the Sabbath table became a welcome obligation and provided an opportunity to compose many new melodies.

The founders of Ḥasidism, R. Israel BAAL SHEM TOV and his disciples, regarded music and dance as the most important means of uplifting the soul and releasing it from the negative world of the *kelippot*. They believed in the existence of a Divine spark even in the most humble or defiled melody, and strove to release it by singing it in sanctity. Melodies were not all of the same value; some were considered simple expressions of joy, others were vehicles of prayer, and the highest NIGGUNIM (melodies) were those created by the TSADDIKIM, the ḥasidic leaders and saints. Wordless melodies were highly esteemed; they were sung to non-semantic syllables, such a *va-ba-bam*, and *doy-doy-doy*. Ḥasidic leaders encouraged the creation of new *niggunim*. Some were themselves gifted musicians and composed melodies for the prayers. Others employed "court" composers. From the mid-19th century, many employed *ḥazzanim* (cantors) and some had choirs whose task was to disseminate the new melodies by teaching them to the pilgrims who flocked to the "courts" during the holiday seasons. Thus different melodies and different performance practices developed at the various ḥasidic dynasties.

Instrumental music was permitted if played for weddings or other life-cycle celebrations and in the festivities of ḤANUKKAH and PURIM. Bands of Jewish instrumentalists developed from the Middle Ages in many countries. Most famous were the East European musicians called *klezmorim* (Yiddish plural of *klezmer*, from the Hebrew *kelé-zemer* "musical instruments"). They developed a unique repertoire of songs and instrumental pieces ranging from simple dance music to virtuoso solos for violin or clarinet, with characteristic embellishments and tone colors. Since most of the music was not notated, much of it was lost when the demand abated. Lately, however, a revival of *klezmer* music has taken place

A group of klezmorim *(musicians) who performed at weddings and other celebrations. Poland, early 19th century.*

in Israel and the United States, some neo-*klezmer* coming from Ḥasidic circles, others from pop-music instrumentalists.

MYSTICISM, JEWISH Ever since the second century CE, there has been a trend in Jewish culture which is not satisfied with traditional ways to approach God through Jewish religious practice and thought, but seeks a closer, more intimate and more meaningful contact between the worshiper and his Creator. The search for such an approach to or union with God was expressed in many ways and those who believed it could not be brought about by intellectual or rational means, developed into the various circles, groups and sects of Jewish mystics. The best-known and most important Jewish mystical movement is known as the Kabbalah, which flourished from the end of the 12th century; however, it was preceded in ancient times by HÉKHALOT AND MERKAVAH mysticism and in the Middle Ages by the Ashkenazi Ḥasidic mysteries (ḤASIDÉ ASHKENAZ).

Jewish mysticism, like Judaism as a whole, believes that the Bible is the source of all truth. Ancient Divine revelations to the patriarchs, to the Jewish people as a whole and to the prophets, embody eternal truth. Mystical truth, therefore, need not be revealed in an individual, visionary manner; it can be gleaned from a mystical interpretation of the ancient texts. Throughout its history, Jewish mysticism has reflected the tension between the tendency to arrive at the mystical truth by an esoteric system of hermeneutical interpretation of biblical verses and talmudic sayings, viewing them as mystic symbols on the one hand and on the other, the drive towards original mystical discovery through visions, dreams, revelations of celestial powers and intuitive reflection. Ancient Jewish mysticism, as reflected in the *Hékhalot* mystical texts, tended to the second alternative and most of the works of these mystics are vivid and colorful descriptions of their visions in the Divine world. The Kabbalah usually tended towards the hermeneutical alternative: its very name means "tradition" and the kabbalists saw themselves as transmitters of ancient secrets, given to them by previous generations or gleaned by them from ancient texts. Still, even within the homiletical and exegetical works of the kabbalists it is possible to trace the elements of an original revelation, an individual mystical experience.

The core of Jewish mysticism is a set of symbols which can be found in its most developed form in the Kabbalah. Mystics, almost by definition, claim that truth cannot be expressed by words, because words denote only what the human senses or intellect experience. If truth is beyond human sensory or logical perception, then it cannot be expressed by language. Yet the Bible is written in words and, being Divinely inspired, these words must contain Divine truth. According to the kabbalists, these words do not denote sensual reality, but symbolize, in a complex way, a mystical truth which is essentially beyond words. God gave the mystics the scriptures as a kind of dictionary of symbols which only the mystic can understand and in this way have some glimpse of the truth beyond these words. The mystics thus read the scriptures in a different, unique way and they can use the symbols — the biblical terms — to express the truth as glimpsed by them. The symbols used by the earliest kabbalistic sources — the *Sefer ha*-BAHIR and the works of R. Isaac the Blind in the late 12th century — became the standard language of the kabbalists, to which each school and each individual mystic added their own terms and their own specific meanings. The ancient Jewish mystics and the Ashkenazi Ḥasidim did not form such detailed systems of symbols as did the Kabbalah, but the basic trend of giving biblical terms symbolical meaning is also present in their writings.

During most of its history, Jewish mysticism developed in the form of small esoteric circles of mystics who dealt with their secrets far from the center of their contemporary culture, even though they themselves were part of that center. The tests of *Hékhalot* and *Merkavah* mysticism are attributed, pseudepigraphically, to R. AKIVA, R. ISHMAEL and other tannaitic sages, and it seems that these mystics were not culturally remote from the centers of talmudic and midrashic culture. Ashkenazi Ḥasidim developed mainly in the school of the medieval German Kalonymus family, which was the most prestigious at that time. The first schools of the Kabbalah, those of R. ABRAHAM BEN DAVID OF POSQUIÈRES in Provence and the Spanish school in Gerona headed by Naḥmanides, were at that time the leading academies of *halakhah* and their heads were the religious leaders of their generation. The Kabbalah of Isaac LURIA developed in the great cultural center of 16th-century Safed and there are several similar examples. Jewish mysticism was not marginal, but it tried to keep its secrets away from the general public and therefore it did not dominate Jewish culture. This changed dramatically in early modern times, when Lurianic Kabbalah spread widely in the 17th century, and the movements of SHABBETAI TSEVI and ḤASIDISM became popular, shaping Jewish culture and religious history.

From the late 12th century, Jewish mystics wrote ethical treatises which did not reveal their mystical views but the content of which itself reflected the message that they thought the general public could and should receive. Both Ashkenazi Ḥasidim and the Gerona kabbalists wrote some of the most influential ethical works which contributed meaningfully to Jewish medieval culture, works such as R. JUDAH HE-ḤASID's *Sefer Ḥasidim* and R. Jonah Gerondi's *Sha'aré Teshuvah* ("The Gates of Repentance"). In the 16th century, kabbalists began to publish kabbalistic ethical works which used openly kabbalistic symbolism and terminology; in the 17th century such symbolism became dominant in Hebrew homiletical literature. In this way, the Kabbalah gradually became interwoven into everyday Jewish religious and ethical practice, especially by giving mystical meaning to the commandments and ethical norms. Modern Ḥasidism continued this trend and brought it to a peak, popularizing mystical symbols and making them central in Jewish life and worship. Hebrew mystical ethical literature was the vehicle by which Jewish mysticism became a dominant force in Jewish culture in the 17th to 19th centuries.

History The history of Jewish mysticism is divided into five main periods, each representing different mystical attitudes and a different position for the mystics in Jewish society and culture: (1) Ancient Jewish mysticism, the mystical schools which developed in late antiquity, the talmudic period. (2) The early Jewish mystical schools in medieval Europe in the 12th and 13th centuries. (3) The Kabbalah in Spain in the 13th to 15th centuries and its spread to other countries in Europe and the East. (4) The Kabbalah after the expulsion from Spain, the center in Safed, the spread of Lurianic Kabbalah, the Shabbatean movement, 16th to 18th centuries. (5) The emergence of Ḥasidism, modern and contemporary Ḥasidic, anti-Ḥasidic, and non-Ḥasidic schools of Kabbalah.

In the first three periods, until the late 15th century, Jewish mysticism was not a central element in Jewish religious culture. Mystical literature developed mainly in close, esoteric circles whose works remained secluded from the general public and interest in it was limited to very small groups. Thus, for instance, among the vast collection of writings in the Cairo GENIZAH only 23 fragments of ancient Jewish mystical works (*Hékhalot* and *Merkavah* mysticism) were found, an insignificant number compared to the tens of thousands of fragments in that collection. On the other hand, the prevalence of references to mystical lore in talmudic and midrashic literature proves that among at least a part of the Jewish intellectual leadership in late antiquity there was an interest in esoteric and mystical speculation. Ancient Jewish mysticism developed on the basis of midrashic interpretations of biblical texts, especially of the first chapters of EZEKIEL and Genesis (CREATION) and the SONG OF SONGS, to which it added ideas and influences from other sources, most notably the Enoch literature of the second century BCE and other apocryphal and apocalyptical sources (see APOCALYPSE; APOCRYPHA). The ancient Jewish mystics were an integral part of the cultural world of the ancient sages, but they developed a specific mystical practice, as well as a literary genre (*Hékhalot* and *Merkavah* literature), and even differed in some linguistic aspects from the general talmudic-midrashic literary and linguistic forms.

The early stages of development of this school of mystics can be found in the second century CE, probably among scholars who developed ideas originating in the school of R. Akiva. Their main aim as mystics was the practice of ascension, which was paradoxically called "descent to the chariot" (*yeridah la-merkavah*). Several pseudepigraphical works attribute this practice to R. Akiva and R. Ishmael, sometimes describing the *tanna* Neḥuniah ben ha-Kanah as the leader of the group. Their main contribution to Jewish mystical thought is to be found in the treatise *Shi'ur Komah* ("The Measurement of the Height") in which God, the Creator, is described as an enormous anthropomorphic figure, each of His limbs having several esoteric names, whose measurement is given as billions of times the size of the cosmos. The mystic attempts to ascend through the seven heavens and the seven celestial palaces in order to reach the throne of glory on which this figure "sits" and participate in the prayers of the ministering angels around this throne.

Hékhalot and *Merkavah* literature is intensely visionary in character, describing in great detail the celestial realm and God's surroundings. It is expressed in poetical language and includes many hymns, some of which were later included in the Jewish prayer book. It does not convey any general religious or ethical message to the people as a whole and, in form and content, remains the concern of the closed circle of mystics.

It seems that this mysticism reached its peak in the fourth century and continued to develop in the fifth and sixth, first mainly in Erets Israel and later in Babylonia. Some anthologies of the works of these mystics were compiled later in the geonic period, but there is no knowledge of original new trends and ideas in the later geonic period. The edited texts of ancient Jewish mysticism served as a starting point for the next stage, the appearance of mystical schools in medieval Christian Europe in the 12th century.

In the second half of the 12th century, two new mystical schools emerged, one in southern Europe, mainly in northern Spain and southern France, and the other in the Rhineland. These two, commonly known as the Kabbalah and Ashkenazi Ḥasidism, were not, at that time, unified schools, but rather several independent groups or even solitary writers, each unaware of the existence of the others. The early Kabbalah includes three different, and probably independent, traditions — the *Sefer ha-Bahir*, composed in the late 12th century and including the symbolism of the ten Divine Emanations, the SEFIROT, the tradition of R. Abraham ben David of Posquières and his son, R. Isaac the Blind, and the third, the *Iyyun* ("contemplation") circle, a group which produced several brief mystical treatises, intensely neo-Platonic in character, which did not know of the symbolism characerizing the other two traditions.

Ashkenazi Ḥasidism flourished mainly in the Kalonymus family, in Spire and Worms, and the three main figures in its tradition are R. Samuel ben Kalonymus he-Ḥasid (the Pious), his son R. JUDAH HE-ḤASID, and the latter's disciple, R. ELEAZAR BEN JUDAH OF WORMS. Besides this central school, there were several other groups and independent writers, such as the school which based its pseudepigraphical traditions on a "Baraita of Joseph ben Uzziel" and the anonymous authors of the *Sefer ha-Ḥayyim*, a theological and ethical work, and *Sefer ha-Navon*, a commentary on the SHEMA. The

Man holding a tree with the ten sefirot. *Title page of Latin translation of work by the Spanish kabbalist, Joseph Gikatilla.*

three "kabbalistic" schools have common elements which differentiate them from the different "Ashkenazi H̱asidic" groups; however, the differences between the several groups in each of them are considerable.

The common element in all these groups is a new concept of the Godhead as representing a unity of several different forces. The simple biblical and rabbinic conception of the unity of God has been broken by all these circles of mystics and in its place a complex system, describing Divine unity as a result of the harmony among several Divine powers, numbering between three and 13, was instituted. From this period onwards, until the present day, the main concern of Jewish mystics has been the description of the inner relationship between the various Divine powers within the Godhead, their division into "masculine" and "feminine" elements, their attitude towards evil, their role in the creation, in the Divine guidance of world affairs, in the fate of the Jewish people and in the future messianic redemption.

After the initial phase, in the last quarter of the 12th century and the first quarter of the 13th, these various groups began to develop into two distinct schools: the Ashkenazi H̱asidic school, headed by R. Eleazar of Worms, and the kabbalistic one, centered in Gerona in Catalonia and headed by Naẖmanides. In these two schools, European Jewish mysticism received its basic symbols and ideas, which shaped Jewish mysticism for centuries to come. Ashkenazi H̱asidism declined after the middle of the 13th century, and many of its ideas were absorbed by the Kabbalah, that spread widely in the second half of the 13th century and established new schools in central Europe, in Italy and in the East.

The third stage was the development of the Kabbalah in Spain from the late 13th century to the expulsion of the Jews from that country in 1492. The most important event in this period was the appearance of the ZOHAR, the main text of the Kabbalah, in the last years of the 13th century. The author of the main part of the Zohar, R. MOSES DE LEÓN, utilized in the composition of his mystical masterpiece the teachings of the various kabbalistic circles that flourished in Spain in the 13th century, especially those of Gerona and the radical teachings of the Cohen brothers, the "gnostic" kabbalistic group of Castile in the second half of the 13th century. In this group the kabbalistic concept of dualism, of a constant struggle between the "left side" and the "right side" in the cosmos, was powerfully expressed, and influenced the Zohar's teachings concerning the *sitra aẖra*, the satanic left side in the Divine and created worlds.

The Zohar emerged at a time when a large group of kabbalists were active in northern Spain, some of them having direct contact with R. Moses de León; some of them may have had some impact on the Zohar itself. Most notable among them: R. Joseph Gikatilla (who was a disciple of R. Abraham ABULAFIA, one of the most original kabbalistic thinkers in Spain), R. David ben Judah the Pious, R. Joseph "of Shushan the Capital," the anonymous author of *Tikkuné ha-Zohar* whose work was included in the Zohar collection and, possibly, the anonymous author of the *Sefer ha-Temunah* ("The Book of the Picture"). These and other kabbalists developed the symbolism of the Kabbalah and assisted in achieving a central place for the Zohar in Jewish mysticism; their work had a great impact on subsequent generations of kabbalists in Spain and elsewhere. During the 14th and the early 15th centuries the Kabbalah in general and the Zohar in particular had increasing influence upon Jewish intellectuals in Germany, Erets Israel, Italy, and Byzantium. From the Byzantine kabbalistic circles came, probably in the 15th century, the books, *Kanah* and *Peliah*, two of the masterpieces of medieval Kabbalah.

The fourth period in the history of Jewish mysticism is directly connected to the crisis in Spain that culminated in the expulsion of the Jews from Spain (1492) and Portugal (1497) and the establishment of new intellectual centers in Italy, Turkey, and Safed. By the 16th century, the teachings of the Zohar had become an integral part of Jewish general culture, used by homilists and writers without any distinct mystical intention. At the same time, an upsurge in the messianic element in the Kabbalah, which had not been central in its previous development, changed its character dramatically (see MESSIAH). Even before the expulsion, a new school of kabbalists in Spain began to write intensely messianic kabbalistic works and this tendency increased in the works written by the kabbalists who lived through the expulsion. R. Abraham be-Rabbi Eliezer ha-Levi, who went to Jerusalem, wrote several mythological-apocalyptical kabbalistic works expressing the new attitude.

The center in 16th-century Safed included kabbalists of different schools and some of the most prominent among them, like R. Moses CORDOVERO, believed in continuing the old Spanish Kabbalah. Cordovero's main purpose was the systemization of zoharic Kabbalah and writing a detailed commentary on the Zohar. However, the new trends were becoming stronger and they found their clearest expression in the revolutionary Kabbalah developed in Safed by R. Isaac Luria (the *Ari*) and his disciples, especially R. Ḫayyim VITAL, in the last third of the century. While using elements found in the Zohar, Lurianic Kabbalah developed a new myth according to which the earthly exile is but a reflection of a flaw in the Divine world which allows evil to flourish. Jewish religious life is intended to correct this flaw and bring salvation first and foremost to the Divine world, but also pave the way for the redemption of the Jewish people. Lurianic Kabbalah transformed Jewish mysticism into an ideology directly relevant to Jewish contemporary problems, thus for the first time enabling Jewish mystics to be historically active in shaping the future of the people as a whole.

This reversal in the attitude of the Kabbalah towards messianism and historical activity served as a spiritual basis for the emergence of the Shabbatean movement in 1665-1666. The messianic theology of Nathan of Gaza, the prophet of Shabbetai Tsevi, developed Lurianic Kabbalah while putting in its center the role of the messiah in the process of the redemption. Shabbetai Tsevi and Nathan of Gaza presented their believers with a new mystical faith, the faith in the redemptive role of the personal messiah who, as one of the *sefirot*, is an incarnation of a Divine power whose role is to correct everything that is flawed in the Divine and earthly worlds. When Shabbetai Tsevi was converted to Islam these ideas were developed further to explain and justify the conversion, creating a paradoxical mysticism of faith in a converted messiah. Various Shabbatean sects in the 17th and 18th centuries developed different versions of this messianic theology, but all of them put in their center the idea of the mystical leader, the Divine power whose responsibility it is to bring salvation to all existence. Shabbateanism turned Lurianic Kabbalah into a theology centered around a mystical leader.

The fifth and last stage in the development of Jewish mysticism, which began in the middle of the 18th century and continues to develop today, is connected with the emergence of the modern Ḫasidic movement, founded by R. Israel BAAL SHEM TOV. Ḫasidism brought about a schism in East European Jewry between the adherents of the many Ḫasidic sects, led by the TSADDIKIM, and their opponents, the MITNAGGEDIM. Both sides in this schism were kabbalists, accepting, in various ways, the basic ideas of the Kabbalah, though many Ḫasidic leaders tended to re-interpret some Lurianic symbols in a new way. The Mitnaggedim were very often devoted to Lurianic concepts in different forms. The main difference between Ḫasidism and its opponents is to be found in the Ḫasidic theory of the *Tsaddik*, the belief in the redemptive role of the Ḫasidic Rabbi as a mystical leader. Some Shabbatean elements undoubtedly had an impact on the development of the theology that gives the *Tsaddik* a superhuman role in redeeming the souls of his adherents and responsibility over their fate both in this world and in the next. The Mitnaggedim fiercely oppose attributing such a role to a human being and uphold the symbols of pre-Shabbatean Kabbalah. This conflict continues into present-day Judaism.

N

NAḤMAN OF BRATSLAV (1772-1811). Ḥasidic leader; great-grandson of Israel BA'AL SHEM TOV and founder of a separate branch of the Ḥasidic movement. As a young man, he established himself in the Ukraine, exercising the role of a TSADDIK, and the pilgrimage which he made to Erets Israel in 1798-9 was later clothed with mystical significance. Though terminated abruptly as a result of Napoleon's campaign against the Turks, this visit made a lasting impression on Naḥman, who was fond of saying: "No matter where I go, it is always to Erets Israel."

Believing that he was destined to revive the authentic ḤASIDISM of his great ancestor, and to combat insincere leadership within the movement, Naḥman became embroiled in controversy almost as soon as he returned to the Ukraine. His revolutionary fervor struck other Ḥasidic leaders of the time as sheer presumption. While living in Zlatopol, Naḥman was denounced by Aryeh Leib of Shpola (1725-1812), known as "the *Shpoler Zeyde*" (Grandfather), who declared that Naḥman's soul belonged to a later generation and had come into the world too soon; Naḥman's reply was that the *Zeyde's* soul belonged to a past generation and had come into the world too late. Such enmity continued to pursue Naḥman while he was consolidating his branch of the Ḥasidic movement in the small Podolian town of Bratslav (1802-10). He finally left Bratslav for Uman in the Ukraine, dying there of tuberculosis at the age of 39. Generations of Bratslav Ḥasidim made his grave in Uman a center of pilgrimage and, in accordance with his instructions, danced around it on his *yahrzeit*.

In his works, Naḥman of Bratslav often mentions the "true *Tsaddik*" of his generation, presumably referring to himself. There is also reason to believe that Naḥman saw himself fulfilling a messianic role. His devoted follower and amanuensis, Nathan Sternhartz (1780-1845), recorded the teachings of the master, but neither he nor any other disciple succeeded him, Naḥman having promised that he would continue to lead his Ḥasidim after his death. Among other Ḥasidic groups, the Bratslavers are therefore nicknamed "the dead Ḥasidim," since they have no living *Rebbe*. Their near-worship of Naḥman was a source of offense to other sections of the movement, as well as to Ḥasidism's opponents, the MITNAGGEDIM.

Nathan Sternhartz, the most effective propagator of Bratslav Ḥasidism, was also responsible for compiling and publishing many of his late master's works. They include *Likkuté Moharan* (Ostrog, 1806), an anthology of teachings which appeared in Naḥman's lifetime, and *Likkuté Moharan Tinyana* (1811), a supplementary volume; *Sefer ha-Middot* (1811); and *Sippuré Ma'asiyyot* (1815), the famous "Tales of Rabbi Naḥman," which are regarded as one of the classics of Yiddish literature.

APHORISMS OF NAḤMAN OF BRATSLAV

Man must lose himself in prayer and entirely forget his own existence.

Solitude is a great virtue. One should set aside an hour each day to be alone with God. Solitude in the open air, in the forest or the desert, is especially important.

Humility for the sake of approval is the worst form of arrogance.

Better a superstitious believer than a rationalistic unbeliever.

One who keeps silent in the face of abuse is a true Ḥasid.

Melody and song lead the heart of man to God.

Nine *Tsaddikim* do not make a prayer quorum, but one common man joining them completes the *minyan*.

The whole world is [like] a very narrow bridge, and the main thing is not to be afraid.

God is present whenever a peace treaty is signed.

Since God is Infinite and man finite, a man is bound to have religious doubts; but like Moses, he should go into the darkness where he will find God.

Toward the end of his life, in Uman, Naḥman met local exponents of Jewish Enlightenment (HASKALAH), from whom he may have derived certain West European cultural ideas. Essentially, however, the *Tsaddik* was an uncompromising anti-rationalist who saw fit to revive the old heresy charge against Maimonides and maintained that "where reason ends, faith begins." Naḥman understood the kabbalistic doctrine of TSIMTSUM to mean that seeking God through reason is utterly futile, since one who reasons exists in the void from which God Himself is absent. The only way to God lies in a simple, uncomplicated faith, by virtue of which man can rise beyond the void to meet his Creator. That is why Naḫman, like his contemporary Kierkegaard, delighted in the paradox of faith and acknowledged the role of doubt in the sphere of religious belief.

NAḪMANIDES (Moses ben Naḫman Gerondi, known by the acronym *Ramban*, 1194-1270). Leading rabbinic authority, Bible commentator, talmudic scholar and communal leader. Born in Gerona in the northern Spanish district of Catalonia, he was a doctor by profession. He was a prolific halakhist whom later rabbis in Spain regarded as their authority, referring to him simply as "the Rabbi." Apart from his influence in Jewish public life in Catalonia and beyond, he was also *persona grata* at the royal court of King James I of Aragon. However, in 1263, a convert to Christianity, Pablo Christiani, challenged him to a public DISPUTATION on the relative truth of Judaism and Christianity, which was held in Barcelona over a period of four days, in the presence of the king and his court, and many ecclesiastical dignitaries. Naḫmanides, who had been granted full freedom of speech in advance by King James, distinguished himself, and was even rewarded by his patron. His victory drew the enmity of the Dominicans who forced him into exile.

Thus, at the age of 70, Naḫmanides left Aragon, eventually arriving in Erets Israel, where he devoted himself to the revival of Jewish religious and community life, which had been virtually extinguished in the wake of the Crusaders. Seven centuries later, the small synagogue established by Naḫmanides in Jerusalem, a few hundred yards from the Western Wall, was rediscovered and restored.

Naḫmanides spent his last days in Acre, where he completed his commentary on the Bible. His deeply emotional love for the Holy Land is evident in all his writings. In an appendix to his Bible commentary, he gives expression to his feelings of loneliness:

> "I am the man who saw affliction. I am banished from my table, far removed from friend and kinsman, and too long is the distance to meet again...But the loss of all else which delighted my eyes is compensated by my present joy in a day passed within your courts, O Jerusalem...where it is granted me to caress your stones, to fondle your dust, and to weep over your ruins. I weep bitterly, but I find joy in my heart. I rend my garments, but I find solace in so doing."

Naḫmanides died in Erets Israel; various traditions place his grave in Haifa, Acre, Jerusalem, and Hebron.

In his youth, Naḫmanides was very much under the influence of French Jewish scholarship. His novellae on many tractates of the Talmud were written in the style of the French tosafists (see TOSAFOT). He helped raise Talmud study to prime importance in Spain. His halakhic works are extensive, representing a synthesis of the piety of the French schools and of the general culture of his Spanish background. When the French rabbis decreed MAIMONIDES' philosophical books as heretical and dangerous, Naḫmanides tried to convince them to modify their hostile anti-Maimonist stance, stressing the virtues and importance of Maimonides' work, while at the same time challenging his position which made philosophy the touchstone of religious truth. Authority, for Naḫmanides, lay in the Scriptures and in rabbinic tradition.

Personal seal of Naḫmanides inscribed: Mosheh (Moses) ben Naḫman of Gerona (his native town); ḫazzak *(be strong).*

Naḫmanides' influential Bible commentary incorporates careful philosophy, aggadic references, and mystical insights. He is guided by the principle, clearly stated at the beginning of his commentary on Genesis: "Moses wrote this book, together with the whole of the Torah, at God's dictation." On this basis he also rejects certain Maimonidean explanations, sometimes quite sharply, as that on Genesis 15:2, where he writes: "These words [of Maimonides] contradict the Scripture text; it is forbidden to hear them, let alone believe them." This shows Naḫmanides as a fundamentalist and as an outspoken defendant of the miraculous origin of the written text. While he approached the Talmud with an incisive dialectic mind, he was opposed to the purely rationalistic approach when dealing with Scripture. His commentary reflects a search for a deeper meaning beneath the literal surface sense. For this he turned to Jewish MYSTICISM. He also set great store by the MIDRASHIM of the ancient sages, finding in them inner hidden meanings. Nonetheless, after quoting a Midrash he frequently adds: "But in my opinion, the plain meaning is..."

His approach to the Bible is drawn on a large canvas. He uses the texts as opportunities to expound his views on many subjects. In dealing with the behavior of the biblical personalities he often displays psychological insight. He also has a historical sense and more than any other commentator, diligently inquires into the connection between the chapters and portions of the Bible. For him, the juxtaposition of the portions of the Bible is neither haphazard nor fortuitous, but meaningful; and in opposition to other teachers (including RASHI), he maintains that there is a chronological sequence and order throughout Scripture, except where the text itself indicates a departure from due order.

NAHUM Seventh book of the MINOR PROPHETS in the Prophetical section of the Bible. The only specific information about Nahum is that he was an Elkoshite, but the place Elkosh is not mentioned anywhere else in the Bible. Based on the evidence of his preaching, he was from the southern kingdom of Judah. The immediate background of the Book of Nahum is the destruction of Nineveh by the Babylonians and Medes (612 BCE), but scholars are divided as to whether the words contained in the Book were first spoken before, during, or after that event. The book contains three chapters and 47 verses. The book's designation, "the burden of Nineveh" in the first verse, is a typical prophetic pronouncement of doom concerning the fate of the nations of the world. Nahum prophesies that an unnamed city, which must be Jerusalem, is told that he who conspired against the Lord, i.e., Assyria, is about to remove its yoke from it. Jerusalem's honor will then be restored, but Nineveh will be destroyed as a punishment for its brutality and intrigue. Nahum also suggests a flood (of the Tigris) as being a major factor in the fall of Nineveh (2:7,9). According to Jewish tradition, Nahum's prophecy came after that of JONAH, for the people of Nineveh had repented at the time of Jonah and the city had been saved. The Hebrew text of Nahum in 1:2-10 contains a partially preserved alphabetical acrostic.

BOOK OF NAHUM

1:1 — 1:10	God's vengeance and punishment
1:11 — 2:3	Threats against Assyria and promises to Judah
2:4 — 2:14	Attack on Nineveh
3:1 — 3:19	Sack of Nineveh

NAMES The significance of the name appears early in the Jewish tradition since the first act of ADAM was to give names to all the animals and birds that God had created (Gen. 2:19-20). In the next chapter (Gen. 3:20), Adam names his wife Eve, and a reason is offered for this particular appellation. The name of an individual thus came to represent the essence of his or her nature. The name was of such importance that when the individual changed in some way, the name had to be changed as well. Examples of this may be seen in the biblical incidents of Abram, Sarai, Jacob, and Hoshea whose names are changed to Abraham, Sarah, Israel, and Joshua.

In ancient times it was not unusual for a name to include the name of a god. As long as the worship of Baal had its impact on the Israelites, they had names such as Ishbaal. When monotheism prevailed, the use of Baal ceased and names began to include the various titles of God — El, Eli, Yeho. This practice has continued to the present, with many contemporary Hebrew names still containing the element of God's name.

"How do we know that the name of a person affects his life?" asks the Talmud (*Ber.*7b). R. Eleazar's answer indicates that God is responsible for the creation of names and this determines a person's destiny. Taking this as a basic principle, the sages of the Talmud provide scores of explanations for the names of individuals, places, and even animals listed in the Bible. Jewish legal codification regarding the spelling of names in marriage and divorce documents and in bills of sale is very exacting. This stems from the talmudic discussions which indicate that the misspelling of a name invalidates a document and the transaction involved.

The naming of a newborn infant takes place on one of two occasions, depending on the sex of the child. A baby boy is named at the CIRCUMCISION ceremony; a baby girl is named in the synagogue on the first time the Torah is read after her birth. As a throwback to earlier stages when the name was considered to have some magical quality, a baby's name was actually kept secret until the public announcement. This was considered a form of protection, a way of warding off evil spirits who might attack an infant just after birth.

The Hebrew form of the name consists of the individual's name followed by "son" or "daughter" of the father (e.g., Jacob son of Isaac [Ya'akov ben Yitsḫak] or Dinah daughter of Jacob [Dinah bat Ya'akov]). This is the form used in all Hebrew documents and also for the "call" to the READING OF THE LAW. In recent years it has become customary in many circles to add the mother's name. The mother's name has been used since the Middle Ages whenever a prayer for a return to good health was offered.

The Talmud said: "The majority of Jews in foreign parts (Diaspora) have heathen names" (*Git.* 11b). However, according to the rabbis, the "children of Israel did not change their names in Egypt; as Reuben and Simeon they entered and as Reuben and Simeon they departed." The tendency of giving children names common in the non-Jewish environment has continued throughout the centuries. Jews bore names reflecting every society in which they lived, some — such as Alexander — becoming accepted Jewish names. Frequently, Hebrew names were translated into other languages; an example is Baruch, which became Benedict. Working the opposite way, foreign names were translated into Hebrew and especially Yiddish. Fabius-Phoebus was translated into Shraga, an Aramaic word for light, and then into Yiddish as Feivel. The dual name Shraga Feivel was common in eastern Europe. Spanish names were likewise taken over by Sephardi Jews.

The practice of changing the name at the time of serious illness derives from the Talmud, which states: "Four things cancel the doom of an individual, namely, charity, supplication, change of name, and change of conduct" (*RH* 16b). The rabbis suggest that changing the name is a way of misleading the ANGEL OF DEATH. A ritual thus arose, still practised in Orthodox circles, in which an additional name is given to an ill person. This extra name is either *Ḥayyim* or *Ḥayyah* or a derivative of that name, which means "life." From then on the individual carries both his original name and the new one. In modern Israel, new Hebrew names have been coined and obscure biblical names revived.

NAPHTALI See TRIBES, TWELVE

NASHIM ("Women"). Third Order of the Mishnah. Its seven tractates (YEVAMOT, KETUBBOT, NEDARIM, NAZIR, SOTAH, GITTIN, and KIDDUSHIN) deal with betrothal, the marriage contract, the faithless wife, divorce, and relations between men and women. It also examines the legal obligation of vows, the freeing of slaves, and the laws of the NAZIRITE. According to MAIMONIDES, the first tractate of this Order should logically be *Ketubbot* ("Marriage Contracts"), but instead *Yevamot* ("Levirate Marriage") is first, because levirate marriage is forced upon a man, whereas marriage itself is not, and what a person is compelled to do should precede that which he is free to decide himself. Every tractate is expanded upon in both the Babylonian and the Jerusalem Talmud as well as in the TOSEFTA.

NASI ("prince," "ruler"). Title used at different periods with varying connotations. In biblical times it denoted the head of a clan or tribe, or a king. In the period of the Israelites' wandering in the wilderness, and in the early days of the conquest of Canaan, the title invariably referred to the head of a tribe who performed a number of functions of a communal nature. Their names are listed in Numbers 1:5-16. It was the *Nesi'im* (pl. of *Nasi*) who were sent by Moses to spy out the land (Num. 13:1-15), and instructed on how to parcel out the land of Canaan once it was occupied (Num. 34:16ff). The title is found frequently in the Book of EZEKIEL, where it denotes the king of Judah in the time of the prophets as well as the rulers of other peoples (Ezek. 12:10; 19:1; 32:29, and more). In chaps. 46 and 47 the prophet lists the rights and duties of the ruler (*Nasi*) who will arise in "the latter days."

In the post-biblical era, coins minted by Bar-Kokhba, who led the revolt against Rome in 132-135 CE, bear the Hebrew inscription "Simon *Nasi* of Israel," a title also found in letters signed by Bar-Kokhba.

Five pairs of scholars (ZUGOT) are mentioned as heading the exposition and administration of Jewish law in the period immediately preceding the TANNAIM in the 2nd-1st centuries BCE (*Avot* 1). According to talmudic tradition, the first of each pair mentioned served as the *Nasi* (President) of the SANHEDRIN. Some scholars view the title as applied here as an anachronism, and regard its use for the President of the Sanhedrin to have begun subsequently, either with HILLEL or with R. JUDAH HA-NASI. All those who held the title were descendants of Hillel. The office, with its prerogatives, continued down to 425 CE when it was abolished by the authorities.

Beginning with R. Simeon ben GAMALIEL II, Roman officials recognized the *Nasi* (Patriarch) as the political head of the Jewish community in Erets Israel. This acknowledgment continued even during the early period of the Christian empire.

As head of the Sanhedrin, the *Nasi*, together with his court, had exclusive jurisdiction in fixing and intercalating the CALENDAR. Diaspora communities recognized the religious authority of the *Nasi*, which made it possible for him to send messengers to the far-flung Diaspora, who were authorized to establish courts and gather funds for the ACADEMIES and scholars of Erets Israel.

Most of the special regulations (TAKKANOT) recorded in the Talmud are ascribed to various *Nesi'im*. The *Nasi*, moreover, had the right to ordain scholars (*Semikhah*, see ORDINATION). A *Nasi* was addressed as *Rabban* (our Master).

The title *Nasi* continued in use through the Middle Ages but in most instances in a purely honorific sense. However, in certain communities, the title indicated an official post as head of the local Jewish community and was recognized as such by the secular authorities. Such was the case in the Fatamid Caliphate where *Nesi'im* were to be found in Jerusalem, Damascus, and Baghdad. In both Christian and Muslim Spain in the Middle Ages, there were Jews with the title *Nasi* who were officials of the Jewish community, exercising a judiciary function.

Since 1948, the title *Nasi* has been used for the President of the State of Israel.

NATHAN Prophet at the time of the kings DAVID and SOLOMON (II Sam. 7; I Chr. 17). Nathan was involved in three events related to the life of David. In the first (II Sam. 7; II Chr. 17), God appears to David, through Nathan the prophet, telling him not to build the TEMPLE, and adding that His favor will not depart from the House of David.

In the second event, after David sins with Bathsheba and causes the death of her husband, Uriah the Hittite, Nathan comes to David and tells him a parable of a poor man whose lamb is stolen. After David rules that the person who stole the lamb from the poor man merits the death penalty, Nathan bravely rebukes David and says, "You are the man." David responds with humility, "I have sinned to God" (II Samuel 12).

The third event takes place when David is old and weak. Nathan, who hears that Adonijah, David's eldest son, has anointed himself king, urges Bathsheba to go to the king and ask him to fulfill his promise that her son Solomon will be the successor. Nathan himself supports Bathsheba's claim before the king. After David announces that Solomon is his heir, Nathan takes an active part in having Solomon anointed king (I Kings 1). Nathan was not just a "court prophet" unquestioningly loyal to the king; he was a true prophet who rebuked the king when he sinned and urged him to fulfill his obligations.

NAZIR ("Nazirite"). Fourth tractate of Order NASHIM in the Mishnah. Its nine chapters deal with the laws of one who takes a NAZIRITE vow (cf. Num. 6:1-21). It is a logical extension of the preceding tractate, *Nedarim* (Vows), since it discusses the vow of self-dedication to God. Some of the subjects covered are the minimum duration of the Nazirite vow, the three things forbidden to a Nazirite, and the procedure if a Nazirite becomes defiled or breaks his vow. The last Mishnah states that both Samuel and Samson were lifelong Nazirites, having been dedicated as such before birth. The subject matter is amplified in both Talmuds and in the *Tosefta*.

NAZIRITE (from *nazar*, "to dedicate"). A person who dedicates himself to God for a specified period of time by remaining in a state of purity for the duration of the vow. The Nazirite vow applied equally to men and women and was voluntarily taken for a minimum period of 30 days. During this time, the Nazirite was forbidden to drink or derive benefit from any product of the grape vine or other intoxicating beverages, to cut his hair, or to approach a dead body. The last restriction applied even to members of one's own family. If for any reason the Nazirite did become defiled by a corpse, the Bible contains a prescription for purification: shave the head, wait seven days, and on the eighth day bring two turtle-doves and two pigeons to the priest as offerings to atone for the sin of defilement. The vow then begins anew. When the days of the vow have been fulfilled, the Nazirite must bring a lamb and a ram as offerings to the Temple, shave his hair and burn it on the altar; he is then allowed to drink wine and return to his former status (Num. 6:1-21).

The Nazirite vow was often taken to express thanks — for example, for recovery from illness or the birth of a child — or simply as an act of spiritual purification. As with other ascetic practices, the Nazirite vow was discouraged by the rabbis (*Naz.* 19a). The laws of the Nazirite apply only in Erets Israel and, ideally, only when the priests are serving in the Temple, but cases have been recorded in the Diaspora as well.

While most Nazirite vows were taken for a limited period, the Bible records two cases of lifelong Nazirites, Samson (Judg. 13:3-7) and Samuel (I Sam. 1:11). The status of the lifelong Nazirite was different, in that the prohibition against defilement by a dead body did not apply. The subject is dealt with in the tractate NAZIR.

NEDARIM ("Vows"). Third tractate of Order NASHIM in the Mishnah. Its 11 chapters deal with the laws of voluntary promises to dedicate or consecrate some object in the service of God, or to express gratitude to Him (cf. Num. 30:2-17; Deut. 23:22-24). The tractate enumerates the different expressions that may be used in making a vow, invalid VOWS, the vows of abstinence from certain food and drinks, and the cancellation of vows. MAIMONIDES states that the tractate *Nedarim* is included in the Order *Nashim* ("Women") because it includes the laws allowing a father to annul the vows of his daughter and a husband to annul the vows of his wife. The subject matter is amplified in both Talmuds and in the *Tosefta*.

NEGA'IM ("Marks of Leprosy"). Third tractate of Order TOHOROT in the Mishnah. Its 14 chapters deal with the laws concerning the infection of leprosy and its treatment by the priest (cf. Lev. 13-14). The subjects covered include: the kinds of leprosy, inspection by the priest, signs in the hair and flesh that determine leprosy, the spread of leprosy, the separation of the leper from the community, and the cleansing of the leper by the priest. The final four chapters deal with the laws of leprosy found in clothing and in the walls of a house, and the requisite sacrifices which the leper brought to complete his atonement. The subject matter is amplified in the *Tosefta*.

NEHEMIAH (5th century BCE). Jewish governor of Judah, appointed by the Persian ruler, Artaxerxes I (464-424 BCE). Nehemiah was Artaxerxes' drink steward, but when he heard of the terrible conditions in Jerusalem, he obtained permission from the king to visit the city for a limited period. He arrived in Jerusalem in 444 BCE, with an appointment as governor of Judah (in Neh. 8:9, he is referred to as the *Tirshatha*, evidently the Persian equivalent of "governor").

Nehemiah's first action was to rebuild the wall of Jerusalem, a project in which all the residents of the city participated. The construction of the wall was met with fierce opposition by the neighboring inhabitants, led by Sanballat, governor of Samaria, Geshem the Arab, and the governors of Ammon and Ashdod. This did not stop Nehemiah, and the construction continued, in which "the builders, each had his sword girded at his side" (Neh. 4:11). The wall was completed in 52 days. Nehemiah also initiated reforms within society: cancellation of the debts of the poor, and populating Jerusalem by arranging for a tenth of the population of Judah to take up residence there. Nehemiah, together with EZRA, reorganized the life of the Jewish community, and made a covenant with the people to separate themselves from foreign nations. In 432 BCE Nehemiah returned to Jerusalem, after an absence of some length. He expelled Tobiah the Ammonite from the Temple, removed foreign wives, renewed the guard rosters of priests and Levites in the

Temple, and ensured that the Sabbath was observed in Jerusalem.

NEHEMIAH, BOOK OF See EZRA AND NEHEMIAH, BOOKS

NEHUTÉ (lit. "those going down"). Aramaic designation for certain talmudic sages who traveled between Erets Israel and Babylonia (or vice versa), bringing *halakhot* and statements from one country to the other. Such communication between the Palestinian and Babylonian ACADEMIES was especially frequent during the third and fourth centuries CE, when *amoraim* of the third and fourth generations were active (see AMORA). The earliest *Nehuté* were Palestinian teachers: not only did they transmit halakhic and aggadic dicta of the Palestinian Academies and sages, but also brought various historical data to the Babylonian Academies and familiarized them with the questions raised in the Academies of Erets Israel. The first to be styled *Nehuta* was Ulla bar Ishmael, a third-century Palestinian *amora* who transmitted Palestinian customs and proverbs. Isaac Nappaha, a near-contemporary of Ulla's, was another such Palestinian *amora*. He transmitted aggadic material in his homilies and he figures in many talmudic anecdotes. Among the Babylonian scholars who later proceeded in the opposite direction was Rav Dimi (or Avdimi). His statements quoting Palestinian teachers are often introduced by a standard formula ("When Rav Dimi came, he said..."). This is also true of Ravin who is mentioned several times in the Jerusalem Talmud; like other Babylonian *Nehuté*, he left Erets Israel because of the deteriorating situation there. It has been suggested that the original purpose of the *Nehuté* was not so much to communicate Palestinian teachings as to raise money for the Palestinian Academies among the wealthier Jews of Babylonia. Even if this was the case, such "wandering scholars" did prevent a fatal split between the two great centers of Torah learning, and it is due to the *Nehuté* that a good deal of "Palestinian" material found its way into the Babylonian Talmud.

NE'ILAH (short for *Ne'ilat She'arim*, "the closing of the [heavenly] gates"). Fifth and concluding prayer service of the DAY OF ATONEMENT, the only day of the year when a fifth service is recited. The *Ne'ilah*, normally said as the sun begins to set, is regarded as the last chance to pray for forgiveness for the previous year, and, as such, is conducted with great solemnity, with its own unique, somber melody. During the cantor's repetition of the AMIDAH, which follows the silent *Amidah*, the ark is left open. This repetition incorporates a number of *piyyutim* (liturgical poems), especially of a penitential nature. Whereas during the previous ten days, the worshiper beseeches God to "write him" in the BOOK OF LIFE, during *Ne'ilah* the words are changed to "seal," indicating the final nature of the hour. In Israel, the priests ascend to bless the congregation. The service ends with the public "acceptance of the Kingdom of Heaven"; all repeat seven times "the Lord is God," recite once the verse, "Hear O Israel, the Lord is our God, the Lord is One," and conclude by reciting three times, "Blessed be the name of His glorious kingdom for ever." The SHOFAR is sounded, and all exclaim LE-SHANAH HABA'AH BI-YERUSHALAYIM, "the coming year in Jerusalem."

The term *ne'ilat she'arim* was originally the name given to the prayer recited at the closing of the gates of the Temple.

NEOLOGY (lit. "new doctrine"). Term originally used to designate the Hungarian version of REFORM JUDAISM. Following the example set by Aaron CHORIN at the beginning of the 19th century, Leopold Löw (1811-1875) and other modernist rabbis exerted pressure for educational, religious, and communal reforms. They also delivered patriotic sermons in Hungarian and gave enthusiastic support to the revolution of 1848. At that time, some radicals proposed establishing a new temple in Pest on German Reform lines, but the Neologists put an end to this scheme in the interests of communal unity. They were, however, in favor of a modern rabbinical seminary and of synods attended by rabbis and laymen which would reorganize and regulate Hungarian Jewish life. Both proposals met with fierce opposition from the Orthodox, most of whom followed the ruling of Mosheh SOFER that innovations (even if halakhically permissible) were to be avoided at all costs. Having passed a law emancipating the Jews of Hungary in 1867, the government joined forces with the Neologists of Pest in convening a Hungarian National Jewish Congress (1868-9) at which the Orthodox delegates found themselves in the minority. After objecting to proposed changes in the communal structure and failing to have the SHULHAN ARUKH (i.e., rabbinic law) accepted as supremely authoritative, most of the Orthodox representatives withdrew and their opponents were then able to run the Congress as they chose.

In 1871, however, a new law was passed authorizing the creation of separatist Orthodox communities. This measure had the effect of splitting Hungarian Jewry into Neologist, Orthodox, and "Status Quo Ante" (non-aligned traditionalist) communities, a division that lasted until 1950. The Neologists, fearing that an unbridgeable gap would separate Jews from one another, now adopted a policy of reconciliation marked by discreet conservatism. At synagogue services, an organ might be played, but women sat apart from men and there was no further changing of the prayer book. Neology also maintained *shehitah* (ritual slaughter) and *kasher* food supervision; and the rabbis trained at its Budapest seminary approximated to those of West European Orthodox congregations in their scholarship, outlook, and attire. Ideologically, differences with Hungarian ultra-Orthodoxy remained, but a further rapprochement between the two camps (in matters of Jewish education and welfare especially) followed the Holocaust. Today, uniquely in Eastern Europe, both trends coexist within one central organization, receiving state support, providing rabbis for other Communist bloc communities, and reestablishing contact with Jews in the outside world.

NEO-ORTHODOXY An ideological trend within ORTHODOXY, combining meticulous observance of rabbinic law and traditional custom with a positive attitude toward modern society and Western culture. Neo-Orthodoxy's first leading exponents were Isaac BERNAYS of Hamburg and his colleague, Jacob ETTLINGER of Altona, who had both acquired a university education and could therefore make a strong impact on German-speaking, questioning young Jews. Initially, such Orthodox "modernists" trod a dangerous path between extremists to the religious left and right. By the mid-19th century, however, social acceptance and the waning appeal of radical REFORM made it easier for Neo-Orthodoxy to gain adherents.

Its principal spokesman and ideologist from that time onward was Samson Raphael HIRSCH, whose religious and educational program, expressed in the doctrine of *Torah im Derekh Erets* ("Torah in harmony with secular culture"), first shaped the community which he headed in Frankfurt (1851-88) and then guided other separatist congregations in Central Europe. The brand of Neo-Orthodoxy created by Hirsch was dogmatic and exclusivist, insisting not only on strict adherence to the SHULḤAN ARUKH and punctilious fulfillment of the *mitsvot* (religious commandments), but also on a policy of aloofness from non-Orthodox Jews in communal matters and from any attempt to engage in academic Jewish scholarship. Yet Hirsch was quite prepared to display liberalism in other spheres: the promotion of German culture, the adoption of Western dress and a Jewish "clerical" garb, an amelioration in the position of women, the fostering of patriotism, and the preaching of the idea of a Jewish "mission" to humanity (the return to Zion being a distant prospect and life in exile a positive reality). Though strenuously pursued, not all these ideals went unchallenged in the Neo-Orthodox camp.

During and after Hirsch's time, certain innovations were characteristic of the modern traditionalism developing in Western lands. They included regular preaching in the vernacular, aesthetically improved synagogue services (with cantor and choir), the issue of new prayer books with translation (into the vernacular) and commentary, full participation in civic, professional, and even political life, and the establishment of RABBINICAL SEMINARIES for the training of religious leaders in Italy (Padua, 1829), France (Metz, 1830), England (London, 1855), and later also in Germany (Berlin, 1873). Neo-Orthodoxy, whether on the German pattern or not, also promoted a centralization of religious authority in a national CHIEF RABBINATE (France, England, Italy, the Low Countries, Denmark, etc.) and in various synagogue "roof organizations." It established an effective Jewish press and gained powerful representatives: Samuel David Luzzatto (1800-1865), Italian scholar; Nathan Marcus Adler (1803-1890), first Chief Rabbi of the British Empire; and Zadoc Kahn (1839-1905), Chief Rabbi of France. Their counterparts in the USA were Bernard Illowy (1812-1871), the only American Orthodox rabbi of his time who had earned a doctorate, and Bernard Drachman (1861-1945), a protégé of New York's Reform Temple Emanu-El, whose studies in Germany converted him into a disciple of Hirsch.

Neo-Orthodoxy did not prove to be monolithic, even in its German homeland. Azriel HILDESHEIMER differed from Hirsch in regard to Jewish communal affairs. A first major split in Neo-Orthodoxy resulted from the Prussian *Austrittsgesetz* ("Law of Secession," 1876), which enabled Hirsch and his supporters to opt out of the communal framework and establish their own separatist congregations. Hildesheimer and others saw no advantage in a move that would disrupt Jewish unity and leave most communities under the control of Reform Jews.

Hirsch's isolationist policy also extended to the Ḥibbat Zion movement (forerunner of the Zionist movement), which the Hirsch camp opposed and the Hildesheimer group supported. Before long, the issue of Political Zionism widened the rift still further, outside Germany as well. Those who followed Hirsch mostly joined the anti-Zionist Agudat Israel organization, where they found themselves in a ghetto-oriented ultra-Orthodox fraternity. Hildesheimer's followers mostly identified with the Zionist camp, and their outlook gave rise to modern or "centrist" Orthodoxy.

NESHAMAH YETERAH ("additional soul"). Popularized talmudic concept of an additional soul which God bestows on the Jew from the Sabbath's commencement to its termination (*Bétsah* 16a). This "extra soul" is thought to reveal itself in the particular sense of well-being and delight which the observant Jew experiences throughout the Sabbath. It was accorded a mystical significance by the kabbalists: in *Yom Zeh le-Yisra'el*, a favorite Sabbath table hymn composed by Isaac LURIA, the Day of Rest is termed "an additional soul for suffering people." Hence, during the HAVDALAH ceremony at the end of the Sabbath, the spices inhaled are said to provide an "aftertaste" of the *neshamah yeterah*, fortifying the individual now saddened by its loss when the Sabbath ends and a new working week begins.

NETILAT YADAYIM See ABLUTIONS

NEVELAH See TEREFAH AND NEVELAH

NEW CHRISTIANS See MARRANOS

NEW MONTH, ANNOUNCEMENT OF See MOON

NEW MOON See MOON

NEW YEAR See ROSH HA-SHANAH

NEW YEAR FOR TREES (also known as Tu bi-Shevat or Ḥamishah Asar bi-Shevat, i.e., 15 Shevat, its Hebrew date, or Rosh ha-Shanah la-Ilanot, the New Year for Trees). Arbor Day, a minor festival in the Jewish calendar. The festival is not mentioned in the Bible and is first referred to in the late Second Temple period. This special day arose as a fixed cut-off date for assessing the TITHE levied on the produce of fruit trees. Fruit grown before the New Year for Trees would be included in the grower's calculations for the old year, while all produced after that date would be taxed for the following year.

The Mishnah (*RH* 1.1) records a debate between the schools of Hillel and Shammai concerning the date for the festival. Both schools agree on the month of Shevat as the time when the winter's departure is signaled by the first tentative signs of rewakened growth in nature; but while the school of Shammai proclaimed 1 Shevat as the correct date, Hillel's disciples maintained that it should be 15 Shevat. This argument may reflect the difference in economic status between the two schools: the Hillelites, being the poorer, would have had experience with land which was slower in its recovery from the winter. At all events, in confirming the 15th of the month as the New Year for Trees, the rabbis brought this minor holiday in line with two other agricultural festivals — Passover and Sukkot — which are also celebrated in the middle of the month.

Two schoolgirls planting a tree in Jerusalem to celebrate the New Year for Trees.

With the destruction of the Second Temple, the laws of tithing were no longer relevant, since they did not apply outside the Holy Land. Yet this minor festival lived on, having acquired a somewhat different meaning. Wherever Jews lived, it helped to preserve their connection with Erets Israel. Even when they were surrounded by the winter snows of exile, Tu bi-Shevat reminded them of the sunnier climate in their ancient homeland. It was retained in the calendar as a day on which fasting was prohibited and the penitential *Taḥanun* prayers were omitted as inappropriate to such an occasion.

During the 15th century, new ceremonies and rituals marking the New Year for Trees were instituted by the mystics of Safed. Under the influence of Isaac LURIA, it became customary to celebrate the festival with gatherings at which prescribed fruits were eaten and specially written hymns and Scriptural passages were recited in praise of the Holy Land and its produce. The ceremony included drinking four cups of wine, as at the Passover *Seder*. This liturgy became popular among Sephardi communities in Europe and Muslim lands, and appropriate readings were published in a work entitled *Peri Ets Hadar* ("Goodly Fruit"), first printed in 1753.

Among the various fruits traditionally eaten on Tu bi-Shevat, pride of place was given to that of the carob tree which grew extensively throughout ancient Erets Israel. Also of special significance to the festival was the almond tree, the first to blossom in Israel after the winter; by the middle of Shevat, it is usually in full bloom, heralding the arrival of spring. In modern Israel, hundreds of thousands of new saplings are planted on Tu bi-Shevat, when schoolchildren are encouraged to participate in this activity.

NEXT YEAR IN JERUSALEM See LA-SHANAH HA'BA'AH BI-YERUSHALAYIM

NEZIKIN ("Damages"). Fourth Order of the Mishnah. Its ten tractates (BAVA KAMMA, BAVA METSI'A, BAVA BATRA, SANHEDRIN, MAKKOT, SHEVU'OT, EDUYYOT, AVODAH ZARAH, AVOT, and ḤORAYOT) deal principally with the laws of damages to property or money in the public or private domain, capital crimes, homicide, setting up courts of justice, and the authenticity of testimony. Also included is a tractate dealing with the laws of IDOLATRY (*Avodah Zarah*) and one which is a collection of moral and ethical maxims by the sages of the Mishnah (*Avot*). In the Midrash, this Order is called *Yeshu'ot* ("Salvations") based on an interpretation of Isaiah 33:6. Every tractate of this Order except for *Eduyyot* and *Avot* is expanded upon in both the Babylonian and the Jerusalem Talmud, and in the *Tosefta*, except for *Avot*.

NIDDAH ("menstrual uncleanness"). Seventh tractate of Order TOHOROT in the Mishnah. Its ten chapters deal with the laws pertaining to a woman's status during and after her menstrual cycle (cf. Lev. 15:19-30). The topics covered include: the period of menstruation and the resulting uncleanness (NIDDAH), the status of a virgin, the transmission of uncleanness, self-examination, miscarriage or abortion, the status of menstruating Gentiles, the tokens of puberty in girls, and the status of a woman who has a flux not during her usual menstrual period. The Mishnah also discusses the menstruant woman and her uncleanness with regard to sacred things, the second tithe, and the priest's share of the dough. This is the only tractate in Order *Tohorot* which is amplified in both Talmuds and the *Tosefta*.

NIDDAH Separation due to menstrual impurity. The term, in talmudic and rabbinic literature, has its origin in the Book of Leviticus. Its meaning of "separation" is reflected in the Aramaic Bible translations of the term. Throughout the Bible, this meaning remains primary, although metaphoric development connects the term to impurity in general and to sin. In Ezekiel the combination *ishah niddah*, a menstruous woman, is found. By the tannaitic period *niddah* referred to a woman who has not been cleansed of the ritual impurity of menstruation and is therefore obligated to remain separate from contact with her husband, as well as from the Temple and objects or foodstuffs which must be kept in a state of ritual PURITY.

Leviticus 15 deals with normal and abnormal genital discharges, the resulting level of ritual impurity, and purification requirements including expiation offerings for the abnormal situations. The female with the abnormal discharge (*zavah*) has prolonged periods or inter-menstrual uterine bleeding. According to the SEPTUAGINT, the male with the abnormal discharge (*zav*) suffers from gonorrhea. From the chiastic structure of this chapter, the resultant levels of impurity transferred by contact, as well as linguistic studies of the terminology, it appears that the abnormal discharges, male and female, parallel each other, while the normal male seminal discharge parallels normal female menstruation. Menstruation was considered female seed in the Book of Leviticus, a fairly common notion in ancient medical theories. Male seed impurity, transferred by contact, including coitus, can be removed by bathing and waiting until sunset. Female seed impurity, also transferred by contact, including to the male through sexual relations during menstruation, requires waiting seven days for the woman and the man who has sexual connection with her, but only bathing and waiting until sundown for one who touches her bedding or chair. The *zav* and *zavah* must wait until their discharge ceases and an additional seven clean days before bringing their sacrifices. In addition, the *zav* must bathe in "living waters" (e.g., a spring).

Although Leviticus 15 warns of contaminating the Sanctuary, it is not considered sinful to be in a state of impurity. Even sexual relations with the menstruant are merely described in terms of impurity, apparently also the view of the Sadducees. However, Leviticus 18:19 forbids sexual connection with a menstruant and threatens excision (KARET) from the people of Israel as the punishment.

The tannaitic material on *niddah*, chiefly MISHNAH, TOSEFTA, and SIFRA, have certain extra-biblical assumptions. The rabbis were agreed on the issue of bathing and assumed it held for women as well. All but the *zav* require immersion in a natural gathering of water (MIKVEH) of a specified minimum volume. Clarification of situations of doubt, for example, color of impure blood, stains, questionable birth or menstrual impurity, retroactive impurity, irregular bleeding due to pregnancy, nursing, menopause, famine, etc., were among the many aspects clarified during this period. Three additional consecutive days of uterine bleeding were considered sufficient for a woman to become a *zavah*. The minimum number of days between the end of one period and the beginning of the next (11 days) was brought as a "law of Moses from Sinai" (see HALAKHAH LE-MOSHEH MI-SINAI), thereby establishing the system by which normal or abnormal bleeding was reckoned. Apparently, internal examinations to check for menstruation were established at this time and concern about distinctions between pure and impure blood became very significant. The destruction of the Temple with the concomitant loss of the normal expiation rites led the rabbis to more restrictive legislation in order that biblical prohibitions not be transgressed.

R. JUDAH HA-NASI, at the end of the tannaitic period, decreed (*Nid.* 66a), presumably because of situations of doubt regarding pure or impure blood or confusion on the issue of counting, that if a woman sees blood for three consecutive days she keep seven clean days because of them. A law in the name of R. Huna (TJ *Ber.* 5.1), about which there was no dispute, states that even if a woman sees a drop of blood the size of a mustard seed she keep seven clean days because of it. This law, in a slightly different form, is found several times in the Babylonian Talmud in the name of R. Zeira. The additional phrase in that version, "The daughters of Israel became more strict with themselves so that even if she saw...," is remarkable in that it seems to be the only case where rabbinic literature attributed such a far reaching legal decision to women. These decrees eliminated the biblical category of *niddah* and placed all women in the more restrictive category of *zavah* with its longer purification period of seven clean days after the cessation of menses. Within a generation or two this custom became binding on Israel as a whole. It forms the basis of the laws of *niddah* in the SHULḤAN ARUKH and determines Orthodox practice today. The SAMARITANS and the KARAITES retain the biblical definition of *niddah*, (seven days), but bathing may be done in bathtubs. Although the ritual purification of the male after genital discharge was kept strictly during the talmudic period, the restrictions on his participation in public worship were loosened over the years so that now those laws are kept only by a tiny minority. The laws of *niddah*, which have come to be known as FAMILY PURITY laws, were kept quite strictly because

Blessing recited at the ritual purification of a niddah. *From a Book of Psalms and Benedictions, Pressburg, 1742.*

of the punishment of *karet.* Observance of these laws has become a distinguishing mark between ORTHODOXY and others. In the 19th century, REFORM JUDAISM, placing them in hygienic categories, disregarded the laws of *niddah* as outdated and not reflective of private bathing facilities common in many homes. CONSERVATIVE JUDAISM has suggested reducing the minimum number of days of ritual impurity from 12 to 11. However, discussion of this commandment maintains a low profile within the movement.

NIGGUN See MUSIC

NIGHT PRAYERS A series of blessings, prayers, and Scriptural verses invoking God's protection during the night, which are recited before going to sleep. The first paragraph of the SHEMA ("Hear, O Israel") is an essential component of these Night Prayers, which are therefore known in Hebrew as *Keri'at Shema (she-)al ha-Mittah* ("the reading of the *Shema* in bed"). Their recitation was prescribed by the rabbis (*Ber.* 4b), who declared that "all the demons of the night flee from one who says the *Shema* in bed" (*Ber.* 5a). A mystical variation of this thought occurs in the Zohar (III, 211a): "How many tyrants are subdued when men recite the *Shema* in bed and seek mercy from the Holy King with appropriate verses!" Two basic elements mentioned in the Talmud (*Ber.* 60b) are the *Shema*'s opening section (Deut. 6:4-9) and the benediction commencing, "Who casts the bonds of sleep on my eyes." In its present form, however, the Night Prayer contains various medieval additions: extracts from the Evening Service introduced by HASHKIVENU; the PRIESTLY BLESSING; verses from the Book of Psalms (90:17, 91, 3:2-9, 121:4, 128, 4:5); and the ADON OLAM hymn as its conclusion. Some prayer books include an introductory meditation and the EL MELEKH NE'EMAN formula prior to the *Shema*. Nowadays, many observant Jews omit a few of the incidental verses. An abbreviated version of the Night Prayer is recited by young children.

FROM THE NIGHT PRAYERS

Blessed are You, O Lord, who makes the bands of sleep to fall on my eyes and slumber on my eyelids. May it be Your will that I will lie down in peace and rise in peace. Let me not be troubled by thoughts or bad dreams or evil fancies, but let my rest be perfect before You.

NINE DAYS Final stage of public mourning for the TEMPLE's destruction which commences on the fast of SHIVAH ASAR BE-TAMMUZ. During the three week period extending from 17 Tammuz until the day after 9 Av (TISHAH BE-AV), observant Ashkenazim practice various mourning customs, avoid places of entertainment, and do not celebrate marriages (see THREE WEEKS). As from the first (New Moon) of Av, these restrictions are intensified and, until the afternoon of the tenth, Ashkenazim forgo meat and wine except on the Sabbath or at a SIYYUM celebration marking the completed study of a talmudic tractate. Many Orthodox Jews refrain from washing clothes and wearing new or elegant attire during this period. In general, Western Sephardi practice throughout the Three Weeks is close to that of Ashkenazim. Other Eastern communities, however, only ban weddings and avoid haircuts during the first ten days of Av, but there are numerous variations in their practice. Most non-Ashkenazim limit their abstention from meat, wine, haircuts, and shaving to the week in which the Tishah be-Av fast day actually occurs.

NISAN (Akkadian, *Nisannu*). First month of the Jewish religious CALENDAR; seventh month of the Hebrew civil year counting from TISHRI. It is a "full" month of 30 days and normally coincides with March-April. Its sign of the zodiac, Aries the Ram, was associated by the rabbis with the paschal lamb. Nisan is called "the first of the months of the year"

(Ex. 12:2), but in the Pentateuch (Ex. 13:4, 23:15, 34:18; Deut. 16:1) it is generally known as Abib (Heb. *ḥodesh ha-Aviv*, "the month of spring"). Nisan was the designation adopted by Jews returning from the Babylonian EXILE. It appears in later biblical sources (Est. 3:7; Neh. 2:1) as well as in the Apocrypha. Nisan's place at the head of the religious calendar may be linked with the Mishnaic statement that its first day is "the new year for kings and festivals" (*RH* 1.1).

The Israelite departure from Egypt took place in mid-Nisan, and in ancient days messengers were dispatched by the SANHEDRIN to announce the precise time for the observance of PASSOVER (*RH* 1.3). Passover is celebrated on 15-21 Nisan in Israel (on 15-22 Nisan in the Diaspora), and the counting of the OMER begins on the second night of the festival. According to the Bible (Ex. 40:17), the Tabernacle was erected in the wilderness on the first (New Moon) of Nisan; on the tenth, a generation later, the Israelites crossed the Jordan to occupy the Promised Land. Traditionally, 15 Nisan marks the beginning of the harvest season in the Land of Israel (*BM* 106b). Holocaust Memorial Day (*Yom ha-Shoah*) is today observed in Israel on 27 Nisan (in Diaspora communities, however, on 19 April). Fasting, funeral eulogies, and public displays of mourning are prohibited throughout the month, since it is *zeman ḥerutenu* ("the Season of our Freedom") commemorating Israel's redemption from slavery.

NISHMAT KOL ḤAI ("the soul of everything that lives"). Opening words of the prayer of thanksgiving recited in the Sabbath and festival morning prayers prior to the conclusion of the PESUKÉ DE-ZIMRA, the "verses of praise" which precede the SHEMA and its blessings. It is recited in all rites, with minor differences in wording.

The prayer, which includes numerous biblical verses, extols the greatness of God and dwells on man's utter inadequacy to praise Him: "Even if our mouths were filled with melody as the sea, and our tongues with song as its myriad waves...we could not thank You, O Lord our God and God of our forefathers...for even one of the thousands and tens of thousands of favors that You performed both for our forefathers and for us." The prayer goes on to enumerate examples of such great deeds: "You, O Lord our God, redeemed us from Egypt, and freed us from the house of bondage. You saved us from plague and from terrible illness..." God is then asked to continue granting His aid as He has done until now. The passage concludes with a lyrical description of God's deeds and of the Jew's pledge to praise Him for all eternity.

Nishmat is mentioned in the Talmud, but parts were evidently added during geonic times. Although the prayer makes no specific mention of the Sabbath or the festivals, it was inserted into the service on these days due to the fact that they are days of rest, which allow more time for introspection and contemplation of God's deeds. The prayer is also recited as part of the Passover SEDER (*Pes.* 118a).

NISSIM BEN REUBEN GERONDI (known as the *Ran*, an acronym of *Rabbenu Nissim*; d. c.1380). Spanish halakhist, talmudic commentator, and physician. The name Gerondi indicates that he was born in Gerona. Rabbi and DAYYAN in Barcelona, Nissim was also head of the community's rabbinic academy (*yeshivah*). He was considered the head of Spanish Jewry, and together with others was imprisoned for a time on an unknown charge. The foremost halakhic authority of his time, he received inquiries from many countries, including Erets Israel. Of the thousand or so responsa he wrote in reply, only 77 have been preserved.

Nissim's fame rests on his commentary on ALFASI's compendium of the Talmud, in which he concentrates on giving the practical legal ruling. He also wrote commentaries on 11 talmudical tractates, the most important being that on NEDARIM, which appears side by side with that of RASHI in most editions of the Talmud. He is the author of a philosophical work containing 12 homilies (*derashot*), and of a commentary on the Pentateuch of which the section on Genesis has been published. He was opposed to the study of Kabbalah, and rebuked NAḤMANIDES for devoting too much time to MYSTICISM.

NOACHIDE LAWS Seven key rules of morality which, in the rabbinic view, are the duty of all mankind to obey as the descendants of a common ancestor. Traditionally imposed on NOAH, these Noachide (or "Noachian") Laws preceded the Torah and the *Halakhah* — the legal system meant only for the Jewish people. According to Maimonides, acceptance — on the basis of the Bible — of the seven universal precepts means that any such righteous Gentile is numbered with "the pious ones among the nations of the world (ḤASIDÉ UMMOT HA-OLAM) deserving a share in the world to come" (*Tosef. Sanh.* 13.2).

NOACHIDE LAWS

(1) civil justice [the duty to establish a legal system];
(2) the prohibition of blasphemy [which includes the bearing of false witness];
(3) the abandonment of idolatry;
(4) the prohibition of incest [including adultery and other sexual offenses];
(5) the prohibition of murder;
(6) also that of theft;
(7) the law against eating flesh ["a limb"] cut from a living animal [i.e., cruelty in any shape or form] (TB *Sanh.* 56a).

Christians and Muslims are regarded by most halakhic authorities as non-idolaters and as having accepted the Noachide Laws.

NOAH Hero of the FLOOD story. Noah, who lived until the age of 950, had three sons: Shem, Ham, and Japheth. At a time when the rest of the world was corrupt (Gen. 6:12), Noah was the only just person who "walked with God" (Gen. 5:9). Noah was instructed to build an ark and to bring into it seven of every type of clean beast and two of every other type of living creature. In the 600th year of Noah's life, God caused a flood in which it rained for 40 days and 40 nights. All living creatures were destroyed except those in the ark. The waters remained at the same level for 150 days. Only then did they begin to subside. Forty days later, Noah sent out a raven and later a dove. The second time the dove was sent, it returned with an olive leaf in its beak. This was a sign that the treetops were uncovered. When Noah was finally able to leave the ark, he built an altar and made an offering of the clean beasts to God. God gave the rainbow as a sign to Noah that never again would a flood destroy the entire earth. God also gave Noah a series of commandments (the NOACHIDE LAWS). In later Jewish tradition these were seen as universal laws for all mankind. Later, after having planted a vineyard, Noah drank wine and became drunk. His son, Ham, "uncovered his nakedness." Once his drunkenness had worn off, Noah cursed Ham and his son Cana'an. Some commentators understood Ham's sin to be homosexuality; it has been suggested that Ham committed incest with his mother, Cana'an being the son of this incestuous relationship. According to critical views this story was told to justify the superiority of the ISRAELITES over the CANAANITES. The classical commentators are divided about the meaning of Genesis 6:9: "Noah was a just man and perfect in his generations." According to one view, this indicates that he was great in spite of the depravity of those around him, while according to another view he was great only in comparison to those of his generation. In parallel flood stories in the ancient Near East, there is no idea that the surviving individual was rescued because of his righteousness and moral superiority.

Noah releasing a dove from the ark. Detail of a mosaic on the ceiling of St. Mark's Cathedral, Venice, 13th century.

NOVELLAE (*ḥiddushim*). Original interpretations of passages in the Talmud. Unlike the running commentaries on the Talmud by RASHI and others, the writers of novellae sought to expound the logic implied in various talmudic passages, or else to explain and solve difficulties in the talmudic text or in the interpretations of the commentators (e.g., the TOSAFOT explain problems found in Rashi's commentary). Novellae could also be occasioned by a difficulty arising from the novellae of a previous writer. To answer these difficulties, a writer would offer his original interpretation of the talmudic passage in question, resolving the question or questions that had been raised.

In effect, some novellae form a super-commentary on those of a previous author. Thus, for example, R. Yom Tov ben Abraham Ishbili (late 13th-early 14th century) frequently takes as his point of departure difficulties in a novella of NAḤMANIDES (1194-1270).

Often the writer of novellae approaches the talmudic text directly and explains why a passage is phrased in what appears to be a peculiar way; for example, a passage that puts a later MISHNAH before one that preceeds it. A favorite method of R. Solomon ben Abraham ADRET (1235-1310) in his novellae is to raise objections to a certain question and answer in the Talmud, and proceed to demonstrate the reasoning behind the discussion. Sometimes he asks why the Talmud answers a question in the way it does when an apparently more convincing answer was available, one which he supplies. He then proceeds to explain why his proposed answer would not fully respond to the original question, and thus justifies the answer given by the Talmud.

A large collection of novellae on five talmudic tractates is to be found in the anthology compiled by R. Bezalel Ashkenazi (Egyptian talmudist, 16th century), entitled *Shittah Mekubbetset* ("Collated System"). Its compiler drew on manuscript material by various talmudists, much of which has never been published. Not the least valuable aspect of these novellae and those mentioned above is the variant readings of the talmudic text they offer. These are now being collated as the basis for a scientifically oriented edition of the Talmud.

NUMBERS Certain numbers appear frequently in the Bible, probably the most common of these being seven, which was regarded as especially auspicious (for example, the SABBATH on the seventh day of the week; the SABBATICAL YEAR each seventh year; the JUBILEE after seven sabbatical year cycles; the seven days of PASSOVER and the seven days of SUKKOT). The number ten appears in ABRAHAM's final appeal to God to save Sodom if there were ten righteous men there; in the TEN COMMANDMENTS; and in the TITHE (tenth part) that had to be given to the Levites and to the poor. Both of these numbers have subsequently been prominent in Jewish practice: seven people are called to the READING OF THE LAW on the Sabbath; seven circuits of the synagogue are made on

HOSHANA RABBAH and on SIMHAT TORAH; ten adult males are required for a prayer quorum (MINYAN); when ten adult males are present an expanded introduction to the Grace after Meals is recited. The number 12 also has special significance as represented in the months of the year, JACOB's 12 sons and the 12 TRIBES. The ZODIAC signs also total 12. Another favorite number is 40, as exemplified by the 40 days of the FLOOD; the 40 days that Moses went up to Mount SINAI (twice); the 40 days between Moses' two ascents; and the accounts in Judges (Judg. 3:11, 5:31, 8:28) in which "the land was tranquil for 40 years" (in fact, 40 may have been used in these contexts for "an extended period" rather than a precise count).

The fact that the letters of the Hebrew ALPHABET are attributed numerical values, and that numbers are written as combinations of letters, was instrumental in the development of GEMATRIA, a form of biblical exegesis in which various words and phrases are added up numerically and interpretations are then drawn from the resulting numbers (also applied in other contexts). This form of interpretation was especially prevalent among the kabbalists.

The Bible attached a certain mystic significance to numbers, as is witnessed by the fact that Jews were not to be counted directly. The census was taken by each person depositing a half-shekel coin, after which the coins were counted. When David counted his people directly rather than indirectly (II Sam. 24), pestilence struck the land and 70,000 people died. To this day, observant Jews do not count individuals for a *minyan* (prayer quorum), but recite a verse containing ten words to calculate whether a quorum is present.

HEBREW NUMBERS

1-א	7-ז	40-מ	100-ק
2-ב	8-ח	50-נ	200-ר
3-ג	9-ט	60-ס	300-ש
4-ד	10-י	70-ע	400-ת
5-ה	20-כ	80-פ	
6-ו	30-ל	90-צ	

NUMBERS, BOOK OF Fourth book of the PENTATEUCH, known in Hebrew as *Be-Midbar* ("In the [Sinai] Wilderness") from the fifth word of its opening verse. The sages, as well as Origen, refer to it as the "*Hummash* [i.e., Pentateuchal volume] of the Numbered," as both at the beginning and toward the end there is a census of the Israelites. Ancient commentators also referred to it as *Sefer Va-Yedabber* ("The Book of 'And He Spoke'"), on the basis of its first word. According to the Masoretic tradition, Numbers contains 36 chapters and 1,288 verses. The Babylonian cycle of readings (which is followed today by all Jewish communities) divides the book into ten pericopes (*sedarot*), but according to the Palestinian TRIENNIAL CYCLE, it contains 32 sections.

The book is divided into three parts, each being related to one of the major camping sites of the Israelites: 19 days in the Sinai wilderness (Num. 1:1-10:10); 38 years between the wilderness and the plains of Moab (10:11- 21:35); and about five months in the plains of Moab (22:1-36:13). Thus, according to tradition, the volume encompasses a period of about 38 1/2 years, from the second year of the Exodus until after the death of AARON.

Included in Numbers are the PRIESTLY BLESSING (6:24-26) and the third paragraph of the SHEMA (15:37-41). Traditionally, verses 35-36 of chapter 10 constitute a separate unit. In the Hebrew text, these verses are preceded and followed by an inverted letter *nun*. According to the Babylonian Talmud, they are not in their proper place and really belong in another section describing how the camp was arranged according to tribes.

THE BOOK OF NUMBERS

1: 1-4:49	The first census; the order of camping and traveling
5: 1-7:89	Various laws and offerings
8: 1-26	Purification of the Levites
9: 1-23	Passover and the fire cloud
10: 1-12:16	The order of travel; complaints
13: 1-14:45	The incident of the 12 spies and the punishments that ensued
15: 1-41	Additional laws of offerings, Sabbath observance, and the *tsitsit*
16: 1-17:28	The Korah rebellion
18: 1-19:22	Duties of the priests and Levites; laws of ritual purification
20:1 -21:35	Israel at Kadesh: the sin of Moses and Aaron, defeat of enemy kings
22:1- 24:25	The story of Balaam
25:1- 18	Phineas the zealous priest
26:1- 65	The second census
27:1- 11	The daughters of Zelophehad
27:12-23	Joshua to succeed Moses
28:1 -30:17	Sacrifices, the laws of oaths
31:1 -54	The war against Midian
32:1 -42	Tribal occupation of land east of the Jordan river
33:1 -35:34	The long journey of the Israelites, the borders of the Holy Land, the Levitical cities and cities of refuge
36:1 -13	Laws of inheritance by daughters.

Jewish tradition maintains that Numbers, like the other books of the Pentateuch, was dictated by God to Moses. According to the Documentary Hypothesis (see BIBLE: SCIENTIFIC STUDY), most of the volume is from sources J or E, as well as a combination of the two (JE). Those sections which deal with sacrifices, the priests, and the Levites, as well as numbers and dates, are all from source P.

NUMBERS RABBAH An exegetical-homiletical MIDRASH on the book of NUMBERS, part of MIDRASH RABBAH. It is divided into 23 sections. The Midrash on the first two Torah portions (*Be-Midbar* and *Naso*) is more than twice as extensive as that on the remaining eight portions of Numbers. This disparity in size indicates that the printed text of the Midrash is composed of two different Midrashim: one on Numbers 1-7 and one on Numbers 9-36.

Many of the homilies of the first part are based on a single theme; others are exegetical in character. Usually, each section opens with an anonymous psalm. Its language is basically Mishnaic HEBREW with clear evidence of an admixture of the Hebrew of the early Middle Ages. The second part is homiletical and contains many parallels with Midrash TANHUMA. The two parts were joined by a 13th-century copyist.

NUSAH (or *nosah*; "arrangement, version, style"). Hebrew term chiefly denoting (a) the liturgical or prayer rite used by a major Jewish community, and (b) the traditional "mode" to which a specific prayer or biblical passage is chanted. The word *minhag* is often employed as a synonym for "liturgical rite" (see CUSTOM).

By the early Middle Ages, various forms of ritual had developed from the ancient Babylonian and Palestinian (Erets Israel) traditions. Essentially, the differences involved those types of liturgical poetry, KINOT, PIYYUT, and SELIHOT, which certain communities had adopted. In the course of time each ritual underwent changes, and "cross-fertilization" between certain groups occurred.

The Babylonian tradition gave rise to a number of separate rituals in Spain, Portugal, and southern France, parts of North Africa, and the Near East. Its most important offshoot was *nusah Sefarad*, the Spanish rite now preserved by SEPHARDIM in Israel, Britain, Holland, the USA, and other lands. Some characteristics of this prayer rite are the arrangement of the Morning Service, the wording of KADDISH and KEDUSHAH, the formulation of the GRACE AFTER MEALS, and procedures for the READING OF THE LAW. Closely related to the Sephardi rite is *nusah edot ha-Mizrah*, the "Eastern" communities' form of worship, which is indigenous to North Africa, Syria, Turkey, and Iraq, and which now largely survives in Israel. This is true also of *minhag Téman*, the Yemenite ritual based on the prayer books of SAADIAH GAON and MAIMONIDES, which the Sephardi tradition clearly influenced. Among other rites that have disappeared was that of Provence, an unusual mixture of traditions that survived until the 19th century.

The Palestinian group had fewer representatives. One, the Romaniot or Byzantine rite (*nusah Romania*), held its own from Turkey to Greece and Sicily until the 16th century, when Sephardi refugees imposed their own form of worship on the indigenous Jewish communities. More tenacious, despite foreign influences, was the Italian or Roman rite (*minhag Italyani*), possibly the oldest in Europe, which is still practised by Italian Jews (including those who have settled in Jerusalem). Some of its characteristics are shared by the Ashkenazi rite, others are found nowhere else. The Italian prayer book was the first of its kind to be printed (1485-86). Two other prayer rites developed in the Carolingian Empire. Of these, the North French rite survived the Middle Ages only in three small Italian communities. The other, *nusah Ashkenaz*, spread with recurrent expulsions of the ASHKENAZIM from the Rhineland and Central Europe to Poland, Lithuania, and Russia; to the west and south of the Elbe; it underwent little change, but to the east it acquired some distinctive features and became known as *minhag Polin*. It is this "Polish rite," styled *minhag ha-Gera* (because of its association with ELIJAH GAON) in Israel, which now has the largest following throughout the Jewish world.

Those Ashkenazi Jews who embraced HASIDISM adopted a modified version of the Sephardi rite, based on that of Isaac LURIA (*Ari*) and therefore known as *nusah ha-Ari*. It incorporates various Sephardi liturgical elements (in the *Kaddish, Kedushah*, etc.), but is still Ashkenazi for the most part. Since 1948, attempts have been made in Israel to evolve a "unified rite" (*nusah ahid*) suitable for Jews of different origins, both a prayer book and a Passover HAGGADAH (issued by the Israel Defense Forces' Chief Rabbinate) having that aim in view. Apart from minor changes (e.g., rewording prayers related to the Temple sacrifices), CONSERVATIVE JUDAISM has retained the traditional Ashkenazi rite. In line with its own theological stand, however, REFORM JUDAISM has made sweeping changes and substitutions over the years, although some omissions are now being restored.

The term *nusah* also has the connotation of a musical style employed in the liturgical rendering of prayers. All existing rites have preserved such melodic traditions, and anyone capable of interpreting them with accuracy and tunefulness is said to "know" or "possess" a good *nusah*. There are standard modes for daily and weekly prayers, special modes for reading the Pentateuch and the Five Scrolls, as well as solemn motifs for portions of the service on festivals and on the High Holidays. See also CANTOR AND CANTORIAL MUSIC; CANTIL-LATION; LITURGY; MAHZOR; MUSIC; PRAYER; and PRAYER BOOK.

OATHS See VOWS

OBADIAH Fourth of the MINOR PROPHETS in the Prophetical section of the Bible. The shortest book in the Bible, it consists of a single chapter with 21 verses. Nothing is known of the prophet himself, not even the name of his father or of his city. According to the Midrash (*Yal. Shimoni* 2.549), he was a descendant of Eliphaz, one of JOB's friends, and a convert (hence his father's name was not mentioned) who preached the downfall of his own country. According to another tradition, he was the same Obadiah who hid the prophets of God during the reign of Ahab and Jezebel (1 King 18:3-7).

The Book of Obadiah contains an anti-Edomite oracle, as well as a Day of Judgment prophecy. When Jerusalem fell in 586 BCE, the Edomites not only exulted in the Judahites' humiliation, but actively assisted their Babylonian foes by intercepting the refugees and occupying the Negev. For Edom's violence against Judah, the prophet prophesies that Edom is to be abandoned by its allies and that God will destroy its wise men and its warriors. Finally, verses 15 to 22 describe the imminent Day of the Lord, when the house of Jacob will acquire the possessions of Edom. Scholarly views on the composition of the book are characterized by two principal approaches: one maintains the essential integrity of the book, while the other regards it as two separate works.

THE BOOK OF OBADIAH	
Verses 1 — 16	The guilt of Edom and its punishment
Verses 17 — 21	The future restoration of Israel

OFFERINGS See SACRIFICES AND OFFERINGS

OHOLOT ("Tents"). Second tractate of Order TOHOROT in the Mishnah. Its 18 chapters deal primarily with two subjects: the impurity caused by physical contact with a corpse and the impurity caused by entering a tent or house containing a corpse (cf. Num. 19:11, 14-16). The Mishnah discusses the uncleanness caused by blood, hair, teeth, and nails, the uncleanness contracted by the house itself and the objects within it, the spreading of uncleanness, the case of a stillborn child and the uncleanness contracted by walking over an unmarked grave. The purification from this uncleanness was carried out by immersion in a ritual bath (MIKVEH) and the besprinkling with the "living waters" mixed with the ashes of the RED HEIFER. The subject matter is amplified in the *Tosefta*.

OLAM HA-BA AND OLAM HA-ZEH See AFTERLIFE

OLD AGE See AGED

OMER ("A sheaf"). The offering of new barley brought to the Temple on the second day of PASSOVER. The Omer measure is one tenth of an ephah (i.e., 2.2 liters), and therefore a relatively modest offering (see Lev. 23:9ff.), but until the Omer had been brought to the priest in the Temple, none of the new produce could be eaten. The biblical instruction is to bring this harvest offering "on the day after the sabbath." This led to a bitter controversy between the Pharisaic rabbis and the SADDUCEES. The rabbis interpreted the term "sabbath" in the text to mean the first day of the Passover festival, i.e., the 16th day of the month of Nisan. For the Sadducees, and later also for the KARAITES, it meant the weekly Sabbath. Since the Bible goes on to instruct that "from the day on which you bring the sheaf of the wave offering — the day after the sabbath — you shall count seven weeks," and that the 50th day shall be the festival of SHAVU'OT, the Sadducees maintained that Shavu'ot always fell on a Sunday, exactly seven weeks after the Sunday following Passover. Because of this controversy, the rabbis gave emphasis to reaping the new grain on 16 Nisan, even if that day itself happened to be a Sabbath. The procedure was carried out with great ceremonial and public proclamations (*Men.* 10.1), and has been revived in agricultural settlements in modern Israel.

With the destruction of the Temple and the cessation of all offerings (see SACRIFICES AND OFFERINGS), the practice of counting the days between Passover and Shavu'ot survived on rabbinic authority only. From the night of 16 Nisan until the end of the seven-week period, every day is counted separately, the number of days and weeks of the Omer period being mentioned. The counting is done at night during the Evening Service (in accordance with the Babylonian custom; in Erets Israel and in Egypt, it was once permissible also during the day). A custom that developed in synagogues was to have a calendar on the wall indicating which day had been reached in the counting of the Omer (*sefirat ha-Omer*). This practice gave rise to a new form of Jewish ritual art (the "Omer counter").

While the origin of counting the Omer is traced to the biblical regulation, various rabbinic interpretations stress its relevance for Jews in the post-Temple era. Maimonides explained that the daily counting of the interval between Passover and Shavu'ot expresses the eagerness of the people to celebrate the latter festival, marking the anniversary of the Revelation and the giving of the Torah. Other teachers, in similar vein, have stressed that the freedom festival of Passover is incomplete without the Torah festival of Shavu'ot, since freedom without law can be destructive. A bridge is therefore needed to connect both festivals, with their joint ideal of freedom with law. The counting of the Omer is such a bridge.

In the course of time, the weeks of the Omer period became overshadowed by sadness and semi-mourning: no new clothes were worn, for example, and haircuts were prohibited. The reasons for this are obscure and they are debated by Jewish scholars. The Talmud gives a possible clue when it refers to the death of 24,000 students of Rabbi AKIVA following a plague which broke out during the weeks between Passover and Shavu'ot. This is said to have occurred during the Bar Kokhba revolt against Rome (132-135 CE). In that case, the extent of the tragedy must have impressed itself on the memory of the Jewish people; but others have suggested that the story of the plague was concocted to provide an opportunity for the commemoration of various tragic events during the Bar Kokhba uprising which could not be marked openly under the Romans.

In rabbinic law, the Omer period is marked by various restrictions: pious Jews forgo haircuts and often avoid shaving, marriages are not solemnized, and public festivities are not held. Exceptions to this rule are the remaining days of the month of Nisan after Passover (although custom varies), the New Moon and LAG BA-OMER (the 33rd day of the Omer), and latterly — among religious Zionists — Israel's INDEPENDENCE DAY (5 Iyyar) as well as Jerusalem Day (28 Iyyar).

OMNAM KEN ("Indeed it is so"). Opening words and title of a penitential poem (*Seliḫah*) which Ashkenazi congregations recite during the KOL NIDRÉ Service on the eve of the Day of Atonement. Structurally a Hebrew alphabetical acrostic of 11 two-line stanzas, this poem acknowledges man's domination by the evil impulse, but asks God to pardon His contrite people, each stanza concluding with the one-word response, *salaḫti* ("I have forgiven"). Its author, Yom Tov ben Isaac of Joigny, left France and settled in York, England. When the small Jewish community there, besieged in the local castle, was offered the choice between apostasy and slaughter, Yom Tov reputedly inspired his fellow Jews to perform an act of mass suicide on 16 March 1190, declaring: "We prefer a glorious death to a shameful life."

ONEG SHABBAT (lit. "Sabbath delight"). The obligation to rejoice on the Sabbath, in accordance with Isaiah 58:13: "You shall call the Sabbath a delight." This is taken to include partaking in three meals during the Sabbath (at the time of the Talmud only two meals were eaten), and making each of them into a festive occasion, replete with the singing of ZEMIROT (table hymns). Special dishes should be served as part of the Sabbath delight. The third meal of the day, the *se'udah shelishit* (see SE'UDAH), is especially a time for singing various *zemirot* and for Torah discourses.

When the poet Ḫayyim Naḫman Bialik (1873-1934) arrived in Erets Israel in the 1920s, he instituted an *Oneg Shabbat* program on Sabbath afternoons, extending into the evening. This included the communal singing of Sabbath songs and communal Bible study, a lecture or discourse on the Bible, and refreshments. This offered an opportunity to enjoy the Sabbath even to the non-observant. Bialik's innovation was adopted in many synagogues and communities.

ORAL LAW (*Torah she-be'al-peh*). Judaism's code of law as recorded in rabbinic literature, based primarily upon rabbinic interpretation of the WRITTEN LAW found in the Pentateuch. The talmudic sages stated, as a principle of Judaism, that the Oral Law, which was to be transmitted by oral teaching from master to disciple, was communicated to Moses by God at Mount Sinai simultaneously with the Written Law. This was based upon their interpretation of the verse (Ex. 24:12): "The Lord said to Moses, Come up to Me to the mountain and I will give you the stone tablets and the Torah and the Commandment which I have inscribed to instruct them." R. SIMEON BEN LAKISH said, "This verse is to be understood as follows: 'the stone tablets' refer to the Ten Commandments; 'and the Torah' refers to the Pentateuch; 'and the Commandment' refers to MISHNAH; 'which I have inscribed' refers to the Prophets and the Writings; 'to instruct them' refers to GEMARA; teaching that all were given to Moses at Sinai" (*Ber.* 5a). The term TORAH, originally applied to the Pentateuch, was later commonly used to cover the entire Written Law together with the Oral Law.

Ongoing interpretation of the written code was a necessity, in light both of the concise nature of the Written Law and changes in circumstances over the centuries. For example, the Written Law prescribes: "You shall not do any work on the Sabbath" (Ex. 20:10); the Oral Law had to define precisely which "work" constitutes a violation of this injunction. As new situations arose, the expounders of the Oral Law, the *ḥakhamim* or SAGES, would apply a particular ruling (*halakhah*) which then became an integral part of the Oral Law.

In the course of time, the content of the Oral Law grew. The changes in Jewish life — from Babylonian Exile to Return to Zion to renewed Exile — necessitated further interpretation of the basic Written Law, as well as the adoption of new regulations for exigencies unanticipated in that code. This proliferating process began in the days of Ezra (mid-fifth century BCE), described as "a SCRIBE [*sofer*] expert in the Torah of Moses" (Ezra 7:6), who "expounded" the Written Law ("Ezra set his heart to expound [*li-derosh*] the Torah" (Ezra 7:10)). From this verb is derived the term MIDRASH, the method employed by the sages to infer from Scripture the rulings (*halakhot*) which comprise the Oral Law. These *halakhot* were designated *divré Soferim*, "the pronouncements of the Scribes," and were given the status of biblical law. Indeed, the sages had to state "The pronouncement of the Scribes are far more precious than the words of the Bible" (TJ *Pe'ah* 2.6 (17a)). This assertion was made to counteract the contention of the SADDUCEES that there is no biblical sanction for the Oral Law.

The Oral Law also includes rulings of rabbinic origin not derived from the expounding of Scripture, such as the observances commanded by the sages for the holidays of PURIM and ḤANUKKAH, and the kindling of CANDLES on Sabbath and Festival eve. The sages added other rulings: some in order to insure the observance of biblical law, known as GEZERAH; others "for the welfare of society," known as TAKKANAH. Also included in Oral Law are certain practices which arose as a matter of community CUSTOM, known as *minhag*.

The Oral Law is not a definitive code; it includes many diverse and even conflicting opinions. Concerning these the sages said, "All of them are the words of the living God" (*Er.* 13a). It was only through discussion and disputation that a definitive ruling (*halakhah*) could be established. HERMENEUTIC laws of deduction were laid down for this purpose.

During the period of the TANNAIM (c. second century CE) several collections were made of rulings inferred from Scripture and appended to the pertinent verses (halakhic *midrashim*), in addition to collections handed down from previous scholars. By the beginning of the third century, halakhic opinions had become so scattered among the various scholars that R. JUDAH HA-NASI decided to gather them and arrange them according to subject-matter in six major divisions (*shishah sidré mishnah*). The result was the MISHNAH, the basic text of the Oral Law. Several disciples of R. Judah gathered tannaitic opinions not included in the Mishnah, in a collection called the TOSEFTA. All the opinions assembled in these collections formed the basis of further discussions of the AMORAIM, in the academies of Erets Israel and Babylonia. By the beginning of the sixth century these discussions were collected and edited in the Jerusalem and Babylonian TALMUDS. These, particularly the latter, became in turn the basis of further discussion in the following centuries (in fact, to this day).

The subsequent literature of the Oral Law can be divided into the following categories: NOVELLAE (*ḥiddushim*) and TALMUD COMMENTARIES; CODES (such as the *Mishneh Torah* of MAIMONIDES and the SHULḤAN ARUKH) with their commentaries; RESPONSA (*teshuvot*) to halakhic queries. Another category of compositions in the medieval period was arranged according to the 613 biblical COMMANDMENTS derived by the rabbis from the Written Law.

Refusal to accept the Oral Law and the intention to rely solely on the Written Law characterized various groups in Jewish history. The SAMARITANS relied solely on the Pentateuch, while the Sadducees and ESSENES rejected the Pharisaic (rabbinic) tradition but had their own ways of interpreting the Written Law. The KARAITES (from the eighth century) relied solely on the Written Law without any subsequent interpretation. Reform Judaism, while not regarding the Oral Law as binding, has veered between respect and rejection. The more recent trend (for example in the responsa of Solomon Freehof) is to regard the Oral Law as a guide providing advice and tradition but not authority. The official relevant body of the CONSERVATIVE movement, the Committee on Jewish Law and Standards, seeks to anchor its decisions on the Written Law although actual practice within Conservative congregations often deviates from halakhic tradition.

ORDINATION (*semikhah*). The ritual transmission of spiritual authority. Traditionally, God gave authority to MOSES who passed it on to JOSHUA. In conformity with the act of Moses (Num. 27:18-23) in investing Joshua as his successor, the laying on of hands is usually part of the ceremony.

The Mishnah (*Avot* 1.1) records the transmission of the authority through Joshua to the Men of the GREAT ASSEMBLY. In time, ordination became a ceremony performed in the SANHEDRIN, with the consent of the PATRIARCH, by the ordinand's teachers. The recipient received the title RABBI and was endowed with full judicial authority. *Semikhah* could be conferred only in Erets Israel: the credentials given by the Babylonian ACADEMIES gave lesser authority and conferred the title *rav*.

Although the original Sanhedrin disappeared with the destruction of the Second Temple (70 CE), ordination continued at the Sanhedrin reconstituted under R. JOHANAN BEN ZAKKAI. After the suppression of the Bar Kokhba revolt (135), ordination was forbidden by the Roman emperor, Hadrian, but persisted for many years — until 425 according to some opinions, until the 11th century, according to others. In the meantime, Jewish communities had become established far and wide, and they needed qualified teachers and judges. This office was denominated differently according to time and place, but the title "rabbi" seems to have become general. It became customary for the candidate to present a diploma signed by one or more Torah scholars. This document became known as *Hattarat Hora'ah* (permission to teach); it is often referred to as *semikhah* but has not the authority of the formal *semikhah*. The diploma was given informally after examination by the teachers at the ordinand's *yeshivah* or by some rabbi of eminence elsewhere. The formula employed would vary, but the phrase *yoreh yoreh, yadin yadin* (he may teach, he may render decisions) was considered essential.

Early in the 19th century, EMANCIPATION began to transform Jewish life in Central and Western Europe. A new style of rabbi was needed, RABBINICAL SEMINARIES with published curricula were established and conferred the title of rabbis. This change of style did not reach the large Jewish communities of Eastern Europe, or the Muslim world, where *yeshivah* training followed by individual ordination remained the rule. This has been followed in Israel.

The American Jewish community sustains every variety of practice (including the ordination of WOMEN among the non-Orthodox), from the East European-style Orthodox, to the elaborate pageantry developed by the Reformers. For the Conservatives the Jewish Theological Seminary does not confer the old-style *semikhah* but the decree of "rabbi, preacher, and teacher" reserving the possibility of ordination with the traditional *yoreh yoreh, yadin yadin* to specialized post-graduate students.

An attempt by R. Jacob Berav of Safed to restore ordination in the plenary sense (1538) failed owing to the opposition of the Jerusalem Rabbinate. Suggestions that a Sanhedrin might be convened, which would also have restored the original *semikhah*, were aired after the establishment of the State of Israel in 1948 but received little support.

The synagogue at Essen, Germany, with an organ behind the Ark. The Synagogue was built in 1913 and destroyed by the Nazis in 1938.

ORGAN Musical instrument which became part of Christian worship in about the seventh century. Prior to 1700, a few rabbis sanctioned the use of an organ in northern Italy and Prague for festive occasions rather than for Sabbath services. It was, however, the regular playing of an organ on Sabbaths and holy days, an innovation first promoted by Israel JACOBSON in Westphalia and Berlin which the Hamburg temple (1818) soon emulated, that was characteristic of the emergence of REFORM JUDAISM and split German Jewry into two opposing camps. Among the halakhic arguments against this departure from tradition, published by Akiva EGER, Mosheh SOFER, and other representatives of ORTHODOXY, were the copying of non-Jewish custom (ḤUKKAT HA-GOY) and the infringement of Sabbath laws when the organ was used on that day. For their part, the early Reformers quoted various precedents, including the *magrefah*, an instrument played in the ancient Temple of Jerusalem, assumed by some to have been a sort of water organ.

By 1850, the installation of an organ had begun to identify Reform synagogues in Hungary, England, the United States, and other countries. While Isaac Noah MANNHEIMER excluded the use of an organ from his Vienna *Stadt-Tempel*, so as to preserve communal unity, some otherwise traditional congregations in France followed the new trend. Many Conservative synagogues in the US now also allow the playing of an organ on Sabbaths and festivals, at least by a non-Jew. Orthodoxy throughout the world maintains its halakhic objection to the practice, but some modern Orthodox congregations (in England, for example, since the late 19th century) do permit organ accompaniment to wedding and civic services held on weekdays.

ORLAH (lit. "uncircumcised" — the fruit of a tree during its first three years). Tenth tractate of Order ZERA'IM in the Mishnah. Its three chapters discuss the laws forbidding the derivation of any benefit from fruit trees in Erets Israel during the first three years of growth (cf. Lev. 19:23-25). The Mishnah describes which trees are exempt from the laws of *orlah*, the law applying to mixtures of *orlah* with other tithes or permitted fruits, and using *orlah*-fruit dye or cooking food over a fire fueled by *orlah*-fruit peelings. The law against using *orlah* is a rabbinic injunction also outside Israel. The subject-matter is amplified in the Jerusalem Talmud and the *Tosefta*.

ORPHAN See WIDOW AND ORPHAN

ORTHODOXY Term applied to the religious beliefs and practices of those Jews in Central and Western Europe who, from the late 18th century, opposed the changes brought about by the EMANCIPATION, Jewish Enlightenment (HASKALAH), and the innovations of REFORM JUDAISM. Traditional JUDAISM is distinguished by "orthopraxy", faithful adherence to the established practices (laws and customs) of the Torah as a Divinely ordained "way of life."

In positive terms, therefore, Orthodoxy is synonymous with classical rabbinic Judaism as developed and reflected by the rabbis through the ages. The Orthodox Jew accepts that the WRITTEN LAW (Torah) is Divinely revealed, that the halakhic process of the ORAL LAW is Providentially guided and therefore authoritative. However, even more than creedal affirmations, Orthodoxy stresses practical adherence to the SHULḤAN ARUKH code, involving a high degree of religious observance in daily life.

In negative terms, Orthodoxy sees itself as the only legitimate bearer of the Jewish tradition, rejecting all other modern Jewish trends as deviations.

Trends in Orthodoxy (1800-1939). The radical changes in Jewish life resulting from the Emancipation were both social and intellectual. For Jews, the most important consequence of the Napoleonic era was the possibility of gaining admission to the social and political life of the outside world, together with the opportunities which this afforded both to escape from the poverty and constrictions of the ghetto and for economic and cultural betterment. In the intellectual sphere, the Haskalah, in its early phases at least, sought to replace the authority of religion with the spirit of free rational inquiry. While offering vastly attractive opportunities to the Jew as an individual, this new age clearly threatened the traditional Jewish way of life. As emancipated German and Hungarian Jews moved into the wider society, their traditional dress, mannerisms, and religious obligations (e.g., the dietary laws and abstaining from work on the Sabbath) became socially burdensome and embarrassing, while various aspects of the traditional mode of worship were viewed as aesthetically and intellectually unacceptable.

Still more alarming to traditional Jewish leadership was the development and growth of the Reform movement. Its most radical exponents, Abraham GEIGER and Samuel HOLDHEIM, not content with ritual and liturgical changes, proceeded to challenge the halakhic basis of Judaism. In the view of the outraged traditionalists, the very nature of Judaism itself was being systematically distorted and misrepresented. Thus, the self-definition of Reform's opponents as "Orthodox" Jews had a twofold significance: the repudiation of what they regarded as an unauthentic version of the Jewish faith coupled with a conscious decision to uphold traditional belief and practice, even if this meant forfeiting some opportunities of the new age. The religious hallmarks of Orthodoxy therefore include strict adherence to Jewish law and to the traditional Hebrew liturgy; rejection of modern Bible criticism; a ban on ORGAN music at Sabbath and festival prayer services; and separate seating for men and women in the synagogue.

From the very beginning, there was little agreement among the Orthodox as to how these various challenges might be countered. Some, rejecting Enlightenment values altogether, proclaimed a ban of EXCOMMUNICATION against the Reformers and urged the faithful to withdraw into even greater isolation from the world outside. This approach was advocated by R. Mosheh SOFER of Pressburg (Bratislava) and characterized much of Hungarian Orthodoxy, as well as the Ḥasidic communities and East European Jewish masses who were not reached by the Emancipation until after World War I. It also found expression in the anti-Zionist Agudat Israel world movement.

Others, while aware of the dangers, also recognized the validity of the values of the modern world and endeavored to incorporate them within the framework of traditional Judaism. Rabbinical leaders of this type, who included Samson Raphael HIRSCH, Azriel HILDESHEIMER, and members of the Breuer and Carlebach families, created the NEO-ORTHODOXY from which modern or "centrist" Orthodoxy was to emerge in the West. A parallel line of development in Eastern Europe can be traced from ELIJAH GAON of Vilna, R. Ḥayyim of Volozhin (1749-1821), and the BERLIN and SOLOVEICHIK families, to R. Isaac Jacob Reines (1839-1915) and Abraham Isaac KOOK who pioneered modern religious Zionism.

The human losses and general destruction wrought by the HOLOCAUST proved especially damaging to Orthodoxy, which had its major demographic reserves in those areas (such as Poland) in which the Jewish communities were exterminated. The religious faith of Holocaust survivors was often shattered by the slaughter of millions of innocent men, women, and children. During and after World War II, some eminent heads of YESHIVOT and leaders of ḤASIDISM managed to escape to North America and Palestine, where they set about reorganizing and rebuilding their institutions.

American Orthodoxy. By 1880, the American Jewish community (then numbering about 250,000) was mostly of German origin, economically well placed, but religiously on the decline. Of the approximately 200 major congregations then in existence, perhaps a dozen were still nominally Orthodox; the rest were Reform. Over the next four decades (1880-1920), some two million Jews, mostly from Eastern Europe, arrived in the United States. Most had lived traditional Jewish lives, but they came without religious leaders or teachers, and were concentrated in New York and other large cities, where economic subsistence and adaptation to American life became their primary concerns. Jewish learning yielded to public school education, which was both mandatory and the key to Americanization; Sabbath observance gave way to economic necessity, Jewish values to those of the dominant society. By the late 1930's, most Jews had left the "ghetto" areas of first settlement for less "Jewish" neighborhoods. The process of assimilation was already under way, and after the Holocaust it seemed to most observers that Orthodoxy in the New World was doomed.

However, Orthodoxy experienced a revival, as a result of a combination of two factors: the arrival of militantly Orthodox scholars, heads of *yeshivot*, and Ḫasidic leaders, coming from Europe immediately before and after World War II; and the growth of an American-born Orthodox vanguard which had survived the "melting pot" process with its traditionalism intact. This was largely due to a number of pioneering *yeshivot* in New York, one being the Rabbi Isaac Elchanan (Etz Chaim) Theological Seminary (1897), the forerunner of Yeshiva University; and also the Young Israel congregational movement (1912).

Torah Umesorah, an Orthodox body established by Rabbi Shraga Feivel Mendlovitz of Yeshiva Torah Vodaath, from 1944 organized a network of Hebrew day schools and post-high school *yeshivot* throughout the USA and Canada. Today, in addition, there are more than 40 *yeshivot* for advanced talmudic studies in the USA.

The most important institutes for the training of Orthodox rabbis and scholars are, first and foremost, New York's Yeshiva University and the Hebrew Theological College in Chicago (1922). The largest Orthodox synagogue body, the Union of Orthodox Jewish Congregations of America, is responsible for the international O-U certification for reliable *kasher* food.

The head of a traditional yeshivah *with his disciples.*

As elsewhere, Orthodoxy in the USA comprises two distinct camps, institutionally as well as philosophically. Unlike the "right wing" (ultra-Orthodox) or traditional group, the modern or "centrist" Orthodox believes in:

(1) Participation in such aspects of general culture as university life, the arts, and science.

(2) Cooperation with all Jews, Conservative, Reform, and secular, in matters of mutual community (but not religious, theological or practical) concern, e.g., through the Synagogue Council of America, the New York Board of Rabbis, and the Presidents' Conference.

(3) Recognition of the State of Israel and participation in the World Zionist Organization.

(4) A more flexible perception of the *halakhah* than previously exercised.

Modern Orthodoxy's religious leadership is to be found in the Rabbinical Council of America (RCA), whose members have long considered Joseph B. Soloveichik to be their guide and mentor.

The institutions of Orthodox Jews in the traditional ("Torah-true") camp include the Union of Orthodox Rabbis (Agudath Harabbonim, 1902), the Rabbinical Alliance (1944), Agudat Israel, all of the Ḫasidic communities from Lubavich (Ḫabad) to the extreme anti-Zionist and anti-Israel Satmar group, and the traditional Lithuanian-style *yeshivot*. Fortified by an exceptionally high birth rate and reducing their involvement in general culture to a bare minimum, they have established large, economically viable communities, each with its own network of social and educational facilities. Current trends suggest that they have not only adapted themselves successfully to the American environment, but are also overtaking the modern Orthodox, who are themselves undergoing a shift to the religious right.

Other Diaspora Communities. Whereas Orthodox Jews constitute the smallest religious "trend" in the USA, the proportion among synagogue-affiliated Jews elsewhere in the Diaspora is much higher, sometimes reaching 80 percent. Traditional Judaism retains its hold among Sephardi-Eastern communities, and in places such as Latin America and certain East European communities, the Orthodox predominate among religious Jews, although in these countries most Jews have no religious affiliation whatsoever.

Alongside the old-established *École Rabbinique* (1829), three or four traditional *yeshivot* have sprung up in France, which now boasts the world's fourth largest Jewish community. Divisions within European Orthodoxy are now more organizational than ideological, and one sign of growing unity and cooperation has been the Conference of European Rabbis established in 1957.

Since the Victorian era, a decorous type of modern Orthodoxy has characterized most synagogues throughout the British Commonwealth. Greater London's United Synagogue (1870) maintains a large network of congregations, a prestigious *bet din* (rabbinical court), nationwide *kashrut* supervision, and a Chief Rabbinate. Parallel bodies, within the same religious framework, are the Federation of Synagogues (1887), the Spanish and Portuguese Jews' Congregation (1701) which now also represents various Eastern synagogues, and other congregations and *batté din* outside the capital. On the traditional right stand the Union of Orthodox Hebrew Congregations (1926), a few Ḥasidic groups, and the *yeshivah* community of Gateshead in northern England. About 65% of Britain's synagogue-affiliated Jews belong to synagogues with an Orthodox commitment although this is not always reflected in their lifestyle. The British pattern is largely reflected in the communities of the British Commonwealth (present and past).

For the State of Israel, see ISRAEL, STATE OF.

OUZIEL, BENZION MEIR ḤAI Rabbi and communal leader in Erets Israel (1880-1953). Born in Jerusalem, he was appointed Chief Rabbi of Jaffa district in 1911. His communal activies also took him to Salonika, where he was made Chief Rabbi in 1921. In 1923, he was appointed Chief Rabbi of Tel-Aviv and in 1939, the Sephardi Chief Rabbi (RISHON LE-TSIYYON) of Palestine.

Ouziel's scholarship found expression in numerous responsa, published in a number of volumes entitled *Mispheté Ouziel* (1935-64); sermons, addresses and writings, published in 1939 under the name *Mikhmanné Ouziel*; a philosophic work entitled *Hegyoné Ouziel* (1953-54) and a two-volume legal work, *Shaaré Ouziel* (1944-50).

Ouziel was an active advocate of religious Zionism and believed that the re-establishment of a Jewish state in the land of Israel was part of God's plan. He preached and wrote tirelessly to encourage Jewish settlement in Israel. Jewish nationalism was, of necessity, linked to faithfulness to the Torah and, in his view, the national structure would have to be built upon the firm foundation of Torah.

Rabbi Ouziel (center), carrying a Torah Scroll, 1918. (Next to him, Chaim Weizmann).

P

PAGANISM See IDOLATRY

PALESTINE TALMUD See TALMUD

PANTHEISM The philosophical doctrine which identifies God with nature. The classical phrase used for describing pantheistic theories is "God is all and all is God." The chief and most systematic philosopher of pantheism is Baruch (Benedict) SPINOZA (1632-1677), a Jew who was excommunicated for his views by the Portuguese community in Amsterdam.

Pantheistic ideas are traceable to early Greek thinkers and their idea of emanation as a theory which explains the origin of the universe. Through Neo-Platonism (see PLATONISM AND NEO-PLATONISM), Jewish medieval scholars were familiar with such writings. Solomon IBN GABIROL in his *Mekor Ḫayyim* has a neo-Platonic system of graded emanation as an explanation of creation from the single source which is God (see SEFIROT). Abraham IBN EZRA wrote, "God is One. He is the creator of all and He is all... God is all and all comes from Him" (Comm. on Gen. 1:26; Ex. 23:21).

Some writers have even claimed to discover pantheistic implications in classical rabbinic theology with its description of God as *Ha-Makom*, "the Place." This teaching could mean more than God's omnipresence, and could point to the actual identification of God with the reality of the material world in every place. PHILO seems to have understood the rabbinic concept in this way, and it can be seen as a derivative of the emphasis on the concept of the immanence of God.

More clearly close to possible pantheistic concepts are ideas put forward by the kabbalists and Ḫasidic theorists (see MYSTICISM). The ZOHAR, and particularly Moses CORDOVERO, explained their systems of the *Sefirot* describing the Divine emanations from the pure spirit to the material world, suggesting a kind of unity between God and the world. Menaḫem Mendel of Liubavich (1789-1866) wrote, "There is no existence whatsoever apart from His existence" (*Derekh Mitsvotekha*). The contemporary philosopher, Hugo Bergman, described Abraham Isaac KOOK's system as "mystical pantheism." Kook taught that all reality is a manifestation of God in a myriad of forms which have no reality without Him.

The Jewish thinker who worked within the framework of Jewish life and thought, and who came the closest to pantheism, was Nachman KROCHMAL (1785-1840). Taking some of the kabbalistic theories, he draws the conclusion that God created the world out of Himself.

However, in spite of all such teachings which seem to leave room for pantheistic concepts, none represents pure pantheism. This is because none of the above Jewish systems identifies God as the universe. To teach that He is the soul or the source or the vital force from which all things emanate still does not say that the emanated world forms a unity with the emanating God. God is immanent, that is, He is ever present and close to all things which He created, but He is still transcendent, that is, over and above the universe which owes its existence to Him. Judaism, in all its varied expressions, is absolute in its theistic emphasis. There is, in Judaism, a transcendental God who acts separately on the world and exercises His separate will on the world.

PARADISE See EDEN, GARDEN OF

PARAH ("Cow"). Fourth tractate of Order TOHOROT in the Mishnah. Its 12 chapters deal with the laws of the choosing, slaughtering and burning of the RED HEIFER (cf. Num. 19:1-22). This animal's ashes mixed with pure spring water were used to purify those who came in contact with the dead. The Mishnah discusses the age of the Red Heifer, its invalidity by the presence of non-red hair, the manner of slaughtering and burning, the procedure for mixing the ashes with the water and the purification of those who were unclean by the sprinkling of this mixture. The mystery of the Red Heifer (which has not existed since the destruction of the Temple) was that it purified those who were defiled, yet defiled those involved in its preparation. Even the wisest of men, King Solomon, could not understand this commandment. Therefore it is reckoned as one of the *ḫukkim* — those commandments which are beyond comprehension by human reason. The subject matter is amplified in the *Tosefta*.

PARASHAH (pl. *parashiyyot*). A section of the PENTATEUCH. Sephardi Jews use the term to denote both the 54 weekly portions of the Pentateuch read in the SYNAGOGUE in the Sabbath Morning Service and the four special sections

(*Shekalim, Zakhar, Parah,* and *Ha-Hodesh*) read on specific occasions (see SABBATHS, SPECIAL). Ashkenazim generally employ the term *sidrah* (the Aramaic of *seder*, "order") to denote the weekly portion and apply *parashah* (or *parshah*) to the sub-divisions into which that portion is divided, for each of which a different worshiper is called to the READING OF THE LAW.

The weekly portions are known by the first or most important word of the opening verse, starting with *Be-Reshit, Noah, Lekh Lékha*. The printed text of the Pentateuch, in which worshipers in the synagogue follow the Torah reading, is marked to indicate the beginning of the various portions read for each person called to the reading. At the Afternoon Service on Sabbath afternoon, the first portion of the coming Sabbath is read; likewise on MONDAY AND THURSDAY mornings (unless these coincide with a New Moon or a fast day).

PARDES Word of Persian origin, meaning an area surrounded by a fence; probably related to the Greek *paradeisos*, which became the English "paradise." It appears three times in the Bible (Song 4:13; Eccl. 2:5; Neh. 2:8). In one of the earliest Jewish mystical passages, it refers to Divine wisdom (*Hag.* 14b). In the Middle Ages, it was used as an acrostic for the four schools of Bible interpretation: P=*peshat* (literal interpretation), R=*remez* (allusive), D=*derash* (homiletical), and S=*sod* (the esoteric or mystical interpretation).

PARENT AND CHILD Jewish law regulates parent-child relationships primarily through a system of obligations. There are two main biblical sources for the child's obligation to the parent. One is the fifth commandment of the Decalogue, "Honor your father and your mother, that your days may be long in the land which the Lord your God gives you" (Exodus 20:12). The second is, "You shall each fear his mother and his father" (Lev. 19:3). The rabbis asked why in the former source, the father came first while in the second, precedence was given to the mother. They answered that in the first source the father is stressed because a child naturally gives more honor to the mother, but in the second, the father is the more feared, and so the mother is mentioned first. The intention is that both parents should be equally honored and feared (*Kid.* 30b-31a). Honor is taken by the Talmud to mean feeding, washing, dressing, helping in and out of the house (and by extension on various errands). The requirement to feed and care for the parent is to be undertaken at the parent's expense. If the parent is lacking in means, then his care takes precedence over any other charitable obligations that would normally devolve upon the child (*Sh. Ar. YD* 240.5) with the son being expected even to beg from house to house if he should lack the means to care for his parent (*Kid.* 32a). Reverence was understood as not sitting in a parent's seat or contradicting him in conversation (*Kid.* 31b).

Nowhere does the Bible command love of parents. Parents are included, however, in the general command to love one's fellow man as oneself (Lev. 19:18), but they are legally differentiated for the child from the rest of society by defined obligations of respect and reverence. The Talmud adds that if a parent instructs the child to violate the *halakhah*, he is to be disregarded (*BM* 32a, *Yev.* 5b). Wounding and cursing a parent are listed in the Bible as capital offenses (Ex. 21:15, 17).

The various obligations cited were not imposed in a spirit of dry compliance with legal demands, but rather were characteristic of the *halakhah's* method of regulating relationships by means of articulating mutual obligations (see below). So the Talmud (*Kid.* 32a) declares that a son may feed his father the finest delicacies and yet lose his share in the world to come if he does so grudgingly, while another may win his portion in the world to come by requesting that his father undertake difficult work, such as grinding flour, if the request is made in a spirit of kindness and respect. The parent has the right to renounce any and all of the child's obligations toward him and is advised not to impose too great a burden upon the child (*Kid.* 30b).

The Talmud and Midrashim go to considerable length in their praise of the honor of parents. Bringing children into the world was considered particularly meritorious, and parents were accorded the status of partners in the creation. Thus one who honored his parents as prescribed, was by extension honoring God Himself (*Kid.* 30b). The *halakhah* presumed that parents loved children, but did not presume that children loved parents.

In general, parental legal obligations devolve upon the father only. In case of divorce, for example, a father has to support his children, a mother does not. If a mother of fatherless children chooses not to rear them, they become wards of the community; the father has no such right. A married mother may not, however, refuse to nurse her newborn child if the father is unable to afford a wet nurse.

The father's obligation toward his child includes all of the child's daily needs. He is also obligated to educate the child to Judaism, to teach a male child a trade, to redeem him if he is the first-born (see FIRST-BORN, REDEMPTION OF) to have him circumcised, and to see to his marriage (*Kid.* 29a). While he is not obligated to see to his daughter's marriage, he is obligated to provide her with sufficient clothing, etc., that she be considered marriageable (*Ket.* 52b).

Child custody in divorce is, in principle, based upon the welfare of the child. Custody is a parental obligation, i.e., a right of the child, not of the parent. Maternal care is considered essential for children under the age of six; thus young children are routinely reared by their mother. After the age of six, owing to their need for education and religious instruction, boys are to be in the custody of the father, who is obligated to provide these. Girls, even after the age of six, normally remain in the custody of the mother so that she can provide guidance in the ways of modesty (*Ket.* 102b-103a).

The father is legally obligated to support all children in the mother's custody, unless the mother has undertaken to support them.

In the State of Israel, questions of custody and child support are governed by Jewish law and administered by rabbinic courts.

Children's obligation to honor and revere parents extends beyond the parent's lifetime. Thus in the post-talmudic period the custom arose for the son to say KADDISH and for sons and daughters to observe the anniversary of a parent's death (YAHRZEIT) as a special mark of respect. Another way of showing respect was for the children to assume responsibility for the debts of their deceased parents.

PARENTAL BLESSING (*birkat banim*). Blessing usually recited by the father for his children of all ages every Sabbath eve after services, either in the synagogue or at home. This custom is not mentioned in the Talmud and probably originated in the Middle Ages.

The text for male children is taken from the blessing of Jacob (Gen. 48:20): "So he blessed them by saying...God make you like Ephraim and Manasseh." To this was added the blessing for daughters: "May God make you like Sarah, Rebekah, Rachel and Leah." The Priestly Benediction is then recited in both cases. A personal prayer may also be added.

A further custom arose at the end of the Sabbath for children to be blessed again by their fathers and students by their teachers.

PARNAS (lit. "provider"). Title given to lay leaders of communities and congregations since early rabbinic times. Both the Targum (Isa. 22:15) and the Mishnah (*Ket.* 7.1) employ this term in the generalized sense of "overseer" or "steward," but in the Talmud it is used to denote any outstanding Jewish leader (*Ber.* 28a; *Yoma* 86b) as well as one appointed to an office of communal responsibility (*Git.* 60a, etc.; see AUTHORITY and COMMUNITY). Such leaders and administrators, who received no payment for their labors, deserved the highest respect but might not impose themselves on the community and had to function by consent (*Ber.* 55a). An overbearing *parnas* should not be tolerated; safeguards concerning any appointment were therefore recommended and a communal leader of gentle temperament was the ideal choice. Affluence and influence, rather than piety and scholarship, enabled — and still enable — many individuals to attain this high office.

Medieval Jewish communities elected *parnasim* to head their synagogues and direct their financial, philanthropic, and other autonomous operations. Among the Jews of North Africa, this communal leader was called *muqaddim* in Arabic. *Parnasim* headed the self-governing *Landjudenschaft* or territorial Jewish assembly of the Holy Roman Empire; they also presided over the "Council of the Four Lands" in Poland and Lithuania (see AUTONOMY). Larger communities (e.g., Cracow) appointed leaders known as *parnasé ha-ḥodesh* ("providers for a month"; cf. I Kings 4:7) who held office in rotation. Western congregations of Spanish and Portuguese Jews elected a council of elders, known as the "*Mahamad*" (see MA'AMAD), headed by a *Parnas Presidente*. Throughout the modern world, *parnasim* exercise far less authority than they once did as lay leaders of entire communities. Democratically elected to office, the contemporary *parnas* is either his congregation's president or its senior GABBAI (warden).

Delegation of parnasim *(community leaders) from Germany at the Council of Constance, 1417. From the Chronicles of the Council.*

PAROKHET The finely woven "curtain" or "veil" that separated the "holy place" in the SANCTUARY from the HOLY OF HOLIES, as commanded in Exodus (26:31-33): "You shall make a curtain [*parokhet*] of blue, purple, and scarlet yarns and fine twisted linen; with cherubim it shall be designed, the work of a skilled craftsman...and it shall serve as a partition between the holy place and the Holy of Holies." A similar curtain was made for Solomon's Temple (II Chr. 3:14), two giant figures of a CHERUB guarding the Ark of the Covenant within the Holy of Holies or "Sanctuary" (I Kings 6:23ff.). The curtain covered the cherubim and, when worshipers thronged to the Temple on Pilgrim Festivals, the curtain was rolled aside so that they might see the cherubim (*Yoma* 54a).

The synagogue ARK which now houses the Scrolls of the Law is considered analogous to the Holy of Holies in the Sanctuary. It is enclosed with doors, sometimes ornamented, as a sign of respect and for protection. In Ashkenazi and many Eastern congregations, an embroidered curtain is hung in front of the Ark doors; this curtain is also styled a *parokhet*, as in the Temple.

While the SYNAGOGUE as an institution in Jewish religious life is often said to have "replaced" the Temple, and was indeed termed a *mikdash me'at* (a Sanctuary in miniature; cf. Ezek. 11:16), no halakhic or theological justification was proposed to give the synagogue either the appearance of the Temple or its pattern of service. Nevertheless, from the earliest recorded dates of synagogue art and procedure, efforts were made to remind the worshiper of the glory and sanctity which the Temple had possessed. The curtain used to divide the Sanctuary from the contents of the Ark remains, in appearance, ornamentation, and function, a shared link between synagogue and Temple.

In both Ashkenazi and Sephardi traditions, the Ark's curtain was made of rich materials such as velvet, brocade, or Italian silk decorated with needlework and embroidery. As in the Temple, the curtain is made by women. The symbolic representations which it incorporates are either of a general or a special type. The former include dedicatory inscriptions (since the curtain may be a private gift to the synagogue), floral and fruit motifs, or a MAGEN DAVID. The latter reflect the particular significance of the curtain as a gateway to the sacred space in which the Torah scrolls rest. They include the KETER ("crown") symbolizing the Torah's majesty as the word of God, flanked by "lions of Judah" which are also symbolic of kingship. Fluted columns and other architectural elements represent the entrance to the Temple. This concept of the "sacred portal" is a universal theme of religious art and frequently appears on ancient Jewish coins. Winged lions and other mythological beasts symbolize the otherworldly spiritual realm and its angelic hosts which minister to God, as did the cherubim in the original *parokhet*.

In place of the normal colored hanging, a white satin curtain is used on ROSH HA-SHANAH, the DAY OF ATONEMENT, HOSHANA RABBAH, and SHEMINI ATSERET. Ashkenazim remove the curtain from the Ark on TISHAH BE-AV as a sign of grief over the Temple's destruction; Eastern Jewish practice is for a black curtain to be hung on that fast day. There is no *parokhet* fronting the Ark in Western Sephardi congregations, the curtain being hung instead within and to the rear of the doors of the Ark.

PARTICULARISM See UNIVERSALISM AND PARTICULARISM

PARVEH See DIETARY LAWS

PASSOVER (*Pesaḥ*). One of the PILGRIM FESTIVALS (with SHAVU'OT and SUKKOT) when Jews were commanded to make PILGRIMAGES to the TEMPLE in Jerusalem (Ex. 23:14). Passover is celebrated for eight days (seven days in Israel and by Reform Jews) commencing on 15 Nisan. Outside Israel, the first two and the last two days are holy days, while the middle four are ḤOL HA-MO'ED, the intermediate working days. In Israel, only the first day and the last day are holy, while the middle five days are working days.

Like the other two Pilgrim Festivals, Passover has both an historical and an agricultural motif. Historically, it commemorates the EXODUS of the Children of Israel from Egyptian slavery. Its agricultural significance is as a spring festival, celebrated at the beginning of the barley harvest.

The various names of the festival point to its different aspects.

1. *Ḥag ha-Matsot*, the Festival of Unleavened Bread (Ex. 12:15). This stems from the commandment to eat unleavened bread (MATSAH) and the prohibition against eating ḤAMETS or leavened food, in commemoration of the Israelites' hasty exodus from Egypt when they had time to prepare only unleavened bread. While the prohibition against *ḥametz* applies to the entire festival, the commandment to eat *matsah* applies, strictly speaking, to the first night only.

2. *Pesaḥ*, Passover. This is related to the biblical record of the angel of death who "passed over" the houses of the Children of Israel when he slew all the first-born of the Egyptians (Ex. 12:27). The term was also applied to the paschal

Houses of Israelites marked with blood of the paschal lamb so the Angel of Death will "pass over" them. 15th-century Haggadah.

lamb (*korban pesaḥ*). In the biblical record, each family was commanded to be prepared with a lamb, a few days before the Exodus. Then, on the eve of the departure from Egypt, the animal was to be slaughtered and some of its blood sprinkled on the doorposts and lintel of their houses as a sign to the ANGEL OF DEATH to "pass over" these houses on his way to slay the Egyptian first-born. The lamb then had to be roasted and eaten in haste that same night, together with *matsah* and bitter herb (MAROR). Subsequently, the ritual of the *korban pesaḥ*, or the paschal lamb, was observed as a sacrificial festal meal on Passover eve in the wilderness (Num. 9:1-5) and throughout the Temple period. The Talmud (*Pes.* 64ff.) gives a detailed description of the laws and customs pertaining to the paschal sacrifice that were prevalent in the period of the Second Temple.

3. *Zeman Ḥerutenu*, The Season of our Freedom. So described, particularly in the festival liturgy, because Passover celebrates the liberation of the Children of Israel from Egyptian bondage, and their emergence as a free nation.

4. *Ḥag ha-Aviv*, The Festival of Spring, marking the beginning of the barley harvest.

The Preparation for Passover. No other festival calls for such extensive preparation. Based on the explicitly strict biblical prohibition against leavened foodstuff from Passover eve throughout the entire festival, Jewish law emphasizes that even the tiniest morsel of leaven is prohibited. The smallest amount of leaven disqualifies a mixture of permitted food, however large. Hence, the care and thoroughness with which the Jewish household is cleaned in preparation for the festival. The single objective is to get rid of every particle of prohibited leaven.

In talmudic law (*Pes.* 35a), the term *ḥamets* applies to any of the following species of grain and their derivatives which, through contact with water, have been subjected to a leavening process: wheat, barley, spelt, rye and oats. Sephardim permit rice and legumes, while Ashkenazim add these to the prohibited list.

The strict rabbinic laws on *ḥamets* exclude the use of all domestic utensils, crockery and cutlery used in the preparation of such food during the year. For the most part, crockery used during the year may not be utilized on Passover on the assumption that earthenware absorbs an element of the *ḥamets* for which it was used. Separate dishes are therefore kept especially for Passover. Metalware, e.g., knives and forks formed of one metal piece, may be "kashered" (rendered fit) for Passover use and so may metal pots which have been used for boiling food. The general method for kashering these items is by dipping them in boiling water after they have been thoroughly and meticulously cleaned. Glassware is non-porous and may be kashered by immersion in water for three days — changing the water each day — followed by a thorough cleaning. The approach of Conservative Judaism is to dispense with the soaking of glassware based on the assumption that a cleaning with modern deter-

Preparation of utensils to be used at Passover by immersion in boiling water. From the Leipzig Maḥzor, *Germany, 13th century.*

gents is equally effective. Metal utensils that have been used for frying, e.g., frying pans, can only be kashered by holding them over fire to burn off every particle of *ḥamets*. However, despite the permissibility of kashering non-porous food utensils, the common observant Jewish household finds it preferable to keep a separate set of such objects especially for the Passover festival.

Today, the composition of some modern materials is so complex that it is hard to determine its porosity or non-porosity. For this reason, certain items of "Corningware" and hard plastic are subject to different opinions by rabbinic authorities. The Orthodox rabbi is usually less willing than the Conservative rabbi to consider these materials "kasherable." In cases of doubt the layman is advised to seek the guidance of his rabbi. Reform Jews do not change their utensils. Other preparations include (1) The search for leavened food (*Bedikat Ḥamets*): on the eve of 14 Nisan a formal search is made for any leaven which is still in the house. This is then put aside and burned on the following morning (See LEAVEN, SEARCH FOR). (2) The sale of the unleavened food (*Mekhirat Ḥamets*): any leavened food, drink, or other commodities which cannot be removed before Passover and which are intended for use after the festival are sold to a non-Jew for the duration of the festival. This done, any leaven in the house of the Jew, strictly speaking, does not belong to him. In this way he avoids transgressing the biblical law against the possession of leaven or its retention in his house during Passover. Because of the legal technicalities in this kind of sale, it is usual for the rabbi to carry out these arrangements on behalf of the community. Leavened food or drink which remains on the premises of a Jew and which has not been disposed of by such a sale is forbidden for use even after the festival.

The *Seder* is the order of the home ritual observed on the first two nights of Passover (in Israel and among Reform Jews, on the first night). This is the most important observance of the festival as well as one of the most widespread among the Jewish people. Its purpose is to dramatically commemorate the slavery and the Exodus. This is done through symbol, ceremony, special readings, and hymns (See SEDER).

Liturgy. The liturgy for Passover contains the statutory festival additions of HALLEL and the ADDITIONAL SERVICE. The readings from the Pentateuch are Exodus 12 (the story of the Exodus from Egypt) on the first day and on the seventh day, Exodus 13-15, which contains the account of the crossing of the Red Sea on the seventh day after the Exodus. A liturgical feature unique to Passover is the prayer for DEW recited before the Additional Service on the first day. The *Yizkor* or MEMORIAL SERVICE is read in Ashkenazi synagogues on the last day.

As on other Pilgrim Festivals, one of the FIVE SCROLLS is read on Passover. On Passover, it is the SONG OF SONGS. The connection is seen in the book's description of the spring season.

Counting of the Omer (*Sefirat ha-Omer*). In accordance with the law recorded in Leviticus 23:15 ff., the OMER is counted from the second night of Passover.

Pesaḥ Sheni (Second Passover). People unable to participate in the festive ceremonies of the paschal sacrifice were permitted to observe the rite one month later, i.e., on 14 Iyyar (See PASSOVER, SECOND).

Me'ot Ḥittim ("money for wheat") is a special charity fund to provide the poor with all the necessities for the Passover celebration (See ME'OT ḤITTIM).

Some Passover Customs. The SAMARITANS in Erets Israel observe the Passover rites on Mount GERIZIM near Shechem. To this day, the slaughter of the paschal lamb is the climax of their ceremony. A number of sheep are set aside on 10 Nisan. On the eve of the 14th they are slaughtered, roasted for six hours in ovens dug in the earth and distributed to the families to be eaten in their homes with bitter herbs, to the accompaniment of song and dance.

The ETHIOPIAN JEWS (Beta Israel) cease to eat leaven three days before the festival, consuming only dried peas and beans until Passover eve. Then they fast until their high priest slaughters the paschal lamb on an altar in the courtyard of the synagogue. The blood is sprinkled around the entrance to the building.

In the Caucasus, the Jews wear clothes of "freedom" with wide, loose sleeves, some with a dagger or even a pistol in their belt. They reenact a drama in which one of their number goes out, knocks on the door and pretends he has just arrived from Jerusalem. All the others ask him for news of the Holy City and whether he has a message of liberation and redemption. Certain Sephardim and Eastern communities also enact a drama, eating the meat hastily, standing, with loins girded and staff in hand, like the Israelites in 'Egypt. Some wrap the *afikoman* in a cloth which they put over their shoulder and leave the room saying, "This is how our ancestors left Egypt."

The secret Jews of Spain and Portugal, the MARRANOS, observed the festival on 16 Nisan in order to avoid suspicion on the previous day. They clandestinely baked unleavened bread on that day and held a secret *seder* at which they consumed a whole roast sheep, while wearing traveling shoes and holding staffs in their hands. Marranos in Mexico smeared their doorposts with the blood of lambs, like the ancient Israelites, and beat the waters of a stream with willow branches to symbolize the crossing of the Red Sea.

PASSOVER —PESAḤ

Other Names: *Ḥag ha-Pesaḥ* (Feast of Passover)
Ḥag ha-Matsot (Festival of Unleavened Bread)
Ḥag ha-Aviv (Spring Festival)
Zeman Ḥerutenu (Season of our Freedom)

Hebrew Dates: 15–21 Nisan (in Israel and among Reform Jews in the Diaspora)
15–22 Nisan (in the Diaspora)

Torah and Prophetical Readings:

1st Day: Ex. 12:21–51; Num. 28:16–25 *(Maftir)*; Josh. 5:2–6:1 (Ashkenazi *Haftarah*) Josh. 5:2–6:1 (Sephardi *Haftarah*)

2nd Day (in Diaspora): Lev. 22:26–23:44; Num. 28:16–25 *(Maftir)*; 2 Kings 23:1–9, 21–25 *(Haftarah)*

Intermediate Sabbath: Ex. 33:12–34:26; Num. 28:19–25 *(Maftir)*; Ezek. 37:1–14 *(Haftarah)*

7th Day: Ex. 13:17–15:26; Num 28:19–25 *(Maftir)*; 2 Sam 22:1–51 *(Haftarah)*

8th Day (in Diaspora): Deut. 15:19–16:17 (14:22–16:17 on Sabbath); Num. 18:19–25 *(Maftir)*; Isa. 10:32–12:6 *(Haftarah)*

Scroll: Song of Songs

Hallel: recited (in full) on first day(s); half-*Hallel* on intermediate and last day(s)

Yizkor recited: on last day; Prayer for Dew recited on 1st Day

Civil dates on which the festival occurs, 1990-2010:

1990/5751	10–16 (17) April
1991/5752	5–11 (12) April
1992/5753	18–24 (25) April
1993/5754	6–12 (13) April
1994/5755	2–8 (9) April
1995/5756	15–21 (22) April
1996/5757	4–10 (11) April
1997/5758	22–28 (29) April

1998/5759	11–17 (18) April
1999/5760	7–13 (14) April
2000/5761	20–26 (27) April
2001/5762	8–14 (15) April
2002/5763	3–9 (10) April
2003/5764	17–23 (24) April
2004/5765	6–12 (13) April
2005/5766	24–30 April (and 1 May)
2006/5767	13–19 (20) April
2007/5768	3–9 (10) April
2008/5769	20–26 (27) April
2009/5770	9–15 (16) April
2010/5771	5–11 (12) April

PASSOVER, SECOND Observance of PASSOVER on 14 Iyyar by those prevented from keeping it on its regular date a month previously. The Bible (Num. 9) relates that a number of Israelites approached Moses and told him that they had not been able to observe the Passover on its proper date because they had been ritually impure. After Moses spoke to God, God informed him of the Second Passover (*Pesaḫ Sheni*), whereby anyone who was unable to bring the paschal sacrifice on 14 Nisan because of ritual impurity or because he was too far away to reach the Sanctuary in time could bring a paschal sacrifice one month later. This privilege was not limited to those prevented by external causes from bringing the paschal sacrifice at the right time. There is one reference in the Bible of a mass offering of the Second Passover at the time of King Hezekiah, when the paschal lamb had not been brought at the proper time because "the priests had not sanctified themselves sufficiently, neither had the people gathered themselves together to Jerusalem" (II Chr. 30:3). In post-Temple times, the only vestigial remnant of the Second Passover is that TAḪANUN is not recited on that day. Some people have a custom to eat unleavened bread during the Second Passover.

PATRIARCHS, THE The three founding fathers (*avot* in Heb.) of the Jewish people: ABRAHAM, ISAAC and JACOB. The lives of the patriarchs are regarded as a paradigm for Jews throughout the ages and the different aspects of their lives are regarded as object lessons for ideal behavior.

All three patriarchs communicated with God and they and their descendants were bound to Him by an eternal COVENANT, physically manifested by CIRCUMCISION. They were promised that their descendants would be uncountably numerous. God promised all three patriarchs the Land of Canaan as the the eternal inheritance of their people.

In the *aggadah*, Abraham represents *ḫesed*, or compassion for others; Isaac represents *din*, or strict justice; and Jacob represents *raḫamim*, loosely translated as "lovingkindness," but more accurately meaning justice tempered with mercy. In that sense, Jacob is considered to be "the Chosen One of the Patriarchs."

The traditional burial site of Isaac marked by a cenotaph, in the Cave of Machpelah, Hebron.

The patriarchs are mentioned in numerous places in prayer. The opening blessing of the AMIDAH, the core element of every prayer service, known as *Avot*, begins with the words, "... God of Abraham, God of Isaac, and God of Jacob." (In recent years, many non-Orthodox congregations have added the names of the MATRIARCHS to this blessing.) Many prayers also appeal to God, using the merits of the patriarchs that stand their descendants in good stead. The sacrifice of Isaac (AKEDAH) plays a prominent part in these appeals.

According to tradition, the patriarchs introduced the daily prayers: Abraham introduced the morning (*Shaḫarit*) prayer; Isaac, the afternoon (*Minḫah*) prayer, and Jacob, the evening (*Arvit* or *Ma'ariv*) prayer.

PATRILINEAL DESCENT CONTROVERSY Controversy over whether a child born of a Jewish father and non-Jewish mother may be automatically considered Jewish or must undergo conversion to be recognized as Jewish. According to Jewish law (*halakhah*), "Your son by an Israelite woman is called your son, but your son by a heathen woman is not called your son" (*Kid.* 68b). Thus, a child who is born of a Jewish mother is considered Jewish irrespective of the religion of the child's father or of the child's level of Jewish observance or knowledge. However, the child born of a Jewish father and a non-Jewish mother, regardless of his Jewish practice or knowledge, is not recognized as a Jew.

In recent years this traditional means of determining a child's Jewish identity has been called into question by the REFORM and RECONSTRUCTIONIST movements. In 1982, the

Reform movement adopted patrilineal descent as a criterion for Jewishness. According to this view, the child of an INTERMARRIAGE between a Jewish father and a non-Jewish mother who is raised as a Jew and observes the duties of the Jewish life-cycle is considered Jewish without undergoing conversion. A child of a Jewish mother, regardless of the father's religion, is also Jewish. The Reconstructionist movement recognized patrilineal descent in 1983.

In response, in May 1984 the Rabbinical Assembly of the CONSERVATIVE movement reaffirmed their sole acceptance of matrilineal descent as the determining factor of a child's Jewishness. The ORTHODOX movement, following *halakhah*, recognizes only matrilineal descent.

Patrilineal descent was adopted by the Reform and Reconstructionist movements for a number of reasons. In light of the high intermarriage rates, it was felt that Judaism could not afford to exclude the children of these marriages as Jews, particularly when they are raised as Jewish. There is no biblical justification for matrilineal descent. According to the Bible, both the priesthood and inheritance are patrilineal. Matrilineal descent favors Jewish women, but penalizes Jewish men who choose to intermarry.

The Conservative and Orthodox movements feel that patrilineal descent goes against not only the *halakhah* but also the concept of KELAL YISRAEL — the idea that all Jews must stand together. Individuals who consider themselves to be Jewish based on patrilineal descent, may some day have their Jewishness called into question.

Fragment of the mosaic floor of a synagogue bearing the inscription "Peace to Israel", found at Usafiya, 6th century.

PEACE The Hebrew word for peace, *shalom*, is derived from a root denoting wholeness or completeness, and its frame of reference throughout Jewish literature is bound up with the notion of *shelemut*, perfection.

In the Bible, the word *shalom* is most commonly used to refer to a state of affairs, one of harmony, tranquillity, and prosperity. *Shalom* is a blessing, a manifestation of Divine grace. Of course, it also denotes the opposite of war, for the absence of war, too, suggests an orderly and tranquil state of affairs.

In rabbinic texts, *shalom* primarily signifies a value, an ethical category; the overcoming of strife and enmity in family, communal, and national life, and the prevention of war. It is still depicted as a manifestation of Divine grace, but in many sayings it appears in a normative context: the pursuit of peace is the obligation of the individual and the goal of various social regulations and structures.

The rabbis went to great lengths in their praise of peace, to the point of viewing it as a meta-value, the summit of all other values. Peace is the ultimate purpose of the Torah, and the essence of prophecy and redemption; *Shalom* is the name of God, the name of Israel, and the name of the Messiah.

Nevertheless, the sages discuss the relationship between peace and other values, such as justice and truth. One view is that peace, justice and truth are fully harmonious and complementary (TJ *Ta'an.* 4.2). However, there are also discussions concerning which value prevails in cases of conflict. In this context, even where peace is given priority it is viewed as an individual, partial value that must compete with other values. Thus, one may lie for the sake of peace (*Yev.* 65b). Furthermore, according to R. Joshua ben Korḥa, strict justice is incompatible with peace; a judge should therefore temper justice with peace, and rule for compromise (TJ *Sanh.* 1.5; TB *Sanh.* 6b; the opposing view is "let justice pierce the mountain," that is, justice at all costs).

The unique development of the philosophical and mystical literature in the Middle Ages is reflected in their portrayal of peace as an ontological principle. Peace was elevated to the level of the cosmic, the metaphysical, the Divine. Peace is the foundation of all being, the principle that harmonizes contending forces within each individual object, and reconciles the separate elements of nature as a whole. Ultimately, peace is the embodiment of the Divine immanence in the world: "God is the ultimate form of the world, and in this He comprehends all and joins and unifies all, and this is the very essence of peace" (R. Judah Löw ben Bezalel, *Netivot Olam*, *Netiv ha-Shalom*, 1).

Peace and War. Jewish sources, from the Bible onward, acknowledge war as a given of human existence. It is a reflection of the real, yet fallen, human condition in history, as opposed to the meta-historical era of the End of Days. War reflects the actual situation of man, but not his destiny.

The post-biblical discussion of this question was greatly influenced by the reality of Jewish powerlessness. Neither

Chart for counting the Omer, *the seven-week period between Passover and Shavu'ot. Paper-cut. Poland, 1876.*

ברוך
אתה יי אלהינו מלך העולם אשר
קדשנו במצותיו וצונו על ספירת
העומר
היום יום אחד לעומר

נדב ההגה הפייש
אופנהיי מקויא יצ
וזוגתו אח מ׳ רעכלי
בת ה׳ כ׳ ברוך רג יצ
שנת
תפה לפק

war nor peace really stood as concrete options for the Jewish people. Only the wars of the Gentiles belonged to historical reality; the ancient wars of Israel were a matter more for theology than for politics. The Jew waged war against the evil inclination far more than he did against any historical foe. Peace, too, was discussed primarily from a utopian perspective, in light of the prophetic vision of eternal peace.

In this context, three different models of peace were put forward. According to the first model, peace will eventually be achieved by a transformation of the consciousness of the individual. Thus, MAIMONIDES viewed intellectual perfection as the guarantor of peace. The apprehension of truth, the universal knowledge of God, will displace man's attachment to illusory goods and destructive impulses, and completely eliminate the irrational factors that cause conflicts and wars (*Yad, Melakhim* 12.5; *Guide* III,11). According to the 11th-12th century Spanish thinker Abraham bar Ḫiyya, on the other hand, man's destructive impulses are to be overcome not by an intellectual change but by an emotional one, namely, by a sense of intimacy and love that will grow among men in the messianic era, once they have all chosen to adopt the same faith and path (*Hegyon ha-Nefesh*, 4).

According to the second view, the people of the world will be made to live in peace by being brought together under a single universal framework. Thus, David Kimḫi (Comm. to Isa. 2:4; Mic. 4:3) and Isaac Arama (*Akedat Yitsḫak*, 46) portrayed the Messiah as a supreme, utopian judge who would make peace between the nations. This vision speaks not of a human society that has risen above all striving and conflict, but rather of a kind of international court whose authority and righteousness are accepted by all. Other thinkers envisioned a kind of Pax Judaica, a single, central government in Zion to which all peoples would be subject (Saadiah Gaon, *Book of Doctrines and Beliefs*, 8.8; Albo, *Sefer ha-Ikkarim*, 4.42).

A third view anticipated the achievement of peace by an internal reformation of the socio-political order. In the teachings of Isaac ABRAVANEL, war was described as a consequence of man's historical and cultural fall, a fall that is embodied preeminently in man's technological civilization, and political tradition and institutions. Ultimate redemption is destined to bring about the demise of materialistic civilization and the disappearance of political structures and boundaries (Comm. to Gen. 3:22, 4:1,17, 11:1 and elsewhere). In the teachings of Isaac ARAMA, on the other hand, peace and war are discussed in relation to the presently operative political and judicial order. The closer the laws and the political order come to satisfying the natural, universal sense of justice, the more peace will tend to overcome war (*Akedat Yitsḫak*, 46, 81, 105a).

The emphasis on peace in Judaism is shown by the fact that all major prayers (including the AMIDAH, the KADDISH, and the GRACE AFTER MEALS) conclude with a prayer for peace, as does the Priestly Blessing (Num. 6:27).

PEACE IN THE JEWISH TRADITION

Peace is the greatest of all blessings.

The whole Torah exists solely for the sake of peace.

Great is peace, for it is to the world what leaven is to dough. If God had not placed peace in the world, all mankind would have been destroyed by the sword and wild beasts.

Be among the disciples of Aaron: Love peace and strive for peace, love people and acquaint them with the teachings of the Torah.

R. Simeon ben Gamaliel said, "The world rests on three things: Justice, truth, and peace." R. Mona said, "These three are one and the same, for if there is justice, there is truth, and if there is truth, there is peace."

Peacemaking, like charity, brings benefit in this world and in the world to come.

Jerusalem will be rebuilt only through peace.

PEACE-OFFERING See SACRIFICES AND OFFERINGS

PE'AH ("corner [of the field]"). The second tractate of Order ZERA'IM. Its eight chapters enumerate the "dues" which a farmer must give to the poor (Lev. 19:9-10; 23:22; Deut. 24:19-22). They are: 1) *pe'ah* — 1/60 of one's field, orchard, or vineyard. 2) *shikhḫah* — the forgotten sheaf of fruit. 3) *leket* — gleaning the fallen ears of grain at the time of reaping. 4) *peret* — gleaning the fallen grapes. 5) *olelot* — leaving the unripe clusters of grapes. 6) *ma'aser ani* — the poor man's tithe (one-tenth of the remaining produce after the first tithe has been separated). (See AGRICULTURAL LAWS). The subject-matter is amplified in the Jerusalem Talmud and the *Tosefta*.

PE'AH See AGRICULTURAL LAWS; LEKET SHIKHḪAH VE-PE'AH

PENITENCE See REPENTANCE

PENITENTIAL PRAYERS See SELIḪOT

PENTATEUCH The first five books of the BIBLE, known in Hebrew as the *ḫumash* (from the Heb. root ḫ-m-sh meaning five) or the TORAH. It would appear that the division into these five books had already been made long before the destruction of the Second Temple. The five books are: GENESIS (*Be-Reshit*); EXODUS (*Shemot*); LEVITICUS (*Va-Yikra*); NUMBERS (*Be-Midbar*); and DEUTERONOMY (*Devarim*). They are also known as the Five Books of MOSES.

The Hebrew names of the books are taken from the first words in each book. In Jewish tradition, each book has also

Parokhet, *(curtain) for the Ark of the Law in velvet with gold thread embroidery.*

another name: Genesis, *Sefer ha-Yetsirah* ("the Book of Creation"); Exodus, *Sefer ha-Ge'ulah* ("the Book of Redemption," i.e., from Egypt); Leviticus, *Torat Kohanim* ("the Law of the Priests"; most of the book deals with law relating to the priests); Numbers, *Ḥumash ha-Pekudim* ("The Book of the Censuses"; both the beginning and the end deal with the numbering of the Israelites); and Deuteronomy, *Mishneh Torah* ("The Repetition of the Torah"; most of the book is a repetition of Exodus, Leviticus, and Numbers).

Modern scholars have linked the Pentateuch to the Book of JOSHUA and have seen the six books as a unit, referred to as the Hexateuch. There are two reasons for this. Firstly, the Pentateuch speaks of the promise to inherit the Land of Canaan and the preparations toward entering the land, and in order to complete the story and to realize the promise, the Book of Joshua, which deals with the conquest of the Promised Land and its division among the tribes, has to be included. Secondly, the Book of Joshua can be shown to be divided according to the same sources as the Pentateuch, so that from a literary-critical viewpoint it appears to be a continuation of the Pentateuch, and part of it.

Opposed to this view is the claim that the Book of Joshua is an organic unit which stands alone. Similarly, the Book of Joshua depends greatly on a number of traditions in the Pentateuch (thus, for example, Josh. 14-21 is dependent on Num. 26:52-56, 34, 35:34).

The historic component of the Pentateuch opens with the creation of the world, deals with the transformation of Abraham's offspring into a nation, their redemption from Egypt, and their wanderings in the desert, and concludes with Moses' death just before the Israelites enter the Promised Land.

The Pentateuch is read in the synagogue from the SCROLL OF THE LAW. In ancient Israel, the Jews completed a cycle of the Pentateuch reading in the synagogue on the Sabbath every three years, and therefore divided the Pentateuch into 154 (or 167, depending on custom) *sedarim* ("orders"). A remnant of this custom is to be found in the letter *samekh* at the beginning of the *sedarim* in the Pentateuch printed in Venice in 1518 (*Mikra'ot Gedolot*). This custom fell out of use, but has been reintroduced in some modern non-Orthodox congregations. The Babylonian custom, which is accepted today throughout the Jewish world, calls for the completion of the Pentateuch reading in the synagogue in a single year, the last section being read on SIMḤAT TORAH. The Babylonian division is into 54 *parashiyyot* (see PARASHAH; READING OF THE LAW).

Traditional View. According to Jewish tradition (*BB* 15a), the entire Pentateuch is a single unit that was given by God through Moses to the Israelites. Moses wrote the words of God, except for the last eight verses (Deut. 34:5-12), which were written by Joshua. Another view (*ibid.*) is that Moses wrote these eight verses as well. Because the Pentateuch is regarded as of Divine origin, it can never change, as stated by Maimonides in his 13 PRINCIPLES OF FAITH: "I believe with perfect faith that this Torah will not be changed, nor will there be another Torah from the Creator." Similarly, according to Maimonides, a Jew must believe "that the entire Torah that we now have in our hands was given to our teacher Moses" (*ibid.*). The talmudic rabbis argue whether the Pentateuch was given scroll by scroll or as a complete sealed Torah. The dispute is whether Moses wrote down a section of the Pentateuch whenever it was told him, and joined the different sections into a single work before his death, or whether, throughout the time in the desert, whenever God told Moses a section he memorized it, and close to his death wrote down the entire Pentateuch (*Git.* 60a).

Jewish tradition sanctified the text of the Pentateuch, not only in terms of its content, but also in terms of each individual letter. Because of its sanctity, the Pentateuch is to this day written by hand by a SCRIBE on parchment made of the hide of a ritually fit species of animal, and is copied from another scroll. The text is checked carefully, and if even a single letter is missing or extra, the scroll is invalid. To insure that no letters were omitted or added incorrectly, there were trained scribes who counted the letters, and thereby prevented errors from creeping in. As the entire Pentateuch is seen as Divine, each word, and sometimes even each letter, has a purpose. The rabbis said that if it appears to a man that a certain word or sentence has no significance, the reason is human ignorance, and not any error in the Torah.

Bible Criticism. At the base of Bible criticism lies the belief that the Pentateuch is not Divine and was not written by Moses. It is, rather, a compilation of various literary sources that were written at different times, and that were later combined by an editor into a single work.

Modern Bible criticism emerged in the 18th century, and became especially influential with the work of the German scholar, Julius Wellhausen (1878). According to this view, the Pentateuch was composed from four main sources:

J — the source which uses the tetragrammaton, transcribed as JHWH (see GOD, NAMES OF);
E — the source which uses the name *Elohim*;
P — the priestly code (primarily Leviticus);
D — the Deuteronomistic source.

Some claim to identify a JE source, one combining the first two listed above, which appears primarily from Exodus on.

The view of different sources for the Pentateuch is based on the duplication of stories, such as the two accounts of the Creation (Gen. 1:1-2:3 and 2:4-24), or the taking of Sarah by Abimelech as recorded in Genesis 20 (E source) and the taking of Rebekah by Abimelech in Genesis 26 (J source). In addition, this system seeks to solve various textual and theological problems. The chronological aspect of this system is based on the hypothesis by Martin de Wette (1805) that the book found by King Josiah in 610 BCE (II Kings 23) was the Book of Deuteronomy. According to de Wette,

Josiah did not find the book, but composed it at the time (D source). This book represents the theological revolution of the concentration of worship in one place, Jerusalem. Therefore all references to decentralization of worship must precede this period, whereas those which stress this principle are later than Josiah's time. According to this theory, the J and E sources preceded the Book of Deuteronomy, whereas the time of the P source is a matter of dispute, and there are those who regard it as dating from the time of Ezra and Nehemiah (Wellhausen).

This form of criticism was called "Higher Criticism," to distinguish it from "Lower Criticism," which provided for the emendations of the text of the Pentateuch (and the rest of the Bible) on the assumption that the received text contains errors. Limited and light changes are to be found in the MASORAH, but these were held to be of ancient tradition and were introduced without touching the text. However, critics who had no inhibitions regarding the sanctity of the text suggested many alternative readings, sometimes based on the ancient translations. In the light of modern scholarship and understanding, much of it by Jewish scholars, some of the more excessive hypotheses have been modified and replaced by more conservative views.

PENTECOST See SHAVU'OT

PERJURY The act of giving false testimony. The bearing of false witness is forbidden by the Ninth Commandment (Ex. 20:13; Deut. 5:17). Perjury applied to a set of witnesses and not to an individual (who, on his own, could not bring about a conviction). Generally, in order to be convicted of perjury under Jewish law, a set of witnesses must be impeached by later testimony in a manner known as *hazamah. Hazamah* occurs when one set of witnesses asserts that a previous set had not been where it claimed, and therefore could not have seen what it testified. Thus, if the first set testifies that it observed one man kill another in a certain place on a certain date, and the second set testifies that it was with the first set in an entirely different place on that date, this is *hazamah*. The second set is believed, and the first set is considered perjurers, or *edim zommemim* (lit. "scheming witnesses"). If, however, the second set testifies that the accused was somewhere else at the time of the murder, or that no murder took place at all, this is called *hakhḇashah* (contradiction), and the testimony of both sets is disregarded (*Mak.* 1.4; Maim., *Yad, Edut* 18.2).

The punishment for bearing false witness is set forth in Deut. 19:19: "You shall do to him as he schemed to do to his fellow." Thus, *edim zommemim* who testify in a criminal case receive the punishment they sought to inflict on the accused; in a civil case, they forfeit the amount of money damages they sought to impose on the defendant. However, there are exceptions to this rule, and in certain cases *edim zommemim* are flogged even though the consequence of accepting their testimony would have been other than flogging (see *Mak.* 2a-b; *Yad, Edut* 18.1, 20.8; *Tur, ḇM* 38:1-3).

All convictions of perjury had to be widely publicized as anyone found guilty was disqualified from ever appearing as a witness again.

PESAḆ See PASSOVER

PESAḆIM ("paschal sacrifices"). Third tractate of Order MO'ED in the Mishnah. Its ten chapters deal with the laws requiring the eating of MATSAH (unleavened bread) and forbidding the consumption of leaven (*ḇamets*) during the festival of PASSOVER (cf. Ex. 12:1-28, 43-50; 13:3-10; Num. 9:1-14; Deut. 16:1-8). The Mishnah also covers the offering of the paschal lamb sacrifice during the era of the Temple and the conduct of the SEDER (service) on the first night of Passover. This tractate also discusses the two different times when one may offer the Passover sacrifice, either on the proper date or on the Second Passover. The subject matter is amplified in both Talmuds and in the *Tosefta*.

PESHAT (plain, literal meaning of a text as contrasted with *derash*, its homiletical meaning). Biblical interpretation by the talmudic and midrashic sages was almost exclusively homiletical. This, however, did not preclude the awareness of the plain meaning of the text.

Bible commentaries generally fall into the literal and exegetical categories. Some commentators adhere to the text's literal meaning while others interpret it midrashically, allegorically, mystically, or philosophically. RASHI, for example, in his commentary on the PENTATEUCH, declares that his purpose is to render the literal meaning of Scripture. Nevertheless, he frequently cites a MIDRASH, especially when this solves some apparent difficulty in the text.

Among Bible commentators, such outstanding figures as Abraham IBN EZRA, SAMUEL BEN MEIR, and David KIMḆI favored *peshat*. Samuel ben Meir did not hesitate to contradict the talmudic, legal interpretation of a verse if, in his opinion, its plain meaning demanded it. See also PARDES.

PESHER ("interpretation"). Exegetical commentary on biblical passages found among the literature of the DEAD SEA SCROLLS. The word is found in Ecclesiastes 8:1 and occurs

Fragment of the Habakkuk *(Habakkuk commentary) from the Dead Sea Scrolls. 1st century CE.*

again in Daniel 4:16 in a context that implies that the interpretation of secret things (such as Nebuchadnezzar's dream interpreted by DANIEL) comes by way of Divine revelation. This is the connotation found frequently in the Dead Sea Scrôlls, particularly in the document entitled *Pesher Habakkuk* (Interpretation of the Book of HABAKKUK).

The men of the Dead Sea sect, believing that the end of time was imminent, produced a text that is an eschatological line by line interpretation of the three chapters of Habakkuk. The interpretation is ascribed to the "Teacher of Righteousness."

PESIKTA DE-RAV KAHANA ("Section of Rabbi Kahana"). An ancient homiletical MIDRASH on the Pentateuch and prophetical synagogue reading for special Sabbaths and festivals. Long before a manuscript of this Midrash was discovered, Leopold ZUNZ demonstrated its existence on the basis of quotations in the YALKUT SHIMONI and in the *Arukh* of Nathan ben Jehiel of Rome. It was published for the first time in the latter half of the 19th century.

Its ascription to R. Abba bar Kahana may be because he is cited in the opening section. The original arrangement followed the cycle of the Jewish calendar. Its redaction took place in Erets Israel some time in the fifth century CE.

PESIKTA RABBATI ("Great Section"). A medieval MIDRASH on the Pentateuch readings for all festivals including H̱anukkah, *Shabbat ha-Gadol* (see SABBATHS, SPECIAL), TISHAH BE-AV, etc. (but there is no Midrash for the Torah readings for SUKKOT). Five sections are identical with those found in the much older Midrash PESIKTA DE-RAV KAHANA. Like the latter, its sources are exclusively from Erets Israel. Many of the homilies are preceded by a halakhic introduction which begins with the phrase *Yelammedenu Rabbenu* ("Let our Masters teach us"). This would indicate that the editor of the Midrash drew on TANH̱UMA YELAMMEDENU. The Midrash is held to be a work from Erets Israel, edited in the sixth or seventh century CE.

PESUKÉ DE-ZIMRA ("Passages of Song"). A sequence of biblical verses and psalms, read in the daily Morning Service, following the MORNING BENEDICTIONS and preceding the BAREKHU summons to public worship. The core of these passages may be found in a group of psalms of praise to the Creator (Ps. 145-150), which probably formed part of the Temple ritual and from which the *Pesuké de-Zimra* evolved. According to the sages, "one should first give praise to God and then approach Him in worship" (*Ber.* 32a); the "Passages of Song" may thus be recited without a prayer quorum since they serve as an introduction to prayer, elevating man's spirit before he recites the SHEMA and the AMIDAH. Though referred to by name in the Talmud (*Shab.* 118b), the *Pesuké de-Zimra* only entered the prayer book in geonic times (*Seder Rav Amram Gaon*, ninth cent.), when their recitation was limited to Sabbaths and festivals. In the Italian, Sephardi, and Eastern rites, these passages are termed *Zemirot* ("hymns" or "psalms") and worshipers recite them aloud. Ashkenazim, however, read them in an undertone, the *ba'al tefillah* (prayer leader) chanting the opening and closing verses only. A widely observed practice is for congregants to stand during the BARUKH SHE-AMAR prologue and the closing sections.

PETIH̱AH ("opening"). Ceremony performed whenever the ARK is opened in synagogue. From ancient times, this honor was reserved for the worshiper who removed the Scroll(s) of the Law from the ark prior to the READING OF THE LAW, and who performed the ceremony in reverse when the Scrolls were returned after reading had been completed. One honored with *petiẖah* on such occasions usually removes the scroll from the ark, transfers it to the reader (who places it on his right shoulder), and then closes the ark before the procession leaves for the reading desk. In some congregations,

Man carrying a Scroll of the Law, to illustrate the prayer recited at the opening (petiẖah) *of the ark for the Reading of the Law.*

however, these honors are separated and may also be reserved for synagogue wardens. It is customary for congregants to stand from the moment when the ark is opened and as the scrolls are borne to and fro. The ark is also opened when the ANIM ZEMIROT hymn is chanted or (especially in Ashkenazi practice) when solemn prayers are recited during the Ten Days of Penitence. The practice may date from the talmudic period, when the ark was taken outdoors and petitions were recited before it in times of national emergency (*Ta'an.* 2.1-2, 15b-16a). Nowadays, in Reform temples, the ark may also be opened for the recitation of a Prayer for the Government.

PHARISEES The spiritual leaders of the Jewish people in the Land of Israel during the greater part of the Second Temple era. The name stems from the Hebrew *perushim* (from the root "to be separate," "set apart"); Greek *pharisaioi.* This party was one of the three or four "philosophical" trends described by the Jewish historian Josephus (the others being the SADDUCEES, the ESSENES, and the Zealot faction).

It has been suggested that the Pharisee ideology had its roots in the days of EZRA and NEHEMIAH (fifth century BCE), who reinstituted a Torah-based Judaism among the Jewish inhabitants of Judah. The most potent instrument for the propagation of the Jewish religious message among the people appears to have been the institution commonly known as the Men of the GREAT ASSEMBLY. These were first and foremost teachers of the people, expounders and interpreters of the ORAL LAW, and custodians of the body of customs and traditions being constantly amassed by the Jews of the Land of Israel and the Diaspora.

The Pharisees constituted the essential lay religious leadership of the people. They were firmly rooted in the mass of the people, which was reflected not only in the vast body of new legislation they enacted, but also in the concern for the common people expressed in Midrash and *Aggadah*. In both aspects, the Pharisees appear in sharp contrast to the Sadducees who represented the thin, upper aristocratic layer of Jewry and, for an extensive period, the High Priestly families.

The Pharisees assumed clear shape and form in the days of John Hyrcanus (ruled 135-104 BCE). They achieved particularly strong political influence during the reign of Salome Alexandra (76-67 BCE) under their leader SIMEON BEN SHETAḤ (according to one tradition, the queen's brother).

After the Romans assumed power (63 BCE), the Pharisees reverted to their original role as expounders of Jewish law and arbitrators of the community's internal disputes. This did not mean that they abdicated their right to speak out and to act upon the political issues of the day, as is evidenced by the pro-revolt stand taken by R. Simeon ben GAMALIEL I and other Pharisee leaders in the early days of the revolt against the Romans of 66-70 CE, and also during the Bar Kokhba revolt of 132-135 CE.

The Pharisee world (unlike that of the Sadducees) was typified by its academies of religious learning. The great schools of HILLEL and SHAMMAI were already flourishing in the first century BCE, and the town of Yavneh seems to have boasted a *yeshivah* (academy of learning), known as Kerem Be-Yavneh, already before the destruction of the Temple in 70 CE. The town with its academy was to assume a central role when the Pharisaic sage, R. JOHANAN BEN ZAKKAI, converted it into a new and eventually great center of study and rabbinic leadership of the community, in place of destroyed Jerusalem. This new bastion of Pharisaism was to take on even greater significance under the presidency of R. Johanan's successor, R. Gamaliel II. The Pharisee-oriented academy took basic and far-reaching decisions in the sphere of Jewish law and practice, among them: decisions affecting the Jewish CALENDAR; giving permanent form to the focal daily AMIDAH prayer; and the decision generally to accept the legal conclusions of the School of Hillel as against those of the School of Shammai (see BET SHAMMAI AND BET HILLEL). The New Testament representation of Pharisee concern as being only with the dry minutiae of Jewish law is refuted by the vast body of Talmud literature, which shows the simplicity of the sages' ways, their concern for their fellow Jews, their belief in man's freedom of choice, the respect in which they held their elders, and their general involvement in the totality of Jewish society. Josephus notes: "Because of these views they are...extremely influential among the townsfolk," and that the "great tribute" paid by the Jewish population to "the excellence" of the Pharisees lies in their practice of the highest ideals, both in their discourse and in their way of living.

The Talmud mentions many differences of approach in the sphere of *halakhah* between the Sadducees and the Pharisees. These include the dating of the Shavu'ot festival; the validity of certain Pharisaically-ordained ceremonies on Sukkot (the festive Water Drawing ceremony, among others); and the punishment of false witnesses, this being an apparent exception to the Pharisees' general leniency in the matter of legal punishment. They also differed on matters of belief, with the Sadducees, for instance, rejecting the belief in an AFTERLIFE, RESURRECTION, and the MESSIAH, which were basic to the Pharisees.

The Sadducees disappeared completely as a force in Jewish life in Erets Israel with the destruction of the Temple, but the Pharisees continued as the dominant spiritual mentors of the Jews for centuries thereafter. It was the Pharisee leadership which laid the groundwork upon which the mainstream of Judaism was founded.

PHILO Hellenistic Jewish philosopher (c.20 BCE-50 CE). Philo was one of the main philosophers of the transition period from Platonism to Neo-Platonism. In his writings, he endeavors to reconcile the world-view of Platonic philosophy with the principles of the Bible, and thereby pioneered in the attempt to forge a synthesis between Greek philosophy and Judaism, which was to later characterize medieval Jewish philosophy.

Philo belonged to a rich and influential Jewish family in Alexandria. Little is known of Philo's life except that he visited Jerusalem and that he headed a Jewish delegation to the Roman emperor, Caligula, in the year 40 CE.

Many of his works have survived, most of them in Greek, and some in Armenian translation. The greatest part of his writings deals with the Pentateuch. Most of these writings, such as his books on the Creation, on the lives of the Patriarchs, *On the Life of Moses*, *On the Decalogue*, and *On The Special Laws*, emphasize the moral and philosophical side of the Pentateuch, which was conceived of as an ideal framework of laws. In his commentary on the first 17 chapters of Genesis, Philo utilizes an allegorical interpretation of the biblical verses to convey his philosophical and mystical views. In his *Questions and Answers on Genesis* and *Questions and Answers on Exodus*, preserved in Armenian translation, he also interprets individual words and verses of the Bible allegorically.

In addition to his writings on the Bible, Philo wrote, apparently in his youth, several works of a completely philosophical nature: *All Just and Good Are Free*, *On Providence*, and *On the Eternity of the World*. Furthermore, Philo composed several works of an historic and apologetic nature: *An Apology for the Jews*, *Contra Flaccus*, and *On The Embassy to Gaius*.

In his writings, Philo explains the Bible in light of Hellenistic philosophical ideas. In his opinion, philosophical truths are concealed in the Bible; Philo uses allegorical interpretation to reveal them. An example of this is Philo's understanding of the first verses of Genesis as referring to ideas and primeval matter. Biblical characters represent, in his opinion, the various moral virtues. Philo possessed a broad knowledge of Hellenistic philosophy; most of the Greek philosophers are mentioned in his writings. His originality is expressed not only in his synthesis of Greek and Jewish philosophy, but also in purely philosophical questions. Philo is a representative of middle-Platonic philosophy, which combines Platonic doctrine with ideas of the Stoics and the Neo-Pythagoreans.

Philo's thought is of a deep religious and mystic character. According to Philo, God is a completely transcendent entity. Although God is beyond human apprehension, man must constantly strive to know Him. The logos, the Word of God, is the wisdom of God, different from God, yet not separate from Him. The *logos* is the force through which the world was created and it mediates between God and man. Following Plato, Philo distinguishes between the transient, material world and the eternal, spiritual world. Man, a creature composed of body and soul, partakes of both worlds and thus, is given the possibility of choosing between them.

Philo commented on the Bible in its Greek translation, the SEPTUAGINT. His knowledge of Hebrew was, at best, minimal, and he might not have known any Hebrew at all. In spite of several similarities between his conceptions and those of the sages, it appears that Philo had no connection with the sages of Israel of his day. Philo's thinking presents a picture of the intellectual Jewish climate of Alexandria, characterized by a world-view imbued with Hellenistic thought, but nonetheless unwilling to deny its own Jewishness.

The CHURCH FATHERS were greatly influenced by Philo's thought, including his allegorical mode of interpretation of the Bible and his doctrine of the *logos*, and they preserved his writings. With the exception of Josephus, Philo is not mentioned in any early Jewish source. The sages and the medieval Jewish thinkers did not know of Philo's writings, and his thought had no influence on Jewish thinking. The first Jewish thinker to revive interest in Philo was Azariah dei Rossi, one of the greatest scholars of the period of the Renaissance.

PHILOSOPHY Traditionally, philosophy is believed to have two tasks, one analytic and the other synthetic. The first consists primarily of a method; the critical application of rational intelligence and logical reasoning to a variety of subject matters with the aim of explicating the meaning of basic concepts and of judging truth claims. The second task attempts to discover answers to metaphysical questions so as to increase man's knowledge of reality.

The religion of Judaism could therefore relate to philosophy in two ways. In the first, the critical analytic method of philosophy could be applied to Judaism. This has been done in different periods by believing Jews while standing within the circle of faith. When perpetrated in this manner, with the conclusions set in advance, the activity is called Jewish theology rather than philosophy. When done by individuals (Jews or non-Jews) who stand outside the circle of faith, the activity is an aspect of the philosophy of religion with only an indirect connection with Judaism.

However, philosophy could also impact on Judaism in relation to its synthetic task. Believers in Judaism may wish to compare and perhaps integrate their religious beliefs with the substantive philosophic teachings of their time. This too has been done in connection with Judaism beginning with the attempt of PHILO of Alexandria (c. 20 BCE-c. 50 CE) to reconcile Judaism with the Greek philosophy prevalent in his day. However, here too what emerges may be seen as "theology." For a full treatment of the subject see THEOLOGY.

PHYLACTERIES See TEFILLIN

PIDYON HA-BEN See FIRST-BORN, REDEMPTION OF

PIDYON SHEVUYIM See CAPTIVES, RANSOMING OF

PIETY Term generally referring to reverence for God, with the emphasis in Judaism on the performance of the COMMANDMENTS andthe devout fulfillment of those duties required by God. Various Hebrew words describe the pious man, such as *Ḥasid*, *yeré shamayim* (lit. "one who fears heaven"), or TSADDIK, but there is no clear line differentiating one from the other. The criterion for proper behavior is often stated in terms of one trying, as far as is possible, to emulate God's behavior (IMITATION OF GOD). Thus, when Jeremiah quotes God as stating "I am pious" (or "holy") (*ḥasid*) the implication is that man must emulate God in this as well. At the same time, the Bible cautions against the danger of irrational and excessive piety, and warns "not to be overpious" (Eccl. 7:16).

The nature of piety is a matter of dispute. RASHI (on Lev. 19:1) states that a person who refrains from violating the commandments is considered as pious. Naḥmanides rejects this view, claiming that one may adhere totally to the law of the Torah and yet be a despicable person. According to him, piety goes beyond following the letter of the law.

The sages offer a prescription for piety based on action rather than on belief, when they quote God as saying: "Would that they [i.e., the Jewish people] forget Me but observe My Torah, for the light within it will bring them back to the proper path" (*Yal. Shimoni* to Jer., 282). They also say that a person should engage in studying (or in performing other commandments) even without the proper intention, because "from these deeds not for their own sake will come deeds for their own sake" (*Pes.* 50b).

The Talmud discusses the HASIDIM HA-RISHONIM, an early group of pietists, "whose level of piety cannot be duplicated in later generations," stating, as an example, that they would spend an hour preparing for each prayer, an hour at prayer, and an hour following it before they resumed everyday pursuits (*Ber.* 32b).

In different eras there were groups and individuals who were known as *hasidim*, or "the pious ones," as, for example, during the late Second Temple period. In the Middle Ages, a movement of *hasidim* emerged in Germany, the HASIDÉ ASHKENAZ, led by R. JUDAH HE-HASID. These pietists adopted numerous stringencies in their daily living. In the 18th century the movement of HASIDISM emerged, which preached that every person, however humble, can attain the greatest of heights through proper devotion and piety when performing the commandments and during prayer, and not only through study.

PIKKU'AH NEFESH ("Consideration for human life"). Hebrew term denoting the paramount obligation to ignore most religious laws when someone's life is endangered. "You shall not stand idly by the blood of your neighbor" (Lev. 19:16) is one traditional source for this rule; another, citing Leviticus 18:5, is the rabbinic view that God's commandments are intended for man to "live by them" and not die through their observance (*Yoma* 85b). The *pikku'ah nefesh* law takes account of numerous emergency situations, especially those calling for "work" normally prohibited on the Sabbath and Jewish festivals, since "consideration for human life" takes precedence over the Sabbath laws (*Yoma* 85a; *Shab.* 132a). In practice, holy day regulations are set aside when a sick person needs medical attention or anyone's health may be imperiled. Expectant mothers or those falling ill should be driven to hospital; the use of a telephone is permitted; the duty to fast on the Day of Atonement is waived; doctors and nurses must see to their patients; and even forbidden food may be consumed if this will preserve someone's life. The law of *pikku'ah nefesh* does not apply, however, in cases involving three cardinal prohibitions — blatant idolatry, murder, and sexual crimes. Here, a Jew must accept martyrdom rather than transgress these commandments (*Sanh.* 74a-b).

PILGRIMAGE The responsibility to go to "the place which the Lord your God will choose" (Deut. 16:16) on the three PILGRIM FESTIVALS. During the period of the judges, the site to which all came was Shiloh (I Sam. 1:3). Later, after the TEMPLE had been built in JERUSALEM, the thrice-annual pilgrimage was made to the Temple, and served as a strong unifying force among the Israelites. However, the period during which the First Temple in Jerusalem served as the focus of Israelite life was a short one, lasting only to the end of SOLOMON's reign. With the accession to the throne of Rehoboam and the revolt of Jeroboam, the tribes were split into two separate nations. In order to prevent the people of the northern Kingdom of Israel from traveling to Jerusalem, Jeroboam established alternate sacrificial venues in Dan and Bethel.

The Bible specified that all (adult) males were required to make the pilgrimage three times a year and stated further that "they shall not appear before the Lord empty. Every man shall give as he is able" (Deut. 16:16-17). This was understood by the sages to refer to the *hagigah* sacrifice (pilgrimage offering) that was an obligatory part of the visit to Jerusalem. The Second TITHE, that could only be eaten in Jerusalem (or, alternately, could be sold and the proceeds used in Jerusalem to buy food to be consumed there) enabled those coming to the pilgrimage festivals to have adequate food supplies during their stay in the city.

An indication of how many people heeded the call in Second Temple times can be seen in the account by Josephus (*War* 6.9) of the Passover celebration in the year 66 CE when, according to this account, no less than 256,500 lambs were sacrificed — and each lamb was eaten by a number of people.

The pilgrimage itself required much advance preparation, both for those coming to Jerusalem and for the inhabitants of the city. Jewish law requires that in Erets Israel the phrase "give dew and rain" be recited in the AMIDAH from the seventh day of Heshvan, 15 days after the prayer for RAIN is recited on SHEMINI ATSERET, at the end of SUKKOT, in consideration for those who came from far-off places, lest the rains begin right away and these pilgrims be forced to travel on muddy roads. This shows that some had to travel for as much as 15 days each way in order to take part in the pilgrimage. In fact, various sources indicate that Jews may have come from even further, for there are references to people arriving in Jerusalem from as far away as Rome.

After the Temple was destroyed, pilgrimages to Erets Israel continued, but their character was entirely different. Now they were sorrowful voyages, made in order to weep at the destruction. Thus, the term "the Wailing Wall" was given by non-Jews to the WESTERN WALL when they saw how the Jews who came there wept. Proper conduct during such visits to the HOLY PLACES was stipulated in Jewish law. One who saw either Jerusalem in its destruction or the site of the Temple which had been razed had to tear his clothes, as must a person in mourning.

Throughout the centuries, Jews made their way to Erets

Tomb of Johanan ha-Sandelar (tanna, *2nd century), in Galilee, to which pilgrims flock each year.*

Israel. In the 17th century, the rabbis of the mystical school in Safed "identified" many graves in Galilee as those of ancient sages and in the wake of this, Jewish pilgrims the world over came to "stretch themselves" over these graves, pray there and light candles. Visiting the Holy Land often involved great difficulties and dangers. The reception of the pilgrims inside the country itself varied in different eras. Frequently the Jews were required to pay large sums of money in order to approach various sites. Various, often arbitrary, restrictions also applied. Even as late as 1948, Jews wishing to visit the Cave of MACHPELAH, the grave of the Jewish patriarchs and matriarchs according to Jewish tradition, were only permitted to descend seven steps on the eastern side of the cave and insert notes with petitions in a hole which led into the cave proper. Only after the State of Israel conquered the West Bank in 1967 were the Jews able to enter the Holy Places.

In Israel today, there are various pilgrimages to different holy sites. Thus, on LAG BA-OMER as many as 100,000 people visit the tomb of R. SIMEON BAR YOḤAI in Meron; on 14 Iyyar (*Pesaḥ Sheni*) the tomb of R. MEIR BA'AL NA-NES in Tiberias is visited. In recent years the grave of Israel Abu-Hatsira ("Baba Sali") in Netivot has become the site of a pilgrimage by Jews of North African origin on the anniversary of his death, on 3 Shevat.

In modern times, many Jews come from all over the world to spend pilgrim festivals in Jerusalem which Israeli Jews visit the Western Wall.

PILGRIM FESTIVALS The three FESTIVALS which the Israelites were commanded to celebrate "in the place the Lord your God will choose" (Deut. 16:16). These are PASSOVER (seven days in the Land of Israel beginning on 15 Nisan), SHAVU'OT (one day in Israel, 6 Sivan), and SUKKOT (eight days including SHEMINI ATSERET, beginning on 15 Tishri). The festivals are referred to in Hebrew as the *shalosh regalim*, the three (foot) pilgrimages, the name being derived from the biblical ordination that all adult (i.e., age 13 or older) males go to the place God would choose, which was eventually JERUSALEM (Ex. 23:17; see PILGRIMAGE). Until the Temple was destroyed, three commandments had to be observed by adult males on the festivals: going to Jerusalem; bringing individual sacrifices known as the *ḥagigah* ("pilgrimage offerings") in addition to those brought on behalf of the nation; and rejoicing on the festival. Each festival had its own requirements for the sacrifices to be brought on behalf of the nation (Num.28,29), and after the Temple's destruction, these were incorporated in the ADDITIONAL SERVICE recited on each day of the festivals.

All three festivals have both agricultural and national significance. Passover is "the festival of the spring," in which a measure of the new barley crop (the OMER) is brought, and it also celebrates the EXODUS from Egypt; Shavu'ot is the "harvest festival," celebrating the end of the barley harvest and the beginning of the wheat harvest, as well as the giving of the Torah at Mount SINAI; Sukkot is "the festival of the ingathering" of crops, and it also commemorates the 40 years the Israelites wandered in the desert.

The laws requiring a pilgrimage to Jerusalem and the bringing of offerings lapsed with the destruction of the Temple. However, the obligation to rejoice on the festivals continued; this was interpreted as the eating of meat, the drinking of wine, and the wearing of new clothes. MAIMONIDES (*Sefer ha-Mitsvot*, Commandment 54) notes that this commandment to rejoice includes insuring that the underprivileged be also provided with the means to rejoice on the festival.

Jews from all over the country visit Jerusalem for the Sukkot festival. Some carry Torah Scrolls.

The Morning Service on each day of the pilgrim festivals includes the recitation of the HALLEL prayer, the READING OF THE LAW, and the *Musaf* (Additional Service). Outside Israel, an extra day is added to each festival (see SECOND DAYS OF FESTIVALS). All work except that connected with food preparation is forbidden on the first and last days (first two and last two outside Israel) of Passover and Sukkot, and on Shavu'ot.

Each festival has its own individual rituals and customs, such as the SEDER on Passover, the all-night study (TIKKUN ḤATSOT) on Shavu'ot, and the FOUR SPECIES on Sukkot. One of the FIVE SCROLLS is also read on each festival: the SONG OF SONGS on Passover, RUTH on Shavu'ot, and ECCLESIASTES on Sukkot.

PILPUL (derived from *pilpel*, "pepper"). A systematic approach to the study of talmudic and rabbinic texts, aimed at the clarification of difficult texts, often involving an intricate halakhic discussion. Initially, it was regarded as a creative and praiseworthy approach, and could involve the application of HERMENEUTICS for the purpose of deriving *halakhah*. *Avot* (6.5) lists *pilpul* as among the 48 virtues through which Torah is acquired. However, when carried to extremes, it became an exercise in hairsplitting and complicated theoretical speculation. As such, it was already decried by the rabbis, who criticized R. MEIR, the outstanding scholar of his generation, for his excessively "pilpulistic" approach (*Er.* 13b).

Following the example set in the 16th century at the rabbinical academy (*yeshivah*) of R. Jacob Pollak in Cracow, *pilpul* became widely utilized in East European *yeshivot* as a tool for sharpening the mind of the student and for developing his powers of logic, often through argument for argument's sake. Divergent, unrelated texts were juxtaposed and artificially forced into a relationship with each other by casuistic and semantic means. The resulting dialogue and derivative techniques were a major source of intellectual stimulation in the limited reality of the East European ghetto. However, it continued to arouse condemnation, as in the words of R. Judah Löw ben Bezalel of Prague: "Those who see the essence of study in sharp-witted *pilpul* show disrespect to the Torah and are spending their time erroneously, and would do better to learn carpentry."

In modern times, the term is generally used in a perjorative sense, implying excessive hairsplitting.

PIRKÉ AVOT See AVOT

PIRKÉ DE-RABBI ELIEZER ("Chapters of Rabbi Eliezer"). MIDRASH composed in the early decades of the ninth century by an unknown author and ascribed by him to R. ELIEZER BEN HYRCANUS, a *tanna* of the late first/early second century CE. Scholars are divided as to whether it was written in Erets Israel or Babylonia. The work enjoyed considerable popularity in Jewish circles and went through more than two dozen editions, including a Latin translation in the 17th century.

Noteworthy are the many similarities as well as the divergences between it and the Pseudepigrapha (see APOCRYPHA AND PSEUDEPIGRAPHA). All the sages mentioned in the work are from Erets Israel, and the Jerusalem TALMUD is frequently quoted.

The book is composite in nature and consists of three originally distinct sections: one describes the occasions when God descended to earth; another gives a detailed account of early rabbinic MYSTICISM as well as the calculation of the CALENDAR; the third is a partial Midrash on the AMIDAH. The first two chapters present a biographical account of the putative author of the book, R. Eliezer ben Hyrcanus. Several chapters appear to be intended as homilies for special Sabbaths (see SABBATHS, SPECIAL). A distinct polemical note emerges in its attitude to certain teachings in the Pseudepigrapha, apparently accepted by some Jewish sects in the author's time.

The Babylonian *ge'onim* are the first to quote the book, and it is occasionally referred to by the *Tosafists* (see TOSAFOT). Some of its midrashic teachings are echoed in the ZOHAR.

PITTUM HA-KETORET ("the compounding of the incense"). Talmudic BARAITA (*Ker.* 6a) listing the various ingredients and the quantity of each that went into the compounding of the incense offerings in the Temple, which is incorporated into the LITURGY.

According to Exodus 30:7-8, 34-38, AARON was commanded to offer up INCENSE in the SANCTUARY twice a day, once in the morning and once toward evening. The practice was maintained throughout the periods of both the First and Second Temples.

Pittum ha-Ketoret first appeared in a prayer book in the Roman rite. From there it was adopted by the Ashkenazi rite where it is recited in the Sabbath ADDITIONAL SERVICE (following *Én k-Elohénu*). Jonah of Gerona (13th century) introduced its recital into the daily afternoon service and this remains the practice in the Sephardi and Yemenite rites. Various reasons have been suggested for its incorporation in the liturgy (including a statement in the ZOHAR that recitation of this prayer prevents death) but none is wholly convincing.

PIYYUT (stemming from a Greek word meaning "poet"; pl. *piyyutim*). Liturgical poem; in a broader sense, the totality of Hebrew religious verse composed from the first centuries CE to the Enlightenment (HASKALAH) period.

At first, the *piyyutim* were intended to replace the obligatory prayers, and thereby to add variety to the service, primarily on the Sabbaths and festivals. Later, when the content and form of the prayers were formalized, *piyyutim* were composed and added to the fixed prayer text.

Most of the *piyyutim* were meant for the main festivals, but in the course of time *piyyutim* were also composed for regular and special Sabbaths, for fast days, and even for ordinary weekdays. *Piyyutim* were also written for family events, such as weddings, circumcisions, and days of mourning. In Erets Israel, they were composed when the fixed prayer texts began to be established.

Ancient versions of the text of *piyyutim* can be found in the Talmud. Certain *piyyutim* were included in the early prayer services and can be identified by their special style and meter. These *piyyutim* do not rhyme.

The development of the *piyyut* is divided into three major periods:

a) The pre-classical period, the era of the anonymous *piyyut*, which ended in about the sixth century, and is marked by a verse with meter but without rhyming. These ancient *piyyutim* are simple in form. Their language is clear, and they are generally arranged in an acrostic alphabetical form, without any indication of the *paytan* (i.e., the author of the *piyyut*). The only *paytan* of this period whose name is known is Yose ben Yose.

b) The classic period in the sixth to eighth centuries, where the rhyme assumes importance. In this period, most of the activity was in Erets Israel, and the authors were famous both by name and by their works. They included Yannai, who wrote *kerovot* (see below) for all the weekly Pentateuch readings (based on the TRIENNIAL CYCLE); Eleazar ha-Kallir, many of whose poems are in the Ashkenazi festival liturgy; Ḥaduta ben Abraham; and Simeon ben Megas. During this era, the classic forms of the *piyyut* were given their standard form.

c) The third period, the late era of the Eastern *paytanim*, most of whom lived outside Erets Israel, was very fruitful.

In the European countries, there were two major schools, one Central European and the other Spanish. The first was centered in southern Italy in the 9th century. Some of the first poets there were Silano, Shephatiah, and his son Amittai. Very few of their *piyyutim* have survived. The poetic activity then moved to central and northern Italy, where *paytanim* headed by Solomon ben Judah the Babylonian were active, and from there it moved in the tenth century to Greece, Germany, and France.

There was a great creative flowering in Germany in the tenth-11th century. The influence of the Erets Israel school is very apparent in all these works, throughout this entire period. At the same time new forms were developed.

Italy and Southern-France Provence were eventually influenced by the Spanish school, which first began to flourish in the mid-tenth century. It was there that Hebrew religious verse reached its zenith, with the great poets, including Joseph Ibn Abitur, Solomon IBN GABIROL, Isaac Ibn Ghayyat, Moses IBN EZRA, and JUDAH HALEVI.

In Spain, various original and bold forms were developed that had not been known by the Eastern *paytanim*. The

Part of the piyyut *"Open the Gates of Mercy", from the Day of Atonement liturgy. From a* Maḥzor, *Germany 1345.*

Spanish school is the most clearly defined of all the schools of *piyyut*. Even after the expulsion of the Jews from Spain in 1492, the writing of Spanish-type *piyyut* did not come to an end, but was renewed in those countries to which the refugees migrated: Turkey, Greece, Erets Israel, etc.

The *piyyutim* may be divided, in accordance with their liturgical object, into a number of types, which differ both in the way they were created and in their development. The most ancient and most important are the *kerovot*, a set of *piyyutim* added to the AMIDAH prayer, and the YOTSEROT, a collection of *piyyutim* added to the blessings before and after the SHEMA of the Morning Service. Parallel to the morning *yotzer* are the MA'ARAVOT, added to the blessings before and after the *Shema* of the Evening Service.

Other examples of *piyyutim* include the *teki'ata* said in the Additional Services on Rosh ha-Shanah, the AZHAROT on Shavu'ot, the SELIḤOT (penitential prayers) on fast days, the KINOT (elegies) on TISHAH BE-AV, and the HOSHANOT on Sukkot. There are also Sephardi *piyyutim* included in the NISHMAT KOL ḤAI section of the Sabbath and festival prayers, known as *nishmatot*; and *piyyutim* to be said before the standard *piyyutim*, known as *reshuyyot*.

The style and vocabulary of the *piyyutim* evolved over the centuries. Those of the ancient anonymous *piyyut* were very similar to the standard prayers. The vocabulary is biblical with certain talmudic elements, and the style is clear and simple. From Yannai onward, Jewish religious verse became more obscure and less respectful of pure forms, and the *paytanim* invented their own vocabulary. These new words and style, which were not in conformity with the classic Hebrew grammar, were later fiercely criticized in Spain. The *paytanim* of the school of Kallir used a complex system of terms, and incorporated much talmudic and midrashic material, as well as various veiled allusions, all of which led to multiple interpretations. Religious verse in Spain based itself on a clear biblical framework, in reaction to these exaggerations. Solomon Ibn Gabirol played a large role in this process of change. This new style influenced the poets of North Africa, Yemen, Erets Israel, Babylon, and Provence. The Eastern European *piyyut*, however, remained faithful in general terms to the Kallir model in language and style.

Already in early times there had been harsh criticism of the *piyyut*, particularly from members of the great ACADEMIES in Babylon. In spite of this, the *piyyut* was given an honored place in the prayers, even in Babylon. The cantor chose which *piyyutim* he wished to use, and a very large number were created.

As time went by, certain *piyyutim* became an integral part of the prayers, and each community decided which *piyyutim* to insert.

PLAGUES, TEN The punishments that were brought upon Pharaoh and Egypt by God, to persuade him to set the Israelites free (see EXODUS from Egypt). The plagues were: (1) the Nile waters turning to blood; (2) the swarming of frogs; (3) lice; (4) probably flies, although traditionally regarded as wild animals; (5) pestilence, afflicting the Egyptian livestock; (6) a skin inflammation; (7) heavy hailstorm; (8) locusts; (9) three days of darkness; (10) death of the Egyptian first-born. The plagues were divided into three groups, each with its own message to Pharaoh. Thus, before the first plague, Pharaoh was told: "By this you will know that I am the Lord" (Ex. 7:17). Before the fourth plague, he was told: "that you may know that I am the Lord in the midst of the earth" (Ex. 8:18). Finally, before the seventh plague, Moses was instructed to say to Pharaoh that the purpose of the plagues was "that you may know that there is none like Me in all the earth" (Ex. 9:14). The messages stated that: a) God is the Lord; b) that He is actively involved in everything that occurs; and c) that He is omnipotent, and there is none but Him. In each group of three plagues, Pharaoh was warned in advance of the first two, while the third was brought about unannounced. This division into three is also found in the mnemonic device of R. Judah, quoted in the Passover HAGGADAH, which separates the ten plagues into groups of three, three, and four. Another division of the plagues is into groups of three, and a final tenth plague. Poetic accounts of the plagues are given in Psalms 78:44-51; 105:28-36. The Midrash contains various fanciful interpretations, some of which are incorporated in the Passover *Haggadah*.

PLATONISM AND NEO-PLATONISM Philosophical systems deriving from Plato (427-347 BCE) in the ancient, medieval, and modern periods. Plato's system was accepted by some religious individuals. In Alexandria, the first-century Jewish thinker, PHILO, sought to provide a rapprochement between Platonism and Jewish tradition by using the allegorical method to interpret the Five Books of Moses.

However, this early attempt had no lasting impact on Jewish thought, and it was not until the Middle Ages that the Neo-Platonic tradition, created by Plotinus and his successors and filtered through Islamic sources, began to affect Jewish philosophy. The Platonic "forms" were identified with the creative thoughts of God, and God was defined as the Good, the First Principle, and "The One," i.e., as absolutely single and self-sufficient. From this ultimate One, the intelligible world of ideas and the lower forms of being descended or emanated down to the material world (see SEFIROT).

The human soul was a particle from a higher realm of being. The Jewish Neo-Platonists labeled this higher realm the Throne of Glory, and it was to this that the soul longed to return. Neo-Platonism offered a basis not just for rational contemplation but also for spiritual and mystical life. In this system the effort to reunite with the ultimate One lay behind all concrete experience. The methodology to be followed was intellectual abstraction, contemplative ascent, in which in the end only God would be left (see THEOLOGY).

Isaac Israeli (c. 850-950 CE) is an early source of Jewish Neo-Platonism. He defined philosophy as assimilation to God according to the human capacity. Ascent of the human soul to the Divine is through three stages, the ultimate stage depicted as becoming angelic or Divine, an experience to which he applied the word DEVEKUT, conjunction. The Neo-Platonic doctrine regarding the unknowability of the first principle is expressed in Israeli's position that only God's existence is knowable and not His essence. This distinction is found in the writings of BAḤYA IBN PAKUDA, Joseph ibn Zaddik, JUDAH HALEVI and Abraham IBN DAUD.

Another major medieval Neo-Platonic Jewish thinker was Solomon IBN GABIROL, whose doctrines are found in his work, *Mekor Ḥayyim*. He stressed that the goal of human existence is the conjunction of the human soul with the supernal world through knowledge and action, specifically intellectual and ethical purification. Ibn Gabirol argued that the study of philosophy offers liberation from death and conjunction with the source of life. The human cannot come to know what Ibn Gabirol labels the "First Essence" because it transcends everything and is incommensurable with the intellect.

In the late Middle Ages, the *Republic* of Plato became known through the writings of the Arab philosopher Averroes. That work was translated into Hebrew by Samuel ben Judah of Marseilles in the 14th century and was widely studied by Jewish thinkers as their introduction to political philosophy. In 1486 Elijah del Medigo translated it into Latin for the Christian mystic, Pico della Mirandola. Del Medigo utilized the work in his treatise on faith and reason, *Beḥinnat ha-Dat* ("An Examination of Faith").

Judah Abravanel or Leone Ebreo, as he was known in Latin, the son of Isaac ABRAVANEL, wove the basic ideas of Platonic philosophy into his *Dialoghi di Amore* ("Dialogues on Love"). In Moses Mendelssohn's *Phaedon*, published in 1767, Mendelssohn's discussion of the immortality of the soul was modeled on the Platonic dialogue of the same title.

Although Neo-Platonism was superseded by ARISTOTELIANISM in the development of medieval thought from the 12th century, it continued to have its impact on mystical speculation. The Kabbalah, which came to the fore in the 13th century, was influenced by Neo-Platonic thought, including the doctrine of emanation (see MYSTICISM).

POLEMICS See APOLOGETICS AND POLEMICS

POLYGAMY See MONOGAMY AND POLYGAMY

POOR and POVERTY Since biblical times Jewish writings have dealt with the treatment of the poor and disadvantaged. They have always been based on the view that the poor and disadvantaged have a right to support and help from those who are more fortunate. Every member of the Jewish community has the responsibility and obligation to contribute to the care of the poor and needy. As the source of all sustenance, God provides the more fortunate with their lot; therefore, just as God has given to them, so they must give to the less fortunate. Furthermore, God has a special concern for the poor and so must the Jewish community. These principles are reflected in the writings and laws governing the treatment of the poor throughout Jewish history.

The Pentateuch recognizes that poverty will always exist and that Judaism has an obligation to the poor. "For there will never cease to be needy ones in your land, which is why I command you: open your hand to the poor and needy kinsman in your land" (Deut. 15:11). This commandment to help the poor is repeated throughout the Bible. It even becomes a source of blessing. The Israelites are told that they will not receive God's blessing if they ignore the poor.

The prophets championed the rights of the poor and called upon the Israelites to heed their plea. They condemned those who shame or oppress the poor, or ignore their needs. At the same time, while they do not blame the poor for misfortune, neither do the prophets idealize or glorify the poor and poverty.

The Bible clearly outlines the rights of the poor, systematically spelling out the minimum sustenance they are to receive from the more privileged members of the Jewish community. When they reap, landowners are commanded to leave the edges of their fields for the needy, and are told to leave the olives, grapes, and sheaves of grain that fall while they are harvesting. They are only allowed to beat the olive trees once; the fruit falling after beating the second time is left for the needy (see LEKET SHIKHHAH VE-PE'AH). The Bible also prescribes a SABBATICAL YEAR every seventh year, when the fields are to lie fallow, and the needy are allowed to come and eat from them. The Book of Deuteronomy calls for the inclusion of the poor in the celebration of the pilgrimage feasts. Finally, the poor are entitled to TITHES, these being given the same name as the tithes for the Levites or for those dedicated to God's service. The implication is that the Jewish community has an equal responsibility to the Levites and to the poor. In addition to these mandatory subsidies, people are encouraged to give other offerings voluntarily.

These basic points continued to form the cornerstone of the rabbinic attitude toward poverty. By the talmudic period, poverty was so endemic and widespread that it was looked upon almost as a virtue. It helped to strengthen one's character. On the other hand, the rabbis also realized that excessive poverty "deprives a man of his mental balance" (*Er.* 41b). The rabbis also seemed to regard poverty as somewhat predetermined and not necessarily reflective of a person's character or efforts. They called upon the people to consider the feelings of the poor when giving, both in terms of how it felt to be poor and how it felt to receive charity. They reminded people that "God stands together with the poor man at the door, and one should therefore consider whom one is confronting" (Lev. R. 34.9). By the third century, the principle of anonymous giving was institutionalized. It was considered improper to give publicly or to let the recipient know the donor's identity.

Giving to the poor in secret: the hands of two persons hidden by a curtain, one giving, the other receiving. Amsterdam, 17th century.

Once the Jews became urbanized, new means of giving to the needy had to be instituted. The biblical principle of the right to support remained the same. However, by the talmudic period, the method had changed. Community institutions collected and distributed funds. All members of the Jewish community were required to contribute. The charity fund (*kuppah*) was for food and clothing. The *tamḥui* (soup kitchen) was for the support of the transient poor. There was also a burial fund (see BURIAL SOCIETY) that was equally available to both rich and poor. The dowry society (*hakhnasat kallah*) provided the dowries and trousseaux for poor brides. In addition, the HEKDESH served as a poorhouse and asylum for the old, the sick, and the stranger. Every Jewish community, however small or indigent, had these institutions.

Although the Jewish community has changed fundamentally in the modern world, the principle of helping other less fortunate members of the community has prevailed. While the institutions and ghettos of the Middle Ages have largely disappeared or been transformed, Jews all over the world continue to contribute to the support of the poor and needy, regarding this as a basic element in their tradition. See also CHARITY.

POSEKIM (sing. *posek*). Rabbinic scholars who decide the HALAKHAH (Jewish law) in specific cases, and whose decisions are regarded as authoritative in the region under their jurisdiction. This limitation arose from the fact that, in making his decision, the *posek* took into account local traditions and customs. The term is used in contrast to the scholar who devotes himself to analyzing the sources of the *halakhah* in rabbinic literature for their own sake.

The authoritativeness of a decision by a *posek* was gauged by his reputation as a master of talmudic learning, and not by any official position he might hold or by the prestige attached to that position. In addition to his learning, the *posek* was expected to have considerable practical experience in rendering judgment in actual cases.

While the Babylonian TALMUD is the most important source on Jewish law, in most instances it summarizes the debate on a topic without giving any definite ruling. From the seventh century onward, queries addressed to rabbinical authorities (initially the *Ge'onim*) requested decisions on points of law, and these were provided in the replies (see RESPONSA). Collections of these decisions began to appear, the earliest including the *She'iltot* of R. AḤAI OF SHABḤA (eighth century). HALAKHOT GEDOLOT AND HALAKHOT PESUKOT were the forerunners of the later literature of the *posekim*.

As the Talmud required systematization, great scholars engaged in the work of CODIFICATION and they often had to give rulings as to what they considered *halakhah*. These authorities included Isaac ALFASI, Moses MAIMONIDES, R. ABRAHAM BEN DAVID OF POSQUIÈRES, R. ASHER BEN JEHIEL, R. JACOB BEN ASHER, R. Joseph CARO, and R. Moses ISSERLES.

Concise volumes of rabbinical decisions were compiled by R. SHNEUR ZALMAN OF LYADY, R. Abraham Danzig (*Ḥayyé Adam*), and R. Solomon Ganzfried ("Abbreviated SHULḤAN ARUKH"). Collections have also appeared relating to specific subjects and in modern times connected with the developments of technology (see HALAKHAH AND TECHNOLOGY). Notable among the 20th-century *posekim* is R. Mosheh FEINSTEIN whose decisions are regarded as authoritative in contemporary Orthodox circles.

REFORM JUDAISM rejected the authority of the *Shulḥan Arukh* and insisted on the right of each rabbi to render his own decisions without being bound by any code. However, advice is often sought, and notable responsa guiding such decisions have been issued by Solomon Freehof.

POST-MORTEM See MEDICAL ETHICS

PRACTICAL KABBALAH Term designating various activities which are akin to "white" magic and which have little or no connection with Judaism's mystical tradition, the KABBALAH proper. From late talmudic times onward, the techniques of "practical" Kabbalah were confined to special individuals and unauthorized dabbling in these techniques was considered a perilous adventure. Whereas mystical contemplation and communion with God was the essence of normative ("theoretical") MYSTICISM, the speculative or "practical" Kabbalah involved manipulation of Divine and angelic names, the use of AMULETS or charms containing magical letter combinations, the protective services of a GOLEM, chiromancy and exorcism (see DIBBUK; DEMONS AND DEMONOLOGY). One who engaged in any of these practices was often known as a BA'AL SHEM ("master of the name" or "Name"). WITCHCRAFT, necromancy and other forms of black magic, all abhorrent to Judaism, were rigorously excluded; alchemy and ASTROLOGY, however, did play an occasional (if peripheral) role. Traces of the "practical" Kabbalah are detectable in Jewish folklore, customs, and SUPERSTITIONS.

PRAYER (*tefillah*). Expression of a relationship with God, either in praise and thanksgiving or through meditation, requests and petitions, entreaties and the CONFESSION OF SINS. Jewish prayer is rooted in the belief that man is able to communicate with God, individually or collectively, and that God hears and responds to man's approach. In the Bible, God is envisaged as a personal Deity who created man in His own image and who therefore has a spiritual connection with him. The Book of PSALMS, widely regarded as the greatest devotional text of mankind, links prayer with the personal search for God and man's yearning to be close to, or at one with, the Creator, Redeemer and Revealer of truth. The ethical and spiritual values associated with the Divine are recognized by the worshiper through a significant change of attitude and conduct on his part.

Although only one of many terms with a similar meaning, the word *tefillah* is most commonly used in the Bible for prayer. It stems from a Hebrew root which means "to think,

Rabbi wrapped in a prayer shawl (tallit) *leading the service in the Bucharest synagogue, Rumania.*

entreat, intercede, judge," and its reflexive verbal derivative (*le-hitpallel*) thus has the sense of "judging oneself" as well as "praying."

Prayer may be formalized or impromptu. The Bible contains more than 80 examples, ranging from the touching five-word plea by Moses on behalf of his sister Miriam (Num. 12:13) to King Solomon's lengthy petition when the Temple was dedicated (I Kings 8:12-53). Initially, however, no prayers were ordained for regular worship. Until the destruction of the Second Temple, prayer was institutionalized through the SACRIFICES AND OFFERINGS that expressed submission to the Divine Will and that were often accompanied by an invocation (Gen. 13:4, 26:25). Since the ritual offering became a highly choreographed, dramatic act of public worship in itself, the biblical laws governing sacrifice made no provision for liturgical rites, the only important exceptions being the pilgrim's declaration on bringing the first fruits to the Temple (Deut. 26:5-10) and the priestly confession on the Day of Atonement (Lev. 16:21-34). The text of the latter has been preserved only in its Second Temple formulation (*Yoma* 3.8). However, an early universalist note was struck in a conception of the Temple by Isaiah (56:7) as "a house of prayer for all peoples."

During the Babylonian Exile (see EXILE, BABYLONIAN), communal prayer in the SYNAGOGUE developed as a replacement for sacrifices. After the destruction of the Second Temple in 70 CE, the rabbis followed this precedent by regulating daily prayer services (see LITURGY). They referred to this new form of prayer as *avodah she-ba-lev*, "the service of the heart" (*Ta'an.* 2a). A talmudic debate over the origin of the three daily prayer services incidentally emphasized the need to retain the personal, spontaneous element in prayer (*Ber.* 26b). The sages taught that making prayer a "fixed duty" or "routine exercise" negated its purpose and effect (*Ber.* 4.4; *Avot* 2.13). One sure antidote to such praying by rote was offering an original prayer each day (TJ *Ber.* 4.3). "God longs for the prayer of the righteous" (*Yev.* 64a), but it must not be uttered "in the midst of sorrow, idleness, laughter, frivolous chatter, or idle talk, only in the joy of [performing] a commandment" (*Ber.* 31a). During the TEN DAYS OF PENITENCE especially, prayer is one of three factors that can annul an evil decree (TJ *Ta'an.* 2.1).

Set formulas of worship are traditionally ascribed to the Men of the GREAT ASSEMBLY (*Ber.* 33a). Congregational prayer services expanded to include the MORNING BENEDICTIONS, the SHEMA and its accompanying blessings, the AMIDAH or *Tefillah* (a central "prayer" of 18 blessings) and the READING OF THE LAW — Torah study and worship combined. (For further details see also MORNING SERVICE, AFTERNOON SERVICE, EVENING SERVICE, and ADDITIONAL SERVICE.) A liturgical pattern for daily, Sabbath and holiday worship thus took shape. To this statutory core, a variety of non-obligatory prayers were added in the form of poetry and prose (see KINOT, PIYYUTIM, SELIḤOT); woven into the fabric of the PRAYER BOOK throughout the ages, these inspired a fresh dedication to public worship. Other forms of prayer (e.g., GRACE AFTER MEALS, HAVDALAH, and KIDDUSH) were ordained for the home.

Attaining the right frame of mind (KAVVANAH) and praying with devotion (*iyyun tefillah; Shab.* 127a) are also stressed by the rabbis, who observed that the ḤASIDIM RISHONIM spent a whole hour "attuning their hearts to God" (*Ber.* 5.1). Although emphasis is placed on forming the words with one's lips and not declaiming them in a loud voice (*Ber.* 24b, 31a), the religious obligation can equally be discharged by listening carefully to the prayer leader (BA'AL TEFILLAH) and responding AMEN. It is best to keep private supplications short (*Ber.* 61a) and to "know before whom you stand" (*Ber.* 61a, 28b). Corporate prayers set in the first person plural, or those offered on behalf of others, have greater significance than private, self-centered prayers. A MINYAN, or prayer quorum of ten, is required for the recitation of BAREKHU, KADDISH, the AMIDAH, and other statutory prayers; if no *minyan* is present, these prayers are omitted.

According to MAIMONIDES, "prayer without devotion is no prayer at all" (*Yad. Tefillah* 4.16). For the medieval kabbalists, *kavvanot* (in the plural) signified "meditations and devotions" concerning the Divine mysteries hidden in the liturgy. ḤASIDISM, which regards prayer as a supreme religious act, developed an emotionally ecstatic expression in worship in order to achieve a mystical communion with an "attachment" to God (*devekut*). Over the centuries, various major sectors of the Jewish people also evolved their own specific "liturgical rite" (see NUSAḤ) and swaying the body in prayer became a pious custom.

From about 1800 onward, as a result of the new civil status that Jews had gained in Western society, REFORM JUDAISM began to question and change large sections of the traditional prayer book. Prayers for the restoration of sacrifices and for the national return to Zion were generally eliminated; others were translated into or composed in the vernacular. To varying degrees, this process continued as other non-Orthodox movements (CONSERVATIVE JUDAISM and RECONSTRUCTIONISM) emerged. Some modern Jewish thinkers, notably Mordecai KAPLAN, have also discountenanced "the use of ritual (i.e., petitions in the *Amidah*, etc.) for the purpose of influencing the course of events" and believe that prayer should be considered a means of attuning oneself to those powers in the universe that make for human self-fulfillment.

Direction of Prayer. Since ancient times, Jews have followed the practice of turning toward JERUSALEM or the TEMPLE in prayer. At the dedication of the First Temple (c. 950 BCE), King SOLOMON anticipated that the prayers of Israel would be directed "toward this place" (I Kings 8:30, 35; II Chr. 6:21, 26). More specifically, he foresaw that the exiles in distant foreign countries would "pray to You in the direction of their land which You gave to their fathers, of the city which You have chosen, and of the House which I have built to Your name" (I Kings 8:48; II Chr. 6:38). DANIEL in Babylonia worshiped three times daily in an upper room of his house where he "had had windows made facing Jerusalem" to the west (Dan. 6:11). By the Mishnaic period, this custom had become a legal norm (*Ber.* 4.5), the sages maintaining that all Jews "should direct their hearts to one place in worship" (*Ber.* 30a). Thus, according to the Talmud, a Jew who prayed in the Diaspora should face the Holy Land; in Erets Israel, the Jew should turn to Jerusalem; in Jerusalem he should face the Temple and on the Temple Mount he should direct his prayers to the Holy of Holies (*Ber.* 30a).

For the Jewish communities of southern Europe and North Africa, turning to Jerusalem meant facing east, toward the sunrise (see MIZRAḤ). This determined the "orientation" of their synagogues and the positioning within them of the holy ark in or next to the eastern wall. Early Christians also worshiped and oriented their churches in line with Jewish practice, while Muhammad initially selected Jerusalem as the Muslim *kiblah* (direction of prayer) before changing it to Mecca. The talmudic rule was later codified by Maimonides (*Yad, Tefillah* 11.2) and the *Shulḥan Arukh* (*OḤ* 90.4). For architectural reasons, not all modern synagogues are correctly "oriented" toward Jerusalem; in case of doubt, a Jew may simply "direct his heart toward his Father in heaven."

SAYINGS ABOUT PRAYER

When praying, cast down your eyes and lift up your hearts.

Do not change the sages' formulations of the prayers.

Let those who are ignorant of Hebrew learn the prayers in their own daily languages, since prayer must be understood.

If the heart does not know what the lips utter, it is no prayer.

Man must lose himself in prayer and forget his own existence.

A poor man's prayer breaks through every barrier and storms its way into the presence of the Almighty.

The gates of prayer are never closed.

Prayer is conversation with God.

PRAYER BEFORE A JOURNEY (*tefillat ha-derekh*). Prayer recited by a traveler on setting out on a journey, in accordance with a talmudic ruling (*Ber.* 29b). The prayer asks God to protect the traveler "from enemy, ambush, bandits, or wild animals on the way." The prayer proper concludes with a blessing to God "...Who hears prayer," but this is often followed by the recitation of various biblical verses, especially those demonstrating God's protection of individuals, and then certain psalms. The prayer is said whether or not danger seems imminent. It is not recited until the traveler has gone beyond the last houses on the outskirts of the

The Prayer on setting out on a Journey illustrated by travelers on horseback and on foot. From a Book of Benedictions, Germany, 1345.

city. There are those who rule that any journey of an hour or longer requires that the prayer be said. When a number of people are traveling together, the custom is for one person to recite the prayer aloud, and for the others to answer "amen" at the end. Generally, the prayer is said only once a day, even if frequent stops are made.

PRAYER BOOK The Jewish prayer book (*seder tefillot, siddur*, or MAHZOR) contains the obligatory and customary LITURGY to be recited in the SYNAGOGUE and at home at appointed times. In addition to the regular congregational prayer service for weekdays, the Sabbath and festivals, the prayer book has traditionally offered an order of service to be conducted by the family around their table (symbol of the Temple altar) including benedictions before and after the meal and Sabbath songs (ZEMIROT). In many cases, *halakhot* (religious laws) concerning prayer are also included, as well as penitential prayers (SELIHOT) for forgiveness, the Psalter for devotional use and biblical and talmudic passages which have become a regular part of the liturgy.

At first, both the terms *Siddur*, i.e., "prayer order" (pl. *siddurim*) and *mahzor*, i.e., "cycle" (pl. *mahzorim*) referred to the book of prayers for the whole year. Later, after PIYYUTIM (liturgical poetry) had been extensively added during the Middle Ages, the Ashkenazi custom arose to distinguish between the *siddur* for daily prayers and the *mahzor* for festivals.

At one time, prayer uniquely belonged to the Oral Tradition. The *tannaim* and *amoraim* of the Talmud speak exclusively of memorized prayers (*Ber.* 5.3-5; *RH* 4.5-6; *Ta'an.* 2.2) because of the prohibition against writing down liturgical texts. "R. Judah ben Nahmani... discoursed as follows:... The words which are written [i.e., the Bible] you are not at liberty to say by heart, and the words transmitted orally, you are not at liberty to recite from writing" (*Git.* 60b). The TOSEFTA, a rabbinic work of the early centuries of the Common Era, records, "Writers of blessings are like those who burn the Torah" (*Tos. Shab.* 13.4). A later generation, guarding against the ultimate loss of the entire Oral Tradition due to the Roman persecutions of the second and third centuries, lifted the ban. "Oral Tradition is not meant to be written down. We say, however, that since its writing down cannot be eliminated, we say 'when it is time to work for the Lord, they may break the law' (Ps. 119:126)" (*Git.* 60a). Written prayer books began to appear in the geonic period. These hand-written manuals for the prayer leaders' use alone were permitted, at first, only on the Day of Atonement and other fast days due to the difficulty in mastering the complex service by heart. License was then extended to include the order of daily prayers and those for the Sabbath and festivals.

The first formulated order of service is found in the talmudic tractate *Soferim*, a work of the eighth century. In the ninth century, AMRAM GAON, a leading Babylonian scholar, compiled the first prayer book, *Seder Rav Amram Gaon*. Created at the request of Spanish Jewry, this prototype of an authorized liturgical manual contained the statutory prayers for the entire year and the *halakhot* that govern them "as they have been transmitted... by the *tannaim* and... *amoraim*," and concludes with a section devoted to lifecycle celebrations. The extensive commentary defined the basic principles of the liturgy as developed by the rabbis and for the first time established the limits of deviation beyond which local custom could not go.

In the tenth century, the *Siddur* of SAADIAH GAON included the pertinent legal background in Arabic for the benefit of the Jews of Egypt and introduced an economical arrangement of the prayer service which, however methodical, failed to become generally accepted. Unlike Rav Amram Gaon's guide for community leaders, Saadiah's prayer book was compiled for actual use by the synagogue worshiper, with notes explaining the appropriate times, modes and postures of prayer. It enjoyed popularity until MAIMONIDES' *Mishneh Torah* included "The Order of the Prayers for the Whole Year."

Mahzor Vitry (The Cycle of Prayers from Vitry), reflecting the 11th-century rite of northern France, repeats many of the legal sections of its predecessors and introduces *piyyutim*. Its editor, R. Simhah ben Samuel, a student of Rashi, appended to his prayer book the Passover *Haggadah*, prayers for *Simhat Torah*, and commentaries to selected prayer texts. From this time it became customary to include the comments of great rabbinic authorities in the margins of prayer books.

The first prayer books to be printed derive from the Iberian Peninsula for use by MARRANOS (crypto-Jews) in about 1475. *Mahzor Roma* and *Siddur Katan* ("Sidorello"), published in 1486 by Nathan Soncino, preserve the Italian rite and mark the beginning of the prayer book's popular accessibility to the individual Jew. The first Ashkenazi *siddur* was printed in Prague in 1512.

The Ashkenazim and the Sephardim have developed distinct prayer book traditions (see NUSAH). Among the Ashkenazim, the categories include the *Kol Bo* ("Everything Within") also known as the *Mahzor Ha-Gadol* ("Great *Mahzor*") with Sabbath and festival prayers for the year, the festival *Mahzor* and the *Siddur*, containing daily and Sabbath prayers. Sephardi prayer books include *Tefillat ha-Hodesh*, for weekdays, Sabbaths, the New Moon, Hanukkah, and Purim; *Mo'adim*, for the PILGRIM festivals; *Rosh ha-Shanah*, for the New Year; *Kippur* for the Day of Atonement; *Ta'aniyyot* for the fast days. Among the best-known prayer books in Europe were Jacob EMDEN's *Siddur Bet Ya'akov* (1769), Wolf Heidenheim's classic *Siddur* (1806), and Isaac Seligman Baer's *Avodat Yisra'el* (1868) which contains a learned commentary.

The Hasidim modified the Ashkenazi prayer book to include elements of the Sephardi liturgy following their adoption in the 18th century of Isaac LURIA's kabbalistic version of the liturgy (*Nusah ha-Ari*) complete with his com-

Four of the Ten Plagues. Top (left) lice; (right) frogs; below (left) murrain; (right) beasts. From the Golden Haggadah, *Spain, 13th century.*

קורע בגדיו

mentary and KAVVANOT. The Arabic-speaking Jews of Yemen refer to their comprehensive prayer book as *Tikhlal*, which remained a hand-written text until published in Jerusalem at the end of the 19th century.

As with the totality of Jewish life, the prayer book, too, underwent fundamental changes in response to Emancipation and Enlightenment at the turn of the 19th century. The earliest reformers were concerned with the form of the synagogue service and only later dealt with the theological underpinnings of the traditional *siddur*. Among the innovations were simplified service and prayers in the vernacular.

The first Reform prayer book, edited by I.S. Fraenkel and M.I. Bresselau in 1819, was the *Hamburg Gebetbuch: Sefer Ha-Avodah*. It contained researched citations in Jewish sources giving support for some of its liturgical reforms, which included the abbreviation of certain texts, the elimination of repetitions and the introduction of both the vernacular language and Sephardi *piyyutim*.

After the Reform Rabbinical Conferences of 1844-46, that attempted to unify the wide variety of liturgical versions developing in Germany at this time, the Berlin community struck out on its own and developed a radically universalist service, predominantly in German with but a few biblical verses in Hebrew.

Prayer book reform in America, following patterns set in Central Europe, included Leo Merzbacher's *Seder Tefillah — The Order of Prayer for Divine Service* (1855), David EINHORN's *Olam Tamid — Book of Prayers for Israelitish Congregations* (1856) and Isaac Mayer WISE's *Minhag Amerikah — The Daily Prayers for American Israelites* (1857). These rituals, in turn, prepared the way for *The Union Prayer Book for Jewish Worship — Seder Tefillot Yisrael* (1894-5), which unified the entire American Reform movement under one spiritual banner. Each successive edition reflected the changing self-image of Reform Judaism, as in 1922, when ceremony and ritual took on new meaning, and in 1940, when the consciousness of Jews as a people with its own culture transformed the posture of Reform worship. The most recent edition, *Shaaré Tefillah: The Gates of Prayer — The New Union Prayer Book* (1975), affirms Jewish tradition and culture, peoplehood and homeland as expressed in its editors' choices of services, prayers, supplementary readings and rituals. The same approach can be seen in the Reform movement's other liturgical innovations: *Shaaré Bayit: The Gates of the House* (1977), *Shaaré Teshuvah: The Gates of Repentance* (1978), and *Shaaré Seliḫah: The Gates of Forgiveness* (1980).

The Movement for Conservative Judaism in America represents a departure from the traditional *siddur* as well, although it adheres more faithfully to the classical structure. Its first publication in 1927, *Maḫzor le-Shalosh Regalim — The Festival Prayer Book*, reveals a marked kinship with the enlightened Orthodoxy of its day. A second edition (1946), entitled *Seder Tefillot Yisra'el le-Shabbat u-le-Shalosh Regalim — Sabbath and Festival Prayer Book*, permitted few textual revisions but introduced supplementary readings and explanatory notes. Since 1961, Conservative liturgical publications have sought to reflect a consensus among the wide spectrum of belief and practice represented within the movement. *Siddur li-Yemot ha-Ḫol — Weekday Prayer Book* (1961), *Maḫzor li-Yamim ha-Nora'im: Maḫzor for Rosh Hashanah and Yom Kippur* (1972) and *Siddur Sim Shalom: A Prayer Book for Shabbat, Festivals and Weekdays* (1985) all preserve a large part of the traditional liturgy and yet speak in popular parlance of the spiritual and moral concerns of the day, with a decidedly Zionist emphasis.

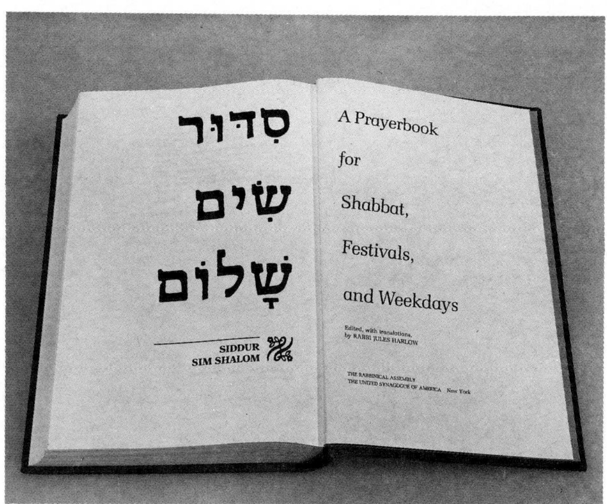

Prayer book (siddur) *in Hebrew with English translation, published by the Rabbinical Assembly. The United Synagogue of America.*

The fledgling Reconstructionist movement, as early as 1945 published *Seder Tefillot le-Shabbat — Sabbath Prayer Book*, and in 1948, *Maḫzor li-Yamim ha-Nora'im — High Holy Day Prayer Book*. These, and their later works of the *Festival Prayer Book* (1958) and *Seder Tefillot li-Yemot ha-Ḫol — Daily Prayer Book* (1963) make extensive use of auxiliary material meant to enhance the traditionally oriented Conservative-style service. The distinguishing features of the liturgy are found in the affirmation of a Judaism without supernaturalism and in the denial of the Jewish people as the Chosen People.

The most popular work in the English-speaking Orthodox community has been Simeon Singer's *Authorized Daily Prayer Book* which first appeared in 1890. Also influential have been J.H. Hertz's 1941 annotated and enlarged edition of the Singer prayer book and Philip Birnbaum's *Daily Prayer Book* (1949) and *High Holyday Prayerbook* (1951). The Rabbinical Council of America has endorsed David de Sola Pool's *Traditional Prayer Book for Sabbath and Festivals* (1960) and the new Art Scroll *Siddur*, that includes prayers for the State of Israel and the Israel Defense Forces. Many

Prayer book cover in leather with silver, enamel and semiprecious stones. Germany, 19th century.

Sephardi congregations worship with Sephardi prayer books edited by David de Sola Pool. Others use prayer books published in Israel. The Syrian Jews of the United States have published a number of prayer books for their own use.

Contemporary prayer books are beginning to show signs of a response to the two most cataclysmic events of Jewish life in this century: the Holocaust and the re-establishment of the State of Israel. As early as 1961, the Conservative and Reconstructionist prayer books included services for the commemoration of these events. Since then, many homemade liturgies have been printed by individual congregations and communities, some in cooperation with Christian churches. Virtually all of the recently published prayer books include memorial services for *Yom ha-Shoah* (Holocaust Remembrance Day) and Sabbath and holy day petitions on behalf of the State of Israel, as well as services for *Yom ha-Atsma'ut* (Israel Independence Day, on 5 Iyyar).

Creative liturgies, with a growing sensitivity to egalitarian language, social issues and a spiritual search, have also been designed and printed for experimental prayer settings. Thematic, orchestrated and choreographed, interreligious and multi-media services have been authored by clergy and laity for congregations and schools, camps and ḤAVUROT. As of the 1980s, the Jewish personnel in the US Armed Forces have a unified prayer book for the first time in American Jewish history. The result of a joint effort on the part of an interdenominational rabbinic commission, this unique and promising volume combines the Hebrew text of the de Sola Pool *Siddur* with interpretive translations and readings in English from the *Shaaré Tefillah: Gates of Prayer*. In Israel Shelomo Tal's *Rinnat Yisra'el* in Ashkenazi, Sephardi, and Ḥasidic versions are widely used.

PRAYER SHAWL See TALLIT

PREACHING See HOMILETICS

PREDESTINATION The theory that man's fate is determined by a force or forces outside his individual will. The theology of predestination is that man's destiny is ordered by the Divine power. Carried to its extreme, the doctrine denies human freedom and asserts that everything that happens to an individual or to a people is the will and plan of God. In Jewish philosophy the subject is mostly dealt with under the title of *hashgaḇah*, or Divine PROVIDENCE.

Jewish teaching on the subject is generally clear in its emphasis on human freedom. Biblical theology stresses the freedom of human choice, and the lesson in the very first story of the Bible, viz. the story of Adam and Eve in the Garden of Eden in which the first humans are given a law to obey and the freedom to keep or reject it, postulates free choice. Moses constantly exhorts the people about the two paths, good and evil, life and death, from which they can choose (cf. Deut. 11:2ff, 30:15). Among medieval thinkers all the major philosophers, with the possible exception of Ḥasdai CRESCAS, argued for the centrality of human freedom to choose, to act, and to bear the results of such choice. In other words, man is the arbiter of his own destiny and there is very little room for the acceptance of a concept of predestination. Following this line of thought, *hashgaḇah* or Divine Providence acts in accordance with the justice of God, rewarding or punishing man in accordance with his choice.

On the other hand, rabbinic literature contains some statements which appear ambiguous, such as the pronouncement of Ḥanina (second century) that, "Everything is in the hands of God except the fear of God" (*Ber.* 33b). Taken literally, the first half of his statement seems to be an affirmation of predestination. The second half, however, asserts the doctrine of human freedom. Either Ḥanina is holding on to both horns of the dilemma, or he acknowledges that he has no way of explaining the problem of the apparent conflict between Divine control and human freedom.

Nearly all medieval philosophers (MAIMONIDES is the outstanding exception) believed in the power of the astrological forces over man's destiny. However, in spite of their belief in ASTROLOGY, most of the medievalists emphasized that man's proper choice for good conduct can overcome the power of his stars. It is only when he makes a bad choice or no choice at all that the astrological forces determine his fate.

In the liturgy for ROSH HA-SHANAH (New Year) and the DAY OF ATONEMENT, the prayer U-NETANNEH TOKEF has often been discussed in relation to the question of predestination. The phrase, "On the New Year it is decreed and on the Day of Atonement it is sealed who shall live and who shall die...," looks like a text implying predestination of man's fate for the coming year. It has however, been interpreted as a meditation on the uncertainty of life.

Modern science has shown that man's fate is influenced by factors of heredity and environment, and to that extent, a man is never the completely free master of his own destiny. However, that is far from the theological concept of predestination which holds that everything that happens to man is previously decreed by God. Against that doctrine, classical Judaism holds firm to its teaching that human freedom is, in normal men, the most powerful factor which molds human character and destiny (see FREE WILL).

PRIESTLY BLESSING (*Birkat Kohanim*). The Scriptural benediction consisting of three short verses, comprising 15 Hebrew words in all, which was ordained to be recited only by the PRIESTS (*kohanim*) as descendants of AARON (Num. 6:22-27). It formed part of the regular Temple service, being pronounced each morning and evening after the daily (*Tamid*) offering. Within the Temple itself, priests combined the three verses (24-26) in a single blessing and pronounced the Tetragrammaton before worshipers from a special tribune or rostrum; outside Jerusalem, the three blessings were recited separately and a Divine Name of lesser holiness (probably *Adonai*) was employed (*Sot.* 7.6; *Tam.* 7.2). However, by the later Second Temple period, uttering God's "Ineffable Name" had become a right vested in the HIGH PRIEST only on the Day of Atonement. It was incorporated in the synagogue liturgy and during the Mishnaic period became known also as *Nesi'at Kappayim* ("raising the hands"); it was then recited at each Morning, Additional, and Afternoon Service, as well as at the Concluding Service on the Day of Atonement (*Ta'an.* 26b).

All traditional rites have incorporated the Priestly Blessing in the penultimate benediction of the AMIDAH, during the reader's repetition, in the Morning Service and the Additional Service. Throughout the Diaspora, however, it is only recited by the reader (not chanted by the priests). Priests customarily recite it during the Additional Service on festivals (except on a Sabbath), on the Day of Atonement, and during the Afternoon Service on fast days. In Israel, priests recite it on weekdays at the Morning Service, on Sabbath, the New Moon, on festivals at the Additional Service, at the Concluding Service on the Day of Atonement and on the afternoon of Tisha be-Av. In Jerusalem, the Priestly Blessing is chanted daily.

Before the recitation, priests in the congregation remove their shoes and walk to the rear of the synagogue, where their hands are ritually washed by the LEVITES (see Ex. 30:17-21); in the absence of a Levite, this duty may be performed by any first-born male. The priests then assemble before the Ark, cover their heads with the prayer shawl (*tallit*) and (after the summons of "*Kohanim!*") chant an introductory benediction: "Who has hallowed us with the sanctity of Aaron and commanded us to bless His people Israel in love." On reaching the last word, they turn to face the congregation with the palms of their hands stretched forward at shoulder height, the thumbs touching each other, and the fingers spread in a symbolic pattern under the prayer shawl. Congregants avert their eyes while the *kohanim* chant each word of the Priestly Blessing after the reader. After each of the three blessings, congregants (not the reader) answer with AMEN; however, when no *kohanim* are present, the response is usually *Ken yehi ratson* ("May this be God's will"). Having concluded this ceremony, the priests turn to face the Ark once again and lower their hands and their prayer shawl.

Sephardi, Italian, and Eastern Jewish communities have preserved a single version of the ritual for all occasions. Ashkenazim (including Ḥasidic Jews), however, reserve a more elaborate form of the ceremony for the Additional Service of festivals. (In Yiddish, reciting the Priestly Blessing is known as *dukhenen*, an allusion to the platform before the Ark which the priests ascend and which symbolizes the raised *dukhan* (platform in the Temple).) Worshipers may recite brief Scriptural verses after each word of the Priestly Blessing as well as a longer supplication at the end, although many authorities condemn such practices.

Only criminality or a severe physical blemish disqualifies a *kohen* from reciting the Priestly Blessing. Some Conservative congregations have abolished the ancient ritual, leaving it to be pronounced by the reader, while Reform Judaism has transformed it into a closing "invocation" by the rabbi. The same biblical formula has been incorporated in the PARENTAL BLESSING and is often recited over a bridal couple under the MARRIAGE CANOPY. Two hands outstretched in the Priestly Blessing may also be engraved on a TOMBSTONE, indicating that the deceased was a *kohen*.

The kohanim *(priests), their heads covered with prayer shawls, recite the Priestly Blessing at the Western Wall, Jerusalem.*

THE PRIESTLY BLESSING

Our God and God of our fathers, bless us with the threefold blessing in the Torah written by Your servant Moses, which was pronounced by Aaron and his sons, the *Kohanim*, Your holy people (as it was said):

May the Lord bless you and guard you. Amen!
May the Lord shine His countenance upon you and be gracious to you. Amen!
May the Lord display kindness toward you and grant you peace. Amen!

PRIESTLY GARMENTS Special robes worn by the PRIESTS in the SANCTUARY and TEMPLE. This attire was stored in special rooms, when not being worn, and could not be taken out of a specific area in the Temple compound. The HIGH PRIEST wore eight garments, four undergarments and four outer garments. Ordinary priests wore special undergarments but not the outer garments.

The High Priest's four undergarments were a tunic, a sash, a headdress, and breeches. The tunic was woven from linen and wool and, unlike those of the ordinary priests, was fringed (Ex. 28:39-40). The sash went around the tunic: that of the High Priest was woven from fine linen and dyed wools (Ex. 28:39, 39:29), while those of the regular priests were fashioned from fine twined linen only. The turban of AARON, the High Priest, was a miter, while ordinary priests wore "decorated turbans for headgear." The breeches were "to cover the flesh of their nakedness, from the hips to the thighs" (Ex. 28:42, 39:28; Ezek. 44:18).

The four rich and splendid outer garments were worn only by the High Priest. They were made of a mixture of dyed wool and fine linen assembled by skillful workmanship. Another characteristic of these garments was the interwoven threads of pure gold and the gold filaments. These expensive substances imparted an even higher degree of holiness to the priestly garments.

The four outer garments were the ephod, the breastplate, the robe of the ephod, and the plate (crown) hanging in front of the miter (turban). These outer garments had the character of royalty since they were woven from gold, blue, and purple wool. They were complemented by the plate. When the High Priest wore all these garments along with the miter, and was in full dress, he was the picture of royalty.

The ephod was worn over the blue tunic, secured by two shoulder straps and a belt in the middle. The straps bore two onyx stones with the names of the 12 sons of Jacob (six on each stone; Ex. 28:5-14). The front of the ephod carried the breastplate, which was either a square tablet or pouch, and which was made of gold, various fibers, and wool. On it were placed the URIM AND THUMMIM, which the High Priests used as oracles for purposes of divination.

The robe of the ephod was worn under the ephod and was therefore longer than the ephod and extended below it. This garment was entirely made of blue wool, and on its hem hung bells of gold and pomegranate shapes made from wool and linen (Ex. 28:31-35). There was much controversy about the number of bells and pomegranates, with the rabbis arguing as to whether there were 72 or 36 (*Zev.* 88b).

The plate, sometimes known as a crown, hung on a blue thread in front of the miter. Fashioned from pure gold, it had two words on it, *kodesh l-Adonai* ("holy to the Lord"; Ex. 28:36-38). During the Second Temple period, only the name of God was inscribed on the plate (Jos., *Ant.* 3.178).

In contrast to the regal attire worn the rest of the year, on the DAY OF ATONEMENT the High Priest wore garments made of ordinary linen; a tunic, breeches, sash, and miter (Lev. 16:4). The ordinary priest wore breeches of regular linen when he ascended the steps of the outer altar to remove the ashes that were left from the sacrifice (Lev. 6:3).

The priestly garments: a. the tunic; b. sash of the tunic; c. turban; d. bells of gold and pomegranates of tehelet *(sky-blue) linen and wool; e. robe of the ephod; f. band of the ephod; g. the breastplate; h. crown around the turban; i. onyx stones with the names of the tribes. Engraving, Germany, 18th century.*

PRIESTS (*kohanim*, sing. *kohen*). Male descendants of the first HIGH PRIEST, AARON, of the tribe of Levi. Unlike in other religions, the priesthood in Judaism is hereditary (through the male parent) and has been continued to the present.

Originally, the priests had clearly defined roles and obligations which differentiated them from the other Israelites. For example, they were assigned to serve in the TEMPLE and it was they who offered the different SACRIFICES brought by the people. The priests were also meant to be teachers of the people and were not to own land (see Num. 18:20).

At the time of the First Temple, the High Priest was anointed with oil and had a status close to that of the monarch. High Priests of the Second Temple period were not anointed. Although the High Priest was anointed with oil when he took office, when the Israelites went out to war, another priest might also be anointed and he would accompany the soldiers and exhort them before going into battle. Once a priest had been anointed, even if it was only to go out to war, his status remained similar to that of the High Priest.

The priests in the Temple wore four specified garments, while the High Priest wore eight such garments (see PRIESTLY GARMENTS). The High Priest was often referred to as "the priest of many garments," to distinguish him from the other priests.

As the priests did not own land, they subsisted upon the "24 gifts to the priests." Thus, each person had to give a fraction of his crop to a priest as a sacred donation (*terumah*: "heave offering"). While by Torah law even the giving of a single stalk is sufficient to exempt an entire barn full of wheat, the rabbis ruled that the *terumah* should be no less than 1/60 of the crop; more magnanimous people would give 1/50 or even 1/40 of their crops. The *terumah* could only be eaten by the priest and his immediate family, including any Canaanite slaves the priest owned. The priests were also given parts of the meat of certain sacrifices, meal offerings that had been brought to the Temple, the first shearing of the wool, the first-born of the flock, and ḤALLAH (part of any dough that had been kneaded).

The priests were organized in 24 MISHMAROT, or guard rosters, each of which took its turn to serve in the Temple for a week at a time. During the week, all the priestly portions of the sacrifices brought to the Temple were distributed among the members of the guard. Among the duties of the priests were offering the daily sacrifices each morning and evening and caring for the MENORAH — the lamp — and the INCENSE burned in the Temple. The priests were also assigned guard duty within the Temple itself. Those priests with visible disabilities were not permitted to perform the sacrifices in the Temple.

The priests sprinkled the BLOOD of sacrifices brought by Israelites on the outer ALTAR. If a woman was suspected of adultery by her husband, she would be given the "bitter waters" to drink by a priest, as a method of proving or disproving the allegations against her (see SOTAH).

The priests were also charged with examining certain types of growths for *tzara'at* — loosely and probably inaccurately translated as leprosy — which had appeared on a person's body, in a building, or on fabric. Based on the criteria spelled out in the Bible (Lev. 13), the priest would then pronounce whether this particular growth was indeed a *tzara'at*; if the verdict was positive, the person or object would have to be quarantined.

The Bible forbids the priest to marry a divorcee or a "harlot," here including any woman with a promiscuous past. Nor may a priest marry a woman who has undergone *ḥalitsah* (ceremony exempting from LEVIRATE MARRIAGE). By rabbinic interpretation, a priest is not permitted to marry a proselyte. Should a priest undergo a marriage ceremony with any of the aforementioned women forbidden to him, the marriage, while unacceptable, is nevertheless binding and a divorce is needed to terminate the relationship. The sons of such a union are considered to be *ḥalalim* (profane) and are not priests. Relying on the fact that such marriages, while unacceptable, are nonetheless binding, the Conservative movement does not forbid a priest to marry a divorcee, but urges that the wedding be unostentatious.

Priests are also prohibited from coming in contact with the dead, for such contact imparts a forbidden degree of ritual impurity (see PURITY AND IMPURITY). Only in the case of the deaths of any of seven close relatives may a priest become ritually impure. These relatives include the priest's father, mother, brother, never-married sister, son, daughter and wife. As priests cannot walk among the graves in cemeteries, it is customary to have the members of priestly families buried close to the road, so that their survivors can visit their graves. If a priest encounters a dead body and there is no one else around to take care of burial, he is duty-bound to bury the body, even though it results in his becoming ritually impure. At funerals of anyone but the seven close relatives listed above, the priests will generally remain outside the funeral chapel, for being under the same roof with the deceased would render them ritually impure. Jewish cemeteries will generally not plant large, leafy trees which overshadow the road, because should they overhang a grave and should a priest walk underneath the tree, he would become ritually impure.

In Israel today, many hospitals have taken steps to separate their morgue from the rest of the hospital by two sets of doors, only one of which can be open at a time. In this way, even if there are dead bodies in the morgue, priests visiting the hospital would not become ritually impure.

Since the destruction of the Temple, rabbinical laws continued to require that priests be shown a certain degree of respect because of their status. Thus, the first person called to the READING OF THE LAW is a priest. Similarly, a priest should be invited to lead the GRACE AFTER MEALS. When a person who is not a priest leads the grace, he sometimes notes, "with the permission of the priests."

In the case of a first-born male, where neither the father of the child nor the father of the mother of the child is a priest or LEVITE, the child must be redeemed on his 31st day (or thereafter, if necessary; see FIRST-BORN, REDEMPTION OF). Any priest can serve to redeem the child. In the ceremony, the priest offers the child's father the choice of "forfeiting" his son or redeeming him for the equivalent of five silver shekels. One other duty which the priests still perform is that of blessing the people (see PRIESTLY BLESSING).

The Reform movement has completely dispensed with all rules and restrictions governing the priests.

PRINCIPLES OF FAITH Authoritative foundations of a dogma. In the Pentateuch, no attempt is made to distinguish between rules and principles among the commandments and to formulate a basic dogma. Even what at first promises to be a declaration of principles ("And now, Israel, what does the Lord your God require of you but to..." (Deut. 10:12)) continues not with essential principles but with the entire Torah program: "...fear the Lord your God, to walk in all His ways, and to love Him and to serve the Lord...with all your heart...to keep the commandments and the statutes." The "ten words on the tablets of stone" (Deut. 4:13) present basic practices rather than principles of Judaism (see TEN COMMANDMENTS).

However, eventually systemization and the determination of basic dogmas were found to be essential. Thus, the talmudic rabbis were not satisfied to establish the exact number of commandments in the Pentateuch but started to divide them into those between man and God and those between man and man (*Yoma* 85b), distinguished between rules and principles and sought to discover the supreme moral principle (*Sif.* Lev. 19.18, *Shab.* 83).

Similarly in the area of creed, the rabbis spoke of a person who denies the existence of God as a *kofer be-ikkar*, "he who denies the root," i.e., belief in God is the basis of the entire Torah (*Ar.* 15b). Responding to the proliferation of heretical views, the rabbis ruled, "these are the ones who are excluded from the world to come: He who denies resurrection, the Divine origin of the Torah, and the EPIKOROS" (i.e., those who deny PROVIDENCE and REWARD AND PUNISHMENT; *Sanh.* 10.1). Since a share in the world to come is promised to "All Israel..." such an exclusion would appear to define the creedal requirements of an "Israelite." In terms of positive affirmation, the rabbis embodied basic principles of Judaism in the text of the liturgy, in the daily SHEMA (the statement "Hear O Israel, the Lord is our God, the Lord is One" can be seen as the fundamental statement of the Jewish faith) and in the High Holiday and festival prayers.

Already the first century philosopher PHILO recognized that the acceptance of Scripture commits the Jew to certain fundamental beliefs such as the existence and unity of God, Divine Providence and the revelation and eternity of the law.

During the Middle Ages, the question of the basic principles of Judaism acquired special importance in the light of the need to set Judaism apart from KARAISM, on the one hand, and from CHRISTIANITY and ISLAM on the other. The fact that other faiths had clear statements of dogma also influenced Jewish thinkers to emulation.

The best known formulation of the creedal principles of Judaism is that of Moses MAIMONIDES (12th century) who enumerated 13 *Ikkarim* ("roots" or "fundamentals") in his commentary on the aforementioned Mishnah in *Sanhedrin* (10.1). As such, his formulation (see inset) had halakhic implications, as it constituted a definition of the necessary and sufficient creedal requirements for membership in the community of Israel.

Maimonides' 13 Principles found their way into the prayer book as the popular hymn YIGDAL and as a supplemental prose recitation after the prescribed Morning Service in the form of a personal affirmation: "I believe in perfect faith that..."

Maimonides interpreted "World to Come" as immortality of the SOUL, which he considered the ultimate spiritual reward or self-fulfillment of the human being. Since he believed that only the rational part of the soul could survive the death of the body, Maimonides found congenial the Mishnah's assertion that "World to Come" was partly dependent upon intellectual perfection and the holding of correct beliefs. Other rabbinic leaders such as Abraham ben David of Posquières, who agreed with Maimonides that all 13 were in some sense significant Jewish religious principles, were not prepared to assert that denial of a principle such as the "incorporeality of God" disqualifies a person for a share in the world to come or for membership in the Jewish community.

The discussion over Principles of Faith continued up to the dawn of the Modern Period. During the 15th and 16th centuries, significant contributions within the traditional framework were made by Simeon ben Tsemaḫ DURAN (*Ohev Mishpat, Magen Avot*), Ḫasdai CRESCAS (*Or Adonai*), Joseph ALBO (*Sefer ha-Ikkarim*), Isaac ARAMA (*Akedat Yitsḫak*) and Isaac ABRAVANEL (*Rosh Amanah*). The differences of opinion found in these works emanate from the lack of recognized criteria for what constitutes a "principle of faith" or what difference a principle makes for the practitioners of Judaism. For example, from a purely philosophical point of view it is very difficult to understand why Maimonides included the principle of "resurrection" or that "God alone is to be worshiped" and omitted a fundamental such as "freedom of the will." Albo suggests that the term *ikkar* ("principle") denotes "something upon which the existence and duration of another thing depends and without which it cannot endure"; in short, the necessary conditions of a faith-system. Albo admits three basic Principles of Judaism (or of any Divine law) but the other principles listed by Maimonides are beliefs incumbent upon every Jew, the denial of which may not entail heresy. In Albo's scheme, each principle can be said to have "branches," thus from God's existence is inferred His knowledge, unity and incorporeality, from Providence is inferred the principles of Messiah and Resurrection, while from "revelation" come "prophecy" and the mission of Moses.

Arama suggests that in discussing the fundamentals of

Judaism, it must be determined which concepts the Torah chose to emphasize. This can be seen in the conceptual elements behind the Sabbath and festivals which yield Creation (Sabbath), God's Omnipotence (Passover), Prophecy and Divine Revelation (Shavu'ot), Providence (Rosh ha-Shanah), Repentance (Day of Atonement), and "World to Come" (Sukkot).

Abravanel rejects the entire notion of differentiating between principles and non-principles in Judaism and claims that Maimonides merely assembled a group of representative beliefs for those unable to perceive the intellectual presuppositions of their commitment to Judaism.

A contemporary treatment of the subject is found in Louis Jacobs' *The Principles of Judaism* (1964).

SOME FORMULATIONS OF THE PRINCIPLES OF JUDAISM

Maimonides

1. God exists
2. God's unity
3. God's incorporeality
4. God's eternity
5. God alone is to be worshiped
6. Belief in Prophecy
7. Moses was the greatest of the prophets
8. God revealed the Torah to Moses
9. The Torah is unchangeable
10. God's omniscience
11. Reward and Punishment
12. Messiah
13. Resurrection of the dead

Ḫasdai Crescas

1. God's omniscience
2. Providence
3. God's omnipotence
4. Prophecy
5. Human free will
6. The purposefulness of the Torah

Simeon ben Tsemaḫ Duran -- Joseph Albo

1. God exists
2. Divinity of the Torah — Providence
3. Reward and Punishment

PROFANATION See DESECRATION

PROMISED LAND See ISRAEL, LAND OF

PROPHETS AND PROPHECY The prophets were charismatic figures, believed to be endowed with the Divine gift of receiving and imparting a message revealed to them by God. Prophecy is the delivery of this message, not the ability to look into the future. The prophet was the intermediary between the Divine Will and the people. The concept was known to other peoples in the ancient Middle East and the ancient Israelites related seriously, for example, to Balaam, the prophet-soothsayer sent by the king of Moab to curse them (Num. 22). The first person to be called a prophet in the Bible was ABRAHAM (Gen. 21:7), while MOSES was regarded as the greatest of the prophets (Deut. 34:10), a belief formulated by MAIMONIDES in his PRINCIPLES OF FAITH.

Once the prophet felt that he had been commanded by God to speak His word, he had to do so (Amos 3:8) and had to convey the message whether or not the people wished to hear it (Ezek. 3:11). Some of the prophets were initially reluctant to serve, such as Moses, Jeremiah and Jonah; the last even tried to run away from his mission. However, the prophet must obey and accept his role as the Divine mouthpiece, frequently beginning his message with the introduction, "Thus says the Lord." Once he prophesies, he is set apart from the other men and must bear the responsibility of being chosen. His message does not concern the being of God, but the Divine plan for the world.

The second section of the Hebrew BIBLE is called *Nevi'im* — Prophets. It is divided into two sections. First come the "Former Prophets" — the books of Joshua, Judges, Samuel and Kings, that are in fact historical works, but contain the stories of the early pre-classical prophets, notably, Nathan, ELIJAH and ELISHA. The second group is the "Latter Prophets," containing the classical literary works. These consist of three major prophets (ISAIAH, JEREMIAH and EZEKIEL) and the twelve MINOR PROPHETS (HOSEA, JOEL, AMOS, OBADIAH, JONAH, MICAH, NAHUM, HABAKKUK, ZEPHANIAH, HAGGAI, ZECHARIAH and MALACHI). The difference between the "major" and "minor" prophets is the length of the book, not their relative importance.

The former books bring mainly biographical details about the prophets, whereas the latter books give the contents of the prophecies. Common to both types is the title "prophet" and the Divine inspiration to deliver a message to the people of Israel in order to preserve their covenant with God.

The early prophets are sometimes called "seers." Some of them, especially Elijah and Elisha, were miracle-workers. In this early prophetic period (up to the eighth century BCE), there were groups or schools of prophets who would gather together and train themselves in the prophetic experience (I Sam.10:5,10). These preclassical prophets fearlessly rebuked the ruler, especially for moral wrongdoing such as adultery and murder in the case of David and Bathsheba (II Sam. 12) and unjust confiscation and murder in the case of Naboth's vineyard (I Kings 21).

The first of the literary prophets was Amos and the last, Malachi. Thus, the period of classical prophecy lasted for about 300 years (mid-eighth to mid-fifth centuries BCE) and spanned the crucial periods of the rise of three great empires, Assyria, Babylonia and Persia, as well as crucial events in the life of the nation — the destruction of the Northern Kingdom by Assyria (722 BCE), the destruction of the Southern Kingdom and the Temple by the Babylonians (586 BCE), the Babylonian Exile and the early years of the Return to Zion with the rebuilding of Jerusalem and the Temple.

The prophets came from many classes of society: aristocracy (Isaiah); priesthood (Jeremiah and Ezekiel); farmers (Amos), etc. They preached on the issues of the day and were fearless in the reproofs they administered to kings and priests, the rich and the powerful, the hostile masses. As a result, they were often persecuted and subjected to great hardships (e.g., Elijah, Jeremiah). However, they also inspired the rulers and sometimes guided them (e.g., Deborah, Samuel, Isaiah).

The prophets would often tell the people what would happen to them and the kingdom. This came out of their conviction that the people's sins would lead to national disaster. In giving this message of impending doom, the prophets believed they were conveying the warning of God. They also interpreted the major international events of their day in the light of their special outlook, seeing God as responsible for the fates of all peoples and for their interrelations.

A characteristic feature of the prophet's method was his employment of symbolic acts to make his message more vivid. Isaiah called his children Shear-Jashub and Maher-Shalal-Hash-Baz. The first means "A remnant shall return" and the second "The enemy shall speedily take away the spoil." He did this so that the people would have a constant, living reminder of their national fate as he saw it. Jeremiah bought up family property when the Babylonians were at the gates, to show his confidence in the return of the people to their ancestral land. Ezekiel engraved the names Ephraim and Judah on two separate sticks and held them together to symbolize his belief in the ultimate reunification of all the scattered tribes of Israel.

All the prophets accepted the Temple cult. Their criticisms were aimed at those who meticulously performed the ritual while being immoral in their everyday lives and disregarding the social and ethical demands of the Divine code. Indeed, they saw the essence of God's demands to lie in the moral and ethical, rather than the cultic, spheres. Ritual was not to be seen as a substitution for moral behavior but only as a reinforcement. This view inevitably led to tensions between PRIESTS and prophets.

Prophetic teaching covers many aspects of the Jewish ethic. It contains a rebuke to the sinner as well as the message of God's love, a burning nationalism and also a universalism and messianism, the threat of punishment as well as the promise of redemption. Above all is an insistence on the centrality of the unity of the One God. In general, all the prophets preached against a background of idolatry, pagan immorality and social corruption. Therefore, while each prophet spoke in his own style and with his own emphases, to a significant extent the prophets displayed a strong unanimity in outlook.

The phenomenon of prophecy formed a central subject in Jewish philosophy and several questions exercised the minds of Jewish thinkers, particularly in the Middle Ages. Who were these people called "prophets"? How did they experience the Word of God? Was the prophetic experience objectively real or only subjectively so?

Two schools of thought emerged regarding these questions. The first was the supernatural school which saw prophecy as a miracle and the prophet as a person supernaturally chosen by God. The outstanding representative of this school is JUDAH HALEVI who insisted that all depends on God's choice. The intellectual qualifications of the prophet are not relevant to that Divine choice. Further, what a prophet sees in his vision or dream is objectively real, although only the prophet with his special gift of prophecy can see or hear it (*Kuzari* I,11,43,79-98; II,49; III,23). Halevi further holds that only Israel as the people of the Torah have true prophets of God (I,27,95,115), while only the Land of Israel can be the site of true prophecy (II,10,12,14). The prophecies of Moses and Ezekiel are seen as true because they related to the Land of Israel.

The second school of thought stressed the natural aspects of the prophetic experience and held that not everyone can be a prophet or even be chosen by God to carry His message. The prophet is a person who is perfect in his mental, spiritual, moral and even physical life. The phenomenon of prophecy is really an extension or overflowing of his qualities of perfection. The second school thus shifts the emphasis from God's choice and the supernatural to the quality of the man and his inherent psychological factors.

MAIMONIDES represents this second school. He devotes nearly one-third of the second book of his *Guide for the Perplexed* to this subject. Essentially, he combines both schools of thought. He says that the prophet is chosen by God; but it is only the perfect man who will be chosen. God cannot choose one who is intellectually or morally inferior (*Guide*), II, 32,36: *Yesodé ha-Torah* VII,5). Further, the prophet must have a perfectly developed imaginative faculty. According to Maimonides, the prophetic experience is not objectively real, but exists only for the prophet. It is only subjectively real and is experienced by his imaginative intelligence (*Guide*, II,41-42). The single exception to this is the prophecy of Moses. While other prophets saw God in a dream at night or in an ecstatic vision by day, Moses saw God "face to face," in a direct prophetic confrontation. Maimonides holds that there is a lesser degree of prophecy among all other prophets because they saw or heard what they saw or heard only in a dream or vision. Among non-Jews, Maimonides allows, there is also a degree of prophecy but it is lower still.

Nearly all Jewish writers on the subject suppose that prophecy ceased with the closing of the Bible canon at the time of Ezra and the rabbis said that prophecy ended with Malachi.

PROSBUL (*Prozbol*), a Greek word meaning either "for the court" or "official notice," used to denote the legal document preventing the cancellation of debts during the SABBATICAL YEAR. By biblical law, all outstanding debts were to be cancelled during each Sabbatical year. Consequently, lenders became wary of lending money as the Sabbatical year approached, even though the Pentateuch specifically warned against such actions: "Beware, lest you harbor the base thought, 'The seventh year, the year of remission is approaching,' so that you are mean to your needy kinsman and give him nothing" (Deut. 15:9). As borrowers found it almost impossible to borrow money under these circumstances, HILLEL, relying on a legal loophole, bypassed the law. As the rule of cancelling debts in the Sabbatical year applies only to debts owed to individuals, Hillel arranged for the use of the *prosbul*, a legal device whereby lenders are able to turn over all their outstanding debts to a law court (BET DIN) before the onset of the Sabbatical year. In this way, as the debt is due for collection by the *bet din* rather than by an individual, it is not cancelled by the Sabbatical year. While there was opposition to the introduction of this system, because of Hillel's authority it was eventually accepted as valid. The *amora* SAMUEL declared that had he the power, he would have annulled Hillel's innovation.

Conservative and Reform rabbis often point to *prosbul* as an example of the rabbis' ability to nullify even an explicit Torah commandment, and they have deduced from this the right of the modern rabbinate to do the same. The Orthodox view, though, is that the device used by Hillel was built into the very fabric of the law and that what Hillel did was to institutionalize a method which had always been available on a particular basis.

The actual text of the *prosbul* states: "I hereby make known to you (the names of the three rabbis involved), in such-and-such a place, concerning any debt owing to me by so-and-so, that I may be able to collect it when I wish." The three judges then sign the form.

PROSELYTES See CONVERSION TO JUDAISM

PROVERBS, BOOK OF Second book in the HAGIOGRAPHA section of the BIBLE. Together with ECCLESIASTES and JOB, it belongs to the genre of WISDOM LITERATURE, prevalent throughout the ancient Middle East, which consisted of advice and wise sayings for the moral conduct of everyday life. The book's 31 chapters and 915 verses comprise various collections of maxims, two of which are ascribed to an author: Agur (30:1-33), and the mother of King Lemuel (31:1-9). The section of 22:17-24:22 has been identified as comprising 11 sayings from the Egyptian Instruction of Amenemopet, and one aphorism possibly from the Aramaic text, Aḫikar. According to rabbinic tradition, Agur was either King Saul or King Solomon, while Lemuel was another name for Solomon.

The biblical claim that Solomon wrote most of the material in Proverbs rests on his reputation for extraordinary wisdom. In addition, he is said to have composed 3,000 proverbs and 1,005 songs (I Kings 5:9-14). According to the Talmud, Solomon wrote the Song of Songs in his youth, Proverbs in his middle age, and Ecclesiastes in his old age (*BB* 15a). It is possible that Solomon may have sponsored the teaching in his court, whereupon his courtiers honored their king by attaching his name to their collected material, just as psalmists associated David's name with numerous psalms.

Although it is difficult to date the various collections that comprise the Book of Proverbs, scholars hold that it should be viewed as an anthology spanning several hundreds of years. There is, however, no reason to doubt the antiquity of many of the ancient proverbs which could well have originated from the Solomonic period. The Talmud dates its editing to the time of King Hezekiah (eighth century BCE, see *BB* 15a).

Many literary forms appear in the Book of Proverbs, but the two major ones are instructions and sayings. Whereas in the individual sayings parallelism is used, one half verse either opposing or repeating in different words the idea in the other half verse, the instructions in chapters 1-9 comprise extended paragraphs devoted to a particular topic.

BOOK OF PROVERBS

1:1 — 1:6	Preface
1:7 — 9:18	The proverbs of Solomon; the value of wisdom
10:1 — 22:16	Further collection of Solomon's proverbs
22:17 — 24:22	The study of wisdom
25:1 — 29:27	Wise sayings ascribed to Solomon
30:1 — 30:33	The words of Agur, son of Jakeh
31:1 — 31:9	The words of King Lemuel
31:10 — 31:31	An alphabetic acrostic in praise of the virtuous wife.

The tone is optimistic and universal. Some favorite subjects are the contrast between wise persons and fools; the importance of discipline, whether from parents or teachers, or self-imposed; the value of eloquence; the dangers of drunkenness, laziness, and gossip; and the threat posed by the "foreign woman." The aim of learning was to know the right word and act for every occasion, hence to master one's life. That goal could not be attained without controlling the passions, especially anger and lust.

The last section of the book, "A woman of worth" (31:10-31), has been incorporated into the Friday night home ritual, and is recited before the KIDDUSH prayer (see ESHET HAYIL).

PROVIDENCE (*hashgahah*). The concept which sees God as having total knowledge and governance of all existence, which He created. Further, not only does He know and control all things, but He loves all His creatures, and cares for them, extending his *hashgahah* or surveillance over them.

In its extreme form, Divine providence extends over everything, and includes not only all human beings but also animal and even plant life. Thus in the teaching of the Muslim *Ashariyah*, God's providence is exercised over the leaves which fall from the tree, deciding which shall fall first and where. A more liberal view of Divine providence holds that God's providence is not particularized, that is, it is not exercised over the individual, but rather over humankind as a whole. In the history of Jewish philosophy, some thinkers were influenced by the *Ashariyah*, and a few others came close to an interpretation of what they thought was Aristotelian teaching and adopted the liberal opinion. Generally speaking, however, the mainstream of Jewish thought holds that Divine providence extends over every individual human being. This teaching, which finds support in the Scriptures, where Divine providence is constantly exercised over the fate of the people of Israel, is constantly repeated in Jewish sources.

This belief is related to other questions such as FREE WILL and REWARD AND PUNISHMENT concerning which it raises a number of serious problems. The first question relates to human freedom. If God knows all, He also knows what each person will do. Where then is human freedom, which is central in Jewish THEOLOGY? Secondly, if providence is exercised over the fate of each person, then the future of that person is also pre-known and pre-determined by Divine providence. It follows then that it is providence which controls each person's fate, and that therefore his destiny may have only little relation to his behavior (see PREDESTINATION). Finally, if all things happen as a result of Divine providence, how can one explain the prosperity of the wicked and the suffering of the just?

In Jewish philosophy these questions have been the subjects of numerous discussions. SAADIAH GAON and MAIMONIDES insist on retaining both God's knowledge and human freedom at the same time. God's knowledge, said Maimonides, is not like human knowledge and is not determinative, i.e., it is a knowledge which comprehends all things, past, present, and future in one "glance." To hold that God knows what man will do, is the same as His knowledge of what man has already done, and in no way does it determine man's choice of actions (*Guide*, 3.30; *Yad, Hilkhot Teshuvah*, 5.5).

With regard to the second question, the Jewish teachers, in a sense, limited Divine providence in a way that still allows for human responsibility for one's actions. This doctrine of human responsibility is rooted in biblical teaching (Ex. 32:32-33; Deut. 11:26-28; 30:15,19; Mal. 3:16; Dan. 7:10) and is given prominence in extra-biblical writings from the Talmud through to the medieval philosophers. Even the latter (with the notable exception of Maimonides) who believed in the influence of the particular star and constellation under which one is born, nevertheless emphasized that the most important factors deciding man's fate are the necessary results of his own conduct coupled with the impact of providence.

The question of reconciling Divine providence with the existence of EVIL is resolved in different ways. Theories are advanced that man does not know the nature of evil or that reward and punishment in this life merely compensate for the temporal good and evil performed in this world, or that the nature of the ultimate good and evil can only be known by God and that all man experiences is an incomplete stage in the total record, because even a painful experience can lead to a greater good.

Jewish teachers realized the unsatisfactory nature of these "solutions," and accordingly gave ample room for the doctrine of reward and punishment in an AFTERLIFE in which the good will be rewarded and the wicked punished.

Thus while the doctrine of Divine providence is retained in Jewish theology, it is general enough to leave ample room for the teachings of human freedom, and reward and punishment.

PSALMS, BOOK OF (*Tehillim*). The first book of the HAGIOGRAPHA section of the BIBLE, incorporating 150 psalms and 2,527 verses. Jewish tradition considers the inscription preceding many psalms as a separate verse, while the Christian Bible considers such inscriptions as part of the following verse; hence, the verse numbering in Psalms often differs between the two Bibles.

The first two psalms function as a general introduction to the entire collection and the final psalm serves as a conclusion. The book itself may be divided into five parts (see outline). Each section is supplied with a concluding doxology (41:14; 72:19-20; 89:52; 106:48; 150). The division into five books seems to derive from an analogy with the Pentateuch. Of the 150 psalms, the majority are attributed to specific authors: one to MOSES; 72 to DAVID; two to SOLOMON; 12 to Asaph; one to Heman and one to Ethan.

The psalms themselves may be divided into three categories based on content: hymns of praise, elegies and those which serve a didactic purpose. Some have identified a fourth category: songs of trust (e.g., Ps. 23, 129).

The hymns usually celebrate God's role as creator and redeemer; they describe the deeds of redemption on Israel's

Illustration of Psalm 113, showing the interior of a synagogue; on the left, the reader holds a Torah scroll. From Barcelona, Haggadah, *14th century.*

behalf with lavish rhetoric. Laments, both individual and communal, bemoan Divine absence or wrath. The sufferer insists that his distress is undeserved and wonders whether God has forsaken him in his need. Structurally, the laments consist of complaint and confession of confidence. Two reasons are offered for this shift to confidence: either the assurance of Divine deliverance or a leap of faith. The confidence is grounded in covenantal faith.

The third type is the didactic poem that may retell Israel's history, offer a reflection on the Torah (1; 19:8-15; 119), or examine the problem of evil (37; 49; 73). Some psalms are written as alphabetic acrostics (9-10; 25; 34; 111-112; 119; 145).

The precise dating of individual psalms is impossible. Only Psalm 137 yields specific clues that would imply a post-exilic date, for it looks back over the period of residence in Babylon.

Different psalms formed part of the service in the TEMPLE and there was a separate psalm for each day of the week (*Tam.* 7:4). The "songs of ascent" may have been sung by pilgrims as they ascended the Temple mount before entering the Temple or perhaps the term alludes to the Levites standing on the steps of the Women's Court of the Temple as they sang these psalms. The Levites sang certain psalms to accompany the offering of various sacrifices (*Suk.* 4:5). Some of the Psalms are headed by technical terms which are not fully understood. They may relate to the musical performance.

According to Jewish tradition, King David composed or edited the Book of Psalms. Scholars have assigned a much later (post-exilic) date to its redaction, while affirming an early date for many of the psalms, based in part on parallels with Egyptian, Babylonian, and Canaanite hymns.

THE BOOK OF PSALMS

1-41	Book I: Psalms of David (except 1-2,10,33)
42-72	Book II: 18 ascribed to David, seven to the sons of Korah, 50 to Asaph, 72 to Solomon, and four anonymous
73-89	Book III: 73-83 attributed to Asaph; 84,85,87 to the sons of Korah; 86 to David; 88 to Heman the Ezrahite; and 89 to Ethan the Ezrahite
90-106	Book IV: 90 attributed to Moses; 101,103 to David; the rest are anonymous
107-150	Book V: 15 psalms attributed to David and one to Solomon. Most of the others have no inscription. 120-134 are called "Songs of Ascent."

In the Liturgy More than any other portion of the Bible, the psalter (the Book of Psalms) was designed for liturgical use. Already prior to the Temple's destruction (70 CE), various psalms had found their way into the LITURGY of the SYNAGOGUE; from the talmudic period onward, there was a steady increase in the number of psalms chosen for public worship, home ceremonies, and other occasions, largely in response to popular demand. The traditional PRAYER BOOK now contains more than 70 complete psalms and well over 200 verse extracts from the psalter which have been woven into other liturgical passages.

The original nucleus is thought to have comprised the HALLEL psalms (113-118) recited on Pilgrim FESTIVALS, the New MOON and ḤANUKKAH, the "Great *Hallel*" (Ps. 136) read on Sabbath and festival mornings and included in the Passover SEDER (*Sof.* 18.2) and the seven daily psalms that the LEVITES used to recite in the Temple.

From rabbinic times until the later Middle Ages, additional psalms entered the LITURGY. Apart from the PESUKÉ DE-ZIMRA sequence, which is expanded on Sabbaths and festivals, these include ASHRÉ (Ps. 145), recited twice each morning and at the commencement of afternoon prayer; Ps. 24 (or 29 on Sabbaths and festivals coinciding with a Sabbath) chanted when the Torah scroll is carried back to the Ark after the READING OF THE LAW; BAREKHI NAFSHI and the 15 "Songs of Ascents" (Ps. 120-134; see SHIR HA-MA'ALOT), read after the Sabbath Afternoon Service during the winter months; Ps. 144 and 67 which, in most rites, precede the Evening Service at the termination of a Sabbath; the psalms introducing GRACE AFTER MEALS (137,126, or 23); Ps. 47, repeated seven times before the sounding of the SHOFAR on ROSH HA-SHANAH. Other psalms are reserved for the MARRIAGE SERVICE, for the DEDICATION of a house, the FUNERAL SERVICE, prayers in a house of MOURNING (especially Ps. 119), *Yizkor* MEMORIAL SERVICES, etc. Among the latest to be added were LEKHU NERANNENAH and the KABBALAT SHABBAT sequence (Ps. 95-99, 29, 92-93, to which Sephardim added Ps. 100), compiled by the 16th-century mystics of Safed.

As a pious and praiseworthy custom, the daily recitation of psalms gave rise to special *Ḥevrah Tehillim* brotherhoods in many parts of the Jewish world. All 150 psalms are still included for this purpose in certain Orthodox prayer books or separate booklets.

THE DAILY PSALMS

Sunday	Psalm 24
Monday	Psalm 48
Tuesday	Psalm 82
Wednesday	Psalm 94
Thursday	Psalm 81
Friday	Psalm 93
Sabbath	Psalm 92

PUNISHMENT The Bible prescribes various penalties for transgressors (which MAIMONIDES explains as being relative to the seriousness of the offense: *Guide*, III, 41). They include: death (see CAPITAL PUNISHMENT); excision (see KARET); EXCOMMUNICATION (*ḥerem*).

Flogging (see Deut. 25:1-3). The Bible prescribes a maximum of 40 lashes, which the rabbis explained as not more than 39 — one-third on the chest and the rest on the back. They prescribed this punishment for transgression of a negative biblical command, and also for one who refused to fulfill a positive commandment (*Ḥul. 132b).*

Retaliation in cases of assault and battery.

Fines and financial compensation were imposed by Scripture in a variety of cases, such as defamation of one's bride's virginity (Deut. 22:13-19), rape (Deut. 22:28-29), robbery (Ex. 22:3) and a person who sells his neighbor's property (Ex. 21:37). The talmudic sages levied fines where technicalities limited the jurisdiction of the courts to impose the penalties prescribed by Scripture (*BK* 84b), or for infractions of rabbinic ordinances (TJ, *Av. Zar.* 1.6 (39d).)

Confiscation of property by the court (*hefker bet-din*) was employed as a means of enforcing compliance with the law. This was based upon the passage in the Book of Ezra (10:8) "that anyone who did not come [to the assembly summoned by Ezra] would, by decision of the officers and elders, have his property confiscated."

Imprisonment was not prescribed by Scripture as a penalty. However, a person was to be held in custody until the court would ascertain his punishment (Num. 15:34; cf. *Ket.* 33b, that one who strikes his neighbor is kept in custody until the effect of his assault is ascertained). Though imprisonment for non-payment of debts was contrary to Jewish law, some Jewish communities in the Middle Ages imposed it, following the custom prevalent among non-Jews.

Maimonides lists 36 offenses demanding capital punishment; 39 for which the Bible prescribes death "at the hand of heaven" but for which courts could impose a flogging punishment of up to 39 lashes; and another 168 which could also be punished by up to 39 lashes. For all capital punishment or flogging sentences, the crime had to be committed in front of eye-witnesses and after the culprit had been prewarned of the punishment involved.

PURIM ("lots"). Minor festival celebrated on 14 Adar (Second Adar in a leap year) to commemorate the deliverance of Persian Jewry from their intended destruction by Haman, the grand vizier or chief minister of King Ahasuerus. Since Ahasuerus is usually identified with Xerxes I, the "Great King" of Persia, all the events related in the biblical Book of ESTHER would have occurred in the mid-fifth century BCE. *Purim* derives from the Akkadian word *pur* meaning "dice" and refers to Haman's casting of lots in order to fix a propitious date (13 Adar) for his planned massacre of the Jews (Est. 3:7-14). The Fast of Esther is now observed on 13 Adar in remembrance of the fast proclaimed by Queen Esther before she interceded with Ahasuerus for her threatened people (Est. 4:16; see FASTING AND FAST DAYS). The next day, 14 Adar, is celebrated as Purim, the Feast of Lots which Esther's cousin Mordecai instituted in commemoration of the Jews' providential deliverance (Est. 9:20ff.). However, although already observed in the Hasmonean era (second cent. BCE), this festival gained its sanction subsequently from the rabbis.

The 15th of Adar is known as *Purim Shushan* (or *"Shushan Purim"*) because the fighting between the Jews and Haman's supporters in Persia's capital (ancient Susa, Hebrew *Shushan*) did not end until the 14th, and Ahasuerus granted the Jews an extra day to vanquish their enemies, which meant that the deliverance could only be celebrated one day later (Est. 9:13-18). Accordingly, the rabbis enacted that in

Jerusalem and other cities that were walled in the days of Joshua, Purim should always be celebrated on 15 (rather than 14) Adar. Since refraining from work is not compulsory, though recommended, Purim has the status of a minor festival in the Jewish calendar. In leap years (when there are two months of Adar), the 14th (or 15th in Jerusalem) of the first Adar is known as Purim Katan, the Lesser Purim, marked by an abstention from fasting, from prayers of supplication, and from eulogies at a funeral.

PURIM —FEAST OF LOTS

Hebrew Dates:	14 Adar (Adar Sheni in leap years) 15 Adar (*Purim Shushan* or "*Shushan Purim*") in Jerusalem and a few other ancient walled cities
Torah:	Ex. 17:8-16
Scroll:	Book of Esther (evening and morning with special benedictions)

Civil dates on which the festival occurs, 1990-2010:

1990/5751	11 March
1991/5752	28 February
1992/5753	19 March
1993/5754	7 March
1994/5755	25 February*
1995/5756	16 March
1996/5757	5 March
1997/5758	23 March
1998/5759	12 March
1999/5760	2 March
2000/5761	21 March
2001/5762	9 March*
2002/5763	26 February
2003/5764	18 March
2004/5765	7 March
2005/5766	25 March*
2006/5767	14 March
2007/5768	4 March
2008/5769	21 March*
2009/5770	10 March
2010/5771	28 February

* These days being a Sabbath, *Purim* in Jerusalem is extended from the regular day elsewhere (Friday) to sunday as *Purim Meshullash*, a "threefold *Purim* festival."

Laws concerning the festival of Purim are detailed in the talmudic tractate MEGILLAH. The central observance is the reading of the Esther scroll at both Evening and Morning Services in the synagogue. A traditional melody is employed for the chanting. In most congregations, Purim is marked by a lighthearted carnival atmosphere: adults as well as children may attend the reading in fancy dress and, whenever Haman's name is mentioned, congregants normally stamp their feet, whirl noisemakers (*greggers* in Yiddish), and otherwise create a joyful din. This age-old practice accords with the injunction to "blot out the memory of Amalek" (Deut. 25:19), who is said to have been Haman's ancestor (Est. 3:1). Amalek's wickedness, a seasonal leitmotif, is first emphasized in the MAFTIR reading (Deut. 25:17-19) for the Sabbath immediately before Purim (*Shabbat Zakhor*; see SABBATHS, SPECIAL) and subsequently in the Pentateuch reading for Purim itself (Ex. 17:8-16). As on the festival of ḤANUKKAH, a short prayer of thanksgiving for the miraculous deliverance (AL HA-NISSIM) is inserted both in the *Amidah* and in Grace after Meals; but the HALLEL psalms are omitted on Purim, since the events which this festival commemorates took place outside of Eretz Israel.

Owing to its uniquely joyful nature, Purim is the occasion for parties and other traditional festivities. According to rabbinic law, these should include the exchanging of food gifts or "portions" among relatives, friends, and neighbors (*mishlo'aḥ manot*); donations to charity; and a special festive meal or SE'UDAH in every home during the afternoon. Purim also has its own traditional dishes, which include fried pastries known as "Haman's ears" (*ozné Haman*), and triangular buns or pastries filled with poppyseed, dates, prunes, etc., which in Yiddish are termed *Hamentashen* ("Haman's pockets"). A standard practice is for parents and relatives to give children *Purim-gelt* ("Purim money"), presents in cash.

A mood of sanctioned frivolity characterizes the celebration. *Barukh Mordekhai* ("Blessed be Mordecai") and *Arur Haman* ("Cursed be Haman"), two phrases taken from the *Shoshannat Ya'akov* ("Lily of Jacob") hymn sung after the reading of the Book of Esther, have the same numerical value (502) in Hebrew. This prompted the rabbis to declare that on Purim it is laudable to become so intoxicated that "one can no longer tell the difference between the two" (*Meg.* 7b). From early times, the staging of masquerades, parodies, and satirical plays (the Yiddish *Purim-shpil*, for example) has been the order of the day; and in *yeshivot* (talmudic academies) one student would be chosen to act as the "Purim rabbi," imitating and poking fun at his teachers. The carnival spirit is particularly evident in modern Israel, where city streets are thronged with revelers and children decked out in an imaginative array of costumes. The best-known carnival parade (held in Tel-Aviv and elsewhere), is the *Adloyada*, a title based on the words *ad de-lo yada* ("until one can no logner tell the difference"; see above).

The celebration of Purim and the historicity of the events

described sometimes aroused criticism. Scholars point out that there is no independent evidence for the Purim story and that this festival does not seem to convey an unambiguous ethical or religious message. Like Ḥanukkah, it has strong national overtones — commemorating a historic triumph of the Jews over their bloodthirsty persecutors and the downfall of Haman, the archetypal anti-Semite. Through Purim's celebration year by year, Jews were able to renew their faith in God as their savior, and to momentarily forget the griefs and perils with which they had to contend in exile (see also PURIMS, SPECIAL).

PURIMS, SPECIAL Just as Jews throughout the world celebrate the festival of PURIM in commemoration of their ancestors having been saved from a hostile decree condemning them to death, so many individual Jewish communities ordained their own Purims, each in its own way, to commemorate their deliverance from various calamities. For example, the Padua Purim, celebrated on 11 Sivan, commemorates the Jews' deliverance from a major fire in 1795; the Florence Purim (27 Sivan) marks the resue of the Jews from a mob in 1790 by the intercession of the local bishop; the Avignon Purim (24 Tammuz) was celebrated each year, although details of the deliverance had long been forgotten; the Baghdad Purim (11 Av) celebrates the conquest of the city by the Arabs and the defeat of the Persians who were treating the Jews badly; the "Snow Purim" (24 Tevet) was celebrated by the Jews of Tunis after a major snowstorm wreaked havoc in the country but left the Jewish quarter untouched; the Kovno Purim (7 Adar II) was instituted when the Jews of Kovno were granted numerous rights in 1783 by King Poniatowski (a special scroll was written, documenting the troubles suffered by the Jews and their deliverance by the king's edicts); and, most recently, the "Hitler Purim" of Casablanca was celebrated on 2 Kislev (11 November 1943), when the city was saved from falling into German hands. Here, a "Hitler Scroll" was written, paraphrasing the traditional one, including the words "cursed be Hitler, cursed be Mussolini," and naming many of the other Nazi and fascist leaders.

PURITY, RITUAL (*tohorah*). A concept in Jewish law indicating the fitness of a person to participate in Temple ritual or of an object for use therein; its opposite is *tumah* ("ritual impurity"). One who becomes *tamé* ("impure") must usually undergo three different stages of purification. These involve: waiting a certain length of time; immersion in a ritual bath (*mikveh*); and offering sacrifices. The chief sources of impurity are dead bodies, leprosy, and issues from sexual organs. Contact with or even being in the presence of a CORPSE results in the highest degree of ritual uncleanness, which can be transferred to a lesser degree to other people, to objects, or to food. Purification in this case was achieved by the person being sent outside the camp for seven days, immersing in a *mikveh*, and then being sprinkled by the priest with the ashes of the RED HEIFER mixed with water. After the destruction of the Second Temple, the latter rite was no longer possible and all Jews have the status of *tamé met* ("corpse uncleanness").

Impurity caused by leprosy (*tsara'at*) is of three types: of man, of clothing, or of buildings. Leprosy as a skin disease is diagnosed by the priest either immediately, or after a one or two-week incubation period. Anyone suspected of leprosy must be quarantined until he is clean. His purification is achieved by the priest sprinkling upon him the blood of a bird sacrifice mixed with water, after which the person must immerse in a *mikveh*, wash his clothes, shave off all his hair, and offer sacrifices (Lev. 14:1-32). The leprosy of clothes and buildings likewise requires isolation for a week or two before diagnosis. The leprosy discussed in the Bible is commonly held to be different from the leprosy diagnosed today by the medical profession. Cases of this biblical leprosy are virtually unknown.

The impurity caused by an issue from the sexual organs is the one case in which many of the laws of purification still apply. A woman during her menstrual cycle (NIDDAH) is considered impure (Lev. 18:19). She must refrain from marital relations and can transfer this uncleanness to others, to food, or to objects. Purification is achieved by waiting for seven days after the cessation of bleeding, and then immersing in a *mikveh*. Other issues by a woman (*zavah*) or by a man (*zav*) require waiting either until evening or for seven days, the offering of a sacrifice (not operative since the destruction of the Temple), and immersion in a *mikveh*.

Any objects may become unclean except those made of stone, unfired clay, dung, and, according to rabbinic decree, wood and bone. Objects which become impure through contact with a corpse must be passed through either fire or water, but earthenware vessels cannot be purified and must be broken.

Food becomes unclean after being detached from the ground and coming in contact with a liquid (water, dew, oil, wine, milk, blood, or honey). This food or drink cannot be purified and may not be used in the Temple. These laws are also no longer in effect. A rabbinic decree requires the washing of the hands before eating bread because of the impurity contracted by the hands through touching ritually unclean objects or parts of the body.

The Talmud often mentions the concept of purity in connection with moral and spiritual development. "Purity is one of the grades on the way to the spirit of holiness" (*Av. Zar.* 20b), and "Repentance and good deeds are conducive to purity and holiness" (*Ber.* 17a) are two examples. Torah study is in itself viewed as a purification. The prophet EZEKIEL said, concerning the time of the Redemption, "I will sprinkle clean water upon you, and you shall be clean; from all your uncleannesses, and from all your idols, will I cleanse you" (Ezek. 36:25).

R

RABBAH BAR NAḤMANI (known simply as Rabbah in the Talmud; c. 270-331 CE). Babylonian *amora* of the third generation, descended from a priestly Galilean family. Rabbah's brilliance as a talmudic dialectician led to his being nicknamed *Oker Harim* ("Uprooter of Mountains"), whereas his colleague and rival Joseph bar Ḥiyya — a man of vast and comprehensive knowledge — was dubbed *Sinai* (*Ber.* 64a). Many halakhic controversies between these two scholars are recorded, the decision nearly always following Rabbah's opinion. In 309, Rabbah was appointed head of the Academy of Pumbedita and retained that position for the next 22 years. As a teacher, he dealt with all aspects of the *halakhah*, including those areas which had no practical application in Babylonia (e.g., the laws of ritual purification). It was under Rabbah's efficient administration that the Academy of Pumbedita attained its golden age. Thousands came to hear him lecture at Pumbedita during the KALLAH months, and Rabbah usually opened on a humorous note before turning to the subject in hand (*BM* 86a; *Shab.* 30b). Tragically, however, the very success of these gatherings provoked official resentment and the civil authorities finally accused him of enabling his students to evade tax payments during the *kallah* months. Rabbah met a lonely and wretched end as a fugitive in the countryside outside Pumbedita.

RABBANITES See KARAITES

RABBI ("my master"). Title of qualified Jewish religious authority and teacher. It was originally, in Mishnaic times, an expression of respect. In the first century CE, it became an official title conferred on ordained members of the SANHEDRIN who were adjudged to have established their reputations as experts in Jewish law. The ceremony at which the title was conferred was known as ORDINATION (*semikhah*). This could take place only in Erets Israel; in Babylonia, sages of similar status received the title *Rav* and never used the term "rabbi." Ordination in the full sense ceased in the fourth century. However, the term "rabbi" continued to be used for any individual who was qualified to make decisions in matters of Jewish law. A limited form of ordination known as *hattarat hora'ah* ("permission to teach"), signed by one or more scholars, developed, especially among Ashkenazi communities. Later, examinations were introduced, either by the YESHIVAH where the candidate studied, or individual authoritative rabbis who granted the title.

Jews settled far and wide, and the regimes under which they lived were dissimilar. Nevertheless, they remained a community bound together by adherence to the laws and teachings of the Talmud. The Gentile rulers allowed them the status of an autonomous corporate entity, and they needed qualified interpreters of talmudic literature. At first, the more expert members of the community undertook this duty on a voluntary basis: rabbis received no payment for their work and earned their livelihoods in other ways. Eventually, especially in the wake of the Expulsion from Spain (1492), when the religious leaders found it impossible to find other means of living, the rabbinate became a paid profession, and the rabbi was a salaried officer of the community. His duties varied from place to place, and the attitude of the non-Jewish authorities (who in some instances insisted on confirming any appointment) might determine the scope of his authority. The common thread included the rabbi's duty to render decisions according to rabbinic law, not only in religious matters but also in civil litigation. In large cities, the rabbi often headed a *yeshivah*, and in all places he supervised religious activities such as ritual slaughter and the ritual bath. His office conferred no special privileges in performance of rituals, and his preaching was usually confined to sermons twice a year, on the Sabbaths preceding Passover and the Day of Atonement (see HOMILETICS).

Sometimes, as in the case of Prague, the rabbi of a major community acquired jurisdiction over a province, but for the most part communities and their rabbis were confined to a town and its environs. Each was independent of the other; there was no institutional hierarchy, but the scholarly reputation of an individual rabbi might lend authority to his pronouncements well outside his own community.

The advent of Enlightenment and EMANCIPATION posed new challenges to the traditional role of the rabbi. In the countries where Emancipation was achieved, the rabbis lost their judicial role, questions of belief and observance needed to be reconsidered, and age-old practices were reformed in growing circles. The need for a rabbi to acquire secular knowledge in addition to Jewish learning was felt in Orthodox as well as Reform circles, and RABBINICAL SEMINARIES in a modern spirit were founded for the training of rabbis from the 19th century. Their curriculum reflected the new responsibilities of the rabbis: less emphasis on Talmud, and concern with subjects which would enable the rabbi to preach and teach in congregations whose members had themselves received a secular education. In the British Commonwealth, in the 19th century, rabbis called themselves "ministers" and took the title "reverend," in imitation of their surroundings. Since World War II, the tendency has been to assume the title "rabbi," leaving "reverend" for those not fully qualified.

The large Jewish communities of Eastern Europe were for the most part unaffected by these changes, and the *yeshivah* continued to flourish. The tsarist regime attempted to force on its Jewish subjects government-appointed rabbis. In the US the rabbinate has been characterized as "a new profession with an old name." The Jewish community dates back to 1654, but almost two centuries elapsed before New York enjoyed the services of its first rabbi. The new structures of Jewish life called for fresh rabbinical images. There was no autonomous corporate entity with judicial power as had existed in the "old world," and functions which, in Europe, had been community matters, were now handled by other bodies. Synagogues multiplied freely, and the rabbis were responsible to a single congregation. The tendencies that emerged (Orthodox, Conservative, Reform, and Reconstructionist) developed their own seminaries, congregational unions, and rabbinical associations, each with its own standard of rabbinical practice. Except among the more extreme Orthodox, the pattern that has emerged is for the emphasis of the rabbi's activities to be pastoral, social, educational, and INTERFAITH.

In the Sephardi and Eastern communities, the nature of the rabbinate changed little, concentrating on its judicial and educational functions. A common title for the rabbi was *marbits Torah* ("spreader of Torah"). In the Ottoman Empire, the millet system assigned to the religious authorities of the non-Muslim communities jurisdiction over religious matters. In Palestine/Israel, this practice was carried over and systematized by the British mandatory administration and then by the government of Israel. This means that in Israel there is an official rabbinate with legal control over matters of personal status (e.g., marriage, divorce, conversion). The rabbis receive their salary from the State for their services as marriage registrars, etc. They are less concerned with synagogue activities than rabbis in the Diaspora, and tend to confine their interests to matters of *halakhah*, without involvement in wider issues such as occupy rabbis in other countries. The official rabbinate in Israel is Orthodox and the rabbis of non-Orthodox congregations have received no recognition.

There is a parallel Ashkenazi and Sephardi CHIEF RABBINATE which, together with the Ministry of Religious Affairs, confirms every rabbinical appointment. The rabbis themselves are graduates of *yeshivot*.

RABBINICAL SEMINARIES The need for modern-style seminaries to train rabbis emerged early in the 19th century as part of the movement for Jewish EMANCIPATION in Central and Western Europe. Up to that time rabbis had come from YESHIVOT which had been geared to Torah study, but in which the professional training of rabbis was, at best, incidental. In the pre-Emancipation communities, the primary task of the RABBI was to expound the law and to judge according to the law, for which he was equipped by a schooling in Talmud and codes. However, with Emancipation, the Jewish communities began to live in the world of the host society, culturally as well as politically. In this situation the intense but narrow training provided by the *yeshivot* was largely irrelevant. The function of the rabbi became comparable to that of the Christian clergyman, and governments, which closely supervised religious bodies, often demanded that Jewish communities appoint spiritual leaders with a modern education.

In 1829 a Collego Rabbinico was established in Padua, then part of the Austrian empire. Support from Italian Jews was limited, and more than once it suspended operations. The latest reopening took place (in Rome) in 1955. Also in 1829, the French École Rabbinique opened in Metz, and moved to Paris in 1859.

Germany offered more fertile soil for the establishment of rabbinical seminaries. Some German Jews hoped that the status and needs of Judaism would be recognized by the establishment at a German university of a faculty of Jewish theology, parallel to the faculties of Catholic and Protestant theology, but this was not conceded by the governments concerned. The need for a Jewish institution was met by the will of Jonas Fränckel, a wealthy Breslau merchant, under whose bequest the Júdische-Theologisches Seminar was opened in Breslau in 1854. In the spirit of its first director, Zacharias FRANKEL (1801-1875), the advocate of "positive historical Judaism," the Breslau Seminary emphasized free scholarly inquiry combined with adherence to traditional Jewish practice. Ordination depended on a prescribed seven-year course of study, and candidates were expected to obtain a university doctorate. The curriculum included the traditional Jewish texts, but was far broader than that of a *yeshivah*: WISSENSCHAFT DES JUDENTUMS (Jewish Science) was the key concept directing its program.

Graduates of the Breslau Seminary served a wide variety of congregations, principally those in Germany, usually denominated liberal, which accepted moderate changes in religious practice. It was the prototype of later institutions, although its standpoint satisfied the partisans of neither ORTHODOXY nor REFORM. The leading exponent of Reform in Germany was Abraham GEIGER (1810-1874), and under his direction the Hochschule für die Wissenschaft des Judentum (Còllege for the Science of Judaism) was opened in Berlin in 1872. (In an act of anti-Semitic malevolence the government in 1883 required *Lehranstalt* [Institute] to be substituted for *Hochschule* [College]). The founders emphasized the need for the institution to be free from state, synagogue, or party ties. By this time Geiger's ardor for change in religious practice had waned, and those who had expected his seminary to become a torchbearer of Reform were disappointed. In 1873 the Rabbinerseminar für das Orthodoxe Judentum (Orthodox Rabbinical Seminary) was opened in Berlin under the leadership of Azriel HILDESHEIMER (1820-1899). Its standpoint was that of the *Torah im derekh erets* (Torah with secular knowledge) school of Samson Raphael HIRSCH, but in the eyes of some of the Orthodox the synthesis diluted the purity of the faith with the heresy of secular study. This divergence came into focus in 1934 when a proposal that the Hildesheimer Seminary transfer to Palestine was quashed immediately by the local rabbinate.

The bitterest opposition to the establishment of a rabbinical seminary came from the Orthodox Jews of Hungary. Nevertheless, with government help, a Seminary was opened by the NEOLOGY movement in Budapest in 1877. It attracted a distinguished staff of scholars and survived both World War II and the subsequent communist regime. The Israelitische Theologische Lehranstalt (Jewish Theological Institute) of Vienna (1893) made less of an impact.

In 1855 Jews' College opened in London. With the Chief Rabbi as president *ex officio*, it has always been an Orthodox institution. To train Reform rabbis the Leo Baeck College was opened in London in 1956.

In Eastern Europe the world of pre-Emancipation Judaism remained substantially intact, and there was little support within the Jewish community for the training of rabbis outside the traditional *yeshivah* mode. However, the anti-Semitic tsarist government sought to impose a modernized rabbinate, establishing seminaries at Vilna and Zhitomir in 1847. The Jews treated them with derision and for the most part ignored their graduates. They were closed in 1873.

With the exception of the Berlin Hochschule, which lingered on until 1942, the Nazis closed the institutions under their control in 1938.

In the United States rabbinical seminaries preceded *yeshivot*. The need for an English-speaking, locally trained rabbinate began to be argued during the period of heavy immigration from Central Europe after 1820, and in 1867 Isaac Leeser (1800-1868) established Maimonides College in Philadelphia. However, it crumbled after his death. Credit for the first successful effort belongs to Isaac Mayer WISE (1819-1900). He had insisted on the need for such an institution from the time of his arrival in the United States in 1846, and became president of the rabbinical seminary Hebrew Union College, when it opened in Cincinnati in 1875. The College, whose first graduates were ordained in 1883, was intended to serve all points of view within the American Jewish community, but events conspired to make it the standard bearer of radical Reform.

As a counter-thrust, a conservative group established the Jewish Theological Seminary in New York (1886). This was reorganized under the presidency of Solomon SCHECHTER in 1902, who assembled a distinguished group of scholars. It was the Seminary that brought together the various elements constituting the CONSERVATIVE movement. Ideologically, though not sociologically, the standpoint of the Jewish Theological Seminary could be compared to that of the Breslau Seminary. In 1922 the Jewish Institute of Religion, which sought to be inclusive but in practice was Reform, was founded in New York by Rabbi Stephen S. Wise.

Hebrew Union College-Jewish-Institute of Religion in Cincinnati.

Jewish Theological Seminary in New York.

Laying the cornerstone for the main building at Yeshiva University's Main Center campus, New York, 1927.

The *yeshivot* responded to the needs of the East European immigrants who transformed the American Jewish community at the end of the 19th century. The Isaac Elhanan Yeshiva, dating back to 1886, was expanded into the wide-ranging Yeshiva University, including a medical school, within which the Rabbi Isaac Elhanan Theological Seminary functions as a college for training rabbis. In 1968 the Jewish Reconstructionist Foundation opened a rabbinical training college in Philadelphia.

Expansion has characterized the history of the American institutions; they reach out into many fields rather than nurture the aloof specialization of their European predecessors. For example, Hebrew Union College took over the New York Jewish Institute of Religion and established branches in Los Angeles, where it has a school of social work, and in Jerusalem, where it has a school of archeology. The Jewish Theological Seminary established the University of Judaism in Los Angeles as well as a Jerusalem branch; in New York it maintains the Jewish Museum and a radio program and a combined program in Judaic Studies with Columbia University.

In 1952 a Seminario Rabbinico was established in Buenos Aires under Conservative auspices, intended to prepare candidates for admission to the New York institution.

RACHEL Wife of JACOB; one of the MATRIARCHS of Israel. She was the younger daughter of Jacob's uncle, Laban. Jacob met her by a well and wished to marry her. Following trickery by Laban, who substituted his older daughter, LEAH, for Rachel on Jacob's wedding night, Jacob was forced to work another seven years, in addition to the first seven he had agreed to work for Rachel's hand.

Rachel was the mother of JOSEPH and Benjamin. It was in giving birth to Benjamin just outside Bethlehem that Rachel died.

When Jacob fled from the house of his father-in-law, Laban, Rachel stole Laban's graven images. Laban pursued Jacob and his camp and searched it for these graven images, but Rachel successfully concealed them from her father.

Rachel is described as being, "of comely appearance and beautiful" (Gen. 29:17); she was Jacob's favorite wife. When Jacob finally met his brother Esau, after a 20-year separation, still fearing his wrath, he placed his concubines with their children first in his camp, followed by Leah and her children and finally Rachel with Joseph. Evidently this was to protect Rachel and her son.

The traditional site of Rachel's tomb has drawn pilgrims at least since the Byzantine era and has been a favorite subject of Jewish folk art. Women, especially those who are barren, come to pray at Rachel's tomb, for it is related that she was barren for a long time before giving birth to her children.

RAIN, PRAYERS FOR Various supplications, hymns, and prayers for rain read in synagogue, notably on SHEMINI ATSERET, the last day of Sukkot. There are numerous biblical allusions to the importance of rainfall in the Land of Israel; it may be granted to the farmer as a Divine blessing (Lev. 26:4; Deut. 11:13ff., 28:12) or it may be withheld as a punishment (Deut. 11:16-17; I Kings 8:35, etc.). According to the rabbis, all men enjoy the benefits of rain but its timely descent can be affected by their conduct (*Ta'an.* 7a-8a). It was customary for the High Priest in the Temple to recite a short petition for "a rainy year" on the Day of Atonement (*Yoma* 53b). Supplications were also prescribed whenever crops might be lost through a drought. This tradition has been maintained by the Jewish communities of Yemen and by Sephardim in Israel, who read special petitions and observe a fast when normal rainfall is delayed.

Talmudic sources mention Sukkot as the time when "the world is judged for water" (*RH* 1.2). This led to the practice of incorporating two separate passages in the daily AMIDAH, an appreciative "reference" and a seasonal "request," the "reference" being delayed until Shemini Atseret and the specific "request" until 7 Ḥeshvan, so that premature rainfall would not interfere with observance and enjoyment of the Tabernacles festival (and the journey of the pilgrims homeward from Jerusalem). *Mashiv ha-ru'aḥ u-morid ha-geshem* ("You cause the wind to blow and the rain to fall") is the first passage, recited from the Additional Service of Shemini Atseret until Passover. Throughout this period, *Mashiv ha-ru'aḥ* is inserted in the second benediction of every *Amidah*. The second passage, *Ve-ten tal u-matar li-verakhah* ("Grant dew and rain for a blessing"), is inserted in the ninth benediction, which gives expression to the hope for a prosperous year. This "request," the length and content of which vary in different prayer rites, is recited in Israeli synagogues from the evening of 7 Ḥeshvan until Passover; in Diaspora congregations, however, several more weeks elapse before it is recited from 4-5 December, the evening of the 60th day following the autumnal equinox.

From the early Middle Ages, with the objective of enhancing the solemnity of these passages, various introductory liturgical poems (*piyyutim*) were recited at the beginning of the Additional Service on Shemini Atseret. Known as *Tefillat Geshem*, the Prayer for Rain (or *Tikkun ha-Geshem* in the Sephardi rite), they closely resemble the *Tal* sequence read on Passover (see DEW, PRAYERS FOR). Few Ashkenazi congregations still read the entire sequence of these old hymns. The standard practice in most Orthodox congregations of the Diaspora is for the cantor to don his white KITEL before the Additional Service and to chant the Prayer for Rain while repeating the first two benedictions of the *Amidah*. It commences with *Af Beri uttat shem sar matar* ("*Af Beri* is the name of the angel of rain"), a two-stanza poem which begs God not to withhold His bounty of rainfall. Then, while the ark remains open and congregants stand, the cantor proceeds to chant *Zekhor av nimshakh aḥarekha ka-mayim* ("Remember the Patriarch who followed You"), an alphabetical acrostic hymn traditionally composed by Eleazar KALLIR. Its six stanzas recall the various miraculous events connected with water that God performed for the Patriarchs, Moses, Aaron, and the twelve Tribes of Israel. After proclaiming "For You are the Lord our God who causes the wind to blow and the rain to fall," the cantor repeats the congregation's threefold prayer that rain will come "as a blessing, not as a curse; for life, not for death; for plenty, not for famine." Apart from *Af Beri*, this ritual is followed in Conservative synagogues, but Reform congregations recite an abbreviated version of the Prayer for Rain.

In Israel, however, the Sephardi practice of avoiding any "interruption" during the *Amidah* has been adopted by most congregations that adhere to the Ashkenazi rite. They accordingly omit all the introductory liturgical poems and recite the *Geshem* hymn immediately prior to the silent *Amidah* on Shemini Atseret (which is also Simḥat Torah). The Diaspora (Ashkenazi) ritual is chiefly maintained in Israel by Ḥasidic congregations.

RANSOM See CAPTIVES, RANSOMING OF

RASHI (acronym of Rabbi Shelomo Yitsḥaki; 1040-1105). The outstanding Jewish biblical and talmudic commentator. Rashi was born in Troyes, northern France where for the greater part of his life conditions for the Jews were generally favorable.

At an early age, Rashi went to study in Worms; he then went to Mainz, the center of learning in Lorraine. His principal teachers were Jacob ben Yakar and Isaac ben Judah, the outstanding students of Rabbenu GERSHOM, *Me'or ha-Golah*.

After some years as a student in Mainz, Rashi returned to Troyes where he established his own academy; he also served as *dayyan* (rabbinic judge), of the community. He earned his livelihood as a vintner.

Rashi had two daughters, Miriam and Jochebed, who married students of their father. His grandchildren were counted among the outstanding scholars of the next generation, the most famous being SAMUEL BEN MEIR (*Rashbam*) and his brother Jacob (TAM).

The last years of his life were saddened by the events of the First Crusade of 1095. In their inflamed state of mind the Crusaders devastated the defenseless Jewish communities of the Rhineland. Rashi was particularly sensitive to the disasters which had befallen his own colleagues as well as the great centers of learning and their scholars. Certain of his comments on the Psalms and other biblical books appear to reflect his anguish over the fate of his people (see Rashi on Ps. 38:1; 38:18; 39:2-5; Isa. 53:9).

These tragic events may well have affected Rashi's health and towards the end of his life he became too weak to write. He dictated some responsa to his grandsons and friends. But by this time his massive works on Bible and Talmud were almost completed. He finished his commentary on the entire Bible, with the exception of the Book of Chronicles. His commentaries on certain tractates of the Talmud were completed by others. Tractate *Bava Batra*, from page 29a onwards, was completed by his grandson, Samuel ben Meir.

In addition to his monumental commentaries on Bible and Talmud, Rashi wrote a few liturgical poems and some 350 responsa in answer to questions on Jewish law addressed to him by Jews from all over Europe. The responsa reveal a great deal about Rashi's personality, particularly his kindliness, gentleness and humility, as well as his rather liberal approach to matters of ritual.

Rashi's great reputation rests on his commentaries on Bible and Talmud. His commentary on the Pentateuch, which was to become the standard text for every student from childhood onwards, was the first Hebrew book to be printed: in 1475, in Reggio, Italy. In his work on the Bible, Rashi set himself a clear aim: to give the plain meaning — PESHAT — of the text. His style is clear and concise and his Hebrew simple. His personal familiarity with many everyday occupations such as that of the farmer, the artisan and the merchant enables him to enliven his explanations with unusual comments illustrating the meaning of the text for his disciples. He often relies on the Aramaic Bible translation of Onkelos in order to pinpoint the literal meaning of the word. In addition, wherever he finds it helpful, Rashi gives the Old French equivalent of a difficult Hebrew word, in Hebrew transliteration. There are about 1,300 such words in Rashi's Bible commentary and 3,500 in the Talmud commentary. Known as *la'azim* (singular, *la'az*) 'in foreign language,' they are extremely valuable to students of Old French. In his search for accurate meaning, it was only natural that Rashi should also have investigated the grammar of

Hebrew words and phrases. As a result, his commentary contains numerous notes which provide a valuable early contribution to the grammar of the Hebrew language.

The central feature of Rashi's methodology is the use of the twin methods of *peshat* and DERASH. The former is the plain meaning; the latter is the attempt to find a deeper meaning in the text which can be drawn upon to illustrate a law or an ethical position. Rashi's declared aim at the outset was to provide the *peshat* (see Rashi on Gen. 3:8; 4:8; 33:20); in fact, however, his commentaries are rich in *derash* and the midrashic folklore thus introduced adds a new dimension to the interpretation, frequently helping to achieve a clearer understanding of the text (see Rashi on Gen. 3:8; 24:67; 25:21-26; 49:22). Although Rashi himself claims to introduce *derash* only when the *peshat* is difficult, he occasionally turns to the *derash* when there is no apparent reason to do so (see Rashi on Gen. 1:1,26; Deut. 27:15ff). He understood that for many people the folklore of the *aggadah* was more attractive than the dry *peshat*. One very important result of Rashi's extensive use of *derash* is that throughout the ages, his countless readers have been introduced into the world of rabbinic folklore, an area of Jewish literature with which they might otherwise have remained unfamiliar.

Rashi's influence extended well beyond the Jewish community. The Franciscan monk, Nicholas de Lyra (1270-1340), read Rashi in the original and in his own Bible commentary, De Lyra frequently cites Rashi and acknowledges his indebtedness to him. In turn, Martin Luther borrowed heavily from De Lyra for his own translation of the Bible. Thus Rashi influenced the Bible translations of the Reformation scholars.

In his commentary on the Talmud Rashi's method is more consistent, as his sole aim was to elucidate for his students the meaning of the text before them. A series of problems made Talmud study difficult: the question of the authenticity of the text, at a time when copyists had produced variant readings; the difficult Aramaic language; the often obscure nature of the talmudic arguments. Rashi proved himself a sure guide in all these areas. Making a few emendations to Rabbenu Gershom's text, he submitted what he believed to be the true text. His emendations were subsequently incorporated into all printed editions of the Talmud. His true genius is evident in his skill as an expositor of the text; he provided Talmud students with the most comprehensive and yet clearest explanations. Without his commentary the Talmud would long have remained a closed book. Modern day students of the Talmud continue to make extensive use of the commentary that has become an indispensible tool for comprehension.

Rashi's work on the Talmud was continued by a school of commentators known as the Tosafists (see TOSAFOT). Founded by Rashi's own grandchildren and disciples, the school continued for about two hundred years. They added commentaries to the text and frequently expanded points of Rashi's own explanation. In all standard editions of the Talmud the comments of the Tosafists appear on the outside column of each page, opposite Rashi's commentary printed on the inside column.

SAYINGS OF RASHI

All the 613 commandments are included in the Decalogue.

Any plan formulated in a hurry is foolish.

Be sure to ask your teacher his reasons and his sources.

Teachers learn from their students' discussions.

A student of laws who does not understand their meaning or cannot explain their contradictions is just a basket full of books.

Do not rebuke your fellow man so as to shame him in public.

To obey out of love is better than to obey out of fear.

RAV (or Abba Arikha, i.e., Abba the Tall, c. 175-247 CE). Babylonian *amora* of the first generation; founder of the ACADEMY of Sura. Born to a well-established Babylonian family, Rav went to Erets Israel to join his uncle the *tanna* R. Ḥiyya and to study at the Academy of R. JUDAH HA-NASI from whom he received limited ORDINATION. There he came in close contact with other *tannaim*; the impact of his years of study in Erets Israel and his ongoing personal connection with colleagues and teachers there is reflected in his legal decisions.

He returned to Babylonia, to the Academy at Nehardea, but went on to found his own center at Sura in 219. Here his ability and teachings soon brought hundreds of students flocking to him at a time when the scholarship of the Babylonian community was not yet on a par with that of the Palestinian centers. His colleague SAMUEL, the head of the Nehardea Academy, was the authority on civil law; Rav was expert in ritual matters. The authority of the two men insured the independent status and prestige of the Babylonian academies. The discussions between Rav and Samuel, and their divergent teachings, form a prominent feature of the Babylonian Talmud. In matters of ritual law, Rav's rulings were generally decisive.

Rav is likewise known for his homiletical discourses and his ethical teachings. The special prayer for the New MOON is attributed to him.

Rav's pre-eminence can be seen in the fact that while technically a member of the first generation of *amoraim*, he was granted the authority to dispute tannaitic pronouncements, a right generally reserved for *tannaim* only.

SAYINGS OF RAV

Arrogance is equivalent to all the other sins.

God Himself prays, "May My mercy overcome My anger."

When your mind is not at ease, do not pray.

In the future world there will be no eating, drinking, propagation, business, jealousy, hatred or competition, but the righteous will sit with crowns on their heads enjoying the brilliance of the Divine Presence.

He who refuses to pray for his fellow is a sinner.

What is improper in public, is forbidden in secret.

Each individual will be called to account in the hereafter for every enjoyment he declined in this world without sufficent cause.

RAVA (Abba bar Joseph bar Ḫama; c.280-352 CE). Prominent Babylonian *amora* of the fourth generation. His teachers were Naḫman ben Jacob (in Maḫoza), Joseph bar Ḫiyya (in Pumbedita), and Rav Ḫisda (in Sura), whose widowed daughter he later married. When ABBAYÉ, his great rival and one-time fellow student, became head of the Pumbedita Academy in 323 CE, Rava settled in his native Maḫoza and gained a formidable reputation through his teaching there. After the death of Abbayé (338 CE), Maḫoza absorbed Pumbedita's teaching staff and, from then until the end of Rava's life, served as the only Academy in Babylonia. The debates between Rava and Abbayé constituted one of the foundations of the Babylonian TALMUD. In all but six cases, the *halakhah* was decided in Rava's favor. He had a brilliant analytical mind, excelling in the detection of analogies, and in his arguments relied on logic and reason where others invoked tradition.

Equally noted as an aggadist, Rava would address large public gatherings on Sabbath afternoons. Torah study was exalted as a supreme value in Rava's teachings. "How foolish people are!" he once observed. "They rise in the presence of a Torah scroll, but not for a great Torah scholar" (*Mak.* 22b). Ethical sensitivity moved Rava to declare that whoever puts someone to shame in public will be denied a share in the afterlife (*BM* 59a). When someone reported that, on pain of death, he had been ordered to kill another man, Rava told him: "Rather allow yourself to be killed than commit murder. Is your blood redder than that other man's? Perhaps his blood is redder than yours" (*Pes.* 25b).

READING OF THE LAW (*Keri'at ha-Torah*). The chanting in synagogue of prescribed sections from the PENTATEUCH; these must be read from a SCROLL OF THE LAW (*Sefer Torah*) in the course of public worship, i.e., only when a MINYAN (prayer quorum) is present. One of the oldest and most distinctive features of the Jewish LITURGY, reading the Law was an integral part of the synagogue service in late Temple times, but traditionally, Moses is its originator (Ex. 24:7; Deut. 31:12). According to the sages, he instituted the practice on Sabbaths, festivals and New Moons, while EZRA utilized it for the purpose of instruction on Mondays and Thursdays (when people came to market) and on Sabbath afternoons (when they had time to study; *Meg.* 31a, *BK* 82a). From Ezra's time, Scriptural passages were translated from Hebrew into the Aramaic vernacular by a METURGEMAN and in some Diaspora communities a Greek translation must have been provided for those who knew little Hebrew.

The Reading of the Law at a bar mitsvah *ceremony. Painting by J. Brandon, France, 19th century.*

Even though early rabbinic sources mention special readings by name (*Yoma* 7.1; *Meg.* 3.4, 29b-31a), also indicating how many worshipers should be called to the Reading of the Law on each occasion (*Meg.* 4.1-4, 21b-23a), texts for the regular weekly portion (*sidrah* or PARASHAH) appear to have been ill-defined until the talmudic period, i.e., after the third century CE. No less than three verses at a time might be read, however, so that a minimum of 21 verses were included in each consecutive Sabbath *parashah*. Eventually, two different Torah reading cycles came to be adopted. The Palestinian (Erets Israel) tradition, that survived until the 13th century, divided the Pentateuch into 175 *sedarot* or pericopes according to the number of Sabbaths that would occur over a period of three years (see TRIENNIAL CYCLE). The Babylonian system, now traditional throughout the world, divided it into 54 longer pericopes for an annual cycle that matched a Jewish leap year. Every *parashah* derives its Hebrew title from a key word in the opening sentence. During a normal year of 52 weeks, various "double portions" have to be read, as allowance must also be made for the postponement of certain regular weekly readings when major festivals and Sabbaths coincide. The twelve-month cycle of weekly readings concludes and begins anew on the festival of SIMḪAT TORAH.

WEEKLY READING OF THE LAW IN SYNAGOGUE

Pentateuch reading		Prophetical reading *(Haftarah)*
GENESIS:		
Be-Reshit	1:1 — 6:8	Isaiah 42:5 — 43:11 (42:5-21)*
No'aḥ	6:9 -11:32	Isaiah 54:1 — 55:5 (54:1-10)
Lekh Lekha	12:1-17:27	Isaiah 40:27- 41:16
Va-Yera	18:1-22:24	II Kings 4:1-37 (4:1-23)
ḤayyéSarah	23:1-25:18	I Kings 1:1-31
Toledot	25:19-28:9	Malachi 1:1-2:7
Va-Yetsé	28:10-32:3	Hosea 12:13-14:10 (11:7-12:12)
Va-Yishlaḥ	32:4-36:43	Hosea 11:7-12:12 (Obadiah 1:1- 21)
Va-Yeshev	37:1-40:23	Amos 2:6-3:8
Mi-Kets	41:1-44:17	I Kings 3:15-4:1
Va-Yiggash	44:18-47:27	Ezekiel 37:15-28
Va-Yeḥi	47:28-50:26	I Kings 2:1-12
EXODUS:		
Shemot	1:1 — 61	Isaiah 27:6-28:13; 29:22- 23(Jer.1:1-2:3)
Va-Era	6:2 — 9:35	Ezekiel 28: 25-29:21
Bo	10:1 — 13:16	Jeremiah 46:13-28
Be-Shallaḥ	13:17-17:16	Judges 4:4-5:31 (5:1-31)
Yitro	18:1 -20:23	Isaiah 6:1-7:6; 9:5-6 (6:1-13)
Mishpatim	21:1 -24:18	Jeremiah 34:8-22; 33:25-26
Terumah	{ (25:1- 27:19	I Kings 5:26-6:13
Tetsavveh	{ (27:20-30:10	Ezekiel 43:10-27
Ki Tissa	30:11-34:35	I Kings 18:1-39 (18:20-39)
Va-Yak'hel	{ (35:1 -38:20	I Kings 7:40-50 (7:13-26)
Pekudé	{ (38:21-40:38	I Kings 7:51-8:21 (7:40-50)
LEVITICUS:		
Va-Yikra	1:1 — 5:26	Isaiah 43:21-44:23
Tsav	6:1 — 8:36	Jeremiah 7:21-8:3; 9:22-23
Shemini	9:1 — 11:47	II Samuel 6:1-7:17 (6:1-19)
Tazri'a	{ (12:1 — 13:59	II Kings 4:42 — 5:19
Metsora	{ (14:1 — 15:33	II Kings 7:3-20
Aḥaré Mot	{ (16:1 — 18:30	Ezekiel 22:1-19 (22:1-16)
Kedoshim	{ (19:1 — 20:27	Amos 9:7-15 (Ezekiel 20:2-20)
Emor	21:1 — 24:23	Ezekiel 44:15-31

* Parentheses indicate Sephardi rite where this differs from the Ashkenazi.

Pentateuch reading		Prophetical reading *(Haftarah)*
Be-Har	{ (25:1 — 26:2	Jeremiah 32:6-27
Be Ḥukkotai	{ (26:3 — 27:34	Jeremiah 16:19-17:14
NUMBERS:		
Be-Midbar	1:1 — 4:20	Hosea 2:1-22
Naso	4:21 — 7:89	Judges 13:2-25
Be-Ha'alotekha	8:1 — 12:16	Zechariah 2:14-4:7
Shelaḥ Lekha	13:1 — 15:41	Joshua 2:1-24
Koraḥ	16:1 — 18:32	I Samuel 11:14-12:22
Ḥukkat	19:1 — 22:1	Judges 11:1-33
Balak	22:2 — 25:9	Micah 5:6-6:8
Pinḥas	25:10 — 30:1	I Kings 18:46-19:21
Mattot	30:2 — 32:42	Jeremiah 1:1-2:3
Masé	33:1 — 36:13	Jeremiah 2:4-28;3:4 (2:4- 28;4:1-2)
DEUTERONOMY:		
Devarim	1:1 — 3:22	Isaiah 1:1-27
Va Etḥannan	3:23 — 7:11	Isaiah 40:1-26
Ekev	7:12 — 11:25	Isaiah 49:14-51:3
Re'eh	11:26 — 16:17	Isaiah 54:11-55:5
Shofetim	16:18 — 21:19	Isaiah 51:12-52:12
Ki Tetsé	21:10 — 25:19	Isaiah 54:1-10
Ki Tavo	26:1 — 29:8	Isaiah 60:1-22
Nitsavvim	29:9 — 30:20	Isaiah 61:10-63:9
Va-Yelekh	31:1 — 30	Isaiah 55:6-56:8
Ha'azinu	32:1 — 52	II Samuel 22:1-51
Ve Zot Ha Berakah	33:1 — 34:12	Joshua 1:1-18 (1:1-9)
Fasts (morning and afternoon days)	Exodus 32:11-14; 34:1 -10	Isaiah 55:6-56-8 (Ashkenazim only at Afternoon Service)
Sabbath and New Moon	Weekly portion; Numbers 28:9-15 (*maftir*)	Isaiah 66:1-24
Sabbath immediately preceding New Moon	Weekly portion	1 Samuel 20:18-42

See also SABBATHS, SPECIAL and the individual festivals for the readings on these occasions.

Whenever the Reading of the Law takes place in synagogue, congregants stand while the Torah scroll is removed from the ark and carried to the BIMAH (reading desk). This is also the procedure when the scroll is returned to the ark. On all such occasions, the chanting of prescribed biblical verses and psalms accompanies the ceremonial procession to and fro, but (in Ashkenazi congregations especially) this ceremonial is most elaborate on Sabbaths and festivals. MI SHEBERAKH prayers are usually recited for each worshiper called to the Reading of the Law and *Ve-zot ha-Torah* (Deut. 4:44) is sung when the scroll is raised after all the readings have been completed. After the reading, the honor of raising the Scroll and displaying it to the congregants is called *hagbahah* ("elevation"). (Among Sephardi, Italian, and Eastern communities, the Scroll is raised prior to the reading.) Another congregant is then honored with *gelilah* ("rolling together"), rolling the Scroll together, binding it, and covering it with its mantle.

On Mondays and Thursdays, Sabbath afternoons, fast days (including Tishah be-Av), Ḥanukkah, Purim and the afternoon of the Day of Atonement, three persons are called to the Reading of the Law; on New Moons and the intermediate days of Passover and Sukkot, four are called; on the pilgrim festivals and Rosh Ha-Shanah, there are five sections; on the morning of the Day of Atonement, the number increases to six and on a regular Sabbath morning, seven persons are called. The Reading of the Law takes place at the end of Morning Service and prior to the Additional Service; on Sabbaths, the Day of Atonement and fast days, special readings are also prescribed for the afternoon. An additional or MAFTIR portion is read on Sabbaths (when the concluding verses of the weekly *parashah* are repeated), major festivals (a selection from Num. 28-29), intermediate Sabbaths of festivals, or Sabbaths coinciding with the New Moon. The worshiper honored with *maftir* usually reads the subsequent HAFTARAH reading from the Prophets. On Sabbath afternoons and the following Monday and Thursday, the portion read is the first section of the next Sabbath's reading.

The honor of being summoned to the Reading of the Law is known in Hebrew as *aliyah la-Torah* (lit. "going up to the Torah"). Until the Middle Ages, everyone chanted his own portion, having memorized the vowels, punctuation and musical accents which are lacking in the handwritten and unpointed scroll of the Law (see CANTILLATION). Once this skill had declined, an expert BA'AL KERI'AH or "Torah reader" was appointed to chant each successive portion (who indicated the place with a YAD or pointer) for those called to the Reading of the Law. However, anyone possessing the required skill may himself read. This has remained the practice among Yemenite Jews and a 13-year-old boy normally chants the *maftir* portion and the *haftarah* on the occasion of his BAR MITSVAH. Otherwise, the person called usually recites the prescribed TORAH BLESSINGS prior to and after the reading of his portion. A prayer-shawl (TALLIT) must also be worn, though (except on Tishah be-Av and the Day of Atonement), not at the Afternoon Service. If, in the course of a reading, some defect is found in the text of a scroll, it must be replaced in the ark (for subsequent correction) and a new scroll is then taken out in which the reader may continue from the point where he discovered the mistake.

An order of precedence in the allocation of Torah honors was developed by the sages (*Git.* 5.8, 60a). A *kohen* (priest) should be called first, a *levi* (Levite) second, and only thereafter a *yisra'el* (any other Jew). When no *levi* is present in the synagogue, the *kohen* also receives the second portion. Should no *kohen* be present, either a levite or a *yisra'el* may replace him, but no levite may be called second if a *yisra'el* has received the first *aliyah*. Certain honors are traditionally reserved for a distinguished scholar or for the congregational rabbi, e.g., the privilege of being called third (*shelishi*), or called for *maftir*. A father and son or two brothers do not receive successive *aliyot* (probably for fear of the EVIL EYE).

Other priorities are determined by the specific occasion. First comes a bridegroom on the Sabbaths immediately preceding and following his MARRIAGE, except if he is a widower or divorced. Among Ashkenazim, this special honor is known in Yiddish as an *oyfruf* (cf. German *Aufruf*, "call" or "summons"). Next in the order of precedence are a bar mitsvah boy; a father wishing to have his newborn daughter named that Sabbath morning or one whose newborn son will be circumcised in the course of the following week; someone observing a YAHRZEIT; a person who has just completed the *shivah* week of MOURNING and then anyone who must recite the GOMEL blessing on deliverance from peril.

Most Reform temples in the United States have either shortened the traditional readings or abandoned them altogether; modifications have generally been less drastic in Europe, where passages are declaimed rather than chanted. A number of American Conservative synagogues have reverted to the long abandoned triennial cycle of readings. In those non-Orthodox congregations where WOMEN are counted in the prayer quorum (*minyan*), they may receive an *aliyah la-Torah* and in this way a girl may also celebrate her BAT MITSVAH. Orthodox opinion is resolutely against such innovations, although some modern Orthodox rabbis have permitted observant women to conduct a Torah reading when they form a *minyan* of their own.

REBBE See ADMOR; ḤASIDISM; TSADDIK

REBEKAH Wife of ISAAC and one of the MATRIARCHS of the Jewish people. She was the daughter of Bethuel who was Abraham's nephew. Abraham sent his servant, Eliezer, to his family in Mesopotamia to select a daughter for his son, Isaac. Eliezer prayed that he would be able to identify the prospective bride by the following sign — when he asked a young woman by the well for water for himself she would of her own initiative offer to water his camels as well. Rebekah appeared and fulfilled this condition. Upon being brought to Bethuel's house, Eliezer immediately informed them of his mission. He received their consent, including that of Rebekah, to take Rebekah back with him.

Isaac was forty years old when he married; no mention is made of Rebekah's age. Their twin sons, JACOB and Esau, were born twenty years after the wedding.

Unlike Isaac, who doted on the first-born Esau, Rebekah favored Jacob. Through her prodding and planning — she went so far as to tell her son (Gen. 27:13), "Upon me be your curse, my son" — Jacob managed to trick his father into giving him the blessing of the first-born. When Esau realized that Isaac had no intention of retracting the blessing given to Jacob, he planned to kill his brother. Learning of this, Rebekah persuaded Isaac to send their younger son to her brother, Laban, in Haran, to search for a wife. She died without ever seeing Jacob again.

Rebekah was buried in the Cave of MACHPELAH, with Isaac.

REBELLIOUS SON (*ben sorer u-moreh*). Term given by the Bible to a son who intentionally rebels against the authority of his parents: "If a man has a stubborn and rebellious son who will not listen to his father's and his mother's voice and though they chasten him, he will not listen to them" (see Deut. 21:18-21). The Talmud states that the designation applies only to sons, not daughters, and limited the applicability of the law to the few months after he became a legal adult (13 years and one day old). Both parents had to be alive and neither could be deaf, dumb, blind, lame or crippled (*Sanh.* 8.4).

The rebellious son is brought to the *bet din* (rabbinical court) only after he has stolen money from his father, in order to buy and consume a certain amount of meat and wine. Furthermore, he must previously have been convicted, whipped, and warned by his parents in front of three witnesses to cease his rebellious ways. He is tried by a court of 23 judges and, if found guilty, stoned to death by the men of the city. Although this punishment appears extreme in relation to the crime, the sages explain that he is punished not for what he is, but for what he will become: If he be allowed to continue to steal from his father, he will consume all his family's wealth and then, because of his lust, will resort to robbing people on highways. Therefore, the Bible states, "Let him die innocent and not die guilty" (*Sanh.* 71a).

This law is not included in the 613 COMMANDMENTS deduced from the Pentateuch. Perhaps this is because of what is stated in the Talmud, "A stubborn and rebellious son never was and never will be. Then why was the law legislated? To receive the reward of studying it" (*Sanh.* 71a). Biblical scholars have suggested that the object of the law was to transfer authority for punishing the son from the head of the family to the discretion of the court.

RECONSTRUCTIONISM An American Jewish movement and philosophy created by Mordecai KAPLAN with the aim of reshaping and revitalizing Judaism. In view of his growing conviction that Judaism was not meeting the challenges of modernity or the needs of contemporary Jewry, and that the Reform, Conservative, and Orthodox movements were not offering viable solutions to the problems, Kaplan began to formulate a program for the reconstruction of Judaism. Since, in his opinion, modern Jews no longer believed in salvation in the afterlife, Judaism needed to offer a means of achieving salvation in this world. He rejected supernaturalism and authoritarianism in favor of democracy.

Reconstructionism is based on the concept that Judaism is an evolving religious civilization. As such, it has a unique language, history, culture, body of customs and folkways, social organization, and attachment to the Land of Israel, imbued by a religious core. As an authentic religion and culture, Judaism has always been dynamic and evolving; during each successive period of Jewish history, Judaism has developed, changed and adapted to its environment without losing its basic identity or continuity.

God, Torah, and Israel form a conceptual triangle, with each element having equal importance for Jewish existence. God is "the power that makes for salvation," the highest possible fulfillment of human beings; God is that complex of forces within the individual and in the universe that makes this "salvation" possible. Torah, which includes both the Hebrew Bible and rabbinic literature, is the creation of the Jewish people and its search for the Divine. It is the record of their experience. The commandments (*mitsvot*) preserved within the Torah are actually the customs and folkways of the Jewish people. As such, they can be changed and are subject to the insights and values of every generation.

Israel, which is both Land and People, is central to Jewish existence. For Judaism to reach its ultimate height, Israel and the Diaspora must be in constant interaction.

Reconstructionism formally became a movement with the founding of the Society for the Advancement of Judaism (SAJ) in New York in 1922. The SAJ synagogue center was the practical application of Kaplan's theoretical model. The founding principles included: working toward freedom of thought in interpreting tradition; developing the synagogue as a Jewish center; democratizing Jewish institutional life; and encouraging the rebuilding of Erets Israel. Currently, the Reconstructionist movement has its headquarters on the campus of the Reconstructionist Rabbinical College in Wyncote, Pennsylvania, USA. The College was founded in 1967. Its curriculum is constructed so as to enable the students to view Judaism as an evolving religious civilization. From its inception, it opened its doors equally to men and women. Affiliated congregations are organized in the Federation of Reconstructionist Congregations and *Ḥavurot*.

Though one of the smallest Jewish movements in America, Reconstructionism exerts an influence well beyond its size. Many of its ideas and concepts have become normative in the life of American Jews: the synagogue center, the ḤAVUROT; and the BAT MITSVAH ceremony, for example, which Kaplan developed.

REDEMPTION The Hebrew roots conveying the meaning of redemption, *padah* and *ga'al*, imply the prior existence of an obligation towards another and were originally used in the context of commercial transactions, indicating release from debt. The word *yeshu'ah*, often translated as "salvation," referred originally to deliverance from difficulties. These terms were extended to refer to triumph over all oppressive conditions and also to the deliverance of the individual from sin. The predominant use of the terms in prophetic and rabbinic literature applies to national restoration and regeneration, as well as to an ultimate ideal state of the universe.

In the Bible, *padah* and *ga'al* are applied to financial "redemption" of ancestral land from another to whom it had been sold (Lev. 25:25,26); financial "redemption" of a member of one's family from servitude to another due to debt (Lev. 25:48-49); as well as "redemption" of a home, field, ritually impure animal, or agricultural tithe which has been dedicated to the SANCTUARY (done by giving the financial value plus one-fifth, in lieu) (Lev. 27).

Ga'al is also employed in relation to a deceased relative who dies childless, whose brethren were obligated to "redeem" the name of the deceased, i.e., save it from extinction, by insuring the continuity of his seed, lands, and thus filial tribute (Ruth 4:1-10; Deut. 25:5-10).

In the case of murder, the *go'el* (redeemer) was the BLOOD AVENGER who sought to requite the wrong in kind, redeeming thereby, if not the soul of the deceased, at least the honor that had been desecrated (Num. 35:12-29).

The original meaning of the root *yasha* (similarly *yeshu'ah, teshu'ah*) is "to make wide," i.e., to deliver from distress caused by enemies. Accordingly, *yasha* and its derivatives express "victory" (as in Judg. 25:12; I Sam. 2:1, 14:54; Isa. 49:8) and the impassioned prayer *hoshi'ah-na* (i.e., "hosanna," Ps. 118:25; see HOSHANOT) should be translated "give victory."

The one who leads to victory is therefore the *moshi'a*, i.e., savior (e.g., Judg. 3:9,15; 6:36,37; I Samuel 25:4; 26; Ps. 44:4; Job 26:2). This "victory," however, is to be found, above all, in faith in God which enables man to triumph over adversity (Ps. 62:2-8; 69:30).

These terms were naturally extended to the activity of God Himself. He is seen as the Redeemer who in His special care for the orphan and widow, the poor and oppressed, liberates the vulnerable from their tribulations (II Sam. 4:9; I Kings 1:29; Job 19:25; Ps. 68:6). He also redeems from sin (Ps. 130:8) even though, as it is seen as the fruit of free will, redemption from sin is generally understood as within the power of the individual to effect through sincere contrition and self-rehabilitation — i.e., returning to God and His paths (e.g., Isa. 55:7; Jer. 4:1; see REPENTANCE). Above all, God was seen as demonstrating His redemptive character in the EXODUS from Egypt, the paradigm of Redemption.

National redemption became the primary focus of the concept in the wake of military defeats, foreign rule and ultimately, the destruction of the Temple and subsequent exile. Inasmuch as the latter events were understood to be a consequence of infidelity to the Divine Covenant, the people's repentance and regeneration are crucial to the redemptive process. Perceptions differ, however, as to whether this activity is itself the initiative for, or the product of, redemption. For example, Amos and Hosea (in keeping with Deut. 30) see the people's repentance as the *a priori* requirement initiating their redemption, whereas in the latter part of the Book of Isaiah and in Micah, only a Divine initiative is viewed as capable of effecting redemption. Even more explicit is the predominant perception in Ezekiel of a national spiritual rehabilitation taking place only after redemption, which is portrayed as emanating not only from Divine initiative, but from the Divine need that God's name be sanctified among the nations (36:22-23).

Jeremiah resolves the tension by portraying a two-way process. While the initiative must come through the people's repentance, redemption can only be brought about fully by God Himself. However, throughout prophetical literature God is seen as the Redeemer who preserves the remnant, ingathers the exiles and restores the people to its inheritance and glory, ultimately ushering in an era of human perfection and universal harmony in a world imbued with His spirit (e.g., Isa. 11:10; 52:10; Zech. 14:9, 16).

The role of the MESSIAH therefore is not that of the Redeemer, for God alone is the Savior. While the messiah was established as shepherd of God's flock (Ezek. 34:23), the national hope for Redemption was centered on God Himself. Notable in this regard is the frequent absence of a messianic personality in prophetic visions of redemption. This is also the case in Apocryphal works such as Tobit and Ecclesiaticus.

The social and political upheavals of the last centuries BCE culminating in the destruction of the Temple in 70 CE stimulated the development of apocalyptic and utopian trends regarding the hope for national redemption which would precede universal salvation. The Dead Sea sect, however, saw itself as the subject of ultimate cosmic redemption through which God brings purification for all.

The rabbis of the Mishnah and Talmud were themselves influenced by these apocalyptic and utopian trends, but generally, they retained a realistic orientation towards a religious-national-political restoration that takes place within history itself. The term *ge'ulah* is used almost exclusively in rabbinic literature in this context. In accordance with biblical prophecy, the rabbis looked forward to a regenerative messianism in which the Israelite monarchy is reestablished, the nation is delivered from foreign servitude, the exiles are ingathered and finally, the Temple is rebuilt. This would then herald a spiritual redemption of mankind as a whole. Perhaps the most notable mystical element that they introduced into the concept of Redemption was the suggestion that the Divine Presence itself is in exile with the people of Israel. Thus in redeeming His people, God, so to speak, redeems Himself (*Mekh. Bo*, 14; *Sif.* Numbers, 161).

The difference of perception regarding the redemptive initiative continues in rabbinic literature (cf. *Sanh.* 97-98). In consonance with the views of Jeremiah is the effort to resolve the tension by portraying redemption as a joint endeavor. Notable in this regard is the passage from *Song of Songs Rabbah* 5.2 in the name of R. Yessa: "The Holy One, Blessed be He, said to Israel: 'My children, open for me an aperture of repentance as small as a needle's eye and I will open for you an opening through which wagons and carriages can enter."

The differing perspectives on the initiative in redemption that ultimately lead to a naturalist or supernaturalist view of the process are also to be found both within Jewish medieval philosophy as well as within Jewish mysticism.

Among the philosophers, SAADIAH GAON, JUDAH HALEVI, NAH̲MANIDES, H̲asdai CRESCAS and Joseph ALBO portray national redemption in supernatural terms. In contradistinction, MAIMONIDES, IBN GABIROL, Abraham IBN EZRA and LEVI BEN GERSHON, strongly influenced by Neo-Platonic and Aristotelian concepts, see personal redemption as a transcendence of the material dimensions of existence through the Higher Intellect, thus developing the spiritual soul and ultimate immortality. In the same way redemption is wrought not only for Israel but for the world through a commensurate corporate raising of the intellect and spirit (cf. Maimonides, *Guide*, 3,11).

The difference in emphasis regarding the initiative in national redemption is also found within Kabbalah. For the kabbalists, exile reflected the impaired condition of CREATION. The redemption of the Jewish people and the universal recognition of God's Presence and Name, would mean full reparation. However, while the Spanish kabbalists saw the redemption as essentially a miraculous event unrelated to human endeavor, the alternative view, identified particularly with the followers of Isaac LURIA, was that redemption is no more than an external manifestation of internal *tikkun* (restitution or reconstitution) which depends upon the deeds of Israel and its way of life. Redemption was thus seen as dependent upon human action which initiates the advent of the Messiah. As it was this outlook that had nurtured the Shabbatean debacle (see SHABBETAI TSEVI), the ensuing Hasidic movement (see HASIDIM), that also embraced Lurianic Kabbalah, sought to mute the inherent dangers of utopianism. This was accomplished by reverting to the traditional teaching of distinguishing between personal and national redemption. The former is seen as concerning solely the mystical redemption of the soul and is divested of any messianic connotations. Accordingly, it is to this realm that human initiative is limited, while the Divine is seen as bringing ultimate national and cosmic redemption.

On the other hand, modern Jewish philosophy (including Herman COHEN, Martin BUBER, Franz ROSENZWEIG) overwhelmingly understood the initiative of personal redemption to be the means by which national and universal redemption are achieved. The latter is thus generally identified with the ultimate triumph of good over evil.

It was also such perception which led Classical REFORM JUDAISM to see redemption primarily in terms of social reform and advancement in modern society. Accordingly, it sought to divest the idea of any particular Jewish national political character. Thus, during the late 19th and early 20th centuries, it opposed the most dramatic modern movement of human activism in the cause of Jewish national redemption, namely, ZIONISM. The latter was also bitterly opposed on the other extreme of the Jewish religious spectrum by ultra-Orthodoxy, which perceived it as an act of rebellion against the Divine Will that alone could initiate redemption.

Religious Zionism, as conceived both by the precursors of the Zionist movement and especially by those who led the various ideological movements, saw Zionism as the expression and initial fulfillment of the Divine calling for human initiative in national redemption, facilitating the ultimate redemption of mankind as a whole.

REDEMPTION OF THE FIRST-BORN See FIRST-BORN, REDEMPTION OF THE

RED HEIFER (*parah adummah*). A cow with a distinctive reddish coat whose ashes, mixed with spring water, were used for the ritual cleansing of persons or objects that had been defiled by contact with a CORPSE (Num. 19:1-22). The animal had to be without physical blemish and must never have been placed under the yoke. Whereas normal SACRIFICES took place at the entrance to the Tent of Meeting (Lev. 17:8-9), and later in the Temple, the Red Heifer had to be slaughtered "outside the camp." According to tractate PARAH of the Mishnah, only the High Priest was entitled to slaughter the animal and then sprinkle part of its blood seven times in the direction of the Holy of Holies. It was burned whole, together with cedar wood, crimson stuff, and hyssop, until all had been reduced to ashes. These were placed in a container, mixed with fresh spring water, and set aside for use as the "water of separation" from impurity (*mé niddah*). Although the "water of separation" purified those who had been defiled (upon whom it was sprinkled on the third and seventh day of their week-long period of contamination), it also had the effect of defiling anyone who prepared or touched it. Priests, slaughterers, and those who burned the Red Heifer were obliged to wash their clothes and bathe, remaining unclean until nightfall. Similar rituals had to be performed by those who collected the ashes or sprinkled the water.

Various theories have been propounded as to the Red Heifer ceremony's background and rationale. All tend to find a symbolic importance in the color red: it is capable of warding off evil spirits, and it is proverbially linked with sin. Many of the sages, however, considered the law of the Red Heifer to be one of the biblical statutes for which there is no rationale: "A corpse does not really defile nor does water really purify; but the Holy One issued a decree and no one has the right to transgress it" (Num. R. 19.4). Others suggested that this law provided a symbolic atonement for the ancient sin of the GOLDEN CALF.

The Pentateuch (Num. 19:9) calls the Red Heifer a "sin-offering," i.e., a cleansing from sin, hence the laws applied to it by the rabbis. Chapter three of tractate *Parah* contains a detailed description of all the minutiae involved in preparing the "water of separation." Clearly, a perfect Red Heifer must have been extremely rare and costly to obtain. The Mishnaic source indicates that only seven (or perhaps nine) Red Heifers were in fact slaughtered from the time of Moses to the destruction of the Second Temple. Thereafter, a dwin-

The Red Heifer from the portion Parah *read on one of the four special Sabbaths. From an Italian Mahzor, 1441.*

dling supply of ritual water may have enabled the purification ceremony to continue until the third century CE. Among the SAMARITANS, this practice actually survived down to the 15th century (see also PURITY AND IMPURITY).

On *Shabbat Parah*, the Sabbath which occurs about a week after the Purim festival, Num. 19:1-22 is the prescribed additional (*maftir*) reading in synagogue (see SABBATHS, SPECIAL). This custom dates from Second Temple times, when it was intended as a reminder to those who had been defiled by a corpse that they should be sprinkled with the "water of separation." Otherwise, they could not enter the Temple for the purpose of sacrificing (and later eating) the paschal lamb.

REFORM JUDAISM Trend in Judaism which rejects the view of the immutability of the WRITTEN LAW and has consequently adapted Jewish thought and practice to accord with contemporary outlooks and requirements. It is also known as Liberal and Progressive Judaism. Moses MENDELSSOHN, although he always remained an Orthodox Jew, helped to create the climate in which Reform emerged. The idea that Jews might live as free and equal citizens spoke with added force because of his advocacy; his teaching that the doctrines of Judaism were derived from reason and were therefore universalist in character made Judaism compatible with ENLIGHTENMENT ideas and encouraged Jews to look beyond the traditional rabbinic outlook and value education outside the narrow rabbinical system.

Except where decreed otherwise by the secular power, the Jewish religious polity is based on the autonomous local congregation, not on any national or transnational hierarchy. Hence the parameters of Reform were not always established definitively, especially as they were often laid down in polemical statements. Some deviation — minor or major — from pre-existing practice was always involved, whether the text of the liturgy, the playing of the ORGAN, the replacement of ancient chants by European style music, the rights of women, or the location of the BIMAH in respect to the ark. The origin of the movement lay in Germany. This was due partly to the pre-eminence of Germany in the spheres of theology and philosophy and the existence of a measure of religious pluralism, along with close government supervision. In the Latin world, both the Catholic and atheist attitude disinclined people to experiment with new forms of religion.

Within a few years of Mendelssohn's death, the French Revolution made EMANCIPATION a practical possibility. Emerging from the ghettos and acquiring secular education, the Jews of Germany were now confronted with comparisons between the condition of Judaism and that of the surrounding churches and their dissatisfaction focused on the style of public worship. In 1810, Israel JACOBSON built a new-style temple at Seesen in Westphalia; when it was closed, at the end of the French occupation there, he transferred his activity to Berlin (1815). As a result of representations made by the ORTHODOX, the services in Berlin were prohibited by the Prussian government (1817); a decree in 1823 forbade the slightest innovation in the language, ceremonies, prayers, or songs in Jewish worship.

In the meantime, a Reform temple was established in Hamburg (1818), with its own revised prayer book. This was a direct challenge to the authority of the Hamburg rabbinate. Due to the curtailment of the autonomous corporate structure of Jewish life, the rabbinate could no longer resort to punitive measures. To bolster their position, the Hamburg rabbis secured opinions from colleagues throughout Europe who were firmly against both changes in the prayer service and the use of the vernacular.

SERMONS in the vernacular, introduced by the Reformers, had been denounced as a violation of Jewish tradition; however, in his *Gottesdienstlichen Vorträge der Juden* (1832), the scholar, Leopold ZUNZ, demonstrated that such sermons were a venerable Jewish institution which had fallen into disuse during the ghetto period. In later works, Zunz showed how the liturgical poetry and ritual customs of the Jews had developed through the ages.

Coincident with the new development of the scientific study of Judaism (WISSENSCHAFT DES JUDENTUMS) came a new approach to the training of rabbis which deemed that their education should no longer be confined to the Talmud and its derivative codes of law. In 1838, the Breslau Jewish community decided that they needed a rabbi of the new school and their choice fell on Abraham GEIGER.

Geiger, who had already achieved a reputation as a scholar, had expressed himself as a decided advocate of Reform. His nomination brought on a long and bitter controversy which not only divided the Breslau community but involved the Prussian government and rabbis throughout Europe. Geiger was not content with the external embellishment of the worship service, but formulated the principles on which the Judaism of the new age must be based. There was no eternal validity to the mass of doctrines and observances which had come down from the past; all were part of a process of evolution, discernible in the Bible as well as in the Talmud, by which the Jewish people gave expression to its belief in ethical monotheism. The Jewish people had gone through a transformation. Now that they were no longer a closed and segregated community, observances of a nationalistic or particularistic character were at variance with real life. Therefore, prayers for a return to Zion or the restoration of sacrifices had no place in the liturgy and furthermore, it was inappropriate that Hebrew should be the language of prayer when German had become the mother tongue of German Jews.

Geiger's practices were far more conventional than his principles. At Breslau, Frankfurt-on-Main and Berlin he ministered to congregations which included a considerable traditionalist element and he recognized that as rabbi, he could not enact reforms which did not enjoy general support.

In this he may be contrasted with Samuel HOLDHEIM, who after becoming the first rabbi of the Berlin Reform Congregation in 1846, eliminated Hebrew and transferred the Sabbath to Sunday. At three rabbinical conferences — Brunswick (12-19 June 1844), Frankfurt-on-Main (15-26 July 1845) and Breslau (13-24 July 1846) — the general attitude and the atmosphere were permissive. The Brunswick conference declared that mixed marriages were not forbidden, provided the State permitted the children to be brought up as Jews. It also declared that the Jew is bound to consider the land to which he belongs by birth and civic conditions as his fatherland and that he must protect it and obey all its laws.

Several resolutions dealt with the Sabbath, reflecting the assumption that the traditional corpus of observance would remain intact. At the same time, they laid the groundwork for future innovation and more radical positions. Emphasis was placed upon "reconsecrating" the spirit of the Sabbath day (primarily in the synagogue but also in the home) and upon the "edifying" celebration of the divine service. In keeping with the patriotic sentiments (and reflecting German veneration of the State), it was specifically noted that "a Jewish official may perform the duties of his office in so far as he is obliged to do so on the Sabbath." At Frankfurt, a majority agreed that the use of Hebrew in prayer was not "objectively" necessary, though its use in certain small quantities was advisable for the time being. This was strongly contested by Zacharias FRANKEL, and he withdrew from the conference. In Frankel's view, changes were not prohibited, but the 'needs of the day' were not a sufficient reason for change; change must proceed from the demands of the people as a whole, acting under the guidance of scholars. This viewpoint, which he called Positive Historical Judaism, was to form the basis for American CONSERVATIVE JUDAISM.

In 1854, a theological seminary was opened in Breslau, with Frankel as director. The Berlin *Hochschule* — a seminary under Geiger's direction — was opened in 1872. That group within German Jewry, which diverted from Orthodoxy and took its inspiration from Geiger and Frankel, adopted the name 'Liberal.' The term 'Reform' connoted for them the radicalism of Holdheim and his Berlin followers which was not well received by a very conservative society. The Union of the Liberal Rabbis of Germany was formed in 1899, followed nine years later by the Union for Liberal Judaism. At its conference in 1912, the Union for Liberal Judaism endorsed a set of "Guide Lines" that had been prepared by the rabbinic group. The document drew strong protest from the Orthodox; at the same time it was unacceptable to the Liberal laity, who considered it too demanding. In popular usage 'Liberal' also came to signify anti-Zionist.

Echoes of German Reform were heard throughout Europe. The program adopted in Vienna — traditional practices, purged of their excrescences and embellished with the eloquence of a Mannheimer and the music of a Sulzer — was the goal. By an odd quirk, it was on the tolerant soil of England that the ecclesiastical authorities excommunicated the earnest founders of a very moderate reformed synagogue (1842). However, by 1856, the independent new community was fully recognized by an Act of Parliament granting it the right to register weddings. For the most part, the Jews of England continued to be satisfied with the moderate Orthodoxy guided by the Chief Rabbinate. However, protest against continuing religious stagnation was voiced from time to time. Among the recurring suggested reforms were Sabbath afternoon services, emphasis on the vernacular and elimination of the MI SHE-BERAKH prayer of the service; musical accompaniment and decorum were also important issues. In 1902, a small but distinguished group founded the more outrightly liberal Jewish Religious Union. In each case, the adoption of a new prayer book was an important step in the public formulation of the religious position.

In Hungary, the 1867 decision of a congress of all Jewish communities to establish a modern rabbinical seminary drove the more rigid Orthodox elements to secede, leaving the majority to adopt a mildly reform position, known as NEOLOGY, which has been maintained to the present time.

Reform in the United States. In the meantime Reform Judaism had become the accepted mode in the United States. The climate was favorable. Separation of church and state and non-discrimination on grounds of religion were decreed by the constitution and there were no long-standing traditions to give prestige to existing churches; religion was an entirely voluntary affair. However, freedom also brought its problems. When the United States came into being, the few existing Jewish congregations practised a watered-down Orthodoxy, following the Sephardi ritual. This could not suffice for the large group of immigrants from central Europe who settled in the country after 1815. Some change was necessary, but there were no trained leaders. The first breath of Reform touched the acculturated Jewish community of Charleston, South Carolina, where a short-lived Reform congregation came into being in 1824. Reforms were later introduced in the Sephardi congregation (1841). It was among the German-Jewish immigrants in the north that the movement spread. In Baltimore, Har Sinai (1842) and in New York, Emanuel (1845) were established as Reform congregations. In 1846 Isaac Mayer WISE arrived from Bohemia; in Albany and later in Cincinnati (from 1854) he was identified with the Reform viewpoint. More than once, however, he showed himself to be ambivalent on the question of Reform. His priority was a "union of American Israel" in which a representative synod would establish a rabbinical seminary, authorize a single prayer book (*Minhag America*) to replace the divergent rituals brought from Europe and sanction changes in practice. Out of the experience of joint action he foresaw the emergence of a form of Judaism particularly suited to the American environment. For this program

Wise secured the support of a conference of rabbis which met in Cleveland in 1855. However, it incurred the bitter antagonism of David EINHORN (1809-1879) and other German-trained rabbis whose commitment to Reform came first. In this controversy, the PRAYER BOOK, which should have been a unifying element within the Reform community, became instead an expression of diversity.

Wise produced his *Minhag America*, a modified version of the Orthodox ritual; Einhorn produced *Olat Tamid*, in effect a new work, in German with a few Hebrew paragraphs, reflecting the position adopted at the Frankfurt rabbinical conference.

Fresh waves of controversy followed in the wake of a conference of Reform rabbis which met in Philadelphia in 1869. Eventually, the Cincinnati laity summoned a conference of congregational delegates which resolved to establish the Union of American Hebrew Congregations (1873). The Union's constitution made no mention of an ideological standpoint and expressly disavowed the right to interfere with the affairs of any congregation. The primary object of the Union was "to establish a Hebrew Theological Institute." Hebrew Union College was inaugurated in 1875, with Wise as president. Like the Union, the college refrained from adopting a particular theological stand, and Wise expressed the hope that it would train rabbis for all sectors of the American Jewish community. The serving of non-kasher food at the banquet celebrating the first ordination (1883) irritated the traditionalists and they withdrew their support. The breaking point came two years later when Wise presided over a rabbinical conference at Pittsburgh which adopted a radical position enunciated by Kaufman KOHLER (Einhorn's son-in-law and spiritual heir), whereby the binding character of "the Mosaic legislation" was denied and the views and habits of modern civilization became the criterion of spirituality.

Nominally, the Pittsburgh Platform was not an official statement, but it gained acceptance as the acknowledged position of American Reform Judaism. "We recognize in the modern era of universal culture of heart and intellect the approach of the realization of Israel's great Messianic hope for the establishment of the kingdom of truth, justice and peace among all men...We recognize in Judaism a progressive religion, ever striving to be in accord with the postulates of reason..." The liberal optimism of the late 19th century spoke through the rabbis at Pittsburgh and it conformed to the feelings of their constituents.

The Pittsburgh Platform formalized the 'Protestantization' of the American synagogue. The year 1889 saw the formation of the Central Conference of American Rabbis, with Wise as president: one of its first tasks was to compile a uniform liturgy. The resultant Union Prayer Book (1895) leaned heavily on Einhorn's *Olat Tamid*; thus, the objectives of Geiger and his colleagues, expressed at the Frankfurt conference, were realized in America. The Pittsburgh Platform served as a license to discard the whole corpus of personal observance and the manifestation of religion was concentrated in the weekly public service in which the rabbi's sermon was an essential element. Synagogues were designed to make the pulpit the central feature of the building. A Sunday school sufficed for religious education.

This pattern, sometimes called "American Judaism" and later "Classical Reform," became the dominant mode among the established German Jews in America. Its eventual influence on the wider community was considerably mitigated with the overwhelming flood of Eastern European Jewish immigration in the latter part of the 19th century (see ORTHODOXY). The newcomers had no affinity for "Classical Reform" and found their religious outlet through their own institutions. In 1903, Kaufman Kohler became president of the Hebrew Union College and his direction strengthened the impress of the "Classical" pattern on the training of Reform rabbis.

A considerable proportion of the student body in the College came from the Eastern European segment of American Jewry and had inherited none of the ideological rejection of traditional Jewish practice characteristic of the German reformers. Moreover, the atmosphere of the Reform temples changed as more and more Eastern Europeans joined them. World War I, the emphasis on Americanization, the economic crisis of the 1930s, rising anti-Semitism and controversies over Zionism blunted the optimism that envisioned in a haze of universalism a world inevitably getting better.

Dissatisfaction with the Pittsburgh Platform eventually led to the adoption by the Central Conference of American Rabbis of the Columbus Platform (1937). Between the new statement and the old there was a marked difference in tone. Now "Judaism is the historical religious experience of the Jewish people...Judaism is the soul of which Israel is the body...." The former rejection of the idea of a messianic restoration to Zion is replaced by an affirmation of the obligation of all Jewry to aid in the upbuilding of Palestine as a Jewish homeland and there was a call for "moral discipline and religious observance and worship in the Jewish home." The Columbus Platform was of assistance to the rabbi who wished to direct the program of his temple along a more traditionalist path; it had less effect on the laity.

Reform continued to develop in other parts of the world, albeit on a smaller scale. In England, the Liberal Jewish Synagogue was founded in 1912. Its spiritual leader was Israel I. Mattuck, who had graduated from Hebrew Union College not long before. He had considerable ability but his adherence to the "Classical Reform" pattern retarded development. As for liturgical modernization, in a society in which the 1662 Book of Common Prayer held sway, there was no keen appetite for such change. The movement became identified with anti-Zionism and this helped to isolate it further. In 1926, the English group, led by Lily Montagu, established the World Union for Progressive Judaism.

World War II brought about the end of an era in Jewish history, crystallizing the growing awareness among the leaders of American Reform that the movement had not responded to the challenges facing it. Dissatisfaction focused on the narrow program of the Union of American Hebrew Congregations. After 1943, when Rabbi Maurice Eisendrath became its Director (he received the title "President" in 1946), the Union exhibited a new dynamism, building up its organization and thrusting into areas from which it had previously held aloof. It developed a strong concern in matters of social action, sometimes to the dismay of its more conservative adherents. The Union had lost influence through being situated in the isolationist Middle West: Eisendrath moved its headquarters from Cincinnati to New York.

Reform Judaism benefited from the "return to synagogue" which characterized the post-war years. Between 1940 and 1980 the number of congregations affiliated with the Union increased from 400 to 730. This expansion was matched by an increase in the number of rabbis ordained by Hebrew Union College. During the period 1940-1981, membership of the Central Conference of American Rabbis increased from 400 to 1,286. Dependence upon teachers from the European seminaries now being out of the question, the College established facilities for post-graduate training. It took over the Jewish Institute for Religion and thus acquired a presence in New York; more recently, it opened a school in Los Angeles to serve the growing Jewish community of the western United States. It has invested heavily in a Jerusalem branch in which American rabbinic students do the first part of their training, and which also has an ordination program for men and women preparing for the Israeli rabbinate. The first Israeli student was ordained in 1980.

Another relatively new direction which has been encouraged by the Central Conference since World War II is the area of personal observance outside the synagogue. Expressions of this direction are the *Gates of the House* (1977) and its companion, *Tadrich LeShabbat* (1972) and the *Gates of Mitsvah, A Guide to the Jewish Life Cycle* (1979).

The Reform Central Synagogue in New York.

The European center of Jewish life had all but disappeared as a result of World War II and the mood among the remnant was not overly receptive to the old program of Reform Judaism. Nonetheless, small but deeply-rooted Reform communities in France, Germany, the Netherlands, Belgium, Sweden and Switzerland continued to develop, each according to its own patterns. For example, the French Reform community dates back to 1903, when the *Union Israélite Liberale* first established the guidelines for the Liberal Temple. The Temple in Rue Copernic, Paris, was dedicated in 1907 and continues to be the central pivot of the French Reform Movement.

The English Liberal community, while divided between the Reform faction, under the leadership of the West London Synagogue, and the Liberals, spearheaded by the St. John's Wood Liberal Jewish Synagogue, did band together to establish the Leo Baeck (Rabbinical) College in 1958. Both English movements have produced numerous innovative prayer books (from 1856); liturgically, the Liberal wing broke new ground with the publishing of *Service of the Heart* (1967) and the companion MAḤZOR, *Gate of Repentance* (1973). The former served as a model for the *Gates of Prayer*, the new version of the *Union Prayerbook* which the Central Conference of American Rabbis issued eight years later.

Reform communities are also found in South Africa, Zimbabwe, Australia, New Zealand, India, South America, Canada and Israel. In 1970, the World Union moved its headquarters to Jerusalem, where the Israel Movement for Progressive Judaism had been founded two decades previously. Reform Judaism has had to wage a constant struggle to gain a foothold in Israel, where its institutions include 15 congregations and two kibbutzim in the Aravah, representing a joint effort of native-born Israelis and recent and veteran immigrants. The educational groundwork previously provided by the Leo Baeck School in Haifa (1939) has been augmented by three kindergartens throughout the country and the early grades of elementary school in Jerusalem.

REJOICING OF THE LAW See SIMḤAT TORAH

REMNANT OF ISRAEL (*she'erit yisrael*). Teaching that after the mass punishment and destruction of the Jewish people for their sins, a faithful few, dedicated to God and His teachings, will survive to maintain and benefit from God's covenant with His people. This remnant would return from exile to its own land and would thereafter live in security and peace. The doctrine is first indicated in Leviticus 26:36-45, but was especially characteristic of the literary prophets. Isaiah addressed the "remnant of the House of Israel" (46:3) and even symbolically named his son "Shear Jashub," i.e., a remnant shall return (7:3). Among the other prophets who expounded the idea were Jeremiah (31:6-7), Ezekiel (11:13), and Micah (5:5-7). The Jews returning from Babylonian Exile considered themselves as constituting the prophesied remnant (Haggai 1:12-14; Ezra 9:8, 14-15; Neh. 1:2-3). The concept also entered the liturgy, while in modern times the phrase "the surviving remnant" was applied to survivors of the Holocaust.

RENDING OF GARMENTS (*keri'ah*) A MOURNING ritual. This halakhic obligation is derived indirectly from a prohibition to AARON and his surviving sons, after the death of his sons Nadab and Abihu, "uncover not your heads, neither rend your clothes..." (*Yad, Hilkhot Evel* 8:1; Lev. 10:6). If the High Priest had to be explicitly forbidden to rend his garments, this implied that other Jews (male and female) were obligated to do so. The sages ruled, based on Leviticus 21:2-3, that one should rend his garments at the death of seven kindred: father, mother, brother, sister, son, daughter, and spouse (*Shab.* 105b). In the Bible, many figures are described as tearing their garments in mourning, reflecting a sense of separation or a feeling of guilt and loss and self-inflicted punishment: for example, Elisha for Elijah and Jacob for his son Joseph thought to have been killed by a wild animal. The *keri'ah* has to be performed at the moment the soul has "gone," or within the 30 days of mourning (SHELOSHIM). For parents there is no time limit, but it should be done as soon as possible. Rending not carried out in the heat of grief and with full emotional involvement, is not considered appropriate (*MK* 24a). The rending, which is performed standing (*MK* 22b), has to be done on the outer garment only, on the right-hand side, and should be at least a handbreadth long. For parents the rent was traditionally made in all the clothes, until the heart was exposed (and therefore it was made on the left-hand side) (Joel 2:12). While for parents the garment is rent by hand, a knife or other instrument may be used for other kindred. The garments may be repaired seven days later except in mourning for parents where it is never repaired. According to several places in both Talmuds, when a sage dies, the whole community rends its garments, because it is "like his family" (JT, *MK* 3:7). In a later development, the Talmud teaches that if one is present at a DEATH, rending is mandatory, even for a person not distinguished by learning or piety. Maimonides (*Yad, Hilkhot Evel* 9.2) mentions other occasions when garments are rent, including over the death of one's Torah teacher or the NASI (patriarch) or the head of the law court, over a burnt Scroll of the Law, on seeing Jerusalem and the cities of Judah in their destruction, and on seeing the site of the Temple. The person who rends recites the blessing "Blessed is the judge of truth".

REPENTANCE (*teshuvah*). Repentance is an integral element of Judaism and the fact that God accepts repentance is considered to be one of His greatest gifts to man.

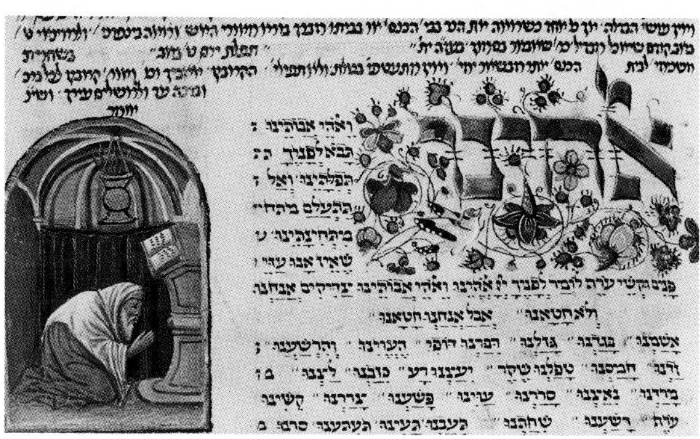

Illustration of Ashamnu *("We have trespassed") recited on the Day of Atonement. Italy, 15th century.*

The sages distinguish two types of repentance: repentance out of fear of the punishment for one's sins and repentance brought about by a deep love of God. Repentance of the first kind transforms all sins committed intentionally into sins committed through oversight or ignorance; this decreases the severity of the offense. Repentance out of love for God goes further; it changes all sins committed intentionally into merits. It is thus not surprising that the Talmud states, "The place occupied by those who have repented cannot be attained by even the most righteous person" (*Ber.* 34b).

The word *teshuvah*, repentance, is derived from the Hebrew root *ShUV*, which means to return — the implication being to return to God. Thus, when the Bible states (Deut. 4:30), "when you return to the Lord your God," the sages understand this to refer to repentance. The concept of "return" also implies that the way of God is the norm and wrongdoing, a deviation.

The Latter Prophets preach constantly about the need to return to God, to turn away from evil and act righteously, as in Isaiah (44:22): "Return unto Me; for I have redeemed you," while 14:2: "Take with you words, and return to the Lord: say unto him, 'Take away all iniquity, and receive us graciously'" and Malachi 3:7: "'Return unto me, and I will return unto you,' says the Lord of hosts." Even stronger is the statement by Ezekiel (33:11), "Say unto them, 'As I live,' says the Lord God, 'I have no pleasure in the death of the wicked; but that the wicked turn from his way and live.'"

Traditionally, whenever a calamity befalls the Jewish community, it is a cause for soul-searching, repentance and, often, fasting. Thus, if there is a drought, a fast day may be declared, with the object of moving the people to repent. By the same token, all the official fast days of the Hebrew calendar are meant to arouse people to consider their actions and repent and not merely to refrain from eating and drinking during the required time.

In order to allow for people to repent properly, ten days are set aside each year — the TEN DAYS OF PENITENCE beginning with ROSH HA-SHANAH and culminating in the DAY OF ATONEMENT, with the climax at the closing *Ne'ilah* Service of the Day of Atonement. According to tradition, during these ten days God makes it especially easy for people to repent.

Penitence is also the theme of the fifth blessing of the daily AMIDAH ("forgive us our Father, for we have sinned ...) and the TAHANUN prayers and especially of the SELIHOT (penitential prayers) said in the morning service of each fast day and before and during the Ten Days of Penitence. The prayers on the High Holidays state unequivocally that "Repentance, prayer and charity avert the severity of the decree [issued by God concerning each man's fate for the coming year]." The Sabbath occurring during the Ten Days of Repentance is referred to as *Shabbat Shuvah* or *Shabbat Teshuvah* (Sabbath of Repentance) and it is traditional for the rabbi to expound on that day on the need to repent.

Pious Jews also set aside the day before each New Moon for what is known as *Yom Kippur katan* — a "minor Day of Atonement," which is devoted to repentance. The sages state that if one sees a sage sinning, he can be sure that the sage has repented by the next day. Some pious Jews examine their deeds at the end of each day and repent immediately for untoward actions that occurred during that day. Indeed, when the sages called to "repent one day before you die," the implication is that since a man may die on any day, he should repent each day.

As defined by the rabbis, there are stages in repentance: first, in any SIN between man and his fellow man, the person must regret his sinfulness and rectify as far as possible the damage he has caused. Thus, if a person stole something, he must return the theft. If the offense was not a monetary one, the offender must do everything possible to appease and reconcile the one offended. In every crime, whether between man and his fellow man or between man and God, the person must acknowledge and confess his sin before God (not before any human being) and must express contrition over his act. Finally, he must resolve never to repeat that sin again. Sins against God may only be forgiven by God.

The concept of repentance has played a prominent role in Jewish religious literature, both theological (see THEOLOGY) and ethical (see ETHICS). MAIMONIDES devoted a whole section of his code to the subject and for the medieval moralists, such as BAHYA IBN PAKUDA, the theme was central. For the kabbalists, repentance assisted God to perfect the divine work of Creation. Religious movements, notably HASIDISM and the MUSAR movement have focused on the concept of repentance as has the contemporary phenomenon of the BA'AL TESHUVAH (literally, the repentant). An important modern treatment of the subject is Rabbi A.I. Kook's *Orot ha-Teshuvah* ("Lights of Repentance") which maintains that the individual is often too weak for the struggle against sin and for the reunion with God implied in *teshuvah* and this struggle requires the collective strength of the entire people of Israel. See also ATONEMENT; CONFESSION.

SAYINGS ABOUT REPENTANCE

It is forbidden to remind the penitent of his former sins, even in jest.

The gates of prayer may be shut but the gates of repentance are always open.

Even if a man has been wicked all his life but repents at the end of his days — he is forgiven.

If a man says "I will sin and repent but then sin again and repent," he will not be given the opportunity to repent.

Each penitent thought is the voice of God.

A Litvak (Jew from Lithuania) is so clever that he repents even before he sins.

They asked of Wisdom : What is the punishment of the sinner? Wisdom replied: evil pursues sinners. They asked Prophecy: What is the punishment of the sinner? Prophecy replied: The Soul that sins shall die. Then they asked God : What is the punishment of the sinner? He replied: Let him repent and he will find atonement.

RESH LAKISH See SIMEON BEN LAKISH

RESPECT FOR PARENTS AND TEACHERS The fifth of the TEN COMMANDMENTS states, "Honor your father and your mother in order that your days may be long upon the land which the Lord your God gives to you" (Ex. 20:12). The Mishnah says that the reward for the fulfillment of this commandment is both in this world and in the world to come (*Pe'ah* 1.1). The Talmud relates that there are three partners in the creation of a child: the father, the mother and God (who gives the soul). When a child honors his parents, it is as if he honors God (*Kid.* 30b).

The ways in which a son must honor his parents include supporting them physically with food and drink, clothing and shelter if they are in need, not insulting them in public and not displaying anger towards them. A son must not occupy his father's seat, contradict him, oppose him publicly in a debate, or call him by his name. A married daughter should also respect her parents and do as much as she can for them, as long as it does not conflict with the requirements of her husband. Even after their death, a child is obligated to honor his parents by reciting KADDISH for eleven months. Once this period has passed, a son must say when speaking of his father, "May his memory be for a blessing, for the life of the world to come" (*Kid.* 31b).

There is one case where respect for parents does not apply and that is when one is commanded by one's father or mother to transgress Jewish law. Then one is obligated not to obey them, and need not fear any reprisals.

A Jew is obligated to honor and fear his teacher even more

than his father. Even though his father has given him life in this world, his teacher prepares him for life in the world to come. Therefore, he must stand up when his teacher (or any wise man) enters the room. If a scholar is also a merchant, his business is given preference by the community and a sage whose main occupation is learning Torah is exempt from taxation and other assessments, even if he is rich. Disrespect or hatred towards those learned in the law is considered a grave sin and the Talmud states that whoever despises the sages has no share in the world to come. See also CHILDREN; FATHER; FAMILY; MOTHER.

RESPONSA (Heb. *she'elot u-teshuvot*, "questions and answers"). Written answers on issues of Jewish law and learning from talmudic scholars to queries from colleagues and lay people or communities. The practice of this form of rabbinical communication began in the talmudic period and became formally instituted in the geonic era.

When the Jewish people became dispersed, the problem arose of maintaining religious unity among the scattered Jewish communities. The practice therefore developed of referring halakhic queries to central authorities whose responses would determine local legal decisions and Jewish practice. Touching on all aspects of Jewish life, the Responsa insured a standardization of Judaism in all Jewish communities and constituted an authoritative body of precedents and decisions consulted to this day by rabbinical scholars when deciding on contemporary issues of religious observance. In addition, the sense of national unity was maintained by the constant flow of communications between the various communities. Not limited to practical matters alone, the Responsa enabled scholars in remote areas to question colleagues in the centers of Jewish learning. Spiritual leadership could be maintained in remote communities and the sense of community among rabbinical scholars was reinforced, despite the vast distances separating them.

The Responsa can be divided into three main periods:

a) Geonic (see GA'ON) (from the mid-seventh to mid-11th centuries). The first major responsa began to appear in the middle of this period. While some of the communications were brief answers expressed in one or two words, others were more substantial, at times reaching the proportions of a monograph. The subject-matter was variegated, ranging from requests for assistance on issues of Jewish religious practice to queries on points rooted in Jewish as well as secular learning. These queries were directed to the Babylonian *ge'onim*, whose replies have become authoritative Jewish religious classics. Unfortunately, the *ge'onim* did not make copies of their replies and many have been lost.

b) RISHONIM (from the 12th to 15th centuries): the subject-matter focuses increasingly on issues of religious practice and the format becomes longer. These became regarded as authoritative sources.

c) AḪARONIM (from the 16th century to the present): In the wake of various expulsions, Jewish communities became more scattered and less homogenous. Problems arose concerning different customs and with regard to communal structures. The emphasis in terms of subject-matter was now on practical, rather than philosophical, matters.

As in earlier periods, the responsa of the 20th century, which are consulted by Orthodox, Conservative, and Reform scholars, rely on previous authorities — the Talmud and the Responsa of previous centuries — in order to grapple with the problems faced by the modern Jew, such as organ transplants and euthanasia. Even during the Holocaust, Jews consulted rabbis to legislate on matters arising from forced existence in the ghettos and concentration camps. With the establishment of the State of Israel in 1948, Jews are now involved — after a gap of 20 centuries — in all aspects of statehood management and a new category of Responsa is required in order to deal with halakhic issues within the context of a sovereign Jewish statehood. The Responsa are also studied today as a major source of Jewish social history, throwing light on the inner workings of the community and on everyday life.

Major projects of compiling and classifying the Responsa have been undertaken by two of Israel's universities: the Hebrew University of Jerusalem and Bar-Ilan University, Tel-Aviv, the latter by computerization.

RESPONSES, LITURGICAL Prescribed words or phrases that are recited or chanted by the congregation, during public worship in the synagogue, and which "answer" portions of the service recited by the reader. In many Western synagogues, a number of these responses are also sung by the choir. Although customs vary between the different prayer rites (especially between Ashkenazi and Sephardi congregations), the major responses are common to all.

Most of these words and phrases can be traced to the Bible, and a few are direct quotations. Three in particular have been current since the era of the Temple; these responses, originally chanted by a choir of LEVITES, are: AMEN, BARUKH SHEM KEVOD MALKHUTO LE-OLAM VA-ED, and SELAH. Though retained in the liturgy, HALLELUJAH no longer serves its analogous function.

The Aramaic KADDISH prayer is a responsive doxology that has formed part of congregational worship since late rabbinic times. Great importance is attached to its central response, *Yehé Shemeh rabba mevarakh le-alam u-le-olemé olemayya* ("May His great Name be praised forever and for all eternity"; *Shab.* 119b). The words *Kudsha Berikh Hu* ("The Holy One, blessed be He") occur in the second paragraph of the *Kaddish*; Ashkenazim repeat the last two words (*Berikh Hu*) as a formal response ("Blessed be He"); *amen* is said after the complete Divine Name in all other rites.

Closely related to the first *Kaddish* response is *Yehi Shem Adonai mevorakh me-attah ve-ad olam* ("Blessed be the Name of the Lord from now and for evermore"; Ps. 113:2).

This phrase occurs in the HALLEL psalms, but is used among Ashkenazim as a response to the invocation recited by one leading GRACE AFTER MEALS. Similarly *Barukh Adonai Ha-Mevorakh le-olam va-ed* ("Praised be the Lord who is [to be] praised for all eternity") answers the BAREKHU summons to public worship and the *Barekhu* invocation recited by a congregant summoned to the Reading of the Law. *Ken yehi ratson* ("May this be God's will"), sometimes used as an alternative to *amen* in the PRIESTLY BLESSING, often endorses a hope or wish.

TABLE OF PRINCIPAL RESPONSES

Aléhem ha-shalom ("Peace be upon them")	after names of the Patriarchs when the first paragraph of the *Amidah* is repeated in synagogue (by Sephardim).
Am kedoshekha ka-amur ("Your holy people, as is said")	after the word *Kohanim* in the sentence introducing the Priestly Blessing; this Sephardi practice has been adopted by some Ashkenazim.
Amen	after Morning Benedictions, each blessing of the *Amidah* (during reader's repetition), phrases of *Kaddish*, each verse of the Priestly Blessing, New Moon blessing, and other benedictions.
Barukh Adonai ha-Mevorakh le-olam va-ed	after the *Barekhu* invocation in daily services and Reading of the Law.
Barukh Hu u-varukh Shemo	after the third word of benedictions; but not during *Kiddush* and *Havdalah*, before and after *Shema*, over sounding of the *shofar* and reading of the Scroll of Esther on Purim, or during Grace after Meals.
Barukh Shem Kevod Malkhuto le-olam va-ed	after the opening sentence of *Shema* (silently, except on the Day of Atonement), following benedictions recited on putting on the *tefillin* (by Ashkenazim), and three times at the end of the *Ne'ilah* Service on the Day of Atonement.
*Barukh tiheyeh** ("May you be blessed")	(a) answer given by a *kohen* to *ḫazak (u-) barukh* salutations after he has recited the Priestly Blessing; (b) answer to congratulations received by one who has been called to the Reading of the Torah or who has performed some other commandment; alternatively: *ḫazak ve-emats* (by Sephardim).
Berikh Hu	in the second paragraph of every *Kaddish* (by Ashkenazim).
Ke-me-az ("As of old")	after the words, "May our eyes behold Your return to Zion in compassion (*Amidah*; by Sephardim).
Ken yehi ratson	after each verse of the Priestly Blessing (instead of *amen*) in certain Ashkenazi and Sephardi congregations.
Selah	concludes a response to *Gomel* blessing; after *Yehi ratson* blessing of the New Moon (by Ashkenazim), etc.
Yehé Shemeh rabba mevarakh la-alam u-le-alemé alemayya	after the first paragraph of every *Kaddish*.
Yehi Shem Adonai mevorakh me-attah ve-ad olam	after the "invitation" to recite Grace after Meals (by Ashkenazim).
Yevarekhekha Adonai ("The Lord bless you")	response to biblical salutation of *Adonai immakhem* ("The Lord be with you"; Ruth 2:4) offered to one called to the Reading of the Law before he recites the first Torah benediction (Sephardi practice, also customary among Italian Jews).

* This is also an Ashkenazi response to *Yishar Koḫokha*, congratulations offered on the performance of any commandment, e.g., after being called to read the Torah.

Standard benedictions, normally answered by *amen*, commence with the three words *Barukh Attah Adonai* ("Blessed are You, O Lord..."; Ps. 119:2). On many occasions, the prescribed response to the third word is *Barukh Hu u-varukh Shemo* ("Blessed be He and blessed be His Name"). A response made to the GOMEL blessing pronounced after rescue from peril or safe return from a long journey is *Mi shegemalekha kol-tov Hu yigmolkha kol-tov, Selah* ("May He who has been gracious to you continue to deal graciously with you for evermore").

Various semi-liturgical responses are also current among Sephardi communities, associated in particular with the Reading of the Law and the Priestly Blessing.

RESURRECTION The belief that the bodies of the dead will rise from their graves and be reunited with their souls. The concept arose in Judaism in post-biblical times (perhaps under Persian influence), and was adopted by the PHARISEES but rejected by the SADDUCEES. The Pharisees reacted by affirming that a person who denied belief in resurrection had no place in the world to come (*Sanh.* 10.1). The second prayer of the AMIDAH addresses God as "He Who resurrects the dead." A prayer prescribed for one who visits a cemetery for the first time after 30 days affirms that God "will one day resurrect departed individuals and return them to the world of the living in a spirit of justice."

MAIMONIDES incorporated belief in the Resurrection of the Dead into his thirteen PRINCIPLES OF FAITH. However, in his other writings, he was ambiguous on the subject, reflecting a basic tension between this belief and the doctrine of the immortality of the SOUL. It was debated in the Middle Ages whether the world to come (*Olam ha-Ba*) refers to resurrection or to immortality of the soul. After Maimonides was accused of not wholeheartedly endorsing the belief in resurrection, he wrote an essay in which he affirmed that resurrection would take place but would not be permanent.

Judaism combined the three eschatological concepts, resurrection, immortality, and the Messiah, into the belief that the soul continues after death and that, after the coming of the Messiah, the body is resurrected and combines with the soul on earth. Generally, the medieval philosophers followed the lines laid down by the rabbis. Saadiah Gaon foresaw two resurrections: the first for righteous Jews, the second for all other men. However, many problems puzzled Jewish thinkers: Will all the dead be revived or only the righteous? Will only Jews be resurrected or all mankind? If there is physical resurrection, will bodily imperfections be retained? Will the resurrection come before or after the Messiah? What is the relationship between the resurrection of the dead and the final judgment?

In modern times, the non-Orthodox have tended to reject the belief in resurrection, except as a metaphor for the immortality of the soul, and they do not take the physical aspects literally. All references to resurrection were removed from Reform prayer books, and Reconstructionists also never accepted it. The Conservative *Sim Shalom* retains the traditional prayer in the *Amidah*, translating it as, "Who gives life to the dead." See also ESCHATOLOGY; TRANSMIGRATION.

RETALIATION The Bible lays down (Lev. 24:20), "Break for break, eye for eye, tooth for tooth: as he has caused a blemish in a man, so shall it be done to him" (similarly, Ex. 21:5; Deut. 19:21). This law of retaliation (*Lex Talionis*) has given rise to much interpretation and nowhere is it stated that it was applied literally. On the face of it, the law seems to imply that whenever a person causes physical injury to another, that same injury is to be inflicted on him (as is found in ancient non-Israelite legal codes). The Oral Law, though, laid down that this verse cannot be taken literally, for there is no way, for example, to insure that the complications caused by the loss of one person's eye will be equivalent to the complications resulting from the destruction of another person's eye. The Oral Law, therefore, interprets the law to refer to financial compensation: the value of an eye for an eye. The person causing the injury is required to make redress for the pain, the actual damage incurred, medical costs, lost income and any embarrassment that may have been caused. Each factor has its own formula, the actual damage caused, for example, being evaluated in terms of how much a slave of comparable age would be worth without the injury as compared to how much his value would be with the injury. Similarly, the payment for embarrassment takes into account the stature of both parties and the circumstances in which the injury was caused.

The only place where *Lex Talionis* can apply is in the case of murder, where the death penalty could be imposed. This is the one case where the retaliation — the taking of life — can be in kind. However, one may also note that, unlike other Middle Eastern codes of the time, the Torah specifically notes that: "The fathers shall not be put to death for the children, neither shall the children be put to death for the fathers: every man shall be put to death for his own sin" (Deut. 24:16). One may compare this verse with the Code of Hammurabi, that states that if a building collapses and kills the owner's child, the builder's child is to be put to death in retaliation.

RETURN TO ZION See ZION, RETURN TO

REUBEN See TRIBES, TWELVE

REVELATION A general theological term referring to the act whereby God shows Himself to man.

Bible. Although to individuals in the midst of personal or national distress, God may appear to be "hiding" (Isa. 45:15, Ps. 13:2, 44:24,25), the essential thrust of the Bible is that God is self-disclosing and wishes to be known by human beings. God reveals Himself, first through His actions in nature and in history. The existence of the world is seen as testifying to its creator, to His goodness, wisdom and power (Isa. 40:26; Ps. 19:1). God's concern for man caused Him to intervene in human history long before the advent of Israel, e.g. in the stories of the FLOOD and the Tower of Babel. Unlike the beliefs of other peoples of the time, God's subsequent revelations to Israel are not the concerns of a national God for His people but the activity of a universal God who relates to a particular people in order to bring about His plan for all people (Gen. 12:1-3, Amos 9:7).

In the biblical account it is not ABRAHAM or MOSES who seek out God but God who accosts these individuals, reveals Himself, and instructs them in the task He has set for them (Gen. 12:1, Ex. 3:2). In his highest development, the Hebrew PROPHET is not the seer who waits to be consulted by men but God's spokesman who has been sent to tell people what they do not wish to hear. The founding actions of God in the history of Israel are the Exodus from Egypt, the Giving of the Law at Mount Sinai, God's sustenance of Israel in the wilderness, and Israel's inheriting of the Promised Land. Each of these "mighty acts" discloses something about the attributes of God, His plan for history, and His expectations from man.

Moses receiving the Tablets of the Law. From the Yahuda Haggadah, *Germany, 19th century.*

Although God is described as appearing to man in dreams and visions (Gen. 15:1, 18:1,2; Ex. 3:2, Gen. 15:1, Ezek. 1), His most characteristic manner of revelation is through speech. The Lord "speaks" and man hears and understands.

Those vouchsafed a revelation of God in the Bible may perceive His "messengers" (*malakhim*) or angels in the form of men (Gen. 18:2, 32:2; Judg. 13:3) or a phenomenon called God's *kavod* ("glory") (Lev. 9:4, 6, 23) or a pillar of cloud (Deut. 31:15).

The biblical assertion, "Man may not see My face and live" (Ex. 33:20) is interpreted as referring to God's essence which is beyond mortal man's sight and comprehension. What God does reveal to man through His deeds and words are evidence of His presence, intuition of His concern and desire to enter into relationship, knowledge of His attributes and, above all, something of His will: His plans, purposes and intentions for the individual, the nation, and mankind.

Talmud. The process by which God communicates with man is called by the rabbis, *nevu'ah* ("prophecy") *ru'aḇ ha-kodesh* (HOLY SPIRIT) or "coming to rest of the SHEKHINAH" ("Indwelling Presence"). The rabbis stipulated that the spirit of prophecy is conferred upon individuals only if they have developed certain moral and spiritual qualities (*Sot.* 9:15, *Shab.* 92a) (see PROPHETS AND PROPHECY). The rabbis linked the cessation of prophecy to the destruction of the First Temple and noted that "with the death of Haggai, Zechariah, and Malachi the Holy Spirit departed from Israel" (*Sanh.* 11a, *BB* 12a). While prophecy in the sense of new legislation was foreclosed, the rabbis continued to believe in the possibility of experiencing the Presence of God and hearing a Heavenly-echo (BAT-KOL) (*Sanh.* 11a, *Avot* 6:12) which, however did not have halakhic authority.

Medieval. Since revelation is the basis of Christianity and Islam as well as of Judaism, the medieval Jewish theologians did not have a problem with the concept of revelation as such, but with the need to show the superiority of the Jewish chain to authentic revelation. This was generally done by pointing to the public nature of the Sinaitic revelations before all the people of Israel (SAADIAH GAON, MAIMONIDES, JUDAH HALEVI). However, belief that this happened relies on belief in the reliability of the Jewish tradition. So that while traditional Judaism is founded on a supernatural origin in revelation, belief in revelation has only the certitude of natural knowledge, i.e., a special form of historical knowledge.

What is the purpose of revelation if, as the medieval scholars believed, human reason could discover these truths on its own? The answer given by Saadiah Gaon and others was a pedagogical one: to make these vital truths available to all men at the beginning of their lives and to avoid the possibility of error. Others such as Judah Halevi argued that the goal of Judaism is not knowledge of God but life with God, immediate communion with Him.

According to Maimonides the phenomenon of prophecy is grounded in the natural connection between the human mind, its intellectual and imaginative faculties, and a cosmological entity called "the active intellect" and comes about as the result of the perfection of certain natural human faculties. However, whether or not a person actually becomes a prophet depends ultimately upon the will of God. For Judah Halevi revelation is primarily a supernatural, non-rational, event unattainable by the individual on his own, an infusion of the Divine Presence from the outside accompanied by a transforming religious emotion of love for God.

In his own analysis of the subject, Joseph ALBO is very close to Maimonides. However in terms of the need for revelation, Albo sides with Judah Halevi and claims that man's own powers are insufficient to provide him with the guidance essential for human salvation.

Modern Jewish Thought. The problem of revelation for the modern Jew is not the intricacies of how God speaks to man but whether it really happened. For naturalistic versions of Judaism such as RECONSTRUCTIONISM and American REFORM JUDAISM (according to the Columbus Platform in 1937) which have no room for the supernatural, the idea of a spiritual God communicating a content of particular commandments to man, is sheer miracle and must be rejected.

Existential Jewish philosophers such as Martin BUBER and Franz ROSENZWEIG have affirmed the reality of a Divine Revelation at the core of the biblical experience at least in the sense of Presence of God if not in the imparting of specific content.

Orthodox thinkers such as KOOK and SOLOVEITCHIK suggest that the individual today can encounter the revelational activity of God in the study of Torah and by personal response to the return of the Jewish people to the Land of Israel. HESCHEL is content to leave the question of the precise manner of the interaction between God and the mind of man a mystery and to focus on the consequences of belief in revelation. Just as the religious importance of the doctrine of creation is to be able to perceive the world as the handiwork of God, so the religious significance of revelation is to be able to see the Bible as reflecting the will of God and as relevant to our lives (*God in Search of Man*, sect. II).

REWARD AND PUNISHMENT The belief that Divine justice will reward the righteous and punish the wicked. In the Pentateuch, God appears as a moral being and JUSTICE is an integral part of morality (see ETHICS); it follows that God acts justly in the world. As a universal principle, justice pertains to all entities, to the individual as well as to the nation. God's governance of the world in accordance with justice is called PROVIDENCE.

As part of their COVENANT with God, the Jewish people as a nation is promised material wealth and prosperity for obedience and is threatened with various punishments (including exile) for disobedience (Deut. 11:13-21). This is emphasized in great detail in the Blessings and Curses passages in the Bible (Lev. 23; Deut. 28).

Promises of rewards for observing individual commandments are generally found in connection with positive precepts which call for the exercise of benevolence and charity. These rewards are described in terms of long life and material blessing (Ex. 20:12; Deut. 15:10).

Already the books of the PROPHETS and the WISDOM LITERATURE contain critical reflections upon the principle of Reward and Punishment. Jeremiah asks, "Why does the way of the wicked prosper?" (12:1) and Habakkuk says, "How long O Lord shall I cry out and You not listen, shall I shout to You 'Violence' and You not save?...therefore the law fails and justice never emerges...For the wicked do beset the righteous, therefore judgment emerges perverted" (1:2-4). The problem is raised in Ecclesiastes and Psalms (37, 49, 73), and receives its most comprehensive and dramatic treatment in the Book of JOB. This problem, called "theodicy" (justifying the acts of God), surfaces when experience is seen to conflict with what man expects on the basis of the principle of Divine Reward and Punishment. If the righteous suffer instead of receiving reward, the moral sense is outraged, as happens also if the wicked go unpunished and are free to oppress the innocent. The prosperity of the wicked offends. One biblical response is to say that the success of the wicked is only temporary. "When the wicked spring up as grass and when all the workers of iniquity do flourish, it is that they may be destroyed forever" (Ps. 92:6).

To the question why Israel's punishment seems to be more severe than that meted out to other nations, Amos replies, "You alone have I known of all the families of the earth; therefore I will visit upon you all your iniquities" (3:2), i.e., precisely because of God's special relation to Israel more is expected of it. At the same time, while other nations may have been utterly destroyed for their sins, the eternal existence of Israel is assured (Jer. 31:34).

For those who interpret the "suffering servant" of Isaiah (53) as referring to Israel, another meaning emerges for the suffering of Israel. It is not punishment for their sins but rather atonement for the sins of others. The justness of such vicarious suffering remains unexplained in the Bible.

Job, as well as other parts of the Bible (Gen. 22:1, Ex. 16:4, Deut. 8:2), presents the concept of *nissayon* ("test" or "trial"). Suffering need not be a punishment, but a means by which God "tests" the faith or character of the individual for his ultimate benefit.

In the last chapters of Job (where God appears to Job out of the whirlwind), Job is humbled before the awesome power of God in nature (38-41). His own egocentric concerns are dwarfed in comparison to the magnitude of the universe (40:3-5). Man cannot comprehend the Divine plan.

Rabbinic Literature. In principle, the talmudic rabbis affirmed the biblical concept of Reward and Punishment, but in certain crucial areas developed the concept in new directions. While there are some allusions in the Bible to life after death (see SOUL, IMMORTALITY OF), nowhere is an explicit connection made between that and the principle of Reward and Punishment. The rabbis concluded that the decisive arena for Reward and Punishment of the individual is in some more permanent existence after death (see AFTERLIFE). R. Jacob said, "This world is like an antechamber to the world to come; prepare yourself in the antechamber so that you may enter into the hall" [i.e., the bliss of the world to come is incomparable to anything experienced in this world] (*Avot* 4.21,22).

Two considerations led the rabbis to this conclusion. The

first was the empirical evidence that the promise in the Bible of material reward for the performance of particular commandments by the individual was not being fulfilled in this world. The rabbis observed: "There is no reward in this world for the fulfillment of commandments" (*Ḥul.* 142a), and that the biblical promise, "that your days may be prolonged" (Ex. 20:12), can refer to some eternal existence of the spirit after the death of the body. Reward for the precepts is not necessarily accorded in this world. The dominant rabbinic view remained that both this world and the world to come were theaters for the Providential application of the principle of Reward and Punishment for every individual in various complicated permutations.

This concept of a "two-stage" human existence helped to alleviate the problem of "the righteous who suffer and the wicked who prosper." The rabbis also cultivated the idea of "afflictions of love" (*Ber.* 5a), i.e., that suffering may not be a punishment but a test and an opportunity for spiritual growth (*Gen. R.* 32.3). While the rabbis thought of various possible explanations for the suffering of the righteous, R. Yannai concluded: "It is not in our power to explain either the prosperity of the wicked and certainly not the afflictions of the righteous" (*Avot* 4.19).

Another factor which led the rabbis to develop the notion of the world to come as the ultimate theater for individual Reward and Punishment was the realization that material reward is not a proper motivation for the worship of God: "Be not like servants who minister to their master in order to receive a reward, but be like servants who minister to their master without the condition of receiving a reward, and let the reverence of Heaven be upon you" (*Avot* 1.3).

Another element developed by the rabbis is RESURRECTION of the dead which, according to one view in the Talmud (*Ta'an.* 7a), will be granted only to the righteous. Ultimate reward and punishment should be visited upon the unity of body and soul (*Sanh.* 91a-b; but see *Lev. R.* 4.5 for an opposite viewpoint).

In their speculations about the nature of the ultimate reward and punishment, the rabbis spoke of *gan eden* (Garden of Eden) as the "place" of reward and *gehinnom* as the "place" of punishment (*Pes.* 54a; *Er.* 19a). The duration of the punishment for sins is given as 12 months. However, for the unrepentant wicked, some stipulate eternal punishment (*RH* 16b), described in physical terms as fire, while the happiness of ultimate reward is described as a wonderful banquet (*Ber.* 34b). Some of the rabbis clearly understood these teachings as purely symbolic (*AZ* 3b; *Ber.* 34b).

In Medieval Jewish Thought. The medieval Jewish theologians who attempted to recast the biblical and rabbinic thought into a coherent whole were compelled to treat the pivotal issue of Reward and Punishment. This was difficult in view of the non-philosophic character of the biblical material on the one hand, and the variety of conflicting opinions in the rabbinic tradition on the other.

The crucial issue on which these thinkers were divided was whether justice and reason require that the body and soul as a unity or rather the soul alone be the recipient of the ultimate Reward and Punishment. Accepting the former as the case, SAADIAH GAON, for example, sketches a system in which after death, the souls of the righteous and the wicked are kept in separate "places" until the major eschatological event, the resurrection of the dead. This will take place after the Redemption and the coming of the MESSIAH that, for Saadiah, are merely preliminary to sorting out the truly righteous and wicked of the Jewish people. Once the body and soul are reunited, judgment will take place, after which a single Divinely-revealed substance will constitute "light" for the righteous and "fire" for the punishment of the wicked. Thus will commence the world to come, consisting of a radically transformed, highly spiritualized "new heaven and new earth" in which the righteous, after being purified of their few sins, will enjoy eternal happiness and the unrepentant wicked will suffer eternal punishment. A similar approach was taken by NAḤMANIDES.

MAIMONIDES, however, followed a different course. His starting point was that the essence of man is his reason and that only the rational soul has a capacity for immortality. The ultimate "reward" for the individual, that is identical with human self-fulfillment, is an all-spiritual existence in the presence of God which the righteous attain immediately after death. This is what is known as "the world to come." The ultimate punishment is the failure of the wicked to attain immortality and thus for them to simply perish in total extinction. Unrelated to these metaphysical events is the Messianic Age that takes place on the historical level and signifies a natural, non-miraculous arena for the reward and punishment of the nations and the establishment of the Kingdom of God.

For Maimonides as well as for others like ALBO, there is nothing in this theory of Reward and Punishment which logically necessitates the doctrine of Resurrection of the Dead. It is, however, included by both of them on traditional grounds. Resurrection, according to Maimonides, will occur sometime after the advent of the Messiah in order for the righteous to further perfect themselves, or in order to provide just compensation for some of the righteous who might have suffered in a particularly cruel manner in times when the forces of evil seemed triumphant. After living a full life in the Messianic Age, those resurrected will die a natural death and resume their eternal spiritual existence in the world to come.

Isaac ABRAVANEL perceived the Resurrection as designed to help bring about the Messianic Age, for it would constitute the single most overwhelming, incontrovertible "wonder," that would have the immediate effect of winning over the people of the world to accepting God's sovereignty.

Albo tries to answer the question of why the Bible itself did not fully and explicitly expound the doctrine of spiritual reward and punishment in a hereafter. The Pentateuch, he says, is essentially the constitution of the Jewish people or the history and provisions of the covenant between God and the nation called Israel. In reference to a people as a whole, which lives its collective life in history, reward and punishment can only be couched in material terms: prosperity, military victory, drought, defeat, exile. There is no such thing as a spiritual hereafter for the nation as such. Hence the Bible, in addressing itself to the destiny of Israel the nation, is silent on the subject of the spiritual salvation of the individual.

In discussing the need for other-worldly rewards, Saadiah makes some modern-sounding existential observations. We find, he says, that even people who reach the highest positions in life still suffer from insecurity and yearn for something higher and better. The experiences of this life with all of its pleasures are simply not satisfying and not sufficient. A just God must therefore have provided for those deserving an "untroubled existence and pure happiness."

Almost all of the medieval thinkers, at least to some extent, subscribed to a doctrine of natural rewards and punishments. Already, the rabbis taught: "The reward of a *mitsvah* is the *mitsvah*" [i.e., the positive effect of the commandment itself upon the doer] (*Avot* 4.2). Reward and Punishment can be seen not as some extraneous condition imposed by a judge to induce compliance or deter violations, but as a natural and inevitable outgrowth of the actual deeds themselves. Similar views were propounded by Maimonides, Naḫmanides, and Albo.

Modern Thought. The principle of Reward and Punishment, together with the concept of Divine Providence, has come under intense scrutiny as a result of the Holocaust and the establishment of the State of Israel. The rise of the State of Israel, with the return of Jewish sovereignty to its land, has led many Orthodox Jews to see these events as the "beginning of Redemption" and the fulfillment of biblical prophecy. For reactions to the Holocaust, see HOLOCAUST: Religious Responses among Victims and Subsequent Religious Thinking.

RIGHTEOUSNESS The value of JUSTICE and right; hence, a good action. The usual Hebrew words *tsedakah* or *tsedek* have the connotation of legal justice, as in the biblical texts "Justice, justice, shall you pursue" (Deut. 16:20) and "Just balances, just weights" (Lev. 29:36), the latter in the context of righteousness in the market place.

In its ultimate ideal, the aspect of righteousness as justice is ascribed to God as in "A God of faithfulness and without iniquity, righteous and right is He" (Deut. 32:4) and "The Lord is righteous in all His ways" (Ps. 145:7).

In addition to having legal implications, righteousness implies loyalty to moral teachings. Already NOAH was described as "a man, righteous and wholehearted" (Gen. 6:9) but it is the prophets who particularly developed the ethical aspects of righteousness. To Amos, these are more acceptable than mere legalism (2:6; 5:12,23). Moreover, social righteousness must be complemented by inner repentance (see SOCIAL ETHICS).

Total human righteousness is regarded by the author of ECCLESIASTES as unattainable: "For there is not a righteous man on earth who does good and does not sin" (7:20), but this may be no more than a counsel of moderation in the spirit of his advice "Be not righteous overmuch" (7:16). However, the later books of the Bible see the perfect world as one of "righteousness," while the DEAD SEA SECT saw their guide and model as the "Teacher of Righteousness."

In rabbinic ethics, as well as among the medieval moralists, the quality of righteousness is even more than conformity to legal and moral norms. It is also a state of deeper piety expressed in a character of deep spirituality, illustrated in acts of true charity. Indeed, the word *tsedakah* is now used especially for CHARITY. Especial esteem attaches to the TSADDIK, the righteous man; the term becomes a title for a pious or saintly man, later to have a unique application in Ḥasidism. The world is sustained by the 36 *Tsaddikim* (see LAMED VAV TSADDIKIM) while the Talmud glorifies the *tsaddik* as the ideal type of man to which all must aspire.

RISHONIM (literally the "early" or "former" ones, as opposed to AḪARONIM, or the "later" ones). The early authorities in Jewish law. The term is generally used for the great talmudic scholars and commentators who lived between the end of the geonic period (11th century CE) and the publication of the SHULḪAN ARUKH by Joseph CARO in 1564-5. In the study of the Talmud in the classical YESHIVOT, the commentaries of the *rishonim* are regarded as of cardinal importance, and each word in these works is considered to be precisely formulated and demanding study and explanation.

RISHON LE-TSIYYON ("First in Zion"). Title given by SEPHARDIM to their "head of the rabbis in Israel." The biblical term from which it derives is "a harbinger unto Zion" (Isa. 41:27). The title of *Rishon le-Tsiyyon*, accorded to the presiding Sephardi rabbi in Jerusalem, dates from the 17th century. Since the establishment of Britain's Palestine Mandate after World War I, Israel has had a dual CHIEF RABBINATE headed by the Ashkenazi chief rabbi and the *Rishon Le-Tsiyyon*.

RITUAL BATH See MIKVEH

RITUAL SLAUGHTER See SHEḪITAH

ROSENZWEIG, FRANZ (1886-1929). German Jewish philosopher and existentialist thinker. He was born in Kassel into an assimilated family, several of whose members converted to Christianity. His relative, Eugen Rosenstock-Huessy, had a profound influence on Rosenzweig, even to the point of bringing him to the intention to convert. However, Rosenzweig changed his mind after attending DAY OF ATONEMENT services in an Orthodox prayer house. The effect on him was dramatic and final. He recognized that he had no need to seek God in Christianity since he had already found Him in Judaism. Further deep reflection led him to the conclusion that for the Christian, the path to God is through adherence to CHRISTIANITY. Rosenzweig was the first Jewish theologian to view Christianity as equally legitimate as Judaism, both having their origin in the Divine. He proposed the doctrine of the Two Covenants which in a mysterious way stand united before God. Christianity as the Judaism of the Gentiles could bring the nations of the world to establish their relationship with God. Judaism and Christianity can recognize each other's integrity, asking for understanding, not change. At the end of time they will be united, but meanwhile, neither must seek to change the other (see INTERFAITH).

In his university years, Rosenzweig studied general philosophy, history and classics. After his decision for loyalty to Judaism, he devoted all his intellectual and spiritual gifts to Jewish and religious studies, teaching and writing. He went to Berlin where he came under the influence of such men as Hermann COHEN and Martin BUBER. He continued a lengthy correspondence with Rosenstock-Huessy during the years of World War I. In the German army he saw service in Eastern Europe where he witnessed at first hand something of the intense Jewish life in that part of the world. This had a deep effect on him.

In 1920, he helped to found the influential *Freies Judisches Lehrhaus* (Free Jewish House of Learning) in Frankfurt. This institution became one of the most important and prestigious centers for Jewish studies and it attracted the most distinguished Jewish scholars in post-war Germany.

Rosenzweig's major work is *Der Stern der Erlösung* ("The Star of Redemption"). The work was begun in 1918 on postcards written home from the war front and completed by Rosenzweig after his return. He teaches that there are three elements in total existence: God, the Universe and Man. Each of them is interrelated through the process of Creation, Revelation and Redemption. The Universe is related to God through Creation: God is related to Man through Revelation and Redemption: Man is related to God through Revelation and Redemption. So too, the Universe is related to God and Man through the triangle of the three forces. When one places the triangles on each other, a star is formed — the Star of Redemption.

For Rosenzweig, the Bible is not the last word of a onetime Revelation. Revelation is an ongoing process of God identifying Himself to the searching individual. The sanctity of the Scriptures and the validity of the commandments must speak to the individual who must open his heart in a love relationship to the Divine teaching: this takes time and patience. When Rosenzweig was once asked whether he prayed with *tefillin* (phylacteries), he replied, "Not yet."

His existentialist approach is also illustrated in his attitude to the Bible. The teachings of the various schools of Bible criticism in no way affected his veneration of the Scriptures. He said that while the story of Balaam's ass is a fairy tale during the rest of the year, it contains the word of God speaking to him when it is read from the Scroll on the appointed Sabbath. For him, the letter 'R' need not stand for "Redactor" who, the Higher Critics held, collated various sources of the Bible text, but for *Rabbenu* (our Master, Moses). Ultimately, it is the religious interpretation which makes the message holy.

Among Rosenzweig's other works are his translation into German of JUDAH HALEVI's liturgical poems and his classic joint work with Martin Buber on the translation of the Bible into German. They reached the Book of Isaiah before Rosenzweig's death and the project was completed by Buber.

In 1921 a progressive paralysis began to affect Rosenzweig and he ultimately lost all power of speech and movement. Nevertheless, he continued his literary work, pointing with a single finger to the letters on a typewriter as his wife pressed down the keys.

ROSH HA-SHANAH The Jewish New Year, a one-day festival in ancient times, now observed for two days (in Israel as well as in the Diaspora) on the 1st and 2nd of TISHRI. It marks the commencement of the annual TEN DAYS OF PENITENCE, which reach their climax on Yom Kippur, the DAY OF ATONEMENT. The Mishnah (*RH* 1.1) records four separate new years in the Jewish CALENDAR: 1 Nisan for kings; 1 Elul for tithing cattle; 15 (or 1) Shevat, the NEW YEAR FOR TREES; and 1 Tishri for calculating the SABBATICAL YEAR and the JUBILEE. In the course of time, however, it was this last date only that came to be known as Rosh ha-Shanah, all of the others being overshadowed by the importance attached to the religious New Year and the penitential season.

The term *rosh ha-shanah* occurs once in the Bible to denote the "beginning of the year" (Ezek. 40:1), although its precise meaning is far from clear. In the Pentateuch, this festival has three designations: *Shabbaton*, a day of "solemn rest" to be observed on the 1st of the seventh month; *Zikhron Teru'ah*, "a memorial [proclaimed] with the blast of the horn" (Lev. 23:24); and *Yom Teru'ah*, "a day of blowing the horn" (Num. 29:1), which indicates its chief observance, namely, the sounding of the SHOFAR (ram's horn). Later, however, the rabbis gave the festival two other names: *Yom ha-Din*, the DAY OF JUDGMENT, and *Yom ha-Zikkaron*, "the Day of Remembrance," when God remembers His creatures.

The concept of "Judgment Day" is rabbinic, deriving largely from statements made in tractate ROSH HA-SHANAH. The Mishnah speaks of all mankind passing before God on the New Year like a flock of sheep (*RH* 1.2). This idea is expanded in the Talmud, which lays emphasis on the New

Year as an occasion for self-examination in the light of Judaism's highest ideals. From the awesome picture of each man or woman standing before the throne of God, judgment on his or her fate for the coming year being entered on Rosh ha-Shanah and the verdict sealed on the Day of Atonement (*RH* 16a), the rabbis went on to visualize "three ledgers opened in heaven: one for the completely righteous, who are immediately inscribed and sealed in the BOOK OF LIFE; another for the thoroughly wicked, who are recorded in the Book of Death; and a third for the intermediate, ordinary type of person, whose fate hangs in the balance and is suspended until the Day of Atonement" (*RH* 16b). Hence the designation of Rosh ha-Shanah and Yom Kippur as *Yamim Nora'im* ("Days of Awe").

These themes dominate both home observance and synagogue liturgy on Rosh ha-Shanah. Festive white marks the appearance of the synagogue and its worshipers. It also symbolizes closeness to God and the ideal of man's cleansing from sin. The ark curtain (*parokhet*), reading desk, and Torah scroll mantles are all decked in white; the rabbi, cantor, and BA'AL TEKI'AH (who blows the ram's horn), as well as some of the more pious laymen in traditional congregations, likewise don a white robe or KITEL.

On both days of Rosh ha-Shanah, except when the first coincides with a Sabbath, the blowing of the *shofar* is a high point of the services. MAIMONIDES explained this biblical injunction as a rousing call to REPENTANCE on the part of each individual: "Awake, you sleepers, and ponder your deeds; remember your Creator, forsake your evil ways, and return to God!" (*Yad, Teshuvah* 3.4). A total of 100 notes are sounded, beginning with 30 blasts immediately after the Reading of the Law. Sephardi, Eastern, and Ḥasidic Jews then blow 30 more during the silent Additional Service AMIDAH, another 30 during the reader's repetition of the *Amidah*, and the remaining notes at the end. In the Ashkenazi rite, however, there is no sounding of the *shofar* during the silent *Amidah*, only in the course of the reader's repetition (30), and at various points thereafter (30), usually concluding with a final sequence of ten blasts prior to ADON OLAM.

Opening of the prayers for Rosh Ha-Shanah (New Year). From the Leipzig Maḥzor, *Germany, 14th century.*

NEW YEAR — ROSH HA-SHANAH

Other Names: *Yom Teru'ah* (Day of sounding the Shofar)
Yom ha-Din (Judgment Day)
Yom ha-Zikkaron (Day of Remembrance/Memorial Day)

Hebrew Dates: 1–2 Tishri

Torah & Prophetical Readings:
1st Day: Gen. 21:1-34; Num. 29:1-6 (*Maftir*); 1 Sam. 1:1-2:10 (*Haftarah*)
2nd Day: Gen: 22:1-24; Num. 29:1-6 (*Maftir*); Jer. 31:2-20 (*Haftarah*)

Civil dates on which the festival occurs, 1990-2010:

1990/5751	20-21 September
1991/5752	9-10 September
1992/5753	28-29 September
1993/5754	16-17 September
1994/5755	6-7 September
1995/5756	25-26 September
1996/5757	14-15 September
1997/5758	2-3 October
1998/5759	21-22 September
1999/5760	11-12 September
2000/5761	30 Sept.-1 Oct.
2001/5762	18-19 September
2002/5763	7-8 September
2003/5764	27-28 September
2004/5765	16-17 September
2005/5766	4-5 October
2006/5767	23-24 September
2007/5768	13-14 September
2008/5769	30 Sept.-1 Oct.
2009/5770	19-20 September
2010/5771	9-10 September

Since Rosh ha-Shanah is a solemn rather than a joyous festival, no HALLEL is recited, but various parts of the service (e.g., the KADDISH) are chanted to traditional High Holiday prayer modes. The liturgy includes numerous liturgical poems (PIYYUTIM), AVINU MALKENU, and ALENU LE-SHABBE'AH (during the Additional Service's repetition), when kneeling and prostration are customary in Orthodox and some Conservative synagogues. The Additional Service *Amidah* includes three groups of ten verses relating to God's kingship (MALKHUYYOT), remembrance of His covenant, mercy, etc. (ZIKHRONOT), and the sounding of the ram's horn (SHOFAROT). The Judgment Day theme looms large in the Ashkenazi prayer, U-NETANNEH TOKEF, which concludes on a hopeful note, with worshipers proclaiming that "Repentance, Prayer, and Charity can avert the evil decree." Also reflected in the New Year liturgy is the rabbinic view of Rosh ha-Shanah as the "birthday of the world" (*RH*, 8a, 10b, 27a).

A custom still widely observed, by Orthodox Ashkenazim in particular, is the ceremony of TASHLIKH, consisting of the symbolic casting of one's sins into a river, lake, or other body of water on the afternoon of the first day of Rosh ha-Shanah (or of the second day if the first coincides with a Sabbath). The traditional GREETINGS exchanged on the festival convey a wish that Jews may be "inscribed for a good year" or "for a good life."

Customs in the home add a poetic, popular touch to the observances. After KIDDUSH, a piece of bread is dipped in honey for the *Ha-Motsi* benediction (see GRACE BEFORE MEALS), a piece of apple is likewise dipped in honey and eaten after a brief prayer that the year ahead may be "good and sweet." Also customary is the eating of a new season's fruit, on the second night of Rosh ha-Shanah, to justify reciting the SHEHEHEYANU benediction on enjoying new things. *Hallah* loaves baked specially for the festival are usually round or with the plaited crust in the shape of a ladder, to signify hopes for a "good round year" or man's effort to direct his life upward to God.

ROSH HA-SHANAH ("New Year"). Eighth tractate of Order MO'ED in the Mishnah. Its four chapters deal primarily with two subjects: the laws for fixing the new month by the *Bet Din* and the laws relevant to blowing the SHOFAR (ram's horn) on ROSH HA-SHANAH (New Year) and the accompanying blessings (cf. Lev. 23:23-25; Num. 29:1-6). Also covered are differences between the celebration of the New Year during and after the Temple period. The first mishnah mentions four NEW YEARS on the Jewish calendar: one for kings; one for tithing animals; one for trees and *Rosh ha -Shanah* — the New Year for years, planting and vegetables, and commemorating the creation of the world. The subject matter is amplified in both TALMUDS and the TOSEFTA.

ROSH HODESH See MOON

RUTH, BOOK OF Biblical book in the HAGIOGRAPHA section of the Bible, telling the story of Ruth, from whom King DAVID was descended. The book contains 85 verses, divided into four chapters. This is one of the FIVE SCROLLS read in the synagogue on special days. Ruth is read on the festival of SHAVU'OT (on the second day of the festival outside Israel.) According to the Talmud, (*BB.* 14b), Ruth is the first book of the Hagiographa, preceding Psalms. This is appropriate, since, by rabbinic tradition, the Book of Psalms is attributed to David.

There are three main characters in the story: Naomi, her Moabite daughter-in-law, Ruth, whose husband has died, and Boaz, Naomi's kinsman, who eventually marries Ruth. Naomi, with her husband Elimelech and two sons, moves to Moab because of famine in Canaan. All three men die, leaving Naomi and her two Moabite daughters-in-law destitute. Naomi decides to return home, and asks her daughters-in-law to remain in their own land. One agrees, but Ruth refuses to leave her mother-in-law, telling her, "your people shall be my people, and your God my God." These words have made her the paradigmatic proselyte to Judaism.

After they return, Naomi instructs Ruth to exercise the right reserved to the poor to glean grain which falls during the harvest (see Lev. 19:9-10; 23:22). In the fields Ruth meets Boaz, who is a relative of her father-in-law. Boaz agrees to marry Ruth and to purchase from the two women Elimelech's field. Most scholars interpret Boaz's marriage to his cousin's childless widow as an example of LEVIRATE MARRIAGE.

Ruth gleaning in Boaz's field. Etching by Ephraim Moses Lilien, Austria, 20th century.

BOOK OF RUTH

1:1 — 1:5	Elimelech's family go to Moab; his two sons marry Moabite women; the three men die.
1:5 — 1:22	Ruth insists on returning with her mother-in- law, Naomi, to Beth-lehem.
2:1 — 2:23	Ruth gleans in the fields of Boaz.
3:1 — 3:18	Following Naomi's advice, Ruth claims kinship with Boaz.
4:1 — 4:12	Boaz gets the next-of-kin to renounce his duties.
4:13 -4:22	Boaz marries Ruth and their descendant is David.

The linguistic features of the Book of Ruth have been invoked in favor of a variety of dates for its composition, from the period of the Judges to the period of Ezra and Nehemiah, but recent scholarship favors an earlier dating. One rabbinic tradition (*BB* 14b) holds that it was written by the Prophet Samuel.

RUTH RABBAH A homiletical MIDRASH on the Book of RUTH. It is divided into eight *parashiyyot* (sections) and opens with a *Petiḇta* (introduction) consisting of six proems. Almost all its material is drawn from the Jerusalem Talmud, GENESIS RABBAH, LAMENTATIONS RABBAH, and LEVITICUS RABBAH. A few homilies derive from PESIKTA DE RAV-KAHANA. There are a few additions in the text that date from the 11th century.

Since the Book of Ruth begins with the phrase "And it came to pass in the days of...", the Midrash cites an ancient homily which declares that whenever the phrase "and it came to pass" appears in Scripture, it portends sorrow for Israel. A lengthy exposition alludes to numerous biblical passages in which the phrase occurs with homiletical explanation of the sorrow in each instance.

Thus on the opening phrase of the Book of Ruth "And it came to pass in the days of the judging of the Judges," the Midrash comments: "Woe to the generation that judges its judges and woe to the generation that has to judge its judges."

S

SAADIAH GAON (882-942). Outstanding scholar of the geonic period and communal leader. Born of humble origins in Upper Egypt, he migrated as a young man to Erets Israel where he settled in Tiberias, then the center for MASORAH studies. From there he moved to Babylonia, but not before he had engaged in a protracted controversy with the Palestinian *gaon* Aaron ben Meir. The immediate issue involved was the authority to regulate the CALENDAR, a prerogative that had long since passed from the ACADEMIES of Erets Israel to those of Babylonia but that ben Meir sought to reclaim. The controversy ended after some years with a victory for Saadiah and the threat to a generally recognized Jewish calendar was averted. The larger issue was the supremacy of the Babylonian over the Palestinian sages.

Upon his arrival in Babylonia, Saadiah was granted the honorific title of *Aluf* (Prince), in recognition of his achievements in Jewish learning. Shortly after his appointment as GAON of the Academy of Sura by the EXILARCH David ben Zakkai, Saadiah became embroiled with the latter in a bitter controversy. The exilarch put Saadiah under a ban and deposed him as *gaon* of Sura, Saadiah responding with a counter-ban of ben Zakkai. For seven years the dispute, that divided the leadership of Babylonian Jewry into two opposing camps, dragged on before a settlement was reached.

These public frays, in Babylonia and Erets Israel, in no way affected either the number or variety of his scholarly works. However, most of his writings are known today by title, with scattered fragments preserved in the Cairo GENIZAH, or from quotations. They reflect originality and a high sense of logical, orderly arrangement rare for his time.

In the area of Hebrew language, Saadiah composed a Hebrew rhyming dictionary (*Sefer ha-Agron*); a listing and explanation of the words that appear but once in the Bible (*hapax legomena*); and a work on grammar. In recent times, considerable portions of his commentary on many books of the Bible (written in Arabic) have been recovered and published with Hebrew translation. His crowning achievement in Bible studies is his Arabic translation of the Bible, with a partial commentary. To this day, Yemenite Jews use this translation and it is printed alongside the Hebrew text together with TARGUM Onkelos in a volume called the *Taj* ("Crown of the Torah").

Saadiah's edition of the PRAYER BOOK incorporated the pertinent laws and customs as well as a number of original prayers.

Saadiah's philosophical work, *Sefer ha-Emunot ve-ha-De'ot* ("The Book of Beliefs and Opinions"), inaugurated medieval Jewish philosophy. Strongly influenced by the Mutazilite school of Islamic philosophy, as well as by Aristotelianism, Platonism and Stoicism, Saadiah offered a rational analysis and proof of the basic theological concepts of Judaism. Reason and revelation, he held, correspond and one cannot refute the other. Throughout the book there is a strong polemical note directed at KARAITES, as well as dualists, Trinitarians and Islam.

In the area of Jewish law, Saadiah pioneered with ten monographs on specific areas, written in Arabic. Only one of the monographs, the *Book of Documents*, a masterly model of logical arrangement, is extant.

Maimonides said of him: "If it were not for Saadiah, the Torah could well have disappeared from among the Jewish people."

SAYINGS OF SAADIAH

The more valuable an objective, the more effort it demands.

Reason has long since decided that God needs nothing, but that all things need Him.

Death is the means of transition to future life, which is the ultimate goal of mortal existence.

In this world we see the godless prosper and the faithful suffer. There must be another world in which all will be recompensated in justice and righteousness.

Any interpretation that conforms to reason must be correct.

Distress is no excuse for disloyalty.

We have two bases of our religion, apart from the Bible. One, that precedes it, is the fountain of reason; the other, which is later, is the source of tradition.

SABBATH (*Shabbat*). The seventh day of the week; the day of rest, one of the central features of Judaism. The basic reasons given in the Bible for the Sabbath are to commemorate it as the culmination of CREATION (Gen. 1 and Ex. 20), to offer an opportunity for servants to rest (Deut. 5), to serve as a sign of the COVENANT of God with, and His consecration of, the people of Israel (Ex. 31). Deuteronomy 5 also connects the EXODUS to the Sabbath. It is the only holy day mentioned specifically in the TEN COMMANDMENTS.

Three basic themes of Judaism characterize the day: Creation, REVELATION, and REDEMPTION. They are seen in the biblical passages which serve as the cornerstone of the Sabbath, and in some of its practices, notably the public READING OF THE LAW.

Biblical sources. The first key text is Genesis 2:1-3: "The heaven and the earth were finished and all their array. And on the seventh day God finished the work which He had been doing, and He ceased [or "rested"] on the seventh day from all the work which He had done. And God blessed the seventh day and declared it holy, because on it God ceased from all the work of creation which He had done." The Bible does not mention that the Patriarchs observed the Sabbath (although rabbinic sources do, e.g., Gen. R. 11.17, or 64.4).

During their wanderings in the Wilderness of Zin and with the introduction of MANNA, the Israelites were first commanded to observe the Sabbath; they were told that five days of the week, they were to collect a single portion of manna, but on the sixth they should collect a double portion, for "tomorrow is a day of rest, a holy Sabbath of the Lord" (Ex. 16:23). When some searched on the seventh day for manna and found none, "the Lord spoke to Moses, 'How long will you men refuse to follow My commandments and My teachings? Mark that the Lord has given you the Sabbath...Let no man leave his place on the seventh day" (Ex. 16:28-29). Three weeks later, the Israelites received the Ten Commandments, the fourth of which is devoted to the Sabbath. The version in Exodus 20:8-11 reads:

> "Remember the Sabbath day and keep it holy. Six days you shall labor and do all your work, but the seventh day is a Sabbath of the Lord your God: you shall not do any work, you, your son or daughter, your male or female slave, or your cattle, or the stranger who is within your settlements. For in six days the Lord made heaven and earth and sea, and all that is in them, and He rested on the seventh day; therefore the Lord blessed the Sabbath day and hallowed it."

The version in Deuteronomy 5:12-5 begins "Observe" instead of "Remember," and concludes: "Remember that you were a slave in the land of Egypt and the Lord your God freed you from there with a mighty hand and an outstretched arm; therefore the Lord your God has commanded you to observe the sabbath day." In both versions, the emphasis is on the Sabbath as a day of rest for the entire household, animals included.

The Sabbath is also a Covenant between Israel and God: "Keep My sabbaths, for this is a sign between Me and you throughout the generations, that you may know that I the Lord have consecrated you...a covenant for all time: it shall be a sign for all time betwen Me and the people of Israel. For in six days the Lord made the heaven and earth, and on the seventh day He ceased from work and was refreshed" (Ex. 31:13-17).

An instance of the death penalty being meted out for transgressing the Sabbath is found in Numbers (15:32-36). A sacrifice was the penalty for unwitting desecration of the day.

Little information is available about Sabbath observance during the First Temple period, although something may be gleaned from statements in AMOS and HOSEA. There is no prohibition against trading on that day in the Pentateuch, but Amos (8:5) implies that it existed in his time. Hosea (2:13) includes the Sabbath in the happy times which will cease. Isaiah (1:13) bears witness to the Sabbath being a national institution. Jeremiah (17:21-22) exhorts the people to observe the Sabbath as it was commanded, for the future of Jerusalem depended on it.

Nehemiah (chap. 10) tells of the covenant he made with the returned exiles, one point of which was not to buy items on the Sabbath. However, upon his return from Persia he saw that the covenant had not been adhered to and introduced changes to insure Sabbath observance (Neh. 13:15-22). Ezra and his disciples began to systematize rules and interpretation of the Bible and tradition to preserve and encourage Sabbath observance. The men of the GREAT ASSEMBLY and the SCRIBES ordained strict observance of the Sabbath. The residents of Jerusalem would not defend themselves on the Sabbath when besieged by Ptolemy I. Some 150 years later, however, during the Maccabean wars Mattathias the Hasmonean ruled that the laws of the Sabbath may be transgressed to save lives, therefore the Jews could defend themselves on the Sabbath (I Macc. 2:40-41).

After the SANHEDRIN began to function, Sabbath laws became more formalized in the HALAKHAH, and the rabbinic laws became the touchstone for all further development of these rules until modern times.

Work prohibited on the Sabbath. The basic feature of the Sabbath is to refrain from "work" (*melakhah*), following the injunction in Exodus 20:10, "The seventh day is a sabbath of the Lord your God: you shall not do any work."

The Pentateuch cites only a few specific types of prohibited work, including kindling a fire (Ex. 35:3), and plowing or harvesting (Ex. 34:21). Exodus 16:29 is the source for prohibiting carrying from domain to domain, and for the rabbinic ruling not to walk more than 2,000 cubits out of one's city or town.

The early rabbis determined that the primary categories of forbidden activities are those involved in the building of the Tabernacle, and they are listed under the name *avot melakhah* (lit. "fathers of work") in the Mishnah (*Shab.* 7). They are: (1) sowing, (2) plowing, (3) reaping, (4) binding sheaves, (5) threshing, (6) winnowing, (7) sorting, (8) grinding, (9) sifting, (10) kneading, (11) baking, (12) shearing sheep, (13) washing wool, (14) beating wool, (15) dyeing wool, (16) spinning, (17) weaving, (18) making two loops, (19) weaving two threads, (20) separating two threads, (21) tying [a permanent knot], (22) loosening [a permanent knot], (23) sewing two stitches, (24) tearing in order to sew two stitches, (25) hunting a deer, (26) slaughtering, (27) flaying, (28) salting, (29) curing a skin, (30) scraping the hide, (31) cutting, (32) writing two letters [of the alphabet], (33) erasing in order to write two letters, (34) building, (35) pulling down a structure, (36) extinguishing a fire, (37) lighting a fire, (38) striking with a hammer [i.e., putting the finishing touch on something), and (39) moving something, i.e., carrying, from one domain to another.

The definition of the categories was elaborated upon in the Talmud, and broadened by including within their scope other types of similar work, which are called *toledah* (pl. *toledot*, "derivatives"). For instance, a derivative of reaping would be to cut flowers or pick fruit. The derivative rulings were to be observed as strictly as the basic category.

In order to prevent from unwittingly transgressing any of the prohibited works, or doing something not in harmony with the spirit of the day, the rabbis enacted further rulings. Examples of these, which serve as a "fence around the law," are: *gezerot* ("decrees"; see GEZERAH). For instance, a tailor should not go out just before sunset with a needle stuck in his clothing, in case he forgets it there until after the onset of the Sabbath and "carries" it (*Shab.* 1.3); MUKTSEH, ("set apart"): certain things should not be touched even if they are not forbidden as such, since this might lead to a prohibited act; *nolad* ("born"), i.e., something which comes into existence during the Sabbath, such as a freshly laid egg, is not to be used; and *shevut*, i.e., an act not in the spirit of the day, for example climbing a tree (*Betsah* 5.2).

Rabbinical sources devote much space to discussing the prohibition on carrying objects. One is not to carry from the public domain to the private and vice versa, and from one point to another within the public domain. Since this may involve effort under certain circumstances, and in order to allow carrying in the areas initially prohibited they formulated an ERUV, i.e., three types of enactments, so that carrying may be permitted within a determined area.

Situations which supersede Sabbath prohibitions. Witnesses of the New MOON, who had to inform the SANHEDRIN or BET DIN, were allowed to do so on the Sabbath. CIRCUMCISIONS are performed on the Sabbath and all the required preparations are permitted; dangerous animals may be killed; one may fight in self-defense; anything necessary to save a life may be done, (see PIKU'AḤ NEFESH), as well as any action to assist a woman in childbirth. A basic rule established by R. AKIVA was that whatever can be done before the Sabbath may not be performed on the Sabbath (*Pes.* 66b).

Contemporary Jewish attitudes. All streams in Judaism have stressed the centrality of the Sabbath. For several decades the REFORM movement was quite distanced from traditional observances and practices, including attempts to transfer the Sabbath to Sunday (an idea which did not succeed). Today, in both CONSERVATIVE and Reform Judaism, the main weekly synagogal service is held on Friday night and/or Sabbath morning. Lighting candles in the home and reciting the KIDDUSH are widely-practiced private rituals. Abstention from commercial activities and gainful employment are encouraged, as is dedication of the Sabbath day to spiritual and contemplative endeavors. Although Reform Judaism does not require fulfillment of all the traditional commandments as defined in the *halakhah*, it stresses the fundamental goals of *kedushah* (holiness), *menuḥah* (rest), and *oneg* (joy) in celebration of the Sabbath day. The specific form of expression given to these values is a matter of contemporary individual interpretation, and not merely the adoption or even adaptation of historical expressions and forms. Conservative, Reform and Reconstructionist synagogues have experimented with and often adopted creative innovations in their Sabbath services.

The Sabbath day. The Sabbath is to be a day of joy, relaxation, spiritual harmony, and a change of pace from workdays. In the home, this is expressed by festive meals with choice dishes, some traditionally associated with the Sabbath (see FOOD, FESTIVAL AND SABBATH). Time is to be devoted to study, rest and conjugal relations are encouraged (the Book of Jubilees and the KARAITES forbid marital relations on the Sabbath). Hosting guests is traditional on the Sabbath.

The Sabbath begins on Friday at sunset. By late Friday afternoon all is in readiness to welcome the Sabbath. Approximately 20 minutes before sunset, CANDLES are lit with the blessing, "Blessed are You, O Lord our God, King

Blessing of the candles on the eve of the Sabbath. Drawing, Russia.

of the universe, Who has hallowed us by Your commandments, and commanded us to kindle the Sabbath light." In some non-traditional congregations with late Friday Evening Services, candles are lit at that time in the synagogue with the same blessing. According to the Mishnah, only one candle is required; however, it has long been customary for at least two to be used (in honor of the "Remember" of Ex. 20:8 and the "Observe" of Deut. 5:12; *OH* 263). In some families, one candle is lit for each member. Kabbalists lit seven candles, one to represent each day of the week. The mistress of the house has the obligation to light the candles. Should no woman be present, a man must do it.

The kindling of the Sabbath lights was considered so significant by the sages that they ruled that if a person in need financially has to choose between buying wine for KIDDUSH or candles for the Sabbath, the candles should take precedence.

Kabbalat Shabbat ("reception", i.e., "welcoming or accepting the Sabbath"). This is the service preceding Friday *Ma'ariv*, traditionally at twilight, generally not later than one half-hour after sunset. It is a late addition to the Friday EVENING SERVICE traced back to the 16th-century kabbalists in Safed who would go out to the fields on Friday afternoon to "greet the Sabbath Queen," the Sabbath also representing for them the Divine presence, the SHEKHINAH. This practice in turn harks back to the custom of the *amora*, R. Ḫanina, who having readied himself for the Sabbath, would stand at sunset and say, "Come let us go forth to welcome the Sabbath Queen," and R. Yannai, who would say, "Come, Bride! Come Bride!" (*Shab.* 119a). These sentiments inspired the Sabbath hymn LEKHAH DODI, written by Solomon ALKABETS, which is a central feature of the service.

In Sephardi rites Psalm 29 and *Lekhah Dodi* are recited. The Ashkenazi rite consists of Psalms 95-99, *Lekhah Dodi*, and Psalms 92-93. The Reform movement in Israel follows the general Ashkenazi form, to which is added the modern Hebrew poet Bialik's Sabbath eve poem, "The Sun from the Treetops." The US Reform prayer book offers a number of alternate services, which include abridged versions of the Psalms mentioned, and the entire *Lekhah Dodi*, to be read in Hebrew and in English. The RECONSTRUCTIONIST service opens with biblical passages (Deut. 5:12-15; Isa. 56:1-2, (58:12-14), proceeds to an invocation and meditation on the Sabbath, and then to the reading of one or more of the psalms mentioned and *Lekhah Dodi*. From *geonic* times it became customary to read BA-MEH MADLIKIN with the Evening Service, either prior to it (Sephardi custom) or after it (Ashkenazi custom).

Evening Service. A special AMIDAH is recited on Sabbath eve, followed by Genesis 2:1-4. The reader then blesses God, after which the paragraph *Magen avot* ("shield to our forefathers") is recited, and then the reader concludes the service.

The prayer book of the Reform movement (*Gates of Prayer*, New York, 1975) offers ten alternate Sabbath Evening Services, none of which includes *Magen avot*, but which do have in addition to abridged traditional texts, other readings, particularly in the English portions of the service.

When a Sabbath coincides with a festival, the festival *Amidah* is recited, with additions referring to the Sabbath. When praying at home these additional paragraphs are not recited.

In some congregations *Kiddush* is recited in the synagogue following the services.

Sabbath evening in the home. In the late afternoon, the table is prepared for the festive Sabbath meal. There is a long-standing custom in many homes for the father to bless the children when they return from the synagogue, with both hands placed on the head of the child, saying, to a boy, "May God make you like Ephraim and Manasseh," and for a girl, "May God make you like Sarah, Rebekah, Rachel, and Leah." The PRIESTLY BLESSING is also said. The Reform movement proposes that any individual blessing may be used.

All present then sing *Shalom Aleikhem*, a hymn which, until recently was part only of the Ashkenazi ritual; it welcomes the Sabbath angels who, according to the Talmud accompany the worshiper home from the synagogue (*Shab.* 119b). Printed versions of the hymn are known from the 17th century and its institution met with some opposition. ESHET ḪAYIL, the verses from Proverbs (31:10-31), singing the praise of the valorous woman, is then recited.

At the table, *Kiddush* is then recited, followed by the washing of the hands and the blessing over bread, over the Sabbath loaves, the *ḫallot* (see ḪALLAH). Two loaves are used, reminiscent of the double portion of manna gathered on Fridays in the desert.

The meal is followed with the singing of table hymns, ZEMIROT, and concluded with the GRACE AFTER MEALS, including an additional paragraph for the Sabbath.

Sabbath morning. The prayers consist of a MORNING SERVICE, a READING OF THE LAW portion (*sidrah*) of the week, a selection from the Prophets (the HAFTARAH), and the ADDITIONAL SERVICE.

In the MORNING SERVICE, the introductory prayers prior to the SHEMA differ in part from those of weekdays, and the *Amidah* is a special one. Seven persons are called to the Reading of the Law, and an eighth for the Prophetical reading. In Orthodox synagogues only men are called to the reading; in the other movements women also participate. The Reform movement's service is abridged and has no Additional Service. Six alternate services are given in the US Reform prayer book (*Gates of Prayer*, 1975, pp. 283-387).

In many congregations it is customary for the rabbi to deliver a sermon, since the Sabbath day is to be used as a day of learning. In some communities the morning services are followed by a congregational *Kiddush*.

On returning home, the Sabbath meal is eaten: the morning *Kiddush* and the blessing over the bread are recited. The pattern of the meal follows that of the evening.

Afternoon Service. The Afternoon Sabbath Service is unique in that the Torah is read prior to the *Amidah*. Three persons are called to the Torah, and the first portion of the Reading of the Law for the following week is chanted.

The rabbis determined that there should be three meals on the Sabbath day (*TB Shab.* 117b-118a). The third meal is known as the SE'UDAH SHELISHIT; it does not include *Kiddush* and should take place late enough to end just in time for the Evening Service. It is accompanied by the singing of ZEMIROT. Under kabbalistic and hasidic influence, the meal is often prolonged out of reluctance to part from the Sabbath, and is known as MELAVVEH MALKAH ("accompanying the [Sabbath] Queen").

End of the Sabbath. The Evening Service is held well after sunset, and is preceded by the recitation of Psalms 16, 144, and 67 by Sephardim and only the latter two by Ashkenazim.

The HAVDALAH service, the ritual ending the Sabbath, is usually recited at home, but in some communities also in the synagogue.

Ceremonial objects and other Sabbath appurtenances. Initially, simple oil lamps, probably made of clay, were used for the Sabbath light. In the Middle Ages, hanging lamps, with a variation of systems for controlling the flow of oil became quite common. It was also from the Middle Ages that candles were used, becoming prevalent in the 17th century. To make them distinctively Jewish, the candlesticks were inscribed with the blessing over the candles, or with "In honor of the Holy Sabbath," or designed with elements symbolizing some Jewish tradition. The cups for *Kiddush* were also artistically designed. Covers made of linen or other fine fabric were used for covering the Sabbath loaves (*hallah* covers). They were often embroidered with words such as "In honor of the Sabbath" or another relevant phrase, decorative floral patterns, or Sabbath themes. Bread knives intended for Sabbath use only, incised with relevant phrases, are also found in many Jewish homes.

In earlier times special appliances for keeping the food warm on the Sabbath were used. As food may not be warmed over an open fire on the Sabbath, in many Orthodox homes a piece of tin or copper is placed over the burning fire on a gas stove.

Innovations. In the US, in the 19th century Liberal rabbis instituted a Friday Evening Service after dinner, since worshipers could not reach the synagogue in time for the traditional hour. This began in 1866 in the Reform movement. Many Conservative and Reform congregations hold a late Friday Evening Service and this includes an address by the rabbi. In some synagogues candles are then lit. Some congregations use this service for creative innovations.

Orthodox synagogues have no instrumental accompaniment to the service, but other movements, particularly the Reform, do. Some congregations in America have instituted a *devar Torah*, a short speech delivered at the Saturday Morning Service, delivered each week by a different congregant.

THE SABBATH

More than the Jews have kept the Sabbath, the Sabbath has kept the Jews.

The Sabbath is the festival of all the earth, it is the birthday of the world.

If you observe the Sabbath, it is as though you have kept all the commandments.

For the duration of the Sabbath, God gives man an extra soul.

The Sabbath is a mirror of the World to Come.

SABBATHS, SPECIAL Sabbaths bearing particular designations on account of the Torah, *haftarah*, and liturgical readings allocated to them, or because of their position in the Jewish religious calendar. Three of them are linked to the beginning of a month: *Shabbat Mevarekhim*, the Sabbath preceding each New MOON (apart from the month of Tishri), on which the precise date(s) are announced and a special formula is recited blessing the month ahead; *Shabbat Mahar Hodesh*, a Sabbath occurring on the eve of the New Moon; and *Shabbat Rosh Hodesh*, a Sabbath coinciding with the start of a month.

Other special Sabbaths, following the order of the Hebrew year, are *Shabbat Shuvah*, which occurs during the TEN DAYS OF PENITENCE between Rosh ha-Shanah and the Day of Atonement; one *Shabbat Hol ha-Mo'ed*, which falls during the intermediate days of SUKKOT; *Shabbat Be'Reshit*, when the new Torah reading cycle begins; *Shabbat Hanukkah* (of which there may be two); *Shabbat Shirah*, the Sabbath on which the SONG OF MOSES is read; four Sabbaths that occur in the spring, *Shekalim, Zakhor, Parah*, and *ha-Hodesh* (see below for origin of names); *Shabbat ha-Gadol*, the Sabbath immediately before PASSOVER; another *Shabbat Hol ha-Mo'ed*, which falls during the intermediate days of Passover; and the Sabbaths preceding and immediately following TISHAH BE-AV (the Ninth of Av fast day) known as *Shabbat Hazon* and *Shabbat Nahamu* respectively.

Reform Judaism has retained only a few of the special Sabbaths: those connected with the New Moon, as well as *Shabbat Shuvah, Shabbat Zakhor*, and the two intermediate Sabbaths of Passover and Sukkot.

Shabbat Mevarekhim ("The Sabbath of Blessing"). Origin of name: The prayer for a good month recited after the Reading of the Law.
Liturgy: Ashkenazim recite *Yehi Ratson*, a formula based on the prayer of Rav (*Ber.* 16b), trusting that "it will be God's will to renew the coming month for good and for blessing." Sephardim begin with four (*Yehi Ratson*) expressions of

hope that "it may be God's will" to reestablish the Temple, rescue His people from all afflictions and disasters, maintain Israel's sages and their families, and grant a month of good tidings. Both rites then continue with *Mi she-Asah Nissim* ("He who performed miracles"), an announcement of the precise date (and sometimes time) of the New Moon, and a concluding benediction. These prayers are recited in Orthodox, Conservative, and (with some modification) in Reform congregations, but not by Reconstructionists. The Italian and Ḫabad (Ḫasidic) rites commence with *Mi she-Asah Nissim.*
Torah Reading: Weekly portion.
Haftarah: Weekly portion.

Shabbat Maḫar Ḫodesh
Origin of name: Falls on the eve of the New Moon (cf. I Sam. 20:18).
Torah Reading: Weekly portion.
Haftarah: I Sam. 20:18-42, describing the covenant between Jonathan and David made on the eve of the New Moon (*Rosh Ḫodesh*).

Shabbat Rosh Ḫodesh
Origin of name: Falls on the New Moon (*Rosh Ḫodesh*).
Liturgy: *Hallel* recited after Morning Service; *Attah Yatsarta* sequence replaces *Tikkanta Shabbat* in the Additional Service *Amidah.*
Torah Reading: Weekly portion; Num. 28:9-15 (*maftir*).
Haftarah: Isa. 66:1-24 (concludes with a repetition of verse 23).

Shabbat Shuvah ("The Sabbath of Return")
Origin of name: Opening word of the *haftarah*, "Return [*shuvah*], O Israel, to the Lord your God." However, as this Sabbath falls during the Ten Days of Penitence, it is also popularly known as *Shabbat Teshuvah* ("Sabbath of Repentance").
Torah Reading: Weekly portion.
Haftarah: Hos. 14:2-10; Joel 2:15-27 (Ashkenazim) or Hos. 14:2-10; Mic. 7:18-20 (Sephardim). Ashkenazim in the Diaspora read Mic. 7:18-20 before the Joel passage.
Customs: Community rabbi devotes a sermon to the theme of repentance.

Shabbat Ḫol ha-Mo'ed Sukkot
Origin of name: Occurs during the intermediate days (ḪOL HA-MO'ED) of the Sukkot festival.
Liturgy: *Hallel* and the Book of Ecclesiastes recited after the Morning Service; special religious poems (*piyyutim*) also recited in some Orthodox congregations.
Torah Reading: Ex. 33:12-34:26; selection from Num. 29 (*maftir*).
Haftarah: Ezek. 38:18-39:16.

Shabbat Be-Reshit ("The Sabbath of Genesis")
Origin of name: Opening words of the Book of Genesis, "In the beginning [*Be-Reshit*] God created...," included in the Reading of the Law for the Sabbath immediately following the Simḫat Torah festival. *Shabbat Be-Reshit* marks the recommencement of the annual Torah reading cycle which was completed on Simḫat Torah.
Torah Reading: Weekly portion (Gen. 1:1-6:8).
Haftarah: Weekly portion.
Customs: Among those called to the Torah on this Sabbath, the congregant chosen as *ḫatan Be-Reshit* ("bridegroom of Genesis") on Simḫat Torah receives an honored place (see BRIDEGROOMS OF THE LAW). He usually provides a *se'udah* or festive meal, sometimes in conjunction with the synagogue ladies' auxiliary, to which all worshipers are invited after the Sabbath Morning Service in traditional congregations.

Shabbat Ḫanukkah (two may occur in the event of the first and eighth days falling on the Sabbath)
Origin of name: Falls during the ḪANUKKAH festival.
Liturgy: *Hallel* recited after Morning Service.
Torah Reading: Weekly portion; Num. 7:1-17 (*maftir*). If Sabbath also falls on the eighth day of Ḫanukkah: Weekly portion (Gen. 41:1-44:17); Num. 7:54-8:4 (*maftir*). If *Shabbat Ḫanukkah* coincides with the New Moon, Num. 28:9-15 is read from a second scroll before *maftir*, for which a third scroll is used.
Haftarah: Zech. 2:14-4:7 (for second Sabbath, I Kings 7:40-50); if New Moon, Isa. 66:1-24 is substituted.

Shabbat Shirah ("The Sabbath of [the] Song")
Origin of name: Song of Moses and the Israelites at the Red Sea (Ex. 15:1-18), included in the prescribed Reading of the Law.
Liturgy: Special religious poems are read in some congregations.
Torah Reading: Weekly portion (*Be-Shallaḫ*; Ex. 13:17-17:16).
Haftarah: Judg. 4:4-5:31 (Ashkenazim); Judg. 5:1-31 (Sephardim).
Customs: *Shirat ha-Yam*, the "Song of the Sea," is read on the seventh day of Passover as well as on *Shabbat Shirah*. All traditional communities reserve a special form of cantillation for "the Song," and there is talmudic evidence (*Sot.* 30b) that at least three modes of rendition were known in ancient times: congregational responses of "I will sing to the Lord" after each verse chanted by the cantor, or the repetition of each verse after him, or the chanting of verses alternately by cantor and congregation. In present-day Ashkenazi synagogues, worshipers stand while *Shirat ha-Yam* is read, but this is not the general practice among Sephardim. On both *Shabbat Shirah* and the seventh day of Passover, Moroccan Jews recite a liturgical poem referring to the eight biblical songs sung by Moses, Miriam, Joshua, Deborah, and other Israelites. Western Sephardi congregations have a double reading of "the Song" to a traditional melody on *Shabbat Shirah*, the verses of Ex. 14:30-15:18 being chanted both prior to and as part of the Torah reading. Orthodox congregations of the United Synagogue in London have borrowed this Sephardi tune for their own cantillation of *Shirat ha-Yam*; elsewhere Ashkenazim use a traditional East Euro-

pean mode. In Israel, communal chanting of "the Song" forms part of the ceremonies held by the shores of the Mediterranean and Red Sea (at Eilat) on the seventh day of Passover.

The *Arba Parashiyyot* ("Four Portions") are read on four special Sabbaths occurring at intervals in the spring. Two occur before the festival of PURIM and two after it. On each of these Sabbaths, in addition to the weekly portion, *maftir* is read from a second scroll. Should one of these Sabbaths coincide with the New Moon, Num. 28:9-15 is read from a second scroll and *maftir* from a third.

Shabbat Shekalim ("The Sabbath of the Shekel Tax")
Origin of name: This Sabbath precedes or coincides with the New Moon, Rosh Ḫodesh Adar (Adar II in a leap year). The Mishnah (*Shek.* 1:1) states that "on the first day of Adar they gave warning of the shekel dues" which had to be paid before the first day of Nisan. The *maftir* chanted deals with the half-shekel levy on the public, which in Temple times went to the upkeep of the Sanctuary.
Liturgy: Special religious poems are read in some congregations.
Torah Reading: Weekly portion; Ex. 30:11-16 (*maftir*).
Haftarah: II Kings 12:1-17 (Ashkenazim); II Kings 11:17-12:17 (Sephardim).
Customs: In many Sephardi congregations the rabbi preaches in favor of contributions to religious institutions in the Land of Israel.

Shabbat Zakhor ("The Sabbath of Remembrance")
Origin of name: On this, the Sabbath before Purim, the additional (*maftir*) portion stresses the obligation to "remember [*zakhor*] what Amalek did to you" (i.e., by a cowardly attack on Israel's rearguard in the wilderness). Haman, traditionally a descendant of Amalek, also planned to destroy the Jews, hence the connection with Purim.
Liturgy: Special religious poems are read in some congregations.
Torah Reading: Weekly portion; Deut. 25:17-19 (*maftir*).
Haftarah: I Sam. 15:2-34 (Sephardim begin one verse earlier).

Shabbat Parah ("The Sabbath of the [Red] Heifer")
Origin of name: On this Sabbath, which precedes *Shabbat ha-Ḫodesh* (see below), the special *maftir* deals with the RED HEIFER whose ashes were used for ritual purification. In Temple times, as Passover drew near, anyone in a state of defilement had to be cleansed so that he could offer (and later eat) the paschal sacrifice.
Liturgy: Special religious poems are read in some congregations.
Torah Reading: Weekly portion; Num. 19:1-22 (*maftir*).
Haftarah: Ezek. 36:16-38 (Ashkenazim); Ezek. 36:16-36 (Sephardim).

Shabbat ha-Ḫodesh ("The Sabbath of the Month")
Origin of name: Opening words of the additional (*maftir*) reading, "This month [*Ha-ḫodesh ha-zeh*, i.e., Nisan] shall mark for you the beginning of the months." This Sabbath precedes or coincides with Rosh Ḫodesh Nisan, the month in which Passover occurs. Laws governing the festival are included in this section.
Liturgy: Special religious poems are read in some congregations.
Torah Reading: Weekly portion; Ex. 12:1-20 (*maftir*).
Haftarah: Ezek. 45:16-46:18 (Ashkenazim); Ezek. 45:18-46:15 (Sephardim).

Shabbat ha-Gadol ("The Great [or Awesome] Sabbath")
Origin of name: Uncertain, but may derive from the last verse of the *haftarah*, "Lo, I will send the prophet Elijah to you before the coming of the awesome [*gadol*], fearful day of the Lord" (Mal. 3:24). *Shabbat ha-Gadol* comes immediately before Passover, and the *haftarah* was selected not only because Elijah is seen as the Messiah's harbinger, but also because of the popular notion that the messianic Redemption will take place in the same month (Nisan) as the Exodus from Egypt (*RH* 11a).
Liturgy: Extensive religious poems are read in some congregations.
Torah Reading: Weekly portion.
Haftarah: Mal. 3:4-24 (concludes with a repetition of verse 23).
Customs: The community rabbi gives a lecture on Passover and preparations for the holiday; should this Sabbath fall on the eve of Passover, the talk is given a week earlier. A portion of the *Haggadah* is also read by worshipers in the afternoon. Among the Sephardim, in communities such as Salonika, pupils of the Jewish school (*talmud torah*) would receive new outfits on this day, which was therefore also known as *Ḫag ha-Halbashah* ("Festival of the New Clothes").

Shabbat Ḫol ha-Mo'ed Pesaḫ
Origin of name: Occurs during the intermediate days (*ḫol ha-mo'ed*) of Passover.
Liturgy: *Hallel* and Song of Songs are recited after the Morning Service; special religious poems are also read in some congregations.
Torah Reading: Ex. 33:12-34:26; Num. 28:19-25 (*maftir*).
Haftarah: Ezek. 37:1-14 (Ezek. 36:37-37:14 in a few congregations).

Shabbat Ḫazon ("The Sabbath of the Prophecy")
Origin of name: The *haftarah* chosen for this Sabbath, preceding the Ninth of Av fast day, speaks of Isaiah's prophecy or "vision" (*ḫazon*) concerning the punishments which will be meted out to a sinful Israel. In geonic times, this Sabbath was known as *Shabbat Ékhah* ("The Sabbath of Lamentation"), a term still used by Yemenite and other Eastern communities.
Torah Reading: Weekly portion (Deut. 1:1-3:22).
Haftarah: Isa. 1:1-27.
Customs: The rabbi or some other learned Jew usually chants

the *haftarah* (much of it to the tune of the Lamentations scroll). Congregants attend synagogue in plainer clothes than on a regular Sabbath. The Ark may be covered by a weekday curtain or even by a black one. Among Ashkenazim, on Friday night, LEKHAH DODI is sung to the tune of the ELI TSIYYON elegy. Social visits are avoided.

Shabbat Naḇamu ("The Sabbath of Comfort")
Origin of name: Opening words of the *haftarah* read on this, the first Sabbath after Tishah be-Av, "Comfort [*naḇamu*], O comfort my people," bringing consolation and the promise of Israel's final Redemption.
Torah Reading: Weekly portion (Deut. 3:23-7:11), which includes the Ten Commandments and the first paragraph of the *Shema*.
Haftarah: Isa. 40:1-26.

SABBATICAL YEAR (*shemittah*). Seventh year of rest for the land. The Bible proclaims every seventh year "a sabbath of the Lord" (Lev. 25:1-7, 18-22) during which the soil of the land of Israel must rest and lie fallow. The farmer is forbidden to plant, sow or plow, but has to rely on the bounty of God to provide him with a threefold harvest in the sixth year to tide him over until the harvest of the eighth year becomes available (Lev. 25:22). The harvest of the seventh year is to be regarded as the common property of all — rich and poor, stranger and slave. When all had had their fill, the remainder was to be left for the domestic and wild animals (Lev. 25:4). All debts were canceled in that year, the creditor being admonished not to dun the debtor or harbor the unworthy thought of refraining from lending him money because the sabbatical year was pending (Deut. 15:1-11). As explained by Rabbi A.I. KOOK, like the Sabbath itself, the Sabbatical year represents a respite from mundane toil, from getting and spending with everything tainted with business, when both land and people can spiritually recuperate — "a foretaste of a utopian world where inequalities are erased" (*Shabbat ha-Aretz*, p. 8).

The Sabbatical year was originally part of a 50-year cycle (Lev. 25:8-17). The climax of this sevenfold seven cycle was the 50th or JUBILEE year when all land was returned to its ancestral owners and Hebrew slaves who had insisted on remaining in service after the biblical six-year maximum, were released (Ex. 21:1-6). The Bible ordained exile as the punishment for neglect of the Sabbatical year; indeed, the Babylonian EXILE was described as extending the "threescore and ten years until the land had paid back its Sabbaths" (II Chr. 36:21). The Jubilee years, however, lapsed with the return of the exiles from Babylonia and the rebuilding of the Temple, as it was regarded as binding only as long as the majority of the Jewish people were settled in Erets Israel and the tribal allocation of land was still in force. Nevertheless, the returning exiles solemnly undertook to "forgo the seventh year crop and the exaction of every debt" (Neh. 10:32). The Mishnah SHEVI'IT reflects the attempts to institutionalize the observance of the Sabbatical year and apply it meticulously to the agriculture of the time. Alexander the Great and subsequent benevolent rulers are recorded as having waived the royal tax during that year. HILLEL circumvented the problem of the reluctance to lend money as the Sabbatical year approached by instituting the PROSBUL. After the destruction of the Temple, rabbinic authorities waived the Sabbatical year observance when dire punishment awaited those who would refuse to pay the tax imposed by hostile rulers during these years.

It was only with modern Zionist agricultural settlement beginning in the late 19th century that the practical observance of the Sabbatical year once again became relevant. The religious Zionist Mizrachi movement committed itself to the fictional *hetter* sale to a non-Jew during the Sabbatical year to allow cultivation to continue "so as not to endanger the whole Zionist enterprise." However, the *hetter* was bitterly opposed by other rabbinical authorities, especially among the non-Zionists. In the State of Israel, the Ministry of Religious Affairs has been invested with the authority to execute the ritual sale of all state lands to non-Jews during these years. Modern agricultural techniques such as hydroponics, pre-sabbatical sowing, and multiple-harvesting varieties of crops have been resorted to, in order to avoid violating the basic biblical prohibitions. Official planting ceremonies do not take place during the Sabbatical year (the last Sabbatical year was in 1986-87). Harvesting and marketing operations of seventh-year produce is done in the name of the Israeli ecclesiastical court and the religious kibbutz movement allocates a percentage of its Sabbatical year produce to welfare causes in order to fulfill the spirit of the biblical ordinance.

1986-7, 1993-4 and 2000-1 are Sabbatical years, running from one ROSH HA-SHANAH to the next.

SACRIFICES AND OFFERINGS The first sacrifices mentioned in the Bible were brought by CAIN AND ABEL. Genesis also records that NOAH and all the PATRIARCHS offered sacrifices, while the EXODUS from Egypt was marked by the first paschal sacrifice.

According to the traditional sources, whenever there was a centralized location for worship, sacrifices could only be brought to that place. Thus, during the existence of the SANCTUARY in the desert, no sacrifices were allowed elsewhere. After the Israelites entered Canaan, the permanent Sanctuary was established in Shiloh. During the brief periods when this was not in existence, sacrifices were offered in various *bamot*, or "High Places." Finally, when Solomon's TEMPLE was completed, the recourse to High Places was permanently forbidden (*Zev.* 18b,112b).

Various explanations have been given for the bringing of sacrifices. The Hebrew for sacrifice, *korban*, implies "bringing closer," and the sacrifices have been seen both as drawing man closer to God and God closer to man. MAIMONIDES, in his *Guide for the Perplexed*, sees the sacrifices as a way of weaning the Israelites away from the common practice of sacrifices prevalent in the region, by having them brought to God Himself rather than used for idolatrous purposes. (The sacrifice of Isaac [AKEDAH] may even be meant to denounce the evidently common practice at the time of sacrificing human beings.) Scholars are divided as to whether this was indeed Maimonides' position, or whether it was merely his answer to the rationalists to whom his volume was addressed. Evidence of a contrary view by Maimonides may be seen in his *Mishneh Torah*, where he dwells at great length on the various laws governing sacrifices, after stating in his introduction to this work that he had omitted all laws which were not applicable for all time. This seems to indicate that he envisioned the restoration of the sacrificial cult in the Temple.

NAḤMANIDES and many other medieval rabbis disagree with the view expressed by Maimonides in the *Guide*. They see the sacrifices as having great spiritual and symbolic value and an intrinsic importance in themselves, and, as such, applicable wherever the circumstances permit. The guilt-offering, for example, is regarded as serving to impress upon the person bringing the sacrifice the enormity of his sin, to the extent that whatever happened to the animal that was sacrificed should by rights have happened to the sinner.

Initially, meat was only eaten following a sacrifice. As the meat of certain sacrifices was eaten by the people bringing the sacrifices and by their families and friends, all of whom had to be ritually pure, some see these types of sacrifices as being primarily directed at elevating the mundane action of eating meat into the worship of God. In this, the act parallels many others in Judaism which serve that end.

Some have claimed that many of the prophets rejected the sacrificial cult, and wished to replace it with a superior moral code of ethical values. Others have argued that a careful reading of the verses indicates that the prophets were not rejecting the practice itself, but the facile manner in which sacrifices were brought, as if they themselves were sufficient atonement for sins. To the prophets, a sacrifice brought without the proper intent of repentance was an abomination.

The sacrifices may be divided into three broad categories: sacrifices brought as a sign of submission to God; those brought as thanks; and those brought as part of the repentance for a sin committed inadvertently, through negligence. A guilt-offering may not be brought for a sin committed deliberately, for in such a case the offering does not serve to atone for the sin. This proviso effectively blocks out the possibility of sinning with the intention of later bringing a sacrifice to atone for the sin. Sacrifices may also be divided into those which are obligatory, such as the daily morning and afternoon sacrifices, and those which are voluntary, offered by individuals for various personal reasons.

In a way paralleling the sacrifices of Cain and Abel, the sacrifices and offerings, as delineated by the Bible, consist of either animals or grain. Certain basic guidelines applied to both types (as offered in the Second TEMPLE). All sacrifices and offerings had to be brought in the Temple, although each was assigned a specific place within it. There were four types of animal sacrifices, with subcategories within each. These were: the *olah*, "burnt offering"; the *shelamim*, "peace" or "well-being" offering; the *ḥatat*, "sin offering"; and the *asham*, "guilt offering."

Animal sacrifices required the animal to be free of any physical blemish; sacrifices of fowl, however, lacked this restriction. Animals which might be used included bulls, cows, sheep, and goats, while only turtle doves and pigeons could be used for an offering of fowl. Certain sacrifices required animals of a particular sex, and there were also age limitations on the animals brought. Animals were slaughtered with a slaughtering knife, while birds were killed by a priest pinching their necks with a specially sharpened thumb nail. Except for burnt offerings or peace offerings brought on behalf of the entire nation, all animal sacrifices required the laying of two hands with all one's might on the animal's head before the slaughtering. Some view this as a means for the bearer to identify the sacrifice with himself. In all cases, the blood of the slaughtered animal or fowl was either sprinkled or poured according to a specified ritual. All parts of any animal or fowl offered as a sacrifice had to be disposed of within a certain limited number of days. For these purposes, unlike the general law in Judaism that a new day begins at night, the day would begin at dawn. Thus, a sacrifice which had to be disposed of within one day would have to be eaten before dawn of the day following the sacrifice.

In the case of sacrifices brought by individuals, the person sacrificing the animal could perform all the actions up to the sprinkling or pouring of the blood by himself, including laying his hands on the animal, lifting it, slaughtering it, flaying the hide, dissecting the carcass, and washing the parts. All subsequent actions, including sprinkling or pouring the blood at or near the altar, arranging the wood on the altar, and burning those parts that were to be burned, were carried out by a priest. The priest who sprinkled or poured the blood was entitled to any priestly portion of a particular sacrifice.

Olah, "burnt offering." No less than 14 types of sacrifices were included in this category, including the daily morning and afternoon (*tamid*) sacrifices; the ram brought by the High Priest on the DAY OF ATONEMENT; the burnt offering of a woman who had given birth, of a *zav* or *zavah* (people who had suffered an abnormal bloody genital emission), of a NAZIRITE who was at the end of his term or whose term was interrupted by his having become ritually impure through contact with the dead, of the *metsora* (a type of skin disease, possibly leprosy), of a convert, and a freewill burnt offering by any individual.

Only male animals (bulls, rams, or he-goats) could be used for the burnt offering, but a fowl might be of either sex. In the case of an animal, the hide belonged to the priest, while the rest of the animal was burned on the altar; in the case of a fowl, the entire fowl was burned.

Shelamim "peace offering." The animal used for a peace offering could be of either sex. The *imurim* (certain portions of the innards, including *helev* (fat), the kidneys, and the lobe of the liver) were burned on the altar, while the meat of the animal was eaten. There were four kinds of peace offerings: a) *shalmei tsibbur*, the "community peace offering," brought on SHAVU'OT; b) *shalmei hagigah* and *shalmei simhah*, the "festival peace offering" and the "festive peace offering," brought by an individual, the former as a way of celebrating a festival, the latter as a way of expressing thanks to God; c) *shelamim* of a *neder* or *nedavah*, a peace offering which had been pledged, either in the form of "I will bring a sacrifice" or in the form of "I will bring this particular animal or fowl as a sacrifice"; d) *shalmei nazir*, the peace offering brought by a Nazirite at the end of his term. In the first case above, the priests ate the meat, while in the other three the person bringing the sacrifice ate it with his family and friends. Similarly, in the first case the hide belonged to the priests, while in the others it belonged to the person bringing the sacrifice.

Hatat, "sin offering." This sacrifice was brought when a person or an entire community, through negligence, violated a commandment, where the punishment for the deliberate violation would have been KARET (being "cut off" from the community). Depending on the specific *hatat* involved, a bull aged two or three years, a year-old he-goat, a year-old female sheep or goat, or a fowl, was offered. Where the *hatat* was to atone for a sin committed by the HIGH PRIEST or by the entire community, the animal or fowl was burned outside the Temple. In all other cases, the PRIESTS ate the meat.

Asham, "guilt offering." There were six types of guilt offerings. a) *Asham gezélot*, the "guilt offering of theft." If a person denied falsely under oath that he owed another person money, he had to return the amount owed plus an additional fifth, and bring this sacrifice, consisting of a two-year old ram. b) *Asham me'ilot*, "the guilt offering of desecration." If a person inadvertently benefited illegally from any of the possessions of the Temple, he had to repay the amount involved to the Temple plus an additional fifth, and to bring this sacrifice, a two-year old ram. c) *Asham shifhah harufah*. If a man had sexual relations with a woman who was half a slave and half free (e.g., if she had been owned by two partners and one had given her her freedom), and who was betrothed to a Jewish slave, he had to bring a two-year old ram. d) *Asham nazir*, the guilt offering brought by a Nazirite who had became ritually impure during the period his vows were in effect by contact with the dead, consisting of a one-year old sheep. e) *Asham metsora*, the guilt offering of the *metsora*, brought on the day that he became ritually pure. A rich person had to bring a one-year old sheep, while a poor person had to bring a turtle-dove or pigeon. f) *Asham talu'i*, "the doubtful guilt offering," brought by a person who was not sure if he had transgressed a prohibition in a case in which, had he indeed done so and had certain other conditions been present, he would have had to bring a *hatat*. In such a case, the person had to bring a two-year old sheep. In each of the above cases, the animal had to be male, and its flesh was given to the priests to eat.

Offerings. This category includes all the different offerings consisting of grain. Six of the nine were known as various types of *minhah*, or "grain offering". Of the nine grain offerings, all except two were made with fine wheat flour. Some of these offerings had to be MATSAH, or unleavened, while others were leavened. With certain exceptions, all were composed of grain, oil, and frankincense. All meal-offerings, like other sacrifices, were seasoned with salt (Lev. 2:13). These offerings included: a) *minhat ha-omer*, "the OMER grain offering," consisting of the barley harvested on the second day of PASSOVER, which was eaten by priests in the Temple courtyard; b) *shetei ha-lehem*, "the two loaves" brought on Shavu'ot, without either oil or frankincense; c) *lehem ha-panim*, "the SHOWBREAD," 12 loaves, which did not contain oil, that were placed on a special table in the Temple each Friday, where they would remain until the following week; d) *minhat havitin*, a type of *matsah* brought daily by the High Priest; e) *minhat hinnukh*, "the grain offering of dedication," brought by a priest on the first day he entered the Temple service; f) *minhat nesakhim*, "the libation grain offering," which might be brought by an individual or on behalf of the entire community, and which did not include frankincense; g) *minhat* SOTAH, "the grain offering of the [suspected] unfaithful wife" which consisted of barley without either oil or frankincense; h) *minhat hotei*, "the grain offering of the sinner," brought without oil or frankincense; and i) *minhat nedavah*, "the freewill grain offering," brought by an individual.

The sacrifice of animals was always accompanied by a libation (*nesekh*) of wine and a meal-offering. The Bible specifies the quantity of wine and of grain for each species of animal sacrificed. The meal-offering could consist of flour by itself, of thin wafers baked in an oven or prepared in either a flat or a deep pot. The latter three meal offerings were made of flour and oil, and, in most cases, frankincense. The wine was poured at the corner of the altar, while a handful of the meal-offering was placed on the altar and the rest was consumed by the priests. Although it was permitted to bring a meal-offering by itself, there was no such provision for an independent offering of wine.

There was also a twice-daily INCENSE offering, burned on a special incense altar in the Temple.

Each special day, such as the Sabbath and the days of each of the festivals, had its own list of sacrifices as prescribed in the Torah. A detailed list of these is to be found in Numbers 28-29.

A different form of sacrifice was that of the FIRST FRUITS, consisting of the SEVEN SPECIES for which Erets Israel is praised: wheat, barley, grapes, pomegranates, figs, olives, and dates.

The species were carried in a joyful procession to Jerusalem, especially for Shavu'ot, but could be brought until Ḥanukkah. Each person who brought his first fruits to the Temple had to make a declaration before a priest, the text of which is recorded in Deuteronomy 26:5-10. Of the six Orders of the Talmud, one entire Order, KODASHIM, is devoted almost entirely to the sacrificial system.

Although PRAYER had become part of the ritual even during the Temple period, once the Temple was destroyed it replaced the different sacrifices, in accordance with the interpretation of Hosea 14:3: "Instead of bulls we will pay [the offering] of our lips." To this end, the preliminary Morning Service includes an account of the daily sacrifices which were offered in the Temple. On Sabbaths, festivals, and on the New Moon, the ADDITIONAL SERVICE (*Musaf*), is said, which describes the additional sacrifice (*musaf*) brought on each of these days.

Orthodoxy regards the replacement of the sacrifices by prayer as nonpermanent, and the AMIDAH prayer contains references to the eventual restoration of sacrifices in the Temple. The Reform movement, on the other hand, has removed all such references from its prayers, as it regards sacrifice as no longer relevant to Judaism.

The standard Conservative Prayer Books, including the most recent editions of the High Festivals and the Sabbath and Daily Prayer Books, put all references to animal sacrifices in the historic past and have omitted all expressions of anticipation for the restoration of the Temple and animal sacrifices. This is in accordance with mainstream Conservative theology which does not accept the notion of a Third Temple and sacrifices as applicable to modern Judaism.

SACRILEGE See BLASPHEMY; DESECRATION; KIDDUSH HA-SHEM AND ḤILLUL HA-SHEM

SADDUCEES A political and religious grouping in Erets Israel during the latter half of the Second Temple era (from the second century BCE to the first century CE). It is generally assumed that the title of *Tsadokim* in Hebrew, *Saddukaioi* in Greek, indicates a connection with the line of the High Priest, Zadok (from the time of King David). As in the case of the PHARISEES, their main ideological opponents, the actual origins of the Sadducees remain unclear.

The Sadducees may well have had their embryonic beginnings already in the pre-Hellenistic era or, more probably, in the years immediately following Alexander the Great's conquests in the region during the fourth century BCE. Sadducean history, however, is spotty and the party apparently could not boast as continuous a history as the Pharisees, at any rate not until the Hasmonean house emerged on the scene.

The ultimate split between the two political-theocratic factions and their open contest for national primacy occurred during John Hyrcanus' reign (135-104 BCE). The Sadducees achieved and maintained supremacy until the reign of Salome Alexandra (76-67 BCE).

The Sadducees are generally and correctly perceived as members and adherents of the aristocratic laity and as being closely involved in the affairs of state of the Jewish people in its homeland. They participated in the highest level of the people's spiritual rule — the HIGH PRIESTHOOD — and consequently, to some extent, in its religious legislative bodies. According to Josephus, the Sadducees, in contrast to the Pharisees, did not believe in the immortality of the SOUL ("they hold that the soul perishes along with the body") and ultimate RESURRECTION of the dead, a cornerstone of Pharisaic belief. The Sadducees accepted the WRITTEN LAW but not the ORAL LAW, that is, the vast body of rabbinic legislation and exegesis.

The Sadducees maintained that fate has no place in the general scheme of things and that man is completely free in his choice of good or evil. Nor was there any place in the overall Sadducean scheme for angelic or demonic spirits. On the subject of everyday social contacts, their interpretation and application of Jewish law was, as a rule, rigid and severe.

However, ancient rabbinical sources would refute Josephus' assertion about the Sadducees' refusal to accept the Oral Law. It seems more accurate to say that they refused to countenance Pharisaic Oral Law as binding on themselves, but there were Sadducee decrees (*gezerot*) which comprised an Oral Law different from the Pharasaic version.

The Sadducee link with the Jerusalem Temple and, in particular, with its High Priesthood, was so strong that the rabbinical sages of the period felt they had to keep an eye on the Sadducee High Priests lest they engage in Temple practices frowned upon or rejected outright by the Pharisee leadership. A method of constant surveillance employed in later years was to have a Pharisaic *segan* or High Priest's deputy at the side of the Sadducee High Priest at all times.

Josephus' stated that the Sadducees were rejected by most Jews and that it was the Pharisees whom they loved and turned to for guidance. However, the Sadducees were not an assimilationist group. They were known for their conservative, traditional character and for their desire to adhere as rigorously as possible to the laws and practices of their forefathers. Their severity in meting out punishment for offenses against biblical law was axiomatic. Although ideologically and in actual practice associated with the Jewish aristocracies of the different periods, they were very much a part of the general political scene of the times and they were thoroughly Jewish, certainly as far as their links with the Temple and Jewish traditions were concerned.

However, they never gained a real foothold among the people. As proponents of the Temple aristocracy and its High Priesthood, they were a force to be reckoned with but they were identified too closely with the aristocracy and sought to ingratiate themselves with the Roman rulers by keeping the populace quiescent. As they were bound up with the Temple cult, the destruction of the Temple brought their demise, leaving the field entirely open for their longtime opponents, the Pharisees.

SAGES Title given primarily to the Bible scholars of Erets Israel of the pre-MISHNAH, Mishnah, and TALMUD periods. They are often referred to in Hebrew as *Ḥazal*, acronym for the phrase, *Ḥakhaménu Zikhronam li-Verakhah* ("Our sages of blessed memory"). The term encompasses the scholars of both Erets Israel and Babylonia. The sages provided the spiritual leadership of the Jewish people during a crucial period when the nation shifted from a temporal power base to a spiritual focus, following the loss of sovereignty and the destruction of the Temple.

Although little has been preserved of the discussions of the pre-Mishnah period SAGES of the last two centuries BCE, some appear in various later collections, such as the Mishnah. The sages of the Mishnah period (to 200 CE), who taught in Erets Israel, are known as *tannaim* (see TANNA), while those of the Talmud period (to 500 CE) are known as *amoraim* (see AMORA). The amoraim of Erets Israel were responsible for the Jerusalem Talmud (c. 400 CE) and those of Babylonia for the Babylonian Talmud (c. 500 CE), although there was a great deal of cross-pollination of ideas and rulings, and each Talmud quotes sages from both countries. Whereas other groups (such as the SADDUCEES) limited themselves to the WRITTEN LAW, the sages (who belonged to the tradition of the PHARISEES) believed in the ORAL LAW which, by tradition, had been given at Sinai together with the Written Law. Therefore, they were willing, for example, to accept an entire corpus of laws relating to work on the Sabbath from a mere allusion in a verse, which, as they themselves admitted, amounted to "suspending a mountain on a hair" (*Ḥag.* 1.8). The formulations of the sages became the mainstay of HALAKHAH.

SALANTER (Lipkin), ISRAEL BEN ZE'EV WOLF (1810-1883), Lithuanian rabbi and founder of the MUSAR MOVEMENT. Born in Zhagare, he attended the *yeshivah* (rabbinical academy) of Tsevi Hirsch Broida in Salant. He was greatly influenced by R. Zundel of Salant whom he described as the light that he followed all his days. At the age of 30, he became head of a *yeshivah* in Vilna, but soon resigned that position to set up his own *yeshivah*. He also formed "houses" for the study of *musar*, the religious ethics of Judaism, in which he delivered his ethical discourses. This type of discourse became the norm of the Salant school.

In 1848 Salanter declined to accept a position in the *yeshivah* which the Russian government had set up in Vilna and, to avoid the pressure brought upon him, went to Kovno where he established a *musar yeshivah*. In 1857 he went to Germany where he published the Hebrew periodical *Tevunah* to which outstanding rabbinic scholars contributed. Towards the end of his life he spent two years in Paris to strengthen Jewish institutions and then moved to Koenigsberg, where he died.

The leadership which Salanter gave in Vilna during the cholera epidemic of 1848 made a deep impression and left its mark upon contemporary and later literature. Fearing that fasting would weaken the resistance of the Jewish population, he ordered the congregation to eat and drink on the Day of Atonement. He set a personal example by ascending the reader's desk during a solemn moment of the morning service, reciting the benediction and partaking of cake and wine.

Salanter, a man of saintly character and altruism, was also active in political and communal affairs. Of wide scholarly interests, he suggested that the Talmud be translated into European languages and taught in universities. His system of *musar*, set forth in his letters, was followed by all the Lithuanian *yeshivot*. Some of his discourses and letters were collected and published by his pupils.

SALT Condiment used in biblical times for a variety of purposes: in the sacrificial ritual, in medicine, and as a preservative for food. Every sacrifice was to be sprinkled with salt (Lev. 2:13) and the Temple housed a salt chamber. Newborn infants were rubbed with salt, apparently as a health measure (Ezek. 16:4). Because of its preservative quality, an everlasting covenant is described as a "covenant of salt" (Num. 18:19). When the Prophet Abijah wishes to describe God's promise that the House of David will rule over Israel forever, he calls the promise "a covenant of salt" (II Chr. 13:4,5).

The lasting effect of salt probably accounts for its use by the prophet ELISHA as a means for purifying the waters of Jericho when he was told by the local townspeople that the "water was bad and caused miscarriage" (II Kings 2:19-22). On the other hand, salt was strewn on the land of a town by a conqueror in order to render it permanently barren (Judg. 9:45).

Among the DIETARY LAWS ordained by the *Halakhah* is the procedure for draining blood from meat before it is cooked by salting it thoroughly. The *halakhah* requires that a little salt be sprinkled on the bread eaten at the beginning of a meal before a benediction is recited over it. This is popularly explained as a symbolic act since a man's table in post-Temple times serves as a substitute for the altar where sacrifices were salted.

SAMARITANS Descendants of the people formed by the mixture of Israelites remaining in the northern kingdom of Israel with other peoples settled there by the Assyrian conquerors (after 722 BCE). The capital of the region was Samaria. The Samaritans observe the Pentateuch but reject the other books of the Bible and the entire ORAL LAW; they do have their own oral traditions regarding various biblical practices.

The Talmud refers to the Samaritans as *Kutim* (Cutheans)

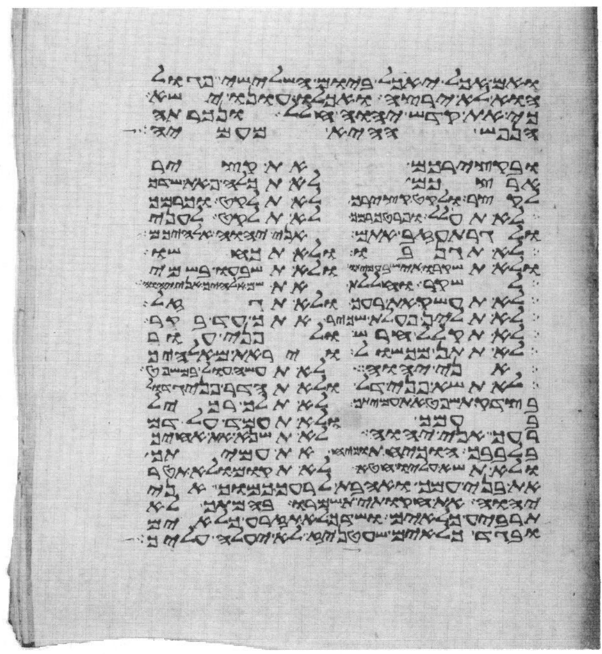

Page of a Samaritan Pentateuch, written in Hebrew, in Samaritan script. 13th century.

and regards them as descended from various non-Jewish tribes which converted to Judaism. The Samaritans, on the other hand, refer to themselves as either *Bené Yisrael* (the "Israelites") or as the *Shomerim* ("those who observe [the Law]"). One of the minor tractates of the Talmud, *Kutim*, is devoted to the laws governing the relationships between Samaritans and Jews. The first statement in that tractate notes that the Samaritans in some ways resemble Jews and in others, non-Jews, yet stresses that in most ways they resemble Jews. As a generalization, the Talmud states that in regard to those laws which the Samaritans do observe, they are more scrupulous than the Jews (*Ḥul.* 4a).

The Samaritan Pentateuch, written in a variation of the old Phoenician ALPHABET, differs in numerous places from the Jewish text, most notably in its references, not found in the Jewish Pentateuch, to Mount GERIZIM, the holy mountain of the Samaritan faith. Unlike Judaism, which regards "I am the Lord your God..." (Ex. 20:2) as the first of the Ten Commandments, the Samaritan Ten Commandments begin with the next verse ("You shall have no other gods before Me") and the tenth commandment, known as "Mount Gerizim," declares this mountain as the site where an altar is to be built to God.

Whereas the Jewish Pentateuch stresses the accuracy of the written text, the Samaritan stress is on the accuracy of the text as it is to be read and different Samaritan scrolls have variant spellings of the same text.

The Samaritan interpretation of the laws of the Sabbath precludes having any warm food on the Sabbath day itself and forbids leaving one's immediate vicinity throughout the Sabbath.

The Samaritan CALENDAR, while observing the seven festival days decreed within the Pentateuch, uses its own method for determining when to add leap months; it is thus possible for the Samaritan and Jewish holidays to be a month apart. The observances of the different festival days differ markedly from the Jewish observances and to this day the Samaritans gather at Mount Gerizim before each PASSOVER to bring the paschal sacrifice. Unlike the Jewish calendar, which has the festival of Shavu'ot on the 50th day after the second day of Passover, the Samaritan calendar always begins the count of the 49 days of the OMER on the first Sunday following the first day of Passover, so that Shavu'ot always occurs on a Sunday. Fasting throughout the Day of Atonement applies to everyone aged one year and up. The FOUR SPECIES mentioned in the Pentateuch in regard to Sukkot are interwoven into the making and decoration of the SUKKAH that is built for the festival. Due to harassment by their Muslim neighbors, the Samaritans began hundreds of years ago to build their *sukkot* in their homes and this has since become their established custom.

The Samaritans assemble on Mount Gerizim near Shechem, for the sacrifice of the paschal lamb.

An important part is played by the high priest, but since the death of the last priest in direct descent, the high priesthood is now occupied by a member of the tribe of Levi, who is selected on the basis of seniority.

The word "Samaritan" appears only once in the Bible (II Kings 17:29), referring to the newly-settled colonists in the north who persisted in their pagan ways. When the exiles returned from Babylonia, they rejected the Samaritan claim to be Jews and refused to let them assist in the reconstruction of Jerusalem and the Temple. They were barred from offering sacrifices at the Jerusalem Temple or to intermarry with Jews. The Samaritans consequently adopted a hostile attitude, which was directed against NEHEMIAH. They then built their own temple on Mount Gerizim. They suffered severely when Shechem was destroyed by Alexander the Great and their temple was destroyed twice, the first time by John Hyrcanus in 128 BCE and the second, in 486 CE. The Byzantine Christian emperor, Justinian, ended their autonomy and as they, unlike the Jews, were not considered the "people of the book" they suffered also under Islam. Samaritans lived in other countries and there is evidence of a Samaritan synagogue in Rome which was destroyed in the sixth century CE and of Samaritans in Babylonia and elsewhere. Eventually, they dwindled to a small group concentrated in Erets Israel. Today, the mother community is located in and around Shechem with a daughter community in Ḫolon, near Tel-Aviv; together they number about 500.

SAMBATYON Name given to a legendary river beyond which the Ten Lost TRIBES of Israel were thought to remain in exile. This river's miraculous nature, hinted at by the Talmud (*Sanh.* 65b), is elaborated in the Midrash: it renders crossing impossible by throwing up stones during the week and only comes to rest on the Sabbath (*Gen. R.* 11.6). Moreover, while the tribes of Judah and Benjamin (i.e., the Jews) are dispersed throughout the world, the Ten Lost Tribes are confined to some area "beyond the Sambatyon" (*Gen. R.* 73:5; TJ *Sanh.* 10.6, 29c). Details of the legend were current in Second Temple times, as Pliny the Elder included them in his *Natural History* (77 CE). R. AKIVA took the existence of the Sambatyon to prove the Divine nature of the Sabbath (*Sanh.* 35b). For most Jews of the Middle Ages, notably Rashi (commenting on *Sanh.* 65b) and Naḫmanides (on Deut. 32:26), the Sambatyon was not a legend but a geographical fact. This belief had been reinforced by Eldad ha-Dani, a mysterious ninth-century traveler, who told the Jews of Kairouan in North Africa that while on weekdays the river (located in Ethiopia) hurled such masses of rock and grit into the air that it could flatten a mountain and be heard a day's journey away, on the Sabbath it rested within a mist protecting the exiles from enemies on the opposite side. Eldad's widely publicized account revived interest in the old tradition, inspiring the Christian tale of Prester John and attempts by Abraham ABULAFIA and others to locate the fabulous Sambatyon. An upsurge of Jewish messianism in the 17th century accounts for the renewed exploitation of the theme by Manasseh Ben Israel (*Spes Israelis*, 1650) and by Shabbateans associated with Nathan of Gaza. (see SHABBETAI TSEVI).

SAMUEL (11th century BCE). Prophet and last of the biblical judges, who led Israel during a transitional period, between the time of the judges and the beginning of the monarchy.

Samuel's father, Elkanah, came from a noble family in Mount Ephraim. His mother, Hannah, was barren for many years. She prayed in the Sanctuary in Shiloh, in the presence of Eli the priest, asking for a son and vowing to consecrate him as a NAZIRITE to the Sanctuary for his entire life. After Samuel had been weaned, he was handed over to Eli the priest. God appeared to him with a prophecy foretelling the destruction of Shiloh and of the House of Eli. After Shiloh had been destroyed by the Philistines and Eli had died, Samuel was appointed as judge and prophet of God. As a judge, he roamed in the area between Bethel, Gilgal, Mitzpeh, and Ramah. As his sons, Joel and Abijah, who also served as judges, judged unfairly, the people demanded that Samuel anoint a king over them, against his wishes but in accordance with God's demand. Samuel anointed Saul of the tribe of Benjamin as king, after warning the people about the disadvantages of a monarchical system.

King Saul disappointed Samuel twice, when he offered sacrifices without waiting for Samuel, and once again in the war against Amalek, when he allowed the Amalekite king to survive. Samuel informed Saul of God's prophecy that the kingship would be torn from him and given to another. Samuel went to Bethlehem and secretly anointed DAVID as king. The prophet never again met with Saul. After Samuel's death, on the eve of Saul's battle against the Philistines on Mount Gilboa, a woman (the "witch of En-dor") who had the ability to raise the dead raised up Samuel's spirit, which prophesied that Saul would suffer a military defeat, and that he would die with his sons.

According to the Talmud, Samuel's importance was equivalent to that of Moses and Aaron. The sages say that the prophet lived for only 52 years (*Tem.* 15a). He judged Israel for 10 years on his own, and for one year together with Saul (*MK* 28a). According to the Bible, Samuel was buried in Ramah. Tradition identifies this location with Nebi Samwil, northwest of Jerusalem.

SAMUEL, BOOK(S) OF The third volume of the Former PROPHETS section of the Bible. In Jewish tradition, the Book of Samuel is a single volume; the SEPTUAGINT and the Latin translation, the Vulgate, divided it into two parts and that division was followed in printed Hebrew Bibles from the early 16th century.

The book, which starts with the birth of the prophet SAMUEL and continues well into the reign of DAVID, may be divided into six units: (1) I Samuel 1:1-7:17, Samuel; (2) I Samuel 8:1-15:35, Samuel and Saul; (3) I Samuel 16:1-II Samuel 1:27, Saul and David; (4) II Samuel 2:1-8:18, David rules over Judah and Israel; (5) II Samuel 9:1-20:26, David's reign; and (6) appendices. The book comprises narratives, prophecies, poems, and lists. They came from different hands and were later edited into a unit.

BOOKS OF SAMUEL

I Samuel	
1:1 — 3:21	The birth of Samuel and his consecration as a prophet.
4:1 — 6:21	The destruction of Shiloh, the capturing of the Holy Ark, and its return.
7:1 — 7:17	Samuel the Judge.
8:1 — 10:27	Saul is anointed as king.
11:1 — 11:15	The victory of Saul over Ammon.
12:1 — 12:25	Samuel's farewell speech.
13:1 — 15:35	Saul's wars against the Philistines and Amalek.
16:1 — 16:23	The anointing of David as king.
17:1 — 17:58	David fights Goliath.
18:1 — 19:10	David in Saul's court.
19:11 — 27:12	Saul pursues David.
28:1 — 28:25	The witch of En-dor.
29:1 — 30:31	David in the camp of Achish and his battle against Amalek.
31:1-II	Sam.
1:27	The battle against the Philistines on Gilboa, the death of Saul and his sons, David's lament.
II Samuel	
2:1 — 4:12	The civil war of David against the house of Saul. David is made king of Judah in Hebron.
5:1 — 5:25	David becomes king of all of Israel; the conquest of Jerusalem.
6:1 — 6:23	David brings the Ark of the Covenant to Jerusalem.
7:1 — 7:29	God does not permit David to build the Temple.
8:1 — 8:18	David's battles against the Philistines, Moab, Zobah, and Aram of Damascus.
9:1 — 9:13	David and Mephibosheth, son of Jonathan.
10:1 — 10:19	David's battles against Ammon and Aram.
11:1 — 12:31	David and Bathsheba.
13:1 — 19:1	The revolt by Absalom.
19:2 — 19:44	David returns to Jerusalem.
20:1 — 20:26	The revolt by Sheba, son of Bichri.
21:1 — 21:14	David, the Gibeonites, and Saul's descendants.
21:15 — 21:22	List of David's warriors.
22:1 — 22:51	The song of David.
23:1 — 23:39	David's last words, list of David's warriors.
24:1 — 24:25	The census.

According to *Bava Batra* 14b, the book was written by the Prophet Samuel and was completed by Gad the Seer and Nathan the Prophet after Samuel's death. Some modern scholars believe that the volume was edited in the sixth century BCE. Part of it is based, according to many modern scholars, on the court chronicles of David or Solomon.

SAMUEL BEN MEIR (known as *Rashbam*; c.1085-1174). Bible commentator and talmudist; grandson of RASHI and elder brother of Rabbenu TAM. Born in Ramerupt near Troyes, France, Samuel studied mainly under Rashi, but also under his father Meir, one of the first Tosafists (see TOSAFOT).

Samuel probably wrote commentaries on all the books of the Bible but only that on the Pentateuch, published in 1881, has been preserved in its entirety. Part of his commentary on Esther, Ruth, and Lamentations has been published (in 1855) and some of his commentaries are still in manuscript; those on Psalms, Ecclesiastes, and Song of Songs, published under his name, are not by him. His commentaries are marked by an extremely literal interpretation of the text (*peshat*), even when this interpretation opposes the *halakhah*. Thus he holds that, according to the literal meaning of the text, it is not necessary to wear phylacteries (*tefillin*), and that the Hebrew day is to be kept from morning to evening, an interpretation criticized by Abraham Ibn Ezra in his *Iggeret ha-Shabbat*. There is no suggestion that Samuel did not accept the *halakhah* as binding; he simply saw no contradiction between the plain meaning of the Torah and the authoritative tradition which functioned according to different principles. According to Samuel, his grandfather, Rashi, admitted that if he had the time he would have had to write another commentary, more in accordance with the literal approach then current. Samuel had a good knowledge of Hebrew grammar, and was conversant with Old French and Latin (he quotes the Vulgate). He attacked christological exposition of the Bible.

A number of Samuel's talmudic commentaries have been preserved. He completed the commentary on PESAḤIM chapter 10, in which Rashi is very brief, and that on the greater part of BAVA BATRA which Rashi had left unfinished. These commentaries, which are lucid but extremely verbose, are included in the standard editions of the Talmud.

SAMUEL, MAR (third century CE). Leading Babylonian AMORA of the first generation, together with RAV. The *Mar* in his name was an honorific title in recognition of his distinction. In addition to his vast rabbinic knowledge, Samuel mastered the contemporary sciences, notably medicine (he was once summoned to Erets Israel to cure R. JUDAH HA-NASI of an eye disease) and astronomy (although he repudiated ASTROLOGY, which was widely accepted in Babylonia at the time). His knowledge of astronomy once led him to exclaim: "The paths of heaven are as familiar to me as the paths of Nehardea" (his native town). He was prepared to fix the first day of each festival based on astronomical calculation, and therefore proposed that the SECOND DAY OF FESTIVALS, observed in the Diaspora because of calendrical doubt (see CALENDAR), be abolished. The Palestinian authorities rejected this.

Samuel succeeded his father, Abba ben Abba ha-Kohen, as head of the ACADEMY of Nehardea. While he enjoyed very amicable relations with Rav, the head of the Academy of Sura, the Talmud records hundreds of halakhic controversies between them which lie at the base of the Babylonian Talmud. In all matters pertaining to civil law, the decision went according to Samuel's opinions. In this area, Samuel established many basic principles which became universally accepted. His declaration that in civil matters "the law of the state [in which Jews live] is to be recognized as valid and binding [for its Jews]" (DINA DE-MALKHUTA DINA), profoundly influenced subsequent Jewish life. Samuel himself was on friendly terms with King Shapur I (243-273), the noted empire-builder of Persia.

SANCTIFICATION See HOLINESS; KEDUSHAH

SANCTUARY ("tabernacle" or "tent of congregation"). Portable shrine, made by MOSES following God's instructions (Ex. 25-27) which traveled with the Israelites in the desert. The sanctuary (*mishkan*) was placed in the center of the camp, with the LEVITES camped around the inner perimeter and the other tribes on the outer perimeter. The sanctuary and all its utensils were portable, and all were transported from place to place by the Levites. The sanctuary stood in an open courtyard 100 cubits (a cubit is about 18") by 50 cubits in size. The courtyard fence consisted of wooden pillars placed every five cubits, from which a cloth curtain was suspended. The middle 20 cubits of one of the short sides of the courtyard was left open, as the entrance. The courtyard was shielded from view by a curtain 20 cubits long, ten cubits distant from the entrance, which was suspended on four wooden pillars.

The sanctuary itself was located in the eastern half of the courtyard, and measured 30 cubits by 10 cubits. Its three walls were made of acacia wood, covered with gold, and one of the short sides had no wall. Silver sockets bound the boards together, and each board had gold rings, through which passed acacia wood bars plated with gold, to give the structure stability. At the end of the sanctuary stood the HOLY OF HOLIES, which was separated from the rest of the sanctuary by a veil hanging on five wooden pillars, into which were woven the likenesses of cherubs. The ARK OF THE COVENANT, surmounted by two cherubs, was kept in the Holy of Holies. The Ark of the Covenant contained the two TABLETS with the TEN COMMANDMENTS. A rabbinical *aggadah* adds that the broken set of the first tablets was also kept there. A large cloth covering, made up of five sections joined together, extended from almost the bottom of one of the two long sides of the sanctuary, over its top, almost like a roof, and down the other side, almost to the bottom of the tabernacle wall. It too had cherubs woven into it. The front of the sanctuary had a covering with cherubs woven into the fabric. Over the "roof" covering lay a larger covering made of twelve goatskin sections. Finally, above this, lay another, made of ram skins and the skin of *teḥashim*, a word usually translated as badgers. According to the *aggadah*, it was an animal which existed only at that time, for the express purpose of the sanctuary.

Imaginary representation of sanctuary in the wilderness. Etching, Holland, 17th century.

Inside, before the Holy of Holies, stood the table upon which the SHOWBREAD was placed, the INCENSE altar, and the MENORAH. In the courtyard stood the outer ALTAR, upon which sacrifices were offered. The courtyard also contained a brass laver, used by the priests to wash their hands and feet before performing their duties.

Once the sanctuary was set up, the different chieftains of the tribes brought identical sacrifices and gifts, each on a separate day, for twelve consecutive days (Num. ch. 7).

Only when Solomon built his Temple in Jerusalem was the sanctuary finally superseded, and the Ark of the Covenant given a permanent home.

SANDAK (or *sandek*; often translated as "godfather"). The man who holds the infant boy on his knees during the CIRCUMCISION ceremony. The word itself is of Greek origin, from words meaning either a patron or a companion to the father. The invitation to be *sandak* is considered an honor. Traditionally, a person who had a great scholar as his *sandak* is regarded as privileged. The honor is often bestowed on one of the child's grandfathers.

SANHEDRIN (from *synedrion*, Greek for "sitting in council"). Higher courts of law during the later Second Temple period and during the following centuries. The actual origin of the institution is obscure despite the Talmud's assertion that its beginnings are to be traced to the 70 elders chosen by Moses (Num. 11:4). It was already in existence by the end of the fourth century BCE (Hellenistic period) and possibly dated back to the previous Persian period.

The institution is known in rabbinic and extra-talmudic sources by different names. In Jewish sources, it is called Sanhedrin, the Great Court in Jerusalem, or the Court of Seventy. In non-Jewish sources, it appears under the name of Council of Elders, *Gerousia* (Council), or Sanhedrin. These alternative names probably reflect its varying composition and authority in response to the changing political and social conditions of the Jewish community of Erets Israel during the course of the Second Temple period. Smaller lawcourts with 23 members (known as "Small Sanhedrins") met in each city (including Jerusalem) and regions with localized jurisdiction.

According to talmudic sources, the Sanhedrin was composed of sages and was headed by a president (NASI). Thus, talmudic tradition has it that the first name mentioned in the five pairs (ZUGOT) of scholars in the period between the Hasmonean revolt and the Herodian era served as the *nasi* of the Sanhedrin while the second in each pair served as "Father of the Court." From New Testament sources an almost totally different picture of the composition of the Sanhedrin emerges. Here (e.g., Acts of the Apostles), the Sanhedrin is described as headed by the High Priest and is composed of "priests and scribes." Historians have proposed a number of solutions to this contradiction. One is that there were three councils: one that met in the Chamber of Hewn Stone within the Temple, consisting of Pharisaic sages (see PHARISEES), which concerned itself with religious matters including the Temple ritual; one was a court that dealt with violators of the law; and one council that occupied itself with the administrative affairs of the city of Jerusalem. Most scholars maintain that there was only one Sanhedrin. Originally, it was composed of priests and headed by the High Priest. These were Sadducean (see SADDUCEES) in their social and religious outlook. Gradually, these aristocratic Sadduceans were displaced by the more democratic Pharisaic sages whose authority was acknowledged even by the Sadducean priests in the closing decades of the Second Temple period. However, the High Priest continued to exercise his traditional function as head of the Sanhedrin in matters that had political overtones even though he had become a regular member of the court. This would account for the conflicting talmudic traditions concerning whether the Sanhedrin consisted of 70 or 71 members.

The authority of the Sanhedrin in a variety of areas was extremely wide and, as the leading institution of the Palestinian community, extended to the far-flung Diaspora. Disputes in matters of *halakhah* that arose in local courts would be referred to the Sanhedrin for a final, decisive opinion. A sage who refused to accept the latter would be branded a "rebellious elder" (see ZAKEN MAMRE). It was the Sanhedrin that served as the legislative body, issuing decrees (GEZEROT) and ordinances (TAKKANOT). Although these laws are ascribed to individual *nesi'im* (pl. of *nasi*), they undoubtedly were discussed and approved by the Sanhedrin as a whole. The Sanhedrin alone exercised the right to fix the monthly and yearly CALENDAR, an important factor in maintaining religious uniformity between Erets Israel and the Diaspora. As the representative body of the people, it had the right to authorize or disallow an offensive war. Theoretically, though not in practice, a king or high priest required the approval of the Sanhedrin before he could be appointed. It was the Sanhedrin that was empowered to take measures — such as imprisonment — against those who engaged in sectarian (including Christian) propaganda activities. While such action was favored by the Sadducean members of the Sanhedrin, the Pharisaic members objected to such stern measures.

A moot point in the history of the Sanhedrin is its authority to try and to execute judgment in cases involving CAPITAL PUNISHMENT. One talmudic tradition states that this authority ceased 40 years before the destruction of the Second Temple, but there is evidence that capital judgments were rendered and carried out up to the year 70 CE. Scholarly opinion is divided as to what limits were placed on the Sanhedrin in this regard.

The actual judicial procedure of the Sanhedrin is vividly described in the Mishnaic tractate SANHEDRIN. No circumstantial evidence, no matter how strong, was admissible. In cases involving capital punishment, the procedure was heavily weighted in favor of acquittal to such an extent that one *tanna* declared that a Sanhedrin that ordered an execution once in 70 years was "a murderous court."

The Sanhedrin reestablished in Yavneh by R. GAMALIEL some time after the destruction of the Second Temple assumed virtually all the prerogatives of the original Sanhedrin in Jerusalem. It, too, was recognized both in Erets Israel and the Diaspora as the supreme representative body of Jewry in regard to both religious and communal matters. With the abolition of the Patriarchate (office of *Nasi*) by the Roman authorities early in the 5th century CE, the Sanhedrin came to an end. The proposal, after the founding of the State of Israel, to reestablish the Sanhedrin in Jerusalem found scant support in the Orthodox Rabbinate, even though it was proposed by Israel's first Minister of Religious Affairs, Rabbi J.L. Maimon.

SANHEDRIN Fourth tractate of Order *Nezikin* in the Mishnah. Its eleven chapters deal with the laws concerning the establishing and functioning of courts of law (cf. Deut. 16:18-20; 17:6-20). Courts of three, 23, and 71 judges were set up in Erets Israel depending on the size of the city and the case involved. The Supreme Court was called the Great

SANHEDRIN and convened in the Hall of Hewn Stone in the Temple. The Mishnah discusses money suits, criminal suits, examination of witnesses, capital crimes, execution and even the rights of the king and High Priest regarding judgment. The subject matter is amplified in both Talmuds and in the *Tosefta*.

SANHEDRIN, "GREAT" See CONSISTORY

SARAH Wife of ABRAHAM, mother of ISAAC, MATRIARCH of the Jewish people. Originally, her name was Sarai, but it was changed by God at the same time that Abram's name was changed to Abraham (Gen. 17:15).

She originated from Abraham's family (Gen. 11:29-31) and she accompanied her husband from Mesopotamia to Canaan. Her beauty was outstanding (Gen. 12:11) and is described in legendary detail in a text discovered among the DEAD SEA SCROLLS. She was coveted by foreign rulers (Gen. 12:10-20;20) and when Abraham came into the territory of Abimelech, king of Gerar, he presented her as his sister. After Sarah was taken by Abimelech, God appeared to the king in a dream and told him that Sarah was Abraham's wife. Abimelech thereupon sent both Abraham and Sarah away with many gifts.

Failing to conceive, Sarah gave her maidservant, Hagar, to Abraham as a concubine and Hagar gave birth to Ishmael when Abraham was 86 years old. Only 14 years later, at the age of 90, did Sarah give birth to Isaac and his very name is based on her comment that "whoever hears will rejoice (*yitsaḥak*) with me" (Gen. 21:6). Seeing the way Ishmael mocked Isaac, Sarah entreated Abraham to send both Hagar and Ishmael away. Abraham was loath to do this, until told by God "whatever Sarah says to you, harken to her voice" (Gen. 21:12). On this, the *aggadah* comments that Sarah's prophetic powers exceeded those of Abraham. Abraham then complied with Sarah's request.

Unlike for the other Matriarchs, the Bible records Sarah's age, both at the time she gave birth to Isaac and at her death at the age of 127 years.

The Midrash claims that Sarah died when she received the report of the sacrifice of Isaac (AKEDAH). The Midrash also lays great stress on Sarah's working alongside her husband in bringing people closer to the realization of the One God, with Abraham being active among the men and Sarah among the women.

When Sarah died, Abraham bought the Cave of Machpelah from Ephron the Hittite for 400 shekels of silver to use as a burial site.

SATAN Originally, the Hebrew noun *satan* in the Bible meant simply an adversary, someone hostile. Thus, for example in I Kings 11:14 "The Lord raised up an adversary (*Satan*) for Solomon in Hadad the Edomite". In later books of the Bible, the noun came to mean a supernatural being who in the heavenly entourage accuses man before God. This role of Satan is made explicit in the prologue to Job (1-2) where Satan challenges the sincerity of Job's piety. Both here and in Zechariah (3:1,2) Satan can act only within the limits set by God and is totally subordinate to Him. It has been suggested that the concept of a heavenly accuser of man grew out of the desire not to ascribe evil to God (compare II Sam. 24:1 where God incites David to take a census of the people with the later I Chron. 21:1 where David is provoked by Satan).

In APOCRYPHA AND PSEUDEPIGRAPHA, the role of Satan is greatly enlarged, as it is in the Talmud and Midrash. Whereas previously he was subservient to God, he now incites man to disobey the will of God. Accordingly, he acquires the name *Mastemah* (Enmity) in the Book of Jubilees. In the Testament of the Twelve Patriarchs he is called Belial; in the Dead Sea Scrolls, the Angel of Darkness. This development in the concept of Satan may have been due to Persian dualism.

He is the subject of many folk beliefs and is also referred to in the liturgy. However, in Kabbalah he is often replaced by other names for the prince of evil.

SAVORA (Aram. for "ponderer, explainer"; pl. *savoraim*). Term designating the Babylonian scholars who, in succession to the AMORAIM, were responsible for various final improvements to the Talmud. Jewish historians long maintained that the *savoraim* were active for no more than 50 years (approx. 500-550 CE). Recent investigation has shown, however, that they flourished well into the period of the *ge'onim* (see GAON), i.e., until around 690 CE. Moreover, it now appears that the *savoraim*, not ASHI and Ravina bar Huna (died 499), were the Talmud's final redactors. About one dozen of these "ponderers" — e.g., Simuna and Rabbai of Rov — are named in geonic sources, and the change in designation (from *amora* to *savora*) has a historical explanation. Under the Sassanid rulers of Persia, Zoroastrian fanaticism led to the closure of talmudical ACADEMIES, the execution of two exilarchs (leaders of the Jewish community), the temporary abolition of the exilarchate (reestablished only after the Arab conquest in 641), and the collapse of Jewish legal autonomy. Deprived of their earlier judicial function, scholars of the time changed from amoraic lawmaking to savoraic clarification of the existing law. They soon discovered that their predecessors, while compiling and organizing the legal material accumulated in the Babylonian Academies, had failed to elucidate numerous obscure points in the text.

This work of reasoned explanation first preoccupied the *savoraim*, who supplied brief connecting phrases to eliminate disparities. Another of their tasks resulted from the many talmudic controversies that provide no clear-cut decision as to which opinion is viewed as the definitive HALAKHAH. On the basis of contemporary practice, the *savoraim* presumably added clarifications of their own. Later generations of *savoraim* went far beyond mere explanatory phrases and editorial notes. They now inserted rather lengthy passages into the talmudic discussion, usually at the beginning of a tractate or chapter. Thus, early geonic authorities indicate that the first few pages of tractate KIDDUSHIN were written by the *savoraim*, and this may be true also of other extended passages where the discussants are not identified by name.

SCAPEGOAT See AZAZEL

SCHECHTER, SOLOMON (1847-1915). Rabbinical scholar and leader of CONSERVATIVE JUDAISM who founded its basic institutions, setting the tone for its ideological development. Born in Romania, Schechter studied at the Vienna rabbinical seminary and then at the *Hochschule für die Wissenschaft des Judentums* in Berlin. After moving to England in 1882, he lectured in Talmud and Rabbinics at Cambridge University (1890-98) and subsequently taught at University College, London (1898-1901). His first major publication, a critical edition of the AVOT DE-RABBI NATAN (1887), remains a classic of modern rabbinic scholarship, but his international reputation was established by the discoveries he made in the Cairo GENIZAH (a depository for worn-out sacred books). Having recognized fragments brought to him from Cairo as part of the lost Hebrew version of the Book of Ecclesiasticus, Schechter traveled to Egypt in 1896 and eventually unearthed some 100,000 pages of medieval manuscripts which were transferred to Cambridge, thus opening up a vast treasure trove of ancient Jewish texts that revolutionized rabbinic scholarship.

From 1902, Schechter headed the Jewish Theological Seminary in New York, where he succeeded in attracting eminent scholars to join the teaching staff. He made the Seminary an internationally renowned powerhouse of Jewish learning with one of the world's greatest libraries of Judaica. Schechter's vision endowed the Seminary with a dual purpose: to create a rabbinical leadership for American Jewry and to function as an institute for modern study of Judaism. He was also responsible for establishing the United Synagogue of America (1913), which became the lay, congregational arm of the Conservative movement. Schechter originally hoped that the Seminary and the United Synagogue of America would cater for all traditionalist communities in the US, allowing room for the rabbinical leaders of moderate ORTHODOXY as well as for those of the "positive-historical" school. This dream was not realized, however, and Schechter's institution became identified exclusively with Conservative Judaism.

Apart from scholarly works of major importance, Solomon Schechter published numerous essays on Judaism, rabbinic theology, and topics of the day. A gifted English stylist, he emphasized the theological aspects of traditional Judaism and excelled as an interpreter of Jewish concepts for the layman. He often took a stand on controversial issues, notably by lending support to Zionism, a cause which the Seminary's anti-nationalist lay leadership opposed. Schechter believed that a reborn Jewish State would be the fulfillment of Jewish religious hopes and in no way contradicted Judaism's universal message. Here, as elsewhere, Schechter defended traditional Jewish values and concepts against the liberalizing, assimilationist tendencies of REFORM JUDAISM. While granting the Reform movement's positive attributes, he denounced its propensity to abandon the essentials of Jewish tradition, whether halakhic or doctrinal. Schechter nevertheless believed in the possibility of change within the framework of rabbinic tradition, and felt that a developing *halakhah* would take into account the opinions voiced by masses of loyal Jews, to which he applied the designation of "catholic Israel."

SCIENCE A body of verifiable knowledge of the empirical world generated by a particular method consisting of observation expressed in mathematical relationships, hypothesis, experimentation, explanation and prediction in order to discover regularities called "natural laws" and to propose theories.

For historical and sociological reasons there is little in the relationship between institutional Judaism and the rise of science in the 16th and 17th centuries that parallels the bitter conflict that developed between the Church and science. However on the theoretical level, modern scientific "discoveries", such as the Copernican Theory and EVOLUTION created problems for Jewish THEOLOGY as well.

Judaism, as reflected both in the Bible as well as in the Talmud, is "this-worldly". Since nature and history are the

Astronomy instrument. From a scientific treatise by Joseph Solomon Delmedigo, a pupil of Galileo. c.1628.

realms in which man is to work out his destiny, he has an obligation to "know" them as well as he can. Study of Bible is to be combined with attention to the practical concerns of this world (*Avot* 2:2).

The Rabbis amassed a considerable amount of specialized knowledge in particular areas: The determination of the calendar required knowledge of astronogy. Many laws encouraged an awareness of the biology of the human body and a knowledge of medicine. The dietary laws stimulated observations of animal anatomy and classification of birds and reptiles. However, lacking the scientific method, the rabbis had no effective way to distinguish "knowledge" from magic and superstition. Thus, astrology was often combined with astronomy and quackery with medicine.

In the Middle Ages, many Jews, some of them rabbis and scholars in Jewish subjects, played a leading role in science (astronomy, mathematics, medicine, etc.) and also in the transmission of Arab science to the Christian world.

Many medieval Jewish philosophers held that human reason is a gift from God so that in principle there could not be a conflict between the conclusions of reason and the content of Divine Revelation. Thus, to the extent that science is reason's report of the real it is reliable and authoritative. Medieval "science" produced little that was in conflict with REVELATION. MAIMONIDES, himself a leading medical authority, remained true to his principles and declared that had the doctrine of the eternity of the Universe been proven by logical deduction from self-evident first principles, he would have been compelled to reinterpret those passages of the Bible which speak of creation (*Guide II*, 25).

Furthermore, according to Maimonides, the only way to observe the crucial commandment of loving God is to study His works which are the various aspects of nature. Only then can man be brought to exclaim: "How manifold are your works O God, in wisdom have you made them all" (Ps. 104:25). Therefore the Jew has an obligation to engage in theoretical science as well as in practical technology.

How does modern Judaism relate to the Science-Religion conflict? Liberal Judaism, because of its qualified attribution of Divine authority to the Bible, does not have to make assertions about the empirical world. Judaism deals only with ends, hopes, values and conduct; religion and science have separate legitimate spheres and there is no area of conflict.

Since Orthodox Judaism, however, affirms the Divine authority of the Bible, it finds that traditional Judaism makes assertions which may be in conflict with the views of the scientific community, for example, concerning cosmology (e.g., the world was created in time in a particular order...), psychology (man possesses freedom of the will to make moral choices...), history (the Jewish people were enslaved in Egypt during a particular period...) and about the authorship of literary documents (the Pentateuch was written by Moses at a particular time...). The response of Orthodoxy in such eventualities has often been to reinterpret the Biblical text in such a way as to eliminate the conflict, the rationale being that difficulty with the literal meaning has always been considered a legitimate reason for substituting a midrashic or non-literal interpretation. Thus, the six days of creation are taken as "six aeons" instead of literal days. There are other Orthodox theologians who when confronted by conflict between the Bible and scientific theory (such as the theory of Evolution) reject the scientific view on the grounds that the evidence in its favor is not conclusive.

SCRIBES (*soferim*) Scholars of the early Second Temple period who expounded the Oral Law and enacted regulations (TAKKANOT) in the light of the Torah; later, writers of holy documents. Experts in the Bible and the oral tradition, the scribes in the post-Babylonian EXILE period assumed leadership of the Jewish nation. The scribes formed a bridge between the prophets and the Pharisees. Historically, the period of the scribes began with EZRA ("the Scribe"), who led Jews back to Judah from Babylonia in the 5th century BCE, and continued until Simon the Just, the last survivor of the Men of the GREAT ASSEMBLY (*Avot* 1.2).

The word for scribe (*sofer*) is related to the verb "to count" and these scholars counted the letters of the Bible and were meticulous in the spelling and pronunciation of each word, making sure that the precise text was passed on to the next generation. In Jewish law, the decrees transmitted by the scribes are called *divré soferim* (words of the scribes), *tikkuné soferim* (corrections of the scribes), or *dikduké soferim* (minutiae of the scribes). The Talmud (*Meg.* 19b) relates that when God gave Moses the Tablets of the Law on Mount Sinai, He also showed him all the decrees which the scribes would make in the future. The later sages emphasized the importance of the scribes as authorities of the Oral Law when they stated, "Be more careful in the words of the scribes than in the words of the Bible" (*Er.* 21b). The scribes enacted laws relating to prayer and blessings and instituted the festival of PURIM. They also emended the text of the Pentateuch in 18 places, usually to avoid anthropomorphisms.

Later, the term "scribes" was used primarily for men who wrote MEZUZOT, phylacteries (TEFILLIN), Scrolls of Esther and the Torah scrolls, as well as DIVORCE documents and formerly, also marriage documents (KETUBBOT). This type of scribe is called *sofer setam* (the second word is an acronym of "scribe of Scrolls of the Torah, *tefillin* and *mezuzot*"). This work requires careful observance of scribal law and proficiency in the use of a quill or bamboo stylus. When R. MEIR told his teacher, R. ISHMAEL, that he worked as a scribe, R. Ishmael said, "My son, be careful in your work, for it is the work of heaven" (*Er.* 13a). If the scribe omits one letter, adds one extra letter, or corrects his writing not according to the halakhic rules, the entire scroll is invalid and cannot be used. A specialist in scribal law is employed to check *mezuzot*, *tefillin* and Scrolls of the Law to insure that they are written in accordance with *halakhah*. Laws for the scribes are laid

A specialist checking a scroll to insure that it is written in accordance with the laws for the scribes.

down in tractate SOFERIM, appended to the Talmud. The SHULḤAN ARUKH code lays down 65 laws containing hundreds of intricate details instructing the scribe how to write and repair his work. (For details see SCROLLS OF THE LAW.)

Because of the spiritual nature of this work, many scribes immerse themselves in the *mikveh* (ritual bath) each day before beginning their work and, when writing the names of God, keep their minds clear of extraneous thoughts. Tradition promises great reward to scribes who do their work honestly and well and equally harsh punishment to those who fail to do so.

SCROLL OF THE LAW (*Sefer Torah*). Handwritten copy of the Five Books of Moses, kept in the ARK of the SYNAGOGUE and taken out for the READING OF THE LAW on each Sabbath as well as on MONDAYS AND THURSDAYS, New Moons (see MOON), FESTIVALS, and FAST DAYS. The scroll must be written on parchment or vellum by a SCRIBE (*sofer*) familiar with all the laws involved. Only parchment obtained from a ritually clean species of animal may be used, although the animal need not have been ritually slaughtered. The parchment, which must be specially treated in advance to insure durability, must be embossed with lines before the scribe begins writing. The ink must be black and it is generally prepared according to a traditional formula. Whereas reed pens were once used, scribes today write with pens with metal nibs. Jewish law defines in great detail the shape of each letter, but there are differences between Ashkenazi and Sephardi rulings on these shapes. The Torah scroll contains no vowels or cantillation marks; nor are there punctuation marks dividing sentences or phrases. Sections (e.g., the two songs in Ex. 15:1-19 and Deut. 32), are marked off by either a blank space equivalent to at least nine letters within a line (*setumah* = "closed"), or the balance of the line being left open (*petuḥah* = "open"). Four lines are left blank within the different books of the Pentateuch. Thirteen of the letters of the alphabet have little lines drawn above them, known as *tagin* or "crowns." Six of the columns must begin with a specific word, but there are no other requirements regarding the layout of the columns, which can have between 45 and 60 lines. Most Torah scrolls, though, begin each column (except for the above-mentioned six) with the letter *vav*. The sections of the parchment are sewn together, using tendons obtained from ritually clean species of animals. Once the entire scroll is ready, it is mounted on two wooden staves, known as the *atsé ḥayyim* ("trees of life"). In Ashkenazi congregations, the full scroll is then tied with a sash and covered with a cloth mantle (*me'il*). In Sephardi congregations, the cover is made of either wood or metal, and is known as the *tik*. In German congregations, it was customary for parents of a newborn child to prepare a sash (wimple) to be used in tying the Torah scroll. This sash was generally embroidered with the name of the child and wishes for his future well-being and donated to the synagogue when the child grew up, sometimes for his bar mitsvah. The Scroll is adorned with the TORAH ORNAMENTS.

If an error of any kind is found in a Torah scroll, such as two letters touching or an error in copying, the scroll may not be used again until the error is corrected by a scribe. If correcting the error would necessitate the erasure of God's name, the entire segment of parchment containing the error must be replaced with a new one. Should three or more errors be found in a Torah scroll, it may not be used again until it has been checked from beginning to end for further errors and all errors are corrected. In Ashkenazi congregations, if a Torah scroll has been found to need repair, the custom is to tie the sash of a Torah scroll over the mantle rather than underneath it, as an indication of the fact that the scroll may not be used until it has been repaired.

The Torah scroll is the most venerated of Jewish ritual objects. It is customary to stand as a sign of respect whenever the synagogue ark is opened and the scrolls become visible to the congregation (see PETIḤAH) and also when a Scroll of the Law is being carried in the synagogue. Similarly, when the open Torah scroll is held up for all to see for the HAGBAHAH (in the Sephardi ritual, before the Torah reading and in the Ashkenazi ritual, after the reading), all rise. Should a Torah scroll need to be removed from the synagogue, it must be wrapped; usually a prayer-shawl (*tallit*) is used for the purpose. A Torah scroll may not be placed on a table, unless the table has first been covered by a cloth. Congregants touch the mantle of the Torah scroll with the edge of their *tallit* as the scroll is carried past them and then kiss the edge of the *tallit*. If fire breaks out in a synagogue, the Torah scrolls must be the first objects to be rescued. Torah scrolls may even be carried outside on the Sabbath,

The first ripe fruits at Shavu'ot. Stained-glass window, London Central Synagogue, by David Hillman, 20th century.

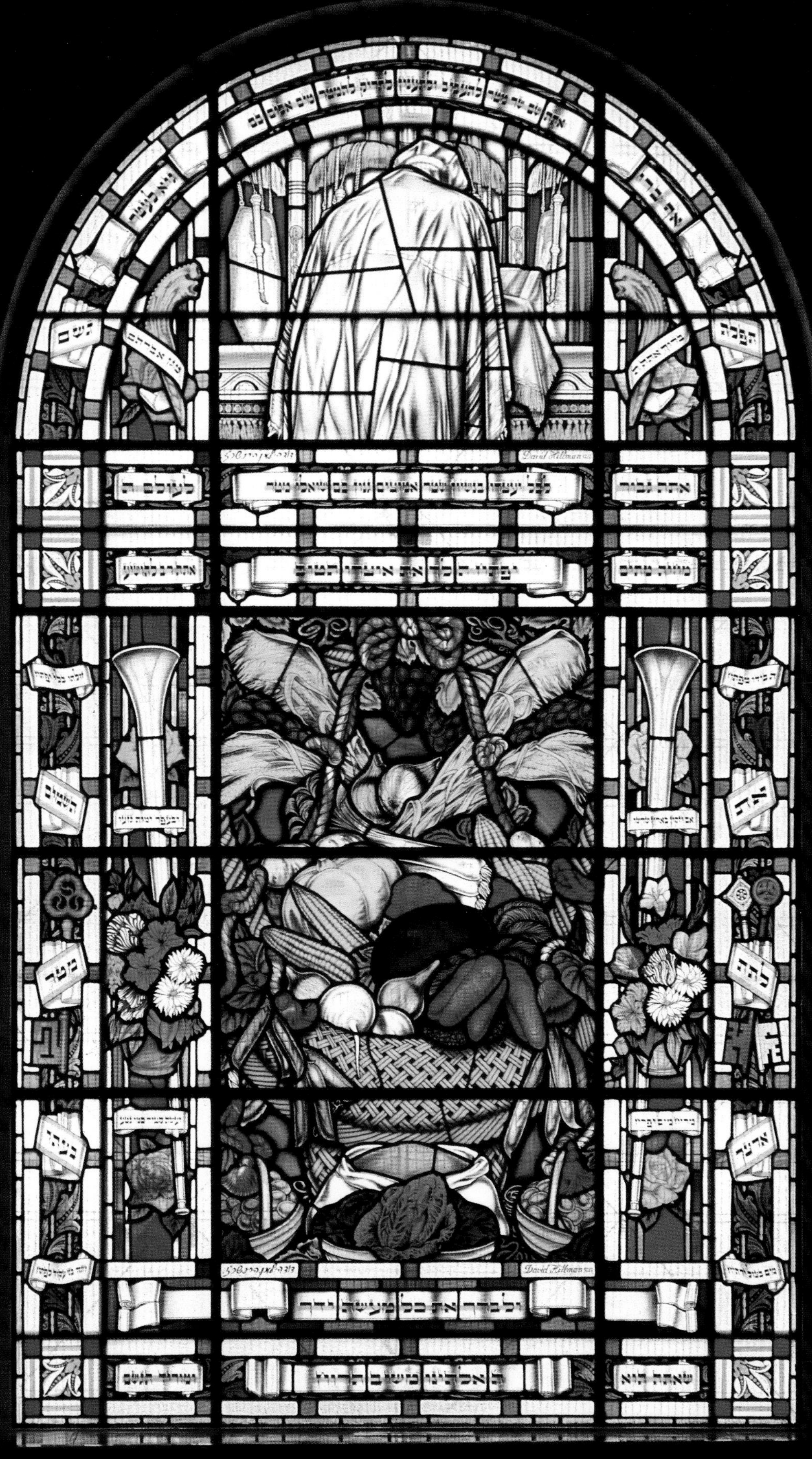
David Hillman
David Hillman

Raising the Scroll of the Law (hagbahah) *in the synagogue. Painting, Holland, 1780.*

should fire threaten them. Should a scroll be burned in a fire, the ashes or remaining parts of the scroll must be given a proper burial in the local cemetery. If a Torah scroll falls, the entire congregation is required to fast. If a scroll is no longer fit for use due to age, it cannot be disposed of summarily, but must be properly buried or placed in a special storeroom (GENIZAH).

On SIMḤAT TORAH (SHEMINI ATSERET in Israel), HAKKAFOT (circuits) are held in the synagogue both in the evening and in the morning, where all the Torah scrolls are removed from the ark and are ceremoniously carried around the reading desk seven times. Ḥasidic custom outside Israel is to have such *hakkafot* on both Shemini Atseret and Simḥat Torah.

The last of the 613 commandments is that each Jew should write a Torah scroll for himself. Practically speaking, very few people do so. There are views that one fulfills this commandment by buying a Torah scroll or even by paying for the writing of a single letter in a Torah scroll. It used to be customary for scholars and affluent Jews to keep a Scroll of the Law in their homes.

By biblical law, the entire Jewish community had to gather on the Sukkot festival in the year following the sabbatical year in a ceremony known as HAKHEL, to hear readings from the Torah scroll, either by the king or, if there was no king, by another notable. The king was required to have his own small Scroll of the Law, which he was to keep with him at all times.

SCROLLS, FIVE See FIVE SCROLLS

SECOND DAY OF FESTIVALS Extra holy day(s) observed by Jews living in the Diaspora on the festivals of PASSOVER, SHAVU'OT, and SUKKOT. They stem from a recurrent problem of Second Temple times — fixing the correct date for each New MOON (and hence for any festival or fast that would occur during the month ahead) in the Jewish CALENDAR. Originally, physical observation of the New Moon was ascertained from reliable witnesses by the Sanhedrin in Jerusalem; once acceptable testimony had been obtained, a chain of beacons relayed the information to other communities and, at a later stage, messengers were dispatched to supply Jews living outside Erets Israel with the relevant information. There is reason to believe that this system of communication broke down as a result of the anarchy prevailing during the last days of the Temple. In order to make doubly sure that they would not observe a festival on the wrong date, Jews in the Diaspora began keeping two holy days (instead of one) at the beginning and the end of both Passover and Sukkot, and two also on Shavu'ot. Once a fixed calendar had been introduced in the fourth century CE, however, the date of each New Moon and festival was known in advance. Jews living in Babylon therefore addressed an inquiry to the sages in Erets Israel, asking if it would not be logical to dispense with these "second festive days" (*yom tov sheni shel galuyyot*). The reply was that a custom hallowed by centuries of usage should still be maintained, even if the reason for its observance no longer applied.

Current practice throughout the Diaspora is to convert the first intermediate day of Passover and Sukkot into a second holy day (*yom tov*) and for ISRU ḤAG (the day after each festival's termination) to become the eighth day of Passover or the ninth day of Sukkot (SIMḤAT TORAH being attached to SHEMINI ATSERET). A second *Seder* is also held on Passover. *Isru ḥag* likewise becomes the second day of Shavu'ot. ROSH HA-SHANAH is the only festival when even in the Land of Israel a second day is added to the biblical one-day festival. This was probably due to the fact that since the New Year falls right at the beginning of the month, even Jews in the Holy Land could have been temporarily uncertain if news of the announcement of the new month (Tishri) did not reach them in time. Nevertheless, there is ample reason to believe that the original practice in Erets Israel was to observe Rosh ha-Shanah for one day only, in accordance with the biblical description, and that the institution of the "second day" was a later innovation. The DAY OF ATONEMENT, however, remains a one-day solemnity in the Diaspora as well as in Israel, because an extension of the fast would prove unduly severe.

Talmudic evidence (TJ *Er.* 3.9) indicates that observance of these "second festive days" was considered a religious penalty for choosing to live in exile (GALUT). Reform Jews do not observe the second day of festivals. The Conservative movement allows its rabbis and congregations freedom of choice in the matter, but the vast majority of Conservative congregations do observe the "second day." Israelis visiting abroad have a religious obligation to conform in public with the Diaspora practice; a Jew coming to Israel from overseas has

Synagogue plaque, shivviti, *taking its name from the first word of Psalm 16:8. Paper-cut, 19th century.*

to observe the second day of festivals unless he envisages *aliyah* at some point in the future.

SECTARIANS See MINIM

SEDER ("order"). The order of the home ceremony observed on the first night (in the Diaspora on the first two nights) of the PASSOVER festival.

In the biblical and Temple periods, the observance of Passover was concentrated on the paschal sacrifice. Following the destruction of the Second Temple in 70 CE, the rabbis had to recast the observance of Passover without the paschal sacrifice, yet maintaining strong connections with their past heritage. In this difficult task they were somewhat assisted by the Bible itself where the instructions relating to the paschal sacrifice clearly stipulate that it is to be eaten in family groups (Ex. 12).

The development of the post-Temple *Seder* took place gradually. The basic ritual is first set out in the Mishnah (PESAḤIM, ch. 10). In the effort to provide a link with the Passover celebration in Temple times, the rabbis may have been influenced by some aspects of the Hellenistic and Roman symposia where discussion and banqueting were enjoyed in convivial company. Reclining at the meal, dipping the food, the serving of *hor-d'oeuvres*, may be elements of the Roman symposium incorporated into the rabbinic *Seder*. If so, they were given special values relating to the Passover story, so that the *Seder* became distinctively a religious rite serving the aim of recalling and celebrating Israel's deliverance from Egyptian bondage. The *Seder* does this with an ordered program of symbol, ceremony, thanksgiving and rejoicing.

Several items are central in the *Seder* celebration:

(i) The HAGGADAH. The name given to the special book containing the order of the ceremonial.

(ii) The special *Seder* dish which contains the following items: (1) A slightly roasted hard-boiled egg. This symbolizes the special festival sacrifice offered in Temple times in honor of the Passover. (2) A roasted bone (*zero'a*). It symbolizes the paschal lamb, eaten by the family in Temple times as the Passover feast. (3) Bitter herbs (MAROR), which symbolize the bitter oppression suffered by the Israelite slaves in Egypt. (4) *Ḥaroset*, a mixture usually made of apples, nuts, wine and cinnamon. In the popular interpretation, it reminds the family of mortar, prepared by the Israelite slaves in making bricks. (5) *karpas*, i.e., parsley or other green vegetable. This is dipped in salt water during the ritual. According to the Talmud it is intended to arouse the interest of the children. Other explanations suggested are that it is eaten in imitation of the *hor-d'oeuvres* of Roman nobility, or that the parsley as it is passed through the salt water is symbolic of the Israelites crossing the Red Sea. (6) Salt water. One theory is that the salt water represents the tears shed by the Israelites in Egypt.

(iii) Three *matsot* (pieces of unleavened bread). Two of these take the place of the two loaves of bread used on Sabbaths and festivals, while the third is required for the extra ritual of the *Seder*. A popularly accepted idea is that the three *matsot* represent the threefold division of the Jewish people, viz., priests, Levites, and Israelites.

(iv) The four glasses of wine. These are central in the *Seder* ritual and are drunk in token of the four terms of redemption mentioned in the Bible (Ex. 6:6-7).

(v) The cup of Elijah. There was a dispute about whether the Bible gives a fifth term for redemption, calling for a fifth cup. Since rabbinic tradition holds that unsolved questions will be resolved by ELIJAH the prophet, a fifth glass is filled in his honor. After the meal, the door is briefly opened and Elijah is symbolically welcomed. In early ages it was customary for the door to be left open throughout the *Seder*, as an invitation for the needy and the stranger to enter and join in celebrating the Passover. However, this practice became hazardous in the Middle Ages when Jews were in danger of attack by their Christian neighbors. Passover occurs around Easter time, and anti-Jewish blood libels at this time were not unknown. Frequently, Jews had to observe the *Seder* in secret, for fear of a violent break-in by their false accusers. However, at one point in the *Seder* the door was opened for a brief moment to welcome Elijah. He is especially important on Passover since traditionally he is the herald of the Messiah and points to the hope for a future time of perfect freedom and peace.

(vi) *Afikoman*. A special piece of *matsah* to be put away at the beginning of the *Seder* which is distributed to all participants at the end of the meal. It is eaten, and intended to symbolize the last meal of the Israelites prior to the Exodus.

True to the literal meaning of the word, there is a clearly stipulated order to the entire *Seder*. The chief elements of this order are found already in the Mishnah, but additions and some rearrangements are of medieval origin.

(1) *Kadesh*. First, as on the eve of all holy days, the KIDDUSH benedictions sanctifying the festival are recited over wine.

(2) *Reḥats*. The hands are washed prior to the performance of the rituals of the *Seder*. It is usual for a special pitcher with water to be placed in a convenient part of the room, or for the water to be brought around to the participants at the table. At this point it is customary for the celebrant only to wash his hands and not recite the blessing.

(3) *Karpas*. Parsley or some other vegetable is dipped in the salt water and is then eaten after the appropriate benediction is recited.

(4) *Yahats*. The middle one of the three ceremonial *matsot* is broken. One half is put aside or hidden for the *afikoman*. An old custom involves the hiding of the *afikoman*, the search for it by the children and the promise of a reward to whoever finds it. This is in the spirit of arousing and sustaining the interest of the children.

(5) *Maggid*. The first part of the *Haggadah* is now read. This includes the FOUR QUESTIONS, the list of the ten plagues that preceded the EXODUS FROM EGYPT, with midrashic comments, an explanation of the paschal lamb, the *matsah* and the bitter herb and the recitation of the first part of the HALLEL psalm. In the course of the readings, the second and third glasses of wine are drunk. It is usual for the leader of the *Seder* to encourage family participation and discussion in an attempt to make the *Haggadah* narrative as interesting and as relevant as possible.

(6) *Raḇtsah*. The hands are washed, as before a meal, this time with the usual benediction for the ritual washing of the hands.

(7) *Motsi Matsah*. Each participant eats a piece of the unleavened bread. The usual benediction for bread is recited and since this is, strictly speaking, the only time when the Jew is obligated by the law to eat the unleavened bread, he pronounces a special benediction, "on eating the unleavened bread."

(8) *Maror*. The bitter herb. Some bitter herb is dipped in the *ḫaroset* and eaten after making a benediction relating to the biblical commandment to eat the bitter herb on the Passover.

(9) *Korekh*. The sandwich. In Temple times, the meat of the paschal sacrifice was eaten with bitter herb. In addition, it was the custom of the famous sage HILLEL (first century BCE) to eat it together with the unleavened bread. Something of this custom is now followed by eating the *matsah* and the *maror* together.

(10) *Shulḫan Orekh*. The festive meal. This is an integral part of the *Seder* celebration just as in ancient times the Passover eve was festively observed by the eating of the paschal lamb.

(11) *Tsafun*. A piece of the *matsah* "hidden" after *Yahats* (no. 4), is eaten as the *afikoman*, (see (vi) above).

(12) *Barekh*. The GRACE AFTER MEALS is recited.

(13) *Hallel*. The remaining *Hallel* psalms are recited. These are followed by a number of medieval hymns. Through the years they have been handed down with jolly melodies, many of which have become part of warm family traditions. Among the best-known are EḪAD MI YODE'A, ADDIR HU, ADDIR BI-MELUKHAH and ḪAD GADYA.

(14) *Nirtzah*. The celebration is "accepted." The *Seder* is concluded with the joyous declaration LE-SHANAH HA-BA'AH BI-YRUSHALAYIM (Next Year in Jerusalem). In Israel the text is amended to *Le-Shanah ha-Ba'ah bi-Yrushalayim ha-benuyah* (Next year in rebuilt Jerusalem).

SEFER TORAH See SCROLL OF THE LAW

SEFIROT Kabbalistic terms denoting the ten emanations through which the Godhead manifests itself (see MYSTICISM). The term *sefirot* is derived from the cosmogonical speculations of the *Sefer* YETSIRAH (third-fourth century), where it denotes the first ten numbers (one to ten) and dimensions of the universe. The early kabbalists adopted this term to refer to their concept of the Divine world as comprised of ten Divine powers, originating from the Godhead (ÉN SOF) in a process of emanation, and together presenting a Jewish version of the gnostic concept of the pleroma. The system of the ten Divine powers is presented in the late 12th-century *Sefer* BAHIR and in the commentary on *Sefer Yetsirah* by R. Isaac the Blind in Provence (late 12th-beginning 13th century). It then became the central system of symbols used by kabbalists. There is no direct connection between this term and the Greek "spheres," that denoted the wheels in which the stars are fixed. In terms of content, there may have been

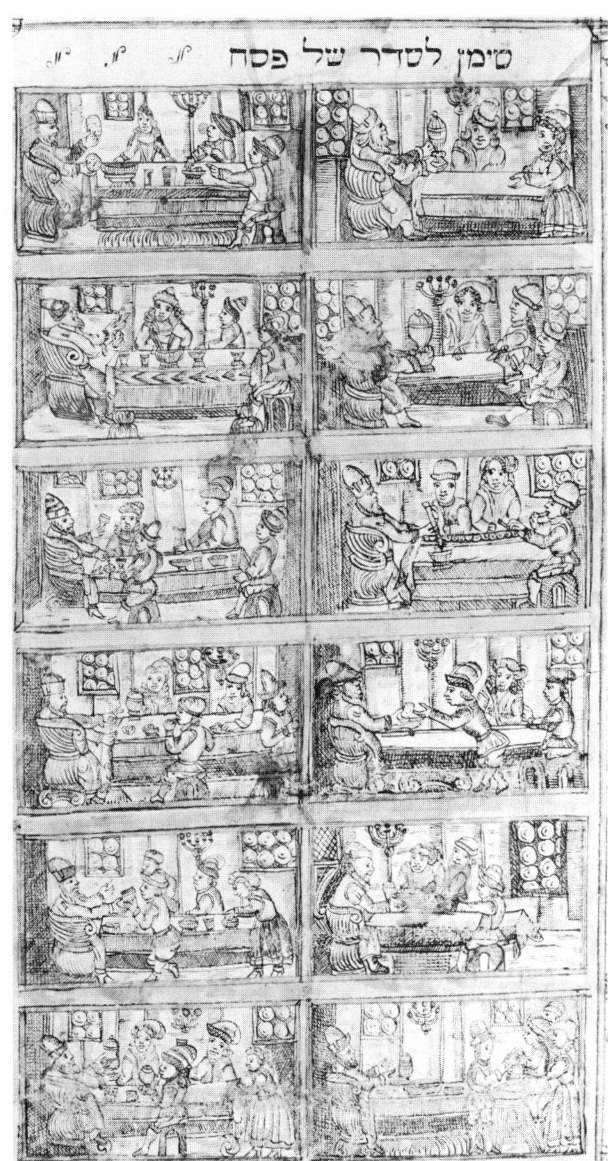

Order of the Passover Seder. *From a* Haggadah, *Germany, 1732.*

some influence of the philosophical system of ethical means by which God governs the world on the evolvement of the *sefirot* in the Kabbalah.

Each of the *sefirot* has a name. The most common names and characteristics (that vary in every kabbalistic work) are *Keter* (Crown), the supreme Divine power that may be identifed with the Godhead and includes the Divine Will and supreme Thought; *Hokhmah* (Wisdom), which denotes the Divine plan for all existence; *Binah* (Intelligence), which is the source or fountain of all existence. These three, in the anthropomorphic symbolism of many kabbalists, comprise the head of the Divine figure. *Hesed* (Charity) is the right arm and the source of Divine goodness; *Din* (Law) or *Gevurah* (Power), the left arm, is the source of strict justice and punishment; *Tiferet* (Beauty) unites the two and represents the Divine body or heart and the Divine mercy. *Netsah* (Eternity) represents the right leg and *Hod* (Glory) the left, both being lower manifestations of *Hesed* and *Din*. The ninth *sefirah*, *Yesod* (Foundation), represents the male organ and the flowing of Divine force in the universe. The tenth, the SHEKHINAH (Presence) or *Malkhut* (Kingdom), is a separate, feminine figure, which includes elements of all the nine *sefirot*, reflects them and governs the created world. Many kabbalists from the second half of the 13th century described the existence of another, parallel, system of *sefirot* of the left side, the forces of evil. (See ADAM KADMON.)

SELAH Hebrew term of uncertain meaning which occurs three times in the Book of Habakkuk (3:3, 9, 13) and 71 times in the Book of Psalms. It is almost invariably placed at the end of a verse. Both the meaning and the purpose of *Selah* remain obscure, although it is generally regarded as some form of liturgical or musical direction to the Levite choir and orchestra in the Temple. Various suggestions have therefore been made — that it indicated a dramatic pause or change of tempo in the levitical recitation of psalms, when the choristers' voices were raised or lowered, a new melody was introduced, or the instrumentalists accompanying them brought the tune to a crescendo or allowed it to fade in a diminuendo. According to the Talmud (*Er.* 54a), *Selah* may be translated as a synonym of "for evermore," while rabbinic exegesis holds it to be a confirmation of the preceding phrase or sentence. It is in this sense that the term was accepted in the Jewish prayer book (see RESPONSES, LITURGICAL).

SELIHOT (sing. *selihah*). Penitential prayers seeking FORGIVENESS (*selihah*) and mercy from God for sins committed. According to tradition, God taught Moses His thirteen attributes by the use of which Moses could always plead for mercy and would not be refused (*RH* 17b). The thirteen attributes, stated in Exodus 34:6-7, are: "The Lord! The Lord! a God compassionate and gracious, slow to anger, abounding in kindness and faithfulness, extending kindness to the thousandth generation, forgiving iniquity, transgression, and sin, remitting punishment." These became the nucleus for all prayers and requests for forgiveness. In the course of time, a whole category of liturgical poems (PIYYUTIM) called *selihot* were written around this theme.

Selihot were originally recited on the Day of Atonement and other fast days but were later extended to other days. From the geonic period on, they were recited every MONDAY AND THURSDAY after the Morning Service AMIDAH. These *selihot* all begin with the thirteen attributes. The SHULHAN ARUKH states that it was customary to rise at dawn in the period between 1 Elul and the Day of Atonement to recite *selihot* and this is still the Sephardi custom. Ashkenazim start this penitential season on the Sunday before Rosh ha-Shanah (if the latter falls on a Monday or a Tuesday, the recital of *selihot* commences on the Sunday of the previous week). Hasidim begin their recitation after midnight on the Saturday night of the said week; others begin before daybreak. Special *selihot* were composed for the different fast days. Different rites (see NUSAH) had varying customs and texts. Separate volumes of *selihot* were published.

Many liturgical poets wrote these penitential poems. Some of the authors are anonymous, while others are noted figures such as the outstanding composer of *piyyutim*, Yosé ben Yosé, R. GERSHOM ME'OR HA-GOLAH, RASHI and R. SAMUEL BEN MEIR. The Spanish poet, Moses IBN EZRA, was so well known as a composer of these poems that he came to be called *Ha-Salah* (i.e., the author of *selihot*).

Many of the *selihot* are based on alphabetic ACROSTICS, but there are also other arrangements, such as reverse alphabetical acrostics. In most cases the name of the author appears acrostically after the alphabetical verses.

SEMAHOT One of the minor tractates of the Talmud (appended to the Order NEZIKIN), dealing with the laws of MOURNING; the name of the tractate, which in translation means "joys," is a euphemism. The work is also known as *Evel Rabbati* ("Great [work on] mourning").

SEMIKHAH See ORDINATION

SEPHARDIM Jews tracing their descent from ancestors who lived in medieval Spain (*Sefarad* in Hebrew). The term has been used more generally to include Jews who follow Sephardi liturgy, legal traditions and customs, even if their ancestors did not actually live in Spain. They are distinguished from the ASHKENAZIM — Jews who originated in central or eastern Europe.

Medieval Spanish Jewry distinguished itself in many areas of endeavor, general and Jewish. They recorded remarkable achievements in philosophy, literature and the natural sciences and contributed to Jewish scholarship in such fields as *halakhah*, talmudic commentary and interpretation, biblical exegesis and Hebrew grammar. Outstanding figures of medieval Sephardi Jewry continue to have profound influ-

A Sephardi couple from Turkey in traditional costume, c.1800.

ence on Jewish learning and thought, e.g., JUDAH HALEVI, Solomon IBN GABIROL, Abraham IBN EZRA, Moses MAIMONIDES, Moses NAHMANIDES, Solomon ben ADRET, and Isaac ABRAVANEL.

After the expulsion of Jews from Spain in 1492 and the decree forbidding Judaism in Portugal in 1496, Sephardi Jewry underwent a dramatic upheaval. Many resettled in the domains of the Ottoman Empire that received them with open arms. Some went to Erets Israel and other locations in the Middle East. Many migrated to North Africa. They re-established themselves as Sephardi communities, following the traditions of the places where they had lived in the Iberian Peninsula. The arrival of large numbers of Sephardim created some problems for the local Jewish communities. Generally, Sephardi language, customs and halakhic rulings came to dominate in those communities where Sephardim were numerous. Where Sephardim came in smaller numbers, or where the local community was strong enough to maintain its own hegemony, Sephardim adapted to the prevailing Jewish culture.

During the 16th and 17th centuries, many MARRANOS — Jews who had been forcibly converted to Christianity in the Iberian Peninsula (and their descendants) — found their way to places where they could openly return to Judaism. They settled largely in western Europe and some went to the New World. These Jews are often called "Western Sephardim." Their traditions and cultural patterns differ from those of Sephardim who settled in Muslim lands. While Sephardim of Turkey, the Balkans, Israel and the north of Morocco spoke JUDEO-SPANISH (Ladino), in some Greek cities they spoke Greek. Those in Arab countries spoke Arabic. Those in Western Europe and the New World came to speak the languages of the lands in which they settled.

The 20th century saw major changes in Sephardi demography. In the early decades, many thousands of Levantine Sephardim migrated to the USA. Others moved to Europe, South America and southern Africa. Many Sephardi communities were exterminated by the Nazis. Sephardim from throughout the Sephardi diaspora settled in Israel, especially after the establishment of the State. Israel is now the major center of Sephardi settlement but communities can be found throughout the world, notably in France, the USA, Canada, Mexico, Latin America and England.

Sephardi communities have made significant contributions to Jewish religion and culture. The mystics of 16th-century Safed created the foundation for the subsequent development of Jewish MYSTICISM. The rabbinic authorities of the 16th century created a vast and impressive halakhic literature, notably, R. Yosef CARO who codified Sephardi religious practice and customs in his SHULHAN ARUKH. Others were halakhists, authors of rabbinic responsa, biblical commentators and authors of ethical tracts. Particularly popular was R. Jacob Huli's encyclopedic Judeo-Spanish biblical commentary, *Me'am Lo'ez*.

Historically, Sephardim avoided splitting into different ideological religious movements. They maintained unified communities which adhered to traditional Jewish law and Sephardi custom. Sephardi culture was generally characterized by respect for individuals and individualism, reverence for tradition and respect for elders. The influence of the Kabbalah on the non-Western Sephardim imbued them with a deep inner piety and sensitivity to symbolism. One of the main differences between the Sephardim and Ashkenazim lies in their prayer rites (see NUSAH). The prayer customs of the Sephardim trace back to Babylonian Jewry, whereas the Ashkenazim are the heirs of the liturgical traditions of the Jews in Erets Israel. Hebrew pronunciation differs, although in recent years — since the Sephardi pronunciation was adopted for everyday Hebrew in Erets Israel — a growing number of Ashkenazi synagogues (and schools) have adopted the Sephardi pronunciation. Sephardi liturgical differences include varying order of prayers, the omission of many of the liturgical poems (PIYYUTIM) for Sabbaths and the festivals, the omission of KOL NIDRÉ in most congregations on the eve of the Day of Atonement and of MEMORIAL SERVICES for the dead on PILGRIM FESTIVALS and the Day of Atonement. The cantillation melody for reading the Pentateuch is different and there is another order of prophetical readings. Sephardi SELIHOT, KINOT and other poems are often not the same as those recited by the Ashkenazim. They also have unique wedding, circumcision and death customs, as well as festival traditions (for example, on Passover Sephardim eat rice which is forbidden to the Ashkenazim). Some Sephardi liturgical practices were taken over in certain East European communities, notably in the Ḥasidic liturgy. The Ḥasidim also adopted a number of Sephardi usages, such as not putting on phylacteries (*tefillin*) on intermediate days of festivals (ḤOL HA-MO'ED).

In Israel, where Sephardi and Ashkenazi communities have lived side by side for centuries, the situation was institutionalized under the British Mandate when the CHIEF RABBINATE was established with both a Sephardi and an Ashkenazi chief rabbi. This duality has been retained in the State of Israal, where there are also Sephardi and Ashkenazi chief rabbis in the main cities.

SEPTUAGINT (often written LXX, i.e., "seventy"). The oldest extant Greek translation of the Bible. It got its name from the story of the seventy elders responsible for the translation, as related in the "Letter of ARISTEAS," in the Talmud and in the works of Philo and Josephus. There are disagreements about the date the translation was carried out, but it is agreed that not all the Bible was translated at the same time and that, except for the Pentateuch, it was not the product of a single major operation. According to the "Letter of Aristeas," it was composed in Alexandria. Ptolemy II Philadelphus (285-246 BCE), who was a bibliophile, heard from his librarian, Demetrius, that the Jewish Bible was worth translating for the king's archives. The king wrote to the high priest in Jerusalem, asking him to send scholars who would be able to translate the Pentateuch into Greek. The high priest sent 72 wise men, whom the king lodged in a building on the island of Pharos, near Alexandria. Each translated only a part of the Pentateuch and after 72 days, at the conclusion of the work, the Greek translations were read before the Jewish community and before the king. All lauded the Jewish Bible and its wisdom and praised the work of the translators.

The Talmud (*Meg,* 9a) states that all the elders translated the entire Bible. According to legend, each made his own translation and when these were compared, they were found to be identical. It is now thought that the project was initiated not by the king but by the Egyptian Jewish community which needed a Greek translation for its own requirements. In fact, it may have emerged through oral tradition in the synagogues of Alexandria. The entire Bible was translated by c.100 BCE.

The word "Septuagint", applied at first only to the Pentateuch, was later applied to the other books as well. The internal order of the books is different from the Hebrew version. In addition to the books of the Bible, there are a number of apocryphal works (see APOCRYPHA AND PSEUDEPIGRAPHA), such as Maccabees and Ecclesiasticus. Various changes and errors are the result of later additions and deletions made to accord with Christian theology, such as the addition of the Hebrew word equivalent for "from the cross" in Psalms 96:10, the incorrect translation of the word *alma* ("maiden") as "virgin" (Isa. 7:14) and others.

The style of the translation is not uniform, because of the different translators involved and the different times of the various translations. The Septuagint is noteworthy for its popular, limited and simple vocabulary. It was because of the Septuagint translation that the rest of the world became aware of the culture of the Jews and, according to Philo (*Life of Moses* 2.7), the Jews of Alexandria held an annual festivity on the island of Pharos on the anniversary of the completion of the Septuagint.

The sages of Erets Israel, on the other hand, regarded the translation as a real danger to the Hebrew language, which they feared would be replaced by Greek. In addition, the translation began to be used as the basis for the allegorical sermons of the Hellenistic Jews, and the Christians, too, began to utilize it in their polemics against Judaism. The sages therefore announced: "The day that the Torah was translated was as terrible as the day that the [golden] calf was made" (*Sof.* 1). The last chapter of MEGILLAT TA'ANIT states: "On the 8th of Tevet the Torah was written in Greek during the time of King Ptolemy, and darkness came to the world for three days."

SERKES, JOEL (known as *Baḥ*, from the initials of *Bayit Ḥadash*; 1561-1640). Rabbi and talmudic commentator in Poland. Born in Lublin, Serkes served as rabbi in Lublin and Brest-Litovsk and as head of the *yeshivah* and *av bet din* (head of the court) in Cracow from 1619. His major work is *Bayit Ḥadash* ("New Home"), a commentary on JACOB BEN ASHER'S *Arba'ah Turim*, which traces the sources of each halakhic decision from the Talmud and the RISHONIM. He also wrote responsa and notes on the Talmud. He strongly opposed philosophy as well as PILPUL and favored study of the Kabbalah.

SERMONS See HOMILETICS AND HOMILETICAL LITERATURE

SE'UDAH ("a meal"). A festive meal held either because of a special day or a special occasion (known as *se'udat mitsvah*, a feast [as the fulfillment] of a commandment).

Festive meals include the three Sabbath meals (see SE'UDAH SHELISHIT), two meals on every festival day, the Purim afternoon feast and the Passover SEDER. The Bible also indicates a feast on the New Moon (see I Sam. 20:5; Isa. 1:13-14). At all the aforementioned meals, except for that on Purim, the person reciting the blessing over the bread must do so over two whole loaves. A Jewish saying runs, "there is no feast without fish, meat and wine," the rest of the meal being merely ancillary.

The idea of a festive meal celebrating an occasion of significance is already found in Genesis, where Abraham made a great meal to celebrate the weaning of his son Isaac (Gen. 21:8). Various such occasions are considered to require a *se'udat mitsvah* — a meal of religious significance — including the day a boy is circumcised or becomes BAR MITSVAH or a girl becomes BAT MITSVAH, at engagement and wedding receptions and throughout the week of SHEVA BERAKHOT, and upon the completion of study of a talmudic tractate.

SE'UDAH SHELISHIT ("third meal"). The third of the three obligatory SABBATH meals (see SE'UDAH). It is also known as *shalosh se'udot*. The meal is generally eaten after the Afternoon Service on Saturday. At each of the meals of the Sabbath, the blessing on bread must be on two whole loaves, but unlike the first two meals of the Sabbath, this meal is not preceded by the sanctification (KIDDUSH). The table melodies sung are generally slow and of a somewhat solemn nature, as the day fades into night and the sacred Sabbath gives way to a regular weekday.

SEVEN SPECIES (*shiv'at ha-minim*). Produce characteristic of Erets Israel. These crops are specified in an idyllic biblical passage describing Erets Israel as "a land of wheat and barley, of vines, figs, and pomegranates, a land of olive trees and honey; a land where you may eat food without stint, where you will lack nothing..." (Deut. 8:8-9). Wheat, the most valuable grain, and barley, source of the average Israelite's daily BREAD, constituted the two most important indigenous cereal crops (see FIVE SPECIES). From the vine, different types and qualities of WINE could be produced; the fig tree yielded a nourishing staple fruit and the pomegranate was a key symbol of the land's fertility (cf. Num. 13:23; Song 6:11, 7:13). Oil of the highest grade, pressed from olives, fed the lamps of the Sanctuary's candelabrum; while honey, though sometimes taken from bees (Judg. 14:8-9; I Sam. 14:27), was more often the sweet juice of dates or figs (Deut. 32:13; Ps. 81:17; II Chr. 31:5).

SEVENTEENTH OF TAMMUZ See SHIVAH ASAR BE-TAMMUZ

SEX The Bible views sex as an essential component of MARRIAGE. The creation of woman is based on the judgment that "it is not good for the man to be alone" and that the woman should be his "fitting helper" (Gen. 2:18). With the creation of woman, man is told to "leave his father and mother and cling to his wife, so that they become one flesh" (Gen. 2:24). Their union is thus closely intertwined with sexuality. The purpose of marriage is twofold: procreation and companionship. It means building a home and family (Gen. 1:28) as well as overcoming loneliness. To marry and have children is, in the Jewish view, a religious act — the very first MITSVAH — reflecting a commitment to transform the world.

Marital relations are the wife's right and the husband's duty. This obligation he must fulfill at specific intervals, which vary according to his occupation and ability (*Ket.* 61b). Should he wish to change from one occupation to another that will demand longer absences from home, he must secure his wife's permission in advance, because a woman prefers less income and a close relationship with her husband to a higher income and separation from him (*ibid.*). The "curse of Eve," that a woman's desire is for her husband and he will rule over her (Gen. 3:16), is said to account for woman's sexual modesty and her inhibition against taking the initiative in sexual activity (*Er.* 100b).

Romantic love does not play the role in early Judaism that it does in later periods: "Isaac then brought her into his mother Sarah's tent, and took Rebekah, and she became his wife; and he loved her" (Gen. 24:67). Love came after marriage, when the couple had assumed their mutual responsibilities. In Rabbinic Judaism, the sexual relationship between husband and wife is governed by intimacy, continuity, and sensitivity to physical needs. Intimacy refers to mutual consent where the law prohibits a husband from compelling his wife to have intercourse with him. The law also prohibits intercourse when either spouse is drunk or when the woman is asleep. Mutual consent implies non-exploitation. The sages insisted that husbands and wives may not withhold themselves sexually, and may not engage in intercourse while in a state of anger toward each other. Sexual favors are not an object for barter. Intimacy also implies exclusivity: the sages forbade a person to have intercourse with his or her spouse while thinking of someone else. Intimacy thus demands a totality of relationship between the two parties.

A second component of marital life is continuity, an awareness of the ongoing character of their union (see FAMILY; FAMILY PURITY). A marriage may not be entered into with the intention of terminating it, for this contravenes the essential pledge of continuity. A married couple should refrain from having intercourse in the fields — not because someone may see them, but because such behavior lacks the essentials of continuity. A third component is sensitivity to physical needs. The sexual component cannot be negotiated out of marriage by mutual agreement, although economic factors can. For example, the partners could agree that the husband will not support the wife but that she will provide for herself, so that everything she earns will belong to her. If, however, a couple should agree to maintain only a platonic relationship, the marriage is invalid; for besides procreation, the aim of marriage is to develop a mature sexual relationship between the parties. Sensitivity to each other's sexual urges should be so fundamental to the relationship that neither partner need verbalize it.

The sages demand modesty and restraint in the sexual act. Overindulgence is to be avoided, as well as unnatural positions (*Sanh.* 37b). Intercourse should take place at night, in privacy, after tender, loving words have been expressed. According to the author of *Iggeret ha-Kodesh*, an anonymous ethical work of the 13th century, sex is "holy and pure when engaged in properly at the proper time and with the proper intentions... Whatever God created cannot possibly be shameful or ugly." It is the misuse of man's body that creates ugliness, since every one of his organs is neutral. Accordingly, "when a husband is united with his wife in holiness, the Divine Presence abides with them."

The preferred time for intercourse is on Friday night, the holiest of the week (*Ket.* 62b). The sages view man's sexual drive as an expression of the *yetser ha-ra* (the evil inclination), bad if uncontrolled but good if channeled. They believe that man is capable of restraining his libido. The ideal is not to deny or suppress a natural urge, but to harness it for consecrated ends — hence the admonitions to engage in conjugal relations within certain parameters that foster intimacy, continuity, and sensitivity to one's partner's sexual needs. Such parameters include the laws of MENSTRUATION (*niddah*). These laws prohibit marital intercourse during the menstrual period and for at least a week thereafter (Lev. 15:19-28).

Sexual Offenses. In Judaism, sexuality is bound up with the establishment of a family, with love and mutuality, and involves a natural act. All sexual acts that are not conducted within the framework of the marital relationship, or which are unnatural, must be shunned. Pre-marital sex is forbidden, according to Maimonides (*Yad, Ishut* 1.4), so as to prevent immoral behavior among Jews. Sex with Gentile women is also banned (*Sanh.* 82a), to prevent lasciviousness, as is visiting prostitutes.

The law forbidding masturbation is usually derived from the Onan story (Gen. 38:8-10). Although this episode seems to indicate *coitus interruptus*, the ban was widened to include any act that rules out procreation, the Talmud calling it "adultery of the hand" (*Nid.* 13b). Female masturbation is not mentioned, as it does not involve a deliberate waste of semen. Ethically, masturbation is prohibited because it occurs outside of the marital relationship and is not conducive to its enhancement and mutuality. This holds true also for pre- and extramarital relations, and for HOMOSEXUALITY. The Bible categorizes extramarital relations by a woman as ADULTERY (Ex. 20:13), while rabbinic law forbids men to indulge in them. Male homosexuality is termed "an abhorrent act" (Lev. 20:13) and female homosexuality — lesbianism — is likewise prohibited (*Yad, Issuré Bi'ah* 21.8).

Rape constitutes a transgression. If a man rapes a betrothed girl, he is put to death; if she is single, he must marry her and she can never be divorced. The woman is put to death only if she is married and was a consenting party, or where she could easily have called for help and failed to do so (Deut. 22:22-29). In the Judaic ethic, sex is held to be an indispensable element of life. It is the means through which men and women find completion; it must be disciplined by rules; it is private and intimate; and, when culminating in procreation, it has cosmic significance.

SFORNO, OBADIAH BEN JACOB (c. 1470-c.1550). Bible commentator, philosopher and physician. Born in Cesena in Italy, Sforno went to Rome where he studied philosophy, mathematics, philology and medicine. Attaining a high standard in Talmud and *halakhah*, he was considered one of the most important Torah scholars in that city. In Rome, he taught Hebrew from 1498 to 1500 to Johannes Reuchlin, the Christian humanist. In about 1525, he left Rome and led the life of an impoverished wanderer until settling in Bologna where he set up a school for higher religious education (*bet midrash*), which he headed until his death.

Sforno's fame rests primarily on his commentary on the Pentateuch and other books of the Bible. Rejecting mystical and forced interpretations, he emphasizes the plain meaning of the text (*peshat*) and takes pains to develop its ethical teachings. Writing succinctly in polished Hebrew, he judiciously quotes from earlier commentators and displays an extensive knowledge of grammar and philology. His introduction to the Pentateuch, called *Kavvanot ha-Torah* ("The inner meaning of the Torah"), deals with the structure of the Pentateuch and the reasons for the COMMANDMENTS.

Sforno wrote the philosophical work *Or Ammim* in which he attacked the views of Aristotle, holding them to be opposed to the principles of Judaism; he expressed surprise that even MAIMONIDES agreed with many of Aristotle's theories. He translated *Or Ammim* into Latin, under the title *Lumen Gentium*, and dedicated it to King Henry II of France.

Sforno also wrote a commentary on AVOT and various letters, sermons and responsa.

SHA'ATNEZ ("Mingled stuff"). Term of uncertain origin denoting any woven material that contains a mixture of wool and linen which Jews are forbidden to wear according to biblical law (Lev. 19:19; Deut. 22:11). Other mixtures of "a diverse kind" (*kilayim*) are also prohibited by the Torah (cf. Lev. 19:19, Deut. 22:9-10; see also AGRICULTURAL LAWS), although no reason is given for these negative precepts. Since priests were exempt from the *sha'atnez* law, Maimonides

Advertisement for a sha'atnez *laboratory in a Johannesburg Jewish periodical.*

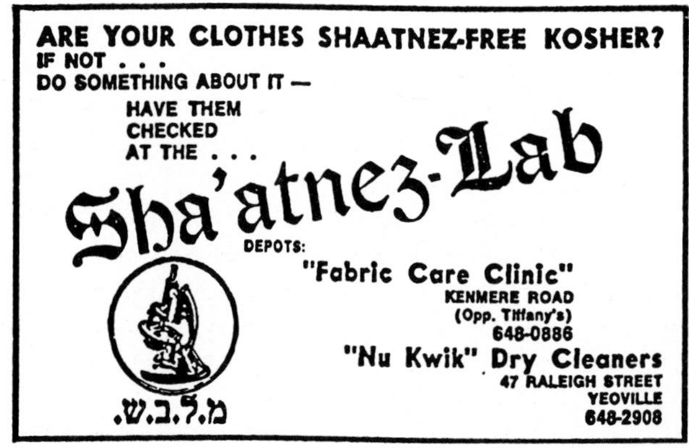

suggests that the use of such a forbidden mixture was associated with pagan worship. Nowadays, strictly observant Jews order their clothing from a tailor or manufacturer on whose premises the necessary checks are made; alternatively, garments may be inspected after purchase in a special "*sha'atnez* laboratory," to insure the replacement of any cloth, sewing thread, or stiffening material that proves religiously unacceptable. Certain clothing manufacturers arrange for a *sha'atnez* test label to be sewn into the lining of a garment after this inspection. Synthetic (e.g., polyester) fabrics and clothing made entirely from cotton need not be checked in this way.

SHABBAT ("Sabbath"). First tractate of Order *Mo'ed* in the Mishnah. Its 24 chapters deal with the types of labor forbidden on the Sabbath, the prohibition of certain categories of work on the eve of the Sabbath, the kindling of the Sabbath candles and miscellaneous laws regarding Sabbath observance (cf. Ex. 20:8-11; 31:12-17; Num. 15:32-36; Deut. 5:12-15). These prohibitions are based on the 39 categories of work traditionally performed in the building of the sanctuary. Because of the Sabbath's great importance in Jewish life and the fact that it is mentioned extensively in the Bible, this tractate appears first in the Order *Mo'ed* (Seasons), that is devoted to the laws of the Jewish holy days. The subject matter is amplified in both Talmuds and in the *Tosefta*.

SHABBAT See SABBATH

SHABBETAI TSEVI (1626-1676). Pseudo-messiah in Turkey; creator of the most powerful and widespread of all Jewish MESSIANIC movements in the Diaspora. Three major factors led to its appearance: the Wars of Religion in Europe (1618-1648); successful propagation of the kabbalistic doctrines of Isaac LURIA; the traumatic effect of the Chmielnicki massacres among East European Jewry (1648-49). Their combined effect was to make Jews everywhere receptive to the idea that a messianic redeemer had emerged from the general chaos of the time.

A gifted scholar, ordained at 18 in his native Smyrna, Shabbetai Tsevi increasingly devoted himself to ascetic exercises and study of the ZOHAR, also attracting numerous disciples. However, throughout his life, he suffered from bouts of manic depression alternating with periods of tranquillity or euphoric illumination. At times he was locked in battle with what he supposed to be demonic powers; at others, he was capable of the most extraordinary and paradoxical irreligious behavior. The fact that he had been born on TISHAH BE-AV, the Messiah's traditional birthday, must have strengthened his belief in his own messianic destiny and led him to begin pronouncing the Tetragrammaton (see GOD, NAMES OF) in 1648. That year was marked by various calamities and was also viewed by kabbalists as one that would herald Israel's redemption. After a period of forbearance, the Smyrna rabbinate expelled Shabbetai Tsevi (c.1651) and over the next few years he wandered through Greece and European Turkey, scandalizing Jews with his antinomian demonstrations and pronouncements.

He later found a more congenial environment in Jerusalem and in Cairo, where (in March 1664) the prophet HOSEA served as role model for his marriage to a girl of doubtful repute named Sarah, who had survived the Cossack massacres in Poland and whom Shabbetai Tsevi dubbed "the bride of the Messiah." A renewed spell of depression made him turn for help to Nathan of Gaza (1643-1680), a brilliant young rabbi; but instead of curing him, Nathan hailed Shabbetai Tsevi as the promised redeemer and cast himself in the role of Elijah the Prophet. Nathan created vast enthusiasm throughout the Jewish world by dispatching a communiqué which told how the Turkish Sultan would be deposed, Israel's Ten Lost TRIBES would return from their exile, and a short-lived rebellion would signal the "birth pangs of redemption" heralding the Messiah's advent.

Many leading rabbis were swept along in the euphoria; those who remained hostile or skeptical were often cowed into silence. From Jerusalem to Aleppo to Hamburg and Amsterdam, communities split over their belief in Shabbetai Tsevi's messiahship. In the Smyrna synagogue, Shabbetai Tsevi abrogated the commandments, performed forbidden acts, and proclaimed himself "the Lord's anointed" (December 1665). Opponents were excommunicated and fled for their lives, the messianic redemption being scheduled for 18 June 1666. Meanwhile, penitential liturgies composed by

Shabbetai Tsevi, the pseudo-messiah, blessing his followers.

Nathan of Gaza heightened the frenzy. Before long, prayers for "our Lord and King, Shabbetai Tsevi" replaced those for the Sultan; major fast days were converted into festivals and Jews, rich and poor alike, sold everything they had in time for the expected redemption.

Shabbetai Tsevi sailed to Constantinople, but this messianic journey ended in his arrest and imprisonment by the Turks (February 1666) in the fortress of Gallipoli. Although reluctant to turn the visionary into a martyr, and even prepared to grant him the facilities of a "court," the Turkish authorities soon realized that imprisonment had not weakened his resolve or the almost hysterical devotion of his followers. When faced with a choice between death and Islam, Shabbetai Tsevi opted to become a Muslim (16 September 1666), although he, his wife and others who followed him thereafter led a crypto-Jewish life. This sudden betrayal, inconceivable to the hitherto loyal masses, drove tens of thousands back to the traditional fold. Others, however, remained faithful "believers," even after Shabbetai Tsevi's death as an exile in Albania (1676).

The Shabbatean Movement. Confronted with the apostasy of the "Messiah," his leading followers sought explanations and had to determine their own future course of action. Nathan of Gaza insisted that by outwardly embracing Islam, Shabbetai Tsevi had succeeded in penetrating the enemy camp so as to do battle with the forces of evil. Far from abandoning his mission to redeem the Jewish people, he had chosen a "messianic exile" in order to hasten the end of Israel's exile. This was only possible because the Messiah, unfettered by the laws of the Torah, could engage in acts which — to an ordinary Jew — appeared strange or paradoxical.

In its major centers (Turkey, Italy, and Poland), the Shabbatean movement faced violent opposition from the rabbinical authorities and went underground. Here and there, during the 18th century, crypto-Shabbateans could be discovered at work even in the rabbinate (see EYBESCHÜTZ, JONATHAN). In Turkey, hundreds of "believers" formally converted to Islam and (between 1683 and 1924) their sect of the *Dönmeh* (Turkish for "apostates") could be found chiefly in Salonika. While rejecting much of the Torah (contracting forbidden marriages, indulging in ritualized sexual promiscuity and observing 9 Av as a festival, etc.), the *Dönmeh* long maintained a separate "Jewish life," they opposed intermarriage with Muslims, had their own prayer houses and cemeteries, developed a Judeo-Spanish form of liturgy and even retained their ancestral (Sephardi) family names.

The *Konyosos*, one subsect of the *Dönmeh*, conducted missionary propaganda and gave rise to the FRANKISTS, a late 18th-century Shabbatean group which embraced Catholicism and spread from Poland to Bohemia and Germany. By 1850, except for the *Dönmeh*, Shabbateanism had practically vanished. From the ranks of the *Dönmeh* several leaders of the revolutionary Young Turk movement emerged in 1909. Until recently, a small *Dönmeh* community existed in Istanbul.

SHADKHAN ("matchmaker"). A person who negotiates a marriage, usually in return for monetary compensation. *Shiddukhin* (arranged marriages) were the usual and preferred method of marrying off young people throughout much of Jewish history. In the Bible, the first *shiddukh* (match) was arranged by Abraham's servant, Eliezer (Gen. 24). His choice of REBEKAH as wife for his master's son ISAAC was based on her kind character and her family's close connection to Abraham (she was his niece). The Talmud emphasizes the importance of *shiddukhin* in stating that although all kinds of work and business transactions are forbidden on the Sabbath, arrangements may be made for the betrothal of young girls on that day (*Shab.* 150a).

The profession of *shadkhan* was firmly established by the early Middle Ages, although sometimes the heads of two families arranged their children's marriage. The rabbis discussed the *shadkhan*'s right to remuneration and its amount. The fee was based on the dowry — two percent in most cases, three percent if the couple lived more than ten miles apart. Originally, the *shadkhan*'s profession was a highly esteemed one in which Torah scholars were commonly employed. A rabbi was the natural go-between since he knew many of the families in the community, and was in a position to recommend a young Torah scholar to a father anxious for a pious, learned son-in-law. R. Jacob MÖLLN, a great scholar of the 15th century, worked as a *shadkhan* because he refused any compensation for his rabbinic functions. Women also entered the profession, especially in Muslim lands.

In the 19th century, the status of the *shadkhan* began to decline. Not all in the profession were honorable, and the *shadkhan* became the butt of numerous jokes and stories in the Eastern Europe *shtetl*. In recent years, the *shadkhan* has been largely replaced by dating services (often computerized). However, *shadkhanim* continue to function to this day with only a few changes, notably in Israel. Fees vary according to the reputation of the *shadkhan* and the ability of the couple to pay. Although some marriages among the very Orthodox, especially the Ḥasidim, are still arranged by parents or rabbis, many are arranged by a *shadkhan*. After the initial introduction, the young people usually meet three or four times, but are free to refuse the match if it is not to his or her liking.

SHAḤARIT See MORNING SERVICE

SHALI'AḤ ("messenger", "emissary"). A person dispatched to perform a specific task, an agent empowered to act on someone else's behalf; an emissary from the Land of Israel to Jewish communities in the Diaspora.

The concept of agency (*sheliḥut*) is of importance in rabbinic sources and the *halakhah*. Thus, a bill of DIVORCE may be handed over or received by an agent (*Git.* 4.1, 62b) and HAMETS (leaven) may be sold to a non-Jew through rabbinical agency before Passover, since "a man's agent is like himself" (*Ber.* 5,5), i.e., acts performed by the *shali'ah* bind the one whom he represents. In the same way, goods and property may be bought and sold and even a marriage contract may be drawn up on the principal's behalf. However, a deaf-mute, an imbecile, or a minor cannot serve as an agent (*Git.* 23a); no Jew can deputize another to fulfill a MITSVAH which devolves upon himself; and "there can be no agency for wrong doing" (*Kid.* 42b), i.e., while a person may not be instructed to commit an offense, the blame for any offense committed on the agent's initiative may not be shifted to his principal.

Another concept is that of the *sheli'ah mitsvah*, someone dispatched to perform a religious function, whom the sages deemed to be safeguarded from harm in the course of his mission since "an errand of mercy is its own protection" (*Pes.* 8a). Listed under this heading is the SHELI'AH TSIBBUR, "messenger of the congregation" or prayer leader delegated to conduct worship in the synagogue. Another is the person who travels far afield, usually to solicit aid for public and religious institutions in the Land of Israel. From 700 CE until modern times, Jewish communities in many lands had a special charity fund available for the traveling Erets Israel emissary, who went by several names: *sheli'ah Tsiyyon*, the "messenger from Zion" (*Bétsah* 25b); *sheluha de-Rabbanan*, the "emissary of the rabbis" (often abbreviated to *shadar*); or *shelu'ah Erets Yisra'el.* Armed with letters of credential, these emissaries were primarily fundraisers who obtained Diaspora Jewry's assistance for YESHIVOT and the poor in the Holy Land. They included eminent rabbis and scholars (e.g., Moses Alshekh and Hayyim Joseph David AZULAI) who often spent many years abroad, also providing spiritual leadership and rendering halakhic decisions.

Nowadays, this type of religious fundraiser is known as a *meshullah*. The contemporary *shali'ah* goes overseas, usually for two three years, as a representative of the World Zionist Organization or other Israeli bodies. He or she may be sent to teach Hebrew and religious subjects in Jewish day schools, to direct Zionist youth activities, to give religious leadership in small communities, etc.

SHALOM ZAKHAR ("peace to the male child"). Friday night festive gathering in Ashkenazi communities of friends and relatives at the home of the parents immediately following the birth of a son. Since the SABBATH is called *Shalom* ("peace"), the name *Shalom Zakhar* is given to this custom. Another explanation for the designation *Shalom Zakhar* is that a woman in the throes of childbirth may feel resentment toward her husband, who is responsible for her pain. With the birth of the child, the pain has subsided, the joy of having a new baby fills the house, and there is once again peace (*shalom*) between husband and wife. A further explanation comes from the talmudic saying "A boy is born — peace comes to the world" (*Nid.* 31b). In Poland and Lithuania, members of the congregation would be invited to the festivity by an announcement at the end of the Friday Evening Service. One folkloric custom was to eat lentils, a sign of mourning, as it was believed that while in the womb, the child had been taught the entire Torah, but as he entered the world, an angel struck him on the lips and he had forgotten everything.

SHALOSH REGALIM See PILGRIM FESTIVALS

SHAMMAI (c.50 BCE-c.30 CE). Sage in Erets Israel and *av bet din* (vice-president) of the Sanhedrin, he and HILLEL were the last of the five "pairs" (ZUGOT) who transmitted the ORAL LAW. In halakhic matters, Shammai — a builder by trade (*Shab.* 31a) — adopted a severer line than Hillel, to judge by the four controversies between them recorded in the Mishnah. His generally conservative approach reflected the older *halakhah* and a literal interpretation of Scripture. Shammai's rigorousness, often attributed to an impatient, irascible nature, is exemplified in his reaction to the Gentile who offered to become a proselyte if Shammai would teach him the whole Torah while he (the non-Jew) was standing on one foot. Angered by this bizarre request, Shammai drove the man away with the stick he happened to be clutching in his hand at the time. Hillel adopted a more conciliatory approach to the Gentile, however, teaching him a version of the GOLDEN RULE (*Shab.* 31b).

These teachers founded rival schools (see BET SHAMMAI AND BET HILLEL), the *halakhot* of Shammai's school presumably originating with him. Nevertheless, on a few occasions, Shammai rejected the line adopted by both schools (opting for a harsher one) and, in another instance, sided with the Hillelites. The measures taken by Bet Shammai to severely restrict contact with the non-Jews may well indicate Shammai's own alertness to the dangers facing the Jewish people in his time. Three of his sayings are quoted in the Mishnah (*Avot* 1.15): "Make your Torah study a regular practice," "Say little and do much," and "Greet everyone with a cheerful face." Like some of the halakhic decisions transmitted in his name, this last saying proves Shammai to have been capable of leniency and benevolence, even if religious zeal often made him severe and belligerent.

SHAMMASH (lit. "servant"). Community or synagogue official. Best known as the paid sexton in the synagogue, the *shammash* could also have been employed by the community and in some instances by the rabbinical courts. The *shammash* played various roles depending on the institution to which he was connected. His varied jobs included: tax collector, bailiff, process server, secretary, messenger, and even grave digger. One known function of the *shammash* was as the *"shulklapper"* who knocked on window shutters as a call to morning prayer, to announce the beginning of the Sabbath, and to awaken people for midnight services and for SELIHOT prayer during the month of Elul.

In the 20th century, the *shammash* continued to be a significant functionary in all countries where Jews lived. In most instances he was responsible for the services proceeding in an orderly fashion, and in some cases he also read the Torah. In recent years the number of synagogues with a *shammash* has declined. Although in some cases he has been replaced by the modern "ritual director," in others the members of the synagogue themselves volunteer to take on the role once held by the *shammash*. In some Reform congregations in North America women serve as *shammash*. In Israel, the *shammash* has retained his importance; all major synagogues have one, and he often serves as the key official since frequently there is no permanent rabbi.

The term is also applied to the ninth light on the HANUKKAH candle, from which the other candles are lit.

SHAS Common designation for the Babylonian TALMUD; an acronym of the Hebrew *Shishah Sedarim*, "Six Orders" (of the Mishnah or Talmud). According to medieval Christian opinion, the Talmud contained defamatory statements about Christianity and fortified Jewish resistance to conversion. Objecting to the word "Talmud," Christian censors appointed to check talmudic literature normally substituted the term GEMARA, but in a few instances supplied the term *Shas*. The first edition of the Talmud to be censored in this fashion was that published in Basle (1578-81), which nearly all subsequent versions have followed.

SHAVING The Bible states, "You shall not round the corners of your heads, neither shall you destroy the corners of your beard" (Lev. 19:27). As explained in the ORAL LAW, the two prohibitions involved here are: removing one's sideburns, thus effectively "rounding the corners (*pe'ot*)" of the head, and "destroying the corners" on one's face, of which there are five, two on each cheek, and one on the chin. The law regarding sideburns enjoins that hair be left on the face down to the beginning of the cheekbone, and that it be at least long enough that it can be gripped between two fingers. Many ultra-Orthodox Jews do not cut the sideburns at all, and either grow sideburns (known as *pe'ot*), or allow the hair to grow long enough to be swept behind each ear. (The *pe'ot* of the Yemenites have a different origin: they were instituted by one of the Yemenite kings as a method to differentiate between Jews and Muslims. The wearing of *pe'ot* later became a matter of pride among this community.) The Oral Law regards the verse, "they shall not shave off the corner of their beard" (Lev. 21:5) which refers to priests, as being a general prohibition applicable to all Jews. It then deduces that the prohibition against shaving only applies when both of these conditions are met: the hair is "destroyed," interpreted to mean closely shaved; and a cutting edge which is in direct contact with the face is used. It is therefore permitted to use an electric razor, since the cutting edge does not come in contact with the skin. A depilatory is also permitted. There are nevertheless many observant Jews who wear beards, regarding it as part of the Jewish heritage and a custom handed down throughout the ages.

There are various periods when it is forbidden to shave or have a haircut. These include Sabbaths and festivals, since this action is considered to involve work. Observant Jews also do not shave for the OMER period between Passover and Shavu'ot and during the three weeks between 17 Tammuz and 9 Av, although there are differences in the Ashkenazi and Sephardi customs in regard to the latter period. A person in mourning is forbidden to shave for at least 30 days, and even longer when in mourning for his parents. Various authorities permit shaving on the intermediate days of festivals and on Fridays (in honor of the Sabbath) during the *Omer* period.

SHAVU'OT ("Weeks"). Second of the three PILGRIM FESTIVALS, known in English as the Feast of Weeks, Pentecost, and Festival of the Giving of the Law; observed in the Diaspora, for two days (6-7 Sivan) and in Israel and by Reform Jews everywhere for one day (6 Sivan).

The name "Weeks" derives from the biblical instruction to count seven weeks from the time of the Passover harvest festival, at the end of which a second harvest festival was to be observed (Ex. 34:22; Lev. 23:15ff.; Deut. 16:9-10). The three days preceding the festival are known as *sheloshet yemé ha-hagbalah* ("Three Days of Preparation"; see Ex. 19:11-12) during which the mourning regulations of the OMER period are suspended. Pentecost is the Greek term for "fiftieth," i.e., the festival celebrated on the 50th day (see below); it was the name adopted by Greek-speaking Jews of the first century. Shavu'ot is also called *Hag ha-Katsir* (the Harvest Festival; Ex. 23:16) and *Yom ha-Bikkurim* (the Day of the First Ripe Fruits; Num. 28:26), when the Israelites were to bring a special thank-offering to the Temple. In talmudic literature the festival is frequently referred to as *Atseret* (*Shev.* 1.1, *RH* 1.2), usually translated as "a Solemn Assembly." The term is used in the Bible, where it is also applied to other festivals (Lev. 23:26; Num. 29:35; Deut. 16:8), but in post-biblical sources it is nearly always restricted to Shavu'ot. For the rabbis, *Atseret* meant "the concluding day of the festival," reflecting their view of Shavu'ot as *Atseret shel Pesah*, the conclusion of Passover. Shavu'ot not only marks the end of the grain harvest commencing at Passover time, but also signifies the culmination of the process of freedom started with the Exodus at Passover, and concluded with the proclamation of the Law at Sinai, traditionally on Shavu'ot. Liturgically, the festival is called *Zeman Mattan Toratenu*, the Season of the Giving of our Torah, which, as the rabbis derived from Exodus 19:1-16, occurred on 6 Sivan. This name relates to the events described in Exodus 19-20 and recalls the central historical event which post-biblical Judaism ascribes to this day. Shavu'ot is the only festival for which no specific date is given in the Bible. Instead, the people are instructed to count seven weeks "from the morrow of the day of rest [the Sabbath], from the day on which you brought the offering of the sheaf [*Omer*] of the waving" (Lev. 23:15). The cutting of the *Omer* of the new barley marked the beginning of the counting period; on the 50th day, the new-harvest festival was observed. For the rabbis, "the Sabbath" referred to the first day of Passover, and the 50th day was therefore always 6 Sivan. The SADDUCEES and later the KARAITES understood the term "Sabbath" in its literal sense, so that the counting began on the Sunday of Passover week; thus the date was variable but the holiday would always fall on a Sunday. (This is also the tradition among the SAMARITANS.) It is possible that the controversy centered around the rabbinic view linking Shavu'ot to the great historical event of the Divine Revelation at Mount Sinai, for which there had to be a fixed date. The Sadducees, however, saw no warrant in the Scriptures for such an association and therefore for them Shavu'ot remained a purely agricultural celebration for which a movable date was entirely appropriate. Ethiopian Jews regarded the "morrow" of the day of rest as meaning the day after the Passover festival and thus observe Shavu'ot on 12 Sivan.

In the Temple period, Shavu'ot was the time when the individual farmer would set out with his neighbors in joyous procession to Jerusalem in order to offer a selection of his first ripe fruits (*bikkurim*) as a thank-offering. The Mishnah contains a vivid account of the farmer's preparation for this offering and the ceremonies connected with it (*Bik.* 3; see FIRST FRUITS).

In post-Temple times, however, the main emphasis shifted to the festival's identification as the anniversary of the giving of the Torah at Sinai, when the TEN COMMANDMENTS were proclaimed to the assembled Children of Israel.

Shavu'ot is less rich in special laws and customs than the other pilgrim festivals. In many traditional communities the world over, the practice of remaining awake during Shavu'ot night is widely observed. R. Solomon ALKABETS and other Sephardi kabbalists of the 16th century originated the custom of TIKKUN *Lél Shavu'ot* (*Tikkun* for Shavu'ot eve) in which a special anthology comprising the beginning and end of each portion of the Pentateuch, the opening verses of each chapter in the rest of the Bible and the opening passage of each of the 63 tractates of the Mishnah, was read. Some lectionaries also contained citations from the ZOHAR, as well as poetic exhortations (AZHAROT) on the theme of the 613 commandments. Today, in those communities in which the custom is observed, a passage of Talmud or other rabbinic literature usually takes the place of this lectionary. Some Diaspora communities followed the practice of reading the Book of Psalms on the second night, in accordance with the tradition that David the Psalmist was born and died on Shavu'ot, but this custom has become rare. It was usual for the Jews of Kurdistan to visit holy tombs on this day, especially the traditional tomb of the prophet Nahum near Moshul.

SHAVU'OT — PENTECOST

Other Names: *Ḥag ha-Shavu'ot* (Feast of Weeks)
Ḥag ha-Katsir (Harvest Festival)
Yom ha-Bikkurim (Day of the First Fruits)
Zeman Mattan Toratenu (Season of the Giving of our Torah)

Hebrew Dates: 6 Sivan (in Israel and among Reform Jews in the Diaspora)
6-7 Sivan (in the Diaspora)

Torah & Prophetical Readings:
1st Day: Ex. 19:1-20:23; Num. 28:26-31 (*Maftir*); Ezek. 1:1-28, 3:12 (*Haftarah*)
2nd Day (in Diaspora); Deut. 15:19-16:17 (14:22-16:17 on Sabbath); Num. 28:26-31 (*Maftir*); Hab. 2:20-3:19 (*Haftarah*)

Scroll: Book of Ruth
Hallel: recited (in full)
Yizkor: recited on 2nd day only in the Diaspora (not by Reform Jews)

Civil dates on which the festival occurs, 1990-2010:

Year	Date
1990/5751	30 May
1991/5752	19 May
1992/5753	7 June
1993/5754	26 May
1994/5755	16 May
1995/5756	4 June
1996/5757	24 May
1997/5758	11 June
1998/5759	31 May
1999/5760	21 May
2000/5761	9 June
2001/5762	28 May
2002/5763	17 May
2003/5764	6 June
2004/5765	26 May
2005/5766	13 June
2006/5767	2 June
2007/5768	23 May
2008/5769	9 June
2009/5770	29 May
2010/5771	19 May

Synagogues are decorated with flowers or plants on the occasion of the festival. Reasons suggested for this widespread custom are that the floral decoration is symbolic of the main summer harvest; that Mount Sinai, where the Divine Revelation occurred, was miraculously covered with vegetation in honor of the great event; that Shavu'ot is thought to be "judgment day" for fruit trees; or that the decorations symbolize the beautifully adorned first-fruit offering brought in Temple days.

Dairy food has long been traditional on Shavu'ot. The simple reason for this may be that Shavu'ot is a summer festival, when light dairy dishes are appropriate. A more traditional explanation is that there was insufficient time to prepare a meat meal on the day of the Giving of the Torah as the entire community was occupied in receiving the Torah. Housewives who baked their own bread customarily made twin loaves for Shavu'ot. The custom probably commemorates the two loaves of bread which, in Temple times, were made from the new wheat of Erets Israel and brought as a communal offering (*Men.* 8.1).

The prescribed readings for the festival include the Ten Commandments preceded by the liturgical poem AKDAMUT MILLIN, on the first day, and YETSIV PITGAM, before the *haftarah* on the second day. The Book of RUTH is also read. Various reasons have been suggested for this. The agricultural background to the story makes it an appropriate choice for Shavu'ot, the Harvest Festival; Ruth's commitment to the people and the faith of Naomi constitutes a timely lesson for Shavu'ot, which itself commemorates Israel's acceptance of the Torah; David, who was descended from Ruth, has traditional associations with the festival.

In keeping with the Sinaitic aspect of Shavu'ot, it has been customary since the Middle Ages to begin the formal Jewish education of young children at this time of the year. Nowadays, in many communities (particularly in America), the festival also marks the graduation of teenagers from the formal synagogue educational framework, or CONFIRMATION in Reform congregations. In the State of Israel, many collective settlements hold a "First Fruits" (*Hag ha-Bikkurim*) celebration on Shavu'ot, at which the "fruits" of the kibbutz — including industrial products — are displayed in a festive procession (see KIBBUTZ FESTIVALS). In Israeli kindergartens, there are special pre-Shavu'ot celebrations to which the children come carrying baskets of fruit and wearing wreaths of flowers on their heads, reminiscent of the harvest festival.

SHE-HEHEYANU ("Who has kept us alive"). Name given to a benediction recited over something new. According to the Mishnah (*Ber.* 9.3), a person acquiring a new house or new utensils should pronounce a blessing, the full text of which reads: "Blessed are You, Lord our God, King of the universe, who has kept us alive [*She-heheyanu*], sustained us, and brought us to this season." It is accordingly recited on moving into a new house or apartment, wearing a new suit or dress, or tasting a new season's fruit. This benediction is also to be said on the first evening of festivals; before the SHOFAR is sounded on Rosh ha-Hashanah; prior to the recitation of BAREKHU on the eve of the Day of Atonement; on taking the FOUR SPECIES before *Hallel* on Sukkot; on lighting the first HANUKKAH candle; before the Scroll of ESTHER is read in synagogue on Purim; and at the Redemption of the FIRST-BORN ceremony. In Israel (but not in the Diaspora), a father also recites *She-heheyanu* at the CIRCUMCISION of his son.

SHEHITAH ("ritual slaughter"). The proper slaughtering of ritually fit (*kasher*) animals as prescribed by Jewish law (*halakhah*). The precise method of *shehitah* is not spelled out in the Written Law, but it is derived from the verse, "You may slaughter as I have instructed you, any of the cattle or sheep that the Lord gives you, and eat it to your heart's desire" (Deut. 12:21). The laws of ritual slaughter are discussed in detail in the tractate HULLIN in the Mishnah and Talmud. Maimonides counts *shehitah* as one of the positive commandments of the Bible and quotes the Talmud in stating that "Moses was instructed in the rules of ritual slaughter when he received the Torah on Mount Sinai" (*Hul.* 28a).

The ritual slaughterer (*shohet*) has to be certified by a qualified rabbinical authority. He must perform *shehitah* at least three times in front of a supervisor before he is certified. After certification, he is advised to review the laws of *shehitah* once a month.

The knife of the ritual slaughterer, called a *hallaf*, is his most important instrument and much of his training is spent in learning how to sharpen it to a perfect edge. If even a small nick is found on the blade, either before or after slaughtering, the slaughter is declared invalid. The *shohet* pronounces a special blessing before slaughtering, and one blessing suffices for the slaughter of many animals at one time. The actual slaughtering is performed by a swift back and forth motion cutting across the throat while the animal is tied up and suspended upside-down by a rope. The *shohet* must not put undue pressure on the neck while cutting, but the greater part of both the windpipe and the gullet must be cut for the *shehitah* to be declared valid. The laws for slaughtering birds are slightly more lenient in this respect.

According to Jewish law, five movements disqualify *shehitah*: (1) *shehiyyah* — the slightest pause or interruption in the action of the knife; (2) *derasah* — pressing the knife downward into the neck instead of moving it back and forth across the throat; (3) *hahlada* — the knife gets stuck behind the gullet that gets cut from the inside; (4) *hagramah* — the cut is not made in the proper place on the throat; (5) *ikkur* — the implement is imperfect and tissues are torn out rather than cut. Soon after slaughtering the animal, the *shohet* must examine the lungs to ascertain whether or not they are defective. If a defect, such as a puncture or a blood clot, is found, the animal is declared *terefah* (unfit) and may not be eaten.

The purpose of *shehitah* has been presented as preventing cruelty to animals (another commandment of the Bible). Experts have stated that *shehitah* is a swift and comparatively painless way of killing an animal. The *Midrash* asks "What difference does it make to God how an animal is slaughtered?" The answer given is that "the *mitsvot* [commandments] were given only to ennoble the people" (*Gen. R.* 44.1), i.e., the commandment to slaughter in a specified manner makes the Jew more compassionate and sensitive.

The blood of birds and undomesticated animals must be covered after slaughtering, since (unlike domesticated animals), they owe nothing to man and their slaughter is all the more shameful. This is done by first throwing sand or soil on the ground, slaughtering the animal or bird and then throwing more sand over the blood.

As early as the 12th century in Spain, a self-imposed meat tax was collected in each Jewish community to help pay for the services of the *shohet* and to insure proper *shehitah*. Later, in eastern Europe, similar taxes were introduced. Often this tax money also helped to finance other communal institutions, such as schools and synagogues. In 18th-century Europe, a rift developed between the HASIDIM and the MITNAGGEDIM regarding ritual slaughter. The Hasidim introduced a new method of sharpening the knife which R. Elijah, the Gaon of Vilna, the leader of the *Mitnaggedim*, did not accept. Subsequently, in 1772, a *herem* (ban) was placed on the ritual slaughter by all Hasidim, their knives and their ritual slaughterers. Nevertheless, the Hasidic movement continued to spread and eventually this ban was lifted.

In the last century, several anti-*shehitah* movements arose in Europe. In Germany in the middle of the 19th century, *shehitah* was officially banned. Among the countries following this example were Switzerland (1893), Norway (1930) and Sweden (1937). The banning of *shehitah* was sometimes a thinly veiled expression of anti-Semitism, but was also often the result of humanitarian concerns.

Today, *shehitah* is practised mainly in centrally located slaughterhouses owned by big meatpacking companies. Usually the *shohet* does only the slaughtering while a *mashgiah* (*kashrut* supervisor) checks the lungs. All meat is then stamped to protect the consumer. A rabbi is often on hand to settle any doubts that may arise. In Israel, the Chief Rabbinate, as well as several private religious organizations, handle the supervision of *shehitah*.

SHEKALIM (annual half-shekel tax). Fourth tractate of Order *Mo'ed* in the Mishnah. Its eight chapters deal with the subject of the half-shekel that every male over 20 years of age was obligated to give yearly for the maintenance of the Temple (cf. Ex. 30:11-16; II Kings 12:5-17). The tractate discusses when and where the half-shekel was offered, who was obliged to give it, the redemption of half-shekels for gold coins, the purchase of Temple offerings and the use of any surplus money at the end of the year. Also mentioned are the names of the 15 officers who supervised the maintenance of the Temple and miscellaneous laws dealing with the disposal of cattle, flesh, or money found in the Temple or in the vicinity of Jerusalem. The subject matter is amplified in the Jerusalem Talmud and the *Tosefta*.

SHEKHINAH A term that, beginning with tannaitic literature, signifies the presence of GOD in the world. The term *shekhinah* does not appear in the Bible. In talmudic literature, in the AGGADAH and in the TARGUMS it refers to God when He is present in a certain place. The *shekhinah*, the presence of God, reveals itself as a heavenly light (*Shab.* 30a, *Ber.* 17a). The sages speak of the "wings of the *shekhinah*," under which the pious and proselytes take shelter and the "feet of the *shekhinah*," that are displaced by the proud and sinners (*Ber.* 43b, *Hag.* 16a). The term is often employed by the sages when they want to emphasize the relationship between God and Israel. Thus, the *shekhinah* goes into exile with Israel and will return with them at the End of Days (*Ber.* 6a). When harmony prevails between man and wife, the *shekhinah* dwells between them (*Sot.* 17a).

Anthropomorphic descriptions of the *shekhinah* may already be found in aggadic literature (see ANTHROPOMORPHISM). A Midrash states, "When the *shekhinah* would leave the Temple, she would turn around and caress and kiss its walls and its columns and cry, saying "Oh farewell my Temple! Oh farewell, house of my kingdom! Oh farewell, house of my dear one! Oh farewell forever! Oh farewell!" (*Lam. R., Petihta* 25). However, the personification of the *shekhinah* in rabbinic literature is not accompanied by a distinction between the *shekhinah* and God.

In later midrashic literature, the *shekhinah* occasionally appears alongside God and this may be evidence for the development of the concept of a separation between God and His *shekhinah*. In medieval Jewish philosophy, it is viewed as a Divine entity separate from God. Jewish philosophers, from SA'ADIAH GAON to MAIMONIDES, identified it with the Divine Glory and saw it as God's first creation. Maimonides speaks of the *shekhinah* as "the created light that God causes to descend in a particular place in order to confer honor upon it in a miraculous way" (*Guide* I, 64). According to Maimonides, it is the *shekhinah* which is revealed to the prophets, not God himself (*ibid.*, I, 21).

The separation between God and His *shekhinah* appears in Jewish MYSTICISM even in the earliest writings. Whereas the philosophers perceived the *shekhinah* as a created entity, the kabbalists saw it as part of the Divine world, identifying it with the lowest of the SEFIROT. This was perceived as the feminine element of the Godhead. The feminine character of the *shekhinah* is portrayed in *Sefer* BAHIR occasionally as a daughter and occasionally as a mother. The concept of the *shekhinah* as a bride is a central image in the ZOHAR, which describes the relations between the *shekhinah* and the *sefirot* above her as husband-wife relations.

Alongside the description of the *shekhinah* as a loving mother, in special relation to Israel, she is also described, particularly in the Zohar, in dark, destructive tones. When the *shekhinah* is distant from her mate, the forces of evil, the *sitra ahra*," gain control over her and make her into a demonic force.

The strengthening of the good or the evil element of the *shekhinah* depends on man's deeds. The *shekhinah* completes the Divine harmony when she is united with the *sefirot* superior to her. This unity, however, does not always take place and the sins of mankind cause the *shekhinah* to be separated from her mate. The talmudic passages emphasizing the attachment of the *shekhinah* to the Jewish people and the exile of the *shekhinah* are understood in the Kabbalah as referring to an internal exile within the Godhead. The repair of this situation is within man's control; through his deeds he can either bring the *shekhinah* closer to her mate or drive them apart. The concept of the redemption of the exiled *shekhinah* and her union with her mate through observing the commandments takes on a central place in the Kabbalah of Isaac LURIA and later, in HASIDISM.

SHELIAH TSIBBUR (lit. "messenger of the community"). The prayer leader or "reader" who conducts public worship in the SYNAGOGUE. Whereas any Jew capable of reciting the prayers might act as the prayer reader — the BA'AL TEFILLAH — on weekdays, the office of *sheli'ah tsibbur* demanded special qualifications. Early references to the *sheli'ah tsibbur*, a title often abbreviated to its acronym, *shats*, can be found in the Mishnah (*Ber.* 5.5, *RH* 4.9, etc.).

Originally, the *sheli'ah tsibbur* was chosen for his knowledge of Sabbath and festival prayer modes (see NUSAH) and for his ability to improvise texts and melodies. He recited the BAREKHU summons to public worship; the KADDISH doxology; the SHEMA and its benedictions and also repeated the *Amidah* with KEDUSHAH, except at evening prayers. He conducted the service for the READING OF THE LAW, and recited MI SHE-BERAKH and MEMORIAL PRAYERS for those called to the Torah. From the 18th century onward, a musically trained professional CANTOR often replaced the *sheli'ah tsibbur* in large urban congregations. Nowadays, he may either be a full-time *hazzan* (cantor) or an unsalaried but qualified "reader," not unlike the *ba'al tefillah*, who serves as the cantor's deputy.

SHELOSHIM See MOURNING

SHEMA Basic statement of the Jewish faith: "Hear O Israel, the Lord is our God, the Lord is one" (Deut. 6:4). As a prayer in the Morning and Evening Services, the *Shema* incorporates three paragraphs: (a) *Shema* (Deut. 6:4-9), which, according to the rabbis, is the acceptance of the Kingdom of Heaven, i.e., acceptance of God as the God of the Jewish people; (b) *Ve-haya im shamo'a* (Deut. 11:13-21), which, while reiterating much of the content of the first paragraph, adds the concept of REWARD AND PUNISHMENT; (c) TSITSIT (Num. 15:37-41), which details the law of the *tsitsit* (fringes) that must be placed on four-cornered garments, and concludes with a mention of God's redeeming Israel out of Egypt.

After the first verse of the *Shema* is recited, the sentence BARUKH SHEM KEVOD... , "Blessed be the name of His glorious kingdom for ever," is added. This sentence is said in an undertone except at the Evening and Morning Services on the Day of Atonement when it is recited aloud by the whole congregation.

All adult Jewish males are required to recite the *Shema* twice daily, based on the statement in its first paragraph: "When you lie down and when you rise up." The earliest time it may be said in the morning is "from the time one can recognize an acquaintance at a distance of four cubits," while the latest is at the end of the first quarter of the day, i.e., one quarter of the time between sunrise and sunset. The evening *Shema* must be said no earlier than nightfall and no later than midnight (the mid-point between sunset and sunrise), although in cases of unavoidable delay it may be said until dawn.

The *Shema* is recited within a fixed pattern of blessings which precede and follow it. In both the Morning and Evening Services, two blessings precede the recital of the *Shema*; one blessing follows it in the Morning Service and two in the Evening Service. The blessing following the *Shema* in the Morning Service, *ga'al Yisrael* — "who redeemed Israel" — must be followed immediately by the silent AMIDAH, thus effectively linking the *Shema* to the *Amidah*.

The *Shema* text contains 245 words. As there are 248 positive commandments in the Torah corresponding, according to the rabbis, to the 248 bones and organs in the human body, three words are added to the *Shema* to make a symbolic connection. In the case of a prayer quorum (*minyan*) praying together, the cantor repeats the last two words and adds the first word of the next prayer, *emet*, thus making up the total of 248 words. In the Sephardi ritual, the same three words are repeated by a person praying on his own. In the Ashkenazi ritual, a person praying on his own adds the words EL MELEKH NE'EMAN ("God, faithful King") before beginning the *Shema*.

In the Ashkenazi *minyan*, the *Shema* is recited by each person individually, whereas among Sephardim the cantor recites all the passages aloud (excluding that in the second paragraph that indicates the punishment for not obeying God's commandments) and the rest of the congregation recites the *Shema* together with the cantor.

The sages put great stress on the correct pronunciation of the words, because of the commandment fulfilled by reciting the *Shema*. The Talmud, for example, gives specific examples of words which end with a certain letter and are followed by words beginning with the same letter, and notes that the

Celebration of Simhat Torah (Rejoicing of the Law) in the Leghorn Synagogue, by Solomon Hart, 19th century.

worshiper must pause between the two in order to enunciate each properly. Furthermore, Jewish law requires special concentration on the meaning of the words of at least the first two verses (and many Jews cover or close their eyes to achieve such concentration). The *Shema* has been accepted universally as the Jewish credo and appears in a number of contexts in part or in its entirety. Thus, the MEZUZAH on the doorpost contains the first two paragraphs. Both TEFILLIN boxes, that of the hand and that of the head, contain four biblical passages, including the same two paragraphs.

THE SHEMA

Hear O Israel, the Lord is our God, the Lord is one.

You shall love the Lord your God with all your heart and with all your soul and with all your might.

These words which I command you this day you shall take to heart. You shall teach them diligently to your children. You shall recite them when you are at home and when you are away, morning and night. You shall bind them as a sign on your hand, they shall be a reminder above your eyes, and you shall inscribe them on the doorposts of your home and upon your gates.

The NIGHT PRAYERS, the non-obligatory prayer said upon retiring, incorporate the *Shema* and are known in Hebrew as *keri'at Shema al ha-mittah* ("reading of the *Shema* in bed"). There is even a view stating that a person who finds it difficult to fall asleep should repeat the *Shema* until he does so.

The prayer recited on a deathbed includes the *Shema*, and pious Jews have sought to die with the prayer on their lips. Throughout the ages, down to the Holocaust death camps, whenever Jews have been put to death, they have recited the *Shema* in their last moments on earth, affirming their belief in the One God.

The first verse of the *Shema* appears in a number of places in the prayers. Thus, it is part of the daily morning benedictions. On Sabbaths and festivals, the verse is recited by the cantor and congregation aloud, as the cantor stands holding the Scroll of the Law, prior to bringing it to the reading platform (*bimah*) for the READING OF THE LAW.

Again, it appears in the KEDUSHAH recited in the cantor's repetition of the Additional Service *Amidah* on Sabbaths and festivals. It is surmised that this particular usage arose from the fact that there was a time when Jews were forbidden by their rulers (who saw in its monotheistic affirmation an affront to their own faith) to recite the entire *Shema* and informers were sent to insure that the passages were not read. As the informers left after the customary time to say the prayer, the Jews instituted the inclusion of at least the first verse in the subsequent *kedushah*.

Finally, as NE'ILAH, the last service of the Day of Atonement, the most solemn day of the Jewish year, comes to an end, the entire congregation, in a demonstration of the communal acceptance of God, recites the verse aloud.

SHEMAYAH AND AVTALYON (First century BCE). The fourth of the five ZUGOT, the pairs of sages who linked the Maccabean era with that of the *tannaim*. Traditionally, Shemayah and Avtalyon were either converts or descendants of converts, tracing their ancestry back to the Assyrian king, Sennacherib (*Git.* 57b). Shemayah was president of the SANHEDRIN (*Nasi*), while Avtalyon was the head of the law court. No halakhic dicta are recorded in their names, but both are quoted in *Avot*. Shemayah stated, "Love labor and shun power, and do not become close to the authorities"(1:10); this may well be a reference to Herod, during whose reign Shemayah lived. Avtalyon declared, "O sages, be careful with your words, lest you incur the penalty of exile, and you will be exiled to the place of bad waters (i.e., heresy). Then the students who follow you will drink and die" (1:11).

SHEMINI ATSERET ("Eighth Day of Solemn Assembly"). Festival observed immediately after SUKKOT (Tabernacles), i.e., on 22 Tishri, as laid down in the Pentateuch: "On the eighth day you shall observe a holy occasion...it is a solemn gathering (*atseret*); you shall not work at your occupations" (Lev. 23:36; cf. Num. 29:35). The term *Atseret* (lit. "concluding festival") is also applied to the last day of Passover (Deut. 16:8) and, by the rabbis, to SHAVU'OT (*RH* 1.2; *Shev.* 1.1). A parallel function may thus have been served, in biblical times, by the *Atseret* of Passover (Shavu'ot) and the *Atseret* of Sukkot (Shemini Atseret). The rabbis treated the eighth day as a festival in its own right, and the liturgy indicates this independent status through appropriate references in the AMIDAH and the KIDDUSH. Shemini Atseret is distinguished from Sukkot also in that the FOUR SPECIES are no longer utilized after HOSHANA RABBAH and *Kiddush* on the eighth day is followed by the special SHE-HE-ḤEYANU benediction, which can only be recited for a new festival and not merely for the conclusion of Sukkot.

By rabbinic decree, the annual cycle of Pentateuch readings is completed and begun anew on Shemini Atseret. For this reason, the festival is known also as SIMḤAT TORAH, the Rejoicing of the Law. Outside of Israel, where two days of Shemini Atseret are observed, the customs of Simḥat Torah are kept on the second day only. Some Sephardi and Ḥasidic communities in the Diaspora, however, also arrange HAKKAFOT processions with the Torah scrolls on the first night of Shemini Atseret, as in Israel. Whenever there is no intermediate Sabbath during Sukkot, the Book of ECCLESIASTES is read on Shemini Atseret.

There are two significant additions to the liturgy on Shemini Atseret. One is the Prayer for RAIN, chanted during the repetition of the Additional Service *Amidah* (but in Israel mostly prior to *Musaf*). Because of this prayer's significance,

Havdalah *spice-box. Silver filigree with biblical scenes on enamel. Western Europe, 18th century.*

the Ark is opened and the (Ashkenazi) reader usually wears the white KITEL associated with the High Holidays. The phrase with which the prayer concludes, *Mashiv ha-ruaḇ u-Morid ha-gashem* ("Who causes the wind to blow and the rain to fall"), must be repeated at every *Amidah* service until the spring festival of Passover. The other special feature is the holding of *Yizkor* MEMORIAL SERVICES after the Reading of the Law in Ashkenazi synagogues.

SHEMINI ATSERET — EIGHTH DAY OF SOLEMN ASSEMBLY

Other Names: *Yom ha-Shemini*; *Ḥag ha-Atseret* (Eighth Day Concluding Festival)

Hebrew Date: 22 Tishri (coincides with *simḥat Torah* in Israel; marks end of Sukkot in Diaspora)

Torah & Prophetical Readings (in Diaspora): Deut. 14:22-16:17; Num. 29:35-30:1 (*Maftir*); I Kings 8:54-9:1 (Ashkenazi *Haftarah*) I Kings 8:54-66 (Sephardi *Haftarah*)

Scroll: Ecclesiastes (if there is no Intermediate Sabbath on Sukkot)

Hallel: recited (in full)

Yizkor: recited (not by Reform Jews); prayer for Rain (*Geshem*)

Civil dates on which the festival occurs, 1990-2010:

1990/5751	11 October
1991/5752	30 September
1992/5753	19 October
1993/5754	7 October
1994/5755	27 September
1995/5756	16 October
1996/5757	5 October
1997/5758	23 October
1998/5759	12 October
1999/5760	2 October
2000/5761	21 October
2001/5762	9 October
2002/5763	28 September
2003/5764	18 October
2004/5765	7 October
2005/5766	25 October
2006/5767	14 October
2007/5768	4 October
2008/5769	21 October
2009/5770	10 October
2010/5771	30 September

SHEMONEH ESREH See AMIDAH

SHEOL See AFTERLIFE

SHERIRA GAON (c.906-1006). Head of the Academy in Pumbedita. Descended from a long line of *ge'onim* (see GAON), he was appointed to the office in 968. Sherira managed to revive and strengthen the Babylonian ACADEMIES, also promoting contact with Jews in other lands. He wrote numerous responsa, many of which were sent to the North African community of Kairouan. Of especial importance was his famous *Letter* (*Iggeret ha-Rav Sherira*), addressed to a representative of that community (Jacob bar Nissim) in 987. R. Jacob had asked Sherira a series of questions about the history and development of the ORAL LAW. By whom (for example) were the Mishnah, *Tosefta*, and *baraitot* written? What was the significance of the various titles bestowed on the sages in the Talmud? Why should the tractates of the Mishnah have been arranged in their present sequence? And in which order of succession were the AMORAIM, SAVORAIM, and *ge'onim* to be placed?

In reply, Sherira wrote at length and answered the questions in considerable detail. Drawing on various records, notably those of the Pumbedita Academy, he supplied chronological lists of names from the talmudic period down to his own. Without this information, the literary history of that entire period would be virtually a closed book. Sherira Gaon's *Letter* was widely circulated throughout Europe and became available in two recensions, one "French" and the other "Spanish." The differences between the two are considerable; scholarly opinion now tends to the view that the "Spanish" manuscript is closer to the original *Letter*. Only fragments of Sherira's Bible commentary have been preserved. He apparently wrote commentaries on individual tractates of the Talmud as well, but these are known only from quotations by later authorities.

A malicious denunciation, resulting in temporary imprisonment, embittered the last years of Sherira's exceptionally long life. In 998, he resigned office in favor of his son, HAI GAON.

SHEVA BERAKHOT See ḤUPPAH; MARRIAGE

SHEVAT (Akkadian: *Shabatu*). Eleventh month of the Jewish religious CALENDAR; fifth month of the Hebrew civil year counting from TISHRI. It has 30 days and normally coincides with January-February. Its sign of the zodiac is Aquarius the Water Carrier. The name Shevat is mentioned once only in the Bible (Zech. 1:7) and once in the Apocrypha (I Macc. 16:14). It was on the first day of Shevat that Moses began reading the last book of the Torah to the assembled Israelites (Deut. 1:3). On 15 Shevat, the process of the earth's renewal is underway and the day marks the NEW YEAR FOR TREES, a minor festival of the Jewish calendar.

SHEVI'IT ("sabbatical year"). Fifth tractate of Order ZERA'IM. Its ten chapters discuss the laws relating to the resting of agricultural land in Erets Israel during the seventh year (cf. Ex. 23:10-11; Lev. 25:2-7; Deut. 15:1-3). These prohibitions cover sowing, pruning, reaping, gathering, selling for profit the produce that grows by itself, etc. The Mishnah also deals with the laws of the "release of debts" during the seventh year (see SABBATICAL YEAR). The subject matter is amplified in the Jerusalem Talmud and the *Tosefta*.

SHEVU'OT ("oaths"). Sixth tractate of Order NEZIKIN in the Mishnah. Its eight chapters discuss two principal subjects: the laws concerning oaths administered both in court and in private life and the rules governing unsuspected ritual defilement and its atonement through sacrifices (cf. Lev. 5:1-13, 20-26; Ex. 22:6-10; Num. 30:3). Also covered are the laws of deposits and the four kinds of trustees. The reasons given for these two very different subjects being found in the same Mishnah is that they are mentioned in adjoining verses in the Bible (Lev. 5:3-4). The subject matter is amplified in both Talmuds and in the *Tosefta*.

SHIR HA-KAVOD See ANIM ZEMIROT

SHIR HA-MA'ALOT ("Song of Ascents"). The superscription given to each of PSALMS 120-134. According to a Mishnaic description of the TEMPLE (*Mid.* 2.5), there were 15 steps (*ma'alot*) leading up to the Court of the Israelites from the Women's Court; on these steps, "corresponding to the 15 *Ma'alot* psalms," the LEVITES played music and sang. This was also their custom when the WATER-DRAWING FESTIVAL took place (*Suk.* 5.4). Various explanations have been offered for the *Ma'alot* superscription: (1) that it actually derives from the Temple steps; (2) that its meaning is "degrees" (on the basis of II Kings 20:9-11), hence "A Song of Degrees" in the Authorized Version; (3) that these were psalms chanted by the returning exiles who "began to go up from Babylon" (Ezra 7:9). Textual evidence suggests, however, that favorite songs chanted on the way up to Jerusalem for the three PILGRIM FESTIVALS constituted the original nucleus of these 15 "Songs of Ascents."

In the Ashkenazi rite, between Sukkot and Passover, the entire sequence is recited at the end of the Sabbath Afternoon Service. For the past 300 years, Ashkenazim have also chanted Psalm 126 — " a remembrance of Zion" and its promised restoration — prior to GRACE AFTER MEALS on Sabbaths and festivals.

SHIR HA-SHIRIM See SONG OF SONGS

SHIR HA-YIḤUD ("Hymn of [God's] Unity"). Poem praising God's unity, which is divided into seven sections, a different one being recited on each day of the week in many Ashkenazi communities at the end of the MORNING SERVICE. Some communities recite only the Sabbath section; others omit it altogether. Its recital was opposed by R. ELIJAH GAON OF VILNA and other authorities who felt that praise of God should not be exaggerated as His glories can never be recounted by man. Its authorship is uncertain but it has been ascribed to R. Samuel ben Kalonymus, father of R. JUDAH HE-ḤASID (12th century, Germany).

SHIVAH See MOURNING

SHIVAH ASAR BE-TAMMUZ ("17th of [the month of] Tammuz"). Fast day commemorating the breach made in the defense wall surrounding Jerusalem in 586 BCE; this led to the capture of the city by the Babylonians under Nebuchadnezzar three weeks later. The historical sources regarding these events, which culminated in the First Temple's destruction, are II Kings 25 and Jeremiah 52. They relate that the armies of Nebuchadnezzar breached the walls of Jerusalem on the ninth day of the fourth month (Tammuz). From this it seems likely that the fast was originally observed on the ninth, and not on the 17th of the month. This was the position until Shivah Asar be-Tammuz — together with other minor fasts, with the possible exception of TISHAH BE-AV (the Ninth of Av) — was abolished after the construction of the Second Temple (cf. Zech. 8:19). With regard to the last days of the Second Temple in 70 CE, Josephus notes that the breach in the walls of Jerusalem was made on the 17th of Tammuz, and that a fast was subsequently established on that date. When all the fasts commemorating the destruction of the First Temple were reintroduced, the rabbis decided that a fast on the 17th of the month would link both historical events.

Tradition also associates other sad events with this day. On the 17th of Tammuz, it is said, the first Tablets of the Law were shattered by Moses when he descended from Sinai and found the Israelites worshiping the Golden Calf. On this same date, the heathen Apostomos burned a Scroll of the Law and placed an idol in the Sanctuary (*Ta'an.* 4.6). Those events probably occurred during the oppressive regime of Antiochus in the era of the Maccabees. The last misfortune associated with the 17th of Tammuz was the collapse of the sacrificial system in 70 CE. The prolonged Roman siege had made it increasingly difficult to provide the animals required and, once Jerusalem's walls had been breached, the daily sacrifices in the Temple came to an end.

The period from the Fast of Tammuz until the Fast of Av, known as the THREE WEEKS, is traditionally observed as a time of public mourning. The minor fast of 17 Tammuz commences at sunrise on the day itself and not on the previous night (see also FASTING AND FAST DAYS). There are no restrictions on bathing or wearing leather shoes, and other laws may be relaxed without question if anyone's health may be affected. Special Torah readings are prescribed for both the Morning and the Afternoon Services. The passages read in the morning are Exodus 32:11-14 and 34:1-10. In the afternoon, these passages are repeated and then followed (in the Ashkenazi rite) by a *haftarah* taken from Isaiah (55:6-56:8).

SHIVVITI Synagogue plaque called after the first word in Hebrew of Psalm 16:8: "I am ever mindful of the Lord's presence," which is part of the daily prayers. It was usually hung on the wall in front of the worshipers and contained the above verse as well as other verses concerning the Torah. These tablets are often the objects of artistic decoration. Some *shivviti* plaques were used as AMULETS and incorporated magical formulas.

SHNEUR ZALMAN OF LYADY (known as *Ba'al ha-Tanya*, "author of the *Tanya*"; 1745-1813). Founder of the HABAD movement in Hasidism. Born in Liozno, near Vitebsk (Belorussia), he soon acquired great proficiency in Talmud and *halakhah*, also becoming familiar with mathematics and astronomy. Against the wishes of his father-in-law, but aided by his wife, Shneur Zalman left home in 1764 to study under DOV BAER, the Maggid of Mezhirech, whose fame had spread as a Hasidic master of prayer. The Maggid, greatly impressed with his new disciple, appointed him tutor to his son, Abraham "the Angel," in the "revealed things," while young Abraham reciprocated by teaching Shneur Zalman the "secret things" — the Kabbalah in its Hasidic interpretation. Subsequently, the Maggid urged Shneur Zalman to prepare an up-to-date codification of Jewish law. Owing to a fire, only part of it was ever published — as *Shulhan Arukh ha-Rav* (1814); noted for its exquisite Hebrew style and clarity, this work is acknowledged as a major halakhic achievement, even by scholars remote from Hasidism.

After the Maggid's death in 1772, Shneur Zalman began to attract followers in Belorussia and Lithuania, the stronghold of the MITNAGGEDIM. Led by ELIJAH BEN SOLOMON ZALMAN, the Gaon of Vilna, these "Opponents" fiercely combated such encroachment on their territory. Elijah Gaon even refused to meet Shneur Zalman and his older colleague, Menahem Mendel of Vitebsk, when they tried to discuss the possibility of reconciling the two mutually hostile camps. With Menahem Mendel's departure for Erets Israel in 1777, Shneur Zalman became the undisputed leader of Hasidism in northern Russia, where he established the Habad movement. For the guidance of his followers, Shneur Zalman wrote a volume of "Collected Sayings" (*Likkuté Amarim*, 1797) which in its complete form was published as the *Tanya* (Shklov, 1814). The *Tanya* was the first work to attempt a systematic exposition of Hasidic doctrine, though with special emphasis on the Habad ideology.

Following the Vilna Gaon's death, Shneur Zalman was accused of being a religious heretic and political danger to the state. In 1798, he was arrested and then imprisoned in St. Petersburg; all charges against him were dismissed, however, and he was released on the 19th of Kislev (5559), a day still observed by the Habad Hasidim as a major festival celebrating the vindication of Hasidism. Thereafter he settled in Lyady, Belorussia, from where he fled south during Napoleon's advance on Moscow; he died in the Ukraine.

Shneur Zalman was succeeded as head of the Habad movement by his son, **Dov Baer** (1773-1827), who moved to the Belorussian town of Lyubavich. There, despite some rival offshoots, the main leaders of Habad resided for generations and each became known as the Lubavicher *Rebbe*. Dov Baer's successor **Menahem Mendel Schneersohn** (1789-1866), was both his son-in-law and his nephew. He wrote a famous volume of responsa entitled *Tsemah Tsedek*. In Habad terminology, Shneur Zalman is known as the "*Alter Rebbe*" ("Old Rabbi"), Dov Baer as the "*Mittler Rebbe*" ("Middle Rabbi"), and Menahem Mendel as the "*Tsemah Tsedek*." The fourth head of the Lubavich dynasty was Menahem Mendel's youngest son, **Samuel** (1834-1882), who was followed by his son, **Shalom Dov Baer** (1866-1920). **Joseph Isaac** (1880-1950), his son and successor, fled to the United States and established his headquarters in Brooklyn after World War II. He was succeeded by **Menahem Mendel Schneersohn** (born 1902), a son-in-law of Joseph Isaac, and, (on his father's side), a direct descendant of the *Tsemah Tsedek*.

APHORISMS OF SHNEUR ZALMAN

Virtue flowing from reason is superior to virtue not founded on reason.

One may not interrupt one's study of *halakhah* for prayer.

Though not itself a food, salt adds flavor to dishes. The same is true of Kabbalah: though scarcely comprehensible — and tasteless — in itself, it adds flavor to the Torah.

There are shrines in the heavenly sphere that may only be opened through song.

Lord of the universe: I want neither Your Garden of Eden nor Your rewards in the hereafter. What I desire is You alone!

The only way of converting darkness into light is by giving to the poor.

Every act of kindness that God performs for man should make him feel not proud, but more humble and unworthy.

SHO'AH See HOLOCAUST

SHOFAR (ram's horn). A kind of trumpet producing distinctive notes and blown ritually during the penitential season. It is first mentioned at the Revelation on Mount SINAI

A Yemenite shofar *(ram's horn) of the 19th century.*

(Ex. 19:16, 19); thereafter, a blast of the *shofar* proclaimed the JUBILEE YEAR (Lev. 25:9-10), summoned the Israelites to war (Josh. 6:4ff.; Judg. 3:27, 6:34, 7:18-22), and marked the anointing of a ruler (I Kings 1:34). It also featured in the TEMPLE service (Ps. 98:5-6, 150:3) and heralded the commencement of each SABBATH (*Shab.* 35b). Ever since the Temple's destruction, however, *shofar* blasts have primarily been associated with ROSH HA-SHANAH, the Jewish New Year, which is designated in the Pentateuch "a day of sounding the horn" (*Yom Teru'ah*; Num. 29:1). According to the Mishnah (*RH* 3.2-3), one may use the processed horn of any ritually fit animal (sheep, goat, antelope, or gazelle), but not that of cattle or oxen, as the latter would call to mind the GOLDEN CALF idolatry. However, since the AKEDAH (Binding of Isaac) episode constitutes the Reading of the Law on the second day of Rosh ha-Shanah, a ram's horn is traditionally sounded.

In standard traditional practice, the *shofar* is blown throughout the month of Elul (except on the eve of Rosh ha-Shanah), toward the end of weekday morning prayers. It is sounded on both days of Rosh ha-Shanah and at the end of the Concluding (NE'ILAH) Service on the Day of Atonement to mark the fast's termination. Sephardim often blow it during HOSHANA RABBAH morning prayers as well. Orthodox and Conservative Jews do not sound the ram's horn on a Sabbath. In many communities 100 notes are sounded altogether.

An "Order of Blowing" was laid down by the rabbis in tractate ROSH HA-SHANAH. Each sequence of blasts should begin and end with *teki'ah*, a continuous rising note that terminates abruptly. This is equal in length to three *teru'ah* notes. Since there was a difference of opinion among the sages regarding the nature of these *teru'ah* sounds (*RH* 4.9), they eventually ruled that separate *shevarim* (three wailing notes) and *teru'ot* (nine staccato blasts) should be sounded on Rosh ha-Shanah. The prolonged *teki'ah gedolah* completes every sequence and is also blown at the end of the Day of Atonement. The Mishnah (*RH* 4.5-6) further prescribes that the *shofar* be sounded after each of three passages — MALKUYYOT, ZIKHRONOT, and SHOFAROT — known collectively as the *teki'ata* (*RH* 30a), in the Additional Service *Amidah* of Rosh ha-Shanah. Ashkenazim do so only during the reader's repetition, but in other rites the *shofar* is likewise blown at intervals during the silent *Amidah*.

Symbolically, the ram's horn calls upon sinners to repent (MAIMONIDES). According to SAADIAH GAON, it also awakens thoughts of God's sovereignty, justice, and redeeming power. The tenth benediction of the weekday *Amidah* expresses the Jew's hope that God will before long "sound the great *shofar*" to herald deliverance and the INGATHERING OF THE EXILES in the Land of Israel. Since 1949, each new Israeli president has been sworn in to the accompaniment of a *shofar* blast.

SHOFAROT Last of the three middle blessings of the AMIDAH prayer at the Additional Service of ROSH HA-SHANAH (New Year). This section stresses the use of the SHOFAR (ram's horn) throughout. (The kabbalistic rabbis laid great stress on the importance of blowing the ram's horn on Rosh ha-Shanah, seeing the action as having the power of transforming God's strict justice to mercy.) After an introductory section which describes the use of the ram's horn at the giving of the Torah at Sinai, ten verses of the Bible are recited which deal with the blowing of the ram's horn, three each from the Pentateuch, the Hagiographa and the Prophets, with the tenth verse again taken from the Pentateuch. The section concludes with a blessing addressing God as "He who hears with mercy the sound of the blowing of the *shofar* by His people Israel." The completion of the section is marked by the blowing of ten blasts on the ram's horn (except on the Sabbath).

SHOWBREAD (*leḫem ha-panim*; Shew bread; "bread of display" in the JPS version). The 12 loaves of bread placed on a golden table in the SANCTUARY in the wilderness, and in the TEMPLE in accordance with Scriptural command (Ex. 25:30; Lev. 24:5-9; Num. 4:7). The latter passage calls the showbread "the regular bread." The number of loaves probably corresponds to the 12 TRIBES of Israel. Each loaf was made of two-tenths of an ephah of flour. Incense was placed alongside the loaves (Lev. 24:7). On being replaced by fresh ones, the loaves of the previous week were distributed among the priests for their consumption. The episode in I Samuel 21:1-7, in which David requests food for his men from Ahimelech, the priest at Nob, and the latter agrees to give them the showbread, accords with the Scriptural laws. The only significant discrepancy lies in the fact that the showbread was eaten by persons who were not priests.

Rabbinic literature describes the baking, the arrangement and the distribution of the showbread among the priests in some detail, according to the practice current in the late Second Temple period. The 12 loaves were arranged on a marble table in two equal rows. Three rods of gold were used to separate the loaves from each other, thus allowing for the circulation of air and preventing mold. Fresh showbread was laid out every Sabbath, and the loaves of the previous week were placed on a golden table and the incense was burned on the ALTAR. The sages decried the fact that the family of

The showbread. Detail from an embroidered Ark curtain. Germany.

Avtinas (Garmu), which was responsible for baking the showbread, refused to teach the art to others.

Loaves of bread were also displayed in ancient Babylonian temples, but these were changed four times a day, in accordance with the four daily meals of the gods.

SHTIBL ("little room"). Yiddish term used by H̱asidic Jews for their own type of SYNAGOGUE, combining the functions of a prayer, study, and social center. As a result of increasingly bitter conflict in the late 18th century with their traditionalist opponents, the MITNAGGEDIM, H̱asidim found themselves excluded from most spheres of religious and communal life in Eastern Europe (see H̱ASIDISM). Unable to worship in the synagogues of the *Mitnaggedim*, and in any case ill at ease with the atmosphere prevailing there, H̱asidim established more informal houses of worship where prayers were conducted according to their own rite. An emotional outpouring of the heart rather than solemnity and decorum typified worship in the *shtibl* (pl. *shtiblakh*), simple, often austere, premises containing a few tables and benches. These were all that the H̱asidim needed for joyful prayer at any hour of the day, for discourses by their spiritual leader or *Rebbe*, and for communal meals or their own mode of study.

SHUL (lit. "school"). Yiddish term employed by Ashkenazi Jews to designate any traditional SYNAGOGUE. Because the educational role of the synagogue was common knowledge throughout the Roman world, Gentiles dubbed the Jewish house of prayer a *schola*; Catholic churchmen later made *schola Judaeorum* ("Jews' school") equivalent to the *synagoga*. In Middle High German Latin term reappeared as *Judenschule*. German Jews fleeing to Poland subsequently retained *shul* in Eastern Yiddish, while others who moved to northern Italy found an analogous vernacular expression in *Scuola*. In Eastern Europe, where Jewish communal life had its focus in the local houses of prayer and study, *shul* was a term normally employed by MITNAGGEDIM. H̱asidic Jews worshiped separately in their SHTIBL. A section reserved for female worshipers, above or to the rear of the main synagogue, was known in Yiddish as the *Vaybershul* ("women's synagogue").

SHULH̱AN ARUKH (lit. "a set table"). The standard code of Jewish law (*halakhah*) written by Joseph CARO of Safed, with supplementary annotations (*Mappah*) by Moses ISSERLES of Cracow. Caro's decision to compose the *Shulẖan Arukh* was influenced by the religio-cultural atmosphere of mid-16th century Safed. Here was an ingathering of exiles from Spain, bringing together in one community the outstanding Sephardi scholars of the time together with the outstanding proponents of the esoteric teachings of the Kabbalah. A feeling of the dawn of the messianic era pervaded the community, prompting the foremost halakhist there, Jacob Berab, to attempt to reconstitute the ancient Sanhedrin. Although the attempt failed, Caro was moved to produce a work that would serve, in lieu of a Sanhedrin, as a central authority for all Jewry.

Caro's *Shulẖan Arukh* is a concise digest of his *Bet Yosef*, a comprehensive commentary on the *Arba'ah Turim* of JACOB BEN ASHER, and thus follows the latter's division of Jewish law into four major areas. He followed the example of MAIMONIDES' *Mishneh Torah* in setting down the law in terse and decisive statements, but unlike Maimonides, he did not include those laws that are in effect only when the Jerusalem Temple is in existence. In his introduction, Caro writes that he was guided primarily by the opinions of Isaac ALFASI, MAIMONIDES, and ASHER BEN JEHIEL , but also took into consideration the opinions of later authorities. Caro could not fail to be influenced in some matters of ritual by the teachings of the Kabbalah. As a Sephardi, he ruled according to the practices sanctioned by Sephardi Jewry.

While Caro was composing his commentary to the *Tur*, Moses Isserles began to compose his own commentary which he called *Darké Moshe*. When Caro's *Bet Yosef* reached Poland, Isserles was dismayed; the work had already been done, and in an exemplary fashion. However, on second thoughts he decided to finish his commentary since *Bet Yosef* ignored many of the rulings and customs of the Ashkenazim. Once Caro published his summary in the form of the *Shulẖan Arukh*, Isserles decided to add to it his annotations (*haggahot*) to set down the Ashkenazi practice. He called these notes *Mappah*, "a tablecloth" to cover Caro's "table." Together they constituted what soon became the authoritative code of Jewish practice, the Sephardim following the decisions of Caro and the Ashkenazim following the decisions of Isserles.

The differences between the two derive from the basic differences between the Ashkenazi and Sephardi approaches to halakhic decisions. Because of the system of PILPUL that dominated the Ashkenazi schools, there was much hesitation among them to make clear-cut decisions where earlier authorities had expressed contradictory opinions, and the rule adopted was always to follow the more stringent opinion. While Caro permits the use of glass vessels for both meat and dairy dishes, provided they are rinsed thoroughly in between, Isserles rules that they may not be used indiscriminately and if a glass vessel was used for non-*kasher* food, it cannot be cleansed for *kasher* use and must be discarded. Isserles gave force of law to many customs (*minhagim*), some of which added restrictions to the matter of marital relations during a woman's menstrual period and to the laws of mourning.

The promulgation of the *Shulḥan Arukh* was greeted at first with the same objections raised against previous codes of Jewish law. The foremost scholars in Poland at the time argued that a digest of the *halakhah* without specifying the sources was insufficient for arriving at a proper decision.

Objections notwithstanding, the *Shulḥan Arukh*, with the *Mappah*, became firmly established as the standard text for every religious leader to consult before rendering a halakhic decision. Moreover, a cluster of commentaries increased with each new edition. A popular 19th-century abridgment was the *Kitsur Shulḥan Arukh* of Shlomo Ganzfried of Hungary.

SHUSHAN PURIM See PURIM

SIDDUR See PRAYER BOOK

SIDRAH See PARASHAH

SIFRA An halakhic MIDRASH on LEVITICUS. In Palestinian sources, the work is known under the title *Torat Kohanim* (The Law of the Priests). Babylonian sources refer to it as *Sifra* (The Book) or as *Sifra de-Vé Rav* (The Book of [the Academy] of Rav). On the basis of the word *Rav* in its title, early authorities (e.g. MAIMONIDES), believed that the work was compiled by the Babylonian *amora* RAV. More recent scholarly opinion holds the view that while the work was studied in the Academy of Rav, he was not its compiler. Various theses have been propounded as to the final editorship, but the subject is still disputed.

The work is frequently quoted in both the Palestinian and Babylonian Talmuds. The quotations in the former are virtually verbatim, but not so in the latter. This has elicited a suggestion that the Babylonian Talmud drew its material from a source other than the known text. The exegetical methods used by the *Sifra* are those of R. AKIVA, and there is common agreement that basically the work emanated from the Academy of R. Akiva even though R. ISHMAEL is frequently cited. The work is divided into sections (*parshiyyot*), each of which deals with a specific subject. Each section is further divided into chapters. Generally, each chapter begins with the first word of the biblical verse to be expounded. The first part of a critical edition by Louis FINKELSTEIN has recently appeared.

SIFRÉ DEUTERONOMY (Aram. "books"). Tannaitic MIDRASH on the Book of DEUTERONOMY. It is both aggadic and halakhic in character. While the bulk of this Midrash emanates from the school of R. AKIVA, some portions, notably paragraphs 1-54, come from the school of R. ISHMAEL. The editor did not hesitate to borrow material from the school of R. SIMEON BAR YOḤAI and from other sources, and this led R. JOḤANAN to declare that anonymous statements in this work should be attributed to Simeon bar Yoḥai (*Sanh.* 86a).

SIFRÉ NUMBERS (Aram. "books"). A tannaitic MIDRASH on the Book of Numbers. While mainly halakhic, the work contains a considerable amount of *aggadah*. Both the technical terms of exegesis as well as the *tannaim* quoted correspond fairly closely with those to be found in the MEKHILTA DE-RABBI ISHMAEL. This has led to the conclusion that the work emanated from the Academy of R. ISHMAEL.

However, on the basis of linguistic criteria as well as the names of the *tannaim* mentioned, it has been determined that certain sections (e.g., par. 78-106) derive from a source other than the Academy of R. Ishmael, probably from the school of R. AKIVA. It has been plausibly conjectured that this section derives from a Midrash in which the material of both schools was utilized.

The current division of the text in accordance with the weekly Torah readings is not found in early manuscripts and is the work of later printers who divided the book to have it conform to the annual cycle of the READING OF THE LAW.

SIMEON See TRIBES, TWELVE

SIMEON BAR YOḤAI TANNA of the fourth generation, one of the outstanding students of R. AKIVA, putative author of the ZOHAR. He spent 13 years at Akiva's academy at Bené Berak and even when Akiva was imprisoned by the Romans, Simeon managed to visit him and engage with him in learned discussion. Despite his great attachment to and reverence for his teacher, he did on occasion disagree with him. Bar Yoḥai's own school was in Tekoa in Upper Galilee and among his students was JUDAH HA-NASI. The basic text of the MEKHILTA DE-RABBI SIMEON BAR YOḤAI on Exodus and SIFRÉ DEUTERONOMY which emerged from the teachings of his academy show the influence of R. Akiva's teachings.

R. Simeon was an uncompromising opponent of Roman rule which he denounced on every possible occasion. His outspokenness after the suppression of the Bar Kokhba revolt brought him into trouble with the Roman authorities who condemned him to death and he, together with his son,

R. Eleazar, had to go into hiding. According to a talmudic report embellished by legend, they hid in a cave for 13 years where they continued to study Torah until the decree of death was abrogated. His uncompromising character was expressed in his disapproval for those who engage in ordinary pursuits other than Torah study. The story of his refuge in a cave and the miracles he performed there probably account for the traditional ascription to him of authorship of the Zohar, something which has long since been proven to be impossible. Nevertheless, his reputation as a sainted miracle worker persists to this day. On LAG BA-OMER, held to be the anniversary of his death, tens of thousands travel to Meron to pray at his tomb, bonfires are lit and special poems about him are recited.

After his emergence from hiding, he eventually became leader of the people and participated in a delegation to Rome to appeal to the Emperor Antoninius Pius to lift the ban on circumcision imposed by the Emperor Hadrian. In this effort, he and his colleagues were successful.

In his method of HERMENEUTICS he established general rules under which various diverse particulars could be subsumed. He interpreted the purpose of the Scriptural law, whether it was explicitly expressed or implied, in order to formulate *halakhah*. His aggadic teachings contain a number of striking statements, some of them uttered in the context of halakhic discussion.

SAYINGS OF SIMEON BAR-YOḤAI

Hatred upsets the social order.

Throw yourself into a blazing furnace rather than shame a neighbor in public.

To honor parents is even more important than to honor God.

God is angry at him who does not leave a son to be his heir.

It is a duty to save a woman from rape, even at the cost of the assailant's life.

It is forbidden to observe a commandment by performing a transgression.

A liar's punishment is that he is not believed even when he tells the truth.

Great is work, for it honors him who performs it.

SIMEON BEN GAMALIEL See GAMALIEL

SIMEON BEN LAKISH (known in the Babylonian Talmud as Resh Lakish; c.200-c.275 CE). Palestinian AMORA of the second generation. In his youth, for lack of other employment, Resh Lakish became a Roman gladiator and his phenomenal strength inspired many legends. Befriended by JOHANAN BEN NAPPAḤA, he studied under him in Sepphoris, married Johanan's sister, and gained fame as one of the leading sages in Erets Israel. A skillful debater, Resh Lakish often challenged his brother-in-law's halakhic rulings and his view was generally adopted in the end. For Simeon ben Lakish, Torah study was man's chief obligation and the education of schoolchildren had the highest priority (*Shab.* 119b). When R. Johanan founded an Academy in Tiberias, Simeon joined him there. Widely respected for his selflessness and exemplary character, Resh Lakish was mortally offended when his brother-in-law made a tactless reference to his gladiatorial past. After Simeon's death, R. Johanan was inconsolable, crying "Where are you, Bar Lakish?" until he too expired (*BM.* 84a).

SAYINGS OF SIMEON BEN LAKISH

Anger deprives a sage of his wisdom, a prophet of his vision.

God lends a man an extra soul on the eve of the Sabbath and withdraws it at the close of the Sabbath.

Synagogues and houses of study are Israel's fortresses.

Great is repentance: it turns sins into incentives for rightful conduct.

Correct yourself first; afterwards correct others.

He who has mercy on the cruel will in the end behave cruelly to the merciful.

SIMEON BEN SHETAḤ (1st century BCE). One of the ZUGOT (pairs of scholars who headed the SANHEDRIN between the Maccabean era and the time of Herod). Simeon served as presiding officer (NASI) of the Sanhedrin during the reigns of King Alexander Yannai and Queen Salome Alexandra; the latter, according to one source, was Simeon's sister. As leader of the PHARISEE party, Simeon ran into conflict with Alexander Yannai, who favored the SADDUCEES, but eventually the two were reconciled. Although he was *nasi* of the Sanhedrin, most of its members were Sadducees; however, during the reign of Salome Alexandra, he was able to bring the Pharisees into a dominant position in the Sanhedrin.

Two important enactments were decreed by Simeon. In one, he was a pioneer in the establishment of schools maintained by the community, insuring that all boys receive a basic elementary education (TJ, *Ket.*, 8.11, 32c). Previously the teaching of the young had been the exclusive responsibility of parents who employed private tutors, which poor parents could not afford.

Simeon's second decree had a far-reaching effect on Jewish marriage customs and is in practice to this day. In his time, a groom was required to deposit a certain sum of money with his intended father-in-law, prior to marriage. Because poor grooms could not afford to do so, many young women remained unmarried. Simeon ruled to replace this practice with a written undertaking by the groom at the time of marriage that he would mortgage all his assets for the payment of a stipulated sum to his wife if he should divorce or predecease her (see KETUBBAH).

As *nasi* of the Sanhedrin, Simeon ben Shetaḥ laid down rules for proper court procedure and the cross-examining of witnesses. During one famous case, in which Alexander Yannai was summoned to stand trial for a murder committed by his slave, Simeon's fellow-members of the Sanhedrin were intimidated by the presence of the king, but Simeon fearlessly charged him with responsibility for the crime (*Sanh.* 19a-b, 2.1).

SIMḤAH ("Joy" or "rejoicing"). A basic element in Jewish religious life. Thus, the Bible, referring to the festival of SUKKOT, declares "you shall rejoice in your festival... and be only joyful" (Deut. 16:14-15); each holiday is an occasion for joyous thanksgiving (Ps. 118:24); and in MIZMOR LE-TODAH the summons is to "worship the Lord in gladness, come into His presence with shouts of joy" (Ps. 100:2). Rabbinic teaching stressed the idea of God's Presence resting not on the man whose frame of mind is gloomy, but on one who "fulfills the commandments with a joyful heart" (*Shab.* 30b). This "joy in the performance of a commandment" (*simḥah shel mitsvah*) was to accompany Jews throughout history, determining their attitude toward and celebration of every festive event. It characterized Sabbath observance (Isa. 58:13; see also ONEG SHABBAT), the three PILGRIM FESTIVALS, ḤANUKKAH, and PURIM; it found expression also in the WATER-DRAWING FESTIVAL and in SIMḤAT TORAH (the "Rejoicing of the Law). "Joy and gladness" on the occasion of a wedding had already become proverbial in ancient times (Isa. 62:5; Jer. 33:10-11), and the rabbis affirmed that "a man who lacks a wife lives a joyless life" (*Yev.* 62b). This *simḥah shel mitsvah* dominates each happy event in the Jewish life cycle, from CIRCUMCISION, to BAR MITSVAH or BAT MITSVAH, and MARRIAGE. The event is a *simḥat mitsvah* and the celebrant is dignified with the title of *ba'al simḥah* ("host of the festivity"). The concept of joy inspired ḤASIDISM and its founder, Israel BA'AL SHEM TOV, insisted that "he who lives in joy performs the will of the Creator."

SIMḤAT BET HA-SHO'EVAH See WATER-DRAWING CEREMONY

SIMḤAT TORAH ("Rejoicing of the Law"). Joyful festival observed when the annual cycle of the Pentateuch reading in the synagogue is completed and a new one begins. In Diaspora communities the festival is celebrated on the day after SHEMINI ATSERET, thus making SUKKOT an extended nine-day celebration. In Israel, the festivities of Simḥat Torah are combined with the observance of Shemini Atseret. Liturgically Simḥat Torah is still referred to as part of the Shemini Atseret festival. No biblical or talmudic source exists for the separate festival of Simḥat Torah and scholars are of the opinion that it was unknown before the geonic era (ninth century CE), by which time an annual cycle of the READING OF THE LAW had become a universally accepted practice. Before then, a TRIENNIAL CYCLE had been customary in Erets Israel for many years. Even so, Simḥat Torah appears to have been observed in the Middle Ages without some of the restrictions generally applied to a festival. For example, there were communities where bonfires were lit and some of the dismantled and disposable parts of the SUKKAH were burned.

The Simḥat Torah festivities in the synagogue are all connected with the joy of Torah reading. In the Evening Service after ATTAH HORETA LA-DA'AT, all of the scrolls are taken out of the Ark and carried around the *bimah* (reader's platform) and the synagogue in a sevenfold procession (HAKKAFOT) accompanied by the special chant, *Anna Adonai hoshi'ah na*, ("O Lord, save, we beseech You!"), followed by an alphabetical doxology. Each procession is usually separated from the next one by an interlude of singing and dancing in which those carrying the Torah scrolls are joined by other members of the congregation in a spirit of joyful religious enthusiasm. Children take part in the processions, carrying Simḥat Torah flags or miniature scrolls. In some synagogues the processions are followed by a reading of part of the next to last chapter of the Pentateuch (Deut. 33:1-17). This is the only time when the Reading of the Law takes place at night.

The next day, Morning Service includes the same *hakkafot* processions, followed by an elaborate Bible reading. The concluding chapters of the Pentateuch (Deut. 33-34) are read and it is customary for all males to be called to the Reading of the Law. In some congregations, several Torah readings are held simultaneously, most of the two chapters being repeated as often as necessary to allow as many worshipers as possible to be called to the Reading of the Law. In others, entire groups are called up at the same time and recite the benedictions together. In many Conservative synagogues, even those which usually do not call women to the Reading of the Law, an exception is made on Simḥat Torah and women then accompany their menfolk to the platform. One special reading is also held for youngsters below BAR MITSVAH age; in modern Orthodox as well as Conservative synagogues, girls under 12 (BAT MITSVAH) also take part. A large woolen prayer shawl is held over the children while they recite Torah blessings and their prescribed section is read. At its conclusion, a special benediction is pronounced over the children quoting the words of Jacob's blessing to his grandchildren (Gen. 48:16). This "calling-up" is known as *Kol ha-Ne'arim* ("All the youngsters"). In Reform Temples men and women participate equally in all aspects of the ritual.

The last section of the reading from the Book of Deuteronomy, which concludes the Pentateuch, is reserved for a specially honored congregant, one of the BRIDEGROOMS OF THE

LAW (*Ḫatan Torah*). Immediately after this reading, a second scroll is taken and the cycle of year-long reading from the Pentateuch begins anew. The first section of the Bible (Gen. 1-2:3) is read and the person honored is called the "Bridegroom of the Beginning" (or Genesis); (*Ḫatan Be-Reshit*). The Prophetical reading for the day is the first chapter of the book of Joshua.

In Israel, it has become customary to hold a "second *hakkafot*" — joyful outdoor celebrations — on the night after Simḫat Torah. Frequently on this occasion, Torah scroll processions are enlivened by bands, instrumentals, choirs etc.

During the 1960s, Simḫat Torah became a major event in the calendar for Jews in the Soviet Union who celebrated the Rejoicing of the Law as a day of identification and unity with others of their people around the world from whom they had been separated for decades. Many thousands who congregated around the synagogues in Moscow and other main cities observed the festival with singing and dancing, especially of Israeli songs.

SOME TRADITIONAL SIMḪAT TORAH CUSTOMS

In Afghanistan, all the scrolls were taken out of the Ark and heaped into a pyramid, almost up to the synagogue's roof. When they were carried around the synagogue, there was a break between each circuit for eating and drinking.

In Cochin, a pyramid of coconut oil lamps was placed in front of the entrance to the synagogue, a carpet laid on the flagstones of the courtyard, and the Scrolls of the Law were carried around the outside of the synagogue.

In Calcutta, one synagogue has 50 Scrolls of the Law. The women, dressed in saris, go from scroll to scroll, kissing them. At the end of the holiday, a beauty queen is chosen at a Simḫat Torah ball.

In Yemen, young children are taken to the synagogue for the first time on Simḫat Torah.

Because the Bible reading on this day tells of the death of Moses, elegies were recited in the synagogues of medieval Iraq; in southern France, two mourners stood on either side of the reader, shedding bitter tears, when he related Moses' death.

In Holland, the Bridegrooms of the Law were escorted home in a torchlight procession, to musical accompaniment.

In medieval Spain, a crown from one of the Torah Scrolls was placed on the head of every man called to the Reading of the Law.

In some places in Eastern Europe, the reader wore a large paper hat decorated with feathers and bells.

SIMḪAT TORAH — REJOICING OF THE LAW

Hebrew Dates: 22 Tishri (in Israel and among Reform Jews in the Diaspora)
23 Tishri (in the Diaspora)*

Torah & Prophetical Readings:
Deut. 33:1-34:12; Gen. 1:1-2:3; Num. 29:35-30:1 (*Maftir*); Josh. 1:1-18 (Ashkenazi *Haftarah*) Josh. 1:1-9 (Sephardi *Haftarah*)

Hakkafot: (Torah scroll processions): evening and morning
Hallel: recited (in full)
Yizkor and Prayer for Rain (*Geshem*) recited in Israel

Civil dates on which the festival occurs, 1990-2010:

1990/5751	12 October
1991/5752	1 October
1992/5753	20 October
1993/5754	8 October
1994/5755	28 September
1995/5756	17 October
1996/5757	6 October
1997/5758	24 October
1998/5759	13 October
1999/5760	3 October
2000/5761	22 October
2001/5762	10 October
2002/5763	29 September
2003/5764	19 October
2004/5765	8 October
2005/5766	26 October
2006/5767	15 October
2007/5768	5 October
2008/5769	22 October
2009/5770	11 October
2010/5771	1 October

* Civil dates in the table refer to the festival's occurrence in the Diaspora only; in Israel it falls one day earlier.

SIN An action which breaks a law or alternatively, the failure to observe a positive COMMANDMENT. In Judaism, emphasis is placed on acts of commission or omission which go against the Divine law, rather than on the theological concept of sin. In every case, the sinner is morally accountable to God, both for sins against man and for infractions of the ritual law.

Nearly 30 different words are used in the Bible to refer to all kinds of sins; of these, three are primary. The most important word is *het*; with its numerous verbal and nominal variations, *het* occurs nearly 600 times in the Hebrew Bible. The root meaning of the word is "to miss the mark." While the word *het* and its derivatives apply to all kinds of sin — social and ritual, deliberate and unwitting — it is the only term which describes the least offensive category of sin: an unwitting transgression of the ritual law.

The second most prevalent term, with all its variations, is *avon*. Usually translated as "iniquity," it implies a sin which is far more deliberate and outrageous than *het*. Although it is occasionally used in reference to ritual sin, it is most frequently connected with punishable crimes against the social law and ethic, e.g., acts of injustice, lawlessness, or perversion.

The third term is *pesha*. The usual translation of its verbal form is "to transgress," but "to rebel" is more accurate. It implies a more serious offense than *avon* and is different from the simple meaning of *het*. Thus, "For he adds transgression [*pesha*] unto his sin [*het*]" (Job, 34:37). *Pesha* is never used to refer explicitly to a ritual sin. According to R. David KIMHI, it always implies "a willful departure from the authority of the master or from the one who has given the command." In the framework of a religious concept, *pesha* usually denotes a deliberate rebellion against God through transgressing His law.

In rabbinic writings the three terms are used in the above order to describe the comprehensive character of sin (*Yoma* 36b). Every sin includes some element of each of the three categories: "missing of the mark" (*het*) with respect to the highest ideal; a deviation (*avon*) from the right and lawful way; and an act of rebellion (*pesha*) against the authority of the law and the lawgiver. In rabbinic theology some sins are, however, more serious than others. For example, sins of commission are more serious than sins of omission. Those sins which go against the law of the Torah are weightier than infractions of rabbinic law. The most serious offenses are idolatry, murder and incest; a person should be ready to die rather than to commit any one of these.

Rabbinic literature also uses the term *averah* to connote a sin. The word means, literally, "a transgression" and generally points to a sin of commission, whether against a ritual or a social law.

In general, Judaism adopts a pragmatic attitude to human failings and the remedy for a breach of the law is largely practical, e.g., the bringing of a sin offering, restitution, and ATONEMENT. In this system of practical religion little is said about the origin of sin, or about any difference in man before and after ADAM's sin. Accordingly, there is no significant recognition in Judaism of the effect of man's first sin on his descendants. In spite of a few ambiguous references, mainly in hasidic and kabbalistic literature, the mainstream of classical Judaism clearly rejects any suggestion that sinfulness in human nature is a legacy from Adam's "original sin." The text that God will "visit the iniquities of the fathers upon the children" (Ex. 20: 5) is not taken as a theological statement of the inevitable transmission of sin from generation to generation. In fact, it does not actually teach that children will be punished for the sins of the fathers but refers to a situation in which the children are also "them that hate Me." The doctrine of individual responsibility that is expounded in Deuteronomy 24:16 and Ezek. 18:1-4 is central in Judaism.

Wherever the rabbis attempted to trace the psychological origin of sin, they ascribed it to the *yetser ha-ra*, the evil inclination, that is innate in human nature. This approach to the "psychology of sin" is also prominent in kabbalistic thinking and in the ethical literature of Hasidism. It is also the meaning of the text, "For there is not a righteous man upon earth who does good and does not sin" (Eccl. 7:26). For with the *yetser ha-ra* there is also the *yetser ha-tov*, the good inclination (see GOOD AND EVIL). Moreover, Judaism insists, as one of its basic teachings, that man is blessed with FREE WILL. The consequence of such freedom is that while he may be overcome, even momentarily, by his evil inclination, which leads him into sin, he can choose to master it. Man is thus free to obey or disobey, to fulfill the commands of God or to reject them, and this is the challenge with which he is faced. In Jewish thought, every normal person enjoys such freedom, at least to that extent which enables him to make a moral choice.

While the Jewish concept of sin often appears to be formal, involving the legal minutiae of the law that has been broken, in its developed and spiritualized form sin is shown to result in a feeling of deep guilt, experienced in man's sensitive conscience. This idealized concept is found in the later books of the Bible. Habakkuk (2,10) describes sin as an "offense against the soul," anything which disturbs man's spiritual equilibrium and causes his alienation from God (cf. Job, 5:6; 18:5-21; 20:4-29; Ps. 38:3; Isa, 48:22; 57:21). Sin is the obverse of the holy and cuts man off from God.

While Jewish philosophers, both medieval and modern, relate to both the biblical and rabbinic concepts of sin, there is less emphasis on sin in the rabbinic sense of *averah* and a greater stress upon the psychological effect of sin as a state of alienation from man's noblest ideal or highest potential.

Throughout the entire literature, it is made abundantly clear that sin can be remedied and that the estrangement of man from God can be repaired by the exercise of sincere REPENTANCE, which alone can restore man's wholeness. (See also CONFESSION OF SINS.)

SINAI, MOUNT (*Har Sinai*). Location of the theophany, where God revealed Himself to Moses and the people of Israel; identified in the Bible as Horeb, "the mountain of God," where Moses had his first encounter with God at the BURNING BUSH (Ex. 3). Within two months of leaving

Egypt, the entire people of Israel encamped on the plain below while Moses went up to the top of Mount Sinai in order to receive the TEN COMMANDMENTS and the other Divine precepts (Ex. 19-20). This historic Revelation is known in Hebrew as *Ma'amad Har Sinai* (see below). When the prophet Elijah fled from the wrath of Jezebel, he found his way to Horeb and there God once more revealed Himself (I Kings 19:1-14). There is no later incident involving the mountain in the Bible.

Although some placed Sinai's location in Arabia, modern scholarship is almost unanimous in locating the mountain in the Sinai peninsula, the "great and terrible wilderness" (Deut. 1:19) between Egypt and the Land of Israel. Various suggestions have been made as to the route of the Exodus and the site of the mountain. The biblical text names the various Israelite encampments en route from Egypt to Kadesh Barnea, but nothing definite can be learned either from such names or from archeological discoveries in the area. Jebel Musa (the "Mount of Moses") in southern Sinai is widely regarded as the place of Revelation, but this is a Christian identification. Byzantine monks first hallowed Jebel Musa as the site of the BURNING BUSH and settled there in the early fourth century CE. The Roman emperor Justinian built the monastery of St. Catherine ("Santa Katerina") in the mid-sixth century.

Jewish tradition has been indifferent toward the problem of Mount Sinai's location, preferring to concentrate on the meaning and implication of the Sinaitic Revelation (*Ma'amad Har Sinai*). That historic event is also known as *Mattan Torah*, "the Giving of the Law" (*Ber.* 58a). Jewish tradition also interprets biblical references to "statutes, ordinances, and laws" (Lev. 26:46, etc.) as indicating that two parallel "laws" were given at Sinai, the ORAL LAW as well as the WRITTEN LAW. All authoritative teachings form part of the Revelation and, according to the Midrash, all future generations of Israel were present in spirit at the Mount Sinai Revelation. Hence the concept of *Torah mi-Sinai* ("Torah from Sinai") formulated in the Mishnah (*Avot* 1.1), of ancient "received tradition" known as HALAKHAH LE-MOSHEH MI-SINAI, and the Ashkenazi corpus of ancient melodies designated "*Mi-Sinai*" *niggunim* (i.e., tunes dating from "olden time").

SIN-OFFERING See SACRIFICES AND OFFERINGS

SIVAN (Akkadian: *Simanu*). Third month of the Jewish religious CALENDAR; ninth month of the Hebrew civil year counting from TISHRI. It is a "full" month of 30 days and normally coincides with May-June. Its sign of the zodiac, Gemini the Twins, is associated by the rabbis with Moses and Aaron, who led the Israelites after the Exodus. There are several biblical references to "the third month," but the name Sivan is mentioned only once in the Bible (Est. 8:9).

On the first (New Moon) of Sivan, the Israelites entered the Sinai wilderness (Ex. 19:1) and the three days of "bounding" (*sheloshet yemé ha-hagbalah*) imposed on them before the Revelation at Mount Sinai occurred on 3-5 Sivan (Ex. 19:10ff). SHAVU'OT, the Feast of Weeks (or Pentecost), which commemorates the Giving of the Law on Mount Sinai (*Mattan Torah*), is celebrated on 6-7 Sivan (in Israel on 6 Sivan only). Originally, Shavu'ot was a harvest festival, when firstfruits of the wheat crop were brought as offerings to the Temple in Jerusalem. Tradition has it that King David died on 6 Sivan. According to one opinion in the Talmud (*BM* 106b), 15 Sivan marks the beginning of summer in the Land of Israel.

SIYYUM ("finish"). The completion of the study of a tractate of the TALMUD or MISHNAH by an individual or a group. The *siyyum* is made in the presence of a *minyan* (prayer quorum), followed by a special prayer called *hadran* and the recitation of KADDISH. Light refreshments or even a festive meal are served and a Torah discourse is customarily delivered. The Talmud states that ABBAYÉ, who was head of the Academy in Pumbedita, made a feast whenever one of his students concluded the study of a tractate (*Shab.* 118b).

It is common for a *siyyum* to be held on the day before Passover. All first-born males have an obligation to fast on that day as a remembrance of the miracle that saved them from the tenth plague in Egypt (see FASTING AND FAST DAYS). However, if they attend a *se'udat mitsvah* (festive meal to mark completion of a commandment, such as a *siyyum*), they are exempt from this obligation. Consequently, it is a custom in most synagogues on the day before Passover for one of the members to make a *siyyum*, thereby exonerating all the first-born present. A *siyyum* is also made upon completion of the writing of a new SCROLL OF THE LAW (called *siyyum ha-sefer*, "conclusion of the book"). Those present fill in the letters of the final verses, and the Scroll is donated to the synagogue by the person who commissioned it. The entire community then joins in a joyous procession, escorting the new Scroll to the synagogue.

SLANDER See LESHON HA-RA

SLAVERY The voluntary or involuntary servitude of one person to another. In the ancient world, slavery was commonplace and human society made no effort to change the situation. According to ancient Greek thought (Aristotle), humanity is naturally divided into free men and slaves.

Judaism did not abolish slavery, but limited it and imposed such stringent conditions on the ownership of slaves that in many cases slavery became paid labor for a specified period of time. The Bible differentiates between the Hebrew slave and the Canaanite slave. A Hebrew became a slave either because he was sold by a law court (BET DIN) to repay a theft he had committed and was unable to repay, or because he sold himself due to extreme poverty and inability to support his family. A person sold by the law court can be sold for no more than six years. If at the end of the set time he does not wish to go free, his ear is pierced with an awl and he then remains a slave until the JUBILEE year. The Talmud explains why the man's ear is pierced as follows: "The ear which heard the words at Mount Sinai, 'for the Israelites are slaves unto me,' they are My [i.e., God's] slaves and not slaves to slaves; yet this person nevertheless acquired a master for himself — therefore his ear is pierced." His master may not separate him from his wife and children and must feed them, although they are not subservient to him and their earnings do not belong to him.

MAIMONIDES in his *Mishneh Torah* (*Yad, Hilkhot Avadim*), lists the obligations of the master to his Hebrew slave, whether the person sold himself or was sold by the *bet din*. First, the sale cannot be a public one. A person who purchases a slave cannot make him do "servile" work, which is defined as unlimited work or work of no value. The owner is forbidden to have the slave perform work of a demeaning nature. The owner is required to supply Jewish slaves, whether male or female, with the same quality of food and drink, clothing and living accommodations as his own, as it states, "for he is happy with you," (Deut. 15:16), which the rabbis interpret as meaning that the master may not eat good quality bread and serve the slave inferior quality bread, that the master may not drink old wine and serve the servant new wine, that the master may not sleep on feathers and the slave sleep on straw. The sages said that one who buys a slave for himself is really buying a master for himself.

A female Jew can only become a slave if she was sold as such by her father. A father may not sell his daughter as a slave unless he has absolutely no land or movable possessions or even clothing on his back. Even in such cases, the father is forced to redeem his daughter, as soon as he is able, because of the blemish to the family. A female may only be sold as a slave by her father while she is a minor and she is freed automatically by the onset of puberty, unless her master has married her. No female beyond the age of puberty can be a slave. The Torah protects the female slave's honor and commands the master either to marry her or to give her to his son in marriage, and if not, "she shall go free, without payment," (Exodus 21:11), i.e., without having to pay for the privilege. A female slave, unlike a male slave, cannot extend her service by having her ear pierced.

The law court is forbidden to sell a Jew as a slave to a non-Jew and one who sells himself to a non-Jew must do everything in his power to redeem himself thereafter. If he cannot arrange for the funds, his relatives must attempt to do so. The law court has the right to force the relatives to redeem him, so that the slave does not become assimilated among non-Jews. If the relatives do not redeem him or cannot afford to redeem him, it is a positive commandment for every Jew to redeem him.

The Hebrew slave who is to return to his family after a number of years of servitude must be given a grant by his former owner, in order to enable him to reestablish himself: "When you set him free, do not let him go empty-handed. Furnish him out of the flock, threshing floor, and vat, with which the Lord your God has blessed you. Bear in mind that you were slaves in the land of Egypt and the Lord your God redeemed you; therefore I enjoin you this commandment today" (Deut. 15:13-15).

A Canaanite slave is the property of his master and is bought for all time. He does not go free in the jubilee year. The Bible states, "Such male and female slaves as you may have — it is from the nations round about you that you may acquire male and female slaves ... These shall become your property. You may keep them for a possession for your children after you, for them to inherit for all time. Such you may treat as slaves" (Lev. 25:44-46).

However, even the life of the Canaanite slave is not totally under the master's control. If the slave was circumcised, he is considered to be a member of the family, and he partakes of the paschal sacrifice together with everyone else. The Bible requires the slave to rest on the Sabbath and to observe the same commandments that a woman must observe. He can be released from his slavery either by being redeemed or by his master freeing him by means of a document to that effect. If the slave suffers any permanent injury to an organ (e.g., his eye or tooth, etc.) by the hand of his master, he is automatically granted the right to his freedom. Killing a Canaanite slave is considered to be murder. It is forbidden to return a runaway slave to his master (Deut. 23:16). Even though the Canaanite slave is formally the property of his owner, "it is pious and wise for a person to act mercifully and not to impose too heavy a burden on his slave and not to mistreat him, and to give him proper food and drink, and not to humiliate him by action or by word, and not to be excessively angry or to shout excessively, but to speak to him calmly and to hear his complaints" (*Sh.Ar., Y.D.* 267.17). A Canaanite slave who had been freed could become Jewish through immersion (*tevilah*) and could then marry a Jew.

The Christian Church at an early stage after coming to power in the fourth century, forbade Jews to own Christian slaves. The owning of slaves ceased among Jews earlier than among Christians.

In the western hemisphere, Jews — like other whites — could be found among slave-owners and slave traders. The period of the US Civil War found Jewish voices on both sides. Rabbi Morris J. Raphall of Congregation B'nai Jeshurun in New York strongly defended slavery, citing the biblical precedent. Rabbi David EINHORN of Baltimore spoke out in favor of abolition, calling slavery "the greatest possible crime against God," and had to flee the city amid riots between rival factions.

SOCIAL ETHICS The Bible, with its this-worldly emphasis, makes its ethical demand compatible with social life, avoiding any suggestion of ASCETICISM or withdrawal from day-to-day living. On the other hand, the maximum measure of justice that can be achieved within the existing reality is demanded with concise and uncompromising clarity, involving a strong emphasis on social ethics.

These are expressed not in abstract principles, from which ethical behavior may be deduced, but in legislation. The Pentateuch commands the defense of the widow and orphan (Ex. 22:21-23); forbids oppression of the (non-Jewish) stranger (*ibid.*, v. 20); requires the humane treatment of slaves (Ex. 21:1-11,26,27; see SLAVERY); prohibits false witness, BRIBERY, and showing judicial favor (Ex. 23:1,3; Deut. 16:18-20; 19:16-17); and demands care for the POOR (Deut. 15:7-11). The thrust of such legislation is the avoidance of harming one's fellow-man and the protection of society's weakest elements. Such concern is also highlighted (perhaps symbolically) in the prohibition of placing a stumbling block before a blind man and of cursing the deaf (Lev. 19:14). The Bible's ethical ideal finds expression in the verse, "You shall not take vengeance; nor bear any grudge against the children of your people, but you shall love your neighbor as yourself" (Lev. 19:18).

While the demand to love one's neighbor as oneself seems to be unique in ancient times to the Bible (see LOVE OF NEIGHBOR), regulations similar to those of the Bible are not unusual in other documents of the period. Thus, many of the Bible's social ethics are not unique in content; but the role of ethics in other ancient Near Eastern cultures seems to be marginal, whereas it is central in the Bible. This centrality is articulated most dramatically in the writings of the later PROPHETS, e.g., "Thus says the Lord: Let not the wise man glory in his wisdom; neither let the mighty man glory in his might; let not the rich man glory in his riches. But let him that glories, glory in this: that he understands, and knows Me, that I am the Lord Who exercises mercy, justice, and righteousness in the earth. For in these things I delight, says the Lord" (Jer. 9:22-23). The ethical aspirations of other ancient cultures are not always a part of the religious cult or social organization, whereas the Bible on numerous occasions makes clear that the observance of ritual commandments is meaningless in a society not governed by ethical principles: "Yea, though you offer Me burnt-offerings, I will not accept them; neither will I regard the peace-offerings of your fat beasts. Take away from Me the noise of your songs; and let Me not hear the melody of your psalteries. But let justice well up as waters, and righteousness as a mighty stream" (Amos 5:22-24).

The sages of the Talmud amplified the Bible's ethical concerns. HILLEL, an early *tanna*, asked to summarize all of Judaism, declared, "What is hateful to you, do not do unto your fellow-man" (*Shab.* 31a). R. Akiva, a later *tanna*, pronounced the command to love one's neighbor as oneself to be the central principle of the Torah, to which his contemporary, Ben Azzai, responded that man's creation in the image of God (an expression of the absolute worth of every human being) is an even more fundamental principle (*Sif.* to Lev. 19:18). The sages also expanded biblical legislation out of concern for the disadvantaged. Thus, for instance, they introduced the KETUBBAH (marriage document) to protect the rights of divorcees and widows, instituted the PROSBUL to help the poor attain loans, and decreed that a woman may not be divorced against her will. They referred to CHARITY by the Hebrew term *tsedakah*, which derives from the word "justice," thus emphasizing the obligatory nature of helping the poor. They ruled that every town must have at least two charity wardens, who must be well-known and honest, and that these should collect money from the people every Sabbath eve and distribute it to the poor. The ultimate outgrowth of this was the various charitable associations that have continued from the Middle Ages until the present (see COMMUNITY).

Application of biblical law is discussed at length in the Talmud, where a principle, known as *lifenim mi-shurat ha-din*, is derived from the biblical text. This means going beyond the letter of the law for the purpose of humane dealing, and various commentators have differed on the extent to which such behavior is obligatory. The importance that the rabbis attributed to this notion may be seen in the assertion that Jerusalem was destroyed because its inhabitants were never willing to go beyond the letter of the law (*BM* 30b).

A similar point, although more radical because it is expressed in the concrete legal framework, is made by the *amora*, Rav, in his ruling in the case of porters who have, apparently by negligence, broken a cask of wine (*BM* 83a). Rav requires the cask's owner not only to return the impoverished workers' clothes, held by the owner against possible damages to his product, but to pay their wages as well. Asked if this is indeed the law, Rav answers in the affirmative, citing the verse, "That you may walk in the way of good men, and keep the paths of the righteousness" (Prov. 2:20).

The Jewish ethical ideal is one of substantive justice, as contrasted with the Western standard of retributive or distributive justice. While the latter is subsumed under substantive justice, it consists essentially of rules of procedure, i.e., how one ought to act. The former is an expression of how things ought to be, and is based upon an ultimate (in the case of Judaism, messianic) ethical vision. Substantive justice seeks full enhancement of human, particularly social, life, and as such is expressed in all institutions and relationships. The image of God is understood as human potential. Contemporary writers have observed that the Bible combines concrete legislation on a case-by-case basis with demands for absolute ethical behavior (such as Lev. 19:18; Deut. 16:20; Jer. 9:22-23). This combination provides a system for dealing with everyday problems as they arise, while pointing the individual and the society toward long-range ethical improvement.

See also BITTUL HA-TAMID; BUSINESS ETHICS; ETHICS; LABOR AND LABOR LAWS.

SOFER (or SCHREIBER) MOSHEH (1762-1839, rabbi, halakhist, and fighter for Orthodox Judaism, known as *Hatam Sofer*, after his main work). Born in Frankfurt where he was a pupil of Phinehas Horowitz and Nathan Adler, Sofer became rabbi of Dresnitz (Moravia), Mattersdorf, and in 1806, of Pressburg (Bratislava) where he remained to the end of his life. His second wife was the daughter of the great talmudist, Akiva EGER. His vast knowledge of talmudic and rabbinic literature brought him questions on all aspects of Jewish law from rabbis in many parts of the Jewish world. A powerful preacher and rabbinic leader, he displayed great energy in the struggle against NEOLOGY, holding that to substitute the vernacular for Hebrew in the prayer book would damage Jewish unity. A guiding principle of Sofer was that all innovation is prohibited. Opposed to any attempt, however slight, to change the *status quo* in religious practice, he was the outstanding leader of Orthodoxy during his lifetime.

His responsa appeared in seven volumes entitled *Hiddushé Teshuvot Mosheh Sofer*, generally known by the intials of the words as *Hatam Sofer*. A prolific writer, he was also the author of two volumes of sermons, novellae on the Talmud, commentaries on the Bible and kabbalistic poems. Many editions of his ethical testament, devoted entirely to the battle for Orthodoxy, have been published.

His eldest son, Abraham Samuel Benjamin Wolf Sofer (1815-1875), known as *Ketav Sofer*, after his collection of responsa, Bible commentaries and talmudic glosses by that name, succeeded his father as head of the Pressburg *yeshivah*. Sofer's second son, Simeon, became rabbi of Cracow, where he established the Orthodox congregation, *Mahziké Hadas*.

SOFER See SCRIBE

SOLOMON (tenth century BCE). Successor of his father DAVID as king over ISRAEL. He was the fourth of David's sons, son of Bathsheba, and is also called Jedidiah (II Sam. 12:24,25). Solomon ruled for 40 years between approximately 968 and 928 BCE. Solomon was anointed while his father was still alive; he was chosen in preference to his older brother, Adonijah, who was also a claimant to the throne (I Kings 1).

After David died, Solomon, by his father's command, killed David's army general, Joab, and exiled Abiathar the priest. His brother, Adonijah, was eliminated after Solomon suspected that he wished to revolt (I Kings 2).

Solomon inherited a large kingdom stretching from Tiphsah on the Euphrates to the Philistine Gaza on the southwestern border. The Bible describes Solomon's era as one of peace and tranquillity. His control over most of the land west of Mesopotamia was made possible as a result of the temporary weakness of Egypt and Assyria, the major powers in the region.

Solomon strove to secure his kingdom through political marriages with the daughters of the kings of the region: Moab, Ammon, Sidon and Heth (I Kings 11:1). Altogether he had a total of 700 wives and 300 concubines (I Kings 10:3). His premier wife was the daughter of Pharaoh, the king of Egypt (I Kings 3:1). It was unusual for the Pharaohs to marry their daughters to foreigners; the marriage is an indication of the strength of Solomon. As a wedding gift, Pharaoh gave his daughter the town of Gezer, that he had conquered and burned to the ground. However, when a political revolution took place in Egypt and Pharaoh Sishak Bel I (945-924 BCE), the first Pharaoh of the 22nd dynasty, ascended the throne, it marked a change in the relations between Egypt and Israel. This pharaoh gave political asylum to Solomon's enemy, Jeroboam (I Kings 11:40).

The Judgment of Solomon. Illuminated manuscript, 15th century.

Solomon had strong friendly ties with Hiram, king of Tyre (980-946 BCE), expressed in the latter's aid to Solomon in building the TEMPLE. In return for wheat, oil and wine, Hiram supplied Solomon with cedar and cypress wood, as well as gold. Hiram also sent Solomon artisans and craftsmen to aid him in building the Temple. Solomon and Hiram cooperated in operating a fleet, whose home base was Etzion Geber, on the Red Sea. Solomon supplied the ships, while Hiram supplied the crews (I Kings 10:11). This fleet sailed to Ophir and Tarshish and brought back gold, silver, ivory, apes, and peacocks (I Kings 10:22).

A spectacular event in his foreign relations was the visit by the Queen of Sheba (in southwest or east Africa; I Kings 10:1-13). The background to this visit was probably the control and the monopoly of international trade, including trade in spices and sandalwood.

In an attempt to unify the Israelite tribes into a single nation, Solomon divided the country into 12 districts (in addition to Judah), run by governors; the borders of these districts did not coincide with those of the 12 TRIBES. Each district had to support the large royal court for one month of the year. The massive building campaign undertaken by Solomon in Jerusalem and throughout the country and the grandeur of his reign constituted a heavy economic burden. This required heavy taxes and resulted in the request by the people addressed to Solomon's son, Rehoboam, to ease the tax burden (I Kings 12:3-4).

Solomon was a great builder and his construction projects included the building of the Temple in Jerusalem, that began in the fourth year of his reign and took seven years to complete. The Temple was part of a building complex which also included the house of the forest of Lebanon, the porch for the throne (of judgment), and the king's palace. All of this took 20 years. Solomon fortified Jerusalem, strengthened its walls, and expanded its area to the north (I Kings 11:27). He built the fortified towns of Hazor, Megiddo, and Gezer, crucial points of his kingdom. He also built Beth Horon (upper and lower), Baalat, and Tadmor, as well as storage towns for provisions during emergencies and towns for lodging horses and for charioteers.

This extensive building activity, in addition to the tremendous cost of maintaining the royal court, imposed a heavy tax burden on the people, as well as widespread forced labor. This caused unrest within the people. Jeroboam of the tribe of Ephraim, who was in charge of the forced labor of the tribes of Joseph (Ephraim and Manasseh), attempted to revolt against Solomon. The rebellion failed and Jeroboam fled to Egypt. After Solomon's death, Jeroboam successfully rebelled against Solomon's son and successor, Rehoboam, and established the northern kingdom of Israel.

Solomon's legendary wisdom is described in a number of instances. In the political realm, Solomon was able to maintain a large empire at peace and his internal policies enabled the nation to flourish economically. On the judicial plane, he was a wise judge, as seen in his judgment of the two women who both claimed motherhood of the same child (I Kings 3:16-28). Intellectually, the Queen of Sheba came to test him with questions and he passed this test successfully (I Kings 10:1-13). Solomon's wisdom is described as being greater than that of all the wise men of his era (I Kings 5:9-11). This wisdom stemmed from God's blessing to him in a dream when he assumed the throne (I Kings 3:5-14). In literary terms, he was known for his parables and for his poetry. The Bible relates that he composed 3,000 parables and 1,500 poems (I Kings 5:12). The Bible also attributes to him the writing of Proverbs and the Song of Songs.

The sages also attribute to him the authorship of Ecclesiastes. According to them, Solomon wrote the Song of Songs in his youth, Proverbs when he was a mature adult, and Ecclesiastes in his old age (Song, *R.* 1:11). One Midrash claims that Solomon was one of the ten authors of Psalms (*Shoẖer Tov* 1:6); another that he knew the language of the animals and birds (*Targum Sheni* on the Scroll of Esther).

SOLOVEICHIK Lithuanian rabbinical family whose members have been among the leading *yeshivah* heads and Torah scholars since the mid-19th century.

Joseph Baer (1820-1892) studied at the Volozhin *yeshivah* under his great-uncle Isaac, son of R. Ḫayyim of Volozhin who founded the *yeshivah*. Soloveichik eventually resigned from his senior post there, however, after a controversy broke out among the students over whether he or Rabbi Naphtali Tsevi Judah BERLIN should head the *yeshivah*. He later served as rabbi of Slutsk (1865-78) and then of Brest-Litovsk (Brisk). Joseph Baer Soloveichik's published writings, entitled *Bet ha-Levi* (1863-91), included his novellae on the Talmud, responsa, and sermons on Genesis and Exodus.

Ḫayyim (1853-1918), son of Joseph Baer, was born in Volozhin, where he later studied at the *yeshivah* and displayed youthful ability as an instructor. In 1880, he was officially appointed to the faculty, retaining his position until the *yeshivah*'s forced closure by the tsarist government in January, 1892. After his father's death, Ḫayyim succeeded him as the communal rabbi, and was known as "Rav Ḫayyim Brisker." From that time onward, Brest-Litovsk attracted leading graduates of the European *yeshivot* who came to study with him.

Ḫayyim Soloveichik initiated a new approach to talmudic study, calling for incisive analysis, exact classification, critical independence, and emphasis on Maimonides' *Mishneh Torah*. His disciples spread his method to *yeshivot* throughout the world where they later taught. R. Ḫayyim was a perfectionist who believed that his novellae had not yet reached a fit state for publication. His novellae on the *Mishneh Torah* were finally issued by his sons in 1936. Many of his talmudic novellae have likewise been published since then, both in authorized and non-authorized editions, based mainly upon the notes and reconstructions of his family and students.

Moses (1876-1941), the eldest son of R. Ḫayyim, studied under his father and held office as rabbi in several White Russian towns. After World War I, he headed the department of Talmud at the Taẖkemoni Rabbinical Seminary in Warsaw; from 1929, he chaired the Talmud faculty of the Rabbi Isaac Elchanan Theological Seminary at New York's Yeshiva College. His erudition and lectures greatly enhanced the level of talmudic study in the then nascent American Torah community.

Isaac Ze'ev (1886-1960), the youngest son of R. Ḫayyim, also studied under his father, whom he succeeded as rabbi of Brisk. Large numbers of *yeshivah* graduates from all over Europe went there to study under "Rav Velvel" and to become proficient in the "Brisker method" of Talmud study. Isaac Ze'ev was active in communal affairs and sternly opposed the Zionist movement and religious innovations.

Together with seven of his children, "Rav Velvel" managed to escape from the Nazis, but his wife and another four children perished in the Holocaust. From 1941, having settled in Jerusalem, he devoted himself to his studies and refused to accept any official appointment. He nevertheless exercised great influence in Israeli Torah circles, especially after the death of Rabbi Avraham KARELITZ, owing to his erudition and family traditions. Isaac Ze'ev arranged for the publication of his novellae on the Torah and Maimonides, while his talmudic novellae were edited by his sons.

Joseph Baer (1903-), the eldest son of R. Moses, was born in Pruzhany, Belorussia, where his maternal grandfather, Elijah Feinstein, was the communal rabbi. Until his early twenties, he devoted himself almost exclusively to rabbinical literature, mastering his grandfather's "Brisker method." He received the equivalent of a high school education from private tutors and in 1925 entered the University of Berlin, where he majored in philosophy and was awarded his doctorate for a thesis on Hermann COHEN's epistemology and metaphysics (1931). A year later, Joseph Baer immigrated to the United States, where he became rabbi of the Orthodox Jewish community in Boston, the city which remained his home. In 1941, he succeeded his father as head of the Talmud faculty at Yeshiva University and thereafter also lectured at YU's Bernard Revel Graduate School, where he served as professor of Jewish philosophy. He continued his teaching and association with Yeshiva University until his retirement in 1985. Soloveichik identified with the Religious Zionists of America (Mizrachi), and was honorary president of the RZA from 1946. He also assumed the chairmanship of the Halakhah Commission of the Rabbinical Council of America in 1952. He became the spiritual mentor of the majority of American-trained Orthodox rabbis, and for decades he inspired students to follow his teachings.

The uniqueness of Joseph B. Soloveichik lay both in talmudic analysis and in philosophical thought. His talmudic methodology was chiefly based on that of his grandfather, but he broadened its scope, expanding its terminology and disseminating it within a larger community. It is, however, in his emphasis on the interaction of *halakhah* and philosophical thought that Soloveichik pioneered a new approach. He affirmed that the halakhic system is rooted in spiritual and ethical realities, and that the construction of a Jewish *Weltanschauung* is only possible through the confrontation of *halakhah* in all its spheres. Many of his discourses and published writings were concerned with these attempts to clarify "the philosophy of the *halakhah*."

As the unchallenged leader of enlightened Orthodoxy in the USA, Joseph B. Soloveichik was popularly designated "the Rav." His main influence was exerted through his lectures and public discourses. As a talmudic and halakhic expositor, he had an unusual gift for explaining difficult technical and theological problems. He was also a noted orator in his native Yiddish, as well as in English and Hebrew. Soloveichik at first maintained his family's reluctance to appear in print, owing to the demands of perfectionism. In later years, however, he both published and allowed others to edit, publish, and translate several volumes of his halakhic novellae, homiletical insights, and philosophical essays.

Aaron (1918-), the youngest son of R. Moses, immigrated with his family to the US in 1929. He studied at New York's Yeshiva College and was also trained as a lawyer. Aaron lectured in Talmud at Mesivta Tifereth Yerushalayim, at the Rabbi Chaim Berlin *yeshivah*, and at the Rabbi Isaac Elchanan Theological Seminary of Yeshiva University. In 1966, he became head of the *yeshivah* and dean of the faculty at the Hebrew Theological College in Skokie, Illinois. Subsequently, he organized his own *yeshivah* in Chicago, which he named "Yeshivas Brisk." In 1986, Aaron Soloveichik returned to the Rabbi Isaac Elchanan Theological Seminary of Yeshiva University in New York, where he succeeded his elder brother as head of its Talmud faculty.

SONG OF MOSES The triumphant hymn of praise sung by Moses and the Israelites after their miraculous deliverance from the chariots of Pharaoh that pursued them into the Reed (Red) Sea (Ex. 14:30-15:18). *Shirat ha-Yam* (the "Song at the Sea"), as it is known in Hebrew, concludes the PESUKÉ DE-ZIMRA in the daily Morning Service. Handwritten in a Torah scroll, the verses of Exodus 15:1-19 form a distinctive visual pattern; and in Temple worship the Levites evidently chanted them in some responsive fashion. Congregations which observe the Sephardi and North African rites have preserved a special melody for *Shirat ha-Yam*. Ashkenazi congregants, who stand while it is recited, have a traditional chant of their own reserved for *Shabbat Shirah*, the Sabbath when this Torah portion (*Be-Shallah̲*) is read in synagogue, and also for the seventh day of Passover (see SABBATHS, SPECIAL). According to Israeli practice, the *Shirah* is sung by groups of worshipers on the last (seventh) day of Passover, when they assemble at the Mediterranean and Red Sea (Eilat) beaches. For pious Jews, reading the Song of Moses day by day fulfills the biblical injunction to "remember the day of your departure from the land of Egypt as long as you live" (Deut. 16:3).

SONG OF SONGS Biblical book in the HAGIOGRAPHA section of the Bible; one of the FIVE SCROLLS read in the synagogue on special days. Song of Songs (also known in English as Canticles and the Song of Solomon), is read in the synagogue on the Sabbath of PASSOVER, the festival of spring. Sephardim recite it after the Passover SEDER, and on Friday afternoons before the Sabbath service, as a way to welcome the "Sabbath Queen". Its name indicates how it was perceived: as the song *par excellence*.

The book consists of 117 verses divided into eight chapters, and it has been the subject of extensive discussion and investigation. The rabbis of the Talmud debated at length whether to include the book in the biblical canon. Their problem was the seemingly secular motifs, without even a mention of God. The book was eventually included in the

The Song of Songs illustrated by Zev Raban, 1925.

canon after R. AKIVA interpreted its contents allegorically, as a love song between God and Israel. The imagery of the bride and groom in the song served as a major theme of the Kabbalah.

While there are numerous allusions to SOLOMON and Jewish tradition credited him with authorship of the Song of Songs, most scholars today do not accept this ascription. On linguistic grounds, with the use of Persian and Aramaic words, the book is generally dated within the late Persian or early Greek periods. The Talmud ascribed it to King Hezekiel and the men of his time (*BB.* 15a).

The consensus among scholars is that the Song of Songs is an anthology of love songs. The songs express the longing and the yearning of the lovers for one another and joy in final consummation, conveyed by expressive monologues and dialogues. The flora and fauna and geographical background of the land of Israel are vividly described within the songs.

Various interpretations have been suggested for the Song of Songs. The following outline is one of these:

SONG OF SONGS

1:1 — 1:8	Songs of the bride
1:9 — 2:7	Dialogue of the lovers
2:8 — 3:5	Reminiscences of the bride
3:6 — 3:11	The wedding parade
4:1 — 5:1	Songs of the youth
5:2 — 6:3	Search for the lost bridegroom
6:4 — 7:10	The bride's beauty
7:11 — 7:14	Love in the vineyard
8:1 — 8:4	Brother and sister
8:5 — 8:14	Various songs and fragments

SONG OF SONGS RABBAH Aggadic MIDRASH on the SONG OF SONGS, also known as *Midrash Hazitah* from the first word of the verse (Prov. 22:29) quoted at the beginning of the work. The Midrash cites homilies on the Song of Songs and follows the biblical text consecutively, sometimes even word by word. Editions subsequent to the first divide the work into eight sections (*parshiyyot*) corresponding to the eight chapters of the biblical text. The sources on which the editor drew are the Jerusalem and Babylonian Talmuds, GENESIS RABBAH, LEVITICUS RABBAH and PESIKTA DE-RAV KAHANA. There are, moreover, a fairly large number of homilies attributed to various *tannaim* and *amoraim* which are not found in these sources.

In keeping with the rule of interpretation of the Song of Songs established by the *tannaim*, the central concept is interpreted allegorically as representing a dialogue between God, the lover, and the People of Israel, the beloved. This method is reflected in the statement in the Midrash (1:1): "R. Johanan said 'Wherever King Solomon is mentioned in this scroll, the reference is to the actual King Solomon; whenever the word "King" appears [on its own], the reference is to God.' The sages say: 'Wherever King Solomon is mentioned the reference is to the King who is (the Lord) of peace; wherever King is mentioned the reference is to the congregation of Israel.'"

The language of the Midrash is Mishnaic Hebrew with an admixture of Galilean Aramaic. Being a work of Palestinian origin, it contains numerous Greek words. Its redaction is dated some time in the sixth century CE.

SOTAH ("wife suspected of adultery"). Fifth tractate of Order NASHIM in the Mishnah. Its nine chapters deal primarily with the laws of a wife suspected of marital infidelity and her trial by the Sanhedrin (cf. Num. 5:11-31; Deut. 20:1-9, 21:1-9). The procedure included bringing an offering to the priest, the mixing of the "holy water" with the dust of the sanctuary, the loosening of the woman's hair, the administering of a special oath and the requirement for her to drink the "bitter waters" before the court. Also covered in this tractate are various laws dealing with blessings or oaths which must be said in the Holy Tongue (Hebrew) and those which may be said in any language, exemptions from military service and the procedure called "breaking the heifer's neck" if a man is found slain outside the city with no witnesses to his murderer (Deut. 21:1-9). The name *Sotah* is derived from the verb *seti* or *satoh* (in Aramaic) which means to stray from the path of righteousness. The subject matter is amplified in both Talmuds and in the *Tosefta*.

SOUL, IMMORTALITY OF The Bible generally speaks of man as a psychosomatic unit, yet it is man's "breath of life" (*nishmat hayyim*; Gen. 2:7), in contrast to his body, which is described as emanating directly from God and which is apparently the element in man that represents

"God's image" (Gen. 1:27). Words such as *nefesh, ru'ah*, and *neshamah*, usually translated as "soul" or "spirit," are seldom used in the Bible to refer to any disembodied or separably "spiritual" part of man. Generally, these terms designate the life or the personality of the individual. The later books, however, contain passages which may be understood as referring to the spirit or soul apart from the body: "Yet the soul of my Lord shall be bound up in the bundle of life with the Lord your God..." (I Sam. 25:29) or: "All go unto one place; all are of the dust and return to the dust. Who knows if the spirit of man goes upward and if the spirit of the beast goes downward to the earth?" (Eccl. 4:20, 21).

For the talmudic rabbis, the soul of man is clearly separable from the body. Thus, they draw an analogy between God's relationship to the world and the soul's relationship to the body: "Five times did David say, 'Bless the Lord, O my soul.' He said this in reference to God and in reference to the soul. Just as God fills the entire world, so does the soul fill the entire body. Just as God sees but cannot be seen, so the soul sees but cannot be seen. Just as God nourishes the entire world, so does the soul nourish the body. Just as God is pure, so is the soul pure... Therefore, let the soul which possesses the five attributes come and praise Him to whom these attributes belong" (*Ber.* 10a). Another version reads: "The soul outlasts the body and God outlasts the world" (*Lev. R.* 4.8). This conception is recited in the morning liturgy in a prayer already found in the Talmud: "My God, the soul which You gave me is pure. You did create it. You did form it. You did breathe it into me. You preserve it within and You will take it from me, but will restore it to me hereafter... Blessed are You O Lord, Who restores souls unto the dead."

The Sadducees denied the immortality of the soul and debated the subject with the Pharisees. According to the rabbis, the soul is the vivifying element in man that is "given" by God and constitutes man's connection with Him. It is to be identified, in some sense, with the individual "self" of the person and seems to be capable of "existing" before and after its embodiment. By acknowledging that the soul as received is "pure," the worshiper assumes responsibility for the moral struggle and its outcome and admits that it is the task of man to surrender unto God, at the end of each day and certainly at the end of his life, a soul unstained and uncorrupted by its contacts with evil.

Beyond this, the rabbis did not develop any psychological theory which might explain the relationship between the soul and the introspectively discernible elements of consciousness such as mind, emotions, memory, will, reason. The medieval Jewish philosophers attempted to combine the essential rabbinic teachings regarding the human soul with an amalgam of Neo-Platonic, Aristotelian and Muslim concepts which was the accepted wisdom of the period. The differing emphases of the Bible and rabbinic treatment of the soul had an analogue in Greek philosophy, in the different approaches of Plato and Aristotle. In the Platonic view, the soul is a distinct entity coming into the body from a different, "spiritual" world and acting on the body by using it as its instrument. According to the Aristotelians, the human is a unitary being whose activity is psycho-physical. In their terminology, all reality consists of matter and form, where "form" is to be understood as that by virtue of which the thing is what it is rather than some other thing. In the case of the human being, the soul is the form of the material body. But since according to this view, individual forms have no separate existence and perish with the dissolution of the matter, it follows that the soul-form of the human being likewise ceases to exist with the death of the body.

For SAADIAH GAON, the soul is created together with the body. It is separated from the body after death but they are reunited for eventual reward or punishment. MAIMONIDES, who generally follows Aristotle, was able to reconcile his philosophy with the theological requirements of Judaism. The soul is essentially one, says Maimonides, but expresses itself in five different activities or through five different faculties: nutritive, sensitive, imaginative, emotional and rational. While the first four aspects of the soul do indeed perish with the death of the body, each person does have an opportunity to achieve immortality by developing his rational faculty, which is initially only a potentiality, into a fully actualized perfected entity which becomes permanent and indestructible. This developmental notion of the soul helps to pinpoint the centrality of human freedom of choice and connects the ultimate reward (immortality of the soul with God) and punishment (complete extinction) of the individual to his own actions. However, the views of JUDAH HALEVI and Hasdai CRESCAS appear closer to the entire thrust of Judaism by teaching that the development of the soul towards immortality, which is communion with God, depends primarily not upon intellectual activity and the attainment of knowledge (rational faculty), but upon moral actions and the love of God.

The Bible itself contains various hints of belief in an AFTERLIFE (II Kings 2; Prov. 12:28; Dan. 12:2), but it has no clear conception of immortality linked to human destiny and Divine justice. In the words of the Bible scholar Yehezkel Kaufmann, "It is not the belief in immortality that came later, but the breakthrough of the soul to God from the realm of death." As the national document of a people and its covenant with God, the Bible concentrated on this-worldly rewards and punishments, such as peace and prosperity or destruction and dispersion, which apply to the nation, rather than immortality of the soul, which applies to the individual only (ALBO).

In the eschatological teachings of the Talmud, a number of different terms refer to the ultimate redemption. Those like *yemot ha-mashi'ah* (the days of the Messiah) or the *ketz* (the end) relate to the historic level and refer to the role of the nation, Israel, in the establishment of the Kingdom of

Heaven on earth. Terms such as *olam ha-ba* (world to come) or *tehiyyat ha-metim* (resurrection of the dead) refer primarily to the problem of theodicy, Divine justice and individual destiny and salvation. Thus, for the rabbis, the World to Come signifies that all-spiritual existence to which the deserving soul ascends after physical death in which "there is no eating or drinking... but where the righteous sit and enjoy the splendor of the Divine Presence" (*Ber.* 17a). The place of the righteous after death is also called *Gan Eden* (Garden of Eden) and the place where the wicked are punished is *Gehinnom.*

Belief in the physical RESURRECTION of the righteous at some time in the future was considered by the rabbis in the Talmud to be a basic principle of the Jewish faith and was prominently enshrined in the liturgy. While Maimonides included resurrection of the dead as one of his 13 PRINCIPLES OF FAITH, he maintained that the righteous who will be resurrected will live a full life and then die a natural death. In his view, the ultimate destiny of the deserving human being is communion with God in a spiritual World to Come.

The concept of resurrection of the dead seems to have been occasioned by the original biblical notion that man is in essence this psychosomatic unity of body and soul, mind and matter, spiritual and physical. Thus, if man lived, sinned and achieved as a psychosomatic entity, justice would seem to require that he be so rewarded and punished (*Sanh.* 91). The eschatological view developed by Nahmanides followed along these lines (*Sha'ar ha-Gemul*).

Many modern Jewish thinkers have stressed the doctrine of the immortality of the soul rather than the resurrection of the dead, although both continue to be fundamental for Orthodox Jews. The Reform Pittsburgh Platform (1885) stated: "We reassert the doctrine of Judaism that the soul of man is immortal, grounding this belief on the Divine nature of the human spirit, which forever finds bliss in righteousness and misery in wickedness. We reject as ideas not rooted on Judaism the belief both in bodily resurrection and in Gehenna and Eden (hell and paradise) as abodes for eternal punishment or rewards."

SPEKTOR, ISAAC ELHANAN (1817-1896). Lithuanian rabbinical scholar, halakhic authority, and communal leader. Born in the province of Grodno, where he first studied with his father, the rabbi of Rozhanka, Spektor was later taught and ordained by Benjamin Diskin of Volkovysk. He went on to serve as rabbi of Izabelin (1837), Bereza (1839), Nesvizh (1850), Novogrudok (1851), and Kovno (1864-96). It was in the last city, a major focus of Jewish life, that Spektor became preeminent on the East European rabbinical scene. He established a graduate school for advanced talmudic study which later enjoyed renown as the "Kovno Kolel," and he helped to change the Russian government's stated aim of abolishing the traditional *hadarim* (Jewish religious elementary schools) in line with the tsarist reform of Jewish education. He was less successful, however, in his efforts to defend traditional rabbis accused of "usurping" the prerogatives of government-appointed "rabbinical" functionaries (see KAZYONNY RAVVIN).

Having declared Jewish settlement in Erets Israel to be a religious duty, Spektor lent wholehearted support to the Love of Zion (*Hibbat Tsiyyon*) movement. He joined R. Samuel Mohilever of Bialystok and R. Naphtali Tsevi Yehudah BERLIN of Volozhin in its spiritual leadership and in influencing the masses to accept its ideology. Jewish pioneers in Erets Israel soon faced the dilemma posed by agricultural labor during a SABBATICAL YEAR (*shemittah*) and, by 1889, the growth of agricultural settlement there made *shemittah* a pressing issue. Spektor's responsum, which allowed the land to be worked after its nominal sale to Muslims for a period of two years, was meant only as a short-term solution, but the precedent has since been followed by other authorities.

He was a prolific author of halakhic works, which included five volumes of responsa: *Be'er Yitshak* (1858), *Nahal Yitshak* (2 vols., 1872-84), and *Én Yitshak* (2 vols., 1889-95). Especially worried by the plight of the AGUNAH, the deserted wife who could not be certain of her husband's death, Spektor published 158 responsa on this tragic issue. With only three exceptions, he managed to devise a halakhic basis for the remarriage of each *agunah*, thereby establishing precedents for various lenient decisions that have been applied since the Holocaust.

Two important *yeshivot*, both founded in 1897, were named in Spektor's memory. The first, Keneset Bét Yitshak, originally formed part of the Slobodka *yeshivah* and continued to flourish in a suburb of Kovno (Kaunas) until after World War I. The other, established in New York as the Rabbi Isaac Elchanan Theological Seminary, evolved into Yeshiva University, America's largest Jewish institute of higher learning.

SPICEBOX Container for SPICES (*besamim*) used in the HAVDALAH ceremony at the conclusion of the SABBATH that includes a special blessing to be recited while inhaling the fragrance of spices. Literary evidence from the 12th century mentions the practice of using a special container (in the given instance, a glass vessel) for the *havdalah* spices. Since, during the Middle Ages, the most frequently used spice for this purpose was the myrtle (*hadas*), the container itself was also called *hadas.*

The earliest spicebox extant today dates from mid-16th century Germany and is made of silver in the form of a tower. As there are no halakhic requirements for spice containers, artists were free to use their creative imagination in their manufacture. There was nothing to stop any imaginative individual from pressing into service any appropriate container that happened to be available. Like other Jewish ceremonial objects, spiceboxes reflect the wide variety of time and place and the changing fashions of style, technique and iconography. They take the form of flowers, fruits, or fish, although the tower has remained the most popular design. Over the centuries, all sorts of architectural detail were added to the spice tower: masonry, balustrades, belfries, spires and domes, turrets, shingles, flags and bells. Some striking 17th-century spice towers from Augsburg have tiny human figures on the corners representing soldiers, musicians and Jews holding various ritual items.

SPINOZA, BARUCH (BENEDICT) Philosopher (1632-1677). He was born in Amsterdam to a MARRANO family from Portugal, who had fled to Holland and returned to Judaism. As a child, he received a formal Jewish education in the *Ets Hayyim* Talmud Torah. Upon completion of his studies, he began to delve deeply into the works of the medieval Jewish philosophers, such as Gersonides and Maimonides, both of whom profoundly influenced his views and philosophic system.

From the age of 22, Spinoza began to draw closer to the Christian circles in his city, and to express an interest in the general sciences. His "atheistical" and heretical views aroused concern both in the Jewish community and in Amsterdam's Calvinistic circles, leading to his excommunication by the Amsterdam Jewish community in 1656. Following this, he left Amsterdam and spent most of the rest of his life in the Hague, earning his livelihood by polishing lenses for reading glasses.

Spinoza's philosophic thought is complex and difficult, combining metaphysics, ethics, psychology, anthropology, political thought, and the philosophy of religion. The religious base is one of its major hubs, as Spinoza offers man an alternative to the established religions.

His first great work was the *Theologico-Political Treatise* (1670), in which he criticized the major tenets of religion, protested the subjugation of the state to religion, and preached freedom of the spirit and thought. He also expounded his views on the Bible, which paved the way for subsequent biblical criticism. The book shook the foundations of traditional theology, and caused a major storm, after which, Spinoza no longer dared to publish his ideas in print and only lectured on them before his faithful disciples.

His most important work, *Ethics*, was published after his death. In it he developed his pantheistic theory, in which he identifies nature with God, as expressed in his famous saying, "*Deus sive natura*", ("God or nature"). Its major thesis is the idea of the unity of all reality. When Spinoza used the term "nature," he was not only referring to the world or to all of physical nature, but to everything that exists. Biblical monotheism apears in Spinoza as if in the highest degree of purity, having been purified of all the historic additions of worship and commandment. In this sense, there is a clear link between his thought and the history of Jewish thought.

Spinoza also identified, clearly and profoundly, the new political reality in Europe, and discussed its significance for the fate of the Jewish people. As a result, he was critical of the Jewish heritage, both from a philosophical and a modernizing viewpoint. His major conclusion was that the laws of the *halakhah* were not in keeping with the new culture, which meant that a change in the status of religion in the life of the individual and the state was required. Because of his views, he was considered a heretic even after his death, and his teachings were proscribed by both Christians and Jews. Only at the end of the 18th century did philosophers begin to study his views, and since then his writings have become an inseparable part of modern philosophy.

STEINBERG, MILTON (1903-1950). U.S. Jewish philosopher, theologian, and rabbi. Born in Rochester, New York, he studied at City College, New York, where he encountered the philosopher Morris Raphael Cohen, whose critical methods and emphasis on reason influenced Steinberg, as did Bergson and Schopenhauer, the subjects of his master's dissertation. He also studied at the Jewish Theological Seminary, where he was particularly influenced by Mordecai M. KAPLAN and his stress on Jewish peoplehood, the need for change, the use of one's critical faculties, and naturalistic approaches to belief. As a congregational rabbi, Steinberg first served in Indianapolis and then, from 1933, at the Park Avenue Synagogue in New York. He was actively involved in communal and educational affairs and in Zionism. His first book, *The Making of the Modern Jew* (1934), was followed by *A Partisan Guide to the Jewish Problem* (1945) and *Basic Judaism* (1947). He also wrote the novel *As a Driven Leaf* (1939), about the scholarly heretic ELISHA BEN AVUYAH.

Following his early death, notes and articles that he left were collected by Arthur A. Cohen in a posthumous volume, *Anatomy of Faith* (1960). Steinberg was active in Jewish RECONSTRUCTIONISM and believed in much of its program and ideology, but disagreed with Kaplan's theological stand. He called for an enlightened modern faith, a belief in God which took into account science and modern knowledge, one far removed from simple, fundamentalist concepts but which left room for God as an active force in the world of men. Reason could not be the sole criterion of judgment, nor could it enable man to penetrate the realm of faith, since God is more than the world he perceives — the essence of all being.

STUDY The study of TORAH, as taken in the broad sense of all the classical Jewish religious texts and commentaries, is of paramount importance in Jewish life. As soon as the Pentateuch was completed, God told Joshua, "Let not this Book of the Teaching cease from your lips, but recite it day and night" (Josh. 1:8). The Mishnah stresses the centrality of Torah study, when it lists various commandments and then concludes, "but the study of Torah is equivalent to them all" (*Pe'ah* 1.1, amplified in *Shab.* 127a). The Talmud debates which is more important, action or study, and decides on study, "for it brings one to action" (*Kid.* 40a). In fact, when a solitary individual studies the Torah, God Himself determines that person's reward (*Avot* 3.3). Ideally, a man should divide his free time between study of the Bible, Mishnah, and Talmud (*Kid.* 30a).

The performance of a commandment is always preceded by the appropriate blessing. In the case of Torah study, which should ideally be carried out throughout the day, the blessing is recited as part of the morning prayers. To insure that the blessing will not have been recited in vain, it is followed by a limited amount of Torah study, including a passage from the Pentateuch containing the Priestly Blessing (Num. 6:24-26), another from the Mishnah (*Pe'ah* 1.1), and a third from the Talmud (*Shab.* 127a).

The obligation to study Torah on a regular basis only applies to men. Under traditional Jewish law women were required to study the WRITTEN LAW and not the ORAL LAW, and only those laws which pertain to them.

According to *Sifré* (*Ekev*), it is the father's duty to teach his son Hebrew from the time the child begins to talk. As the *lingua franca* at the time was Aramaic, the implication is that the child must be taught Hebrew even if this will not be his mother tongue. More specifically, a Mishnah in *Avot* spells out a study regimen: "at five years old, it is the age to study the Torah; at ten, the Mishnah; at 15, the Talmud" (5.25). Yet *Ecclesiastes Rabbah* (7) points out that not every person is capable of following such a plan, and that "of 1,000 who enter [the study of Torah], only 100 attain [the study of Mishnah], and only ten reach [the study of] the Talmud."

Sifré (Ha'azinu) offers practical advice on how to study, stating that a person should devote himself to general principles, which can then be applied elsewhere, rather than to individual facts, which cannot be easily translated into an operable hypothesis. The rabbis advocated setting aside a fixed daily time for study and stressed the advantages of studying with a fellow-student or students. The BET MIDRASH (study house) was a permanent feature of all communities.

Study session in a synagogue in Yemen.

The importance of study may be summed up in one of the pictures drawn by the sages of the World to Come, where "the righteous will sit with their crowns on their heads," while studying Torah directly with God Himself.

See also EDUCATION; TALMUD TORAH.

SUICIDE Judaism regards all life as given by God and sacrosanct. Man is not the absolute owner of his life, but is its guardian. As such, he has no right to dispose of it as he sees fit, and suicide is considered as murder. The verse, "But for your own life-blood I will require a reckoning" (Gen. 9:5) is regarded by the rabbis as forbidding suicide.

Generally, as human life is considered of paramount value, one may not forfeit his life in order to avoid breaking the laws of the Torah. Thus, the sages comment on the verse in Leviticus 18:5, "You shall live by them [the commandments] and not die by them." Only in three cases is the rule that one must be willing to die rather than violate the law: when forced into idolatry, murder, or sexual immorality.

Although there have been cases of mass suicide, such as following the fall of Masada to the Romans in 73 CE, the *halakhah* does not approve of this step, regardless of the circumstances.

According to *halakhah*, a suicide is to be buried in a separate part of the cemetery, and is not to be mourned by his next-of-kin. Generally, rabbis seek to mitigate the severity of these provisions, by ruling that the deceased took his own life while in an unstable state of mind, and is therefore technically not a suicide.

SUKKAH The booth (or tabernacle) erected for the SUKKOT festival in compliance with the commandment, "You shall dwell in booths for seven days; all Israelites shall dwell in booths" (Lev. 23:42). The rules governing the *sukkah* are given in the Mishnah tractate of SUKKAH, with commentary in both Talmuds.

The *sukkah* itself must be a temporary abode, meant to remind the Jew of the booths in which the Israelites lived in the wilderness after they left Egypt. Although the walls may be strong, the covering at the top must be thin enough to enable one to see the stars at night, but thick enough to mask sunlight during the day. The roof covering (known as *sekhakh*) must be made of cut vegetation, such as tree branches or bamboo poles. The material used must not be linked to the ground, so that the branch of a living tree cannot serve as the roof of the structure. A *sukkah* is not valid if the covering is located under a roof or a ceiling.

The *halakhah* specifies that the *sukkah* must be big enough to hold "the head and majority" of the body of one person, together with a table at which to eat, and it translates this as at least seven handbreaths (about 28 in.) by seven handbreaths in size. The covering must be at least ten handbreadths (about 40 in.) from the ground. There is no limit to the maximum size, but it must not be over 20 cubits

Singing table hymns in a sukkah *("booth").*

(approximately 30 ft.) high from the ground, for then "the eye cannot grasp it."

The walls must be strong enough to withstand a "normal wind," and they can be made of wood, stone, or even canvas over a metal framework. Two of its walls must have a minimum length of seven handbreadths each, and part of a third wall of at least one handbreadth (four in.). It is not required to have four walls.

All adult males must eat (at the least) products made of flour in the *sukkah*, including bread and other baked goods or pasta. Each time one eats anything substantial in the *sukkah*, one must pronounce the blessing, "... Who has commanded us to reside in the *sukkah*." There are those who are more stringent and do not eat anything outside the *sukkah*, and the *halakhah* enjoins sleeping in the *sukkah*. As this is a "time-related" commandment, women are exempt from the obligation to eat and sleep in the *sukkah*, but they may do so out of choice. During bad weather, one is exempted from sitting in the *sukkah*.

In Israel, the *sukkah* is used throughout the biblically ordained seven days of the festival, but outside Israel customs vary: the MITNAGGEDIM eat in the *sukkah* on the eighth day (SHEMINI ATSERET) as well, but do not pronounce the blessing on residing in the *sukkah*. The Ḥasidim recite KIDDUSH (prayer of sanctification) in the *sukkah* on the eighth day, but eat inside the house on that day.

Special prayers are often recited when first entering the *sukkah* at the beginning of the festival, and when leaving it at the end of Sukkot, and it is customary to recite the USHPIZIN daily.

SUKKAH ("booth"). Sixth tractate of Order MO'ED in the Mishnah. Its five chapters concern the laws of building and dwelling in the SUKKAH during the seven days of the festival of SUKKOT (Tabernacles) and the regulations regarding the FOUR SPECIES which every male is required to wave on the festival (cf. Lev. 23:33-43; Num. 29:12-38; Deut. 16:13-15). The last chapter describes the joyous WATER-DRAWING FESTIVAL which took place in the Temple during the festival. Also mentioned are the 70 special sacrificial offerings brought during Sukkot. Throughout the Mishnah, the Festival of Tabernacles is called simply *Ḥag* (Festival), which is also its designation throughout the ORAL LAW. The subject matter is amplified in both Talmuds and in the *Tosefta*.

SUKKOT Festival of Tabernacles, observed during the week commencing 15 Tishri. Outside Israel, in the Diaspora, the first two days are celebrated as full holidays (see FESTIVALS and SECOND DAY OF FESTIVALS) while the last day, SHEMINI ATSERET (the "Eighth Day of Solemn Assembly"), is also kept as a holiday, followed by SIMḤAT TORAH ("the Rejoicing of the Law"). This amounts to a continuous observance of nine days. In Israel, only the first and eighth days are full holidays, Shemini Atseret and Simḥat Torah being combined. The middle five days (six in Israel) are ḤOL HA-MO'ED, intermediate days of the festival when work is permissible but a festival framework is maintained (for example, in the liturgy).

Sukkot is one of the three PILGRIM FESTIVALS when, in ancient times, the Jews made pilgrimages to the Temple in Jerusalem. Like Passover and Shavu'ot, Sukkot has both historical and agricultural significance. Its historical meaning is indicated in the Bible, which links it with Israel's 40-year journey through the wilderness en route to the Promised Land. During that time, they lived only in "tabernacles" or booths, in commemoration of which the Bible instructs the Jew to "live in booths for seven days" (Lev. 23:42-43). However, as an agricultural event, occurring in the fall harvest season, Sukkot was also observed as a festival of thanksgiving for the bounties of nature granted during the past year (Ex. 23:16; Deut. 16:13).

The various names given to this festival provide a comprehensive explanation of its purpose:
(1) *Ḥag ha-Asif*, "the Festival of the Ingathering [of crops]" (Ex. 23:16,34:22), pointing to its agricultural importance; (2) *Ḥag ha-Sukkot*, "the Festival of Tabernacles" (Lev. 23:34; Deut. 13,16), commemorating Israel's experience in the wilderness under God's protection; (3) *Ḥag*, "the Festival" (Lev. 23:39-41; Num. 29:12), a name popular with the rabbis, as if to suggest that Sukkot was the holiday *par excellence*; and (4) *Zeman Simḥatenu*, "the Season of our Rejoicing" (cf. Deut. 15:14-15), a liturgical designation reflecting the Bible's commandment to "be altogether joyful."

In older books of the Bible, Sukkot is the only holiday given considerable attention, indicating that it was the main festival of the time. Its centrality disappeared, however, when Jews mostly lost contact with agriculture after the destruction of the Second Temple. The main observance of the festival involves "dwelling" in the SUKKAH. Today this is a very temporary structure built especially for the festival in one's yard or garden, or on a balcony, patio, etc. It is not roofed over but covered with detached foliage or other natural growth, through which the stars can be seen at night. The ETHIOPIAN JEWS (Beta Israel), who also observe Sukkot, never made booths, probably because they live in huts all year round. While the *sukkah* was originally a reminder of Israel's journey in the wilderness, the rabbis suggested that its insubstantial nature symbolizes man's reliance on Divine protection. All meals during the festival are eaten in the *sukkah*, unless bad weather makes it impossible to do so.

USHPIZIN, a 16th-century custom which originated among the kabbalists, is still part of the religious observance in the *sukkah*. The word *ushpizin* means "guests" and refers to seven notables in Jewish history (Abraham, Isaac, Jacob, Moses, Aaron, Joseph, and David) who are symbolically welcomed into the *sukkah*, one each day.

Central to the festival are the FOUR SPECIES, plants (one being a fruit) which are held together and waved at different points in the festival service, in accordance with the biblical injunction to "rejoice before the Lord" (Lev. 23:40). These Four Species (*arba'ah minim*) are the *lulav* or palm branch, the *etrog* or citron, the *hadassim* — three myrtle twigs, and the *aravot* — two willow branches. "Taking the *lulav*" applies to all four species, which are arranged in a bouquet. On the first seven days of the festival, apart from the Sabbath, the *lulav* is taken and during the HALLEL it is waved in all four compass directions, as well as upward and downward, to acknowledge God's omnipotence and sovereignty over the entire universe. Appropriate to the joyous character of Sukkot, the "full," unabridged *Hallel* (Ps. 113-118) is recited each morning. The book of ECCLESIASTES is prescribed reading for Sukkot. It may be that the pessimistic outlook of Ecclesiastes was thought suitable for the fall, when people began to anticipate the winter rains and colder months ahead.

Congregants waving the Four Species at Sukkot. From the Salzbach Mahzor.

SUKKOT — TABERNACLES

Other Names: *Hag ha-Sukkot* (Festival of Booths)
Hag ha-Asif (Feast of Ingathering)
Zeman Simhatenu (Season of our Gladness)

Hebrew Dates: 15–21 Tishri (in Israel and among Reform Jews in the Diaspora)
15–22 Tishri (in the Diaspora)

Torah & Prophetical Readings:
1st Day: Lev. 22:26-23:44; Num. 29:12-16 (*Maftir*); Zech. 14:1-21 (*Haftarah*)
2nd Day (in Diaspora); Lev. 22:26-23:44; Num. 29:12-16 (*Maftir*); I Kings 8:2–21 (*Haftarah*)
Intermediate Sabbath: Ex. 33:12-34:26; Num. 29:17-31 (*Maftir*); Ezek. 38:18-39:16 (*Haftarah*)

Scroll: Ecclesiastes (*Kohelet*) recited on Intermediate Sabbath; otherwise, on 1st Day of Sukkot (Israel) or Shemini Atseret (Diaspora)
Hallel: recited (in full)

Civil dates on which the festival occurs, 1990-2010:

1990/5751	4–10 October
1991/5752	23–29 September
1992/5753	12–18 October
1993/5754	30 September–6 October
1994/5755	20–26 September
1995/5756	9–15 October
1996/5757	28 September–4 October
1997/5758	16–22 October
1998/5759	5–11 October
1999/5760	25 September–1 October
2000/5761	14–20 October
2001/5762	2–8 October
2002/5763	21–27 September
2003/5764	11–17 October
2004/5765	30 September–6 October
2005/5766	18–24 October
2006/5767	7–13 October
2007/5768	27 September–3 October
2008/5769	14–20 October
2009/5770	3–9 October
2010/5771	23–29 September

Opposite page. Top: Wooden synagogue in Zabludow, Poland, mid-17th century. Below: Kaifeng Synagogue, China (reconstructed model). Overleaf. Left: Interior of Shaarey Zedek Synagogue in Southfield, Michigan. Right: Interior of the Great Synagogue in Jerusalem.

As on all other holy days, an Additional Service *(Musaf)* follows Morning Service and the Reading of the Law. On the first seven days of the festival, a procession takes place around the synagogue to the accompaniment of HOSHANOT prayers and hymns. The *hosha-na* refrain means "Save, we beseech You!" and this ceremony recalls the daily circuits made around the altar on this festival in the Temple. On a Sabbath, the prayers are recited but no procession is held.

Seven circuits (HAKKAFOT) take place on the seventh day of the festival, HOSHANA RABBAH (i.e., "the Great *Hoshanah*"). Traditionally, Hoshana Rabbah marks the conclusion of the solemn season and this is reflected in various customs: the Ashkenazi reader wearing a KITEL and chanting High Holiday prayer modes, the SHOFAR being sounded during the processions in Sephardi congregations. Finally, all of the Four Species are exchanged for a bundle of *"hoshanot"* and this is struck three times until some leaves fall off; it has been suggested that this is symbolic of the resurrection, as the denuded branches of a tree bud with new life in due season.

A characteristic feature of the eighth day, Shemini Atseret, is the Prayer for RAIN to fall in the Holy Land, a blessing that is essential for a fruitful year. In Israel on that day (and in the Diaspora on the following day) Simḥat Torah marks the conclusion of the annual Torah reading cycle and the beginning of a new cycle (for details, see SIMḤAT TORAH).

In ancient days, the joy of Sukkot was further enhanced by the WATER-DRAWING FESTIVAL, *Simḥat Bet ha-Sho'evah*, when water libations were ceremoniously poured over the altar to highlight the petitions for rain that had been offered on Sukkot. Joyous festivities and merrymaking linked with these ceremonies, took place in ancient Jerusalem. In modern Israel, special "Water-Drawing" festivities are held by religious circles during the intermediate days of Sukkot and have also been revived in kibbutzim.

The ancient ceremony of HAKHEL, prescribed in Deuteronomy (31:10-13) and described with more detail in the Mishnah (*Sot.* 7.8), has also been revived. In Temple times, when the people were assembled during the Sukkot following the end of the SABBATICAL YEAR, portions of the Torah were read aloud by the king or, when no king ruled, by the religious leader. In the *Hakhel* ceremony's modern form, the President of Israel publicly reads from the Torah to a mass assembly gathered at the WESTERN WALL.

One of the prophetical readings for the festival is chapter 14 of Zechariah, where it is said that all the nations will someday go up to Jerusalem" to keep the feast of Tabernacles" (verses 16-19). A total of 70 bullocks were sacrificed in the Temple on the seven days of the festival (Num. 29:12ff.) and the rabbis suggest that this number corresponded to the 70 nations of the world (*Suk.* 55b).

SUN, BLESSING OF (*birkat ha-ḥammah*). Blessing recited once every 28 years when the sun completes its cycle and returns to the place in the universe where, according to tradition, it began, on the fourth day of creation. A rabbinic commandment, this event is observed by reciting the blessing, "Blessed are You, Lord our God, King of the universe, Who makes the work of creation" (*Ber.* 59b). The reckoning of this 28-year cycle is based on the calculation of the talmudic sage SAMUEL, who estimated the length of a year as being 365 days, six hours (see CALENDAR).

According to the Talmud, the turning point of this 28-year sun cycle occurs at the vernal equinox on a Tuesday evening (the first in the month of Nisan) at six p.m. in Jerusalem. However, since the sun is not visible at that time in all parts of the world, the sages ordained that the blessing be recited the next morning at sunrise. A prayer quorum is not necessary, but it is the preferred custom to say this blessing in a large assembly. The blessing is said while standing, and the sun must be visible. The accompanying prayers include selections from the Zohar, Bible, Prophets, and Psalms. The last date for the blessing of the sun occurred on 8 April, 1981; the next one will be 8 April, 2009.

SUPERSTITION The Bible (Deut. 18:9-11) forbade Israelites to engage in "the abominations of the nations" whose land they were to inherit, specifically singling out "any one that makes his son or his daughter to pass through the fire, or that uses divination, or is an observer of times, or an enchanter, or a witch, or a charmer, or a consulter with familiar spirits, or a wizard, or a necromancer". Various prophets also denounced superstition. Thus Jeremiah stated, "Do not hearken to your prophets, nor to your diviners, nor to your dreamers, nor to your enchanters, nor to your sorcerers" (Jer. 27:9). Nevertheless, various superstitions have prevailed at different times. The Talmud, for example, discusses ASTROLOGY, and R. Joshua ben Levi implies that persons born on a specific day of the week all share certain character traits, although R. Johanan rejects the idea that there are various times which are more fortuitous than others. The idea of auspicious or inauspicious times is contained in the *Shulḥan Arukh* (*OH* 551:1), which states that "from the beginning of the month of Av, a Jew who is involved in a legal case with a non-Jew should attempt to postpone it, because the time is not auspicious."

The Talmud (*Sanh.* 65 a-b), in discussing the verses in Deuteronomy 18, explains some of the superstitions which are involved. Thus "an observer of times" (*me'onen*), according to R. Akiva, is one who offers propitious times for leaving on a journey, or for purchasing objects, or for harvesting one's crops. "An enchanter" (*menaḥesh*), is one who sees omens in various everyday events, such as dropping one's bread or staff, or having a deer cross one's path, all of these being considered bad omens.

The Talmud mentions various other superstitious practices, to some of which it gives credence, while others it finds senseless. In certain instances, the practices are condemned as being against Jewish law. R. Akiva, in a list of those who

Chapel of the U.S. Air Force Academy, Colorado Springs.

have no share in the World to Come, mentions a person "who whispers [verses of the Bible as charms] over a wound" in order to heal it (*Sanh.* 10.1). MAIMONIDES nevertheless writes in *Mishneh Torah* (Laws of Idolatry 11:11) that "if a person was bitten by a scorpion or by a snake, one is permitted to whisper on the wound ... in order to calm him down and strengthen his heart, even though it is utterly valueless, for given the fact that his life is in danger, [the sages] permitted it, so that he should not go out of his mind."

The Talmud lays down certain actions which, to the modern mind, would seem to be needless superstition, such as forbidding a woman to walk between two men. Great attention is also paid to the implications of DREAMS, and an entire literature developed on how to "rectify" bad dreams.

Other areas of superstition revolve about the EVIL EYE. The Talmud and especially the Kabbalah have many references to evil spirits and DEMONS, and their effects. Maimonides dismisses all of these references by stating that demons do not bother any person who ignores them. In order to ward off evil events, the Talmud discusses the comparative efficacy of various AMULETS.

Throughout the Middle Ages superstitions either remained or were added, to the extent that R. JUDAH HE-ḤASID, in his *Sefer Ḥasidim* (Sec. 59), gave a list of different practices which were unavailing and even against Torah law. These superstitions included not eating eggs on the night after the Sabbath and not taking fire twice from the same source if there was a sick person or a woman who had given birth in the house. Yet, *Sefer Ḥasidim* also lists many practices and omens which it claims are valid; for example, if a new house is built on the same site where another had stood earlier, care must be taken to insure that the doors and windows in the new house be in exactly the same place as the old one, for otherwise "one's life is in danger from the demons or the angels."

Certain customs which are practiced to this day have also come under attack as being superstition, although many classic sages have been in favor of such practices. These include the TASHLIKH ceremony on ROSH HA-SHANAH, where all one's sins are figuratively thrown into the water, and KAPPAROT before the DAY OF ATONEMENT, in which sins are figuratively transferred to the hen or rooster which is used in the ceremony.

SYNAGOGUE (*bet keneset*). The central religious institution of Judaism, the center for public PRAYER and for other religious and community activities; the prototype for analogous institutions in Christianity and Islam.

Origins. Although sources (Josephus, Philo, the New Testament, the Talmud, and archaeology) confirm the existence of the synagogue as a stable institution already in the first century CE, its origin is unclear. A number of relatively late sources, e.g., the Midrash (*Yal.* Ex. 408), the New Testament (Acts 15:21), and Josephus (*Contra Aapionem* 2, 175), ascribed its establishment to Moses. However, this was a homiletical attempt to predate its actual origin. Many authorities feel that the events culminating in the emergence of the synagogue are to be dated to the Babylonian EXILE (after 586 BCE). Scholarly speculation is that the exiles met from time to time, perhaps every Sabbath, to seek consolation over the loss of their land, to study Scripture, and perhaps to pray. Some prayers may even have been written at this time. As evidence, passages in Ezekiel, prophet of the exiles, are cited to indicate meetings of elders (Ezek. 8:1, 14:1, 20:1). The Talmud (*Meg.* 29a) finds a direct reference to the synagogues of Babylonia in Ezekiel 11:16: "Thus said the Lord God: I have indeed removed them far among the nations, and I have scattered them among the countries, and I have become to them a small sanctuary in the countries to which they have gone." The phrase "small sanctuary" was in the course of time often applied to a synagogue. Other theories have dated the origin of the synagogue to First Temple times, to the Hellenistic age, and to the Hasmonean period.

Ancient Period. With the return of the exiles from Babylonia and the rededication of the TEMPLE, synagogues, or proto-synagogues, probably developed in Erets Israel. The Mishnah tells of a synagogue on the TEMPLE MOUNT, beside the Temple itself (*Sot.* 7.7-8; *Yoma* 7.1). The Jerusalem Talmud (*Meg.* 3.1) claims that there were some 400 synagogues in Jerusalem at the time of the destruction of the Second Temple, a figure that may be exaggerated but points to their multiplicity. Nevertheless, development of the synagogue in the Diaspora may have outpaced that of Erets Israel. The first concrete evidence of synagogue building comes from Egypt in the third century BCE. Philo (first century), mentions the synagogues of Rome, the existence of which has been confirmed by archaeology; the Book of Acts mentions Paul as preaching in synagogues in Damascus, Asia Minor, and Cyprus; and the Talmud refers to the magnificent Diaspora synagogue in Alexandria (destroyed in the Diaspora revolt, 115-117 CE). Early synagogues are known to have existed in various Mediterranean communities. By the end of the first century CE, wherever Jews lived they had their synagogues, and this was to prove vital to the people's success in surviving the destruction of the Temple and reconstructing Jewish life.

With the destruction of the Temple, the central role of the synagogue in Jewish life became firmly established. Certain Temple rituals were transferred to the synagogue for the sake of continuity, while others were specifically prohibited to emphasize the distinction between the two institutions. Prayer was considered a replacement for sacrifice, and prayer services were fixed to correspond to the regular communal offerings that could no longer be brought to the Temple. The forms and procedures of synagogue service established at that time have remained constant to this day. Unlike the Temple, where the ritual was carried out inside the SANCTUARY by the priests, the only requirement for a synagogue service was a quorum (MINYAN) of ten men, while any layman could lead the service. Thus the shift from synagogue to Temple represented a historic transformation in the role of the individual in the ritual. The phenomenology of man's relationship with God became more personalized, and less a matter of participation in the collective, although the element of communal worship in the synagogue prevented the complete individualization of the ritual. Inasmuch as Jewishness has ethnic, communal, and cultural dimensions not directly rooted in the liturgy, the synagogue, from its inception assumed additional roles. Throughout history, it has continued to do so with varying emphases in different ages.

Both *halakhah* and *aggadah* ascribed unique importance to the synagogue. All synagogues are considered to partake of the holiness of the Temple. They were seen as extraterritorial parts of Erets Israel, and it was believed that at the End of Days all would be miraculously transported to the Holy Land (*Meg.* 29a). The *halakhah* circumscribed this holiness with specific regulations. Frivolity, gossip, and idle chatter were prohibited. One could not eat or sleep in the synagogue, although one could eat and sleep in a BET MIDRASH (study hall). Thus synagogues were sometimes built with the intent of giving them the status of study halls in order to allow for these activities. Even in communities where men did not cover their heads at all times, it became customary to cover one's head in the synagogue (see COVERING THE HEAD). The holiness of the synagogue remains in force even when it is not longer in use, and even when it is in ruin. The sale of a synagogue is permitted only under specific circumstances and generally requires consultation with a competent halakhic authority.

The oldest extant structures thought to have served as synagogues are located in Erets Israel, and have been discovered by recent archeological investigation. They are found at Masada, in the Judean Desert, at Herodion to the south of Jerusalem, and at Gamla in the Golan Heights. They all predate the destruction of the Temple in 70 CE.

After the destruction of the Temple, synagogue construction was prohibited by the Romans. Subsequently, however, such activity resumed at an impressive pace. Over 100 synagogues dating from the third to the eighth century CE have been identified so far in Israel. The Jewish population had shifted largely to Galilee in the north, where the earliest concentration of structures is to be found. These follow several different prototypes. Most common is the basilica form, consisting of a long hall divided by two rows of pillars into a central nave and two aisles. Benches line the internal walls, and the pillars probably supported a gallery; all are oriented towards Jerusalem. There is no definite evidence of separate sections for women in the synagogues of this period. Exteriors tend to be impressively constructed and ornamented, making the synagogue by far the most imposing structure of the settlement, and whenever possible situated at the town's highest point or close to a water source. Interiors tend to be plain and unornamented, presumably to avoid distracting worshipers from the service. Among the finest examples of this type of synagogue are those at Baram in central Galilee, and at Capernaum on the shores of the Sea of Galilee. At a particular stage, mosaic floors were introduced, first with only geometrical designs, and later with representations of human and animal figures, depictions of Bible stories, the fruit of Erets Israel, Temple implements, the Zodiac, and mythological figures borrowed from the general culture of the time. An impressive example of a mosaic floor is the synagogue discovered at Bet Alpha in the Jezreel Valley.

Remains of synagogues from this period have also been discovered in the Diaspora. Some of the earliest are located in Greece and Asia Minor. Among the most impressive are the synagogue at Sardis in western Turkey, a basilica some 400 feet long, accommodating 1,000 worshipers; at Dura Europos, Syria (completed 244 CE), with four walls covered with 58 depictions of biblical scenes; and the synagogue in Hammam-Lif, Tunisia, whose central mosaic is now on display at the Brooklyn Museum in New York.

Middle Ages. During the Middle Ages, the synagogue was the center of Jewish life, and Jews tried to live as close to one as possible. In many communities, it was constructed so as to be inconspicuous (following the regulations imposed on the community) in the heart of the Jewish quarter of the city. The synagogue was in use at all hours, many men attended services three times a day, and almost all of them came on Sabbaths and holidays. The atmosphere differed from the solemn decorum of the contemporary church. Prayers, with the exception of the silent AMIDAH, were recited in a loud voice, conversation, although not sanctioned, was not uncommon, children were given a fair amount of freedom. Worshipers felt that they were indeed carrying on a dialogue with the Creator, with Whom their relationship was close and familiar. Relative to the surrounding society, the synagogue was a democratic institution. All were counted for the quorum, and being called to the READING OF THE LAW or leading the service was not conditional upon any particular qualifications or status. Any congregant with a significant grievance could stop the service during the Sabbath Reading of the Law and prevent its resumption until satisfaction was obtained. All types of communal activity were pursued in the synagogue; the local rabbinic court might convene there, classes were conducted in the sanctuary or in an annex, solemn oaths and bans of excommunication were pronounced there. Communal offices, the ritual bath, a library, ovens for the baking of unleavened bread, a hospice for travelers, a social hall, the GENIZAH, etc., might be located in synagogue rooms or adjacent structures.

Throughout the Middle Ages synagogue architecture continued to reflect prevalent styles, particularly influential being the Romanesque and Gothic. In this period, the use of representational art diminished. Special sections for women became standard. The reader's platform (BIMAH) at

The former Toledo synagogue founded in 1203, later Santa Maria la Blanca Church.

the center of the synagogue took on greater significance and, together with the ARK on the wall facing Jerusalem, constituted the architectural and artistic focus. In Ashkenazi communities seating arrangements changed: the surrounding benches in the style of the ancient synagogues were abandoned for the more capacious arrangement of parallel seating facing forward. Since synagogues were not permitted to be taller than neighboring churches, many synagogues in Europe were constructed with their floors below street level to obtain maximal internal height. Impressive synagogue structures were built by Spanish Jewry, showing the influence of Moorish architecture. With the expulsion of the Jews in 1492, all Spanish synagogues were confiscated and many were turned into churches. In Italy, from the 16th century, the building of synagogues was limited when the Jews were restricted to ghettos. However, within their somber surroundings, magnificent synagogues, reflecting the achievements of the Renaissance, were constructed, as, for example, in Venice. In Rome, where 14 communities originally existed, the Jews were allowed only one synagogue building in the ghetto, but overcame the problem by constructing five synagogues within the structure.

A unique phenomenon in synagogue architecture was the wooden synagogues of Poland. These developed from the mid-17th century onward and spread all over Eastern Europe. The interior decorations, covering every inch of wall and ceiling space, were a unique expression of Jewish folk-art. Another special type of synagogue was the "fortress" building, enabling the Jews to defend themselves in the event of attack.

The synagogues of the Ḥasidic movement (from the 18th century) were small and informal (see SHTIBL). There are generally no salaried positions in Ḥasidic synagogues; worshipers assume their administration and lead the services.

In Muslim lands, Jews had to face discriminatory laws ranging from periods of destruction of synagogues to the ordinance that they should be higher than the lowest mosque in the town. Generally, the Jews built modest structures in the hope that their worship would not be disturbed, although regulations were sometimes circumvented and imposing synagogues were built (e.g., in Aleppo, Egypt, Djerba in Tunisia, and Baghdad). Multiple ARKS were a special feature of Eastern synagogues; triple Arks were usual but sometimes there were even more, as synagogues often had many Scrolls of the Law. In some places, under the influence of Muslim customs, Jews removed their shoes before entering the prayer hall.

Modern Period. In the 19th century, major innovations were introduced by the REFORM movement. Partially influenced by contemporary churches, Reform synagogues were usually large imposing buildings, impressively equipped and furnished. They were referred to as temples. ORGANS were introduced and the women's section was abolished as men and women were seated together. Decorum and aesthetic values were emphasized. Covering the head for both men and women was not required in most Reform congregations. The reader's platform was no longer in the center of the building, but contained within the space in front of the Ark (a change adopted in many Orthodox congregations).

In their turn, Orthodox congregations in Western countries also started to place more emphasis on decorum and aesthetic considerations, and to construct more imposing synagogues. The design of these, however, was limited by the strictures of *halakhah*, such as the need to separate men and women. In Western countries, especially in North America, most synagogues today have reassumed the role of social community center as in the Middle Ages. They often have social halls for the celebrations of weddings, *bar mitsvahs*, etc.; religious schools, including Sunday and sometimes weekday afternoon classes; men's clubs and women's clubs (often called sisterhoods) and sponsor a wide range of educational, social, and recreational activities. Design of the buildings and their appurtenances is innovative, and outstanding architects and artists, Jewish and non-Jewish, have been commissioned to beautify the synagogue. Recent developments include the founding of *ḥavurot*, or small groups who work together on developing their own ritual (see HAVURAH), and the participation of WOMEN in all levels of synagogue activity in the non-Orthodox congregations.

In the Diaspora, synagogue membership is one of the chief means of Jewish identification, and many Jews join synagogues even if they do not attend the services regularly. In Israel, on the other hand, Jewish identification may be achieved in numerous different ways, and therefore the synagogue's role as a community center is minimal, and it is almost exclusively a place for prayer and religious study.

T

TA'ANIT ("fast day"). Ninth tractate of Order MO'ED in the Mishnah. Its four chapters discuss the laws of declaring a public fast day in the event of drought, epidemic, or invasion by a foreign army (cf. Num. 10:9; I Kings 8:35-39). Also included are various laws related to the fixed fast days: the 17th of Tammuz, the Ninth of Av, and the Day of Atonement. The subject matter is amplified in both Talmuds and the *Tosefta*.

TABERNACLE (MISHKAN) See SANCTUARY

TABERNACLES FESTIVAL See SUKKOT

TABLETS OF THE COVENANT Two stone tablets received by MOSES from God on Mount SINAI; also known as "two tablets of the law" or "two tablets of testimony." Moses was summoned by God to ascend Mount Sinai in order to receive "the tablets of stone and the Torah and the commandments which I have written" (Ex. 24:12). Upon these stone slabs was inscribed "by the finger of God" (Ex. 31:18) the TEN COMMANDMENTS, "on both their sides; on the one side and on the other...and the writing was the writing of God" (Ex. 32:15,16).

When Moses saw the Children of Israel worshiping the GOLDEN CALF, he smashed these two tablets (Ex. 32:19). He was subsequently called by God to carve a second pair, identical to the first, and to ascend to the mountain top where Moses would again inscribe the words of the first tablets (Ex. 34:1-4). These two tablets were brought down by Moses and were eventually deposited in the Ark of the Covenant (Deut. 10:2) that Solomon housed in the First Temple (I Kings 8:1-10), remaining there until the destruction of the Temple by the Babylonians in 586 BCE.

In the talmudic period, the two tablets of the covenant took on symbolic meaning, representing not only the WRITTEN LAW and all 613 COMMANDMENTS, but the ORAL LAW as well (*Ex. R.* 46:1). Rabbinic debate is recorded concerning the order of the Decalogue engraved on the tablets (TJ, *Shek.* 49d), their form, and the differences between the first two tablets and the second. They were the subject of much Midrash and legend. One Midrash identifies the first tablets with the text of the Decalogue in Exodus 20 and the second with the version found in Deuteronomy 5.

The Tablets of the Covenant flanked by two lions over the Ark in the Berlin Synagogue, 19th century.

In the late Middle Ages, the two tablets of the covenant came to be used as a Jewish religious symbol. In 19th-century Central and Western Europe, they were often displayed on the exterior of the synagogues, being regarded as a more universal symbol than the *menorah*. They continue to adorn Jewish ritual objects, especially synagogue arks, art and jewelry, often guarded on either side by the lions of Judah and decorated with a shield of David. The tablets are depicted as two connected rectangular slabs with rounded tops and are usually inscribed with the first ten letters of the Hebrew alphabet, Roman numerals, or the first words of each of the commandments.

TAḴANUN ("supplication"). Penitential prayer added after the reader's repetition of the AMIDAH of the weekday Morning and Afternoon Services. It contains a number of devotional supplications seeking Divine mercy. It is not recited on days with any degree of festivity and in the case of the Afternoon Service, is also not recited on days preceding any day of festivity. Taḫanun includes *nefilat appayim*, ("falling upon the face"), during which the worshiper lays his forehead on his left hand (unless he is wearing phylacteries on that hand, in which case he rests his forehead on his right hand) and recites II Samuel 24:14, which has a reference to "falling into the Lord's hands." Originally the worshiper completely prostrated himself, a custom still followed in France in the 13th century. The verse from Samuel is followed by Psalm 6:2-11 in the Ashkenazi ritual and Psalm 25 in the Sephardi. At the Morning Services on Mondays and Thursdays, *nefilat appayim* is supplemented by extensive prayers of a supplicationary and penitential nature. On fast days and during the TEN DAYS OF REPENTANCE, both the Morning and Afternoon *Tahanun* prayers are preceded by the prayer, AVINU MALKENU ("Our Father, our King").

The *Tahanun* is not recited on the Sabbath and festivals, the New Moon, throughout the entire month of Nisan, 14 Iyyar, on Lag ba-Omer, from the beginning of the month of Sivan until the ninth of the month (an alternative custom is until the 14th of the month), from the day preceding the Day of Atonement until the second day after Shemini Atseret (another custom is until the month of Heshvan), on Hanukkah, Tu bi-Shevat, Purim and Shushan Purim, and the 14th and 15th of I Adar. Nor is *Tahanun* said on Tishah be-Av, the national day of mourning for the destruction of both Temples, for the sages state that the day will eventually become a festival. In Zionist circles, it is not recited on Israel Independence Day and Jerusalem Day, since these are regarded as days of Divine deliverance. It is also not said in a house of mourning during the week of *shivah*, if there is a bridegroom in the synagogue within the first week after his marriage, or if the father, *mohel* (circumcisor) or *sandak* (godfather) of a child to be circumcised that day is present.

TAHARAT HA-MISHPAHAH See FAMILY PURITY

TAKKANAH (pl. *takkanot*). Regulation or ordinance instituted either by the sages of the Talmud and obligating all Jews, or by communal leaders for the members of their community (*Takkanot ha-Kahal*), or by the members of an association to regulate their own affairs. *Takkanot* were enacted by the sages primarily to accommodate Jewish life to new situations, e.g., the *takkanot* of JOHANAN BEN ZAKKAI after the destruction of the Second Temple (*RH* 4.1-3); or to improve the economic security of the wife by clauses inserted in the KETUBBAH (marriage contract; *Ket.* 4.7-12); or to expedite the extension of loans by the document (PROSBUL) which Hillel instituted (*Git.* 4.3). In ancient times, other *takkanot* were instituted by municipal authorities to regulate the assessment of taxes and the collection and distribution of alms, as well as to regulate labor relations (*BM* 7.1; *BB* 7b-8b). *Takkanot* of a prohibitive nature, such as the 18 measures of BET SHAMMAI limiting contact with the Romans so as to "remove the danger of transgression," were known as *gezerot* ("decrees"). For regulations meant only for a specific emergency and lacking permanent effect, see HORA'AT SHA'AH. Throughout the Middle Ages, the elders of Jewish communities, in conjunction with their rabbinical leaders, instituted *takkanot* to regulate both the religious and the fiscal affairs of the community; their binding force was recognized by the *halakhah*, although certain *takkanot* (e.g., those of Rabbenu GERSHOM ME'OR HA-GOLAH and Rabbenu Jacob TAM) were accepted only by Ashkenazim. In modern times, Sephardi and Eastern Jewish authorities continued to exercise this right, while Ashkenazi rabbis were reluctant to do so. In Israel today, the Chief Rabbinate has limited its power of instituting *takkanot* to the regulation of the Israeli rabbinical courts, leaving the regulation of civil affairs to the Knesset. For further details, see GEZERAH and HALAKHAH.

EXAMPLES OF TAKKANOT

One who divorces his wife for misconduct is forbidden to remarry her.

Elementary school teachers must be appointed in every community (R. Joshua ben Gamla, first cent. CE).

Gentiles are entitled to participate in the poor man's allocation of the harvest.

Jews are not to engage in pig-breeding.

One should not give way to extortion when ransoming Jewish captives.

Bigamy is forbidden (*Herem de-Rabbenu Gershom*, 11th cent.).

A woman may not be divorced except with her own consent (Rabbenu Gershom).

A Jew forced to convert to another faith, but who has returned to Judaism, may not be put to shame (Rabbenu Gershom).

Unauthorized reading of someone else's letters is prohibited (*Herem de-Rabbenu Gershom*).

All litigation between Jews must be referred to Jewish courts (Rabbenu Jacob Tam, 12th cent.).

Informers and those requesting Gentile intervention in the community's internal affairs are subject to excommunication (Rabbenu Jacob Tam).

No conversation is permitted in the synagogue during the *Amidah* and the Reading of the Law (*Takkanot Shum*, 13th cent.).

Lavish celebrations and ostentatious jewelry or costume are to be avoided (Sumptuary laws of both Ashkenazim and Sephardim, 13th-18th cents.).

Where money is owed to both a Jew and a non-Jew and the debtor is able to pay only one of them, the non-Jew must receive payment first.

TAL See DEW, PRAYERS FOR

TALLIT A four-cornered, fringed garment worn during certain prayers, in fulfillment of the commandment of fringes (TSITSIT; Num. 15:38). This garment is often referred to as the *tallit gadol* ("large *tallit*") as opposed to the "*tallit katan* ("small *tallit*") or *tsitsit*, which is customarily worn under the shirt. The blessing upon donning the *tallit* is *le-*

hitattef be-tsitsit, "...Who has commanded us to wrap ourselves in *tsitsit*." After the blessing, a person should wrap himself entirely in the *tallit*, covering his head, and remain that way "for the time it takes to walk four cubits" (about two yards), and only then arrange the *tallit* around the shoulders. Only males are required to wear the four-cornered garments, because the commandment is time-related (and therefore women are exempt), being restricted to the daytime. In the Sephardi and German communities, the *tallit* is worn by all males; however, many Ashkenazi Jews do not begin to wear the *tallit* until after marriage. Even among those communities where the *tallit* is worn before marriage, it is customary for only married men to cover their heads with the *tallit* during prayers.

In general, the *tallit* is worn for every Morning Service and each Additional Service when there is one, except on TISHAH BE-AV when the *tallit* is put on for the Afternoon instead of the Morning Service. On the DAY OF ATONEMENT, the *tallit* is worn for all five prayers. On days when TEFILLIN are worn, the *tallit* is put on before the *tefillin*.

The reader wears a *tallit* at the Afternoon Service, and in some communities at the Evening Service as well. A person not wearing a *tallit* who is called to the Reading of the Law must put one on before reciting the Torah blessings.

When the priests ascend to bless the people, they place their *tallit* over their head and hands, because God's Divine Presence is said to rest on their hands when they pronounce the PRIESTLY BLESSING.

Wool prayer shawl (tallit) *with silk embroidery. Italy, 18th century.*

Ideally, the *tallit* should be made of wool, but other materials, such as silk, may be used; the fringes must be made either of wool or of the material of which the garment is made. Each of the four corners of the *tallit* must have a fringe consisting of four threads doubled over, giving eight threads. These are then tied in a distinctive manner, with one thread, which is longer than the others, wound round the other seven and then double-knotted. A common custom for the preparation is a double knot followed by seven, eight, 11 and 13 windings, each winding followed by a double knot, giving a total of five double knots.

Although the wool *tallit* has customarily been woven with black (sometimes white) stripes, the wave of interest in Judaism which began in the 1960s and 1970s has led to the introduction of hand-woven *tallitot* (pl. of *tallit*) with stripes of various colors and with other motifs woven in.

The feminist movement has been involved in the question of the wearing of the *tallit*, and women in the Conservative, Reform, and Reconstructionist movements, as well as a number of Orthodox women, now wear the *tallit* during prayers. The Conservative movement demands that all women in its rabbinic program pledge to keep all the commandments incumbent on the male, including the wearing of the *tallit* during prayers.

TALMID ḪAKHAM (lit. "a disciple of the wise"; pl. *talmidé ḫakhamim*). Mishnaic term for a learned Jew, particularly a rabbinic scholar. A "disciple of the sages" served his apprenticeship through "attendance on the sages" (*Avot* 6.5), accompanying a recognized scholar in order to observe and learn from all his ways (*Ber.* 47b). The Jewish ideal was to attain scholarly rank, thus qualifying one to join the "aristocracy of learning." The tannaitic rabbis differentiated between various levels of attainment, from the student who uncritically absorbed everything to the one who retained only essential knowledge (*Avot* 5.5).

A *talmid ḫakham* was granted certain privileges (e.g., not having to pay taxes or shoulder communal tasks), but the duties imposed on him were far more extensive. He had to be genuinely and exceptionally pious, considerate, forbearing, polite, moderate and refined in his habits; careful about his dress and appearance (*Ber.* 43b; *Shab.* 114a); serving as an example to others (*Suk.* 21b; *Sif.* to Deut. 33:2). The true scholar was humble in the presence of colleagues (*Er.* 54a), but hard as iron in debate (*Ta'an.* 4a); his questions and answers must always be to the point (*Avot* 5.7), and he was expected to deal with halakhic problems anywhere and at any time (*Shab.* 114a).

The sages naturally tended to idealize the scholar as well as his obligations. A *mamzer*, one born of a forbidden union, who attained the rank of a *talmid ḫakham* had precedence over an ignorant High Priest (*Hor.* 3.8, 13a; *Meg.* 28a). If necessary, a man should sell off his possessions in order to marry a scholar's daughter (*Pes.* 49a); insulting a *talmid ḥakham* made one liable to a heavy fine (TJ *BK* 8.6) or even to EXCOMMUNICATION (*MK* 15a). On the basis of a Scriptural verse (Isa. 54:13), the rabbis also declared that "Torah scholars promote peace in the world" (*Ber.* 64a; cf. *Yev.* 122b). In modern times, any Jew well versed in rabbinic law and literature is described as a *talmid ḥakham.*

TALMUD The authoritative body of Jewish law and lore accumulated over a period of seven centuries (c.200 BCE-c.500 CE) in Erets Israel and Babylonia. The word Talmud derives from *l-m-d* ("study" or "teach"). The Talmud incorporates the MISHNAH and the rabbinical discussions of the Mishnah, known as the Gemara. There are two Talmuds, the Jerusalem (or Palestinian) Talmud (*Talmud Yerushalmi*) and the Babylonian Talmud (*Talmud Bavli*). For many centuries, the former was largely neglected and the term "Talmud" came to be applied exclusively to the Babylonian Talmud, while the word "Gemara" was also used for this work in its entirety. When the Talmud was censored by Christian censors in the 16th century, they almost consistently substituted the word "Gemara" for "Talmud." Another common designation of the Talmud is SHAS, the Hebrew acronym for the six Orders (*shishah sedarim*) of the Mishnah.

The ORAL LAW, traditionally given to MOSES on Mount SINAI, was codified in the Mishnah, c.200 CE, while the Gemara presents the discussions during the following two centuries in Erets Israel and three centuries in Babylonia.

The talmudic period is consequently divided into two periods, that of the Mishnah and that of the Gemara. The reason for this division is not merely literary. HALAKHAH, which is the totality of Jewish law, is based on a hierarchy of sources; the older the source, the greater its authority. Thus, laws mentioned explicitly in the Bible have more authority than those mentioned in the Mishnah; laws in the Mishnah carry more weight than those found in the Gemara, laws quoted in the Gemara are more authoritative than later halakhic decisions, and so on. In keeping with this division of authority, the rabbis of the different periods were given different titles: the rabbis of the Mishnah are called *tannaim* (pl. of TANNA), i.e., those who teach; those of the Gemara are called *amoraim* (pl. of AMORA), i.e., those who explain.

The Mishnah was devoted almost exclusively to *halakhah*, and contains only the end result of rabbinic debate and discussion; the arguments, the proofs, and the lengthy discussion of supporting biblical texts are on the whole absent. While the Mishnah is the preeminent collection of rabbinic statements from its period, it is not the only one. The old method of studying the Oral Law was preserved in four volumes of MIDRASH HALAKHAH. MIDRASH is the term for any rabbinic comment on or interpretation of a biblical text; the anthologies of Midrash statements are also called by this title. *Midrash Halakhah* refers to the rabbinic interpretations of the biblical law texts.

Many of the rabbinic statements of law and biblical exegesis were not included either in the Mishnah or the *Midrash Halakhah*. These statements are called *baraitot* (pl. of BARAITA). A collection of these *baraitot*, called the TOSEFTA, was edited a number of generations after R. Judah ha-Nasi edited the Mishnah. It parallels the structure and format of the Mishnah. Yet even the *Tosefta* is not a complete compilation of all the rabbinic statements which were not included in the Mishnah. Innumerable *baraitot* were preserved in the second, larger section of the Talmud called the Gemara (from Aram. *gemar*, "that which is learned from tradition").

Despite the tendency of historians to divide history into neatly delineated periods, the line separating the two stages of talmudic history is hazy. Indeed, the publication and subsequent wide circulation of the Mishnah changed the way the Oral Law was studied. Instead of formulating new *mishnayyot* (laws from the Mishnah), the rabbis, beginning with the colleagues and students of R. Judah ha-Nasi, began to analyze the Mishnah.

While the Land of Israel was the preeminent spiritual center of world Jewry in the Mishnaic period, a second center was rapidly gaining prominence. Jews had lived in Babylonia since the exile following the destruction of the First Temple. By the time R. Judah ha-Nasi published the Mishnah, the Babylonian ACADEMIES were gaining rapidly in reputation and influence. As a result, the Gemara developed separately in the two centers.

Talmudic Methodology. Wherever the rabbis gathered to study the Mishnah, whether in Israel or Babylonia, their basic methods and purposes were the same. Unlike the Mishnah, which resembles an encyclopedic anthology of law aphorisms, the Gemara texts preserve the proceedings of the Academies. The most outstanding aspect of the Gemara is the record of the give-and-take, the debate, and the discussion which took place concerning a Mishnah, a biblical text, or a point of law. The editors expanded the discussions by combining material which originated in different Academies or in different centuries. The primary purpose of the discussions is to elucidate the Mishnah text. A typical chapter of Talmud opens with a single Mishnah, usually not longer than a paragraph. This is followed by the Gemara. On rare occasions, the Gemara text is only a few lines long as well most of the time, the Gemara discussions cover numerous pages. Then another Mishnah is quoted, followed by the relevant Gemara discussions.

The Gemara text is broken up into units, each of which is called a *Sugya* (a topic). The *Sugya* immediately following the Mishnah usually begins by analyzing the language of the Mishnah text. This analysis and the subsequent discussion take the form of questions and answers, which sometimes appear anonymously, though more often the author's name is mentioned. Typically, the discussion then proceeds to discovery of the biblical verse or verses which are the source for the law under review. The next step is to compare and contrast the Mishnah with similar texts from other *mishnayyot* or from a *baraita*. In harmonizing the Mishnah with a *baraita*, the Gemara sometimes claims that the Mishnah is missing a detail, the insertion of which changes the meaning of the Mishnah, thus removing the conflict between the two texts. Since the *amoraim* were not allowed to disagree with an accepted law from the Mishnah, the Mishnah is sometimes used as the basis for attacking a position held by an *amora*. If the Mishnah statement is an anonymous one, the *amora* can defend himself by attributing it to a particular *tanna*, while he himself sides with a different *tanna* on this point of law.

The discussions in the Gemara are not limited to the contents and style of the Mishnah. Since the rabbis employed associational logic in addition to linear logic, they frequently extended the discussion to other laws, verses, or topics, sometimes only vaguely related to the original subject. They did not limit themselves to those laws which had daily application. There are extensive debates in the Gemara about purely theoretical matters, such as the sacrifices or the Temple, which by then was no longer in existence. Sometimes, the Gemara discusses at great length opinions which are not accepted as law.

Unlike the Mishnah, the Gemara is not limited to matters of law. Intermixed with the law debates are large sections of Midrash (discussion of the biblical text), AGGADAH (rabbinic stories about the characters and events in the Bible), stories about the rabbis, medical advice, science, philosophical debates, and demonology.

While the starting-point of the Gemara discussions is the analysis of the Mishnah, the end point is the decision as to what is to be accepted as law. Very often, a new principle of law is established along with the final law decision. On occasion there is even debate as to which opinion is to be accepted as normative practice. Not every *Sugya* comes to a conclusive decision on the law. Some end with the word "*Téku*," an acronym meaning that the problem appears insoluble and that the prophet ELIJAH will resolve it when he returns to earth to announce the coming of the Messiah.

Over the years, the political, social, and economic milieu in Erets Israel deteriorated faster than in Babylonia. Thus, the rabbis were forced once again to commit the Oral Law to writing. By 425 CE, the first edition of the Talmud (Mishnah and Gemara) began to circulate. Since it was the product of the Erets Israel Academies, it was called the *Talmud de-Vené Ma'arava* (Talmud of the Western People, Erets Israel being west of Babylonia). In later generations, it was called the *Talmud Yerushalmi*.

Jerusalem (Palestinian) Talmud (*Talmud Yerushalmi*). Despite its name, the Jerusalem Talmud was not the product of a Jerusalem rabbinic academy. During the period it represents, the Jewish population of Erets Israel was concentrated in the northern half of the country. Thus, the "Jerusalem" Talmud was edited in the rabbinic academies of Caesarea, Sepphoris, and Tiberias.

The Jerusalem Talmud, which is only about a third the size of the Babylonian Talmud, does not include Gemara on the entire Mishnah. There is no Gemara on the last two Orders of the Mishnah, viz. KODASHIM (laws of the Temple and the sacrifices) and TOHOROT (laws of ritual impurity). Despite various theories, scholars have yet to offer a satisfactory explanation of this anomaly. Some modern scholars have tried to prove the existence of a Jerusalem Talmud text on these two Orders, but their arguments are considered inconclusive. On the other hand, the Jerusalem Talmud does include Gemara on the entire first division of the Mishnah, ZERA'IM, dealing with agricultural laws. Despite the destruction of the Second Temple and its connection to the land through the agricultural laws and sacrifices, the Jews in Erets Israel still observed those agricultural laws that were not directly connected to the Temple (including laws of tithes and priestly dues). Thus, the laws contained in the Order *Zera'im* were studied in their academies for their practical relevance.

Gemara of the Jerusalem Talmud is written in a Galilean dialect of Western ARAMAIC. A small amount of Hebrew is mixed in, along with some Latin and Greek, much of which appears in corrupt form. On the whole, the discussions are short and incisive. Approximately one-sixth of the Jerusalem Talmud deals with non-halakhic matters. The reason for this is the development in the Palestinian academies of separate anthologies of Midrash (e.g., the MIDRASH RABBAH on the Pentateuch and the FIVE SCROLLS) and *aggadah* (e.g., the PIRKÉ DE-RABBI ELIEZER).

The rabbis studying in the Palestinian academies did not work in a vacuum. There was constant movement of teachers and students between these academies and those in Babylonia. Despite the constant cross-fertilization of ideas and legal opinions, the Palestinian Talmud was an attempt to preserve the proceedings of the academies in Erets Israel before they were lost to posterity because of the rapidly deteriorating political situation in the country. While the rabbis labored hastily in Tiberias to produce the first complete Talmud, the rabbis in Babylonia were still debating the law. The Jerusalem Talmud received its final form c.400 CE. Much of the credit belongs to the third-century R. JOHANAN BAR NAPPAḤA, although the final redaction was long after his time.

As the Babylonian *ge'onim* declared the Babylonian Talmud authoritative, the Jerusalem Talmud was long neglected. SAADIAH GAON was one of the few authorities to quote it in his RESPONSA. It was, however, studied in Erets Israel, North Africa, and southern Italy. Medieval Spanish talmudists, beginning with MAIMONIDES, turned to it and cited it far more frequently than their Franco-German contemporaries. The first known (partial) commentary comes from a 16th-century Spanish exile in Erets Israel, R. Solomon Sirillo. The *aggadah* from the Jerusalem Talmud was published separately in 1590 by R. Samuel Yafeh Ashkenazi. The 18th century witnessed a revival of interest particularly by Lithuanian talmudists, including R. ELIJAH, the GAON OF VILNA. In the 20th century, scholars including Saul LIEBERMAN, Louis GINZBERG, and Adin Steinsalz have written on and published editions of the Jerusalem Talmud.

Babylonian Talmud (*Talmud Bavli*). This second version of the Talmud is very different from the first. Its Gemara is about 50% Hebrew and 50% Eastern Aramaic. Greek and Latin terms are used as well, but not in the mutated form found in the Jerusalem Talmud. The discussions in the Babylonian Talmud are more expansive and more tangential material is included. Only about one-third of the Gemara relates to *halakhah*, while almost two-thirds are Midrash and *aggadah*.

The Babylonian Talmud contains Gemara on the first book in the Mishnah division of *Zera'im*, dealing with the laws of prayer, but since there was no obligation to observe the agricultural laws outside Erets Israel, it contains no Gemara on the rest of the Order *Zera'im*, which is devoted to those laws. On the other hand, it contains Gemara on each of the books in the Order *Kodashim* (laws pertaining to sacrifices), despite the fact that the material was theoretical by then. It has Gemara on only one book in the last Order, *Tohorot* (laws of ritual impurity), namely, tractate *Niddah* dealing with the laws relating to menstruating women, which remained applicable. Altogether, the Babylonian Talmud contains about two and a half million words, on almost 5,900 folio pages (two sides of a single sheet of paper in the standard printed edition), in 36 separate tractates.

The Mishnah text which appears in the Babylonian Talmud includes many variants from that in the Jerusalem Talmud. Scholars disagree about the sources of these variant readings. Some feel that they stem from earlier and later editions of the Mishnah, with the Jerusalem Talmud using a later, updated version. Others say that the Babylonian version reflects the different way the Mishnah was studied in the Babylonian academies. The rabbis in Babylonia were more critical of the Mishnah text and had no compunction about emending that text. Only rarely are the variants so different that the resulting law is affected.

The two Talmuds differ significantly in language, style, content, scope and range of subject matter, date of redaction, and ultimately in the authority each has in matters of law. When the Babylonian Talmud was finally edited, there was no public decision to accept it and its rulings as definitive, yet over the years and centuries, that is what happened. The Babylonian Talmud includes much material which originated in the academies of Erets Israel. So much so, that later halakhic authorities claimed that the Babylonian Talmud includes all the accepted halakhic rulings made in the Erets Israel academies.

Traditionally, it was held that the Babylonian Talmud was edited by Rav ASHI and Ravina. This has now been questioned and it is felt that the process of editing and arranging the material took place in a number of stages over a period of several generations. It may have been the work of anonymous editors living after the death of R. Ashi (425), who would have set the standards, and concluded the work about 500 CE. Even subsequently the later scholars, the SAVORAIM, did not hesitate to insert brief explanatory notes into the text.

In the centuries after its final redaction, the Babylonian academies grew in size, prominence, and influence. The Babylonian communities became the center of world Jewry. As a result, less than two centuries after its completion, the *ge'onim* used the Babylonian Talmud as the basis for their authoritative rulings. As time went on, the great codifiers of Jewish law, Isaac ALFASI, Moses Maimonides, R. ASHER BEN JEHIEL, and Joseph CARO, determined the preeminence of the Babylonian Talmud as the halakhically accepted version of the Talmud.

Editions. Only a small number of handwritten manuscripts of the Talmud predating the 16th century are extant today. This is probably the result of the long battle waged by the Roman Catholic Church against the Talmud, which resulted in numerous burnings of the Talmud, the most famous of which took place in Paris in 1242. The Church continued with periodic attacks and burnings well into the 16th century.

The first complete edition of the Babylonian Talmud was printed in Venice by the Christian publisher, Daniel Bomberg, in the 1520s. He also printed the Jerusalem Talmud shortly thereafter. Since then the Talmud has been published numerous times. The authoritative edition used today was published in Vilna before the turn of the century. Modern printings are usually offset from the Vilna edition.

Translations. The first translation of the Babylonian Talmud into a European language (German) is that of Lazarus Goldschmidt (1897-1909). The Soncino Press in London published the first complete English translation which was edited by Isidor Epstein (1935-1952). A translation into modern Hebrew is being undertaken by Jerusalem scholar Adin Steinsalz. A new English translation is being published by Jacob Neusner.

Influence of the Talmud on Jewish Life. The Talmud is a written edition of the Oral Law as it developed over a 900-year period. That fact alone is sufficient to guarantee its overriding influence on Jewish religious observance throughout the ages.

The STUDY of Talmud achieved such importance that the commandment of Torah study (see Deut. 6:7 and 11:19) was interpreted to apply primarily to Talmud study. To this day, Talmud study remains the primary occupation in rabbinic academies throughout the world.

The Babylonian Talmud, in particular, is more than a law book. It is a treasure trove of Jewish thought, history, Bible exegesis, folklore, and much more. Ultimately, the Talmud shaped the very nature of Judaism and Jewishness and its laws transformed Judaism into an all-encompassing way of life. See also TALMUDIC COMMENTARIES.

TALMUDIC COMMENTARIES

Babylonian Talmud. In the geonic period, no need was felt for a commentary on the TALMUD. Both its language (ARAMAIC) as well as its *realia* were thoroughly familiar. Hence, with the exception of a commentary on the Order TOHOROT ascribed to HAI GAON and an interpretation of a talmudic word or phrase here and there, no comprehensive commentaries were written in that period. The situation was different in both North Africa and in the Franco-German center by the 11th century. In neither place was Aramaic the spoken language, while everyday *realia* were completely different. This explains the motivation to write talmudic commentaries during that period.

In the early 11th century, Rabbenu GERSHOM BEN JUDAH wrote a commentary on several tractates. These are actually an anthology of explanatory notes on the talmudic text by a number of commentators. At the same period, R. Hananel ben Ḥushi'el of Kairouan in North Africa wrote a running commentary on a significant number of tractates. There is evidence that his commentary covered the entire Talmud, but only parts are extant. He made liberal use of the Palestinian Talmud to illuminate the text of the Babylonian Talmud. His commentary is found in standard editions of the Talmud.

The commentary of RASHI on the entire Talmud (with the exception of a few tractates erroneously ascribed to him, e.g., *Ta'anit* and *Mo'ed Katan*) remains unsurpassed in all ages for both its comprehensiveness and its clarity. Drawing on the traditions of the school of Rabbenu Gershom and his own teachers in Worms where he had studied, he succeeded in illuminating abstruse passages. From his commentary, it is evident that Rashi did not intend it for the beginning student, for he takes it for granted that its readers are familiar with the more common vocabulary of both Hebrew and Aramaic, although an unusual word or phrase in Aramaic will elicit from him two or more synonyms in Hebrew. Where a Hebrew synonym is not available, Rashi offers a French translation. Without Rashi's commentary, it could be surmised that the Talmud might well have remained a sealed book.

Rashi's own pupils are the authors of the TOSAFOT, who clarify points still found puzzling after Rashi's commentary. Rabbenu NISSIM BEN REUBEN (Spain, 14th century) was the author of a highly lucid commentary on the tractate NEDARIM, found in all standard editions of the Talmud.

Jerusalem Talmud. The first known commentary on the Jerusalem Talmud is by R. Solomon Sirillo, written in Erets Israel about 1530. Lacking a printed text of the Talmud, the author bases his commentary on a manuscript and hence frequently offers better readings than those of the printed text. At about the same time, another scholar, R. Eleazar Azikri of Safed, composed an extensive commentary (*Sefer Ḥaredim*) on a number of tractates, some of which are to be found in the standard (Vilna) edition of the Jerusalem Talmud. R. David Fränkel (Germany, 18th century) was the author of an extensive commentary on the Orders ZERA'IM and MO'ED, entitled *Korban Edah*, and additional notes entitled *Shiyyaré Korban*.

The most comprehensive commentary, covering the entire work, is by R. Moses Margolies, a Lithuanian talmudist (d.1780). The commentary is divided into two parts; *Pené Mosheh* and *Mareh ha-Penim*. The former is a running commentary; the latter, a series of novellae. The author was the first to make use of the TOSEFTA in interpreting the Jerusalem Talmud. Said to have been a teacher of R. ELIJAH GAON OF VILNA, R. Margolies' interest may have led R. Elijah to write copious notes on the Jerusalem Talmud. To these must be added the commentaries *Sha'aré Yerushalmi* by R. Dov Berish of Slonim; *No'am Yerushalmi* by R. Joshua Isaac Schapiro; and *Nir* by R. Meir of Kodrin. The most recent commentary (on the first five tractates) was composed in Soviet Russia by R. Isaac Krasilchikof of Moscow. The manuscript was smuggled out of Russia on microfilm and published in Israel in 1980.

TALMUD TORAH ("study of Torah"). Name given to community schools, especially in Eastern Europe. The Talmud Torah, unlike the ḤEDER, had various classes, each taught by its own *rebbe* (master). Also, unlike the *ḥeder*, the Talmud Torah was often a venture funded by the community. Various community edicts were enacted to finance the Talmud Torah, and it was common to tax all householders and not only those with children, in support of the school. Taxes might also be imposed at rites of passage, such as births, marriages, and funerals, with the local Talmud Torah as the beneficiary. The student clientele varied with the location. The Amsterdam Talmud Torah, which was founded in the 16th century, catered to all pupils, both rich and poor. In Eastern Europe, on the other hand, the Talmud Torah was generally patronized only by those children whose parents could not afford to engage a *rebbe* of their choice. The Talmud Torah was generally the responsibility of the *Ḥevrat Talmud Torah*, or Talmud Torah Society, which raised the required funds and paid the teachers. Because the Talmud Torah was sponsored by the COMMUNITY, there was often community supervision of the EDUCATION. The studies in the Talmud Torah were exclusively of the classic Jewish texts, and much attention, especially in the younger grades, was given to learning by heart, including the rote translation of the Pentateuch into Yiddish. Older students concentrated on the Talmud. Secular studies were non-existent. The hours in the Talmud Torah were long, and students often arrived home considerably after dark. Students who completed their studies in the Talmud Torah might go on to study in a *yeshivah*, but the vast majority would enter the labor market. The old-style Talmud Torah has largely disappeared as an institution (except in ultra-Orthodox circles), but the name is still used for afternoon schools.

TAM, RABBENU (Jacob ben Meir; 1100-1171). The most distinguished of the French Tosafists (see TOSAFOT). Rabbenu ("our master") Tam was given the name on account of his piety and erudition, after the rabbinic interpretation of Genesis 25:27: "Jacob was a scholarly man (*tam*) dwelling in tents." A wine merchant and financier, he was almost killed by Crusaders during the Second Crusade, his life being saved by a passing nobleman who promised the mob that he would convert him to Christianity. The son of RASHI's daughter and her husband Meir ben Samuel, Tam studied under his father, his brother SAMUEL BEN MEIR (*Rashbam*), and Jacob ben Samson, Rashi's pupil. He headed the rabbinical academy (*yeshivah*) in his birthplace of Ramerupt. Tam was recognized as the greatest scholar of the age, and halakhic questions were directed to him from all parts of the world. At one time more than 80 Tosafists enrolled at his academy, attended by the best scholars of the generation.

R. Tam's explanations pervade the *tosafot* on the Babylonian Talmud. His main work, *Sefer ha-Yashar*, also contains *tosafot* and decisions as well as responsa. Wherever possible he gives lenient decisions within the framework of the *halakhah*. Unlike his brother Samuel ben Meir, R. Tam was strongly opposed to emending the talmudic text, which he always attempted to justify.

The author of liturgical poems, R. Tam corresponded in rhyme with Abraham IBN EZRA. He approved the introduction of *piyyutim* (liturgical poems) into the liturgy, not regarding them as interruptions of the prayers. As a result of his dispute with his grandfather Rashi on the order of the four biblical sections placed in the TEFILLIN, some pious Jews to this day put on two pairs of *tefillin*, one pair containing the order of the sections according to the opinion of Rashi and the other the order of the sections according to the opinion of Rabbenu Tam.

TAMID ("Continuous Offering"). Ninth tractate of Order KODASHIM in the Mishnah. Its seven chapters discuss the daily burnt-offering in the Temple brought by the priests every morning and afternoon (cf. Ex. 29:38-42; 30:7,8; Num. 28:3-8). Rather than merely listing the laws regarding the daily offering, the Mishnah describes the actual performance of the ritual. Included is a description of the removal of the ashes from the altar, the arrangement of the firewood, the drawing of lots among the priests for duties, the procedure for slaughtering the lamb and bringing it to the altar, the daily morning prayer, the music that accompanied the sacrifices, the cleaning of the candelabrum and the offering of INCENSE on the inner altar. The subject matter is amplified in the Babylonian Talmud.

TAMMUZ (Assyro-Babylonian: *Duzu* or *Dumuzi*). Fourth month of the Jewish religious CALENDAR; tenth month of the Hebrew civil year counting from TISHRI. It has 29 days and normally coincides with June-July; its sign of the zodiac is Cancer. There are several biblical references to "the fourth month," but the name Tammuz occurs in the Bible only as that of a Mesopotamian deity, better known to the Greeks as Adonis (Ezek. 8:14). Jews returning to Judah from the Babylonian exile introduced the use of Tammuz (modified Dumuzi) as the name of their fourth month and it later appears frequently in rabbinic literature. Traditionally, Tammuz marks the beginning of summer in the Land of Israel (*Shab.* 53a). The fast of 17 Tammuz (SHIVAH ASAR BE-TAMMUZ) commemorates the breaching of the walls of Jerusalem by the Babylonian army in 586 BCE on 9 Tammuz (II Kings 25:3-4); in 70 CE, the Roman legions of Titus did so again on the 17th. This fast ushers in the mournful THREE WEEKS culminating in TISHAH BE-AV. According to Zechariah (8:19), this "fast of the fourth month" will nevertheless be turned into a joyful occasion in time to come, along with the three other biblical fasts.

TAMMUZ, SEVENTEENTH OF See SHIVAH ASAR BE-TAMMUZ

TANAKH See BIBLE

TANH̱UMA A number of Midrashic works on the Pentateuch attributed to R. Tanẖuma bar Abba, a Palestinian *amora* of the fourth century CE. The *Tanẖuma* is based on the TRIENNIAL CYCLE of Pentateuch reading observed at that time in Erets Israel. Various texts have been published under the name of *Tanẖuma* or are available in manuscript form, all having certain common elements, but it is difficult to determine whether all are derived from a specific root text or whether any single one of the extant texts is the original. Among the known texts, one may be the oldest Midrash in existence; parts of it are even quoted in the Talmud. Another, known as *Yelammedenu Rabbenu* ("let our teacher teach us") based on the introductory words to many passages, is quoted in medieval sources, but there is no single complete text of the work. In addition to these two versions there is a third version popularly known as the *Midrash Tanẖuma*, based on a manuscript in Oxford, which differs in many ways from the other collections. In addition, there are numerous manuscripts in existence, none containing a complete volume, which again offer different material from the others.

TANNA ("teacher," from an Aram. verb meaning "to study" or "repeat"; pl. *tannaim*). Designation for scholars of the ORAL LAW whose period of activity extended from around 20 CE until the days of JUDAH HA-NASI (c.200 CE). Their immediate predecessors were HILLEL and SHAMMAI, although some claim that the earliest *tanna* was Simeon the Just, one of the survivors of the GREAT ASSEMBLY (c.330 BCE; *Avot* 1.2). The *tannaim* were responsible for first setting down the ORAL LAW in writing: the MISHNAH (by Judah ha-Nasi), the

TOSEFTA, the BARAITA, and the MIDRASH HALAKHAH. Over 120 *tannaim* are mentioned by name in the Mishnah; others are referred to in the extra-Mishnaic *baraitot*. With few exceptions, they were all Palestinian by birth and education.

Five generations of *tannaim* are usually distinguished, the first headed by R. GAMALIEL the Elder and R. JOHANAN BEN ZAKKAI, whose teaching center was Jerusalem. After the Second Temple's destruction in 70 CE, it was chiefly through the efforts of R. Johanan that tannaitic learning revived in Yavneh and the fabric of Judaism emerged unimpaired. Subsequently, other teaching centers were established in Erets Israel (for details, see ACADEMIES). Leading *tannaim* of the next generation included R. Gamaliel II and R. Eleazar ben Azariah of Yavneh, ELIEZER BEN HYRCANUS, and JOSHUA BEN HANANIAH.

Anti-Jewish persecution under the Roman emperor Hadrian and the collapse of the Bar Kokhba revolt in 135 CE, only two generations after the loss of the Temple, had a profound influence on tannaitic activity and scholarship. As spokesmen for the Jewish community of Erets Israel, R. Gamaliel II, R. Joshua, and R. Eliezer journeyed overseas to make contact with Rome's growing Jewish community and to intercede with the Roman authorities. So did R. AKIVA, a third-generation *tanna*, who also visited other Diaspora communities. Together with R. ISHMAEL BEN ELISHA and R. Hananiah ben Teradyon, Akiva was among the TEN MARTYRS of the Hadrianic era. The halakhic Midrashim (MEKHILTA, SIFRÉ, etc.) stemmed from the Academies of R. Akiva and R. Ishmael, both of whom also formulated principles of HERMENEUTICS for the interpretation of Scripture which promoted the development of rabbinic law (HALAKHAH).

Akiva's pupils, *tannaim* of the fourth generation, included SIMEON BAR YOḤAI, YOSÉ BEN ḤALAFTA, and MEIR (who had also studied under R. Ishmael). They, together with R. Simeon ben Gamaliel II and JUDAH BAR ILAI, gave a fresh impetus to rabbinic learning after 135 CE. Judah ha-Nasi was the outstanding fifth-generation *tanna*, and with his redaction of the Mishnah this period of scholarship is said to have ended. A sixth, transitional generation may have flourished, however, between the Mishnaic era and that of the talmudic rabbis (see AMORA). It is thought to have comprised younger contemporaries of R. Judah such as Ḥiyya Rabbah and Bar Kappara who collected halakhic material and *baraitot*.

The word *tanna* also designates a class of "interpreter" (METURGEMAN) who had memorized long sections of the Oral Law and who recited them aloud for the benefit of students in amoraic times (*BM* 76b).

TANNA DE-VÉ ELIYYAHU ("A *tanna* of the school of Elijah"). A moralistic Midrash whose date and place of composition is uncertain. Suggested dates and places run from the fifth to the tenth century and from Erets Israel to Italy. Its title derives from a story in the TALMUD (*Ket.* 106a) that on two occasions the prophet ELIJAH came to the second generation Babylonian AMORA Rav Anan and taught him. The Talmud terms the first session *Seder Eliyyahu Rabbah* (the larger teaching of Elijah) and the second, *Seder Eliyyahu Zuta* (the shorter teaching of Elijah); both are in the existing text. The first part of the book (*Seder Eliyyahu Rabbah*) consists of 31 chapters written in an elaborate Hebrew style abounding in synonyms. The content is varied: explanations of commandments, homilies on complete chapters of Scripture with numerous parables and examples, descriptions of the ultimate destiny reserved for the righteous, prayers, lamentations, calls for repentance and the study of the Torah and a variety of ethical exhortations. The author's universal outlook is reflected in the statement: "I call heaven and earth to witness that whether Israelite or Gentile, whether male slave or female slave, whether man or woman, the Holy Spirit rests upon everyone according to his deeds." The Midrash is first quoted at the end of the 11th century.

The second part of the work, *Seder Eliyyahu Zuta*, consists of 25 chapters of which the first 14 resemble the first part of the work in both style and content. Subsequent chapters are devoted to a variety of unrelated subjects, pointing to a late redaction.

TARGUM The ancient ARAMAIC translations of the Bible. The word comes probably from the Hittite *tarkummai*, "proclaim, explain, translate." They began to be composed several centuries before the Common Era, in a period when Aramaic was the dominant language of the Near East, including Judea. The Targums provided a translation, and often an interpretation, of the Hebrew Bible in the Jewish Aramaic vernacular.

The earliest extant manuscripts of Targum were discovered among the DEAD SEA SCROLLS, and are dated to the mid-second century BCE. These are fragments of a Targum to Leviticus 16:12-21, and of two Targums to the Book of Job. Since there are no records of Job having been read in the synagogue, this early manuscriptal evidence suggests that the Hebrew Bible was translated not only for synagogal-liturgical purposes, but also as an aid to private or public study. Indeed, the many quotations from Targums in classical rabbinic literature lend support to this conclusion.

The Targums may be divided into two major dialectal groups and into several distinct literary genres. Targumic activity flourished in Erets Israel as well as in Babylonia, with translations produced in Galilean (or Jewish Palestinian) Aramaic and in Babylonian (or literary Jewish) Aramaic. The Babylonian and Palestinian schools differed in their literary approaches no less than in their dialects. Whereas the Targums edited in Babylonia tend to be literal word-for-word renderings of the Hebrew original (with some exceptions), the Palestinian Targums are often paraphrastic and expansive with interpretive passages that do not exist in the Hebrew base text. These interpretations are usually evoked by some difficulty in the Hebrew verse, and almost always have parallels in early rabbinic literature. Another important difference between the Palestinian and Babylonian Targums lies in their interpretation of legal passages. Such variations reflect the different halakhic schools of R. ISHMAEL and R. AKIVA respectively. The Babylonian Talmud, which is the major source of normative Jewish law, sanctions the Pentateuchal Targum ascribed to the proselyte Onkelos (2nd century CE) as having been composed under the aegis of R. Eliezer and R. Joshua (disciples of R. Akiva), and it refers to Targum Onkelos as "our Targum." This official recognition eventually led to the total displacement in the synagogue of the expansive and creative Palestinian Targum of the Pentateuch by the more pedantic and literal Onkelos.

When a Targum chooses to diverge from the literal translation in favor of a paraphrastic rendition, it is usually for an accountable reason. The Targums often identify people and places that are anonymous in the Hebrew Bible. They harmonize contradictory passages and provide a single common translation for slightly variant phrases. They update legal passages to coincide with later halakhic practice, occasionally reverting to an anti-sectarian polemic. Anthropomorphic descriptions of God that attribute to Him human form or emotions are often (but not consistently) avoided or ameliorated. Likewise, embarrassing passages related to the Patriarchs or the ancient Israelites are frequently altered to protect the dignity of these figures. The Palestinian Targums often insert lengthy aggadic (legendary) passages into the biblical narratives. Among these expansive Targums are many messianic interpretations of biblical verses.

Targum Onkelos was read in private devotion after twice reciting the original Hebrew version of the weekly Bible reading (*shenayim mikra ve-eḇad targum, Ber.* 8a) and it is the Targum that is still chanted in Yemenite synagogues during public worship (see METURGEMAN).

There are Targums to the entire Hebrew Bible, except for those books which were originally composed partially in Aramaic (Daniel, Ezra-Nehemiah). The Pentateuch has the largest number of Targums: these are Onkelos, the Palestinian Targums, and the Pseudo-Jonathan Targum which is a late conglomerate of the former two and the most expansive of all. Onkelos is preserved in hundreds of medieval manuscripts; the Palestinian Targums are known from tens of fragments, primarily from the medieval hoard discovered in the Ben Ezra Synagogue in Old Cairo (see GENIZAH). Other Targumic genres include a) anthologies or extracts (called "fragment-Targums") of the Palestinian Targums and of Onkelos (unpublished), which are comprised of selected verses and phrases; b) collections of expansive passages (*Toseftot*) taken from the Palestinian Targums; c) liturgical collections of Palestinian Targum containing the synagogal readings for special Sabbaths and festivals; and d) Targumic poems introducing, or inserted within, the latter.

The Talmud attributes the composition of the Targum to Prophets to the *tanna* Jonathan ben Uzziel. It is therefore called Targum Jonathan. The Targum to the Former Prophets follows Onkelos in both language and dialect as well as in its generally literal approach. There are, however, many expansive passages of midrashic embellishment (*toseftot*) that are either written in the margins of manuscripts or that have been inserted into the text. These expansions are usually set apart from the running Targum by the heading "*Tosefta*" or "Targum Yerushalmi."

The Targums to the Latter Prophets and to the Writings show greater affinity to the Palestinian Targums, in varying degrees. They too contain many *Toseftot*. There are two or more distinct versions of Targum for some books. For example, the Targum to Job from Qumran is quite different from the traditional text preserved in European manuscripts and early printed editions. Likewise, there are two traditional Targums for the Scroll of Esther (Targum Rishon and Sheni) and possibly a third version reflected in manuscripts. The Targum to Proverbs appears to contain secondary elements, not translated directly from the Hebrew version, but possibly based upon an earlier Syriac translation.

There has been wide-ranging interest in the Targums among Jewish and Christian scholars alike. Targum texts serve as an important source for the study of ancient Semitic languages, and especially of the various Aramaic dialects. They provide a view of the ancient synagogue and the liturgical use of Bible in early times. They have an important place among the rabbinic sources of biblical exegesis, often preserving interpretations that differ from those that later emerged as normative.

TARGUM SHENI ("second translation"). A Midrashic paraphrase in Aramaic of the Book of ESTHER. In addition to the numerous older Palestinian and Babylonian sources on which the author draws, there is some material that reflects his own imaginative creation. Some of the motifs are borrowed from the Koran; this points to the late seventh or early eighth century as the time of its composition. The language is Western Aramaic, with a large mixture of Greek words.

The prolixity of the author is illustrated by his comments on the text — "when King Ahasuerus sat on the throne of his Kingdom" (Est. 1:2), which prompts a long, elaborate and highly detailed description of the throne of SOLOMON. He then proceeds to write a fulsome panegyric on Solomon's might and wisdom.

One of the author's favorite methods is to create extensive conversations between the various characters in the Book of Esther. In one of these conversations, Haman gives a fairly accurate description of Jewish practice but interprets it maliciously in order to denounce the Jews. The author likewise composes a number of prayers which he puts in the mouth of Esther and Mordecai.

TARYAG MITSVOT See COMMANDMENTS, THE 613

Casting sins into the water (tashlikh). *Lithograph, Poland, 1824.*

TASHLIKH Ceremony performed on the first afternoon of Rosh ha-Shanah (the New Year) unless this falls on a Saturday, in which case it is postponed to the next day. The ritual consists of going to a body of water and throwing in a few crumbs while reciting verses from the prophets Micah and Isaiah. The verse in Micah 7:19 states "you will cast [*tashlikh*] all their sins into the depths of the sea"; hence the name of the ceremony.

The earliest reference to the custom is found in the 15th-century *Sefer ha-Maharil* by R. Jacob MÖLLN of Germany. Although he forbade the use of breadcrumbs in the ceremony, his prohibition was not heeded.

Unusual variants include a Kurdish custom of jumping into the water to observe the ceremony. Kabbalists shake their garments as a way of freeing themselves from the "shells" of sins that have formed during the year. Their act is based on the talmudic statement that the cleanliness of garments is a sign of moral purity. Sephardi and Eastern Jews appear to have observed *tashlikh* since the 16th century. Syrian Jews created a pool of water by running hose water; their ceremony includes many citations from the Zohar.

Some rabbis rejected the custom of *tashlikh* as a superstition with non-Jewish origins.

TEFILLIN ("phylacteries"). Two small quadrangular black leather boxes (or *batim*, sing.: *bayit*) containing four biblical passages which the male Jew from the age of 13 wears on the left arm (*shel yad*) and on the head (*shel rosh*) during the weekday MORNING SERVICE.

Originally, the *tefillin* were worn throughout the day and there are sources which attest to women wearing them as well (*Er.* 96a). The Bible does not describe *tefillin* nor offer instruction regarding how they are to be made; the details were specified by the rabbis (*Men.* 34a-37b).

The *tefillin* consist of parchments which are taken from the outermost hide of a ritually fit (*kasher*) animal, inscribed with permanent black ink and placed in a square box upon which is written the Hebrew letter *shin*. The boxes have a wider base and an opening through which the straps pass. The strap of the head is tied with a knot in the shape of the Hebrew letter *dalet* and that of the arm in the shape of the letter *yud*. These three letters, *shin, dalet, yud* combine to form one of the names of God, *Shaddai*.

The injunction to wear *tefillin* is based upon four paragraphs in the Bible (Ex. 13:1-10; 11-16; Deut. 6:4-9; 13-21). These are written by a SCRIBE on one piece of parchment and inserted into the box for the arm, and on four separate pieces of parchment for insertion into four parallel compartments for the head. The biblical portions define the foundations of Judaism in terms of God's unity and the acceptance of Divine rule, as well as God's providence and faith in the world's redemption, as symbolized by the Exodus from Egypt. Thus, the act of binding oneself with the *tefillin* serves as a regular reminder to the Jew to be bound up in service to God, with heart, mind and might.

Tefillin are worn daily for the Morning Service and are removed on the New Moon at the beginning of the Additional Service. They are not worn on the Sabbath nor on major festivals since these holidays are deemed adequate reminders in themselves of the Jew's reponsibilities to God. They are also not worn on the first day of mourning, by a groom on his wedding day, by a leper, or by one who has been excommunicated. On Tishah be-Av, they are worn for the Afternoon instead of the Morning Service.

A discovery at Qumran on the shores of the Dead Sea has revealed considerable variations in first-century custom con-

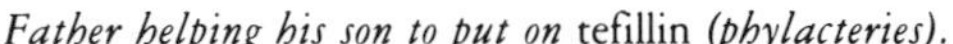

Father helping his son to put on tefillin *(phylacteries).*

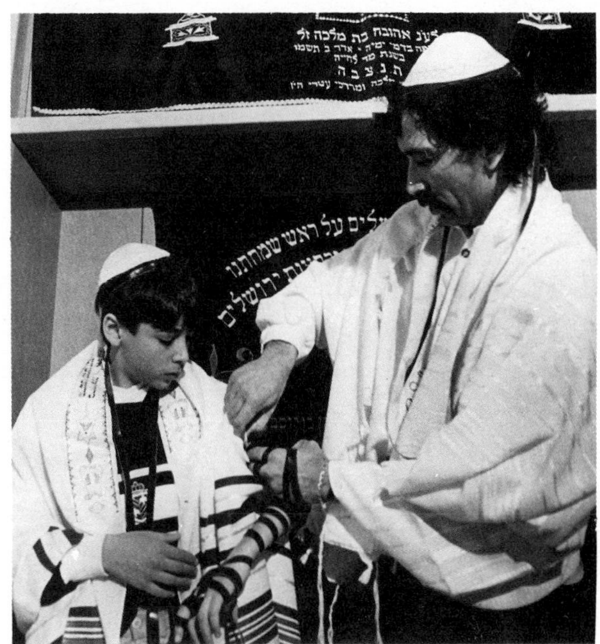

cerning the order and addition to the four basic paragraphs of the *tefillin* (some included the Ten Commandments). Although in the second century there was uniformity regarding the texts, two different traditions remained and persisted concerning the order of the paragraphs. In the Middle Ages, these differences took the form of a dispute between RASHI and his grandson, Rabbenu TAM, which certain pious Jews, including some Ḥasidim and Eastern Jews, resolved by donning two sets of *tefillin* — one according to Rashi's order, the other according to Rabbenu Tam — each morning in order to be certain that they were following the precept properly. *Tefillin* are to be examined once every seven years by a scribe.

Abraham GEIGER, the 19th-century Reform pioneer, claimed that *tefillin* were originally pagan amulets and set a precedent for their exclusion from Reform worship which lasted until their reappearance in the most recent prayerbook (*Gates of Prayer*, pp. 48-49). They were, however, advocated by Leopold ZUNZ and remain a part of the Conservative daily Morning Service. They have been taken up by some Jewish feminists as a symbol of their egalitarian religious status; they base their practice upon selected precedents in Jewish tradition. For example, the sages say that Michal (Saul's daughter) wore *tefillin* and they did not protest (*Er.* 96a).

HOW TO DON TEFILLIN

1. The hand *tefillin* is placed on the muscle of the inner side of the left forearm ("opposite the heart"); the benediction is recited which concludes, "to lay the *tefillin*"; the strap is tightened and wound seven times round the arm between the elbow and the wrist and three times around the middle finger. Left-handed people place the *tefillin* on the right forearm. (Ashkenazim wind it anti-clockwise, in an inward manner; Sephardim and Ḥasidim wind it clockwise.)

2. The head *tefillin* is placed on the head so that the front edge of the case lies just above the spot where the hair begins to grow and directly above the space between the eyes. Its strap circles the head and is fastened by a knot at the nape of the neck, allowing the two loose ends to hang down in front. The benediction for the binding of the *tefillin* is recited while this is done, followed by the words, "Blessed be the name of His glorious kingdom forever."

3. The remaining part of the strap of the hand *tefillin* is bound around the palm forming the Hebrew letter *shin*, while Hosea 2:21-22 is recited.

4. When the *tefillin* are removed at the close of the service, the order is reversed; the head *tefillin* is removed before the hand *tefillin*.

TEḤINNAH (pl. *teḥinnot*; "supplication"). Private supplication recited by the individual worshiper, usually in addition to the prescribed prayers, in accordance with the teaching that prayer should never become a fixed routine but rather a supplication before God for mercy (*Avot* 2:18). Such entreaties are known from biblical times (Jer. 37:20; Ps. 55:2). During the talmudic period, improvised *teḥinnot* were said privately by the individual worshiper after the AMIDAH, but these were later replaced by the fixed TAḤANUN prayer, with an opportunity left for individual supplications in the framework of the *Amidah*.

In the course of time, many private devotions, by known rabbinic figures and otherwise unknown persons alike, have been incorporated into the corpus of the regular prayer book. A well-known example of this is the *Yehi Ratson*, with which RAV used to conclude the *Amidah* prayer and which now serves as a preamble to the blessing for the New Month.

Large numbers of *teḥinnot* have been composed throughout the Jewish world, in varying styles and vernaculars: these include kabbalistic devotions identifiable by the opening phrase "May it be Your will" or "Master of the Universe"; ingenious compositions in which every word begins with the same letter of the alphabet; prayers to be said before lighting the Sabbath candles or crossing an ocean or when visiting a cemetery; supplications couched in sophisticated and fluent Hebrew, in Aramaic, and in the Judaic dialects of the various Diaspora communities. While some *teḥinnot* are preserved in the prayer book, the vast majority are collected in separate volumes. Brochures of devotional prayers for women in Yiddish were known as *tekhines* (i.e., *teḥinnot*).

TEKHELET ("blue"). A blue-green dye used in priestly and royal garments (Ezek. 23:6). By biblical law, a strand of this shade is to be included in each set of the fringes of the TSITSIT (Num. 15:38). The sages state that *tekhelet* resembles the sea, which resembles the sky, which in turn resembles the color of God's seat of glory (*Men.* 43b). Thus, the *tekhelet* in the *tsitsit* serves as a reminder of God's presence everywhere. According to the Talmud, *tekhelet* is derived from a kind of snail, referred to as *ḥillazon*, found in the sea off the northern coast of Erets Israel (*Sanh.* 91a). The process to obtain the dye was lengthy, and hence expensive. The Mishnah mentions a dye named *kela ilan*, evidently indigo, which gave a color close to *tekhelet* (*Men.* 42b). As the two were almost indistinguishable, the sages recommended that *tekhelet* threads be bought only from an expert (*ibid.*). Later on, the process involved was evidently forgotten, and as Jewish law does not make *tekhelet* obligatory, the fringes used for *tsitsit* were all white. In the 19th century, a Ḥasidic rabbi, Gershon Ḥanokh Leiner, known as the Radziner Rebbe, claimed that the dye needed to produce *tekhelet* could be obtained from the cuttlefish. Rabbi Isaac Halevi HERZOG identified the source of *tekhelet* as a species of snail which rarely comes near the shore. Ḥasidim of the Radziner sect adopted the findings of the Radziner Rebbe, and their *tsitsit* contain a dyed blue thread. Most prominent rabbis, however, do not accept his argument, and the vast majority of observant Jews continue to use only white fringes in their *tsitsit*.

TEMPLE Central sanctuary of Jewish worship, situated on Mount MORIAH (the *har ha-bayit*, TEMPLE MOUNT) in JERUSALEM. The First Temple was built by King SOLOMON c.960 BCE and destroyed by the Babylonians under Nebuchadnezzar in 586 BCE. The Second Temple was dedicated c.520 BCE and destroyed by the Romans under Titus, 70 CE.

First Temple. Originally, King DAVID had wanted to build the Temple, but God, through Nathan the prophet, rejected this wish, evidently on the grounds that he had shed blood. Instead Nathan informed David that his son, Solomon, would build the Temple (II Sam. 7:12-13).

When Solomon became king, he enlisted the aid of his ally, Hiram, the king of Tyre (980-946 BCE), in the construction of the Temple. In return for wheat, oil, and wine, Hiram supplied Solomon with cedar and cypress wood, as well as gold. Hiram's servants floated the wood down on rafts to Jaffa. Hiram also sent Solomon artisans and craftsmen to aid him. Construction began in the fourth year of Solomon's reign (c.964 BCE) and took seven years.

The Temple itself was a magnificent structure, made of the finest materials. It was a stone building standing within a royal compound which also housed the palace, a Hall of Judgment, the Hall of Cedars, and a house for Solomon's wife, Pharaoh's daughter. The Temple was 60 cubits (90 feet) long, 20 cubits (30 feet) wide, and 30 cubits (45 feet) high (one cubit = c.18 inches). It was faced by the patio of the forecourt, which added ten cubits to its length. The main structure was surrounded by a three-story building divided into chambers, with the stories connected by trapdoors. These probably served as storerooms for the Temple treasures. The main building was divided into an inner room, the HOLY OF HOLIES (the *devir*) on the west, measuring 20 by 20 cubits, and an outer room (the *azarah*) measuring 20 by 40 cubits on the east. Around the Temple was a walled-in compound. The entrance to the Temple was through the porch, on each side of which stood a massive bronze pillar. The two pillars had names: Jachin and Boaz.

The inner walls of the Temple were paneled with cedar wood. The floor of the Holy of Holies was likewise of cedar wood, while that of the outer room was of less expensive cypress wood. The walls were decorated with carvings of gourds, cherubs, palm trees, and flowers in bloom, and were encrusted with gold. There were doors to both the outer room and the Holy of Holies. The walls of the latter were decorated on both sides, and its floor was plated with gold (I Kings 6:29-30). The Holy of Holies was entered only once a year, on the DAY OF ATONEMENT, by the HIGH PRIEST.

The most important object in the Temple was the ARK, which was installed within the Holy of Holies. Inside the ark stood the two TABLETS OF THE COVENANT with the TEN COMMANDMENTS. The ark linked the Temple historically to the Shiloh SANCTUARY, which had existed for 369 years, as well as to the Sanctuary which had accompanied the Israelites in the desert. Two wooden cherubs with outspread wings surrounded the ark, symbolizing the Divine Presence.

In the outer room stood the main implements of the Temple's daily worship: an INCENSE altar, the table for the SHOWBREAD, and ten lampstands (see MENORAH). These were all made of gold or gilded. In front of the Temple stood a "sea," an immense bronze water basin supported by 12 bronze cattle. Along the east front of the building stood ten smaller water basins, each on its own wheeled stand, five to the north of the entrance and five to the south. A bronze ALTAR also stood in the courtyard, which was used for the various SACRIFICES, both communal and individual.

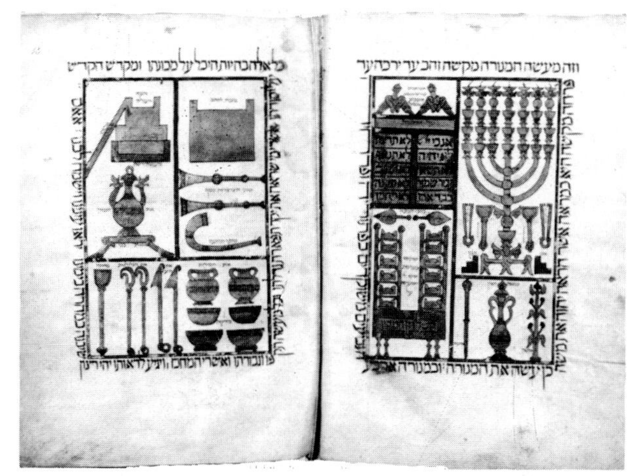

The Temple implements. Illustration from a Bible, France, 1299.

Within the Temple compound were three enclosures for specific groups: the *ezrat kohanim* (the priestly enclosure) for the PRIESTS working in the Temple; the *ezrat yisra'el* (the enclosure for Israelites) for male worshipers; and the *ezrat nashim* (the women's enclosure) for female worshipers.

During Solomon's reign, the Temple was the focal point of all Jewish ritual, and pilgrims came to it from all the tribes of Israel (see PILGRIMAGE; PILGRIM FESTIVALS). However, at the time of the reign of Rehoboam, Solomon's son, the Temple's unique position was challenged. Jeroboam, who revolted and established the northern kingdom of Israel, taking with him ten of the Twelve Tribes, set up two other temples, in Dan and Bethel, to prevent his people from coming to Jerusalem. Although later kings of Israel who were allied with the kings of Judah relaxed the prohibition against going to Jerusalem, the First Temple never again regained its centrality for all the Twelve Tribes.

The Temple itself served as the site for PRAYER and for the bringing of sacrifices to God. In addition to the different communal sacrifices offered daily and the additional communal sacrifices brought on the Sabbaths, festivals, and the New Moon (Num. 28-29), individuals offered their own sacrifices, either in thanks or as part of their atonement for sins committed through negligence.

The Temple was the site to which the OMER (the first barley measure, harvested on the second day of Passover) and the FIRST FRUITS (on Shavu'ot) were brought. On Passover eve, all families were required to come to Jerusalem to offer the paschal sacrifice, the lambs being sacrificed in the forecourt of the Temple. Many of the PSALMS were originally composed for use in the Temple.

During its history of four centuries, the Temple was repaired numerous times and changes were introduced in its structure and furnishings. Thus King Joash ordered that the money brought to the priests be utilized for repairing the breaches in the Temple and for refurbishing those implements that required repair (II Kings 12). Similarly, King Josiah was responsible for renovations (II Kings 22). On the other hand, under Kings Manasseh (possibly as a concession to the king of Assyria) and Amon, the worship of other gods was introduced to the Temple.

Second Temple. The Second Temple was dedicated in Jerusalem sometime between 521 and 517 BCE, some 65-70 years after the destruction of the First Temple. Its rededication followed Cyrus' decree permitting the return of the exiled Jews from Babylonia to Judah. Virtually the entire period between his decree and the dedication was marked by adamant efforts on the part of the country's non-Jewish populace from the Samaria region to prevent the Temple's reconstruction. Spurring on the Jews in the project of rebuilding were the prophets HAGGAI and ZECHARIAH, whose encouraging words were directed in the main toward the people's leaders, Zerubbabel of the Davidic line and the High Priest Joshua (or Jeshua as he is referred to in the later books of Ezra and Nehemiah). The rebuilt Temple at this stage, however, was but a shadow of its former glory.

The Zadokite line now resumed the High Priestly role its original forebear, the High Priest Zadok, had assumed under King Solomon roughly 450 years earlier (I Kings 2:35).

Approximately 70-80 years after its rededication, the Second Temple, in the period of EZRA and NEHEMIAH, resumed its central status in the history of the people. Ezra and Nehemiah saw to it that priestly and Levite genealogy was carefully reappraised and that the various Temple duties and personnel were reapportioned.

Over two centuries later, in the year 200 BCE, the Seleucid monarch, Antiochus III, instructed his local governor, Ptolemy Thraseas, as a sign of his appreciation of the local Jews' assistance in his military campaign, to insure the sanctity of the Temple and its adjoining areas. The king even included a listing of unclean animals which may not be brought into the city precincts (Jos., *Ant.* 12.138ff.).

The Temple's fortunes took a dramatic turn for the worse upon the accession of Antiochus IV (Epiphanes) to the Seleucid throne. With the assistance of certain Hellenizing elements among the Jewish High Priestly and lay aristocracy, the Temple was converted into a place of pagan worship. This and other acts of brutal repression of the Jewish faith, brought on the revolt of the HASMONEANS which eventually led to the restoration of the Temple's exclusively Jewish character by JUDAH MACCABEE. The date of the Temple's rededication (in 164 BCE), 25 Kislev, is commemorated in the ḤANUKKAH festival.

The last non-Maccabean High Priest, Onias IV, whom events compelled to flee his exalted station and homeland, was responsible for the establishment of a temple on Egyptian soil (in the 60s of the second century BCE).

The first of the Hasmoneans to don the High Priestly vestments was Judah's brother, Jonathan, about the year 150 BCE, and with this the eight-centuries-old Zadokite line was brought to an abrupt end. The Hasmoneans retained the High Priesthood for over a century until the accession of Herod to the kingship. High Priests were now installed and deposed at the whim of King Herod and his successors, and with the prodding and connivance of Roman procurators and governors. When the Revolt against Rome erupted in 66 CE, one of its initial acts was to end Temple sacrifices on behalf of the Roman emperor and his family.

Structure. The Bible, the Talmud, and Josephus, as well as the more recent archeological excavations, account for the bulk of the available information on the Second Temple structure. No real picture is available of the structure during the time of the prophets Haggai and Zechariah, or even that of Ezra and Nehemiah, other than that during all this period the Second Temple was but a faint reflection of its former glory. Not much is known either of the Temple structure during the years that followed and under the Hasmoneans.

The overall picture is that of the greatly enlarged and magnificent building begun by Herod in 20/19 BCE. Although the rebuilt Temple was formally dedicated a year and a half later, work on the structure continued for decades, with the last finishing touches being made only some two years before the beginning of the Revolt in 66 CE.

The Temple Mount was now surrounded by massive walls. The outer forecourt or Temple esplanade was a greatly enlarged quadrangle, with another rectangle space, the forecourt proper, inside the quadrangle area. Entrance to the forecourt was by a flight of steps, around the base of which ran a railing (*soreg*) with warning inscriptions in Greek and Latin, affixed at regular intervals, banning the entrance of non-Jews beyond this area on pain of death.

Access to the inner and outer forecourts for Jews as well was subject to certain restrictions, particularly in the sphere of ritual impurity. The Mishnah tractate of MIDDOT distinguishes between five areas and their correspondingly ascending degrees of sanctity: the Temple Mount; the *hel* (i.e., the space within the aforementioned railed off area); the court of the women; the court of the Israelites; the court of the priests. The Holy of Holies remained the most sacrosanct part of the Temple compound. It was actually one of two chambers in the Temple proper, lying immediately beyond the antechamber which contained the incense altar, the candelabrum (*menorah*), and the showbread table.

Rabbinical sources indicate that the seat of the Great SANHEDRIN was located inside the inner forecourt of the Temple Mount. Some sort of SYNAGOGUE was also in use there. Josephus describes the Temple's exterior coating of massive plates of gold with their brilliant reflection of the sun's rays, while the rabbis enthused over the magnificence of the Second Temple: "He who has not seen the House of Herod [i.e., the rebuilt Herodian Temple], has never in his life seen a beautiful structure."

Ritual. The main ministrants at the Temple service were the priests and the LEVITES, the latter assisting the priests in the daily service, while also assuming the functions of Temple singers (see MUSIC AND SONG), gatekeepers, and Temple servants. The highest ranking member of the priestly hierarchy was the High Priest. There was also the highly important post of *segan* or Temple captain who had supreme charge of order in and around the Temple area. It would appear, at least during the latter years of the Second Temple period, that the *segan* was also there to keep a watchful eye on Sadducee High Priests in case they strayed from Pharisaic Temple ritual. In addition to these highest ranking officiants, there were several categories of officialdom, including Temple treasurers and lesser ranking captains.

The entire priesthood was subdivided into 24 groups (see MISHMAROT AND MA'AMADOT) who took weekly turns to enable all its members to participate in the ministrations at one time or other. Each priestly group had a corresponding Levitical group. There was a further subdivision of the priestly groups into "fathers' houses" (*baté avot*), with each such house responsible for a specific number of days of Temple service. There was also a Temple physician, a choirmaster, and a special officer in charge of the priestly vestments.

Sacrificial worship took place daily, including the Sabbath day and on the various festivals. Present at these daily Temple services was a "stand-by" group of lay Israelites (*ma'amad*) who represented their brethren from the various sections of the country. The entire Jewish population was divided into 24 such *ma'amadot* to correspond with the priestly and Levitical groups. This innovation provided the entire people with a sense of participation in the Temple service. For the sacrificial system see SACRIFICES AND OFFERINGS.

Although the Bible contains no references to prayers during the sacrificial services, the Second Temple did have prayers, blessings, and readings from the Pentateuch. At the conclusion of the incense offering, the priests blessed the general assemblage (the PRIESTLY BLESSING is still recited in synagogues throughout the world).

Music and song contributed to the beauty of Divine worship. At various points in the daily sacrifice ceremonial, the Levites would join in with song and string music and the sounding of the silver trumpets. At each of these trumpet soundings, the people would prostrate themselves in adoration of the Almighty. In addition, the Levites would chant a special Psalm for each day of the week.

After the Destruction. The rabbis taught that the First Temple was destroyed because of the sins of immorality, idolatry, and bloodshed, while the Second Temple fell because of causeless hatred among Jews. The destruction of the Second Temple affected virtually every aspect of religious thought and practice. On the one hand this was expressed in mourning practices, on the other, by undying hope and expectations of its rebuilding.

The mourning was expressed in various ways. Thus, the *halakhah* determined that when a Jew whitewashes the interior of his house, he should leave a square cubit uncovered as a reminder of the Temple. The Talmud decreed that he who sees the ruins of the Temple should make a tear in his garments, the traditional sign of mourning. The kabbalists instituted a prayer service (TIKKUN ḪATSOT) which includes elegies on the destruction of the Temple. The annual fast of TISHAH BE-AV is observed in memory of both Temples. The sense of mourning found expression in folklore. It was a practice to daub the forehead of a groom with ashes. The breaking of a glass by the groom at the conclusion of the MARRIAGE ceremony was also popularly interpreted as an expression of mourning for the destruction of the Temple.

The sense of hope was incorporated in the LITURGY. The AMIDAH was emended to include a plea for the restoration of the text of the 17th benediction of the Temple and the sacrificial service, while the Mishnah, after a detailed description of the sacrificial system, in the tractate TAMID quotes the prayer, "May it be God's will that the Temple be speedily rebuilt in our days, Amen." R. Ishmael ben Elisha, aware that he had violated a rabbinic prohibition, wrote, "When the Temple is rebuilt, I will bring a fat sin-offering." Throughout the centuries, descendants of the priests studied the Temple ritual against the time when they would be recalled to their functions.

This speculation received a new relevance for certain Jews after the Old City of Jerusalem fell under Jewish sovereignty in 1967. The issue of whether a Jew may enter the Temple area, while in the state of ritual impurity in which all Jews have been since the destruction of the Temple, has led to controversy over the location of the "Temple area." According to the *halakhah* various preconditions must be met before the Temple can be rebuilt. These include: the majority of Jews must be living in Erets Israel; there must be conditions of peace; the desire for a Temple must stem from a genuine religious feeling among the Jewish people; a supernatural token of Divine approval must be given; and a true prophet must order the rebuilding. According to MAIMONIDES, the Third Temple will not be built by human hands but has been constructed in heaven, from where it will miraculously descend at the appropriate time.

TEMPLE MOUNT (*Har ha-Bayit*). Elevated area in the southeastern corner of the Old City of JERUSALEM, site of the First and Second TEMPLE. The area recognized today as the Temple Mount is enclosed by four large retaining walls built during the reign of Herod the Great (first century BCE). The dimensions of this enclosure significantly exceed the dimensions of the Temple Mount mentioned in the Mishnah (*Mid.* 2.11) which are those of the sanctified area of the Temple Mount. The sanctified area was augmented by constructing the retaining walls and filling in the gaps formed between the walls and the original slope with a system of domed vaults which was then covered by earth. The eastern retaining wall, parts of which predate Herod, and part of the southern retaining wall were incorporated into the wall that surrounds the entire Old City when it was reconstructed in the 16th century. Archeologists as well as halakhic authorities disagree regarding the precise location of the Temple and its various precincts on the Temple Mount and the sensitive status of the area precludes the possibility of excavation or other *in situ* investigation.

The Bible recounts that the binding of Isaac (AKEDAH) occurred on a mountain in the Land of Moriah and from an early period, Mount MORIAH was identified as being the mountain upon which the Temple was subsequently built (II Chr. 3:1). After the Temple was constructed by SOLOMON, the Temple Mount was recognized by Jews as the holiest place on earth. Since the seventh century (except for an interlude of Crusader occupation), it was in the possession of Muslims for whom it was also a holy site. More than 100 Muslim buildings now stand on the Temple Mount, most prominent of which are the Mosque of El Aksa and the (Golden) Dome of the Rock.

Jewish sources relate to the holiness of the Temple Mount primarily through a system of restrictions and commands. The Mishnah (*Kel.* 1.6ff.) reports that the Temple Mount is holier than the rest of Jerusalem, which is in turn holier than other walled cities in Erets Israel, which are holier than the rest of the Land, which is itself holier than the rest of the earth. Each one of these levels of holiness is demonstrated by its own set of regulations. The holiness of the Temple Mount is expressed in the prohibition against entry to individuals in certain states of ritual impurity. The Mishnah continues to detail ascending gradations of holiness within the Temple Mount itself, each with its attendant regulations, and concludes that the holiest place is the HOLY OF HOLIES, which could be entered only by the High Priest during the Yom Kippur service. Out of respect for the Temple Mount, the Mishnah forbade one to enter "with his staff, or wearing

Aerial view of the Temple Mount, Jerusalem.

his shoes, or with his feet dust-stained; nor should he make of it a short cut, and spitting [is forbidden]" (*Ber.* 9.5). With the exception of mourners and the excommunicated, the Temple Mount was always entered from the right side and always departed from the left (*Mid.* 2.2).

With the destruction of the Temple in 70 CE, the holiness of the Temple Mount became an issue. The majority of halakhic authorities held that the holiness of the Mount and its various precincts remained in force even after the destruction. The main implication of this discussion pertained to the permissibility of entrance. Since in the post-Temple period everyone is considered to be impure and since lacking the ashes of the RED HEIFER (see Num. 19) it is impossible to shed this status, most halakhic authorities agree that since the destruction, entrance to the Temple Mount is prohibited (see, e.g., Maimonides, *Yad, Bét ha-Beḫirah* 6.14-16) and, as a rule, Jews have refrained from entering. Moreover, as it became impossible to identify the precise location of the Temple within the precincts of the platform, it became impossible to know the exact site of the Temple and, especially, of the Holy of Holies, which may not be approached. After the Six-Day War in 1967, the issue arose again. The Chief Rabbi of the Israel Defense Forces, Shlomo Goren, claimed to have identified an area within the Temple Mount enclosure that was definitely outside the actual bounds of the sanctified portion and in theory it would be permissible to enter this area. It remained, however, a minority opinion.

Immediately upon the 1967 reunification of Jerusalem,

the Israel government decided to ban Jewish worship on the platform, in the framework of its protection of the holy places of all faiths and in order to avoid a confrontation with the Muslim world. Jews attempting to worship have been prevented from doing so. Today, the Temple Mount is administered by the Muslim Religious Council (*Wakf*).

TEMURAH ("Exchange") Sixth tractate of Order KODASHIM in the Mishnah. Its seven chapters deal with the laws of the exchange of objects (animals, money, etc.) dedicated to the Temple (cf. Lev. 27:9,10,32,33). The Mishnah discusses who may make an exchange, what may be exchanged, a mistaken dedication, the offspring of a dedicated animal and the lost or blemished sin-offering. The tractate also covers other laws connected with offering sacrifices including the difference between individual and congregational offerings, what may or may not be offered on the altar, and which animals may be used for the Temple upkeep. The subject matter is amplified in the Babylonian Talmud and the *Tosefta*.

TENA'IM See BETROTHAL

TEN COMMANDMENTS (or Decalogue; *Aseret ha-Dibrot*). The injunctions spoken by God from the top of Mount SINAI, addressed to the Children of Israel, seven weeks after the EXODUS from Egypt. Subsequently, they were inscribed by God upon the two stone TABLETS OF THE COVENANT and handed to MOSES to be placed in the ARK OF THE COVENANT in the SANCTUARY and later in the TEMPLE built by SOLOMON. According to the Bible, the Ten Commandments are the terms of the COVENANT between God and the Israelites at Sinai (Ex. 34:27-28). To impress upon them the unique and profound importance of this REVELATION of God's commands, the Israelites were told to prepare themselves by sanctifying themselves, cleansing themselves and their garments, and refraining from sexual intercourse. To further enhance the event, the words were accompanied with thunder and lightning and blasts of the SHOFAR (ram's horn) (Ex. 20:15-16).

Before his death, Moses enjoined the Israelites, "Take to heart these instructions [i.e., the Ten Commandments] with which I charge you this day. Impress them upon your children. Recite them...when you lie down and when you get up" (Deut. 6:6-7). Accordingly, Jews used to recite them every morning and evening. However, with the rise of certain sects which taught that only the Ten Commandments were Divinely proclaimed and that they were more important than the other COMMANDMENTS, the sages substituted the twice-daily recital of the SHEMA for the Ten Commandments to show that the rest of the Torah was equally Divinely inspired (TJ *Ber.* 1.5).

The Ten Commandments are at the core of Judaism, constituting the basic moral and ritual code later expanded by the other commandments. An indication of their special significance is the custom for the congregation, which is generally seated during the Reading of the Law, to rise when the Ten Commandments are read (both within the regular reading cycle and on SHAVU'OT). Furthermore, when read in public, a special cantillation joining each commandment into a single verse is intoned by the reader instead of the ordinary cantillation.

The Ten Commandments have been the subject of extensive comment by the classical Jewish commentators. Noting that in the first two Commandments God speaks to the people directly in the first person, while in the others God is referred to in the third person, the sages concluded that the Israelites heard only the first two and that the others were transmitted to them by Moses (*Mak.* 24a). They also suggested that since the first five, inscribed on one tablet, contain the name of God, they deal with relations between man and his Maker; whereas the second five, inscribed on the second tablet, which do not mention God, deal with relations between man and his fellow-man. Furthermore, God did not want His name inscribed on the tablet dealing only with capital sins.

The words of the Ten Commandments are recorded twice in the Pentateuch: in Exodus 20:2-14 and, as recapitulated by Moses, in Deuteronomy 5:6-18. Several explanations are suggested for the differences between the two versions. For example, in the second version, 40 years after the Exodus, in regard to the fourth commandment ordaining Sabbath observance, it was appropriate to remind the people of their bondage in Egypt; this was not necessary in the first version, spoken only seven weeks after the Exodus, which gives the rationale for the Sabbath as "For in six days the Lord made heaven and earth... and on the seventh day He rested."

There are differences in the numeration of the Commandments. Following the MEKHILTA, Jews generally understood the opening "I am the Lord your God...", as the first commandment. However, some regard this as introductory, and take "You shall have no other gods" as the first command, and "You shall make no graven images..." as the second.

The rabbis stated that the Tablets on which the Ten Commandments were inscribed were prepared before Creation and that therefore the Decalogue is of universal application, outside time and place. They also suggested that when God spoke the words it was simultaneously translated into 70 languages so that all peoples could understand.

The *aggadah* relates that God first appeared to the Edomites, Moabites, and Ishmaelites, offering them the Torah. However, upon hearing the injunctions against murder, theft, and adultery, they refused the offer, claiming that such restrictions would interfere with their life style (*Sif.* to Deut. 33:2). Later, Judaism's daughter-religions, Christianity and Islam, accepted the importance of the Ten Commandments, although not in the same basic role as in Judaism.

THE TEN COMMANDMENTS
(Exodus 20:2-14)

God spoke all these words, saying:
1. I am the Lord your God who brought you out of the land of Egypt, the house of bondage: You shall have no other gods besides Me.
2. You shall not make for yourself a sculptured image, or any likeness of what is in the heavens above, or on the earth below, or in the waters under the earth. You shall not bow down to them or serve them. For I the Lord your God am an impassioned God, visiting the guilt of the parents upon the children, upon the third and upon the fourth generations of those who reject Me, but showing kindness to the thousandth generation of those who love Me and keep My commandments.
3. You shall not swear falsely by the name of the Lord your God; for the Lord will not clear one who swears falsely by His name.
4. Remember the Sabbath day and keep it holy. Six days you shall labor and do all your work, but the seventh day is a sabbath of the Lord your God: you shall not do any work, you, your son or daughter, your male or female slave, or your cattle, or the stranger who is within your settlements. For in six days the Lord made heaven and earth and sea, and all that is in them, and He rested on the seventh day; therefore the Lord blessed the Sabbath day and hallowed it.
5. Honor your father and your mother, that you may long endure on the land that the Lord your God is assigning to you.
6. You shall not murder.
7. You shall not commit adultery.
8. You shall not steal.
9. You shall not bear false witness against your neighbor.
10. You shall not covet your neighbor's house: you shall not covet your neighbor's wife, or his male or female slave, or his ox or his ass, or anything that is your neighbor's.

TEN DAYS OF REPENTANCE (or Penitence; *aseret yemé teshuvah*). The ten days beginning with the NEW YEAR (1Tishri), through the DAY OF ATONEMENT (10 Tishri), considered the most solemn period of the year, during which all mankind is judged and its fate determined for the coming year. The Talmud (*RH* 16b) states that on the New Year, those who are perfectly righteous are inscribed in the BOOK OF LIFE, those completely evil in the Book of Death, and the cases of all others remain pending until the Day of Atonement. Consequently, it is during this time that efforts must be made to improve oneself. The High Holiday prayers spell out how this is to be done: through REPENTANCE (*teshuvah*), PRAYER (*tefillah*), and CHARITY (*tsedakah*). During the Ten Days of Repentance, various additions are incorporated in the prayers, primarily of the Morning Service. Before the Morning Service, penitential prayers (SELIHOT) are said. Various additions are made to both the silent AMIDAH and the reader's repetition; these primarily stress God as King, and ask Him to grant life in the coming year. The reader's repetition of the *Amidah* is followed by the AVINU MALKENU ("Our Father, our King") petition. In some congregations it is customary to recite Psalm 130:1 ("Out of the depths ...") in the Morning Service. As this period is one of repentance, Jewish law requires each person to beg forgiveness of anyone whom he has wronged during the past year. As defined by Jewish law, true repentance consists of undoing, wherever possible, whatever harm has been done, confessing the sin aloud (not to another person) in words, and resolving not to commit such a sin again. It is a custom to visit the graves of close relatives before the Day of Atonement. In some communities (in Western Europe and among Sephardim) the custom arose of flagellation while reciting the CONFESSION of sins on the eve of the Day of Atonement. The Sabbath between the New Year and the Day of Atonement is referred to as either *Shabbat Shuvah* (*Shuvah* being the first word of the prophetical reading for that day), or *Shabbat Teshuvah*, namely the Sabbath of Repentance (see SABBATHS, SPECIAL).

TEN MARTYRS Ten Jewish sages in the second century who, traditionally, were tortured and martyred on the orders of the Roman emperor, Hadrian. The account is based on several *midrashim*, especially the medieval Midrash, *Eleh Ezkerah*. According to this, the Roman ruler asked the rabbis what Jewish law prescribes as punishment for one who kidnaps and sells a fellow-Jew. The rabbis informed him that the Bible stipulates that the criminal be put to death. The emperor then brought up the case of Joseph who was kidnapped by his ten brothers and sold as a slave to Egypt. He argued that since the brothers were not sentenced to death, ten sages of Israel must be put to death in their place. The ten included the most distinguished scholars and leaders such as R. AKIVA, Hananiah ben Teradyon, Eleazar ben Shammua, Hananiah ben Hakhinah, the High Priest Ishmael, and the president of the Assembly, Simeon ben Gamaliel.

Historically, there are many inaccuracies in the Midrash. The ten listed martyrs did not all live at the same time; although some of them met their death at the hands of the Romans, they were murdered on other pretexts and in other circumstances than those described; others were not murdered at all. Tannaitic and early talmudic literature does not have the story at all, other *midrashim* contain only partial accounts and several contradict each other in important details, including the identity of the martyrs. Most authorities conclude that the story has little historical basis.

Nevertheless, while the story may not be historically true, it portrays the tragic situation of the Palestine Jews under Roman oppression, particularly in the period of the Hadrianic persecutions following the unsuccessful revolt of Bar Kokhba (132-135 CE). It was a time of the severest persecutions, when the Romans issued repressive edicts prohibiting the study of the Torah and the practice of Judaism and many Jewish leaders were indeed martyred.

The story, in poetic form, found its way into the Day of Atonement liturgy, where it is read during the Additional Service (*Eleh Ezkerah*). Conservative synagogues have supplemented this section of the liturgy (the Martyrology) with the inclusion of readings from Holocaust literature which memorialize the martyrdom of six million Jews in Germany and Nazi-occupied Europe during World War II. The story of Jewish martyrdom is thus continued in the modern liturgy and made more relevant for the contemporary age.

The story of the Ten Martyrs also found its way into the liturgical KINOT (elegies) for TISHAH BE-AV (*Arzé Levanon*). During the Middle Ages, when extensive Jewish martyrdom at the hands of Christian persecutors was a fact, it assumed a mystical dimension.

TEN PLAGUES See EXODUS FROM EGYPT

TEREFAH U-NEVELAH (lit. "torn" and "carcass"). Terms used to denote the flesh of an animal or fowl permitted for food by the DIETARY LAWS which it is nevertheless forbidden to eat. Jewish law requires all *kasher* animals to be slaughtered according to appropriate halakhic provisions (see SHEḤITAH). Following the ritual slaughter, an animal must be examined to insure that it is free of a number of specific defects, any of which would have led to its death within less than a year. If it is found, for example, that it had a hole in the lung, the animal is referred to as a *terefah*, and its flesh is not to be eaten. If an animal died by any means other than ritual slaughter (e.g., of old age or by another slaughtering method), the carcass is known as a *nevelah*. If the ritual slaughterer does not kill an animal according to all the laws, the animal is, in this case too, considered a *nevelah*. Halakhically, the only difference between a *nevelah* and a *terefah* is that the former imparts ritual impurity, while the latter does not. The word *treif(e)* has since been extended to refer to any food which may not be eaten (e.g., a mixture of meat and milk), even though by strict definition the term is inappropriate.

TERUMOT ("heave offerings"). Sixth tractate of Order ZERA'IM in the Mishnah. Its 11 chapters deal with the laws of separating the priest's share of agricultural produce (cf. Lev. 22:12; Num. 18:8, 11, 12, 24-32; Deut. 12:6; 18:4). This 1/50th was the first "gift" which had to be separated and none of the food could be eaten before this was performed. The Mishnah also discusses the mingling of *terumah* with common produce, the prohibition on non-priests eating *terumah*, and the prohibition against using *terumah* for other purposes (see TITHES). The subject-matter is amplified in the Jerusalem Talmud and the *Tosefta*.

TEVET (Akkadian: *Tebitu*). Tenth month of the Jewish religious CALENDAR; fourth month of the Hebrew civil year counting from TISHRI. It has 29 days and normally coincides with December-January; its sign of the zodiac is Capricorn. There are several references in the Bible to the "tenth month," but as Tevet it is mentioned only once (Est. 2:16). Traditionally, it marks the beginning of the winter rains in Erets Israel (*Er.* 56a). On 10 Tevet, the Babylonian armies of Nebuchadnezzar laid siege to Jerusalem (II Kings 25:1; Ezek. 24:1-2) and this is commemorated by ASARAH BE-TEVET, the "fast of the tenth month" (Zech. 8:19; *RH* 18b). In Second Temple times, other fast days were also observed during Tevet: one on the eighth, for example, bewailing the completion of the SEPTUAGINT, the Greek translation of the Bible (*Sof.* 1.7).

TEVET, TENTH OF (*Asarah be-Tevet*). Minor fast commemorating the beginning of the siege of Jerusalem by the armies of the Babylonian king Nebuchadnezzar (II Kings 25:1). This siege was the prelude to the destruction of the First Temple in 586 BCE.

The fast commences at dawn and lasts until nightfall (see FASTING AND FAST DAYS). The special liturgy includes penitential prayers (SELIḤOT) and a reading from the Pentateuch (parts of Ex. 32 and 34) dealing with the worship of the Golden Calf and Moses' intercession for God's forgiveness. The same passage is read in the Afternoon Service with the addition of a prophetical reading from Isaiah 55 and 56.

The Israel Chief Rabbinate has designated the Tenth of Tevet as the remembrance day for the victims of the Nazi Holocaust. It was suggested that KADDISH be recited on this day for the six million victims. The date was chosen because it seemed appropriate that the day which commemorates the first national tragedy should also commemorate the most recent disaster. Outside Israel, however, and even within the Jewish State, the Tenth of Tevet is hardly known as a day of memorial for the six million martyrs, and *Yom ha-Shoah*, the Holocaust Memorial Day on Nisan 27 is the more widely observed commemoration.

TEVUL YOM ("One who has bathed in the ritual bath"). Tenth tractate of Order TOHOROT in the Mishnah. Its four chapters deal with the status of one who was unclean and immersed in a ritual bath (*mikveh*) before sunset on that day (cf. Lev. 11:32, 22:6,7). Until sunset, he was called *sheni le-tumah* (second degree unclean) and could impart third degree uncleanness by physical contact. The Mishnah explains the laws related to the *Tevul Yom*, produce touched by a *Tevul Yom*, and the status of the priest's due and other tithes touched by a *Tevul Yom*. Although the *Tevul Yom*'s uncleanness is less stringent than that of one who had not immersed in the ritual bath, the former is still not allowed beyond a limited distance into the Temple. The subject matter is amplified in the *Tosefta* but not in the Talmuds.

THANKSGIVING OFFERING See SACRIFICES AND OFFERINGS

THEFT Theft is forbidden in the verse: "You shall not steal" (Lev. 19:11). The equivalent verse in the TEN COMMANDMENTS (Ex. 20:15) was interpreted as referring not to theft, but to kidnaping, i.e., the theft of a person. Theft implies an action carried out surreptitiously, where the thief makes every effort not to be observed. By contrast, robbery involves a direct confrontation between the robber and his victim. The thief who is caught must repay twice the value of what he stole as a fine. If he stole a head of cattle and sold or slaughtered it, he must pay back four or five times the value, based on the type of cattle stolen. A thief who voluntarily returns his theft is not required to pay the fine. Unlike the thief, a robber who is caught must only make restitution, but need not pay any fine. The sages explain that the reason for the difference is that the thief is worse than the robber. The robber, by his actions, shows that he fears no one. The thief, on the other hand, shows fear, which is why he avoids confrontation, and if that be the case, he should at least show equal fear of God. MAIMONIDES in his *Mishneh Torah* (*Hilkhot Genévah*, 1) writes: "Whoever steals anything worth a penny or more, transgresses a negative commandment... It is irrelevant if one steals from a Jew or a non-Jew, from an adult or from a minor... It is even forbidden to steal as a jest or to steal with the intention of returning the object, or with the intention of paying for the object." By biblical law, a man who has stolen and does not have the wherewithal to repay the theft (as opposed to the fine involved) may be sold into slavery for up to six years to pay for the theft. However, a woman cannot be sold into slavery in such circumstances. The Bible also prescribes that if a person finds a thief in his home at night, he may take any necessary measures, including killing, in order to defend himself, for the presumption is that a thief who is caught in the act may be willing to kill in order to save himself. *Halakhah* stresses that *genévat da'at* — literally, "theft of the mind," i.e., deceiving another — is also considered to be theft. It is forbidden to buy stolen property, for this aids the thief to function. The Talmud puts it descriptively: "It is not the mouse that steals, but the hole which does so." A person who consciously buys stolen property must return it to its original owner and cannot receive payment for the object. If such stolen property is bought inadvertently, it must be returned to the original owner, provided the owner recompenses him for the money spent.

THEODICY See REWARD AND PUNISHMENT

THEOLOGY Theology is the systematic reflection on religious beliefs. Generally, religion is first experienced and only later contemplated. The Bible is overwhelmingly a record of primary religious experience. As such it contains very little theological reflection. This is true of the first two divisions of the Jewish Bible, the Pentateuch, which is the most authoritative portion containing the legislative core of JUDAISM, and the books of the Prophets. However, the last division, the Hagiographa, in which the human response is more dominant, contains the beginnings of reflection in areas where experience seems to clash with cherished religious beliefs. Although traces can already be found in the later Prophets, it is the books of Job, Ecclesiastes, and some of the Psalms that contain a sustained grappling with the problem of theodicy, an attempt to understand the justice of GOD in the face of the suffering of the righteous.

While the Bible itself does not contain a theology, there are hints at the possibility of theology. The fact that there is no immediate Divine rejection of Abraham's (Gen. 18:25), Moses' (Ex. 32:11-13), or Job's questioning of God's moral nature, indicates that God's moral will is accessible to human comprehension and to human criticism. This paves the way for theology.

There is considerable theological reflection in the Talmud; however, it is scattered throughout the corpus and not developed systematically. Instead of engaging in formal argumentation, the rabbis expressed their thought in terse epigrams in which fundamental religious insights are compressed into a single general saying. Thus on the question of FREEWILL versus Divine omniscience: "Everything is foreseen, yet permission is given; the world is judged with mercy yet the verdict is according to one's deeds" (*Avot* 3.15). Theological reflections were left in a fluid form and wide differences of opinion were tolerated. The basic premise of talmudic Judaism remained that the Torah represents Divine REVELATION so that all parts of biblical law, both its moral and its ritual portions, are equally binding and authoritative and are to be meticulously observed.

In certain areas of vital religious experience, the rabbis explored and broadened their understanding of basic concepts. Thus the Bible calls for both the fear and love of God (Deut. 10:12). The rabbis asked: What does that mean? How is this to be achieved? Do not fear and love conflict? Do religious deeds require proper intention and purity of motive? Even on the control principle of Divine Revelation, nuances of approach developed as the rabbis probed the mysteries of God's communication with man, having important implications for their understanding of the nature of the Torah. Sometimes they engaged in speculation unrelated to a biblical text: "For two and a half years the schools of Hillel and Shammai debated whether man would have been better off if he had not been created..." (*Er.* 13b).

The talmudic rabbis did not fix the contents of the Jewish faith in the form of dogmas. However, it was clear to them that acceptance of the Bible implies belief in a moral God, PROVIDENCE, REWARD AND PUNISHMENT, MIRACLES, REPENTANCE, revelation, and REDEMPTION. They insisted upon these norms of faith even though their exact formulation was not reduced to a catechism.

Beginning with PHILO of Alexandria (25 BCE-50 CE), a new and external pressure arose to stimulate Jewish theology: contact with foreign philosophic thought. The great cosmopolitan city of Alexandria in Egypt was at that time the place where Greek-speaking Jews could receive full exposure to the rich Hellenic culture. Convinced that both Hellenic wisdom as the fruit of God-given human reason, and the Bible as the word of God, represented the truth, Philo set about to show both his fellow-Jews as well as the Greeks that the teachings of the sacred Jewish tradition were in conformity with Greek philosophy. He did this by freely applying the allegorical method of interpretation to the biblical text in a systematic and thoroughgoing way. Thus, he developed the concept of the Divine Logos (Word) or Wisdom of God, that he identified with God's attributes of JUSTICE and MERCY, and with the realm of the ANGELS, as the intermediary between the abstract, metaphysical God and the material world. Man has access to this spiritual world by means of intuition or mystical apprehension for which he can prepare himself by ascetic living. While remaining on the whole faithful to the religious principles of Scripture, such as human freedom and revelation, Philo's theology tended in the direction of a personal mystical vision. By wedding Scripture to PHILOSOPHY and its highest forms to morality, Philo made clear the universal thrust of Judaism.

Philo has been called "the first theologian." His historic significance has been characterized as follows: "Between a philosophy which knew not of Scripture and a philosophy which tries to free itself from Scripture, European thought for 17 centuries was dominated by what is generally called 'medieval philosophy.' Philo is the founder as well as the direct and indirect source of this type of philosophy" (H.A. Wolfson).

The inclination to theologize did not arise again until the Middle Ages. This time the movement lasted from the beginning of the ninth century until the 15th century and found expression in religious poetry, biblical exegesis, popular sermons, as well as in special philosophical works.

Instead of being considered as simply "a handmaid" of traditional Jewish thinking, in the Middle Ages philosophy became the central Jewish value for wide circles. The stimulus to theologize was again involvement in a foreign culture, that of Islamic-Arabic civilization which through the common medium of the Arabic language brought Jews into contact with the highly developed Islamic Kalam theology and, through it, with Greek philosophy. This time, however, theology was needed to defend Judaism against direct intellectual attack from a number of different quarters. A Jewish sect called Karaism (see KARAITES), which acknowledged only the authority of the Bible and grew popular in the ninth century, attacked the reliability of the rabbinic tradition. The expanding religions of ISLAM and CHRISTIANITY, in order to justify their rupture with Judaism, conducted an aggressive attack on the mother religion. The fact that all three faiths were revealed religions only sharpened the controversy. Judaism had to refute the arguments that the revelation given to Israel had been abrogated by the one given to Muhammad or had been fulfilled by the appearance of Jesus. In this variegated and tolerant Islamic-Arabic civilization was also heard the voice of the dualistic Parsee religion that attacked all monotheisms and particularly the doctrine of CREATION.

In the midst of such intellectual ferment, naive faith in traditional authority was most difficult to maintain. Reason remained the only arbiter in the face of conflicting claims to exclusive truth. In order to "answer the heretic" both within and without, Jewish thinkers were compelled to reexamine Judaism in theological terms. However, as in the case of Philo centuries earlier, the given components from which the theology was to be formed were not only the biblical and rabbinic traditions, but a certain philosophic content, which the intellectual climate of the time assumed to be the indubitable print of human reason. Therefore, the task of Jewish theology in the Middle Ages was not merely analytic, i.e., a matter of applying reason to a body of received religious doctrine in order to clarify meaning, systematize concepts, eliminate inconsistencies, and justify truth claims, but it was also asked to reconcile two separate contents: the religious tradition and a contemporary "philosophy." The latter was believed to be the product of reason employed in the synthetic mode, i.e., metaphysical speculation.

In this period, the contemporary philosophy was represented by the Kalam theology in its Mutazilite version, as well as by NEO-PLATONISM and ARISTOTELIANISM as interpreted by the Islamic commentators.

The major figures and works in medieval Jewish theology start with SAADIAH GAON of Egypt and Babylon (882-942) and his *Sefer ha-Emunot ve ha-De'ot* ("Book of Beliefs and Opinions"); Solomon IBN GABIROL (c.1026-1050) of Spain, a great religious poet who worked out a metaphysical system along Neo-Platonic lines, and his *Fons Vitae* ("Fountain of Life"); and BAḤYA IBN PAKUDA (early 12th century) and his *Ḥovot Ha-Levavot* ("Duties of the Heart"), a devotional work designed to intensify the inner religious experience, the opening chapters of which contain a theological treatment of the concept of God, His existence, and His unity. Abraham bar Ḥiyya of Barcelona (first half of 12th century), in his *Megillat ha-Megalleh* ("Scroll of the Revealer"), introduces a concern for history in his expanded Neo-Platonism. JUDAH HALEVI of Toledo (1085-1141) was a religious poet who wrote *Kuzari*, a philosophic work in the form of a dialogue between the KHAZAR king and a Jewish scholar. Abraham IBN

DAUD (d. c.1180) of Toledo, wrote *Emunah Ramah* ("The Exalted Faith") based primarily on Aristotle. Moses MAIMONIDES (1135-1204) of Cordova, Fez, Fostat (Egypt), author of the major philosophical work, *Moreh Nevukhim* ("Guide for the Perplexed") was the leading philosophical figure of this period, who created the most comprehensive and penetrating synthesis of Judaism and Aristotelianism. LEVI BEN GERSHOM (Gersonides; 1288-1344) of Southern France, wrote *Milḫamot Adonai* ("Wars of the Lord"), a scholastic and technical discussion of major problems of religious philosophy using the Arab philosopher Averroës' version of Aristotle as starting point. Ḫasdai CRESCAS (1340-1410), in his *Or Adonai* ("Light of the Lord") analyzes the basic doctrines of Judaism according to their dogmatic importance; and another Spanish thinker, Joseph ALBO (d. 1444), in his *Ikkarim* ("Basic Principles"), discusses the dogmas of Judaism, adopting an eclectic position that incorporates aspects of Maimonides, Halevi, and Crescas.

Common to all medieval theologians, Jewish, Muslim, and Christian, although they obviously developed their ideas in different ways, was the major premise that God has provided man with two sources of truth: Scripture, which embodies God's revelation; and human reason, with which some men discovered the same truths found in Scripture as well as others which, while not found therein, do not contradict Scripture. These latter truths are called philosophy. Since God is source of both types of truths, there can be no conflict between them. Misunderstanding Scripture or mistakes made in reasoning can cause apparent conflict. Scripture must be interpreted in the light of what is known to be true from reason, while human reasoning has to be checked by the information given in Scripture.

In defending Judaism against the attacks of the Karaites and the other revealed religions, Jewish theologians were compelled to find a rational answer to the questions: Why believe in Judaism rather than in some other religion? Wherein lies the superiority of the Sinaitic revelation? In order to do this effectively, it was essential to have a general theory of knowledge. This meant involvement in the field of general philosophy.

All of the issues relating to the concept of God, His unity and uniqueness, the nature of His attributes, the conflict between God's omniscience and man's freedom, and His relationship to time and space and to the world of nature and man, are thoroughly discussed by all the medieval Jewish theologians.

Some shortcomings of medieval Jewish theology emanated from the historical fact that important philosophical questions were intertwined with empirical ones. In many instances, this theology could not rise higher than the limited astronomical or physical or biological views upon which the philosophical issues were based. Thus the medievals' views on PROPHECY or on immortality of the SOUL were shaped by their understanding of psychology, while their perception of creation and miracles was affected by their understanding of physics. Some of these Jewish thinkers were able in certain cases to challenge the assumptions of the times. Maimonides contested the theory of the eternity of the universe on logical grounds. Judah Halevi acknowledged that philosophy can lead to knowledge of God, but that only religion (Judaism) can develop the special religious disposition of man and bring him to life with God, i.e., communion with Him. Ḫasdai Crescas provided a thoroughgoing critique of Aristotelianism and described a Judaism freed of Greek distortions: Positive attributes may be ascribed to God; the primary content of the idea of God is goodness and not thought; love of God results from joy in His goodness.

Not all Jews were happy with the achievements of Jewish theology. Once the philosophic works of Maimonides were translated into Hebrew and spread throughout the Jewish world, a violent controversy erupted which continued throughout the 13th century. Some of the specific charges leveled against Maimonides, such as criticism of his treatment of the doctrine of RESURRECTION of the dead, were misguided. Other criticism was directed not against any of Maimonides' specific teachings, but against his general rational method, which many felt would be misused by the general untrained Jewish public and lead to a weakening of their faith. Some scholars, such as NAḪMANIDES, stood above the controversy, but took serious issue with some of Maimonides' biblical interpretations as well as with the reasons given by the latter for the commandments.

Moses MENDELSSOHN (1729-1786), the first modern Jewish philosopher, was also a major theologian of Judaism. Beginning with the German Enlightenment, the unity of Jewish culture and the insularity of the Jewish community was shattered, at least for some Jews. The challenge was no longer narrowly intellectual, but social and cultural in the broadest terms. In this philosophical milieu, in which reason still held sway, the tendency was to find a justification for the principles of universal religion. Unlike his medieval forebears, Mendelssohn had broad philosophic interests and contributed in the general areas of metaphysics, psychology, and aesthetics. However, such was the philosophical climate of the age that his general philosophic efforts to justify belief in the existence of God and immortality of the soul were quite in keeping with traditional Judaism.

Mendelssohn makes use of medieval theology's approach to argue for the superiority of the Jewish revelation over the Christian and Muslim revelations that are based on miracles. However, he rejects the medieval notion that revelation delivers both religious and rational truths. Since all men are in need of eternal truths such as the existence of the One omnipotent God and the immortality of the soul, the source of these truths could not be a particular revelation to a particular people. Secondly, historical events, no matter how impressive, cannot import rational conviction. Therefore, according to Mendelssohn, revelation presupposes rational truth which is available to the Jews, as it is to all men in the universal religion of reason. Judaism, therefore, is not a revealed "religion" but a revealed law which prescribes proper behavior for the Jewish people; it is of eternal validity. The TORAH presupposes and represents the universal religious truths so that the Jewish people has the mission, "by its very existence to proclaim them unceasingly unto the nations, to teach, to preach, and seek to maintain them." On this view, Judaism consists of three levels of belief: eternal ideas concerning God, Providence, and the soul which are provable by human reason and hold universally; historical verities about the Jewish past established by historical evidence; and commandments known and authorized by revelation.

The radical and extreme changes in the condition of the Jewish people called the Enlightenment and Emancipation created enormous social pressures for religious change. An increasing number of Jews found themselves oriented to a life which was essentially secular, a small portion of which was allotted to "religion." While Mendelssohn could still believe that he had reconciled traditional Judaism and philosophy, the next generation began to demand that Judaism itself be westernized.

In the early part of the 19th century, mainly in Germany, a group of scholars, each in his own way, began to work out a theology of Judaism which in their view could be reconciled with the advanced thought of their time, and which constituted the ideology of the REFORM movement. These included Solomon Ludwig Steinheim (1790-1866), Samuel HOLDHEIM (1806-1860), and Abraham GEIGER (1810-1874). Steinheim suggested that not all of the Bible was Divine Revelation and that each age must develop its own criteria of selectivity. Holdheim maintained that even laws Divine in origin may be given only for particular circumstances. Geiger identified Judaism's national development as being in the direction of UNIVERSALISM with the elimination of all particularism and rationalism which goes with the concepts of CHOSEN PEOPLE, Zion, and personal MESSIAH. A similar theology was formulated by Kaufman KOHLER in 1885 for the American Reform Movement.

Generally, the leaders of traditional Judaism were removed from the philosophic ferment that seized Germany in the late 18th and 19th centuries. Whatever theologizing took place was in terms of medieval categories. An exception was Samson Raphael HIRSCH (1808-1888), who was the first major spokesman for a traditional position ready to theologize in a modern key. Considered to be the founder of Modern or NEO-ORTHODOXY, Hirsch believed that Judaism obligated the Jew to learn the physical and social sciences, since God manifests Himself in nature and in history. He was, however, critical of Mendelssohn and Maimonides, claiming that both had permitted an exaggerated regard for the philosophy of their day to distort their perception of Judaism. Judaism must be understood "from within itself" in order to appreciate as objectively as possible what it is, what it demands, and what it is trying to achieve.

A centrist position was staked out by Zacharias FRANKEL (1801-1875), a rabbi and critical scholar who founded what has been called the "positive-historical" school, which in America evolved into the CONSERVATIVE movement. In terms of practice, this school was opposed to drastic changes and urged retention of the tradition. However, it sought to ground ultimate religious authority not in the interpretation of a Divine document by an elite, but in the sentiments of the totality of Israel (KELAL YISRA'EL). This approach was continued in America by Solomon SCHECHTER (1850-1915).

Associated with Conservative Judaism is the theology of Mordecai M. KAPLAN (1881-1983) called RECONSTRUCTIONISM. In common with the former is his emphasis on traditional behavior and the significance of the Jewish community. Influenced by the sociological theory of Emile Durkheim and the philosophy of John Dewey, Kaplan reinterpreted the fundamentals of Judaism, God, Torah and Israel, in thoroughly naturalistic terms. God is not a personal Deity, but the totality of natural forces in the universe making for the moral good. Torah is not Divine Revelation but "a recall of the struggles of the Jewish people to educate its own conscience," and Israel as a group and as a community is the dynamic creator of Judaism which is essentially "the advancing civilization of the Jewish people."

Of great influence in recent Jewish theology has been the work of the German thinkers, Hermann COHEN (1842-1918), Franz ROSENZWEIG (1886-1929), and Martin BUBER (1878-1965) who remained outside the denominational framework of Judaism. Although for Cohen God remained a regulative idea and not a reality while religion was only a historic presupposition for ethics, his writing remains a source of great value in the explication of the ethical content of Judaism (see ETHICS).

Both Rosenzweig and Buber were able to break out of the mind-set of speculative idealism and affirm the reality and independence of God, the world, and the individual. Using the new "existentialist" thinking, Rosenzweig was able to speak meaningfully of the biblical categories of creation, revelation, and redemption. Similarly, Buber, on the basis of his "I-Thou" dialogical philosophy, provided a basis for a real relationship between the individual and God, the Eternal Thou. Also Buber's emphasis on the metaphysical significance of inter-subjective "relationships" worked to demonstrate the importance of the notion of community as a key to appreciating both the Ḫasidic and the Zionist movements.

More recently, Jewish theology has been enriched by the works of the thinkers who span the denominational spectrum and who address themselves not only to the perennial problems but also to the *novae* of our day, the HOLOCAUST and the establishment of the State of ISRAEL. These are Abraham Joshua HESCHEL, Joseph Baer SOLOVEICHIK, Eliezer Berkovits,

Emil Fackenheim, Louis Jacobs, Andŕe Neher, Abraham Isaac KOOK, Arthur A. Cohen and Jakob J. Petuchowski.

THERAPEUTAE Semi-monastic sect of the first century CE which stressed the meditative life. The group was especially numerous around Alexandria in Egypt, although it also existed "in many places in the inhabited world" (Philo, *On the Contemplative Life*, 21). The name, stemming from the Greek *therapeuein*, denotes both "healing" and "worship." The former connotation refers to them as healers of men's souls, while the latter attests their worship of God.

Philo speaks admiringly of this group. The simple houses of these settlers contained a room set apart for their meditations and study of the Holy Scriptures and other devotional works from sunrise to sunset. Twice daily, at dawn and eventide, they prayed and composed hymns and psalms to God. This solitary existence was relaxed somewhat on the Sabbath day, when they met in the synagogue where both men and women, in partitioned areas, sat and listened to sermons. They fasted daily until sunset, except for the Sabbath day when they relaxed somewhat, allowing themselves little more than bread and water. This asceticism extended even to their dress, which only sufficed to protect them against extreme heat and cold.

A striking feature was the festal meeting or "chief feast" held by the order, apparently on the Shavu'ot holiday. The occasion consisted of prayer, Bible discourse, a frugal repast and choral song and dance.

Philo contrasts the contemplative life of the Therapeutae to that of the ESSENES "who persistently pursued the active life." Philo nowhere suggests how members were recruited into the community or their source of subsistence. While some see a possible relationship between the Essenes, the Dead Sea Sect and the Therapeutae, the majority view is that the Therapeutae and Essenes, at any rate, were distinct and separate communities.

THREE WEEKS The period beginning with the 17th day of Tammuz, on which the walls of Jerusalem were breached by the Babylonian army under Nebuchadnezzar, and the ninth of Av, the date associated with the destruction of the Temple. This period is generally known in Hebrew as the period *bén ha-metsarim* ("between the straits") in accordance with the verse in Lamentations (1:3), "all her persecutors overtook her between the straits." Traditionally, this is the saddest time of the Jewish calendar. Various customs serve to bring home the loss for the Jewish people, there being differences between Ashkenazi and Sephardi practices. Generally, as the days grow closer to the ninth of Av, the severity of the signs of mourning increases. Throughout the three weeks, one may not get married nor, according to Ashkenazi custom, may one shave or cut one's hair. In Sephardi practice, these restrictions only apply from the first day of Av. Throughout that time, it is also forbidden to take any action which would require the recitation of the SHEHEḤEYANU blessing, such as eating a kind of fruit not yet eaten that season or wearing new clothes. Beginning with the first day of Av, the Ashkenazi custom is not to eat any meat or drink wine until after the ninth of Av, while Sephardim refrain from meat and wine from the Sunday preceding the Ninth of Av. This prohibition does not apply on the Sabbath, for no mourning is permitted on that day. On TISHAH BE-AV itself it is not permitted to eat or drink, wear leather shoes, anoint with oil, wash (except where required), or engage in marital relations. As the Temple continued to burn throughout the ninth of the month and to midday of the tenth, certain actions are forbidden until the latter time, including shaving or cutting one's haircut, and eating meat or drinking wine. On each of the three Sabbaths during the Three Weeks, a special prophetical passage (*haftarah*) is read, the three *haftarot* being referred to collectively as *Telata de-Poranuta* — "the three (*haftarot*) of calamity" (Jer. 1 and 2, and Isa. 1).

THRONE OF GOD The concept of GOD as sitting on a throne, which symbolizes the power of His rule, is common in the Bible, while the idea of the Throne of Glory is repeated in rabbinic literature, in poetry (PIYYUT) and in the HÉKHAL literature.

The description of God as sitting on a "lofty and exalted throne" (Isa. 6:1) appears in the Bible primarily in prophetic visions. Prophets, visionaries and later mystics, had a vision or even experience of ascending to God's throne, graphically portrayed as a chariot in the first chapter of Ezekiel. The Throne of God is listed by the rabbis as one of those items which existed before the creation of the world and "the souls of the righteous are kept underneath the Throne of Glory" (*Shab.* 152b). In rabbinic literature, there is mention of the Throne of MERCY and the Throne of JUSTICE, that express the different attributes of God. When God "sees that the world deserves to be destroyed, He gets up from the Throne of Justice and sits on the Throne of Mercy" (*Av. Zar.* 3b). Some places in rabbinic literature, which are close to the *hékhal* literature, give descriptions of God's Throne and its dimensions (*Ḥag.* 13a; *Midrash Proverbs* ch. 10). Descriptions of the Throne of God are frequent in the mystical *hékhal* literature, which discusses a number of God's thrones, identified with the *merkavah* (chariot). According to this literature, the Throne sings praises to God and invites God to come and sit on it — "and three times each day His Throne of Glory prostrates itself before Him and says, 'O Radiant God, the God of Israel, honor me and sit on me, O Glorious God, because Your sitting is cherished and precious to me, and is no burden to me'." The throne-chariot of Ezekiel was a basic subject of early Jewish MYSTICISM and the rabbis limited its study to those they felt were mature and learned.

In the Middle Ages, there were certain reservations about the anthropomorphic picture of God as sitting on a throne and the philosophers and kabbalists gave it allegorical, symbolic interpretations. SAADIAH GAON regarded the description of God sitting on His Throne as a special vision, which came to the prophets to verify their prophecies (*Emunot ve-De'ot*, 2.10). The ninth chapter in the first part of MAIMONIDES' *Guide for the Perplexed* is devoted to an interpretation of the significance of the Throne. According to Maimonides, the Throne shows the greatness and essence of God, that are inseparable from Him: "The word 'Throne' denotes God's greatness and essence." He wrote that *Ma'aseh Merkavah*, used for throne mysticism, really meant philosophy.

The kabbalists, too, regarded God's Throne as part of the Godhead and understood it as a symbol of one of the SEFIROT. According to the *Sefer* BAHIR, the Throne of Glory symbolizes the *sefirah* of *binah* (understanding): "The Throne of Glory that is adorned and complete and praised and pleasing is the home of the world to come and its place is in wisdom" (para. 146). According to the Zohar, the throne symbolizes the *sefirah* of *malkhut* (majesty) and God sits upon the *sefirah* of *tiferet* (glory). God's sitting on His Throne indicates harmony in the world of the Godhead: "When is there perfection above? When God sits on His Throne. And until He sits on His Throne, there is no perfection" (III:48a).

TIKKUN See LURIA, ISAAC AND LURIANIC KABBALAH

TIKKUN ḤATSOT (lit., "midnight institution"). A ceremony, primarily among kabbalists, in which lamentations and prayers are recited at midnight, in order to mark the myth of the exile (GALUT) of the Divine Presence (SHEKHINAH) and its redemption.

The custom of rising at midnight and reciting hymns and praises already existed at the time of SHERIRA GAON and was considered a pious practice. HAI GAON linked this custom to a talmudic legend according to which God mourns throughout the night for the destruction of the Temple and the exile of the Jewish people (*Ber.* 3a). ASHER BEN JEHIEL (13th century) stated that "it is fitting for every God-fearing person to be grieved and distressed at midnight, and to lament the destruction of the Temple" (commentary on *Ber.* 3a).

The kabbalists adopted this pious custom and regarded it as a *tikkun* — a human action which affects and restores the Godhead. The Zohar regards midnight as an appropriate hour for the pious to awaken and study the Torah, this having a beneficial influence on both those who study and on the upper worlds. At the same time, the Zohar does not use the phrase *Tikkun Ḥatsot*, nor does it give a list of lamentations to be said at midnight for the Divine Presence in exile.

The fixed text for *Tikkun Ḥatsot* was composed by the 16th-century kabbalists in Safed. According to the custom of the followers of Isaac LURIA, *Tikkun Ḥatsot* includes two parts, reflecting two aspects of the Divine Presence: *Tikkun Leah* and *Tikkun Rachel*. During *Tikkun Rachel*, which symbolizes the Divine Presence in exile, certain mourning rites are practiced and Psalms 137 and 89, the last chapters of Lamentations, and lamentations which were composed in Safed and in Jerusalem are recited. *Tikkun Leah*, which follows *Tikkun Rachel*, also includes the recitation of psalms and the reading of various *piyyutim* (religious poems) and stresses redemption and consolation. This custom later spread from Safed to other Jewish communities.

TISHAH BE-AV ("Ninth of [the month of] Av"). Fast day commemorating the destruction of the First TEMPLE by the Babylonians under Nebuchadnezzar in 586 BCE and the destruction of the Second Temple by the Roman legions of Titus in 70 CE. Although Tishah be-Av is usually bracketed with the other minor fasts which recall the Babylonian siege and destruction of Jerusalem, its associations and mode of observance are uniquely significant. Whereas the other historical fasts commence at sunrise on the day itself, the Fast of Av (like the Day of Atonement) commences at sunset on the previous night and lasts for over 24 hours. It is governed by various restrictions (see FASTING AND FAST DAYS); should the Ninth of Av fall on a Sabbath, the fast is observed from Saturday night. Unlike those other minor fasts which commemorate the period of the destruction of the First Temple, Tishah be-Av was not discontinued after the return from Babylon and remained in force throughout the period of the Second Temple.

Associating the destruction of both Temples with the Ninth of Av raises a question of dating. The Bible mentions both the seventh and the tenth of the month as the date on which the First Temple was destroyed (II Kings 25:8-9; Jer. 52:12-13); there is no mention of the ninth. As far as the Second Temple is concerned, ancient opinion was unanimous in fixing the tenth of the month as the day on which the calamity occurred, and there was an apparent eagerness to mark the same date as the anniversary of the First Temple's destruction. Josephus, the chief non-rabbinic source for the history of the Second Temple, makes this point when he writes: "And now that fatal day was come according to the revolution of the ages; it was the tenth of the month of Av, upon which [the Temple] was previously burned by the king of Babylon" (*War*, VI, 248-50). The weight of rabbinic evidence is likewise for the tenth as the date of the destruction. The Talmud (*Ta'an.* 29a) resolves the difficulty by suggesting that, in the last days of the First Temple, the enemy entered the holy precincts on the seventh of Av, attacked the building on the eighth, started the conflagration on the ninth, and the Temple burned to the ground on the tenth. In view of the fact that the fire was actually started on the ninth, that day seemed appropriate for commemoration by fasting and prayer. Later, when the Second Temple was likewise destroyed, the original fast day observed on the Ninth of Av served to commemorate both disasters, in accordance with a rabbinic dictum that later sorrowful events may be ascribed to a date saddened by an earlier calamity.

NINTH OF AV — TISH'AH BE-AV

Other Names: *Tsom Tish'ah be-Av* (Fast of the Ninth of Av)

Hebrew Dates: 9 Av

Torah & Prophetical Readings:
Morning: Deut. 4:25-40; Jer. 8:13-9:23 (*Haftarah*)
Afternoon: Ex. 32:11-14, 34:1-10; Isa. 55:6-56:8 (Ashkenazi *Haftarah*) Hos. 14:2-10, Micah 7:18-20 (Sephardi *Haftarah*)

Scroll: Book of Lamentations (*Ekhah*) chanted in evening; in morning also in some congregations

Civil dates on which the festival occurs, 1990-2010:

1990/5751	31 July
1991/5752	21 July*
1992/5753	9 August*
1993/5754	27 July
1994/5755	17 July
1995/5756	6 August
1996/5757	25 July
1997/5758	12 August
1998/5759	2 August*
1999/5760	22 July
2000/5761	10 August
2001/5762	29 July
2002/5763	18 July
2003/5764	7 August
2004/5765	27 July
2005/5766	14 August
2006/5767	3 August
2007/5768	24 July
2008/5769	10 August
2009/5770	30 July
2010/5771	20 July

* Postponed from the previous day (a Sabbath)

The Ninth of Av has associations with many dark chapters in Jewish history. In 135 CE, Bar Kokhba's last surviving fortress, Betar, fell to Hadrian's legions, and traditionally this occurred on Tishah be-Av. On 18 July 1290 (coinciding with the Fast of Av), Edward I signed the edict banishing all Jews from England. Similar associations were made with the expulsion from Spain, the last professing Jew having left Spain four days earlier. Thus, by coincidence or design, Tishah be-Av became the gloomiest date in the Jewish calendar, synonymous with oppression and exile.

In the course of time, Jewish law and custom evolved several degrees of public mourning from SHIVAH ASAR BE-TAMMUZ. The subsequent THREE WEEKS culminate in the NINE DAYS beginning on the New Moon of Av and reach a climax on the eve of Tishah be-Av, when the last meal is frugal, an egg symbolizing the mourner's traditional fare (some Eastern communities dip the food in ashes as a sign of mourning). Thereafter, eating and drinking are forbidden during the fast day; other prohibitions ban shaving, bathing, and marital relations; wearing leather shoes, engaging in work, or even indulging in normal Torah study. The appearance of the synagogue during Tishah be-Av bears witness to the melancholy historical associations of this date. At nightfall, the curtain is removed from the Holy Ark (in many Sephardi congregations which have no Ark drape, a black curtain is hung for Tishah be-Av), the cloth is taken away from the *bimah* (reading desk), and the lights are dimmed. Congregants, in cloth or rubber footwear, sit on low stools or on the floor and do not greet one another. The synagogue's whole atmosphere is in fact transformed, the joyous house of prayer having become a place of mourning.

Mourning the destruction of the Temple on Tishah be-Av.

As if to banish the last vestige of joyous ceremonial, the *tallit* (prayer shawl) and *tefillin* are not worn at the Morning Service, these being considered religious "ornaments" inappropriate to so mournful an occasion (although Syrian Jews don them at home before going to synagogue). On this one day in the year, however, they are worn later at the Afternoon Service and then removed before evening prayers. Normal seats are occupied in the afternoon; an abbreviated *havdalah* is recited at the end of the fast if Tishah be-Av occurs on Sunday; and no meat meals are eaten until the following day.

The special scroll reading for Tishah be-Av is the Book of LAMENTATIONS (*Megillat Ékhah*), which describes the destruction of Jerusalem and the Temple in poetic and moving terms. The scroll and all but the last two verses of the morning *haftarah* are chanted to a plaintive melody. *Ékhah* is read in all synagogues on the night of the fast; some congregations also include it in the Morning Service after the Torah reading. Also unique to Tishah be-Av are the KINOT (elegies), a collection of religious poems which, in the Ashkenazi rite, include a series of "Odes to Zion" by JUDAH HALEVI. They evoke the Jewish people's constant yearning for Zion and conclude with ELI TSIYYON VE-AREHA, sung by worshipers to a more lively tune. Other poems in this collection were inspired by the horrors of the Crusades and other tragic episodes in medieval Jewish history. A few *kinot* are recited at the end of the Evening Service, but most are read the next morning.

Despite the gloomy atmosphere prevailing throughout the Ninth of Av, hope for Israel's redemption has never been absent from this day. It is held that, like the other fasts, Tishah be-Av will eventually become an occasion for rejoicing (Zech. 8:19) and the rabbis identified it with the birthday of the Messiah.

The observance of this fast day was abandoned by Reform Judaism as an anachronism. Latterly, however, Reform congregations have often changed their attitude, seeking contemporary relevance in Tishah be-Av even if they do not keep it as a fast.

In the State of Israel, thousands attend services at the WESTERN WALL below the Temple Mount and Tishah be-Av is observed as a day of public mourning. All restaurants and places of entertainment are closed, while radio and television programs emphasize various aspects of the occasion.

TISHRI (or Tishré; Akkadian: *Tashritu*). Seventh month of the Jewish religious CALENDAR; first month of the Hebrew civil and chronological year. Tishri has 30 days and normally coincides with September-October. Libra the Balance, Tishri's sign of the zodiac, was associated by the rabbis with Divine justice and the weighing of man's deeds, since the New Year (ROSH HA-SHANAH) on 1 Tishri is traditionally a Day of Judgment for the whole world. Tishri is not mentioned in the Bible, although there are many references to "the seventh month" which is also called Ethanim (I Kings 8:2). According to rabbinic sources, Tishri marks the beginning of fall in the Land of Israel.

Most of the significant dates in Tishri are linked with the biblical festivals. Rosh ha-Shanah is celebrated in both Israel and the Diaspora on the first two days of the month. The Fast of GEDALIAH, instituted after the Babylonian conquest and originally called the "fast of the seventh month" (Zech. 8:19), is observed on 3 Tishri. The TEN DAYS OF PENITENCE commencing with Rosh ha-Shanah reach a solemn climax on the DAY OF ATONEMENT (Yom Kippur) on 10 Tishri. SUKKOT, the festival of Tabernacles, is celebrated on 15-23 Tishri in the Diaspora (15-22 Tishri in Israel). It includes HOSHANA RABBAH on the 21st and ends with SHEMINI ATSERET and SIMḤAT TORAH (the Rejoicing of the Law). Simḥat Torah is not a biblical festival and dates from post-talmudic times; in the Diaspora it is observed after Shemini Atseret, as an extra holiday on 23 Tishri, but in Israel the two festivals are combined on 22 Tishri.

TITHE (*ma'aser*). A tenth part of agricultural produce or livestock which was "holy to the Lord" (Lev. 27:30-32). The Bible specifies various percentages of the crop that the farmer must allocate in accordance with given criteria as a religious offering to particular individuals. The custom of tithing is of ancient origin, as Abraham gave a voluntary tithe to Melchizedek (Gen. 14:18-20; cf.28:22). As part of the commandments "dependent on the Land [of Israel]," these tithing regulations are only applicable to produce grown there (*Kid.* 1.9). Such laws applied to the first six years of the seven-year cycle during which crops were grown; no tithes were given in the seventh SABBATICAL year (*shemittah*) during which the fields had to remain fallow.

Initially, the farmer was required to give *terumah* (a "heave offering" or contribution) to the PRIEST (Ex. 29:28; Num. 18:8). There is no specification as to which particular priest must receive the *terumah*, and the decision as to whom it should be given was left to the farmer. Regarding the quantity involved, biblical law requires only that *terumah* be given and does not mention any minimal amount. Thus, the sages declared that giving "a single ear of wheat is enough to exempt an entire barn." By rabbinic decree, however, *terumah* had to be no less than 1/60 of a farmer's crop: according to the Mishnah (*Ter.* 4.3), the average person gave 1/50, while generous people would give 1/40. The relevant laws are discussed in tractate TERUMOT of the Mishnah, *Tosefta*, and Jerusalem Talmud.

Each year, after the separation of *terumah*, the farmer had to set aside one-tenth of his crop for the LEVITES as the regular "first tithe," *ma'aser rishon* (Num. 18:21,24). Which Levite actually received this first tithe was left to the farmer's discretion. Since the Levites, unlike the other tribes, were not given agricultural land of their own but lived in cities, the tithe enabled them to subsist and discharge their primary function — teaching Torah to all Israel. Tractate MA'ASEROT of the Mishnah and Jerusalem Talmud (known as *Ma'aser Rishon* in the *Tosefta*) indicates the rules for this tithe.

The Levites were required to give one-tenth of the tithes they received, or one percent of the original crop, to the priests. This allocation was known as "a tithe of the tithe" (*ma'aser min ha-ma'aser*, Num. 18:26), or *terumat ma'aser* (*Bik.* 2.5). According to the Talmud (*Yev.* 86b), when EZRA returned to Erets Israel from Babylonia, he found that the Levites had mostly not heeded the call to join the other returning exiles. In response, Ezra penalized the Levites by allowing the Israelites to give their first tithe to the priests, who were also descended from the tribe of Levi. Some have interpreted this talmudic passage to mean that the Israelites were actually required to give their first tithe to priests, and to withhold it from the Levites. This situation prevailed throughout the period of the Second Temple.

In the first, second, fourth, and fifth years of the seven-year *shemittah* cycle, the farmer had to set aside one-tenth of his remaining crop as the "second tithe," *ma'aser sheni*. This produce had either to be brought to Jerusalem and eaten there, or, if that was too difficult, it could be sold and the money used to buy food which had to be eaten in Jerusalem (Deut. 14:22-26). The law of the second tithe enabled Israelites who "went up" to Jerusalem for the three PILGRIMAGE FESTIVALS to maintain themselves during their stay in the city. Detailed regulations concerning this tithe are to be found in tractate MA'ASER SHENI of the Mishnah, *Tosefta*, and Jerusalem Talmud. The tithe of animals (Lev. 27:32) was, according to the rabbis, also consumed in Jerusalem.

In the third and sixth years of the *shemittah* cycle, the "poor man's tithe" (*ma'aser ani*) replaced the normal second tithe (Deut. 14:28-29, 26:12). This had to be distributed to the Levites, to the WIDOW AND ORPHAN, to Gentile sojourners, etc., but a cash equivalent might be given instead of the actual produce.

Untithed produce, known as *tevel*, might not be eaten until the appropriate tithes had been separated. The talmudic sages feared that an unlearned person (AM HA-ARETS) might only give *terumah* and not the remaining tithes. They therefore ruled that any "suspect" produce bought from such a farmer also had to be tithed (see DEMAI).

While these various laws were no longer observed by Jews living in the Diaspora after the destruction of the Second Temple, rabbinic law still requires the tithing of produce grown in Erets Israel. Accordingly, some observant Israelis separate a very small amount from produce they have bought from other Jews, recite a prescribed benediction and then destroy this *terumah* (for a parallel custom, see ḤALLAH). According to a formula devised by R. Avraham Yeshayahu KARELITZ (*Ḥazon Ish*), however, the different tithes are merged. Slightly more than one percent of the produce is set aside and its sanctity is then transferred to a specially reserved coin. Since tithes are no longer allocated to priests and Levites but may be fed to animals, those taken at source (e.g., by major food distributors and cooperatives) are sent to the different zoos in Israel. Processed Israeli foodstuffs exported abroad are usually tithed by the rabbinate, that endorses these products as religiously fit (*kasher*). Raw fruit and vegetables, however, are not necessarily tithed before export.

Two notable effects of the tithing system in ancient Israel were an emphasis of Jerusalem and the Temple as focal points of the Jewish religion and an aroused awareness that generous consideration had to be given to the less fortunate. Even today, a legacy of the *terumah* and *ma'aser* regulations may be seen in the symbolic allocation of up to one-tenth of one's income for the purpose of charitable donations.

TOHORAH See PURITY, RITUAL

TOHOROT (Cleannesses). Sixth and last order of the Mishnah. Its 12 tractates (KELIM, OHALOT, NEGA'IM, PARAH, TOHOROT, MIKVA'OT, NIDDAH, MAKHSHIRIN, ZAVIM, TEVUL YOM, YADAYIM, and UKTSIN) deal with the susceptibility, transmission and purification of ritual uncleanness. In the course of the order, four general categories of uncleanness are mentioned: 1) associated with human issues, menstruation and childbirth; 2) transmitted by food and drink; 3) associated with disease (leprosy); 4) transmitted by a corpse or carrion (see PURITY). Since the destruction of the Second Temple, most of these laws have been inoperative. Only the tractate *Niddah* is expanded upon in the Babylonian and Jerusalem Talmud.

The name is also given to the fifth tractate of the Order. Its ten chapters deal with the rules of the lesser degrees of ritual uncleanness which take effect only until sunset of the day they are contracted (cf. Lev. 11:34). The Mishnah discusses the uncleanness transmitted by the carrion of birds and cattle, uncleanness regarding food and drink, the persons engaged in the preparation and consumption of the food, and the vessels which contain the food. Also mentioned are cases of doubtful uncleanness. The title, *Tohorot*, is euphemistic as the contents deal with impurity. However, as MAIMONIDES states, the Mishnah speaks in a "clean language" and furthermore, it instructs on how to purify oneself. The subject is amplified in the *Tosefta* but not in the Talmuds.

TOMBSTONE A marker erected over a grave to indicate the site of BURIAL. The first biblical mention of a tombstone was the one which Jacob erected over the grave of Rachel (Gen. 35:20). During talmudic times, it appears that one of the major purposes of tombstones was to prevent priests from coming in contact with the burial places of the dead, for such contact would result in their ritual defilement. Along the same lines, the Mishnah (*Shek.* 1.1) indicates that the public authorities were required once yearly, in the month of Adar, to mark out the graves in their areas, to prevent the ritual defilement of people on their way to bring the paschal sacrifice. A later *mishnah* in that tractate (2.5) indicates that if money were collected for the burial of a person and there was a surplus, it should be used for a tombstone on the grave, evidently as a memorial. On the other hand, the Jerusalem Talmud (*Shek.* 2.5) notes an opinion that tombstones are not to be placed over the graves of the righteous, for their sayings are their memorial. This ruling is also codified by MAIMONIDES (*Yad, Hil. Avel,* 4.4). Further, Joseph CARO rules (*Sh. Ar. YD* 364) that tombstones are not obligatory. The kabbalist Isaac LURIA, on the other hand, regarded the tombstone as imperative, even seeing it as important for the wellbeing of the deceased. In recent centuries, it has been an universally accepted Jewish custom that the grave of the deceased is marked by a tombstone.

Tombstone of Judah Touro in Newport cemetery, Rhode Island.

Practices differ concerning the position of the tombstone and the date on which it is erected. The Ashkenazi custom throughout most of the world is to have a vertical tombstone at the head of the grave. The Sephardim, as well as the Ashkenazim in Israel, have a horizontal tombstone over the entire grave. In Israel, the custom is to dedicate the tombstone 30 days after death, but in the rest of the world this is usually done only after the first year.

The ceremony that has evolved for the consecration of a tombstone generally includes the recitation of verses in Psalm 119 (which is an alphabetic acrostic) to spell out the name of the deceased, followed by verses to spell out the Hebrew word *neshamah* (soul). This is followed by EL MALÉ RAḤAMIM — a prayer invoking God's mercy on the deceased — and the mourners' KADDISH.

Generally, epitaphs on Jewish tombstones have been engraved in Hebrew and the first line has customarily been an abbreviation for the Hebrew words "Here lies." The last line of the tombstone has generally offered a prayer for the soul, using a standard formulation such as "May his/her soul be bound up in the binding of life," "May his/her memory be a blessing," or "May he/she find rest in Eden" (i.e., Paradise). Since the 19th century, other languages have been used in addition to, or in place of, Hebrew.

Various artistic motifs appear on tombstones, including different animals or birds. When the person's name was that of a specific animal (e.g., "Dov Ber" = bear, "Aryeh" = lion), a representation of that animal might be carved on the tombstone. Another motif, especially on the graves of those who died young, is that of interruption, symbolized, for example, by an incomplete pillar or a chopped-down tree. When the deceased was a priest, it is customary to have on the tombstone two hands held in the priestly blessing, while the tombstones of Levites show water being poured, a reference to the duty of the Levites to wash the hands of the priests before the priestly blessing.

In some places, elaborate structures ("tents") are put up for distinguished or wealthy individuals (and sometimes as a family grave). For great scholars or saintly individuals, especially in Muslim lands and in Ḥasidic circles, an *ohel* (tent) was erected over the grave, which became a center of pilgrimage. In certain communities, when visiting a grave it is customary to place a stone on the tombstone, as a sign of respect for the deceased.

TORAH The word "Torah" is derived from the Hebrew root *yaroh* ("to teach") and is best translated as "teaching" or "instruction." The term "law," by which "Torah" is often translated, follows the Greek rendering *nomos* but gives the false impression that the Torah as a whole is legalistic.

In the PENTATEUCH, the word "Torah" is often used in conjunction with a particular subject such as "the Torah of the Nazirite" (Num. 6:21) or appears alone in the plural as the sum total of such particular doctrines (Gen. 26:5; Ex. 16:28). However, in Deuteronomy the word "Torah" appears in the singular with the definite article and seems to refer to the Mosaic legislation as a whole: "This is the Torah which MOSES set before the Children of Israel" (Deut. 4:44, 29:20, 30:10). The term occurs in the later Books of the Bible as "the Torah of the Lord" and the "Torah of Moses" and thus distinguishes the Pentateuch from the rest of the Bible (Josh. 1:7; Ezra 3:2, 7:10; Neh. 8:8; Mal. 3:22). Thus, the primary connotation of the word "Torah" is the Pentateuch.

To designate the Pentateuch as "the Torah" in this sense has traditionally implied that it is a unified work of Mosaic authorship and that its entire contents all express the nature of the COVENANT between God and His people Israel. The Pentateuch ends with the death of Moses and with the people of Israel poised to enter the Promised Land. Because of Moses' supreme stature as prophet and spokesman for God (Deut. 34:10), the designation of the Pentateuch as *Torat Mosheh* means that therein alone is to be found the legislative core of Judaism. By extension, however, all of the written BIBLE, i.e., the Jewish canon consisting of 24 books is sometimes referred to as "the Torah" (Dan. 9:10-13). These books were judged to be written with the aid of the HOLY SPIRIT (*ru'aḥ ha-kodesh*) that is a form of Divine or prophetic inspiration. However, the distinction between the three divisions in terms of this relative holiness, level of prophecy and, therefore, level of authority, was vigorously maintained in traditional Judaism (*BB* 14,15; *Ta'an* 8; *Shab.* 88a). Thus the authorship of both the Book of Jeremiah and the Book of Lamentations were ascribed to Jeremiah, but only the former was deemed to be the word of God speaking through His prophet and therefore included in the division called *Nevi'im* while the latter was judged to be the personal expression of an individual and was incorporated in the canon but grouped together with the Hagiographa.

Originally, in order to maintain the distinction between

the written Torah (see WRITTEN LAW) and various traditional interpretations, customs, and practices, the rabbis forbade the commitment to writing the additional material. However, when it became too voluminous and chaotic conditions made oral transmission too uncertain, the ban was lifted and the material organized and transcribed in the form of the MISHNAH, the TALMUD, and other rabbinic works. The rabbis expressed the view that "two Torahs" were given at Sinai, a Written Torah and an Oral Torah (see ORAL LAW) and that at least some of the oral traditions relating to the meaning of basic biblical concepts were as authoritive as the written text (see HALAKHA LE-MOSHEH MI-SINAI). In a sense, the Oral Torah came to be regarded as more important than the Written Torah inasmuch as the explanation and understanding of the latter depended upon the former. A third meaning of the word "Torah" therefore includes elements of the Oral Torah which are considered authoritative or *de-oraita* — "from the Torah."

Finally, in its broadest sense, the word "Torah" is sometimes used to refer to the entire corpus of *halakhah* and *aggadah*, Written and Oral, from the Bible up to and including the latest responsa and homiletical interpretations of the rabbis.

The authenticity of both the Written and the Oral Law depends upon the reliability of the chain of TRADITION. Therefore, the recording of its different stages was considered important: "Moses received the Torah [Oral tradition] on Sinai and handed it down to Joshua; Joshua to the elders; the elders to the prophets and the prophets handed it down to the Men of the GREAT ASSEMBLY" (*Avot* 1.1). The recording of the transmitters of the Oral Law remained an important type of Jewish historical writing (see HISTORIOGRAPHY).

While the issue of the "truth" of Moses' prophetic revelation is a theological and philosophical question, the claim of Mosaic authorship for the entire Pentateuch is a literary-historical one which in the modern period has generated much controversy (see BIBLE).

Two different approaches have been noted among the talmudic rabbis regarding the interpretive possibilities of the Torah and the manner of its revelation. The first emphasizes the human recipients of the Torah, sees it as written in human language, favors a literal reading of the text acknowledging its Divine source and perceives it as embodied in a historic document given under particular historic conditions (R. ISHMAEL). The second approach tends to emphasize the Divine giver of the Torah and stresses its metaphysical aspects. It too affirms its Divine origin but feels that its language requires interpretations (R. AKIVA). Thus the first view asserts that the entire Torah was made known to Moses on Sinai and he revealed it on different occasions in accordance with God's instructions. Another view, more in keeping with the literal text, asserts that the Torah was given "section by section" (*Git.* 60a), some in Egypt, some on Sinai, some from the Tent of Meeting in the wilderness and some on the plains of Moab. Both these traditional approaches affirm the Divine origin of the Torah.

The concept of a Divinely-revealed Torah encouraged the belief that there is much more to be found in the text than the literal meaning of the words and sentences. The rabbinic use of MIDRASH regarded as a special, Divinely-sanctioned method of extracting additional meanings from the text, was based on this belief.

A modern school of thought arose in the 19th century and can be identified with the Historical School of Judaism, often bracketed with the CONSERVATIVE MOVEMENT. According to this teaching, the Pentateuch contains the revealed message of God, but, like the Bible critics, holds that the words were written down by different authors at different times, and only later was the Pentateuch gathered together and edited into a uniform work. The important thing, however, is that in their search for God, Moses and the great religious teachers of Israel experienced the message of God, so that the written Torah is their record of Israel's meeting with God. The actual words of the Torah are not of Divine origin; it is the inspired and revealed message, including the laws, which has the stamp of Divine authority.

Preexistence. Many rabbinic teachings speak of the Torah as existing in Heaven prior to the creation of the world (*Pes.* 54a; Gen. R. 1:4; Lev. R. 19:1). The biblical basis is derived from Proverbs 8:22-31, "The Lord made me [Wisdom, identified with Torah] as the beginning of His way, the first of the work of old. I was set up from everlasting, from the beginning or even the earth was." According to another Midrash (Gen. R. 1:1) the Torah served as the blueprints of the universe which God consulted as He created the world.

For PHILO and others in the tradition of Greek philosophy, these doctrines were influenced by Plato's notion that ultimate reality consisted of the world of Ideas of which the experienced world is only a poor reflection. The Kabbalists adopted this notion of the pre-existence of the Torah to their general theory of Emanations (SEFIROT), perceiving the Torah as one of the "instruments" or early expressions of God. Another Kabbalistic view claims that the entire Torah is made up of names of God (Zohar, *Yitro* 87.1), i.e., that the letters of the Torah can be reordered to form strings of the Divine names. This imputed great spiritual power to the Torah as well as the possibility of discovering hidden meanings. It also suggested that the same letters of the Torah can be rescrambled in messianic times to accommodate a new reality. Indeed there are rabbinic teachings to the effect that in the days of the Messiah certain changes may take place in the Torah (Ecc. R. 11:8; Lev. R. 13:3).

The rationalist thinkers of the Middle Ages did not accept this belief literally but interpreted it metaphorically as indicating that God created the world wisely (SAADIAH GAON) or that the Torah predated the world in a teleological sense, i.e., that the Torah is the very purpose of creation (JUDAH HALEVI).

Eternity of the Torah. This concept of the Torah as a pre-existent metaphysical entity which served as the spiritual model of the universe implied, at least to Philo, the eternity of the Torah, i.e., that it will remain valid and effective for all time. In the Pentateuch itself, there are passages whch hint at its perpetuity (e.g. Ex. 31:16; Lev. 3:17; Deut. 13:1, 29:28) but these are not conclusive.

With the rise of CHRISTIANITY and ISLAM which acknowledged the original authenticity of the Torah but argued that it had been superseded by Jesus and Muhammad, the question of the eternity of the Torah became crucial. During the Middle Ages, the doctrine of the eternity of the Torah was generally upheld, with MAIMONIDES including it as the ninth of his 13 PRINCIPLES OF FAITH. A more flexible view is presented by Joseph ALBO. In terms of its Divine origins and state purpose, the Torah is perfect. As an unconditional covenant between God and Israel it continues to be valid and binding. However, men and society do change. It is at least conceivable that as history wears on and human society draws closer to the messianic age, some changes in the Torah way of life imposed on the Jew may be indicated. Albo concludes, therefore, that it is possible for a Jew to believe that a new Torah can come from God. It will, however, command consideration only if it is revealed in the same public manner as the original Torah (*Ikkarim* III 19).

A contemporary Reform view of Torah is presented in *Reform Judaism: A Contemporary Perspective* (1976) of the Central Conference of American Rabbis: "Torah results from the relationship between God and the Jewish people ... lawgivers and prophets, historians and poets gave us a heritage whose study is a religious imperative and whose practice is our chief means to holiness...for millennia, the creation of Torah has not ceased and Jewish creativity in our time is adding to the chain of tradition."

According to Reform theologians, the Oral Torah developed by the rabbis of the first and second centuries CE transformed biblical Judaism, and made it applicable to new unforeseen situations. It established the process of change that could be carried out by any generation of learned Jews. Reform Judaism holds that God's will can be known by people in every age, and not merely through documents and precedents of ages past. Torah can change, if necessary, radically. Torah is dynamic, and its interpretation individualistic. Moreover, according to Reform Judaism, for all the virtues of tradition and the benefits of scholarly guidance, the individual Jew must be the final arbiter of what is living Torah.

TORAH BLESSINGS (*Birkhot ha-Torah*). Special benedictions recited daily in the Morning Service or when called to the READING OF THE LAW in the synagogue. Each Morning Service contains a sequence of three introductory benedictions "on studying the Torah" which were formulated by the rabbis (*Ber.* 11b). These benedictions praise God for the bestowal of His precepts and the privilege of "occupying ourselves with the words of Torah," pray that gaining and spreading religious knowledge may be a pleasant duty for "the house of Israel," and thank God for having assigned the Torah to His CHOSEN PEOPLE. The second benediction, *Ve-ha'arev na*, expresses the hope that all study of Torah may be performed *li-shemah* — "for its own sake" (see ALTRUISM), namely, to gain wisdom rather than some fancied merit. The third benediction in this sequence is identical with the initial blessing pronounced by one who has been called to the Torah reading (see below). The blessings recited each morning are complemented by sections from the Pentateuch (Num. 6:24-26), the Mishnah (*Pe'ah* 1.1), and the Talmud (*Shab.* 127a).

BENEDICTION PRIOR TO THE READING OF THE TORAH

Praise the Lord who is [alone to be] praised!

Praised be the Lord who is [to be] praised for all eternity.

Blessed are You, Lord our God, King of the universe, who has chosen us from among all peoples and given us His Torah.

Blessed are You, Lord, Giver of the Torah.

BENEDICTION FOLLOWING THE READING OF THE TORAH

Blessed are You, Lord our God, King of the universe, who has given us the Torah of truth and implanted eternal life within us.

Blessed are You, Lord, Giver of the Torah.

When summoned to the Reading of the Law, a worshiper first recites the BAREKHU invocation and then repeats the congregational response. In the Sephardi, Eastern, and Italian rites, a person called to the Torah recites an additional formula before *Barekhu* — *Adonai immakhem* ("The Lord be with you!") — to which those standing next to him reply, *Yevarekhekha Adonai* ("The Lord bless you!"). This exchange of greetings is a direct quotation from the Book of Ruth (2:4); see also RESPONSES, LITURGICAL. After the reader (using a YAD or pointer) has indicated the place in the Torah scroll, the individual called touches that section of the parchment with the edge of his prayer shawl (or with the Torah binder), kisses it, and then (if the scroll is mounted on staves) grasps both wooden rollers, winds them together, recites *Barekhu* and the first Torah blessing, and unwinds the scroll for his portion to be chanted. Once this reading has been completed, he again winds the rollers together and holds them as he recites the second, concluding benediction. It is at this point that the father of a boy who has just been called to read the Torah for the first time, as a bar mitsvah, recites the BARUKH SHE-PETARANI formula.

The first benediction over the Torah emphasizes God's choice of Israel as His holy nation (cf. Ex. 19:5-6; Deut. 10:15, 14:2) and the recipient of His Torah. In the second benediction, emphasis is laid on Israel's thankful acceptance of God's Law and of Judaism's spiritual responsibilities. According to JACOB BEN ASHER, the phrase "Torah of truth" stands for the Written Law, while "eternal life" refers to the Oral Law. In most prayer rites, the wording of each separate benediction is identical. Two exceptions should, however, be noted. Sephardim and other Eastern Jewish communities modify the second blessing's text to read: "Who gave us His Torah, the Torah of truth." In the case of the first blessing, Jews belonging to the Reconstructionist movement, which has theological objections to the concept of a Chosen People, read: "Who has brought us close to His service" in place of "Who has selected us from among all peoples."

TORAH ORNAMENTS The desire to honor the Torah and to protect it has found expression among Jewish communities in the artistic objects used to decorate the SCROLLS OF THE LAW.

The ARK, where the scrolls are kept, was in most cases decorated to the best of the community's ability. Its location along the wall facing Jerusalem, indicating the direction in which to turn in prayer, made it the subject of adornment with the symbolic motifs that characterize Jewish ART.

The scroll has a cloth mantle and a metal breastplate is often hung over the cloth mantle. The rollers (*atsé hayyim*) to which the parchment scroll is attached are made of wood and are often topped with metal finials (*rimmonim*, lit., pomegranates). Torah scrolls are frequently adorned by a KETER ("crown"), which fits over the two rollers, and a Torah scroll may have both *rimmonim* and a *keter*.

The use of Torah ornaments developed gradually over the generations. Already at the time of the Talmud, there is written evidence of the existence of beautiful silk coverings which were placed around the Torah scroll. Archeological findings testify to the existence of decorative Holy Arks.

When the Torah scroll is taken out of the ark and taken to the reading platform (BIMAH) for the reading, the artistic decorations are removed and only the YAD (the "hand" used as a pointer) remains in use.

Evidence for the custom of affixing a breastplate to the Torah goes back to the 17th century. This tradition developed due to the need to identify the Torah scrolls for the various festivals for which they were used. The breastplates were used primarily in European countries and many were made of precious metals with inlaid precious and colorful stones. The most prevalent motifs are pillars, a crown, lions, eagles, griffins, roses, trees of life, seven-branched candelabra and the Two Tablets of the Covenant. Sometimes the pillars are accompanied by two figures symbolizing Moses and Aaron. In the last century, the *magen david* (Shield of David) has also been very common.

The decoration of the *rimmonim* is found as of the 15th century. This was preceded by engravings on the upper portion of the rollers themselves, but later the *rimmonim* became independent artistic objects. Some of the Italian *rimmonim* contain exquisite designs of fine metalwork which extend to a considerable height and which include miniature bells.

The *keter* (crown) is already mentioned in the Middle Ages, but most of the extant examples trace back to the 18th and 19th centuries. The form of the *keter* is derived to a large extent from the style of the crowns used by the kings of Europe. The *keter* decorates the Torah like a queen. The most noteworthy artisans in the manufacture of crowns were from Italy, Germany and Eastern Europe. In the 18th and 19th centuries, especially interesting examples were made in Poland. They are characterized by various layers, one on top of the other, and their designs include lions, eagles, birds, griffins, messianic elements, zodiacal signs and floral motifs.

Many Torah mantles were made of velvet and their designs often resembled those on the PAROKHET (ark cover). The Torah containers used in Islamic lands and in India show evidence of fine and complex art work. Some are made of silver with inlaid precious stones, while others are carved of wood. These Torah containers protected the scroll even during the READING OF THE LAW.

The preparation of the Torah wrapping from the swaddling clothes of infants is an Ashkenazi custom. Families would decorate the cloth with pictures or embroidery, including wishes for the future of the infant. Once the child grew up, the cloth was dedicated to the synagogue.

Breastplate hung over the mantle of the Torah Scroll.

TORAH READING See READING OF THE LAW

TOSAFOT ("additions"). Series of commentaries on 30 of the tractates of the TALMUD; scholars have debated whether the word *tosafot* is meant to imply an "addition" to the talmudic text, or, what is more likely, to RASHI's commentary on the Talmud.

The *Tosafot* were not written by a single individual, but were the product of an entire school of scholars, known as the Tosafists, numbering about 300 individuals who lived in France and, later, Germany, between the 12th and the 14th centuries. About 100 of these are known by name. The school of the Tosafists began with Rashi's two sons-in-law, R. Meir ben Samuel and Judah ben Nathan, although the leading Tosafist was R. Meir's son, Rabbenu TAM. The *Tosafot* were the product of discussions in the different academies (*yeshivot*) of the Tosafists which were recorded by various individuals and then edited and re-edited over an extended period of time, with various emendations added during the process.

Unlike Rashi's commentary on the Talmud, which is a running elucidation of the talmudic text, the *Tosafot* deal with individual topics. The topics, many of which take Rashi's commentary as their starting point, seek to elaborate on the meaning of the text and the passage, often by juxtaposing passages in other tractates which appear to contradict the passage at hand. In dealing with the different passages, the *Tosafot* often arrive at alternate explanations to those offered by Rashi. The opening comment by the *Tosafot* on many tractates deals with the specific language with which the tractate commences and explains the choice of words.

An entire genre of books was developed by authors who attempted to defend Rashi against the questions posed by the *Tosafot*.

The accepted practice in printing the Talmud is to have the Talmud text in the center of the page, with Rashi's commentary on the inner margin of each page and the *Tosafot* on the outer margin (see TALMUDIC COMMENTARIES).

Using the same techniques employed in their commentary on the Talmud, the Tosafists also composed a commentary on the Bible, known as *Da'at Zekenim mi-Ba'alé ha-Tosafot*.

TOSEFTA ("addition"). Collection of tannaitic teachings supplementing those in the MISHNAH. The *Tosefta*, which is about four times as large as the Mishnah, is divided along the same lines. It, too, contains the same six "Orders" and their sub-division into the same tractates (although the Mishnah has at least three tractates — *Tamid, Middot,* and *Kinnim* — for which there is no *Tosefta* counterpart, while AVOT OF RABBI NATAN may or may not be the *Tosefta* equivalent of *Avot*). The Tosefta is composed of *baraitot* (tannaitic teachings not included in the Mishnah; see BARAITA), which are a major source for the talmudic discussion on any topic. Some of them are alternative versions of the Mishnaic text; others explain the Mishnah; while still others either add to the Mishnah or deal with fresh material.

The authorship of the *Tosefta* and the criteria for inclusion of its material have long been debated. The Talmud (*Sanh.* 61a) attributes the work to R. Nehemiah and states that the Mishnah is the work of R. MEIR. If this were true, it would explain the many similarities between the two works, for both men were students of R. AKIVA. There is, however, no clear evidence regarding R. Nehemiah's authorship. Also, many scholars seem to regard the collection as eclectic, perhaps made by compiling various traditions from different sources, even when the sources are mutually contradictory. Like the Mishnah, the *Tosefta* often brings two sides to a dispute, without determining the final decision.

Recent research has suggested that the *Tosefta*, as handed down, was unknown to the authors of either the Jerusalem or the Babylonian Talmuds, for there are numerous instances where the Talmud seeks to clarify questions which are clearly explained in the *Tosefta*. Nevertheless, it appears that the author or authors of the *Tosefta* were located in Erets Israel, for the style and substance of the *Tosefta* is much closer to that of the Jerusalem Talmud than to that of the Babylonian Talmud.

The *baraitot* contained in the *Tosefta* often offer the same text as the Mishnah, but there are instances where the two differ, sometimes only in wording but at other times also in content. On many occasions, the material found in the *Tosefta* has no counterpart in the Mishnah. As a rule, the Talmud accepts the Mishnah as the prime source for any interpretation and where a *baraita* argues with the Mishnah, the Mishnah is generally accepted as authoritative. Where there is a lacuna in the Mishnah, the *baraita* is generally regarded as binding. The definitive edition of the *Tosefta* is that of Saul LIEBERMAN, *Tosefta ki-Peshuta*.

TRADITION (*Masoret*). The complex of legal norms and folkways handed down orally from one generation to another, from teacher to disciple. The sages gave credibility to these oral traditions, not based on the Bible but accorded similar validity, anchoring them in the halakhic code (see ORAL LAW). Many of them are recorded in tractate EDUYYOT of the Mishnah. The rabbis said, "Tradition is a fence around the Torah" (*Avot* 3.13); that is to say, the oral tradition safeguards the observance of biblical law. To enhance the credibility of these traditions, many were imputed to have a Mosaic origin (HALAKHAH LE-MOSHEH MI-SINAI). However, talmudic commentators agree that in some instances this is not to be taken literally, the expression merely indicating that the tradition is of long standing and is universally accepted.

In a narrower sense, the term *Masoret* was employed by the sages to designate a deficient spelling in the Scriptural text, as opposed to MIKRA, the traditional manner in which the script was read (e.g., *s-k-t* [Lev. 23:42] can be read in the singular *sukkat*, but was read in the plural, *sukkot*; *Sanh.* 4a). Another term employed by the sages for the oral tradition is *kabbalah*.

In time, tradition came to encompass non-halakhic customs (see CUSTOM), which were considered as binding as rabbinic injunctions, as in the adage, "Israel's custom is (tantamount to) Torah," asserted by medieval authorities. Latter-day authorities, especially Ḥasidic, impute sanctity to traditions in dress, folkways at religious ceremonies such as circumcisions and weddings, special dishes for the various festivals, and traditional chants at synagogue services.

TRANSMIGRATION OF SOULS The concept of the soul's reappearing after death and entering a new body is first found as a positive idea in a Jewish context in the early works of the Kabbalah, from the late 12th century. It is absent in ancient Judaism, while the early Jewish medieval philosophers who mention it, do so to oppose it (SAADIAH GAON, Abraham bar Ḥiyya). The earliest work of the Kabbalah, the Book of BAHIR, presents it as God's way to give man another opportunity to atone for his sins and attain salvation after spending his first life as a wicked person. R. Isaac the Blind, the leading kabbalist in Provence in the late 12th-early 13th century, was reputed to be able to distinguish between an "old" and "new" soul, knowing the history of each soul through his supernatural powers. Almost all kabbalists from the 13th century, including the Zohar, used this concept in many ways and developed a specific terminology for it, the most common term being *gilgul* (an abbreviation of *gilgul-neshamot*).

The use of this concept in kabbalistic literature peaked in the 16th century, after the expulsion from Spain, in the kabbalistic center in Safed. The anonymous author of *Galya Raza* ("Revealer of Secrets") forcefully emphasized the element of the process of transmigration of souls as punishment for sins — the being into which one is transformed is determined by the nature of one's sins. The idea that man's soul can reappear in animals became common and Isaac LURIA identified a certain fornicator in a large black dog in Safed.

The most systematic treatment of this subject is found in the works of R. Ḥayyim VITAL, Luria's disciple. According to Vital's psychology, every one of the five parts of the soul migrates from body to body independently; thus every soul is a combination of elements which have lived several times in the past in different places and circumstances, each needing some form of *tikkun* (improvement). The influence of Vital's works made the concept of transmigration common in early modern Jewish mystical thought, including in the movement of SHABBETAI TSEVI. (See also DIBBUK for a related, though different, concept.)

TREE OF LIFE Tree, the eating of whose fruit confers immortality. The tree of life is referred to three times in the course of the story of ADAM in the GARDEN OF EDEN. In describing the latter, it is said "with the tree of life in the middle of the garden" (Gen. 2:9). After Adam's disobedience, God says "...what if he should stretch out his hand and take also from the tree of life and eat, and live forever!" (Gen. 3:22). Finally, after the expulsion of Adam and Eve from the Garden, God stations "the cherubim and fiery ever-turning sword, to guard the way to the tree of life" (Gen 3:24).

Many scholars see in the biblical tree of life an echo of a widespread myth in ancient Near Eastern literature of the existence of a magical plant the consumption of which would endow one with immortality, and "trees of life" are to be found in Sumerian and Egyptian literature. In the Garden of Eden story the implication appears to be that had Adam not disobeyed by eating the fruit of the tree of knowledge, he could have eaten of the tree of life and thereby gained immortality. The story gave an etiological explanation of human mortality.

The magical quality of the tree of life captivated the imagination of the authors of pseudepigrapha and the sages of the MIDRASH. According to the Midrash, the tree of life gave shade to the entire region and possessed no less than fifteen thousand tastes. It was so huge in diameter that it would take a man five hundred years to encircle it. From beneath its roots, there flowed the water that irrigated the earth and then flowed into the four rivers mentioned in the story of the Garden of Eden.

The writers of pseudepigrapha transplanted the tree, so to speak, from the Garden of Eden to paradise in the afterlife. This notion is not to be found in the older rabbinic literature, but is taken up by later Midrash. Generally speaking, the rabbis of the Midrash as well as the authors of apocrypha and pseudepigrapha took the story of the tree of life literally. The single exception among ancient writers was PHILO, who interpreted it allegorically. Beginning with the Arab period and the spread of philosophy among Jewish scholars, the tree of life as well as the Garden of Eden story as a whole is interpreted allegorically, notably by MAIMONIDES. The KABBALAH, while accepting the actual existence of the Garden of Eden, interprets the Tree of Life in a mystical-allegorical manner.

TRESPASS OFFERING See SACRIFICES AND OFFERINGS

TRIBES, TEN LOST The ten "lost" tribes consisted of the tribes of Reuben, Simon, Dan, Naphtali, Gad, Asher, Issachar, Zebulun, Ephraim, and half of Manasseh. They constituted the northern kingdom of Israel, that broke away from the kingdom of Judah after the death of King Solomon. In 722 BCE, the kingdom of Israel fell to the Assyrians under King Shalmaneser, who deported many Israelites to Halah and Habor by the river Gozan and to the cities of Medes (II Kings 17:6; 18:11). Not all Israelites, however, were deported (see II Chr. 35:17-19).

Although it was generally believed that the Israelites who were "carried away into Assyria" (II Kings 17:3) assimilated, a passage in I Chronicles 5:26 suggested that the lost tribes continue "unto this day." This belief was kept alive by prophetic utterances that God would gather in the "remnants of Israel" from the four corners of the globe (Isa. 11:12). Ezekiel (37:15-28) spoke of his vision of the union of Israel and Judah who would together partake of the blessings of messianic times (Zech. 8:13).

Belief in the continued existence of the "lost" ten tribes is maintained in the talmudic and midrashic literature. They were generally thought to reside on the other side of the legendary Sambatyon river, whose waters run regularly, though fiercely, during the week but rest on the Sabbath. Rabbis made attempts to identify the localities to which the ten tribes had been carried away. In the Jerusalem Talmud it is stated that only a third of the exiles live beyond the Sambatyon river, but all will eventually return (*Sanh.* 10:6, 29c). One opponent of this view was R. Akiva who stated that "the ten tribes shall not return again" (*Sanh.* 10:3).

Particularly during messianic periods, though intermittently until today, reports have been received of the "discovery" of lost tribes. The ninth-century traveler, Eldad ha-Dani, claimed to be a member of the tribe of Dan. He is generally thought to have originated in Ethiopia, although some scholars have associated him with Jews as far afield as China. In the second half of the 12th century, the Spanish traveler, Benjamin of Tudela, described the four tribes of Dan, Asher, Zebulun, and Naphtali who dwelt near the river Gozan. He also mentioned the tribes of Reuben, Gad and half of the tribe of Manasseh as living in Khaibar in Yemen. Similar references are found in the letters of the legendary Christian figure, Prester John. Reference to Prester John, the Sambatyon river and the lost tribes can be found in a 1488 letter by R. Obadiah di Bertinoro. In the 16th century, David Reuveni, purportedly of the tribe of Reuben, claimed to be the descendant of King Solomon and the brother of Joseph, the king of the descendants of the tribes of Reuben, Gad, and half of Manasseh, who were living in the desert of Khaibar (Habor) in Arabia. He claimed he was sent on a mission to Rome by the king of the "lost" Israelites in order to hasten the era of the redemption.

In 1644, Aaron Levi de Montezinos reported to Manasseh Ben Israel in Amsterdam that the Indians in South America were of the lost tribes. Ben Israel used this, and reports of other Jews dispersed the world over, as an argument to Oliver Cromwell to allow Jews to live in England on the grounds that the dispersal of Jews to all countries would bring the messianic return of Jews to the Holy Land. He published the idea that the Twelve Tribes will be joined together in the messianic age in his book, *Hope of Israel* (1650).

In the 19th century, many Jewish emissaries left Erets Israel for remote parts in order to search for the "lost" tribes. Noteworthy among these are Jacob Sapir (1822-1888), who visited Yemen and India and reported upon their dispersion in those countries, and Benjamin II (1818-1864), who emulated the medieval traveler Benjamin of Tudela.

Today, legends of descent from the "lost" ten tribes abound. Jewish communities of Kurdish, Bokharan and Indian (the Bené Israel) origin claim their forefathers were exiled from the Kingdom of Israel, while the Israel Chief Rabbinate has decided that the Jews of Ethiopia are from the tribe of Dan. In addition, a wide range of non-Jewish tribes and groups claim descent from the Israelites, ranging from sections of the Nigerian Yoruba tribe to the "Manipur Jews" from northeast India, who claim to be of the tribe of Manasseh. Fifteen million Pathans spread over Afghanistan and Pakistan (and Kashmir) are divided into sub-tribal groupings with names such as Reubeni (Reuben), Efridar (Ephraim) and Ashuri (Asher), leading to the suggestion that they come from the lost tribes. The British Israelites derive the word "British" from the Hebrew "*berit-ish*" (man of the covenant).

TRIBES, TWELVE The tribes into which the Israelites were originally divided. Traditionally, the tribes trace back to Jacob's 12 sons, born to him by his two wives and their maidservants. They were: Leah's sons Reuben, Simeon, Levi, Judah, Issachar, Zebulun; her maidservant Bilhah's sons Dan and Naphtali; Rachel's sons Joseph and Benjamin; her maidservant Zilpah's sons Gad and Asher.

The references to the Twelve Tribes do not always refer

The emblems of the Twelve Tribes. Beth El Synagogue, New Rochelle,

to the same 12. On occasion it is indeed to the 12 as listed above, whereas on other occasions, Joseph is counted as two tribes, Manasseh and Ephraim, in accordance with Jacob's statement to Joseph: "Your two sons, Ephraim and Manasseh... as Reuben and Simeon, they shall be mine" (Gen. 48:5). When Ephraim and Manasseh are counted as two tribes, the tribe of Levi is omitted from the count, because Levi was different from the other tribes in being delegated to serve God and teach the people and did not receive its own territory (see LEVITES). In the desert, the tribes were further divided into clans and the clans subdivided into families. The tribes were headed by *nesi'im* (pl. of NASI), variously translated as princes or chieftains. The tribes played an important role in the desert — a representative of each tribe helped Moses take the first census (Num. 1,2,4) and one man from each tribe was chosen to spy out the land of Canaan (Num. 3:2-15).

Once the tribes conquered Canaan, they occupied their own territories — accounts of the apportionment are found in the book of JOSHUA, 13-21 — and evidently formed a loose confederation without a central leader. They were bound together by their common belief in one God. Only with the inauguration of the kingdom under Saul came the first attempt at unification of all the tribes. This continued during DAVID's reign. In what was apparently an attempt to rid the tribes of their clannishness, SOLOMON divided his kingdom into 12 districts which often cut across tribal lines.

Later, the tribes split into two kingdoms; the southern kingdom of Judah included only Judah and Benjamin and the northern kingdom of Israel included the other ten tribes. The Levites were not included in either division and there were Levites and PRIESTS (who are also part of the tribe of Levi, tracing back to AARON), in both kingdoms. There were periods in which the two kingdoms were allied with each other, while in others they even went to war against each other. The existence of two kingdoms ended in 722 BCE, about 200 years after the split, when the Assyrians conquered the northern kingdom and exiled its inhabitants (see TRIBES, LOST TEN). Those who remained in the country assimilated among the other peoples living there; the SAMARITANS may well be the remnants of these assimilated peoples.

Twice in the Pentateuch all the tribes are blessed: first (Gen. 49), when Jacob blesses his sons just before his death, second (Deut. 33), when Moses, also before his death, blesses the tribes in the desert.

Certain schools of biblical scholarship have questioned the biblical account of the common origin of the 12 Tribes and suggest that they were individual groups thrown together by historical circumstances.

TRIENNIAL CYCLE The READING OF THE LAW in the synagogue based on completing the Pentateuch every three years. The practice of the reading in ancient Erets Israel developed gradually. The first stage consisted of reading on the Sabbath a short selection from each *Seder* (portion). In the second stage, the minimum number of verses to be read on any SABBATH was set at 21. Accordingly, it took between three and three and a half years to complete the entire Pentateuch, depending on the number of Sabbaths in the year.

The Triennial Cycle is reflected in the divisions to be found in a number of early Palestinian MIDRASHIM, notably LEVITICUS RABBAH. It is also reflected in the early Palestinian PIYYUT (religious poetry) whose themes conform to the cycle of reading as practised in Erets Israel.

While the Babylonian annual cycle of Pentateuch reading became the standard practice in the DIASPORA, the Triennial Cycle long remained in vogue in certain places. The traveler Benjamin of Tudela reported (c.1165) that in Cairo a synagogue frequented by Jews originating from Erets Israel still followed the Triennial Cycle. MAIMONIDES also referred to the practice but noted that it was not widespread.

In the 19th century, the German REFORM movement proposed the reinstitution of the Triennial Cycle. The suggestion, however, was not adopted. Instead, it became the practice in Reform synagogues to read approximately a third of each regular weekly Torah portion (*parashah*). It is this practice, or some variation of it, that is followed in Reform synagogues and in a number of Conservative synagogues in the United States.

TRUTH In Judaism, truth is represented as an ultimate ethical value both for the individual and for society as a whole. The rabbis teach, "The world exists on three things, on truth, on JUSTICE, and on PEACE" (*Avot* 1.18), for where there is truth, justice will necessarily follow and then will come peace — the greatest blessing for society. A similar idea is expressed in a comment on *emet*, the Hebrew word for truth, as containing the first, middle and last letters of the Hebrew alphabet; this is taken to indicate that from beginning to end, all basic personal and societal values are ideally built on truth. In Jewish ethics, truth is bracketed with other supreme human values.

Jewish ETHICS uncompromisingly stress the value and importance of truth in thought, speech and deed. However, recognizing that an individual's judgment may not always be reliable, the advice is not to judge as an individual but to strive for truth through a majority opinion. Further, since no one can be absolutely certain that his personal view represents the truth, a man should consider the alternative view before making his final assessment. This seems to have been the approach of the School of Hillel in their debates with the School of Shammai. It was because the Hillelites also studied the opinions of their opponents that their own conclusions had the stamp of greater truth (*Er.*, 13b).

While truth is a central value, Jewish ethics recognize that in certain circumstances there could be even higher values, for example, the preservation of life. In the case of a conflict between life and truth, life takes precedence.

Facade of the Herodian Temple. Part of a scale-model of the Holy City in Second Temple times, Jerusalem.

The rabbis were aware of the impossibility for man's finite mind to comprehend total truth. Total truth belongs to God alone. Thus, they declare that "the seal of God is truth" (*Shab.* 55a). Within this framework of ideas, Franz ROSENZWEIG said that truth is a value which can only be associated with God.

The characteristic direction of Jewish ethics is essentially practical in nature. Consequently, even while acknowledging that only God is truth, it submits the ethic of the IMITATION OF GOD, with its ideal for man to follow the "ways of God" and, as far as is humanly possible, to live with the practical details of a life of truth.

TSADDIK (pl. *tsaddikim*; "righteous," "just," and "charitable"). An individual outstanding in piety and faith; later, a Ḥasidic rabbi.

In the Bible, a *tsaddik* is contrasted with a *rasha* (wicked man), as in Genesis 18:25, when ABRAHAM argues with God against His destroying the righteous of Sodom and Gomorrah together with the wicked. Although God Himself is described as a *tsaddik* in the Bible (e.g., Deut. 32:4, Jer. 12:1, Ps. 11:7), the term usually denotes one who imitates God by embodying the ideal type of religious morality. The prophet Habakkuk says "the righteous man is rewarded with life for his fidelity" (2:4), while Isaiah envisions the Jewish people as righteous at the End of Days and thereby fit to reclaim their ancient homeland for all time (60:21).

The rabbis employed the term for one whose prayers are so fervent and sincere as to have the power to avert Divinely decreed disasters (*MK* 16b). The Talmud notes that the world rests upon the righteousness of 36 *tsaddikim* without whom it would collapse (see LAMED VAV TSADDIKIM). Several personalities from Scripture are deemed by the rabbis to have been *tsaddikim* and are so entitled whenever mentioned: Noah, Joseph, Samuel, Mordecai, and Esther (*tsaddikah*).

The kabbalists imbued the *tsaddik* with Divine power (including clairvoyance) and ascribed to him the role of intercessor between God and the Jewish people. Following this tradition, Ḥasidism crowned their charismatic dynastic leaders with this title, regarding them as the channel through which the Divine was communicated to the common people, and ascribing supernatural powers to them. They were regularly visited by their followers in pursuit of saintly advice and *segullot* (formulae for success or recovery from illness) who in return would make donations directed to charity or to the *tsaddik*'s personal income. Some lived in opulence; other confined themselves to a simple life, characterized by charitable acts. In general, the title was hereditary. In modern Ḥasidic communities, the title has been generally replaced by the Yiddish *Rebbe* ("Rabbi"), with the exception of those living in Israel who refer to their leaders as *Admor*, a Hebrew acrostic for "our lord, our teacher, and our rabbi."

TSADDIK, JOSEPH IBN (1075-1149). Spanish philosopher and poet. Little is known of his life, except that he was a *dayyan* in Cordoba from 1138. He wrote a considerable amount of poetry, but little has survived to the present. His major extant work, *Olam Katan*, or "Microcosm," has come down in a Hebrew translation of the original Arabic. It pictures the human being as a microcosm of the universe, uniting its corporeal and spiritual elements. Maimonides was greatly impressed with the author, whom he had known in his early days in Cordoba, although he evidently never saw this work. There is a marked similarity between Ibn Tsaddik's and Maimonides' conceptions of man. Ibn Tsaddik also wrote a work on logic, which has not survived.

TSEDAKAH See CHARITY

TSE'ENAH U-RE'ENAH (lit., "Go forth and behold", from Song of Songs 3:11). Title of a collection in Yiddish of various homiletic sources on the Pentateuch, composed in the 16th century specifically for women by Jacob ben Isaac Ashkenazi of Janov, Poland. The book is based on the Talmud, Rashi's commentary and the commentary of R. BAḤYA BEN ASHER. The book achieved immense popularity and was for centuries a staple for women throughout Eastern Europe, to be found in virtually every home. Some opposed the work, for it dealt with the material homiletically rather than in terms of the literal meaning of the text, but this opposition did not lead to any loss of popularity.

TSIDDUK HA-DIN See BURIAL

TSIMTSUM See LURIA, ISAAC AND LURIANIC KABBALAH

TSITSIT ("fringes"; also known as *arba kanfot*, "four corners"). Four-cornered fringed undergarment worn by observant Jewish males, based on the commandment, "They shall make for themselves fringes on the corners of their garments for all generations..." (Num. 15:38). It became customary for Jewish boys to begin wearing *tsitsit* at age three to accustom them to this *mitsvah*. Part of this commandment is to put a blue thread on each fringe (see TALLIT). The *tsitsit* is commonly made of wool or linen.

Until the 13th century, Jews traditionally wore a four-cornered garment on which the *tsitsit* was attached, and from then on they wore a special garment called the *tallit katan* ("little prayer-shawl") under the shirt. The fringes are prepared as on the *tallit gadol* ("large prayer shawl").

The obligation to wear *tsitsit* applies only to the daytime and women are exempt. In the reading of the SHEMA it is customary to take out the *tsitsit* at the relevant paragraph and to kiss the fringes at every mention of the word *tsitsit*.

TU BE-AV See AV, FIFTEENTH OF

TU BI-SHEVAT See NEW YEAR FOR TREES

Torah Scroll finials, partly gilt silver. Padua, Italy, 18th century.

U

UKTSIN (Stems of fruit and produce). Twelfth and last tractate of Order TOHOROT in the Mishnah. Its three chapters add further details to the laws of the susceptibility to uncleanness in food stated in previous tractates (KELIM, TOHOROT, MAKHSHIRIN). The Mishnah specifically deals with the parts of a fruit or vegetable (stem, stalk, shell, etc.) which do or do not protect against ritual uncleanness, the minimum amount of food necessary to impart food-uncleanness, the pit of the fruit, egg-shells, and rinds as conveyors of uncleanness, and the intention to eat the fruit and its susceptibility to uncleanness. As this is the last tractate of the Mishnah, it concludes its discussion of fit vessels with words of inspiration: "Rabbi Simeon ben Ḫalafta said. "The Holy One, blessed be He, found no vessel that could hold blessing for Israel except for peace, as it is said, 'May the Lord give strength to His people; may the Lord bless His people with peace'" (Ps. 29:11). The subject matter is amplified in the *Tosefta*.

U-NETANNEH TOKEF ("Let us declare [the utter holiness of this day]"). Opening words and name of a liturgical poem chanted in Ashkenazi congregations, during the reader's repetition of the Additional Service AMIDAH, on ROSH HA-SHANAH and the DAY OF ATONEMENT. It contains various dramatic motifs associated with these Days of Awe: "The great SHOFAR is sounded; the still small voice is heard; the angels are dismayed; fear and trembling seize hold of them as they proclaim: 'Behold the Day of Judgment!...'" God's decree concerning the fate of all mankind, recorded on the New Year and sealed on Atonement Day, is then elaborated, but there is also an assurance that "Penitence, Prayer, and Charity may avert the edict's severity."

According to a medieval Jewish folk tradition, *U-Netanneh Tokef* was first recited by R. Amnon of Mainz, a legendary German martyr, whose hands and feet had been cut off at the behest of a local archbishop when he refused to embrace Christianity. Having been carried into the synagogue on Rosh ha-Shanah, Amnon asked the cantor to pause before the KEDUSHAH and then chanted this prayer with his dying breath. Three days later, he appeared in a vision to R. Kalonymus ben Meshullam Kalonymus and taught him the poem; since the 11th century it has formed part of the Ashkenazi High Holiday liturgy.

The fact that an early manuscript version of *U-Netanneh Tokef* was discovered in the Cairo GENIZAH points to about 800 CE as its date of composition. The subsequent link with "R. Amnon of Mainz" was presumably intended to heighten the poem's martyrological importance for Ashkenazim during and after the Crusades.

UNIVERSALISM AND PARTICULARISM The religious concern for mankind as a whole as contrasted with the concern for those belonging to one's own faith. Jewish perspectives since biblical time have expressed both these tendencies, often with ambiguities and tensions. The very opening of the Bible is written from a universalist perspective, concerned with the origin of mankind and with God's concern for humanity. The corollary of its fundamental proclamation of the unity and fatherhood of God is the brotherhood of man.

A strong element of particularism entered with the COVENANT with ABRAHAM. However, while, as the result of the covenant, Abraham and his descendants become the people of God, the universalistic element is not forgotten when God explains "Through you and your descendants will be blessed the families of the earth" (Gen. 28:14).

The polarity continues throughout Jewish tradition. The Pentateuchal Code develops the particularistic aspects, Israel must remain distinct — in its worship, work and leisure, its diet, dress, family life and general conduct. Its origins and historical recollections are unique, in particular, the Exodus from Egypt and, at a later time, the messianic hope. However, Israel's special conduct is universalist because it is to be seen as exemplary. The nations of the world should exclaim, "Surely that great nation is a wise and discerning people. For what great nation is there whose God is so near... and has laws and rules as perfect as all this Teaching that I set before you this day?" (Deut. 4:6-8). The Pentateuchal Code, while concentrating on the inner life of the people, warns against particularistic prejudices and tendencies and stresses a humane social ethics to be applied to all men, Jew and non-Jew, notably the resident non-Jew, for "you shall not oppress or crush the alien; you know how he feels for you yourselves were aliens in the Land of Egypt".

It is in the words of the prophets that the universalist message of the Scriptures shines out most clearly. Isaiah and

Micah describe the End of Days when all nations shall say, "Let us go up to the mountain of the Lord, to the House of the God of Jacob who will teach us His ways and we will go in His paths... Nation shall not take up sword against nation and they will never again know war" (Isa. 2:3-4). Amos directs his prophecies not only to Israel but to the surrounding nations. The Book of Jonah is an outstanding example of a universal message with its contrast of the good faith of the pagan sailors and the repentance of the men of Nineveh with the bad faith and selfishness of the prophet of Israel.

Both tendencies are found in the early rabbis. The universalists stress that God's message is intended to reach the rest of the world. The many blessings recited by the Jew each day express a firm faith in God as the universal king. The most eminent of the *tannaim*, HILLEL, taught, "Be of the disciples of Aaron... loving all beings and attracting them to the Torah." The rabbis sought to attract proselytes to Judaism (see CONVERSION TO JUDAISM) and the third-century rabbi, Eleazar ben Pedat taught that "God exiled Israel among the nations only in order that they should add proselytes to their numbers" (*Pes.* 87b). The rabbis developed the concept of the basic natural laws, the NOACHIDE LAWS, which, if observed by non-Jews, would bring them life in the World to Come without the necessity to adhere to Judaism. This was in contrast with the narrower, particularistic teaching of salvation by CHRISTIANITY. Man, in rabbinic imagery, was created from dust gathered from all parts of the world so no one could claim superiority; the Torah was given to Israel in a no-man's land where all can come to share it; and it was delivered in 70 languages so that all mankind could understand it. At the same time, the rabbis expressed particularistic, nationalistic emotions, often directed against their oppressors. As in the Bible, God is seen as delivering the Israelites from their enemies. Israel's enemies are God's enemies.

Eventually, external circumstances dictated the internal balance in Jewish outlook between universalism and particularism. Christianity and ISLAM both claimed to have arrogated to themselves the Jewish "chosenness" and both sought to convert the Jews. Attempts by Jews to win proselytes was now a capital crime for both the Jew and the potential convert. Jews were excluded from the surrounding society and lived in virtual isolation. Under these circumstances, their particularistic tendencies came to the fore. They devoted themselves to their own culture, ceased attempts to win souls for Judaism, and in their anger and frustrations, developed anti-Gentile manifestations. Nevertheless, when they occasionally attained situations of comparative freedom, universalism came to the fore, and consolation was found in the thought that Christianity and Islam were extensions of Judaism. Thus, MAIMONIDES wrote: "All the matters concerning Jesus and Muhammad were only to lay out a path for the Messiah and to rectify the whole world to serve God together. The whole world is now filled with the idea of the Messiah, of Torah, and of the commandments". His basic attitude towards non-Jews was expressed in the belief that "God demands the heart, that things are to be judged according to the convictions of the heart, and that is why the sages said that the pious of all nations have a place in the World to Come if they know what is fit to be grasped of the knowledge of God and if they live a life of basic virtue." However, more prevalent throughout the Middle Ages was a strong particularism: the suffering was only explicable by contrasting Israel's election with the cruel world of the non-Jews. The frequently-expressed contempt for the Gentile and the pejorative expressions used were partly a defense mechanism.

The era of EMANCIPATION and Enlightenment, starting in the 18th century in Western and Central Europe, evoked a resurgence of universalism. Moses MENDELSSOHN identified the metaphysical content of Judaism with the universalized "religion of reason." Jews and non-Jews are both entitled to Divine love and salvation, while Judaism remained the private concern of the Jews. Now, released from the ghetto, the ancient concept of the Jewish MISSION to mankind, in which the Jews brought a theological message with a strong ethical stress, became the main thrust of REFORM JUDAISM, which removed from its liturgy all references seen as particularistic. This meant the omission of any mention of election and the chosen people, a personal messiah who would redeem the people of Israal, the link with the Land of Israel and any hope of a future return, or REWARD AND PUNISHMENT after death. Israel's chosenness lay in the moral message it conveyed to the rest of mankind. In the 20th century, Reform Judaism retreated from its extreme universalism, largely under the impact of the Nazi HOLOCAUST which dimmed the enthusiasm for universalism, brought a sense of self-reliance and, together with the establishment of the State of Israel, an intensive consciousness of Jewish peoplehood.

The Zionist movement also reflected the dichotomy between universalism and particularism in a basic argument over its ultimate objectives. One viewpoint held that the goal of the Jews' return to their own land was a process of normalization, expressed in the biblical phrase that Israel should "be like all other peoples (Ezek. 25:8). Others held that the restored people in Zion should be a "light to the nations" (Isa. 42:6), i.e., provide a universal inspiration. The development of the State of Israel has continued to reflect this ambiguity and conflict. Its official religious life is strongly particularistic and this contrasts, and potentially clashes, sharply with the predominating universalism or cosmopolitanism of most of Diaspora Jewry.

UNLEAVENED BREAD See MATSAH

URIM AND THUMMIM (etymology unclear). An oracle worn by the HIGH PRIEST inside his breastplate, used for discovering God's judgment. The Bible commands (Ex.

28:30), "Inside the breastplate of decision you shall place the Urim and Thummim," but it does not explain what they are. The breastplate in which the Urim and Thummim were placed was one of the eight garments worn by the High Priest and included four columns of precious stones, upon which the names of the 12 tribes were engraved (see PRIESTLY GARMENTS).

According to a rabbinic tradition, through the Urim and Thummim certain letters would light up on the breastpiece, and the high priest could then form these letters into an answer to his questions. Scholars believe that it was a form of divination by the use of lots.

The Bible mentions many cases of questions addressed to the Urim and Thummim, primarily regarding going to war, but also in other matters. God commands Moses to appoint Joshua, "He shall present himself to Eleazar the priest, who shall on his behalf seek the decision of the Urim before the Lord. By such instruction they shall go out and by such instruction they shall come in, he and all the Israelites, the whole community" (Num. 27:21-22; Deut. 33:8).

Also, when it came to dividing the land among the tribes, the lots drawn were authenticated by the Urim and Thummim (Deut. 33:8). King Saul turned to the Urim and Thummim when he wanted to know his fate (I. Sam. 38:6). There is no mention of their use after the time of David. After the return of the exiles from Babylonia, the priests were ordered not to eat of the most holy things until a priest "with Urim and Thummim" could confirm that they were truly of priestly descent (Ezra 2:63).

USHPIZIN (Aram. "guests"). The seven mystical guests who, according to Jewish MYSTICISM, visit the tabernacle (SUKKAH) every day during the festival of SUKKOT; they are ABRAHAM, ISAAC, JACOB, JOSEPH, MOSES, AARON, and DAVID. The source for this visitation is the verse in the ZOHAR which says, "When one sits in the *sukkah*, Abraham and six righteous men come to share his company" (Zohar 5.103b). Each one in turn is seen as leading the others into the *sukkah* on successive nights of the festival.

It is customary to invite these seven guests into the *sukkah* each night with a special request, reading in part, "May it be Your will, Lord my God, and God of my fathers, that the Divine Presence will dwell in our midst...I hereby invite these exalted guests to dinner — Abraham, etc." This custom, originally adopted by the kabbalists and later by the Ḥasidim, has now been adopted by many Orthodox Jews. The sages said that to merit the visit of these seven distinguished guests, one must also invite guests of flesh and blood from among the poor, and it was a custom to invite a needy student to sit at the head of the table to deputize for the special *ushpizin* guest of the evening. In the Kabbalah each of the guests corresponds to one of the SEFIROT (attributes of God). Each day, it is held, one of these attributes dominates the atmosphere of the *sukkah*. It became customary to include among the decorations of the *sukkah* a plaque mentioning the seven "guests."

USURY Lending on interest. The Pentateuch (Ex. 22:24) stresses that no interest may be exacted on a loan to "the poor of your people". This is extended (Lev. 25:35-37) to the prohibition of usury on a loan given to the resident alien and a loan of food. A further passage (Deut. 23:20-1) however permits the taking of interest from a non-Israelite.

The law is explainable in terms of an agrarian society in which a loan was aimed to tide a farmer over until his next crop and is regarded as a deed of kindness. The non-Israelite envisaged in the last passage is probably the itinerant merchant who used the loan for commercial purposes.

Scripture uses two terms for interest, *neshekh*, literally "bite", and *tarbit*, i.e., "increase". Scholars tried to determine whether there is a difference between the two. According to the Talmud, there is no difference, and the use of two terms is meant to teach that a person who takes interest violates two negative commandments. The WISDOM books of the Bible warn against the moral offense of taking interest. The prophets (e.g., Ezek. 22:12) bracket it with such offenses as taking a bribe and spilling blood.

The Talmud gives the biblical law a wide application. Accordingly, not only he who exacts interest is guilty of violating the law but so are the creditor, the scribe who wrote the note of indebtedness, as well as the witnesses who affixed their signatures to it. Moreover, the Talmud develops a whole category of acts which it calls *avak ribbit* ("the dust of interest") which are forbidden. This category includes acts by which the creditor may benefit in any way from his loan.

The development of commerce in the talmudic-age made these laws particularly onerous, and various legal means were devised in order to circumvent them. One of these was the arrangement whereby the creditor became a partner in the debtor's commercial enterprise and shared in its profits and was guaranteed against any loss. In the Middle Ages, a legal device was established (*hetter iskah* — literally, "permission of business") whereby the lender becomes a partner in the borrower's business, shares in its profits, and is guaranteed against loss. Under this arrangement, the borrower receives a nominal sum for his services.

VAKHNAKHT See SHALOM ZAKHAR

VIDDU'I See CONFESSION OF SINS

VIOLENCE Unlawful use of force to injure a person or a resort to intimidation by threatening such action against others. The first crime recorded in the Bible is the slaying of Abel by Cain (Gen. 4:8), and the first crime listed in the Ten Commandments is MURDER. The great FLOOD was a Divine punishment for lawlessness and violence (*ḥamas*; Gen. 6:11-13), while Jacob condemned his sons Simeon and Levi for their ruthless violence against the men of Shechem (Gen. 34:30, 49:5-7). The Day of Atonement liturgy at its climax, in the NE'ILAH (Concluding Service), affirms that this day was given to Israel "so that we should cease from violence" (*oshek*).

Jewish law nevertheless recognized that to act violently or aggressively is human, and a blanket pacifism was never endorsed. Realizing that it could not eliminate this tendency, Judaism sought to confine violent action within a framework of holiness and dignity. A stand must be adopted between aggressors and victims, and the sages were unanimously in favor of self-defense: "If one comes to slay you, slay him first" is the rabbinic formulation (Num. R. 21.5; *Sanh.* 72a). One forfeits one's own life, however, by becoming an aggressor. When someone told RAVA that he had been ordered to kill another man or forfeit his own life, Rava answered: "Better let that official kill you. What makes you think that your blood is redder than his [the intended victim's]? Perhaps his blood is redder than yours!" (*Pes.* 25b).

Faced with violence, Jews could react in four different ways: by self-defense (whenever possible), by choosing martyrdom, by taking flight, or by seeking an accommodation (the MARRANO solution). As far as a resort to violent action is concerned, the *halakhah* permitted extreme violence only as a means of preserving life. Limited violence was allowed to defend one's religious convictions or property, but killing a burglar is permitted only when the householder has reason to fear for his own life. In defending oneself or others, where life can be saved through wounding the aggressor it would be murder to take his life (*Sanh.* 72b). This principle is derived from the biblical law on housebreaking and robbery (Ex. 22:2).

Under no circumstance is violence permitted for the sake of revenge, although violent action may be lawful when dealing with criminals. Here, a standard example is the use of force to liberate persons held in captivity and whose very lives are at stake; operations against kidnapers, hijackers, and "skyjackers" would be the modern equivalent (see CAPTIVES, RANSOMING OF). See also WAR.

VIRGINITY The state of being a virgin (in Hebrew, *betulah*), a girl who has not had sexual intercourse with a man. In Jewish tradition, virginity is an ideal for all unmarried women. The High Priest could marry only a virgin (Lev.21:14); the other priests could also marry widows but not divorced women.

An engaged girl was regarded as a virgin between the time of BETROTHAL — *erusin* — and MARRIAGE — *nissuin*. If a man married a woman presumed to be a virgin and proved that she had ceased to be a virgin due to intercourse with another man during the betrothal period (*Sanh.* 7:4), the woman was put to death by stoning (Deut. 22: 20-21). If his charge of unchastity against her was proven false, he had to pay a fine to her father and could never divorce her (Deut.22:19). The wedding of a virgin usually took place on a Wednesday, for if the husband wanted to accuse her of not being a virgin, he could take his case to court which used to sit on Thursdays (*Ket.* 2a). In the marriage contract (KETUBBAH) which a groom gave his bride at the wedding ceremony, it was stipulated that if she was a virgin, his estate would provide a minimum of 200 *zuz* for her sustenance upon divorce compared to a minimum of 100 *zuz* provided if he married a widow.

A girl below the age of three who was sexually abused does not thereby lose her virgin status (*Nid.* 5:4). It is also assumed that all girls are virgins prior to marriage, a testimony to the morality practiced in ancient times.

The Talmud records situations where foreign rulers exercised the right of first act of sexual intercourse with Jewish brides. The sages changed the wedding day from Wednesdays to Tuesdays in order to anticipate such an action and thereby protect the brides.

VISITING THE SICK (*bikkur ḥolim*). To visit and comfort the sick and attend to his needs is a major commandment in the Jewish tradition. The Talmud states that visiting a sick person takes away 1/60 of his sickness, while failing to do so may lead to the sick person's death (*Ned.* 39b). According to the Midrash, God Himself visited ABRAHAM when the Patriarch was recovering from his circumcision.

According to the rabbis, when in the presence of the sick, one should not sit on a high chair, or on the bed, or above the patient's head. One may ask the sick man what are his requirements and whether he needs financial assistance (*Kol. Bo*, 112). In his will, R. Eleazar the Great wrote: "My son, pay careful attention to visiting the sick, because one who visits him lessens his illness. Entreat him to return to his Creator, and pray for him, and then leave. Let not your presence be a burden to him, because he has enough of a burden with his illness. When you go to visit a person who is sick, enter joyfully, because his eyes and heart are directed to those who enter to visit him." The 12th century *Sefer Hasidim* (361) has this to say: "If a poor man is sick and a rich man is sick, and people go to visit the rich man in order to show him respect, go you to the poor man, even if the rich man is learned, because there are many people present with him, and no one goes to visit the poor."

The highly organized Jewish communities of earlier periods contained special *bikkur holim* societies, whose members visited the sick and attended to their needs.

VITAL, HAYYIM (1542-1620). Kabbalist, who studied in Safed with Moses Alshekh. When Isaac LURIA came to Safed in 1570, Vital became his most prominent student and follower, and Luria said that no one understood his teachings better than Vital. After Luria's death, Vital claimed that he alone possessed accurate notes on his teacher's doctrines, and disqualified other versions. He also believed that the spirit of the Messiah Ben Joseph had passed from Luria to him. He achieved a reputation as a wonder-worker and many turned to him to exorcise DIBBUKS. From 1577 to 1585, he headed a *yeshivah* in Jerusalem. In his lifetime, he refused to publish any of his works, but when he was ill, others managed to remove manuscripts from his possession and copy them. They included his account of Luria's teachings, eventually published under the title *Ets ha-Hayyim*, regarded as the basic work of Lurianic Kabbalah. Vital spent his last years in Damascus.

Allegoric picture from The Tree of Life *by Hayyim Vital. Manuscript, Central Europe, 18th century.*

VOWS AND VOWING A commitment to God to perform a particular act or to abstain from committing something otherwise permitted. A vow can be undertaken by a solemn oath, although the term "oath" is taken to refer especially to an understanding made in a law court, while in the Bible an "oath" carries with it the implication of a curse, if the oath proves false or is violated.

Vows are discussed in Numbers 30:1-16, which includes the regulation: "When a man vows a vow to the Lord or takes an oath imposing an obligation upon himself, he shall not break his pledge; he must carry out all that has crossed his lips." The passage also contains provisions for a husband to cancel the vows of his wife and for a father to cancel the vows of his minor daughter. The inviolability of a vow is reflected in the story of King Saul who sent his soldiers to pursue the Philistines under a vow to refrain from eating until evening. When his son Jonathan unknowingly violated the vow, Saul's decision was to put him to death and this was only averted by the demand of the people (I Sam. 14:24-45). A more tragic denouement resulted from Jephthah's vow to sacrifice the first thing he would see emerging from the door of his house. When his daughter came out, he kept his vow (Judg. 11:30-40).

The most common vow in ancient times was a pledge to bring a sacrifice (votive offering) and the Pentateuch describes the procedure for such a SACRIFICE to the Temple (Lev. 7:16-17). Such vows would be made in situations of danger or distress (Ps. 66:13-16). The vow may be conditional upon God's granting a favor. Thus Hannah vowed that if she had a male child, he would be devoted to the service of God (I Sam. 1:11). A specific type of oath was of some form of abstinence, notably in the case of the NAZIRITE. However, the Bible warns against taking vows which possibly cannot be fulfilled: "Better not to vow than to vow and not pay" (Eccl. 5:3-4).

Jewish law uses three terms for the vow: *neder*, the most general term; *nedavah*, the freewill offering, pledging a gift to God; and *shevu'ah*, the oath undertaking to pursue or not pursue certain courses of action. The *neder* and *nedavah* pledging a sacrifice or dedicating property to the Temple have been inoperative since the destruction of the Temple; the subject is discussed in the Mishnaic Order, *Kodashim*. Vows and their annulment are the subject of Tractate NEDARIM (the Nazirite oath is dealt with in Tractate NAZIR).

The sages of the Talmud, recognizing the problem of

vows made in haste and subsequently not fulfilled, disparaged the taking of vows, with Samuel going so far as to declare "Even when one fulfills his vow he is called wicked" (*Ned.* 22a).

The *halakhah* recognizes the possibility of annulling a vow retroactively. The procedure involves searching for factors which the individual had not taken into account or facts unknown to him at the time of taking the vow.

As a result of the Talmud's negative attitude on vowing, the practice has largely disappeared, although the *Shulhan Arukh* (*YD* 203:7) permits it for the purpose of ridding oneself of bad habits. The one widespread exception is the practice of vowing a contribution to the synagogue or to some charity upon being called to the READING OF THE LAW. Another custom that arose was the practice of annulling vows each year on the eve of ROSH HA-SHANAH. The formula for this involves making a declaration before a panel of three regretting any vows taken during the year, whether intentional or unintentional. The three then pronounce the vows annulled. At the same time, the individual declares that it is his intention that nothing he may say over the course of the coming year receive the force of a vow. The KOL NIDRÉ formula recited on the eve of the DAY OF ATONEMENT concerns the annulment of unwitting or rash vows.

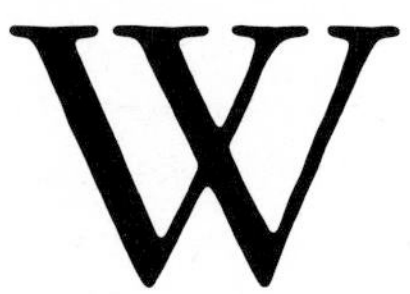

WAR Armed conflict between states and peoples which, in the ancient world, also involved their respective gods. If a nation was defeated, so was its deity. The Bible thus portrays Israel's God as "the Warrior" (Ex. 15:3), "valiant in battle" (Ps. 24:8), who "goes forth like a man of war, a fighter" (Isa. 42:13), and marches at the head of His army (Ps. 68:8). Israel's wars are God's wars, hence the symbolic appearance of the Ark of the Covenant, which is carried onto the battlefield in the days of Moses (cf. Num. 10:35-36) and, later, in the period of the monarchy (I Sam. 14:18, II Sam. 11:11). Battles fought against the Amalekites, who had cut down the stragglers of Israel's rearguard in the wilderness, were also considered to be God's battles: not only had the Amalekites violated His laws of compassion for the weak, they had even dared to attack His people (Deut. 25:17-19). These two aspects could be separated, however, as God and His devotees would declare war on Israelites who lapsed into idolatry (cf. Ex. 32:25-29; Deut. 13:13-19). This is the primary issue in the Book of Deuteronomy's regulations concerning war. All idolators, whether Canaanite or Israelite, were to be uprooted from God's land. Since the Israelites had entered into a covenant with God, the terms of which made them vassals owing Him allegiance, they could be destroyed if they flouted that covenant by transferring their allegiance to another overlord (a provision characteristic of the covenantal treaties entered into by ancient Near Eastern empires).

The laws of warfare are spelled out in Deuteronomy (20:1-20) and amplified in the Mishnah (*Sot.* 8). Before going into battle, soldiers are exhorted by the priests not to panic at the sight of the enemy's might. Officers then grant exemption to four categories: men who had built a new home but not yet dedicated it; those who had planted a vineyard but not yet tasted its fruit; those who had betrothed a wife but had still to consummate the union; and anyone whose faintheartedness might weaken the army's morale. In addition, both the soldiers and their camp had to be in a state of holiness (Deut. 23:10-15). Before a town is stormed, its inhabitants should be offered peace terms; their fruit trees are not to be cut down, even in the event of a prolonged siege. If any Canaanite town refuses to surrender, all of its inhabitants must be annihilated, a measure aimed at preventing the likely spread of idol worship were these pagans to remain alive. In the case of towns captured far away, where permanent occupation is not envisaged by the Israelites, only adult males are to be killed; everyone else may be taken as the spoils of war.

It was Israel's firm belief that God could never be defeated. If, therefore, Israel should suffer a reverse, it had to be the outcome of faithlessness, of a betrayal of God's covenant with His people. Thus, when they tried to enter the Promised Land against His will and were promptly routed by their enemies (Num. 14:45), God had in fact been vindicated. Similarly, in the era of the Judges, any shift in the fortunes of war is attributed not to military prowess or the number of troops involved but to Israel's religious faithfulness or disloyalty. Significantly, however, David was precluded from building God's holy Temple because he had "shed much blood" as "a man of battles" (I Chr. 22:8, 28:3). The task of building a Sanctuary in Jerusalem, the City of Peace, had to await a more tranquil age and a ruler whose very name — Solomon — voiced the concept of PEACE (*shalom*).

Three categories of war are designated in the Mishnah (*Sot.* 8.7): *milḫemet ḫovah*, "obligatory" because of enemy aggression; *milḫemet mitsvah*, "commanded by God" and the Torah; and *milḫemet ha-reshut*, an "optional" war of political significance only. Campaigns of the first type, limited to the destruction of Amalek and the Canaanite nations, were historically obsolete. Wars falling under the third category, for the purpose of extending Israel's borders or improving the economy, could only be waged by the king after he had obtained the consent of a 71-member Sanhedrin. The second category, wars of self-defense and national survival, had the only remaining practical application. For such a war, even the biblical exemptions (see above) had to be suspended: a newly married couple must take part in the fighting as a sacred duty; and Sabbath prohibitions could also be waived in the interests of national defense (*Tosef. Er.* 4.5-9).

While this concept of a "holy war" proved vital in Hasmonean times (cf. I Macc. 3.21), most of the sages, when the Jews no longer enjoyed independence, had no firsthand knowledge of warfare. A dress sword worn on the Sabbath they considered not an "ornament" but a disgrace, and they tended to explain away military allusions found in the Bible. One amoraic scholar believed that the weapon of the hero in Ps. 45:4 meant "the sword of the Torah." The wars and battles of the Bible had faded into a distant past, and now the struggle against Rome was also becoming a vague memory. Talmudic analysis and codification of the laws governing war must thus be regarded as largely theoretical.

During the Middle Ages, a horror of warfare became ingrained in Jews because of their suffering at the hands of various conquering armies, particularly the European crusaders. Jewish participation in military operations was limited to Arabia and the Maghreb, where Judaizing tribes fought unsuccessful battles against the Muslims; to Ethiopia, where the Beta Israel ("Falashas") were eventually defeated by native Christians; and to southern Russia and the Caucasus region, where Judaizing KHAZARS formed a wedge between Christian Byzantium and Muslim Persia. Another rare instance of generalship was displayed by Granada's Jewish vizier, Samuel ha-Nagid (993-1056), the statesman and poet who led his armies against rival Muslim principalities and who died in the midst of one such campaign.

The process of Jewish emancipation, from the late 18th century, together with new sociopolitical conditions in Europe and America, had the inevitable effect of converting military service into a live issue for Jews, who now fought under many banners. Halakhic authorities such as Moses SOFER dealt with the question in their responsa: a minority concluded that a Jew should not risk his life in non-Jewish wars, but the weight of halakhic opinion was in favor of Jews discharging their civic duty and serving in the army of the motherland. Rabbi Israel Meir Kagan (ḤAFETS ḤAYYIM), for example, noted that all the enactments applying to Jewish kings also apply to non-Jewish rulers whose maintenance of law and order benefits their Jewish subjects. However, there is consistent and unanimous condemnation of any Jew opting to serve as a mercenary.

Israel's War of Independence (1948-49) was regarded in most Orthodox religious circles as a *milḥemet mitsvah*, a justified war. The same approval was given to Israel's later wars. However, the 1982 Lebanon War led to a division of religious views, some authorities defining it as a *milḥemet ḥa-reshut*, an optional war, undertaken for purposes beyond legitimate defense.

Since the early years of the State, a consensus of opinion has been achieved within Israel regarding matters of national security. This finds religious expression in the directives issued by the military rabbinate governing conduct in time of war and the waiving of Sabbath prohibitions, etc., in an emergency situation that involves "danger to life" (see PIKKU'AḤ NEFESH).

WASHING OF HANDS See ABLUTIONS

WATER-DRAWING FESTIVAL Ceremony held in the TEMPLE on the night following the first day of the SUKKOT festival and thereafter on each night of the festival. It celebrated the water libation which followed the morning sacrifice on each day of the festival. The water libation was a matter of dispute between the PHARISEES, who regarded it as being an oral tradition handed down from Sinai, and the SADDUCEES, who saw no basis for it. The name "water-drawing ceremony" is derived from Isaiah 12:3: "Joyfully shall you draw water from the fountains of triumph." King Alexander Yannai, a Sadducee, deliberately poured the water on his feet as a sign of his contempt for the entire ritual, and was pelted by the people with the citrons used for the Sukkot festival (*Suk.* 34a). Probably because of the opposition of the Sadducees, great emphasis was placed by the Pharisees on celebrating the water libation, which was an exceptionally joyful time. The Mishnah states: "He who has not seen the rejoicing of the water-drawing ceremony (in the Temple) has never seen rejoicing in his life" (*Suk.* 5.1). The great sages joined the festivities, and R. Simeon ben Gamaliel I was reputed to have juggled with eight lighted torches at the water-drawing ceremony, without allowing a single torch to touch the ground (*BB.* 53). The sages danced with the people to music supplied by the Levites and would not sleep the entire night, but would doze off on each other's shoulders. To add to the festivities, huge bonfires were lit throughout Jerusalem, lighting up the entire city. In Israel's contemporary kibbutzim, attempts have been made to revive the festival in a modern form.

WAVE OFFERING See SACRIFICES AND OFFERINGS

WEDDING See ḤUPPAH; MARRIAGE

WEEKS, FESTIVAL OF See SHAVU'OT

WESTERN WALL (*Ha-Kotel ha-Ma'aravi*). A portion of the western retaining wall of the TEMPLE MOUNT in JERUSALEM, most important of Jewish HOLY PLACES. During the reign of Herod the Great (first century BCE), the Temple Mount was expanded by closing the perimeter with great retaining walls, filling in the gap formed between the retaining walls and the original slopes with a system of domed vaults, leveling the top of the peak, and covering the vaults with earth. The longest of the retaining walls was the western one, measuring 1,580 feet (485 meters) from north to south. That portion of the wall revered today as a holy place is a 195ft. (60m.) strip located toward the southern end. It cannot be determined precisely when it became customary to offer prayers exclusively at this spot.

The wall was constructed of enormous stones, most of which weighed between two and eight tons, although some weighed as much as 40 or 50 tons and a few weighed more than 100. Today, seven rows of the original Herodian stones may be seen above ground level; above these are another four or five rows of somewhat smaller stones added at the time of the construction of the El Aksa Mosque (early eighth cen-

The Western ("Wailing") Wall of Herod's Temple showing the typical Herodian masonry of the Temple enclosure.

tury CE). Several layers of smaller stones which cannot be dated with any accuracy lie above these, while the top three rows of white stones were added by the Muslim Religious Council in recent years as part of general repairs to the Temple Mount.

According to the Midrash (*Ex.R.* 2.2; *Num.R.* 11.2; *Lam.R.* 1.31), the "western wall" was never destroyed because the Divine Presence (SHEKHINAH) rests there. Interpretation of this tradition is difficult, since on the one hand, no original wall of the Temple itself remains, while all four retaining walls can still be seen. Since the retaining walls were not endowed with any particular holiness, it is difficult to imagine that the sages were referring to the western retaining wall. It has been suggested that perhaps the western wall of the Temple was originally left standing by the Romans and was only later destroyed, or alternately, that the reference is symbolic — since the Divine Presence resided on the western wall (of the HOLY OF HOLIES) and since the Divine Presence never departed, it is as though the western wall was never destroyed. In any case, the walls of the Temple Mount seem to have taken on greater importance after the destruction, since they were the only concrete remnants of the Temple, and it is the application of the midrashic tradition to the western retaining wall that is responsible for the special place that it ultimately assumed in Jewish consciousness.

The significance of the present site seems to be relatively recent. During the geonic period, the preferred place of assembly and prayer was the Mount of Olives. Benjamin of Tuleda (12th century CE) mentions the western wall, but none of the other medieval visitors to Jerusalem nor scholars who lived there refers to it. Only after the Ottoman conquest of Palestine (1517) is the Western Wall mentioned as an important holy place. It has been suggested that the site's location within the city walls and its easy accessibility from the Jewish quarter helped raise its status at this time. From then onward, the site became increasingly revered by Jews, who began to identify it with ancient traditions. It became famous among Jews throughout the world, with representations appearing in synagogues, books and on various ritual objects. Jewish pilgrims to Jerusalem always visited it, now believing the Western Wall to be the holiest place in Judaism short of the Temple Mount, which was in any case forbidden to entry. It was at this time also that non-Jews began referring to the site as the "Wailing Wall" after witnessing the Jews there mourning the destruction of the Temple. During this entire period, only a small area approximately 91 ft (28 m.) by 11.5 ft (3.5 m.) was available to worshipers.

Toward the end of the 19th century, the Wall also began to symbolize the Jewish people's nationalist aspirations. As such, it became a point of contention between the Muslims and the Jews. The two communities struggled over such issues as whether it was permitted to sound the SHOFAR at the Wall or to introduce benches or a table from which a SCROLL OF THE LAW could be read. It was during this period also that the Western Wall replaced the eastern or southern retaining walls in Muslim tradition as *al-Burak*, the place where Muhammad had tethered his horse while he ascended heavenward from the Temple Mount.

Prayer offered at the Western Wall is deemed to be particularly efficacious. R. Jacob Ettlinger (19th century) wrote: "Since the gate of Heaven is near the Western Wall, it is understandable that all Israel's prayers ascend on high through there." A common custom is to write requests on slips of paper and place them in the wall.

Many other customs have developed around the Western Wall. At one time those visiting the Wall would remove their shoes. People going on journeys would break off small pieces of the Wall to take with them, although this practice was frowned upon. Pious women would draw lots for the honor of cleaning the area of the Western Wall. However, these and many other customs have fallen into disuse.

When the Jewish quarter of the Old City surrendered to the Arab Legion in 1948, the Western Wall came under the control of the Hashemite Kingdom of Jordan. According to the armistice agreement, Jews were to be permitted access to their holy places within Arab-held Jerusalem. The Jordanian government did not, however, honor this agreement and not until 7 June 1967, when Israeli paratroopers captured the Old City, were Jews again able to worship at their holiest place. A large plaza was cleared in front of the Wall and it became a formal place of worship, with separate areas for men and women. Many boys from Israel and the Diaspora celebrate their BAR MITSVAH there. The Western Wall is the focus of national as well as religious sentiment. National ceremonies are held there and certain units of the Israel Defense Forces are sworn in at the Wall. The site is administered by the Israel Ministry of Religions.

WHOLE-OFFERING See SACRIFICES AND OFFERINGS

WIDOW AND ORPHAN Beginning with the Bible, Judaism has always recognized the special needs of the widow and the orphan. Both the widow, a married woman whose husband has died, and the orphan, a child whose mother or father has died, are frequently classed together in the Bible, for they are among the helpless in society. Therefore, the Bible warns: "You shall not ill-treat any widow or orphan" (Ex. 22:21). This theme is reiterated in the prophets, "Uphold the rights of the orphan; defend the cause of the widow" (Isa. 1:17). The Psalmist cries to God for retribution from the wicked for "they kill the widow and stranger; they murder the fatherless" (Ps. 94:8). Special legislation is enacted for their protection (Deut. 24:7).

The sages express similar sensitivities regarding the widow and the orphan. R. Yosé said: "Anyone who robs a widow or an orphan, is as if he robbed God" (Ex.R. *Mishpatim* 30.8). "Who is one who performs charity continuously? He who raises an orphan" (*Ket.* 50a).

Aside from expressing their concern, the sages legislated a variety of laws which benefit the widow and orphan. Since the widow does not inherit her deceased husband's estate (it reverts to the children), the rabbis found it necessary to safeguard the widow financially and instituted the KETUBBAH, the marriage contract, which served as an insurance policy which was paid to the wife after her husband died (*Ket.* 4.2). If her deceased husband was owed money, the debt is to be paid to the widow (*Ket.* 9.2).

The Talmud also reflects the problems a widow encountered in finding a home. At times, she returned to her father's house. Under other circumstances, she went to live with her in-laws or she became the guardian of her children and remained in her deceased husband's home. As guardian, she was required to report to the local court concerning the expenses paid from the estate incurred in feeding and clothing her children (*BB* 9.6). If the widow lives alone, she must be careful not to take in lodgers, for people might suspect her of licentious behavior (*A.Z.* 22a).

A person who has lost either a father or a mother and is incapable of fending for him- or herself is considered an orphan in Jewish law. There is no age limit to this status (Maimonides, *Yad, De'ot* 6.10). If a young girl is given in matrimony by her father and then divorced before she reaches her majority, she is given the status of orphan, even though both of her parents are alive (*Ket.* 73b). The community is obligated to assist an orphan in paying for a marriage celebration. A girl orphan takes precedence over a boy orphan in receiving such assistance (*Ket.* 67a).

Widows play a secondary role in two further commandments. The first is the obligation of a brother-in-law to marry the widow of his brother if the latter died without leaving any children (LEVIRATE MARRIAGE). The purpose of this commandment is to insure that the name of the deceased will not be blotted out. The second commandment is that which prohibits the HIGH PRIEST from marrying or having intercourse with a widow. Here the focus is on the High Priest. He is obligated to marry a virgin and is prohibited from marrying any woman who is not a virgin.

MAIMONIDES in his *Sefer ha-Mitsvot*, Negative Commandment no. 256, writes: "It is forbidden to deal harshly with fatherless children and widows, whether by word or by deed. We must speak to them very gently and kindly, treat them as well as we possibly can, show the most favorable disposition toward them, and set ourselves a very high standard in all these matters."

WINE The Bible ascribes to Noah the first vineyard, from whose fruit he made and drank wine (Gen. 9:20-21). Wine was one of the products of the Land of Israel, which the Pentateuch cites as a sign of the land's fertility and abundance (Gen. 49:11; Deut. 33:28). Widespread production of wine in ancient Israel has been confirmed by archeological finds.

As a beverage, it regularly accompanied the main meal of the day. Wherever the Bible mentions "cup" — for example, "my cup brims over" (Ps. 23:5) — the reference is to a cup of wine, which is said to "gladden the heart of man" (Ps. 104:15).

Wine played a prominent role in ritual and religious usage. The Torah stipulates the amount of wine to be poured on the altar as a libation in connection with each type of sacrifice (e.g., Num. 28-29). It was the practice, later developed into a ritual, to offer mourners a cup of wine. The practice is reflected in the verse "Give... wine to the bitter in soul" (Prov. 31:6).

This widespread use of wine inevitably led in some instances to drunkenness, a state strongly condemned in the Bible and already occurring in the stories of Noah (Gen. 9:21-24) and Lot (Gen. 19:31-38). The Rechabites, maintaining the ancient traditions of their nomad forefathers, refrained from drinking wine (Jer. 35:2ff.). During his period of naziriteship, a nazirite was enjoined from drinking wine and even from any liquid in which grapes had been steeped (Num. 6:13).

In the talmudic epoch, both the cultivation of vineyards and the production of wine were a prominent feature of the economy and a number of sages were vintners. While the Bible speaks of only three types of wine, at least ten varieties have been identified in talmudic sources. Some of these were mixed with different spices. It was customary to dilute wine before drinking by adding one-third water. The main meal of the day, taken in the evening (only breakfast and supper were eaten in talmudic times), consisted of two courses, with each of which a cup of wine was drunk.

Glass bottle for Kiddush *wine inscribed with verses from Genesis.*

Several basic religious rituals were marked by the drinking of one or more cups of wine over which a special benediction was recited: "...Who creates the fruit of the vine." The rabbis said, "There is no rejoicing without wine" (although they warned against over-indulgence — except on PURIM). At a CIRCUMCISION, one cup of wine was drunk. At a MARRIAGE ceremony, since it consisted in post-talmudic times of two parts, two cups of wine were used from which both the bride and groom sipped. Mourners in their seven-day period of mourning were given ten cups of wine, a practice that was abandoned in the post-talmudic period. Sabbath and festivals were greeted by the recitation of the Sanctification (KIDDUSH) over a cup of wine. In the ceremony marking the end of the Sabbath or festival (HAVDALAH), a cup of wine is used, while a characteristic feature of the Passover SEDER service is the drinking of four cups of wine. Four cups of wine are also drunk in the Tu bi-Shevat *seder* developed by Isaac LURIA (see NEW YEAR FOR TREES).

Since wine was widely used in idolatrous worship, the sages forbade the consumption of such wine, known as *yén nesekh*. The prohibition forbade wine that had been so much as touched by a non-Jew. It was extended to include any wine produced by a non-Jew, even if not intended for idolatrous worship. The Law Committee of the CONSERVATIVE movement has removed the latter ban, which was never accepted by the REFORM movement.

WISDOM (*ḥokhmah*). Wisdom has always been highly regarded in Judaism. The Pentateuch (Deut. 4:6) describes how, when the other nations of the world will learn of the Torah's statutes, they will say, "Surely, that great nation is a wise and discerning people." In the WISDOM LITERATURE wisdom is extolled and even personified as in, "Say to Wisdom, 'You are my sister,' and call understanding a kinswoman" (Prov. 7:4). In the Bible, King SOLOMON's wisdom is especially stressed.

Throughout the generations, the highest Jewish ideal has been the TALMID ḤAKHAM, the wise scholar erudite in Torah scholarship. By the same token, the ignoramus, the AM HA-ARETS, has always been regarded with scorn, one reason being "an ignorant person cannot be pious" (*Avot* 2:6), for he lacks the requisite knowledge to fulfill the commandments properly. Respect for the wise is not limited to those wise in Jewish learning. A special blessing is prescribed upon seeing a man who is exceptionally wise in other fields. This blessing thanks God for "having given of His wisdom to flesh and blood." The comparable blessing upon seeing a *talmid ḥakham* is "who has apportioned of His wisdom to those who fear Him."

ON WISDOM

The beginning of wisdom is: Acquire wisdom.

Wisdom cannot reside in the evilhearted.

Never talk to a fool for he despises words of wisdom.

Wisdom increases with years — but so does folly.

Wise men repeat what they have seen: fools what they have heard.

Make your home a meeting place for the wise — and drink in their every word.

Who is wise? He who learns from everyone.

Since the destruction of the Temple, the wise have taken the place of the prophets.

As important as is wisdom, it must be tempered with the fear of God, and "The beginning of wisdom is fear of the Lord" (Ps. 111:10). Furthermore, "A man whose fear of sins is greater than wisdom — his wisdom will endure; and the man whose wisdom exceeds his fear of sin — his wisdom will not endure" (*Avot* 3:11).

Innate wisdom is regarded as a gift from God, and as such

not praiseworthy in itself. It is what the person does with this ability which makes the difference: "Let not the wise man glory in his wisdom ... but only in this should one glory: In his earnest devotion to Me" (Jer. 9:22).

The Midrash differentiates between secular wisdom, which it calls *ḫokhmah*, and Torah wisdom, stating that if one is told that the other nations have *ḫokhmah*, he may believe it, but he should not believe if told that the other nations have Torah (Lam. R. 2.17).

In the Kabbalah, one of the ten SEFIROT or attributes of God, is *ḫokhmah*, wisdom.

WISDOM LITERATURE Category of ancient literature which praises WISDOM and offers guidance on everyday living. In the Bible, these include the Books of JOB, PROVERBS, some of the PSALMS, and ECCLESIASTES. The first three are commonly refer to in Hebrew as *Sifrei Emet* — lit., "books of truth" — where the word *emet* is an acronym of the Hebrew names of the three books. In the apocrypha, Ecclesiasticus and the Wisdom of Solomon also belong to Wisdom literature (see APOCRYPHA AND PSEUDEPIGRAPHA).

Wisdom literature, with its proverbs and apothegms, belongs to an international tradition. Parallels to minor collections are well known, including to Sumerian and Babylonian proverbs and the Egyptian Instruction literature. Foreign authors are acknowledged for two brief collections in Proverbs (Agur, 30:1-7; Lemuel's mother, 31:1-9), and a number of instructions from the Egyptian King Amenemopet appear in Proverbs 22:17-24:22. The truths preserved in such succinct sayings are universal, and the problems examined in Job and Ecclesiastes were experienced throughout the ancient Near East. Hence this body of literature has nothing specifically Jewish until Ecclesiasticus. It is often addressed to the young and is pragmatic in tone, offering the young the benefit of the experience of their elders. The oldest books within the wisdom books were addressed to children in the home (as in "my son" in Proverbs), but later ones functioned in the royal court as advice on how to advance, and in schools, which are first mentioned in Ecclesiasticus (about 190 BCE). The books themselves employ a variety of literary devices to make their points, including similes, metaphors and allegories. Sometimes, two opposites are contrasted, as the righteous and the wicked in Psalm 1. The Wisdom literature is remarkably free of references to Jewish ritual as such, and is thus quite universal in character. By tradition, Solomon wrote both Proverbs and Ecclesiastes, Proverbs with its optimistic view of life in middle age, and Ecclesiastes in his old age.

WISE, ISAAC MAYER (1819-1909). Pioneer of American REFORM JUDAISM and first president of Hebrew Union College. Little is known of his early years. He studied at *yeshivot*, but it is uncertain whether he received rabbinic ordination. In 1846 he emigrated to America, where he was appointed rabbi in Albany. His Reform tendencies and personal conflicts led to his ouster in 1850, whereupon he organized his own congregation. In 1854 he moved to Congregation Bnai Jeshurun, Cincinnati, remaining there for the rest of his life.

Wise had no difficult in introducing reforms in Cincinnati, but wider horizons had captured his attention. Within weeks of settling there, he started first an English weekly, *The Israelite*, and then a German supplement, *Die Deborah*. He founded Zion Collegiate Institute, intended to train rabbis. He took the initiative in summoning a rabbinic conference in Cleveland (1855), establishing an American Jewish synod to publish a uniform prayer book and pronounce on changes in Jewish practice.

The college was stillborn; the conference left behind it a trail of personal recrimination. Wise's principal concern was to unify American Jewry and in order to conciliate the Orthodox he introduced into the platform adopted at Cleveland a clause accepting the Talmud as the only legitimate interpretation of the Bible. This was denounced by the doctrinaire reformers as treachery.

Of his own accord Wise proceeded to publish a PRAYER BOOK — *Minhag America* (1856) — which was a revision of the traditional prayer book. After the Civil War he seemed to be realizing his objective of a broadly based conference, when his Reform rivals stole a march by convening a conference, limited to rabbis committed to Reform, to lay down a set of Reform principles (1869). Wise participated and seemingly accepted its radical position, but later backed away and resumed his own project. Again he became the center of a storm and it was only through the lay leaders of the Cincinnati community that action ensued. They called together representatives of congregations in the south and west and established the Union of American Hebrew Congregations (1873). Among other projects, the Union was to set up a "Hebrew Theological Institute," but it was expressly enjoined from exercising any religious supervision.

This was something less than the authoritative synod Wise had sought, but he accepted the compromise. He became president of Hebrew Union College when it was established in 1875 and in 1883 he ordained its first graduates. Hebrew Union College had been intended to serve all sections of the American Jewish community, but Wise's endorsement of the Pittsburgh Platform (1885), a Radical reform statement, helped to narrow the College's standpoint, while large-scale immigration from eastern Europe produced a second Jewish community for which nothing other than a traditional *yeshivah* sufficed. Tensions among the non-Orthodox abated sufficiently for the Central Conference of American Rabbis to be established in 1889.

WISSENSCHAFT DES JUDENTUMS (German, "Science of Judaism"). Name given to the critical study of Jewish history and culture which developed among the Jews of the German-speaking world in the 19th century. With the arrival of EMANCIPATION, the Jews began to make themselves at home in secular studies. Until then the Jewish past had been known only through the uncritical exegesis of sacred texts. The scientific study of the Jewish past, it was then felt, would bring Jewish culture on a par with that of the German environment, intensive scholarship would reveal the richness of the Jewish past which would restore the Jews' pride in their heritage and raise their standing in the eyes of the Gentile world. The *Wissenschaft* scholars sought to devote themselves to pure scholarship, detached from the subjective feelings aroused by the contents. Their goal was to understand Judaism in its widest context and determine its place in human cultural evolution. This involved a liberation from theological preconceptions, both Jewish and Christian. The Church had negated Jewish post-biblical creativity which the *Wissenschaft* sought to rehabilitate. Its determination to achieve total objectivity led to an open break with the past. The rationalistic bias of the *Wissenschaft* scholars restricted them to the study of rationalistic currents and led to a disregard for or bias against other trends, notably MYSTICISM in all its forms down to and including ḤASIDISM.

The most prominent founding figure in the movement was Leopold ZUNZ. It had been the hope of Zunz and others that their work would receive official recognition through the establishment of a department of Jewish studies at a Prussian university, but this was refused. Instead, such studies were cultivated through seminaries for the training of rabbis (see RABBINICAL SEMINARIES). Another outcome of the movement was the establishment of scholarly journals. The *Monatsschrift für Geschichte und Wissenschaft des Judentums* ("Monthly Journal for Jewish History and Science") appeared in 1851. It was established by Zacharias FRANKEL and continued to appear until suppressed by the Nazis in 1939. The *Révue des Études Juives* dates from 1880 and the *Jewish Quarterly Review* from 1888. Learned societies also came into being and they supported the scholarly journals.

The situation of the large Jewish communities of Eastern Europe did not produce the concern for *Wissenschaft* which spread in Central Europe; *Wissenschaft* did not attain the status there that it enjoyed in Central Europe, while in the rabbinic world it was tainted with heresy.

Wissenschaft was criticized for its apologetic tendencies — its determination to demonstrate that Jews were not culturally inferior; its wish to show that Judaism had evolved in various forms in its history and therefore degrees of reform were in keeping with a long Jewish tradition; its stress on archival research at the expense of tendencies and meaning; its benign 19th-century pseudo-universalism; and for its indifference to nationalistic, particularly Zionist, currents.

However, it made a lasting impact and in the 20th century merged into what came to be called "Jewish Studies." Certain outgrowths of the European scholarship tradition developed in the early 20th century. US scholarship, initially based on European-trained scholars, began to make contributions (such as the *Jewish Encyclopedia*) at the beginning of the century. The Jerusalem school of scholars emerged with the founding of the Hebrew University in 1925, although here, too, the first generation consisted of scholars from Europe. After the European centers were destroyed in the Holocaust, these two outgrowths of the European school found themselves on their own, with no more external resources, but succeeded in advancing to independent maturity, each producing native-born Jewish scholars and centers for Jewish scholarship and academic teaching.

Until the 19th century, Jewish subjects were taught in universities only within Christian contexts. The 20th century has seen a proliferation of academic Jewish teaching programs so that not only Bible, but Rabbinics, Jewish mysticism, Jewish thought, etc., are subjects of scientific research and teaching in many universities, offering for the first time an alternative to the traditional institutions of Jewish learning. Outside Israel and ultra-Orthodox circles, a training in scientific scholarship is now basic to rabbinical education.

WITCHCRAFT Several categories of witchcraft and sorcery are described in the Bible. In Exodus 22:17 it is commanded that "You shall not let a witch live." Diviners and soothsayers are forbidden in Leviticus 19:26 and Deuteronomy 18:10; turning to ghosts and spirits in Leviticus 9:31 and 20:27, Deuteronomy 18:11; being an augur or sorcerer in Deut. 18:10. The Bible calls for the individual's wholehearted allegiance to God and therefore all contact with various forms of witchcraft and sorcery is prohibited (Deut. 18:13). Furthermore, the crime of witchcraft is equated with the crime of human sacrifice (Deut. 18:10) with the same punishment designated for both (Lev. 20:27). Despite the prohibitions, witchcraft was obviously used, as shown most graphically by King Saul's visit to the "witch of En-dor" to consult the spirit of the prophet Samuel (1 Sam. 28).

The Mishnah deals with the various forms of punishment for witchcraft (*Sanh.* 7.4). The Talmud suggests that witchcraft was mostly prevalent among women, citing the story of SIMEON BEN SHETAḤ ordering the execution of 80 witches on the same day (*Sanh.* 6.4). The Talmud lists other forms of witchcraft, all punishable by whipping, namely *niḥush*, reading things into certain occurrences; *kesem*, telling fortunes from sands and stones; *onanut*, astrological forecasts and *ḥever*, reciting formulas to promote healing (*Sanh.* 65b). (See MAGIC; SUPERSTITION)

WOMEN The role of women in Judaism has been bound and influenced by its patriarchal nature. *Halakhah* (Jewish law) has also shaped the Jewish attitude toward women. The rabbis displayed a certain ambivalence between appreciation and the retention of stereotyped notions. In the contemporary period, women have challenged the traditional attitudes especially within non-Orthodox frameworks.

In the biblical world. There are two biblical accounts of the creation of woman. In the first (Gen. 1:27), woman was placed on a par with man, both being created in the image of God. Together they were given domination over the animal world and the task of procreation. In the second (Gen. 2:21-25), woman was created from man's rib to be his helper; man is told to leave his parents and cling to his wife. These two accounts are understood as prescribing MARRIAGE between man and woman, both for reproduction and for mutual interdependence and happiness. Later, in the Garden of Eden (Gen. 3:16), woman was told that for her disobedience, she would be subservient to man.

In ancient times, Judaism was clearly a patriarchal religion, within the context of the general patriarchal society of the Middle East. Social roles were usually prescribed according to one's sex. Following biblical prescription, the leadership class in Israelite society, such as the priesthood and (with exceptions) the monarchy, were male. A woman's primary role and means of self-expression were childbearing and homemaking. As Israelite society became more institutionalized, women were increasingly excluded from the public sphere and the power positions. On the other hand, women play prominent roles such as the MATRIARCHS, Miriam, Deborah the judge, and Huldah the prophetess; Ruth, Jael and Esther; while Salome Alexandra ruled the country in the Maccabean period.

At the same time, Israelite women in some ways fared better under biblical law than women in surrounding cultures. Many of their rights were safeguarded and their freedom preserved. For example, a woman had to be properly provided for by her husband. However, she was, in some sense, her husband's property, and although MONOGAMY was the ideal, biblical law sanctioned polygamy.

The prevailing sentiment was that she belonged in the home. Women bore children, and were responsible for family life. The panegyric to the "woman of valor" in Proverbs (31:10-31) refers to "buying and selling" as part of the woman's role. However, she was not considered morally or emotionally mature enough to occupy power positions in Israelite society.

Rabbinic attitudes. During the rabbinic period, although women were often appreciated and even protected by rabbinic law, negative statements were made about women. On the one hand, the Talmud states that man is incomplete without woman. A man without a wife lives without joy and blessing; and a man should love his wife as himself, and respect her more than himself. The rabbis also claimed that each generation would be redeemed because of the righteous women of that generation. On the other hand, various rabbinic statements refer to women as being frivolous, greedy, and gossipers, and a source of temptation.

Comparable to the biblical period, Jewish women fared better under Jewish law than their non-Jewish counterparts. The Jewish woman could not be married without her consent. The KETUBBAH (Jewish marriage contract) was a legally binding document that provided for her and guaranteed her a monetary settlement in the event of a divorce. A woman's husband was not allowed to deny her sex for long periods of time.

According to *halakhah*, womanhood is considered a separate juristic status with its own specific sets of rights, obligations, and restrictions. In terms of religious obligation, women were classed with slaves and children, disqualified as witnesses, excluded from the study of Torah, and possibly segregated in Temple and synagogue. For biological reasons, they were regarded as ritually impure for long periods (see NIDDAH). On the other hand, within the family and home, they enjoyed respect, admiration, and considerable authority. Three positive commandments are specifically assigned to women. They must separate a piece of dough from the kneading bowl to give to the priests as ḤALLAH. They must light the Sabbath CANDLES. And they must uphold the laws of FAMILY PURITY. As a general principle, the *halakhah* exempts women from positive time-bound commandments.

Key casket with scenes showing traditional duties of a Jewish woman: lighting the Sabbath lamp, mikveh, *baking bread.*

Consequently, they are not obliged to perform those that must be performed at a specific time such as SHOFAR (blowing the ram's horn), sitting in the SUKKAH, wearing a fringed garment (TALLIT or TSITSIT) and fixed PRAYER, although there were exceptions to this principle, e.g., HANUKKAH lights and the PURIM *megillah* which were obligatory for women. The purpose of this seems to have been to exempt women from those commandments that might require them to forgo their household responsibilities in favor of performing a *mitsvah*. There developed an ambivalence between their generally inferior role in ritual and other matters to an idealization stretching from the feminine personification of Wisdom in late Bible times to the projection of the feminine into the Godhead in medieval Kabbalah.

The contemporary period. The exemption of women

from time-related commandments presents a problem in the contemporary period as women seek equal access to the observance of Judaism. In general, the *halakhah* seems to suggest that a woman may voluntarily choose to perform a *mitsvah* even if not so obliged.

In the contemporary period, a growing number of women have called for equal consideration in Judaism. The traditional principles are no longer being accepted by many Jewish women today, especially in non-Orthodox circles. Contemporary Western society is increasingly granting equality to women and recognizing that even the "separate but equal" principle is inherently inequal. Hence, many Jewish men and women are calling upon the Jewish community to reexamine its attitudes regarding women.

Due to its halakhic framework, Orthodoxy has been unwilling or unable to make basic changes. As stated by one authority, Rabbi J. David Bleich, *halakhah* is a self-contained system which follows its own internal logic. It has created its own ideal values for women and the values of the non-Jewish world constitute no cause for change. Certain Orthodox circles have increased women's involvement in worship and study and have restructured the synagogue partition (*mehitsah*) so that women are no longer confined to the back of the hall. Several modern Orthodox synagogues in the U.S. have even welcomed women's prayer quorums (MINYANIM) in which women act as readers and are called to the Torah. However, such changes remain within the traditional male-female roles, with no major alteration in *halakhah* or ritual. There is no suggestion of calling women to the Reading of the Law or being counted in a prayer quorum at a regular service, and certainly not of ordaining women as rabbis. In Israel, women have been selected to boards responsible for the appointment of rabbis, despite strong objections in many Orthodox quarters.

Non-Orthodox movements have been more responsive to the new demands and to the influence of feminism. Women have gained increasing status in Jewish ritual in Reform, Conservative, and Reconstructionist congregations. The Hebrew Union College (Reform) ordained the first American woman rabbi in 1972. The Reconstructionist Rabbinical College has accepted women to its rabbinical program since its opening in 1967. In 1983, the Jewish Theological Seminary (Conservative) voted to admit women to its rabbinical program (although its Cantors' Assembly declined to admit women cantors). In all three groups women are counted in a *minyan* (although among Conservatives, this is left to the decision of the individual congregation). Under the impact of feminism, some liturgies have been altered in non-Orthodox trends (e.g., by defining God in neutral rather than masculine terms and by mentioning the Matriarchs along with the PATRIARCHS). The BAT MITSVAH ceremony has taken its place alongside the BAR MITSVAH (also in Orthodox circles but not as part of the regular synagogue service) and new rituals have been developed to welcome baby girls into Judaism.

WORLD TO COME See AFTERLIFE

WRITTEN LAW (*Torah she-bi-khetav*). The PENTATEUCH, traditionally dictated by God to MOSES; by extension, the entire BIBLE. Rabbinic tradition distinguishes between the Written Law and the ORAL LAW that, taken together, form the source of all basic Jewish legislation. On Leviticus 26:46, "These are the statutes and ordinances and *torahs*, which the Lord made between Him and the children of Israel on Mount Sinai by the hand of Moses," the *Sifra* (54.11) comments: "The use of *torah* in the plural shows that two *Torahs* were given [by God to Moses], one written and one oral." The Oral Law consisted of verbal explanations of the Written Law, traditionally transmitted together with it by God to Moses. Formally, only the Pentateuch may be considered Written Law, since the rest of the Bible, the PROPHETS and the HAGIOGRAPHA, are considered to have been written under a less intense level of inspiration. Moreover, the legal material in the Prophets and Hagiographa were called by the rabbis "tradition" (*divré kabbalah*). Nevertheless, the term Written Law is sometimes used for the entire Bible.

In rabbinic tradition, the Written Law was never meant to stand alone and could be understood only through the authoritative interpretation of the Oral Law (*Shab.* 31a); MAIMONIDES (*Introduction to the Mishnah* 1) wrote: "Every commandment was given with its explanation."

Ark of the Italian Synagogue in Jerusalem, shown open with three Torah Scrolls inside.

לא תרצח
לא תנאף
לא תגנב
לא תענה
לא תחמוד
לכבוד ה' ולזכר
נשמת הגאון כמוהר"ר
נתן אוטולינגו זצ"ל

Y

YA'ALEH VE-YAVO ("May [our remembrance] arise and come...[before judaiYou]"). Key words and title of a special paragraph inserted in the three daily AMIDAH prayers (although not in the Additional Service) on New Moons and Pilgrim Festivals, including the intermediate days of Passover and Sukkot. On all of these occasions and on Rosh ha-Shanah, it is also inserted in the third paragraph of GRACE AFTER MEALS. Scriptural authority for this petition was found in Numbers 10:10; it must have been composed in talmudic times, as the sages mention its inclusion in the *Amidah* (*Ber.* 29b; *Sof.* 19.7) and in the statutory Grace (*Sof.* 19.11). The essence of *Ya'aleh ve-Yavo* is a prayer that God may call to mind the forefathers and the entire House of Israel, His promised Messiah and Jerusalem, His holy city, so that "deliverance, mercy, life, peace" and other blessings will be granted to the Jewish people on this festive day. When recited aloud, the three brief petitions that follow are answered by a congregational response of *amen*.

YAD (lit. "hand"). Pointer used to keep the place while reading from the SCROLL OF THE LAW. Direct contact of the hands with the parchment of the scroll was forbidden on penalty of their becoming "unclean" (*Yad* 3.2). Also, as a gesture of respect, the rabbis warned against handling a "bare" Torah scroll (*Shab.* 14a; see READING OF THE LAW). It therefore became customary to attach a pointer to the Torah scroll, usually hung on a chain from the roller. The *yad* as a special ceremonial object is first mentioned in 1570. In Sephardi communities, it is also the custom to point with a cloth or with the fringes of the prayer shawl (*tallit*). The *Yad* generally takes the form of a rod or shaft culminating in a "hand" with an outstretched or curled index finger, or sometimes an elongated "finger". It can be made of almost any material. In the course of time, it became an object of artistic creativity. Sometimes the pointers are encrusted with semi-precious stones such as coral cuffs and coral finials, bracelets and rings. There are often inscriptions on the *yad* which are sometimes dedicated to the donor. Others have verses appropriate to the occasion of reading the Torah such as: "The instruction of the Lord is lucid, making the eyes light up" (Ps. 19:9) or "This is the Torah that Moses set before the Israelites" (Deut. 4:44).

Engraved and pierced Torah pointer (yad) *from Poland, 1855.*

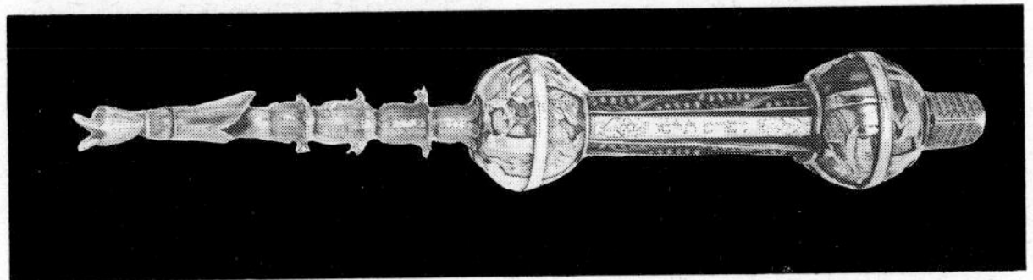

YADAYIM ("hands"). Eleventh tractate of Order TOHOROT in the Mishnah. Its four chapters deal with the uncleanness of the hands and their purification. The Mishnah describes how the hands can become ritually unclean (either first-degree or second-degree uncleanness), the quantity of water needed to cleanse them, the kinds of vessels which may be used, the ways of pouring water over the hands and cases of doubtful uncleanness. The last chapter discusses the validity of various offerings, the tithes given by Jews outside the Land of Israel and several disagreements regarding RITUAL PURITY and TITHES between the PHARISEES and the SADDUCEES. The subject matter is amplified in the *Tosefta*.

YAHRZEIT ("anniversary"). Yiddish name for the death anniversary of a parent or other close relative whom one is obligated to mourn. The Hebrew date on which the death occurred is observed each year as the *yahrzeit*. Rituals associated with this observance were first instituted by Ashkenazim in 15th-century Germany and then spread to other parts of the Jewish world. In particular, there was a mystical belief that saying KADDISH on every successive *yahrzeit* would be conducive to the "elevation of the departed soul" to higher spheres of immortality and repose. This also accounts for the now standard practice of kindling a MEMORIAL LIGHT (*ner neshamah* or *yahrzeit* candle) which burns for 24 hours in the home.

Mourners recite *Kaddish* within the framework of a *minyan* (prayer quorum) at the three daily services on a *yahrzeit*. Some Sephardim begin to recite *Kaddish* from the preceding Sabbath. Should the *yahrzeit* coincide with a Monday or Thursday, Ashkenazi mourners are called to the READING OF THE LAW, otherwise they are called on the previous Sabbath. On weekdays a MEMORIAL PRAYER is chanted by the reader after the mourner's Torah portion has been com-

The signs of the zodiac and medallions with inscriptions linking the subjects of the pictures with the promise of redemption. Detail of the ceiling of the Chodorow Synagogue, Poland, 18th century.

pleted. Sephardi mourners are usually called to the Torah on the Sabbath before or after the death anniversary. Already in talmudic times, children abstained from eating meat or drinking wine on the anniversary of a parent's death (*Ned.* 12a; *Shev.* 20a). This later gave rise to the custom still practiced by some Orthodox Jews, of fasting on a *yahrzeit*, unless it falls on a day when the TAḤANUN supplications are omitted from daily worship (see FASTING AND FAST DAYS). Similarly, when the date of a *yahrzeit* coincides with a CIRCUMCISION or Redemption of the FIRST-BORN ceremony, exemption from fasting is granted to the father of the boy who is to be circumcised or redeemed, as well as to his godfather (*sandak*), circumciser (*mohel*), and the priest taking part in the redemption ceremony. It is a widespread practice to visit the grave of a departed close relative on the occasion of a death anniversary. Stanzas from Psalm 119 commencing with the letters of the deceased person's Hebrew name are usually recited.

Among Eastern Sephardim, an alternative designation for the *yahrzeit* is *naḥalah* ("inheritance"). Spanish and Portuguese Jews often call it *meldado*, a "study session" in memory of the departed to which relatives and friends are invited. Afternoon and Evening services form part of the *meldado*, which concludes with the serving of a light meal. At one time, *meldado* observances took place at home, but nowadays they are usually transferred to the synagogue.

Traditionally, 7 Adar is observed by members of a BURIAL SOCIETY and other pious Jews as the anniversary of the death of Moses. LAG BA-OMER marks the putative *yahrzeit* of R. Simeon bar Yoḥai, celebrated in Meron, Israel, with mass pilgrimages to his grave and the lighting of bonfires. Ḥasidic Jews celebrate the *yahrzeit* of their ADMOR or REBBE, while North African Jews conduct a joyful observance (HILLULA) at the grave of revered rabbis.

YALKUT MAKHIRI ("Makhir's compilation"). An anthology of homiletic *midrashim* on various parts of the Bible compiled in the 14th century by R. Makhir ben Abba Mari, a resident of Southern France. He drew upon the homiletical literature found in TALMUD and MIDRASH, which he rearranged according to the biblical sequence of chapter and verse. Like YALKUT SHIMONI, its importance lies in the variant versions of ancient sources. Sections that have been published cover the Books of Isaiah, the Minor Prophets, Psalms and part of Proverbs.

YALKUT SHIMONI ("Simeon's compilation"). A comprehensive anthology of MIDRASH and HALAKHAH composed in Germany during the early decades of the 13th century by R. Simeon Rava, known as R. Simeon ha-Darshan (the Preacher). The anthology follows the biblical text in its entirety from Genesis to Chronicles. The compiler draws from virtually the whole body of rabbinic literature, from the Talmud through the ge'onic period. The work enjoyed wide popularity and, from the 15th century, it was frequently cited. Today its importance is twofold: it often provides variant readings of its sources and also quotes *midrashim* that have been lost and are otherwise known only by name.

YAMIM NORA'IM See HIGH HOLIDAYS

YEKUM PURKAN ("May salvation [from heaven] arise"). Opening words and name of two Aramaic prayers which, in the Ashkenazi rite, follow the *haftarah* prophetical reading on all Sabbath mornings apart from High Holidays. The first, invoking Divine protection of rabbis, students, and communal leaders, may be recited also by one praying alone, whereas the second — a prayer for the synagogue worshipers — may only be said with a quorum (*minyan*). The first *Yekum Purkan* is the older: it refers to the heads of the ACADEMIES, scholars, and exilarchs of the Babylonian Diaspora, and to the sages and "holy community" of Erets Israel. Having entered the liturgy in Erets Israel, *Yekum Purkan* was adopted by the earliest Italian rite and then incorporated in the medieval French *Maḥzor Vitry*. The first paragraph is sometimes omitted on festivals coinciding with a Sabbath, and the Conservative prayer book includes only the second *Yekum Purkan* (with an abbreviated translation).

YESHIVAH (pl. *yeshivot*). An institution dedicated to advanced rabbinic study. Its curriculum consists almost entirely of the study of texts, chiefly those of the TALMUD. Traditionally, RABBIS have pursued their studies in a *yeshivah*, but *yeshivot* are not institutions for professional training.

Yeshivot are related to the ACADEMIES of Erets Israel and Babylonia that flourished from at least the third century CE until about the middle of the 11th century. These academies, also known as *yeshivot*, served not only as teaching institutions but also as rabbinic courts and centers for the dissemination of rabbinic RESPONSA, whereas the later *yeshivot* served primarily as institutions of learning. Changing conditions in Iraq together with the growth of Jewish communities outside of Babylonia led to the decline of the Babylonian academies and a corresponding rise in the importance of other *yeshivot*. None of these, however, ever gained the centralized authority and influence of the Babylonian institutions.

In the tenth century, a *yeshivah* existed in Jerusalem. This was apparently the last remnant of the great academies of Erets Israel and was probably transferred to Jerusalem from Tiberias. The Jerusalem *yeshivah* was moved to Damascus after 1071; other important centers of learning existed in Damascus and Aleppo until the end of the 12th century.

A legend that appears in Abraham IBN DAUD's *Sefer ha-Kabbalah* (mid-12th century) tells of four scholars on their way to study in Babylonia around the year 990 whose ship was seized by pirates. One of the scholars was never heard from again, but the three others were sold as slaves, each in a different port, one in North Africa, one in Egypt, and one in Spain; all three succeeded in establishing *yeshivot* which became famous. This story reflects the fact that from the tenth century onwards, *yeshivot* could be found in most Jewish communities as well as the fact of continuity between these and the Babylonian academies.

Yeshivot existed in North Africa from the eighth century; the first great one, believed to be founded by Hushiel ben Elḥanan, was the Kairouan Academy. It reached its peak in the tenth century, and with its decline in the 11th century the *yeshivot* of Fez in Morocco and Tlemcen in Algeria became the leading institutions of the region. An important *yeshivah* existed also in Fostat (near modern Cairo).

One of the first important *yeshivot* to appear in Spain was located in Cordoba and was founded by Moses ben Ḥanokh in the 10th century. The *yeshivah* of Lucena, which counted among its students JUDAH HALEVI, and the Barcelona *yeshivah* were among the earliest rabbinical academies in the country. Numerous *yeshivot* existed in Spain up to the time of the expulsion in 1492, and many of the important Spanish scholars, e.g., NAḤMANIDES and Solomon ben Abraham ADRET, headed their own *yeshivot*.

A great intellectual contribution was made by the Ashkenazi *yeshivot* of northern Europe, these institutions being largely responsible for such major authorities as GERSHOM BEN JUDAH MA'OR HA-GOLAH (early 11th cent.), RASHI (late 11th century), and the Tosafists (see TOSAFOT). The Ashkenazi *yeshivah* bore little resemblance to the great academies of old. The function of the rabbinic courts was practically non-existent. The *yeshivot* were small, with usually less than 100 students, who often lived together with the head of the institution and studied in a room in his home. The scholar who headed the *yeshivah* was responsible for the financial requirements of the institution, with some support from the local community. Students from wealthy families were expected to pay for their upkeep. Those attending such *yeshivot* were generally accomplished scholars who had previously studied privately. MOSES BEN JACOB OF COUCY noted that the students of the French *yeshivot* were so dedicated to their studies that they often slept in their clothes. In the *yeshivot* of northern France there existed a system somewhat akin to the granting of degrees, with the title of *ḥaver* (fellow) as the first recognition of accomplishment and the title *morenu* (our teacher) signifying real command of the field studied and qualification to head one's own school. The golden era of French *yeshivot* ended with the expulsion of Jews from France in 1306.

By the middle of the 16th century, a new type of institution, the *yeshivat ha-kahal* (community *yeshivah*) appeared. Detailed regulations for these communal *yeshivot* were promulgated by the general councils of entire areas. In Italy and Germany, scholars studied together with small numbers of students in little synagogues. This arrangement was known as *klaus* in German. Communities were expected to maintain these *yeshivot*, and the students had their meals at private homes on a rotating basis. Studies centered around discussion and disputation; as a result, the chief literary product of these institutions was glosses and commentaries. The main center of *yeshivot* moved to Eastern Europe, especially Poland, in the 16th century. A significant intellectual development was a method of study known as PILPUL. It involved a dialectic reasoning based upon minute distinctions and differentiations, which took primarily the form of oral discussion, and very little written material remains.

The *yeshivot* of the Ashkenazi centers experienced a decline in the 17th and 18th centuries due to a number of factors. In Polish regions, the Cossack rebellion of 1648 destroyed many communities along with their *yeshivot*. For some time, the system of *yeshivot* in these areas was not revived apparently due to economic hardship and perhaps due to the spread of ḤASIDISM which had a somewhat different approach to learning. Not until the early 19th century was there a signfiicant revival (and reformation) of the *yeshivah* system.

The modern era in the development of the *yeshivah* began in 1802 with the opening of the Volozhin *yeshivah*, White Russia, founded by Ḥayyim of Volozhin, a leading disciple of ELIJAH BEN SOLOMON, THE GAON OF VILNA. This followed the Vilna Gaon's method of study which negated *pilpul*. As the school expanded, it constructed its own building — the first structure in modern times to be built solely for a *yeshivah*. Its golden period was under Naphtali Tsevi Judah Berlin (from 1854) when over 400 pupils were attracted to the school from all over the greater Russian area. Other noted *yeshivot* flourished at Mir, White Russia; at Slobodka and Kovno, which became a center of the MUSAR MOVEMENT, with a daily half-hour session devoted to the study of ethical texts, a revolutionary introduction in a world concentrated solely on the Talmud; and at Telz, Lithuania. These and many other *yeshivot* attracted thousands of students, some of whom became rabbis and teachers, others looking on it as a higher education before going on to secular occupations. In Ḥasidic Poland, most *yeshivot* were associated with particular Ḥasidic courts and only their Ḥasidim studied there. The largest and most important *yeshivah* in Hungary was the Yeshivat Ḥatam Sofer in Pressburg (Bratislava), founded in 1806 by R. Mosheh SOFER. The largest *yeshivah* in Germany was organized in Frankfurt in 1890 by Solomon Breuer, son-in-law and successor of R. Samson Raphael HIRSCH. The great European *yeshivah* center ended abruptly and brutally with the Nazi Holocaust. Survivors reestablished some of the famous *yeshivot* elsewhere: that of Slobodka in Israel, of Mir in Brooklyn and Jerusalem, of Telz in Cleveland, Ohio.

Before World War II, the development of *yeshivot* in North America had not been very successful, apart from Yeshiva University which grew from a merger in the late 19th century of Yeshivat Ets Ḥayyim and Yeshivat Yitshak Elhanan. Since the war, those founded include the Rabbi

Ner Israel Rabbinical College in Baltimore, Maryland.

Aaron Kotler Institute for Advanced Studies in Lakewood, New Jersey, Torah Vo-Da'as in New York, and Ner Israel in Baltimore. Although none of these institutions permits secular studies as part of their curriculum, many of their students pursue university studies alongside their *yeshivah* courses.

By far, the leading center of *yeshivot* today is in the State of Israel. Already in the 16th century, *yeshivot* again flourished in the country, the new impetus being provided largely by Jews expelled from Spain in 1492, who settled in the Holy Land. Some 18 *yeshivot* existed in Safed, which was perhaps the most important center of Jewish learning of that period. There were also important Sephardi and Ashkenazi *yeshivot* in Jerusalem. From the end of the 16th century on, however, there was a serious decline until the 18th century.

In 1840, the Ets Ḥayyim Yeshivah was established in Jerusalem, the first Ashkenazi *yeshivah* in the country, founded on a Volozhin-type model. Other early examples of this type followed. The growth of the Jewish community after World War I brought about a concomitant growth of *yeshivot*. A real turning point was reached, however, when, in the wake of the Nazi Holocaust, numerous outstanding Torah scholars found their way to the Holy Land, staffing existing institutions, founding new ones, and re-establishing some of the great *yeshivot* of pre-war Europe. It has been estimated that there are more full-time *yeshivah* students studying in Israel today than there were in pre-war Europe.

The willingness of the State of Israel to defer the army service of anyone studying full time in a *yeshivah* has permitted the *yeshivot* to develop rapidly. According to government figures, some 18,000 young men were availing themselves of this opportunity in the late 1980s.

Among the *yeshivot* catering to older students in Israel, three main categories can be distinguished: the "Lithuanian *Yeshivot*," continuing the model created at Volozhin, where Talmud is studied to the exclusion of almost every other subject; the Ḥasidic *yeshivot*; and the Zionist *yeshivot*, best-known of which is the Merkaz ha-Rav in Jerusalem founded by Rabbi A.I. KOOK. The religious kibbutzim have established their own central *yeshivah*. It is estimated that 11,000 students study in these higher *yeshivot*. There are also *yeshivot* at junior high and high school levels. A unique form is the *yeshivat hesder* where students combine *yeshivah* training with their army service.

YETSIRAH, SEFER ("Book of Creation"). Hebrew treatise on cosmogony and cosmology, originating from the third or fourth century. Several versions of the work are extant, differing considerably from each other. Its purpose is to present the basic principles by which God created the world and by which the world continues to operate. Yet, some mystical elements can be found in it and the author's terminology served as a source for symbols for the medieval Jewish mystics (see MYSTICISM).

The world was created, according to this work, by the combination of two principles: The ten NUMBERS from one to ten and the 22 letters of the Hebrew ALPHABET. Ten Divine utterances brought about the existing cosmos and the combined force of the numbers and letters contains in it all existence. The ten numbers are called in this work SEFIROT, an original term, and they are described as the five infinite dimensions or ten directions of the cosmos — East, West, North, South, Up, Down, Beginning, End, Good and Evil; they are also the stages by which the three elements (Fire, Water and Air) evolved. The *sefirot*, however, are also entities which worship God and kneel before His throne.

The letters of the alphabet are divided by the author into three groups: Three "mothers" — *aleph, mem,* and *shin*, representing the three elements; seven "double" letters, i.e., ones which can be pronounced in two different ways — *bet, gimel, dalet, kaf, peh, resh* (in the Bible, the *resh* is several times punctuated with a *dagesh kal* which is used to change pronunciation) and *tav*; the remaining 12 are "simple" letters. In succinct sentences, the author describes the meaning of each group of letters in cosmic existence, in the realms of anthropology and psychology.

Sefer Yetsirah is the earliest Hebrew presentation of a grammatical system, long before Jewish scholars, following Arabic models, systematized Hebrew linguistics. According to *Sefer Yetsirah*, all Hebrew words are based on two-letter roots, of which there are 231. Creation and the existence of the world are based on combinations and permutations of these roots.

It is not clear whether the book was intended to serve as a manual for scholars and mystics in creating various beings. Many medieval commentators used it to direct their readers on the creation of a GOLEM. The earliest commentators, however, employed it as a work of science — SAADIAH GAON, Shabbetai Donolo, Judah HALEVI (*Kuzari*, 4) and others —

until, in the late 12th and 13th centuries, it was taken over by mystics, both kabbalists and Ashkenazi Ḥasidim, and became one of their main sources for mystical symbolism.

YETSIV PITGAM ("Steadfast is our praise"). Opening words of an Aramaic liturgical hymn which most Ashkenazi congregations in the Diaspora recite on the second day of SHAVU'OT. Inserted after the first verse of the *haftarah*, it has a lengthier counterpart in the AKDAMUT MILLIN hymn read on the first day. *Yetsiv Pitgam* comprises 15 lines, the initial Hebrew letters forming an acrostic of the author's name: Ya'akov be-Rabbi Meir Levi. A hymn of praise to "the eternal King," *Yetsiv Pitgam* depicts the Sinaitic revelation and Israel's age-old devotion to the Torah. It ends with a prayer that God will defend and strengthen all those who uphold His teachings, that His blaspheming enemies may be confounded and silenced.

YEVAMOT (levirate marriages). First tractate of Order NASHIM in the Mishnah. Its 16 chapters deal mainly with LEVIRATE MARRIAGE (*yibbum*), the obligation of a man to marry his deceased brother's wife if she has not borne the deceased any sons (cf. Lev. 18:6-18; Deut. 25:5-10; Ruth 4:5-10). The tractate covers the laws of those obligated to the levirate marriage, who is exempt, and the ceremony called *ḥalitsah*, where the surviving brother can exempt himself from marrying his brother's widow. The Mishnah also discusses permitted and forbidden marriages with reference to priests, minors and Gentiles, as well as cases of rape or seduction. The last two chapters cover the laws of a women who has remarried on the basis of an erroneous report of the death of her husband. The subject matter is amplified in both Talmuds and in the *Tosefta*.

Opening of the tractate Yevamot *from Asher ben Jehiel's commentary on the Mishnah. Germany, 14th century.*

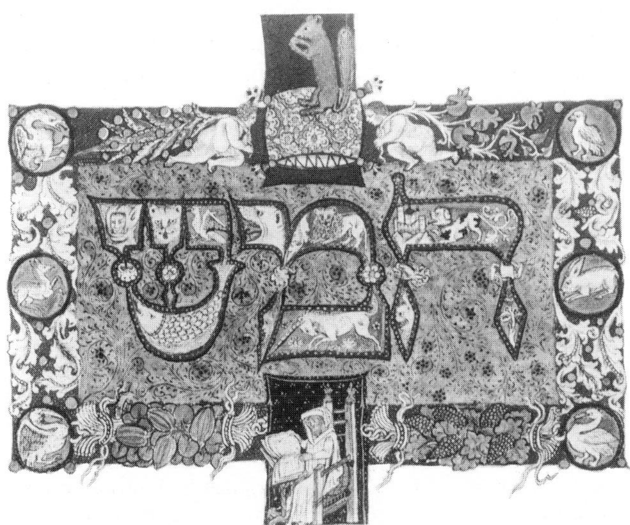

YIBBUM See LEVIRATE MARRIAGE

YIDDISH (contracted form of *Yidish-daytsh*, "Judeo-German"). The everyday language of most ASHKENAZIM from the early Middle Ages until recent times. From the early 11th century, Rhenish Jews and others leaving France gradually adopted the Old High German and Middle High German speech of their Christian neighbors. Hebrew terms and expressions were introduced in conversation and Hebrew characters were employed (rather than a Latin alphabet associated with clerics) to set this Germanic language down in writing. As large numbers of Ashkenazi Jews moved east to Bohemia and Poland in order to escape recurrent waves of persecution, their *Yidish-daytsh* tongue absorbed and was influenced by the Slavonic parlance of old-established Jewish communities which they encountered there. Around 1500, Yiddish split into diverging branches, a Western (*Juden-deutsch* or Judeo-German) patois spoken in Germany, Alsace, Holland, and Switzerland, and an Eastern Yiddish that became the mother tongue (*Mamma-loshn*) of Jews living beyond the Prussian frontier. Terms and concepts relating to synagogue worship, the dietary laws, and other traditional practices characterized both forms of this Ashkenazi Jewish language.

Passover Seder *plate inscribed with good wishes for the holiday, in Yiddish in Hebrew letters. Delft, Holland, 18th century.*

From its earliest beginnings, in the 14th century, Yiddish literature was strongly religious and didactic, catering for the less educated and intellectual type of Jew. Among the dozens of Bible translations and paraphrases which brought such readers a knowledge of talmudic lore and authoritative rabbinic exegesis, two outstanding examples were the *Taytsh-Ḥummash* (1590), a Yiddish version of the Pentateuch. and Jacob ben Isaac Ashkenazi's late 16th-century *Tsenerene*, (see TSE'ENAH U-RE'ENAH), the enormously popular commentary on the Pentateuch synagogue prophetical readings (*haftarot*), and the Five Scrolls that became staple reading for pious women on the Sabbath. Also dating from this period was the *Ma'aseh Bukh* (1602), an anonymous collection of 255 instructive and entertaining stories, legends, and folktales; mostly drawn from the Talmud and Midrash, these stories glorified the HASIDÉ ASHKENAZ and greatly influenced the development of Yiddish prose. Epic treatments of various biblical figures and events, written in the 15th century, culminated in two narrative masterpieces: the *Shmuel Bukh* (1544), a heroic interpretation of Israel's history from Samuel to David, and the *Melokhim Bukh* (1543), a sequel extending to the Babylonian Exile. Many biblical plays were written and staged from the 16th century, including the *Purim-Shpil* monologues, satires, and comedies performed annually down to World War II in Eastern Europe (see PURIM).

Liturgical works in Yiddish were mainly translated from Hebrew. Such *piyyutim* often had the specialized form of *tekhines*, devotional prayers and supplications for the use of women especially, a Yiddish translation appearing next to the original Hebrew. *Got fun Avrohom* ("God of Abraham") is a related kind of devotional chant composed in the 17th century; recited by Jewish housewives at the Sabbath's outgoing, it reflects all the uncertainties and concerns of everyday life in the Russo-Polish *shtetl*. Medieval HAGIOGRAPHY was revived in Ḥasidic literature, notably the Hebrew-Yiddish *Tales of Rabbi* NAḤMAN OF BRATSLAV, and a multitude of Yiddish songs grew out of Ḥasidic piety and folklore. Perhaps the best-known example of the latter is a dramatic "plea to God" entitled "Levi Yitskhok's *Kaddish*." Biblical and religious themes have also played a major role in recent Yiddish literature. For example, I.L. Peretz wrote tales idealizing the Ḥasidic rabbis; Chaim Grade's verse and prose glorified the scholarly milieu of the Lithuanian MITNAGGEDIM; while Yehoash (Y.S. Bloomgarden) completed a translation of the Bible (1922-27) that is now widely regarded as one of the outstanding literary achievements in Yiddish. Biblical heroes in Itzik Manger's lyrical works are transposed to the Ashkenazi heartland of Eastern Europe and his *Megille-Lider* (1936), an imaginative version of the Esther scroll and *Purim-shpil*, gained enormous success as an Israeli musical in the 1960s.

Of the nearly 11 million Jews who spoke Yiddish in 1939, a vast number perished in the Holocaust. *Yeshivot* and ultra-Orthodox Ashkenazi circles are now prominent among those forces helping Yiddish to survive throughout the world, especially in Israel and the United States.

YIGDAL ("May He be magnified"). Opening word and title of a popular liturgical hymn. Its authorship is generally attributed to Daniel ben Judah of Rome (fl. 1300). A metrical version of Maimonides' 13 PRINCIPLES OF FAITH, this hymn often appears twice in prayer books of the Ashkenazim — first, before *Adon Olam*, at the beginning of the Morning Service and later, at the end of the Evening Service for Sabbaths and festivals, where it is usually sung. Unlike all other major prayer rites, that of Ḥasidic Jewry does not include *Yigdal* in any synagogue service. The Ashkenazi version comprises 13 lines, each corresponding to a successive article in Maimonides' credo, and a single rhyme is used throughout; the Sephardi and Eastern version includes two additional lines, the last being partly a repetition of the 13th.

YISHTABBAḤ ("Praised [Your Name] shall be"). Opening word of the prayer concluding the PESUKÉ DE-ZIMRA ("Passages of Song") in every Morning Service, also included in the Passover *Seder* service. This paragraph contains 15 synonyms of praise to God, traditionally linked with the 15 Psalms of Ascent (120-134) which the Levites recited while climbing the 15 steps of the Sanctuary (see SHIR HA-MA'ALOT). The text in most rites is virtually identical, but Sephardim only count the first 13 words of praise which (according to the Zohar) correspond to the 13 Divine Attributes. Worshipers recite *Yishtabbaḥ* while standing, no interruption being permitted, so as to attain an appropriate mood before the BAREKHU summons to public worship.

YIZKOR See MEMORIAL SERVICES

YOM HA-ATSMA'UT See INDEPENDENCE DAY, ISRAEL

YOM KIPPUR See DAY OF ATONEMENT

YOM KIPPUR KATAN (literally "minor DAY OF ATONEMENT"). The day before each New MOON, according to a custom originated by the kabbalist R. Moses CORDOVERO of Safed. According to the kabbalists, each New Moon is a time of forgiveness for sins. Therefore, by repenting fully on the day before the New Moon, the new month can be entered completely free of sin. The day itself is marked by fasting (either for part of the day or the entire day), special penitential prayers composed for the day, and even Torah reading if there are ten adult males fasting for the entire day. The reading is that of fast days, and at the afternoon service the fast day *haftarah* is read. While popular in Europe in previous centuries, the custom is not observed today, with few exceptions. The authoritative code, the SHULḤAN ARUKH, makes no mention of the custom.

YOM TOV See FESTIVALS

YOMA ("The Day," i.e., Day of Atonement). Fifth tractate of Order MO'ED in the Mishnah. Its eight chapters deal with the High Priest's preparation and performance of the special Day of Atonement Service in the Temple (cf. Lev. 16:1-34; 23:26-32; Num. 29:7-11). Rather than a dry recitation of laws, the tractate narrates the High Priest's service in a detailed and dramatic way, culminating in the delicate and awesome ritual in the HOLY OF HOLIES. The last chapter enumerates the laws of Yom Kippur (DAY OF ATONEMENT) itself which includes fasting for 24 hours, not washing, not wearing leather shoes, and abstaining from marital relations.

The name *Yoma* (in Aramaic) was abbreviated from the name *Yoma Raba* ("the Great Day") by which the Day of Atonement was known. The subject matter is amplified in both Talmuds and the *Tosefta*.

YOSÉ BEN ḤALAFTA (c.100-c.160 CE). *Tanna* in Erets Israel of the fourth generation; one of the last students of R. AKIVA; called simply "R. Yosé" throughout talmudic literature. His statements are quoted over 300 times in the MISHNAH and in various *baraitot*. Like his colleague, R. JUDAH BAR ILAI, he played a leading role in the reestablished SANHEDRIN and was a teacher of R. JUDAH HA-NASI. The latter always showed great respect for Yosé ben Ḥalafta's opinion when arriving at a legal decision, and in halakhic disputes Yosé's view prevails over those of Judah bar Ilai and R. MEIR. He earned a livelihood as a tanner of hides in Sepphoris, where he established a law court and a rabbinical academy. His five sons were all noted scholars.

SAYINGS OF YOSÉ BEN ḤALAFTA

Whoever honors the Torah is himself honored; whoever dishonors it, is himself dishonored.

Ever since creation, God has been busy arranging marriages, a task as onerous as dividing the Red Sea.

One should never open one's mouth to Satan [i.e., "Talk of the Devil and he's sure to appear!"].

One pang of conscience outweighs many lashes.

It is not the office that bestows honor on the person, but the person who gives distinction to his office.

In the Messianic era, all nations of the world will of their own accord take shelter under the wings of God's Presence.

A chronological work ascribed to Yosé ben Ḥalafta is the *baraita* entitled *Seder Olam Rabbah*, which records dates from the period of creation down to the author's own time. This compilation is of importance for Second Temple history, since it lists events of that era not mentioned elsewhere (see HISTORIOGRAPHY). R. Yosé evidently took part in religious debates with Christians and pagans who challenged the fundamentals of Judaism. In the theological sphere, his dictum that "the Holy One is the Place [*ha-Makom*] of the world, but the world is not His place" (Midr. Ps. 90:1), was meant to emphasize God's transcendence. He enacted the ruling that no one may be condemned to death unless two witnesses had previously warned him against committing the offense (*Mak.* 1.9; *Sanh.* 56b).

YOTSEROT (sing. *yotser*). A series of liturgical poems (PIYYUTIM) which embellish the two blessings before and the blessing after the recital of the SHEMA of the MORNING SERVICE. They are recited in many communities on the festivals and on special Sabbaths. The word is derived from the opening words of the first blessing before the *Shema*, "*yotser or*" ("creator of light"). The *yotserot* are among the most ancient forms of the *piyyut*.

The classic series of *yotserot* is composed of 7 sections:

1) The *yotser*, before the verse, "Holy, holy, holy ..."

2) The *ofan*, before the verse, "Blessed be the Lord from His abode." Its name derives from the reference to *ofanim*, a certain type of angel.

3) The *me'orah* or *me'orot*, recited before the first blessing preceding the *Shema*, the blessing which ends "*yotser ha-me'orot*" ("creator of the luminaries").

4) The *ahavah*, read before the second blessing preceding the Shema, which concludes "*ohev amo Yisrael*" ("Who loves His people Israel").

5) The *zulat* or *zulatekha*, recited before the words, *én Elohim zulatekha* ("there is no God other than You") concludes the first paragraph after the *Shema*.

6) The *mi kamokha* ("Who is like You?"), named after the verse containing those words, which is also part of the blessing after the *Shema*.

7) The *Adonai Malkenu* ("Our Land, Our King"), based on the prayer text in the Sephardi ritual. Among Ashkenazi Jews, this section is known as *ge'ulah*, because the blessing concludes *ga'al Yisrael* ("Who redeems Israel").

The *yotserot* for semi-festival days, such as Ḥanukkah, Purim, the New Moon, the intermediate days of the festivals, fast days, etc., are composed of five *piyyutim* (numbers 3-7 of the above list). In modern times, the *yotserot* are not usually recited.

Z

ZAKEN MAMREH A "rebellious elder" who, by biblical law, is sentenced to death (Deut. 17:12). According to the rabbis, various conditions must be fulfilled for this rule to be implemented. First, it only applies to an ordained Torah scholar. Second, he must deliberately refuse to accept the decision of the SANHEDRIN. Third, the elder must have ruled that others act in accordance with his views. Teaching his views is not grounds for punishment. Fourth, he must be aware that the other sages have ruled differently and nevertheless persevere in his ruling. Fifth, his refusal to accept the ruling of the other sages must relate to a law for which the punishment for negligence is a sin offering, and for deliberate violation the punishment is KARET, "cutting off" from his people. An example of such a case would be where the Sanhedrin decrees that a certain year is to be a leap year, which means that an extra month is added before Passover. If the "rebellious elder" refuses to accept this ruling, his decision will mean that those following him will celebrate Passover a month early, and when it came to the official Passover, would be guilty of the sin of eating leaven, for which the punishment is *karet*.

The purpose of this law was to preserve the unity of the Jewish people, and the rule is therefore that in such a case, even where the Sanhedrin would be willing to be conciliatory, it has no right to commute the death sentence.

ZAVIM (discharges). Ninth tractate of Order TOHOROT in the Mishnah. Its five chapters deal with the subject of the cleanness or uncleanness of a man (*zav*) or a woman (*zavah*) suffering from running issues (Lev. 15: 1-15, 25-30). The Mishnah describes the qualifications of a *zav* (or *zavah*), the counting of the clean days, ritual immersion in a ritual bath, and the offering of a sin-offering and a burnt-offering. The tractate also discusses the transmission of uncleanness by a *zav* or a *zavah*, and the conveyance of uncleanness through contact with a dead animal. The subject matter is amplified in the *Tosefta*.

ZEBULUN See TRIBES, TWELVE

ZECHARIAH One of the Minor Prophets in the Prophets section of the Bible. His first prophecy was made in the second year of the reign of Darius I Hystaspis, i.e., 520 BCE. Zechariah was a contemporary of Zerubabbel the governor, Joshua the high priest, and HAGGAI the prophet. He prophesied for about two years. Along with Haggai, he exhorted the people of Jerusalem to resume work on the rebuilding of the TEMPLE.

BOOK OF ZECHARIAH

1:1 — 1:7	Call to repentance
1:8 — 1:17	Vision of the horses
2:1 — 2:4	The four horns and the four smiths
2:5 — 2:16	The man with the measuring line; promise of restoration
3:1 — 3:10	The cleansing of the priesthood
4:1 — 4:14	The lamp and the olive tree; promises of deliverance
5:1 — 5:11	The flying scroll and the woman inside the bushel
6:1 — 6:8	The four chariots
6:9 — 8:23	The messianic age
9:1 — 9:8	Punishment of neighboring nations
9:9 — 9:17	Redemption of Israel
10:1 — 10:12	Ingathering of Israel's exiles
11:1 — 11:17	The punishment of the evil shepherds
12:1 — 14:21	Apocalyptic oracles; end of days.

The Book of Zechariah is the 11th of the 12 Minor Prophets. It belongs, together with Haggai and MALACHI, to a group of prophecies after the Babylonian EXILE. The Book contains two different parts: the first eight chapters are explicitly ascribed to the prophet and give a clear account of the date of his prophecies. The remaining six chapters, eschatological in content, are written in an obscure style with allusions to a background that is unclear. Authorship and date of composition of this part are unknown. Although the whole work is attributed to one prophet, most modern scholars contend that the author of these chapters cannot be the same prophet and that the oracles stem from a later period. The Book of Zechariah is the longest of all the Minor Prophets, and the book contains 211 verses. After the return from Babylonian exile, the people of Jerusalem were a poor and dispirited community (8:10). Adding his voice to that of Haggai, Zechariah urged them to continue building the Temple as a necessary prelude to the messianic kingdom. The result of their combined efforts was the completion of the restoration of the Temple (Ezra 6:15) in 516 BCE. The first six chapters contain eight visions which are recorded as having taken place in a single night. The connecting theme of these visions is the assurance that the messianic age is about to begin despite appearances to the contrary. The last chapters of the book deal with various aspects of the messianic age. Both sections of the book contributed greatly to the later literary genre of apocalypticism.

ZEKHUT AVOT

See MERIT

ZEMIROT

(from the Hebrew root *zmr* "to sing"). Table hymns sung during and after the SABBATH meals. The commonly used texts are poems and *piyyutim* written over the ages by various Hebrew poets; some are by well-known poets, the authors of others remain anonymous. Most are in Hebrew, a few are in Aramaic. The subject matter includes Sabbath laws, observances, and customs, the rewards due the Sabbath observer, references to the prophet ELIJAH, and praise of God. The topics used and the allusions to biblical phrases perhaps developed from the ancient custom of discussing Torah subjects at meals.

Sefer Ḥasidim (ed. Wistinetzki, 722) states that it is commendable to sit and sing praises on the Sabbath, citing Psalm 92:1-2. *Siddur Rashi* (534) states that the recital of *zemirot* at the conclusion of the Sabbath is a proper custom; in the same manner as citizens of a country accompany the excursions of the king with voices and lutes and harps, so Jews accompany the exit of the Sabbath Queen in joy and songs.

The kabbalists of the 16th and 17th centuries wrote several liturgical poems in honor of the Sabbath; they include some of the most popular *zemirot*, such as *Yom Zeh le-Yisrael* and *Yah Ribbon Olam*.

Some 25 *zemirot* became the core of the table hymns among Ashkenazim, and they were divided into three groupings, each one associated with a specific Sabbath meal, Friday evening (eight), Sabbath morning (eight), and end of the Sabbath (nine), particularly at a MELAVVEH MALKAH. Some are already to be found in the *Maḥzor Vitry* (11th century). While collected by Ashkenazim, the authors include Spanish Hebrew poets, such as Dunash Ben Labrat, JUDAH HALEVI and Abraham IBN EZRA. The Sephardim did not determine a fixed collection of *zemirot*, but rather poems and songs, *zemer* or *pizmon*, which are sung in both synagogue and home.

There is no rigid rule requiring that any specific number be sung. A wide variety of tunes developed, some identified with particular Jewish communities, others more generally known as Ashkenazi or Sephardi. New tunes still continue to be introduced.

Ḥasidic communities found a venue of expression for their spiritual elevation and enthusiasm in the creation of new melodies for the *zemirot*, sometimes in the form of adaptations of tunes absorbed from their host countries.

A recurring theme in the *zemirot* sung at the end of the Sabbath is Elijah, as herald of the Messiah and the final redemption.

Today in many homes and particularly at communal meals, songs fitting the themes of the Sabbath day, but not part of the traditional *zemirot* per se, are also sung at the Sabbath table, all leading to the creation of a special Sabbath spirit at the meal.

ZEMIROT

	Author	Date
Friday evening		
Kol Mekaddesh Shevi'i ("Whoever Hallows the Seventh Day")	Moses (family name unknown)	Early Middle Ages
Menuḥah ve-Simḥah ("Rest and Joy")	Moses (family name unknown)	Early Middle Ages
Mah Yedidut ("How Beloved is your Restfulness")	Menahem (family name unknown)	Early Middle Ages
Mah Yafit ("How Lovely")	Mordecai ben Isaac	Early Middle Ages

	Author	Date
Friday evening		
Yom Shabbat Kodesh Hu ("The Sabbath Day is Holy")	Jonathan (family name unknown)	Early Middle Ages
Yom Zeh le-Yisrael ("This Day is for Israel")	Isaac LURIA	16th century
Yah Ribbon Olam ("God, Master of the Universe")	Israel Najara	16th century
Tsur Mi-Shelo ("Rock — from Whom we have Eaten")	Unknown	16th century

	Author	Date
Friday evening		
Tsamaḫ Nafshi ("My Soul Thirsts")	Abraham IBN EZRA	12th century
Sabbath morning		
Barukh Adonai Yom Yom ("Blessed be the Lord every day")	Simon bar Isaac	10th century
Barukh El Elyon ("Blessed is God Most High")	Baruch of Mainz	13th century
Yom Zeh Mekhubbad ("This Day is Honored")	Israel (last name unknown)	Middle Ages
Yom Shabbaton ("Day of Rest")	JUDAH HALEVI	12th century
Ki Eshmerah Shabbat ("If I keep the Sabbath")	Abraham Ibn Ezra	12th century
Shimru Shabtotai ("Keep My Sabbaths")	Solomon (last name unknown)	Middle Ages
Deror Yikra ("Freedom He shall Proclaim")	Dunash ben Labrat	10th century
Shabbat ha-Yom la-Adonai ("Today is Sabbath to the Lord")	Samuel (last name unknown)	Middle Ages
Sabbath afternoon (SE'UDAH SHELISHIT)		
Bené Hekhla ("Members of the Sanctuary")	Isaac Luria	16th century

	Author	Date
Sabbath afternoon (SE'UDAH SHELISHIT)		
Mizmor le-David (Psalm 23)		
Yedid Nefesh ("Beloved of the Soul")	Eliezar Azikri	16th century
End of Sabbath		
Ha-Mavdil ("He Who distinguishes")	Isaac the Younger	11th century
Eliyyahu ha-Navi ("Elijah the Prophet")	Unknown	Middle Ages
Be-Motsa'é Yom Menuḫah ("At the End of the Day of Rest")	Jacob de Lunel	12th century
Haddesh Sesoni ("Renew my Joy")	Unknown	Middle Ages
Agil ve-Esmaḫ ("I shall Rejoice and be Happy")	Eleazar (last name unknown)	Before 1545
Elohim Yisadenu ("God will give us support")	Abraham (last name unknown)	Middle Ages
Eli Ḫish Go'ali ("My God, Speed my Redemption")	Naḫman (last name unknown)	Middle Ages
Addir Ayom ve-Nora ("Mighty, Formidable, and Awesome")	Unknown	Middle Ages
Ish Ḫasid Hayah ("There was a pious man")	Jesse bar Mordecai	Early Middle Ages

The *zemirot* are to be found in most comprehensive prayer books as well as in special collections which include the Grace after Meals. The collections of table hymns generally open with *Shalom Alékhem* which is part of the Friday evening ceremonies but not of the *zemirot*.

ZEPHANIAH One of the Minor Prophets in the Prophets section of the Bible. Zephaniah was a descendant of Hezekiah (Zeph. 1:1), presumably King Hezekiah of Judah. In that case, he was distantly related to King Josiah during whose reign he prophesied. If this is true, one can understand how the prophet railed against the nobility, with whose lifestyle he was personally acquainted. According to Jewish tradition, Zephaniah was a contemporary of the prophet JEREMIAH and the prophetess Huldah. According to a tradition, Jeremiah preached in the markets, Zephaniah in the synagogues, and Huldah before the women.

The Book of Zephaniah is the ninth book of the 12 Minor Prophets. It consists of three chapters, with 53 verses. It contains three oracles by Zephaniah delivered during the early years of the reign of King Josiah (640-608 BCE). The first oracle castigates the people of Judah for idol worship, for adopting non-Israelite practices (1:8). Their punishment is

BOOK OF ZEPHANIAH

1:1 — 1:18	Denunciation of idolatry in Judah and pronunciation of judgment
2:1 — 3:7	Nations called to repentance
3:8 — 3:13	After judgment of the wicked, the remnant will be delivered
3:14 -3:20	Deliverance of Israel.

to be a cataclysm, which, like other prophets before him, Zephaniah refers to as the Day of the Lord. Because his descriptions of this event are so vivid, Zephaniah is often called "the prophet of the day of the Lord." The second oracle is a call for repentance, evidently aimed at Judah. Zephaniah's final oracle denounces Judah's political and religious leaders. God promises to bring against them an army of people from all over the world composed of devotees of God. The surviving remnant of Judah will include ingathered exiles, and it will be characterized by justice and humility; it will be the pride of all humanity.

ZERA'IM (Seeds). First Order of the Mishnah. The opening tractate, BERAKHOT, deals with the laws of prayer and the blessings said over food and drink. The remaining ten tractates (PE'AH, DEMA'I, KELA'IM, SHEVI'IT, TERUMOT, MA'ASEROT, MA'ASER SHENI, ḤALLAH, ORLAH and BIKKURIM) deal with agricultural laws such as separating tithes, sowing mixed seeds, letting the land lie fallow, and bringing the first fruits to the Temple. Most of these laws apply only in Erets Israel. Maimonides explains that *Zera'im* is the first Order because it is concerned with food, and a man cannot live and serve God without eating. The tractate concerning blessings begins the Order because before eating the produce of the land, one must first bless the Creator, whose existence makes all plant and animal life possible. All of the tractates in Order *Zera'im* are expanded upon in the Jerusalem Talmud, but only *Berakhot* is covered in the Babylonian Talmud as well.

ZEVAḤIM (sacrifices). First tractate of Order KODASHIM in the Mishnah. Its 14 chapters deal with the laws of slaughtering and sprinkling the blood of animal and bird sacrifices in the Temple (cf. Lev. 1: 1-17; 2:1-4; 4:27-31). The Mishnah discusses the seven classifications of offerings, intention when offering a sacrifice, the correct procedure in *sheḥitah* (slaughtering), receiving and tossing the blood, the separation of the priest's portion of the offering, and the cleaning of garments and vessels stained with the blood of a sacrifice. The subject matter is amplified in the Babylonian Talmud and the *Tosefta*.

ZIKHRONOT (lit. "remembrances"). Name given to the second of the three middle blessings of the AMIDAH prayer in the ADDITIONAL SERVICE of ROSH HA-SHANAH. This section evokes "remembrances," where God is ultimately asked to remember His covenant with the Jewish people. After an introductory section indicating how God remembers everything, ten verses of the Bible are recited which mention God as remembering, three verses each being taken from the Pentateuch, the Prophets and the Hagiographa, with the tenth again from the Pentateuch. Among these "remembrances" are the flood, the Jews' slavery in Egypt, and God's promise to remember His covenant with His people. Ten blasts on the SHOFAR mark the completion of the section.

ZION One of the names for the city of JERUSALEM, or a part of it. Early biblical references to the name are quite specific, though changeable. "David took the stronghold of Zion, that is, the city of David" (II Sam. 5:7, also I Chr. 11:5). The reference here is to the small hill, now southeast of the present city walls, which was the site of the first Jebusite settlement of Jerusalem. The name Zion, sometimes called Mount Zion, was extended to cover the biblical city, enlarged by David and subsequent kings of Judah. In Micah 4:7 ("the Lord will reign over them in Mount Zion") and 4:8 ("daughter of Zion"), and especially in Isaiah and Psalms, Zion served as a synonym for the whole of Jerusalem.

In time, the name Zion came to mean the whole land of Judah ("O my people who dwell in Zion," Isa. 10:24), and, even more generally, the people of Israel rather than any particular place ("and saying to Zion 'You are my people';" Isa. 51:16).

The word "Zion" inside a Magen David *on the finials of a Torah Scroll from Persia.*

Later usage was both more specific and more general. In the late biblical and early post-biblical period the name Zion came to refer to the TEMPLE MOUNT (Joel 3:17, I Macc. 7:33). Its final geographical identification was to the western hill just south of the present walls of the Old City. It was David's tomb, traditionally (but improbably) located there, which made this identification permanent.

The connection with David was also responsible for the generalization and broadening of the name Zion. As David was seen as the ideal king presiding over a golden age, so Zion, the city of David, was the idealized Israel. For centuries the Jewish people dreamed and prayed for a return to Zion (rather than to Jerusalem, or the land of Israel). The Mourners of Zion (*avelé-tsiyyon*), a group of mystics and ascetics, lived in Jerusalem from the time of the destruction of the Temple, and in many communities of the Diaspora well into the Middle Ages. JUDAH HALEVI, medieval Hebrew poet and philosopher, wrote his most famous poems as "Songs of Zion." The modern national revival and return of the Jewish people to its homeland bears the name "Zionism." See ZION, RETURN TO.

ZION, RETURN TO (*shivat tsiyyon*). The desire of Jews in GALUT (exile) to return to the Land of Israel (ZION, a synonym of JERUSALEM, being applied to the whole land, hence the modern term "Zionism"). Already Abraham and Sarah were told by God, "Your seed shall be a stranger in a land that is not theirs..and in the fourth generation they shall come back here [i.e., to Canaan]" (Gen. 15:13-16). The punishments threatened by God to the Israelites if they did not keep His commandments were exile from their land and scattering among the nations, but these are coupled with the promise that eventually "The Lord your God will bring you back from captivity...and gather you again from all the peoples..and will bring you into the land which your fathers possessed and you shall possess it" (Deut. 30:1-5). This theme was taken up by the prophets who preached reform under threat of exile but coupled with the promise of ultimate return (e.g., Ezek. 11:17-20; Hos. 8:10,13,11:11; Amos 9:14-15; Mic. 4:6.

The term "Return to Zion" was first applied to a historic event some 50 years after the destruction of the First Temple when Cyrus, the Persian conqueror of Babylonia, proclaimed to the Jews in the Babylonian captivity: "Whosoever there is among you of all His people, his God be with him, let him go up..." (Ezra 1:3; II Chr. 36:23). From expressions such as this the use of the term ALIYAH ("going up" or "ascension") developed, denoting immigration of Jews to the Land of Israel).

The Bible records the various small waves of immigration under Zerubabbel, Ezra, and Nehemiah that "went up" and refounded Jewish life in Judah. Most of the exiles, however, chose not to return, and the rabbis, in retrospect, said that the destruction of the Second Temple was already foreshadowed in this refusal of the exiled Jews of Babylon to return *en masse* (*Yoma* 9b). It was after the destruction of the Second Temple, in 70 CE, the concomitant loss of sovereignty, and the growth of the *Galut* that the yearning for the Return to Zion became a major factor in Judaism.

The collective Jewish consciousness of a Return to Zion resulted from a combination of nostalgic memory, utopian vision, and a sense of religious obligation.

(1) There was first the natural longing of exiles for the familiar landscapes, flora, and fauna of home and birthplace. Even later generations, who had not known the Land at first hand, maintained a constant consciousness of its physical features. Widespread Jewish literacy in the Bible disseminated knowledge of the hills and valleys, cities and springs of the Holy Land, the setting of the events and stories in the Bible which kept alive the natural attachment and love of the people for their land. This was enhanced by the liturgical tradition of facing Jerusalem during prayer, praying for rain according to the seasonal needs of Erets Israel, and thrice daily petitioning God for a return to Zion.

In leaving the house of a mourner, the Jew says, "May the Almighty console you among the mourners of Zion and Jerusalem." In the GRACE AFTER MEALS, he says, "Rebuild Jerusalem , the holy city, speedily in our days..." while every AMIDAH prayer contains the petition: "Let our eyes behold Your return in mercy to Zion..."

(2) An essential component of the Jewish belief-system is the ultimate redemption of mankind on the historical level called "the days of the MESSIAH". This will include utopian elements such as the restoration of the lost institutions of the national and religious life to the Jewish people such as territory, sovereignty, national leadership, Temple, and Sanhedrin. Thus a religious motivation for returning to Zion is to complete the original though interrupted task given to Israel to fashion a national state in accordance with the ideals of the Prophets which might serve as a "light to the nations" (Isa. 42:6). What is unclear, and what has remained a matter of dispute among religious Jews to this day, is the amount of human activism to be exercised in the fulfillment of these prophecies. The question is whether the Divine assurance of Israel's return to the land means that the exiles must wait patiently until God brings them back or whether they are to make efforts on their own to return. Some argue that since Exile was an act of Divine punishment, Israel must wait for a clear sign that its sins have been expiated. Indeed the rabbis spoke of an oath exacted from Israel that they would not forcibly break the Exile and fight their way into the Land (*Ket.* 111a). However, Jewish messianism was bound up with the concept of the Return to Zion, even by the use of force. The proof of the genuineness of any claimant to messiahship must be that he will lead the Jews back to their own land. The MESSIANIC MOVEMENTS that emerged over the centuries were based on this premise.

(3) The return to Zion has been incorporated into Jewish law as a religious obligation of the individual Jew. While the authorities differ as to the precise status of the obligation, its juridical force is seen in a cluster of rulings, as for example that the refusal of a spouse to accompany husband or wife in a move to the Land of Israel is a cause for divorce (*Yad*,

Hilkhot Ishut 13). As a formal halakhic obligation, return to Zion became subject to all sorts of qualifications. Thus if travel to or living conditions in Erets Israel are life-threatening, then the obligation to preserve life stands higher than the commandment of moving to Erets Israel. Until the middle of the 19th century, actual conditions were such as to render the practical force of the halakhic obligation to return to Zion quite tenuous.

The religious quality of living in Erets Israel was considered superior to life elsewhere. In spite of the existence of important biblical academies in Babylon, individual sages continued to immigrate from there to Erets Israel throughout the talmudic period. Not only could more *mitsvot* (positive commandments) be observed in Erets Israel but even those not dependent upon the Land had greater religious significance when observed in Erets Israel. Also, it was held that the SHEKHINAH, the indwelling Presence of God, never departed from Jerusalem, implying that a living experience of God was more likely in Erets Israel. Even death and burial in the Holy Land had its privileges, and those who had no choice but to be buried in the Diaspora tried to arrange that a bag of soil from the Holy Land be buried with them.

The rabbis had no illusions about the vagaries of the Jewish commitment to a return to Zion. "Judah has gone into exile...she dwells among the nations and finds no rest" (Lam. 1:3) to which the rabbis comment: "Had she found rest, she still would not have returned". Also, "So great is the day of the INGATHERING OF THE EXILES and so difficult that it would seem as though God Himself must literally take hold of each one with His hand to bring him out of his place" (Rashi on Deut. 30:3).

Historically, the constant trickle of Jews who returned to Zion over the centuries was religiously motivated, and included a number of distinguished rabbis. Groups of refugees arrived from Spain and Portugal after the expulsions of the late 15th century and some of them established the great kabbalistic center in Safed. From the end of the 18th century groups of Ḥasidim and disciples of ELIJAH BEN SOLOMON, the Gaon of Vilna, settled in the Holy Land, especially in the "Holy Cities" of Jerusalem, Hebron, Tiberias, and Safed. Most of them spent their time in religious study and many went to the country so as to be buried in holy soil.

In the 19th century, the concept of the Return to Zion underwent two radical transformations, one on the part of REFORM JUDAISM and the other by political Zionism. Reform Judaism, which was the first reinterpretation of Judaism in response to the challenge of modernity and the changed conditions brought about by the EMANCIPATION, stated in its Pittsburgh Platform of 1885: "We consider ourselves no longer a nation but a religious community and therefore expect neither a return to Palestine... nor the restoration of any of the laws concerning the Jewish State."

According to this view, the dispersion of the Jewish people is not to be seen as Divine punishment but as an effective

Kurdistan immigrants carrying Torah Scrolls descending the plane bringing them to Zion.

opportunity to disseminate the values of prophetic morality worldwide. The development of a universal transnational culture to which Jews would contribute would establish "truth, justice and peace among men" and would constitute the realization of Israel's messianic hope. Since then, historical developments have led to changes in Reform ideology. The Columbus Platform in 1937 affirmed the obligation of all Jewry to aid in the upbuilding of a Jewish Homeland in Palestine as a refuge for the oppressed and as a center for Jewish cultural and spiritual life. In recent years the Reform movement joined the Zionist Organization, and has actively endorsed immigration to Israel.

The ideology of the modern Zionist movement whose goal was the return of the Jewish people to Erets Israel, drew upon a number of different strands to change the overall complexion of the concept of Return to Zion from philanthropic to political, from messianic to utopian, from religious to secular-centered. The rise of nationalism throughout Europe prompted Jews, who did not lack a sense of historic and ethnic identity, to reclaim their patrimony in Erets Israel. For some (Moses Hess) the Jewish national spirit could contribute to a materialization of the world social revolution as they proceed to build their own society. For others (Leo Pinsker, Theodore Herzl) a Jewish State could solve "the Jewish Problem" in countries like Russia and Germany where anti-Semitism had created grave concern. Still others were critical of the pallid "Mosaic persuasion" developed by assimilated Jews in Western countries and called for a renaissance of Jewish national culture beginning with Hebrew language and literature, cultivation of Jewish history and philosophy, which could only be achieved in a national homeland (Aḥad Ha-Am). Under the impact of modernity, the traditional messianic idea of Return to Zion was rationalized into a realistic program by Judah Alkalai (1798-1878) and Tsevi Hirsch Kalischer (1795-1874), and became the basis for religious Zionism. However, the large masses of

Orthodox Jewry in Europe before World War II rejected and opposed political Zionism for preempting Divine intervention to bring the Jews back to their own land and for its secular leadership. Most of these Jews perished in the Holocaust and the survivors (with exceptions) cooperate with the State of Israel (see ISRAEL, STATE OF). These ultra-Orthodox groups did not question the belief in the Return to Zion, but only the means by which it was to be realized.

ZODIAC The imaginary twelve-part division of the sky, through which the sun, moon, and planets pass as they move. At an early period, each Hebrew month was assigned one of the zodiacal signs, the names given to each sign being the exact Hebrew translation of the Latin signs. While the Talmud makes no mention of the zodiacal signs, later Jewish literature does on occasion. Zodiacs are often portrayed in Jewish art, ranging from mosaics in ancient synagogues in Eretz Israel to prayerbooks to painted ceilings in 18th century Polish wood-built synagogues. Parallels are sometimes made between the zodiacal sign and the Jewish content of a month. Thus it is suggested that the zodiacal sign of *Tishri* is *moznayim* (i.e., *libra* — the scales), for in that month God weighs each human being's virtues and sins. Presumably because both the zodiacal signs and the tribes of Israel number 12, there is reference (in *Yalkut Shimoni*) to each tribe being linked to a specific zodiacal sign. Even earlier, *Sefer Yetsirah* spelled out a correspondence between the 12 zodiacal signs and the 12 organs of the human body. See also ASTROLOGY.

ZODIAC

Latin name	English name	Hebrew Name
Aries	Ram	Nisan
Taurus	Bull	Iyyar
Gemini	Twins	Sivan
Cancer	Crab	Tammuz
Leo	Lion	Av
Virgo	Virgin	Elul
Libra	Scales	Tishri
Scorpio	Scorpion	Heshvan
Sagittarius	Archer	Kislev
Capricorn	Goat	Tevet
Aquarius	Water Carrier	Shevat
Pisces	Fishes	Adar

ZOHAR ("Book of Splendor"). The major work in Jewish MYSTICISM; the most influential work of the Kabbalah. The Zohar was written in Castile in the last third of the 13th century, and it is first quoted in kabbalistic works after 1291. The main author of the work was R. MOSES DE LEON, but two sections, *Ra'aya Mehemna* ("Loyal Shepherd," meaning Moses) and *Tikkuné ha-Zohar*, were written by a later anonymous kabbalist early in the 14th century.

Moses de Léon wrote the main part of the Zohar as a hermeneutical commentary on the Pentateuch, a section to each PARASHAH (division). He used the ARAMAIC language in a creative manner, virtually inventing an original version of that language suited to his needs. The *midrash* of the Zohar is presented as the concerted effort of a group of *tannaim* (Mishnaic sages), headed by R. SIMEON BAR YOḤAI and his son R. Eleazar. Besides the tannaim, several fictional figures appear in the Zohar, like the mysterious Sava ("Old Man") and Yenuka ("Child"), who disclose heavenly secrets. R. Simeon and his group are described in many stories and anecdotes, denoting their supernatural knowledge and powers. The midrashic and narrative elements are interwoven into a masterly literary unity.

The literary framework combined with the unusual strength of the Zohar's mystical symbolism made a lasting impact on Jewish culture. The author of the Zohar derived many of his symbols from the works of earlier kabbalists, especially the *Sefer ha-*BAHIR, the kabbalists of Provence and Gerona, and the brothers Jacob and Isaac ha-Kohen in the second half of the 13th century, but all these sources were used in a creative manner, and Moses de Léon added to them his own mystical visions and speculations.

Five central myths are presented in the Zohar:

(1) The myth of the cosmogonical process, the initial evolvement of the ten Divine powers (the SEFIROT), from the eternal Godhead;

(2) The detailed myth of the dynamic interrelationship within the realm of the Divine emanations, especially between the elements of *Din* (Justice) and *Ḥesed* (Mercy, Charity);

(3) The sexual symbolical myth of the relationship between the masculine and feminine elements in the Divine world, the latter represented by the SHEKHINAH;

(4) The myth of the struggle between the holy Divine realm on the right and the evil system on the left, the *Sitra Aḥra* ("The Other Side," meaning the left side), the realm of the satanic powers;

(5) The messianic myth, the apocalyptic description of the REDEMPTION, the role of the MESSIAH, and the role of R. Simeon and his group in that process.

Many kabbalists in later generations did not accept all these mythical symbols, and some tried to moderate them; LURIANIC KABBALAH in the 16th century, however, intensified them even further.

The Zohar is a library rather than a book. Besides the later additions, the *Ra'aya Mehemna* and *Tikkuné Zohar* (the latter usually printed as a separate, fourth volume, following the three volumes of the Zohar itself), it includes an early stratum, Rabbi Moses's *Midrash ha-Ne'elam* ("The Esoteric

Midrash"), written partly in Hebrew and including some undisguised medieval terms. Separate sections are dedicated to the commentaries on the Song of Songs, the creation story (*Sifra de Tseni'uta*, "The Book of Concealment"), Ezekiel's chariot, and others. Of special importance are the *Idra Zuta* and *Idra Rabba* ("The Lesser Assembly" and the "Larger Assembly"), in which dramatic congregations of the group of mystics are described, and secrets are disclosed. The author developed specific styles and literary forms to many of these different parts. A fifth volume was later added to the Zohar, the *Zohar Ḥadash* ("New Zohar"), a collection of authentic material, belonging to many parts of the work, which was not included in the first editions.

While the centrality of R. Moses de Léon in the authorship of the Zohar cannot be doubted, it is possible that other kabbalists had some part in its composition, especially R. Joseph Gikatilla, R. Moses's close associate; it is possible that the teachings of other contemporary kabbalists found their way into the Zohar.

The Zohar was printed twice in the 16th century (Cremona, 1559-1560, and Mantua, 1558-1560, in three volumes; the Mantua edition was the basis for all subsequent editions), amid a controversy which engulfed kabbalists and non-kabbalists. One of the motives for its publication was messianic: the belief, founded in some sections of the Zohar itself, that the knowledge of the Zohar is part of the messianic process. The Zohar joined the Bible and Talmud in the triad of the most sacred books of Judaism.

ZUGOT ("Pairs"). Hebrew term designating the five pairs of teachers and transmitters of the ORAL LAW enumerated in the opening chapter of tractate *Avot* (1.4-15). Each pair was contemporaneous: tradition regards the first member of each *zug* as president (NASI) and the second as vice-president (AV BET DIN) of the great SANHEDRIN that met in the Temple's Chamber of Hewn Stone. Their period of activity constitutes a transitional stage between just prior to the Maccabean Revolt and the era of the TANNAIM. The five pairs were:

1. Yosé ben Yo'ezer and Yosé ben Johanan (before 160 BCE). They lived during the period of the Maccabean Revolt and the Talmud records their decree (*Shab.* 15a) aimed at discouraging emigration to "heathen lands."

2. Joshua ben Peraḥyah and Nittai (or Mattai) of Arbel (c. 130 BCE). Some of their ethical sayings have been preserved in *Avot*, while a few ancient *halakhot* are mentioned in the name of Joshua ben Peraḥyah.

3. Judah ben Tabbai and SIMEON BEN SHETAḤ (c.100-75 BCE). At some point the two men exchanged office. The former reputedly fled to Alexandria during the persecution of the PHARISEES by King Alexander Yannai, while the latter was protected by his sister, Queen Salome Alexandra.

4. SHEMAYAH AND AVTALYON (late first century BCE). Both are said to have been descended from proselytes.

5. HILLEL and SHAMMAI (end of the first century BCE-before 30 CE). Each founded an important tannaitic school; for further details, see BET SHAMMAI AND BET HILLEL.

ZUNZ, LEOPOLD (Yom Tov Lippman; 1794-1886). One of the founders of the "Science of Judaism" (WISSENSCHAFT DES JUDENTUMS) and pioneer of the scientific study of Jewish literature, liturgy, and religious poetry. Born in Detmold, Germany, Zunz attended the University of Berlin, and in 1821 received his doctorate from the University of Halle. He obtained his rabbinical title from Aaron CHORIN.

In 1818 Zunz published his first major work on Jewish literature, *Etwas über die rabbinische Literatur*; in it he argues that Jewish literature should occupy a dignified place in the universities. With others, he founded the *Verein für Cultur und Wissenschaft der Juden* in 1819, and became editor of the *Zeitschrift für die Wissenschaft des Judentums* (1823), in which he wrote three articles, one on Rashi. This was the first time that a biography of a Jewish scholar had been scientifically presented.

In 1820 Zunz became preacher in the New Synagogue in Berlin, but resigned from the position two years later. He was then sub-editor of the Berlin daily newspaper, *Haude und Spenersche Zeitung*, and director of the newly founded Jewish Communal School, but his main interest continued to be research into Hebrew literature. In 1832 there appeared his *Die gottesdienstlichen Vorträge der Juden historisch entwickelt* in which he showed that preaching had always formed part of the prayer services of the Jews and that the sermon was usually in the vernacular (see HOMILETICS AND HOMILETICAL LITERATURE). When in 1836 a royal decree forbade Jews to use German first names, Zunz, commissioned by the Jewish community, wrote *Namen der Juden* to prove that Jews had always used foreign names. His other great works include *Zur Geschichte und Literatur* (1845) and a triology on the PIYYUT, the *seliḥah* (see SELIḤOT), and the different rites. In order to write these works, Zunz visited the libraries of London, Oxford, Paris, and Parma. He was denied access to the Vatican Library because he was a Jew.

INDEX

The entries preceded by an asterisk indicate articles in the body of the Encyclopedia.

C

L

M

N

O

P

S

T

U

V

W

ACKNOWLEDGMENTS

The Publishers wish to express their appreciation to the following individuals and institutions for their help:

Mr Ralph Abadir of Color Print Graphix, C.V., Antwerp, for the printing and binding; Scanli Ltd., for the color separation; Printon Ltd., for the black and white films; Keter Enterprises Ltd. for the film setting run;

Margalit Bassan paging; Suzan Fogg for proof-reading; Sarah Lewis for setting; Hannah Golan and Yacov Polak;

For the color illustrations:
Jacket: (top) Yad Vashem Coll. Jerusalem; (below) IMJ; (*back*) Jewish Theological Seminary Library, N.Y.; *p.17* Coll. IJM. Photo Studio Tanaka; *p.18* Coll. IMJ. Photo IMJ/Pierre Alain Ferrazini; *p.35* Coll. IMJ. Photo D. Harris; *p.36* Photo N. Garo; *p.54* JPH/Photo D. Harris; *p.71* Courtesy G. Wigoder; *P.72* Coll. IMJ/Photo D. Harris; *p.121* The British Library; *p.122* JNUL; *p.139* Wolfson Museum Hechal Shlomo Synagogue, Jerusalem. Photo D. Harris; *p.140* Coll. IMJ. Photo IMJ/D. Harris; *p.197* Tel Aviv Museum; *pp. 197-199* IMJ/Shrine of the Book. Photo Alain Ferrazini; *p.200* Coll. IMJ Photo IMJ/D. Harris; *p.241* Coll. IMJ. IMJ/Photo D. Harris; *p.242* JNUL. Photo D. Harris; *p.259* Coll. IMJ Photo IMJ./Moshe Caine; *p.260* Coll. IMJ. Photo IMJ; *p.301* Coll. Eric Estorick, London. Photo IMJ/Nachum Slapak; *pp. 302-303* Coll. Schocken Library, Jerusalem. Photo D. Harris; *p.304* IMJ Stieglitz Coll.Photo IMJ/Arie Ganor; *p.393* IMJ. Photo IMJ/Yoram Lehman; *p.394* IMJ. Stieglitz Coll.; *P.411* JNUL, Photo D. Harris; p.412 Coll. of the artist (Arie Ophir). Photo IMJ/Nachum Slapak; *p.445* JNUL. Photo D. Harris; *p.446* JNUL, Photo D. Harris. *p.463* IDAM/Photo D. Harris; *p.464* IMJ Photo IMJ; *p.545* Coll. IMJ Photo IMJ/Yoram Lehman; *p.546* Coll. IMJ Photo IMJ/Nachum Slapak; *p.563* British Library;

p.564 IMJ Stieglitz Coll. Photo IMJ/Avi Ganor. *p.629* Photo Sonia Halliday Weston-Turville. Coll. Central Synagogue, London; *p.630* IMJ. Photo IMJ/Nachum Slapak; *p.647* Coll. Jewish Museum, N.Y. Photo Art Resources, N.Y.; *p. 648* Coll. Wolfson Museum Hechal Shlomo, Jerusalem. Photo D. Harris; *p.673* (top and bottom) Beth Hatefutsoth, Tel Aviv/Photo Michael Horton; *p.674* Union of American Hebrew Congregations, Southfield, Mich. *p.675*. Photo David Harris; *p.717* Photo JPH/D. Harris; *p.718* IMJ. Photo IMJ/D. Harris; *p.735* Italian Synagogue Jerusalem. Photo D. Harris; *p.736* Beth Hatefutsoth, Tel Aviv, Photo Michael Horton.

For the black and white illustrations:
Aaron: The British Library; *Ablution*: IMJ Photo IMJ/D. Harris; *Abraham*; JNUL/Laor Coll. Photo D. Harris; *Abravanel*: Coll. Royal Library, Copenhagen; *Abulafia*: Vatican Library, Rome; *Acrostics*: The British Library; *Adultery*: Würtebergische Landesbibliothek, Stuttgart; *Aggadah*: Hessische Landes-und Hocschul bibliothek, Darmstadt; *Agricultural Laws*: Archeology Museum Istanbul, (copy) IDAM Photo IMJ/Hillel Burger; *Akiva*: Courtesy Israel Lewitt; *Al Ha-Nissim*: Coll. IMJ Photo IMJ/D. Harris; *Alphabet*: IMJ/Shrine of the Book; *Aliyah*: Government Press Office; *Angels*: Coll. IMJ. Photo IMJ/Reuven Milon; *Anthropomorphism*: Coll. IMJ. Photo IMJ/D. Harris; *Antisemitism*: Germanisches National Museum, Nürnberg; *Apocrypha*: Coll. IMJ Photo IMJ/D. Harris; *Apostasy*: Coll. IMJ Photo IMJ/D. Harris; *Aramaic*: Coll. IMJ Photo IMJ/David Harris; *Ark*: (left) Photo Amiram Harlap; (right) Courtesy Congregation Mishkan Israel, Hamden, Connecticut; *Ark of the Covenant*: Government Press Office; *Ashkenazim*: Coll. IMJ Photo IMJ/D. Harris; *Assimilation*: Courtesy Beth Hatefutsoth, Tel Aviv; *Asylum*: IDAM/Photo D. Harris; *Avot*: Coll. Wolfson Museum Hechal Shlomo, Jerusalem. Photo D. Harris; *Ba'al Keriah*: Archives des Jésuites de Paris, Chantilly; *Ba'al Shem Tov*: JNUL. Photo Beth Hatefutsoth, Tel Aviv; *Ba'al Teki'ah:* Government Press Office, Jerusalem; *Bahya ben Asher* JNUL, Jerusalem; *Bar Mitsvah*: Photo R. Kneller; *Benedictions*: Royal Library, Copenhagen; *Bet Midrash*: IDAM Photo IMJ/Kurt Meyerowitz; *Bible*: (p.118) Coll. Ben Zvi Institute, Jerusalem; (p. 120) IDAM. Photo IMJ/D. Harris; *Bible Commentaries*: (p.127) Coll. Ben Zvi Institute, Jerusalem, (p.128) JNUL, Jerusalem; *Bimah*: Courtesy Mrs Sarah Shammah in memory of her parents Tera and Ezra Shammah, (center and right) IMJ Archives; *Birth*: IMJ.Photo IMJ/D. Harris; *Bread*: IDAM; *Bridegroom of the Law*: IMJ.Photo IMJ/D. Harris; *Buber*: Photo R. Kneller; *Burial*: JPH/Photo D. Harris; *Burial Society*: Jewish Museum, London. Photo Ronald Sheridan; *Burning Bush*: Photo Zev Radovan; *Candles*: Photo Lea Greenberg, Courtesy Jerusalem Post Archives; *Caro, Joseph*: IMJ.Photo IMJ; *Cemetery*: IMJ Ethnography Archives; *Cherub*: IDAM Photo IMJ/Nachum Slapak; *Children*: Photo Karen Benzian; *Christianity*: Offentliche Kunst sammlung Basel; *Church Fathers*: Bibliothèque Nationale, Paris; *Circumcision*: IMJ Photo IMJ/D. Harris; *Community*: State Jewish Museum, Prague; *Creation*: Coll. Sarajevo National Museum; *Daniel*: Library of the Armenian Patriarchate, Jerusalem; *David*: Photo Museum for Music and Ethnology, Haifa; *Day of Atonement*: Coll. IMJ.Photo IMJ; *Dew, Prayer for*: JNUL; *Dietary Laws*: Vatican Library, Rome; *Divorce*: IMJ/Shrine of the Book. Photo IMJ/Nir Bareket. *Dowry*: Photo IMJ/Hillel Burger; *Ecclesiastes*: British Library; *Education*: Royal Library, Copenhagen; *Eḫad mi Yodeah*: Coll. Bill Gross, Tel Aviv; *Elijah ben Solomon Zalman*: JNUL/Schwadron Coll. Photo D. Harris; *Emancipation*: JNUL; *Essenes*: Photo D. Harris; *Ethiopian Jews*: Beth Hatefutsoth. Photo Doron Bacher; *Eulogy*: State Jewish Museum, Prague; *Evil*: IMJ Photo IMJ/Reuven Milon; *Exodus*: Museum of Jewish Art, Jerusalem. Photo D. Harris; *Ezrat Nashim*: IMJ Photo IMJ/D. Harris; *Family*: (right and left) IMJ Ethnography Collection; *Family Purity*: Stadts-und Universitäts bibliothek, Hamburg; *Festival*: IMJ/Stieglitz Coll. Photo IMJ/Avi Ganor; *First-born, Redemption of*: IMJ Photo IMJ/D. Harris; *First Fruits*: IMJ. Photo IMJ/Hillel Burger; *Four Species*: IMJk Photo IMJ/D. Harris; *Funeral*: State Jewish Museum Prague; *Gamaliel*: IMJ Photo IMJ/D. Harris; *Gemilut Hasadim*: IMJ Photo IMJ/D. Harris; *Genesis*: IMJ.Photo IMJ/D. Harris; *Genizah*: Beth Hatefutsoth, Tel Aviv; *God, Names of*: IMJ Photo IMJ/D. Harris; *Golden Calf*: Rijksmuseum, Amsterdam; *Government, Prayer for*: IMJ.Photo IMJ/Reuven Milon; *Grace After Meals*: IMJ Photo IMJ/Reuven Milon; *Ḫabad*: Photo Reuven Milon; *Hakkafot*: Government Press Office; *Hallah*: Drawing Flora Vainer; *Hallel*: Saul Raskin, New York; *Hanukkah*: IMJ Photo IMJ/D. Harris; *Hasidé Ummot Ha-Olam*: Photo JPH/Moshe Caine; *Ḫasidism*: IMJ Photo IMJ/Hillel Burger; *Hasmoneans*: Reifenberg Coll. on loan from Bank Leumi. Photo IMJ; *Haskalah*: Coll. IMJ PHoto IMJ/D. Harris; *Hebrew*: Cambridge University Library; *Heder*: IMJ Ethnography Coll.; *High Priest*: IMJ Photo IMJ/Hillel Burger; *Hillel*: IMJ Photo IMJ/D. Harris; *Holocaust*: Coll. David Geffen, Jerusalem; *Holy of Holies*: IMJ Photo IMJ/D. Harris; *Holy Places*: IMJ Photo IMJ/D. Harris; *Hospitality*: IMJ Photo IMJ/D. Harris; *Idolatry*: Bibliothèque Nationale, Paris; *Incense*: IDAM; *Ingathering of the Exiles*: IMJ Photo IMJ/Yoram Lehman; *Islam*: IMJ Photo IMJ/Nachum Slapak; *Isserles, Moses*: JNUL.Schwadron Coll. Photo D. Harris; *Jacob*: Wolfson Museum, Hechal Shlomo, Jerusalem. Photo D. Harris. *Jacob ben Asher*: Vatican Library, Rome; *Jeremiah*: Bibliothèque Nationale, Paris; *Jerusalem*: (p.382) Coll. Teddy Kollek; (p.383) JNUL; *Jewish Languages*: IMJ. Photo IMJ/Hillel Burger; *Job*: IMJ Photo IMJ/D. Harris; *Jonah*: New York Public Library, Spencer Coll.; *Joshua*: Oestereichische National bibliothek; *Judah Halevi*: Library of the Jewish Theological Seminary, New York; *Judeo-Spanish*: Museum of Jewish Art, Jerusalem. Photo D. Harris; *Kallah Months*: Beth Hatefutesoth, Tel Aviv; *Kapparot*: Royal Library, Copenhagen; *Karaism*: Beth Hatefutsoth, Tel Aviv. Photo Micha Bar-Am; *Kosher*: From *Lev Tuviah* (ed. by Joel Ziff, 1988). Courtesy David Geffen; *Kibbutz Festivals*: (left) Photo David Harris, (right) Hakibbuts Haartzi Hashomer Hazair Haggadah, drawing and lettering

Shmuel Katz; *Kiddush Cups*: IMJ/Stieglitz Coll. Photo IMJ/Avi Ganor; *Kimḥi, David*: Bodleian Library, Oxford; *Kook, Isaac*: General Zionist Archives; *Lag ba-Omer*: (left) IMJ/Photo IMJ/Reuven Milon, (center and right) Government Press Office, Jerusalem; *Lamentation*: IMJ Photo IMJ/D. Harris; *Leaven, Search for*: IMJ Photo IMJ/D. Harris; *Leviathan*: Karl-Marx Universitäts bibliothek, Leipzig; *Levirate Marriage*: IMJ Photo IMJ/Nachum Slapak; *Leviticus*: Royal Library Copenhagen; *Lilith*: IMJ Photo/IMJ Hillel Burger; Luria, Isaac: Royal Library Copenhabgen; *Luzzatto, Hayyim*: Courtesy Israel Lewitt; *Magen David*: Photo JPH/A. Van der Heyden; *Magic*: Royal Library Copenhagen; *Maḥzor*: Royal Library, Copenhagen; *Maimonides*: Library of the Jewish Theological Seminary, N.Y.; *Maimuna*: IMJ Photo IMJ/J. Sadeh; *Manna*: IMJ Photo IMJ/D. Harris; *Maror*: Royal Library, Copenhagen; *Marranos*: IMJ Photo IMJ/D. Harris; *Marriage* (p.462) IMJ, (p.466) (left) IMJ, (right) Photo Yehiel Haiby; *Matsah*: Coll. Italian Synagogue, Jerusalem; *Meir Ba'al Ha-Ness*: Photo D. Harris; *Memorial Light*: Photo P. Gaudard, National Film Board, Canada, Courtesy McClelland and Stewart Ltd.; *Mendelssohn*: Zentralbibliothek, Zürich; *Menorah*: IDAM, Courtesy Prof. Avigad; *Messiah*: IMJ Photo IMJ/PHoto Hillel Burger; *Mezuzah*: IMJ Photo IMJ/D. Harris; *Mikva'ot*: IMJ Photo IMJ/D. Harris; *Mishmarot*: IDAM; *Mishnah*: JNUL; *Moon*: Coll. Erica and Ludwig Jesselson, New York; Photo IMJ/Reuven Milon; *Mother*: IDAM; *Music*: IMJ Photo IMJ/D. Harris; *Mysticism*: JNUL; *Naḥmanides*: IMJ Photo IMJ/D. Harris; *New Year for Trees*: Government Press Office, Jerusalem; *Niddah*: Photo Courtesy Christie's Amsterdam; *Noah*: Photo Erich Lessing, Vienna; *Organ*: Photo Städtbildstelle Essen; *Orthodoxy*: Photo Gadi Geffen; *Ouziel*: General Zionist Archives; *Parnas*: Coll. Rosengarten Musem Konstanz; *Passover*: (p. 541) Karl Marx Universitäts bibliothek, Leipzig, (p. 540)Schocken Library, Jerusalem. Photo D. Harris; *Patriarchs*: Photo/JPH. A. Van den Heyden; *Peace*: IDAM; *Pesher*: IMJ/Shrine of the Book. Photo IMJ/D. Harris; *Petihah*: Library of the Jewish Theological Seminary, New York; *Pilgrimage*: Photo Werner Braun; *Piyyut*: Vatican Library, Rome; *Poor and Poverty*: Jewish Museum, London. Photo Ronald Sheridan; *Prayer*: Government Press Office, Jerusalem; *Prayer before a Journey*: JNUL, Jerusalem; *Prayer Book*: Photo D. Harris; *Priestly Blessing*: Photo Reuven Milon; *Priestly Garments*: Rheinisches Bildarchiv; *Psalms*: British Library; *Rabbinical Seminaries*: (p. 581) left, Hebrew Union College (left) Photo Jewish Theological Seminary, N.Y. (p. 582) Yeshiva University, N.Y.; *Reading of the Law*: IMJ Photo IMJ/D. Harris; *Red Heifer*: Schocken Library, Jerusalem; *Reform Judaism*: Photo Yoram Lehman; *Repentance*: IMJ Photo IMJ/D. Harris; *Revelation*: IMJ Photo IMJ/D. Harris; *Rosh ha-Shanah*: Karl Marx Universitäts bibliothek, Leipzig; *Ruth*: IMJ.Photo IMJ/D. Harris; *Sabbath*: IMJ Photo IMJ/Nachum Slapak; *Samaritans*: (left) New York Public Library, (right) Photo Werner Braun; *Sanctuary*: Coll. Teddy Kollek. Photo D. Harris; *Science*: National Library Canada/Lowy Coll.; *Scribe*: Photo Werner Braun; *Scroll of the Law*: Bildarchiv Photo, Marburg; *Seder*: IMJ.Photo IMJ/D. Harris; *Sephardim*: A. Rubens Collection, London; *Sha'atnez*: Courtesy G. Sivan; *Shabbetai Tsevi*: Coll. Teddy Kollek. PHoto D. Harris; *Shofar*: Wolfson Museum Hechal Shlomo, Photo D. Harris; *Showbread*: IMJ Photo IMJ; *Solomon*: IMJ Photo IMJ/D. Harris; *Song of Songs*: IMJ Photo IMJ. *Study*: Photo Yehiel Haiby; *Sukkah*: Photo Gadi Geffen, Jerusalem; *Sukkot*: IMJ Photo IMJ/Reuven Milon; *Synagogue*: Photo Ronald Sheridan; *Tablets of the Covenant*: Bildarchiv Photo, Marburg; *Tallit*: Coll. Mrs Morpugo Sde Eliahu. Photo IMJ/D. Harris; *Tefillin*: Courtesy Genya Markon, Photo Mark Haziza; *Tashlikh*: IMJ PHoto IMJ/D. Harri; *Temple*: Bibliothèque Nationale, Paris; *Temple Mount*: Photo Werner Braun; *Tisha be-Av*: IMJ Photo IMJ/Nachum Slapak; *Torah Ornaments*: IMJ Stieglitz Coll. Photo IMJ/Avi Ganor; *Tombstone*: Courtesy G. Wigoder; *Tribes, Twelve*: Courtesy Stanley Irving Batkin; *Vital, Hayyim*: Wolfson Museum Hechal Shlomo; *Western Wall*: JPH/Photo D. Harris; *Wine*: IMJ.Photo IMJ/D. Harris; *Woman*: IMJ Photo IMJ/D. Harris; *Yeshivah*: PHoto Guill, Baltimore. Courtesy Ner Israel Rabbinical College. *Yevamot*: Bibliothèque Nationale, Paris; *Yad*: IMJ Stieglitz Coll. Photo IMJ/Avi Ganor; *Zion*: IMJ Ethnography Coll. Photo Richard Lobell. *Zion, Return to*: Photo Edi Hirshbain.

Charles Scribner's Sons, for the use of the essay on "Peace" by Prof. Aviezer Ravitzky from *Contemporary Jewish Religious Thought* by Arthur A. Cohen and Paul Mendes Flohr (1987). Weindefeld and Nicolson Ltd., for the translation of Alénu le-Shabbeaḥ from *A Jewish Book of Common Prayer* by C. Raphael (1986).

IMJ = Israel Museum, Jerusalem; JNUL = Jewish National and University Library, Jerusalem; IDAM — Israel Department of Antiquities and Museums.